ADVERTISING
THE BUSINESS OF BRANDS

An Introduction to Careers & Concepts in Advertising & Marketing

by Bruce Bendinger, Ann Maxwell, Beth Barnes, Susan Alessandri, Elizabeth Tucker, Anthony McGann, Robert Gustafson, Marian Azzaro, Carla Lloyd, Laurence Minsky, Joe Marconi, Kevin Adler, Susan Jones, Jim Avery, Tom Fauls, Alice Kendrick, Joe Bob Hester, Dennis Ganahl, and James Marra.

Fourth (Media Revolution) Edition

MEDIA
REVOLUTION
EDITION

Advertising & the Business of Brands
Fourth (Media Revolution) Edition

ISBN: 978-1-887229-38-8

17 16 15 14 13 12 11 10 09   12345

All rights reserved. Printed in the USA

Published by The Copy Workshop

A division of Bruce Bendinger Creative Communications, Inc.

Cover Design: Gregory S. Paus

For further information contact: The Copy Workshop

2144 N. Hudson • Chicago, IL 60614

773-871-1179 • FX 773-281-4643

www.adbuzz.com

thecopyworkshop@aol.com

©2009 The Copy Workshop

ADVERTISING

THE BUSINESS OF BRANDS

MEDIA
REVOLUTION
EDITION

Welcome To

A NEW KIND OF INTRODUCTION to a world that's in the middle of a revolution – **a media revolution**.

This book is a collaboration from a team of experts in marketing communication – professors who teamed up to teach you about that changing world.

However, it may not seem like a revolution to you.

We'll talk about some of the new things going on, and you may say, "What's new about that?"

Because the revolution we're going to tell you about is one that you've grown up in. But that's good news. Because it means this book will have one more expert – you.

This book will look at the massive changes in business and society that are shaping the exciting jobs of tomorrow.

We'll focus on the specific areas of advertising and marketing communications, but, as you'll see, it's all connected.

And the goal of this book is to help you make the connections that just could lead you to an interesting career.

So, welcome to a textbook, a history book, a map to the future, and a guide to the fast-changing world of the Business of Brands. It's part of a global marketplace that we're all a part of.

Welcome to a history book that's probably not like any other history book you've ever read.

Because, with this history, you're going to do more than read about it.

In the years to come, you're going to be making it.

The Winds of Change

…are blowing everywhere.

And they're changing the world all around the world.

Remember your first computer? How about that first video game? They've changed, right?

Well, those same kinds of changes have had an impact on the worlds of business and marketing communications.

Some businesses have gotten a lot faster and a lot smarter. Others have been blown away.

And now you're getting ready to set sail for a career in that world. Throughout this book, we're going to try to show you which ways the winds are blowing as you set a course for the future.

What are you waiting for?
Turn the page.

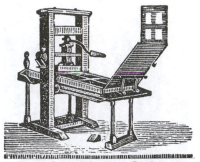

The Gutenberg Galaxy

When the printing press was invented, it did more than make books and newspapers available – it changed mankind.

It quite literally expanded our consciousness.

That's right, the printing press and the mass availability of books changed European civilization and helped power the American Revolution.

No longer did a narrow priestly class have a lock on all knowledge.

Marshall McLuhan pointed out aspects of our own history we'd always taken for granted in his first book, *The Gutenberg Galaxy*.

He showed us how a change in media leads to a change in society.

That's the message of the media – it's not the call on the cell phone in your pocket – it's the fact of all the cell phones connecting us.

That kind of change is revolutionary. And it's just one example.

Now there's another revolution just as profound – a computer-driven media revolution. McLuhan predicted it. And we're living it.

The Media

ONCE UPON A TIME, there was a limited amount of media – books, newspapers, magazines, the radio, and TV.

Today, there's media all around you. It's everywhere.

It's on your desktop.

It's in your pocket.

Inside your mailbox.

Inside your brain.

It makes music.

It takes messages.

It changes channels.

It isn't just your TV and radio.

It isn't just magazines and newspapers.

It isn't just billboards and posters on the sides of buildings.

It's everywhere.

It's inside your computer

And, in many ways, it's inside your head.

Media Today.
You don't just consume it.
You create it.

But unlike every other generation – you no longer just consume media. You create it.

You text it.

You blog it.

You attach it.

You Google it.

And the media becomes an extension of you – an extension of what you do and the brand new world we live in.

As McLuhan observed, media changes us.

The printing press changed us.

The telephone changed us. And now that new complicated, interconnected, digital, mobile environment that's growing around us is taking us all somewhere we've never been.

Extensions.
Media can change the way you see the world around you.

Revolution.

WHAT, YOU HAVEN'T NOTICED? Why would you?

The Media Revolution grew while you were growing up.

That's right, you grew right along with the revolution.

Computers got faster. Computer games got better.

TV added more channels – and, along the way, you found more ways to get information.

Once upon a time, there was only Freedom of the Press for those who owned a newspaper. Even that has changed.

Today, you can make it happen on a blog, in a viral video, or in a 'zine you published yourself.

Communication is no longer a one-way street.

Now it's a two-way highway taking us into an exciting future.

And, as you look for a job, and maybe a career, you'll see old business models shut down as new ones open up. Our mission is to help you understand what's going on and how to make the most of it.

It won't be a problem-free future, but it will be full of opportunity for those who prepare for it.

This billboard helped change governments. A few years later, the ad agency that did it, Saatchi & Saatchi, changed the entire advertising business.

You've grown up with Google. It may seem simple to you – but it's changed the way we're all connected.

The World is Flat

This thought-provoking book by Thomas Friedman gives us insight into all the factors feeding into The Media Revolution – part of a revolution that's changing the world all around the world.

Friedman's metaphor is that these things are "flattening the world."

Very briefly, here are some of the examples he mentions:

The invention of the Internet and Web browsers like NetScape. And what he calls "The Steroids," which are making everything become digital, mobile, personal, and virtual.

As you search for a term paper using Google and Wi-fi, you're taking part in it. Soon, you'll be doing more than just consuming media and information – you'll be part of creating it – maybe you're doing it already.

Four People Who Are Changing Your Life.

You may have never heard of them – and some are no longer with us. But their ideas are affecting your life every day.

You'll meet them early on in this book, but here's a sneak preview.

Joseph Schumpeter

An Austrian economist who got the heck out of Austria before World War One. His observation on our economy is critical for anyone looking for a job today. Creative Destruction. As new industries are created, old business models are often destroyed.

Gordon Moore

Founder of Intel. Ever hear of "Moore's Law?" It impacts your computers, your mobile phones, and your future. Every eighteen months chip capacity doubles and the cost is cut in half. Wow!

Marshall McLuhan

Media guru. His observations about how our society interacts with media were profound. Media evolution is key to the changes going on in our world right now. Understanding McLuhan helps us understand media and that helps us understand The Media Revolution.

Paul Roemer

An award-winning economist – and, if you like to think, he has some good news for you.

You can read more about his thinking in Chapter One.

Instructions:

We're guessing that you've probably read a book before.

But this one is just a little bit different. So hang on.

First, despite language that's pretty easy to read, about halfway through the second chapter, your head may feel a little bit stuffed with information. And you'll only be at Chapter Two.

Helpful Hint #1.

OK, here's the first hint.

Read the Introduction twice – maybe three times – pay attention to the part that outlines the whole book.

Because if you can kind of get the complete outline of the book in your head, all of the details to come will start to make sense – and you'll know where to put them.

With a lot of books, the Introduction is just where the author thanks a lot of people – we do that in the back of the book.

The purpose of this Introduction is to get your head ready for all the information we're going to serve up. You'll thank us later.

The Game behind the Game.

They say, you can't judge a book by its cover.

This book says it's about "advertising," which seems pretty simple – after all, you've been seeing ads for as long as you can remember. Well, it's really about what goes on behind the scenes – to make the ads, the decisions, the strategies, and all the other things that go into making "The Business of Brands" operate.

Concepts and Careers.

You might notice that the subhead of this book is "An Introduction to Careers and Concepts in Advertising and Marketing."

Why is this important? Because we're pretty sure that most of you are interested in earning a good living after you graduate.

In fact, we think it's so important that we added a "Careers" chapter to help you with that important marketing campaign for "The Brand Called You."

Because, more and more, marketing is the way "business does business."

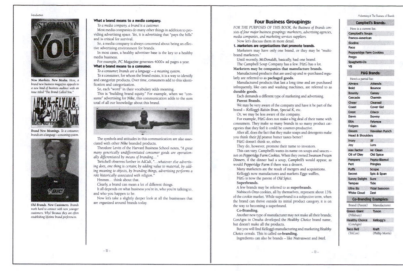

The Look of the Book. It's easy. The main part goes down the middle. Along the sides are ad examples, profiles, and stories to help make it interesting.

How to Read This Book.

IT'S SIMPLE. The key points in each chapter go down the middle, with supporting material featured along the sides.

Each Chapter Starts with...

Each chapter starts with brief profiles of real people who work in the area covered by that chapter. We start with people, not theory.

Here's why. At this stage of your college career, you're still "job-shopping." Real examples help you do that. Then we'll tell you…

"How This Chapter Is Organized."

Next, we outline the areas to be covered in the chapter.

Along the way, the sidebars provide ad examples, "Ad Facts," stories, lists, and statistics to put things in context. The sidebars help make each chapter more interesting and help you connect.

Each Chapter Ends with Concepts & Vocabulary.

At the end of each chapter, you'll find a list called "Concepts & Vocabulary." This list serves two important purposes.

First, if you understand most of the words and concepts, you'll know there's a pretty good chance you understand the chapter.

Second, you can use it for studying. In fact, you can even download a text file of this section from the adbuzz.com Web site.

In Conclusion... It's Easy, but It's Tough.

We worked hard to make this book easy to read.

But… we're writing about a complex, fast-changing business – so even though it's easy to read, it still may not be all that easy.

There's a lot to learn, and sometimes it may feel like your head is bursting with new information.

But look at it this way… if it were easy, they wouldn't need you.

Good luck. And have fun!

This book is dedicated to Tom Jordan,
ad man, educator, father, and friend.
[1941–1998]

ADVERTISING
& The Business of Brands
CAREERS & CONCEPTS IN ADVERTISING & MARKETING.

Introduction.

READ THIS FIRST. It introduces you to the book's key concepts:
- The development of the brand as an organizing idea
- The four business groupings in "The Business of Brands"
- Marketing, communications, and integration = IMC
- The process that "manufactures" marketing = PIE
- The speed of change and the importance of new ideas

This intro will give you a "roadmap" for the rest of the book.

I. The Evolution of Advertising.

THIS SECTION COVERS THE DEVELOPMENT of the American marketplace and its consequences in our lives today.

It begins with the innovations of early advertisers and the rise of new media forms. Then, it shows you how the forces of marketing are changing today's marketplace.

Finally, we'll discuss how advertising has become a major force in both American business and American culture.

1 From Advertising to Marketing.

THE 20TH CENTURY BEGAN with modern advertising. You'll meet innovators and their innovations as the mass consumer market grows. Midway through the century, you'll see a new way of doing business emerge from advertisers and from their advertising agencies – *marketing*. **38**

2 The Modern Marketplace.

THE WORLD OF MARKETING keeps changing.

Today, marketing is a driving force almost everywhere.

In this chapter, we'll examine how the growing importance of marketing has reshaped the entire American marketplace and we'll look at the next evolution – *Integrated Marketing Communications (IMC)*. **92**

3 Advertising & Society.

ECONOMICS, ETHICS, RULES, AND REGULATIONS. This chapter discusses how advertising in our society affects us all, whether we are citizens, consumers, marketing professionals, or advertising students. **138**

The First American was an Ad Man.
Benjamin Franklin, known as "The First American," was not only an inventor, patriot, and publisher, he was also a marketer, advertising copywriter, and publisher of the biggest newspaper in the Colonies – The Pennsylvania Gazette. He's one of the first members of the Advertising Hall of Fame.

From Manufacturing to Marketing.
Brands began as names for manufactured products. They've evolved to become the core concept of marketing organizations.

*ON ANY SUNDAY, you'll see marketers like Campbell's advertising in the **FSI (Free Standing Insert)** section of your local newspaper.*

*These ads are for **promotions**.*

In some cases marketers will spend two or three times more on promotions than they do on advertising!

National Advertising.

This reaches the mass – a large national audience. Some examples:

Network TV: ABC, CBS, Fox, etc.

National Magazines: *Newsweek, People, Time, TV Guide*

National Newspapers: *The Wall Street Journal, USA Today*

Local Advertising.

This reaches people in a specific area or region. Here are some examples:

Local Television
Newspapers
Outdoor
Radio

Niche Advertising.

This reaches a narrow group – either nationally or within a market.

Here are some examples:

Cable Networks: BET, ESPN, Lifetime, MSNBC, MTV, Telemundo

Trade Journals & Special Interest Magazines: *AdWeek, Chain Store Age, PC Monthly, Modern Bride*

Black America's Brand of Choice.

Ads for Advertising.

This is the cover of a sales kit for BET, the Black Entertainment Network.

A media company uses materials like these to communicate the advantages of their media channel to potential advertisers and to other important audiences – such as cable carriers.

II. The Business of Brands.

MARKETERS, AGENCIES, MEDIA, MARKETING SERVICES.

These four unique business groupings make up The Business of Brands. You'll see how these different companies are organized and the many different career opportunities they offer.

4 Marketers & Advertisers.

MARKETING AND ADVERTISING DEPARTMENTS are organized around the brands they market.

In this chapter, you'll be introduced to the ways marketers and advertisers do business. We'll cover their internal responsibilities and the way they work with outside suppliers – like ad agencies and marketing services firms. **188**

5 Advertising Agencies.

BRAND-BUILDING COMMUNICATIONS are the unique product of advertising agencies.

It's a business based on ideas – the bigger the better.

You'll see the many types of agencies, how they work, and the many jobs needed to make an ad agency successful. **231**

6 The World of Media.

MEDIA HAS MANY ROLES IN OUR SOCIETY.

This chapter will focus on the business behind the media – the business of delivering audiences to advertisers and the marketing of *entertainment brands*.

We'll look at the different types of media and how they market themselves to audiences, advertisers, and agencies as well as how this affects us as citizens and consumers. **282**

7 Marketing Services.

MARKETING HAS MANY FUNCTIONS.

In this chapter, we'll survey the specialized companies that supply marketing services: sales promotion, public relations, direct marketing, event marketing, media buying, marketing research, and more. This is an exciting growth area. **340**

III. The Brand-Building Process.

MARKETING. COMMUNICATING. INTEGRATING.

This section will cover the planning, implemenation, and evaluation of advertising in today's marketplace.

You'll see how marketers, agencies, media, and marketing services all work together to build brands.

8 Marketing & the Planning Process.

PLANNING & STRATEGY DEVELOPMENT is the focus of this chapter. Planning begins with evaluation.

You'll see how marketers and agencies work together to define and refine objectives and then develop strategies.   **382**

9 Creativity & Communication.

FROM IDEA TO IMPLEMENTATION. This chapter will cover the key element of implementation, the way an ad agency creates, presents, and then produces the communication.

It's one of the most fun parts of advertising.   **422**

10 Media & the Marketing of Messages.

MEDIA IS THE CRITICAL CONNECTION. It delivers the message in the marketplace. Media costs are usually the largest part of an advertising budget.

This chapter will cover the ways agencies determine the most effective way to deliver their brand's message.

Today, the rapidly changing world of media makes this area a tremendous creative opportunity all by itself.   **481**

11 Evaluation & Integration.

BRAND BUILDING IS an ongoing process of learning, evaluating, and improving – in a continual dialogue with the marketplace.

This chapter will survey the way programs are evaluated – providing critical information as the process begins anew.

You'll see how marketers improve their programs by integration – coordinating the full range of marketing activities for further improvement.   **530**

The full range of marketing activities…

Marketing Plan.

The Marketing Plan is a document that describes *what* a marketer wants to accomplish for a brand.
It covers:

Product
Pricing (and budgets)
Distribution (place)
Promotion (this includes all aspects of IMC – including Advertising)
Marketing Objective and Strategy
Ad Objective and Strategy
and more

Creative Strategy.

The Creative Strategy describes *how* you will achieve your advertising objective – areas such as:

Brand Essence or Personality
Target Audience
Consumer Benefit

To help develop creative work, there may be some sort of "creative brief" which briefs the creative department on the task and target.

There may also be strategies in areas like sales promotion and PR.

Media Plan.

The Media Plan includes:

A Media Objective – a goal which focuses on a target audience.
A Media Strategy – how you will meet that objective in terms of reaching the target audience.
A Media Plan – tactics (media buys) to help you achieve your goals.

Ad Campaign.

The advertising itself is a result of all this planning. Each ad is a *tactic* that helps achieve the advertising objective. The advertising may be:

A TV or Radio Commercial
Print Advertising
Direct Mail
Or a combination of all the above.

& More…

Today, advertising is more than advertising. A complete marketing program for a brand might include event sponsorship, a sales promotion event, and product publicity.

More Power to You. *The PowerBar is just one example of what can happen when an individual with a new idea builds a brand-new brand in the marketplace.*

The Dragon – Bringing Your Product to Market. *The Careers section is an organized resource for helping you find that first job in The Business of Brands.*

Where will you be sitting a few years from now? *Our Mission is to help you prepare for The Business of Brands. The rest is up to you.*

IV. You & the Marketplace.

THIS SECTION IS ABOUT YOU.

The Business of Brands keeps changing.

So do your career opportunities.

If you're considering a career in marketing or advertising, this isn't the end of this book – it's only the beginning.

12 The Power of New Ideas.

NEW PRODUCTS, NEW MARKETS, new media, and new technology.

They're all part of the modern marketplace.

We'll show you how new ideas enter the marketplace as marketers, agencies, media companies, and marketing services create new brands and develop new ways to build brands.

You'll see new products, new ad agencies, new media opportunities (like the Internet), and other exciting new job opportunities – the kind that are opening up every day. **563**

Conclusion: You & Your Career.

THIS IS ABOUT "THE BRAND CALLED YOU." It's about how to find your place in today's marketplace.

If you who think you might want to work in advertising or marketing, this section is for you.

It's about how to make the connections that result in new opportunities in The Business of Brands. **599**

Your Marketing Plan...

This final section will help you work through a four-stage process that can help you do a better job marketing yourself. Your first marketing plan has a very specific objective – Get a Job!

❶ **Understanding Yourself as a Product.**

First, we'll help you evaluate "The Brand Called You."

❷ **Understanding Your Market.**

Second, we'll discuss finding ways to match yourself with the part of the market that will value your abilities.

❸ **Increasing Your Market Value.**

Third, we'll talk about ways to increase your abilities – and your value in the job market.

❹ **Bringing Your Product to Market.**

Finally, we'll talk about ways to market and advertise yourself as you work to earn your first job in The Business of Brands.

Good luck!

Index   645

Start here... > > >

This is a brand. Starbucks.

Scott Bedbury when he was at Starbucks. Before that, Nike. Before that, Scott was at a small agency. Before that, it was sauerkraut!

While Scott was at Nike, this was one of his favorites – a TV commercial that inspired the movie Space Jam. It also helped develop another world-famous brand – Michael Jordan!

Psst... Don't Skip This
Introduction.

LET'S START WITH four true stories.

Do It. Then Brew It.

In 1980, **Scott Bedbury** was looking for a job.

After graduating with a degree in advertising from U of Oregon, Scott thought he wanted to be an advertising copywriter.

But that first job isn't always what you want.

The best job he could get was working for a small company in Portland, marketing pickles, relish, and sauerkraut – their entire ad budget was $200,000.

Scott also helped load pickles and sauerkraut onto the trucks.

Then, he moved to a Seattle ad agency – as a junior account executive. Scott spent a few years learning the ad business.

His next job was with a small, but growing company that seemed to have a lot of potential – a little shoe company called Nike!

There, Scott played a part in revolutionary marketing that not only changed the shoe industry but had an important impact on all athletics – including the growth of **sports marketing**.

After a transitional period, he moved to Seattle – to become Marketing Director of Starbucks, a company revolutionizing the marketing of a product that had been around for centuries – coffee.

Scott worked to turn his brand new brand into a **superbrand**.

Then he left to write a book about the world he had discovered and the brands he helped build.

The book title?

It's a New Brand World!

The Five Ps of Marketing are Product, Price, Promotion, People, and Place – which is distribution. Starbucks products are distributed through Starbucks' own stores, at bookstores like Barnes & Noble and Borders, on United Airlines flights, and in grocery stores. You can even get some of their products by mail. Many products are part of the Starbucks brand – coffee beverages, beans, mugs, ice cream, and even special CDs.

A Nice After-School Job.

After graduating from the University of Texas in 1971, **Roy Spence** and five other UT students formed an ad agency where they'd gone to school – Austin.

They'd enjoyed creating advertising for student projects and had even done work for a few small local clients.

Steve and Bill Gurasich, Roy Spence, Jim Darilek, and Tim McLure decided to call their agency **GSD&M** (Judy Trabulsi, who is the media director and also one of the founders, says she's the "&").

A Mattress under the Art Table…

They had a one-room office, and, for the first two years, lived on virtually nothing. For a little while, Roy Spence even slept on a mattress under the art table.

Thirty-five years later, their agency is one of the largest in the Southwest, billing over $1.5 billion.

They serve national brands like AT&T, Southwest Airlines, John Deere, MasterCard, *BMW*, and the U.S. Air Force.

And they still keep their Texas heritage.

As you can see by the logo on the right, even a state can be treated like a brand.

Their one-room office blossomed into a brand new building – "Idea City," still in Austin.

Every once in a while, GSD&M founder Roy Spence would sleep over at a big White House, where his friend Bill Clinton worked – instead of under the art table.

Before. Steve Gurasich, Tim McLure, Judy Trabulsi, Bill Gurasich, and Roy Spence in the early years.

After. Tim McLure, Steve Gurasich, Judy Trabulsi, Bill Gurasich, and Roy Spence.

*"Big Ideas Generate
Big Results."*

*"When Our Clients Win,
We Win."*

Welcome to Idea City.

"We designed this place to foster entrepreneurship, creativity, community. It's playful, yet serious. It's eclectic, and yet there's a purpose behind everything we did."

Before. 1971 – GSD&M's first office on Peach Street.

After. 1995 – GSD&M's brand-new "Idea City" in Austin, TX.

Robert L. Johnson, founder of BET – Black Entertainment Television.

Bob's Brand New Brand. The Charlotte Bobcats – an entertainment brand now playing in the NBA.

A Very Good BET.

Robert L. Johnson graduated from the University of Illinois in 1970. Then he received a master's in public affairs from Princeton.

In 1976, after working on the staff of Walter E. Fauntroy, the Congressional delegate from the District of Columbia, he took a job as VP of Government Relations for a media group that was still in its infancy – the National Cable Television Association.

He became aware of cable's ability to reach "niche" markets.

He saw how cable was changing the dynamics of media – with **niche marketing** in broadcasting on a national scale.

Johnson believed these marketing principles could be applied very effectively to the African-American market.

He developed a business plan for a cable network he called *BET – Black Entertainment Television –* a 24-hour programming service targeting Afro-Americans. It's mission was *"To become the preeminent diversified media company serving African-American consumers."*

He did it! With a $15,000 investment and a $500,000 loan from cable magnate John Malone, he made that media dream a reality.

Growing a Brand.

Johnson didn't stop there. He understood media synergy. He developed additional cable channels, including BET OnJazz and BET Movies/Starz, a joint venture with Encore Media.

BET Holdings also tried to leverage its brand identity with BET Publications featuring *Emerge: Black America's News Magazine, BET Weekend,* an entertainment and lifestyle magazine, and *Arabesque,* a line of African-American themed romance novels.

For the wired segment of their target group, there is BET.com.

A Big Deal and a New Brand.

With an initial investment in the thousands, Robert Johnson built a brand worth billions. Literally.

He sold BET to Viacom for $2.3 billion in stock!

Now Johnson has a new brand to grow – the Charlotte franchise of the NBA. It all began with an idea and the right media.

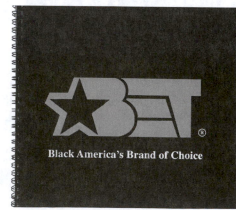

BET Sales Points:

• *The BET Audience reaches some 50 million homes, including 90% of all black cable households.*

• *The African-American middle class is growing and becoming more attractive to retail marketers.*

• *BET brands are emotionally attached to Black America, which gives you instant credibility.*

• *BET is the most recognizable brand in Black America.*

A Sales Presentation – presenting some of the reasons for advertising on BET.

Making Marketers Smarter with Marketing Services.

In 1975, Lisa Fortini decided to go to grad school. She had a B.A. in psychology from Ohio State, but she wanted to know more.

After getting an M.A. in journalism, she received her Ph.D. in communication theory, research methodology, and consumer behavior from the University of Washington. (She was also a regional AAU Power-Lifting Champion!)

From there, she went to Chicago, working in the research department of the Leo Burnett ad agency.

In a few years, she moved up to Research Director at the small Chicago office of a large national agency. Then, to a bigger agency with more responsibility as Research Director of Y&R/Chicago.

Then, to Office Manager of Hal Riney Chicago.

Along the way, she became **Lisa Fortini-Campbell.**

Then, Lisa made one more big move – she left the agency business to become a professor and marketing consultant.

Her consulting firm – The Fortini-Campbell Company – became one of the many specialized companies working for large marketers as suppliers of **marketing services.**

Her service – consumer insight research – is a key component in planning and evaluation for marketers and their agencies.

Her reputation grew. The Fortini-Campbell Company was retained by major marketers around the country – Aetna, Kraft/General Foods (KGF), Hewlett-Packard (H-P), IBM, IDEO, Nuveen, Seagram's, and Spiegel. Then, around the world.

She wrote a book, *Hitting the Sweet Spot: How Consumer Insight Can Inspire Better Marketing and Advertising.* Companies like Leo Burnett, IBM, GM, and P&G use it.

She taught consumer behavior at Northwestern University in the Medill School of Advertising and Integrated Marketing Communications, as top marketers hired her to help them develop better consumer insights.

Today, she travels the world helping clients improve their abilities to develop better consumer insight – a valuable marketing service.

Dr. Lisa Fortini-Campbell, *President, The Fortini-Campbell Company – a market research firm specializing in consumer insight.*

A Smokeless Moment…

Even the most successful careers can have their early bumps.

Lisa remembers…

"At Y&R, we handled the Silver Creek smokeless tobacco account. (You put a pinch between your cheek and your gum and then periodically spit – hopefully into a cup rather than on the floor or yourself.)

"It was an annual review where senior executives visit the branch offices. As the planner, I was in charge of telling them about our work for Silver Creek.

"So, to give these New Yorkers an idea of how to use the product, I decided to demonstrate. I put a pinch of Silver Creek in my mouth – about three times as much as I was supposed to – and began to present.

"I'd never had nicotine before in my life, and rather than spit, I swallowed.

"By the end of the presentation, I looked absolutely green and felt like the top of my head was going to come off.

"As I left the room, the rest of the account team, who'd been watching from the A/V room, had pitchers of water, towels, and buckets… and they had to walk me around the office for half an hour. It was an experience I'll never forget… neither will anyone else who was there."

Data > Information > Insight > Inspiration

Dr. Fortini-Campbell's Secret Formula. Most marketers have lots of data. That data has to be turned into useful information. Based on that information, you work to find an insight that will be the inspiration for more effective marketing and advertising.

Interesting Jobs:

Chris Smith started as a copywriter – just one of the entry-level jobs you can find in The Business of Brands.

Here are a few more examples of entry-level jobs:

Marketer:
Brand Assistant
Marketing Staff Assistant
Marketing Research Assistant
Assistant Marketing Director
Corporate Communications
Field Marketing Representative

Advertising Agency:
Junior Copywriter
Copywriter
Assistant Art Director
Digital Production
Broadcast Traffic
Media Buyer
Electronic Pre-Press
Assistant Account Executive
Receptionist
Media Billings
Research Assistant
Assistant Account Planner

Media:
Media Rep (Sales Representative)
Production Assistant
Promotion Assistant
Sales Assistant
Online Activities
Web site Maintenance

Marketing Services:
Direct Marketing Account Exec
Event Marketing Coordinator
Sales Promotion Account Exec
Public Relations Assistant
Market Researcher

Different Jobs. One Thing in Common.

Scott Bedbury worked for Starbucks, a **marketer.**

Roy Spence helped start GSD&M, an **advertising agency.**

Robert Johnson's BET is a **media** company.

Lisa Fortini-Campbell supplies **marketing services.**

They all have something in common. Each of their jobs, and each of their companies, is part of The Business of Brands.

How This Book is Organized.

We're going to go over this twice. So read this quick summary first, and then we'll take you through it in greater detail.

• **Part One – The Evolution of Advertising.** You'll see how **marketing** became a part of almost every business during the 20th century – and you'll see how advertising helped make it happen.

• **Part Two – The Business of Brands.** You'll find out about the many different jobs in the many different companies that make up our modern marketplace.

• **Part Three – The Brand-Building Process.** We'll cover the stages that "manufacture" marketing and advertising.

• **Part Four – You & the Marketplace.** Here, we'll talk about change in today's fast-changing marketplace and some of the things you can do to get yourself ready.

One of Those Jobs Could Be Yours.

In the conclusion, "You & Your Career," we'll help you sort through all you've learned to focus on the opportunity that's best for you.

After all, not too many years from now, you may find yourself working at a job that plays an important role in that marketplace – just like the people you'll meet in The Business of Brands.

This Introduction Will Cover:

Every chapter begins with a brief section that tells you the main topic areas in the chapter and the sequence of those topics.

Each chapter ends with a list of key concepts and vocabulary. We'll do the same thing here.

This introductory section is designed to give you a better understanding of the book in its entirety. Then, you can focus on each successive chapter knowing how it fits in the whole framework. Got it?

Here are the topics we'll be talking about for the next 30 pages. Most will be key concepts throughout this book.

• **How This Book Is Organized**

• **What's a Brand?** Our definition.

• **Four Business Groupings.** This is important.

• **The Brand-Building Process.** This is important, too.

And two topics that will have great impact on the business world you'll be working in.

• **The Challenge of Change**

• **The Importance of Ideas**

Let's go!

How This Book Is Organized.

This Book Has Twelve Chapters.

Each chapter should take about a week of class time.

Each chapter covers one aspect of The Business of Brands.

The brand has become the organizing concept of modern advertising and marketing. It has also had its impact on our culture overall.

First, let's take a quick tour through the book.

- Twelve chapters. Four sections.
- What's a brand?
- Four business groupings
- The brand-building process and IMC
- The challenge of change
- The importance of ideas

I. The Evolution of Advertising.

WE'LL START WITH a brief history of advertising and marketing. Then we'll cover the evolutions and the revolutions that are going on right now. We'll also look at the ways that advertising relates to society at large. It'll take three chapters:

Chapter One – From Advertising to Marketing.

We'll look at the early history of advertising and how that evolved into marketing.

Chapter Two – The Modern Marketplace.

Think of this chapter as "Current Events." You'll see how marketing and Media Evolution are reshaping our world.

Chapter Three – Advertising & Society.

Now it's time for a bit of perspective. We'll discuss how all that advertising affects us and what it means to all of us.

II. The Business of Brands.

THE SECOND SECTION covers the four kinds of companies that work together to "manufacture" marketing and advertising:

Chapter Four – Marketers & Advertisers.

These are the companies – like manufacturers and retailers – that create and own the brands.

They pay for the advertising you see.

Chapter Five – Advertising Agencies.

These are the specialized companies that "manufacture" ad messages. They create the advertising you see.

Chapter Six – The World of Media.

These are the companies that "distribute" advertising by delivering audiences for brand messages.

Chapter Seven – Marketing Services.

These specialized businesses provide a variety of unique services to marketers, agencies, and media companies. You'll learn about sales promotion, public relations, direct marketing, event marketing, and more.

Unique Ideas. Sharp thinking from entrepreneurs like King Gillette helped develop America's earliest brands.

Unique Individuals like Leo Burnett helped build advertising agencies.

Unique Media Forms. Every time the media changed, advertising changed.

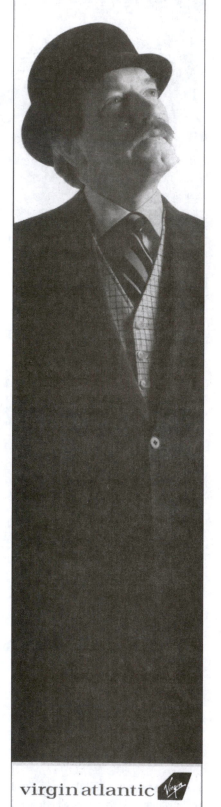

III. The Brand-Building Process.

THE THIRD SECTION is about the process that "manufactures" marketing and advertising; how people and companies work together to plan, implement, and evaluate advertising.

Two Interconnecting Concepts.

There are two connecting concepts in the next chapters:

1. The Three Fundamental Functions of "IMC."

A key part of the brand-building process is something we call "IMC" – **Integrated Marketing Communications.**

The three fundamental functions of IMC are: **marketing, communicating,** and **integrating.**

2. A Three-Stage Cycle. Easy as "PIE."

P.I.E. is an easy way to remember the ongoing cycle of **planning, implementation,** and **evaluation.** Here's how the section works:

Chapter Eight – Marketing & the Planning Process.

This chapter introduces you to what is involved in setting objectives and developing strategies for marketing and advertising.

Chapter Nine – Creativity & Communication.

This chapter will also introduce you to creativity in advertising as well as sales promotion, PR, and direct.

Chapter Ten – Media & the Marketing of Messages.

This chapter covers the unique process of placing those messages in the media in the most effective way.

Chapter Eleven – Evaluation & Integration.

It's critical that marketers make the most effective use of marketing dollars. This means finding out (evaluating) how you did and then prioritizing (integrating) your resources for their most effective use – which leads to the next cycle of planning, implementation, and evaluation. And so on…

Many People. Many Jobs.

Through it all, you'll see many people with many specialized jobs. This will lead into the last section.

IV. You & the Marketplace.

THE FOURTH SECTION will deal with the constant change in the marketplace and ways you can connect with those changes.

Chapter Twelve – The Power of New Ideas.

We'll talk about how marketers, ad agencies, and marketing services deal with new opportunities. And we'll talk about the new medium that's changing everything – the Internet.

Conclusion – You & Your Career.

Finally, we'll focus on how you can prepare yourself to get that first job in The Business of Brands.

This course will last a semester. Preparing yourself for a career will probably last for two years or more.

What's a Brand?

THE BRAND CONCEPT originally developed out of trademarks.

The word **brand** is from the Old English verb *biernan* (to burn). The meaning grew to include making a mark on something by burning (to brand).

It was used on cattle, criminals, and packing crates.

From Verb to Noun.

The word became a noun for something burned on – an identifier.

Harley Procter, one of the founders of Procter & Gamble (P&G), burned a moon symbol onto his soap crates for easy identification on the shipping dock.

A brand became an identifier, primarily for business purposes, and sometimes for legal protection of an invention.

With the American Trademark Act of 1870, it became a legal symbol of good will.

The Trade Mark Association became official in 1878.

In 1905, Congress passed legislation establishing trademarks as the first evidence of ownership.

A brand was *"a name, term, symbol or design – or a combination of these elements that is intended to clearly identify and differentiate a seller's products from a competitor's products."*[1]

Originally, brand names came from four general areas: family names, locations, patriotic symbols, or synthetic names.

From Noun to Verb.

Over time, this original, narrow definition grew to include the process of marketing these branded products or services.

To "brand" something or "put your brand on it" was a positive affirmation of product quality.

"Brand new" meant right from the manufacturer.

John Philip Jones, an internationally known ad professor, describes this evolution: *"the branding process developed a purpose and importance beyond this simple legal role… it suggested a guarantee of homogeneity and product quality to buyers of a brand."*[2]

From Noun to Verb to Concept.

Today, the concept of "brand" has grown even further.

Today, the concept of brand encompasses everything from products more than 100 years old to cutting-edge marketers whose products are **"intellectual property."**

A brand can be an idea. An idea can be many things.

Today, a brand can be a worldwide media conglomerate, a rock band's logo, the latest Web site, or a box of detergent that may have the same basic formula but a different brand name – depending on the country where it's marketed.

Brands do more than differentiate – they add meaning.

They even seem to add life and personality. As French ad executive Jean Louis Dru noted, *"When you go from a product to a brand, you're moving from an object to a person."*[3]

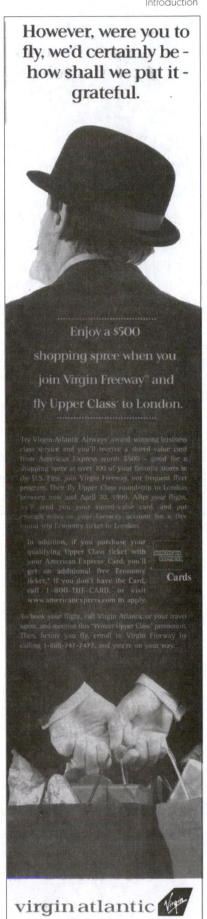

Brand Equity.

Marketing author David Aaker notes:

"Brand equity is an accumulation of intangibles."

Brand equity is *"a set of assets and liabilities linked to a brand, its name, and symbol that add to or subtract from the value provided by a product or service to a firm and/or to that firm's customers."*[4]

Adding up the Intangibles.

Many things contribute to brand equity: Some aspects are *fact-based* – like price and size.

Some aspects are *visible* and *tangible* – such as the styling of an automobile or a fashion item.

Some are *historical* – reputation or our own previous experience.

Some are *subjective* – feelings about the ads, whether or not we like cheese, or someone else's opinion (and your opinion of that opinion).

"Some Useful Groupings."

Aaker groups brand factors and benefits in this way:

Brand Equity Factors:
- Brand Loyalty
- Name Awareness
- Perceived Quality
- Brand Associations (in addition to perceived quality)
- Other Proprietary Assets: Patents, Trademarks, Channel Relationships.

Equities Add Value to the Customer By Increasing:
- Confidence in the Purchase
- Use Satisfaction
- Enhanced Integration and Processing of Information.

Equities Add Value to the Marketer By Increasing:
- Brand Loyalty
- Prices/Margin
- Brand Extensions
- Trade Leverage
- Competitive Advantage
- Overall Efficiency and Effectiveness of Marketing Programs.

A brand is more than a name that identifies and differentiates. Today, it is an idea – a **concept**.

Our modern definition is this: *"A brand is a conceptual entity that focuses the organization of marketing activities – usually with the purpose of building equities for that brand in the marketplace."*

A brand is not just a product. A brand is more than a name or a trademark. *A brand is a concept.*

More Than Just Talk.

A brand isn't just what you say it is (if only it were that easy).

A brand is who you are, what you do, why you do it, and how. All those things add up to **brand equity**.

The Need for Building Brand Equity.

Each brand works at marketing itself. This involves adding equity in a variety of ways – building **brand equity**.

- Increasing sales builds equity. The brand sells more and it's worth more. Big brands are worth a lot.
- To the brand's owners, it also means adding equities such as greater profit margins or market share.
- It may be improving the functional qualities of the brand (taste, price, or product performance). Often, a brand's success is rooted in some sort of **functional superiority**.
- Building equity may be adding meaning to the brand through advertising, event sponsorship, or some other form of relationship building with the consumer.
- To accountants, this relationship with the marketplace is called **goodwill**. With big brands, this can show up as a big number on the balance sheet.

For all these reasons, a brand may have a value far greater than its sales. A number of years ago, Kraft was purchased for $13 billion – *this was 600% more than book value!*

Think about that. Less than 20% of the purchase price was for factories and inventory. Over 80% was for the current and future value of Kraft brands. Wow!!

Negative Brand Equity.

Sometimes, equities can be negative or mixed.

After unfavorable news reports, Audi took years to overcome perceived product negatives that seriously affected its ability to charge higher prices for its cars.

Though its name clearly communicated low fares, ValuJet had to abandon its well-known brand name after a dramatic plane crash and much negative publicity.

Negatives so outweighed positives that starting over with a new name was judged a better marketing strategy than rebuilding a brand that had literally gone down in flames.

Do you know their current brand name?

As the reputation of Japanese manufacturing quality grew, the value of a brand name was clearly dramatized. A TV with the Hitachi name on it was sold for $20 more than the same TV with the General Electric name on it.

In this product category, a Japanese brand name had more positive equity than an American one. Times change.

What Does a Brand Mean?

A BRAND CAN MEAN DIFFERENT THINGS to different audiences. But the key is that it has meaning. As James Twitchell said in *AdCult USA*, "*Advertising is the folklore of a commodity culture.*"

It all depends on your perspective.

What a Brand Means to a Marketer.

To a marketer, a brand is a business unit.

Modern marketers are often organized around more than one of these "conceptual entities." They're usually located within the marketing department and called **brand groups**.

Origin of the Brand Management System.

This **brand management** system was first put forth by **Neil McElroy** at Procter & Gamble in 1931. At the time, he was a young marketer working on P&G's "second soap," Camay.

McElroy proposed developing a brand management team for each brand – the groups would actually compete with each other.

This system was adopted by a few multibrand marketers.

It did not become common until 20 years later.

If the organization has only one brand, then the brand and the marketing department may be the same thing.

Some brands, such as Virgin, now go across a number of product **categories** – with totally separate business units. (Why not go to the 'Net and look up all the different businesses that are part of the Virgin brand?)

Once, Apple meant computers. Then, they expanded the brand into music and phones. Now, what does the Apple brand mean to you?

Marketing has become more important at every company, and a brand is recognized as a key asset.

What a Brand Means to an Advertising Agency.

To an agency, a brand is a client.

To an agency, the marketer or the marketer's brand will be an "account." When asked, "What accounts do you work on?" agency people may list the names of the brands that they work on – or the name of the multibrand marketer.

Developing communications for brands is the most important thing an ad agency does. When done right, these communications in themselves can add value to the brand.

As Twitchell observes further, *"If goods are hardware, meaning is software, and advertising writes most of the software."*

The channel for these brand communications is the media.

These companies have their own view of brands.

Neil McElroy. In 1931, as a young marketer on P&G's "second soap," he proposed the brand management system that became the model for modern marketing organizations. In 1957, President Eisenhower put him in charge of the Defense Department.

Design as Strategy.

One reason for Apple's success is performance at the design level.

GUI.

The Graphic User Interface made Macs easier-to-use – even after Microsoft went GUI with windows.

Typography.

Better use of type gave Apple a foothold in desktop publishing and graphics.

Cool Products.

It's obvious, isn't it?

New Markets. New Media. Here, a brand-new business magazine appeals to a new kind of business audience with an issue titled "The Brand Called You."

Brand New Meanings. To a consumer, brands are a language – a meaning system.

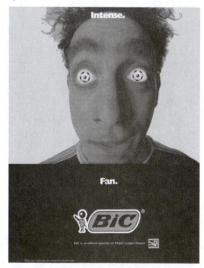

Old Brands. New Customers. Brands work hard to connect with new younger customers. Why? Because younger consumers are often establishing lifetime brand preferences.

What a Brand Means to a Media Company.

To a media company, a brand is a customer.

Media companies do many things in addition to providing ad space. Yet, it is advertising that "pays the bills."

That's why a media company is always concerned about being an effective advertising environment for brands.

In most cases, a healthy advertiser base is the key to a healthy media business. At one time, *PC Magazine* generated 4,000+ ad pages a year. Then the business changed. Even though almost as many read the magazine, it ran into trouble because there were fewer advertisers. Media often play an intermediate role between their reader base and their advertiser base.

A Unique Type of Brand – an Entertainment Brand

There are some brands that you can't exactly buy at a store – yet they may be some of your favorites.

Your favorite rock group or sports team – or that cool new movie with the souvenir cup you kept after visiting a fast food restaurant or a convenience store – these are **Entertainment Brands.**

What a Brand Means to a Consumer.

To a consumer, brands are a language – a meaning system.

To a consumer, for whom the brand exists, it is a way to identify and categorize products. Brands are signs with meaning. Over time, consumers add to this identification and categorization.

So, each "word" in their vocabulary adds meaning.

This is "building brand equity." For example, when we "consume" advertising for Nike, this communication adds to the sum total of all our knowledge about this brand.

The symbols and attitudes in this communication are also associated with other Nike branded products.

Some of these symbols, like Michael Jordan, have become hugely valuable brands in their own right.

In his book, *The Marketing Imagination,* Harvard's Theodore Levitt notes, *"A great many generically undifferentiated consumer goods are operationally differentiated by means of branding…"*

Twitchell observes further in *AdCult, "whatever else advertising does, one thing is certain; by adding value to material, by adding meaning to objects, by branding things, advertising performs a role historically associated with religion."*

Hmmm … makes you think, doesn't it?

Clearly, a brand can mean a lot of different things.

It all depends on what business you're in, who you're talking to, and who you happen to be.

Now let's take a slightly deeper look at all the businesses that are organized around brands today.

Four Business Groupings

THE BUSINESS OF BRANDS consists of four business groupings: marketers, advertising agencies, media companies, and a group we characterize as marketing services suppliers.

Understanding these four business groupings is one of the keys to understanding this book. The fourth grouping, marketing services suppliers, features public relations, sales promotion, direct, event marketing, and other specialties, such as promotional products.

Now let's discuss them in more detail.

1. Marketers Are Organizations that Promote Brands.

Marketers may have only one brand, or they may be "multi-brand marketers." Until recently, McDonald's, basically, had one brand.

Recently, they purchased other restaurant brands. *Chipotle*, for example, is currently operated by the McDonald's Corporation, but it is a separate brand, with most business functions, including marketing, totally separate.

However, the organization is still able to leverage their skill and experience in many areas of restaurant and franchise operations.

The Campbell's Soup Company has a few brands. P&G has a lot.

Marketers May Be Companies that Manufacture Brands.
Manufactured products that are used up and repurchased on a regular basis are referred to as **packaged goods.**

These products usually come in a package.

Manufactured products that last a long time and are purchased infrequently, like cars and washing machines, are referred to as **durable goods.**

Each demands a different type of marketing and advertising.

Parent Brands.

We may be very aware of the company and have it be part of the brand – Kellogg's Raisin Bran, Special K, etc.

Or, we may be less aware of the company.

For example, P&G does not make a big deal of their name with consumers. They make so many brands in so many product categories that they feel it could be counterproductive.

After all, did the fact that they make soaps and detergents make you think Jif peanut butter tastes better?

P&G didn't think so, either. (Recently, they sold Jif to Smuckers.)

This can vary. Campbell's wants its name on soups and sauces – not on Pepperidge Farm Cookies. When they owned Swanson Frozen Dinners, if the dinner had a soup, Campbell's would appear, as would Pepperidge Farm if there was a dessert.

Campbell's Brands:

Here is a current list:

- Campbell's Soups
- Franco-American
- Godiva
- Goldfish
- Pepperidge Farm Cookies
- Prego
- Spaghetti-Os
- V8

P&G Brands:

Here is a partial list:

Always	Attends
Bold	Bounce
Bounty	Camay
Cascade	Charmin
Cheer	Clairol
Clearasil	Cover Girl
Crest	Dawn
Dreft	Downy
Era	Febreze
Folgers	Gain
Gleem	Hawaiian Punch
Head & Shoulders	
Ivory	Joy
Max Factor	Mr. Clean
Oil of Olay	Old Spice
Pampers	Pepto-Bismol
Pert	Pringles
Puffs	Scope
Secret	Spic & Span
Sunny Delight	Sure
Tampax	Tide
Vidal Sassoon	Zest

Get some fun out of life

Co-Branding Examples:

Brand (Parent)	Manufacturer
Green Giant (Pillsbury)	**Tyson**
Healthy Choice (ConAgra)	**Kellogg's**
Taco Bell (YUM Brands)	**Kraft** (Phillip Morris)

Co-Branding. Starbucks Ice Cream

Retail Brands.

Retail sub-brands may be either products sold by the parent company or alternate retail channels run by the parent company.

Gap, Inc.	Old Navy
	Gap
	Banana Republic
Sears	Craftsman
	Die Hard
	Kenmore
Wal-Mart	Sam's Club
	Sam's Choice
	White Cloud
	(bought from P&G!)

Franchises & Bottlers.

Here, the parent company controls brand communications, although local companies, dealers, or distributors often fund the programs.

Ace Hardware

Anheuser-Busch

Amoco

Baskin-Robbins

Coca-Cola

Holiday Inn

Kinko's

Pepsi-Cola

YUM Brands:

    KFC, Pizza Hut, & Taco Bell

True Value Hardware

VISA

The California Raisin Growers *built their brand – raisins – with the pop tune* "I Heard It through the Grapevine." (You can view it in the Theater at www.adbuzz.com)

Many marketers are the result of mergers and acquisitions.

Kellogg's now manufactures and markets Eggo waffles, and P&G is now the parent of Old Spice.

Superbrands.

A few brands may be referred to as **superbrands**.

Nabisco's Oreo cookies, all by themselves, represent about 13% of the cookie market. While superbrand is a subjective term, when the brand can thrive outside its initial product category, it is on the way to becoming a superbrand.

Co-Branding.

Another new type of manufacturer may not make all their brands; ConAgra in Omaha developed the Healthy Choice brand name, but doesn't make all the products.

But you will find Kellogg's manufacturing and marketing Healthy Choice cereals. This is called **co-branding.**

Ingredients can also be brands – like Nutrasweet and Intel.

Marketers May Be Groups of Companies.

Pepsi-Cola and their bottler groups around the world and McDonald's and their franchisees are examples.

VISA and MasterCard, which may include competing banks, are cooperative marketing organizations.

Gasoline companies were early practitioners of this approach, as were certain other licensed products, like Roman Meal bread.

The Role of Field Marketing.

Often, these companies practice a type of marketing that demands implementing programs in local markets or "in the field."

This is known as **field marketing**.

Beverage companies like Pepsi-Cola, Coca-Cola, major beer companies, and franchise organizations like McDonald's will have a national network of **field marketing representatives.**

Sometimes their ad agencies also have **"field reps."**

Marketers May Be Service Providers.

Airlines, banks, insurance companies, or wireless carriers are examples. This is a unique type of marketing because the product may be an **intangible,** such as a service.

As a college student, you will find many service marketers eager to offer you credit cards and phone service.

Marketers May Be Retailers.

Although they may also sell branded products, retailers are brands in themselves – with their own marketing activities.

Many even have their own brands – often called **private label** – such as Sears Craftsman tools. Or Wal-Mart products like Sam's Choice Cola or Walgreen's Dandruff Shampoo.

Retailing is a marketing category undergoing major shifts.

Better information, such as **UPC codes** (those bar codes you see getting scanned at the checkout counter), has made retailers smarter and more powerful marketers.

Meanwhile, the rise of retailer brands is causing marketers like Sears to consider the right emphasis between their overall brand name (Sears) and their well-known sub-brands (Craftsman, Kenmore, DieHard, etc.).

Walgreen's now has an advertising campaign that features their private label products. Their theme is "The *brand* America trusts."

Retailers are changing all the time. Once the Gap was a small chain of clothing stores that featured Levi's and other casual clothes. Today, they can set fashion styles on their own – and the company now has more than one retail brand.

Marketers May Be Organizations.

In today's world, agricultural co-operatives and industry groups may be brand marketers. The California Raisin Growers, the California Orange Growers (Sunkist), the National Pork Council (*"The Other White Meat"*), the Dairy Council (*"Got Milk?"*), and the Cotton Council (*"The Fabric of Our Lives"*) are examples familiar to most of us.

Marketers May Be Government Bureaus.

Countries, states, and regions may also have "brands," particularly where tourism is important. Examples are countries like Jamaica and the Bahamas, and state tourism boards.

They all use brand marketing tools.

So do other product categories, such as milk (the milk mustache campaign is audited by the US Department of Agriculture) and orange juice (the Florida Citrus Board).

As the result of lawsuits, tobacco companies now fund anti-smoking campaigns.

Nonprofit Groups Are Marketers.

The Red Cross, United Way, or Children's Miracle Network (an innovator in **cause marketing**) are brand marketers.

On the local level, organizations such as local arts groups are trying to establish their brands in their communities.

Politicians Are Marketers.

Like it or not, elected officials, and those who want to be elected, are involved in marketing and advertising.

Think about it. The competition for consumer "votes" at the cash register is similar to the competition at the ballot box.

The American marketplace is a natural outgrowth of the open marketplace of ideas central to our concept of democracy – where people and ideas compete.

So, for better or worse, the techniques of brand marketing are an integral part of the electoral process. Candidates' organizations treat their candidate in much the same way that brand groups treat their brands.

"ReBranding Britannia."

"New Labour, new Britain … Tony Blair's first act as Britain's new prime minister was to launch an international campaign to rebrand the UK as a nation for the 21st century.

"Out go bowler hats and fox hunting; in comes fashion, new media, and multiculturalism."

Here are some of the brains behind Britain's image makeover:

Geoff Mulgan – his book, *Britain™*, argued that Britain should rebuild itself by rebranding itself.

Mark Leonard – *Britain™* co-author is "unofficial rebrander-in-chief." He's a researcher who states, *"The key priority is to define a shared ethos – and shared stories – to reflect the best of what Britain has become…"*

British Brand Stories.

Here is their new brand position:

- A hub of fashion and design.
- A destination for entrepreneurial immigrants.
- A tradition of "fair play" makes it a good place to do business.

There's Even A New Slogan.

It's out with *"Rule Britannia."*

Now it's *"Cool Britannia."*

Other British Brand Managers.

Others also play a part:

Lord Melvyn Bragg – one of the first media peers – hosts a TV arts show.

Waheed Ali – an openly gay Asian businessman, Lord Ali is co-founder of *Planet 24*, a TV production company and media advisor to the prime minister. He sits on Panel 2000 – a committee to promote business and tourism.

Noel & Liam Gallagher of the British rock band Oasis, supported Blair's winning campaign.

Another New Brand – Spain.

Spain rebranded itself – using modern art!

Juan Miro's painting *España* became the national logo – a bright, friendly modern look for post-Franco Spain.

Now, even nations are brands competing in the international marketplace.

Wired, Oct. 1998
Fast Company, Feb.-Mar. 1999

HuckChuck

Here, Republican candidate Mike Huckabee uses humor and traditional ad techniques to give his endorsement by movie star Chuck Norris extra likability.

Remember, in today's major elections the bulk of campaign funds that are raised go for… advertising.

And some nights, the major political story is some new ad from some old candidate.

And, in today's major elections, the bulk of campaign funds go for… advertising.

Even Rock Bands Are Brands.

Think about your favorite band. There's probably a cool logo and some merchandise you can buy. Bands have been viewed as brands ever since the Beatles, who became TV shows, movies, lunch boxes, and, of course, music.

Today, concert tours, sponsorships, and merchandising are all part of a band's brand marketing.

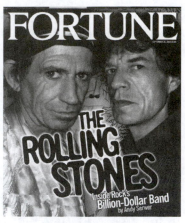

Bands are Brands.

This will continue as entertainment and entertainment brands become an even more important part of our economic product.

Now, even celebrities, like Michael Jordan, are brands.

Finally, You Are a Brand.

In *Fast Company*, management guru Tom Peters described what it takes for success in today's marketplace. The title of his article – "The Brand Called You."

"Regardless of age, regardless of what business we happen to be in, all of us need to understand the importance of branding. We are CEOs of our own company: Me Inc. To be in business today, your most important job is to be head marketer for The Brand Called You."

We'll cover this in our conclusion – "You & Your Career."

2. Advertising Agencies Are the Most Important Suppliers of Brand-Building Communications.

It's changing, but advertising is still one of the most important ways we get information about products and their benefits.

It is also one of the most important ways we add "meaning" to brands. John Philip Jones notes, *"A brand is a product that provides functional benefits plus added values that some consumers value enough to buy."* Most advertising is done by ad agencies.

Advertising agencies are unique organizations.

Their primary "product" is advertising, but they also provide other types of marketing communications and marketing services.

In fact, advertising agencies were the birthplace of much of modern marketing.

Advertising Adds Value to Brands.

More than fifty years ago, James Webb Young of J. Walter Thompson noted the benefits of *"the use of advertising to add a subjective value to the tangible values of a product – for subjective values are no less real than tangible ones."*

A product has a functional purpose; a brand offers something more – ranging from a guarantee of superior quality to the feelings of those who use the product.

Building brands costs a great deal of time and money.

Those best at accomplishing this have been ad agencies.

Advertising agencies will be covered in Chapter Five.

3. Media Companies Are Brand Information Channels.

Historically, media have been viewed as an independent force in our society, with the mission of providing information (and entertainment) to our society.

But … *media also have a key role in marketing.*

Communicating through media channels is an integral part of the branding process. And media companies compete fiercely with each other for audience share and advertising revenue.

Today, the vast majority of American media are supported by income from advertising. *In many ways, their mission has shifted from delivering media content to audiences to delivering audiences to advertisers.*

Carol Marin, a respected TV news anchor, made these comments: *"There is so much emphasis on marketing and demographics. When you decide the target of the information before it's information at all, the news-gathering process is already perverted."*

Marin continued, *"When you zone a newspaper, when you target a TV audience, then you start thinking what do women 18 to 40 want.*

The problem I have is that it automatically narrow-casts.

In the process, you begin to dumb down the news."[5]

This is yet another type of media evolution. We'll talk about it more in Chapter Three, "Advertising & Society" and Chapter Six, "The World of Media."

Most American Media Are 100% Advertising Supported.

This group includes: television networks, local TV stations (except public TV), commercial radio (AM and FM), advertising-only media such as outdoor, and other "out-of-home" advertising.

This group also includes "niche" magazines (sent free of charge to select reader targets) and local free newspapers.

All these media vehicles are free to us because 100% of their revenue comes from advertising or similar sponsor support.

Some Media Depend on Ads for More than 50% of Income.

This group includes most newspapers, most magazines, and some cable TV. Their revenue is provided in varying proportions by readers and subscribers, as well as advertisers.

Some cable TV channels are supported by viewer fees, some are partially supported by those viewer fees, and some are advertiser-supported and provided free to cable carriers.

And when the advertising environment shifts, there are big changes in the media world. For example, newspapers' size and influence is shrinking as resources move to the Internet and other new media.

One result of that is that traditional divisions between the editorial and business sides of newspaper operations are eroding.

A few years ago, in a reorganization of the *Los Angeles Times*, former publisher Mark Willes stated, *"I have suggested strongly that the newsroom needs to know and understand the people in our advertising*

Big Media Brands.

Question: What do all of these media brands have in common?

Answer: they're all part of the Walt Disney Company – where almost 35% of revenue is from "creative content."

Bonus: What TV network is owned by Disney?

Answer: ABC.

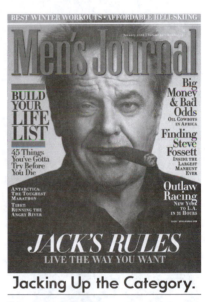

Jacking Up the Category.

Some categories go up.

Some categories go down.

In 2007, ad pages in the Men's Lifestyle category were up 13%.

Men's Journal was up 16%.

"I'm a Batman Slut."

Batman isn't just a comic book super-hero – he's a Time-Warner entertainment brand.

Joel Schumacher, director of not-one-of-the-best Batman movies, *Batman and Robin*, said, *"I'm a Batman slut. I'm new to the world of marketing and tie-ins, but I embrace it."*

Kenner Toy executives sat in on meetings to plan their toy line.

Batman and Robin included deals with Kellogg's, Taco Bell, Pepsi, Apple, Kenner, and Amoco. Schumacher noted, *"Without marketing dollars, it may never have been made."*

These franchises are so valuable, even after some not-so-successful movies, this entertainment brand came roaring back with *The Dark Knight*.

Entertainment Brands Build Winning Promotions.

Maybe you won't run right out for an Iron Man Slurpee cup, but they add news and entertainment value, as well as decor – with movie poster–like promotions.

department." He continued, *"And there has been more than one person who has pointed out the wall between the newsroom and the advertising department. And every time they point it out, I get a bazooka and tell them if they don't take it down, I'm going to blow it up!"*

This was a dramatic change in the public statements of newspaper management. It didn't work. But it signals that the media world is changing dramatically.

As media evolves you will continue to see these sorts of activities as media works to meet the needs of a changing world.

Today, even public TV and radio derive significant support from some sort of paid sponsorship.

Other Media Channels.

Although it may not have occurred to you, your telephone and mail-box are media channels. So are your computer and cell phone.

New media vehicles, like the Internet, are beginning to depend more and more on marketing for revenue.

In total, advertising dollars pay for a high percentage of the media you "consume."

Media Vehicles Are Also "Brands."

Media must market itself to be able to "deliver" audiences to advertisers. Think about that next time you get a magazine subscription renewal, watch a promo for a TV show, or see a billboard for your favorite radio station.

Big Media. Big Brands. "Entertainment Brands."

Media companies have been growing and merging.

Some examples are Rupert Murdoch's News Corporation (which includes FOX Network, the other Fox cable channels, and a number of other media properties), ABC/Disney, and the mega-media entity called Time-Warner.

Time-Warner includes print media such as *Time, People,* and *Sports Illustrated,* as well as broadcast properties like HBO and Turner Network (TBS, TNT, CNN, Cartoon Network, and others). New ventures like the CNN/SI cable channel combine two brands – CNN and *Sports Illustrated.*

Music, movies, and book publishing make Time-Warner a player in virtually every part of the entertainment world.

Look at how Time-Warner leverages a property like Batman – an **entertainment brand.** This will be covered in more detail in Chapter Six, "The World of Media."

4. Marketing Services – Part of the Marketing Marketplace.

The Business of Brands has one more component – with a lot of different pieces. This category covers a wide range of unique companies that have one thing in common – providing a necessary service for marketers, ad agencies, or media companies.

Here are some of the types of companies we'll look at:

- **Direct marketers**
- **Event marketers**

- **Market research firms**
- **Media buying companies**
- **Public relations (PR) firms**
- **Sales promotion firms**

While most are hired by marketers, these companies may hire each other. For example, a sales promotion firm like Frankel might hire a PR firm to help make its name better known to prospective clients.

Example: Media Companies

Media companies may use a number of specialists in programming, research, sales, graphic design, and ad campaigns.

You may have noticed the same ads and "ID package" for a different radio station in a different city.

The ad campaign may even be part of a larger package – the entire radio format.

We'll look at this interesting range of specialized suppliers in Chapter Seven, "Marketing Services."

How Big Is The Business of Brands?

WITH ALL THOSE DIFFERENT BUSINESSES, let's try to wrap our minds around some of the dollar amounts that go for marketing in the US economy.

About $850 Per Person.

In 2007, total expenditures for advertising alone were estimated at $283.9 billion. (You can get the latest update at www.mccann.com.)

Looking at it by media, 23% is TV (national, local, and cable), 15% is newspapers, and over 21% is direct mail.

Just think of the cost of your media consumption – your TV and radio, the stuff in your mailbox, and so on.

We have a population of about 301 million. Let's do the math…
It comes to about $942 for every person in the US!

And that's not all…

Promotion Expenditures.

There's another very important type of marketing expenditure – **sales promotion**. Promotional expenditures include such things as coupon redemptions, trade discounts, contest prizes, premiums, and costs related to event marketing.

In some categories, the total figure for trade promotion can be almost three times bigger than the amount for advertising!

It's a lot of money. For example, think of automobile rebates.

Other Marketing Expenditures.

There are other costs, as well. A company's sales force can be a very big part of the marketing effort.

So are all the costs of marketing department salaries, computers, marketing information, and meetings – like trade shows.

For some small companies, salaries for sales and marketing staff will be a high percentage of the total marketing budget.

Virgin – a "SuperBrand."

Richard Branson dropped out of high school at 16 to start a magazine called *Student*. Over the next 30 years, he built the brand we know as Virgin.

Virgin is a *superbrand* – a group of companies that includes movie theaters, "mega-stores," an airline, a travel agency, tour packagers, hotels, trains, a cola… even a mutual fund.

(Continued on next page)

Virgin (cont.)

The first *Student* magazine was a failure. So was a second. Then he built a mail order record business called Virgin (picked because he and his partners were novices at business).

Over the next 14 years, it became one of Britain's best-known record labels. Then, he began to diversify.

First, Virgin Airlines, using a name already well-known and popular with many Britons.

He sold the record company to build a war chest for his airline, and then he expanded aggressively, with outrageous publicity stunts (his balloon exploits are best known), numerous investment partners, and a single brand name – Virgin.

Time observes, *"Despite the bravado, Branson is as traditional as high tea when it comes to the most critical asset of the company: the brand.*

"He absolutely believes in the power of brands, much the way that P&G or Coke does.

"This belief is at the core of the empire, and the reason the Virgin name has been extended to businesses as different as vodka and insurance."

Branson says, *"Consumers understand that all the values that apply to one product – good service, style, quality, value, and fair dealing – apply to the others."*

This power has attracted investors. Core assets are brand awareness, a winning image, and an ability to add brand values to a variety of ventures.

Businesses include everything from a blimp company to a one-stop bridal shop – Virgin Brides.

Virgin Direct offers financial services with a lower cost base, and there's even a railroad! *(continued)*

See how it adds up? The total for The Business of Brands is huge!

Marketing isn't just an important part of overall economic activity, it's critical for virtually every company that does business.

"World Brands" and "Superbrands."

Some brands that are familiar to us are also familiar around the world. McDonald's, SONY, Mercedes-Benz, and Nike are examples of brands that have become **world brands.**

Other marketers, such as P&G, UniLever, and GM market around the world with a variety of brand names.

For example, the design of GM's Pontiac LeMans was from their Opel Division and manufactured in Korea. US car. French name. German design. Made in Korea.

Virgin is another fascinating example. It shows how far you can go with a brand concept.

Superbrands.

We know a superbrand when we see one.

It's usually a very well-known and popular brand. Often, the brand name can be used across product categories. Calvin Klein, Jack Daniels, and Oreo are superbrands.

Nike has become a superbrand.

So has the NBA. David Stern of the NBA had this to say: *"We believe that we have 30 sub-brands: the NBA and 29 teams. Say 'NBA,' and it means different things to different people. If, for instance, you're in Italy and say 'NBA,' people might think Michael Jordan and the Chicago Bulls… or Grant Hill and the Pistons."*

What's a Brand?

As you can see, the brand idea has evolved dramatically.

Today, it's a product. It's a concept. It's a way of thinking.

And, it's a way of doing business.

Today, as Richard Branson demonstrates, it's almost anything you want it to be.

Key Concepts

Okay, we're going to stretch your brain a bit.

Don't worry, you can handle it.

We're going to introduce you to key concepts that will show up, in various aspects, throughout the book. They are:

Brand-Building and IMC. There are a number of ongoing processes here – and they're usually all going on at once.

The Challenge of Change. In today's marketplace, we have to deal with change that's faster than ever. Understanding change and working in a changing environment is something you'll have to become comfortable with.

Evolution and "The Media Age." One of the biggest changes is happening in the media world that we all swim in. This, all by itself, is having a huge impact on The Business of Brands.

The Importance of Ideas. Thoughts can be as important as things – often even more important.

As you might imagine, many of these key concepts are connected, but let's try to discuss them one by one…

Brand-Building & IMC.

THE THIRD SECTION OF THIS BOOK will focus on how all these different companies work together to build brands.

Three Interrelated Concepts.

Three interrelated concepts are key. We mentioned two already:

• **The three fundamentals of "IMC"**
• **A three-stage cycle of planning, implementation, and evaluation**

Now here's a new concept to think about…

• **"Creative destruction"**

This concept is critical for understanding today's ever-changing marketplace.

Creative Destruction.

The Austrian-born economist **Joseph Schumpeter** was the first to describe this driving force of capitalism and the marketplace.

Think about it. As we create things in our marketplace, other things are destroyed. As we create an automobile industry, the horse and buggy industry must change or die.

This cycle of change is a reality you must understand.

Your career may begin with a growing company that's creating exciting new opportunities.

Then, ten years later, when everything seems wonderful, you may find a new idea, a new company, and a new industry changing your fortunes almost overnight.

In The Business of Brands, the constant is change.

Some companies and brands can last for a century – others can't. Hold that thought.

Okay, now we'll look ahead to Section Three.

Joseph Schumpeter

The Three Fundamentals of IMC.

The three fundamentals of Integrated Marketing Communications (IMC) are marketing, communicating, and integrating.

▲ **Marketing** – goal-setting and strategy development.

● **Communicating** – developing and executing the communication tactics needed to meet marketing goals.

■ **Integrating** – coordinating, prioritizing, and optimizing all the activities needed to meet marketing goals. This is the best way to describe the process. Simply put, smart marketing is "spending your marketing dollars more effectively than your competition." That's the heart of integration.

Almost all marketers are doing all three things – usually all at once.

Virgin (cont.)

Branson likes to *"take on Goliath and give a pretty good value for the money."* He looks for *"industries that are over-charging the customer and a bit flabby."*

The Value of Publicity.
"He understands that a picture is worth a thousand words. And that newspapers don't have many interesting photos."

His hope? *"I'd like Virgin to become one of the most respected brands in the world."* He just might do it.

Source: "Of All That He Sells, He Sells Himself Best," *New York Times,* 6/1/97
"Many Times a Virgin," *Time,* 6/24/96

The Hindu God Shiva.

A creative force of destruction and genesis that is part of the ancient Hindu religion – and modern economics. Joseph Schumpeter described one of the key aspects of our economic system as *creative destruction.*

IMC – A Graphic Representation.

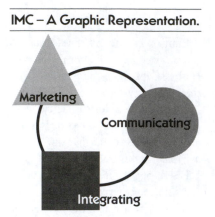

This might be helpful…

▲ **A vertical hierarchy** – prioritizing and objective setting. Deciding what is most important – that's **marketing**.

● **A circular loop** – sending the message, receiving input from the target. Connecting, getting feedback, and improving the message – that's **communicating**.

■ **A solid square** – finding the most effective footing for the program. Looking at all options and opportunities and then building it into a solid coherent program – that's **integrating**.

"Victory is my objective.
War is my strategy."
— Winston Churchill

The Three-Stage Cycle. "Easy as PIE."

These three fundamentals (marketing, communicating, integrating) operate in an ongoing cycle of planning, implementation, and evaluation. (Just remember PIE.)

This constant cycle is a driving force of all marketing activities:

• **Planning.** Decide what to do.

• **Implementation.** Do it.

• **Evaluation.** Measure what was done.

Then, figure out how to do it better. And start over.

Repeat.

The result of this is constant change in the marketplace. And, hopefully, constant improvement. Companies get smarter.

Planning becomes more effective.

Implementation becomes more efficient.

Evaluation becomes more accurate. And so on.

In this way, companies have integrated and internalized a controlled form of creative destruction into their operations.

Creative Destruction and Competition.

Today, this is the way almost all companies do business – from the smallest start-up to a huge multinational marketer.

Not only do these companies compete with other companies, they often compete within the company.

That was one of the innovations in Neil McElroy's brand management approach. At P&G, brand groups compete with each other as well as with the brands of competitors.

It's like that everywhere.

The result is ever-increasing improvements, greater efficiency, greater difficulty (because your competition is getting smarter, too), and virtually constant change. The more everyone tries to win, the more it changes the game.

As Kevin Kelly observes, *"Innovation is a disruption. Constant innovation is perpetual disruption."*[6]

It's a concept as old as the Hindu god Shiva and as new as tomorrow's hot new dot-com.

Section Three. From Planning to Implementation to Evaluation.

With that in mind, take another look at the sequence of Section Three:

Chapter Eight – Marketing and the Planning Process – this will show you how planning works in the real world.

Chapters Nine and Ten are about two kinds of implementation.

Chapter Nine – Creativity and Communication – is about creating effective messages for advertising and more.

Chapter Ten – Media and the Marketing of Messages – will show you how even the placement of those messages demands planning and creative skills.

Chapter Eleven – Evaluation and Integration – will show you ways that evaluation can stimulate more new thinking – and more integration. And that takes you back to planning again.

An Ongoing Process.

As you learn how The Business of Brands works, you'll see that decision making is an ongoing process, with programs in an almost constant state of evaluation and improvement.

The Challenge of Change.

IT'S ALL ABOUT CHANGE.

Since the world we're writing about changes every minute, here's how we'll try to help you keep up.

A Fast-Changing Present. A Faster-Changing Future.

It's easy for a textbook to cover what's already happened.

Predicting the future is tougher. But we'll try.

New Marketers, Agencies, Media, and Marketing Services.

Chapter Twelve will be about – "The Power of New Ideas."

We'll show you some of the latest changes in The Business of Brands and the power of ideas to affect that change.

But it's still hard for an old-fashioned technology like a textbook to keep up with all those changes. So…

Welcome to www.adbuzz.com.

Here we'll tell you how to find out more about what's happening now with a technology that updates easily and efficiently.

Want to know the latest? Check out www.adbuzz.com.

There are readings, resources, message boards, and study questions – even practice tests! And, of course, there's always Google.

The Speed of Change.

The marketplace has become one of the central drivers of change in our society. This is a major shift from the way businesses were run just a few decades ago.

Once upon a time, manufacturing capability was the key.

You'll see examples like King Gillette's razor blades and the Campbell Soup Company. The technology of manufacturing was once the basis for branded products. Today, it's marketing.

And, as Regis McKenna observes, *"Marketing Is Everything."*[7]

From Millennia to Months.

How fast are things changing? Look at it this way. Mankind began as hunter-gatherers – many thousands of years ago.

The Agricultural Revolution (approximately 8000 BC) dramatically changed how people lived. It lasted for thousands of years. During that time, empires rose and fell, but life for the average person went pretty much unchanged.

The Industrial Revolution was the second revolution.

It started a few hundred years ago – and its effects are still being felt in many parts of the world.

That revolution dramatically changed the life of the average person. Life was different for everyone. Work was different, too.

Now we're in a new revolution.

The Post-Industrial Revolution is the third revolution – with services and information increasing in importance.

Here are some of the different types of strategies used in The Business of Brands:

Marketing Strategy
Advertising Strategy
Media Strategy
Public Relations Strategy
Packaging Strategy
Sales Promotion Strategy
Alternative Strategy

The Gap transformed retail fashion by doing better on marketing basics – product, price, place, and promotion. They developed a strategy and then implemented it – growing their company from a $430 million chain of blue-jean shops to an $11 billion global enterprise!

Stronger Stores.

The Target brand successfully combines upbeat contemporary fashion and old-fashioned value.

Starbucks Family of Specialty Drinks

Cappuccino
(CAP-OO-CHEE-NO)

In-Store Communication.

Starbucks transformed the coffee experience by transforming the Five P's of coffee marketing. How did they address each of the Five P's?

"Creative Content."

When we pay for a movie ticket, we're paying for the "information" that's up on the screen

It began in the middle of the 20th century – primarily in the US, Europe, and Japan. It's going on right now – almost everywhere.

Author and futurist Alvin Toffler calls it *"The Third Wave."*

Now, each decade, each year, brings dramatic change.

Acceleration is almost exponential.

Moore's Law.

The pace of change is breathtaking.

One of the things driving change is the amazing growth of computing power. Do you know about "Moore's Law"? It's a surprisingly accurate prediction first made by **Gordon Moore,** former CEO of Intel.

Moore observed that computing power would double every 18 months while the cost of that power would be cut in half. And he was right!

Look at the change in price and performance of computer equipment, and the addition of computing power into cell phones, iPods, and automobiles.

Meanwhile, speed is affecting many other things.

For example, the success or failure of movies costing a hundred million dollars is measured in a few weekends.

And marketing, a process that feeds on change and information, has become one of the driving forces. It's "everything."

PowerShift – the Growing Importance of Information.

Now, as we begin the 21st century, we see amazing forces are at work as new technologies sweep across the globe.

In *PowerShift,* Alvin Toffler notes that the value of information is becoming as great or greater than the value of things.

Think about it. On a Friday night, the cost of a movie ticket is for the "information" that goes up on the movie screen. Disney calls it "creative content."

The value of the newspaper that provided you with the movie listings was the information in that newspaper, not the ink and paper. Movie companies paid media companies to deliver that information to you. (And, what happens if they're all the same company? Well, that's another big change.)

Driving Information.

For example, the car you drive is becoming "information rich."

More and more of the cost of a car is for the information in the microchips to tune radios, make engines more efficient, and power the tooling machinery and assembly robots.

Today, cars are becoming "chips on wheels."

From the phone at your ear to your TiVo to the computer on your desk, it's estimated that there are four times as many microprocessors as there are people on this planet.

And, as we add to this mass of technology and information, our society, our products, and our lives become "smarter."

Changing Channels.

Some of you may remember a time before there was a VCR or DVD player in virtually every home. Your parents can remember when you had to get up from your chair to change the channel.

Not that long ago, the average TV received only three or four channels. Not that long ago, the average student didn't have a computer, a modem, or an e-mail address!

But today, you take all these things for granted.

How do we say this? We're in the middle of a revolution that's changing the world, and you kind of think it's normal.

Well, believe us, this change is profound – nothing like it has happened before. It has done a lot more than change the way we listen to music and watch TV.

Media philosopher **Marshall McLuhan** made the point that as media evolves, so do we. Which brings us to our next key concept.

Evolution & "The Media Revolution."

You're familiar with the concept of evolution. It happens with animals, it happens with civilizations, and it happens with media.

In the case of media, technology tends to drive that evolution – but the impact can be revolutionary.

For example, the printing press.

As a society, it became possible for all of us to become readers – before that, books were precious. For the most part, we were "listeners" instead of "readers." And knowledge was in the possession of a very small and powerful group.

The evolution was to books, but the revolutions were larger than that. It changed Europe. It changed the world.

The Reformation happened, in many ways, because books could be written in the common language, and the Bible was no longer in the possession of a priestly class speaking in Latin. Literature became possible, as books could be printed in quantity.

And, across the Atlantic, the American Revolution was powered by the printing press, including those owned by one of the most successful businesspeople in that new land – Benjamin Franklin.

A quick review of the history of advertising shows an evolution of media from newspapers to magazines to radio to television. The evolving technology of media changed advertising.

And today, digital media is driving an evolution that's revolutionary.

The Impact of the Internet

As media evolves, every previous media form is impacted as well.

For example, since the First Edition of this book, we've seen newspapers go through two major changes in every market.

First, there has been a decline in the traditional "cash cow" of classified advertising.

The McDonald's Idea.

As one of the world's most powerful brands, their plans are built on delivering QSCV (Quality, Service, Cleanliness, Value) – and lots of advertising. This classic spot uses two NBA icons – Bird and Jordan.

The Nike Idea.

Keep pushing the barriers. This time – police barriers. Communications that connect are critical to Nike's success. So is a business plan that builds big ad budgets into every pair of shoes.

The Gap Idea.

Creative leaps for business breakthroughs. The Gap produced their own fashions and their own advertising – this gave them even more control over product, price, and promotion.

The Edsel...

was a Ford car in the '50s that was a resounding (and expensive) failure.

It missed on product, price, and people. Because of that, there was little that advertising could do to make it a success.

At the same time, a little car called Volkswagen had the right product, the right price, and the right advertising.

Think small.

The Volkswagen.

Innovative advertising that broke the mold was part of Volkswagen's successful brand-building.

The campaign was developed by the revolutionary creative ad agency Doyle Dane Bernbach.

Second, virtually every newspaper is working to develop Internet-based services.

Example: The Decline of Classified Revenue

If you wanted to rent, buy, or sell a house, the real estate section of your local newspaper was your primary media choice.

The same for puppies and pick-up trucks.

And, traditionally, classified advertising was very profitable for the newspaper.

Today, Internet search engines provide this service in every market and, for more specialized sales, other services such as eBay provide an efficient sales channel for specialty items.

Not surprisingly, this has had major impact on newspaper revenue.

The Addition of Online Editions

Newspapers have been working to develop new income streams based on the Internet.

For the most part, they have been more successful in developing the service than the revenue stream, but this is all still in process.

Most newspapers have some sort of online presence, and they have been working to provide some of those Internet-based classified services. Often, the traditional classified ad now also includes an online listing.

It's not necessarily great news for newspapers – but, then again, we don't have to cut down forests full of trees just to print classified ads – and that's not such a bad thing.

It's all media evolution at work.

Swimming in a New Media Environment.

This new technology also changes us.

When McLuhan said, "the medium is the message," he meant that it was not the individual telephone call, it was the overall concept of telephones – connecting us all. And now, with new mobile phones, that's changing us again, as we find ourselves in touch 24/7, with new media opportunities represented by those larger than ever screens and those more powerful than ever handheld computers we call mobile phones.

We're changing in other important ways as well.

The printing press changed us from listeners into readers.

The television changed us into viewers.

The copy machine and desktop technology lets us become publishers.

The Internet has allowed us to become broadcasters.

See what's going on? You've grown up with it.

So you don't always think about it, because the media is almost like the air we breathe. We swim in it. We navigate through it. We figure out the best way to get our messages to connect – whether it's checking with a friend for dinner when we're running late – or planning a major marketing communications campaign using all the powerful tools that are now available.

And all of that is making the world of media more exciting than it has ever been before.

It truly is The Media Revolution.

Convergence.

So, how will the next revolution turn out? It's hard to say, but we're seeing it now – and part of that process is called **convergence.**

Today, cable contains all TV plus movies and a bit of radio (the previous media forms).

As your TV converges further, it will merge with your mailbox (the e-mail version) and your computer.

So the Internet, TV, the news, magazine articles, and your favorite music will all be contained within the next media form.

Convergence is going on in many places. For example, the financial industry is converging as banks, brokerage firms, credit card issuers, and insurance companies each work to become full-service financial suppliers.

A few of them probably sent you a mailing this week.

Changing the Workplace.

Work and home will converge as fax and e-mail combine to make location less critical for many information workers.

The technological change now plugged into virtually every home in America has also impacted the workplace.

Look at any industry and you'll see dramatic change – from new biological technologies in agriculture to computerized machine tooling and shorter development cycles in manufacturing.

A driving force of all this change has been an explosive electronic evolution powered by silicon wafers that hold amazing amounts of processing power. Moore's Law at work.

From Steel to Oil to Silicon.

In the 19th century, steel was the measure of a country's might.

In the first half of the 20th century, oil and energy were driving forces, and new jobs grew from this shift.

Today, it's ideas. Electronics and information are reshaping our world. More than ever. Faster than ever.

What does that have to do with marketing? One of marketing's main forces is the implementation of information and technology for competitive advantage.

Improved technology (or a new idea – improved mental technology) is one of the ways you gain a competitive advantage.

That's why increased information is powering the cycle of planning, implementation, and evaluation.

Everywhere you look, traditional services, such as banking and accounting, are undergoing unprecedented change.

Your doctor and the local hospital are changing as market dynamics and the information revolution come to medicine.

Your grocery store now scans the UPC code of every item – and makes use of that information.

The Speed of Change – Computerized.
With computers, product life cycles are measured in months – instead of years.

"Marketing Is Everything."

In this classic *Harvard Business Review* article, Regis McKenna notes:

• Marketing is being transformed by the power of technology.

• Programmable computing power makes possible almost unlimited customer choice.

• Many companies will succeed by becoming "marketing partners" with their customers.

• Marketing is no longer just a function, it's the primary way everyone does business.

• Marketing is similar to quantum physics. A fad, for example, is like a wave that dissipates and becomes a particle.

• The line between products and services is eroding. Products, for example, have higher information content – a service. Meanwhile, services are working to turn their services into products.

• Marketing is moving from monologue to dialogue. Technology lets information flow in both directions.

• Marketing is now becoming everyone's job.

To Find Out More…

For a reprint of the complete article, ask for *Harvard Business Review* reprint #91138.

An Important Book.

Powershift by **Alvin Toffler** makes an important point. The value of information in our economy is becoming greater than the value of things. There has been a shift of power from manufacturing things to the creation of information – such as software or entertainment.

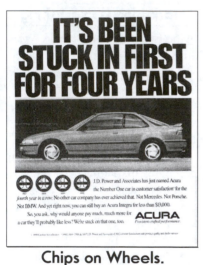

Chips on Wheels.

Today's cars are now "information rich."

That cozy bookstore is now a book/video/software superstore – or maybe it's a Web site. Your neighborhood drug store is now part of a network that tracks your prescriptions as it prepares the health insurance paperwork.

Good News for You.

At the same time, all of this convergence and technological change is making it more possible to respond to the needs of individuals.

Now you have more ways to "have it your way."

Marketing Evolution.

Regis McKenna noted that marketing has become an all-pervasive way of doing business and technology is causing marketing to evolve. *"Marketing evolves as technology evolves."*[8]

We'll see manufacturers evolve into marketers.

We're seeing marketing evolve from mass marketing to market segmentation to a diverse range of strategies.

Now, thanks to Dell and Gateway, you can have your computer the same way you have your pizza – made to order.

Changing Competition.

In every sector of the economy, there's more competition. And the driving force of more competition is – more marketing.

Fast as you can say "new and improved," marketers market new changes and others respond to those changes.

Changing Problems.

All of this generates new problems as it generates new opportunities. For example, information overload is a growing problem – and it's getting worse.

Today, it's easier than ever to generate the information, but can we understand it? That job may be getting harder.

And there are new shortages – time and attention.

Meanwhile…

It's a marketplace full of both uncertainty and excitement.

The bad news comes to those who work for a company undergoing "restructuring." The good news is the thrill of a new venture – and seeing your new home page, live and in color, on the Web.

The Importance of Ideas.

CREATIVITY is more than a clever commercial. It's about creating new brands and new businesses. It may be fun, but it's not easy.

Constant Tension.

In advertising and marketing, there's constant tension between "tried and true" and "brand new."

Every marketer is continually judging when to repeat current programs and when to do something new.

Jaded consumers who say "been there, done that" can make marketing a scary business. And it's always tempting to stick with what got you there (you hope).

But some of the greatest brand success stories have been based on ideas – major strategic and creative "leaps."

Successful Business Creativity.

Here are some interesting marketing examples:
- *Apple* changing the music industry with the iPod
- McDonald's expansion through franchising and "QSCV"
- Chrysler developing the minivan
- Gatorade broadening its brand from a narrow base
- Nike changing the game in athletic shoes
- The Gap and Calvin Klein changing fashion marketing
- Microsoft rapidly embracing the Internet
- Starbucks transforming the coffee experience

Each idea transformed the marketplace.

Let's look at them a bit deeper.

Ideas in Action!

- *Apple* put some simple controls on a flash drive and created the iPod. It changed listening habits and the music industry.

- McDonald's organization and operations integrate an unprecedented range of advertising programs that touch virtually every part of their target market. The creative leaps of the Big Mac and breakfast made huge business breakthroughs – these breakthroughs were first developed by franchisees.

- Lee Iaccoca, Chrysler's new chairman, was part of a campaign that reshaped the company's image – with new products as proof of that change. Though, in the automobile business, success might not last much more than one model year.

- Gatorade's involvement with the emerging sports marketing industry resulted in a powerful publicity program that reached virtually every athlete of every age.

- Nike reshaped how we view athletes with exceptional advertising from both Wieden & Kennedy and Chiat/Day. Just as important, they re-configured their "Five P's" to totally change the game of sports marketing.

- The Gap and Calvin Klein created innovative fashion imagery that touched us in new ways – without an ad agency!

- Microsoft opened new windows – expanding their brand to include a whole cable network – MSNBC.

While some may think they were aggressive to a fault, they survived and prospered in an industry littered with casualties.

- Starbucks produced an in-store environment that reinforced the concept of a cup of coffee as a personal "third place" between home and work.

So, even though marketing is full of risk-averse executives, one of the riskiest things to do in business is to miss a powerful new idea. Of course, the other riskiest thing in business is to pick the wrong new idea. Edsels anyone?

The Importance of Information.

The way businesses make judgments is with information.

That's why various types of marketing research, from discovering consumer insights, to understanding UPC scanner data are key for building brands.

New Channels. *They help create new businesses and new brands.*

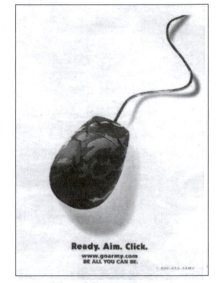

More Microprocessors Than People.
Here, an ad for the US Army.

It May Look like a Bus Bench.

But it's really a highly targeted media tactic for a Denver Internet service.

So, who's the bookstore of the future?

We have more titles than any other online bookseller. With over 8 million titles, we are nearly twice as large as amazon.com. Plus, you can save up to 40% off selected titles. So get online and get your book.

If we don't have your book, nobody does.

barnesandnoble.com
aol keyword:bn

New Distribution Channels. Change. Competition. More Change.

Here, a revolution on the Internet and a revolution in book retailing collide. Who will win? Everyone who likes to read.

You'll also see how the gathering and evaluation of information is, in itself, a creative and challenging task – not to mention a whole set of interesting career opportunities.

The Importance of Insight and Inspiration.

Finally, you need more than information. A smart marketer only looking at marketing information for the coffee industry a few years ago, would not have been able to see much potential.

The information would have shown a declining category, aging consumers, and a lot of price competition.

Yet Howard Schultz, in a Milan espresso bar, saw it so clearly that he was able to commit to his vision and create a vital new product category and an exciting new brand – Starbucks.

And, in his own small way, he changed the world.

Every insight, every improvement, changes things.

The good news is we make our brands better.

The bad news is we make it tougher for the next guy.

Well, now you've been introduced to this book. Let's have a quick review. And then you'll be ready for Chapter One.

Summary

HAVING READ THIS INTRODUCTION, you should have a clearer understanding of the following topics:

- **The Organization of this Book.** This introduction gave you a clear overview of the organization of the 12 chapters of this book. You know what's headed your way.
- **The Brand Concept.** We've discussed how brands have grown from a simple way of labeling goods to an organizing concept of business.
- **The Business of Brands.** You should know the four kinds of businesses that make up The Business of Brands: Marketers, Ad Agencies, Media, and Marketing Services.
- **The Brand-Building Process.** You've been introduced to the fundamental functions of IMC (marketing, communications, and integration) and the ongoing process of planning, implementation, and evaluation.
- **The Challenge of Change**. As the speed of change increases, we all have to understand that managing change has become a constant in business, in our economy, and your career path.
- **The Media Age.** One of the biggest changes is the current explosion of media forms – particularly the 'Net.
- **The Importance of Ideas.** As information becomes a more important part of our economy, new ideas become an even more important source of growth.

These are the things that the rest of this book will be about.

They may also be the things that the rest of your career will be about – in The Business of Brands.

About This Book...

RAPID CHANGE MAKES IT HARDER than ever to keep up.

It's true for people. It's true for textbooks.

That's why this book is also evolving with technology.

Because it's a book and it's a Web site: **www.adbuzz.com**.

Additional readings, news of important changes, hot links to Web sites you should visit, and even practice tests are all located at our Internet study hall – www.adbuzz.com.

From Grandfather Clocks to Digital Watches.

When your great grandfathers started their careers, chances are, their jobs didn't change much.

Chances are, your great grandmothers stayed at home with jobs that also stayed pretty much the same.

With each generation, change has come faster than ever.

Chances are, some of your parents, your friends' parents, or some of your relatives have been caught up in that change.

Sometimes for the better. Sometimes not.

That change will be a part of your life. Like it or not.

Career = a Sequence of Jobs.

Your career will be a sequence of jobs.

Sometimes they will be at one company; sometimes not.

Jobs come and go; a career grows. You'll have to grow, too.

You may need very different skills ten years from now than the ones you'll need for your first job.

What this book will do is provide you with an accurate picture of the "playing field" of marketing and the marketplace as this book went to press.

Keeping up with the changes will be up to you.

At the End of Each Chapter.

Most chapters will contain:
- A Summary of Key Points.
- Discussion Questions
- Exercises
- Concepts & Vocabulary

Your adbuzz.com Web site has:
- *Extra Readings*
- *A Message Board*
- *QuickTime Videos of TV Spots*
- *An Ad Gallery*
- *Study Tips – Like Text Files of Concepts & Vocabulary*
- *Links to Other Useful (and cool) Advertising Web Sites*

A Winning Team. *You have twelve top professors working with you. Here are three of them: Ann Maxwell of Oregon, who worked with the American Ad Museum for your history chapter; Jim Avery of Oklahoma, who is author of* Advertising Campaign Planning *and a member of the National Advertising Review Board; and Alice Kendrick of SMU, co-author of* Successful Advertising Research Methods.

Jim Marra – Your Career Counselor. *He's a professor, author, and former Head of the Temple Ad Sequence.*

Jim supervised the careers section. It's full of contributions from graduates making their mark in The Business of Brands. Take his advice and maybe you'll be in the next edition!

Discussion Questions:

Here are a few thoughts to get you started:

1. Brands.

Aside from the names of products, what examples of branding come to mind? Look around your dorm room or classroom. Any hats or T-shirts? What brand messages did you see on the way to class? What messages did you see when you went out last night?

2. The Business of Brands

Name four companies – each in a separate business type – in The Business of Brands.

3. The Brand Called You.

If you were a brand, how would you implement the three stages of the brand-building process to build your brand?
First, what planning would you do?
Second, what tactics would you implement?
Third, how would you evaluate your success?

4. The Challenge of Change.

What changes will you have to manage to prepare yourself for a business career?

5. The Media Age.

In your lifetime, list some examples of how your own media use has evolved.
What media have you used in the last 24 hours?
We discussed how newspapers have been affected by the Internet – how have other media channels changed?
List some ways in which the Internet has allowed all of us to become "broadcasters."

6. The Power of Ideas.

Name some ideas that have affected your view of things.
Give it some thought. Certainly you have some new ideas of how things work and what you want to do. What ideas – or products based on ideas – have changed your life?

7. Careers.

Name some jobs that might interest you working in The Business of Brands. Make a list.

Concepts & Vocabulary:

AT THE END OF EACH CHAPTER, you'll find a "Concepts & Vocabulary" review – because one of the best ways to understand any business is to understand the words they use.

For example, this is a list of some of the key words and concepts that were introduced to you in this introduction.

In just about every chapter, if you understand all of the concepts in the concept and vocabulary review, you have a pretty good handle on the chapter's contents.

A Few Words of Caution.

Many of these concepts are larger than these basic definitions. Use them as starting points.

Also remember that these definitions only apply to these words as advertising and marketing concepts. Many of these words mean other things in other places.

For example, look at the words "position" and "reach."

"Position" has more than one definition in the industry, while "reach" is a very specific technical measure.

Get in the habit of reviewing these definitions at the end of each chapter – they might be on the test.

In fact, you can probably count on it.

Here are key words and concepts from the introduction – in alphabetical order:

Advertiser – The company that pays for the advertising.

Advertising – Marketing messages in paid media.

Advertising agency – A company that specializes in creating and placing advertising. Advertisers are their clients.

Agricultural Revolution – 10-8000 BC. Development of *primary economic activity* – farming, mining, and simple manufacture.

Brand – 1. A name, term, symbol, or design – or a combination of these elements, intended to clearly identify and differentiate a seller's products from competitors'. 2. A conceptual entity that focuses the organization of marketing activities – usually with the purpose of building equities for that brand in the marketplace. 3. A verb representing activities – usually marketing activities – on behalf of the brand.

Brand equity – "Assets and liabilities linked to a brand, its name and symbol that add to or subtract from the value provided by a product or service to a firm and/or to that firm's customers."[9]

Brand group – Pretty much what it says. A group of professionals in a marketing organization with primary responsibilities for a brand.

Brand management – A form of marketing organization for multiple brands. First proposed and implemented by Neil McElroy at P&G. Now the industry standard.

Exercise: Tilapia Fishing for a New Name.

You know it as the "Kiwi Fruit."

Some clever marketers in New Zealand figured that the "Chinese Gooseberry" needed a new name.

So they called it the "Kiwi Fruit," and the more appealing name helped establish its popularity.

Your assignment: develop a new and more appetizing brand name for a farm-raised fish from Africa.

Right now, it's called Tilapia.

Think about what your client, The Tilapia Farmers of America, might want to call this fish to make it more popular and appetizing.

Along the way, what else might you do as a marketer to make your product more popular?

Think about it.

That's how brands are built.

"The Slimehead Is Good Today."

Or perhaps you'd like some Patagonian Toothfish? Not likely.

So these two fish were re-named – or re-branded.

The New Zealand Marketing Board, who renamed Chinese Gooseberries, went to work on Slimehead.

The result? Orange Roughy!

As for the Patagonian Toothfish… how does Chilean Sea Bass sound?

Yes, It Will Be on the Test.

In every chapter, basic concepts and related vocabulary will be a principle part of the tests.

Here are some study hints:

• **Flash Cards** – you can download a text file of vocabulary from the Web site and make your own study tools.

• **Practice Tests** are on the Web site – you can take them and see how you did.

• **Send us a message** – you might have a thought of your own to share.

You'll see a place in the lower right corner to click and send us an e-mail.

Reading/Resource List:

Each chapter will feature books and resources that will tell you more about the topics in this chapter.

In some cases, the same books will be mentioned in more than one chapter.

Generally, we will provide only title and author name, which is enough for today's search engines.

Some books mentioned are out-of-print, but available.

AdCult: The Triumph of Advertising in American Culture
by James Twitchell

An important book – we will refer to it throughout this book.

The Marketing Imagination
by Theodore Levitt

An important marketing thinker shares his thoughts.

What's in a Name? Advertising and the Concept of Brands
by John Philip Jones

A former JWT executive, now a professor of advertising at Syracuse, Professor Jones offers some of the most cogent thinking on modern advertising and how it works.

Category – Short for *product category*.

Cause marketing – Marketing activities that connect a brand with a cause or social movement.

Channel – 1. In terms of distribution, a series of relationships and logistics that result in a product becoming available. Example: the retail channel is a complex relationship of distributors, shipping, warehouses, and financial arrangements. 2. In media terms, it may be specifically a television broadcast channel or, in general, a way of reaching people.

Co-branding – Brand venture where two companies cooperate in the marketing of a product – usually one company manufactures another company's brand.

Communicating – Transmitting information from source to receiver.

Concept – In advertising, this refers to the idea behind the ad or ad campaign. In marketing, this refers to a brand's reason for being or its basic business strategy.

Convergence – The merging of a previously separate variety of technologies. For example, convergence has made your computer a typewriter, a printing press, a video editing machine, and an audio studio.

Copy – 1. The words in an ad. 2. Imitate. 3. Duplicate.

Copyright – Legal registration of intellectual property to protect ownership.

Copywrite – To create the words (copy) in an advertisement.

Durable goods – Products that last and are purchased (and re-purchased) infrequently. Examples: refrigerators, TVs.

Entertainment brand – Media-based brand that sells content as the product. Entertainment brands work to extend across numerous product categories and media channels.

Field marketing – Form of marketing organization and service that results in hands-on implementation of local marketing programs – commonly used by beverage companies and franchise organizations at both marketers and agencies.

Field marketing representative (field rep) – Person who works to implement local marketing activities, i.e., "in the field."

The Five P's – Basic elements of marketing: product, price, promotion, people, and place (distribution).

Goodwill – An accounting term related to placing a tangible dollar amount on intangibles, such as brand equity or the estimated lifetime value of the customer base.

Implementation – Doing it – the act of making it happen.

Industrial Revolution – About 1800 AD. Development of *secondary economic activity* – mass manufacture.

Intangible – Usually refers to a service, or something else that exists, but that you can't exactly touch.

Integration – Planning, prioritizing, coordinating, and managing a range of marketing functions in a holistic way.

Integrated Marketing Communications (IMC) – Management of the marketing function so as to optimize the range of marketing communications tools available.

Intellectual property – Ownable ideas or unique expressions of that idea. This means they have some sort of legal protection, such as a patent or trademark.

Internal audience – A company's employees and other key individuals who work for or with the company.

Marketer – Person or company involved in marketing products or services. Today, most companies are marketers.

Marketing – Organized system of bringing products to market.

Marketing plan – A structured document that presents marketing activities (tactics), the thinking that leads to these recommendations (strategies), and what they wish to accomplish (objectives).

Marketing services – Generic term for wide range of services used by marketers. Includes: event marketing, market research, media buying, public relations, sales promotion, and more.

Media – Collective noun for communications channels.

Medium – Singular of media. Radio is a medium. (And a media form.) An individual station is a *vehicle*.

Multi-brand marketer – Company marketing more than one brand.

Niche market – Specialized segment of a larger market.

Niche marketing – Act of marketing to that segment.

Objective – A clear statement of what you want to accomplish.

Out-of-home – Term for advertising media that exist outside the home. Examples: outdoor, transit advertising (like bus shelters).

Packaged goods – Products that are used up (consumed) in a relatively short time frame and then repurchased.

Planning 1. Act of organizing future actions based on current information. 2. Short for account planning.

Position – 1. As defined by Trout and Ries, it relates to a place "in the mind of the consumer." 2. As commonly used by marketers, it means relative place within a competitive category. 3. As used by media professionals, it relates to a certain place within a media environment, such as a magazine.

Post-industrial Revolution – About 1950 AD. Development and dominance of *tertiary economic activity* – services and information. (Also called *The Third Wave*)

References (cont.)

Managing Brand Equity: Capitalizing on the Value of a Brand Name
by David A. Aaker

Building Strong Brands
by David A. Aaker

Brand Leadership
by David A. Aaker & Erich Joachimsthaler

Aaker is the leading author on contemporary brand management.

You will find his writings useful, particularly if you decide to go into brand management.

Two Books by Toffler.

Alvin Toffler wrote two books that addressed the sweeping historical changes affecting today's modern marketplace.

PowerShift: Knowledge, Wealth, and Violence at the Edge of the 21st Century
by Alvin Toffler
The Third Wave
by Alvin Toffler

Both books should be readily available in both hard cover and paperback – new and used.

End Notes:

1. John Philip Jones, *What's in a Name? Advertising and the Concept of Brands.*
2. *The Portable MBA.*
3. Jean-Louis Dru, *Disruption.*
4. David A. Aaker, *Managing Brand Equity - Capitalizing on the Value of a Brand Name.*
5. "For Marin, Issue Is More Than TV," *Chicago Tribune,* 6/6/97.
6. Kevin Kelly, "New Rules for the New Economy," *Wired,* Sept. 1997.
7. Regis McKenna, "Marketing Is Everything," *Harvard Business Review* reprint #91108.
8. McKenna, "Marketing is everything."
9. David A. Aaker, *Managing Brand Equity.*

(NOTE: Today's search engines no longer need publisher or copyright information. Information provided is sufficient to find original source material.)

Names You Should Know:

Some names from the introduction:

Neil McElroy

Executive. Invented the brand management system while a young executive at P&G.

Rose to become chairman of P&G.

Later appointed by President Eisenhower as Secretary of Defense.

Harley Procter

Founder of P&G – Procter & Gamble. Early believer in advertising.

Joseph Schumpeter

Austrian-born economist. He developed concept of "creative destruction" as part of his landmark work in economics.

Gordon Moore

Former CEO of Intel. Predicted "Moore's Law."

Marshall McLuhan

The media guru who showed us the profound relationship between media and society.

Private label – Also called *house brand.* A branded product made for a retailer. The retailer maintains exclusive distribution rights.

Promotion – 1. One of the Five P's representing all marketing activities designed to stimulate sales. 2. Short for *sales promotion,* the use of incentives to stimulate sales. 3. A specific sales promotion program.

Sales promotion – The use of an incentive to stimulate sales. The three main consumer incentives are: Save (provide discount), Free (provide added value), and Win (offer chance at a prize).

Situation analysis (also called background review) – A marketing document that summarizes the current state of the marketplace as it relates to a specific brand.

Sports Marketing – Marketing efforts associated with sports teams.

Strategy – An approach to how an objective will be achieved.

Superbrand – A large, well-known brand. The brand name is usually strong enough to work across several product categories.

Tactic – Specific action, usually based on objective and strategy.

Trademark – Registered name or symbol used to protect ownership. Trademarks may be unique names that can be owned across a wide range of product categories (IBM), or the trademark may only apply to a certain product category. For example, Eagle is a brand name for different companies in different product categories – cars, shirts, snacks, condensed milk.

UPC code (Universal Product Code) – These are the "bar codes" you see being scanned at the checkout counter. They provide price information at the cash register and valuable sales and inventory information for marketers and retailers.

Value – A combination of price and quality.

World brand – A brand that is known and marketed in many countries – with similar product functions and brand values.

The Evolution of Advertising

THIS SECTION COVERS THE DEVELOPMENT of the American marketplace and its impact on our lives today.

It begins with the innovations of early advertisers and the rise of new media forms. Then it shows you how the forces of marketing are changing today's marketplace.

Finally, we'll discuss how advertising has become a major force in both American business and American culture.

1 From Advertising to Marketing.

THE 20TH CENTURY BEGAN with modern advertising. You'll meet innovators and their innovations as the mass consumer market grows. Midway through the century, you'll see a new way of doing business emerge from advertisers and their agencies – **marketing**.

2 The Modern Marketplace.

THE WORLD OF MARKETING keeps changing. Now marketing is a driving force almost everywhere. In this chapter, we'll examine how the growing importance of marketing has reshaped not only advertising, but the entire American marketplace.

And we'll look at the next evolution – **IMC**, that's short for **Integrated Marketing Communications**.

3 Advertising & Society.

ECONOMICS, ETHICS, RULES, AND REGULATIONS. This chapter discusses how advertising in our society affects us all, whether we are students, citizens, consumers, or marketing professionals.

Some People You'll Meet:

The Kid from Galveston.

He came to Chicago, lost money in a crooked dice game, and decided to stay awhile.

When he was done, **Albert Lasker** had helped invent the grass on golf courses, the organization of major league baseball, and modern advertising. In his spare time, he helped elect a president and stimulate modern medical research.

Son of an Ad Man.

His dad was in advertising, but when he followed in his father's footsteps, he did it in Nikes.

Dan Wieden helped build the Nike brand as he told the world to "just do it!"

The Girl from Left Field.

Janet Champ wanted to change the world 30 seconds at a time.

She wrote a commercial for Nike called *"If you let me play…"*

The Revolutionary.

Did you know that advertising had a revolution in the '60s?

Bill Bernbach, and his agency Doyle Dane Bernbach, inspired a whole industry to change the way it created advertising.

1

This chapter was written by Ann Maxwell, Professor in the Advertising Sequence at the U. of Oregon – a school that was active in the establishment and operation of the

original American Advertising Museum in Portland, Oregon. She is also the co-author of How to Produce Creative Advertising. *Additional material for this chapter was contributed by Editor Bruce Bendinger, who is a long-time student of advertising history.*

"Advertising is salesmanship in print."

— John E. Kennedy

From Advertising

ONE FRIDAY NIGHT IN 1897, a young reporter had a date.

He was also assigned to cover a play that night. Familiar with the play, he wrote the review ahead of time – and went out.

Next morning, **Albert Lasker** discovered two things.

First, the theater had burned down the night before.

Second, he needed to find a new career.

His father suggested advertising.

➤ In 1911, a young woman from Covington, Kentucky, took the train from Cincinnati to New York with the man she would marry. Together, **Helen** and **Stanley Resor** would grow the world's largest ad agency.

➤ In 1940, after graduating from NYU and working as a writer for the head of the 1939 World's Fair, **Bill Bernbach** got his first advertising agency job. There, the young writer became friends with a young graphic designer named **Paul Rand**.

Rand had a new approach to combining words and pictures.

A few years later, Bill Bernbach applied this approach at his new agency, Doyle Dane Bernbach. The result was "*The Creative Revolution*" – a dramatic change in the way advertising was created.

➤ In the '60s, two Portland, Oregon, ad executives, Homer Groening and "Duke" Wieden, would occasionally meet and wonder if their young sons would ever amount to anything. Homer's kid, Matt, was always drawing cartoons.*

Duke's kid, **Dan Wieden**, followed in his father's footsteps – with a local shoe account – Nike.

All these people, and many more, play an important role in the history of advertising.

---

*
Ever hear of *The Simpsons*, dude?

*"Let us blaze new trails.
Let us prove to the world that
good taste, good art, and good writing
can be good selling."*

— Bill Bernbach

to Marketing.

THE CORE OF OUR HISTORY CHAPTER will be people and ideas.

In this chapter, you'll become acquainted with…

1. Some Unique Individuals.

Advertising is a business where people can make a difference. This history is as much about people as brands.

We've selected key individuals from each decade.

2. The Development of Ideas.

Advertising is also a business of ideas.

We'll talk about how and when key concepts were introduced and established. And we'll show you the advertising that was a part of those changes.

And you'll see one big change – a shift from advertising to marketing. You'll see that one of advertising's biggest ideas was the idea of marketing – a way of doing business that has changed virtually every business.

Both advertising agencies and the marketers who were the leading advertisers of the day led the way in developing the discipline of marketing.

One Fascinating Book.

We really like this book on the history of advertising – *The Mirror Makers*, by Stephen Fox.

We'll be referring to it during this chapter.

You can find out even more about some of the people you'll meet in this book. It's a great read!

The current edition is available through the University of Illinois Press.

You May Like This Book Even Better.

It's *Twenty Ads That Shook the World* by James Twitchell – a behind-the-scenes look at ads that changed America.

You can find two of the stories, and more, in the Chapter One Readings section on www.adbuzz.com.

Advertising Began Thousands of Years Ago…

as innkeepers, merchants, and tradesmen posted signs to tell the public what they had for sale.

But we did not have modern mass advertising until we had mass manufacturing, mass communication, mass distribution, and mass education.

Ten Dollars Reward.

RAN AWAY from the Subscriber, on the night of the 15th instant, two apprentice boys, legally bound, named WILLIAM and ANDREW JOHNSON The former is of a dark complexion, black hair, eyes, and habits. They are much of a height, about 5 feet 4 or 5 inches The latter is very fleshy freckled face, light hair, and fair complexion. They went off with two other apprentices, advertised by Messrs Wm. & Chas. Fowler When they went away, they were well clad—blue cloth coats, light colored homespun coats, and new hats, the maker's name in the crown of the hats, is Theodore Clark. I will pay the above Reward to any person who will deliver said apprentices to me in Raleigh, or I will give the above Reward for Andrew Johnson alone.

All persons are cautioned against harboring or employing said apprentices, on pain of being prosecuted.

JAMES J. SELBY, Tailor.
Raleigh, N. C. June 24, 1824   26 3t

Marketing Began During the 20th Century…

as manufacturers looked for better ways to bring their products to market.

Though the principles have been around as long as the marketplace, marketing is a relatively recent 20th century phenomenon.

Oil for Lamps & Machinery

A fine article of Clarified Pig's Foot Oil, equal to sperm. At a low price and in quantities to suit buyers. • Neat's foot oil ditto. • Also No. 1 & 2 soap. • Palm and shaving ditto. • For Sale by Procter & Gamble Co. East Side Main Street 2nd Door off 6th Street.

This two-inch ad appeared in the Cincinnati Gazette in 1838. (Hey, you have to start somewhere.)

Charter Member of the Advertising Hall of Fame.

One of our Founding Fathers was an advertising man.

Benjamin Franklin made his money selling newspapers and selling ads. It helped make him one of the richest individuals in the American Colonies.

Franklin's creativity, entrepreneurial spirit, and steady support of democratic principles played a key role in shaping our new nation.

Among his specific contributions as a pioneering direct marketer:

• He published a "Catalogue of Choice and Valuable Books," one of the earliest mail order efforts in the Colonies.

• A Guarantee. Franklin assured mail order buyers they could count on "the same justice as if present."

• Integrated marketing. He ran a store and published the *Pennsylvania Gazette*. The paper advertised goods sold in the store.

• Distribution. As colonial postmaster in 1737, he opened up the mail to all periodicals (his predecessor, a rival publisher, had restricted the mail to all but his own publications).

• In 1774, he established what would become the US Postal Service.

Benjamin Franklin was a model for the clever and innovative behavior that is both profitable and useful to society.

He proved you could be a good citizen and a good businessperson.

Evolution = Revolution

The Reformation. The 30 Years War. The American Revolution.

Do you know what was responsible? The printing press!

A major shift in media behavior can have far-reaching impact in all of society.

When books and newspapers became part of everyday life, the change was profound. No longer was information in the control of a priestly class or ruling nobility. Literacy was no longer a luxury and literature was no longer limited to odes recited by traveling bards.

Marshall McLuhan argues that there was a change in consciousness in society. We think he's probably right. And there's no doubt that, because of the printed word, the world we live in changed.

As you read this first chapter, you will see that small evolutions of media forms drive large revolutions in advertising – which is media-based communication.

We'll begin with newspapers and posters and a society coming to grips with the new abundance of the Industrial Revolution. It will end with a magic box that has the power to transform society – television.

OK, there's a lot in this chapter – so pay attention.

A History of Ideas.

AMERICAN ADVERTISING HISTORY is the story of the cultural and economic developments of our nation.

It parallels the development of the modern American economy as it became the most prosperous in the world.

Four Necessities for Modern Advertising.

While advertising in a limited form has been around for centuries, there were four necessary prerequisites for modern advertising:

❶ **Mass-Produced Goods.** We had to have mass-produced goods so that there was something to advertise.

This happened as a result of the Industrial Revolution.

In 1860, for example, there were 7,600 patent applications.

❷ **Mass Communication.** We needed mass communication.

Inventions and improvements like the typewriter, linotype, and better printing presses helped make this possible.

❸ **Mass Distribution.** Goods had to be generally available.

We needed a good national transportation system to move goods and people from one place to another.

Distribution was also necessary to allow mail order to function.

❹ **Mass Education.** We needed education – so that media and advertising could be read by the masses.

Education also meant more prosperity for more people.

After all, advertising cannot exist without consumers who are willing and able to purchase.

Just before the turn of the century, these were all in place. Then Americans added one more key ingredient – individual initiative.

Industrialization and Individualism.

Industrialization was the driving force in the initial movement toward manufacturing branded products.

But the driving force behind the products themselves was most often a single creative individual – or two partners who shared a vision. You will see this time and time again.

At the same time, a combination of technology and enterprise developed the media to carry ad messages.

But, before we start our journey, let's talk about ideas.

First, the idea of America, which is hundreds of years old.

Second, some brand new ideas in economic theory.

American Ideals and New Ideas.

America was an idea before it was a country.

Ideas about the rights of man, the right to have new thoughts and express them, and the idea that government's power resides in the hands of the people are all part of the fabric of our system.

This willingness to encourage and accept new ideas helps explain why these things happened in America.

Think about it – even before there were things to sell in America, Americans were selling ideas.

Early American Thought.

While resting on abundant natural resources, the early colonial American economy depended upon human resourcefulness to take full advantage of them.

Imagination and perseverance – qualities recognized by some as essential to a developing economy – were abundant in the early days of America. And virtually every immigrant brought these qualities with them.

"The First American" Was Also an Ad Man.

Benjamin Franklin, called by some "the first American," was a creative entrepreneur who became one of America's richest men despite humble beginnings.

He wrote ads, virtually invented promotion, and helped develop early print communications in the colonies with his *Pennsylvania Gazette* and *Poor Richard's Almanac.*

The Importance of Persuasion and Opportunity.

A small persuasive pamphlet, *Common Sense* by **Thomas Paine,** "sold" the idea of independence. Virtually everyone in Colonial America read it – or had it read to them.

The thoughts of **Alexander Hamilton** and others as to how government should be an active and benevolent business partner were not unknown; the British certainly took that view.

But in America, government support for business was implemented in a way that led to an abundance of opportunity for the common man and the small businessman – not just the privileged few.

This was a dramatic departure from anything before in history.

These ideas and opportunities attracted people who wanted to make the most of them. As you watch our history unfold, you will

---

The Revolution's Right Hand Man.

Alexander Hamilton, who was George Washington's *aide de camp* during the Revolutionary War, played a key role in identifying the economic foundation for a modern America.

His vision of a dynamic industrial society was prescient at a time when we were still an agrarian society dominated by large landowners.

Here are some of his contributions:

• Co-author of *The Federalist Papers,* which promoted the Constitution.

• First Secretary of the Treasury – he managed the difficult task of getting the new republic on a sound financial footing – internally and with the nations of Europe.

• *The Report on Manufacture* – this controversial document outlined our future as a commercial and industrial power. It argued against the dominant agrarian view and proposed policies to encourage the development of commerce and industry.

• Hamilton promoted a vision of government which was run as a responsible business and behaved like a good business partner.

And that's why he's on our $10 bill.

Sharp Thinking.

King Gillette was a turn-of-the-century inventor and entrepreneur. (Yes, that was his real name.)

The Idea?

He had an idea – the initial idea was for a disposable product – one people would use up and then repurchase. *This is the basic concept of packaged goods.*

Gillette focused on the perfect expression of that idea – a razor blade sharp enough on both sides to provide a good shave, yet cheap enough to be thrown away when dull.

His invention was to replace straight hollow-ground razors – made to last forever but needing sharpening after each use.

A Ten Year Struggle…

Gillette struggled for over ten years. He had trouble finding investors and someone to work on the prototype.

He was told by cutlers, metal-workers, and experts at MIT that a blade made to his specifications was impossible. But he did it.

It was four years before he could give himself a shave with the world's first throwaway blade and six to get the product on the market – Gillette.

Maintaining an Edge!

Fifty-one razor sets were sold the first year, for $5. Second year sales leapt to 90,844, an increase of more than 180,000 percent. In the third year, sales went up 304 percent and the revolution in shaving had arrived.

In 1904, the US Patent Office granted Gillette a seventeen-year patent. More than 300 competitors sprang up, but only Gillette had the patent on the double-edge blade.

Foreign counterfeits flooded the market with names such as *Agillette, Billette,* and *Gillotin.*

Gillette's plan to incorporate the entire world never caught on – but his disposable razor blade certainly did.

see new groups and new individuals enter the stage.

Many of them were immigrants attracted to the idea of America.

The American Economic Idea.

Our economic system – capitalism and a free market – operates on a few basic assumptions:

❶ **Supply and Demand**. The principles of supply and demand help regulate the pricing of goods. Over-abundance drives prices down; scarcity drives prices up and also provides the environment for the growth of new opportunities for the development of lower-cost alternatives.

❷ **Access to Information**. Everyone in the market has equal access to information. Within America's democratic system, commercial speech, like other forms of speech, is protected to some degree under the First Amendment.

❸ **Caveat Emptor**. "Buyer beware" assumes the consumer is a knowledgeable buyer able to make rational decisions.

❹ **Reasonable Behavior**. Reasonable men and women participating in this system cause it to work.

Entrepreneurs and Opportunity.

This was a powerful combination: resources, a resourceful population, and an economic and political environment that encouraged individual initiative and achievement.

Their names live on in the brands they founded.

➤ Immigrants such as **Heinrich Steinweg**, who moved to America and brought traditional craft skills to the new world in the form of the Steinway piano.

➤ Adventurers like **Levi Strauss,** who sailed to the California gold rush with a small stock of dry goods, including some rough canvas intended for sale to miners for tents. Then he had the idea of making rugged canvas trousers – Levi's!

➤ Entrepreneurs such as **Joseph Campbell** and **Abraham Anderson,** who formed the Campbell's Soup company in 1869.

And others with new ideas, like **King Gillette** (see sidebar).

Now let's turn to "the dismal science," economics. A major shift is taking place in economic thinking. And it's not dismal at all.

A Major Shift in Economic Theory.

IN A 1930 ESSAY, **John Maynard Keynes** claimed market economies had seen their best days. This idea had been around a while.

During the 1800s, David Ricardo proposed that scarce land and diminishing returns would be our future. And today, many thoughtful people raise concerns about other limits – clean water, biodiversity, and environmental resources, for example.

But for years, most economic thinkers did little to address a resource which is virtually infinite – ideas, or, to use a current phrase, **intellectual capital.**

Ideas are a driving force in our economy.

Today, **Paul Romer,** an economist at UC Berkeley, uses theoretical mathematics to show this power.

To Romer, our economy is not bound by scarcity and limits on growth.

To him, new ideas breed new products, new markets, and new possibilities for abundance. Romer sees new ideas and technological change driving economic growth. And he notes that "there is a difference between idea-based products and physical goods."

Paul Romer

He encourages us to revise the bleak future economists have so often predicted and embrace the power of ideas and technology.

A Break with Tradition.

Traditional economists separated the world into wants and physical objects. Since physical objects were subject to scarcity, economists concluded that the only real decision was how to allocate scarce resources to maximize wealth.

But in the 1950s, Nobel Laureate Robert Solav noted the power of ideas and technology to generate economic growth.

Romer divides the world into physical objects and **ideas.**

Objects are scarce and subject to the law of diminishing returns. Objects alone cannot fuel economic growth; ideas can.

Humans, says Romer, possess a nearly infinite capacity to reinvent physical objects and their uses. As for ideas, *there is no scarcity at all.*

Romer's emphasizes the abundance of the human imagination as the source of economic growth.

We will see the power of ideas at work throughout the development of branded products and the history of advertising.

Early American Advertising.

FROM BENJAMIN FRANKLIN and the *Pennsylvania Gazette* through the 19th century, most ads merely notified readers of the arrival of goods or the availability of new items.

Most advertising was local and resembled current-day classified notices in newspapers.

Infrastructure Requirements.

Manufacturing, transportation, and communication systems had to arrive before national advertising was possible.

In the 1880s, the US economy was based on agriculture and the manufacture of things like flour, lumber, and textiles – products that could be made into bread, homes, and clothing.

Most goods were sold as unbranded commodities.

Wholesalers dominated the distribution system.

But the catalysts for change were in place: industrialization, education, and improvements in transportation and communication.

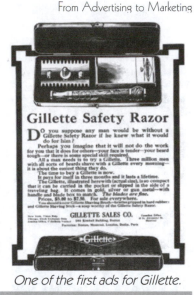

Gillette Safety Razor

One of the first ads for Gillette.

1880-1900.

During this period we saw the growth and development of:

- Low-cost, mass manufactured consumer products
- Mass communication vehicles
- Distribution infrastructure
- A large market of educated consumers with disposable income

This is the maid of fair renown
Who scrubs the floors of Spotless Town.
To find a speck when she is through
Would take a pair of specs or two,
And her employment isn't slow.
For she employs

SAPOLIO

This is the butcher of Spotless Town.
His tools are bright as his renown.
To leave them stained were indiscreet.
For folks would then abstain from meat.
And so he brightens his trade you know
By polishing with

SAPOLIO

Ads for an early consumer brand.

BEAUTIFUL Women Chew **Primley's** CALIFORNIA FRUIT Chewing Gum

Improving Technology Improving Communication

Improvements in everything from manufacturing to printing processes drove growth in the American marketplace. With that growth, new products emerged along with new ways to sell them.

Patent Medicine Ad – a sure cure.

*New Products. New Habits.
New Markets.*

Growth in Manufacturing.

Between the Civil War and World War I, the American economy featured important growth in manufacturing.

During the 1880s, inventors developed machinery that made **flow production** possible in the manufacture of goods like soap, cigarettes, matches, breakfast cereals, and canned goods.

As mass-produced consumer products became available, manufacturers looked for ways to tell people about them.

An early form of communication consisted of lithographed advertising cards. They live on as baseball and trading cards.

In 1900, the **linotype** was invented, producing a full line of typography in metal pieces that could be set quickly and accurately, speeding up newspaper and magazine production.

Mass media could now be manufactured more efficiently.

The Beginnings of the American Consumer.

Between 1870 and 1900, America entered a period of economic boom. US wealth quadrupled – from $30 billion to $127 billion. This period featured the invention of electric lights, the telephone, phonograph, and motion picture camera.

Other inventions allowed mass production, industrial production, and distribution. The sale of packaged goods and foods grew in volume. And so did advertising.

Changing Households.

Americans were changing, too. Household routines evolved into making fewer things and purchasing more.

Consumption of all kinds of items, including canned or processed food, became part of almost every household.

Toothpaste, cornflakes, chewing gum, and safety razors fostered new rituals and habits. Americans began to eat, drink, clean with, and wear products made in factories.

In the 1890s, four brands began to advertise on a large scale. Three were soaps: Sapolio, Pear's, and Ivory (made by Procter & Gamble). The fourth was Royal Baking Powder.

New companies and their brands joined this list: Quaker Oats, Armour, American Tobacco, P. Lorillard, and Remington Typewriters.

In just two decades, the advertising expenditures of manufacturers had grown rapidly, and the types of manufacturers making those expenditures had changed dramatically.

Advertising Cleans Up Its Act.

In 1893, half the companies spending over $50,000 a year on national advertising were patent medicine manufacturers.

They accounted for most of the advertising dollars placed in magazines and newspapers.

In 1904, *Ladies' Home Journal* published a series of articles exposing patent medicines as deceptive fraudulent products.

The articles also exposed the advertising – showing an ad claiming that Lydia Pinkham was working in her laboratory next to a photo of her tombstone (she'd died 22 years earlier).

In 1906, Congress passed the **Pure Food and Drug Act.**

Twenty years later, all but seven of those companies had disappeared from the list.

Department Stores – The First Large Local Advertisers.

By the 1880s, department stores in large cities had adopted fixed pricing. They began selling items in the newspapers.

They announced goods and prices through local newspaper ads – it worked. Consumers began using the information in department store ads as guides for shopping.

By 1900, brand-named nationally advertised goods began to gain more importance in department stores such as Macy's in New York City and Wanamaker's in Philadelphia, but the retailer was still the primary advertiser.

Today, retailers are still the primary users of newspapers.

A Philadelphia agency, **NW Ayer & Son**, pioneered the placement of newspaper advertising and became the first major national agency.

They're still in business today, *"Keeping Everlastingly at It."*

Growth of National Brand Advertising.

Ayer's improvement made it easier to advertise nationally.

Soon, two-thirds of the revenue for newspapers came from advertising, and advertising for national brands in newspapers had surpassed regional and local retail advertising.

But a change in the media was about to change advertising.

Magazines – The First National Media Form.

With the advent of popular national magazines, there was now a real place to advertise nationally to a large audience.

In the beginning, "polite" magazines took pride in not including advertising among their pages. (Remember, much of the advertising at that time was for those patent medicines.)

Two magazines that did merely sold their back covers to the Great American Tea Company and limited advertising to less than a page per issue.

J. Walter Thompson Has a Big Idea.

A young ad man noticed that most magazines ran only a page or two of advertising.

J. Walter Thompson thought it amazing that no one had thought to use these prestigious publications as an advertising medium.

He approached the literary monthlies, who found the thought of extra income quite persuasive. By 1876, *Scribner's* was carrying twenty pages of advertising per issue.

J. Walter Thompson (JWT) specialized in magazines and soon monopolized the field. His success led him to buy the business from his boss – for $500 – and put his name on the door.

JWT became known for the "Standard List" of 25 to 30 of the best magazines in America under its exclusive contract.

Just as newspapers helped establish NW Ayer, the growing magazine industry helped establish J. Walter Thompson.

Products Change.

But department stores and other retailers are still primary users of newspapers.

The Commissioner.

Cyrus H. Curtis of Curtis Publishing encouraged the development of advertising agencies by promoting the agency commission system.

Kellogg's gives their marketing a push – with aggressive sampling.

But a magazine publisher was about to make an even bigger change. His idea would create a whole industry – the modern advertising agency.

That person was **Cyrus H. Curtis.**

Cyrus Curtis Has a Bigger Idea.

Cyrus H. Curtis of Curtis Publishing had a different attitude about the media and advertising. It was revolutionary.

In many ways, Curtis invented both the modern American magazine and the American advertising industry.

Growth in the media and the increase in the number of nationally advertised products got things growing. But it was the establishment of **the commission system** that led directly to the growth of advertising agencies.

Curtis believed in advertising. He believed advertising was an investment – and for him it paid handsomely.

His advertising brought increased circulation – which attracted other advertisers and enabled him to lower costs to subscribers.

Most important, with this policy Curtis created an enthusiastic sales force – advertising agencies.

The Commission System.

As publisher of the *Saturday Evening Post* and the *Ladies' Home Journal,* Curtis established an unbreakable commission system – 10% commission to responsible agencies on advertising space cost, plus 5% discount for cash payment. Agencies were to charge advertisers the full rate for services. And, of course, they did.

In 1883, he started the *Ladies' Home Journal* – a magazine based on articles initially written by his wife. By 1895, Curtis achieved a circulation of 750,000.

From 2,200 to 2 Million.

Curtis then purchased the *Saturday Evening Post,* which he grew from 2,200 to 2 million subscribers in just ten years.

These magazines featured the latest fashions and fiction, and provided news of the latest products, with advertising.

A National Advertising Medium for National Advertisers.

The American magazine audience was an advertiser's dream.

They were educated, had money to spend, and paid attention to the ads. Now manufacturers could speak to huge numbers of potential customers at one time.

A National Marketing Infrastructure.

The infrastructure was now in place:

- **National transportation**
- **National brands**
- **National media vehicles**
- **An educated and affluent audience**

The Final Component Was New Thinking.

There was just one thing left to do.

It needed an idea to make this infrastructure more effective.

It was time for someone to invent modern advertising.

That person was **Albert Lasker.**

"The Age of Lasker."

BETWEEN 1900 AND 1920, advertising and marketing were defined by an important group of new thinkers: **Claude Hopkins, Elmo Calkins, John E. Kennedy, Charles Coolidge Parlin, Cyrus Curtis, Henry Ford, Albert Sloan, W.K. Kellogg,** and most important, **Albert Lasker.**

Almost from the beginning, there was controversy.

Two Schools of Thought – "Hard Sell/Push" & "Soft Sell/Pull."

Two schools of thought emerged regarding advertising messages. We'll refer to them as "Push" and "Pull."

Push marketing pushes product into the distribution channel.

Pull marketing works to stimulate demand, which pulls product off the shelf.

Successful marketing often has some of both.

"Hard Sell" Pushes the Advertising Message.

Push advertising – more commonly referred to as "hard sell" and "reason why" – emphasizes pushing a rational selling proposition at the consumer consistently and often.

It counts on people remembering that proposition, whether they like it or not, and choosing brands based on logic and residual memory.

"Soft Sell" Pulls You into the Advertising Message.

Pull advertising – commonly referred to as "soft sell" and "image" – emphasizes pulling consumers into the message with a clever, engaging, or entertaining presentation.

It counts on people getting involved with the ad and thinking well of the brand because of values communicated along with the ad message (humor, for example). Consumers choose the brand based on an emotional as well as a logical connection.

Each approach can point to dramatic success.

It's a debate that continues to this day.

Early Advertising Innovators.

From its earliest days, advertising has been a personality-driven business. Several individuals left their mark on this period with ideas that set the tone for decades to come.

Charles Coolidge Parlin Invents Market Research.

For example, look at how marketing research originated.

Charles Coolidge Parlin worked for Curtis Publishing at the turn of the century. In 1902, he attempted to persuade Campbell's Soup to advertise in the *Saturday Evening Post;* he was told only working people who made their soup from scratch read the "Post."

Parlin collected samples from Philadelphia garbage routes and proved Campbell's customers also lived in these blue collar areas.

Campbell's contracted for ads 52 weeks a year, with this condition – ads must appear on the first page after the reading matter in the magazine. This became the "Campbell's Soup Position."

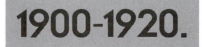

This period will cover:
- The "idea" of modern advertising developed by Lasker and others
- The development of two schools of thought, Push and Pull
- The beginnings of marketing

Before Lasker.

Look at this early ad for Quaker Wheat Berries – with unfocused metaphors and slogans.

And a little Pull with attractive art.

Calkins' Approach

This was the popular "Phoebe Snow" campaign for the Lackawanna Railroad – essentially, an extension of lithographed European poster art.

The sales proposition, *The Road of Anthracite,* referred to the railroad's use of hard coal which resulted in less soot – a real problem at the time. Dressed in white, Phoebe Snow personified the benefit!

After Lasker.

No more "Wheat Berries." Now it's Puffed Wheat and Puffed Rice.

Now it's "Shot from Guns!"

Quaker now has tightly focused claims – with "Airy Nut-Like Morsels" as the result of this unique manufacturing process.

Lasker's copywriter – Claude Hopkins – puffs up Quaker with "reason why" copy. Even cereal can be full of facts and figures.

It is one of the earliest examples of marketing emanating from the world of advertising – but not the last.

Elmo Calkins and "Artful Advertising."

Elmo Calkins and Ralph Holden began the first "creative driven" advertising agency.

Calkins, deafened by a childhood illness, was a copywriter.

However, he ultimately made his greatest impact with art and the design of advertising.

Dissatisfied with the appearance of the common look of ads, Calkins brought fine artists and illustrators into his agency to help create ads with more aesthetic appeal.

He often claimed his greatest satisfaction was in *"improving the physical appearance of advertising."*

The Core Idea of Modern Advertising.

An early copywriter, **John E. Kennedy**, gave us the first definition of modern advertising: "salesmanship-on-paper," or, as it is more commonly used, *"salesmanship in print."*

This is the core idea of modern advertising.

Up to that time, the advertising business was about selling space, not about making the most of what was in that space.

This single concept made all the difference.

Kennedy was an ex-Mountie who had already had a huge impact in Canada. He was hired by Lord & Thomas.

As their chief copywriter, he first described "reason-why" advertising. *"True reason-why copy is Logic, plus persuasion, plus conviction all woven into a certain simplicity of thought – pre-digested for the average mind."*

Kennedy believed in finding a place to have rational dialogue, but not talking over the public's head.

These early concepts still have application today. His successor was **Claude Hopkins** – America's first great copywriter.

Claude Hopkins and "Scientific Advertising."

Hopkins had considered the ministry but discovered that his true calling was writing advertising.

Hopkins loved everything about it. He liked writing for mail order and using coupons and premiums.

He liked testing advertising. And he got results.

Hopkins wrote about his methods in *Scientific Advertising,* which some call *"the greatest advertising book ever published."*

Hopkins and Kennedy worked for a man who became not only the most powerful (and wealthiest) person in advertising, but an important influence on American society and culture.

In 1908, Hopkins made $185,000 a year, probably equivalent to $5 million today. His boss made more.

His boss was Albert Lasker.

Albert Lasker.

Advertising has often welcomed new people with new ideas.

Albert Lasker is a classic example. He was born in the boom town of Galveston, Texas, in 1880.

His father, Morris Lasker, was a successful businessman.

Reflecting his father's entrepreneurial spirit, he began his own weekly newspaper at the age of 12 – the *Galveston Free Press.* Albert solicited advertising published for over a year – at a profit.

But two events changed his life. The first happened when he was just 16 – already working full-time for the *Galveston News.*

Albert is the young reporter at the beginning of this chapter – the one who filed the review of the play he *didn't* see!

Familiar with the play, he wrote the review ahead of time, skipped the performance to go out on a date, and then discovered the next morning that the theater had burned down!

With this embarrassment following him, Lasker moved to New Orleans, then Dallas, all the time working as a reporter.

Then he decided to try his fate in New York. His father opposed this idea and Albert's newspaper career.

So Morris Lasker made a deal with his son, as fathers will.

If young Albert would try working in advertising for three months, he could then go to New York.

Lasker Joins Lord & Thomas.

Through business dealings, Morris Lasker had met D.M. Lord of the Lord & Thomas advertising agency in Chicago.

He arranged for Albert to work there for $10 a week. Initial responsibilities included sweeping floors and emptying cuspidors.

A Roll of the Dice...

Now the second twist of fate. One night after work, Lasker lost $500 in a craps game – a huge sum at the time.

The gambler demanded payment immediately. Albert persuaded Ambrose Thomas to loan him the money. Lasker's dream of moving to New York ended. A larger one began.

At the age of 19, Albert went on the road as a salesman for Lord & Thomas. He quickly acquired $50,000 of new business and persuaded an existing client to increase both the ad budget and the commissions paid to the agency if the agency wrote the copy.

Albert hired a newspaper friend to write the copy.

Agency income on the account went from $300 to $3,000 a month. Lasker was on his way.

John E. Kennedy had the idea...

Claude Hopkins made it work. He made $185,000 in 1908 – at a time when cars were under $1000 and no income tax!

This is the man who paid them.
Albert Lasker owned America's largest ad agency by the time he was 32.

Sunkist Oranges.

Drinking orange juice as a regular habit was Lasker's idea.

He'd heard growers were chopping down orange trees as a result of over-production. This ad, written by Hopkins, helped create demand.

Today, Sunkist is still a client of Lasker's successor agency, FCB.

A Short List of Lasker's Accomplishments.

Some major contributions were:

• **Improved Ad Effectiveness**

He understood the value of saying the right thing in an advertisement.

He increased the importance and effectiveness of advertising copy.

• **Improved Measurement**

An efficient tracking of results, as part of a system of improving the effectiveness of client's advertising.

• **Improved Techniques**

Lasker, along with Hopkins, developed a number of techniques that are still used today.

One example was **"preemption,"** a technique of developing (and owning) a unique claim that may actually be generic to the product category. Saying Lucky Strike's tobacco was "toasted" is an example.

Techniques such as sampling, coupons, free trial offers, and money-back guarantees were implemented with new effectiveness.

• **Radio Programming**

Lord & Thomas pioneered in sponsored radio programming, helping to develop America's first free fully sponsored medium.

• **Contributions to Society**

Throughout Lasker's life, he used his fortune and influence in a wide variety of enterprises.

Lasker was an activist in public affairs. (An uncle in Germany was a leading politician.)

Lasker even helped elect a president! Though, in retrospect, Harding's election was not exactly a high point.

(Continued on next page)

Then he ran into one of those ideas that changes everything...

Lasker Gets Lucky.

Now Lasker's luck really started to turn. He met John E. Kennedy and was exposed to the new concept of advertising. Kennedy had called upon the agency to meet Mr. Thomas.

Thomas sent Lasker down to the lobby. This was a defining moment. Literally.

This meeting marked the first time anyone had provided the modern definition of advertising, *"salesmanship in print."*

Kennedy so impressed Lasker that he hired him on the spot.

Lasker already believed in the power of the written word, and he understood the importance of this simple idea.

This also points up another key aspect of the nature of ideas.

Clearly, Kennedy had the original idea. Just as clearly, Lasker's follow through transformed it into a stunningly profitable reality.

By the age of 24, with a $50,000 salary, Lasker bought a quarter interest in the agency. Eight years later he bought out his partners – owning the biggest agency in advertising at the age of 32.

Printer's Ink reported, *"Mr. Lasker enjoys a degree of confidence and an initiative that have probably been given to no man of his few years in publishing and advertising affairs."*

The

PENALTY OF LEADERSHIP

IN every field of human endeavor, he that is first must perpetually live in the white light of publicity. ¶Whether the leadership be vested in a man or in a manufactured product, emulation and envy are ever at work. ¶In art, in literature, in music, in industry, the reward and the punishment are always the same. ¶The reward is widespread recognition; the punishment, fierce denial and detraction. ¶When a man's work becomes a standard for the whole world, it also becomes a target for the shafts of the envious few. ¶If his work be merely mediocre, he will be left severely alone—if he achieve a masterpiece, it will set a million tongues a-wagging. ¶Jealousy does not protrude its forked tongue at the artist who produces a commonplace painting. ¶Whatsoever you write, or paint, or play, or sing, or build, no one will strive to surpass, or to slander you, unless your work be stamped with the seal of genius. ¶Long, long after a great work or a good work has been done, those who are disappointed or envious continue to cry out that it can not be done. ¶Spiteful little voices in the domain of art were raised against our own Whistler as a mountebank, long after the big world had acclaimed him its greatest artistic genius. ¶Multitudes flocked to Bayreuth to worship at the musical shrine of Wagner, while the little group of those whom he had dethroned and displaced argued angrily that he was no musician at all. ¶The little world continued to protest that Fulton could never build a steamboat, while the big world flocked to the river banks to see his boat steam by. ¶The leader is assailed because he is a leader, and the effort to equal him is merely added proof of that leadership. ¶Failing to equal or to excel, the follower seeks to depreciate and to destroy—but only confirms once more the superiority of that which he strives to supplant. ¶There is nothing new in this. ¶It is as old as the world and as old as the human passions—envy, fear, greed, ambition, and the desire to surpass. ¶And it all avails nothing. ¶If the leader truly leads, he remains—the leader. ¶Master-poet, master-painter, master-workman, each in his turn is assailed, and each holds his laurels through the ages. ¶That which is good or great makes itself known, no matter how loud the clamor of denial. ¶That which deserves to live—lives.

Cadillac Motor Car Co. Detroit, Mich.

Lasker's Accomplishments.

Lasker accomplished a great deal. From the development of basic advertising techniques used today to the organization of major league baseball, Lasker's influence is still with us.

And he made a lot of money doing it. His country estate was sold long ago, but you can still drive through it.

It's the Chicago suburb of Lincolnshire. The whole thing.

The "Pull" of Calkins and MacManus.

While Lasker built an empire on the "reason why" of Kennedy and Hopkins, **Elmo Calkins** of Calkins and Holden took pride in bringing art into advertising.

He was also having some success at it.

With the influence of the European posters popular at the time, art-nouveau inspired layouts strived to create a feeling of class – a feeling very much in tune with the aspirations of the growing American middle class, now buying automobiles and consumer goods in unprecedented numbers.

By 1910, a new "atmospheric" style of advertising emerged. A prime mover was the copywriter **Theodore F. MacManus.**

His ad, "The Penalty of Leadership" (shown above) was one that influenced businessmen and copywriters for years.

The Penalty of Leadership.

This favorite ad of the times, created by Theodore F. MacManus, was an inspiring piece of "atmospheric" copy written for Cadillac, but with no mention of the client's name.

The ad indirectly addressed a problem with a faulty engine by talking about the problems with being first and in the limelight.

The ad ran only once, January 2, 1915, but for years, over 10,000 reprints were sent out annually.

In 1945, *Printers' Ink* magazine asked readers to choose the all-time outstanding advertisement.

"The Penalty of Leadership" won by an overwhelming margin.

The ad was finally repeated in the 250th anniversary issue of the *Saturday Evening Post* in 1967 – 62 years after it initially ran.

Lasker's Accomplishments (cont.)

Other contributions include:

- **Art.** Bringing great modern art to our museums.
- **Medical Research.** The Lasker Foundation provided important support to a number of groups, including the American Cancer Society and Mary Sanger's work on birth control. He brought focus to the need for medical research.
- **Sport.** He influenced major league baseball's organization (he was part-owner of the Cubs). He told his partner to change Cubs Park's name to Wrigley Field. *"It will do your chewing gum sales a lot of good."*
- **Golf.** Development of the grass on your local golf course (basic work was done at Lasker's estate).
- **Politics.** Lasker served in a major capacity in the administration of the president he helped elect –Warren Harding.
- **And More.** Planting the tulips in Central Park. (Mary Lasker was also active in these activities, with her own contributions.)

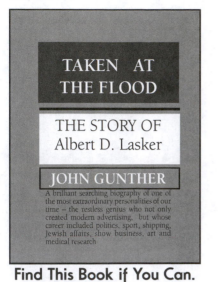

TAKEN AT THE FLOOD

THE STORY OF
Albert D. Lasker

JOHN GUNTHER

A brilliant searching biography of one of
the most extraordinary personalities of our
time – the restless genius who not only
created modern advertising, but whose
career included politics, sport, shipping,
Jewish affairs, show business, art and
medical research

Find This Book if You Can.

Originally published in 1960, this book is long out of print, but if you can find a copy at a used book store, get it. It's a fascinating read.

As the cover says, it's about, "…*one of the most extraordinary personalities of our time – the restless genius who not only created modern advertising, but whose career included… politics, sport, shipping, Jewish affairs, show business, art and medical research.*"

Ned Jordan. Client and Copywriter!

Ned Jordan was a copywriter – but he was something more – he was also an automobile manufacturer.

Above is a classic ad for a roadster that he manufactured – the Jordan.

Not only was his business successful, but Jordan had the foresight to sell his business and save his money just before the stock market crash of 1929.

Somewhere West of Laramie

SOMEWHERE west of Laramie there's a broncho-busting, steer-roping girl who knows what I'm talking about. She can tell what a sassy pony, that's a cross between greased lightning and the place where it hits, can do with eleven hundred pounds of steel and action when he's going high, wide and handsome.

The truth is—the Playboy was built for her.

Built for the lass whose face is brown with the sun when the day is done of revel and romp and race.

She loves the cross of the wild and the tame.

There's a savor of links about that car—of laughter and lilt and light—a hint of old loves—and saddle and quirt. It's a brawny thing—yet a graceful thing for the sweep o' the Avenue.

Step into the Playboy when the hour grows dull with things gone dead and stale.

Then start for the land of real living with the spirit of the lass who rides, lean and rangy, into the red horizon of a Wyoming twilight.

JORDAN
JORDAN MOTOR CAR COMPANY, Inc., Cleveland, Ohio

Times were good. Sales were good. The economic boom lifted spirits, the stock market, incomes, and ad budgets.

Somewhere West of Laramie.
Hard sell and soft sell coexisted, but not peacefully.

While reason-why proponents believed people were persuaded systematically, MacManus argued that this assumed all men were fools and that he held the public in higher esteem.

One example of this "atmospheric" approach is this ad for the Jordan motor car – a roadster manufactured by a copywriter.

As printing techniques improved and ad budgets grew, Calkins-influenced ads became more common in American magazines, providing income for a new generation of illustrators and artists like Maxfield Parrish and Norman Rockwell.

Advertising Gets Organized.

Printer's Ink, an advertising trade magazine, was first published by **George Rowell** in 1895. (We'll tell you about him in Chapter Five.)

This period also saw the emergence of industry organizations.

The first was the Associated Advertising Clubs of America (1904), which included manufacturers, media, and agencies as members.

In 1914, the large advertisers left this organization and formed the Association of National Advertisers (ANA), which addressed their needs more specifically.

A few years later, agencies followed and became the American Association of Advertising Agencies (4A's).

This basic structure continues to the present day, with the ANA representing advertisers, the 4A's representing agencies, and the American Advertising Federation (AAF) representing local ad clubs.

Advertising Goes to War.

Meanwhile, other advertising experts helped President Woodrow Wilson "sell" the war to the American people.

The famous recruitment poster by James Montgomery Flagg is one example – a very hard-selling bit of "soft-sell."

Companies that had previously used the reason-why approach, found it awkward to promote non-essential products while the country was at war.

MacManus' "atmospheric" approach was the solution.

More Consumer Products and Evolving Consumers.

During this same time, manufacturers were inventing foods such as cereals (e.g., Shredded Wheat and Puffed Rice) and toothpaste (e.g., Pepsodent).

At the same time, advertisers were inventing reasons to buy them – like plaque, body odor, and halitosis.

As American consumers became more and more familiar with these new products, advertising evolved from the informational approach to a focus on **benefits.**

By 1920, not only had the products represented by advertising diversified, almost eliminating patent medicine, but advertising had established a better reputation through the success of its efforts to help during World War I.

Growth of National Agencies.

THE WAR OVER, AMERICA WAS BACK IN BUSINESS. President Calvin Coolidge set the tone for the times with this quote: *"The business of America is business."* And it was.

Business was robust. Improvements in manufacturing made goods more available than ever.

This competitive environment of plenty required a more important place for advertising – now advertising was needed to ensure enough demand for the increased production.

GM – The Beginnings of Multi-Brand Marketing.

Branding also evolved through advertising.

The Art of Propaganda. *Advertising helped recruit all the talents of society – including artists.*

Changing Roles. *Advertising reflects social values – compare this World War I poster with the famous World War II poster "We Can Do It" on page 63.*

1920-1929.

This period will cover:
- The beginnings of multi-brand organization at General Motors
- The growth of advertising agency professionalism
- The initial growth of two key national advertising agencies – JWT and BBDO

Leading Brands in 1923.

Take a look at this list – it shows how some brands can last.

Cameras/film	Eastman Kodak
Canned fruit	Del Monte
Chewing gum	Wrigley
Cookies	Nabisco
Razor blades	Gillette
Soft drinks	Coca-Cola
Soup	Campbell's

Driving Competition
– from low price and no choice…

… to more choice and more features.

As people became more familiar with products, advertising began to be less instructive and stress product advantages – benefits.

A Drive for Change.

Up to this point, Ford had dominated the automobile market with vertically integrated mass production techniques and a low price. But choice was limited.

Henry Ford was fond of saying you could have a Model T *"in any color you wanted, so long as it was black."*

Albert Sloan applied what was then revolutionary thinking to the automobile industry. (Read the whole story in Peter Drucker's business classic, *The Concept of the Corporation.*)

General Motors (GM) initiated the idea of changing tastes with the introduction of model changes and different automobile "brands" at different price points.

GM was essentially the first large multi-brand marketer, with an innovative organizational model that worked.

Better customer focus was another GM advantage.

While Ford introduced installment buying for automobiles, GM improved upon it.

By 1925, three-fourths of car sales were made on time payments.

And GM had become the #1 auto manufacturer.

The Marketplace of Ideas Keeps Changing.

This dramatizes another key point about ideas.

A good idea may not stay a good idea.

Market responses, or other change, can alter the competitive environment – sometimes very quickly..

One car for everybody was a good idea when Ford first had the idea. He made it good. He made it cheap. He made it black.

Then the marketplace said, "Been there. Done that."

As the automotive market evolved, the GM concept became an idea whose time had come.

Advertising Agency Professionalism.

The ad industry became more professional during this decade.

Advertising Awards.

The first advertising awards contest, the Harvard Bok award, was launched in 1923. It was established by Edward Bok of the *Ladies' Home Journal,* and administered by Harvard Business School.

During the seven years these awards were given, Barton, Durstine and Osborn (BDO) won more awards than any other agency. (We'll tell you about them shortly.)

Advertising Publications.

Advertising Age was launched at the end of the 1920s.

Franklin D. Roosevelt (FDR), then governor of New York, said he'd choose advertising as a career because *"it is essentially a form of education and the progress of civilization depends upon education."*

FDR's high regard for advertising illustrates the attitude toward advertising in the 1920s.

Mr. Lasker Goes to Washington.

Lasker's involvement in Harding's campaign should be noted. This was, in many ways, the first modern media political campaign.

Harding, a handsome man, was presented in ways designed to appeal to the newest part of the electorate – women.

His "front porch" campaign was a series of media events designed to feed well-crafted stories to reporters as they camped out (and were wined and dined) in the candidate's home town.

As Harding took the high road, a nasty anti-Wilson, anti-League of Nations campaign generated lots of negative press.

The result was a landslide of massive proportions – 61.6%!

Lasker, a primary strategist and member of the "Kitchen Cabinet," was rewarded with an important government post. As he journeyed to Washington, others came to the forefront.

Helen & Stanley Resor.

The Original Account/Creative Team.

Stanley Resor and **Helen Lansdowne Resor** became advertising's premiere account/creative team.

Under their leadership, JWT became the largest agency in the world.

It Began in Cincinnati.

Stanley Resor was hired in 1908 to open a Cincinnati branch of JWT. When he opened the office, he brought along a copywriter he'd previously hired at Procter and Collier, P&G's "house" agency. Her name was Helen Lansdowne.

Helen Lansdowne's Influence.

Stanley liked to coin brand names and persuade the middle class to imitate the habits of the rich. Helen was in touch with women.

Miss Helen Lansdowne

She wrote ads for products used by women, preferring a more intuitive approach to Stanley's more "scientific" approach.

Ads created under Helen Lansdowne's guidance were beautiful to see and had emotional appeal. She combined the reason why of Hopkins with the visual appeal of Calkins.

Some of her most memorable work was for Woodbury's soap and Pond's cold cream.

In 1921, her ads for Woodbury's Facial Soap reflected a return to luxury and romance with *"A Skin You Love to Touch."*

JWT gained the reputation of the "Women's Agency" due to the number of clients with advertising directed at women and the many women on staff. (They wore gloves to work and hats in the office.)

The Lasker Ticket.

Working with William Wrigley, "the chewing-gum king," the candidates were featured in news releases, speeches, newspaper advertising, and billboard poster displays.

They won with 61.6% of the vote.

Mrs. Helen Lansdowne Resor. *Though not even given the title of vice-president, her impact and influence helped shape JWT into the world's largest advertising agency.*

Helen's Touch. *The famous Woodbury's campaign, "A Skin You Love to Touch" – emotion combined with reason why.*

Star Value. JWT's advertising for Lux Soap *helped establish it as a leading brand. The campaign ran for 20 years.*

Ad for Campbell's Soup created by long-time agency BBDO.

Mr. & Mrs. Resor.

Helen Lansdowne and Stanley Resor married in 1917.

Though Helen was not even given the title of vice-president, it was clear to all that Stanley consulted her in most aspects of the agency business.

Her most obvious influence was in creative style, though there is evidence she was a principal policy maker, as well.

Remember, these were different times. At the beginning of the century, women did not yet have the vote. In fact, one of Helen's major outside activities was the Suffrage movement.

"The University of Advertising."

Advertising agencies were beginning to become a source for marketing as well as advertising.

Stanley Resor implemented training that caused JWT to be thought of as *"the university of advertising."*

To further his ambition to professionalize advertising, Stanley hired **Paul Chirington**, a Harvard University marketing professor, as director of research.

He began the formal study of consumer choices with surveys using questionnaires designed "to elicit the truth."

This was one of the first steps to establish agencies as leaders in the emerging discipline of marketing.

Chirington was followed by the well-known behavioral psychologist, **John B. Watson**. Watson had no impact on JWT's advertising, except that his credentials impressed clients.

Bruce Barton
The AdMan Nobody Knows.

Though little known today, one of the better known leaders of this period was **Bruce Barton**, a founder of BDO (Barton, Durstine and Osborn). He was a best-selling author and a US congressman (R/NY) who also ran for the Senate.

Torn between advertising and what he thought of as more serious writing, he ended up doing both.

The son of a liberal Protestant circuit-riding minister, Barton's tolerant attitude toward religion was demonstrated in his *The Man Nobody Knows*, a best-seller about an everyday Jesus Christ.

Barton saw advertising as *"the handmaiden of business."*

A graduate of Amherst, he led BDO in the creative area with an emphasis on beauty and quick, succinct copy.

He would remind employees that *"you're not talking to a mass meeting, you're talking to a parade."*

BDO was a hot agency, hiring college grads *"with salesmen's minds and some writing ability"* and consistently winning awards.

The BDO account list included General Electric in 1920 and 1923; General Motors in 1922; and Lever Brothers in 1924.

BBDO.

In 1928 BDO merged with Batten to become Batten, Barton, Durstine and Osborn. (Radio comedian Fred Allen commented that the name sounded like a trunk falling down the stairs.)

Most people just used the initials. BBDO was now a $32 million agency competing with JWT and NW Ayer.

Lasker Returns...

During the beginning of the Harding administration, Albert Lasker played an important role helping to sell off excess war material. He was, as usual, quite successful.

The same could not be said of the Harding Administration, which was notoriously corrupt.

Tired of Washington, D.C., its politics, and his own great disappointment, he returned to Lord & Thomas in 1922.

Claude Hopkins had led the agency during that time, and, in Lasker's opinion, had mistakenly moved away from reason why. Lasker was going to move them back.

Lasker Gets Luckies.

To restore Lord & Thomas' leadership, Lasker acquired American Tobacco Co.'s Lucky Strike account and its rather eccentric client, **George Washington Hill.**

Hill really believed in the power of advertising.

In 1929, Lucky Strike spent $12.3 million – more than had ever been spent advertising a single product.

Hill liked testimonials. Succumbing to Hill's wishes, ads were created with opera stars claiming Luckies helped their singing.

In January 1930, the Federal Trade Commission demanded American Tobacco stop running endorsement ads if the endorsers had not used the product. That didn't stop Hill.

He developed a new selling strategy, aimed at a new target, coining the phrase *"Reach for a Lucky instead of a sweet."*

A Plain Brown Wrapper

Kotex and toothbrushes were new products that resulted from WWI. Prior to WWI, only 26% of the population took care of their teeth. After the war, it was 40%.

Nurses at the battle-front discovered that cellucotton bandages, produced from wood fiber, were a good replacement for the re-washable cloth then used for menstruation.

Kotex became a new Lord & Thomas client. As the story goes, Lasker asked his wife for marketing advice.

The result was one of the earliest examples of consumer insight developing a better marketing approach.

Kotex eliminated the awkward moment of asking a male druggist for the product by stacking boxes of the product, wrapped in plain brown paper, on the counter. The customer came in, took a box, and left the money on the counter.

Some of this money went directly to Lasker, as he became a major investor in the company, which became Kimberly-Clark.

The most widely advertised product of the time – Lucky Strike cigarettes.

A major strategic insight resulted in "Luckies" being advertised successfully to women – positioning cigarettes as an alternative to sweets and other fattening foods.

Odorono.

This controversial ad by James Webb Young was refused by a number of publications of the time. Two hundred women cancelled subscriptions to a magazine that ran it.

But enough magazines ran the ad to help build a new product category – deodorants. Times change.

"Often a bridesmaid, never a bride."
Listerine dramatizes (and names) the
problem – "halitosis" – a scientific word
for "bad breath."

1930-1939.

This period will cover:

- Y&R, the first modern agency
- The emergence of organized marketing research
- The growth of radio, the first 100% ad-supported medium
- Beginnings of consumerism

Campaigns and Controversies.

Campaigns of this period include *Listerine's* "halitosis," Absorbine's "athlete's foot," and *Lifebuoy* soap's "body odor."

This new public discussion of bodily functions caused public dismay similar to that associated with contemporary Calvin Klein or Benneton advertising efforts.

One of the more controversial ads was an Odorono ad that seems to our eye a fairly restrained piece titled *"Within the Curve of a Woman's Arm."* James Webb Young of JWT wrote it, but a number of magazines refused to run it.

Pushing cultural barriers for commercial gain has often been a part of advertising's communication job.

Other product innovations – tile, porcelain, and linoleum – replaced wood and cast iron materials in the bathroom.

This led to lifestyle changes, improvements in both cleanliness and health – and the growth of personal care products.

The Queen of Rumania.

Toward the end of this decade testimonials reached new heights – or lows. The Queen of Rumania seemed to support herself on fees paid for her endorsements and testimonials.

In one issue of *Liberty* magazine, actress Constance Talmadge endorsed eight different products.

It was 1929. The good times were about to end.

Rubicam & Radio.

AFTER THE CRASH OF 1929, the economy was in dire straits.

So was advertising. The exhilarating growth of the '20s was over.

Annual advertising volume dropped from $3.4 billion in 1929 to $2.6 billion in 1930 and $2.3 billion a year later, bottoming out at $1.3 billion in 1933.

Unemployment grew from 4 million in 1930 to 8 million in 1931 and 12 million in 1932. One worker in four was out of a job.

Hard Sell for Hard Times.

Advertising agencies were forced to lay off personnel.

Copywriter's salaries were slashed from $230 to $60 a week. Lasker cut salaries by 25%.

Though overstaffed, BBDO tried to carry its people.

Hard sell, reason-why copy came back into favor.

This established what would become a recurring pattern – hard sell in hard times.

Raymond Rubicam.

IF THERE WAS EVER A CASE FOR A "GREAT MAN" THEORY of advertising history, suggests *Mirror Makers* author Stephen Fox, **Raymond Rubicam** is it.

On his own at an early age, he began writing freelance features in Philadelphia. Then he landed a job as a newspaper reporter. A desire to make more money motivated him to try selling cars.

Then he discovered advertising. Rubicam found a career that combined both his interests – writing and selling.

Young Meets Rubicam.

Rubicam's first job was at F. Wallis Armstrong, an ad agency with a reputation for tyrannical leadership.

There, he learned about copywriting by studying ads produced by JWT and others.

At the Armstrong agency, Rubicam met **John Orr Young**, an account executive and new business man. They became friends.

Rubicam moved on to NW Ayer. Shortly thereafter, he brought over Young. Their friendship grew.

At NW Ayer, Rubicam created a campaign for Steinway piano. During the '20s, radios and Victrolas had cut into piano sales.

Using Rubicam's slogan, *"The Instrument of the Immortals,"* sales for Steinway soared 70%.

Young & Rubicam.

In 1923, these two friends opened their agency in Philadelphia – Young & Rubicam – without a client to their name. (This in an industry where stealing clients was common.)

They wrote *"Clients none. Cash meagre. Hopes high."*

The Rubicam Style. "Resist the Usual."

During a time of hard sell, Raymond Rubicam believed in the pull of stylish persuasion.

He had the talent to make it work – even in tough times.

He was committed to well-crafted, visually-attractive ads that sometimes used humor.

For the first time in advertising history, creative control was given to those who were doing the actual creating: artists and copywriters – the account man was forbidden to revise an ad to suit himself or a client. Revolutionary. But it worked.

And it was not surprising that this revolutionary new agency, Y&R, became an oasis for creatives.

Ray Rubicam hired unconventional people. He created an open, friendly, informal atmosphere full of people dedicated to creating original work.

He said, *"Our job is to resist the usual."*

The Gallup Influence.

Y&R creative had another secret ingredient – research.

Another unique individual Rubicam attracted to Y&R was **George Gallup,** then a professor at Northwestern University.

Gallup had surveyed over 40,000 people to determine which part of the print media was most noticed by the audience.

His research gathered incredible attention, and he was sought after by many agencies. He said he went to work for Rubicam because Rubicam was the only person he'd met who was interested in learning more about how advertising worked.

Two friends go into business.
Ray Rubicam and John Young.

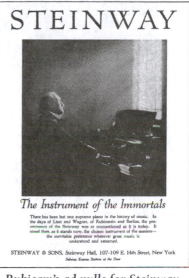

Rubicam's ad pulls for Steinway.

An advertising agency advertises.
This ad appeared in the very first issue of LIFE in 1939. It still looks modern.

Elsie the Cow.

One of the first memorable advertising "critters."

She gives the Borden's brand a warm and friendly personality as she ties together a range of Borden's dairy products.

Y&R at Work.

Part of a long-running series of ads for Jell-O – part of a long-running relationship with General Foods.

Gallup discovered that quality and sexual appeals were most persuasive for men and that women responded to appeals based on sexuality, vanity, and quality.

After Gallup's work, more nudity and sex appeals began appearing in advertising along with more comic strip formats – another popular form with people in the survey.

Unlike John B. Watson at JWT, Gallup had a major effect on Y&R's product. In fact, his research findings had an effect that reached far into the industry.

And agencies continued to grow as a source of marketing knowledge and information.

Y&R Leadership.

During the decade of economic depression, Y&R moved up to second place in annual billings, behind only JWT.

Rubicam believed, *"A company which must hire leaders from the outside either doesn't hire good employees or doesn't train or treat them properly."* Putting that into practice, Y&R grew its own people.

In its first 25 years of business, nobody left the agency with an account. Many people stayed with the agency, despite offers of higher salaries elsewhere.

Some who did leave returned at a smaller salary.

Rubicam stood for ethical restraint and would not solicit clients by preparing speculative work.

The head of the Consumers' Union said, *"When Ray Rubicam was in the room, one could think of advertising as a profession."*

Y&R at Work.

General Foods liked Y&R's work for Postum and Grape Nuts so much they lured them from Philadelphia to New York promising more business. With the move came Jell-O, Sanka, and other General Foods products. Jell-O is still a Y&R account today.

Soon, other clients followed: Travelers Insurance, Arrow Shirts, and Borden's for whom they created Elsie the Cow.

The Consumer Movement Begins.

Y&R'S SUCCESS, while exhibiting higher standards, ran parallel to the success of the **consumer movement**.

Publication of Thorstein Veblen's *Absentee Ownership* and the Lynd's *Middletown* fanned the flames of consumerism.

Consumers' Research, an organization with the purpose of informing and lobbying for the consumer, was launched. In 1927, its membership was 1,200 strong; by 1933 it was 45,000.

Simultaneously, advertising was attacked for promoting waste at a time when there was nothing to spare.

Other Consumer Groups.

Other consumer groups emerged. The Consumers' Union, the League of Women Voters, the PTA, American Home Economics Association, and many other groups organized for the purpose of some aspect of consumer protection.

In 1934, *Printer's Ink* noted, *"There is in progress a consumer rebellion of a kind that almost nobody seems to have anticipated."*

The Copeland Bill.

The growth of the consumer movement was accompanied by a move to give more power to the Food and Drug Administration in the form of the **Copeland Bill**, finally passed in 1938.

This bill gave the FDA power to establish grades and standards for all food products and extend regulation of food product, drug, and cosmetic product labels and advertising.

It granted the FDA new power over the manufacture and sale of drugs. But it contained no compulsory standards for foods and said nothing about advertising.

Though the Copeland Bill did nothing about regulating advertising, the Wheeler-Lea Amendment and the Federal Trade Commission Act, also passed in 1938, did.

Both declared deceptive acts of commerce unlawful.

Consumerism Grows...

Between 1938 and 1940, the FTC handed down eighteen injunctions to stop advertisers from making false claims.

Among those were Fleischmann's Yeast, Lifebuoy, Lux soap, and Borden's dairy products.

By the end of the decade, Consumers' Union grew to 80,000 members, and Consumers' Research reached 60,000 members. A Gallup poll revealed one in four people had read a consumer book.

Then the World Changed... Again.

The consumer movement was quickly overshadowed by World War II. Activities shifted from a focus on advertising to wartime conservation measures.

The FTC stopped pursuing deceptive claims. For example, the FTC gave up its challenge to Listerine for making false claims about curing dandruff and colds.

The consumer movement would not re-emerge for decades.

The Age of Radio.

RADIO SURGED AHEAD. Although the first radio commercial was broadcast in 1922, it was nearly a decade before the medium hit its stride.

In some ways, radio was perfect for the tough times of the '30s.

The First Free Entertainment Medium.

For the cost of a radio and a bit of electricity, America's finest entertainers performed in your kitchen or living room.

By 1932, Americans owned 15 million radios, and an estimated 10 million were tuned in every day.

The Consumer Movement...

was in many ways a reaction to ads like these. Here, Fleischmann's Yeast claimed to cure constipation and pimples.

Hey Kids...

just eat three cakes of yeast a day until your skin clears up. That's what this advertisement recommended – until an FTC injunction.

On the Veranda of the Country Club

WHERE Radio apparatus, like a professional entertainer, must meet the test of satisfying really discriminating people, Magnavox is certain to be installed.

The first requisites—tone clearness, pitch and quality—are fulfilled by the Magnavox Reproducer; the addition of a Magnavox Power Amplifier supplies the other requisite, volume.

Magnavox Products can be had from good dealers everywhere. Our interesting new booklet will be sent on request.

The Magnavox Co., Oakland, California
New York: 370 Seventh Avenue

MAGNAVOX Radio
The Reproducer Supreme

It began as a luxury. But soon, virtually every household in America had a radio.

The Further Adventures of Benton & Bowles.

After Benton "retired" at 36 he became an educator, businessman, politician, publisher, international statesman, ambassador, and author.

After WWII, he became Assistant Secretary of State for Public Affairs and helped establish UNESCO.

Chester Bowles became governor of Connecticut. In 1949, Governor Bowles had to appoint a senator to fill a vacancy. He picked Benton, who ran for re-election in 1950 and won.

Both made important contributions to their country – in addition to founding a leading US ad agency.

[www.adbuzz.com]

Go to the Chapter One Study Hall and look up Text Resources. Click on *"The Most Important Commercial in the Twentieth Century"* by James Twitchell from *"20 Ads That Shook the World."*

Radio manufacturers, the telephone company, newly formed radio networks, ad agencies, advertisers, and Hollywood all had a hand in the creation of this exciting new medium.

A New World for Agencies and Advertisers.

Early sponsorship occurred by advertisers underwriting entire radio shows. Eveready Batteries began this trend by sponsoring a one-hour show in 1923. Other manufacturers followed.

Generally, agencies and sponsors produced the most popular shows. Popular performing talent boosted the ratings of these shows, while networks produced high-minded sustaining shows such as the *Mercury Theater* of Orson Welles.

Benton & Bowles.

Benton & Bowles was a new advertising agency founded by two young men, **Charles Benton** and **Chester Bowles**.

It opened in 1929, just before the Great Crash.

Only a few months later, facing bankruptcy, they were given the opportunity to produce *The Maxwell House Showboat*, which became the top rated show by 1934. Benton & Bowles created two other shows that made it into the top four.

But the Depression-created fear of hiring too much additional staff, as well as the unrelenting demands of a weekly program deadlines, led Benton to quit two years later on his 36th birthday. Bowles quit a couple of years after that.

It was said they never listened to the radio again.

Even as business boomed, there was tension. As agency-produced programming brought more listeners to radio, radio networks raised the fees charged to agency clients.

More Push and Pull.

New techniques were developed – singing commercials, jingles, were now possible, and commercials could be woven into the plot of the radio show (which already included the sponsor's name).

The same debate over the MacManus soft-sell approach vs. the Hopkins hard-sell approach confronted those who were trying to work with this new audio medium.

Radio shows did not reflect the economic crisis. Comedy, variety hours, and dance bands offered welcome escape.

Programs developed by both Y&R and Benton & Bowles, using the soft-sell approach, became the most popular.

Y&R had their first "prime-time" hit with its Jell-O sponsored *Jack Benny Comedy-Variety Show.*

Lucky Strike's Hit Parade lasted into the early days of TV.

The Invention of the Soap Opera.

Daytime radio developed. **Frank Hummert** and his assistant, **Anne Ashenhert**, created the "soap opera."

They believed human interest stories like those found in newspapers would appeal to homemakers. Hummert kept ownership of these shows, which ultimately made him more powerful than his clients or the networks.

In 1937, he was the best paid man in advertising.

Then the World Changed… Again.

In 1939, Europe entered what was to become World War II.

Eventually, everyone went to war – including advertising.

Advertising Goes to War.

ADVERTISING HAD PROVEN ITSELF A HERO in WWI. It helped recruit people into the armed forces and persuaded people to support other issues important to the country's well-being.

Now, the ad industry mobilized for WWII.

The War Advertising Council.

Industry leaders such as Helen Resor and James Webb Young of JWT were asked to join the War Advertising Council.

The advertising industry ended up donating about a billion dollars in time and space to the war effort.

The Treasury Department ruled that advertising could continue during the war, in reasonable amounts.

Those advertisers who did advertise often connected their product to the war – either by advertising its use in the war effort or by recognizing the people who were fighting in it.

Women Join the Labor Force.

During WWII, American women played a major role on the home front.

Two million went to work in heavy industry – as welders, riveters, lathe operators – in shipyards and factories. In total, more than six million women entered the work force.

This new American woman was encouraged by the War Advertising Council through ads like this one – *"We Can Do It."*

Women joined the work force at home. Companies like Campbell's manufactured special products for the Army and Navy.

But that didn't stop all progress, and even though the company was forced to cut back on production, they managed to introduce a few new products – like Franco-American Macaroni.

Change & Growth.

THERE WAS A WAR GOING ON. But other things were going on as well. The economy was growing – and so was advertising.

Slow Growth in Agency Income.

Between 1941 and 1945, US ad volume grew from $2.2 billion to $2.9 billion – still a half billion dollars below its 1929 peak.

JWT led all agencies in billings, and Y&R followed.

In 1947, JWT became the first $100 million agency.

Early Positioning.

In 1932, Plymouth's *"Look At All Three,"* created by J. Sterling Getchell, appealed to a country recovering from the Great Depression.

Featuring Walter Chrysler as the spokesperson, it positioned *Plymouth* alongside *Ford* and *Chevrolet*.

Three months after the ads first ran, *Plymouth* sales were up 218%!

1940-1949.

This period will cover:

- Advertising's involvement with the war effort
- Management changes at major agencies
- The transfer of military experience to American business

Propaganda Goes to Work.

Advertising encouraged the habits necessary for a nation at war.

Patriotic advertising during World War II.

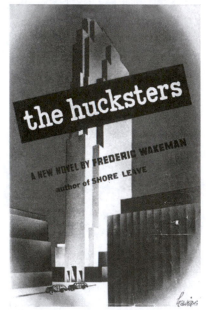

Ford in Your Future. 1944. *Gas was being rationed and no new cars were being built. This is how Ford advertised.*

The Hucksters – *also appearing on late-night TV, starring Clark Gable.*

Growth in Consumer Spending.

After WWII, soldiers returned to their jobs and people began spending all the money they'd saved during the war.

Their return from the war and the accompanying personal abundance set spending in motion. The Post-war Boom was beginning.

Meanwhile, the agency business was changing leadership.

The Changing of the Guard.

Ray Rubicam retired in 1944.

Bruce Barton ran for the Senate in 1940, but lost. He returned as president of BBDO, but in 1946 turned the agency over to the street-smart **Ben Duffy** (shown here on the cover of *Forbes*), aggressive about new business and the power of television.

One of BBDO's more prominent clients was General Dwight D. Eisenhower.

Duffy provided major assistance in both of Ike's campaigns and led the charge into TV. BBDO put 80% of its budgets into this new medium. Billings quadrupled!

Lasker Liquidates – Forms FCB.

Albert Lasker tried to find a replacement for himself but failed. Men he chose either died or left Lord & Thomas.

When his son finally said he wouldn't go into the ad business, Lasker liquidated his stock for $10 million, selling his agency to three senior employees, the managers of the New York, Chicago, and LA offices: **Emerson Foote, Fairfax Cone,** and **Don Belding.**

The agency reopened in 1943 as Foote, Cone & Belding.

Growth in Agency Services.

The traditional agency commission was still 15%.

But after the war, clients began to expect more for their money.

Agencies began to add staff to cover other areas of expertise not offered clients before the war. The list included: market research, merchandising, publicity, media, and, in many cases, marketing.

As overhead went up, profits came down.

Some smaller agencies merged with larger ones to meet this increased demand for services.

Birth of "the Brainstorm."

The wartime experience had re-shaped American business.

Even creativity developed a paramilitary game plan.

In 1940, **Alex Osborn** of BBDO created **brainstorming.**

His books, such as *Applied Imagination,* were quite popular. And many of Osborn's basic principles – such as the thought that idea generation should be done without the discouraging effect of judgment – are still used today.

By 1956, BBDO participated in 401 brainstorming sessions which produced 34,000 tentative ideas. Of these, 2,000 were considered worthy.

One of the most memorable was Campbell's *"Soup on the Rocks."*

The Growth of Qualitative Research.

About this time, **Ernest Dichter,** a Freudian psychologist, created **motivation research.** Motivation research had a significant impact on creative work and on the public's perception of advertising in general.

Soup on the Rocks – *product of a BBDO brainstorming session.*

Dichter applied projective tests to discover consumer's hidden motives. As awareness of motivation research grew inside and outside of the industry, the controversy raged. Many industry people dismissed it as "hocus pocus."

Outside, it fueled suspicion about advertising and led novelists to a favorite new villain – "the advertising man."

And a Little Literature.

In stark contrast to how advertising was viewed in the 1920s, fiction of this time portrayed advertising as a false world filled with long hours, questionable ethics, and villainous people.

The advertising man was portrayed in moral conflict.

Frederic Wakeman's *The Hucksters* launched this trend.

His antagonist was suspiciously similar to George Washington Hill, the infamous tobacco baron – Wakeman wrote this novel while working on the Lucky Strike account.

It became a best-seller, was picked up by the Book-of-the-Month-Club, and made into a motion picture starring Clark Gable. (Sidney Greenstreet is the George Washington Hill character. Adolphe Menjou's part is based on Emerson Foote.)

Now, you can see *The Hucksters* on late-night TV.

Meanwhile, another change in the media was about to change advertising – and the world.

Advertising was about to turn on television.

Osborn & "Brainstorming."

by Don Parente

Alex Osborn, a pragmatic and very successful businessman, thought of himself as a creative person.

He is the father of **brainstorming** and the "O" in BBDO.

"Creative Imagination."

He strongly believed in the ability of people to stimulate, enhance, and expand their creativity.

He developed exercises, procedures, drills, and ideas to develop this "creative imagination."

He wrote seven books on creativity, including his classic *Applied Imagination.*

Six Stages of Brainstorming:

Brainstorming sessions can take many forms. Most practitioners follow some variation of these six steps:

1. The Problem. The leader states the problem.

2. "How to…" Restate the problem in a "how to" format.

Restatements are posted on large sheets of paper.

3. "How Many Ways…" The group selects the first restatement to be "brainstormed." Initial solutions are called out and written down.

4. Warmup – "Other Uses for…" After initial thoughts, a short session which steps away from the problem.

For five minutes, group members warm up on another idea – like how many other uses for a paper clip.

5. Brainstorm! Now the group refocuses on the problem to be solved.

Ideas are continually written down and "built on."

6. The Wildest Idea. After the storm slows down, the group takes the "wildest idea" and tries to turn it into something useful.

Ninety minutes to two hours is good for a first session.

[Donald Parente is a Professor in the Ad Sequence at Middle Tennessee State and an Alex Osborn expert.]

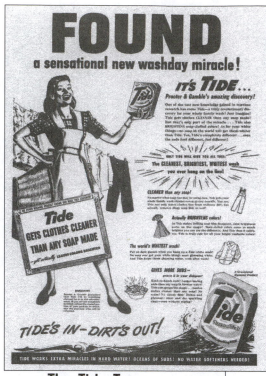

The Tide Turns.

Detergents, a by-product of wartime munitions chemistry, enter the market with a better way to clean clothes.

The brand management system enters the market with a better way to manage multiple brands.

The inventor/creator – Secretary of Defense Neil McElroy.

Automobile Culture Goes into Overdrive.

New car models become national events. Futuristic styling announces the arrival of the modern age.

The Age of Television.

TELEVISION WAS THE EVENT OF THIS DECADE.

After the war, the United States lived in a prosperity that hadn't been seen since the 1920s. Or ever.

Advertising expenditures tripled – from $1.9 billion in 1945 to $5.7 billion in 1950. This still represented 2.9% of consumer spending in 1950, the same as in prewar 1940.

But consumer spending was going through the roof!

And underneath, the nature of advertising was changing.

Because advertisers were changing.

The Growth of Marketing.

During the 1950s, P&G reached the billion dollar mark. Half their revenue came from new products invented during this decade.

General Foods sold $300 million worth of products a year during this same time period.

Brand Management.

Though not yet widely implemented, the **brand management** system proposed by **Neil McElroy** at P&G was becoming the industry standard.

President Eisenhower named McElroy Secretary of Defense.

The booming post-war university population was discovering new classes in the relatively new discipline of marketing.

The same military structure that had always been a part of the manufacturing side of business now became part of the marketing side of business.

The same "can do" attitude that brought victory in WWII was there to bring victory in the post-war marketplace.

The '50s Marketplace Goes into Overdrive.

There was not only a Baby Boom, but a construction boom and an automobile boom. An interstate highway system was built.

Automobiles became the most heavily advertised products, with GM passing P&G as the leading national advertiser.

The only other manufacturer among the top ten advertisers that did not make automobiles was Coca-Cola.

In this period, motor-vehicle registration began its leap – from $31 million in 1945 to $78.8 million in 1960.

The $100 Million Agency Club Grows.

BBDO and Y&R became $100 million agencies in 1951.

McCann-Erickson joined this elite group in 1954.

By 1957, all four agencies passed $200 million in billings.

More Marketing Services from Agencies.

Agencies, looking for ways to serve clients better, gradually added more and more marketing services.

Agencies now had marketing departments, which assisted clients in such things as budgets and marketing plans.

While clients like P&G and General Foods had solid skills, the more experienced marketers were often at ad agencies.

Agency marketing people had the benefit of being involved in marketing plans for all their clients, whereas many clients were still new to the disciplines of marketing. Furthermore, these companies, with a manufacturing focus, usually lacked the agency's more sophisticated resources and broader experience.

Stability and International Growth.

While everyone was prospering, some things stayed the same.

JWT stood for stability in the remodeled Graybar Building in New York City. Its reception room resembled a stately library lined with books chosen by noted author Lewis Mumford.

The agency rarely lost business, but when it did, jobs were found for those previously assigned to the departed account.

JWT also prospered because it was international – just as American business was beginning to expand.

Rumors had JWT offices used as CIA staging areas during this period. Ed Wilson, a top exec in JWT's New York office had been a high-ranking official in the OSS – the CIA's wartime predecessor.

By the end of WWII, JWT had 15 foreign offices.

By 1960, JWT was billing $120 million abroad, about half the agency's total domestic billing.

Y&R expanded into Canada and Great Britain.

McCann and BBDO also grew in this period.

In 1957, McCann-Erickson moved its office of 1,100 employees – the largest office move ever by an agency.

Marion Harper, McCann, and Interpublic.

By 1959, McCann trailed only JWT in domestic billings. McCann, known for its organization, was also thought of as the research agency and as an account management agency.

Then, they made a revolutionary change that was decades ahead of any other agency – the result of one person's vision.

Marion Harper, Jr. went from office boy to president of McCann-Erickson in nine years. Harper was an empire builder.

He placed emphasis on an international presence and turned McCann into the first American agency in the Far East.

He bought other agencies and kept them separate from McCann until 1960. Then he announced a reorganization and formed a new conglomerate, Interpublic. It was a bold new idea at the time.

1950-1959.

This period will cover:
- The growth of American advertising agencies worldwide
- The establishment of the brand management system
- The rise of television and a new kind of advertising – "The Spot"

Advertising Icons.

In 1957, Leo Burnett invented the *Pillsbury Doughboy, Tony the Tiger,* and the *Jolly Green Giant.*

Marketing Disaster.

In 1957, the Ford Motor Company introduced the Edsel.

Agency research into what the American public wanted in a new car caused the production of a choice that straddled 18 models and became one of the greatest product disasters of all time.

Coke and Interpublic.

Marion Harper organized Interpublic to service Coca-Cola's marketing needs around the world.

The USP.

Here's Reeves' original USP definition from his *Reality in Advertising.* In many ways, it's a made-for-TV version of Claude Hopkins' reason why.

Proposition.

1. Each advertisement must make a proposition to the consumer. Not just words, not just product puffery, not just show-window advertising.

Each advertisement must say to each reader, *"Buy this product and you get this specific benefit."*

Unique.

2. The proposition must be one that the competition either cannot, or does not, offer. It must be unique – either a uniqueness of the brand or a claim not otherwise made in that particular field of advertising.

Selling.

3. The proposition must be so strong that it can move the mass millions, i.e., pull over new customers to your product.

Interpublic held McCann-Erickson and McCann-Marschalk, both traditional agencies; an international agency; and Communication Affiliates, Interpublic's research, public relations, sales, and promotional services arm.

One of the main benefits of this move was the ability for what was the previous "McCann" to handle competing accounts under the same corporate roof.

America Turns on TV.

IN 1950, SOMEONE SAID, *"...television affords little profit for advertising agencies since most TV appropriations are small compared with those of other media."*

Ben Duffy didn't agree. In 1949, he was already spending 80% of BBDO's media time on TV and only 20% on radio.

In 1948, the FCC refused to license any new stations until signal interference among the existing 108 was worked out.

Even so, the ad industry's total TV business grew from $12.3 million in 1949 to $40.8 million in 1950, to $128 million in 1959.

It had taken radio 16 years to reach that level.

CBS made its first net profit in 1953.

One year later, TV was the largest advertising medium in the world.

In the beginning, advertising agencies owned the shows and produced them for their single-sponsor clients.

Shows bore the name of the advertiser. The *Voice of Firestone* debuted along with *Texaco Star Theater* with Milton Berle, *Kraft Television Theater,* and *Goodyear TV Playhouse.*

The network provided facilities, air time, and censorship.

Often, the sales pitch was integrated into the entertainment, particularly in comedy and variety shows. And the sponsor could demand changes. In the early days, they did.

When a contestant named Ford appeared on Groucho Marx's quiz show, the DeSoto car company, which was sponsoring the show, asked the contestant to use another surname. A gas sponsor changed the phrase "gas chambers" to "chambers."

From Sponsorship to Spot.

When a single sponsor was responsible for a whole show, it felt responsible for the manner and frequency of the ads. They were in a whole new business, producing TV shows, which had little to do with manufacturing cheese, tires, or gasoline.

Eventually, the networks began offering multiple sponsorships and took control of programming. This also changed advertising.

Push on TV – The USP & "the Spot."

A new force on television was the Ted Bates agency, which created some of the most memorable, though not most-beloved, advertising campaigns.

Bates became known as "the spot agency" for its hard-hitting, intrusive, and repetitive commercials.

This was the beginning of a new type of commercial – the **spot.**

Rosser Reeves, mentored in the Hopkins reason-why tradition, was the mind behind the work at Bates.

Reeves conceived the **Unique Selling Proposition** or **USP.**

He strongly believed only one idea or concept could be made memorable in an ad. Some claims the agency made for their client's product pushed the limits of propriety and the law.

Commercials of "personal" products were banned by the National Association of Broadcasters' television code.

Bates continued to run ads for Preparation H. The NAB had no power to enforce their code, but the FTC did, stepping in to force Bates to drop false claims being made on five client's products.

Reeves was insulted. He wrote a full-page rebuttal, placing it in seven major newspapers. But, a few months later, the offending campaigns were off the air.

Reeves and "The Man from Abilene."
Modern television advertising entered politics in a big way during the 1952 presidential campaign.

Reeves was hired by the Republicans to create commercials for Dwight D. Eisenhower. The result, a classic case of presidential packaging, was *The Man from Abilene.*

It was the first clear demonstration in politics of the power of TV combined with the tools of advertising.

Meanwhile, the marketplace was full of demonstrations of the power of television and the USP to build brands. On the spot.

USPs at Work.
Here are some classic Bates USPs. Some are still in use:

✓ *"Wonder Bread helps build strong bodies 12 ways."*

✓ *"M&Ms melt in your mouth, not in your hands."*

✓ *"Colgate cleans your breath while it cleans your teeth."*

As television added more messages to daily life, messages became shorter. Vivid visuals were used to get attention.

Research Grows in Importance.
Research had earned a place in advertising.

All big agencies now had research departments.

Marketing's importance grew, with more emphasis on research. Now demographics and statistics backed up marketing decisions.

The Advertising Research Foundation (ARF) was founded in 1953.

More and more, research worked to measure ad effectiveness.

Motivation Research.
Another research school of thought emerged.

"The Most Disliked Ad of the Decade."

Reeve's ad for Anacin raised sales from $18 million to $54 million in just eighteen months!

The visual included three boxes in a head: a vibrating tension line, a pounding hammer, and sparking electricity.

Though Reeves acknowledged it was *"the most hated ad in history,"* he pointed out the ad made money for the client. And wasn't that the point?

[www.adbuzz.com]

Go to Chapter One Study Hall, look up Text Resources. Click on "How Would You Like a Hammer in the Head?" by James Twitchell from *"20 Ads That Shook the World."*

"Does She or Doesn't She?"

Shirley Polykoff's slightly naughty (but not really) copy line built Clairol's business.

Read a terrific Malcolm Gladwell piece at www.malcolmgladwell.com, "True Colors. Hair dye and the hidden history of postwar America."

The Hidden Persuaders.

In 1957, Vance Packard's *The Hidden Persuaders* was a bestseller.

He wrote about advertising's efforts to shape purchase decisions.

He based much of his "exposé" on interviews with Ernst Dichter and James Vicary, self-styled creator of **subliminal advertising.**

Dichter's work included things such as the most appealing colors and designs for lipstick packages –hardly subversive. But even the phrase "motivation research" fed Packard's Machiavellian view.

Vicary claimed to have created a means of applying imperceptible visual messages that were unconsciously persuasive.

Though never demonstrated, the National Association of Broadcasters stepped in and banned them – effectively outlawing something which never really existed.

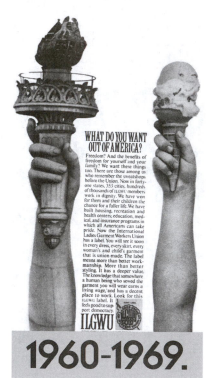

WHAT DO YOU WANT OUT OF AMERICA?

1960-1969.

This period will cover:
- Social change in advertising
- The Creative Revolution – a new style of advertising creativity with writer/art director teams
- Three individuals: Bill Bernbach, Leo Burnett, and David Ogilvy

Motivation research advocates thought the qualitative approach would illuminate the more subtle aspects of communication needed to sell some products.

Leo Burnett and Foote, Cone & Belding enthusiastically embraced this type of research, adding "MR" departments.

Rosser Reeves at Bates dismissed it as "the Freudian hoax."

Other industry people remained fearful or skeptical.

Alfred Politz, a psychologist and also a prominent marketing researcher, criticized the methodology.

One thing was certain. Research was here to stay.

But business was good and it was time for another change in advertising – it came from the creative department.

The Creative Revolution.

THE '60s WERE A TIME OF CONFLICT AND CHANGE. These changes occurred both inside and outside advertising.

Social Change.

As Stephen Fox observed, *"Since the 1920s, advertising functioned as a mirror responding to the culture, more than shaping it."*

American society was opening to greater cultural diversity.

An Irish Catholic, John F. Kennedy, was elected president.

The WASP (White Anglo-Saxon Protestant) establishment began to be challenged on social, political, and economic fronts. Conflict on issues concerning equality, consumer protection, civil rights, and the war in Vietnam dominated the decade.

The Civil Rights and woman's movements pressed for equal treatment of all in the workplace. Some unions, like the International Ladies Garment Workers (ILGWU), began to advertise.

The Congress on Racial Equality (CORE) and the New York City Commission on Human Rights monitored the progress of business as well as the ad industry in the hiring of blacks and their accurate representation in the media. The National Organization for Women (NOW) did for the same for women.

From WASP to Ethnic.

These changes affected advertising. The creative revolution was, in many ways, an ethnic revolution with the WASP stronghold finally giving way to broader representation.

But increased representation did not come easily or evenly.

Though Albert Lasker was Jewish, advertising generally trailed behind related fields in admitting Jews and other minorities to positions of high authority. (An exception has been women, where agencies have tended to be at the forefront.)

JWT, BBDO, Y&R, Ayer, and McCann-Erickson were WASP agencies, largely dominated by white, Anglo-Saxon males.

Doyle Dane Bernbach (DDB) emerged from Grey, one of the few Jewish agencies of any size. They influenced the entire industry.

As **Jerry Della Femina** said at the time, *"It doesn't hurt to be born Italian or Jewish in the streets of the City of New York,"* reflecting the fact that the Creative Revolution was led by Jewish copywriters and Italian art directors.

There were other changes as well.

Smoke Signals.

In 1964, the Surgeon General's landmark report identified the use of cigarettes as harmful to health.

The first warning sign was a 1957 *Reader's Digest* article. Soon after the article had appeared in print, BBDO resigned the $1.6 million *Reader's Digest* account in what appeared to be deference to the $15 million American Tobacco account.

Two years later, TV personality Arthur Godfrey mentioned on his program that smoking made him "feel badly." Lorillard immediately stopped sponsoring his show. (Godfrey later died of lung cancer.)

These events made the message quite clear to agencies. As late as 1988, a Northwest Airlines commercial cheerfully announced an end to smoking on flights. This caused the "offending agency" to lose substantial non-tobacco billings from the parent company – which was also a cigarette marketer.

But some agencies stepped up to the issue. After the Surgeon General's report, the *New Yorker* banned cigarette advertising. O&M and DDB announced they would no longer accept cigarette accounts.

Tobacco Fires Back.

The tobacco industry quickly reacted by adopting their own advertising code. In it, they agreed to stop pitches aimed at young people and to adhere to the newly outlawed claims against stating that smoking "was good for health."

All the while, television budgets for cigarettes continued to grow.

Responding to pressure, Congress banned cigarette ads from TV and radio, beginning January 1, 1971.

Cigarette accounts now emphasized print – primarily magazines and outdoor – and tobacco profits continued to grow.

Industry Debate and Regulation.

As early as 1961, industry leaders were admitting to themselves, if not to one another, that self-regulation was not working.

Fairfax Cone wrote the head of the Federal Communication Commission in Washington, D.C., complaining that there was too much tasteless programming and too much advertising for products of little interest.

On the West Coast, **Howard Gossage** publicly asked *"Is advertising worth saving?"* He described advertising as *"a billion dollar hammer on a ten cent thumb tack"* and voiced concerns on issues ranging from automobile safety, to outdoor billboards, to the agency commission system.

NARB Is Formed.

In 1971, the **National Advertising Review Board** (NARB) was formed as an extension of the Better Business Bureau.

The NARB consisted of a five-member panel with three members representing advertisers, one member representing an agency, and

Social Change for Creative Impact. As always, cosmetics and fashion sell using the cutting edge of change. Here, for the "liberated" fragrance – Charlie.

A Resistance to Change. The tobacco industry used sophisticated marketing and vast resources. Here, quasi-medical appeals and a war hero's endorsement.

How to
get your husband
to fasten his
Rover 2000
safety harness:

Tell him it's a Sam Browne belt
and he looks like a World War I aviator

How the Nazi Car Came to the Jewish Agency.

by Dennis Altman

Volkswagen was to be Hitler's gift to the German working class. The "people's car" was born as a political promise and almost died on the battlefields of WWII.

By 1948, the war was over. German industry was struggling to its feet, and the Marshall Plan was starting to work.

It was also critical that West Germany make reparations payments to the new state of Israel.

At the US State Department, the Volkswagen problem came up often.

Could the free world, just after the fiercest days of WWII, be convinced to buy a German car?

And even then, who could do it?

In New York, DDB was still an advertising secret. Their work for Ohrbach's was highly regarded, but the agency was far from mainstream.

Client Connections.

But DDB's clients were not so limited. Nathan Ohrbach sat on the board of a hot young Wall Street investment firm – Dreyfus.

Agency scuttlebutt said he'd introduced DDB to Dr. Edwin Land of Polaroid and to the synthetic fiber people at Chemstrand Corporation.

The Ohrbach-Dreyfus connection, also much concerned with Germany being able to make payments to Israel, reached to Washington. If the buzz in the DDB hallways was to be believed, VW would go to an agency with no ties to Detroit and no possible link to Nazi anti-Semitism.

DDB's client list was essentially soft goods and cameras and two of the agency's principals were Jewish.

Nathan Ohrbach's experience with the agency was probably the deciding factor. And so Hitler's "people's car" was eventually parked at the very unlikely address of 20 West 43rd Street in New York City.

A bit later, Dreyfus also became a DDB client.

one member representing the public.

In the first ten years of its existence, 1,845 cases were heard; 42% resulted in modification or discontinuance of advertising.

We'll cover the NARB at greater length in Chapter Three.

From the Social Revolution to the Creative One.

Advertising created for an ugly little car – the Volkswagen, a relic from Nazi Germany – by an agency with Jewish founders and many ethnic employees led the Creative Revolution.

Copy written by **Julian Koenig** told the truth and made advantages of the car's deficiencies, such as its basic functional nature (cheap to buy, cheap to run) and low horsepower (high mileage).

Art direction by **Helmut Krone** innovated advertising design by the use of "white space," a more realistic photographic style, and a new handling of typography.

VW advertising became the most admired, most influential campaign of the early '60s and brought national attention to DDB.

It was part of the advertising that changed advertising.

Bernbach, Burnett, & Ogilvy.

THREE INDIVIDUALS WERE AT THE HEART of the Creative Revolution. Each began their journeys over a decade before.

Bill Bernbach (pronounced Burn-*back*) opened Doyle Dane Bernbach in 1949 with a vision – a new way to create advertising.

Leo Burnett opened his agency in 1936 because he thought there was *"entirely too much dull advertising in Chicago."*

David Ogilvy opened Hewill, Ogilvy, Benson & Mather in 1948 largely because he believed no reputable agency would *"hire a middle-aged rolling stone like me."*

Once again, advertising demonstrated that it was an industry where individuals with a vision could make a difference.

Bill Bernbach.

SHORT AND UNATHLETIC, William Bernbach studied English, music, and philosophy at New York University. He liked to quote Bertrand Russell. A favorite was *"Even in the most purely logical realms, it is insight that arrives at what is new."*

Bernbach arrived in the advertising business through the mail room at Schenley. Then he worked as a ghostwriter for the head of the 1939 World's Fair.

From there he went to the Weintraub agency where he met and worked on Ohrbach's (which became one of DDB's first clients) with the influential designer **Paul Rand**.

Together, Rand and Bernbach talked of combining writing and art and looked for new ways to integrate two creative forces that had been in opposition.

At Grey, Bernbach continued that pursuit. He believed people would respond to fresh, original ideas presented in arresting ways.

He said, *"…advertising is persuasion, and persuasion is not a science, but an art."*

He respected audiences.

He said, *"It's true that there's a twelve-year-old mentality in America – every six-year-old has it. We're a smart people."*

He put it all to the test in 1949.

Doyle Dane Bernbach (DDB).

Ned Doyle did account work.

Maxwell Dane handled finance and administration.

All but one founding principal came from Grey – as did their first account – Ohrbach's.

The creative department was Bernbach, **Bob Gage,** and **Phyllis Robinson.** Gage was influenced by Paul Rand and his design teacher, Alexey Brodovitch of *Harper's Bazaar.*

Phyllis Robinson had grown up wanting to be a writer – preferably someone like Dorothy Parker.

DDB's client list grew slowly during the '50s, with campaigns for Ohrbach's, Levy's, Polaroid, and El Al, Israel's airline.

Billings grew to $8 million by the fifth year.

The next year they doubled. By 1957, DDB passed $20 million.

In 1958, DDB took five of the eight gold medals awarded by the New York Art Director's Club.

By 1965, the agency billed $130 million and dominated every advertising award show.

The Writer/Art Director Team.

Bernbach's collaboration with Rand and then Gage established a new working relationship for creative problem solving at an ad agency – the **creative team.**

Artists and writers worked as equals with a sense of joint responsibility for their work.

It was the culmination of a tradition that began with Y&R. In fact, on Raymond Rubicam's 85th birthday, Bernbach said, *"…you taught me the importance of saying the right things in an ad. But more than that, you taught me… the importance of saying those things artfully."*

Early DDB. Big impact on a small budget. The ad above was done by Bernbach and the Paul Rand-influenced art director, Bob Gage.

Paul Rand.

From his 20s on, Paul Rand was widely influential in the design field.

His 1946 book, *Thoughts on Design,* revolutionized the industry.

He worked out a new way of communicating based on juxtaposing visual forms and words.

The Art/Copy Team.

His collaboration with Bill Bernbach became the prototype art/copy team.

He noted, *"Bernbach was the first writer I met who could think visually."*

They collaborated on Ohrbach's.

It became DDB's first account.

A practical headline juxtaposed with a frivolous visual.

The Ohrbach's ad on the left was done a few years later at DDB by Rand disciple Bob Gage.

Corporate Identities.

Rand influenced Bernbach and Bernbach influenced advertising.

Rand's other major influences were in graphic design and corporate identity – most design programs emphasize Rand's importance the way we emphasize Bernbach's.

Rand created corporate identities that are still familiar today: like ABC, IBM, UPS, and Westinghouse.

He was also conscious of the cultural role of the designer in upgrading taste rather than playing to the lowest common denominator.

In this, he and Bernbach were also very much kindred spirits.

Verbal surprise with a simple photo – to dramatize VW quality control.

Visual surprise dramatizes El Al's new faster planes.

You don't have to be Jewish

to love Levy's
real Jewish Rye

Surprise Surprise. A juxtaposition of surprising words and visuals create a new kind of advertising.

Avis is only No.2 in rent a cars. So why go with us?

We try harder.
(When you're not the biggest, you have to.)
We just can't afford dirty ash-trays. Or half-empty gas tanks. Or worn wipers. Or unwashed cars. Or low tires. Or anything less than seat-adjusters that adjust. Heaters that heat. Defrost-ers that defrost.
Obviously, the thing we try hardest for is just to be nice. To start you out right with a new car, like a lively, super-torque Ford, and a pleasant smile. To know, say, where you get a good pastrami sandwich in Duluth. Why?
Because we can't afford to take you for granted.
Go with us next time.
The line at our counter is shorter.

Lemon.

This Volkswagen missed the boat.
The chrome strip on the glove compartment is blemished and must be replaced. Chances are you wouldn't have noticed it; Inspector Kurt Kroner did.
There are 3,389 men at our Wolfsburg factory with only one job: to inspect Volkswagens at each stage of production. 13000 Volkswagens are produced daily; there are more inspectors than cars.)
Every shock absorber is tested (spot checking won't do), every windshield is scanned. VWs have been rejected for surface scratches barely visible to the eye.
Final inspection is really something! VW inspectors run each car off the line onto the Funktionsprüfstand (car test stand), tote up 189 check points, gun ahead to the automatic brake stand, and say "no" to one VW out of fifty.
This preoccupation with detail means the VW lasts longer and requires less maintenance, by and large, than other cars. (It also means a used VW depreciates less than any other car.)
We pluck the lemons; you get the plums.

Bernbach's Management Style.
Though his style was loose, he saw every ad before it left his agency. When hiring, he looked for those with the potential to do something inspiring.

He was a great teacher.

One insider referred to DDB as *"sort of an adult Summerhill."*

And, in fact, many DDB alums went on to either found their own agencies or lead other major agencies – from coast to coast.

Always Trying Harder…
DDB continued to provide inspiration and surprise.

Other notable campaigns were for Avis (*"Avis is only No. 2 in Rent-a-Cars. So why go with us? We try harder."*), American Airlines, Jamaica, and Chivas Regal. And more.

It was advertising that would change advertising.

A Lasting Influence…
As you will see in Chapter Two, Bill Bernbach and his agency did more than create great ads.

They created a new standard – one that virtually every creative department aspired to.

Though viewed as revolutionary at the time, the DDB approach became the industry standard – at least as far as the creative department was concerned.

For example, even though Volkswagen is now at another agency, the spirit of their advertising is from the agency that created the original campaign.

...Worldwide.

That influence was not confined to the US ad industry.

You can see the influence of DDB's work in the advertising industry of every major industrialized country.

Agencies in every country honor his memory and his standards.

The power of the idea. The strength of surprise.

And the creation of advertising where words and visuals work in a unique partnership.

DDB created a new language for the creation of advertising.

Leo Burnett.

NOT YOUR TYPICAL ADMAN – modest, physically unassuming, and lacking the stereotypical creative ego. He was Leo.

Leo's Motto: *"If you reach for the stars, you may not get one. But you won't come up with a handful of mud, either."* That was Leo.

A 1914 Michigan grad, he first worked for Cadillac, writing for an in-house magazine distributed to dealerships.

He joined Cadillac right after Theodore MacManus had written *"The Penalty of Leadership."* Leo was deeply influenced by Mac-Manus' philosophy – *"the power of truth, simply told."*

Leo Comes to Chicago.

As he neared the age of 40, he was hired as the creative head of the Chicago office of the Erwin Wasey agency.

He brought along his friend, **De Witt (Jack) O'Kieffe.**

On arrival, he noted that Chicago could use better advertising. After a few years, O'Kieffe announced he was taking a job in New York unless Leo would open his own agency. So Leo did it.

The Leo Burnett agency launched in 1936 with $50,000, a few accounts, and a half-dozen people from Wasey's creative department.

Years later, the Burnett agency wrote a campaign that saluted the power of *"creative flair and business acumen."*

That flair came from Leo's creative department. The acumen came from the tough-minded account execs led by O'Kieffe.

Apples in the Lobby.

It was 1936. The Depression was still going on. People told Leo he'd soon be selling apples on a street corner. With typical flair, he decided to make the apple his symbol. From that moment on, there was always a bowl of apples in the lobby.

The agency reached $10 million in billings by 1946, $22 million in 1950, $55 million in 1954, and $100 million by 1959.

Growth was spearheaded by Richard Heath, a merchandising expert from Detroit. He landed business from Pillsbury, Kellogg's, Campbell's, the Tea Council, and P&G.

Leo had few interests other than advertising. His only day off was Christmas. His agency was a reflection of that spirit – everyone lived and breathed advertising.

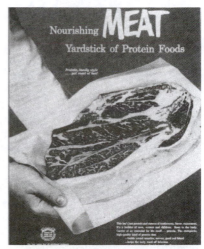

Visual Power. *Red meat. Red background.*

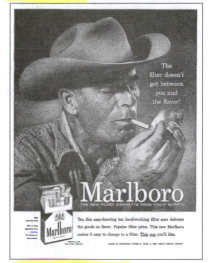

The Power of Image. *Leo Burnett's instincts tied American masculinity – the cowboy – with a filter cigarette.*

The Power of Imagery. *A magical creation – the Jolly Green Giant – adds mythology to the American marketplace and power to a can of peas.*

The man in the Hathaway shirt

The Man Behind Hathaway Shirts.

Here, Ogilvy added "story value" to his ads with a model who wore an eye patch.

Repetition with restraint builds image. Ogilvy started by running these ads in *The New Yorker,* a medium that added its own sense of class and style.

The Man from Schweppes Arrives!

When You Find Something that Works, Use It Again.

Here, Ogilvy personifies the brand with Commander Whitehead as, *"The Man from Schweppes."*

Seems a bit like the Hathaway approach doesn't it? In Ogilvy's view, this was a good thing.

And they made money at it – a Leo Burnett Christmas bonus was usually equal to a month's pay – for everyone in the agency.

"Inherent Drama."

This dedication also had a spirit – Leo believed ads should illuminate an inherent drama that lived within every product.

He believed ads should be written in the vernacular, using a warm and friendly tone. Thus evolved the "Chicago School" – focusing on simplicity, clarity, and people-talk.

"Glacier-like Power."

Leo's campaigns lasted. They created the Jolly Green Giant for the Minnesota Canning Company.

It was so successful they changed their name to the Green Giant Company.

Burnett also created the *Pillsbury Doughboy, Tony the Tiger, Charlie the Tuna,* the *Keebler Elves,* and the Marlboro cowboy – one of the longest running ad campaigns in history.

Leo called it, *"the glacier-like power of friendly familiarity."*

Burnett over Bernbach?

In voting for the Ad Man of the Century, *TIME* magazine picked Leo Burnett over Bill Bernbach. There was some controversy.

The argument was that while Bernbach had most certainly created a style and an industry-wide influence, if you really looked at who had done a better job at creating lasting brands – it was Leo.

David Ogilvy.

WAS AN ENGLISHMAN FASCINATED BY AMERICA. He first came over to study American advertising on behalf of his English employer, the British agency Mather & Crowther.

Before he began his journey, he visited an acquaintance at NBC's London office and asked for introductions. With these, he managed to meet almost every important person on Madison Avenue.

Perhaps one of the most profound meetings happened when he met Rosser Reeves. Ogilvy developed a keen admiration for him.

Reeves' influence on Ogilvy was long-lasting, but perhaps even more influential was the copy of Hopkin's *Scientific Advertising,* which Reeves gave him.

Ogilvy proclaimed it the best book on advertising ever written.

Ogilvy became a Reeves disciple and eventually his brother-in-law when he married Reeves' wife's sister.

A Research Background.

Ogilvy first took a job in research, working for George Gallup.

In three years, he conducted over 400 national opinion surveys and began to connect with the consumer.

During WWII, he served in the British embassy in Washington, D.C. In 1948, he began his own agency – Hewill, Ogilvy, Benson, & Mather – with $6,000 of his own and a few British accounts, including Helena Rubenstein and Guinness Stout.

Ogilvy Takes Reason-Why for a Ride.

British style and wit for Rolls Royce and a headline that came from a car magazine review: *"At 60 miles an hour, the loudest noise in this new Rolls Royce comes from the electric clock."*

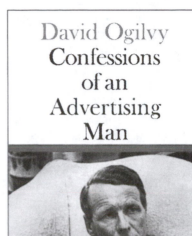

David Ogilvy
Confessions of an Advertising Man

Read All about It.

This was Ogilvy's new business presentation disguised as a book.

It sold over 400,000 copies.

It's still popular – and still a good read. Though many think his second book, *Ogilvy on Advertising*, is even better for the beginning ad student.

Ogilvy's Influences.

Ogilvy was influenced by three American copywriters: Hopkins, MacManus, and Rubicam – both push and pull. The result was quite unique. For example, he believed in both the short-term and long-term effects of advertising.

Short term, he wished for the response of a Hopkins ad.

Long term, he believed *"every ad is an investment in the long-term image of a brand."*

Ogilvy's Ads.

The first of his campaigns to receive wide recognition was one for Hathaway Shirts, a Maine clothing company.

Ogilvy had a distinguished looking spokesman wearing an eye patch. It gave the ad both image and "story value."

The ad first appeared in the *New Yorker* on Sept. 22, 1951, and ran only in the *New Yorker* for four years.

The Hathaway campaign was followed by one for Schweppes Tonic Water and another for Rolls Royce.

All three were created in Ogilvy's new "image" tradition.

The Alka Seltzer Story.

In 1967, Mary Wells and her staff were looking for ideas for Alka Seltzer when she asked the chemists at Miles Laboratories, *"If you take two Alka Seltzers, will it hurt you?"*

They answered, "No."

She suggested a package change that featured two-tablet foil packs. Sales increased as consumers started using two tablets instead of one.

Years later, they developed the ad campaign, *"Plop, plop, fizz, fizz. Oh, what a relief it is."*

Another First.

The first commercial for Alka Seltzer was also what may have been the first "vignette" commercial – a series of short scenes that humorously presented different stomachs.

No matter what shape…

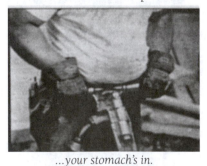

…your stomach's in.

Read All About It.

A Big Life in Advertising.
by Mary Wells.

All three were huge hits.

Ogilvy Rules.

Paradoxically, Ogilvy's recognition came from work he did in the MacManus-image tradition while he was developing a set of rigid Lasker/Hopkins-inspired rules.

Here are some of them:

1. **use the brand name in headline;**
2. **don't be clever;**
3. **avoid analogies and superlatives;**
4. **write sentences less than 12 words;**
5. **make at least 14 references to people per 100 words;**
6. **avoid humorous copy;** and
7. **use photography, not illustration.**

You can read more in Ogilvy-influenced books such as *How To Advertise* or in his own *Ogilvy on Advertising*.

Ogilvy's "Confessions."

Even with these visible campaigns, Ogilvy and Mather didn't move into the top one hundred agencies until the '60s.

It was a book that helped him achieve this goal.

In the summer of 1962, Ogilvy wrote *Confessions of an Advertising Man.* It contained 10 how-to chapters and 16 lists.

He expected to sell a few thousand copies. It sold over 400,000.

The book and its popularity made David Ogilvy the best known advertising professional outside of the industry.

By 1964, billings grew from $58.5 to $77 million.

He bought an Amish farm and a French chateau.

Ogilvy, Benson & Mather merged with Mather & Crowther becoming Ogilvy & Mather, with Ogilvy as chairman/CEO.

Two More Books…

Ogilvy on Advertising and *How to Advertise,* by Ogilvy exec Ken Roman, have also become industry standards.

David Ogilvy wasn't the only advertising person who ended up in a French chateau. The Creative Revolution produced a number of other fascinating individuals.

Jerry Della Femina, for example, wrote a book titled *From Those Wonderful Folks Who Gave You Pearl Harbor.*

And then there was Mary Wells…

The Queen of the Creative Revolution.

There were many talented people who rose to prominence during this time. But one deserves particular mention – **Mary Wells.**

Not only did she set new standards for individual performance, she established trends that would reshape the industry.

Along the way, she became the richest, most celebrated woman in the history of advertising.

Mary Wells arrived in New York from Youngstown, Ohio, at the age of 18 and began writing copy for Macy's.

Then she joined DDB.

Think different.

From DDB...

She worked seven years at DDB, becoming associate copy chief and head of new business. Her copy attracted attention. So did she.

Bright and beautiful, "Bunny" Wells exuded poise and was easily at home with clients and upper management.

... to InterPublic...

In 1963, Marion Harper paid her $60,000 (a lot of money at the time) to move to Jack Tinker & Partners, a unique creative-only shop.

There, she supervised Dick Rich and Stewart Greene, creators of the Alka Seltzer campaign famous for the theme line *"No matter what shape your stomach is in."*

The Alka Seltzer jingle actually became a minor hit, reaching number 13 on the Billboard chart.

When Jack Tinker had a heart attack, Mary was passed over as the choice for head of the agency.

She left Tinker – taking with her two other top creatives.

...to Wells Rich Greene...

A few months later, Mary Wells, Dick Rich, and Stewart Greene opened their own shop with the Braniff airline account.

The "Braniff Air Strip" commercial shown here showed off the new outfits Mary had designed for the stewardesses.

Though some of their advertising might seem frivolous, the thinking behind it was not.

Their goal was to become *"the most profitable agency in history with the smallest possible staff."* And they did it.

Wells Rich Greene established a new pay and profit standard deeply attractive to salary and profit-hungry agency executives.

The agency specialized in television and contracted out for other services as needed. She organized the agency like DDB, with writer/art director teams who were paid generously.

Higher standards...

Both the FTC and NARB held advertising to higher standards of honesty and disclosure.

And competitor's got tougher.

Listerine & Anacin

The FTC ordered Listerine to spend $10 million in corrective advertising, saying it did not prevent either colds or sore throats or lessen their severity.

Anacin was required to spend $24 million to tell consumers Anacin "would not relieve tensions" as previously claimed.

Heinz vs. Campbell's

Heinz reported Campbell's for faking photographs by placing marbles in the bottom of a bowl of soup, forcing the vegetables to the surface.

The FTC forced Campbell's agency, BBDO, to stop the practice.

A few years later, a division of Campbell's purchased a large amount of Heinz Ketchup for a restaurant subsidiary and found mold.

Campbell's report to the FDA resulted in the seizure of 224 cases of Heinz Ketchup.

By George!

These ads are by **George Lois** – one of the terrific art directors to come out of DDB. *The Nauga* (Hey, where do you think Naugahyde comes from?) shows how his thinking can hit an ordinary product.

Lois was also a leader in political ads and activism.

Like this piece for a fundraising event for Rubin "Hurricane" Carter.

1970-1979.

This period will cover:
* The growing importance of marketing in advertising
* The growing importance of advertising in politics

Women in Advertising.

Historically, advertising is a business where women have done well.

In addition to Mary Wells, agency principles include Shirley Polykoff, Jane Trahey, Janet Marie Carlson, Paula Green, Jo Foxworth, Lois Ernst, Joyce Hamer, Adrienne Hall, and Joan Levine.

The largest agency headed by a woman, Advertising to Women, billed nearly $50 million in 1980.

In 1973, Reva Korda became head of Ogilvy & Mather. Yet, in 1976, a sexual discrimination case was filed at O & M.

Over the next six years, representation of women in professional agency jobs leaped from 40% to 57%.

An increasing number of women entered the market in both agencies and marketing.

Today, Shelley Lazarus is CEO of O&M, following Charlotte Beers.

As women's numbers grew inside the industry, other trends followed, such as a move to a more accurate representation of women. This also coincided with changing roles.

We have come a long way.

In 1969, she emerged as the highest paid executive in advertising at the time – $250,000 a year.

In five years, WRG reached $100 million in US billing, the fastest growth record in advertising history.

...to France.

She married Harding Lawrence, head of Braniff Airlines.

They lived a jet-set lifestyle with homes in Dallas, Arizona, Acapulco, the East Side of Manhattan, and the French Riviera.

Shortly after her marriage, WRG dropped Braniff and exchanged it for TWA. Their client list grew to include P&G, Phillip Morris, Miles Laboratories, Hertz, American Motors, and the State of New York (*"I Love New York"*).

New Agencies. New Issues.

OTHER LEGENDARY AGENCIES started during this decade were Papert, Koenig, Lois; Ally Gargano; McCaffry & McCall; Della Femina Travisano & Partners; Scali, McCabe & Sloves; and Rosenfeld, Sirowitz & Lawson – virtually all were located in New York. Many had DDB alumni as principles.

A New Standard.

In 1960, 100 creative directors were polled to identify the 10 best campaigns of the previous decade.

Leo Burnett won two – Pillsbury and Marlboro.

Ogilvy won three – Hathaway, Schweppes, and Rolls Royce. (These were Ogilvy's first three campaigns.)

DDB won four – Ohrbach's, Polaroid, El Al, and VW.

Sixteen years later, *Advertising Age* asked a panel of industry professionals to name the best ads they'd ever seen.

Volkswagen was listed in 60 of the 97 replies.

A Change in Compensation.

Ogilvy changed his agency's method of compensation.

He placed Shell, Sears, KLM, American Express, and IBM on fee contracts – the cost of operating the account plus 25%.

It was the first time agency compensation had changed since 1868. This switch to fees anticipated big changes to come.

The Marketing Revolution.

THE '70s WERE DRIVEN BY MARKETING. Spurred by a recession that began in 1971, the pendulum swung from a creative emphasis to an emphasis on marketing.

Another trend had also taken hold – more and more advertisers were now full-fledged marketers.

A Change in Marketing.

The art of marketing had been developing.

There were three major changes in marketing thinking – they each related to each other and all became dominant.

These key marketing concepts were:
* **Market Segmentation**

- Marketing-Driven Manufacturing
- Positioning

A final result was a shift to client control of marketing decisions.

Market Segmentation.

Through the mid-20th century, industry had been driven by the idea of product standardization. Manufacturing growth came from more assembly lines and more efficient output.

Then along came the concept of **market segmentation.**

In 1956, the concept was defined by Wendell R. Smith as a response to people's differing needs. Product differentiation focuses on something about brands that is preferable to all buyers. For example, cleaning power in a detergent.

In contrast, market segmentation looks at a market, including people with many different demands, and sees it as many smaller, homogeneous markets. Now, different claims are made for products aimed at different groups of buyers.

Example: P&G Detergent Positioning

P&G had now formalized detergent positionings – matching product formulizations with market segment positionings – though, in fact, the detergents were not all that different.

Tide had a powerful cleaning position (the most important attribute) with a strategy of continued formula improvements.

Bold, a new brand, was for colors – with a formula that featured color brighteners.

Gain, a new brand with enzymes, emphasized stain removal.

Dreft was for baby's diapers.

Dash was concentrated.

And Cheer, a traditional "whiteness" brand (Blue Cheer contained a bit of bluing) was reformulated and repositioned as All-Temperature Cheer. This **repositioning** connected Cheer to the new fabrics that needed different washing temperatures. With this positioning, Cheer became the #2 detergent brand.

From Production-Driven to Marketing-Driven.

The inventions and manufacturing techniques of the early part of the century resulted in a production-driven focus.

Quite naturally, a company sold what it could make.

But now, a company could make pretty much anything – or have it made by someone else. The manufacturing technology was there – and so was the manufacturing capacity.

The concern shifted from making it to selling it.

Or, to be more accurate – the key was marketing it.

This new type of thinking had a powerful influence on how products were made and what products were made.

The Importance of the Consumer.

Most importantly, the point of view taken is that of the consumer, not the manufacturer. Instead of just selling what they made, manufacturers paid more attention to making what people wanted – and then sold it based on those strengths.

From Production-Driven to Marketing-Driven. By appealing to segments, marketers can increase sales. Here, a look at all of the "flankers" for Tide.

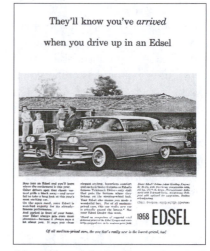

"An Oldsmobile Sucking a Lemon." The ill-fated Edsel – a failed attempt by Ford to launch a new brand.

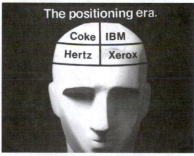

Positioning Occurs Inside the Mind of the Consumer. There is too little room in-side the mind for too many brands.

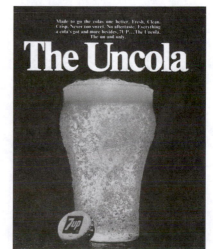

Early Positioning: 7Up

The Japanese Invasion.

Japanese brands made great inroads in the American market during this period. They took over the home electronics industry – stereos to TVs.

SONY brought the videocassette to the market, along with the Walkman and Trinitron Color TV. Yamaha and Honda entered with motorbikes.

Toyota and Datsun (now Nissan) began importing cars with a lower price and greater dependability than most American models of the time.

Their fuel efficiency coincided with gasoline scarcity and higher gas prices, making them fierce competitors with American-made cars. Chrysler almost went out of business, but was bailed out with a government loan.

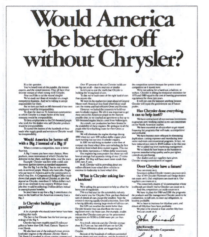

American manufacturers eventually rose to the challenge.

At the end of this period, a number of Japanese brands had become major American brands – and, in the process, helped turn Los Angeles into a major advertising center.

From Production-Driven to Marketing-Driven.

This shift from production-driven thinking to marketing-driven thinking is a major change.

Note how it affected P&G's detergent formulas.

Recognizing that not everyone wanted the same product qualities led to huge innovations in production, marketing, and advertising.

With segmentation in place, greater emphasis began to be placed on the consumer. The idea of marketing segmentation had taken hold in most companies by 1970.

Now marketing, rather than manufacturing, began to become the core function of more and more businesses.

Example: The Edsel

As the dramatic failure of the Edsel demonstrated, it was not enough to make a product – it had to be right for the market.

The Marketing MBAs Take Over.

As MBAs schooled in marketing took over at virtually every major company, this was now the new point of view.

One of the most popular expressions of this new point of view was **positioning**.

Positioning.

Al Ries and **Jack Trout** claimed, *"Today creativity is dead. The name of the game on Madison Avenue is positioning."*

They promoted the concept of positioning – emphasizing a product's place in the mind of the consumer.

The idea, which originated at GE, emphasized naming a product memorably, then focusing on one specific selling point, similar to Rosser Reeves' USP.

Too Many Products. Too Many Messages.

It was also a response to another new reality of the marketplace – too many products, too many messages.

The new problem of the American marketplace was competition and abundance.

More and more products were at parity with the competition.

Differences were minor.

Product improvements were more easily matched.

With increased quality manufacturing capacity, "private label" and "generic" products became more common on retailer's shelves.

Positioning was a way of simplifying the marketing task in an increasingly complicated market.

It was a way of thinking that connected the new realities of marketing segmentation and marketing-driven thinking all the way through to the advertising message.

Big Changes Begin…

Major ad agencies, influenced by their largest clients, began to regard themselves as marketers who specialized in advertising.

Creative shops struggled. Cutting-edge creative work was in conflict with growing bureaucracies of risk-averse marketers.

And costs were going up – for everything.

As the stakes got higher and client marketing sophistication grew, creative marketing thinking became as important as creative advertising thinking – perhaps more important. Because now you absolutely had to do the marketing before you could do the advertising.

More Marketing Muscle.

Ogilvy's agency and Leo Burnett, which had added marketing muscle, grew as they connected with client marketing operations.

Marketing-driven companies producing packaged goods increasingly relied on marketing strategies rather than advertising strategies.

In an attempt to reduce risk, research was used as much as possible – from initial concepts to copy testing of finished commercials.

Not all were unhappy about this trend, which harkened back to the 1950s hard-sell style. David Ogilvy said, *"Today, thank God, we are back in business as salesmen instead of pretentious entertainers. The pendulum is swinging back our way – the Hopkins way."*

Agencies Go Public…

The agency business became more of a business.

As agencies evolved, some turned to Wall Street.

Papert Koenig & Lois (PKL), with George Lois at the helm, was the first agency to sell stock to the general public.

By 1969, JWT, FCB, DDB, Grey, and O&M had all gone public.

At this time, the industry began to see itself as a service business with talent as the major resource, not capital.

Advertising and Politics.

WITH THE FINAL BREAKDOWN of big city political machines and the impossibility of organizing suburbanites nationally, advertising became a more important part of politics on every level.

A few aspects are worth mentioning.

The Nixon White House and the Tuesday Team.

Before becoming White House Chief of Staff, **H.R. Haldemann** was head of JWT/LA. He was a major player in Nixon's political recovery. (After his defeat by Kennedy in 1960, Nixon had also lost a race for governor of California and dropped out of politics – he went to work for Pepsi-Cola's law firm and gave speeches.)

Other JWT staffers also moved up. **Ron Ziegler** went from an account exec to White House press secretary.

In addition, the technology of advertising from initial focus groups to last-minute media buys became institutionalized.

For decades, the Tuesday Team, led by **Pete Dailey** of LA's Dailey & Associates, had a once-every-four-years mobilization of top ad industry professionals. It gave the Republicans an instant agency.

Their advisory board read like "Who's Who in Advertising."

Meanwhile, the Democrat's advertising efforts were in continual disarray at the national level.

Only Jimmy Carter, with the street smart **Jerry Rafshoon** as his advertising advisor, was able to mount a winning campaign.

The "Daisy" Commercial.

In 1964, Lyndon Johnson was running against Republican Barry Goldwater.

A commercial by DDB (with sound by Tony Schwartz) featured a cute little girl counting daisy petals.

The counting changed into a rocket countdown, a missile fires, a mushroom cloud fills the screen.

It blew Goldwater out of the water.

Entertainment. Politics. Marketing.
Here, Ronald Reagan, future president, promotes an upcoming movie as he pitches V-8.

Mikey likes it. This Life Cereal *ad kept running, even after the agency was fired!*

Children.

Consumer activism in the 1960s had overlooked one group – children.

Advertising's responsibilities toward children were asserted by a Boston group called Action for Children's Television, led by Peggy Charen, Evelyn Sarsen, and others.

Recognizing that advertising spent over $200 million on products aimed at children (toys, cereal, candy) and that the average child saw 20,000 30 second spots a year (three hours of television a week) the group petitioned regulatory agencies to limit and improve commercials aimed at kids.

Their victories included:

• The withdrawal of vitamin ads appealing to children

• The reduction of commercials during the weekend on children's programs

• A ban on hosts or stars making pitches – an activity that blurred separation between programming and advertising

• Providing public service spots on good nutrition habits

• A prohibition of appeals urging children to ask parents to buy products

• An agreement that commercials aimed at children could not exaggerate the size or speed of a toy

Much support for these demands came from psychological research demonstrating that children under the age of eight cannot distinguish between programming and ads. (Not until around 6th grade do children become skeptical of advertising.)

We'll cover this further in Chapter Three, "Advertising & Society."

P&G also maintained a presence. **Bryce Harlow** (Secret Service code name: "Soap Suds") was a key presidential advisor.

"The Second Toughest Job in America."

A few veterans of the Creative Revolution, notably **George Lois,** stayed involved in politics.

One of the first political advertising gurus was **David Garth.** (The advisor in Robert Redford's *The Candidate* is based on Garth.)

With savvy media advisors such as former Robert F. Kennedy aide Jeff Greenfield (now a network political commentator), Garth provided specialized advertising help that included positioning the entire political campaign.

One successful example was New York Mayor John Lindsey's re-election campaign. Way behind in the polls, bold television ads had Lindsey admit mistakes while reminding New York City voters that this was *"The Second Toughest Job in America."* Lindsey won.

A Brother in Advertising. And a Job in Advertising.

A former movie actor (and former president of the Screen Actors Guild) had fallen on tough times. His movie career was over, and he was reduced to trying to work up a Las Vegas act – with little hope of long-term success.

Though he'd made some money as an actor, his best earning year had occurred when marginal tax rates on large incomes were as high as 90%. Fortunately, he had a brother in advertising.

The successful brother was **Neil Reagan,** a management supervisor at McCann-Erickson in Los Angeles. He got his brother a job working for McCann client Borax as host for *Death Valley Days.*

From there, **Ronald Reagan** moved on to host *GE Theater,* where he met the Orange County Republicans that promoted his candidacy for governor of California. The rest is history.

Big Changes Begin.

THE FINANCIAL MARKETPLACE was also changing. The same forces creating conglomerates were beginning to affect agencies.

Interpublic bought Campbell-Ewald and SSC&B. Ogilvy bought Scali, McCabe & Sloves, the hottest new agency of the 1970s.

Wells Rich Greene absorbed Gardner, a St. Louis agency.

Bates bought Campbell-Mithun in Minneapolis.

They didn't just buy advertising agencies. The three biggest public relations firms were acquired by JWT, Y&R, and FCB.

With increased emphasis on the bottom line, a tougher-minded business approach was also emerging. Here is an example – Y&R.

Y&R Gets Tough.

Ed Ney, Y&R's Chairman and CEO, and **Alex Kroll**, then the Chief Creative Officer, formed a management team and made decisions others quickly emulated.

They fired half the New York office, cut staff and expenses, and announced creative work with discipline.

Kroll said, *"We believe that creativity is tactical. It should be measured by the cold, gritty eye of the marketplace."*

Y&R then grew by acquiring agencies. They acquired Sudler & Hennessey – an agency specializing in healthcare advertising – and Wunderman, Ricotta and Kleine – a direct marketing company – which allowed them to pass JWT in total US billings, the first time anyone had done this since the 1920s.

In 1979, Y&R acquired Marstellar, bringing in $306 million, replacing JWT as the leader in world billings, though the real age of mergers was yet to begin.

Tough Times for the Creative Revolution.

Meanwhile, Creative Revolution agencies faced tough times.

In 1970, DDB lost its first major account – Alka Seltzer.

By 1973, DDB had lost Lever Brothers, Whirlpool, Sara Lee, Quaker Oats, and Cracker Jack.

How tough was it? In 1971, DDB created *"Mikey,"* a TV spot for LIFE Cereal, which became an instant classic. Sales increased 20%.

In 1974, Quaker moved their LIFE Cereal account to BBDO and kept running the DDB-created advertising. Tough.

Minor Minority Progress.

Overall, Blacks made little progress in the industry.

There had been 5% representation in 1967 – by 1976, it had increased to 13%. They appeared more often as actors in public service and promotional spots than in ad industry management.

However, an increased interest in more effective targeting resulted in the support and funding of new Black-owned agencies by major advertisers such as Coke, McDonald's, AT&T, and Phillip Morris. "Doing good" may have been part of it, but it was also good business.

Work done by minority agencies such as Vince Cullers, Burrell Advertising, Mingo-Jones, Zebra, and others was not only effective with Black Americans, it was effective, period.

Burrell's commercials for Coke and McDonald's were consistently among the best for those brands. Kentucky Fried Chicken's long-term theme "We Do Chicken Right" originated with Mingo-Jones.

One exceptional leader was **William Sharp,** a JWT/Chicago exec. Sharp started a basic advertising class for minority students.

He identified talented individuals and provided initial training.

From there, Sharp went client side, where he played an important role in Coke's advertising department.

Sharp also chaired the AAF, and after leaving Coke, founded his own agency in Atlanta and taught advertising at Emory.

Early graduates of Sharp's advertising course included Alma Hopkins, now an Executive CD at Burrell Advertising, and Carol Williams, later named Chicago Ad Woman of the Year, who now heads her own agency in Oakland, California.

Comparison Advertising – Marketing Gets Aggressive.

Competitiveness – a driving force of American marketing increased dramatically. Advertising became much less polite.

Comparison ads had been discouraged by major agencies, large advertisers, and trade groups.

Changing Social Values. Bill Cosby becomes one of the first Black spokespersons appealing to a general audience.

Tough-Minded Marketing. For years, Pepsi *kept hammering away at their preference in taste tests. It built share for* Pepsi *and caused* Coke *to respond with New Coke – a marketing disaster!*

Agency Principal, Tom Burrell. His agency, Burrell Advertising, stressed "variables" inherent in African-American experiences. The result – quality work with a quality client list.

WHO CARES
WHERE THE BEEF IS?

Frank Perdue Plays Tough.

He builds a huge business by differentiating and then branding a commodity – chicken.

Smart marketing gets Perdue a premium price – that's not chicken feed. And it funds a top-notch ad campaign, *"It Takes a Tough Man to Make a Tender Chicken."*

"I Want My MTV!"

MTV achieved virtually 100% distribution with cable carriers using a pull advertising campaign created by George Lois.

The theme was *"I Want My MTV!"* and famous rock stars, like Mick Jagger, encouraged teens – their target group – to call cable operators and lobby for the channel.

Lois borrowed the idea from himself – a decades earlier campaign had famous athletes like Mickey Mantle, Willie Mays, and Wilt Chamberlain crying and saying, *"I Want My Maypo."*

But they were supported by the FTC and consumers because they supposedly reported more facts and used less "puffery."

NBC dropped its ban on comparative ads in 1964.

By 1972, both ABC, CBS, and the 4A's agreed.

The Supreme Court gave advertising legal standing as protected speech under the first amendment in 1976.

Ries and Trout claimed that comparison advertising was one of the best ways to position a product, since positioning a product *against* a leader allowed your brand to connect with what was already in the consumer's mind.

Finally, the marketplace was becoming more and more crowded. Often, the only way to quickly communicate what was unique about your product was to compare it to another.

Comparison advertising became one of the most characteristic advertising techniques of the '70s.

By 1980, one in four commercials on ABC drew comparisons.

Deregulation.

The economy took an additional step toward more competition with deregulation. By the end of the decade, there was a general trend toward deregulation in industry after industry.

Advertising was thought to be an aid to competition.

In 1980, Congress removed the FTC's power to stop unfair advertising, restricting the FTC to monitoring deceptive ads.

More choice and better prices were two of the results – another result was cutthroat competition.

The Cola Wars.

Memorable campaigns of the decade include "Uncola" for 7Up, Coke's *"It's the Real Thing,"* and *"The Pepsi Challenge."*

Pepsi took on Coke with their *"Pepsi Challenge"* taste tests and began the "cola wars." This was a marketing campaign that resulted in increased share for Pepsi.

One result was Coke's development of "New Coke." This was a short-term marketing failure, which dramatized the importance of a consumer's connection with a brand. Even though blind taste tests demonstrated that consumers preferred the taste of New Coke, when the labels were on, results were dramatically different.

A few years later, a refocused and reinvigorated Coca-Cola Company counterattacked, winning back share and building an even more powerful Coca-Cola brand.

Advertising Tries Harder.

Comparison advertising was so prevalent that DDB relaunched their Avis *"We Try Harder"* campaign.

Scali McCabe & Sloves used the Frank Perdue in a campaign for Perdue chickens: *"It Takes a Tough Man to Make a Tender Chicken."*

This was not just great advertising, it was great marketing.

The poultry business was, indeed, a tough one, but Frank Perdue knew how to work the "Five P's" to his own advantage.

He had a great product (he even fed chickens flower petals to give the skin a differentiating yellow tone) and used advertising to stimulate distribution and justify his slightly higher price.

Marketing Drives More Change.

AS ADVERTISING BECAME MARKETING-DRIVEN, the pace of change accelerated. New computer-based technology, new lifestyles, and a faster interaction with change kicked in.

With higher costs, agencies needed to be more "productive."

Other aspects of the advertising business were also changing:

• **Changing media channels**
• **Changing consumers**
• **A changing marketplace**

By the middle of the decade, advertisers were too concerned with these new issues to place much concern on agency mergers.

Changing Media Channels and Changing Habits.

The emergence of new media alternatives slowly began to have an impact. By 1986, network television advertising by the top 100 American advertisers fell nearly 3%, though total advertising expenditures increased.

The early '80s witnessed the introduction of VCRs and cable television. *CNN* was created by Ted Turner and landed two important sponsors, Procter & Gamble and General Foods. *MTV* was introduced. And by 1986, *ABC, CBS,* and *NBC* were starting to have trouble selling commercial time for sports programs.

Rates dropped 15% from the prior year.

By 1987, half of all the US households were wired for cable.

We'll cover these changes in more detail in Chapter Two.

Changing Consumers – "YUPPIES & DINKS."

Consumers profited from the abundance of the '80s. And marketers recognizing social trends and increased income potential began to segment and target specific groups. Two acronyms signaling the '80s were YUPPIE, which stood for "young urban professional," and DINKS, representing "double-income-no-kids" households.

A Changed Marketplace.

As the decade came to a close, marketing decisions and marketing-driven thinking such as "positioning" had become the dominant values in advertising.

Marketing, which had begun as a minor service ad agencies offered clients, had become the driving force of American business.

Client marketing departments were now in charge.

The brand, which began as something to put on the label, had become the organizing force of marketing departments.

And for more and more businesses, marketing had become the core function. The modern marketplace had arrived.

As we said, we'll cover this in Chapter Two.

Meanwhile, in Portland, Oregon.

Advertising has always been a business where new people with new ideas can make a difference, even in this tough new world of marketing-driven forces.

References:

Here are some of the better titles covering this era. Many go in and out of print – and have been published by different publishers.

They are now easily found using an Internet search engine. For this, all you need is the title and author.

The 100 Greatest Advertisements
by Julius Watkins

The Ad Men and Women:
A Biographical Dictionary of
Advertising
Edited by Edd Applegate

Bill Bernbach's Book: A History of
the Advertising that Changed the
History of Advertising:
by Robert Levenson

(Continued on next page)

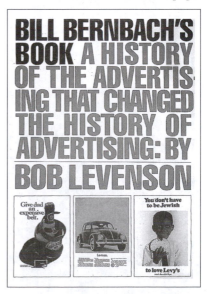

References (Cont.)

Applied Imagination
by Alex Osborn

The Benevolent Dictators
by Barton Cummings

The Branding of America
by Ronald Hambleton

Confessions of an Advertising Man
by David Ogilvy

*From Those Wonderful Folks Who
Gave You Pearl Harbor*
by Jerry Della Femina

George, Be Careful!
by George Lois

The Hidden Persuaders
by Vance Packard

How to Advertise
by Kenneth Roman and Jane Maas

The Hucksters
by Frederick Wakeman

Is There Any Hope for Advertising?
by Howard Gossage
  (Also available as *The Book of
Gossage* from The Copy Workshop)

The Man Nobody Knows
by Bruce Barton

The Mirror Makers
by Stephen Fox

(Continued on page 91)

One of the major influences of the decades to come was growing up in Portland, Oregon.

Son of an Adman…

Throughout the '50s, '60s, and '70s, one of the mainstay agencies in Portland was Gerber Advertising.

It was one of the local agencies typical of the time, with ads for retailers and small Oregon-based companies.

One of the top account people at Gerber was "Duke" Wieden.

His son, **Dan Wieden,** wanted to have a very different kind of agency, doing a very different kind of work.

Dan graduated with a degree in journalism from the University of Oregon and found his first writing job at Georgia-Pacific in 1967. He left to freelance and eventually took a position at McCann-Erickson's Portland office.

There, he met **Dave Kennedy**, a talented art director who'd spent his early career in Chicago and wanted to end up in Colorado.

Dave overshot the mark a bit and ended up in Oregon.

Dan and Dave clicked.

Stepping Out…

Wieden and Kennedy left McCann in 1980 to help launch William Cain, Inc., a new Portland agency that hoped to establish itself in the Howard Gossage tradition. There, they began working on Nike.

Two years later, they left to form Wieden + Kennedy, with Nike as their only account. Their relationship with their main client helped shape a casual yet competitive corporate culture that has attracted the best creative people in the industry.

In the early days, Wieden and Kennedy worked out of a basement, using a pay telephone – austere circumstances they shared with their Nike client, **Phil Knight,** who started out selling running shoes to athletes from the trunk of his car.

Together, agency and client helped build Nike into the largest shoe brand in the United States, and then the world.

Setting Trends…

Wieden + Kennedy became part of a vital new trend in American advertising – the rise of regional agencies. No longer would New York be the only place where great advertising was created.

Together, agency and client would help redefine the way the game is played in the modern marketplace.

But that's another chapter. Coming right up.

Review Questions:

Take a pause… refresh your brain. We've just covered over 100 years of advertising history. There's a lot to remember.

1. People

On the next pages, we've put together a list of all the names that were in boldface in Chapter One.

See how many you recognize.

2. Push and Pull

Briefly review the chapter in your mind (think decades).

When was there primarily push?
When was there more pull?
When were both in contention?

3. Politics and Economics

How was advertising a reflection of political and economic developments in American society?

Match the advertising people and the presidents.

Videos: watch, *The Candidate*, *Power*, and *Speechless*.

See if you can find *The Hucksters* on late-night cable.

Concepts & Vocabulary:

Here are some of the key concepts from this chapter. They may also be mentioned in other chapters.

AAAA (American Association of Advertising Agencies, 4A's) – An organization of leading US advertising agencies.

AAF (American Advertising Federation) – An association of advertising clubs, advertisers, agencies, media, and allied companies, with the objective of making advertising more effective for business and more useful to the public.

ANA (Association of National Advertisers) – A national organization of advertisers with a membership made up mostly of larger manufacturers.

Brainstorm – A technique invented by Alex Osborn of BBDO in 1940 where participants begin the creative idea generating process by sharing ideas in an uncritical atmosphere. The only judgments allowed are positive ones. Osborn pioneered the idea of separating the creative process from the evaluation process.

Brand management – System of running competing brands of products within the same company, first proposed by Neil McElroy at P&G. Each brand group is a team that operates as a relatively independent marketing organization within the larger organization while utilizing common resources.

Caveat emptor – In Latin, "let the buyer beware." This principle is a key component of capitalist theory and holds that the buyer alone is responsible if dissatisfied.

Commission system – This is the way advertising agencies have been paid since 1895 when Cyrus Curtis, publisher of the *Saturday Evening Post* and the *Ladies' Home Journal,* began offering an unbreakable 10% commission to responsible agencies on advertising space they retain plus a 5% discount for cash payment. Agencies charge advertisers the full rate for service.

Comparison advertising – A controversial method of advertising first discouraged by major agencies, larger advertisers, and trade groups, but supported by the Federal Trade Commission and consumers. It was legalized in 1980 when Congress restricted the FTC's power to monitoring deceptive ads.

Names in Boldface...

may be on tests and quizzes, as they represent key figures in the history of advertising. Here are names in this chapter which appear in boldface:

Abraham Anderson
Anne Ashenhert
Bruce Barton
Don Beldin
Charles Benton
Bill Bernbach
Chester Bowles
Tom Burrell
Leo Burnett
Elmo Calkins
Joseph Campbell
Professor Paul Chirington
Fairfax Cone
Cyrus Curtis
Pete Dailey
Maxwell Dane
Jerry Della Femina
Ernest Dichter
Ned Doyle
Emerson Foote
Henry Ford
Benjamin Franklin
Bob Gage
George Gallup
Dave Garth
King Gillette
Howard Gossage
H.R. Haldemann
Alexander Hamilton
Marion Harper, Jr.
George Washington Hill
Claude Hopkins
Frank Hummert
W.K. Kellogg
Dave Kennedy
John E. Kennedy
Phil Knight
Julian Koenig

(Continued on next page)

Names (Cont.)

Alex Kroll
Helmut Krone
Albert Lasker
George Lois
Theodore F. MacManus
Neil McElroy
Ed Ney
David Ogilvy
DeWitt O'Kieffe
Alex Osborn
Thomas Paine
Charles Coolidge Parlin
Harley Procter
Jerry Rafshoon
Paul Rand
Neil & Ronald Reagan
Rosser Reeves
Helen Lansdowne Resor
Stanley Resor
Al Ries
Phyllis Robinson
Paul Romer
Raymond Rubicam
Joseph Schumpeter
William Sharp
Albert Sloan
Heinrich Steinweg
Levi Strauss
J. Walter Thompson
Jack Trout
John B. Watson
Mary Wells
Dan Wieden
John Orr Young
James Webb Young
Ron Ziegler

Agencies...

Some agency names you should know:
NW Ayer (& Son)
BBDO
Benton & Bowles
Leo Burnett
Doyle Dane Bernbach (DDB)
Foote Cone & Belding (FCB)
Interpublic
Lord & Thomas
McCann-Erickson
Ogilvy & Mather (O&M)
J. Walter Thompson (JWT)
Wells, Rich Greene
Young & Rubicam (Y&R)

Consumer movement – Launched in 1927 when **Consumers' Research**, organized with the purpose of informing and lobbying for the consumer, emerged and grew to 45,000 members by 1933.

Copeland Bill – Passed Congress in 1938, giving the Food and Drug Administration power over the manufacture and sale of drugs. The advertising industry opposed the bill for almost a decade because it originally threatened to extend the FDA's regulatory power over product labels and advertising.

Creative team – Approach to creating advertising using a combination of writer and art director who develop advertising concepts in which the visual and verbal elements reinforce each other in such a way that the result is greater than the sum of its parts.

Flow production – Manufacturing machinery that enabled factories to turn huge amounts of raw materials into goods like soap, cigarettes, matches, breakfast cereal, and canned goods.

Hard sell – Advertising style that relies on a structured argument as opposed to an emotional appeal. Referred to as *push* advertising or *reason why.*

Ideas – James Webb Young's definition, *"An idea is a new combination of old elements."* Paul Romer's economic models demonstrate the power of ideas to grow our economy.

Image – Advertising style that relies heavily on aesthetics and often includes an emotional appeal. Also referred to as *pull* advertising and *soft sell.*

Inherent drama – Leo Burnett's approach to creative development that finds the essence of the product and dramatizes that essence. *"There's almost always something there, if you can find the thing about the product that keeps it in the marketplace."*

Intellectual capital – Value derived from ideas, patents, trademarks, and other information-driven content. The increasing value of conceptual content has become one of the driving forces in our economy, powering industries such as software and entertainment.

Linotype – system of setting type in which strips of metal are cast for each line of type. This technology revolutionized print media.

Marketing-driven – The shift in emphasis from selling what is produced to designing and selling products that satisfy a consumer need or market demand.

Market segmentation – Viewing a large market of people with different demands as many smaller homogeneous markets.

Motivation research – study of consumer behavior and motivation.

Multi-brand marketing – Simply put, marketing more than one brand. GM first did this, offering car brands in different price ranges.

NARB (National Advertising Review Board) – Final arbiter of complaints registered against national advertisers – part of industry's self-regulation. Uses moral suasion to stop undesirable practices.

Positioning – A marketing approach that considers how consumers perceive a product relative to competitive offerings. There are a number of definitions: 1. Marketing communication approach that focuses on where the product resides (or could reside) within the mind of the consumer. 2. Marketing that looks at the relative place of a brand in relationship to the competitive environment. 3. The relationship between the perceptual attributes and benefits of a product and the primary target's lifestyle.

Preemption – An early advertising approach first used by Claude Hopkins whereby a product feature common among all products in a category is claimed by a single manufacturer as the feature that distinguishes its brand.

Production-driven – As capacity for flow production increased, manufacturers produced more products to sell. Early advertising helped manufacturers inform consumers about these products and move them out of the manufacturer's warehouses.

Pull advertising – More commonly referred to as *soft sell* and *image*, the style emphasizes attracting consumers by pulling them into the message with an engaging or entertaining presentation.

Pure Food and Drug Act – Passed in 1906, this forced product labels to list active ingredients. The law did nothing to sanction deceptive advertising.

Push advertising – More commonly referred to as *hard sell* and *reason why*, a style that emphasizes building a strong logical sales proposition and pushing that message at the consumer often.

Reason why – A style of advertising developed by John E. Kennedy where *"logic, plus persuasion, plus conviction [are] all woven into a certain simplicity of thought-predigested for the average mind."*

Repositioning – When products within the category change because of new technology, product positions can also shift. This may require the advertising to shift the product's position in the mind of the consumer as planning takes into consideration the changes in benefits offered.

Soft sell – A style of advertising introduced by Theodore F. MacManus referred to as "atmospheric" because the layouts are more artful and the copy more reflective, personal, and less direct than the reason why style.

Subliminal advertising – A discredited theory that advertising that appears below perceptual levels (brief flashes of type or barely audible words) can be unconsciously persuasive. It does not exist.

USP (Unique Selling Proposition) – The central selling idea for an ad or commercial; a selling point matched with consumer benefit, expressed in a unique way. Developed by Rosser Reeves.

War Advertising Council – The advertising industry effort to help out during World War II, an effort which accounted for approximately $1 billion in agency time and media space.

References (Cont.)

Ogilvy on Advertising
by David Ogilvy

Positioning: The Battle for Your Mind
Al Trout, Jack Ries

Reality in Advertising
by Rosser Reeves

Scientific Advertising
by Claude Hopkins

Taken at The Flood:
The Story of Albert D. Lasker
by John Gunther

They Laughed When I Sat Down
by Frank Rowsome, Jr.

When Advertising Tried Harder
by Larry Dobrow

A Big Life in Advertising
by Mary Wells

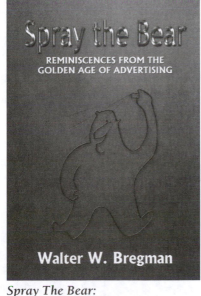

Spray The Bear:
Reminiscences from
the Golden Age of Advertising
by Walter W. Bregman
Hilarious! Available from The Copy
Workshop @ www.adbuzz.com

2

*This chapter was originally written by **Dr. Beth Barnes,*** *now Director of the School of Journalism and Telecommunications at the University of Kentucky. It was updated by **Dr. Susan Alessandri,*** *who teaches advertising and public relations at Suffolk University. Her research focuses on organizational visual identity, branding, and trademark issues. Dr. Barnes is co-author of* Strategic Brand Communication Campaigns, *a leading book on IMC – integrated marketing communication. Dr. Alessandri and Dr. Barnes were colleagues at Syracuse University.*

NOTE: If you have comments or suggestions on this chapter, please send them to: thecopyworkshop@aol.com

*Many attribute this quote to the American retailer John Wanamaker. He said it, but he was actually quoting Lord Leverhume.

"Half the money I spend on advertising is wasted. The only trouble is, I don't know which half."
— William Hasketh Lever
Lord Leverhume, Founder of UniLever*

The Modern & Marketplace

IN 1980, AN EX-P&G BRAND MANAGER named **Steve Ballmer** left the world of packaged goods marketing to work with a friend from college days. His friend had dropped out of Harvard to start a small software company with big ideas – Microsoft.

Mark Goldstein began in a traditional ad agency creative department, then he became President of an agency conglomerate. Today, he's in charge of something called "Integrated Marketing Communications" for BBDO.

Beth Uyenco joined DDB after graduating from MSU. She's seen a revolutionary change as she watched DDB's media department become part of a big new media agency – OMD.

And when **Megan Stockton** first plugged in her computer, she didn't know it would plug her into a whole new career.

Marketers, agencies, media, and marketing services – each has experienced new challenges and new opportunities that are part of revolutions in the modern marketplace.

This Is a More Complicated Chapter.

Chapter One was clear and upbeat. It showed the growth of a major industry – with interesting people and examples.

Chapter Two will be more **complicated and difficult.**
Bad news alternates with good news. Revolutions can be like that.

You'll see complex forces at work – some have nothing to do with advertising – some are changing as you read about them.

When this chapter was first written, Steve Ballmar of Microsoft was having great success in the marketplace. Since then, his business life has had good days and bad – sometimes during the same day. A good day in the US, a bad day in Europe. And that's the point.

No, We're Not Making This Chapter Easier. Sorry.

It's going to stay difficult because that's the way business is.

The simple fact is you have to get ready for it.

So pay attention as we cover the changes creating today's fast-changing marketplace. Ready? Hang on!

1984. This is the Apple commercial that started it all – with advertising that was more than advertising – part of an integrated event.

"The New Advertising."

THE ADVERTISING YOU SEE MAY SEEM THE SAME, but the business behind advertising has changed dramatically.

In Chapter One, you saw an evolution from an emphasis on advertising to an emphasis on marketing, and then the media revolution changed marketing.

"1984" – More than Advertising.

Some mark the official change to this new way of doing things with the famous Apple "1984" commercial.

That one commercial was the most noticeable part of an integrated campaign for this new computer brand.

It ran only once during the Super Bowl.

But today, almost everyone knows about it and has seen it.

It was more than advertising. It was an event.

It was marketing where everything worked together.

Apple's Integrated Campaign Included:

➤ **Public Relations** – primarily product publicity, with lots of lead time, press events, and the building of relationships with software developers, computer editors, and other key industry people.

➤ **New Media Vehicles** – the brand helped create three new magazines: *MacWeek*, *MacWorld*, and *MacUser*. These new media vehicles supported a range of software and hardware marketers and served a new target – Mac users.

➤ **Point-of-Purchase** – a coordinated program of POP displays, product literature, and packaging was distributed through a national retail channel.

➤ **Sales Promotion** – a dramatic *"Test Drive a Macintosh"* program designed to induce trial at the retailer.

➤ **Advertising** – including a high-impact eight-page insert in national magazines, targeted print ads, and unique TV commercials which highlighted product benefits.

This was a classic example of the integration of all elements of marketing communications.

A room full of drones sits passively before a face on a giant screen. They're interrupted by a blonde with a hammer. She tosses the hammer, shattering the screen... and the message appears...

And you'll see why 1984...

...won't be like "1984."

On January 24th, Apple Computer will introduce Macintosh. And you'll see why 1984 won't be like "1984."

Well, now it's 2004. You can see the whole commercial in QuickTime on www.adbuzz.com.

Think Different.

Apple goes back to Chiat/Day for a breakthrough campaign. Business growth is solid, but not spectacular.

Think Again.

Steve Hayden, who wrote the original Apple spot, now hammers out advertising on IBM for O&M.

Twenty Years Later.

iPod and endurance take Apple into a solid business position.

But though Apple's ads were powerful and the program superbly executed, underlying marketing problems remained.

One year later, Apple followed their Super Bowl triumph with a commercial called "Lemmings." That commercial, and their failure to crack the business market, was judged harshly.

Eventually, Apple changed agencies – in a business that was changing dramatically. Ten years later, they changed back.

Often, their advertising was superb. But today, it takes more than great advertising. It takes great marketing.

Finally, with an emphasis on design, a dominant new product (the iPod), and a market that kept growing, so that Apple's relatively small share became a larger business, they achieved solid success. It took 20 years.

Tough Competition. Fast Changes.

In contrast, just north of Seattle, a small software company was moving relentlessly forward.

Though the advertising wasn't as flashy, tough-minded marketing helped drive Microsoft to a dominant position.

And key members of the Apple team went to create IBM's ads.

Meanwhile, older brands, their marketers, and agencies were dealing with a growing list of problems.

Relationships that had lasted decades were changing.

These were the growing pains of the modern marketplace.

And that's what this chapter is about.

How This Chapter Is Organized.

In this chapter, we'll cover five topics:

➤ **How Advertising Changed**

Financially driven agency mergers had a huge impact on the ad agency business. A wide range of other changes each, in their own way, changed the advertising business dramatically.

➤ **The Rise of Regional Agencies**

Important new agencies began doing breakthrough creative work across the country. This was a revolution that had its roots in new marketing realities and the '60s Creative Revolution.

➤ **Why Advertising Changed**

We'll survey underlying changes in the marketplace – you need to understand them because they might affect your future.

➤ **A New World for Marketing Communications**

We'll look at the evolution from advertising to IMC – and the new businesses that have grown out of that evolution.

➤ **A New World for Advertising**

Finally, we'll take a look at all the new opportunities in today's marketplace – some may have a big impact on your career.

Ideas and Information – A Driving Force.

Economist Paul Romer's theories on how ideas are a driving force in our economy are now demonstrated every day.

Throughout, you'll see examples of people and companies dealing with change as they build their careers, companies, and brands.

In fact, change is coming so fast that some of this chapter may have gone out of date by the time you finish it – better hurry.

But, before we start, how about one more revolution?

Evolution = Revolution #2

WHAT? ANOTHER REVOLUTION? You bet.

Chapter Two begins with another magic box – one that may transform society even more – the computer.

Actually, it's the chip inside that box that's doing the heavy lifting, and the cable or WiFi signal that connects you to... the Internet.

That little computer chip is doing more than providing easier word-processing and e-mail. For example, it's turning your telephone into a combo camera, text-messager, calendar, address book, and, oh yes, telephone.

Remember Moore's Law? Computing power doubles every 18 months while the price is cut in half. Think of your first computer compared to the one you're using now.

Better. Faster. Cheaper. Amazing. But there's more.

Computers are changing the nature of media.

Up 'til now, it's been pretty much one way.

The media sends the message. We receive it. No surprise there.

But now, sitting on our desktop, we can turn that communication into a two-way dialogue. We send a simple signal when we search for information. And we do more than send simple signals.

How many of you reading this – and how many of your friends – have already posted a video on YouTube? We don't have to tell you all the things that are going on – you're a part of them.

Think about what a big change this is.

Hundreds of years ago, the printing press turned us into readers – and that changed the world. Now it's changing again.

The computer now lets us be publishers.

The television set turned us from readers into viewers.

And now we can all be broadcasters.

When you think about it, that's pretty amazing.

And it's in the process of changing our world.

What does "The Medium Is the Message" Mean?

As Marshall McLuhan notes, *"It's not the telephone call, it's the telephone."* The larger reality of a telephone network – the medium – has a profound effect on human society.

Think of the changes in your behavior – and your friends and family – when phones became mobile.

McLuhan wants us to think about the water that we swim in.

When you think about it, you realize that our media environment, something we sort of take for granted, is changing around us.

And does that change us?

What do you think?

A Quick Note on "Hot" vs. "Cool" Media.

To McLuhan, a "hot" medium was one that was involving and engaging. A "cool" medium was one that we were more removed from.

Back then, he called TV cool. But, remember, he was talking about Canadian TV in the early '60s. Black and white. Small screens.

Now, with color, bigger screens, and more aggressive audio/visual presentation, it's much, much hotter.

Using today's temperature, you might want to rank your own media choices – "Cool" to "Hot."

**New Relationships.
New Advertising.**

The Coca-Cola Polar Bear ads were not done by an advertising agency. A Hollywood talent agency – Creative Artists Associates – hired independent creative suppliers. Good ads. No agency!

**New Advertising.
New Consumers.**

This United commercial begins with employees having to wait for a "Training Session." This advertising was based on research that showed frequent travelers hated being kept in the dark by airlines.

Advertising with happy people in happy airplanes just irritated them more – demonstrating the airline didn't have a clue about what they went through.

The new United campaign, from their new agency, worked to connect with more experienced (and cynical) consumers.

Ten Years Later.

United, a company hit by high costs and low-priced competitors, decided to have their ads done by the creative team at Fallon. So, they hired the team and fired the agency.

How Advertising Changed.

LARGE AGENCY MERGERS MADE HEADLINES in the 1980s, but other fundamental changes were also going on:

➤ **Financially Driven Agency Mergers**
The financial marketplace had a major effect on advertising agencies as businesses.

➤ **Agency-Client Relationships**
Issues and trends that began in Chapter One continued as marketing moved to the forefront.

➤ **Effectiveness Questions**
There was an underlying change in advertising effectiveness – particularly in mature product categories.

➤ **More Competitive Markets**
Bigger budgets. Smaller impact. As the marketplace became more competitive, costs rose and marketing options expanded, squeezing margins used to fund advertising.

➤ **Media Evolution**
The media kept evolving, but, unfortunately, the business models did not progress so steadily.

Let's take these changes one at a time.

Financially Driven Mergers.

THE BIG NEWS OF THE '80S WAS AGENCY MERGERS. They reconfigured the industry in an important way and had a profound effect on agency-client relationships.

At the beginning of the decade, thousands of agencies, large and small, dotted the business landscape. Then the mergers started.

Mergers Hit Clients First.
"Mergermania" first resulted in the consolidation of client businesses, whether voluntarily, by necessity, or forcibly.

One example of client consolidation came in 1988 when Philip Morris purchased Kraft for $13 billion. This new company, which also included General Foods and Miller Brewing, replaced P&G as the largest national advertiser.

This decimated the smaller, local agencies. No longer were there local banks, hospitals, hardware stores, and specialty retailers in every market. Every merger meant one less client. Then something else started happening to the big national agencies.

From Eighteen to Eight.
Some of the oldest and largest agencies became part of large holding companies such as IPG, WPP, Omnicom, and Publicis.

Other agencies, such as Foote Cone & Belding and Leo Burnett, merged to accumulate the size needed to remain competitive, but, as it turned out, it wasn't enough.

At one count, 18 formerly well-known agency names had been reduced to eight due to mergers. Thousands of ad agency careers were affected by these consolidations.

Certainly, the desire for more size and efficiency played a role, but, just as the information contained in the UPC code changed the power relationship in retailing, something barely related to advertising turned the agency world upside down – stock values and P/E ratios.

P/E Ratios & the Saatchi Brothers.

In 1970, two brothers in their mid-20s, **Maurice Saatchi** and **Charles Saatchi,** started a London agency.

By 1979, Saatchi & Saatchi was the largest British ad agency and fifth in the world. Their clients included the prime minister of England and the ruling Conservative Party.

They wanted to have *the largest advertising agency in the world.* And they did it. Briefly.

The mergers that made this happen began when the two Saatchi brothers discovered one interesting financial fact.

A Difference in P/E Ratios.

They noted that the P/E ratio (price/earnings ratio), a measure of stock value, was almost twice as high for ad agency stocks in London as it was in New York. Apparently, the London Stock Exchange valued agency stocks more highly. So here's what the Saatchi brothers did. It was pretty clever.

Using this bit of trans-Atlantic financial leverage, they secured financing and began to buy American agencies.

They could offer the American owners more than they would receive in the US and still have a higher share price once the stock became part of the British company – Saatchi & Saatchi.

In 1982, the Saatchis purchased Compton, an American agency three times their size, for $29.2 million.

In 1986, they purchased Ted Bates Worldwide for $450 million and became the largest agency in the world. Briefly.

The Omnicom Bomb.

After buying Ted Bates, Saatchi & Saatchi reigned as the largest agency in the world – for two weeks.

Concerned about these mergers, BBDO, Doyle Dane Bernbach, and Needham Harper Worldwide joined together to form a $5 billion agency – Omnicom – one too big to be bought by someone else.

Their concerns were genuine.

WPP = Wire Plastic Products?

Can anyone do this trick? Well, not anyone, but if you happen to be **Martin Sorrell,** a key financial player for the Saatchis, you can give it a try. Here's what he did.

Sorrell bought a British shopping cart manufacturer, WPP –Wire Plastic Products. It was a very small company with one very big asset – a London Stock Exchange listing.

Winning Advertising. This campaign by Saatchi & Saatchi helped Margaret Thatcher and the Conservative Party win in Britain, beating the Labour Party.

'80s Agency Merger Timeline:

March 1982 – British agency Saatchi & Saatchi buys Compton Communications – enters US market.

June 1985 – Benton & Bowles and D'Arcy MacManus Masius merge to become D'Arcy Masius Benton & Bowles (DMB&B).

January 1986 – Bozell & Jacobs and Kenyon & Eckhardt become Bozell Jacobs Kenyon & Eckhardt (BJK&E).

February 1986 – Saatchi & Saatchi's Dorland and Dancer Fitzgerald Sample merge into DFS/Dorland.

April 1986 – Doyle Dane Bernbach and Needham merge into DDB Needham, then join with BBDO to form Omnicom.

April 1986 – Saatchi & Saatchi buys Backer & Spielvogel.

May 1986 – Saatchi buys Ted Bates.

June 1987 – Saatchi & Saatchi/DFS/ Compton formed.

July 1987 – WPP Group, a British holding company, buys JWT.

July 1987 – Young & Rubicam (US), Eurocom (France), and Dentsu (Japan) create joint venture – HDM.

May 1989 – WPP buys O&M.

The Third Saatchi Brother.

Martin Sorrell, Financier
Founder of WPP, former accountant
for Saatchi & Saatchi.
(We'll hear more from him later.)

AdvertisingAge's

AGENCY REPORT MARKET SHARE PIE

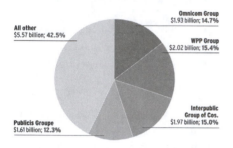

All other
$5.57 billion; 42.5%

Omnicom Group
$1.93 billion; 14.7%

WPP Group
$2.02 billion; 15.4%

Interpublic
Group of Cos.
$1.97 billion; 15.0%

Publicis Groupe
$1.61 billion; 12.3%

Numbers rounded. Source: Ad Age DataCenter estimates. Copyright © 2007 Crain Communications Inc.

Mega-Agency Dominance.

Here's a chart from adage.com

As you can see, four mega-agencies account for more than 50% of US billings.

Clearly, as marketers merged and global marketers emerged, these fewer, larger clients would want to deal with fewer, larger agencies.

Global agency networks are better able to provide more comprehensive services for multi-national clients.

WPP's Martin Sorrell notes that global clients view the range of marketing services from mega-agencies much the same as they used to view full-service agencies.

Quick as you can say "hostile take-over," Sorrell became the owner of Ogilvy & Mather and J. Walter Thompson.

More recently, Y&R became part of this agency group.

Meanwhile, the first of the mega-agency groups, Interpublic (started by Marion Harper) also grew – Marion Harper was right.

New realities – some of which had nothing to do with advertising – had totally reshaped the agency business.

And there were more changes.

Agency-Client Relationships.

AGENCIES WERE GETTING BIGGER and some global relationships were strengthening, but agency-client relationships did not necessarily change for the better.

There has been a fundamental, and seismic, shift in the relationships between clients and their advertising agencies.

Traditionally, agencies have been the intermediary between consumers and the advertising they consume. In the not-so-distant past, the client viewed their agency as a trusted partner, an equal, in the stewardship of the brand. Often, as a leader.

Once, the agency housed the best and the brightest people.

Now this dynamic was changing.

A Source of Marketing Knowledge.

Agency research staffs spent considerable time studying consumer behavior, mapping out how people interacted with the products.

Clients trusted that agencies were not just advertising experts, but communication experts. Agencies had the ability to translate product features into selling benefits and dramatize these benefits with effective, long-running campaigns or media that was, relatively, cost-effective.

As a result, client-agency relationships were long-standing.

Most clients recognized and respected that relationship. Agencies viewed themselves as protectors and defenders of the brand.

A Shift of Power.

But, as we discussed in Chapter One, there had been a shift of power to client marketing departments.

Once upon a time, top agency executives had been the marketing experts.

Now client-side marketers were catching up and, in many ways, passing the marketers on the agency side.

Client Training Grounds.

Client training grounds such as P&G, General Foods, Unilever, and Pepsico were turning out bright, well-trained marketers.

Many "graduated" to join marketers of other brands – often, as the head of marketing or advertising.

Steve Ballmer left P&G, where he'd been working on Duncan Hines Cake Mixes, to go to business school. Then, he left B-school for his friend's brand-new software company. (See the sidebar on the next page). Steve's story is both exceptional and typical.

Many top agency people moved to the client side. **Mike Miles,** had been a Leo Burnett account executive. He became head of Kraft/General Foods (KGF) and then Phillip Morris.

Newer companies, like Nike and Starbucks, recruited younger agency people, like Scott Bedbury.

Growing Size and Resources.

Client marketing departments grew in size, sophistication, and resources – they no longer needed to depend on agency expertise.

Former agency people, like Lisa Fortini-Campbell, began offering their services directly to clients.

Less client dependency put more pressure on the commission system, since commissions had paid for these extra services.

How deep was the shift to marketing? The world's largest manufacturer, General Motors (GM), brought in a new chairman – **John Smale,** former head of P&G. Smale was extremely influential in implementing a deep-rooted change in GM management.

Example: United Airlines

United Airlines' switch was a good example. First, they hired a non-agency research group to get at frequent flyer attitudes.

When the agency did not respond to the implications of this outside research as the client wished, United put its $120 million account in review. The account had been at Leo Burnett for 31 years. Had they been doing a bad job? Not really.

"Fly the Friendly Skies" with Gershwin's *Rhapsody in Blue* was some of the more memorable advertising in the category.

However, it was not connecting with the target.

A competing agency described it as *"the world's best irrelevant advertising."* That agency, Fallon, won the business.

United's explanation for firing Burnett hinged on the agency's failure to connect with today's airline passengers. They felt they needed more than a catchy slogan and memorable music.

"The world is changing in dramatic ways, and the rules of success are different," said Pat Fallon, chairman of the Minneapolis creative shop Fallon McElligott which was hired as lead global agency for United. *"If a client understands that before an agency, an agency can get into real trouble."*

And, if business gets worse, things can change again.

Saddled with high costs and new lower-priced competitors, United went in and out of bankruptcy. One of their cost-cutting moves was to hire Bob Barrie and Stuart D'Rozario (now of Barrie D'Rozario Murphy). Previously, they had been the award-winning creative team at United's "new" agency, Fallon – now their former agency.

Things were tough all over.

More Account Changes.

The United review started a trend. Delta Airlines fired their agency a few months later, ending a 51-year relationship. They hired Leo, United's old agency – it only lasted 3.5 years.

From Cake Mix to Marketing Mix.

Steve Ballmer had to make some dramatic shifts when he moved from P&G to Microsoft.

As an assistant brand manager on Duncan Hines Cake Mixes, he was learning at one of the premiere packaged goods marketers in the world.

He worked on a traditional brand with a traditional target. From there, he went to a business that constantly re-invented itself.

Today, he's facing the challenge of managing one of the world's largest new brands. In addition to well-publicized legal issues, here are some of the marketing issues:

• **Customer Satisfaction.** A whole re-organization will be put in place – organized around customer needs.

This also means a boost to customer support and sending engineers into the field to meet with corporate customers.

• **Corporate Software Sales.** He'll focus on increasing share in the corporate database and e-commerce businesses.

• **The Web Business.** This has been a tough road for Microsoft.

• **Small Is Smart.** With over 27,000 employees, Steve will try to get everyone focused on customers.

It's a big change from bundt cake.

Absolut Shift.

The client changed agencies – the advertising stayed the same. When Absolut Vodka switched ownership, the advertising went to a new agency – but stayed exactly the same.

Their success continues with a campaign that is now part of traveling art shows and even a book!

Zyman Sez...

"I think ad agencies are essential to producing good TV commercials. But I also think that ad agencies are self-important, fixated on the wrong things, and overrated," says Sergio Zyman, former Coke Marketing Director in his book *The End of Marketing As We Know It.*

"This change is about finding cost efficiencies within our organization," said Vicki Escarra, Delta's chief marketing officer. *"We have recently expanded our marketing group to support the advertising and communications programs which Leo Burnett helped establish over the last three-and-a-half years."* From 51 years to 3.5 years.

Major reviews and account shifts are now constant. One client-agency relationship, Kodak-JWT, had lasted since the turn of the century. No more. Today, it would be pointless to list the changes – they are continual.

A study from the American Association of Advertising Agencies found that agency-client relationships had dropped to just over two years on average from 7.2 years in 1984.

That's nearly a 75% decrease – and the changes broadened.

The reduced effectiveness of advertising put more CMOs (Chief Marketing Officers) at risk as well. Top marketing jobs also became more volatile.

The New Reality: More Vendors, Fewer Partners.

The new reality is this – more and more clients now view agencies as relatively easy-to-replace vendors, not partners.

In fact, even purchasing departments are starting to get involved.

Unbundling Begins

Large clients regularly split their account among several agencies – even splitting tasks – with one taking creative responsibility while another handles media buying.

Even when a client has a lead agency, other shops may be brought in on project work. McDonald's agency of record was Leo Burnett – then DDB – with several other agencies for specialized targets, products, and promotions.

No longer did sophisticated agencies allocate resources for unsophisticated clients. The clients were putting in new ground rules.

Example: Coca-Cola

In 1993, Coca-Cola's Chief Marketing Officer, **Sergio Zyman**, engaged as many as 24 separate sources to work on Coke Classic. McCann-Erickson still placed media.

This was the *"Always"* campaign, which has been judged as successful marketing – Coke's share went from 40.7 to 43.9.

While many advertising professionals cited Pepsi for better and more consistent advertising, market results were somewhat at odds with this evaluation.

Again, strong marketing beat strong advertising.

Coke continued to unbundle, trying newer "cutting edge" agencies like Wieden+Kennedy, and hired CP+B (Crispin Porter + Bogusky) for Coke Zero. Creative destruction indeed.

Four Additional Pressures...

The agency-client relationship shifted for other reasons, too.

Advertising agencies work under unique pressures of their own – they are very unusual businesses.

Pressures came from everywhere – including from within the agencies themselves. Each caused further change.

The four major pressures were:

➤ **Client Mergers**
➤ **Compensation**
➤ **Costs**
➤ **Challenges for Improved "Creativity"**

Let's take them one by one.

Client Mergers.

As mentioned, mergers had also been sweeping the marketplace on the client side.

It started well before the agency mergers – and kept on going.

This merging of marketers had two effects on agencies.

First, fewer clients. Second, more financial pressures.

Fewer Clients.

With every merger, an "agency re-alignment" was sure to follow.

The result was fewer "clients" overall, even if the number of brands remained the same.

Regional Shrinkage.

Again, as mentioned, agencies in smaller markets were decimated. Mergers of local banks and hospitals simply resulted in fewer clients.

Powerful national retailers like Wal-Mart and Walgreen's wiped out hundreds of local and regional retail accounts.

However, some regional agencies prospered – like GSD&M, located near Wal-Mart and Southwest Airlines. (More on this later.)

More Financial Pressure.

With the new financing that usually accompanied the merger, there were more pressures on the bottom line.

Marketers had to keep looking for savings. This contributed to another huge change – how agencies were paid.

Compensation.

The media-commission-based system which had been around since the beginning of the century – no more.

Lower Commissions. More Fees.

First, clients reduced the percentage paid on commissions. Agency reviews usually resulted in a lower commission for the "winner."

Fee-based compensation became more and more common.

A few agency people, notably David Ogilvy and San Francisco ad rebel Howard Gossage, had long argued that the commission system sent the wrong signals.

Agencies were paid for expenditures rather than results. It encouraged a tolerance for inflated media rates and a drive for bigger "commissionable" billings – as opposed to other possibilities.

Clients agreed. Fees became more common.

Once, they only occurred where commissions were not appropriate – such as in new product development. Now they were standard.

Starting today a new agency, Kick-Back Corporation* at 451 Pacific, San Francisco, 415-YUkon 1-0800 will place advertising, prepared by the advertiser, other agency, or creative group. The charge will be 5% of the medium's quoted rates. The remaining 10% will be returned to the originator of the advertising.

Howard Gossage
Freeman & Gossage, Inc.*

Gossage Speaks the Unspeakable.

Some trade publications refused to run this announcement for "Kick-Back Corporation." Years later, this became standard practice, as clients negotiated reduced commissions from their agencies.

Advertising Revolutionary.

In the '60s, Howard Gossage's agency was in a San Francisco firehouse.

His criticism of the agency commission system inflamed agencies coast to coast.

Today, more agencies agree.

Unbundling in Action

Here's a listing of Media Agencies and their US revenue (millions) in 2007:

1. MindShare Worldwide — $302
2. OMD Worldwide — 299
3. StarCom USA — 259
4. Mediaedge:cia — 243
5. Zenith Media USA — 215
6. Icon International — 200
6. MediaVest USA — 200
8. MediaCom — 175
9. Novus Print Media Ntwk — 150
10. PHD — 141

Source: Ad Age Agency Report 2008

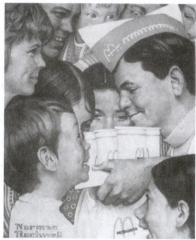

McDonald's Agencies.

McDonald's feeds a lot of agencies. Here's a current list:

DDB (OmniCom)
Agency of record

Leo Burnett
Kids, other major projects

Burrell Communications Group
African-American consumer public relations and marketing

Arc
National sales promotion

(Burnett, Burrell, and Arc are now all part of Publicis)

Alma DDB
Hispanic marketing

And that's just for the US.

Results-Based Compensation?

Despite much rhetoric and a few attempts, results-based compensation was never adopted on a significant level.

Though it seemed a good idea, greater agency control was always an implicit part of any results-based arrangement.

Most clients were reluctant to surrender this kind of control. Occasionally, a "performance bonus" became part of compensation.

Unbundling Continues.

Another result was a further **"unbundling"** of services.

Agency research was no longer "free," and the media part of the account was no longer taken for granted.

Clients became bigger players. With client consolidations and improving media "clout," marketing executives expected, and got, the same consideration previously paid to agencies.

Anheuser-Busch and GM formed "in-house" media buying services. In other cases, media buying specialists, such as Western International Media (now Initiative), emerged. Agencies began to promote media capabilities as a separate service.

Now it wasn't just creative that was volatile. Soon, almost half of the biggest accounts up for grabs were media-only reviews, and the stakes kept getting higher.

That was just the beginning. Reviews for AT&T's $1 billion, Nestle's $1.5 billion, and P&G's $2.5 billion media accounts are more recent examples.

With that kind of money in play, unbundling became a way for an agency to turn its media department into a profit center, and the head of the media department – or, more commonly, the **media agency** – was a more and more important part of the agency business.

Costs.

Even with all this pressure, costs kept rising. For example, top agency management felt they should be compensated on a level with top client executives.

Additional cost pressures came with these higher salaries.

Salaries for top creative people rose, particularly for agencies desperately needing to improve "creative."

Fewer Agency "Extras."

In the good old days, agencies were consumer experts.

When mergermania hit advertising in the '80s, personnel cuts hit research departments hard. Only a handful of large agencies still had sizable research staffs.

By largely abandoning research, agencies lost one of their claims to superior consumer expertise.

The emphasis on the bottom line that came with mergers led many agencies to start offering certain services à la carte.

Now virtually all major agencies allow their media departments to solicit business from clients who are using other agencies to do their creative work.

Once an agency begins unbundling services, it effectively says, "It doesn't matter who does your creative, we can do your media" (or your creative, or your package design, etc.).

It's not hard to see how today's more sophisticated clients might begin to view agencies as easily interchangeable.

Bigger Is Not Always Better.

Finally, many large clients seem to view the mega-agencies as dinosaurs, at least when it comes to their creative product.

Medium-sized shops are seen as far edgier, much more likely to produce breakthrough creative. And, quite often, they are.

Welcome To The Ad Store

The Media Revolution has created new agency opportunities – worldwide. The Ad Store is an excellent example.

After a successful agency career, Paul Cappelli wanted to return to the core business of creating brand-building ideas. And he did – with some talent, a computer, and an easy-to-remember

Internet address – www.adstore.com

His philosophy? *"The AdStore gives you the freedom you've always wanted but couldn't get from traditional agencies shackled by outdated overhead operations."*

Their current clients include: Zappos.com, Centrum Multivitamins, Hyatt Hotels, Jimmy John's Sandwiches, and Diapers.com.

And now, in addition to their office in New York City, there are now offices in: Athens, Barcelona, Brussels, Bucharest (Romania), Cyprus, Hamburg, Papeete (Tahiti), Parma (Italy), Washington D.C., and Zagreb (Croatia).

They deliver. Their GoDaddy.com spot made a controversial appearance during the Super Bowl in 2005.

Challenges for Improved Creativity.

New small agencies based on talent and technology are just one of many opportunities in today's new marketplace.

Big or small, memorable creative work became the mark of a successful agency and something clients looked for.

Just as one strong creative idea can often have a dramatic impact, so can a few talented creative people.

An Agency Strength.

A few fashion industry clients – such as Calvin Klein and all brands at The Gap (The Gap, Banana Republic, Old Navy) were able to develop very good job in-house creative operations. So did Target.

But though there were exceptions, doing ads was one thing most clients could not do well. This was what an ad agency did, and it demanded some fairly non-traditional skills. A few good people and some breakthrough campaigns were all you needed.

Now agencies of every size were considered by clients looking for fresh ideas. Small agencies with unique creative talent grew dramatically. This was one of the key factors that fed the rise of creatively driven regional agencies.

GoDaddy

This rude, blatantly sexist spot from The AdStore was actually quite successful. Go figure.

It appealed to a young male target and broke through the SuperBowl ad environment..

Despite protests in certain circles - some of which the client and agency used as additional publicity leverage, the results for godaddy.com in terms of awareness and new customer sign-ups was excellent.

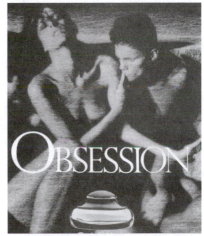

In-House Advertising

As you can see, it's no longer a barrier to breakthrough creative work – like this example from Calvin Klein's in-house advertising department.

**Scrambling for Sales
with Scrabble.**

Games are just one of the sales promotion devices McDonald's uses to stimulate sales – Happy Meal toys and movie tie-ins are two other sales promotion tactics used.

The Cost of Promotion.

Twinkies offers 25¢ and 35¢ coupons, *and* they'll buy you a half gallon of milk (with conditions).

They paid for the FSI and who knows what else.

Effectiveness Questions.

IN CHAPTER ONE, WE SHOWED example after example of business success led by smart and effective advertising. Today, it's difficult to identify the immediate effects of most mass media advertising.

While clients can quickly see the impact of sales promotion, count responses for direct marketing offers, and count the hits on Web sites, the same can't usually be said for advertising.

Run an FSI coupon on Sunday and start counting coupons.

Pay $500,000 or more to run a 30-second image commercial, and you may wonder what impact it had. What happened?

"Brands in Trouble."

This has been a growing concern. As far back as 1991, *Ad Age* featured an article titled "Brands in Trouble." The essence of the story was that brand loyalty was becoming a thing of the past and that marketers and their agencies needed to take drastic steps.

Part of the criticism was directed at advertising for failing to maintain brand identities, but much of the blame was attributed to **sales promotion** and retailers' activities. (More on those later.)

Then again, more experienced consumers and better quality from lower-priced "house" brands had its own effect.

Sales Promotion and Competition for Resources.

As the task of advertising became more difficult, sales promotion – using incentives to stimulate sales – became more important.

Sales promotion efforts, such as discounts and other incentives, became a larger part of marketing budgets – another result of more and more mature categories.

These incentives produced short-term gains, but not always profits. The cost of these effective-but-expensive programs strained marketing budgets further.

The Going Gets Tough.

Technological advances, such as supermarket scanners, led a drive for much more accountability in all marketing efforts. It also served to make retailers even tougher customers. Now they had the data – straight from the cash register.

Combine this with a few other factors:

• **Fragmenting Media.** To state the obvious, there are more media choices. Many of the new media choices, like surfing the 'Net, or playing video games are very different from previous medial models.

• **Fragmenting Audiences.** This results, in the main, with more, smaller audiences. Again, some, like those watching HBO, are no longer in the traditional advertising universe.

• **Tougher Customers.** Today, we are, more and more, a "been there, done that" type of customer. Sure, we may get excited about something dramatically new, but it's hard to move us with "same old same old."

- **Tougher Competitors.** The weaker players have left the room. Those doing business in the 21st Century know what they're doing. An example – "big box" retailers like Home Depot and Lowe's, Barnes and Noble and Borders, and Office Max and Staples, have eliminated smaller competing hardware stores, book stores, and office supply stores in virtually every market. Some entire retail categories, such as record and CD stores, have been virtually eliminated.

With all that, there are some additional concerns that have a very specific impact on advertising effectiveness. Pay attention.

Advertising's Three Biggest Problems:

We call it the "Triple Whammy" – three big challenges affecting ad effectiveness:

1. Media Efficiency.

For years, media costs have risen faster than inflation. It isn't just fragmentation – every little bit costs more.

Rising CPM (cost per thousand) reduces the effectiveness of media dollars. Simply put, it costs more to reach the same number of people. If your ads aren't more effective – to keep up with rising costs – well, that means they're less effective, simply because they cost more. Ouch.

2. Category Maturity.

Do you understand what a "mature category" is? Think about your cell phone. Once, that was a growth category. Then, everybody got one. Now you're a tougher customer. You've been burned by a cell phone bill once or twice and you've got a contract, which makes you much harder to switch.

Mature categories tend to compete with price and promotion.

Advertising tends to be less effective. Customers are experienced. Preferences are now well established.

Competitive product changes are often matched quickly.

Getting consumers to switch brand habits is much more difficult.

3. Consumer Message Overload.

Think of every ad message as a snowflake. It's a blizzard out there.

With so many messages competing for attention, consumers have to become more selective in responding to messages.

Add it up. It's more expensive (CPM) to do something more difficult (switch brands in mature categories) with consumers who are more selective (message overload).

That's three problems that are hard to overcome for most advertisers. But, of course, this is a business that attempts the difficult on a regular basis. In the sidebar, we'll briefly discuss some of the ways smart marketers are facing up to these factors.

A Search for New Answers.

This all brings marketers and agencies alike to one big question: does advertising really work anymore?

That's "advertising" as in traditional, mass media, mass audience advertising.

How to Beat "The Triple Whammy."

Advertising is "a business of spectacular exceptions."

Understanding these factors that impact advertising effectiveness can help smart marketers and advertisers succeed in a tough marketplace.

Here are some sample strategies:

- **Improve Media Effectiveness.** Essentially "free" Internet-based media like Web sites and e-mails can dramatically alter ROI (Return on Investment). Lower CPM media like outdoor has received renewed consideration, as have more targeted media approaches. After all, if it costs more to talk to everybody, perhaps we should try to talk to just the right people. Effective direct marketing does just that.

- **Do Mature Category Marketing.** This means placing more value on your existing customers and increasing the incentives necessary to motivate purchase. Relationship marketing and sales promotion are two of the basic techniques that address the challenges common to marketers in mature categories.

- **Relevance, Salience, and "Stickiness."** Remember, everyone is trying to "cut through the clutter." Adding to the noise level may not do much. However, using basic understanding of the target to develop relevant messages, leveraging consumer insight to develop communication approaches with high degrees of "salience," and designing Web sites with what Web designers call "stickiness," are each examples of ways that we can make our messages some of the few that are noticed and engage the consumer.

Your message may be beautiful, unique, and well-crafted.

Well, so is a snowflake.

When it's a blizzard out there, one more snowflake rarely makes a difference. You need to find ways to get out of the storm.

Trying to Bank on Traditional Promotion.

Kraft brands, like Oscar Mayer, are well-known and well-liked in the marketplace.

But they're not new – so it's hard to get a big sales bump economically.

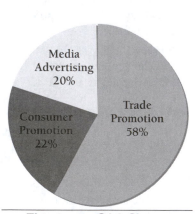

This is an Old Chart.

But it still makes a very important point – trade promotions are a big part of almost every marketing budget.

Plus – as much money is spent on Consumer Promotion as on Advertising.

Remember, there's a lot of marketing investment that you don't see.

Consumer Product Expenditures.
Source: Nielsen's "8th Annual Survey of Trade Promotion Practices," 1998

Many clients have been wondering about that for a while now. While chances are that most *marketing* people on the client side see benefit in advertising, financial people (the ones who control the budgets) have become increasingly difficult to persuade.

It isn't just an agency problem.

Marketers on the client side are feeling pressure as well.

When she was the CEO of Kraft, Betsy Holden, reluctant to cut staff, tried to grow the company out of a difficult business situation with a bold $200 million marketing program.

Good people did their best.

It didn't work. Holden left and staff cuts began.

Today, it's a tougher world for CEOs and CMOs as well.

The reduced effectiveness of advertising is a huge concern.

But wait, the bad news in this chapter isn't over yet.

It's going to get tougher before it gets better.

More Competitive Markets.
A Smaller Piece of the Pie.

While overall advertising spending keeps climbing, in many companies advertising gets less of the marketing budget pie than retailer-directed sales promotion, consumer-directed sales promotion, and even direct marketing.

To make matters worse, the continual increase in media rates, and media fragmentation, has decreased efficiencies further.

So, for many marketers, there's been a decrease in advertising spending relative to other forms of marketing communications. Advertising is now a smaller proportion of budgets.

This isn't obvious, because advertising is the part you see, and it's hard to see things like trade allowances.

But take a look at the chart on the left – it shows how much of the marketing dollar you don't see for consumer products.

Add-On Services – Mixed Success.

Some agencies have responded by offering sales promotion and direct marketing services – but with mixed success.

In most cases, agencies find themselves fighting for even the budget increases needed to keep up with the rising media costs.

Clients respond by squeezing compensation even more.

The Growth of Promotional Expenditures.

Take another look at that breakdown of advertising and promotional spending. It shows you the size of the squeeze.

For consumer products tracked by Nielsen, advertising is just 20% of the picture. Consumer promotions are big, and trade promotions are even bigger – over half the expense.

These are huge budgetary pressures that every marketer faces, particularly those who deal with strong retailers.

A Vastly Different Marketplace – for Everyone.

This combination of relationship changes, unbundling of marketing services, reduced advertising effectiveness, and shrinking budgets has created a vastly different marketplace – much different than the one we saw in Chapter One.

Shrinking and Growing.

That's why, today, you will simultaneously find some parts of the marketing and advertising job market shrinking and under great stress while other parts are expanding rapidly with almost unlimited opportunity.

This is the result of some major changes in the marketplace, changes that present challenges to all would-be brand builders.

Media Evolution.

By now, you're certainly familiar with how media has evolved to include your computer, e-mail, Web sites, and more.

You can remember renting videotapes and taping TV shows. And then you can remember that first DVD player.

All of this is evolving media.

The Search for a New Business Model.

And, though you may have been a little too young to read the business pages, while you were playing video games, the media business was playing games of their own.

Introducing new business models – some successful like Amazon and eBay, and many not very successful at all.

And the big question, as media behaviors changed and network audiences shrank and newspapers lost revenue to online classified services and search engines, is "how do we make money?"

And, that question did not get answered very well.

Certainly, a few online retailers, software suppliers, and agencies specializing in Web-based solutions did very well.

But while inventing a new online business model – like Google and "search" – was great for those who worked for Google or invested in the stock, this did not translate into a dependable business model for everyone concerned.

Steady Growth in Revenue. An Unsteady Industry.

Overall, a simple business based on steadily growing ad revenues, dependable results from traditional media, and being well-paid for effective marketing solutions became steadily less dependable.

Advertising, an industry that had managed to grow and prosper with every media evolution, was having a little trouble figuring this one out. At least the traditional agencies were.

Yet there were mixed signals. If you looked at ad expenditures overall, growth seemed to be consistently on the rise. Increased spending from categories like pharmaceuticals kept revenues growing. And, with most agencies reluctant to report anything that looked like shrinking income, it would be hard to look under the hood of the industry and see if a gradual reduction in fees and commissions as business shifted from general agencies to media agencies could be measured.

Over a Billion!

In 2007, the Top 100 Advertisers, who represent 41% of total ad spending, shifted $1 billion to the Web from TV and newspapers.

As Big as Radio.

In 2008, online revenues were as big as those for radio – with more growth to come.

For the latest information, check in with the IAB (Interactive Ad Bureau) at www.iab.net.

Yo, Alex!

He's our hero! Now he's on magazine covers and feature articles. Cool!

Alex Bogusky, the second-generation designer from Florida, understands The Media Revolution, and his agency, Crispin Porter + Bogusky, is showing the way.

Even though they're in Florida, they know how to get noticed in a snowstorm! For example…

Their high-profile work on the Mini and Burger King attracted clients like American Express, Volkswagen, Coke Zero, Sprite, Domino's, and more.

Then again, Nike came and left. It's hard to stay hot – even in Florida.

Here's one of their insights.

They actively seek out "the psychological, social, categorical, or cultural tension."

In a risk-averse business like advertising, CP+B has the courage to go for ideas that startle.

Billings Rise in the West.

Some examples of the new importance of West Coast marketers:

Automobiles.

In 1980, Honda announced sales of one million cars in America.

Advertising that drove this growth was created by Chiat/Day, which later became Nissan's agency.

When GM wanted to build a brand to compete with these cars, they looked West as well.

Hal Riney developed the Saturn brand – then moved it to Goodby, another San Francisco agency.

Ford's Mercury went West as well.

Computers.

In 1982, Apple computer, also a Chiat/Day client, began an aggressive ad campaign to change the image of what was thought to be a complex and mysterious electronic machine, the personal computer.

And up in Seattle, Microsoft kept on building their brand.

JUST BECAUSE YOU'RE A NICE GIRL DOESN'T MEAN YOU CAN'T HAVE EVIL LEGS.

Fashion.

Levi's, Nike, the Gap, and others showed that powerful trendsetting fashion advertising no longer had to originate in NY.

& Entertainment.

As movie production budgets rose, so did movie marketing budgets.

Soon, big movies took their place among the largest advertisers. And the largest ad medium, television, was becoming a West Coast business.

"It's hard to read the label when you're inside the bottle."

Could you really blame shorter client tenure and increased volatility of accounts on something as ephemeral as the evolution of media? Since the entire industry had a vested interest in things as they were, it would be hard to find that opinion voiced by any but those who were making money on new digital projects.

But if you took a step away, and, instead of looking at all the confusing detail, you considered the broad shift in media-based business and the fairly rapid behavioral shift in media consumption by consumers, it was actually pretty easy to see that this was exactly what was going on. Easy to see from the outside. But not from the inside.

It was just kind of hard to see when you were in the middle of it, with a business model that had been working for somewhere between fifty and a hundred years and with businesses which, troubled or not, were still pretty darn big.

Rising to the Challenge.

For example, in the midst of all these problems, advertising created another fresh new revolution.

In a business that was becoming more challenging, a whole new generation of agencies grew and prospered.

It's time for some good news.

The Rise of Regional Agencies.

REMEMBER DAN WIEDEN from Chapter One? In the somewhat out-of-the-way city of Portland, Oregon, he and Dave Kennedy built an agency reflecting the values of their main client – Nike.

In Austin, Roy Spence and his friends at GSD&M, who we met in the introduction, were hitting their stride. And, more recently in Miami, Crispin Porter + Bogusky started demonstrating new ways to make an impact.

It was a regional revolution.

A Regional Creative Renaissance.

The '70s had seen a creative renaissance in mid-size markets.

The creative revolution of the '60s was born and nurtured in Chicago and New York City.

This new creative era was diffused across the country.

Strong work emerged from Austin, Boston, Dallas, Milwaukee, Richmond, San Francisco, and Minneapolis, as well as Portland.

New York's share of US ad billings shrunk from 49% in 1974 to 44% in 1984. David Ogilvy observed that smaller agencies and clients with small budgets were willing to take more risks.

Three Major Factors.

Three major factors fueled the rise of these regional agencies.

➤ **Major Marketers outside of New York**
➤ **A "Download" of Creative Tools and Technology**
➤ **Bill Bernbach's Influence**

All this changed advertising once again.

Major Marketers in Non-Major Markets.

As companies merged and new powers emerged, not all major marketers were headquartered on the East Coast.

On the West Coast, Japanese auto manufacturers and Silicon Valley's emerging computer industry fueled explosive growth in what was once a small advertising market with few big clients.

Unique breakthrough companies with innovative marketing – like 3M in Minneapolis, Timberland in Boston, Southwest Airlines in Texas, and Nike in Portland – connected with cutting-edge creative agencies in their markets.

Other new clients with new needs emerged. Powerful regional marketing forces, ranging from state tourism boards and lotteries to healthcare providers, needed provocative creative to compete.

What clients want, clients get.

Tools & Technology.

Now sophisticated typography, fine photography, and quality broadcast production were available pretty much everywhere.

Agencies now set their own type on computers, good photographers were now in every market, and local TV stations had video capabilities once restricted to high-cost specialists.

Bad news for old-line type houses as they went out of business.

Schumpeter's creative destruction was still at work.

However, it was good news for Adobe, Apple, H-P, and all the other new companies supplying the computer-based tools of high-tech creative departments.

Bill Bernbach's Influence.

Craft and technology were good partners. A whole generation aspired to the standards of the creative standard bearers – primarily Bill Bernbach. Award books were learning libraries.

In every market, local ad clubs and award shows saluted local and regional work built on Bill Bernbach and Paul Rand's stunning new combinations of words and visuals.

Minneapolis Becomes an Ad Center.

Ron Anderson was credited as the fountainhead, but it was **Tom McElligott** and **Nancy Rice** of Fallon, McElligott, Rice who received industry attention.

Minneapolis? Suddenly this pleasant Midwest city was winning national creative awards for Federal Express, *Rolling Stone,* Hush Puppies, *The Wall Street Journal,* and Porsche.

And it wasn't just one agency, it was the whole city.

The Minneapolis/St. Paul Advertising Club Award book (called "The Bible") now rivaled that of any New York show.

Pat Fallon, the agency's business leader, set out to attract twenty-five blue chip clients. He also attracted top agency execs like **Dave Lubars, Mark Goldstein, Bill Westbrook,** and **Rob White.**

Changing Perceptions.

An early trendsetting Minneapolis campaign was Fallon McElligott's work for *Rolling Stone,* evolving the brand image from '60s "protest" to one more mainstream.

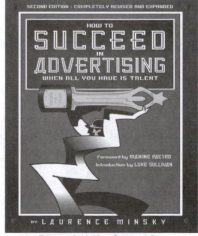

"Geezer Chic"

Bartles & Jaymes wine coolers, created by Hal Riney. Their sort-of slogan: *"Thank you for your support."*

You felt it was from a small, folksy company. It was from Gallo!

Read All about It.

Connect with 18 top US creatives.

Their stories and advice for young ad people are featured in *How to Succeed in Advertising When All You Have Is Talent.*

Goodby, Silverstein & Partners
The First Team.

Rich Silverstein and *Jeff Goodby* teamed up to build a billion dollar agency that features: HP, Comcast, Emerald Nuts, *"Got Milk,"* Hyundai, Starbucks, and more.

The Power of Creativity.

With competitive clutter at an unprecedented level, creativity is the deciding factor for big brands like Discover, H-P, and Budweiser.

And that's why Rich and Jeff's agency has grown – through a commitment to those kinds of messages.

The Power of Storytelling.

Their secret? Look at their reel.

Every commercial tells a story.

"We are classic storytellers," says Silverstein. *"We look for timeless story-telling, honest scripts, and players that reflect that script."*

You can see it in something as simple as a poster for milk. Got it?

got milk?

Smaller Minneapolis agencies such as Carmichael/Lynch and Clarity Coverdale attracted business nationwide.

San Francisco Becomes a Major Advertising Market.
San Francisco featured a number of important individuals.

Hal Riney grew O&M in San Francisco into his own agency with a unique "heartland" style that often featured his distinctive voice as an announcer – it was even used for Reagan's re-election.

There was Riney's "geezer chic" for the entirely fictitious duo, Bartles & Jaymes – made by the very real Gallo Brothers.

And, of course, his work for GM's Saturn introduction.

Jeff Goodby, **Rich Silverstein**, and **Andy Berlin** left Riney to found an agency dedicated to the memory of Howard Luck Gossage. Luck, however, had little to do with it.

The creative skill of Goodby Berlin & Silverstein (now Goodby Silverstein & Partners) helped grow a $1 billion agency with a client list that included Budweiser, e-Trade, H-P, Polaroid, and the popular *"Got Milk?"* campaign.

Saturn left Riney to park their business with Goodby. Then, when Saturn moved on, Hyundai quickly came to take its place.

At FCB in San Francisco, **Mike Koelker** wove some of America's favorite advertising for Levi's.

Millie Olson and **Lydia Pearson** formed Amazon Advertising.

And there were many more examples.

As quality and quantity grew, more clients (never reluctant to fly to San Francisco for a meeting and dinner) came looking for an agency. They were not disappointed.

And More…
Many other first-rate creative agencies emerged:

- **David Martin** and **Harry Jacobs** of the Martin Agency in Richmond, Virginia, helped lead the renaissance in the South.
- **Stan Richards** and The Richards Group in Dallas.
- GSD&M (**Roy Spence** and his friends in Austin).
- Boston featured Hill Holliday, Connors Cosmopulos, and then Arnold Advertising and the Mullen Agency. Hill Holliday copywriter Bill Heater gained national attention with an ad that featured himself in the first of a powerful *"Real Life. Real Answers"* series for John Hancock.
- And Crispin Porter + Bogusky heated things up in Miami – now with an office in Boulder, Colorado.

All these were influential. But, in the beginning, the two with the most powerful influence were Chiat/Day and Wieden + Kennedy.

Chiat/Day.

In 1962, **Jay Chiat** and **Guy Day** met to discuss merging their two agencies. They created Chiat/Day, with a few small local accounts.

Jay Chiat's stated philosophy was to *"take the best people you can find, create an environment that encourages their best work, and then stick up for them when they do it."* Chief among them was:

• **Lee Clow,** a California surfer turned to brilliant art direction.

He majored in advertising and design at Long Beach State and joined Chiat/Day in 1972.

C/D Gets Account Planning.

After seeing account planning's impact in the UK, Chiat hired planners from England and became the first major US agency to use the process.

He brought over **Jane Newman** as their first planner.

Chiat/Day led the way to bringing the power of account planning into the advertising development process in the US.

Chiat/Day produced work for Honda, Porsche, Nissan, Yamaha, Pizza Hut, American Express, Nike, and Apple's *"1984."*

Their work had a bold tone and an unmistakable style.

"Agency of the Decade."

Ad Age named Chiat/Day "Agency of the Decade" in 1989, based on their growth, award-winning work, and blue-chip client list.

They continued to receive agency-of-the-year awards.

Other influential creative people worked at Chiat/Day: **Steve Hayden,** of the famous "1984" commercial (now handling IBM for O&M), film directors **Jeff Gorman** and **Gary Johns,** and **Bob Kuperman,** a former DDB art director who proved top creatives can be top executives – he became Chiat/Day's president.

In addition to bringing account planning to the United States, their "virtual office" was one of the more interesting innovations in American business.

See their "I love LA" musical commercial featuring Nike billboards during the LA Olympics.

Wieden + Kennedy.

IN 1979, A SMALL AGENCY IN PORTLAND began working on advertising for a small, little-known athletic shoe brand – Nike. After they teamed up, neither shoes nor advertising would be the same.

Early Days.

It was work for Honda Scooters that first indicated W&K would be something different. Supermodel Grace Jones and rocker Lou Reed added their unique looks and music.

The early Nike work was handsome and well done – aiming to reach runners and other dedicated athletes.

A Democratic Approach.

Just as Dan wanted to remove artificial barriers in communication (he didn't even like calling it advertising), they tried to do the same thing at work.

So when it was time to present a campaign idea for a new Nike shoe, the winner was a young assistant in the production department. She thought the Beatles song "Revolution" would project the right attitude. And it did. She went on to become a major creative at W+K.

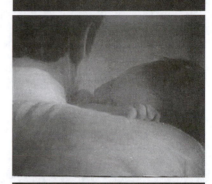

Real Life.

Bill Heater used his own life for a commercial for John Hancock – a campaign created by Hill Holliday in Boston.

German Car. Minneapolis Agency.

Michael Goes to Mars.

The range of brand equity values grew – from dunking, to heroic imagery, to a warm recognizable persona – at home with other superstars, starting with Spike Lee's Mars Blackmon.

Bo Meets Bo.

Bo Jackson was a multi-sport athlete (football and baseball).

The "Bo Knows" campaign built on versatility, cross-training, and a sports-wise audience.

Adding pioneer rocker Bo Diddley was the punch line.

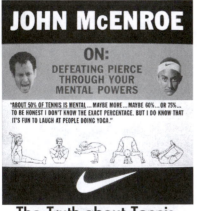

The Truth about Tennis.

Again, Nike gives appropriate personalities – and truths – to their sports star endorsements. Here, the tough-minded competitiveness of tennis player John McEnroe.

The Personal Truth.

Runners are special people – with a personal focus and dedication to excellence. This attitude was at the core of Phil Knight and his growing shoe company.

To touch that target audience, W+K searched for what Dan

called "the personal truth," something that the audience would identify with as true about them.

For long-distance runners, that truth might be one thing, for tennis players another, and for basketball players…

The Kid from North Carolina.

Today Michael Jordan is one of the most recognized personalities on the planet. But it wasn't always that way.

Talented and personable, he was a basketball player – not a brand. But **Jim Riswold** and **Spike Lee** changed all that.

Jim Riswold was a philosophy major turned to copywriting – typical of the unique talents at W+K.

He connected with Michael Jordan as a fan and got Spike Lee, then a little-known young director, to connect with Jordan as Mars Blackmon, Lee's character in his first feature, *She's Gotta Have It*.

The chemistry was perfect. It allowed Jordan to evolve from a slam-dunk highlight into a real person.

This not only set the stage for Jordan and Nike, it set a new standard for Nike's use of athletes. David Robinson in Mr. Robinson's neighborhood, Charles Barkley with *Godzilla* (the original one), and multi-sport athlete Bo Jackson in "Bo Knows" with Bo Diddley.

Each commercial seemed to top the previous one – like athletes going for their next personal best.

Just Do It.

As the work grew, three little words at the end of Nike spots grew along with them – *"just do it."*

As Dan described it, each of the feelings, each of the "personal truths" in each spot, would feed into these three words.

And the Nike logo and theme transcended advertising and entered into the culture. Now people paid extra to wear the logo and ad theme on their T-shirts and sportswear.

As the campaign grew, so did Nike.

Learning from Mistakes.

Even the missteps resulted in better work.

Briefly, Nike added Chiat/Day (the Olympic "ambush" outdoor campaign was the main result). But W+K won the business back. More recently, Nike tried CP+B for a project, but came back to W+K.

A Major Marketing Mistake.

Nike's first effort to sell women's shoes and sportswear failed.

Initial work featured female jocks – with an attitude similar to work aimed at men – pull Michael, stick in Mary. It didn't work.

Ambush!

Though Nike was not an official sponsor of the 1984 Olympics, Chiat/Day placed high-impact outdoor boards throughout LA and made them look like the sponsor.

But they learned – and got better.

What W+K and Nike learned was that women's idea of sport and fitness was an entirely different personal truth.

For women, it's about your own personal best.

The result was, again, even better work – a stunning print campaign that spoke to the heart – what it was like to be the last girl picked in gym class – what it means to exercise.

The first work was done by a writer/art director team **Janet Champ** and **Charlotte Moore**.

Most Valuable Players.

Soon, everyone wanted to "be like Mike," and W+K's client list grew to include (at various times) Microsoft, Miller, and Coke.

The smart and funny ads for ESPN SportsCenter come from that little agency in Portland. So do the ads for PowerBar.

Just as Bill Bernbach and his team created a generation of DDB wannabees, Wieden + Kennedy, in some minds, managed to move the center of advertising to Portland, Oregon.

But they did go to New York to be honored as the new members of the Art Director and Copywriter Hall of Fame.

Miami Advice – "Use Surprise Wisely."

The hot new agency is **Crispin Porter + Bogusky** in Miami – making noise nationwide, with unique award-winning non-traditional work for Burger King, Mini Cooper, and then VW.

Their bold, raw anti-tobacco campaign "Truth" first drew national notice, and they followed with more innovative work.

CP+B combines creative excellence with media smarts, making big impact on a small budget. Sometimes, a mini-budget.

The Mini Cooper Campaign.

CP+B's unique introduction of BMW's Mini is an example.

"One reason that people come to us is our ability to break through the clutter with smaller budgets," says Jim Poh, CP+B's Director of Creative Content Distribution.

"One of our main tenets for the Mini campaign is that if it seems like something another car advertiser would do, we don't want to do it. The car is unique, and should be doing things no other advertiser is doing."

Taking Mini to the Max

After winning the account, CP+B had to figure out how to introduce the Mini with a budget barely 10% of what VW spent on their new Beetle.

CP+B's answer was outdoor and unique inserts such as:

• a first-ever advertising centerfold appearing in *Playboy*;

• a make-your-own cardboard toy Mini insert;

• a piggyback display with a little Mini on an SUV; and

• a lot more cool outdoor.

You can see CP+B's design heritage at work – they paid attention to every piece of work on the brand – from the advertising to the stickers in the car dealership.

Lighting Fires for the Mini.

A crazy little fable for IKEA… "Lamp."
See it on www.cpbgroup.com.

Smoking out tobacco with "Truth."

The Irony Age.

One characteristic of post-modernism is self-referential ironic humor.

Done right, the result is an unspoken connection with the target.

One of the more successful examples is CP+B's use of the phony and slightly creepy "King" character for Burger King.

Originally developed as part of a kids' program, CP+B found ways to use the character – mask, crown, tights, and all, as part of some very hip and very funny ads that target young adults.

A guy wakes up with The King in his bed - and we sell breakfast.

Computer graphics swap The King for a winning NFL quarterback, and our hero scrambles for a winning touchdown – celebrate at Burger King.

An attitude like that helps Burger King become the choice with its target - young adults, primarily male, who are heavy fast food users.

Unböring.

That was the theme for IKEA. CP+B planners noted normal people keep furniture forever – a huge barrier to selling new furniture.

To see what they did about it, go to www.cpbgroup.com and take a look at their Grand Prix spot by Spike Jonze – "Lamp."

Passion.

Alex Bogusky, Exec Creative Director, describes CP+B's approach: *"There's a point where you fall in love with the product, when you want to buy what you're selling. Then you've arrived at the right place."*

They got Molson to add a twin label to generate "bar talk."

"One thing we try to do," Bogusky observes, *"is answer the question, 'What's really going on here?' If you step outside your culture you can get an angle on what's really going on inside it."*

Post-Modernism.

CP+B is a very media-savvy agency. *"Media and creative cannot be separated,"* says CP+B Agency President Jeff Hicks. *"The play between the departments creates the creative content."*

That environment led to their creation of the Subservient Chicken, their curious contribution for Burger King's Chicken Sandwich – at www.subservientchicken.com.

Currently appearing on his/its own Web site. Weird, kinky video plays to a simple proposition, "Chicken, just the way you like it." A post-modern play on "Have It Your Way."

The ironic use of the phony, plastic Burger King character is another example. One more way CP+B takes it to the next level.

Why Advertising Changed.

ALL AGENCIES, NEW AND OLD – from regional shops with a creative orientation to one of the originals (now merged into mega-agencies to serve global brands for international marketers) – have had to come to grips with a dramatically changing marketplace.

The New World for Brands.

It's a tough world out there for brands. Even though many of today's category leaders are the same brands that topped sales charts 20 or 30 years ago, the marketplace is dramatically different.

Plus, there are important categories that didn't exist 20 years ago.

There have been major changes in four key areas:

➤ **Media Evolution** – an expanding media landscape crowded with new players and new media options. New niche players appealing to ever more narrow audiences and powerful media brands growing across many media platforms.

➤ **Consumer Changes** – we've grown up with advertising and marketing. We've been a target audience since we were old enough to recognize a cereal box. Today's marketplace is full of consumers, like you, who are savvier than ever. This presents both challenges and opportunities.

➤ **Competitive Changes** – there's been a major remapping of the competitive playing field. It's tougher and faster, with some big new players in the game.

➤ **Globalization and World Brands** – it's a new world all around the world. The globalization of brands, marketers, and agencies is another important influence.

Each of these factors has affected the way advertising and other marketing communications efforts are planned and implemented. Let's take them one by one.

Media Evolution.

It's complicated, but let's start with these factors.

* Mass Audience Erosion
* Niche Audience Explosion
* New Media (and Agency) Opportunities
* New Interactive Opportunities
* Old Answers Are New Again

The media industry is exploding with more and more "niche" media.

Mass Audience Erosion.

For many marketers, "mass" media is something of a misnomer in today's marketplace. As a group, the top three networks' (ABC, CBS, and NBC) combined viewership is lower every year.

Other curious things happen as the mass audience erodes. Weird single-year bumps occur. In 2003–04 there was a tremendous drop in viewership by single males. Video games? Internet? Sports bars? The only thing certain was they watched less.

The big truth – everyone's audience is smaller.

With network television ratings trending lower, you might wonder whether brands can still establish dominance through advertising? Perhaps, but at a high price.

Mass media marketers now need massive budgets to do the job.

Niche-Audience Explosion.

Of course, not every brand needs to reach a mass audience.

Many brands – rent-a-car companies, for example – depend on a relatively small group of customers for a large part of their business.

In the world of media, there has been a tremendous growth and a new world of exciting opportunities. The rise in the number of niche-oriented publications and cable television channels has been a boon to such brands, but proliferation pains are being felt there as well.

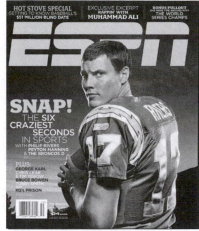

Media Evolution – Finding Their Niche.

ESPN is an excellent example of an emerging media brand: three cable channels – ESPN, ESPN2, and ESPN Classic – a sports radio network, theme sports bars, and a new sports magazine.

Changing Consumers Create Changing Markets.

Campbell's has to accommodate new habits changing who eats soup and how it's prepared.

Kellogg's wrestles with a world that has less time for breakfast.

Little changes like this mean even big brands have new challenges.

"Pushing Water Uphill."

Campbell's works hard to connect its traditional products with new emerging trends, but even the smartest marketing has its limits.

US Brand Leadership:

In 1988, Landor Associates asked 1,000 consumers which brands they were most familiar with and liked best. Here were the top 20:

1. *Coca-Cola*
2. *Campbell's*
3. *Pepsi-Cola*
4. *AT&T*
5. *McDonald's*
6. *American Express*
7. *Kellogg's*
8. *IBM*
9. *Levi's*
10. *Sears*
11. *Disney*
12. *Hershey's*
13. *NBC*
14. *MasterCard*
15. *Tylenol*
16. *Kentucky Fried Chicken*
17. *Kodak*
18. *Windex*
19. *Kleenex*
20. *Budweiser*

Twenty years later, many brands are still leaders, but the world has changed.

More Changes.

KFC has removed "fried" from its name. Levi's, once the brand of the youth culture, became "your father's blue jeans."

AT&T is wrestling with the worlds of cable and wireless where their heritage has less meaning, and Kodak finds itself in a world of digital imaging – with new challenges and competitors.

Even for already well-established brands, it's a new world. And many of these problems cannot be fixed by advertising alone.

Mature Market/New Audience.

Markets change. Baby Boomers, once a big market for blue jeans are now the target for retirement funds and pharmaceuticals to fight aging.

And the price of gas can suddenly make a big market like automobiles a brand new ballgame.

Technology made it easier to create a new magazine. Survival? Well, that's something else.

Recently, there were at least six sports-themed magazines targeted at women either being published or in development.

If *Columbia House* CD Club wants to prospect for new members on cable television, it might need to advertise on one or more of the MTV channels, VH-1, CMT (Country Music Television), Fuse, and BET (Black Entertainment Television) at a minimum (other networks also offer some music programming).

Even its "special introductory offer" might need to feature very different musical styles for each cable network.

Then again, is anyone buying CDs any more?

All this means that the role of media planning today is much different and much more difficult than it used to be.

New Media (and Agency) Opportunities.

Let's assume the ad agency media department (or the media agency) is staffed by people who have a good handle on standard media options.

They know the difference between *Seventeen, YM,* and *Sassy.*

They know when syndicated episodes of *Friends* air in every major market in the country.

They even do a pretty good job of guessing which of the new fall broadcast network series will win in each and every time slot.

As you'll realize when you get to the chapters on media, that's already asking a lot. But, in today's marketplace, it's still not enough.

And, with every new media form, a new kind of agency springs up, with that media or target group specialization their reason for being. As media evolves, advertising evolves, and so do advertising and marketing organizations.

The Rise of Media Planning

Today, sifting through consumer media choices is becoming an art in itself. Those who can do it well are in demand.

In Chapters Six and Ten we'll tell you more about the revitalized area of Media Planning, which is becoming "the other" critical agency service.

Today, marketers look for creative skills and media expertise – sometimes from different agencies. Some creative agencies, like Crispin Porter + Bogusky, look at media (they call it "creative content distribution") as an integral part of their approach.

From Media Planning to "Communication Planning"

There's one more bit of evolution in this area that may be profound. It's a shift to "Communication Planning." The leading practitioner, as of the writing of this book, is a company with the somewhat startling name of Naked. Beginning in Britain, this combination of media planners, consultants, and iconoclasts is "media agnostic."

They do not necessarily believe advertising is the answer. For a major British drug chain, Boots, interested in developing a prescription referral business, they recommended pulling all advertising.

Instead, Boots personnel were instructed to tell all customers currently waiting in line for their prescriptions about the service.

This focused marketing response to a specific problem was far more effective than advertising.

If you'd like to know more about Naked and their approach, we've posted some very informative articles on AdBuzz – in the Chapter 2 section.

New Interactive Opportunities.

What about interactive advertising media?

Should the brand have its own Web site?

If so, where should that Web site be advertised?

Maybe this brand would benefit from sponsorship tie-ins. And what about the "third screen" – your more-capable-than-ever mobile phone.

Now, we don't just buy other people's tied-in properties, we may create them ourselves – Web sites, blogs, videos, 'zines. And each offers some degree of interactivity – from a Web cookie to the database marketing of a frequent buyer program, complete with e-mail updates.

Obviously, there are new opportunities. But there are also new decisions to make. And to make things tougher still, there is more to do, but not necessarily additional resources. Every marketer's budget decisions are tougher than ever.

But they're making those tough decisions. As we noted, in 2007, the Top 100 Advertisers switched $1 billion from old media into digital activities – building Web sites, blogs, banners, and more.

Example: *Samsonite Luggage*

Perhaps your target is people who do a lot of traveling by air, so in-flight magazines, ads on CNN Airport, and airport displays and demonstrations might be considered.

Leo Burnett did this to good effect for their client Samsonite.

They added airport displays and luggage demonstrations aimed at reaching frequent travelers. This was a dramatically different way for a large agency to approach media.

The point is, in addition to the proliferation of traditional media vehicles (magazines, networks, programs), there is a vast array of new media types out there – and new media opportunities.

Old Answers Are New Again

Likewise, sampling, an old-fashioned marketing technique gone out of fashion, mostly due to cost considerations, has re-entered the repertoire of a number of sophisticated marketers.

Outdoor has also made a resurgence in many media plans.

Consumer Changes.

As things move faster, it's difficult for an agency, even one with a research department, to keep up with those "been there, done that" consumers. Today, that's just about everyone.

Let's talk a bit more about the various roles new consumer habits and attitudes are playing in the modern marketplace.

Tougher Customers.

"Samurai consumers" expect more than ever. That means every marketer has to keep improving on past performance. McDonald's had to step up to declining store sales. They did.

They invested huge amounts of money to change their kitchens, introduced new products – including salads – and, after a worldwide advertising competition, chose a new campaign, *"I'm Loving It,"* developed by their German agency.

Dave Thomas
Founder of Wendy's

Tougher Competitors.

As you get better, so does your competition. Wendy's focus on product quality in ads and operations made solid inroads with adults.

Then their founder died and they hit a rough patch. How it goes.

Better competitors make customers tough to get and tough to keep – many switch from brand to brand, based on price differences, new products, or promotional offers.

[adbuzz note]

Read the classic article "The Boston Tea Party – Part Two" by David Nichol, of Canadian retailer Loblaw and find out about the Samurai Consumer.

Go to the Study Hall. Go to Chapter Two and Text Resources for the article. Posted by permission.

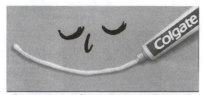

Smile, You're a World Brand.

Colgate uses this image around the world – a simple message that communicates everywhere.

Marketing Evolution from 1950-2000.

Here are some of the big changes that reshaped the world of marketing:

1950–70.
Marketing becomes widespread throughout American business:
- Domestically driven
- A market of shortages
- Growing consumer wealth

1970–80.
The Japanese change the game:
- Building quality into the product (vs. make the product/use it up)
- Internationally driven
- A market of surplus

1980–2000.
The marketer now has technology:
- Capturing and using data
- Digitalization of the world
- New forms of communication

The 21st Century.
Customer now has technology:
- Customer will be the change agent.

Source: based on notes from a speech by Don Schultz

Rocking Competition Worldwide.

When Pepsi used Michael Jackson, they did it around the world.

Back then, this global entertainment figure made a huge impact in many markets, such as Japan.

Savvier Consumers.

In the US marketplace, and in many other developed countries, consumers view advertising, sales promotion, and other forms of marketing communications as givens.

They take it for granted. They know what advertising is all about, they know marketers want their money, and they tend to ignore far more messages than they heed.

Business Week described today's consumers as *"a generation skeptical of any sales pitch and insatiable in its hunger for nonstop entertainment."* Persuading these consumers is a real challenge.

In many ways, these consumers are far less brand loyal. Many switch from brand to brand, largely on the basis of price differences or promotional offers. Many see few differences among brands within any given product category.

Today, it's the "Samurai Consumer," a tough, experienced veteran of the marketplace who expects both quality and value.

Changing Loyalties.

Loyalties can change quickly. When this book was first written, leading consumer brands Nike, Campbell's, Levi's, Microsoft, and McDonald's each found themselves big brands with big problems.

Some found major competitors with improved marketing. Some, like Campbell's, saw new consumer habits.

Nike hit a rough road with third-world suppliers. Levi's lost favor with a new generation of jeans wearers. And Microsoft saw its dominant share and aggressive practices generate legal problems.

Each was, to some extent, the victim of success.

This is often true as today's marketers work hard to match competitors' product improvements – resulting in a rising level of product parity. Things get better. Things get tougher.

Example: Levi's

Levi's, a symbol of the youth culture, had become an adult brand as their loyal customers aged. Many new jean customers were not necessarily going to go with their parents' brand.

As sales of the flagship jeans line slipped, Levi's gave more attention to its Dockers and Slates brands, products designed to better fit their target of aging Baby Boomers.

"Pushing Water Uphill."

How about Campbell's backing away from condensed soup?

Changing meal habits made selling condensed soup *"like pushing water uphill."* So they decided to focus on full-strength soups as the growth area. This is a major business decision: the condensed line represented 66% of Campbell's Soup sales.

But, with consumers becoming more convenience-oriented, Campbell's faced up to the consequences – backing off on their condensed line in favor of their newer ready-to-serve soups.

Store Brands and More Brands.

Many are increasingly likely to choose store brands – like Wal-Mart's Equate – over manufacturers' brands.

Many of them actively distrust advertising; others rely on recommendations from magazines like *Consumer Reports* or the advice of friends when selecting a brand. Successful store brands, for example, have had a huge impact on jeans sales.

Consumers Have Learned How to Get What They Want.
Meanwhile, more consumers simply hop on the Internet to read what others have to say about a particular product or service.

Add it all up and you have a very smart group of people who know what they want, know how to track down information, and know all the tricks of the advertising trade. Tough customers.

It's going to take something more than a pretty 30-second TV commercial to get them to buy. On top of that, today's consumers, whether they're Baby Boomers or twenty-somethings, don't like to be treated as a homogeneous group.

They're individualists. They seek out products that foster self-expression. So, with the right product mix, a discount retailer like Target can market itself as a destination for unique taste and quality – and develop a unique position in the marketplace.

Expanding Options for Everyone.

Many product categories are crowded with niche brands.

Take a look below at the brand lineup for children's fashions in a large regional shopping mall.

Children's Clothing Brands:

Charney's (Regular & Husky)	Limited Too
The Children's Place	Mothertime
The Disney Store	Noodle Kidoodle
Gamekeeper	Old Navy
GapKids	Rugged Bear
Gymboree	Talbots Kids
Kay Bee Toys	Warner Bros. Store
Learningsmith	Weebok

Today's consumers have a lot of options.

How Many Niches?
The drive to increasing segmentation has opened up many opportunities for marketers and their agencies. It also brings challenges.

How do we find these people and communicate with them? What product/service mix do they really want? How can we differentiate our brand offering from that of competitors?

All the while knowing that, if we're successful, other companies will be attracted to our niche, with newer, possibly better, products.

And, if the niches get too small, how do we make money?

Look at how premium coffee has attracted competition to Starbucks' niche – from high-end brews to McDonald's and Dunkin" Donuts.

Competitive Changes.

A third area giving marketers and their agencies headaches is an increasingly complicated competitive landscape.

Introducing training wheels for the feet.

Agility by Weebok

Baby Needs a New Pair of Shoes.

Every marketplace niche now has smart, tough competition – or if it doesn't, wait a week.

Better stay on your toes – or they'll walk all over you.

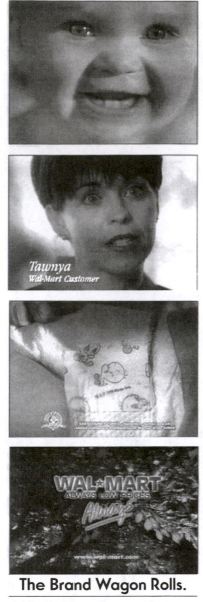

The Brand Wagon Rolls.

Wal-Mart's brand of diapers – White Cloud – used to be a P&G brand of toilet paper.

Now it's an advertised Wal-Mart brand in both categories. This TV commercial features Warner Brothers characters.

Competition Worldwide.

Many companies are now selling globally and facing different sets of competition in each market where they operate.

That's part of the reason why many multi-national companies look for advertising agencies with offices around the world, seeking help from agencies already familiar with a particular country's competitive structure. Here, agencies can add genuine value.

Good News for Global Agency Networks.

As a result, stabilization of client-agency relationships seems to be happening around the world, though it's volatile in the US.

Citibank, SC Johnson, and Ford are just a few examples of global clients that now use their agencies on a global scale.

Even United Airlines, which picked a regional creative shop for their US business needed a global mega-agency, Y&R, for their international business.

Sometimes, good local, national, and regional agencies pay a price. P&G, which had been a loyal long-term client, terminated their relationship with RSCG Tatham in Chicago – not because the work wasn't good, but because the global synergies weren't there.

Competition on the Home Front.

Let's set aside the global aspect of competition for a moment and refocus on the US. Some other curious things are occurring.

Say you're working on the Head & Shoulders shampoo account for P&G. It's the top brand of medicated shampoo and ranks high in overall shampoo sales as well.

So, your primary competition is other brands of medicated shampoo like Selsun Blue and Denorex, with secondary competition of shampoo brands in general, right? Only in part.

What's going on here?

One of your major competitors is also your biggest customer!

Wal-Mart sells their own version of dandruff shampoo – Equate. Walgreen's has its own brand, too.

As with many private label products, the Equate package looks very similar to Head & Shoulders in shape and color.

Ingredients are also similar – the primary difference is price, with Equate selling for less than Head & Shoulders.

As you probably know, Wal-Mart is now the top US retailer by a healthy margin. P&G's sales to Wal-Mart are higher than their total sales to Japan.

So, P&G clearly has a vested interest in keeping Wal-Mart happy as a customer. Yet, P&G's product managers also have to view Wal-Mart as a competitor.

To make it even more confusing, P&G sold one of their brands to Wal-Mart – White Cloud – so that they now have an even bigger competitor in paper products.

That's the new competitive reality, and there are similar situations in other product categories. Your biggest partner and your biggest competitor may be the same company.

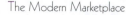

UPC and the Rise of the Retailer.

One of the culprits behind this change in the competitive landscape is those little bars on the back of the package – the **UPC (Universal Product Code)**. UPC information at the checkout counter generates scanner sales data which provides an unprecedented amount of information to retailers.

Armed with this information, retailers have been able to become smarter marketers – it's added a new dimension to the competitive landscape.

Often, this means squeezing extra margin out of the manufacturers – while offering competitive products at the same time.

Instant Competition.

Another competitive element to be considered is that, today, competitors can come from anywhere. Almost instantly.

A number of years ago, large appliance retailers changed the retail music industry almost overnight.

They began offering the most popular CDs at deep discounts. The loss of sales volume was devastating to the CD stores.

It caused many music-only retailers to close their doors.

And, if that weren't bad enough, Napster and others were a virtual death blow to companies like Tower Records, as sales volumes were further depressed due to illegal downloads.

The growth of online music providers, such as iTunes and MusicNow is changing the competitive playing field further.

The book superstores like Borders and Barnes & Noble have changed the book business.

Meanwhile, Amazon.com is introducing more and more people to the advantages of shopping for books, CDs, videos, and more online.

Last but not least, Wal-Mart is having its own impact, generating large volumes and pressuring prices and profit margins on the high-volume best sellers critical to industry profitability.

Competition is coming faster than ever.

The Good News…

The good news is that we all benefit – as a society.

Though there are certainly many dislocations, the net effect seems to be one we like. Even though it's also tougher for everyone.

Despite the changes in the worlds of books and music, there is more selection for more people than ever before in history.

We have more available to us at the beginning of the 21st century than was available for even the richest of the rich at the beginning of the 20th century.

And for all the inequality and unfairness that still exists, there is a flow of information and opportunity across borders and barriers like never before. Now, a computer programmer in India can scan Silicon Valley want ads in the online edition of the *San Jose Mercury News*.

Globalization and World Brands.

Another consideration for today's advertisers is **globalization**.

For many companies, the US is only one part of the marketplace.

Smile. Your Competition Just Got Smarter.

UPC information has made retailers smarter about brands.

Rocking the Competition.

Appliance retailers changed the CD market by offering them as "loss leaders" – products with low margin, or no margin, designed to stimulate sales traffic and volume.

Combined with file-sharing programs like Napster, it helped to put music stores out of business.

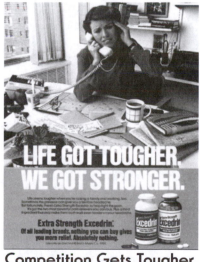

Competition Gets Tougher. We Get Smarter.

That's how it works – like it or not.

When you win, it's great. When you don't, it's a headache – or worse.

Word of Mouth: Old is New Again

Remember the last time you had terrible customer service?

Did you share your story with friends and family?

Chances are, you did, and chances are that you mentioned the brand or the name of the store.

You might believe you were merely sharing a story, but you were actually engaging in "word of mouth."

Word of mouth, of course, is as old as speech itself. But now marketers are trying to harness "word of mouth marketing."

They even have their own marketing association! WOMMA!

Word of mouth marketing is defined by WOMMA (Word of Mouth Marketing Association) as "the art and science of building active, mutually beneficial consumer-to-consumer and consumer-to-marketer communications."

The key is giving consumers something positive to talk about.

Example: Sony Ericsson

A classic example occurred just before every cell phone came equipped with a camera.

Sony Ericsson hired actors to pose as tourists at well-known attractions, such as the Empire State Building.

The actors worked in pairs, asking passersby to take their picture in front of the attraction.

When the passerby agreed, the Sony Ericsson actors would hand over their cell phone, which could double as a camera.

Those asked to take the picture would be intrigued by the combination phone and camera, so they naturally asked questions about the brand and where to buy it.

This generated instant – though slightly artificial – word of mouth marketing.

They're also trying to sell their brands in other parts of the world. Will the same message work everywhere?

The short answer is "It depends."

It depends on market conditions, competition, and, most critically, on whether consumer wants and needs and attitudes and behaviors are similar across cultures.

For some products, the similarity is probably pretty high.

Think about an airline promoting business travel.

Whether a frequent business traveler is Korean, American, or Australian, when it comes to air travel the needs are pretty much the same: safety, flight availability, and, of course, price.

Now think about a company selling food products. From culture to culture, that company may encounter very different consumer taste preferences and food preparation habits.

It's a challenge that many marketers face as they search for global sales growth. Globalization also impacts how we eat. Curry, for example, is now one of the favorite types of food in Great Britain.

New Problems, New Opportunities.

Now the good news/bad news cycle is global. A change in valuation with the Euro may make your trip to Europe more expensive. But it's a boon for foreign tourism in the USA.

A company like Dell sees many opportunities. Michael Dell comments, *"we're not going to find a billion new computer users in the US. We see major growth opportunities overseas."*

Many product categories that are "mature markets" in the US are growth markets overseas. That's good news for advertising and it might be good news for many US companies.

Similarities and Differences – Worldwide.

As Barry Day, Worldwide Creative Director for LINTAS, points out, *"People are becoming more and more dissimilar within regions and more and more similar across regions."*

That is, people in Georgia, Kansas, and California were once more different from each other and more similar to their neighbors. The same would be true with people from Quebec and Brazil.

But today, aerospace executives in Marietta, Georgia, Wichita, Kansas, or Long Beach, California, may have much more in common with each other than with their next-door neighbors.

Likewise, executives working for aviation companies in Canada (Montreal is headquarters for Bombardier) or Brazil (headquarters for Embraer) may have more in common with people who speak different languages than with their fellow countrymen.

Kenichi Ohmae, formerly of McKinsey/Japan, observed that European, American, and Japanese teens, once you factor out language and facial characteristics, are all pretty much the same.

Teens in these sophisticated consumer societies have very similar tastes in music, fashion, and attitudes.

These are examples of the concerns and opportunities facing marketers as they work to build "world brands."

Job Opportunities for You. Worldwide.

Some of you may find yourselves working for marketers or ad agencies in the emerging economies of Eastern Europe, where young Americans are valued for their experience with the most amazing economy in the world.

And, whether it's good news or bad, the trends we've discussed – evolving media channels, savvier consumers, increased competition, and globalization – will continue.

A More Competitive World.

Change is everywhere. Happening faster than ever. Rapidly evolving media forms are changing the way we consume information.

As consumers, we react in very human and powerful ways. The more we're marketed to, the harder we are to reach and persuade.

And now we're interacting and competing globally.

All that competition is creating a level of competition and change like the world has never seen.

A New World for Marketing Communications.

THERE HAVE BEEN OTHER CHANGES – other marketing communications techniques have gained acceptance and success.

Bigger Markets. More Marketing.

As the marketplace expands, so has the range of marketing communications techniques being used by today's marketers.

The four biggest areas being used are:

➤ **Marketing Public Relations**
➤ **Sales Promotion**
➤ **Direct Marketing**
➤ **Event Marketing**

Here again, in the area of marketing services, you will also find many companies experiencing exciting growth.

Marketing Public Relations.

In many categories, such as high-tech, effective marketing public relations (MPR) is the driving force of successful marketing.

High-Tech Marketing.

While you may be familiar with the larger and more established high-tech firms, that industry is one that demands a high degree of marketing-oriented public relations programs as part of a successful marketing effort for high-tech companies of every size.

When Steve Ballmer joined Microsoft, he had to manage a marketing process far different than the one at P&G. The importance of marketing PR is one of the major differences.

Nonprofit. Big Business.

Every community has an infrastructure of charitable and nonprofit organizations – from large ones like United Way and Children's Miracle Network through local ones like museums and zoos.

Busy as Beavers.

Cause marketing, event marketing, non-profits, and governmental organizations are carving out new marketing opportunities.

High-Tech MPR.

Here are some marketing public relations activities for a small high-tech firm:

- **Press kits**
- **Product reviews**
- **Trade shows**
- **Investor relations**
- **Trade channel relations**

With the growth of the high-tech sector, MPR opportunities have grown. We'll cover this in Chapter Seven – "Marketing Services."

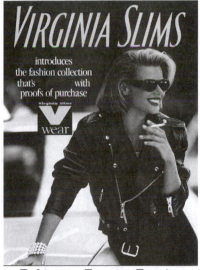

Tobacco Target Tactic.

Cigarette marketers became increasingly targeted and increasingly promotional in their approach.

Here, they used a frequency device (proof of purchase) to increase the lifetime value of their customers.

Lifetime value? Hmmm…

These programs come and go – Marlboro Miles and Camel Cash are no longer active.

Building Healthier Sales Figures.

Short-term, consumer promotions work. Marketers are concerned with rising costs and long-term benefits.

Direct Measurement.

Once marketers connect, they work to maximize the relationship. It's CRM, Customer Relationship Marketing.

Trade Promotions That Fit.

An ad for a Lee sales conference.

Quite simply, these organizations must market to survive.

Fund-raising events and programs are a big part of the operation of these groups – just one more small example of the big role public relations plays in marketing.

The Value of Publicity.

Finally, these tried-and-true tools of public relations have continued to demonstrate their value in brand-building.

As Al and Laura Ries note in *The Fall of Advertising and the Rise of PR,* publicity is a key part of introducing a successful brand. Ries asserts that, while advertising can still be effective in maintaining an existing brand, it is often spectacularly unsuccessful in introducing them.

For many high-tech marketers, PR such as software reviews, trade shows, and word-of-mouth from industry opinion leaders are critical elements of a successful marketing program.

Direct Marketing.

In 2008, direct was estimated at over $63 billion.

However, if you add up all the related expenses, the DMA (Direct Marketing Association) estimates that marketers (commercial and non-profit) spent $173.2 billion. The payoff is even bigger.

The DMA estimates that as $2.025 trillion in incremental sales – about 10% of US GDP.

A lot of people work in the industry – from marketers to shipping and fulfillment professionals. Telemarketers, too. There are an estimated 1.6 million direct employees in the US.

Direct is an important part of the Business of Brands.

And now it's going digital, with everything from database and CRM technology becoming more accessible to small companies to digital delivery mechanisms – from e-commerce to customer service becoming more cost-effective due to computer technology.

Let's take a quick look at why it's such an important part of the modern marketplace.

Two Benefits of Direct Marketing.

Direct marketing has many benefits; two stand out.

1. **Customization.** Direct marketing techniques make it possible to customize messages to small segments of consumers, and, in some cases, to customize to the individual. That fits neatly with the changes in consumer behavior outlined earlier.

2. **Accountability.** Direct marketing is highly accountable because its effects can be measured quickly and easily.

How many people call in response to a televised product offer? How many people mail back a postcard requesting more information on a product or service?

So, direct marketing is highly personal, and highly measurable, making it a very strong player in the marketplace today.

This will be covered further in Chapter Seven.

Sales Promotion.

Sales promotion offers an *incentive* to change purchase behavior.

Usually, sales promotion either temporarily lowers the price of the product or service or adds value in some way.

Two Audiences.

There are two audiences for sales promotion:

1. **Consumers** – those who purchase the product.
2. **"The Trade"** – those who get the product to consumers: retailers, wholesalers, and sales people.

Consumer-directed sales promotion includes techniques such as coupons, rebates, sweepstakes, and premiums.

Trade-directed sales promotion includes trade allowances and "spiffs" (sales incentives).

Two Primary Reasons for Sales Promotion Growth.

Both types of sales promotion became very popular with brand marketers. There were two primary reasons:

1. **Measurability.** Like direct marketing, sales promotion is highly measurable.
2. **Fast Results.** Sales promotion activities generate relatively quick results in the marketplace.

The explosion in sales promotion spending was also triggered by the widespread introduction of scanners at the checkout line.

Scanner-collected data allows the tracking of sales to clearly document the effects of sales promotions.

Issue a coupon, sales go up. You can prove it almost instantly.

Put that couponed product on display, sales go up even more. You can prove that, too.

Sales Promotions Promote Careers and Stock Prices.

Brand managers quickly became enamored with sales promotion for its sales-generation capabilities.

The key to success in brand management is regular and frequent job advancement. The way you get promoted is simple – increase sales. Sales promotion increases brand sales. So...

Couple that with the fact that most US companies are publicly held and that the stock market rewards sales growth.

So, the impetus for sales promotion efforts also came from brand managers as a way to forward careers and from corporations as a way to improve the stock price.

The Bad News...

Unfortunately, for all its short-term benefits, sales promotion does appear to have some long-term drawbacks.

First, it can be hard to make money this way. The cost of sales promotion programs can be quite high – the cost of each new sale may be greater than the available margin.

That's just the beginning.

Strategic Brand Communications.

As Beth Barnes was writing the first version of this chapter, she was also working on a new book with Don Schultz – *Strategic Brand Communications*. It had been called *Strategic Advertising Campaigns*.

Why the name change?

Most of what companies are doing isn't just about advertising anymore.

They're creating, managing, and protecting brands.

It's All about Integration.

The front of the book talks about what's going on in the marketplace today – all the stuff mentioned in this chapter.

Then, a planning framework:

* **Segmenting your customer base;**
* **Developing a strategy;** and
* **Using a return-on-customer-investment approach.**

Next, we cover the areas of:

* **Advertising;**
* **Trade sales promotion;**
* **Consumer sales promotion;**
* **Public relations;** and
* **Direct & interactive marketing.**

Behavioral Segmentation.

A key SBC element is **behavioral segmentation**. We look at customers not just on who they are (demographics and psychographics) but on how they use a brand.

After all, you might want to tell a loyal user something different than a brand switcher.

Customer Value.

Another element is an emphasis on **customer valuation**. How much are current customers worth and how much might they be worth if managed more effectively?

Awareness is nice, but if people aren't buying, it isn't worth much.

We recommend making spending decisions based on how much you think you can get back in sales. We call it return-on-customer-investment–based spending and evaluation.

It's an approach that addresses the needs for accountability that so many clients have these days.

Check it out!

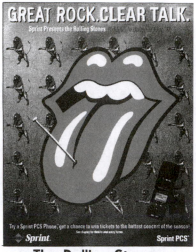

The Rolling Stones Connect with Sprint.

This was part of a concert tour tie-in. Sign-up for Sprint and get concert tickets. Visit the Sprint PCS store and get a free poster.

Breakthrough Checklist:

Here are some of the ways people and companies are making changes for the better in our modern marketplace:

New Strategies: look for new ways to win – new ways to change the game.

New Tactics: Domino's did it with delivery, LensCrafters did it with eyeglasses in an hour. Boots did it by shifting from advertising to in-store contact.

New Technologies: Computers have changed everything. How can you leverage that change?

New Categories: Coffee was an old category, now it's new again.

New Media: New magazines and new media channels, such as mobile phones and the Internet, are all generating their own kind of change.

New Insights: What's your vision of the future? Insights and visions put people and businesses ahead of the curve and lead us into the future.

Looking for a breakthrough?
Look for opportunities in any or all of these areas.

Now everyone promotes. Newspapers, TV, products, services... everyone. Consumers have been trained to expect coupons and rebates, to know every brand will eventually go "on special."

Some argue that manufacturers themselves created this large group of brand-switching consumers through sales promotion.

Traditional sales promotion also seems to do little to enhance a brand's image, unless the desired image is that of a price brand.

P&G has tried to scale back both trade and consumer sales promotion efforts in favor of increases in brand-building advertising. Whether that approach will be successful remains to be seen.

What is clear is that sales promotion is here to stay and will likely continue to challenge advertising for budget resources.

This will also be covered further in Chapter Seven.

Event Marketing and Sponsorship.

The new kid on the block, at least in terms of receiving serious budget consideration, is event marketing, defined as "corporate sponsorship of lifestyle-related programs and events."

By either sponsoring existing events or creating their own, brand marketers can draw consumers into close interaction with the brand, tying it to enjoyable, involving activities.

While it's difficult to get a precise estimate of the size of the event marketing industry, it's clear marketers are investing heavily.

A Big Business.

The undisputed event king is the Olympics. The 1996 Olympics in Atlanta netted $40 million in sponsorship payments. Total Olympic-related spending was estimated at $5 billion.

US ad spending for the 2008 Olympics was over $1.5 billion.

The 2008 Presidential Election added an estimated $3 billion.

The Super Bowl is another example. It's not only a well-watched commercial fest interrupted by a football game, it's the centerpiece of many sweepstakes and related promotions.

The cost of a spot on Super Bowl #1 was $42,500. By the mid-1980s it was up to $600,000. In 2008, $2.6 million.

It seems as though every sporting event has at least one sponsor attached, and usually many more than one.

Watch a NASCAR race and see if any driver is ever mentioned without a sponsor reference. The same is increasingly true for museum exhibits, concert tours, and so on.

Event marketing does not offer the precise measurability of direct marketing and sales promotion. Although attendance at events can generally be counted fairly easily, what's not usually known is the direct impact event participation has on sales.

Still, event marketing is viewed by many as a good way to reach consumers who are increasingly hard to get via traditional media – college students, for example.

Furthermore, as traditional media efficiencies decline, these environments may offer additional value for certain sponsors.

We'll cover this area further in Chapter 7.

Madison & Vine:
Advertising and Entertainment Converge.

There are dramatic changes taking place; advertisers have to work harder than ever to reach smaller audiences that now have the technology to "time shift" their favorite shows and fast-forward through ads.

Undeterred, advertisers have found a new way to reach consumers while they're watching: by packaging ads as entertainment.

By partnering to deliver content, advertisers ensure their messages are seen, while entertainment producers ensure that advertising revenue will continue to support their programming.

A Combination of Techniques.

The concept of Madison & Vine encompasses a number of techniques that refer to entertainment vehicles (such as television and films) that have an embedded advertising message.

If you've ever seen a brand prominently displayed in either a television show or movie, you've experienced a product placement, which refers to an advertiser paying to have the brand featured in an entertainment context.

The advent of reality TV brought the practice of placing branded products in entertainment vehicles to the forefront: the castaways on *Survivor* would compete for the privilege of winning a bag of Doritos, and the Target Bulls Eye logo was prominently displayed on crates the castaways used for stools. This promotion was obvious, but audiences stayed tuned in to be entertained – and were advertised to in the process.

An Historic Intersection.

If you're curious and wondering how the idea of converging advertising and entertainment got its name, you need to look no further than two streets in New York City and Hollywood.

Historically, the largest and most famous New York ad agencies were located on Madison Avenue, and in Hollywood, the legendary center of the movie and radio industry was the corner of Vine Street and Hollywood Boulevard – Hollywood & Vine.

We suspect they'll be doing more business at this location.

Product Placement in Action.

Marketers broke down barriers on network TV, placing their products on shows like *Survivor*, *Heroes*, *American Idol*, *Dancing with the Stars*, and, in the case of Pontiac, giving away cars to everyone lucky enough to be at that particular show.

Building Brands with UPCs

Brands are always looking for ways to build relationships with their customers.

A New Generation CMO.

Starting with traditional agency jobs in Chicago and Washington, DC, Mark Goldstein evolved into a Chief Marketing Officer – first Fallon in Minneapolis, and now Lowe in New York.

Here's his take on key success factors for today's ad agency.

"The agency business is actually very simple. It's about two things: winning the right clients and hiring the right people.

"But most agencies get greedy in pitching business or don't set the hiring bar high enough, and so they rapidly race towards mediocrity.

"You need to be maniacal about only having great clients and great people."

Did it work? Fallon grew from $185 million to nearly $1 billion while Mark was there.

Today, as Chief Marketing Officer and Vice Chairman of BBDO North America, one of his concerns, just like most CMOs, is growth through winning new business. He is credited with helping to land more than $1 billion in billings at BBDO, including eBay, Lowe's Home Centers and Bank of America, among others.

The New World for Advertising.

ONCE UPON A TIME, COPYWRITERS WROTE ADS. They wrote print ads, television ads, radio ads. Occasionally, they wrote a brochure or a headline for an outdoor board.

Art directors had the same limits. So did agencies.

The commission system that paid agency bills also constricted agency creativity. Not so much in what they said, but in where they could say it. That's changing. Big time.

Need more than 30 seconds for your product? Today, you can have a 30-minute infomercial or offer a videotape.

You can publish your own magazine.

Or, no surprise, you can set up your own Web site.

The same visual and verbal techniques used for advertising can now be used for all marketing communications.

Three Core Components:

This new world has three core components:

➤ **A Broader Range of Communication Options**
➤ **A Wider Range of Clients for Marketing Services**
  (And they need more of them.)
➤ **New Advertising Agency Opportunities**
  Let's see what this new world looks like.

A Broader Range of Communication Options.

As we've said more than once, advertising isn't just advertising anymore. Public relations, sales promotion, direct marketing, and event marketing each need high degrees of creativity.

And each is creating new options and opportunities.

More than Just Coupons.

Sales promotion is now more than just coupons.

"Drink Pepsi. Get Stuff" is an example. Every summer, you see soft drink companies implementing promotions designed to make you thirst for whatever they're offering.

Now virtually every major marketer is involved in some sort of promotion. Today, marketers look for promotions that support the brand's values – so that they add value even as they offer a discount.

Starbucks chose to get involved with reading and music – things that many people do when they have a cup of coffee.

Go to any Starbucks and you'll see brand-value-enhancing promotions – involving books and music – that enhance that "third place" that revolves around a cup of coffee.

Direct in Many Directions.

Direct marketing now exists in all media forms: mail, print, radio, television, and the Internet.

Coffee is more than Starbucks. Gevalia Coffee is another example of a marketer turning a traditional category into a direct marketing business.

Ads for Land's End, Nordic Track – anything with a coupon or 800 number – are building brands with direct.

Some successful new advertisers are running direct campaigns – such as those ads for Bose Wave radios. They need profitable levels of response to justify each ad.

Even Richard Branson's Virgin, now a global "super-brand," began as a direct marketing record business.

Direct marketing can be a great way to learn marketing – it forces you to deal with results and reality.

Amazon.com is another example. With more transactions on the Internet, the world of direct is growing – and it will use all the great creative and smart marketing it can.

Event Marketing on a Roll.

A little earlier, we showed a graphic for the *Rolling Stones* and Sprint. A surprising combination? No longer.

Now entertainment, media, and marketing find new combinations every day. As we said, it's "Madison & Vine."

When James Bond drives a car in one of his movies, it becomes part of that brand's advertising. Now most contemporary movies have placements and promotions. We've come to expect it.

In fact, this publisher even got a screen credit when their books appeared on Meg Ryan's desk a few years ago in *Kate and Leopold!* (Sorry, even if you squint, you won't be able to see them. Sigh.)

A Wider Range of Clients.

Even as mergers have made fewer large multi-brand marketers, something else has emerged – more marketing.

And, in an important way, there are now even more clients.

More Opportunities – Big and Small.

Today, every small retailer, every Internet provider, and every new rock band can use the same tools the big boys use.

The marketing technology download continues.

Today, someone with the right computer program and good taste can generate top-flight design – almost for free.

Convergence at Work.

Switch programs and your small business can have access to a database covering the entire US – again, almost for free.

Television advertising was once affordable for only national and large local advertisers. Today, cable TV and new computer-based video editing and graphics programs make it possible for small businesses to have their own TV commercials.

And not all the opportunities are small.

Marketing Is More Important for Every Company.

For years, some big businesses were quite successful without doing much in the way of marketing. Those days are gone.

Entire industries, such as healthcare, have undergone revolutionary change as they've entered the market economy.

Service industries, like banking, and the accounting and legal professions each need new and different marketing solutions for their changing industries.

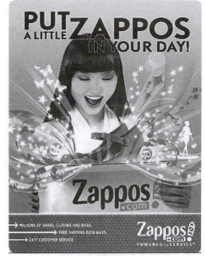

The Ad Store:

Paul Cappelli decided that ad agencies didn't work – at least, big, top-heavy ad agencies didn't work.

So, he created The Ad Store.

Madison Avenue to Main Street. The Ad Store works for clients on a project basis. Cappelli offers *"store-front advertising with 'Madison Avenue quality at Main Street prices.'"*

They're small, but they have some pretty big clients – like Zappos.com, JetBlue, goddaddy.com, Mike's Hard Lemonade and more.

They pull in talent from all over and work for clients from all over. Technology and The Media Revolution is creating a new kind of agency.

Going Global.

The Ad Store began in New York.

There are now offices in Athens, Barcelona, Brussels, Bucharest, Cyprus, Hamburg, Parma, and Washington DC.

The Italian Ad Store just won some major international design awards.

And at a Web Site Near You.

It's a new way of doing business.

If you want to take part in edgy discussions on what does and doesn't work in advertising, or if you want to see other opinions on what's hot and what's not, make The Ad Store's Web site a regular stop.

It's at www.adstore.com.

Media Extensions.
Brand Extensions.

In many ways, consumers give you clues about what your brand means to them.

For example, music is an integral part of the Starbucks experience.

So it's not surprising that it became part of Starbucks' integrated marketing program.

All those people with their laptops is another clue… right?

Exercise:
Look for the Insight.

Next time you come across an ad you like – one that catches your mind as well as your eye – see if you can work backwards through Dr. Fortini-Campbell's framework.

Inspiration.
The ad represents the inspiration – what is that inspiration?

Insight.
What do you think was the insight that drove that execution?

Information.
What kind of information do you think sparked the insight that inspired the creative idea?

Data.
Keep looking for more examples.

By analyzing how companies developed ads you like, you can start to develop the habits that will help you find those insights on your own.

The consumer insight approach is successful because it's a rich way of linking the consumer with the brand.

With this change and dislocation comes something else – a need for more marketing. Because marketing is how companies deal with change. It also means additional job opportunities.

CEOs who once came from manufacturing or finance now come from marketing. And all CEOs now have to be smart marketers as the future becomes more marketing-driven.

As marketing becomes a core business function, opportunities for smart marketers keep growing in companies of every size.

New! More Big Opportunities.

As the marketplace changes, new opportunities emerge. The marketplace always seems to make a place for those with the vision, the insight, or the great new idea that leads the way.

Names we all know, like Java and Starbucks, are relatively new.

Today, we take it for granted that there's a big video rental store nearby – and probably a bagel shop. Wait! That video store might have gone out of business because of Netflix and TiVo.

Michael Jordan was a basketball player who endorsed a shoe – nothing new. He and Nike became a whole new brand. And now he's helping Robert Johnson manage their NBA entertainment brand, the Charlotte Bobcats.

Two of the biggest brands in computers – Gateway and Dell – built their business through direct. They saw opportunity. Dell was able to keep growing. Gateway hit a wall.

And all these businesses need advertising and marketing communications – more than ever.

This is one of the most exciting aspects of the modern marketplace – though it sometimes takes your breath away.

It's also one of the major opportunities for exciting new jobs.

That's why we'll devote a whole chapter to the importance of new ideas in the marketplace at the end of this book.

New Advertising Agency Opportunities.

Branding and brand stewardship are hot topics. And advertising has always been recognized for its brand-building capabilities.

So even though it's a volatile industry, people are hiring.

The advertising industry today is now operating under a very different set of ground rules than in the "good old days."

But that doesn't mean there isn't opportunity.

The Good News: Response to Changes.

Reviewing the forces creating today's marketplace, you now see what we mean by Schumpeter's term "creative destruction." You see how technology growing according to Moore's Law is giving us greater capabilities. And we're doing it all in the middle of a McLuhan-style media revolution.

Many things have changed. Yet, in many ways, "Advertising and The Business of Brands" is larger than ever.

Because things once done only by advertising agencies are now done by the whole new world of marketing communications.

More Media. More Marketing Services.

In terms of job opportunities, two of those changes have been the emergence of new media vehicles for a more "information rich" society, and the many new suppliers of marketing services.

In these two areas alone, there has been huge growth and many new job opportunities.

Those opportunities go from entry-level all the way to top jobs like Mark Goldstein, who was Chief Marketing Officer at Fallon, when the agency won United Airlines. Now he has new challenges at BBDO – still one of the most successful agencies, they need marketing more than ever.

As marketing grows in importance, the number and importance of marketing jobs grows as well.

Many agencies have met the challenge with some unique and successful responses.

A New Generation of Thinking.

The ad industry, as well as marketing, faces difficult challenges. And, just as so many other industries must, it's responding.

Some of the most intriguing responses are account planning, consumer insight, and computer-based jobs.

Account Planning. Media Planning. Communication Planning.
On the agency side, account planning is one way agencies are regaining their sense of today's new consumer.

An account planner is *"one person who is charged single-mindedly with understanding the target audience and then representing it throughout the entire advertising development process – thereby ensuring that the advertising is both strategically and executionally relevant to the defined target."*

Account planners use various research techniques to develop a thorough understanding of the consumer and how that consumer interacts with the brand.

The planner then carries that knowledge back to the agency and applies it to the development of the creative strategy and the ads that result from that strategy.

Account planning goes beyond traditional research.

It's not just a support function, it's an integral part of the advertising development process.

Many agencies, like Chiat/Day, Goodby & Silverstein, and Fallon are having success in winning accounts and developing effective campaigns using account planning.

And, as we mentioned earlier, media agencies are now using an account planning approach to help them deal with consumers' wider range of media choices.

New "media-agnostic" planning groups, like Naked, are providing new models for successful marketing communications in an exciting new world.

A New Media Person.

One of those involved in today's new media thinking is Beth Uyenco, US Director of Strategic Research and Analysis at media agency OMD.

She joined DDB after earning a master's degree from MSU and was recently named a Media All-Star in Research by *MediaWeek*.

We asked her what she thinks of today's new media world.

What are the three biggest changes you've seen during the time you've been in media research?
"First, accounting for media's contribution to a brand's business.

"Second, getting beyond ratings to quantifying the value of a vehicle.

"Third, the rapid deployment of computer systems for media planning/buying: helping users like planners and buyers adapt to systems for channel planning."

What do you feel is the biggest challenge facing agency media people today?
"From management's perspective, the biggest challenge is the increased competitive environment – as agencies have moved to unbundling media.

"From my perspective, proving one's USP – the unique selling proposition – is the biggest challenge. It has to be operationalized in terms of having unique tools for planning and buying media."

What are the most valuable tools at the media planner's disposal?
"Tools which help draw insights about the target in ways other than the conventional cross-tabulation of media."

(Continued on next page)

New Media Person (Cont.)

"Tools which go beyond counting eyeballs or noses and instead provide an understanding of how much better a vehicle or medium delivers the message at the right time, place, and context."

What are the most important skills for an agency media person starting in the business today?

"Being extremely perceptive about how consumers make brand choices."

10 years from now, what do you think will be the three most dominant forms of media?

"Definitely electronic. One will be Internet-based, delivered through a TV/PC appliance that provides vast streams of information in different forms: e-commerce, promotion, direct, etc.

"Television will still be dominant, as there will always be a universal need for passively consumed entertainment, but it will have the ability to provide additional streams of information, which the viewer may opt to attend to in the course of his or her passive viewing.

"More importantly, content will be increasingly on demand as viewers are able to view what they want whenever they want to.

"In response, marketers will be deploying brand messages in ways other than 30-second spots. There will definitely be more content integration of brand messages. Today we call this 'branded entertainment.'

"The ability to reach consumers through media in more meaningful ways will increase the importance of channels that have previously been considered 'unconventional' media.

"These are vehicles which consumers will encounter during their daily activities. A good example of this will be the use of mobile communications."

"Magazines will continue to be dominant due to their low-tech, convenient packaging of content relevant to different consumer segments. However, their electronic versions (websites) will become almost as important as the printed copies because of the value of their editorial content."

Thanks, Beth.

Consumer Insight.

A related client-side research approach on the marketer's side is generally termed "consumer insight."

Lisa Fortini-Campbell is a leading advocate. She argues that *"all of our marketing efforts, from product design through advertising, are successful only to the extent that they connect with a real, live human being – a consumer… it demands that you go beyond just knowing who your consumer is to something deeper – understanding, respect, and empathy."*

A marketer succeeds in "hitting the sweet spot" when an insight into the consumer – who she is, what she cares about, what makes her act and react – is tied to a brand insight, something unique and relevant within the product.

Example: Starbucks, a "Third Place"

When Scott Bedbury went to Starbucks, he brought along one colleague from Nike – a consumer insight person.

They determined that one of the driving forces of Starbucks was that it provided a "third place" between home and work.

It wasn't just the coffee, it was being removed from those other two places and having your own private time – to think, read, listen to music… whatever. With that insight, a whole range of complicated marketing decisions became easier.

Data → Information → Insight → Inspiration.

That's Dr. Fortini-Campbell's conceptual framework.

Data provides the fact base on the target market.

Information comes through data analysis and interpretation.

Insight is the intuitive hypothesis about what the consumer's hot button might be relative to the brand that emerges from studying the information.

Inspiration activates – the result is some means of communicating the insight back to the consumer.

"Mac Jockeys" and WebMasters.

Agency creative departments have some new players, too.

As computer technology has become a part of the process, a state-of-the-art computer network is now in virtually every agency creative department. That means new jobs and new skills.

Print production work is now done in-house with a new breed of "electronic pre-press" specialists.

In other creative operations, from design to videotape editing, to preparing materials for printing, new team members with new skills are now a part of agency creative departments.

And, of course, Web design has created not only new jobs, but it has created new agencies specializing in Web sites.

There are even more changes going on at agencies – the creative department isn't the only one being challenged.

New Media Thinking.

What's a media department to do in the frightening world of more media choices and audience fragmentation? One thing they might do is become a free-standing "media agency."

At the media department at DDB Worldwide's media agency, OMD, people like Beth Uyenco think about media from the consumer's point of view.

They've come up with two important media planning concepts that recognize that the consumer must be at the heart of media planning. Here's a quick overview.

Consumer Aperture™

DDB defines Consumer Aperture as *"when, where, and under what circumstance the customer's mind is most receptive to the selling message."* This is a trademarked name.

For example, your pizza "aperture" on radio might be late drive time or right before a sporting event. The media planner has to do some thinking to identify the ideal aperture.

Aperture considerations are all about delivering *sales* messages that try to spark a response. That's an important way to increase advertising effectiveness.

Personal Media Network (PMN).

Your personal media network is *"the combination of media vehicles a customer individually selects to satisfy his or her individual needs."*

DDB maps out PMNs for target segments, looking at when various types of media are used and whether they're used for information, for entertainment, or as background (in the case of television and radio).

From there, it's a question of matching up aperture points with the corresponding PMN-identified media usage to determine where the advertising message should appear.

Brand Contacts.

Another related concept comes from work being done in the area of Integrated Marketing Communications, a customer-driven approach designed to affect consumers' brand behavior.

Brand contacts *"occur whenever customers or prospects have contact with a particular brand or organization over time. Every exposure has the potential to provide some new information or message to the consumer about what the brand is, how it is used, who uses it, when it is relevant, and on and on."*

The brand contact concept recognizes ads as only one source of consumer information, and not necessarily the most influential.

Organizations that conduct brand contact audits try to identify the most important contact points for their brand in order to better manage their consumer communications.

Thinking about Media?

Ask yourself these questions.

What's the best time and place to reach your target consumer?
In the '20s, Dr. Pepper tried it with 10-2-4.

In the 1920s, Dr. Walter Eddy at Columbia University studied the body's metabolism.

He discovered that a natural drop in energy occurs about 10:30 a.m., 2:30 p.m., and 4:30 p.m.

He also discovered that if the people in his research study had something to eat or drink at 10, 2, and 4, the energy slump could be avoided.

After Dr. Eddy's research findings were released, Dr. Pepper challenged its advertising agency to come up with a theme that would suggest that Dr. Pepper should be that 10, 2, and 4 drink which would keep the energy level up.

The result was one of the most enduring of Dr. Pepper's advertising themes: Drink a bite to eat at 10, 2, and 4.

What's Your Personal Media Network?
Take a minute to think about your own media consumption.

What's the best time, place, and media channel to reach you?

For many of us, mobile phones have added a "third screen" to our own media network.

What's Your Brand's Media Network?
How and when does your brand reach consumers?

In advertising? On a store shelf? On the street?

Today, with multiple media channels and an increasingly noisy communications environment, it's increasingly difficult to develop those moments.

You need to be increasingly aware of brand contact points.

Connecting with Expectant Mothers.

Megan and Her Latest Creative Project. In today's marketplace, you can connect with your own objectives.

Here, a new service offers computer-based ordering for upscale "time-poor" consumers. Not every new venture will succeed – but some will – and, in today's marketplace, everyone has a chance.

Database Marketing.

One of the recent growth areas in direct marketing has been in database marketing, which is designed *"to help identify a marketer's target audiences and facilitate the ongoing relationship between the target audience and the marketer."*

To understand the importance of database marketing, it's critical that you realize that to "identify a marketer's target audiences" means finding out who the *individuals* are who buy your product or are prospects for your product and gathering demographic, psychographic, attitudinal, and behavioral information on them.

The basic precept, as described by David Shepard, one of the leaders in the field, is: *"recognition of the fact that not all customers have the same needs, nor have they the same potential, and therefore they should not all be treated the same way."*

As such, database marketing moves the brand builder from old demographically defined segments like "Women 18–44" into a new world of truly customized marketing.

Database at Work.

Airline frequent flyer programs are some of the original database marketing applications. Now you get "points" when you go to the supermarket or use certain credit cards.

Many other products, including some consumer products packaged goods brands, are actively working to gather customer information and develop databases.

Database marketing can be used to help increase advertising effectiveness through indicating customer needs and pinpointing attitudes and behaviors.

Example: Megan & the Welcome Addition Club

This example isn't just about marketers, it's about careers.

Our example is Megan Stockton, an art director.

After graduating from Eastern Illinois with a degree in graphic design, she started on the interactive side, producing "Ernie," a Web site for the accounting/consulting firm of Ernst & Young.

Then, she felt she needed to develop her traditional graphic skills as well, and got a job as Creative Supervisor on the Welcome Addition Club, a relationship program for mothers – developed for Similac baby formula.

She worked on a communication program that provides information for mothers at each stage of pregnancy and early infancy. With infant formula, the brand choice is often made before the baby is born. So, the earlier the better.

The program begins with useful prenatal information. After the baby is born, a variety of materials is sent depending on whether the baby is formula or breast-fed and whether the formula is Similac or a competitor. It's behavior-based.

Megan designed and produced the full range of materials.

She even helped develop the Web site.

She also became involved with Peapod, an online shopping service – working on ways to connect with customers and introduce them to shopping in a brand new way.

Then she left the company she worked for – but kept working on the projects. Today, she's freelancing out of her own home on a combination of relationship programs and Web designs.

With the right computer programs, she and her writing partner can connect with clients across the country.

Her high-tech capabilities have given her the skills to be in demand for a changing marketplace and the options to be able to do it from her own home – just in time for some big changes.

Megan just started getting Welcome Addition Club mailings addressed to her. And she now has a career that lets her raise a family at home – high tech with old-fashioned values.

That's just one more example of the new options and opportunities emerging in today's modern marketplace.

Summary:

While the changes that have affected the traditional way in which advertising agencies operated won't be undone, the marketplace keeps creating new opportunities:
- New opportunities for brand-building
- New ways to connect with the customer
- New ways to make the cash register ring

Because even with all the changes, that's still what it's about.

Today, most agencies realize accountability is the new watchword as they work to find new ways to generate brand success.

Then again, it stands to reason.

Because it's a business based on change. More than ever.

It's a business where every day brings new challenges and new opportunities in the modern marketplace. Enjoy the ride!

Review Questions:

1. Marketplace Changes.

Given the marketplace changes discussed in this chapter, how might Apple's campaign for Macintosh be different if the computer were being introduced today?

2. Your Personal Thoughts.

How has marketing changed during your lifetime?

Can you predict what new techniques we might experience in the next 10 years? 20 years?

3. Financial Factors.

Discuss some of the major ways that financially driven client mergers affected the advertising agency business.

4. Regional Renaissance.

What forces led to the renaissance of regionally based, creatively driven advertising agencies that won major accounts?

References:

Here are some other books you might find enlightening.

Type in these titles on a good bookstore search engine and you'll get all you need to know.

Chiat/Day: The First 20 Years

An album of their work. Page after page of some of the best pure ad campaigns done since DDB.

Emperors of AdLand
by Nancy Millman

An hilarious, but slightly frightening look at what MergerMania did to New York agencies in the '80s.

Integrated Marketing Communications
by Lauterborn, Schultz, Tannenbaum

Here's the book that helped start it all – providing the IMC framework.

Inventing Desire
by Karen Stabiner

A year with Chiat/Day. You'll get a feel for what it's like to work at this cutting edge agency.

MaxiMarketing: The New Direction in Advertising, Promotion, & Marketing Strategy.
by Stan Rapp & Tom Collins

One of the first to get a handle on IMC. They start with a direct perspective and then show you how they grow that perspective across a range of marketing communications.

Strategic Brand Communications
by Beth Barnes and Don Schultz

Of course.

Whatever Happened to Madison Avenue?
by Martin Mayer

Some of the emerging problems are examined here from the agency standpoint.

5. Integrated Marketing Communications (IMC).

Describe the major components of IMC.

6. Word-of-Mouth Marketing

Discuss any ethical concerns associated with using word-of-mouth marketing. What was your opinion of the Sony Ericsson example where actors introduced tourists to cell phone cameras?

7. Your 21st Century Crystal Ball...

A. How do you think ad agencies will change in the next 10 years? Try to come up with three basic changes that might take place.

B. How do you think advertising will change? List three changes that you think will impact you as a viewer and consumer.

Concepts & Vocabulary:

Account planning – Agency function with the responsibility for representing the voice of the consumer in all decision making – particularly creative development.

Added value – Extras beyond the actual product or service that provide additional benefit to the customer.

Aperture – (See **Consumer aperture**)

Behavioral segmentation – Looking at customers not just based on who they are (demographics and psychographics) but more on how they use our brand.

Brand contacts – Occur whenever consumers, customers, or prospects have contact with a particular brand or organization over time. Every exposure has the potential to provide some new information or message to the consumer about what the brand is, how it is used, who uses it, when it is relevant, and on and on.

Communication planning – A "media-agnostic" approach to achieving marketing communication goals.

Consumer aperture – When, where, and under what circumstance the customer is most receptive to the selling message.

Consumer insight – In-depth knowledge of the consumer that makes it possible to identify product benefits that will motivate purchasing behavior.

Consumer promotion – Sales promotion activities directed at end users of the product or service; includes such things as couponing, premiums, sweepstakes, and frequent-buyer programs.

Database marketing – Planning and marketing system that involves collecting and analyzing data on customers and prospects, particularly behavioral data.

Direct marketing – Describes a range of activities involving personalized contact with a customer or prospect, usually with the intent of generating some sort of measurable response.

Event marketing – Corporate sponsorship of lifestyle-related programs and events.

Globalization – The notion that products can be marketed in essentially the same way throughout the world because of growing similarities between consumers, regardless of their native culture.

In-house – Term for a marketer who develops advertisements (and other promotional messages) using an internal staff rather than an outside agency.

Loss leader – Retail marketing tactic where a popular item is sold at or below cost to stimulate store traffic.

Loyalty program – A marketing program with incentives based on repeated use of the product. For example, frequent flyer programs where fliers collect "miles" and those where customers save proofs of purchase and redeem them.

Marketing public relations (MPR) – Public relations activities used in support of selling a particular product or service; techniques include press kits, product reviews, and trade shows.

Media buying services – Specialty firms that focus on placing advertisements across a variety of media types. Media buying services argue that their high-volume buying nets their clients lower prices than full-service advertising agencies.

Media planning – Today, a new definition is emerging, with account planning style techniques being used to help deal with the increased number of media options.

MergerMania – Term for rash of mergers that hit agencies in the '80s.

Niche audience – A small group of consumers, viewers, etc., who have some very specific things in common.

Price to earnings (P/E) ratio – A financial yardstick which measures the value of a stock (the price) relative to how much a company makes (the earnings).

Personal media network – *"The combination of media vehicles which a customer individually selects to satisfy his or her individual needs."*

Personal truth – Concept espoused by Dan Wieden – a search for a person's inner feeling about the product category or their feelings in a larger sense – something that feels very real and important to them.

Private label – Products similar to major branded items manufactured by the retailer to compete with that item at a lower price. For example, Wal-Mart's Equate shampoo competes with P&G's Head & Shoulders, which is also sold at Wal-Mart.

Return on investment (ROI) – A financial yardstick which measures the profit on a project relative to the investment.

Sales promotion – The use of incentives (either a decrease in price or increase in value) to spark an immediate purchase of the promoted product.

Scanners – Electronic devices that read UPCs, capturing data on products purchased in retail stores.

Spiffs – Incentives given to retail sales people by manufacturers to encourage promotion of particular brands.

Sponsorship – Process where a marketer underwrites some or all of the costs of an event in exchange for promotion of the marketer's product or service in the event context.

Strategic brand communications – Term for the contemporary marketing communications task.

Trade promotion – The use of incentives focused on some aspect of the sales and distribution channel. Some examples are trade discounts, display allowances, and "spiffs."

Unbundling – Process where a full-service advertising agency spins off pieces of its operation as separate profit centers free to compete for business in their area of expertise (most often, media planning and buying).

Universal product code (UPC) – A system used to identify products and manage inventories efficiently.

World brand – A product sold under the same name and substantially the same image in more than one country.

3

This chapter was written by Eliza-beth M. Tucker, Ph.D., when she was the Director of the Texas Media Program at the University of Texas at Austin. Before earning her doctorate, she worked for seven years in the advertising industry on all sides of the business: agency, client, and media. She has been Director of Strategic Planning for Tribal DDB, specializing in new media and is now working on some unique intellectual property.

Nike: If You Let Me Play 30:TV

Girl: If you let me play…
If you let me play sports.
I will like myself more…

"All of us who professionally use the mass media are the shapers of society.
We can vulgarize that society. We can brutalize it.
Or we can help lift it onto a higher level."
— Bill Bernbach

Advertising & Society

JANET CHAMP WANTED TO MAKE A DIFFERENCE with the advertising she wrote. She wanted to do advertising that not only sold products and entertained people, but had a message that made the world a better place. She wrote a commercial for Nike called *"If You Let Me Play Sports."*

In 1949, **Frank T. Smith, Jr.** graduated from Texas A & M and got a job at NBC. Today, he's President of Gulf Coast Broadcasting in Corpus Christi, Texas. One day he found himself at the center of one of the biggest ethical controversies in advertising.

When **Ivan Preston** was a graduate student at Michigan State University, he decided he wanted to study the ethics of advertising – though some suggested he wouldn't find any. Recently, Professor Preston published his latest book, *The Tangled Web They Weave*, and testified before the FCC on **puffery.**

James Desrosier graduated from Kenyon College and went to work at Grey Advertising. Today, he's a visionary helping determine the course of e-business on a global scale – and a member of the National Advertising Review Board.

Each of these people plays a role in the way advertising interacts with society at large.

Advertising Touches Everyone.

Whether we work in advertising and marketing or merely "consume" advertising, it's a part of our world. It's pervasive.

As James Twitchell says in his book *AdCult USA*, *"If goods are hardware, meaning is software, and advertising writes most of the software."* It exerts a major influence on our society.

Advertising professionals must understand this power and how to manage it. As citizen "consumers," we also have a say in how we allow advertising to behave in our society.

Economics, Ethics, Rules, & Regulations.

THIS CHAPTER HAS THREE SECTIONS. Each section will introduce you to a group of important issues.

These are condensed summaries; each could be a book in itself. In fact, each has been the subject of many books.

Here's how we'll try to do it:

➤ **Economic Arguments.**

We'll discuss ideas about how people think advertising works in our economy and how that affects us as a society.

We'll discuss two economic perspectives on advertising:

• advertising as an agent of market power, and

• advertising as an agent of market information.

➤ **Ethical Arguments.**

Ethics deals with "good" and "bad." We'll look at the question: "In what ways is advertising good or bad for society?"

We'll see examples of despicable behavior, admirable corporate citizenship, and many things in between.

We'll cover arguments, criticisms, defenses, policies, and beliefs. All these perspectives can make for lively class discussion, and perhaps even some after-class discussions.

➤ **Rules and Regulations.**

Our government has been making judgments about advertising for more than 100 years. We'll discuss ways we regulate the **commercial speech** of marketers and summarize some of the most important names and dates.

➤ **And More.** If you'd like to dig in a little deeper, we've packed a lot more into our Web site: **www.adbuzz.com**.

Two More Points:

Point #1. We can feel strongly both ways.

We can like an ad, but despise advertising in general.

Don't worry if you have mixed feelings.

We can think most ads are bad because they try to make things more attractive than we know they are, but still like an ad that's really well-done, cute, or funny.

Some ads give us hope – like Nike's "If You Let Me Play Sports." And some outrage us. Advertising's conflicting intentions, executions, and consequences make judging very difficult.

Point #2. Most judgments about advertising are based on one of two things:

• **economic effects,** and

• **ethical evaluations.**

We'll discuss both, starting with the economics.

Girl: I will have more self-confidence
If you let me play sports
If you let me play…
I will be 50% less likely to
get breast cancer.
I will suffer less depression.
If you let me play sports.
I will be more likely to leave
a man who beats me…

Girl: I will be less likely to get pregnant before I want to…

Girl: I will learn… I will learn what it means to be strong… (to be strong)

Girl: If you let me play sports… (play sports…)

Girl: If you let me play sports…

The Economics of Advertising.

MUCH CRITICISM ABOUT ADVERTISING stems from economists. So, to get a grip on the way advertising affects society, we need a small bit of applied understanding of economics.

You'll recall Professor Maxwell established a few basic points in the first chapter on advertising history:

- America's unique political and economic heritage;
- Paul Romer's concept of the economic power of ideas; and
- the need for an infrastructure (mass production, media, distribution, and an educated population) to make modern advertising possible and necessary.

You may also recall the second chapter, where evolution of media and the growth of new market forces helped to create a more complicated world.

Now let's talk about a few more facts of economic life.

Economics – Monopoly & Competition.

As a society we believe monopolies are bad. While we have a few, such as local utilities (power and water), in the main, our society values competition – unless, of course, it causes someone we know to lose their job.

Arguments against Monopolies.

One argument against monopolies is that they can charge more money for something than they could if substitutes were available in an open market.

Another argument is that monopolies give consumers no choice.

We believe monopolies reduce innovation, result in poor quality goods, and generally offer lower quality of life than a competitive environment. That's why, in general, we believe in encouraging competition – at the gas pump, at the grocery store, and even in parts of government – e.g., the bidding process for highway and defense projects, privatization of garbage collection, and now prisons and schools.

Telephone answering machines were not available until the early '80s, not because we didn't have the technology, but because Ma Bell, a monopoly at the time, didn't want her lines tied up. The courts broke up the Ma Bell telephone monopoly.

When the First Edition of this book went to press, the Justice Department was giving Microsoft a hard time related to monopolistic practices. (A decade ago, they were giving IBM a hard time for similar reasons.) As the Second Edition went to press, it was the European Union giving Microsoft a hard time. Now it's oil prices giving everybody a hard time.

This commercial by Janet Champ is an excellent example of how advertising can touch the best in people. Nike captures the larger benefit for women of playing sports as it touches all of us. With "effective surprise" they present us with very adult and lifelong issues as they dramatize the importance of play and healthy exercise for young girls. Applause.

The objective is to increase competition, offer consumers more choice, lower prices, and improve service.

The "deregulation" of tele-communications and energy are current examples of this attitude toward monopolies, actual or potential, and our encouragement of competition.

The Marketplace of Ideas.

We also believe in the competition of ideas and rewarding those who have the best ideas.

In Nature it's a Miracle. In Legal Circles it's Called Infringement.

That's why we have our patent and copyright offices – to protect **intellectual property.**

In some ways, the owner of those copyrights has a monopoly on those ideas – or at least on the unique expression of them.

The Walt Disney Company does not own the idea of a cartoon mouse. But they very definitely own Mickey Mouse – a unique expression of that idea.

This process is in a constant state of flux, readjustment, and debate.

The American Tradition of Competition.

Since the Industrial Revolution, government and industry in English-speaking countries have been a bit at odds.

This conflict is sometimes an expression of popular sentiment; sometimes, in the opinion of some, it seems almost force of habit. (Regulators need something to regulate or they'd have no job.)

If behavior becomes viewed as excessive and a need for regulation is perceived, voters (consumers) speak up, and consumer movements are born. It happens all the time.

This, too, is competition in the American tradition.

You can see some of this conflict expressed in the historical sequence of rules and regulations later in this chapter.

The Power of a Free Press.

Another critical difference between the US and other countries is the degree to which media is unhindered by government. In many other societies, the media are a part of government, either owned and operated or tightly controlled.

In the US, advertisers have many media choices available.

The Power of Competition.

So what does all this have to do with advertising?

Advertising is one of the major ways companies compete in the marketplace. It's viewed as a major force.

Example: Professional Services

Many professional groups such as lawyers and doctors restricted or closely regulated all advertising by members.

Tobacco & TV.

There is a law that says tobacco companies can't advertise on TV.[2]

The law seemed necessary given the Senate's long-standing view that TV advertising is powerful, much more powerful than advertising in magazines or newspapers.

The reasoning was that if people couldn't learn about cigarettes from TV they'd be less likely to smoke.

However, there was a second purpose for the tobacco advertising ban, less publicized and less well known, yet very powerful.

The second purpose of the law was to *"maintain the tobacco industry."*

In 1970, seven states depended on the tobacco industry as a major source of jobs and revenue. So it's understandable that Senators from those states would support a bill that made it easier for those companies to make money – and keep the Senators looking good to the public.

Since advertising is an expensive competitive tool, the tobacco companies were probably delighted when Congress passed the law that said they no longer had to spend millions of dollars in advertising.[3] The results, tracked for almost 20 years indicate that smoking didn't decline – it actually increased between 1970 and 1980, and tobacco companies became profitable enough to diversify into the single most addictive substance known to man: food. In June of 2000, Phillip Morris bought Nabisco – one of the largest food companies.

The Disney Business.

Intellectual property is their business. And they take it seriously.

Extending Copyright Protection. As a result of extensive lobbying, copyright protection for properties such as Mickey Mouse has been extended past 75 years (from the 1998 Disney Annual Report). Mickey Mouse is a copyrighted property of The Walt Disney Company.

ADVERTISING MAKES THINGS COST MORE, RIGHT?

We admit it. Advertising has a tremendous impact on prices. But you may be surprised by what *kind* of impact.

In addition to being informative, educational and sometimes entertaining, advertising can actually lower prices.

It works like this: Advertising spurs competition which holds down prices. And since advertising also creates a mass market for products, it can bring down the cost of producing each product, a savings that can be passed on to consumers.

Moreover, competition created by advertising provides an incentive for manufacturers to produce new and better products.

Which means advertising can not only reduce prices, but it can also help you avoid lemons.

ADVERTISING
ANOTHER WORD FOR FREEDOM OF CHOICE.
American Association of Advertising Agencies

A SIMPLE LESSON IN ECONOMICS FOR ANYONE WHO BELIEVES ADVERTISING RAISES PRICES.

1965 Calculator—Over $2,000.00   1984 Calculator—Under $10.00

In the beginning there was the calculator.

It was a new idea. It had never been advertised. And it cost a fortune.

Then the people who sold calculators started to advertise them. That was hardly a new idea. But it, too, cost a fortune.

Now, you might think all that expensive advertising would drive the price of a calculator to incalculable heights.

But no. What happened was exactly the opposite.

It doesn't make sense. How can something as costly as advertising end up saving you money?

It's really quite simple. Advertising spreads news. When it spread the news of the calculator, people started to buy.

As more calculators were sold, more were produced. As more were produced, the cost of producing them came down. And because advertising creates competition, their quality and sophistication went up.

So today, using an electronic calculator is almost cheaper than counting on your fingers. And advertising helped make it happen — just as it has for countless other products.

In fact, with a little effort you could probably figure out precisely how much money advertising has saved you over the years.

But don't try it without a calculator.

ADVERTISING.
ANOTHER WORD FOR FREEDOM OF CHOICE.
American Association of Advertising Agencies

(Ads in these areas are a relatively recent occurrence.)

The stated argument was "professionalism."

The real reason was to prevent price competition.

Throughout this chapter you'll see a collision of economic forces – with some significant change in advertising as the result.

Let's look at a few of the arguments…

Economic Arguments on Behalf of Advertising.

The American Association of Advertising Agencies (4A's/AAAA) produced a series of ads to address common objections to advertising.

On the following pages, we'd like to show you how the techniques of advertising were used to argue on behalf of the economics of advertising.

Then, we'll look at some additional thoughts and counterarguments.

Here are the ads and some commentary.

Advertising Lowers Prices #1:

This first AAAA ad presents an argument you'll see a few pages from now.

Advertising = Market Information.

It demonstrates that the result is more consumer choice and better prices.

Advertising Lowers Prices #2:

This second ad, using electronic calculators as an example, explains how expensive advertising can lower prices.

It does this by using a simple principle of economics – when volume goes up, prices come down – and advertising can be the catalyst.

Advertising Saves Money:

This third ad shows the most obvious way advertising saves Americans money.

It pays for much of the media we watch, read, and listen to.

It uses the magazine as an example – pointing out that, without advertising, the magazine in which the ad appears would cost twice as much and probably offer less.

It implies, but doesn't mention, that TV and radio are free to the public because of advertising, nor does it mention that a newspaper would probably cost two to five times more than it does with advertising.

Advertising Saves Time:

This ad uses the work of a popular cartoonist to illustrate the benefits of using advertising to get an idea across quickly.

It shows how advertising helps spread news so that a company with a better product can get the product to people faster.

It doesn't tell you one other important point – that good advertising will put a poor product out of business.

People will try it once, but not buy it again. Few businesses can survive by only selling their products once; they must have repeat business.

As Bill Bernbach observed, *"Nothing will kill a bad product faster than good advertising."*

The ad does not mention that publicity, sampling, and "word of mouth" are also critical factors in product success.

DESPITE WHAT SOME PEOPLE THINK, ADVERTISING CAN'T MAKE YOU BUY SOMETHING YOU DON'T NEED.

Some people would have you believe that you are putty in the hands of every advertiser in the country.

They think that when advertising is put under your nose, your mind turns to oatmeal.

It's mass hypnosis. Subliminal seduction. Brain washing. Mind control. It's advertising.

And you are a pushover for it.

It explains why your kitchen cupboard is full of food you never eat. Why your garage is full of cars you never drive. Why your house is full of books you don't read, TV's you don't watch, beds you don't use, and clothes you don't wear.

You don't have a choice. You are forced to buy.

That's why this message is a cleverly disguised advertisement to get you to buy land in the tropics.

Got you again, didn't we? Send in your money.

ADVERTISING
ANOTHER WORD FOR FREEDOM OF CHOICE.
American Association of Advertising Agencies

ISN'T IT FUNNY HOW STEREO ADS ARE BORING UNTIL YOU WANT A STEREO?

We admit it. There are times when advertising isn't especially interesting.

For instance, stereo ads when you're not looking for a new stereo. Or insurance ads when you're not looking for a new insurance company. Or detergent ads when you're not looking for a new detergent.

But suppose your stereo breaks down. Or your insurance rates go up. Or your laundry comes out gray.

All of a sudden, stereo ads, insurance ads and detergent ads start looking a lot more interesting.

It's one of the basic truths of advertising. We try to be entertaining, but that's not really our job. Our job is to help you make the right choices

when you're in the market for any kind of product or service.

Of course, when you're not in the market, we recognize that advertising may seem beside the point. In that case, you're free to pretend it isn't there.

In fact, you're free to ignore advertising for as long as you choose.

Right up until your stereo breaks down.

ADVERTISING.
ANOTHER WORD FOR FREEDOM OF CHOICE.
American Association of Advertising Agencies

Advertising Doesn't Make Us Do What We Don't Want to Do:

The idea that advertising tells us what to buy and what to believe is generally thought to be true, until we ask people if they have personally been influenced to buy something.

The answer is almost always no.

This ad uses a clever photograph to make the point.

Advertising Is Informative:

This ad shows advertising can be useful.

It may only be interesting to those who are looking for the products or services that are being advertised, but, eventually, almost everyone will have an interest in some advertising, some of the time.

Subliminal Advertising Does Not Exist:

This advertisement, showing a mixed drink in an old-fashioned glass with ice and a cherry makes light of subliminal advertising claims.

The ad points out that subliminal advertising simply does not exist and that what you see is in your own mind.

But this book does.

Ice Cube Sex, by Jack Haberstroh is an engaging history of the frauds, exaggerations, and legends of subliminal advertising. (Still available through Cross Roads Books, P.O. Box 506, Notre Dame, IN 46556.)

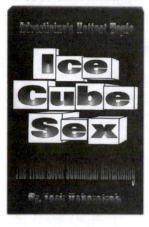

Advertising Myths:

This ad exposes some advertising myths and summarizes the arguments in the AAAA campaign with a bit of reverse psychology.

The "lies" set up the arguments about what advertising does for society and individuals.

This series of ads is a good example of an advertising campaign.

There are, of course, counterarguments.

Stop American Excess
1 800 663 1243

Bull in a China Shop
Thirty-second
"Uncommercial"

"For years, people have defined the economic health of a country by its Gross National Product…
Trouble is, every time a forest falls, the GNP goes up.…
with every oil spill, the GNP goes up…
every time a new cancer patient is diagnosed, the GNP goes up.
If we are to save ourselves, economists must learn to subtract."

WTO/Seattle
Sixty-second
"Uncommercial"

"At this month's World Trade Organization meeting in Seattle, are the world's biggest economic problems really on the agenda?
An unregulated global casino.
A growing underclass.
Overproduction. Overconsumption.
A world awash in chemicals.
Is economic progress killing the planet?
Let's go to Seattle and put those questions on the WTO agenda. www.adbusters.org"

This commercial serves up the agenda for the 1999 Seattle WTO protest.

On the Other Hand…

Here are a few advertisements from *AdBusters*, a group dedicated to counteracting the effects of advertising – often using some of advertising's same techniques.

On the left, they show a pig in the middle of North America, dramatizing our high levels of consumption.

AdBusters is…

THE LEADING BRAND OF advertising protest. Based in Canada, they have been a leader in bringing issues of commercial culture to our attention – issues that will not get play by paid sponsors.

In fact, when AdBusters tries to pay money to media companies to run their "uncommercials," they are consistently refused. So you'll probably have to go to their Web site to see the QuickTime version.

They publish a magazine and other items, like posters and post cards, to publicize their message. Their website is adbusters.org.

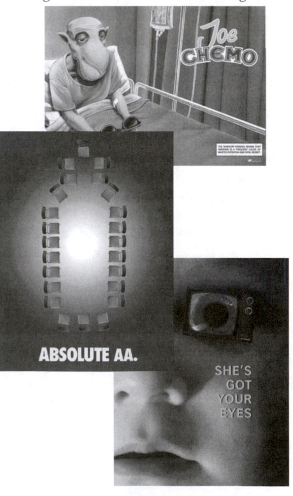

Obsession Fetish

Thirty-second "Uncommercial"

*"obsession… fascination…
obsession…. fascination… fetish…
Why are 9 out of 10 women dissatisfied with some
aspect of their bodies?"*

(Cut to bare back of a woman. She is swaying rhythmically, moaning. The camera pans around. The woman vomits into a toilet.)

"The beauty industry… is the beast."

Why the Canadian Broadcasting System would not run this spot.

According to Mike Darley of CBC, the "Obsession Fetish" TV uncommercial *"violates CBC's standards of taste policy"* and the images in the TV spot *"comprise unacceptable exploitation of sex and nudity."*

Buy Nothing Day

Thirty-second "Uncommercial"

*"The average North American consumes 5 times more than a Mexican, 10 times more than a Chinese person, and 30 times more than a person from India. We are the most voracious consumers in the world…. a world which could die because of the way we North Americans live…
Give it a rest.
November 27th is Buy Nothing Day."*

www.adbusters.org

If you'd like to look at these spots, and find out more about AdBusters, go to their Web site.

You can watch the commercials in Quicktime, or order them for home viewing or class screenings and discussions.

TV Turnoff Week

Thirty-second "Uncommercial"

*"Your living room is the factory.
    The product being manufactured… is you.
    TV Turnoff Week –
    April 22nd through the 28th –
    when no one is for sale."*

Advertising = Power or Information?
Two Ways of Looking at Advertising.

These two pages show two basic ways of looking at how advertising affects the economic well-being of consumers.

Each is a theory about what happens to key economic variables when advertising is added to the marketing mix.

As we go through some of the more popular criticisms later in the chapter, refer to these models, and you should be able to recognize many of the underlying assumptions.

Figure 1. Advertising = Market Power.

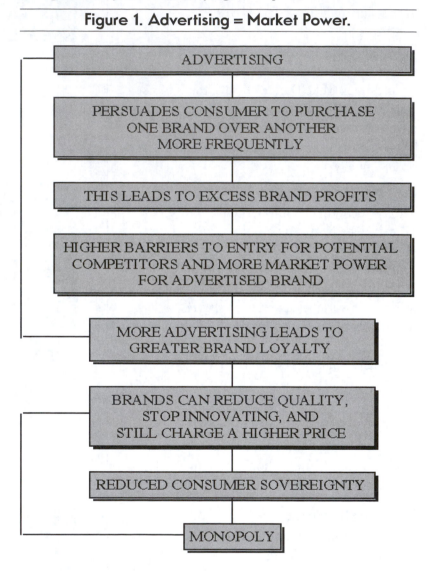

Market Power.

For years, many economists viewed advertising as a tool that encouraged monopoly.

Figure 1 depicts an historic viewpoint of the economic impact of advertising.

As you can see by the sequence in the chart, this view maintains that advertising tends to reduce consumer sovereignty and restrict choice.

AdFact:

For decades, the official FCC regulator's stance on advertising was to think of it as a necessary evil, tolerated only because it supported the mass media system.

As a necessary evil, advertising was considered by most lawmakers to be an "uninvited, and unwelcome guest" in the American home.[4]

The Result – Ongoing Debate.

One more note… each of the theories, Advertising = Power and Advertising = Information, is merely that. The "true" economic effects of advertising are still being debated.

There is so much going on in our modern marketplace that an intelligent person can easily cite an example that "proves" virtually any point of view expressed.

That is called **anecdotal evidence**, which is not "proof."

It is also true that individuals who do a superior job of advertising and marketing can have great impact for specific companies. And no one can determine what happens overall.

Figure 2. Advertising = Market Information.

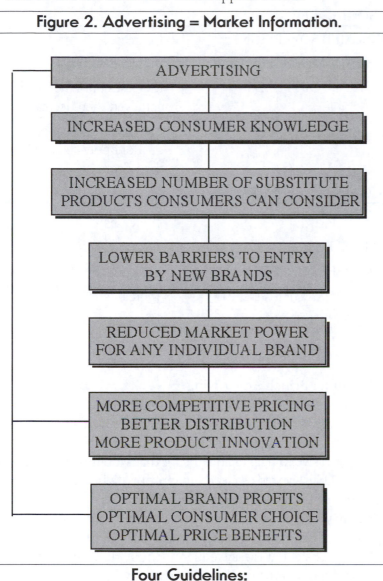

Market Information.

Figure 2 depicts the more modern theory: Advertising = Market Information.

In this model, you can see that advertising conveys information that makes consumers more powerful.

It's the same argument as the one offered in the lemonade stand ad a few pages earlier.

This theory also acknowledges that advertising is not the only source for information in the marketplace.

This is more in keeping with current IMC models that use "brand contact points."[6]

Four Guidelines:

We may not have answers, but we have some guidelines. Rotzoll, Heafner, and Sandage provide four guidelines to help understand the biggest limitations to definitive answers.

1. The actual effects of advertising are not clearly known, e.g., there is no direct one-to-one advertising-to-sales ratio, with no consistent, direct relationship between ads and behaviors.
2. The advertising process has varied intentions and effects. This makes general criticisms hard to substantiate.
3. Highly disparate interpretations are possible, which is the root of most advertising controversies. Always note who is being critical and where they are seeing problems.
4. Advertising must be considered in light of cultural expectations.

"Anecdotal Evidence."

When one uses a story (an anecdote) to make a point, this is called "anecdotal evidence."

For example, a story about someone liking or not liking an ad.

The story may very well be true, but a single example does not necessarily prove the point.

In a subjective field such as advertising, you will find many examples of anecdotal evidence.

Note: There is no such thing as "antidotal evidence." This is incorrect usage – unless, perhaps, it is proof of a cure for something.

Table 3. Advertising and Economic Effects

ADV = MARKET INFO		ADV = MARKET PWR
	SOCIAL EFFECTS	
Increases	CONSUMER SOVEREIGNTY	Decreases
Increases	ABUNDANT SOCIETY	Increases slowly
Increases	QUALITY OF GOODS	Increases until monopoly achieved then decreases
Increases	INNOVATION	Increases until oligopoly or monopoly achieved then decreases
	ECONOMIC EFFECTS	
Decreases	PRICE	Increases
Increases	PRICE ELASTICITY	Decreases
Lowered	BARRIERS TO ENTRY	Raised
Increases	ECONOMIES OF SCALE	Increases
Increases	COMPETITION	Decreases

Here's another easy way to compare the two theories: Market Power (on the right) vs. Market Information (on the left).

"Functional Superiority."

Professor John P. Jones has examined the economic effects of advertising.

He notes that advertising works best when the product that is advertised has some sort of "functional superiority."[7]

It may be performance superiority or something else, such as a better price or better value.

Whatever that superiority, in case after case, only superior products could be advertised profitably and successfully over the long term.

If a product underperformed versus its competitors, no amount of expense or cleverness seemed to be able to build a successful brand.

This is evidence of natural market forces at work.

Example: British Advertising

You can see this cultural difference in British advertising.

Though we share the same language, the advertiser is viewed as even more of an uninvited guest and selling too hard is unseemly.

Aggressive, bragging advertising that would be little noticed in the US is viewed as clearly inappropriate in the UK.

To Further Complicate the Discussion...

What may be true about advertising in general may not be true of specific ads and campaigns. And vice versa.

With hindsight, it is easy to identify individual brands and programs where advertising clearly increased sales.

And it seems obvious that the vitality of the American economy and the uniquely American approach to advertising are somehow related. Easy to understand. Hard to prove.

Making fun of restrictions. That's the approach taken by this British cigarette advertiser. What do you think of this?

The Ethics of Advertising.

JUST AS WE NEED TO TEMPER OUR EXPECTATIONS about what can be known about the economic effects of advertising, we also need to temper what can be proven about advertising's social effects.

When I Was You...

When I took this class as an undergraduate, no one told me what ethics really were or how to evaluate whether advertising was good or bad – I had to rely on my own judgment.

Later, as I was preparing to teach an advertising and society course, I found many students shared my feelings.

Together, over several semesters, we discovered a few ways to understand and evaluate the ethical effects of advertising.

An important part of the ethics of advertising consists of the assumptions we make, as a culture, about life and what makes us happy. The way we answer these important questions explains our fundamental orientation toward life.

Opinions and Proof.

People often think their opinions "prove" advertising is bad or advertising is good. Opinions are easy. Proof is tough.

It's difficult enough for science to provide answers about tangible, physical phenomena, much less the intangible and complex nature of advertising's effect on society. In other words, *the jury is still out.*

The American Political and Ethical Tradition.

The roots of modern advertising, like most American institutions, stem from the earliest beginnings of our society.

The Protestant Ethic and American frontier society were a powerful combination. As a haven for religious minorities, American society gradually developed a tolerance for new ideas – new ideas in religion and new ideas in enterprise.

This was a gradual process. In the early years, religious minorities were often intolerant of other religious minorities.

Philadelphia, with strong Quaker influence, was one of the first real havens for freedom of religion and thought.

It was no accident that this tolerance gave room and freedom for individuals like Benjamin Franklin to flourish. Nor was it accidental that a practical and industrious attitude was part of American society.

Most of these behaviors were based on popular philosophies of the time, and by basing our government on those philosophies, they have become our present cultural orientation towards life, the universe, and advertising.

You Are Invited...

...to a discussion group.

For a deeper understanding of these issues and the philosophical and logical basis for this thinking, go to the adbuzz.com Web site for extra background readings.

Janet Is a Champ.

How do you write important advertising? It starts just like real life.

After earning a degree in English lit, Janet wandered around wondering how to make a living at poetry.

Someone in Boston mentioned the word "advertising" to her, and she fled back to her native Portland, determined to do something meaningful – like work in a mall.

Administrative Aide.

But hunger and a nasty roommate who insisted Champ pay half the heating bills led her to a little place called Wieden + Kennedy, where she got a job as an administrative aide.

After three years, Janet asked if she could be a copywriter. They let her.

At Wieden + Kennedy, her poet's soul helped discover "personal truth" for Nike's women's fitness products.

A Higher Level.

This advertising adds value to society and the reader as well as the brand.

As Bill Bernbach said, *"All of us who professionally use the mass media are the shapers of society, We can vulgarize that society. We can brutalize it. Or we can help lift it onto a higher level."*

Janet's work has done just that – helped lift communication to a higher level. Looks like she ended up writing poetry after all.

TOYNBEE VS. BERNBACH ON ADVERTISING:

Is it immoral to stimulate buying?

 Arnold J. Toynbee, the eminent British historian who has leveled broad-scale attacks against advertising, was asked by Printers' Ink to express his views more specifically. His comments are presented here along with a response by William Bernbach, president of Doyle Dane Bernbach

TOYNBEE: Advertising is moral mis-education

"It is argued that marketing—including the kinds of new products introduced, the design of those products, and advertising—reflects public wants and tastes rather than shapes them." I have been asked whether I believe this to be true. I do not believe that. If advertising were just an echo of desires that were already in the housewife's mind, it would be a superfluous expense of time, ingenuity and money. It would be nothing more than a carbon copy of a housewife's own shopping-list. I believe that advertising does have an effect. I believe it stimulates consumption, as is suggested in the second point put to me:

"It is argued that personal consumption, stimulated by advertising, is essential for growth and full employment in an economy of abundance." If this were demonstrated to be true, it would also demonstrate, to my mind, that an economy of abundance is a spiritually unhealthy way of life, and that the sooner we reform it the better. This may sound paradoxical to modern Western ears. But if it is a paradox, it is one that has always been preached by all the great religions. In an article published in PRINTERS' INK on October 20, 1961, Mr. James Webb Young dismisses the example set by St. Francis of Assisi. "Americans today," Mr. James Webb Young writes, "see little merit in these medieval hairshirt ideas." St. Francis got his ideas from a pre-medieval teacher, Jesus. These ideas cannot be dismissed without rejecting Christianity and all the other great religions, too.

The moral that I draw is that a way of life based on personal consumption, stimulated by advertising, needs changing—and there are dozens of possible alternatives to it. For instance, we could still have full employment in the economically advanced countries if we gave up advertising and restricted our personal consumption to, say, the limits that present-day American monks and nuns voluntarily set for themselves, and if we then diverted our production to supply the elementary needs of the poverty-stricken three-quarters of the human race. Working for this obviously worthwhile purpose would bring us much greater personal satisfaction than working, under the stimulus of advertising, in order to consume goods that we do not need and do not genuinely want.

But suppose the whole human race eventually became affluent; what then? Well, I cannot think of any circumstances in which advertising would not be an evil. There are at least three bad things intrinsic to it:

▸ Advertising deliberately stimulates our desires, whereas experience, embodied in the teaching of the religions, tells us that we cannot be good or happy unless we limit our desires and keep them in check.

▸ Advertising makes statements, not in order to tell the truth, but in order to sell goods. Even when its statements are not false, truth is not their object. This is intellectually demoralizing.

▸ Advertising is an instrument of moral, as well as intellectual, mis-education. Insofar as it succeeds in influencing people's minds, it conditions them not to think for themselves and not to choose for themselves. It is in-

tentionally hypnotic in its effect. It makes people suggestible and docile. In fact, it prepares them for submitting to a totalitarian regime.

Therefore, let us reform a way of life that cannot be lived without advertising.

BERNBACH: Only people are moral or immoral

Mr. Toynbee's real hate is not advertising. It's the economy of abundance or, as we have all come to know it, capitalism. This is perfectly all right if only he would make clear the real target he is shooting at. There are many things about capitalism that need correcting, and Mr. Toynbee would be doing the world a great service if he could persuade us to make these corrections. But he's never going to do that if he throws up smoke screens with tirades against a tool that happens to be used by big business in its efforts to sell more goods.

Advertising, like so many techniques available to man, is neither moral nor immoral. Is eloquence immoral because it persuades? Is music immoral because it awakens emotions? Is the gift of writing immoral because it can arouse people to action? No. Yet eloquence, music and writing have been used for evil purpose.

Only recently we were asked to prepare an advertisement by the National Committee for a Sane Nuclear Policy. We conceived an ad featuring Dr. Spock. Its purpose was to discourage nuclear testing. If Mr. Toynbee will agree that this is a good purpose, then he must also agree that in this case at least, advertising was not an instrument of "moral mis-education." He would also be happy to learn that here was an advertisement so persuasive that it prompted one of the chairmen of SANE to telegraph his congratulations for "by all odds the most powerful single statement I have seen over the imprint of SANE."

For the past two years we have run advertising for Volkswagen cars with the purpose of persuading Americans that simplicity, craftsmanship and low price were available to them in an automobile. These were ads that conveyed facts simply and honestly to the consumer. They seemed to sell the country on filling their automotive needs modestly and with good taste. Would Mr. Toynbee call this effort evil merely because advertising was involved? The Volkswagen was built to give the buyer the greatest value in automotive transportation. Isn't advertising performing a valuable function by making that fact clear to the buyer?

No, advertising is not moral or immoral. Only people are. I can cite many instances in commercial advertising that would prove Mr. Toynbee's point of view. I can cite just as many that would disprove it.

If Mr. Toynbee believes a materialistic society is a bad one (and I am not saying he is wrong in that belief), then he owes it to mankind to speak to the point. He owes it to mankind to speak out against such a society and not merely against one of the tools that is available to any society. He may even find that nothing will "sell" his point as effectively as advertising.

Here's Bill Bernbach in a print debate with Arnold J. Toynbee, an eminent British historian. What do you think of the points they make?

The Ethics of Persuasion.

Bill Bernbach noted that *"Advertising is essentially persuasion. And persuasion is an art, not a science."* You might enjoy reading his defense of advertising on the opposite page.

A persuasive pamphlet written by Thomas Paine, *Common Sense,* was a critical factor in the "selling" of the American Revolution. Persuasion has power.

Persuasion is also an ethical issue in its own right.

Persuasion is an act of communication that seeks to change, resolve, or formulate other people's opinions, feelings, or actions through the deliberate use of argument, reasoning, or entreaty.

This definition also illustrates how persuasion is distinct from coercion or inducement.

Since most advertisements try to be at least somewhat persuasive, a discussion about our cultural expectations should help us understand why we perceive some ads to be unethical and why others seem OK.

Caveat Emptor.

Our marketplace expectation for products and services is **caveat emptor,** or "let the buyer beware." We accept skepticism, recognizing that a seller will seek to highlight advantages while hiding (or failing to mention) flaws and disadvantages. It's up to us to evaluate the ad and draw our own conclusions

A Two-Way Street.

In our society, persuasive communication is two-way: this questioning on the part of the audience is the moral duty called **reasonable skepticism.**

Persuasion in and of itself is not inherently unethical.

Persuasion is part of how we communicate and progress in human society. Without it, we'd have to discover fire, the wheel, and toothpaste for ourselves, generation after generation.

"Bless That Chicken!" Participating in welcoming the Pope on a visit to New Orleans, local advertiser Popeyes, whose slogan was "Love That Chicken," worked with a local TV station and outdoor company to create a welcoming promotion that went a bit beyond "normative expectations." Popeyes? Or Pope Yes!

"Normative Expectations."

Normative expectations are just "what we think."

The correlation is that we usually believe thinking that falls outside those "norms" is not OK.

Isn't It Ironic?

Recently, tobacco companies have agreed to pay billions of dollars in a settlement.

Millions of these dollars will be going into anti-smoking ads.

Irony #1.

The first irony is that the one method shown to be actually effective at persuading kids and teens not to smoke – making fun of the tobacco companies – was specifically disallowed in the written agreement.

In an attempt to promote "teen" rebellion against the tobacco establishment, new campaigns in Florida remind teens that tobacco companies are big companies with authoritative type personas and agendas.

Irony #2.

Meanwhile, the tobacco industry seems to be performing a public service with a campaign "against" smoking by those under 18.

The advertising makes the point that smoking is for adults and it's against the law to sell cigarettes to minors.

Major factors in youth smoking are wanting to be more "adult" and rebellion against authority.

So what is the real point of the "anti-smoking" advertising and what kind of persuasion is really going on with the target market?

Hmmmm.

A Helpful Graphic.

This little chart can help you predict how people are likely to react to any given ad – even if it is truthful – at least according to two dimensions:

• Product Harmfulness
• Target Susceptibility

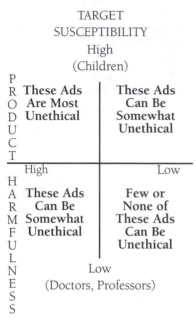

TARGET
SUSCEPTIBILITY
High
(Children)

	High	Low
P R O D U C T	These Ads Are Most Unethical	These Ads Can Be Somewhat Unethical
H A R M F U L N E S S	These Ads Can Be Somewhat Unethical	Few or None of These Ads Can Be Unethical

Low
(Doctors, Professors)

Guidelines for Evaluating Ethics of an Ad or Advertising Practice:

1. Does the ad contain truthful, relevant information that makes rational, significant choice possible?

2. Does the advertiser offer the brand as part of an identifiable set of alternatives?

3. Does the ad allow us sufficient information to reflect, consult with others, and respond, or does it demand immediate action?

4. Does the ad contain a presentation of the best reasons or benefits, rather than just those the persuader thinks will work on us?

5. Can we see that the advertiser respects us as capable of making rational choices, rather than as dupes useful for generating profits or as objects of paternalistic concern?

(Adapted from Jaska and Pritchard)

The Profession of Persuasion.

Persuasion is something also done by politicians, philosophers, ministers, reporters, and college professors. (It's also curious to note how many ministers' sons went into advertising.)

We all do it when we want something.

Since we cannot escape persuasion, and indeed benefit from it in terms of time and money, certain normative ethical expectations have been culturally accepted.

If an advertiser does not take these considerations into account, consumers are likely to feel their ethical expectations have been disappointed and that the ad is unethical.

Most of these expectations stem from the normative statement: *"We want to believe that people are honest."*

That's the reason people believe that, although advertisers may not be honest, their ads, for the most part, are.

The ethics of persuasion and the consumers' judgment of the goodness or badness of an advertisement rest on the extent to which a persuasive message allows the audience to make free choices about the issue presented.

Therefore, it's the audience's ability to use reason in evaluating the message, as well as the content of rational information in the message, that determines ethical evaluations of the message.

In Summary.

Our judgments about how good or bad advertising is for society are the result of a complicated set of cultural philosophies, personal expectations, and preferred methods of ethical reasoning.

There are many other ethical arguments related to advertising – some more persuasive than others.

We'll cover those next.

Cool ad, huh? Hey, you're smart. You're not susceptible.

And we bet you probably aren't thinking of the potential hearing loss caused by "too loud." Then again, when it becomes a problem, you'll be "too old" to do anything about it.

An Advertising Debate.

ADVERTISING HAS BEEN REVILED BY SOME as "the most profoundly subversive force at work in America today."

It has been accused of corrupting our youth, fostering rampant materialism, and causing the demise of the nuclear family.

Advertising has been called deceptive, manipulative, intrusive, offensive, sexist, boring, irritating, offensive, and an unnecessary added expense to already overpriced goods.

Even those with a more positive view acknowledge advertising's immense power. James Twitchell notes: *"Advertising is not part of the dominant culture. It is the dominant culture... it has become the dominant meaning-making system of modern life."*

A Criticism and Debate Format.

It's important that you become familiar with some of the most prevalent arguments. (They'll help you defend your career choice against scornful roommates and mortified parents.)

Using a debate format, the main criticism will be stated first and several supporting arguments presented.

Then, to challenge these criticisms, counterarguments will follow. You'll have to make up your own mind about which side wins or is most persuasive.

The criticisms we'll discuss are:

1. **Advertising takes away free choice.**
2. **Advertising interferes with democratic process.**
3. **Advertising exerts powerful controls over media.**
4. **Advertising is intrusive and violates personal privacy.**
5. **Advertising molds social values.**

And remember, if you have additional questions or issues you want to discuss – come visit us at our Web site.

Criticism: Advertising Takes Away Free Choice.

Support #1. Advertising is inherently deceptive.
Because all advertising, even thoughtful instructive ads, cannot provide complete information, it misleads consumers into making uninformed and therefore irrational choices.

Since the advertiser has more money, expertise, and resources than the consumer, consumers are duped into buying products and brands created merely to advance the advertiser's financial situation, without regard for consumers' scarce financial resources.

Support #2. Advertising creates an artificial social agenda.
Advertising artificially limits the scope of social debate.

This criticism stems from the notion that people can only keep so many things in mind at one time.

Since advertising keeps that space filled with brands and benefits, it's impossible for most people to think about the more socially important, yet unadvertised, issues such as volunteerism or the sustainable development paradigm.

Deontological vs. Teleological

There are two types of ethical theories: teleological and deontological.

Deontology/Intentions.
Deontological perspectives assume there is a universal "right" behavior under all circumstances.

Deontologists determine how "good" an action is based on the intention of the actor.

The consequences of an action are not an issue, only the intention.

What consumers believe about the intention of an advertiser can determine their judgment of the ad.

Teleology/Consequences.
Teleologists determine what is ethical based on the foreseeable consequences of an action.

Decisions that result in the most beneficial consequences for society are best from the teleological perspective.

The intention of the actor is not an issue, only the results of an action.

What someone believes about the consequences of an ad will determine his or her judgment of the ad.

Now that these positions are distinct, we can examine specific methods of ethical reasoning.

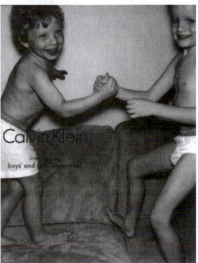

Intentions and Consequences. Some believe that Calvin Klein counts on controversy to generate publicity and word-of-mouth to supplement its ad expenditures.

Bruce's Raindrop Analogy.

Rain is good.

At the right time and place, it helps grow our crops, power our industry, and satisfy the thirsts of our fellow man.

When there's no rain, nothing grows.

Now, think of every ad as a raindrop.

Plop. A tiny bit of water to help grow sales, power our industry, and satisfy the thirsts of our fellow man.

Pretty little raindrops. Plop plop.

This also explains why it's hard to determine advertising's results.

After all, it's hard to measure the effect of a few raindrops when it's raining. Plop plop plop.

Are you with me so far?

Well, what happens when you really turn on the rain machine?

A Non-Stop Deluge.

Here's where our analogy gets messy.

Suddenly, our friend the raindrop multiplies into a raging flood that can wash away everything in sight.

There's nothing wrong with any particular raindrop, but when you get too many, things start to happen.

Look around.

Marketing dollars turn pro sports into contests about player salaries. It washes away the connection between fans and players.

Children turn into targets for sugar-coated snacks and our place in society is measured by high-priced logos – icons of our "spending power."

An Itch We Can't Scratch.

Meanwhile, attractive and creative messages tell us that *things* solve problems. That can create a different problem – one we might not notice.

It can create a nagging need for all those things we don't have.

It's an itch we can't really scratch.

And we end up with a distorted perspective – for there are few clever commercials to tell us that people are more important than things.

Though we know better. (Don't we?)

Unadvertised Alternatives.

Now think about having a conversation with a friend, hugging a kid, or just stopping for a minute and taking a deep breath (we'll wait).

(continued next page)

Furthermore, advertising "choices" are essentially meaningless. Your choice of cereal, toothpaste, or pizza may have great meaning for marketers, but in terms of your life or our society, they are trivial. Yet, these trivial products have been invested with great meaning.

It is, as Howard Gossage noted, *"a billion-dollar hammer pounding a ten-cent thumb tack."*

The social status of "public goods" such as education and political activism are likely to be considerably lower than the social status of an advertised brand.

People are persuaded that owning a BMW is more important than education since BMW advertises and schools do not.

A car commercial humorously suggests buying the car instead of paying for college tuition. What signals does that send?

Support #3. Persuasion subjugates consumer autonomy.

Advertising creates and manipulates consumers' desires by persuading them they need all sorts of superfluous products (e.g., scented kitty litter or sixteen kinds of lemon-lime soda).

Critics, after dividing advertising into two types (informational and persuasive), have determined that persuasive ads are more dangerous because they manipulate consumers' desires through imagery and suggestion rather than information.

Persuasive advertising tries to evoke psychological desires and link ideas about how to satisfy those desires to a brand.

Most women have an emotional desire to be attractive. Cosmetic ads use this to sell their brands by employing beauty to imply the message: *"If you use this brand, you'll be beautiful, too."*

So, even rational women, who know that all brands of cosmetics are very similar in terms of actual ingredients and performance, are, on some levels, convinced of two things:

First, that they must use cosmetics to be beautiful.

Second, that they must use a certain brand.

Finally, whether individual ads persuade us or not, the cumulative effect of a constant barrage of messages that tell us products solve problems and make us happier has a subtle, but powerful effect on our personal values.

Support #4. Advertising creates monopoly power.

Because big brands have a great deal of money, they also have a great deal of power over what consumers know.

Big brands have the power to keep important or damaging information about the brand out of the media.

They have money to conduct research and learn all the negatives as well as the positive nature of brand use.

However, the information they uncover is hardly likely to be voluntarily distributed to the consumer – especially if it's unpleasant. The tobacco industry is certainly a relevant example.

All this makes big brands even more powerful, and serves to stifle competition.

They have the money to pay for powerful expertise to create and deliver advertising messages.

Unchecked, they can manipulate people by withholding valuable information about brand performance, brand quality, or even dangerous aspects of product use.

There is certainly evidence that the tobacco industry withheld evidence of the dangers of their products.

Defense: Advertising Enables Consumers to Make Choices.

There are some powerful defenses to these arguments.

Support #1. Advertising distributes market information.
Advertising provides society with information and ideas about what products are available, when they are available, how much they cost, and what they do.

In terms of economic theory, advertising's primary function is to provide market information. This is one of the basic mechanisms that ensures consumer sovereignty in the marketplace.

Free and open advertising permits competing product and service information to reach the consumer.

This increases market entry, providing more competition, which lowers prices and reduces the market power of any single producer.

Support #2: Advertising helps create and sustain an abundant society.
The abundant society is one where the majority of citizens have moved beyond the satisfaction of physiological needs and are able to enjoy the benefits of industry and art.

Advertising helps create abundance.

Abundance is the concept of diverse choice. In its role of economic engine, advertising provides an important way for producers to "win" in the marketplace.

Since winning is a fabulous incentive for investment, people are all encouraged to participate in the production and distribution of goods and services. This results in a highly competitive, diverse economy and social abundance.

The idea of social abundance is not limited to the number and diversity of products and brands available for consumption.

It is also applied to the marketplace of ideas and opinions.

As more people worry less about when they will eat next, they can turn their minds to a wider variety of pursuits. And, quite frankly, many of those pursuits are material.

James Twitchell makes this observation:

"Human beings like things. We buy things. We like to exchange things.

"We steal things. We donate things. We live through things.

"We call these things 'goods' – as in goods and services.

"We do not call them 'bads.' This sounds simplistic, but it is crucial to understanding the power of AdCult.

"Still going strong, the Industrial Revolution produces more and more things not because production is what machines do, and not because nasty

Raindrop (cont.)

Well, those things, with all their benefits, don't have an ad budget.

Understand the problem?

Since there's no ad budget, we don't hear those messages quite as often as the paid ones.

Thunder and Lightning.
And, to keep the analogy rolling, it's really raining out there. That marvelous thing we call the marketplace is awash with opportunity.

It's turning into the mother of all thunderstorms – handing out rain checks to every consumer in sight.

That thunder and lightning can distract us from other things – particularly when much of it is so marvelously well done.

And it's everywhere.

Catchy commercials catch our attention, taking our attention away from... what? I wonder. Do you?

Well, we all know what tomorrow will bring – more raindrops. Plop plop plop ploploploploploplop...

It's in our mailbox, on our TV, and crawling across our computer screen.

All the world a media opportunity.

Today, we can even bend and shape the media itself – to do what?

To shake out a few more raindrops.

Don't Forget Your Umbrellas.
As a professional rainmaker, this bothers me once in a while – when I'm not enjoying the splash of my own ads hitting the marketplace – or admiring my latest rainbow, with congratulations for a job well done.

See, I've got these mixed feelings.

Hey, rain is good.

You can even prove it.

But you can also prove there can be too much of a good thing – that's something we ought to think about.

So even though we all need a little rain to make things grow, this message was brought to you by things that don't have an ad budget, or a logo – like exercise, family, fresh air, sunshine, and good friends.

Give those brands a hand.

And come in out of the rain.

End of analogy.

The Truth Campaign.

Funded by the tobacco companies (they lost a lawsuit), it features hard-hitting work by Crispin Porter + Bogusky aimed at, and partially created by, teens.

See it at www.thetruth.com.

You've probably seen a good bit of the work. Well, here's a bit of the story behind it.

First, understand that tobacco marketers are very, very smart about persuasion. They also know, from research, that if you smoke early, well… they gotcha.

So, look at the tobacco industry ads.

Essentially, they say, "Don't smoke until you're a grown-up."

On the surface, seems responsible.

But think about it. One of the motivating factors for young people smoking is to feel more adult – with a bit of rebellion against adult authority thrown in.

So let's look at that message again. "Don't smoke until you're a grown-up." See what's going on?

One More Thing.

The tobacco companies understood that one of the most damaging (and effective) approaches was to portray tobacco executives – and the tobacco industry – in a negative way.

In fact, they had it written into the agreement – that the money could not be spent to disparage the tobacco industry. CP+B did it anyway.

We haven't seen any correspondence or complaints – but we think it should be noted that, in addition to doing some effective advertising, Crispin Porter + Bogusky showed something else that isn't all that common in the advertising industry.

Courage.

Good going, guys.

capitalists twist their handlebar mustaches and mutter 'More slop for the pigs,' but because we are attracted to the world of things.

"Madonna was not the first material girl…

"The Marxist balderdash of cloistered academics aside, human beings did not suddenly become materialistic. Our love of things is the cause of the industrial revolution, not the consequence.

"Man (and woman) is not only homo sapiens, or homo ludens or homo faber, but also homo emptor."

Support #3. Persuasion helps us manage choices in an abundant society.

Persuasion is a necessary and important aspect of society because it solves an important problem: our lack of self-sufficiency. We are not interested or motivated to be experts in every field.

This means we need advice on all sorts of issues from doing our laundry to acquiring adequate automobile insurance. While we can call Mom for advice on laundry, unless she is also an insurance agent, we need to go to someone else, a professional, for advice about car insurance.

When we ask Mom for help in getting that stain out of our favorite shirt, we believe she'll give us the best information and experience that she has available. She has no profit motive (especially when she is paying for our clothes).

So we trust she will emphasize the method of stain removal that will work best. Much in the same way a good insurance agent will supply a client with the best information she or he has available while emphasizing the benefits of using a plan that will work the best for the client and also benefit the agent.

As a professional, the agent may have access to information about the insurance plans of other companies for comparison value, but will have the most information about her or his own products.

When we call an agent we know that agent is interested in selling us insurance and we hope that she or he is ethical enough to tell us what plans can or cannot meet our needs.

Support #4. Advertising exerts social control without social responsibility.

Ads teach people basic values, ideas, and lifestyles without being answerable to any authority and without a comprehensive plan.

As we all know, advertising helps teach cultural norms, in terms of dress (Doc Martens), language ("Whassup?"), and behavior (squeezin' the Charmin).

Critics say dress styles, idiomatic speech, and the cultivation of conspicuous consumption habits are merely commercial norms, not necessary and, in many cases, not beneficial.

Others believe these consumerist norms are very dangerous, that they are destroying real culture, and that they will ultimately lead to our social demise.

However, there is evidence to suggest that even pluralist commercial enterprises can engage in progressive enculturation.

Since the 1980s, advertisers have moved toward normalizing social interaction between the physically disabled and mainstream society (K-Mart, McDonald's, and Levi's ads).

Advertising has been credited with helping create patriotic society. Just think about those Saturn ads, where the folks all got up early to watch TV and see the first Saturns imported into Japan. Smokey the Bear helped the National Forest Service reduce deadly forest fires by increasing awareness and prevention techniques (though Howard Gossage had a different point of view).

These are all examples of advertising's ability to teach positive, progressive cultural norms.

Advertising can also act as an agent of economic control (and thereby social control), especially when providing price and availability information.

While we should acknowledge that no single advertisement is the consumer's best friend, advertising in general is an indispensable source of product information.

Thomas Jefferson noted free speech is the "bulwark of liberty," meaning it is the basis and strongest support of free enterprise.

Without free speech, there can be no free economy.

Applied to commercial activity, advertising, with all its competitive, repetitive, and sometimes even irritating information, helps reassure us that we are not being taken advantage of by unseen or undetectable manipulators.

Criticism:
Advertising Interferes with Democratic Processes.

The presidential campaigns of Harding and Eisenhower are certainly examples of advertising experts having a major impact on elections. Let's look at the major criticisms.

Support #1. Although political advertising is the most protected form of free speech, it can often disrupt the election and campaign process.

Negative advertising, intended to inform the voter about the flaws of the other guy ends up alienating everyone.

Many believe this has led to the political apathy evidenced in low turnout of regular voters.

Support #2. Advertising has become so important that fundraising to pay for advertising has become one of the most important aspects of campaigning.

"The Bulworth Argument."

In the 1998 movie *Bulworth*, Warren Beatty's character notes how money for ads has made politicians captives of big money interests. It's an old movie, but it's still true.

As discussed in Chapter One, the advertising-hungry media-driven infrastructure of modern political campaigns grew as the earlier political infrastructures withered.

The result has been a major change in electoral politics. Campaign spending is critical – and that spending is for ads on TV.

An Argument against Smokey the Bear.

"Smokey was the American ad industry's gift to the nation, the symbol of their vaunted public service campaign, which had the stated purpose of reducing forest fires.

"Howard Gossage was aghast at the very idea that the advertising industry, which was responsible for so much of the glut and waste of consumerism, and which had made of the country one giant depository for throwaway products, including the automobile, so piously purported to be lending a helping hand to Old Mother Nature.

"In fact, Howard said, Smokey the Bear was inept and potentially disastrous in his job. Gossage had amassed considerable statistics to argue that the forests were better off when people weren't breaking their matches, as Smokey so often told them to do, because numerous small forest fires were part of the state of nature, and the 'improvement' rendered by the anti-forest fire campaign had produced a situation where the forests were imperiled by larger and more ruinous blockbuster forest fires."

From *The Gospel According to Howard Gossage*, by Warren Hinckle (former editor of *Ramparts* magazine).

Reprinted from *The Book of Gossage* (The Copy Workshop).

Jesse Ventura Action Figure!

Advertising allows non-traditional candidates entry into the political arena.

Shown above is a satirical commercial for the "Jesse Ventura Action Figure," which was part of a winning campaign for this "entertainment brand" turned politician.

Ballots Not Included.

"The Man from Abilene."

Let's take you back to 1952.

An indifferent campaigner, Dwight D. Eisenhower (Ike) was packaged for the American people by "hard sell" ad man Rosser Reeves.

Reeves was one of the first to understand the power of the "sound bite."

He wrote short punchy answers for Eisenhower, who delivered those answers looking down and to the left.

Then, Reeves grabbed people off the street to ask the questions that fit Ike's best answers. He had these people look up and to the right – so it seemed as though Eisenhower was responding to the people and answering their questions.

For the time, it was incredibly sophisticated and effective advertising.

And Rosser Reeves turned Ike, the war hero, into a TV action hero.

Defense: Advertising Is a Democratic Imperative.

Support #1. In the United States, the mass media are free from governmental interference and restraint.

Negative advertising is nothing new – particularly in politics.

Mass media has replaced often corrupt political machines.

Our mass media are not supported by the government; we have no "Ministry of Public Information."

Advertising pays the way for our "free" speech.

This freedom from governmental restraint allows the media to act as watchdogs, on guard against corruption.

And, in fact, this often happens.

The Watergate investigation, which started with a small news story about a break-in at a political headquarters, led to the downfall of the most powerful person in the country, as well as changing the way media covers politics.

(It is also worth noting that these exposés are often the result of leaks and tips to the media from those with an axe to grind, rather than nose-to-the-grindstone political reporting.)

A free media system is necessary to democracy.

That free media system is supported by advertising.

The price for this freedom is paid by advertisers. Advertisers pay large sums to get their messages in front of the audience.

This revenue permits magazines, newspapers, and television networks to select and run material they believe people want to see. As new needs develop, the marketplace responds.

This freedom allows mass media to act as a government watchdog, never letting necessary, even embarrassing, information escape public scrutiny.

Support #2. Politics has always had mudslinging.

Negative ads, especially negative political ads, permit us a well-rounded view of both candidates and issues.

We can tell a lot about a candidate by what sorts of mud he slings.

Those mandatory "approved by" lines euphemistically referring to some committee to re-elect or citizen's group, add volumes of information to those ads.

The same goes for "issue" ads.

Just knowing who sponsored an ad is enough to form a meaningful evaluation of the information it contains.

Political advertising is necessary to get a true and well-rounded picture of who and what we're voting for.

We may have added more sophisticated electronics, but the negative content of many political messages is as old as democracy.

For better or worse, it also allows non-traditional candidates entry into the political arena.

Criticism:
Advertising Exerts Powerful Controls over the Media.

Support #1. Advertisers interfere with editorial decisions.

This criticism has gained more credibility since federal media regulation relaxed a bit in the '80s, especially given the recent explosion of new media.

Called media fragmentation, the '90s witnessed a population explosion of magazines, the startling development of literally hundreds of television networks, the birth of the World Wide Web and its growth into millions of sites.

Through this boom, advertisers have gained unprecedented access to the public, as well as gaining additional power over the media.

Now, if an advertiser threatens to pull advertising money from a magazine or a newspaper because of a potentially damaging story, the story has a much greater chance of getting killed to save the ad revenue.

Before this fragmentation, the media had relatively more power. Now that advertisers have so many more options, media may be more likely to surrender editorial control to maintain profitability.

Support #2. Advertisers inherently interfere with editorial content.

Some argue that whether or not any individual advertiser complains about a story is quite beside the point. The influence of advertising has changed media in important ways.

First, the dynamic of being served by a medium such as your newspaper has been altered by the needs of that medium to deliver you (the audience) to their advertisers.

As Gossage and others point out, an important shift occurs. The audience is no longer served, but delivered to advertisers.

As Twitchell says in *AdCult*, "*All the mass media are behaving like one vast delivery system.*" This has an influence on content. The "*tabloidization*" of news is one example. As Gossage noted, "*The hot dog vendors take over the football game.*"

The effect is pervasive. Pandering to a lowest-common denominator mass-audience forces all media to focus on sensationalism of the Monica and O.J. Simpson variety.

The comment by Carol Marin in the introduction is worth repeating: "*There is so much emphasis on marketing and demographics. When you decide the target of the information before it's information at all, the news-gathering process is already perverted.*"

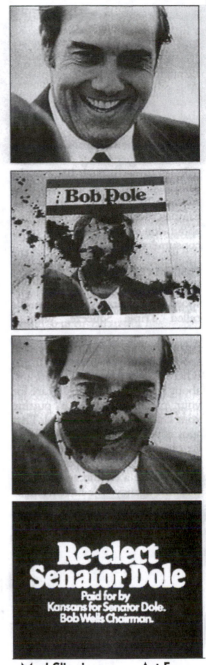

Mud-Slinging as an Art Form.

Here, a skilled candidate presents a commercial that criticizes his opponent for slinging mud – and deftly manages to throw mud back while seeming to take the high ground.

Notice we just show the visuals, you don't have to hear the words to get the point.

In fact, the words probably don't matter. How about that?

Questions for Debate:

1. Given that we all know tobacco is not good for our health, should tobacco advertising be allowed?

2. Given our concern with AIDS, should we allow condoms to be advertised on television, where younger children might be exposed to the message?

3. Make a list of all the tie-ins for Will Ferrell's *Semi Pro.* Based on this, debate, defend, or condemn the following:
   • Old Spice
   • Miller Beer

CBS & Diet Coke.

Spring 1997, *CBS* refused to run a series of Diet Coke ads because they starred actor Dennis Franz as a police officer very similar to his *NYPD Blue* character. *CBS* said it didn't want to contribute to promoting a competitor's program. (*Inside Media,* March 1997)

AdFact:

One out of three high school students has some article branded by a cigarette logo.

Adweek, April 20, 1998

Debate Points:

1. Advertising improves our standard of living.

2. Advertising makes kids more violent.

3. Advertising is cultural brainwashing.

4. Advertising is opium for the masses.

Defense: Advertising Encourages an Ever-Widening Diversity of Media.

Support #1. Advertisers just want a way to reach their target audiences.

Advertising-supported media now exists for even the most narrow of interest groups. By supporting an ever-widening pool of media outlets, advertising provides the voice to many viewpoints previously ignored by media owners and programmers.

Television programming aimed at social minorities and programming that incorporates unpopular opinions have materially enriched our viewing alternatives.

This includes an increase in news coverage, with dedicated networks like CNN, and an increase in network news shows like *Dateline.*

Support #2. Media fragmentation makes control virtually impossible.

We no longer have a few TV networks and a major newspaper controlling a majority of the messages. Blogs, alternative networks, and TV programs looking to stir up controversy all serve to make control over messaging more than difficult – it's impossible.

Even countries with many more controls and restrictions than the US are having difficulty. The free media environment in the US makes that control, over the long term, impossible. Though, one can certainly argue that, over the short term, it is possible to give events strategic "spin."

Criticism: Advertising Is Intrusive and Violates Personal Privacy.

Support #1. Advertising is ubiquitous and unavoidable.

According to this view, the mass media, especially television, are invited guests into our homes.

By turning on the set and changing the channel, we are actively asking for a specific program to enter our living room.

However, along with the invited guest comes the less welcome and more annoying uninvited crasher: advertising.

When we turn the TV on we know that ads will be delivered, but we don't know which ones. Neither can we guess or estimate

An Ever-Widening Diversity of Messages. More media outlets and more marketers mean more new ways to connect with customers. Periodically, gasoline, auto, and alcohol marketers will promote safety as part of their communications strategy.

the manner in which the message will be delivered: humorously, seriously, perhaps evoking fear or anxiety?

These unpredictable visits can be annoying, and many times embarrassing. How many of us have been uncomfortable in a mixed gender group, forced to endure a feminine hygiene commercial?

People, as sovereigns of their own domain, have a right to be free from this intrusion, while still being able to benefit from the entertaining and informational content of the mass media.

Howard Gossage was particularly critical of outdoor advertising for this reason. It intrudes without any permission.

Defense: Advertising Encourages People to Think.

Support #1. For the most part, media consumption is voluntary. Advertising serves to make media more affordable.

In many cases, particularly in events like the Super Bowl, it is part of the entertainment. As Gossage said, *"People read what interests them. Sometimes it's advertising."*

Support #2. Ayn Rand's theory of objectivism provides a somewhat bald defense of advertising based on the premise that all human activity is based on self-interest.

From this perspective, advertising is completely ethical because it initiates consumers' thinking processes and enables them to actively, rationally evaluate their options and make choices in their own self-interest.

In this way, Rand's theory supports advertising as a moral practice not because it serves the "greatest good for the greatest number," but because it serves the self-interested individual by helping them achieve their self-interested goals.

Criticism: Advertising Molds Social Values.

Support #1. Advertising creates unattainable ideals for physical beauty, which systematically harm women both psychologically and physically.

This has been a popular criticism in recent years, most notably in a book by Naomi Wolf called *The Beauty Myth*.

Advertising has created impossible beauty standards and images few real women can meet. Supermodel Cindy Crawford commented, *"Even I don't look as good as Cindy Crawford."*

Airbrushing, sophisticated lighting techniques, and soft focus are all mechanical tools advertisers use to enhance the desirability of their products by enhancing the desirability of the models who embody their brand's image or attributes.

Even though we may rationally recognize that advertising idealizes beauty, and that those standards aren't realistic and shouldn't be applied to real people, it happens nonetheless.

From the Middle Ages through the early 20th century, female beauty was robust, not waif-like.

A plump visage and a decent complexion indicated good health and some degree of wealth.

Advertising Has Helped Make Society Safer.

By encouraging the socially beneficial habit of fastening your seat belt, this campaign has had a positive impact on society.

A Benefit to Society? Or the State?

Ads for gambling products are big business, and gambling has become an important source of state revenue.

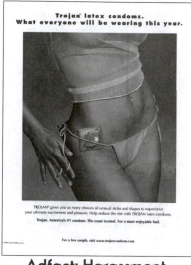

**Trojan latex condoms.
What everyone will be wearing this year.**

TROJAN® gives you so many choices of sensual styles and shapes to experience your ultimate excitement and pleasure. Help reduce the risk with TROJAN latex condoms.
Trojan. America's #1 condom. The most trusted. For a most enjoyable feel.

For a free sample, visit www.trojancondoms.com

Adfact: Harassment.

Many Americans believe that sexually charged advertising promotes sexual harassment (24% of men and 39% of women) (Walsh 1994).

Empty of Value?

Some ads have satirized the waif trend.

"Emptiness consumes me," says the skinny young girl.

"Then eat something" says the spokesman for Boston Market.

AdFact: Privacy.

There is no specific "right to privacy" provided for in the US Constitution.

However, personal privacy is protected by both Supreme Court doctrine and state legislation.

Two legal theories have been used to claim a right to privacy.

1. The right to be free from intrusion (your home is your castle).
2. The property value of your publicity. In other words, what is your personal information worth?

So, the next time you hear someone use the term "my constitutional right to privacy" you'll know they aren't fully informed.

It wasn't until the Roaring Twenties that slim was in. Throughout the following decades, the trend toward slenderizing ideal beauty was evident in the popularity of several female icons: Katherine Hepburn, Marlena Dietrich, Audrey Hepburn, Twiggy, and, more recently, Kate Moss.

However, this trend was not without its exceptions, most notably Marilyn Monroe and Elizabeth Taylor.

While mass media advertising has helped popularize these new perceptions of beauty, modern medicine has also helped.

Research findings that people with lower body fat are at less risk of heart disease, hypertension, and cancer have provided the impetus for two multimillion-dollar new industries: fitness and organic health foods.

So it's clear that advertising alone didn't create today's vision of "Ideal Beauty." However, as one of the main types of content found in our mass media, advertising perpetuates, reinforces, and perhaps extends that vision.

The real harm of this ideal is that it's unattainable, and this produces cognitive dissonance much more often for women than for men. Several of the psychological effects of exposure to unattainable beauty standards have been examined: depression, loss of self-esteem, and poor self-image.

Physical effects, such as anorexia nervosa and bulimia, have also been attributed to advertising's pervasive and unattainable portrayal of ideal beauty. However, as you'll see in the Dove example on the next page, even problems can create opportunities.

Defense: Advertising Is Capitalistic Realism.

Support #1. Advertising teaches us how to live in our world.
"Advertising is the folklore of a commodity culture."

Advertising is the reflection of a common symbolic culture. America is a consumer nation. Advertising reminds and reinforces our social identity as a market economy.

Ads teach us how to live in our culture, use the products and services available, and how they fit into everyday lives.

In this way, advertising helps build social cohesion.

People used to stand around the water cooler talking about the latest episode of *Cheers* or *Seinfeld*, but given the fragmentation of television viewing habits, nowadays they are just as likely to be discussing that Levi's ad where the guy is rushed into the emergency room, dies, and then his heartbeat comes back to the vivid bass line of "Tainted Love."

Advertising, by delivering the same message to everyone, ensures that even disparate groups have common references.

Twitchell again: *"The idea that advertising creates artificial desires rests on a wistful ignorance of history and human nature… Once fed and sheltered, our needs have always been cultural, not natural."*

Support #2. Advertising provides and reinforces ideals that help us strive to be our best.

Classical liberalist business scholars like Theodore Levitt support this idea. Levitt said that advertising is at its most moral when it is embellishing and exaggerating reality.

A startling statement, but true, according to Levitt, because people are always rational and discerning and they want to be uplifted from the mundane everyday world.

Like art and poetry, advertising provides examples of what can be attained, so we know what to strive for.

Furthermore, the Dove "Real Beauty" campaign was able to generate positive sales and a positive response by connecting to the issue of "ideal" body types.

Years ago, Bernbach noted that some of the most effective advertising was "sociological."

By connecting to the "cultural tension" associated with this issue, Dove was able to form a bond between their brand and "real" consumers. They were also able to generate a level of interest that led to such things as Dove models appearing on the Today Show.

The Next-to-the-Last Word…

We'll let Twitchell have the next-to-the-last word in our debate here – something to think about: *"By adding value to material, by adding meaning to objects, by branding things, advertising performs a role historically associated with religion."*

The Last Word.

It's yours.

Debate these points in class – or after class.

And look for more discussion at our Web site.

Rules & Regulations.

MOST ADVERTISERS ARE HONEST BUSINESS PEOPLE. But the exceptions, such as the early patent medicine advertisers, have made rules necessary, such as the Pure Food and Drug Act of 1906 and early postal fraud laws.

Dove. Real Beauty.

Bill Bernbach observed that being "sociological" can provide a creative leverage point. More recently, CP+B look for "psychological, social, categorical, or cultural tension."

The marketers at Unilever, and their agency, Ogilvy & Mather, with both good intentions and an excellent strategic sense, saw a growing opportunity in society – an opportunity that had, in some ways, been created by advertising that portrayed a very narrow version of "beauty."

The DOVE Campaign for Real Beauty is a global effort launched in 2004 to serve as a starting point for societal change and act as a catalyst for widening the definition and discussion of beauty. The campaign supports the DOVE mission: to make more women feel beautiful every day by widening stereotypical views of beauty.

Listening to Women.

The DOVE Campaign for Real Beauty was inspired by a major global study – the *Real Truth About Beauty: A Global Report*. The study validated the hypotheses that the definition of beauty had become limiting and unattainable, as if only thin, young, and blond were beautiful.

DOVE found the current narrow definition of beauty was having a profound effect on the self-esteem of women:

- Only 2% of women around the world describe themselves as beautiful.

- 81% of women in the US strongly agree that "the media and advertising set an unrealistic standard of beauty that most women can't ever achieve."

new Dove Firming.
As tested on real curves.

Dove
Firming Range

Regulatory Power

From High...
Private Policy

Government Forces:

Supreme Court
Reviews laws and regulations for constitutionality. Applies Central Hudson Test to decide if regulation on advertising is constitutional.

Food and Drug Administration (FDA) Oversees advertising, packaging, and labeling for food, drugs, and therapeutic devices.

Federal Communication Commission (FCC)
Regulates advertising indirectly through license renewal process and media clearance department.

State Regulators
For example: Michigan Consumer Protection Act of 1976 - administered by Michigan's Consumer Protection Division.

National Association of Attorneys General (NAAG)
State attorney generals address issues not covered by federal regulations. States may join together in some litigations.

Organized Market Forces:

Media Clearance
Magazines
Broadcasters
CATV

Industrial Self-Regulation
NAD / NARB
AMA - Medicine
ABA - Lawyers

Consumer Organizations:

Mothers Against Drunk Driving
Consumers Union

Natural Market Forces:

Supply and demand
Consumers

...to Low

Attempts to mitigate the harmful effects of advertising on individuals and society take the form of regulation.

Two Main Purposes.

There are two main purposes for advertising regulation:

- To protect competition
- To protect consumers from economic or physical harm

Three Main Areas.

Ad regulations are typically concerned with three areas:

- Deceptive or unfair advertising content
- How advertising is delivered to consumers
- Protection of susceptible groups, like children

Many Forms.

The regulation of advertising takes many forms: federal, state and local laws, regulations that are administered by both federal and industrial agencies, consumer groups, and private enterprises, such as the media and ad agencies.

With such a complicated environment, keeping the do's and don'ts straight can be confusing and costly.

How This Section Is Organized.

This third section is organized according to the scope or power of each particular form of regulation.

Regulatory Power Continuum – Five Levels.

There are five main forces that occupy different positions along the power continuum of advertising regulation:

1. **Natural market forces (consumers' demand)**
2. **Organized market forces**
3. **Self-regulatory forces**
4. **Governmental forces**
5. **Private policy**

Power exerted by lone consumers resides at the lower end of the power continuum – but not because it isn't the most effective.

The Supreme Court is second from the top because it has the broadest scope.

And at the very top is private policy – those doing the work taking it upon themselves to act responsibly

The following text goes from low to high – you should understand how they work in both directions.

Let's review them one by one.

1. Natural Market Forces.

Market forces reside at the lower end of our power continuum because their scope is limited to individual actions – even though these market forces can be extremely powerful.

Historically, there was little advertising regulation before the 20th century. The phrase **caveat emptor** or "let the buyer beware" was the prevailing philosophy. This left advertising regulation to the natural forces of the free-market economic system.

According to natural market forces, businesses that engage in deceptive or unfair advertising practices will be driven out of business because no one will believe their ads or make repeated purchases of inferior products.

In a healthy marketplace, competitors create better products and use more truthful ads to tell consumers their goods are better than those of the competition.

Accordingly, poor performers would be forced to upgrade products and correct their ads or go out of business.

This is also called **laissez faire** regulation (or "hands off").

The underlying assumption of natural market forces are described as the "invisible hand" type of regulation.

Laws of supply and demand drive the quality of advertising. Nondeceptive advertising increases demand and keeps competition strong.

While deceptive ads may result in short-term and unreproducible profits, they will ultimately drive inferior brands out of the market. As Bill Bernbach said, *"Nothing will kill a bad product faster than a good ad."*

A Few Problems.

There are a few problems with relying on natural market forces to regulate advertising.

- First, natural market regulation is a long-term solution; in the short run, consumers can be severely harmed, financially and even physically, by deceptive or misleading ads.
- Second, society suffers as a whole when consumer sovereignty is diminished.
- Finally, natural market forces provide no help or compensation to consumers harmed by unethical practices. Short of a civil lawsuit, consumers who weren't "beware" are left bereft.

The consequences of natural market regulation offered the basis for finding new ways to manage advertising.

So, things got organized.

2. Organized Market Forces.

ONE OF THE MORE RECENT DEVELOPMENTS is using organized market force to support socially responsible practices. There are three major forms of organized market forces:

- **Consumer groups**
- **Media forces**
- **Industrial self-regulation**

As you will see, this type of regulation has more power than natural market forces.

Consumer Groups.

Consumer groups have been active since the 1930s.

Groups such as Consumers' Union and Consumer Research founded a movement called **consumerism.**

Even an advertising agency can have questions about advertising. Here, DDB expresses some of those concerns.

Girl Meets Boycott.

This powerful billboard (the fur leaves a bright red trail of blood) was one of many media tactics that had a powerful effect on the fur industry.

The campaign had heavy celebrity involvement and caused many to stop wearing furs.

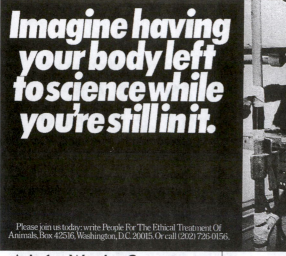

Ads for Worthy Causes.

Often, they result in powerful creative efforts due to the inherent drama in the problem.

The FCC and the "Fairness Doctrine."

The FCC regulates advertising indirectly, through licensure and the renewal of broadcast licenses.

The most notable and direct example of its regulation occurred during the middle 1960s, when the FCC suddenly applied the "Fairness Doctrine" to tobacco advertising.

Prior to this, it had been applied only to "issues of public debate" where political candidates from opposing viewpoints might be denied equal access to the broadcast media.

But the FCC widened the scope of the application, deciding that cigarette advertisements *"did contribute to the public debate on smoking"* (9 FCC 2d 921, 1961).

This application of the doctrine raised the level of anti-tobacco advertising to an unprecedented high.

It was a level that the FCC was unwilling to maintain.

A few years later, after being ordered to apply the doctrine to other advertisements, they made an abrupt about-face, stating that *"ordinary product commercials do not make a meaningful contribution to public debate"* (48 FCC 2d 1, 1974).

Aaker defines this as *"an evolving set of activities of government, business, independent organizations and concerned consumers that are designed to protect the rights of consumers."*

Other groups such as the Center for Science in the Public Interest are a relatively new force in this movement.

Consumers recognize they may not be able to make fully informed decisions as individuals and need the protection of a group.

The major methods employed are lobbying and **boycotts.**

Lobbying for Legislation.

Consumer groups lobbied for protective laws, such as the Fair Packaging and Labeling Act of 1965 and the Consumer Credit Act of 1988.

A powerful, well-organized group – Action for Children's Television (ACT) – helped write the Children's Television Act of 1990.

Boycotts.

Product and brand boycotting have successfully promoted change.

More media options, combined with sophisticated media techniques, have expanded opportunities to create this type of activity.

With the flickering attention span of the public, a certain tenacity is necessary – a few celebrities on your side won't hurt, either.

Example: "Dolphin Safe" Tuna

What began as a small consumer boycott helped change the commercial fishing industry.

Publicity informed the nation that tuna fishing regularly caught and drowned dolphins. Canned tuna sales plummeted.

Then, producers changed fishing methods and began to promote "dolphin safe" labeling.

However, one prevalent problem with relying on this type of organized market force is the length of time it takes to get action.

In addition, business is likely to ignore small groups, and without the economic threat of a serious reduction in profits, has little incentive to change.

Self-Regulatory Forces.

Industrial self-regulation is another organized market force.

To avoid government interference, advertisers monitor the activities of one another to investigate, prevent, and discourage false and unreliable advertising practices.

This is known as **enlightened self-interest.**

Self-regulatory forces try to maximize the ability of consumers to make good decisions by encouraging the use of truthful, relevant information in advertising.

Professional Associations and Self-Regulation.

Industrial self-regulation generally occurs when an industry committee is established with codes, review boards, policies, and standards that must be met in order to maintain good standing within the community.

An example of single industry self-regulation is found in several professional associations such as the American Bar Association and the American Medical Association.

Many of these organizations have stringent rules about what type of advertisements are appropriate and acceptable.

Professional boards insisted that these rules were necessary to protect consumers from unscrupulous practitioners. (The assumption being that any professional who would stoop to advertising was no gentleman… or lady.)

Punishment for infraction of the professional restrictions could be severe. Fines, expulsion from the group, and even loss of practitioner's license were all possible penalties.

While these regulations sounded like they were intended to protect consumers, a number of empirical studies indicated that they served the professionals more than the public.

Disadvantages to Consumers.

The economic disadvantages experienced by consumers due to advertising bans are clearly illustrated in several instances.

Example: Optometrists

One study found the Optometrists Board of Nebraska's restrictions on advertising increased the price of eyeglasses from 25 to 100% compared with areas where advertising was permitted.

Save up to 650%!

Another study indicated that prescription drug prices varied up to 650% between states where retail pharmacy advertising was restricted and those where it was permitted.

Social disadvantages were also illustrated. These were based on the common sense notion that limiting sources of information about anything, a brand or a political candidate, necessarily decreases the amount of information a consumer can access within a given budget of time and money.

When sources of information are restricted, consumers with limited budgets of time or money (generally those consumers in a lower socioeconomic strata) must make decisions with less than optimal information.

This perpetuates social stratification and creates consumer inequity. And, it attracts litigation.

As a result of several Supreme Court decisions, professional organizations no longer have the power to ban advertising, and many of the trade practices of these organizations are now overseen by the FTC.

Industrial Self-Regulation.

Industrial self-regulation operates differently from professional self-regulation. It works only when a group of producers and manufactures get together in an effort to promote truthful advertising.

In 1971, the Association of National Advertisers and several large

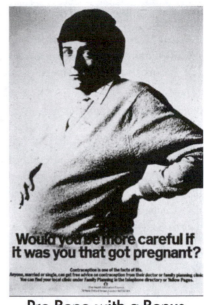

Pro Bono with a Bonus

The advertising industry supports worthy causes with work that often wins advertising awards.

A Pro Bono Bonus!

The Better Business Bureau.

The Better Business Bureau was the result of a suggestion by the Cleveland Ad Club.

Using Network Clearance as a Publicity Vehicle.

Internet marketer godaddy.com submitted several versions of their risqué Super Bowl spot to network clearance – even though they knew the spots would not be approved.

The purpose – publicity. They received press coverage and publicity for their actions – and their brand. Not exactly ethical. But it worked. And yes, you can still find them on the Internet – promoting their "banned" commercials.

advertising agencies agreed to support the nonprofit **Council of Better Business Bureaus** (www.bbb.org) in the creation of a department called the **National Advertising Division** (NAD). The Better Business Bureau handles all administration and funding for the NAD.

The NAD – Complaints and Claim Substantiation.

The purpose of the NAD is *"serving the public interest by sustaining high levels of truth and accuracy in national advertising."* The function of the NAD is to investigate complaints about advertising.

Complaints can come from anywhere – consumers, advocacy groups, even competitors.

The NAD also monitors the advertising landscape and initiates investigations on its own. The scope of these investigations is mostly limited to evaluating whether the advertiser had enough information or a good justification for making the disputed claim.

This is known as **claim substantiation.**

Advertising to Children.

A special department of the NAD called the Children's Advertising Review Unit (CARU) is dedicated to protecting the special interests of children.

3. Self-Regulatory Forces.
Media Clearances.

The most powerful enforcement among organized market forces is the media clearance process.

Individual broadcaster licensees are responsible for denying access to unacceptable advertising content and practices.

License Renewal and the "Public Interest."

Broadcast licenses are awarded and renewed based on the FCC's determination of how well the station's management served the *"public interest, convenience, and necessity."*

The FCC's historical perspective on advertising addresses only its lack of tolerance for "excessive" airing of commercial matter.

The NAB – Clearance Procedures.

For almost 50 years, broadcasters regulated advertising according to guidelines set out by the National Association of Broadcasters' (NAB) Code of Broadcaster Responsibility. This code dictated how much advertising time a station could sell, "clutter" limits, and limited the acceptance of advertising for certain legal products.

Example: *Maidenform*

One example of an unacceptable advertising practice was showing lingerie ads with live models. The Maidenform woman would have been out in the cold, and the Hanes ads showing the little boy wandering into the bathroom with his dad looking on fondly wouldn't have had a chance with the NAB.

According to the NAB, responsible broadcasters could not air advertisements for condoms (or other methods of birth control), nor for liquor. Truthful advertisements for many of these legal products are still denied network time.

Some parts of this code are still honored, although it was found to violate the Sherman Anti-Trust Laws in 1982.

Liquor Advertising.

It is not illegal to advertise liquor.

The industry association called DISCUS (Distilled Spirits Council of the United States) has a code of behavior for its members that expressly forbids the use of television advertising.

There are several reasons why DISCUS took the anti-television stand, but mainly it stems from tradition.

In 1934, newly elected FCC Commissioner Anning Prall told Congress he believed advertising liquor was contrary to the public interest and broadcasters airing such ads would be sanctioned.

Of course, in 1934, there were no powerful companies to lobby on behalf of the liquor industry, and radio had plenty of sponsors.

Companies that did exist really had no need to advertise – the recent legalization of alcohol after 14 years of Prohibition created more demand than existing producers could handle.

But things were different in 1996. Liquor sales were declining and brands scrambled to maintain market share in the face of reduced consumption.

The distilled spirits industry was becoming more competitive. So Seagrams decided to break with tradition and advertise on TV.

That's where Frank Smith entered the picture.

In Frank's case, he had long been an advocate of liquor as a source of advertising revenue.

The point here is that you can be moving along in your advertising career and suddenly find yourself at the center of a legal and ethical crisis – that's why we all have to be prepared.

On whichever side of an issue you find yourself, you will quickly find that you have to know more about the other side.

This wasn't Frank Smith's first experience with liquor advertising and it was, in many ways, a result of his own view of what was ethical and proper. In August of 1982, Frank had signed a local Corpus Christi liquor retailer to run an entire schedule of ads using brand names and prices.

It was an experiment to see if anyone would object. The station received only minimum prices for the spots, but ran over 300 30-second spots in every time slot (except Saturday morning) over the next three months.

Frank set up a monitoring system with local stores to track complaints, but during the entire course of the campaign less than 20 complaints were received.

Even when a convention of more than 5,000 Baptists came to town, complaints were practically non-existent.

But the distributors got nervous, and when the campaign ended, they made no plans to follow up.

Advertising & Addiction.

Products that are part of addictive consumption behaviors may or may not be in a special category.

In comparing tobacco usage in regulated and unregulated countries, it is not clear that regulating advertising has much impact on established smoking behavior.

However, it is also unclear what the effect is on underage non-smokers being exposed to attractive adult imagery for cigarettes.

Other practices are also cause for concern.

For example, direct mail marketing by casinos to heavy gamblers – many of whom have severe gambling problems.

Marketing to these people clearly does them a disservice. Yet, on the other hand, it is merely the traditionally accepted marketing practice of mailing to your best customers.

Another related issue is the fact that these addictive behaviors generate substantial tax revenue, as tobacco, alcohol, and gambling (through both casinos and state lotteries) are now major sources of revenue for states.

Award-Winning Advertising.

The advertising industry does some of its best work for the liquor industry. This classic was created by Doyle Dane Bernbach.

Laws Affecting Advertising.

1890 Sherman Anti-Trust Act
Prohibits monopolies and any contract, conspiracy, or combination involving restraint of trade.

1906 Pure Food and Drug Act
Prohibits misbranding of food or drugs, including labeling.

1914 Clayton Act
Prohibits price discrimination.

1914 Federal Trade Commission Act
Established the Federal Trade Commission. Prohibits unfair methods of competition.

1934 Federal Communications Act
Created Federal Communications Commission to regulate broadcasting.

1936 Robinson-Patman Amendment to Clayton Act
Prohibits price discrimination that lessens competition or helps to create a monopoly.

1938 Wheeler-Lea Amendment to Federal Trade Commission Act
Prohibits unfair or deceptive advertising.

1939 Wool Products Labeling Act
Created labeling requirements for wool products, including fiber content, condition, and manufacturer.

1947 Lanham Trademark Act
Protects brand names and slogans from infringement. Directs US patent office to register names, slogans, and identifying symbols.

1952 Fur Products Labeling Act
Created labeling requirements for fur products, including species and manufacturing details.

1958 Automobile Information Disclosure Act
Requires car manufacturers to itemize new car stickers, including base costs, extras, and freight.

1960 Textile Fibers Product Identification Act
Created labeling requirements for cloths and other materials manu-factured in the US.

1966 Fair Packaging & Labeling Act
Created "truth-in-labeling" law, stipulating manufacturers disclose contents and volume on packages.

In 1995, one of Frank's friends, Phil Block, the owner of Block Distributing was called into a Seagrams' marketing meeting. They were complaining that they wanted to use television but couldn't find a network or affiliate to take the ads. Phil knew who to call.

"It was a mess," said Frank, *"Seagrams had ads they'd run overseas, but nothing for the US; no creative, no positioning."*

Despite that, by early June they had a spot ready, and Frank had the perfect time slot – right after an NBA playoff game.

The media attention was remarkable. Seagrams had a press conference in the KRIS offices with the *Wall Street Journal*, UPI, API, CNN, and 17 other news organizations in attendance.

Advertising Age reported that a total of 17 news broadcasts devoted more than nine minutes to the story, while 10 major daily newspapers printed more than 2,500 words covering the report.

KRIS received a total of 77 letters, mostly local, complaining or commenting on the ads. From all evidence, it appears the real controversy about running liquor ads on TV is at the national level – it doesn't seem like the local population was disturbed at all.

TV was the beginning. Liquor ads are now also on the radio for the first time since 1934.

4. Governmental Forces.
State Regulation – Two Types.
Every state has its own laws and regulations affecting advertising. There are two main types of state laws.

Several states have "mini FTC" laws – aimed at preventing unfair business practices rather than protecting consumers.

Other states have consumer protection laws that also can be used to protect competition.

Some states permit individual citizens to collect monetary damages from companies that advertise deceptively. (Check your state to see if they have a "price-scanner law" requiring stores to pay up to 10 times the difference between the stated and scanned price.)

As federal regulators moved away from active participation, state regulations, and the power of state regulators, increased.

State regulation is a complex and increasingly important area of concern for advertisers.

NAAG.
The National Association of Attorneys General (NAAG), is comprised of states attorneys who have banded together to create regulatory policy where the federal agencies have not.

Several states work through this organization to combat mail fraud (e.g., YOU HAVE JUST WON $1,000,000), illegal sweepstakes, telemarketing scams, and other deceptive business schemes.

NAAG has also played an important role in the recent indictment of tobacco marketers as well as creating "green guidelines."

Federal Regulation.

Federal Trade Commission.

The Federal Trade Commission (FTC) was created in 1914 by Congress as part of the Federal Trade Commission Act in an attempt to limit unfair and deceptive business practices. Section 5 of the act states that *"unfair or deceptive acts or practices in or affecting commerce are illegal."*

In 1938, a consumer protection component was added to the original law with the enactment of the Wheeler-Lea Amendment. Section 12 forbids any false advertising likely to induce the purchase of goods, drugs, devices, or cosmetics.

Functions of the FTC.

Today, the functions of the FTC are two-fold.

First, to protect business from unfair competition.

Second, to protect consumers.

This second function, originally incorporated to serve the first, was intended to make sure people weren't forced to make decisions based on misleading information and to stop or limit practices that were morally objectionable, exploitative, inequitable, or seriously detrimental to consumers and society.

The Domain of the FTC.

The federal government has jurisdiction over all matters that affect the country as a whole. The court gains jurisdiction over issues that are affected by interstate travel or, as in advertising, interstate communication.

Because of a Supreme Court ruling regarding interstate commerce, Congress, through the FTC, has the power to regulate advertisers, products, and any firm that sells, supplies, airs, or transports across state lines.

This power is loosely interpreted.

In today's world, virtually everything crosses state lines, which invokes federal jurisdiction, somewhere along the line of commerce.

If the FTC really wants to go after a company, they can claim jurisdiction based on as tangential a relationship as a company's salesperson having purchased gasoline that had been trucked in from another state!

Powers of the FTC.

The FTC adjudicates complaints on a case-by-case basis.

Complaints can come from any source: competitors, consumers, or even from members of the FTC staff.

NAAG. NAAG. NAAG. The National Association of Attorneys General played an important role for their states in the recent successful tobacco litigation.

1966 Child Safety Act
Prohibits marketers from advertising potentially dangerous products and enables FDA to remove dangerous products from the marketplace

1966 Highway Beautification Act
Restricts placement of billboards along public highways.

1968 Truth-in-Lending Act
Requires full disclosure of consumer credit costs in ads.

1970 Public Health Cigarette Smoking Act
Prohibits broadcasters from accepting money for tobacco advertising. Requires a health warning on all cigarette packaging.

1971 Federal Election Campaign Act
Requires political candidates to disclose ad sponsorship.

1975 Magnuson-Moss Warranty Act
Requires manufacturers to honor product warranties – implied or explicit.

1978 Copyright Act
A revision of the much older act, this clarified the protection of copyrighted materials.

For example, it added the "SR" copyright for the music industry. SR stands for Sound Recording, and now musicians can copyright the performance (vocal style and arrangements) as well as the song.

This virtually eliminated cheap "sound-alike" productions, which copied the sound and performance of hit records.

1980 Federal Trade Commission Improvement Act
Empowers the Federal Trade Commission to create trade rules and regulations.

1990 Children's Television Act
Restricts the amount of time that can be sold for advertising during children's television viewing times.

Professor Ivan Preston.

Profile of an Ethical Career.

After graduating from the College of Wooster in Ohio and serving in the Army, Ivan joined Ketchum, the leading Pittsburgh ad agency during the Golden Age of advertising.

Ivan wasn't satisfied. He saw serious ads that were untruthful, unethical, or downright untenable.

He decided to change the industry he'd chosen. And he has.

With his 1964 Ph.D. in Communication from Michigan State, he began a lifelong effort to improve ad trustworthiness and truthfulness.

He did it in the classroom and with books, articles, and speeches.

He actively participated in developing regulation that would not only protect business from predatory competitive practices, but laws and rules that help protect everyday consumers. Like us.

In the early '70s, Dr. Preston began investigating "puffery."

Ivan believes that "puffing," while technically legal, is detrimental to both consumers and the ad industry due to its insidious ability to make us doubt all advertising claims.

His prolific and persuasive arguments finally landed him in Washington, DC, where, as a consultant to the FTC's Division of Advertising Practices, he advocated change on behalf of consumers.

He remains a leader in the fight to improve the ethics of advertising and is viewed as the conscience of our industry.

His most recent efforts to change advertising practices are contained in his two books, *The Tangled Web We Weave* and *The Great American Blow-Up* – both available from the University of Wisconsin Press.

After a complaint is lodged, the FTC evaluates whether the claim made in the ad is deceptive. Sidebars on pages 178 and 179 list types of claims that may be deceptive and evaluation guidelines.

Example: *Campbell's Soup*

Here is an example of how visual distortions can create a net impression that may be viewed as deceptive.

It involved Campbell's Soup, a brand we'll be featuring throughout the book.

In the Matter of Campbell Soup Co., 77 FTC 664 (1970).

A Campbell's Soup television commercial, intending to make Campbell's soups look inviting and hearty, created the **net impression** that the brand had more ingredients than was actually true. By putting clear marbles at the bottom of a bowl of soup, the carrots, potatoes, peas, and onions in the soup rose to the surface and were highlighted.

"Advertisements which purport to demonstrate or offer evidence of the quantity and abundance of solid ingredients in a can of Campbell's Soup (actually relies on) a number of clear, glass marbles which prevent the solid ingredients from sinking to the bottom, thereby giving the soup the appearance of containing more solid ingredient than it actually contains, a fact that is not disclosed.

"The aforesaid demonstration exaggerates, misrepresents and is not evidence of the quality or abundance of solid ingredients in a can of Campbell's Soup; therefore the aforesaid advertising is false, misleading and deceptive."

The Campbell Soup Company responded that, due to the limitations of the medium, television, these photographic techniques were necessary to illustrate the richness of the soup and merely allowed consumers to see the ingredients which were, in fact, in the soup.

However, the commission was not persuaded, and the soup company was ordered to cease and desist using the ads.

Puffery.

Though the FTC sidebar lists what we know about defining deception, there's still quite a bit of controversy surrounding the issue. Much of it focuses on the differences between deception and exaggeration or "puffery."

Puffery is the use of terms that cannot be precisely determined. As the term itself suggests, puffery is considered by the courts and other regulators to be acceptable, yet nonsensical verbiage that rational consumers can clearly disregard.

However, if there is the possibility that a consumer might place some credence in these claims, or if they have a tendency or are intended to be interpreted as true, they are deceptive.

The use of puffery in an ad typically refers to statements of opinion, exaggerations, overstatements, and the use of superlatives. Examples of puffery are: "out of this world flavor," "Coke is the real thing," and "the world's best beer."

Puffery is often less identifiable than the courts and regulators assume. The difference between statements of fact and statements of opinion are often the topic of fierce debate.

Example: Dannon Yogurt

This kind of debate ensued between the FTC and Dannon Yogurt about the claim: *"Dannon is known as nature's perfect food that science made better."* Dannon's point was everyone knows there really isn't such a thing as a perfect food and the claim was clearly hyperbole. In other words, no rational consumer could possible take it seriously.

The commission didn't see the claim in the same light.

The FTC concluded that the claim was a misrepresentation of fact, *"given the present day emphasis on dieting, health, and nutrition, to make the claim that a food is perfect far exceeds puffing or exaggerations of qualities."*

The Reasonable Consumer and Material Claims.

The crux of whether a claim is deceptive or mere puffery seems to rely on the likely interpretation by a consumer.

The FTC created a "test" to consider it from the viewpoint of reasonable consumers. The FTC looks at the ad from the viewpoint of a reasonable consumer (not an expert) who is acting reasonably under normal circumstances.

The heart of the matter in using this "reasonable consumer" test is to define "reasonable." The FTC defines reasonable consumers as average people acting normally in normal situations. They also evaluate audience susceptibility.

This refers to the level of expertise the typical consumer has in regard to the product, its use, or purchase.

For example, the FTC is not likely to perceive medical doctors as highly susceptible to ad claims or as consumers who are in great need of regulation. (Remember our chart on page 148?)

The commission will, however, apply a much stricter standard when the intended target of an ad is somehow disadvantaged, such as children.

For some consumer groups, "acting reasonably" does not include reading the fine print. An example might be an audio warehouse company offering "10 CDs for a penny."

You know you'll have to buy another six at "regular club prices," but nowhere, except in the fine print, does it say those prices are far greater than retail and shipping and handling fees might constitute a 40% addition to the cost of each CD.

Since these ads are typically aimed at teens and pre-teens with limited purchasing experience, and virtually no experience with legally binding agreements, it's reasonable to conclude the ad is likely to mislead a substantial number of consumers (millions of teenagers) or a significant portion of the target audience (30% of all teenagers). This ad might fail the reasonable consumer test and therefore be accountable to the FTC for deceptive practices.

Advertising Regulators.

Some governmental entities that regulate advertising:

BATF – Bureau of Alcohol, Tobacco, and Firearms
Regulates advertising of controlled substances and dangerous goods.

CAB – Civil Aeronautics Board
Regulates airline advertising.

Federal Election Committee
Regulates political advertising.

FTC – Federal Trade Commission
Regulates all facets of interstate commerce.

FCC – Federal Communications Commission
Regulates radio, television, and telephone providers.

**FDA –
Food and Drug Administration**
Regulates advertising, labeling, and branding of all food, drugs, and health devices.

Library of Congress
Registers copyrighted materials: books, music, computers, software, ads, and other published materials, such as patents and trademarks.

NAAG – National Association of Attorneys General
Each state has its own attorney general. This person is charged with making sure state laws are fairly enforced, as well as defending the state and its citizens from all unlawful activity.

For example, the Texas attorney general named four international tobacco companies in an anti-racketeering suit. The State of Texas claimed Phillip Morris, RJ Reynolds, and others had acted together as a group to harm the citizens of Texas.

SEC – Securities & Exchange Commission
Regulates advertising of stocks, bonds, mutual funds, and other securities.

United States Supreme Court
Possesses the authority to evaluate the constitutionality of any law or regulation restricting free speech, including commercial speech.

Evaluating Deception.

All advertising can, under some circumstances, be considered deceptive. We consumers could evaluate it the same way the FTC does, but that seems awfully time-consuming and exhausting.

What we really need are some criteria for evaluating how much deception can be tolerated.

Here is a summary of the most important criteria which could be drawn from the FTC and NAD policies.

An ad is intolerably deceptive based on how it performs along the following dimensions:

The Nature of the Deception.

If the ad permits or encourages physical harm of any kind, it cannot be permitted.

The same is true for significant economic damages.

False Beliefs.

Any claim or net impression that permits or encourages consumers to hold or create a false belief about a product, service, or brand is deceptive.

So is any false or misleading claim that encourages or allows consumers to purchase a brand they would not have if the claim had been absent.

Calculating Damages.

Is the nature and the extent of the damage likely to be caused significant and/or meaningful?

A 5¢ problem affecting 50 people is less cause for regulation than a $5 problem affecting 500 people.

Self-Correction.

Is the claim or practice self-corrected? If people try a brand expecting superior quality and are disappointed, they won't buy it again. This is an acceptable criteria only when the nature and extent of the damage is minimal.

Intention.

Is the advertiser trying to mislead consumers into a purchase? Or was the claim the result of a mistake, such as a typo or a printing error?

Material Claims.

However, even deceptive claims aimed at susceptible audiences may not be censored by the FTC. If the claim is not material, no harm has been done.

"A material claim is any claim that affects a consumer's choice or behavior, or that makes injury likely."

The materiality of a claim differs according to product category and audience, just as assessments of reasonableness differ.

Claims that might be material for one product category may be inconsequential for another.

Claim Substantiation.

The FTC requires advertisers to provide adequate substantiation for any claim made in an ad.

The claim substantiation policies insist that advertisers have a "reasonable basis" for making claims. This means advertisers must have information supporting the claim on hand before making the claim in an ad.

The NAD and the NARB rely on the standards set by the FTC for their own self-regulation efforts.

Substantiation of Claims.

There are several important steps advertisers must take to ensure that claims are adequately substantiated:

1. Make sure the ad has been examined by several people, not just the copywriter and art director, but accounting and legal departments. Use their expertise as a preventive measure.

2. What type of claims are made? There is a long history of regulating certain types of claims. Are these types of claims made in your ad? Is that exaggeration really just puffery?

3. Have you done enough research to make the claims appearing in your ad? Have you claimed four out of five dentists agree, when you only interviewed five dentists?

Remedies for Deceptive Advertising.

If an ad is found to be deceptive, there are remedies:

* **Cease and desist orders**
* **Corrective advertising**

Let's review them in more detail.

Cease and Desist Orders.

If the ad clearly violates either Section 5 or 12, as defined by the FTC, a cease and desist order may be issued.

This is legal notification to stop running an ad, and, if violated, fines are approximately $5,000 per exposure.

While this is the most powerful punishment the FTC has at its disposal, sometimes it's not powerful enough.

Sometimes this makes non-compliance attractive to unethical advertisers. Some companies make many times the fine each time a deceptive ad runs, choosing to pay the fine rather than pull the ad.

Some companies may fail to comply with orders, but the stakes do get higher when the FTC finds non-compliance. Fines can increase and, in a few cases, there has even been jail time.

Civil Offenses – Not Criminal Offenses.

Advertising regulations are not criminal offenses with a prison penalty attached for violation; they are civil offenses.

Typically, offenders do not end up in jail, unless they are found to be in contempt of court during the proceedings.

Contempt = Jail.

However, the FTC may sue the advertiser in federal court, and theoretically a judge can jail an advertiser for contempt.

Still, identifying and catching an offender is often the biggest problem for regulators.

Corrective Advertising.

A drastic remedy, no longer as popular as it once was, is **corrective advertising.** This allows the FTC to order advertisers guilty of deceptive advertising to correct material beliefs held by consumers caused by the deceptive advertising.

The FTC reasoned that, if a brand's deceptive advertising practices had contributed to consumers' erroneous beliefs about an important brand attribute or benefit, the advertiser should correct that belief by allocating a portion of future advertising budgets to consumer re-education.

Example. *Listerine*

The most famous "corrective" case involved Listerine mouthwash.

"*Kills Germs That Cause Colds*" was a famous slogan that had dominated the mouthwash's advertising since 1879. Variations on the theme for almost 100 years had taught consumers well.

The FTC initially ordered approximately $10 million to be spent correcting this false claim by clearly and conspicuously disclosing the following language: "*Contrary to prior advertising, Listerine will not help prevent colds or sore throats or lessen their severity.*"

On appeal, the brand was permitted to drop the humiliating phrase "contrary to prior advertising" but was still required to include the rest of the information in all ads.

The philosophy behind corrective has been applied by federal courts in comparison advertising cases and included in out-of-court settlements. It is no longer used by the FTC.

Affirmative Disclosure.

The remedies presented above are methods typically applied to deceptive practices after they have occurred.

In addition to these remedies, **affirmative disclosure** is the FTC's remedy for future harm. The principle behind affirmative disclosure rulings is that consumers need all the information, not merely the attractive information, to make good decisions.

Affirmative disclosure rulings direct businesses to include necessary, yet sometimes unappealing, information. They force businesses to include health and safety information, credit terms and agreements, product ingredients, and warning labels.

A Humorous "Guarantee."

Is this humorous and good-natured claim honest or deceptive?

Trade Regulation Rules.

The FTC has created rules requiring specific industries to meet certain criteria in advertising and marketing:

Franchise and Business Opportunities Rule.

Requires giving prospective buyers a disclosure document containing specific information about the franchise and any earnings claims made.

Funeral Rule.

Requires funeral directors to disclose price and other information about funeral goods and services.

Telemarketing Sales Rule.

Requires telemarketers to disclose information that would affect a purchasing decision before the consumer agrees to pay for any goods or services the telemarketer is selling.

1996 Environmental Marketing Claim Guidelines

The FTC has created broad guidelines for all industries using "green claims."

This is one of few instances where the FTC has created guidelines which did not result from case adjudication.

Please see the FTC's Web site at: www.ftc.gov for a full text version of the *Guides for Use of Environmental Marketing Claims: Publication of Revised Guides* (October 1996).

Types of Claims That May Be Deceptive:

1. False Oral or Written Statements.

These are explicit claims that are factual misrepresentations—specifying attributes, characteristics, or benefits not achievable by most consumers or under most circumstances:

- Fresh Choice really was frozen orange juice
- Listerine doesn't really kill germs that cause colds

2. Untrue Claims Are Not Necessarily Deceptive.

- Fantasy claims: e.g., *Coke adds life!*

3. Implied Claims.

- Claims that imbue a product or service with a quality or characteristic that it cannot or does not have. Such as, "You too can look like Arnold if you eat / drink this ..." or, perhaps, you can *"Be Like Mike."*
- Innuendo: Profile Diet Bread claimed "only 46 calories per slice" implying others had more calories, which is false. Most breads have 45 to 50 per slice.
- Using foreign language, jargon, or technical language intended to confuse or intimidate consumers into thinking your product is better or different.

4. Net Impression of the Ad.

The FTC looks at the whole ad, not just a collection of statements.

If the impression is misleading, even though individual statements are accurate, the FTC may find the ad misleading in its entirety.

5. Distortion of the Facts.

You can't make a factual claim that your product is the "best" at something when you haven't actually tested.

There must be some chemical, physical, or function changes to use the term "improved." Not new colors on the label.

However, there is still much distortion possible with "puffery," and relative claims such as "best ever!"

(continued on next page)

Disclaimers.

The example of affirmative disclosure we see most often is the **disclaimer.** It is intended to clarify claims made in the body copy.

This policy is intended to provide consumers with the most relevant, truthful information possible to aid decision making.

The information can be used to clarify an offer or to inform consumers about product performance.

Disclaimers are not always an effective method of avoiding consumer deception. Some people are likely to be confused or deceived no matter how much information an ad provides; sometimes more information creates more confusion. In fact, many believe advertisers word this information in such a way as to maximize confusion.

The small type used in disclaimers supports these suspicions, but research indicates fine print isn't really the problem.

According to a study by Foxman, Muehling and Moore, the type size used in a disclaimer does not significantly assist consumer comprehension (i.e., big type doesn't always equal better understanding).

They also found that 5 to 20% of all consumers are unable to discern true claims from false ones, no matter how much information is provided or what size type is used.

While for the most part, disclaimers do not change beliefs or brand preference, they can change understanding about implied and express warranties contained in main advertisement copy.

Laws Regulating Advertising.

Comparative Advertising.

Today, the practice of naming competitors is widely used to let consumers know your brand is better than others in the category.

From many consumer perspectives, as well as ethical points of view, comparison ads are socially beneficial.

Useful information comparing meaningful attributes is viewed by many as advertising at its best.

In fact, this is exactly how consumer groups and services, such as *Consumer Reports,* treat categories of goods, from automobiles to toaster ovens – by comparing them.

Until the 1970s, comparative advertising was rare.

"Brand X."

Competitors were seldom named. Many advertisers viewed naming competitors in ads as "giving away advertising."

Network advertising guidelines prohibited direct comparisons, allowing only comparisons to "Brand X" in ads.

Many advertisers were afraid they'd confuse consumers.

But there were two larger motivations behind the reluctance to use comparison ads:

1. Advertisers' fear that competing brands would sue for disparaging their brand or violating their trademark.
2. A concern among large advertisers that it would create a harping, negative, and argumentative tone that, once started, might be quite difficult to stop.

Procompetitive Practices.

The FTC, in an effort to promote consumerism, strongly urged the "procompetitive practice."

The commission helped assuage advertisers' fears by persuading networks to change their policies and by teaming up with industry organizations such as the American Association of Advertising Agencies to create comparative advertising guidelines.

Lanham Trademark Act.

Comparison ads found a boost in support from the 1988 revision of the Lanham Trademark Act of 1946.

The act, which allows competitors to sue each other for trademark infringement, was originally passed to prevent misrepresentation of a brand "causing some trade (profits) to be diverted" from the rightful company.

In this original form, it was used by brands whose name or likeness had been usurped by another company.

1988 Revision of Lanham Act.

Liberal application in support of comparative advertising led to a revision of the act in 1988.

The revisions create the basis for a civil suit, "disparaging another person's goods, services or commercial activities." This is the only means available for competitors to sue rivals for false advertising.

Supreme Court.

The Supreme Court on "Commercial Speech."

Noting that people are often more interested in information of economic value than in political value, the Court ruled that the flow of commercial information should not be restricted.

The opinion reads, in part: "*[I]nformation is not in itself harmful… people will perceive their own best interests if only they are well enough informed and that the best means to that end is to open channels of communications rather than to close them… it is precisely this kind of choice, between the dangers of its misuse, if it is freely available, that the First Amendment makes for us.*"

The United States Supreme Court has the power to uphold laws and regulations as constitutional or to strike them down as violations of the federal constitution. Some of its decisions affect advertising in important ways. Here are examples:

Example: Bigelow v. Virginia

Until 1975 no advertising regulation had been struck down as unconstitutional by the Supreme Court. That year the Court handed down its first opinion to change that in a landmark case known as Bigelow v. Virginia.

Ad regulations typically try to stop, ban, or reduce advertising, prevent advertising placement in various locations, or dictate ad copy or content.

Bigelow, a newspaper editor, was convicted of violating Virginia's anti-abortion laws by publishing an ad for a New York women's clinic. The ad informed Virginia residents of the clinic's services.

6. Use of the Word "Free."

The consumer can be under no obligation for further action.

The consumer must not be required to purchase something else to get the free item or service, unless that purchase is clearly included as part of the free claim.

7. Use of Small Print Disclosures.

These cannot offset the main headline.

They may clarify or limit an offer, but they cannot unreasonably limit the main claim so that it is unachievable or too complicated to understand.

8. Uniqueness Claim Substantiation.

In order to have a truly unique product, you pretty much have to be able to qualify for a patent.

9. Performance Claims.

Claims that discuss how a brand will work must be substantiated more than any other types of claims.

Advertiser Responses.

Once an advertiser is confronted with an FTC review, it may take any of the following actions:

- **Comply with the FTC cease and desist order**
- **Fight the FTC in administrative hearings**
- **Fight the FTC in federal court**

Note: If the advertiser chooses to fight at either the administrative or legal level, it must take into consideration that fines continue to be assessed each time the disputed ad runs.

The Central Hudson Test.

Here is the four-part Central Hudson test as it applies to advertising:

1. **The restrictions are directed at ads concerning a lawful activity or product and are not misleading.**

2. **The state must have a substantial, legitimate, or compelling interest in regulating the speech.**

3. **This action must advance that legitimate or compelling interest.**

4. **The restriction may not be so broad as to affect other speech.**

The Parameters of Comparison Advertising.

Originally, trademark law only applied in situations where a competitor tried to palm-off an inferior product by associating it with a trademarked one.

The Lanham Act of 1946 was passed to prevent loss of goodwill or profit when a competitor unfairly used a trademark.

A. Benefits of Comparative Ads:

1. Provides greater information.
2. Stimulates comparison shopping.
3. Encourages product improvement and innovation.
4. Fosters a competitive business environment.

B. Risks of Comparative Advertising Perceived by Businesses:

1. Bad publicity for your brand.
2. Possibility of misinformation.
3. Your brand might be misidentified as the poor performer.

(continued on next page)

The Court overturned the conviction, saying that *"just because the information was contained in an ad, that fact was not enough to strip it of all its First Amendment protection."*

The Court ruled that the ad contained information relevant to an issue of social importance and granted advertising limited First Amendment protection.

Pharmacy Retail Restrictions.

The protection offered to advertisements was widened further when the Court examined a law restricting purely commercial information.

In this case, the Court ruled that retail pharmacy restrictions prohibiting the listing of prices actually caused economic harm.

The Central Hudson Test.

In 1980, the Court backed off from the absolute protection offered in the Virginia pharmacy case. The Court created a four-part test, which is covered in the sidebar.

The Central Hudson test is now used to evaluate the constitutionality of advertising regulations.

It provides limited protection for speech that "proposes a purely commercial transaction."

The first criteria of this test is that the restrictions are directed at ads concerning a lawful activity or product and are not misleading. Obviously, the public interest is not served by protecting deceptive advertising.

Advertising regulation is only acceptable when the state has a substantial, legitimate, or compelling interest in regulating the speech. In addition, the regulation must directly advance the state's interest.

The restriction may not be so broad as to affect other speech. This test clarified the limited level of protection that commercial speech had been granted. The Virginia Pharmacy and Central Hudson cases are landmarks in advertising protection.

Since stating this test, the Court has applied it a number of times. However, its reasoning has not always been consistent.

Example: Puerto Rico & Gambling

One example of this lack of consistency is Posadas de Puerto Rico Associates v. Tourism Co. of Puerto Rico.

Here, the Court allowed a ban on truthful ads for a legal product based on Puerto Rico's substantial interest in keeping its residents from gambling.

The Puerto Rican government sought to prevent its citizens from wagering in the local casinos, possibly inflicting irreparable damage to their economic well-being.

Therefore, it banned ads for casinos inside Puerto Rico.

The ban went so far as to include printed matchbook covers advertising casinos and monograms stenciled on plates.

The Court, while recognizing the restriction on matchbook covers as excessive, upheld Puerto Rico's interest in preventing its citizens from learning about casinos through advertising.

Warranty as Strategy. Hyundai established quality with a dramatic warranty.

Administration of Advertising Regulations.

The Supreme Court, while the highest judicial power in the US, does not actually regulate and administer advertising regulations. That responsibility has been delegated to executive administrative agencies previously discussed – the Federal Trade Commission and the Federal Communication Commission.

Even the Bureau of Alcohol, Tobacco, and Firearms exerts some power over advertising in certain categories.

Other Laws Affecting Advertising.

The Magnuson-Moss Warranty and Federal Trade Commission Improvement Act of 1975.

This act, administered by the FTC, constitutes another effort to use information as a remedy for deceptive ads. It deals with implied or explicit brand warranties and guarantees.

Warranties and Guarantees.

Warranties and guarantees are different types of claims.

A **warranty** is a promise of performance, attributes, or benefits made by a manufacturer.

It becomes a contract between the manufacturer and the consumer upon purchase of the product.

Many claims made in an ad are warranties, e.g., Kodak claims their film is free from defects in materials and workmanship.

Express and Implied Warranties.

An actual claim of performance, attributes, or benefits is considered to be an **express warranty**.

An **implied warranty** is any claim (audio or visual) made that, although not specifically stating a claim, implies one.

"Merchantability."

The most important type of implied claim is **merchantability**. This means the product will perform as claimed if it is properly used for the purpose it was manufactured and intended.

Advertising claims are often used to substantiate product liability claims, which can be among the most expensive types of suits for manufacturers to defend.

Guarantees.

These are also covered under Magnuson-Moss.

A **guarantee** is a promise that if something goes wrong with a product, the manufacturer will make it right.

- **Coverage.** Advertised guarantees must set forth the nature of the guarantee in terms of coverage: full, limited, or conditional.

Comparison Adv. (cont.)

4. Information is narrowed to focus on only a few comparable product attributes and benefits.
5. Publicizes the competition.
6. Potential legal problems.

C. Public Policy Intentions in Regulating Comparative Ads:

1. Fosters more and better information.
2. Seeks to slow the flow of false and misleading ads.
3. Protects business from unfair competition.

D. The FTC Has Stated:

Ads that disparage competitive products, but are not deceptive, are not illegal. Discouraging or forbidding direct comparison advertisements is considered to be prohibiting free trade by restricting free flow of information.

False Representations.

Today, the Lanham Act is used by companies likely to have been injured by a false representation in a competitor's ad. The company claiming injury must show the following:

1. The ad made a false representation about the competitor's product;
2. The claim was false; and
3. There exists either potential or current irreparable damage to its firm, profits, or brand image.

Lanham Actions Are Very Powerful:

1. Immediate injunction bars the ad from further use.
2. Immediate access to substantiating data from the competitor is made available.
3. Monetary damages of up to three times the actual or potential damages caused, with proof of actual damage, may be awarded by the court.

Follow Instructions:

Here are actual label instructions that appeared on consumer goods:

On a Sears hair dryer...
Do not use while sleeping.

On a bag of Fritos...
You could be a winner!
No purchase necessary.
Details inside.

On a bar of Dial soap...
Directions: Use like regular soap.

Frozen dinners...
Serving suggestion: Defrost.

On hotel-provided shower cap...
Fits one head.

On Tesco's Tiramisu dessert...
(Printed on bottom of box.)
Do not turn upside down.

On bread pudding...
Product will be hot after heating.

On an iron...
Do not iron clothes on body.

On children's cough medicine...
Do not drive car or operate machinery.

On Nytol (a sleep aid)...
Warning: May cause drowsiness.

On Korean kitchen knife...
Warning: Keep out of children.

On Chinese-made Christmas lights...
For indoor or outdoor use only.

On Japanese food processor...
Not to be used for the other use.

On Sainsbury's Peanuts...
Warning: Contains nuts.

On a packet of nuts...
Instructions: Open packet, eat nuts.

On a Swedish chainsaw...
Do not attempt to stop chain with your hands.

- **Conditions.** Guarantees must state how far the firm will go to correct problems, and must also set forth conditions of coverage, e.g., restricting coverage to original owners only.
- **Limitations.** Guarantees must set forth the extent or duration of the guarantee, including time and wear limits.
- **Performance.** Guarantees must set forth the manner in which the guarantee will be performed, such as product replacement, repair, or refund.

Example: *Kodak*

Kodak guarantees the full refund of purchase price if consumers are not satisfied with their film.

The consumer is the key to this guarantee.

Only the consumer can determine satisfaction with the film, not a professional photographer or the manager of the store where the film was purchased.

5. Private Policy.

This is listed as the highest form of control because it is *internal* rather than external. In many ways, the motivation is to avoid the problems associated with the previous four levels of rules and regulations.

Advertiser and Agency Procedures.

All advertisers, advertising agencies, and media organizations engage in rule-making about:

- types of advertising they will utilize;
- professional, creative, and ethical standards;
- processes used to ensure guideline compliance; and
- who, within the organization, is responsible for execution and oversight.

Two Reasons for Review Procedures.

Advertisers often have complicated review procedures to ensure that they won't find themselves in regulatory hot water.

The function of internal review procedures are twofold:

- First, to prevent or reduce litigation or regulatory action against their clients
- Second, to increase consumer trust in advertising

Types of Policies.

There are guidelines to ensure internal review policies succeed, such as: claim substantiation, creative standards on content (including racial and sexual stereotyping), sexual explicitness and language, and technical issues, like computer retouching.

It's widely recognized that the formality, complexity, and flow of an organization's clearance process depends on the organization.

With a recent trend toward big companies hiring small agencies, policies and procedures seem a necessary ounce of prevention.

Issues related to ethical and legal review policies must be clarified early on and, ideally, put in writing. And, with luck, problems will be something that happen to others, not to us.

Summary:

The materials covered in this chapter are important to you, whether you are a future ad practitioner or a consumer, for these reasons:
- To increase your professional awareness
- To prepare you to discuss advertising with ad professionals and critics: e.g., family, peers, philosophers, regulators, etc.
- To give you a practical understanding of ad regulation

Now here are some things to help you get ready for the test.

Discussion Questions:

1. Persuasion.
Why is persuasion acceptable in our culture?

2. Economic Effects.
What are the economic effects of ad regulations?

3. Market Power and Market Information.
Discuss the two major perspectives on how advertising effects society – Market Power and Market Information.

4. The Lanham Act.
Why is the Lanham Trademark Act important to advertisers?

Concepts & Vocabulary:

Advertising – A paid message concerning a legal product or service placed through the media by an identified sponsor.

Advertising practice – A recurring practice in advertising. The use of pretty models to sell products and the use of small print to obscure the details of car costs are all advertising practices.

Affirmative disclosure – The FTC uses affirmative disclosure rulings to force businesses to include health and safety information, credit terms and agreements, product ingredients, and warning labels. These rulings are designed to prevent deception before it can harm consumers.

Anecdotal evidence – The use of a story (an anecdote) to make a point. The story may very well be true, but a single example does not necessarily prove the point.

Caveat emptor – Latin for "let the buyer beware."

Cease and desist order – Legal order issued by an agency or court with jurisdiction that an ad must stop running immediately or fines will be assessed.

Commercial speech – A legal term for paid communications, primarily advertising.

Commercial speech doctrine – The series of Supreme Court cases that have resulted in the current level of protection offered to advertising.

Consumerism – Movement concerned with rights of consumers.

Copyright – The copyright act of 1976 is intended to "promote the progress of science and the useful arts" by protecting the creator's

Source Notes:

Ekeland & Saurman (1988), *Advertising and the Market Process*, PRIPP: CA.

Public Health Smoking Act 1970; Schuster, Camille P. and ChristinePacelli Powell (1987), "Comparison of Cigarette and Alcohol Advertising Controversies." *Journal of Advertising* 16 (2): 26-32.

Documents in American Broadcasting, 4th edition (1984), Frank J. Kahn, ed. Englewood Cliffs, Prentice-Hall.

Rotzoll, Haefner and Sandage (1986), "Five Institutional Views of Advertising," in *Advertising in Contemporary Society*.

Schultz, Don and Beth Barnes (1999), *Integrated Campaign Management*.

Jones, John Philip (1995), *When Ads Work*.

Lantos, G. (1987), "Advertising: Looking Glass or Molder of the Masses?," *Journal of Public Policy and Marketing* 6: 104-28.

Jaska, J. and A. Pritchard (1986), *Communications Ethics: Methods of Analysis*. Belmont CA: Wadsworth Publishing, 1988.

Beauchamp, T.L. and N.E. Bowie (1988), *Ethical Theory and Business*, 3rd ed. Englewood Cliff, NJ, Prentice-Hall.

Ogilvy, David (1985), *Confessions of an Advertising Man*

Twitchell, James (1997), *AdcultUSA*.

Galbraith, K.B. (1957), *The Affluent Society*.

Velasquez, Manuel (1992), *Business Ethics*.

Kirkpatrick, Jerry (1986), "A Philosophic Defense of Advertising." *Journal of Advertising*, 15, (2): 3-12.

Jefferson, Thomas (1794), in *The Federalist Papers*.

Rand, Ayn (1964), "The Objectivist Ethics," in *The Virtue of Selfishness*, New York: New York Library.

Wolfe, Naomi J. *The Beauty Myth*.

Levitt, T. (1970), " The Morality (?) of Advertising," *Harvard Business Review*, July-August, 84-92.

Smith, Adam (1794), *The Wealth of Nations*.

(continued on next page.)

Source Notes: (cont.)

Aaker, David (1973), *New Consumerism: Selected Readings,* Columbus Ohio: Grid Inc.

Benham, Lee (1972), "The Effect of Advertising on the Price of Eyeglasses," *The Journal of Law and Economics,* 15 (2): 337-52.

Wilcox and Hovland (1990), *"Advertising in Society: Classic and Contemporary Readings on Advertising's Role in Society."*

Lichtenberger, J.L. (1987), *Advertising Compliance Law.*

FCC: Public Service Responsibility of Broadcast Licensees, 1946; *Documents in American Broadcasting,* ed. Frank Kahn (1985).

In the Matter of Campbell Soup Co., 77 FTC 664 (1970).

Preston, Ivan L. (1975), *The Great American Blow-up: Puffery in Advertising and Selling,* Madison: University of Wisconsin Press; Ivan L. Preston (1994).

The Tangled Web They Weave: Truth, Falsity and Advertisers. NAD Case Report 10/17/83; also, Lichtenberger p. 49.

Fueroghne, Dean (1995), *Law & Advertising: Current Legal Issues for Agencies, Advertisers and Attorneys.* Chicago: The Copy Workshop.

Foxman, Ellen R., Darrel D. Muehling, and Patrick A. Moore (1988), "Disclaimer Footnotes in Ads: Discrepancies between Purpose and Performance," JPP&M.

Beck-Dudley & Williams (1989), "Legal and Public Policy for the Future of Comparative Advertising: A Look at U-Haul v. Jartran," JPP&M.

Virginia Board of Pharmacy v VA Citizens Committee, 47 CFR § 1.

Wiener, J.L. (1988), "An evaluation of the Magnuson-Moss Warranty and FTC Improvement Act of 1975," JPP&M.

right to all profits. Copyright protection is limited to the life of the author plus 50 years (to provide for heirs: think Elvis and Lisa Marie). Copyright is thought to provide an incentive to create.

Corrective advertising – Advertising designed to correct a previous misrepresentation. This can be the result of major legal action or a store notifying you of a misprinted price in the paper.

Disclaimer – A written statement intended to clarify claims made in the body copy of an advertisement.

Deontological ethics – The evaluation of right and wrong based on intentions, regardless of outcomes. Deontological = intent.

Economics – The study of enterprises and relationships involved in the exchange of goods and services.

Ethics – The study of how people judge their own and others' conduct in terms of right or wrong.

Guarantee – A guarantee is a promise by the manufacturer to correct defects according to the stated terms. Advertised guarantees must set forth the nature of the guarantee in terms of coverage: full, limited, or conditional. They must state how far the firm will go to correct the problems and set forth the conditions of coverage (e.g., original owners only). They must also set forth the extent or duration including time and wear limits, as well as the manner in which the guarantee will be performed (e.g., product replacement, repaired, or monies refunded).

Idiomatic speech – The use of slang or jargon in everyday speech.

Intellectual property – Unique expressions of ideas or concepts that are protected by law, primarily patent, copyright, or trademark.

Laissez faire – Status quo, leaving the status of the matter alone and choosing not to act in a manner to change it.

Merchantability – The implied claim that the product will work as expected if correctly used. Software is an interesting exception to this rule. Software is often shipped with bugs, and these bugs often prevent the software from fulfilling its promised function. (This might also be called "fraud.")

Mitigate – To reduce or lessen an effect.

Material claims – Any claim that affects a consumer's choice or behavior.

Normative expectations – What a reasonable person might normally expect.

Persuasion – An act of communication that seeks to convince another to voluntarily change, resolve, or formulate their opinions, feelings, or actions through the use of argument, reasoning, or entreaty.

Physiological needs – The basic requirements of life, including shelter, clothing, food, air, and water.

Policy – A form of unofficial guidelines that private firms, individuals, and organizations create for internal (and in some cases, external) conduct. (Policy is not regulation.)

Puffery – Obvious exaggerations and outrageous statements about a product or service made by the seller, not intended to be taken seriously. The use of puffery in an ad typically refers to statements of opinion, exaggerations, overstatements, and the use of superlatives. Examples of puffery are: "out of this world flavor," "Coke is the real thing," and "the world's best aspirin."

Reasonable basis – A rationale (or foundation) for making claims that advertisers must have prior to making any claims about a product or service.

Reasonable consumer – A standard of judgment. The crux of whether or not a claim is deceptive or merely puffery often relies on the consumer's likely interpretation. The FTC created a "test" to make sure they consider questions of advertising deception from the viewpoint of reasonable consumers. This is pretty much a circular definition – a reasonable consumer is one who is acting reasonably (not as an expert nor as an idiot) at the time under normal circumstances.

Reasonable skepticism – The process of persuasive communication is two-way. The persuader has a moral duty to inform using rational techniques, and the audience has the moral responsibility for questioning the presentation. This questioning on the part of the audience is the moral duty called "reasonable skepticism."

Regulation – Rules imposed by governmental entities to manage the conduct, or economic or social effects of a business or service. In our context, this means advertising. In the US, government does not tell advertisers what they may say in ads, only what cannot be said.

Society – The organization of a group of individuals with traditions that have evolved into a culture. Society maintains itself by providing rules of behavior for individuals within what are called "norms." Our society includes government, economy, and class structure.

Sovereign consumers – The assumption that consumers are rational, calculating, and deliberate and thus able to sort through competing messages to arrive at a reasoned choice that will maximize their own benefits. According to this assumption, sovereign consumers are not at the mercy of advertisers and do not need to be protected from any type of information.

Susceptibility – The level of expertness or sophistication the typical consumer has in regard to product use or purchasing. For example, the FTC is not likely to perceive medical doctors as highly susceptible to advertising claims and in great need of regulation to remedy any problem. However, the commission will apply a much stricter standard when the intended target of an ad is somehow disadvantaged (or susceptible), such as the elderly or children.

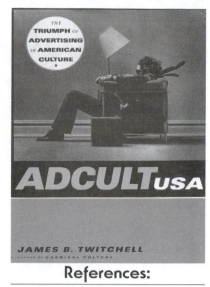

References:

AdCult USA:
The Triumph of Advertising
in American Culture
by James Twitchell

Advertising in
Contemporary Society
Edited by Kim Rotzoll and others

Advertising, The Uneasy Persuasion:
Its Dubious Impact
on American Society
by Michael Schudson

The Book of Gossage
by Howard Luck Gossage, Jeff
Goodby, Kim Rotzoll, et al
The Copy Workshop

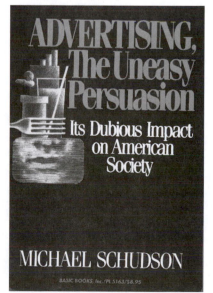

References:

The Great American Blow-Up
by Ivan Preston

The Tangled Web They Weave
by Ivan Preston

Law and Advertising: Current Legal Issues for Agencies, Advertisers, and Attorneys
by Dean Fueroghne

Mythmaking on Madison Avenue: How Advertisers Apply the Power of Myth and Symbolism to Create Leadership Brands
by Sal Bandazzo

Advertising: The Uneasy Persuasion: Its Dubious Impact on American Society.
by Michael Schudson

AdCult: The Triumph of Advertising in American Culture
by James Twitchell

There is current discussion in this area related to ads for casinos and lotteries and people with gambling problems.

Teleological ethics – The evaluation of right and wrong based on the social benefits derived by the outcome of an action without regard for the intention of the action. Teleological = results.

Warranty – A promise of performance, attributes, or benefits made by a manufacturer. It becomes a contract between the manufacturer and the consumer. For example, Kodak advertisements say that their film is free from defects in materials and workmanship.

An **express warranty** is a warranty based on an actual claim. An **implied warranty** is any claim (visual or verbal) that, although not stating a claim, implies one.

Your Own Advertising Library:

AS ADVERTISING AND MARKETING have become more important in our society, books that offer new perspectives on this increasingly important force in our society have begun to appear more frequently.

Here are a few of the ones we like:

Twenty Ads That Shook the World: The Century's Most Groundbreaking Advertising and How It Changed Us All.
by James B. Twitchell

Our friend from *AdCult* is at it again. Disguised as a University of Florida English professor, he tells us the fascinating stories behind some of the most important advertising in history.

The Sponsored Life: Ads, TV, and American Culture.
by Leslie Savan

Did you know the *Village Voice* had an ad critic? Well, it's true. Savan writes on topics from Helvetica (that's a font) as an expression of context-free post-modern communication, to… well how would you like to read an article called "The Brand with Two Brains?"

Those are just two examples. A very provocative book.

The Conquest of Cool.
by Thomas Frank

This is about the real revolution that shook American business – how youthful revolutionaries were joined by the forces of advertising.

Today's hip commercial culture is the result – with the rhetoric of revolution co-opted by the forces behind all those clever 30-second TV commercials. Cool.

II The Business of Brands

MARKETERS, AGENCIES, MEDIA, MARKETING SERVICES.

These four unique types of businesses make up The Business of Brands. You'll see how these different kinds of companies are organized and the many different careers they offer.

4 Marketers & Advertisers.

MARKETING AND ADVERTISING DEPARTMENTS are organized around the brands they market.

In this chapter you'll be introduced to the ways marketers and advertisers do business. We'll cover their internal responsibilities and the way they work with outside suppliers – such as ad agencies and marketing services firms.

5 Advertising Agencies.

BRAND-BUILDING COMMUNICATIONS are the unique product of advertising agencies.

You'll see the many types of agencies, how they work, and the many jobs needed to make an ad agency successful.

6 The World of Media.

MEDIA HAS MANY ROLES IN OUR SOCIETY.

This chapter will focus on the business behind the media – the business of delivering audiences to advertisers and the marketing of entertainment brands.

We'll look at the different types of media and how they market themselves to audiences, advertisers, and agencies as well as how this affects us as citizens and consumers.

7 Marketing Services.

MARKETING HAS MANY FUNCTIONS.

In this chapter we'll survey the specialized companies that supply marketing services sales promotion, public relations, direct marking, event marketing, media buying, marketing research, and more.

Other Marketing Services can also be valuable brand-builders. Above, the logo for Harley-Davidson's 95th anniversary celebration – part of a marketing public relations program that helped build their image as one of America's premiere brands.

FASTER THAN A SPEEDING CIVILIZATION.

A Driving Force...

Today, marketing is a bigger part of every company's activity. And virtually every company is concerned with building the equity of their brands.

Entertainment Brand Meets Service Brand.

Here, Jerry Seinfeld, a hot "entertainment brand" adds his unique brand value to the American Express brand of financial services.

The Brand-Building Experts.

Advertising agencies have more experience building brands than most companies – because they work to build more of them.

Here, Burrell Advertising helps Coke connect with the African-American market.

4

*"We believe that advertising is the most effective
and efficient way to sell to the consumer.
If we should ever find better methods of selling
our type of products to the consumer, we'll leave
advertising and turn to those other methods."*
— Howard Morgens, ex-President, P&G

Marketers & Advertisers

"ELVIS ADVERTISING" WAS DAVID PEACOCK'S student agency at the University of Kansas where he competed in the AAF/NSAC. Today, he's still competing – working for another King – the King of Beers – developing strategies and programs for Anheuser-Busch.

Competitions don't stop. In the Effie competition, **Bridgette Heller** accepted an award for the job she and her brand management team did on Gevalia. From there, she has moved up to become head of a major division of Johnson & Johnson.

Adam Seever liked sports. First, he got into sports marketing with a leading sales promotion firm. Then, he got a job competing with one of the biggest teams in marketing – Coca-Cola.

Every working day, **Todd Holscher** takes the field. After graduating, he took a job in field marketing for Frito-Lay.

Steve Hill was working in retail planning at GM when he asked a few college buddies if they'd like the employee discount.

They're all making their mark in the world of marketing.

How This Chapter Is Organized.

In this chapter, you'll see how each of their jobs fits into the growing world of marketers and advertisers. We will cover:

❶ **The Marketing Function.**

We'll look at the five critical decisions that shape the strategies that shape the success of a brand. The Five P's.

❷ **The Marketing Department.**

We'll look at how marketing departments are organized and some unique jobs and responsibilities.

❸ **The Marketing Process.**

We'll see the cycle of Planning, Implementation, and Evaluation as companies market their brands, particularly the fourth "P" – Promotion.

❹ **Marketing Challenges.**

We'll look at the challenges facing marketers of the future. After all, one of them might be you.

*This chapter was written by
Anthony McGann, who was Editor
of the* Journal of Advertising, *and
President of the American Academy
of Advertising. He teaches at the
University of Wyoming where he
served as Chair of the Department of
Management and Marketing.*

*Additional contributions were made by
Jim Avery, Professor of Advertising at
Oklahoma University.*

THIS CHAPTER IS AN INTRODUCTORY MARKETING COURSE. It's one of the most important chapters in this book.

Because today, whatever role you play, whatever job you have, you absolutely must understand the principles of marketing.

The Marketing Function.

MARKETING HAS MANY DEFINITIONS, all related to "bringing a product to market." For example, the American Marketing Association defines it as *"the process of planning and executing the conception, pricing, promotion, and distribution of ideas, goods, and services to create exchanges that satisfy individual and organizational objectives."*

We've listed some other definitions in the sidebar. More important, let's take a look at a few of the many different kinds of marketers.

Many Different Kinds of Marketers.

WHATEVER BUSINESS YOU'RE IN, MARKETING IS IMPORTANT. It's critical for virtually every company and every brand.

Marketing is Targeted Thinking.

Marketers think in terms of markets or **target markets**.

Primary Target. The **primary target** is the consumer – the person who uses (or purchases) that product.

Secondary Target. There is often an important **secondary target** group, such as a retail channel or sales force.

The idea of a target means you need to aim your thinking.

Peter Drucker observes, *"The aim of marketing is to know and understand the customer so well the product or service fits him and sells itself."*

Let's take a look at some different types of marketers.

Consumer Product Marketers.

These companies market products people use – we're most familiar with these marketers and their brands.

Packaged Goods and Durable Goods.

Some products are consumed in a relatively short period of time – there is always a new market for them.

These products are generally referred to as **packaged goods** as they usually come in packages, like soup, detergent, and cereal.

Campbell's, Procter & Gamble (P&G), Kraft/General Foods (KGF), and PepsiCo are examples of this type of marketer.

Some products are purchased more infrequently.

Examples of these types of products would be automobiles, washing machines, televisions, and tires. Volvo, GE, SONY, and Michelin are good examples of these types of brands.

These products are generally referred to as **durable goods**.

Since much classic marketing was developed with the manufacturers of consumer products, particularly packaged goods, this chapter will tend to emphasize that type of marketer.

But there are many other kinds of marketing.

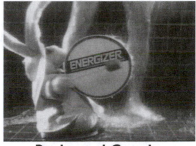

Packaged Goods.

Products like Energizer batteries are purchased frequently – even if they do keep on going... and going...

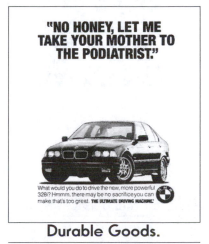

"NO HONEY, LET ME TAKE YOUR MOTHER TO THE PODIATRIST."

Durable Goods.

These are relatively costly products – like BMW – that are purchased infrequently.

They are usually what marketers call a "considered purchase."

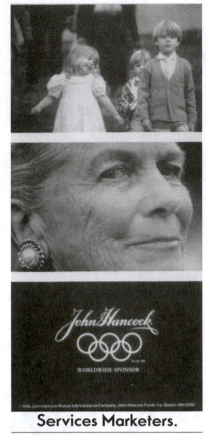

Services Marketers.

John Hancock sells components that you understand, but they are, in many ways, "intangible."

Products and Services Mixed.

Here, both the paint and the professional painting are part of the services offered.

Services Marketing.

Services are also products. As our economy has evolved from a manufacturing economy to a service and information economy, these "products" have become more and more important.

Regis McKenna notes, the line between services and products is fast eroding. For example, some years GM makes more money from the service of financing cars through GMAC than it does manufacturing the cars themselves.

Categories like financial services, airlines, and the hospitality industry are examples of this type of marketing.

Smaller professional services suppliers, such as lawyers, dentists, and accountants are also services – a reminder card from your dentist is, in a basic way, an example of services marketing.

While service offerings are similar to more tangible products, such as packaged goods, they do differ in important ways.

Intangibles.

Services generally contain **intangibles,** components you can experience and understand, but can't physically touch. Like "time."

For example, cellphone service provides for the consumption of a particular kind of time.

In renting a hotel room, one buys the time to use the room as well as the support services that make certain you have clean sheets and a mint on your pillow.

The service can sometimes be thought of as the product.

Products offered by companies like American Express, Citicorp, and Sprint/Nextel are examples of this type of marketer. These companies and their services have now become brands.

Products and Services Mixed.

Products and services are often mixed. The car is a product. The insurance, maintenance, and financing are services.

The oil is a product; having it changed is a service.

Food, whether fast food (often referred to as QSR [Quick Service Restaurants]) or a meal in a sit-down restaurant, is a combination of both. Next time you visit a fast food restaurant, think about which is which – tangible and intangible.

Service marketers are deeply concerned with marketing because their product is so intangible.

In many ways, it is the marketing itself that gives a services product tangibility. The logo on the sign, coupons in your mail, and advertising for Jiffy Lube are a big part of what is tangible – besides the visit itself.

Other Marketing Specialities.

Most industries have some unique marketing aspects. Here is a quick summary of some of the major types of marketing:

- **Agricultural Marketing** – High-tech marketing, where your sophisticated target audience is wearing overalls.

    American Cyanamid and John Deere are examples. Other agricultural groups, like milk producers, advertise to us.

- **Cause Marketing** – From national charity groups, like the Children's Miracle Network, to local charities and community groups, marketing is an important part of keeping these groups operating.

    Think about that next time you receive a fund-raising mailing. Save the Children and United Way are examples.

- **Entertainment Marketing** – We'll cover this and "entertainment brands" in more detail in Chapter Six.

    The NFL, Walt Disney, and the University of Wyoming sports program are examples of this type of marketer.

    If you think about it, each supplies a fairly unique "benefit" to a very different target – even if that target is the same person.

    For example, I connect in very different ways to an NFL game on TV, a Disney movie at the CinePlex, and going to my home team's big game on Saturday – Go Cowboys!

- **Financial Services Marketing** – Banks, brokers, and insurance companies are each involved in the marketing of things having to do with money.

    CitiCorp, Fidelity, and MasterCard are examples.

    Brokers and insurance companies are each involved in the marketing of things having to do with money.

    And you are seeing these businesses begin to overlap – as changing regulations allow them to evolve into full-service financial marketers.

    This overlapping process is called **convergence**.

- **Healthcare Marketing** – This is a dynamic and growing field, involving hospitals, health insurance, pharmaceuticals, and other health providers.

    Pfizer, University of Chicago Physicians Group, and Blue Cross/Blue Shield are examples of this type of marketer.

- **High-Tech Marketing** – A growing and exciting field that has heavy components of public relations and "MarCom," which is short for marketing communications.

    Dell, Intel, and Cisco are examples of this type of marketer, as is every high-tech start-up.

- **Hospitality Marketing** – This category includes various types of travel and lodging.

    United Airlines, Hyatt, and Hertz are examples.

Types of Marketers.

Match the marketer with the type of marketing they do:

1. Hyatt
2. CitiCorp
3. John Deere
4. General Motors
5. Procter & Gamble
6. University of Wyoming Cowboys

A. Hospitality Marketing
B. Agricultural Marketing
C. Entertainment Marketing
D. Durable Goods Marketing
E. Packaged Goods Marketing
F. Financial Services Marketing

Answers: 1A, 2F, 3B, 4D, 5E, 6C.

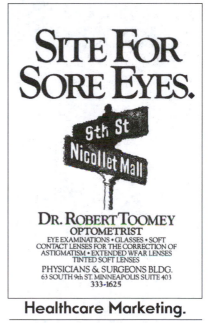

Healthcare Marketing.

It's national, regional, and local.

Hospitality Marketing.

This is a very unique type of product – ways to spend your leisure time.

Media Marketing.

It often markets to other marketers.

Small Marketers.

They need marketing, too.

Got Marketing?

Agriculture has to market, too.

- **Media Marketing** – This is becoming an even larger part of the marketing world. We'll discuss it in Chapter Six. *ESPN, Nickelodeon,* and *Forbes* are examples of this type of marketer.
- **Retail Marketing** – Every retailer is deeply involved in marketing. Even store location is a marketing decision. The Gap, Home Depot and Wal-Mart are examples of this type of marketer – as is every store in your community

Some of these specialties fall into a larger category – "B2B."

"B2B" (Business to Business) Marketing.

Many companies market to other companies.

For example, a manufacturer of baking equipment markets to those who operate bakeries. This industry has its own industry group, trade show, and at least one trade magazine.

This type of marketing is referred to as **business to business.**

One-third of Total Marketing Dollars.

Some estimate B2B as 33% of total marketing dollars.

It is characterized by highly specialized subcategories and marketing that may include heavy dependence on such things as trade shows and personal selling.

"IMC" before There Was "IMC."

As IMC guru Don Schultz observes, these marketers have been practicing integrated marketing communications (IMC) for years.

They prioritize and coordinate a wide variety of marketing tasks: advertising (22%), sales force (23%), sales promotions (6%), direct marketing (6%), trade shows (5.5%), public relations (2.6%), premiums (2%), and more. [Source: Business-to-Business Census. *Ad Age's Business Marketing.*]

DuPont, GE, and Silicon Graphics market business to business.

Marketing Agencies, Bureaus, and Organizations.

There's another interesting subgroup that is almost pure marketing – state tourism bureaus and agricultural groups like the American Dairy Association or the Cotton Council have marketing as their primary reason for being.

Their tasks might also include lobbying, a PR function which is, in some ways, marketing to a very, very small target.

Even our government is involved in marketing to us, urging us to be *"Army Strong"* or reminding us to *"Click It or Ticket."*

While there are similarities within product categories, each marketer has a marketing situation that is unique to them.

But even with all these differences, basic marketing tasks remain surprisingly similar. And virtually everything marketers do is based on five fundamentals.

Five Critical Marketing Decisions.

FIVE CRITICAL DECISIONS shape the marketing strategies and, ultimately, advertising messages. These five decisions – The Five P's – are:

- **Product**
- **Price**
- **Place** (physical distribution)
- **Promotion.** This includes most marketing activities you're familiar with – including advertising.
- **People.** Many marketers add this fifth P, since customers, employees, and others also play a role.

For our purposes, we will focus on the four most traditional areas of marketing decision making. But keep in mind that each is influenced by that fifth P.

Other P's?

Some people use **packaging** as a fifth P. However, important as it is, we consider it to be part of the product or, in some cases, an element of promotional activities.

The Five P's of Marketing.

By now, you should know that these are the Five P's of marketing. Memorize them. They will be on the test.

Let's quickly review the impact they can have on a brand.

1. Product.

It begins with the product.

As we spend the rest of the book focusing on how to promote and advertise our products and brands, do not lose sight of the basic truth that success in the marketplace depends on a good product. Bill Bernbach observed, *"Nothing will kill a bad product faster than good advertising."*

Functional Superiority.

As John Philip Jones notes, advertising works best when the product itself has "functional superiority." That is, the product has some useful advantage which the consumer recognizes.

P&G agrees. Its basic business principles include:

- Sell a better product
- Ensure there is consumer acceptance for your product and your product is not at a competitive disadvantage

Example: Mini-Van

The rise of the mini-van was a good example. Chrysler recognized a changing need and changing perceptions by consumers.

They reconfigured an existing automobile platform.

This offered a functional superiority to other configurations available. Note that this superiority has to be valued by the customer – not the engineering department.

Product Vision.

Often, the product is a result of a visionary individual – such as King Gillette and his razor blade.

John Dorrance had a vision – condensed soup. This would save on shipping. The consumer adds water.

This vision, and the commitment to make it come true, was key to the success of Campbell's Soup.

Product as Hero.

The initial vision of Absolut included packaging and advertising.

The added value of advertising is critical in a product that is essentially colorless and tasteless.

The Importance of Vision.

"Many of the great strategies are simply great visions.

"And great visions can be a lot more inspirational and effective than the most carefully constructed plan."

— Henry Mintzburg
The Rise and Fall of Strategic Planning

What's in a Name?

In addition to avoiding already registered names, a new brand name should emphasize attractive product attributes or features.

Allstate connotes widely available insurance products. Timex is the product's purpose. Jaguar says agility and speed.

Then again, would you choose a forgotten foreign racecar driver with a hard-to-pronounce name for a popular car brand? Yet…it's Chevrolet!

Brands and Brand Extensions.
The best brand names can be surprisingly long-lived. They pay off for those who practice persistence.

They accumulate goodwill that translates into future sales.

They also permit their success to be amplified as *brand extensions*.

Leveraging Equity.
Once, P&G had a new brand name for virtually every new product.

Today, with the cost of establishing a brand name greater than ever, more marketers look to leverage the equity of already existing brand names.

What's in a brand name?

More equity than ever.

Your friend just got friendlier.

Great taste + vitamins and minerals

Extending the Extension.

Over the years, Coca-Cola has added several flavors (cherry, lemon, vanilla, and lime) to its #1 brand extension, Diet Coke. Now, they've also added vitamins and minerals to make Diet Coke Plus.

And then, of course, in our competitive economy, others note the success and develop products as good or better – looking for a new version of "functional superiority."

"Added Value" and Brand Equity.
Like Campbell's, it often begins with a product concept but evolves into a brand concept. As the brand concept develops, added values take on increasing importance and build equity for the brand.

These added values are not a substitute for functional performance. They are in addition to that performance.

The stronger a brand becomes, the stronger these added values become. As it becomes easier for competitors to match functional characteristics, these added values become more important.

Another name for this collection of attributes is **brand equity.**

Smith-Kline, for example, has brand equity managers. This serves to focus the whole organization on its mission and, to some extent, it protects brands against short-term volume objectives that may not be in the brand's long-term interest.

Product Concept.
Howard Schultz, founder of Starbucks, began with a product concept which combined product and environment – *"the goal was to add value to a commodity typically purchased on supermarket aisles."* This was their functional superiority.

The opportunity might not be obvious. For example, Schultz's "Milan epiphany" of Italian-style coffee bars was not apparent by studying the US coffee market. It needed a product and a service vision.

Brand Name and Brand Concept.
Finally, an important part of the product is what you call it – the brand name. Russell and Lane define a brand as:

"A name, term, sign design, or a unifying combination intended to identify and distinguish the product or service from competing products or services."

At first, this name may not mean much, but its value can grow. Aspects of the product may change, but the brand will endure – an asset that can grow over time.

Jones observes, *"A brand enters the world naked and must rely almost solely on its functional properties for its initial survival. The majority of the large number of new brands that do not succeed fail precisely because of their functional weaknesses.*

"Old and successful brands build up a large stock of added values in the goodwill of their users, so a new brand whose manufacture has ambitions of overtaking them must start off with a generous margin of functional superiority to make any progress."

Packaging.
For packaged goods, this is another critical dimension – some even consider it a separate P. It covers factors such as package graphics, size, shelf presence, and usage information.

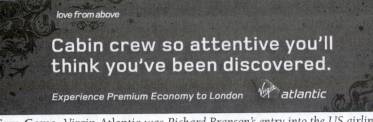

Fare Game. *Virgin Atlantic was Richard Branson's entry into the US airline market. In mature categories, experienced consumers may begin to view certain products, such as a plane trip, as more of a commodity. When that happens, price can re-emerge as a defining factor.*

Already positioned as the low-price option for "Premium Economy" flights, Virgin Atlantic stresses service and amenities in some of its recent ads.

A Branded Product Is More Than the Product Itself.

Over time, a brand becomes a mixture of physical attributes, the customer's perceptions and experience, and a legal identity that links the firm with its offerings.

2. Price.

Henry Ford's success with the Model T was not merely a triumph of manufacturing technology. He lowered the car's price to make it affordable for a larger number of Americans.

In turn, this larger market helped make profitable mass production possible. In many ways, the price was the Model T's functional superiority.

Then, as we discussed in Chapter One, GM came close on the price while offering better styling, more variety, and easier financing. This was their functional superiority.

The *New York Sun* initially charged 1¢ per copy for a similar reason. It used this low price to build a large circulation base.

Today, many new products fail when a minor increase in performance is not judged worth a major price differential.

In this case, the superiority is not functional.

As you can see in the sidebar, Dell Computer began with a price advantage based on their distribution (place) strategy, but evolved to add superior customer contact as a brand value. As the business becomes more challenging, they are trying to evolve further.

The Importance of Margin.

Another important aspect of pricing is **margin.** Margin is the difference between selling price and the seller's cost of goods.

Gross margin counts the entire difference. **Net margin** is reduced to reflect the cost of any value added by the seller.

Example: Apple

Apple Computer kept its margins high by keeping its prices high. Unlike Microsoft, Apple restricted licensing of its software (their operating system), making it available only through its own brand of hardware (its computers).

Over the short term, Apple made quite a bit of money.

Dell – Price & Place.

Michael Dell decided to sell his computers direct. It was a defining part of his strategy.

Dell takes orders, manufactures, ships product direct, and maintains a support system customers can access directly.

No wholesalers. No retailers.

Additional Advantages.
The cost of finished inventory sitting in the trade channel was eliminated.

The speed of product change in the computer industry made Dell look even smarter in retrospect.

And More Strategic Advantage.
Dell's initial strategy was based on the cost advantages of direct sales and manufacturing to order.

Over time, contact with customers became a further strategic advantage as they moved from the initial sale to a long-term relationship.

Strengthening customer relationships, Dell grew even stronger – no longer competing on price alone.

This is a classic example of a marketer thinking strategically – using one or more of the Five P's to achieve competitive advantage.

In this case, price and place.

But Shifts Happen.
Due to some product problems, tougher competition, and customers making the move to laptops, which they wanted to see and touch before buying, Dell ran into rough road.

Michael Dell became re-involved. He is working to rebuild marketing momentum, with much of this new growth coming from overseas.

Why don't you look for a recent story on Dell and see how he's doing?

PC vs. Mac

A lower price differential makes it easier to emphasize other aspects of Apple's functional superiority.

Stretching for More Margin.

Nike is a very competitive company that used margin as a weapon to hammer the competition.

They used that margin to fund celebrity athlete endorsements and the heaviest ad support in the history of the shoe category.

That wasn't all. Nike also used margin to add an important new member to the team – the retailer – that key secondary target that helps them make the final sale.

It was a win/win proposition.

Brewing Extra Margin.

Plenty of margin in every cup was part of **Howard Schultz's** strategy for Starbucks. This allowed Starbucks to pay for prime retail locations and provide a slightly better-than-average package of employee benefits.

More Margin Brews Up More Competition.

Starbucks' success was not lost on McDonald's and Dunkin' Donuts – two franchise operations that already served a lot of coffee. It motivated them to produce improved offerings.

Over the long term, weaknesses in this pricing strategy caught up with them. Apple's share of market was relatively small.

Apple was not an attractive market for software developers. The higher price and smaller software selection scared away potential new customers while providing few if any reasons for current PC users to switch – particularly since PCs were priced much lower than Macs.

Now, with a lower price differential, Apple is able to get more leverage with other functionally superior aspects of its products.

Margin as Competitive Advantage.

In the '60s, Phil Knight of Nike bet that joggers would pay a premium for high-quality running shoes.

This meant extra money for a better product and extra margin for better marketing – particularly to fund advertising and pay for the signing of star athletes to use in that advertising.

As sales grew and costs were reduced by less expensive overseas manufacturing, Nike was able to leverage increased margin to fund high-powered marketing and sponsorships.

In each case, from Model Ts to Apples to Air Jordans pricing decisions were a critical part of their marketing.

And when Howard Schultz brewed his first Starbucks, he put plenty of margin into each cup. Now, he's finding more competitors attracted by those good margins.

Margin Starvation – A Common Problem.

Many products "starve" in the marketplace because there is not enough margin to support marketing activities.

The brand can get stuck in a difficult situation – sales without promotion are too low and sales with promotion are too expensive. It's a tough spot for a brand – and quite common.

In many cases, this problem may be compounded by a lack of functional superiority.

The brand is not perceived as worth the extra cost which would generate the margin necessary to fund advertising.

And, because the brand is not supported with advertising or sales promotion, these perceptions are difficult to change. As a result, the brand starves for lack of adequate communication with the potential buyer.

Price as Product Information.

Pricing can also communicate additional information about the product to sophisticated consumers – and most consumers are sophisticated.

A high price can mean many things. So can a low price.

Conventional economic theory says high prices are bad and low prices are good, but you may have noticed that conventional economists do not buy high-priced cosmetics.

The comparison table below shows some additional meanings for high and low prices.

Consumer Connotations of High and Low Price:

High Price	Low Price
High quality	Low quality
Finest ingredients	Lowest cost ingredients
Scarce amounts available	Surplus amounts available
Highly fashionable	Low/poor fashionability
Perishable	Long shelf life
Durable	Wears out quickly
High technology	Low technology
High resale value	Low resale value
Poor consumer value	High consumer value
Few product substitutes	Many substitutes
High social visibility	Low social visibility

Setting the Price – A Key Management Decision.

The consequences of a price decision must also be anticipated and managed.

A few poor matches will illustrate this point:

- Discounted or very low price for a high-fashion women's brand of wristwatch could easily damage the image of exclusivity that advertising messages carry.
- High prices for in-season navel oranges or everyday household cleaning products can disrupt an ad message that these items are good values.

Price and Competition.

In addition, price can attract or repel competitors.

It can act as a "barrier to entry" or an invitation.

It can provoke or forestall governmental regulation.

Price can even reflect the stage of a particular product's life cycle, since many products cost more when they're first introduced and are sold at lower prices as economies of scale are reached and development costs are recovered.

The computer industry has been a fascinating example of this dynamic, exhibiting all these characteristics far faster than we've ever seen before.

"Milking."

Firms sometimes continue to sell a product long after advertising and other support has been discontinued – or reduced to the barest minimum.

This "milking" typically occurs in the mature phase of a product's life and may continue on into product "old age."

Selling Quality.

Keeping quality perceptions high can be a critical marketing task since those perceptions are critical in commanding a premium price from both customers and distributors.

Working to Change the Bottom Line

Can you change the world's perception of shoes with a single ad? Can you get enough margin to make enough money to pay for more advertising?

Changing the Price by Changing the Place.

People usually want to try shoes on before they buy. But Zappos made a strategic decision to use the Internet.

Small Profit. Big Business.

Wal-Mart's Mission: to buy in massive amounts, cut prices to the bone, distribute efficiently, and earn a small profit on huge quantities at low prices.

Channels. Sometimes Your Place is a Pipeline.

Another way of thinking of "Place" is by thinking about channels – your distribution pipeline.

They can also offer an opportunity for competitive advantage.

As we discussed, the marketplace continually creates new opportunities as it destroys others.

This is particularly true when it comes to channels – both media channels and distribution channels.

Distribution Channels.
Computer companies like Dell grew with direct channel marketing.

Starbucks grows their own distribution location by location, while Gevalia Coffee does it all by mail.

Please accept this elegant free gift in hunter green just for trying Gevalia® Kaffe. Or...

GEVALIA KAFFE
FINE COFFEES OF EUROPE

Catalog companies are now opening their own retail stores, and retailers are developing new catalogs.

And just about everyone is open for business on the Internet.

(Continued on next page)

By relying on the lingering effects of past advertising, margins may be retained in whole or part, even though this process may doom the brand in the long term.

Price and Profitability.
Finally, price is an essential element in the calculations that determine the brand's profitability.

Price the product too high and you have plenty of margin but small volume, a small share, and small (or no) profit.

Price the product too low and you may sell a lot but your product won't be very profitable unless enormous volumes can be sold. (Peter Drucker observes, *"Volume solves a host of problems."*)

Get stuck in the middle and you may have another set of problems. It's relatively easy to understand the basic principles of pricing – making them work can be very difficult.

3. Place – Physical Distribution.

This is another critical element of marketing decision making.

It is also a major cost and a major challenge for the brand.

The cost of putting a common grocery item on the shelf can be substantial. It is more than merely transportation.

As mentioned in Chapter Two, retailers have become bigger players in packaged goods marketing – often marketing their own private label products in competition with established brands which they also sell.

For examples, Coca-Cola dramatically reconfigured its global bottling operation to give the company substantially more distribution and marketing impact. This distribution focus even included converting an entire country – getting a leading Pepsi bottler (Venezuela) to become a Coke bottler.

"The Slotting Allowance."
By tracking UPC data, many sophisticated retailers are able to calculate the worth of the real estate on their shelves.

With new products and, in some cases, established products, they may charge a **slotting allowance** so that manufacturers must pay for the privilege of being on the shelf.

Getting adequate distribution is a critical part of every company's marketing. Physical distribution is that part of marketing responsible for moving product from maker to user.

Keeping distribution is another challenge. If a certain sales level is not maintained, a brand will often lose distribution. (The UPC data provides this information to the retailer.)

Two Elements – Transportation and Channels.
In general, physical distribution consists of two elements, transportation and channels of distribution.

Transportation is what it seems; it's the cost of moving goods from place to place. It is not, however, as simple or as isolated an activity as it might first seem.

Remember those shipping and handling charges that were added on to your last mail order? In fact, shipping and handling are a portion of the retail price of virtually everything we buy, even when these costs are not identified for you.

The Supply Chain.

Simply put, one part of price is getting things from here to there.

Marketers call it **the supply chain**.

Pick a situation – let's say one of your favorite restaurants – look at everything there. The menu items each come from a unique source. The paper products, the components of your favorite beverage – whether bottles and cans or dispensed through a machine that needs regular maintenance. The paper products. The posters on the wall. Get the picture?

Each comes from somewhere and shows up in, hopefully, a cost-efficient manner. And, as you might imagine, efficient management of the supply chain is part of what it takes to deliver the meal you want at a competitive price.

This is one of the aspects where Internet-based systems have brought real efficiencies into the system. Computerized inventory control – re-ordering, and providing a wider range of products and services with improved efficiency has delivered a wide range of benefits.

At the same time, many invested in less efficient aspects of the supply chain have found themselves in a difficult situation – another example of creative destruction providing benefits at the same time it delivers bad news to certain segments of the marketplace.

Distribution as Competitive Advantage.

Efficiency in this area can also create competitive advantage.

A key factor in the growth of Wal-Mart was a cost-efficient system of distribution. This enabled Wal-Mart to virtually wipe out smaller competitors who were dealing with smaller volumes and higher per-item costs.

Fed Ex is an example of an entire business founded on a distribution strategy. (FedEx founder Fred Smith first proposed a national air freight company with a hub in Memphis in a business school term paper. He only got a C.)

As discussed, Dell achieved initial success eliminating the entire retail channel. But markets change. Now they are adding retail partners and abandoning two core principles – exclusive online sales and owning their own factories.

Returns.

Even the cost of returning unsold items can be a factor.

In the book industry, for example, publishers often ship product to retailers on what amounts to a consignment basis.

This is especially common with large chain distributors.

The terms call for "payment (to supplier) on sale," and while the retailer contributes value in the form of a retail setting, the publisher bears the financial risks of the book inventory.

Channels (Cont.)

Media Channels.
You're well aware of all the new media channels opening up – cable and the Internet are two examples.

Consumer Channels.
Now every consumer has his or her own finance system – a credit card.

And every consumer now has a multi-media communication system – a TV, wireless and landline phone, computer, and mailbox.

Connecting through these channels will become more important.

Expanding Brands.
Today, manufacturers, direct sellers, retailers, and media companies are invading each other's "turf" as they expand their brands.

Each uses the P of place to search for competitive advantage.

Changing the Game.

As a wave of gourmet coffees hit the marketplace, the Gevalia brand team took another look at their strategy.

Their new promotional campaign shifted from free gifts to the exclusivity of the Gevalia European product.

Playing the Field.

After graduating, Todd Holscher started at a small Kansas City agency.

When a big client left, Todd had a chance to re-evaluate his career path. He decided he wanted more control over actual marketing.

Clients suggested Frito-Lay – a place where you could "learn a ton."

Todd applied and was hired.

On the Truck.

Field marketing at Frito-Lay starts with getting on a truck and running a route – for about 18 months.

What drove Todd to do it?

"I was beginning to understand the importance of shelf display.

"Brand equity is good – but you need 'pounds on the floor.'"

"I also liked feeling that instant feedback you get when you're doing it out there in the real world."

"Jim Roy."

We asked Todd what Frito-Lay had taught him. He said: "Jim Roy."

Actually, that stands for GM/ROI.

GM is gross margin.

ROI is return on investment.

It's how Todd learned to think about generating the best results.

The W/ITS Formula.

The "W" stands for Who – the target.

"I" is for Inventory – the amount you have on the shelf or on the floor.

"T" stands for Turns – the number of times your inventory turns in a year. Get more turns, and the same shelf space becomes more profitable.

"S" stands for Share – the result of Inventory times Turns.

Promoted to district manager, Frito-Lay helped pay for his MBA.

Todd's career moved him on to new fields, but his time in the field at Frito-Lay served him well.

The music industry also works this way. CDs and audio cassettes are often distributed in this manner.

Doing business this way isn't easy – for the producers or the retailers. When appliance discounters began using top-selling CDs as loss leaders to stimulate traffic, it had a disastrous impact on CD retailers – causing many to go out of business.

This had a subsequent effect on the CD manufacturers, who now had fewer retail distribution points in their channel.

Then Napster hit – a double disaster.

Three More Points about Distribution.

Three more points about these "middleman" functions.

First, these functions need to be performed, whether or not independent firms do them. If a company decides to sell directly, it must do the jobs usually done by other companies in the distribution channel – including generate customers.

Second, firms in many categories can compete with each other by performing the physical distribution differently. Gevalia Coffee and Bose are excellent examples.

Finally, if you're successful with this strategy, like Dell, expect competition – like Gateway.

Apple has also gone through a few channel-based evolutions, starting with exclusive retail relationships, then looking to maximize sales (and margins) with more emphasis on direct sales.

Then, shifting again, with Apple stores, while still selling through existing chains.

Gateway opened stores. Then they closed them.

The game keeps changing.

Place – Physical Location.

In some cases, the cost of distribution is even greater – because you have to build the distribution point yourself.

For example, with a restaurant chain such as McDonald's the cost of distribution includes real estate and construction.

McDonald's created a national brand for hamburgers by running their stores right. They also put them in the right place.

Kinko's early growth was based on finding locations near a campus. Their business strategy evolved into including small businesses and home offices. Now, they're a part of Fed Ex. Clearly, this will create more change in their location-based operating strategy.

For retailers, this is one of the most critical marketing decisions – an initial real estate decision can be the difference between success and failure. It can be very difficult to market your way out of a bad location. In retail, it is worth saying again that the three most important things are location, location, and location.

There's even a type of marketing that focuses on local markets and local distribution outlets – it's called **field marketing.**

A Great Source of Entry-Level Jobs. Field marketing helps make marketing happen in individual markets. Follow-up is key – to make sure the program that was planned at headquarters is implemented in the field. Below, Little Caesars' advertises for regional managers with five years minimum experience. Jobs! Jobs!

Field Marketing.

Many larger marketers – particularly franchise organizations and beverage companies (beer and soft drinks) – use field marketing to strengthen local marketing.

A national network of "field reps" operates as virtually a second marketing force. This often involves working with franchise groups, distributors, local outlets, or special promotional partners.

Here are some typical field marketing activities:

- Working with local media – TV, radio, and outdoor.
- Coordinating national or local marketing programs, such as marketwide events and in-store programs.

For example, many campus events you've experienced probably had a field marketing person behind the scenes.

- Developing specific marketing tactics, such as producing and placing direct mail programs.
- Working with or developing promotional partners.
- Entertaining important clients.

Field marketing is an excellent source of entry-level marketing jobs. It provides an introduction to a wide variety of marketing activities and can provide real responsibility.

4. Promotion.

Finally, there's promotion. This is an initial overview.

Much of the rest of the book will cover this "P."

Promotion Is More than Advertising.

The promotional activity we're most aware of is advertising.

As discussed in Chapter Two, there are many other ways marketers promote their brands, particularly as we enter a new world of emerging media. Here's an initial list:

- **Direct Marketing**
- **Direct Sales**
- **Event Marketing**
- **Merchandising** (including package design)
- **Public Relations and Publicity**
- **Sales and Retail Relations**
- **Corporate Giving**
- **Sales Promotion**
- **Trade Shows**

Experiential Marketing.

There's a new kind of marketing that seeks to grow and deepen the brand experience in new and innovative ways – experiential marketing.

A-B's "Bud World" is an example.

It turns the brand itself into an event – with aspects of presence and lifestyle marketing mixed in.

Experiential marketing takes a true 360 degree approach to the brand – literally immersing consumers.

A-to-S Ratios.

One of the more interesting statistics in marketing is the A-to-S Ratio. This stands for Advertising to Sales.

It measures the relative proportion of the advertising budget as part of the overall sales volume.

It can be high, as with distilled liquor, or low, as in cold-rolled steel.

Here are some examples:

Product Category	Ad $ as % of sales	Ad $ as % of margin
Ag chemicals	1.7	4.7
Amusement parks	7.0	14.3
Apparel	5.1	11.1
Beverages	7.3	11.6
Cosmetics	7.4	16.1
Dairy Products	1.4	6.3
Distilled liquor	15.6	25.9
Eating places	3.1	11.8
Grocery stores	0.9	3.2
Household A/V Equip	5.3	41.8
Retail stores	3.7	8.6
Steel works	0.2	0.8
Sugar & confections	5.9	17.2
Watches	9.3	18.2
Wine, brandy	3.6	10.6

2007 data from adage.com

Changing the Game

Reed Hastings of Netflix, inspired by a massive late fee for an overdue DVD and the flat monthly amount he paid for his gym membership (regardless of how much he worked out), wondered what the rental business would be like if customers could pay only a monthly rental fee and skip the video store by doing business through the mail.

The business model worked. Netflix now has over 8 million subscribers.

The Right Chord.

Finding the right combination of marketing communication and getting everyone to play in harmony can be a challenge.

IBM has been a leader in this area, evolving their strategy from selling business machines to selling software and services. To do this, one of their key ingredients has been the fifth P – people.

We'll be covering most of these additional "non-advertising" promotional activities in Chapter Seven, "Marketing Services."

Promotion/Sales Promotion.
All of these disciplines are "promotion" in the larger sense – they promote the brand. Throughout this book, when we refer to any promotional activity or any combination of promotional activities, we may call this "promotion."

When we are specifically referring to sales promotion, we will attempt to refer to it as exactly that – sales promotion.

However, once you leave this book, you will enter a world where people may say "promotion" when referring to sales promotion.

Marketing Communications, also known as "MarCom."
We call this array of activities marketing communications. Some, particularly on the West Coast, refer to it as "MarCom."

With such a wide variety of choices, it is necessary that efforts be prioritized (few brands have enough to do all they wish to do). Most marketers try to coordinate or integrate these activities for the best result.

IMC = Integrated Marketing Communications.
The declining effectiveness of traditional advertising and the rising cost and declining profitability of sales promotion has led marketers to take another look at virtually every marketing option.

That's why, today, so many are concerned with the practice of integrated marketing communications (or IMC). This approach requires that the firm's marketing communications be coordinated and performed as an integrated activity.

Often, the promotional activities themselves must also be coordinated and integrated. For example, an event might also need advertising and public relations support in the beginning and follow-up afterwards. Support may also include staffing the booth which promotes the brand and developing a Web site for sign-ups.

As marketing departments and marketing budgets have all become larger, this has grown into a major issue.

However, it is not usually a problem for brands with small budgets and one-man departments. They have their own sets of problems, but integration isn't usually one of them.

Don Schultz, author of *Integrated Marketing Communications,* notes that many smaller marketers, particularly those in industrial marketing, have been "integrated" for years.

However, for large brands and major marketers, coordinating the efforts of ad agencies, sales promotion, and public relations specialists, as well as a sales force, can be daunting.

As audiences fragment and communications channels multiply, this is becoming one of the most critical tasks in marketing.

To maximize the benefits of effective promotion, it is necessary that these activities be coordinated with the other P's.

The product must deliver on the functional superiority communicated in the promotional message.

The product must be in place – so it can be purchased.

The price must include enough margin to pay for the necessary promotional programs. And one more thing. People.

5. People – The Fifth P.

For years, there were the Four P's of Marketing.

Yet many noted there was a Fifth P – people.

In most cases, this is the consumer. But, there may also be internal "consumers" – like a sales force or service employees.

Howard Schultz gives his people a lot of credit for Starbucks' success, calling the baristas "the best ambassadors for the brand."

Here are some of the ways smart marketers try to add this fifth dimension to their marketing:

- **Sales Analysis** – Consumers tell marketers a lot by their purchasing patterns. By analyzing current sales and competitive sales results, marketers can develop a more accurate picture of their market.
- **Market Research** – There is an entire industry dedicated to developing additional information on the marketplace.
- **Consumer Insight and Account Planning** – Understanding people is an art as well as a science. Using intuitive techniques, anthropology, ethnography, and traditional market research, consumer insight professionals help marketers develop a deeper understanding of their customers – present and future.
- **Communications Marketing** – The classic example. Naked, a cutting edge communications consultancy, told the British drug chain Boots to stop advertising a prescription service. Instead, they told Boots to train their in-store staff to sell the services to those wanting to fill their prescriptions. Increased success. Reduced marketing costs. People make the difference.

Product, price, place, promotion, and people – you now understand the Five P's. Now, how do you combine them?

The Marketing Mix.

PUTTING ALL THESE THINGS TOGETHER in just the right way is a complex process – this is the "marketing mix."

But there's a simple word for it – **strategy.**

Strategy is a term borrowed from military science. In military circles, it means the science of planning and directing large-scale operations, capable of having decisive influence on the overall outcome of a war.

It places special emphasis on maneuvering forces and positioning resources so as to achieve the desired outcome before actually engaging the enemy.

Marketing Ingredients.

With the Five P's as a background, you can now understand some of the concepts that marketers deal with as they try to get the right "mix."

Here are some examples:

ACV.

All Commodity Volume. The total volume of all products in a category – key for planning and computing volume and dollar share.

ADI.

Area of Dominant Influence. A geographic and media coverage approach that divides the US into media-based marketing territories. For example, the Chicago ADI includes parts of Indiana.

A-to-S Ratio.

Advertising to Sales Ratio. A numerical concept useful for both planning and budgeting. On page 195, we listed A-to-S ratios for a number of different industries. Some are low. Some are relatively high.

BDI.

Brand Development Index. A measure of the relative usage level of a brand in various regions (usually by ADI). For most brands, you will find areas of high and low BDI. Sometimes it is by geography, sometimes by demography, and sometimes by seasonality – often, by all three.

OOS.

Out of Stock. Usually a reflection of a distribution problem. It may be great success (product flying off the shelves), great failure (the product sitting in warehouse, retailers not re-ordering), or something in between (mismatch with manufacturing).

SKU.

Store Keeping Unit. If a product comes in a number of different sizes, usually with a different price and a different number of packages per carton, each of these is an SKU, even though the brand may be the same.

Some products, such as diapers, have a huge variety of SKUs. Others have a smaller number of SKUs.

Strategic Innovation.

Corporate strategy guru Gary Hamel observes a number of factors that help to stimulate strategic innovations:

New Voices.

Innovators listen for new voices – not the same people reinforcing existing perceptions.

Whether the customer's voice or previously unheard voices within a company, here is one key source of new perspectives.

New Connections.

Howard Schultz of Starbucks made his in a Milan coffee shop.

For the owners of Caribou Coffee, it happened in Alaska as a herd of caribou thundered by.

At its root, connections are based on *pattern recognition*, the perception of relationships and opportunities that occurs before they're obvious to everyone.

It's one reason innovations tend to elude rational analysis.

New Perspectives.

Seeing business a new way can help a company leap past the status quo. Michael Dell saw a way to cut costs while matching the speed of change in the computer market.

Then he saw how his company's direct connection could leverage a new level of customer service.

New Passions.

Starting a new business needs more than a new business plan, it needs total commitment of key players.

A passion for fashion was a critical part of The Gap's change from one more store in the mall to a complete fashion and value statement.

Experimentation.

In the beginning, a strategy is an hypothesis – a vision. (Remember Gillette's original idea of a product you would use and throw away?)

Success is often a result of keeping at it till you get it right – and making your vision come true.

To get that vision, you may need some stimulation – to recognize that pattern before everyone else does.

In business, strategy involves planning, pre-positioning, and assaying your resources in a way that correctly anticipates competitor actions and customer response and allows the firm to achieve its desired overall result.

In contrast, tactics (both military and business) involve the way you put that strategy into action.

As Churchill said, *"War is my strategy. Victory is my objective."*

Marketing Strategy.

A marketing strategy is a configuration of the Five P's that is believed will maximize the brand's opportunities for success in the marketplace.

Remember, a strategy is an hypothesis – a best guess – and then a blueprint as to how to do it best.

In his classic book *The Mind of the Strategist*, Kenichi Ohmae, head of McKinsey/Japan observes…

"In business as on the battlefield, the object of strategy is to bring about the conditions most favorable to one's own side.

"In strategic thinking, one first seeks a clear understanding of the particular character of each element of a situation and then makes the fullest possible use of human brainpower to restructure the elements in the most advantageous way…

"…a breakthrough to the best possible solution can come only from a combination of rational analysis based on the real nature of things, and imaginative reintegration of all the different items into a new pattern, using non-linear brainpower."

The Right Combination. The Right Strategy.

It's as true in marketing as it is in cooking – the right mix of ingredients is not the same for every company. For example, take a basic cake mix which, if made following instructions on the box, produces a conventional cake.

However, if more shortening is added, the mixture can produce a waffle. If more flour is added, the result could be a cookie. If the proportion of other ingredients is changed, it's possible to make all sorts of different baked goods.

Are these variations "wrong?"

It depends on the intentions of the cook.

Even big companies can capitalize on mistakes – an early manufacturing error resulted in a batch of Ivory Soap being made with too much air. When Harley Procter received requests for "the soap that floats," he had the instincts to make the most of it.

In a similar process, each company's marketing ideally should be a unique combination of the right amount of each P, chosen to produce the intended result.

There's More than One Strategy.

Practitioners use the term strategy in a variety of ways.

One often hears terms like **copy strategy**, **research strategy**, and **pricing strategy**.

These are subsets of a key document – the **marketing strategy**. But the core business strategy may be a much simpler thing – a broadly visionary perspective.

To be effective in today's fast-changing marketplace, a dimension of innovation is often necessary to achieve success. More innovation may be necessary to maintain success.

Most often, the story of successful marketers and successful brands is both the story of functionally superior products and of innovative business and marketing strategies.

Strategic Innovation.

Marketing guru Gary Hamel defines strategy innovation as *"the ability to reinvent the basis of competition within existing industries and to invent entirely new industries."*

Strategic innovation may be linear – such as Henry Ford building a better, cheaper car with early mass production techniques, or Wal-Mart lowering overhead, improving distribution, and locating in smaller markets with higher-priced competition.

More and more, Hamel notes, strategic innovation will come from *"re-inventing the basis of competition."* We agree.

In retailing, Home Depot invented itself and The Gap re-invented itself to create new wealth for their companies as they captured increased share of their categories.

In the intensely competitive clothing business, The Gap, under the leadership of Mickey Drexler, went from 1.2% to a 4.6% share in less than ten years. This is huge. They evolved from featuring other brands to becoming their own brand.

With a new "superstore" concept for the category, Home Depot's share rose from 0% to 12.5% over this same period (1988–1997).

Example: The Importance of Vision

By having a larger vision of his brand, Richard Teerlink turned a nearly bankrupt company with a storied brand into a profitable powerhouse. People now wait months for his product – even with plenty of lower-priced competition to choose from.

Customers feel like a part of the company.

In a world of give-away T-shirts, people pay hundreds of dollars for clothing with the company's logo on it.

The brand? Harley-Davidson!

Luck Helps.

Strategic innovation can also be the result of luck as well as foresight. Howard Schultz of Starbucks and Phil Knight of Nike each had a vision – so did King Gillette at the turn of the century – their vision came true.

Fred Smith thought that the bulk of their business would be things like pharmaceuticals and critical oil-field equipment – not documents. He started FedEx a few critical years before everyone had a fax machine. By the time the fax machine was common, FedEx had enough volume to remain a viable business.

Innovation by Accident.

The Jobe's Tree Spikes Story.

One night, a guy at the fertilizer plant left the mixer on too long.

In the morning, there were all these hard clumps of fertilizer in the bottom of the mixing bin.

Instead of throwing them out, one of the supervisors looked at the lumps thoughtfully. He took a few to an agricultural expert he knew.

"What," he asked, *"would happen if you stuck one of these clumps near the roots of a tree or shrub?"*

About a year later they discovered they had a new long-term fertilizer delivery system – and Jobe's Tree Spikes were born!

Accidents happen – sometimes there's a good idea hidden inside – even inside fertilizer!

An Earlier Lucky Accident.

Something like this happened many years earlier.

A workman at Harley Procter's soap factory over-mixed some soap, causing air bubbles to get in the mixture. As a result, the soap floated.

"It Floats!" became the slogan for Ivory Soap, helping to make it a best-seller for many years.

CEO & ROI.

The power of the CEO to impact operations is dramatized in the performance of the Coca-Cola Company.

When Robert Goizueta took over in 1980, he embarked on a strategy that transformed the company.

Strategy for the 1980s.

That was the title of the plan he handed out – a mission focused on achieving a meaningful Return On Investment (ROI) in every division.

When Goizueta started, the company had many divisions, some not worth the time, attention, and capital used. If superior ROI could not be achieved, the division was sold off.

CEO Goizueta forced the Coca-Cola Company to focus on what was important. In this case, ROI.

Find out more in *I'd Like the World to Buy a Coke: The Life and Leadership of Robert Goizueta,* by David Greising.

As Gary Hamel observes, *"Foresight doesn't occur in a sterile vacuum; it emerges in the fertile loam of experience, coincident trends, unexpected conversations, random musings, career detours and (even) unfulfilled aspirations.*

"Strategy needs to be a way of understanding what's going on in your industry." And then *"…turning it on its head and envisioning the opportunities that fall out."*

That's the future. Meanwhile, all young marketers need to learn the basics of making a marketing plan year after year – and the place you do that is in a marketing department.

Let's take a look at how they're organized.

The Marketing Department.

MANY MARKETING FUNCTIONS were once performed by ad agencies on behalf of their clients – companies that had manufacturing expertise but (with a few notable exceptions) little marketing expertise. Today, that is no longer true.

From Advertising to the Modern Marketplace…

As discussed in Chapter One and Chapter Two, modern marketing is, in many ways, an outgrowth of advertising and agencies. That was then; this is now.

Today, marketers and marketing departments are the dominant force with their own internal expertise and resources.

More and more, marketing is becoming their core function.

As our marketplace has become more sophisticated, marketing has grown in importance and marketing departments have grown in size and complexity.

Advertising – Still Important.

Once, the primary function of the marketing department was to supervise the advertising and some trade relations.

Now, for many companies, it's only one part of a larger process – though, in many cases, still one of the most important. Here's why:

- It's usually a large amount of money.
- It's a company's main contact with consumers and a major part of its "public face."
- It is a variable that is under the control of the marketer – many other variables may not be.
- It is incredibly "elastic." That is, the difference in possible performance of very good or very bad advertising could be ±300%. This is a huge variability factor – making it inherently risky and attractive at the same time.

Let's Get Organized.

First, let's look at the organizational structures used by marketers to do those jobs. Then we'll look at who does what and for whom.

This will help you understand the process and visualize where you might fit in working for a marketer.

Overall Organization – Part One.

Most large companies have a marketing department. It's one of the most important – just one step down from top management.

CEO, COO, CFO, CIO, CMO – The Initials at the Top.

In a large company, the **CEO** (chief executive officer) oversees large issues related to a company's performance.

The **COO** (chief operating officer) is in charge of day-to-day operations, with major department heads reporting to the COO.

The **CFO** (chief financial officer) has major responsibilities and involvement in anything to do with money and is in charge of keeping the financial records in order.

With the increasing importance of information technology (IT), the **CIO** (chief information officer) is now a new player at the top. The CIO's specialty is MIS (management information systems).

Now it is becoming more and more common to refer to the chief marketing officer as the **CMO**. This reflects the growing importance of marketing within companies – as marketing has become a more central function of every business.

As the marketing function grows in importance, deep involvement by the CEO and COO is also more and more common.

For example, PepsiCo's 1997 decision to sell its restaurants in order to focus on its marketing struggle with Coke seems to have been the personal decision of their CEO, Roger Enrico.

Much of Coke's marketing was the result of the strategic leadership of CEO Robert Goizueta working with CMO Sergio Zyman.

More and more, top players at every company are concerned with marketing. Those are the players – and the initials.

Now let's talk about you. Where might you find a place to get started in a marketing organization?

Starting at the Bottom of the Chart – Or... off the Chart!

Though both are now key members of marketing departments, both Adam Seever at Coke and David Peacock at Anheuser-Busch began in low-level positions at agencies.

Adam started in sports marketing at Frankel – one of Coke's sales promotion agencies – and David started as an Assistant Media Planner at one of A-B's advertising agencies.

In retrospect, David sees that companies like A-B are always looking for people. *"We have a pipeline into local markets,"* he says. *"Our field marketing operations are like a farm team – always looking to identify prospects with potential."*

Now let's take a look at those organization charts.

Top to bottom. And side to side.

Horizontal & Vertical Organizations.

THE TWO PRIMARY WAYS to organize marketing and brand management are vertical and horizontal. Initially, marketing departments developed the traditional way, adding levels as the department grew.

The result was a vertical structure.

Brewing up Double-Digit Growth.

This is Bridgette Heller when she was VP general manager of Gevalia Coffee, at Kraft/General Foods.

She helped build KGF's mail-order gourmet coffee business to more than $150 million.

Growth rates continued to perk – in double digits.

The Gevalia Team.

KGF has a traditional vertical structure (General Foods – the GF in KGF – was a brand management pioneer).

At the time they won their Effie, Gevalia was led by Bridgette Heller, VP general manager.

Global President –Baby Care, J&J From coffee to baby oil - Bridgette Heller now runs one of Johnson & Johnson's most innovative marketing units – baby care.

Her prior experience in direct marketing at Gevalia helped at J&J, as the division has grown with an online Baby Center unit and opened 10 new markets worldwide.

Division growth has been 8% over the last two years – so her new baby is still growing.

Vice President General Manager Bridgette Heller

Category Business Director Steve Mason

Senior Brand Manager Maria Scarlata

Gevalia Brand Group

Life after Elvis –
Building Bud Budgets.

After leaving Kansas University (and Elvis Advertising), David Peacock looked for an opportunity on consumer packaged goods.

Though he thought he might like to write ads, he took the best job he could find – as an Assistant Media Planner at DMB&B in St. Louis.

On the Move.

As David said, "I walked in through the media door." It was a good move. He moved up to Planner.

Then, when A-B, the agency's biggest account, took their media in-house, David watched as A-B hired almost the whole department.

He had a chance to go client side and join the Busch Media Group.

He took the chance.

He moved up through the A-B organization, but not in a straight line. He moved from the media group to sales promotion, working in the Bud family. Then, to Senior Manager for all brand promotions.

That latest promotion took him into financial planning.

Since marketing is such a large part of A-B expenditures, his experience has made him valuable at a new level in corporate management. In 2007, he was named VP of Marketing – it was a long way from Elvis.

From the King to King of Beers.

More recently, more fluid, and often more highly technical enterprises have developed using a horizontal structure.

And, you might not be surprised that some organizations may operate with aspects of both.

Let's look at the vertical structure first.

Vertical Structure – Brand Management/Ad Management.

The concept of a vertical organization dates back to the earliest days of modern industrialization and much earlier forms of governmental and military organizations.

As departments grew, traditional consumer goods companies, especially the largest among them, commonly organized the marketing function into vertical hierarchies.

The Most Common Organizational Unit Is the Brand.

As brands grew in number and as families of brands were extended, the organizational chart became deeper and wider.

A simple organizational chart for a well-established marketing department might look something like this.

Marketing Department – Vertical Organization:

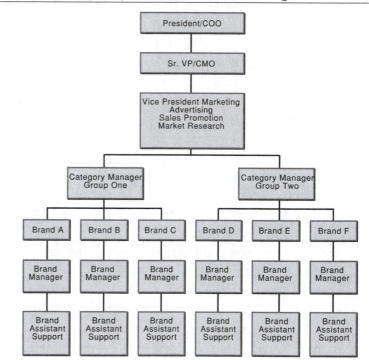

Brand Support Staff.

Depending on the size of the brand, support staff might consist of one **brand assistant** or a whole **brand group** with brand assistants, a dedicated market research person, and perhaps some sort of sales promotion resource.

The vertical structure fixes clear responsibility and a command structure that is central to department operations.

Sales promotion and market research may be separate groups, or specialists may be assigned to the brand groups.

Remember our definition from the beginning of the book? *"A brand is a conceptual entity that focuses the organization of marketing activities."* Hold that thought.

Example: Anheuser-Busch

Now look at how this definition from the beginning of the book impacts Anheuser-Busch's marketing organization.

Even though they compete in only one large category – beer – the needs of their brands created a very sophisticated marketing organization with four large groups:
- Brand Management,
- Media and Sports Marketing,
- Retail Marketing (A-B's name for Field Marketing), and
- Sales.

There are also two smaller groups:
- Ad Traffic and Talent Payment and
- Marketing Operations, a research function.

Here's how it looks.

Remember "Whassup?"

A-B works to develop entertaining ads that appeal to their primary target – young male beer drinkers.

Much of the work for Budweiser also ends up supporting Bud Light, the primary brand extension.

As you can see, advertising is just a part of what the department does.

Anheuser-Busch Marketing:

Working Together across Divisions.

Even though the reporting lines go up and down, day-to-day, all the groups work together to move the brands ahead.

Example: Bud Bowl

A-B's Super Bowl efforts are an excellent example.

Nationally, they plan Bud Bowl with NFL sponsorship.

Locally, retail marketing creates on-premise programs.

The Sales Promotion Group develops support materials.

Busch Media plans media buys.

Promotional Products creates special items.

Image Development even creates a special Super Bowl neon sign.

Organizing across Categories.

Some marketers, like P&G, compete in many product categories.

At the top of their organization, they have **category managers**. At P&G, Category designations are: Baby Care, Beauty Care, Fabric and Home Care (formerly Packaged Soaps and Detergents), Feminine Protection, Food and Beverage, Health Care and New Ventures, and Tissue and Towel.

Unique Brand Needs.

The unique needs of a brand can have a dramatic impact on the organization of brand management.

For example, think of something as simple as signage.

Image Development.

The cumulative value of A-B signage in bars and restaurants is quite large.

In fact, there is an entire department dedicated to the design, and production of signage.

Presence Marketing.

Another unique marketing function is what A-B calls Presence Marketing.

This covers participation in music and other lifestyle events like festivals.

Ethnic Marketing.

Once a separate division, ethnic marketing programs are now integrated into A-B brand management.

Working to Make it Simple.

Telecommunications is a complex business. Sprint may seem like one brand to you, but it's actually two companies – Sprint PCS, a growing wireless network, which subsequently merged with Nextel, and Sprint, which ranges from traditional local phone service to Internet connections.

Headphones and Media.

Pam Kramer, as Sprint Director of Advertising, had responsibility for the consumer long-distance business – like their Nickel Nights program.

Previously, she worked on projects like their NFL headphone program – where NFL coaches wore Sprint headphones on the sidelines.

She also supervised media buying with Sprint's agency – a big job, since they spend over $200 million.

In Charge of Everything Else.

The rest of Sprint's long-distance business, such as the one that targets small business, was run by Roger Crisman.

He helped with the original launch of Nickel Nights and Sprint Extra.

Now he has new challenges.

Ongoing Evolution.

At Sprint (now Sprint Nextel), re-assignments, re-alignments, and changing responsibilities are all part of the career path.

Jobs change. Organization charts change. Even brand names change.

In fact, the company you work for today may be a totally new company tomorrow – even when the brand name is the same.

Problems Associated with Vertical Organization.

One drawback to a vertical organization is duplication. In a company with 10 major brands, there may be quite a bit of overlap.

Layers of organization are expensive and can remove top management from the marketing. People will not be of equal quality.

For these and other reasons, some prefer a different structure.

Horizontal Marketing Department Structure.

An alternative is the horizontal, or flat, company structure.

This method is often associated with recently formed firms in high-tech product areas and with firms that market a range of services with shared technologies – like telecom or finance.

Often, the organizational chart can be wider than it is tall.

A horizontally organized company might look like this.

Organizational Chart for a Horizontal Firm:

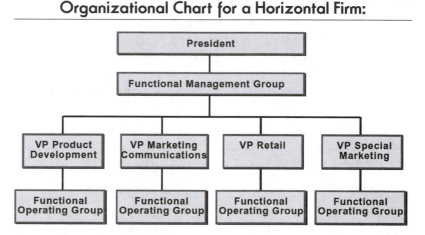

As coherent business units or functions evolve, so do the functional groupings. The company may begin with a small functional grouping called the marketing department.

As business grows, new product teams will develop. As new functions are needed, new groupings will develop.

Unlike the vertical structure, these departments or groupings will work together, but in these more fluid cultures, it tends to be more of a "work with" rather than a "work for."

The Horizontal Advantage.

The principal advantage to the horizontal organization is its ability to evolve relatively smoothly as needs and resources shift.

Just as marketing works to meet consumer needs, the horizontal organization changes to fit the changing needs of the brand.

Evolutionary Organization.

Just as a brand may be in a constant state of growth and change, marketing organizations may be doing the same thing.

For example, Sprint, which is one brand, has a number of separate business units – long distance, local, DSL, and phone cards.

One division, Sprint PCS, is even a separate company – from headquarters to stock market symbol to marketing organization.

Microsoft is a good example of this style of organization.

Founder/CEO Bill Gates says that there are really only four layers in the firm's hierarchy. And it keeps changing.

Overall Organizational Structure for Microsoft:

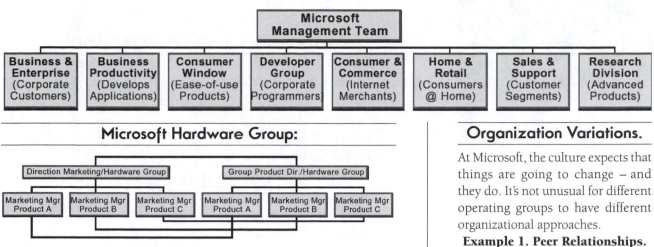

Microsoft Hardware Group:

Microsoft president Steve Ballmer re-organized the company in a new way – not around products but consumer groupings.

So don't be surprised if this chart is already out-of-date.

Horizontal/Vertical – Pro/Con.

Horizontal Disadvantages.

Horizontal structures have weaknesses, too. For example, divisions will have their own marketing budgets and authority.

Coordinating programs for different divisions and maintaining a coherent brand message may be challenging.

This is one weakness of a horizontal structure – low control.

There is diffused responsibility for marketplace performance.

When things go poorly, it can be hard to get that control.

A common behavior is one group blaming another. Advertising might blame poor sales on poor product design or pricing (set by a different department). This is a problem in any type of organization, but it can be compounded when lines of control are spread out.

Another weakness is that this structure depends on having more capable people – those with good judgment and initiative.

The command structure of a vertical organization lets more experienced leadership direct what needs to be done – and expect results. It depends more on people who will take orders and then do a good job doing what they're told.

In contrast, giving authority to someone who does not have what it takes to do the job and is in over their head, is bad for the entire organization. With diffuse responsibilities, a weak link in the chain can affect performance for years.

Nevertheless, many newer companies are organized horizontally – they feel the advantages in specialization, efficiency, and flexibility outweigh the disadvantages.

Horizontal Advantages.

Another significant reason for the growing popularity of the horizontal structure is that it is empowering – more chiefs. Today's employees may dislike working in a deeply vertical organization.

Organization Variations.

At Microsoft, the culture expects that things are going to change – and they do. It's not unusual for different operating groups to have different organizational approaches.

Example 1. Peer Relationships.

The Hardware Group has been in a number of different divisions.

They've developed an organization based on peer relationships.

The product director (who has P&L – profit and loss – responsibilities) and the director of marketing operate on the same level.

Below them, it's parallel structures, with a Microsoft Mouse product manager and a Microsoft Mouse marketing manager working together, but reporting to different bosses.

Example 2. Desktop Applications Category Manager as COO.

This is a large and important group. Though the titles vary, the head of this division is essentially a category manager, with major operational and P&L responsibilities.

The group product manager and the director of marketing are simply direct reports.

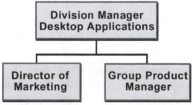

Organizing to Meet Needs.

Horizontal organizations are a fluid reflection of the current needs of the organization.

Microsoft continually re-invents itself and their constantly evolving marketing structures are an ongoing reflection of that change.

Cola Warrior.

Adam Seever worked his way up to helping Coke and its brands compete worldwide.

Here's his advice for tomorrow's brand warriors.

Get an Internship!

Any internship is better than nothing. One at an agency offers exposure to what's out there.

Get an Agency Job!

Agencies offer a cross-section of what the marketing mix is made of… and, again, will enable an alert person the opportunity to get a handle on what is available as a professional.

Get Your Hands Dirty.
Sweat Blood!

In an interview, I was asked why several people had called to show support for me. I said because they know *"I'd sweat blood for the cause."*

Call Contacts. Engage Them.

Very few people got to where they were without help. Good people will be happy to help.

They might not have a job for you, but they almost always know more contacts.

Sponge, Sponge, Sponge.

Soak up any and all information available… read industry journals and publications, research the fields and jobs you're interested in.

Hold Relationships Sacred.

Send thank you letters, follow up, return phone calls.

Help others if you can.

Never, ever burn a bridge!

Different Structure. Similar Jobs.

Whether a department is organized vertically or horizontally, once marketers get to work, their jobs are much the same.

Marketing Job Descriptions.

Here are the primary jobs in a marketing department:

- **Director of Marketing or CMO**
- **Advertising Director or Ad Manager**
- **Category Manager**
- **Brand Manager**
- **Brand Assistant**
- **Sales Promotion Specialist**
- **Market Research**
- **Field Marketing**
- **Other Staff Positions**

Let's take them one by one. We might meet a few interesting people (and interesting jobs) along the way.

Director of Marketing or CMO.

This is the top marketing job in most companies. It often includes the title of vice-president or senior vice-president.

In a large company, many category managers and advertising directors would report to the director of marketing.

More and more, this job has the title of Chief Marketing Officer – or CMO.

Directors of marketing, finance, and manufacturing are usually the top three operational jobs in a company.

Depending on the company's history and business model, one of these three functions may dominate.

Advertising Director or Ad Manager.

Though the reporting structure may vary, an advertising director will have responsibility for the development of the advertising for the brand or brands, usually working with an ad agency.

Though this job has the responsibility for ad development, final approval authority for major efforts is usually at the director of marketing/CMO level – sometimes the COO is involved.

Advertising director is an exciting job but a tough one – this person is often stuck in the middle.

In some cases, this job is done by an Ad Manager, a title with a lower level of authority, though responsibility for and supervision of advertising development is usually part of it.

In many other cases, the development of advertising for individual brands is moved to the brand manager. Then, the advertising director becomes more of a manager of the internal approval process.

Category Manager (Group Product Manager).

A category manager (CM) supervises a number of brands, usually grouped within a product category.

One expert says that the major benefit of using a category manager is to add a strategic level to the management of a brand group.

In theory, a category manager can provide an overview of the business that individual brand managers do not.

A brand manager must pay very close attention to the tactical management of the assigned brand and will pay less attention to the strategic effect of each brand in the group on the marketing success of the entire category.

This is the category manager's responsibility.

The Brand Manager.

The brand manager manages the brand.

On a day-to-day basis, he or she is the key player.

The brand manager is responsible for planning and implementing the marketing plan for the brand.

This marketing plan sets the general course for product offerings and specific product designs, promotions, prices and physical distribution for the assigned items.

The brand manager is often supported by a staff that may include assistant brand manager(s), technical specialists such as a market research person and liaisons with sales and production, and outside experts such as an advertising agency and some sort of sales promotion resource.

Within broad policy guidelines and specific review procedures, the brand manager is responsible for making marketing decisions for the assigned brand.

Assistant Brand Manager (ABM).

This job is sort of a "brand manager in training."

Some companies rotate brand managers with some regularity and others keep people on the same brand for years.

However, the ABM is usually having his or her performance judged by upper management to see whether she or he has the skills to be promoted to brand manager.

Brand Assistant(s).

Larger brands may have two or three assistants working on the brand.

Typically, one assistant could be responsible for media planning, another for sales promotion, and often the newest assistant in the brand group will work on special projects or new products as he or she gets acquainted with the brand, the brand group, and the company.

Big Brands. Big Staff.

A big brand like Tide may have a number of brand assistants, each working on a separate project – such as this out-of-home media project.

The Successful Brand Assistant.

Before a brand assistant is ready for sales training at P&G, she or he must consistently demonstrate three skills essential for a successful career in brand management.

1. The Ability to Get Results.

She or he makes regular, measurable contributions to the brand's progress by getting projects done well and on time.

Work is of professional quality, characterized by thoroughness, accuracy, and solid thought content.

The ability to affect the progress of a brand by initiating, executing, and evaluating key projects are the primary basis for evaluation.

2. The Contribution of Business-Building Ideas.

She or he has taken the effort to learn about everything going on with the brand – even areas where she or he is not directly involved.

Having gained this broad knowledge, she or he now contributes new ideas on a regular basis.

These ideas are simple, soundly grounded in principle, practical, and of sufficient importance to hold the promise of improving the brand's business.

3. The Mastering of Good Communications.

She or he has learned to communicate effectively both orally and in writing.

Memos are clear, simple, logical, well organized, and neat.

At P&G, the principal means of communicating with management is in writing. Great care will be taken in presenting each proposal as effectively as possible.

Oral presentations, both prepared and extemporaneous, exhibit the same recognition of the values of simplicity, clarity, and organization.

From *Brand Manager's Guide to Training the Brand Assistant* – P&G training document.

Souping It Up!

Paul Alexander, Campbell Soup's VP of global advertising has been cooking up a menu that includes:
- New products
- Innovative packaging
- New marketing programs
- Even a new in-store fixture.

Double-Boiler.

He implemented a two-pronged product and marketing strategy.

New products and packaging, like Soup at Hand in microwaveable, easy-open bowls, and a delicious high-quality line extension called Select, broadened selection for adults.

Meanwhile, more new products and a kid-oriented campaign called "Mouth Fun" helped build business in that key sector. Batman Soup anyone?

The IQ Organizer.

In-store, merchandising has always been important for Campbell's and this new dispenser made Campbell's varieties easier to find – with each flavor getting a mini-billboard three times the size of a can of soup.

Over 15,000 have gone into stores so far – with a healthy sales increase resulting virtually every time.

Souper!

Field Marketing.

Part of a field marketing program for Coke. It was conceived on the national level and implemented on the local level, using field marketing to enlist participation in each market.

Staff Functions.
Sales Promotion, Media, & Market Research.

Sometimes, brand groups include specialists in sales promotion, media, and market research, but more often these functions reside in separate groups or departments.

These are normally referred to as "staff functions" and, with the exception of legal services, are normally within the marketing department. Here are some things you should know about their role.

Sales Promotion.

This group is set up to aid the brand group in sales promotion.

It could be either trade or consumer, depending on the needs of the brand. The group will plan and organize everything from a major national event to a local sponsorship.

At Anheuser-Busch, David Peacock worked in a department in which each A-B brand had a dedicated sales promotion staff.

At Coke, Adam Seever works across a range of markets to deliver programs at a local level worldwide.

For all major marketers, sales promotion is a bigger part of their budgets and their marketing organizations.

Media.

Remember, media expenses are a big part of the budget of a major marketer. Any time there's a lot of money involved, it pays to have people keep track of it.

Some marketers have media specialists in their department – this was one of Pam Kramer's responsibilities at Sprint.

This may involve only simple bookkeeping, or it may involve negotiating with networks including sophisticated allocation of GRPs (Gross Ratings Points) among target audiences, seasons, or geography.

Some large marketers, like GM and Anheuser-Busch, have actually taken much of the media function from agencies.

Phil Guarascio at General Motors was one of the most powerful people in marketing. He supervised GM's media, negotiated major media deals, like the Olympics, and was the force behind GM MediaWorks.

However, most marketers, even GM and A-B, continue to rely on their agencies for most aspects of media expertise.

GM uses GM Planworks, a division of Starcom Mediavest.

A-B uses Busch Media Group.

Market Research.

The purpose of this group is to provide the brand groups and the entire marketing department with information, such as who the people are who are most likely to buy the brand, why they make decisions, what their attitudes are toward the brand and competitors, and finally how the brand is used.

Often, these responsibilities include managing research projects using outside suppliers. Brigette Heller at J&J has ongoing shopper-marketing efforts for her baby-care division.

We will describe these companies very briefly in Chapter Seven and discuss the whole process more completely in Chapter Eleven – "Evaluation and Integration."

Legal Services.

Some marketers may have a full-time lawyer within the department. Or, as is more usual, they may call on the company lawyer or legal department to do this job.

Addressing the legal aspects of marketing and advertising is an important part of the job for every company's legal staff.

Sales.

The majority of this book is dedicated to the non-personal selling of brands – primarily advertising.

However, there are a whole lot of jobs out there that involve a more personal involvement in the sales process.

From a marketer's perspective, the two most important are:

• **Field Marketing**
• **Personal Sales**

Field Marketing.

As mentioned, some industries have a long tradition of field marketing – the beer industry has done this kind of marketing for years, working with local taverns (on-premise) and retailers (off-premise) since the early days of "beer drummers."

Many marketers see a strategic advantage in having marketing resources more focused on specific local and regional markets. As a result, local marketing staffs are growing in many categories.

Examples: From Cellular Phones to McDonald's

A recent example is the wireless telephone industry, where the major telecom companies assign field marketing reps to supervise efforts in local markets.

In 1998, McDonald's reorganized a large section of its marketing department into five US regions to improve execution at the local level and work with franchisees more closely. Their new national director of marketing had previously been head of one of the five regions.

Field marketing has always been an important entry-level job. In some cases, it may now be the road to the top.

Personal Sales.

Sales is also a part of marketing – an important part.

Historically, many companies had a sales force that evolved into a marketing department.

In many companies, the sales department is still a large and critical part of the organization.

Often, there are more people in sales than marketing.

For example, Campbell's Pepperidge Farm sales force is a large and important part of the Pepperidge Farm marketing process, with in-store activities being critical to the brand's success.

In business-to-business marketing, the sales force accounts for 23% of marketing expenditures.

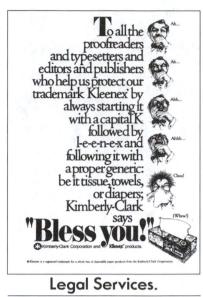

Legal Services.

Protecting trademarks is a key responsibility of a legal staff.

"I'm with the Band."

Along with the debut of Usher's fifth album, *Here I Stand*, he added one more major player – Sony Ericsson.

Usher teamed with Sony for the introduction of the new Walkman music phone in the US, Canada, and 20 European countries – quite a tour!

The campaign will allow music fans access to exclusive content and contests to meet Usher on a video shoot and win VIP tickets for the tour.

The phone will come loaded with Usher ringtones and album downloads.

Sony Ericsson will also engage in joint marketing activities with AT&T, their exclusive US wireless operator.

As marketers look to connect in a crowded marketplace, more and more, they want to say, "I'm with the band."

The Promotion Process.
Connect, Inform, Persuade.

While marketers have to do many things, they find that managing the promotion function is usually the most demanding.

The above commercial frame for C|Net demonstrates the complexity. Somehow, in 30 seconds, the C|Net marketing team had to connect with a computer-literate audience and inform them of C|Net's service in a persuasive manner.

This is the task with the highest degree of variability and challenge.

Let's look at it step by step:

1. Connect.
First, marketers must connect. There are many types of connections.

• They must connect with (and retain) current customers.

Ads often confirm the wisdom of a purchase to a buyer.

For example, the most frequent readers of ads for cars are the recent purchasers of that brand.

• They must also connect efficiently with potential new customers.

2. Inform.
Informing customers may be relatively straightforward.

Or, consumers may need to be taught about the product.

Finally, there may be emotional information: a contemporary fashion image or security and confidence are examples of emotional information.

3. Persuade.
This requires an understanding of what it takes to accomplish that persuasion – the factors that influence purchase behavior.

Summary.
While there may be many ways to accomplish these tasks, they remain constant for virtually every product category and marketer.

The Marketing Process.

THIS SECTION WILL COVER the ongoing marketing process.

Remember, we're trying to do in a single chapter something that can fill big books and years of business school. However, this one chapter will give you an accurate introduction and overview.

Briefly, marketing activities usually include the following tasks:

Planning
1. **Setting overall marketing strategy** (including advertising strategy)
2. **Developing the annual marketing plan**
3. **Calculating the annual marketing budget**
4. **Assigning the marketing tasks**

Implementation
5. **Supervising internal functions**
6. **Overseeing external services** (such as advertising, public relations, sales promotion, event marketing, etc.)

Evaluation
7. **Measuring and tracking efforts**
8. **Reporting performance to top management**
9. **Integrating results into planning**

Now let's take the process step by step.

Planning.

THE FIRST STAGE OF THE PROCESS involves determining objectives, strategies, budgets, and responsibilities.

1. Overall Marketing Strategy.

Marketing strategy is used to develop the overall plan for how the company will attract and retain customers.

It specifies who the customers are, what will be offered, how the offerings will be differentiated from those of competitors, and how this differential advantage will be developed and maintained.

It specifies expected returns to the firm. In short, it is the rationale for why the company is in business.

As such, it may also include a mission statement.

2. Developing the Annual Marketing Plan.

This is a comprehensive document outlining the short-term program for accomplishing the firm's marketing objective.

Strategy development is a key part of the process.

We will cover this in somewhat more detail in Chapter Eight –"Marketing and the Planning Process."

The **annual marketing plan** details the expenditures the firm will make and the expected results of this effort.

It's an important document – there's a lot riding on it.

The overall marketing strategy states the firm's ultimate business destination – the marketing objective. The annual marketing plan contains marching orders for how the company will get there – or at least make one year's progress toward that goal.

3. Calculating the Annual Budget.

Developing and then approving the marketing budget is a critical activity of the marketing department. It is often the largest amount of discretionary spending in the entire company.

It also involves specific procedures, such as an annual budgeting process, for the brand and then periodic reviews to see if the brand will "make its numbers."

The brand manager's authority to approve expenditures will also be contained within fairly specific procedures and guidelines.

It is a cornerstone of company operations.

Marketing Budgets.

A proposed budget is the result of past performance and a prediction of the future. It is one of the most critical tasks a marketer does, yet it is always open to question.

There are a number of ways that companies arrive at budgets. Here are the most common standards:

* **Previous performance** – last year's budget is often a good indicator of this year's budget, plus or minus a few percent.
* **Percent of sales (or case rate)**
* **Affordability, objective, and task** – for example, the brand objective might be to maintain a certain **share of voice.**

Other more scientific methods of setting the advertising budget rely on payback requirements.

DAGMAR – An Advertising Budget System.

One popular system is DAGMAR - Defined Advertising Goals for Measured Advertising Results, formalized by Russell H. Colley for the Association of National Advertisers.

The marketing budget may be done first, encompassing all tasks, and then assigned to the various groups. Or the process works upwards, with departments and brand groups determining the amount they need and then making their case with upper management.

Ongoing Negotiation.

In either case, ongoing negotiation is often the name of the game, since the forecasts may or may not match up with the actual sales figures.

Advertising Budget.

The advertising budget is a subset of the marketing budget. It will usually contain two basic dollar amounts:

* How much will be spent overall on a campaign
* How much will be spent in each medium used

Campaign Spending.

Spending categories vary from marketer to marketer.

Some include coupon redemptions and department salaries.

Some budgets do not include these categories.

Some budget advertising and promotion together and allocate to each from the same Advertising and Promotion (A&P) budget.

Others budget these two major expenses separately.

Auto Sales' Jump Starter.

When Steve Hill, director of retail planning at GM offered two college buddies the GM employee discount, it was enough to get his two friends to change their auto choice.

He sold two cars for GM and he started to think. "Would this work on a broader scale?"

Initiate.

He shared his thoughts with others in GM management and, as luck would have it, there was a National Dealer Council meeting the next day. The dealers bought into it the next day.

Accelerate.

In less than a month, they put the program together, including 1.2 million employee pricing stickers and 454 miles of tape to stick them onto the windows.

Celebrate.

It was a huge success for GM, reducing GM inventories by 50%.

Sales rose 41% in June. In July, they rose another 20%.

Duplicate.

Not only that, but Chrysler and Ford quickly followed with similar programs – which shows you how quickly a good idea can travel.

"Bundles of Benefits."

Products are bundles of benefits and features: color, weight, taste, etc.

Consumers select products on the basis of these features and the benefits these features deliver.

Attributes and Features.

Benefits are generally based on features or attributes.

Attributes tend to be inherent.

Features tend to be manufactured.

Tomato soup is made from tomatoes. This is an attribute.

Apple's Graphic User Interface (GUI) makes the computer easier to use. This is a feature.

Benefits can be based on either.

Product Attributes.

Product attributes can be divided into physical and perceptual. You can easily list the physical attributes of a particular product.

Perceptual attributes are more difficult – perceptions vary.

For example, Campbell's Soup.

For working mothers, it may be "Quality Convenience." For single, retired persons it might be "Wholesome Comfort."

Segments, Niches, & Positioning.

Market segmentation is useful here.

Different demand for different features (color, size, taste, calories) is often a key reason for *product line extensions.*

Competitors use such differences to justify entering markets that are not saturated or satisfied.

Marketers may find unserved "niches" that need attributes not yet available – like the mini-van.

Perceptual or psychological differences may be used in product positioning. For example, Volvo's safety emphasis combines physical and perceptual attributes that appeal to a certain segment.

It's all how you bundle it.

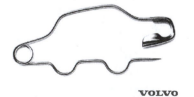

VOLVO
A car you can believe in.

With more marketing communications tasks on the menu, budgeting all possible activities is becoming more complicated.

Media Spending.

Media expenditures are usually the biggest part of the advertising budget. Managers generally look at three factors:

• How large an audience does the medium have?

• How representative of product buyers is that audience?

• Is there compatibility with product purchase and use?

Answers to these or similar questions allow advertisers to rate media and apportion the budget accordingly.

And, in fact, media planning begins with budgeting.

We will cover the media plan further in Chapter Ten.

4. Assigning Tasks and Responsibilities.

The jobs that need to be done in the approved marketing plan will be done by a combination of inside and outside resources.

For example, a marketing study may be supervised by the marketer's marketing research supervisor, executed by an outside research company, and the results used by the ad agency.

Some assignments may have budget implications, so bidding may be part of the process, with necessary budget adjustment.

Implementation.

ONCE THE BUDGET IS APPROVED, the plan has to be executed.

The next part of the process is executing the tasks in the plan that have been approved and budgeted.

There is often a marketing calendar with critical timelines and due dates to organize department activities.

In general, here's what's involved.

5. Supervising Internal Functions.

As marketing departments get larger, their internal operations get more complex. A lot of the business of a marketing department is running itself – seeing that the right people are on the right task.

Accountability is another related issue – each part of the marketing department will usually have accountability for some portion of the budget.

6. Overseeing External Services.

Here are just some of the suppliers that might be used in the course of a year by a marketer:

Advertising Agency.

Of all outside vendors of marketing services, ad agencies are perhaps the best known. In simplified form, they:

• Develop messages by which firms contact customers

• Select and purchase media to carry these messages

• Verify that the messages were, indeed, carried

• Evaluate the success of this communication

We'll cover agencies in more detail in Chapter Five.

Sales Promotion Agency.

Sales promotion carries the firm's contact with consumers to the place where relevant transactions are completed.

There is usually an incentive involved.

With the maturing of product categories, there has been a growth in agencies that specialize in sales promotion.

It is also often a large part of the budget – it can be as big as (or bigger than) the ad budget.

However, many of these "expenditures" are in the form of trade or consumer discounts and are more of an internal financial matter.

Marketers often retain one or more sales promotion agencies to plan and implement various sales promotion activities.

We'll cover this important marketing function in a bit more detail in Chapter Seven – "Marketing Services."

Marketing Public Relations.

Specialists are retained to generate favorable publicity.

Publicity, unlike advertising, is not paid for by the firm.

Rather, it is information judged to be "newsworthy" by the news staff of a mass medium – for example, a marketer appearing on the *Today* show or *Oprah*. Properly used, this can be a relatively small expense that has a substantial payoff.

We'll also cover this in Chapter Seven.

Marketing Research Firms.

Market research firms produce a broad assortment of information products. At the high end are customized, extensive measurements of consumer demand and lifestyles related to advertiser brands.

To broaden its customer base, many market research firms have developed proprietary research products which are sold, in whole or part, to many customers.

Use of these services may be on a one-time basis or ongoing. IRI and Nielsen are two prominent companies.

Media Research.

Media research products can also be purchased from a variety of firms. Some are so prominent that their products have assumed a generic status.

Example: "Nielsens"

This usually means the electronic media ratings generated by the A.C. Nielsen Company for TV programs.

The audience percentage is computed into "points."

This has become the standard way to buy television.

Other Media Research Products.

In a similar way, the Arbitron Corporation is the principal measurement service for radio audiences.

For print media, especially magazines, Simmons Market Research Bureau (SMRB) and Mediamark Research, Inc. (MRI) both use consumer panel data to measure primary (paid) as well as secondary (or pass-along) audiences.

Sales Promotion Agencies.

TLP, a Dallas-based sales promotion agency, helped Pepsi and Mountain Dew put together this "Choose Your Music" promotion, working with Time Warner.

Agencies like TLP are valuable partners in assembling and co-ordinating the logistics of promotional programs like this one.

Another sales promotion agency, GMR, is helping Pepsi take their Pepsi Challenge back on the road with event-style marketing efforts.

The Pepsi Challenge.

Now promoting at a mall near you.

P&G Principles.

Historically, one of the most successful practitioners of marketing has been P&G – Procter & Gamble.

They are, in many ways, a learning organization, where the lessons learned, sometimes at great expense, are integrated into a guiding set of principles.

Here, from historic documents, are some of their business and marketing principles.

Business Principles.
1. Plan all action in advance.
2. Base all action on facts.
3. Always know the objective of your actions.
4. Sell a better product.
5. Make a reasonable profit.
6. Spend advertising and promotion money to build business.
7. Spend big money only against proved techniques.
8. Spend some money to test possible improvements.
9. Whenever possible, limit our activities to those in which we are specialist.
10. Generate competition between our own brands.

Marketing Principles.
1. Base all your business on the consumer, not the dealer.
2. Ensure there is consumer acceptance for your product and that vis-a-vis competition your product is not at a disadvantage.
3. Ensure consumer trial of your product.
4. Ensure that your advertising is building prejudice for your product on one specific performing characteristic – essentially the one which constitutes your edge over competition.
5. In advertising, the proved techniques are best.

(Continued on next page)

Media Buying Services and Advertising Checking Services.
Media buying services are a special kind of limited service ad agency – they buy media. More and more marketers are making use of these services. We'll also cover them in Chapter Seven.

Specialized Marketing Services: Cause Marketing, Sponsorships, Event Marketing, Sports Marketing, Etc.
The growing range of marketing communications tactics has made it all a much more complex process.

Each of these suppliers has to do their own planning, implementation, and evaluation.

Advertising: The Most Critical Task.
Yet, with all of these new opportunities, implementing advertising remains one of the most critical marketing tasks.

Later in the book, we'll be focusing on how an ad agency plans and develops strategies and then creates and places ad messages.

Evaluation.
AT EVERY STAGE, some sort of evaluation plays a part. In initial strategic development, determining budgets, and implementing programs, information is a critical decision-making tool.

At the end of the cycle, as part of developing next year's plan, a number of evaluation efforts take place.

7. Measuring and Tracking Efforts.
It is possible to follow the success of an advertising campaign by following the exposure the ads get and by following the patterns of sales during the campaign.

To monitor ads in television, most advertisers use A.C. Nielsen to give them estimates of how large the audience was. Several other companies sell estimates for radio audiences.

Print advertising audiences are gauged by Audit Bureau of Circulations and Starch/INRA/Hooper.

These organizations offer reliable data about the size of paid circulation, and some measure reader interest in particular ads.

8. Reporting Performance to Top Management.
As results come in, the marketing department is responsible for reporting results of the marketing effort to senior management. They, in turn, owe an assessment to shareholders and other interested stakeholders.

Depending on the industry, these figures may be daily, weekly, monthly, or quarterly. Some of this depends on the nature of the business and the quality of the sales reporting systems.

For example, Frito-Lay gets sales data on a virtual daily basis from its own sales force, who use hand-held computers that download their data to a mainframe every evening.

Retailers with scanner technology integrated into their cash registers can also get prompt sales information. K-Mart transmits sales data daily from over 2,000 stores to its Troy, Michigan, headquarters for oversight and analysis.

Example: Yield Management

In industries like hotels and airlines, reporting on occupancy rates and load factors is often an ongoing function.

This information combined with the ability to make rapid price adjustments is called "yield management." It allows managers with high fixed costs (airplanes, hotel facilities) to maximize sales revenue by the use of flexible pricing.

More Variables = More Difficulty.

Manufacturers who are dependent on distribution systems and sales from a wide variety of vendors with a wide variety of reporting systems have a much more difficult task.

Multi-product marketers have this problem multiplied by the number of brands in their portfolios.

Nonetheless, every brand and every marketing department works to get the numbers and report them to management.

9. Integrating Results into Planning.

The modern marketplace demands an ever-improving level of performance. Here is where information plays a critical role.

When you understand the amount of data generated, it's easy to see why the CIO has become a key executive at most large companies.

This information is a key factor in the continuing improvement of every company's marketing process.

Marketing Challenges.

IN THE NEXT DECADE OR TWO, marketers will face profound changes and challenges. Some are extensions of trends and issues first introduced in Chapter Two.

Here are some of the biggest challenges:

1. **Increasing fragmentation of media**
2. **Increasing sophistication and fragmentation of consumers (and audiences)**
3. **Increasing importance of the marketing function**
4. **Global "hyper-competition"**

1. Increasing Fragmentation of Media.

The revolution is rolling.

There's a cataclysm underway in traditional ad media.

Newspaper publishing now operates for a shrinking, aging readership – even while new alternative weeklies pop up in almost every major market.

Television, once a simple, three-network system, has fragmented into many channels, each with much smaller audiences.

Out-of-home advertising, though constrained by a growing number of restrictions such as zoning, is growing again with kiosks and flat-screen technology.

Direct advertising, while it continues to stuff our mailboxes, is challenged by rising postal costs and the new opportunities on the Internet, with an inherently lower delivery cost.

Priceline.

Here's a business plan built on yield management.

They realized that a certain percentage of airline and hotel capacity could be deeply discounted, and that airline and hotel companies would accept these lower prices.

After all, a small price was better than an empty seat or an empty room.

P&G Principles (Cont.).

6. Know which consumers represent your market (usually housewives for our products) and ensure that your advertising is aimed at them.
7. Ensure that distribution is adequate in marketplace and that stocks are high enough.
8. Plan promotions to encourage display in the store and increase consumer off-take.
9. Push successes before trying to jack up failures.

Sophisticated Consumers.

Here, Sprite makes fun of other soft drink advertising and promotion as they work to connect with sophisticated young consumers with ironic humor and a post-modern attitude.

Harder-to-Persuade Consumers.

What does it take? Harder-to-persuade consumers mean Burger King has to give it away simply to get you to try their fries.

And, since consumers are less brand loyal, they're harder to keep.

As a result, marketing costs keep rising and efficiency keeps declining.

The Internet is also drawing consumer time and interest away from all the older media.

Interestingly, the Internet may have a revolutionary impact on traditional ad agencies by actually replacing them with firms that design and manage Web sites and develop Internet-based communication strategies as opposed to mass-media-based strategies.

What will remain is an inescapable need for marketers to get consumers to buy or try their products and, in general, to connect, inform, and persuade customers.

The good news is there are more tools than ever.

However, that's also the bad news.

How to manage the growing range of tasks successfully will present enormous challenges and comparable opportunities.

2. Increasing Sophistication of Consumers.

Consumers have not gone unaffected by all of these new tools and media opportunities.

Americans under 40 cannot remember a time when they were not a target for some marketer. This has an effect. The post-modern trend of ironic humor in advertising is just one result.

Now everyone is an experienced consumer of advertising.

One result has been sophisticated, sarcastic, self-referential advertising. The campaign for Burger King, which makes fun of its own brand icon, is a well-known example of this approach.

Another result is that what it takes to persuade these consumers has become greater than ever.

Marketers are now looking at marketing and promotion budgets that, more and more, are not equal to the task, which is, not surprisingly, making marketing more difficult.

In some cases, there is a decline in brand loyalty. In others, new alternatives arise. Once-common habits, like going to the video store, are replaced by new behaviors. And, those sophisticated consumers are quicker to adapt – the rise of MP3 and DVD formats are two examples.

In this new world, tried and true marketing techniques may no longer be as effective.

3. Increasing Importance of the Marketing Function.

Still, marketing departments keep growing, and marketing is becoming a greater and greater part of the business of business.

More and more, *"Marketing Is Everything."*

Companies like Sara Lee are even getting out of manufacturing – letting others do what was once a company's core function.

Now, the core function is marketing their branded goods.

As this becomes a greater part of each company, there is the danger that marketing, too, will create its own crowded marketplace.

For example, as larger and larger marketers tap into the same information sources, they may be making similar decisions.

And, again, the task of marketing becomes increasingly difficult.

This is showing up in some statistics – increasing discontent among CMOs with agency performances and increasing management discontent with CMO performance.

Some CMOs are having surprisingly short careers.

The increased importance and difficulty of successful marketing is, itself, a cause for concern.

Peter Drucker, the noted business writer observed that *"no institution can possibly survive if it needs geniuses or supermen to manage it. It must be organized in such a way as to be able to get along under a leadership composed of average human beings."*

Maybe so – but clearly, it is the geniuses and innovators that are having success.

One more concern.

4. Global "Hyper-Competition."

Economic competition is usually viewed as a good thing. It's viewed as good for consumers because competition usually produces a bigger assortment of better products at lower costs.

Compared with monopolies (one seller) or oligopolies (a few sellers), an industry which has many sellers competing with each other serves consumers well.

However, too many aggressive competitors in a market category can be a bloody business.

For example, the worldwide auto market is now in the grips of **hyper-competition.** Moreover, India and China are becoming major car manufacturing (and consuming) markets.

Competent management is no longer the exclusive domain of American, European, and Japanese companies. The "BRIC" countries – Brazil, Russia, India, and China are each bringing world-class competition into major categories.

Factory overcapacity and a business situation that may truly be life or death can lead to a competitive situation where too many marketers fight for share in a market too small for all of them.

Take an industry with chronic overcapacity and governments committed to supporting these major sources of jobs, and you can feel bottom lines crunching worldwide.

Then, a sudden increase in something like fuel prices, will add new levels of difficulty in a situation that was already daunting.

In many categories, from computers to pizza parlors to running shoes, we may actually see a case of "too much marketing."

In some cases, particularly those related to agriculture or energy, we find that governments are already deeply involved, using loans and subsidies to support important industries.

This creates even more pressure in the marketplace.

We already see this in trade agreements, new agricultural products on your grocer's shelf, and all the consequences of moving manufacturing to lowest-cost providers overseas.

For some marketers, the future may be grim, yet a change in fortunes may be only one innovative idea away.

FASTER THAN A SPEEDING CIVILIZATION.

Full Speed Ahead or Heading for a Crash?

Driven by massive overcapacity, some marketers, such as auto manufacturers, may be forced into increasingly desperate circumstances. (We predicted this in our first edition.)

A Tradition of Innovation.

Good old Tide still keeps coming up with product improvements. In fact, that's part of its brand heritage.

Here, Tide addresses a new consumer concern – bacteria.

And, here in billboard form, an older concern – bird business.

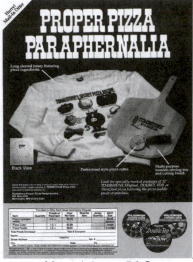

How Many P's?

How many P's do you want on your pizza? How will you differentiate?

How will you compete?

Remember, strategy is about choice. So, what do you want on your pizza?

Here, Tombstone tries to get you to buy their frozen pizza with a high-value promotional offer.

From Ball State to The Peoples' Republic.

Many of our pizza chains have an interesting background.

Tombstone Pizza started in a Wisconsin tavern across the street from a cemetery.

Domino's began as a multi-level sales organization, with store managers putting new stores, run by former assistants, into business and collecting a piece of the franchise fee.

Papa John's Product Strategy.

In 1983, at the ripe old age of 22, "Papa" John Schnatter, armed with a business degree from Ball State, decided that there was room for a national pizza chain that delivered a superior quality pizza.

That simple focus was the basis for Papa John's.

He knocked down the broom closet in his father's tavern, sold his Camaro, and, with $1600 worth of used restaurant equipment, put his strategy into action – Better Ingredients. Better Pizza.

Today, Papa John's has built that strategy into a chain of 3000 restaurants worldwide – including operations in the People's Republic of China.

The Need for Innovation.

As Paul Romer noted, new ideas have the power to add value – a power to make everyone's lives better – a power to create new jobs and even new industries.

Companies managing change so as to create a better world for both their customers and their employees is marketing at its best.

That's why innovative strategy will be so critical for the survival and prosperity of marketers and advertisers in the coming years. They must invent and develop new markets and new categories – not just fight over yesterday's markets. And that's why Chapter 12 is called "The Power of New Ideas."

So that The Business of Brands, and all the opportunities that marketers can create, continues to grow.

Discussion Questions:

1. **Packaged Goods and Durable Goods.**
   a. Name your two biggest packaged goods suppliers. How much do you spend with this marketer every two months? How much per year?
   b. What was you or your family's latest durable goods purchase. How much was spent? Was there financing? What is your best guess of the length of the purchase cycle?

2. **Services.**
   What services marketers are currently looking to recruit you?

3. **Products and Services Mixed.**
   Think of your last meal out – or your last vacation trip. What were products you bought? What were services?

4. **Price and Margin.**
   Think of your most recent purchases. What, on judgment, was the purchase where the marketer had the highest margin? What, on judgment, were the reasons for your willingness to pay that price?

5. **Place/Distribution.**
   Make a list of the different places you've made a purchase in the last month.

6. **Promotion.**
   a. What promotional tactics have you experienced in the last week?
   b. Which, on judgment, were most effective?

7. **People.**
   To what marketers are you, perhaps, a high net worth customer?

8. **Marketing Strategy/Marketing Mix.**
   If you were a director of marketing, how would you prioritize the various MarCom tools? What tactic would you use first?

9. **Vertical/Horizontal.**
   In your own words, how would you describe the differences between vertical and horizontal marketing organization?

10. Marketing Departments.

What entry-level jobs interest you most?

A Tasty Exercise!

Here's a product category you're familiar with – pizza! It will give you a chance to review the basic principles discussed in this chapter.

1. Background.

* How is pizza currently marketed to that high-consumption target you know best – college students?
* What are the major brands – local, regional, and national?
* Who are the marketers behind these brands?
* What tactics are being used in your market to reach that key pizza-eating target audience – you.

2. The Five P's.

* How are the Five P's being used by different marketers?
* Who is competing on price, who on product, who on place (distribution), and how are they all promoting?
* How can the fifth P – people – make a difference?

3. Marketing Strategy.

Now, try to be a strategic innovator – think of opportunities to reshape the pizza market for each of the following groups of prospective buyers:

* **College students**
* **Young adults**
* **Pre-teen children**
* **Yuppies**
* **Single parents**
* **Vegetarians**

4. Hyper-Competition.

There are probably a lot of pizza places in your market.

* How do you propose to meet the growing challenge of hyper-competition in pizza in your market?

This should be an assignment you can sink your teeth into!

Concepts & Vocabulary:

Here are some of the words you need to know in the world of marketers and marketing:

ACV (All Commodity Volume) – A number that looks at the relative importance of volume in a category through different distribution channels. It is a valuable planning and evaluation tool.

Added value(s) – Intangible attributes of a brand beyond function.

ADI (Area of Dominant Influence) – Marketing territory determined by a combination of geography and media coverage.

Advertising – Paid communication in mass media by an identified sponsor, designed to inform and persuade.

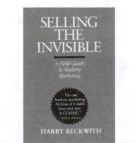

This Little Book is a Delight.

It's called *Selling The Invisible: A Field Guide to Modern Marketing*.

It's one of those books that you keep around, open up… and there, in a page or two, the author (Harry Beckwith) offers a tremendously valuable bit of marketing wisdom.

Get it. It helps you "get it."

References:

Here are some books that can give you useful insights into the world of marketers and marketing:

Winning with the P&G 99: 99 Principles and Practices of Procter & Gamble's Success by Charles L. Decker

Building Strong Brands by David A. Aaker

The Marketing Imagination by Theodore Levitt

Marketing Warfare by Jack Trout & Al Ries

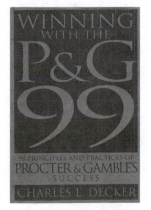

Books by Tom Peters.

He's got his own web site.

You might want to dip your toe in the water.

The Pursuit of Wow might be a good place to start.

It contains 210 numbered observations designed to get you thinking.

His longer books were big in the '90s, and his classic piece "The Brand Called You" is highlighted in our Careers section. You can still grab it off the 'Net from the *Fast Company* Web site – it was one of their early cover stories.

Passion for Excellence

This, his second book, profiles companies that "get it right."

Though some of them didn't stay that way.

Agricultural marketing – The marketing process finely tuned to matters as diverse as pork bellies and crop hybrids.

Annual marketing plan – A key document for marketers. It contains the background, the budget, and the rationale for the upcoming year. At year's end, results are compared to the plan.

Attributes – An inherent characteristic of a product, either physical, such as what the product is made of, or perceptual, such as the way the product is thought of by the consumer.

A-to-S Ratio (Advertising to Sales Ratio) – Measurement used for both budgeting and comparison with competition.

BDI (Brand Development Index) – Calculated index of the percentage of a brand's total sales that occur in a given market, as compared to the percentage of the total population of the market.

Benefits – Positive results that come directly or indirectly from a product based on attributes, features, and functions, both real and perceived.

Brand – The unique name or symbol used to identify a product or service in order to distinguish it from the competition.

Brand assistant – Support staff position within the brand group, usually reporting to the brand manager.

Brand equity – The collection of product attributes that results from accrued added values for a brand over time.

Brand group – Management and support staff, sometimes including research and sales promotion personnel, assigned to a particular product brand.

Brand manager – The individual in an organization responsible for decision making surrounding the planning, developing, implementing, and controlling the marketing of a brand. Sometimes called "product manager."

Business to business (B2B) – The marketing of products or services between companies, rather than from a company to an individual as the ultimate consumer.

Category manager – Marketing executive who works for a multi-brand marketer, responsible for a particular product category. These responsibilities may cover a number of brands, products, or services.

Cause marketing – Advertising and "selling" charities, public and community service groups, and other "issues-oriented" organizations.

CEO (Chief Executive Officer) – Top management officer responsible for overall big-picture performance of a company.

CFO (Chief Financial Officer) – Managerial position responsible for financial affairs within the company.

CIO (Chief Information Officer) – Managing officer charged with directing data collection and processing systems within the company.

CMO (Chief Marketing Officer) – Managing officer with responsibility for a company's marketing function.

Communication Strategy – type of strategy usually consisting of objective statement, target definition, and desired message emphasis.

Convergence – Tendency of technologies and business categories to merge, duplicate, compete, and overlap. For example, banks, brokers, insurance companies, and your credit card are all converging with overlapping and competitive financial services.

COO (chief operating officer) – Managing officer with responsibility for day-to-day operations. Reports to CEO and board.

Copy Strategy – (See **Communication Strategy**)

Core Business Strategy – A single statement of the organization's business purpose.

Direct mail – Form of advertising sent to prospects through the US Postal Service or some other mail service.

Direct sales – Personal presentation, demonstration, and sale of products and services to consumers, usually in their homes or place of employment.

Durable goods – Products with a long life span, like cars and TVs. Unlike packaged goods, they are purchased infrequently and do not require frequent replacement. These are usually major cash expenditures or credit charges and are "considered purchases."

Entertainment marketing – The promotion and sale of products as diverse as spectator sports, music concerts, and movies.

Field marketing – Marketing at a local level; i.e., "in the field."

Financial services marketing – The competitive provision of monetary services by banks, brokers, insurers, and others to consumers in the marketplace.

Functional superiority – Actual, inherent advantage of a product or service as compared to another within the same category.

Gross margin – The difference between the base manufactured cost and the price charged.

Hospitality marketing – Marketing of travel, lodging, convention, and catering services.

Hyper-competition – Over-saturation of a particular market with too many products and not enough room for product marketers to compete for market share.

Intangibles – These are aspects of the brand that cannot be actually touched but which nonetheless do exist. They may be within the product – such as speed of service. They may be within the

References: (Cont.)

Positioning: The Battle For Your Mind by Jack Trout and Al Ries

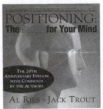

The 22 Immutable Laws of Branding: How to Build a Product or Service into a World Class Brand. by Al Ries and Laura Ries

If you find you're interested in marketing, here are a few more business books you might enjoy:

The Mind of the Strategist. By Kenichi Ohmae.

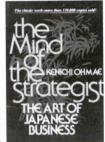

This is our particular favorite. Is it because it's the best book or is it because we read it just as we were beginning to understand the importance of strategy?

Hard to say. Nonetheless, Ohmae offers some thoughts that many find particularly helpful.

The current subtitle is "The Art of Japanese Business," though it was originally "Business Planning for Competitive Advantage."

Whichever copy you acquire, it offers useful observations on the mental flexibility necessary to be truly exceptional at strategic development.

References: (Cont.)

On Competition. By Michael E. Porter, Harvard Business School Press.

Porter is "widely accepted as the world's most influential thinker on business strategy." That said, you may or may not find the answers here.

But, if you want to develop a well-rounded view of the field, it's one of the books you should probably have on your bookshelf.

Management Challenges for the 21st Century.

By Peter F. Drucker.

Generally recognized as "the Dean of Business Writers," Drucker's career spanned the latter half of the 20th Century.

Here, he offers some prescient thoughts on what he believes is headed our way.

Whether or not he is right on all the issues, the clarity of vision and the consistent strength of his writing offers lessons for us all.

You are just beginning your business career.

Before you're done, you're sure to have a few Druckers on your bookshelf.

Marketing Myths That Are Killing Business.

By Kevin Clancy & Robert S. Shulman

In addition to the books that tell you what to do, there are a number of good books that tell you what not to do. This is one of the better ones.

consumer – such as reputation. They may be a combination – such as expectations of a problem-free experience.

Line extension – The strategy of applying an existing brand name to another product in the same category, usually with the objective of increasing total category sales.

Margin – The difference between the cost of the seller's goods and the price of the product paid by the ultimate consumer. *See also* **gross margin** and **net margin**.

Market research – Systematic gathering, development, and analysis of new information used in marketing and advertising decisions.

Market segmentation – Division of a market into distinct groups with common needs that respond similarly to marketing actions.

Marketers – Those who bring goods and services to the marketplace.

Marketing – Process of planning and executing the conception, pricing, promotion, and distribution of ideas, goods, and services to create exchanges that satisfy individual and organizational objectives.

Marketing budget – The discretionary funds utilized in implementing the overall marketing strategy.

Marketing plan – Written document describing the overall strategy developed to market (or promote) a particular brand, organization, or product.

Marketing Strategy – "[T]he process of bringing about conditions most favorable to one's own side" (Kenichi Ohmae) – usually consisting of developing the optimal configuration and/or emphasis of the following elements (the Five P's): product, price, place (distribution), promotion, and people.

Media – Vehicles for the widespread, non-personal communication of advertising to the public, whether by broadcast, print, computer, cable, or outdoor advertising.

Milking – The practice of continuing to sell a product in reliance on lingering effects of previous advertising long after advertising and other promotion support has been either discontinued or reduced substantially. The marketer "milks" the remaining profit and value from the brand.

Net margin – The calculation of margin that factors into the equation the cost of added value of the product provided by the seller.

OOS (out of stock) – Lack of availability of a product at the retail level, whether through manufacture, transportation, or labor problems, or because the product is not in demand by consumers.

Packaged goods – Products consumed, usually repeatedly, in a fairly short period of time, creating a cycle of need, purchase, use, need. There is always a new market for them.

Packaging – The physical appearance and characteristics of a product's container or wrapping.

People – One of the Five P's of Marketing, referring to a range of people involved with the brand, including the brand's target consumer group, employees, etc.

Physical distribution – A set of activities and organizations that deliver product from maker to consumer.

Place – One of the Five P's of Marketing, referring to the distribution of the brand.

Positioning – 1. Marketing communication approach that focuses on where the product resides (or could reside) within the mind of the consumer. 2. Marketing which looks at the relative place of a brand in relationship to the competitive environment. 3. The relationship between the perceptual attributes and benefits of a product and the primary target's lifestyle.

Price – One of the Five P's of Marketing, referring not only to the price of the product, but the margins available to fund brand activities and still deliver a profit.

Pricing Strategy – type of strategy usually consisting of overall business volume and profit objectives taking into consideration the competitive set, costs, and desired margins.

Primary Target – The consumer, the person who purchases or uses the product or service.

Product – One of the Five P's of Marketing, referring to the brand itself – the product or service provided and the benefits that product or service delivers.

Promotion – One of the Five P's of Marketing, referring to the set of activities designed to advance goods and services in the marketplace. Promotion includes advertising and sales promotion as well as other marketing communications activities.

Public relations – Communication concerned with promoting the public's conception of issues, products, organizations and companies, and personalities.

Publicity – Attempts to receive favorable media coverage of a product, service, organization, or person. Typically this is achieved by use of media through press releases, press conferences, product literature, pamphlets or materials, celebrity appearances, or sponsored events.

Research Strategy – type of strategy usually consisting of learning goals and research methodology.

Retail marketing – The sale of a product directly to the ultimate consumer through a store set up for that purpose.

Sales promotion – Use of an incentive to encourage purchase of a product. Examples include: price reductions, like coupons, value added offers, like "2 for 1," and other extras, like sweepstakes. These may be provided to the sales force, distributors, or consumers. All have the same objective – stimulate immediate sales.

References: (Cont.)

These two former Yankelovich executives tap into a wealth of marketplace knowledge to offer a wide range of observations about traps to avoid in the modern marketplace.

New and Improved. The Story of Mass Marketing in America
By Richard S. Tedlow

The history of successful businesses can be a lesson in itself. Perhaps we can't do today what made for yesterday's success, but maybe we can.

We can see the rise of important companies that are still around today, like GE.

We can learn from the ongoing battle between Coca Cola and Peps.

And can think about the rise and fall of once powerful brands like A&P. (Did you know it was once the largest retailer in the world?)

The Rise and Fall of Strategic Planning.
By Henry Mintzberg

We really like this book. So does management guru Tom Peters.

At great length, Mintzberg makes observations such as the one that marketers don't usually create marketing – rather, they create plans.

And that while they are often disguised as strategies, they all too often generate numbers rather than ideas.

If you decide to go deep into a business and marketing career, you might want to own a copy of this book, and occasionally contemplate Mintzberg's cautionary observations.

References: (Cont.)

Strategy Bites Back: It Is Far More, and Less, Than You Ever Imagined.

 By Henry Mintsberg, Bruce Ahlstrand, and Joesph Lampel

Mintzberg had a strategy. His book was too long and hard to read.

So he came back with this brash, slightly non-linear, collection of interviews (including one with Richard Branson), observations, bits of graphic, and even a speech by Mao Tse Tung.

Here is a favorite review, "This is a naughty book, a really cheeky little brat of a book which ought to be spanked soundly and sent to bed without any supper, Except that, if you did that, you would be missing out on a delightful entertaining smorgasboad of advice, insights, red herrings and jokes that altogether make up a classic text for business leaders."

Our Strategy for this Collection of Books.

For the few of you who decided to read this little section, we wanted you to know that business books can be interesting.

And, if you decide to go into the marketing side of business, you may find it very stimulating and intellectually challenging – and worth filling your brain cells with some of the thoughts in some of these books.

Secondary target – A retail channel or sales force (distinguish from **primary target**).

Services – The provision of time, advice, space, care, information, or other intangibles such as hotel lodging, insurance, or healthcare (distinguished from tangible products).

Share (of market) – The percentage of the market "owned" by a brand. This information is usually provided by a syndicated research service, such as Nielsen or IRI.

Share of voice – Percentage of media weight a brand has relative to the media spending of all competitive brands in that category.

Slotting allowance – A fee charged by retailers for placement of a manufacture's product on retail shelves.

SKU (store keeping unit) – The measurement of product based upon packaging by size or count, usually at difference prices.

Strategy – A cohesive plan for directing a course of action; a guide for decision making designed to bring about a certain (hopefully favorable) outcome.

Tactics – Specific marketing actions.

Target market – The group of potential consumers at which marketing efforts are aimed (See also **primary target** and **secondary target**).

5

This chapter was written by Robert L. Gustafson, who was a VP Management Supervisor at Ogilvy & Mather (O&M) in Chicago. He is now an Associate Professor at Ball State University. While at O&M, his client responsibilities included Ameritech Cellular Phones, Eagle Food Stores, Parker Pen, Museum of Science and Industry, Sears, Toro, and Western Publishing. He previously held marketing positions at Midas International, Cunningham & Walsh, and Wells Rich Greene.

"BIG IDEAS, that's what advertising is all about."
— David Ogilvy

Advertising Agencies

AFTER READING THIS CHAPTER you should understand and be able to explain the following: what advertising agencies do, how they started, the ways different types of agencies are organized, and some of the career opportunities they offer.

As you will see, advertising agencies grew with the traditional media of newspapers, magazines, radio, and television. And now, thanks to the Media Revolution, this business is changing again.

You'll also understand how agencies are responding to the trends affecting the future of the agency business and how they are opening up even more new opportunities – and new agencies.

You'll see that this is an exciting time for everyone working in advertising and marketing communications. It's not problem-free, but it's exciting. Seismic changes are happening in the traditional-media, Internet, and entertainment industries.

These changes are dramatically affecting the advertising business and how ad agencies are organized and positioned for future growth. Even the term "advertising agency" may fade away.

There are changes everywhere. Many agencies are repositioning themselves more broadly as a marketing communications company, a brand consultancy, or a media entertainment agency.

Service offerings are growing to include product placement, event sponsorship, and entertainment programming. Media interactivity and engaging creative will rule the day. And handling the Internet will be as important as creating a good TV commercial.

Four Michigan Avenue Neighbors.

Let's start with a quick introduction to four ad professionals you'll meet during this chapter – **Jodi Cary, Stephanie Buzan, Bernie Pitzel,** and **Mairee Ryan.** Each have worked at Chicago advertising agencies – but their jobs are as different as their agencies.

Jodi Cary is an Account Supervisor at a large agency – Ogilvy & Mather (O&M). She received her degree in marketing from Michigan State University.

www.mccann.com.

McCann-Erickson is an agency with a long tradition of innovation. Their site is one of the best sources for up-to-date ad industry information.

It provides the following:

- **Insider's Reports.** Robert J. Coen, Sr. VP-Director of Forecasting, has made his data available – including full twice-yearly reports on ad spending containing predictions, summaries, and analyses.
- **Annual Advertising Spending Details (1935 to date).**
- **Advertising and the Economy (1929 to date).** Ad spending relative to US Gross Domestic Product.
- **Annual Advertising Spending Totals (1776 to date).** This report goes all the way back to 1776, ad spending estimated at $1.2 million!

Advertising Can Be Fun.

George Rowell thought advertising was fun – and no wonder.

In 1865, he left his job as an ad solicitor with the *Boston Globe* and invested his life savings of $1,000 to develop his own rate card, with circulation estimates and pre-negotiated rates which included his commission – up to 75%! In his first month, he billed $2,000 and kept $1,400. Wow.

His next step was buying space and reselling it. But he couldn't keep from

 sharing his secret – he told others how to do it.

Then George founded the ad industry's first trade magazine – *Printer's Ink.*

Jodi started as an assistant in the media department at one agency, transitioned into account management at another, and then moved up to her job at O&M.

Two Blocks Away...

Stephanie Buzan, a graduate of Ball State's advertising program, works in an agency media department, figuring out how to spend those media billings.

She works as a Media Supervisor at DraftFCB, one of the country's largest agencies, with billings of over $9.5 billion. Stephanie will describe one of her typical days working on the S.C. Johnson account.

Over in the West Loop...

In 2003 Bernie Pitzel opened his agency, Romani Brothers (Romani was his mother's maiden name), when a long-term relationship turned into a request to start a new agency.

Meanwhile...

Mairee Ryan has gone freelance – moving from Account Coordinator at a small agency to project manager for agencies and clients as more and more look for help on a project basis.

How This Chapter Is Organized.

Agencies are fascinating and complex businesses. Here's a quick roadmap of how we'll cover the advertising agency business.

Major discussion areas covered in this chapter will be:

➤ **How Agencies Started**
➤ **The Agency Business Today**
➤ **Types of Agencies**
➤ **The Agency's Role**
➤ **Agency Structure and Functions**
➤ **How Agencies Generate Revenue and Profit**
➤ **The Business of Agency New Business**
➤ **Starting and Managing a Small Agency**
➤ **Agency Trends**
➤ **Vocabulary**
➤ **Suggested Reading and Viewing**

All this is about an industry that started about 150 years ago.

How It Started: A Brief Agency History.

YOU'RE ALREADY FAMILIAR WITH AGENCY HISTORY from the material in Chapter One. Now let's revisit some of the ground you covered, this time focusing on how agencies make money.

Advertising goes back to ancient times when shopkeepers' signs would identify their trade.

But advertising agencies, as we know them today, did not develop until the introduction of printing technology, the spread of literacy, and the production of branded products.

The First Advertising Agents.

Most historians credit **Volney Palmer** with starting the first advertising agency in 1841 in Philadelphia. Palmer, like other "agents" of his time, acted as a space broker or sales representative for various newspapers.

He would contact publishers and offer to sell advertising space in their newspapers for a commission.

Since there were no published rate cards or circulation figures, agents could set the price at whatever the traffic would bear. Commission rates varied. Some were as high as 50% – or higher!

During the 1850s, **George Rowell** helped bring some stability to the advertising industry. Rowell paid cash to publishers for large blocks of space at low, discounted rates. He then resold the space in smaller lots to advertisers at a profit.

Rowell was the first agent to guarantee payment to the publishers. In 1869, he published the *American Newspaper Directory* which, for the first time, listed advertising rates and estimates of circulation.

As the volume of advertising grew, and the media expanded with more newspapers and magazines, competition increased.

And the first modern advertising agency opened for business.

The First Modern Advertising Agency.

In 1875, **Francis Ayer** founded NW Ayer & Son. The Ayer agency departed from the limited-space broker role, establishing the agency-client business relationship. Ayer offered to bill advertisers for what was actually paid publishers – less a fixed commission – if advertisers placed all their advertising through his agency.

About the same time, NW Ayer and J. Walter Thompson (JWT) began writing copy and designing advertisements for their clients. Ayer did more newspaper work, while JWT emphasized magazines.

Agencies learned that some ads were more effective than others. This was particularly true of Albert Lasker's agency, Lord & Thomas, with copy by Claude Hopkins.

By developing more effective advertising, agencies became more competitive in attracting new clients.

The Commission System Is Formalized.

In 1917, thanks to Cyrus Curtis and others, the traditional method of agency payment became a 15% media commission.

Publishers found that the commission system encouraged agencies to sell space, yet left them free to sell other space at full price.

Growth from the Role of Agent.

As responsibilities and services expanded, the role of the agency evolved from that of "agent."

As discussed in Chapter One, agencies became the original resources of marketing expertise. This service was funded by the growing income from media commissions.

Then, clients developed marketing expertise of their own.

First, let's take a quick industry snapshot.

COASTING is the term given by bicycle riders to their practice of taking the feet from the pedals and allowing the machine to run with the momentum acquired from previous effort.

This is the season when many business men are tempted to try "coasting" with their Newspaper Advertising.

The newspapers themselves however do not "coast." They are regularly issued, and regularly read, and the advertisers who have learned that

Keeping Everlastingly At It Brings Success

are regularly represented therein. They would no more "coast" with their advertising than with their employees, or any other every-day business necessity.

Coasting is a down-grade exercise. Success is an up-hill station. We have been there ourselves. We have gone there with many successful Newspaper Advertisers. We will be glad to start with you.

Correspondence solicited.

N. W. AYER & SON,
Newspaper Advertising Agents,
Philadelphia.

The Story of NW Ayer "& Son."

Francis Ayer established an ad agency in Philadelphia in 1875.

He named the agency NW Ayer & Son. He was the son, but there was no Ayer senior at the agency.

He did this because he was a very young man in his early 20s and had the good judgment to recognize that some clients would want to work with someone older.

While he never let them see the founder, some clients felt better knowing there was a more mature professional in place.

Young Ayer also established the concept of a client-agency partnership. He billed advertisers exactly what he was billed from the publications.

There was a substantial savings to the advertiser, so Ayer required that the client agree to place all their advertising through his agency.

These were the first exclusive contacts. Over 125 years later, we are still using his innovations.

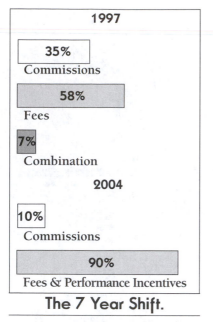

1997	
35%	Commissions
58%	Fees
7%	Combination

2004	
10%	Commissions
90%	Fees & Performance Incentives

The 7 Year Shift.

This shows the big change in agency income in the 7 years between 1997 and 2004 – a massive shift toward fees and performance incentives. (Source: Morgan Anderson Consulting & AMA News.)

From 3 to 510 (at last count)

Even in tough times, good agencies can grow. Goodby Silverstein & Partners started with one small account and now has offices around the world and over 500 employees. Half their output is digital.

You can visit their Web site at: www.goodbysilverstein.com

The Agency Business Today.

THE ORGANIZATION AND SCOPE of advertising agencies ranges from small companies employing one to ten people to mega-agencies that employ thousands globally.

5,000 Agencies… or More… or Less.

The Bureau of Labor Statistics estimates over 18,000 firms, mostly small ones. The *Standard Directory of Advertising Agencies* listed nearly 5,000 agencies headquartered in the United States.

AdWeek publishes an agency directory with fewer names.

Ad Age measures only 457 US-based shops for its annual report.

No one source can accurately list all the advertising agencies in the US, as most are small and individually owned.

In addition, new agencies are founded almost daily. That's one challenge finding an agency job – tracking down new agencies.

183,800 People. 1.2 Million People.

Advertising agencies used to employ about 243,000 people in 1994.

In March, 2008, it was estimated that 183,800 people work for agencies. The Bureau of Labor Statistics lists "advertising and related industries" at over 450,000 jobs. But, when you include the other marketing communications disciplines and media companies, the ad industry employs 1.2 million people.

That number may be lower with recent industry downsizing, or higher when there is a surge in start-ups. The point is, there are still many entry-level jobs and significant numbers of part-time, self-employed, and freelancers.

$284 Billion = $16.56 Billion.

Until recently, when people discussed the size of the industry or an agency, they would refer to **media billing**. Now this is less the case. With the growth of mega-agencies and the fee system, the common standard of measurement is now **income**.

In 2007, US media expenditures totalled $284 billion. (For more information on ad expenditures, check www.mccann.com.) Income registered by agencies for advertising and media services was estimated at $28.2 billion – about 10% of expenditures.

An Urban Industry.

Industry jobs are heavily concentrated in greater New York and California – an estimated one in five firms and one in five employees.

However, due to computerization, increased use of telecommunications, the Internet, and personal lifestyle changes, there are now sophisticated regional ad agencies everywhere.

But whatever their size and wherever they are located, their functions are remarkably similar.

Four Functions of a Full-Service Agency.

Full-service agencies fulfill four basic functions:

❶ **Account Management**
❷ **Creative**
❸ **Media Planning and Placement**
❹ **Research**

Full-service agencies come in many shapes and sizes. In addition, there are many variations on the full-service standard – particularly with new media start-ups.

Types of Agencies.

Here are the major types of agencies we'll cover.

➤ **Mega-Agency Groups.** These are world agency "brands." Many names will be familiar to you from the history chapter.

➤ **Independent National, Regional, and Local Agencies.** These agencies operate as independent entities.

➤ **Specialized or Niche Agencies.** These usually rely on some unique specialty – such as industry or ethnic expertise.

➤ **Digital Agencies.** While virtually all types of agencies are working to add digital capabilities, there are some very exciting new agencies who feature emerging digital media solutions as their primary service. Some are divisions of larger groups. Others are free-standing organizations.

➤ **Other Suppliers of Agency Services.** Agency services can be provided a number of other ways. Full-service agency functions are available "unbundled" by individuals and companies:

• **In-House Agencies.** Some marketers have an agency (or parts of one) inside their marketing department.

• **Marketing Consultants** provide some of the strategic thinking that is offered by account management.

• **Creative Boutiques and Design Houses,** these provide creative services as well as some other marketing assistance.

• **Media Agencies (Media Buying Services)** provide many of the things offered by an agency media department.

• **Research** may be provided by a wide variety of marketing research suppliers.

Agency services come in many configurations and many sizes.

Mega-Agency Groups.

MERGERS RESHAPED ADVERTISING.

During the late 1980s and continuing into the 1990s, the advertising industry, like many others, experienced some dramatic changes due to major corporate mergers.

Saatchi & Saatchi.

As we discussed, Saatchi & Saatchi, a small London-based agency, took advantage of British tax laws and differing price-to-earning ratios on agency stock between the New York and London Stock Exchange.

Combined with ample bank financing, they rapidly expanded to (temporarily) become the world's largest agency network – acquiring a number of large US agencies including Ted Bates and Campbell-Mithun Esty. (Read about it in *Emperors of Adland*.)

For a variety of reasons, including its large financial debt and ventures into unfamiliar businesses, such as consulting, Saatchi's billings declined. (Read about it in *Conflicting Accounts*.)

Before and After.

First, *Emperors of Adland* by Nancy Millman, a fascinating historical document of this revolutionary moment in agency history.

Then, *Conflicting Accounts: The Creation and Crash of the Saatchi & Saatchi Empire* by Kevin Goldman.

Bean Counter to Visionary.

Sir Martin Sorrell has pulled off three of the top ten mergers and acquisitions in advertising history.

Previously, he worked with the Saatchi brothers, where he was known as "the third brother."

Here are the deals:

1. WPP/Y&R	$4.7 billion
4. WPP/O&M	864 million
8. WPP/JWT	566 million

For his thoughts on the future of advertising and WPP, look at his comments on the future of the agency business in the sidebar at the end of this chapter.

OMNICOM $12.7 Billion.

Here's a look at the various divisions of Omnicom.

Three Global Networks:

BBDO Worldwide	2.39 billion
DDB Worldwide	2.62 billion
TBWA Worldwide	1.78 billion

Six Primarily US Agencies

Element 79 Partners	46 million
Goodby Silverstein	84 million
GSD&M	114 million
Martin-Williams	42 million
Merkley Partners	64 million
Zimmerman Partners	175 million

Two Media-Buying Specialists

OMD	859 million
PHD	170 million

13 CRM Specialists

This includes: Agency.com, GMR Marketing, Integer Group, Rapp-Collins, Javelin, and others

CRM Total	4.69 billion

Six Public Relations Firms

This includes: Fleishmann-Hilliard, Ketchum, Porter-Novelli, and others

PR Total	1.27 billion

28 Specialty Marketers

This includes: Corbett Healthcare, Dieste Harmel & Partners, Doremus, Harrison Star Business Group, Ketchum Directory Advertising, and others

Specialty Total	1.31 billion

(Source: *Advertising Age,* 2007 Revenue Ranking)

After much discord, this group was renamed Cordiant, and the Saatchi brothers left, taking a few key people and accounts.

Omnicom.

About the same time as the Saatchi acquisitions, three more large agencies, Batten Barton Durstine & Osborne (BBDO), Doyle Dane Bernbach (DDB), and Needham Harper Worldwide, merged to form the mega-group known today as Omnicom.

Originally, there were two major agencies, BBDO and DDB Needham (now DDB). Omnicom has grown to include TBWA/Chiat Day, Goodby Silverstein & Partners, Ketchum, and a wide range of agencies in marketing services and new media.

WPP.

Following suit, another British company, WPP, led by former Saatchi chief financial officer, Martin Sorrell, acquired two of the world's largest agencies – JWT and O&M. In addition, it acquired one of the country's largest public relations firms, Hill & Knowlton.

WPP acquired Y&R, briefly becoming the largest mega-agency group. But, of course, that changed again. Burnett (Bcom3) became part of Publicis, and FCB (True North) became part of IPG.

IPG & Publicis.

Years earlier, Marion Harper had developed a prototype for these groups – Interpublic (IPG), which also had renewed growth during this period.

Led by Maurice Levy, Publicis, a leading French agency, also took the mega-group route and grew to include Leo Burnett Worldwide, Fallon Worldwide, Burrell Communications, and Starcom MediaVest, to name a few.

Accounts were won and lost. Here's the latest scorecard.

Top Mega-Groups by Income – 2007:

Omnicom Group	$12.69 billion
WPP Group	12.38 billion
Interpublic Group of Companies (IPG)	6.55 billion
Publicis	6.38 billion
Dentsu (Japan)	2.93 billion
Aegis Group	2.22 billion
Havas Advertising	2.09 billion

(Source: *Advertising Age* 2007 Agency Report)

Agency mergers and the formation of mega-groups were also fostered by client mergers and globalization.

As these clients grew, mega-agencies now provided these multinational accounts with more integrated marketing services, such as direct response, sales promotion, and public relations.

Mega-Agency Benefits.

In addition to offering more services in more countries, mega-agencies offer clients other benefits:

- They provide clients with an expanded talent pool of communication specialists.

- They provide increased negotiating clout when buying media time and space.

For the agency, mega-size brings status and financial rewards. In some situations, staff may be reduced to eliminate redundant positions, saving money and improving efficiency.

The high cost of competitive new business presentations can be funded a bit more easily. And account losses are less threatening, with international relationships recreating the feeling of partnership between client and agency.

Still, it's a "people business," and problems can still occur if an agency grows too impersonal or focuses too much on size and profitability rather than creativity. And, of course, when client management changes, all bets are off.

Example: The late WRG

This was demonstrated dramatically with the complete disappearance of WRG (originally Wells Rich Greene).

They had a blue chip client list that included P&G, Alka-Seltzer, Clairol, Heineken, and Phillip Morris.

Mary Wells retired to France and exits accelerated.

As key people left, relationships ended and clients left.

In two years, an $880 million agency disappeared from sight!

Conflicts.

Sometimes mergers bring about a **conflict of interest.**

This happens when the newly formed agency has two accounts that compete with each other for business.

These conflicts usually necessitate either some organizational realignment or the resignation of one account.

Another Example: *Budweiser*

A particularly unfortunate example occurred with DMB&B.
The New York media group was selected to place media for client Kraft General Foods (KGF), and the assignment enlarged to include placement for related Phillip Morris companies (PM owns KGF), which included Miller.

The star account of DMB&B's St. Louis office was Budweiser – a treasured and long-term account. A-B, the parent of Budweiser, felt that the whole matter was improperly handled.

This was aggravated by the fact that competition and bad feelings between A-B and Miller were fairly high.

A-B's discontent was such that they pulled the entire account from DMB&B St. Louis, despite well-regarded work, such as Budweiser's "Frogs" commercials.

Example: A Stroke of Luck

Conflicts can sometimes be a stroke of luck.

During the Omnicom merger, which resulted in DDB/Needham, the LA office of Needham had an automobile account, Honda, which was in conflict with the long-standing DDB/NY account, Volkswagen. Something had to give.

Plop. Fizz. Lose the Biz.

DDB had Alka Seltzer, with award-winning ads like *"I can't believe I ate the whole thing,"* and *"That's a spicy meatball."* And lost the business.

Then it was a Wells Rich Greene account – with *"Plop. Plop. Fizz. Fizz."* But key people left and the biz left – along with the fizz.

Great Work Isn't Enough.

You also need strong client relationships. The Budweiser frogs moved on to another agency, where their peaceful life was interrupted by Louie the Lizard, created by Goodby Silverstein & Partners.

Be it ever so Honda.

Good Work. Good Client. And Good Luck.

When DDB and Needham merged, they helped turn the Los Angeles office of Needham into Honda's agency – Rubin Postaer and Associates.

Even though they were small, strong client relationships and solid work were enough for Honda.

Since then, they shrunk the name and enlarged the agency. Now named RPA, they've become the third-largest independent agency in the US.

Top 25 US Agencies.

Here's a ranking of the top 25 agencies by income for 2007.

1. **McCann-Erickson Worldwide**
2. **BBDO Worldwide**
3. **JWT**
4. **Y&R**
5. **DDB Worldwide**
6. **Ogilvy & Mather Worldwide**
7. **Grey**
8. **Campbell-Ewald**
9. **DraftFCB**
10. **TBWA Worldwide**
11. **Saatchi & Saatchi**
12. **Leo Burnett Worldwide**
13. **Publicis USA**
14. **Zimmerman Advertising**
15. **Euro RSCG Worldwide**
16. **Richards Group**
17. **Doner**
18. **Hill Holliday**
19. **Arnold Worldwide**
20. **Deutsch**
21. **Cramer-Krasselt**
22. **Mullen**
23. **RPA**
24. **GSD&M's Idea City**
25. **Crispin Porter & Bogusky**

The LA office's chief account exec, Gerry Rubin, and creative director, Larry Postaer, found themselves virtually handed their own agency. Today, Gerry Rubin & Postaer, now RPA, is still the agency and still doing excellent work for Honda.

Luck doesn't always go both ways, DDB lost VW soon after.

Agency Brands.

The concept of branding is so central to advertising that many agency executives may refer to their own companies as brands. Indeed, agencies often develop a reputation, style, and philosophy that differentiate themselves.

An agency's scope, including its resources and expertise, also serves to set it apart and define its business interests. There are **global agencies** that can handle their clients' business around the world. They are likely to have hundreds or thousands of employees stationed in many different countries.

These agency mega-groups also own other agencies. Omnicom Group, Interpublic (IPG), Publicis, and WPP, each own a number of different marketing communications companies in an attempt to satisfy all their clients' promotional needs on an international scale.

Example: SuperStar Brands

When McCann-Erickson purchased publicity powerhouse PMK, they pointed out PMK's line-up of stars – like Tom Cruise, Tom Hanks, Michelle Pfeiffer, and Matt Damon.

"Celebrity icons are brands," noted McCann CEO John Dooner. *"There may be opportunities to work with like-minded brands in the corporate world."*

Example: You'd Better Understand the Business You're In

It doesn't always work. When Saatchi & Saatchi went into management consulting, it was a large, expensive mistake.

More recently, IPG ran into huge financial troubles as the result of owning an event marketer – a European racing promoter – that generated huge losses unknown to top management.

International Agency Brands.

O&M, for example, has 275 offices in 66 countries to serve its 1,500 clients. For larger client companies, if an agency does not have the resources to help that company's marketing effort on an international scale, they will turn to another agency.

That's exactly what happened when P&G ended an otherwise very satisfactory relationship with Tatham-Laird in Chicago.

National, Regional, and Local.

Around the world, there are **national agencies** that focus on one country's culture and business environment.

Throughout the US, there are thousands of **regional** and **local agencies** that work closely with clients, often retailers and service providers, within smaller areas.

Many of these national and regional agencies may be part of a larger agency group. (Locals are usually independent.)

Examples: Borders Perrin & Norrander and CMF&Z

For example, Borders Perrin & Norrander in Portland, Oregon, was a strong regional agency. They were responsible for the clever and effective ads for Columbia Outerwear. They became part of True North – now a part of IPG.

Wes Perrin, one of the founders of that agency, has some advice to share later in this chapter.

CMF&Z, with offices in Des Moines and Cedar Rapids, had a strong agricultural client base and expertise in that area. They became part of Y&R's family of agencies.

Regional Alliances.

Most of the strong regionals discussed in Chapter Two, such as Goodby Silverstein and Hal Riney in San Francisco, Fallon and Carmichael-Lynch in Minneapolis, and GSD&M in Austin, now belong to larger agency groups.

For the most part, these agencies operate as independent companies, often competing with other agencies within the same mega-agency group for new clients and, because each has autonomy, handling competitive clients.

But, whatever the size and whatever the country, full-service agencies are remarkably similar in their primary roles and organization, providing clients with the four core agency functions as well as auxiliary marketing services.

But there are a few other types of agencies.

The Small Versus Big Agency Debate

Throughout the modern history of advertising, thoughts and trends have varied about small agencies versus big agencies. In the past five years, a number of smaller, independent agencies have been very successful by creating some brilliant campaigns for their clients and, thus, have rekindled the debate about which approach works best in today's business environment.

Major factors influencing the debate today are the need for corporate "organic growth" and new technologies. The large communication holding companies and mega-agencies are entering a new phase. One reason is there is not much left to consolidate. In 2005, the top four holding companies accounted for over 57% of spending on advertising media and marketing in the US. Rather than grow through acquisitions, the holding companies must find ways to "organically" grow their existing businesses. They have to find ways to be more nimble and to keep their creative product fresh – two areas that don't benefit from sheer company size.

Scott Donaton observes, "*New media technologies disintermediate established business very violently. If media companies can deal directly with marketers, or consumers with manufacturers, why allow a middleman (advertising agencies) between them?*" New interactive technologies will affect whether certain agencies and job functions exist a few years from now. Agencies of every size will need to adapt to remain competitive.

"B to B" Agencies.

US South advertises pre-paid phone cards to the sales promotion industry. Trade publications are a primary channel for B-to-B advertising.

Design Houses & Internet Agencies.

Web sites and Internet strategies are two growing marketing needs that are driving business for these two types of specialized agencies.

A New Kind of Agency.

In 1977 Robert Greenberg began as specialist in computerized film production. Today, R/GA is one of the leading digital agencies. You can visit them at www.rga.com.

#6, #13, and #1!

When Melissa Lammers presented in the finals of the AAF National Student Advertising Competition, her team (University of Florida) came in sixth.

She went on to lead the #1 agency in the 13th largest US market – Puerto Rico – as Senior VP and General Manager for Y&R Puerto Rico, Inc.

Her office is both an ethnic agency, specializing in a Spanish-speaking market, and an important office of an international agency network.

She credits her education as a major contributor to her success. *"I was extra-ordinarily well-prepared for a career in advertising."*

Today's multi-national clients want world-class marketing thinking executed with a local touch – for the greatest effectiveness in each market.

Kang & Lee for AT&T.

Find out more in Chapter 12.

Recently, the pendulum seems to have swung from the "big is better" side to the "creative ideas rule" side. Advertising Age proclaimed, "Smart beats big in today's marketing world. And smarter, smaller, nimbler shops are going to eat their bigger brethren's lunch if the leviathans don't learn some new tricks." For any agency to survive, it must nurture ideas. Great thinking and creative ideas will always be the currency of the advertising business regardless of an agency's size.

One independent, medium-size agency that has been producing breakthrough ideas is Crispin, Porter + Bogusky in Miami, Florida. They created the highly acclaimed launch of BMW's Mini-Cooper. The success of that advertising led to Volkswagen offering them its much larger account in 2005, which they accepted after resigning Mini-Cooper (due to the competitive conflict of handling two competing car accounts). The agency's superb creativity has won it a number of large national accounts including Miller Lite, Coca-Cola's Sprite and Coke Zero, and Burger King.

Crispin's edgy work for Burger King, which is featured throughout this book, is credited with improving sales. Crispin's latest efforts involve developing entertainment content and partnering up with clients. It is planning to produce a full-length movie about a character who lives in an apartment above a Burger King restaurant. The agency was partly motivated by the success of *Napoleon Dynamite*, which cost $400,000 to make and earned over $44 million.

Specialized or Niche Agencies.

Not all agencies offer the four functions of a full-service agency. Many small-to-medium-sized agencies offer specialized services or expertise in a market niche.

The basic types of specialized agencies and services are:
➤ **Business to Business**
➤ **Creative Boutiques and Design Houses**
➤ **Ethnic Agencies**
➤ **Digital Agencies.** This is a new type of agency. It is also a new service offering for traditional agencies.

Let's take a closer look at these agencies.

Business-to-Business Agencies.

Many agencies, like HSR Business to Business in Cincinnati, specialize in developing marketing and advertising programs for companies that sell products or services to other businesses.

Business-to-business advertising may require technical product knowledge, understanding of a particular industry, or simply the kind of service that only comes with proximity and long-term familiarity. For example, Sullivan Higdon and Sink, based in Wichita, an aerospace center, has great expertise in that area.

Identifying prospects, key company decision makers, and ways of reaching them through trade and business publications, direct mail, or other media, differs from mainstream consumer marketing.

Smaller business-to-business clients tend to have even more need of IMC services. Agencies for clients of this size often become valuable extensions of their marketing department.

Creative Boutiques & Design Houses.

The most common specialized agencies are **creative boutiques**. These agencies tend to be small and limit their involvement to the conceptualization and production of creative executions.

Boutiques employ talented creative specialists such as art directors, copywriters, designers, and broadcast producers.

Creative boutiques usually work directly with the advertiser, but they may also work with other full-service agencies on an as-needed, freelance basis.

A related type of company is the **design house**. These also tend to be small companies, though a few are quite large, that specialize in such things as logo and package design, promotional materials, and annual reports. They also do advertising.

As mentioned, virtually every agency is working to add some sort of Internet or digital capability.

Opportunities for Growth.

Some of these companies can grow quite large.

The Richards Group, now the largest independent agency in the US, began with designer Stan Richards adding advertising to his small design practice.

Wieden + Kennedy began as a small creative boutique. How small? They used the pay phone in the lobby.

A new entry is Romani Brothers in Chicago. Creative director Bernie Pitzel opened for business with an airline client he had helped at a number of agencies – ATA. They helped him take off as an independent. Now he's doing it on his own. (We'll hear from Bernie a bit later in this chapter.)

Ethnic Agencies.

Agencies specialize by market niches including ethnic groups. For example, there are agencies that offer expertise in advertising to African Americans, Hispanics, and Asians.

These agencies may be full-service or specialized even further by limited creative or media service. They may create their own advertising for their clients or modify campaigns from other agencies in order to better target them to a specific ethnic group.

Burrell Communications in Chicago (now a part of Publicis) is one of the leading agencies focusing on African Americans. Bromley Communications in San Antonio (also a part of Publicis) is a leading Hispanic agency, and a number of new agencies, such as Kang & Lee (now a part of Y&R), specialize in marketing to Asian Americans. (You'll meet Kang & Lee in Chapter Twelve.)

Muse Corduro Chen in Los Angeles features a very diverse management team. They do work on multiple ethnic groups.

are you a jean or a khaki?

Are You an In-House?

Some of the innovative creative work for Target is done by their in-house ad group. Other work is done by Wieden + Kennedy.

A survey of Association of National Advertisers (ANA) members finds 42% have in-house agencies or MarCom departments.

In-House Agency Advantages.

Familiarity & Specialization. Highly technical industries often use in-house agencies.

GE and Apple Computer are two examples of marketers who have been active in-house.

Staff can be hired with specialized technical backgrounds or receive thorough training in company products.

Confidentiality. Some companies feel more secure by keeping new product designs and marketing plans internal.

Some industries, such as fashion, are vulnerable to copycats.

Cost Savings. Companies may be able to save money by eliminating agency profit margins and by cutting some other overhead costs. However, the company needs to manage additional staff, office space, and equipment.

In-House Tasks. Per the ANA survey, in-house agencies typically handle:

POS and/or Brochures – 92%
Internal communications – 82%
Internal/company videos – 69%
Design/brand identity – 66 %
Direct mail – 65 %
Web site creation and upkeep – 65%
Media planning – 35 %
Media buying – 24 %

A Digitas Portfolio:

Some examples of Digitas' work:

A rich media online promotion for American Express promotes 5% cash back from AmEx Blue.

Interactive online e-booklet for the SAAB 9.3. Click and it animates.

Pontiac's online GTO introduction.

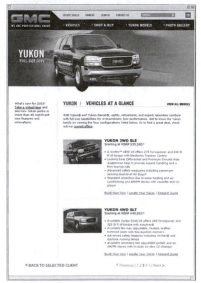

A microsite for the GMC Yukon.

Internet Agencies.

ADWEEK NOW HAS A TOP 50 ranking of interactive agencies in a section called *IQ,* which stands for *Interactive Quarterly.*

Their first issue of 2004 celebrated the fact that marketers spent $2.2 billion in the 4th quarter of 2003 – the best quarter ever.

It was even better than *"before that legendary bubble went 'pop.'"*

Revenue for the Top 50 grew 14% – another sign of renewed health for this new but growing segment of the ad industry.

50 Agencies – from 24 to 1200.

Of the top 50 agencies, two-thirds had over 100 employees. This ranged from #1 Euro RSCG Interaction, a division of Havas, with an estimated 1225 employees to #50, HSR Business to Business, an independent agency in Cincinnati with 240 employees.

Better yet, in an industry that has had its ups and downs, 47 of the 50 agencies had "up" years – with increases ranging from 5% to 84%. This included one of the oldest of the "new" agencies, SBI.Razorfish, now in Salt Lake City, with an increase of 60%.

Agencies of the Year.

Let's look at the two winners of *IQ's* "Agency of the Year" award:
• **Digitas** – *IQ* **Independent Agency of the Year**
• **R/GA** – *IQ* **Affiliated Agency of the Year**

And a third, mainstream agency that's also evolving into a digital powerhouse.

As you see what they do and how they do it, you'll get a feel for what this new sector of the agency business is turning into.

Example #1: Digitas.

With a client list that includes AmEx, AT&T Wireless, FedEx, GM, and Morgan Stanley, Digitas offers what *AdWeek* calls *"…laserlike focus on accountable marketing."*

This plays to the accountability that is built into interactive.

You can count "hits" to find out if you have a hit.

This was particularly good news as Digitas was one of the agencies that had to ride the roller coaster. Predicting a 25% increase in 2001, they saw an 18% decline instead – with huge losses.

But both their business and their stock rebounded (from $3 a share to $10) as they kept to their business of building Web sites, crafting rich-media ads, and executing online promotions.

The big change they perceive is that interest in online success is now coming from the CEOs and CMOs of major marketers.

"Clients are realizing 'this is really going to change the business I'm in today,'" notes Digitas CEO David Kenny.

Example #2: R/GA.

One of the pioneers of computer graphics as been Robert Greenberg of R/GA.

"Bob defines the cutting edge," says Bank of America client Catherine Bessant. *"And not in an impossible way, but in a really functional way that really enables application of the cutting edge to real-world situations and real-world opportunities."*

They began in film. Some of the great computer graphics and titles in *Superman, Alien, All That Jazz, Gandhi, Ghostbusters, Mission Impossible, Predator* (one of the few movies starring two future governors), *Home Alone,* and *Silence of the Lambs* got R/GA its start.

But he was soon discovered by advertising – creating commercials for *Bell Atlantic, Diet Coke, John Hancock, Kodak, Mobil, Shell, Timex,* and even the opening sequence for *Saturday Night Live.*

Check the time line on their Web site – www.rga.com

In the mid-90s, Greenberg evolved his company from films and broadcast to a focus on digital design. As the technology evolved, so did R/GA, becoming the supplier of choice for cutting-edge marketers and a division of True North, which merged into IPG.

This made R/GA the digital hub for IPG's relationships with many of their major clients.

Today, R/GA's client list includes: Bank of America, Levi's, Nestle Purina, Nike, Verizon and more. Some through IPG, but many more through R/GA's growing reputation.

These are just two of the new agency brands making the Internet a more interesting place every click.

Example #3: Goodby, Silverstein & Partners

One of the brightest of the traditional agencies has gone more and more digital. With high-tech clients like HP and Adobe, and a San Francisco base, they worked to increase the percentage of work that went into the digital space. Today, half of the agency's output is some form of digital work.

How to Find out More.

The *Standard Directory of Advertising Agencies* (also known as "The Red Book") lists agencies specializing in the following categories:

- **African American**
- **Asian**
- **Business to Business**
- **Entertainment**
- **Food Service**
- **Health Care**
- **Internet**
- **Infomercials**
- **Resort and Travel**
- **Sports Marketing**
- **Agriculture**
- **Automotive**
- **Direct Response**
- **Financial**
- **Gay and Lesbian**
- **Hispanic**
- **Industrial**
- **Recruitment**
- **Sales Promotion**
- **Technical**

If you have some specialized skill, interest, or background, one of these types of agencies might have a special opportunity for you.

Other Suppliers of Agency Services.

As discussed in Chapter Two, it has become more and more common to "unbundle" agency services. Today, one agency may be in charge of creative; another may place media.

Ironically, as marketing has become more integrated, a wider variety of options has dis-integrated the services of full-service agencies. There are now many interesting niches for those who specialize in providing partial agency services.

An R/GA Portfolio:

Some examples of R/GA's work:

One of the many Web sites R/GA creates for Nike.

Online work for Levi's.

Bank of America rich-media ad with animation. *"It probably costs you $53 a year in stamps to pay bills."*

"Use our free on-line bill paying service instead.

A GS&P Portfolio.

The Got Milk site:

A site for Comcast's "Slowsky's":

In-House Agency Disadvantages.

Objectivity.

A key responsibility of independent agencies is to provide clients with objective recommendations. When you're in-house, that can be easier said than done.

Expertise.

Outside agencies have experience with many different industries. This helps them provide new insights and perspective on client business.

Marketers' major critique is that most lack "a depth of strategic thinking."

Fresh Ideas.

In-house creative may become stale after awhile.

At independent agencies, copywriters and art directors are often rotated from one account to another to keep things fresh.

This is not possible with a small in-house staff focused on one client.

Half the marketers said it was hard to come up with fresh ideas with internal teams.

The Best of Both.

Many companies use both in-house and independent agencies.

Sears, for example, uses Y&R to handle its national campaigns, while using its own in-house advertising department to handle much of the local promotion of its stores.

Even Nike and Apple, with outstanding agencies, have some in-house capabilities for sales materials for dealers and other corporate communications projects.

Source: Association of National Advertisers. Online research. August 2008

Here are a few of the major agency-like options:

➤ **Freelancers and Consultants**
➤ **In-House Agencies**
➤ **Media Agencies** (aka Media Buying Services) These are also covered in Chapter Seven)

Let's take a quick look at these interesting businesses.

Freelancers and Consultants.

In the advertising business there are also many individuals who work for themselves – **freelancers** and **consultants.**

Both sell their services to advertisers and ad agencies. They're hired when there is a project suited to their special talents or when staff is too busy to take on another assignment. With tighter staffing, this has become a more common practice many places.

They may be hired on a project basis, on a day rate, or they may receive long-term contracts and even have office space.

Freelance Suppliers.

These days, it's quite common for companies to hire freelance copywriters, art directors, Web designers, producers, and researchers.

For example, in Chicago, firms such as Paladin, Artisan, Aquent, Copy Desk, and Portfolio provide these services to a wide range of clients and agencies.

Consultants – More than Creative.

Additionally, advertisers and agencies often hire marketing consultants and strategists who have highly developed knowledge of a specific industry or a special marketing technique such as new product development.

Some high-end creative people also serve as consultants – working on overall strategies and agency organization in addition to creating individual ads.

Naked, out of London, now with offices in the US, is an example of an emerging type of strategic consultant dealing with the growing range of communication options.

In-House or "House" Agencies.

An in-house advertising agency exists when an advertiser owns and operates its own agency or department equipped with the resources necessary to create its advertising.

House agencies may create all of a company's advertising or they may be responsible for a portion of the campaign and use outside advertising agencies for the rest.

Many in-house agencies have been very successful.

Some in-house agencies have become independent. For example, LINTAS began as Unilever's house agency – Lever International Advertising Services.

A lot of fashion advertising, such as work for Calvin Klein and Target, comes from in-house operations.

Some overall advantages and disadvantages of in-house agencies are covered in this chapter's sidebars.

Media Agencies (Media Buying Services).

Another form of agency specialization is media buying.

Media agencies offer clients their expertise in media planning as well as buying clout in negotiating rates and placement.

Originally, media buying services worked directly for advertisers or provided services to smaller agencies without the staff or resources to handle media placement for their clients.

But, as discussed in Chapter Two, with unbundling, this has changed dramatically. Now, every mega-agency group has one or more divisions specializing in media.

Even though it is a high-volume/low-margin business, it's one that has grown dramatically. And, since media expenditures are often the largest part of the marketing budget, it's one that is of great attention and concern.

If media interests you, you should know that this is an area full of interesting job opportunities.

We'll also cover these unique businesses in a bit more detail in Chapter Seven, "Marketing Services."

What Agencies Do.

AGENCIES ALL DO VERY SIMILAR THINGS. Let's look at how the American Association of Advertising Agencies (4A's) defines it.

"An advertising agency is an independent organization of creative people and business people who specialize in developing and preparing advertising plans, advertisements, and other promotional tools.

"The agency purchases advertising space and time in various media on behalf of different advertisers, or sellers (its clients) to find customers for their goods and services."

To do this, an agency employs a variety of people with different responsibilities and skills that, to date, has been primarily concerned with the creation and placement of advertising for its clients. As media evolves into more and more digital opportunities, agencies are, not surprisingly, evolving as well.

Here's how we'll cover this next section:
➤ **The Two Primary Roles of an Agency**
➤ **IMC Evolution & Digital Revolution**
➤ **Four Major Departmental Functions**
➤ **Seven Primary Services of a Full-Service Agency**

We'll see how agencies organize to fulfill those functions, and we'll talk to Jodi, Stephanie, Bernie, and Mairee about their jobs.

We might even meet a few more people.

Two Primary Roles.

Successful agencies are characterized by two things:
• **Big ideas**
• **Big, successful brands**

That's why advertising agencies have two primary roles:

1. **Idea generation** – Also known as "creativity."

Brand Stewardship at Ogilvy & Mather.

The following excerpts are from *O&M's Views on Brand Stewardship*. If you'd like to read more, check out their site at www.ogilvy.com.

What Is It?

Brand stewardship is based on the crucial understanding of the difference between a product and a brand.

O&M believes *"the brand is the relationship a product has with the consumer."*

That's what makes *Kodak* more than film and *IBM* more than computers.

"Our job is to build and enhance the relationship between the consumer and the product.

"We do this by keeping our resources squarely focused on all aspects of the brand/consumer relationship.

"We are not merely producers of ads, we are keepers of the understanding that will help our brands thrive, no matter where the marketplace, no matter how competitive, no matter what size, no matter the medium used."

The First Step – Know Your Brand.
First, know your brand inside out.
• The product details
• The consumers
• The competition
• The environment

The Second Step – Brand Audit.
The Brand Audit is a skillful and exhaustive analysis of the consumer's perception of the brand.

The Third Step – Brand Probe.
The Brand Probe is an array of research techniques specifically developed by O&M to help provide the deeper insight and understanding necessary to answer the Brand Audit.

The Fourth Step – BrandPrint™.
The BrandPrint™ is O&M's vivid statement of the unique relationship between the consumer and a brand.

The Fifth Step – Use What You Know.
The BrandPrint™ is used to guide every single marketing decision.

The Pillsbury Idea.

The *"inherent drama"* of *Poppin' Fresh Dough* and the *Pillsbury Doughboy* is an idea that has helped Pillsbury introduce fresh product ideas that are already friendly and familiar –demonstrating what Leo Burnett called *"the glacier-like power of friendly familiarity."*

The Absolut Idea.

Tasteless, odorless, and colorless – yet Absolut sells for 50% more and at one time captured a 50% share of the premium category.

That's the power of an idea.

2. Brand building, which can be an agency-wide function and an organizing philosophy, like O&M's Brand Stewardship.

Advertising Agencies Manufacture Ideas.

An agency is organized around the process of manufacturing ideas – the bigger the better.

When David Ogilvy said, *"Big ideas, that's what advertising is all about,"* he wasn't kidding.

Agencies first manufacture the thinking that goes into the advertising – the strategy, the advertising plan, and the advertising itself. Then they produce and place the advertising.

Ideas are the lifeblood of an advertising agency.

Creating Intellectual Capital.

Ideas are the products that agencies manufacture and sell to make a profit and stay in business.

The quality of an agency's ideas (and how well they are produced) are what set it apart from the competition.

This is a classic example of Paul Romer's economic thinking – ideas add value. That's why one of the key departments in virtually every agency is the creative department.

Agencies Create and Sell Different Kinds of Ideas.

Many are related to designing the advertising itself – television and radio commercials, magazine and newspaper ads, outdoor billboards, and promotional materials.

Other ideas involve finding ways to identify and reach prospective consumers through the mass media or by some other method. (That's one reason agencies are interested in the Internet.)

Still others include marketing ideas such as packaging, distribution, pricing, and promotional opportunities.

Inside the agency, creativity and idea generation are not the sole property of the copywriters and art directors in the agency's creative department.

Everyone in the agency organization, every job title in every department, is responsible to some degree for generating ideas and solutions to client marketing problems.

For example, O&M agency management often challenges staff to come up with one (unsolicited) new idea a week for clients. The best "business-building" ideas are recognized with awards.

The Other Role – Brand Building.

Another major role of an advertising agency is **brand building** or, as it is termed at O&M, **Brand Stewardship.**

This book's title, *Advertising and The Business of Brands*, is meant to emphasize the central importance of branding and effective brand management to the advertising process.

The Need for Leadership.

Typically, a brand needs a single architect, someone who can create, implement, and coordinate a synergistic strategy across multiple marketing communications disciplines, media, and markets.

Traditionally, the agency has been the lead candidate for this role. It acts as the keeper of the faith and torch carrier in terms of resisting any unnecessary tampering with the brand's strategy and equity.

Inherently, agencies provide a strong link between strategy and execution in the marketplace due to the high media visibility of their work.

The Growth of the Brand-Building Process.

As discussed in Chapter Two ("The Modern Marketplace") and Chapter Four ("Marketers and Advertisers"), marketers are now assuming a more primary role in brand stewardship.

As companies come to appreciate the asset value of their brands, their commitment to brand building will also grow.

Agencies, however, remain the primary source of ideas that reach consumers through media channels.

The essence of the agency business is to add *perceived value* to the product or service of its client.

The agency's purpose is to create and direct communication about a product or service so the brand is perceived to have a unique value or brand personality.

Whether originating from client or agency, leadership and vision are critical. Successful marketers and successful agencies are visionaries.

Sharing the Brand Vision in a Changing World.

Today, there are a number of marketing communication disciplines that a brand can use to reach target audiences.

These disciplines represent the various methods marketers have to communicate with their customers and prospects. Often described as the **promotion mix,** alternatives usually include:

- **Advertising**
- **Sales Promotion**
- **Personal Selling**
- **Public Relations**
- **Direct Response Marketing**
- **Packaging**

Today, the brand-building process for most large marketers is a combination of advertising and other techniques, such as sales promotion, and marketing public relations.

So, it is not surprising that many advertising agencies now offer a variety of promotional services under one roof, or with an affiliated division. It's brand building in today's marketplace.

The agency may have separate departments or corporate subsidiaries that offer public relations, direct marketing, sales promotion, and additional specialized communication services.

The IMC Evolution.

For all the reasons discussed, today's advertising agency may be quite a different place than it was 20 years ago – or, if the agency has decided to stick to its specialty, then the client and agency will be dealing with many more marketing partners.

Because that's what it takes to run today's brands.

The Mini Brand Vision.

CP+B's brand vision included a media philosophy, reinforcing the Mini's unique size with an anti-SUV, pro-hot-rod stance.

IMC Evolution.
Cigarette Marketing.

As legal restrictions closed down traditional ad channels, cigarette marketers became some of the leaders in IMC.

Whatever your attitudes toward smoking, programs like this Benson & Hedges promotion stand out as some of the best examples of integrating a brand across marketing channels.

Because it's a habit, tobacco sales promotion efforts often focus on the "heavy user," using frequency programs where smokers save UPC codes and then redeem them for brand-appropriate gifts.

This helps tobacco marketers maximize the "LTV" (Lifetime Value) of their brand-loyal consumers at the same time lives are shortened by the use of their product.

A "Pressure Cooker" Business.

As dramatized by this frame from the classic Federal Express "Fast Talker" TV commercial, the agency business is competitive, demanding, and fast-paced.

It's a service business; a client pays the bills for services rendered. A high level of performance is expected.

Clients must be satisfied or suppliers are quickly fired.

Competitive and Subjective.
The pressure is compounded by the somewhat intangible "products" an agency sells: ideas, ads, and promises of success.

Advertising is a subjective business. End-results can be hard to measure. Meanwhile, clients may explore business relationships with competing agencies by putting their account up for review. As mentioned in Chapter Two, average client tenure has shortened and dissatisfaction has risen.

There is relatively little job security in the agency business. Nonetheless, some agencies have been around for over 100 years and many enjoy long, rewarding careers.

Lean Staffing Is the Rule.
At an agency, the internal pressure is also due to working with a lean staff.

By hiring the best people it can, an agency strives to hold down staff size to improve profitability and avoid layoffs if clients cut their budget or leave the agency.

It's more pressure, but when you succeed, there's absolutely positively no doubt that you were a part of it.

From Ad Agency to "IMC" Agency

As we've discussed throughout this book, one of the major industry trends has been **Integrated Marketing Communications** (IMC).

Though, we must repeat, not everyone calls it that.

Many who practice IMC simply call it "marketing."

Whatever you call it, one result is that agencies and marketers' organizations are changing in order to facilitate closer planning and more synergy across the communications disciplines.

John Siefert, O&M's worldwide Client Service Director for American Express, observes, *"Increasingly, you're seeing more of a blur between disciplines. There's more accountability for brand advertising to generate a response."*

WPP's Martin Sorrell notes that more and more of their business is coming from areas "outside advertising."

Customer Focus.
According to Don Schultz, Professor of Integrated Marketing Communications at Northwestern University, IMC is the process of developing and implementing various forms of persuasive communications programs with customers and prospects over time.

The goal of IMC is to influence or directly affect the behavior of the selected communications audience.

IMC considers all sources of brand or company contacts which a customer or prospect has with the product or service as potential delivery channels for future messages.

In sum, the IMC process starts with the customer or prospect and then works back to determine and define the forms and methods through which persuasive communications programs should be developed.

Done right, IMC is the planning and implementation of the various communications disciplines as a single, overall communications system – making all the channels work together.

Easier Said than Done.
It sounds simple, but in practice it isn't. Plans must be set well in advance in order to coordinate all the efforts for maximum effect. (And, as we've noted, the pace of business has accelerated as well, making longer lead times quite difficult.)

In many instances, communication disciplines may actually be in a different corporate department, may involve several different outside supplier companies, and, most importantly, may involve different budgets and different ways of getting paid. So, you have very serious "turf" and control issues complicating the process further.

Traditionally, these different departments and suppliers compete with one another for a bigger slice of the marketing budget.

Even with all these complications, the evolution continues. Because the campaigns of the future will be integrated campaigns, making the most effective use of all available marketing tools.

Cross-Discipline Skills in Demand.

Effective integration calls for people who have developed a cross-disciplinary perspective. That's why there's an increasing demand for those with experience in two or more IMC disciplines.

For example, they may have worked at an ad agency and then a direct-response firm. They understand how each communication technique can best be used to solve a client's problem.

Agencies will need managers who understand the different communications disciplines and treat them equally without prejudice. People who can integrate objectives and strategies across IMC disciplines will be in demand, as will those creatives who know how to "think IMC."

Similar Jobs. Similar Responsibilities.

Keep in mind that other types of marketing communications companies – such as direct response, sales promotion, and even public relations firms – have functions, organizations, and job responsibilities very similar to agencies.

IMC is creating more career mobility and crossover desirability than many people realize. It's not uncommon for people to change jobs between these industries.

For example, Bob Levin, who you'll meet in Chapter Six, left a job in account management at DDB and became marketing director at SONY Entertainment, where he was responsible for marketing entertainment brands like *Godzilla* and *Men in Black*.

Different Functions. Different Strengths.

Even though you might not end up working in an advertising agency, it's still useful to study how they're organized.

Take a look at the chart below.

Take a Stand for Your Brand.

Today, the key for agency success is to identify your strengths and focus on that as your strategic advantage.

Simple to say, but hard to do. Agency consultant Tim Williams shows you how in this tough-minded book from The Copy Workshop.

Strengths & Weaknesses: Five Forms of Marketing Communications.

Factor	Advertising	Public Relations	Direct Response	Sales Promotion	Personal Selling
Timing	moderate/long	long	short	short	immediate
Control of Message Delivery	total	little	moderate	moderate	little
Control of Message Content	total	minimal	high	high	moderate
Ability to Target	high	low	very high	moderate	moderate
Type of Contact	non-personal	non-personal/personal	personal/non-personal	non-personal	personal
Typical Appeals	emotional/rational	image/news	rational/personal	rational	rational
Adds Perceived Value	high	high	moderate	low	low
Credibility	low	high	low	moderate	moderate
Closes Sale	low	low	moderate	high	very high
Trade Acceptability	high	low	moderate	very high	N.A.
Expense	high	low	high	moderate	high
Accountability	low	very low	very high	very high	high
Profit Contribution	moderate	low	moderate	high	moderate

Entertainment Brand IMC.

One extremely successful example of entertainment branding is Star Wars. With multiple products and multiple communication channels it's also an excellent example of IMC in action.

Consider the films, characters, toys, games, books, cross-promotions with other retailers, and the full range of marketing communications – from on-pack design, through publicity programs, to tie-in sales promotions, to paid advertising.

Here, you can compare some of the relative strengths and characteristics of the various marketing communications disciplines.

As other disciplines evolve, you can see why marketers are in constant evaluation and re-evaluation of the priorities involved in determining the marketing mix.

The modern advertising agency must be aware of these relative strengths and weaknesses – whether or not they offer them as part of agency services.

The Digital Revolution

As you know, agencies and advertising evolve as media evolves. The rapid expansion of digital media opportunities has resulted in an equally rapid expansion of agencies specializing in digital solutions. Some began as production or design houses, others as departments of existing agencies.

Some were small companies purchased by mega-agencies and others were small departments that grew to play an expanding role in the agency they called home.

At present, most are evolving as it matches up with new opportunities.

Understanding that this is an exciting business environment – one of constant change – we can still take a quick look at three basic trends that are driving this expansion.

• Expanding Bandwidth
• Expanding Media Opportunities
• The Evolving Digital Marketplace

Later, we'll take a look at one free-standing digital agency, RGA, and the way two cutting-edge agencies – Goodby Silverstein and Crispin Porter + Bogusky are successfully coming to grips with these new digital opportunities.

Expanding Bandwidth.

Just as Moore's Law is a part of ever-expanding chip capacity (and reduced processing cost), the digital pipeline going in and out of our computers is growing as well. Every day, with cable, DSL, Wi-Fi, and other technologies, individuals can receive (and send) more and more digital information faster and faster.

Quite simply, this means we can do more.

In a very short time, we've evolved from slow dial-up connections that could only send e-mail and surf the 'Net very slowly, to fast, smooth, connections that let us receive (and send) audio, video, and more.

Expanding Media Opportunities.

Now, fast as you can say YouTube, your computer can access video, and, if you're so inclined, send some out so others can see it.

But you know there's more to it than that.

The latest digital billboard on a street corner, at the movie theater, or even in an elevator, is offering opportunities that didn't exist a year ago. Or maybe two years ago.

Today, many new business models have a media component.

Social networking, cool new Web sites promoting the latest movie or the latest ad campaign, sponsored search engines, or blogs with banners are all examples of that expanding – and rapidly evolving – media environment.

The Evolving Digital Marketplace.

One of the most interesting aspects of all this is that our own behaviors are changing.

When we search for a car or an apartment, the Internet is now often a part of that behavior – instead of the newspaper classifieds.

Now, more and more, we shop online for books, CDs, DVDs, and items we might not find nearby. We may sell a bit on eBay.

These are new behaviors and they are creating a marketplace that is changing before our eyes. Recognizing these new patterns of behavior – and even anticipating them – is now an exciting part of our world.

And, more and more, managing digital information in terms of Web sites, videos, automated responses, e-mail, text messaging, downloads, and all the other new behaviors has become a vital and growing part of the agency business.

Certainly it's not all agencies, but, historically, agency-style organizations have been some of the quickest to pick up on new opportunities.

Even with the new range of opportunities for the digital revolution, four services are at the core.

Four Major Departmental Functions.

Earlier, we noted how agencies may specialize by the services they offer (e.g., creative, media buying) or the type of industries they serve (e.g., agricultural, health, ethnic).

Now let's focus on four functions and responsibilities.

A **full-service agency** is one with the size, staff, and resources to provide the four major departmental functions necessary to develop and implement a complete advertising campaign.

These departmental functions are:

❶ **Account Management**
❷ **Creative Services**
❸ **Media Planning And Buying**
❹ **Research**

These are the four key functions. As we've discussed, additional marketing services may also be offered by other departments within the agency or by other corporate subsidiaries as part of the brand-building services offered to clients.

And, like any business, a full-service agency will also have its own internal office management departments such as human resources, accounting, and legal.

Seven Primary Services of a Full-Service Agency.

Some or all of the four major departmental functions work together to provide these seven primary services. In some cases, client marketing organizations will perform aspects of these services as well – particularly if there is an in-house operation.

How to Be a More Effective Account Manager.

by Robert Gustafson

Here are a dozen tips on how to be a more effective account manager.

These tips apply to account management in most marketing communication disciplines.

1. Learn to Be a Leader. Leadership can be learned. Learn to set goals, meet deadlines, share praise, and accept blame.

Find out how to motivate your associates to do their best work.

Don't be afraid to be a critic. Stand up for your convictions and *don't ever accept work that is not on strategy.*

2. Know Your Client's Business. Get to understand your client's business as well as they do – maybe better. Become a respected partner and confidant. Know your client's goals and how they measure success. Be profit-conscious for your client, as well as for your own company.

3. Set High Standards. Always strive to exceed expectations.

Give people more ideas, information, and options than they expect and you'll be a treasured partner.

4. Show Clients You Care. Demonstrate that you appreciate and respect their problems and expertise.

Listen to what they "mean" not "say." Caring also manifests itself in hard work and a commitment to excellence.

5. Be a Good Salesperson. Selling intangible ideas is tough. Rise to that challenge.

Resiliency is critical in any service business. Grow skin thick as an alligator's. Use it for armor when needed. Never stop selling.

6. Communicate Early and Often. By avoiding surprises, you can avoid problems. Move the business along steadily and constantly.

Don't wait until the end to get suggestions or approval. Keep people informed and involved. Put it on paper. Keep words to a minimum.

(Continued on next page)

More Effective (Cont.)

7. Become a Better Communicator.

Communications and persuasion are your business.

Look for ways to become a better writer and presenter. Attend a seminar. Take a class. Read a book.

You might want to read this book: *What Do You Mean I Can't Write? A Practical Guide to Business Writing for Agency Account Managers*, by Norm MacMaster.

For years, this book was an underground legend – passed from hand to hand. Now you can have your own copy. From the Copy Workshop.

8. Be an Honest Diplomat.

Many times the account person is the go-between. Where do loyalties lie?

Sometimes client-versus-agency responsibilities require a balancing act. Practice diplomacy, but be honest and offer your best advice.

Stay out of client politics.

9. Help Your Clients Look Good.

The better they look, the better you look in the eyes of management.

Let clients know about resources and networking capabilities. Offer help in any way.

10. Think Out of the Box.

Ideas are your business. Not just advertising or PR ideas – all kinds of ideas and solutions to problems.

They may be related to product, packaging, distribution, or the corporate organization.

Great account people will read something totally unrelated to their client's business and then make an insightful connection.

Try sending your client one new idea a week. That will gain their attention and appreciation.

11. Require an Annual Evaluation.

Ask for client feedback on agency performance.

(Continued on next page)

As you review them, keep in mind the cycle of planning, implementation, and evaluation.

Note that the process often begins with evaluation.

1. Complete a Market Analysis – Identify major problems and opportunities facing the brand, its target audience, competitive strengths and weaknesses, and most compelling appeals.

Account management, research, and the client brand group are deeply involved in this part of the process. Market research suppliers and services may also be called in.

2. Develop an Advertising Plan – Provide clients with a recommended plan of action including objectives, strategies, budget, timetable, and means of evaluation.

Today, this may be more of an IMC Plan, with advertising a part of it. Depending on capabilities, the client marketing department or account management will take the lead.

3. Integrate Other Marketing Communications – Work with other departments and suppliers for a cohesive IMC campaign.

The timing of this IMC stage varies, depending on the scope and sophistication of the campaign plan.

Larger client companies are more likely to oversee and manage the IMC effort themselves. However, as agencies have grown their IMC and "below the line" capabilities, there are more and more instances where clients are moving this task back to agencies.

4. Prepare a Creative Strategy – Set down what advertising is expected to accomplish, how the brand is to be positioned in the consumer's mind, and how the advertising can add perceived value that sets the brand apart from competition.

Here, the Creative Department takes the lead.

Moreover, since the expansion of media opportunities has opened up new creative opportunities, it is not unusual for the creative department to become involved at an earlier stage of the process – where creative opportunities determine the IMC options.

This is certainly the case with CP+B, where Alex Bogusky and his Creative Department make decisions that drive the entire IMC process.

5. Create Advertising Executions – Conceive and produce the recommended creative materials, such as television and radio commercials, print advertisements, outdoor billboards, etc.

This creative responsibility uses a variety of Production Services people as well as outside suppliers.

Again, what were once exclusively advertising opportunities are now a greater range of creative opportunities. So an agency like Goodby Silverstein will look for ways that their work for H-P will also make an appropriate impact on the Internet.

6. Develop and Implement a Media Plan – Determine what media and media vehicles most effectively and efficiently reach the target audience, negotiate the best possible rates, positions, and merchandising during the media buying process.

This is a core responsibility of the Media Department and/or the media buying service involved. This may be the agency's own service or it may be outsourced.

And, as this edition was being prepared, we were seeing a response to the growing range of communications options with high-end message consultants like Naked. In addition, sophisticated marketers, such as Lever Brothers, P&G, and Kimberly-Clark are taking another look at how they are spending the bulk of their marketing dollars.

7. Handle Billing and Payments – According to the client and agency contractual agreement, bill the client as appropriate for handling payments for media time and space, print and broadcast production, and other types of suppliers.

That's what agencies do.

Now let's take a look at how they're organized to do it.

Agency Organization.

AN AGENCY MAY RANGE IN SIZE from one or two people working out of their home or garage to thousands of employees in offices spread around the world.

Agency Structure and Functions.

How an advertising agency is organized, functions, and the number of services it offers depends on its size and the kinds of clients it serves.

As mentioned, today's emerging media – especially the Internet – have led to the start-up of many small agencies specializing in these new digital technologies.

Small Agency = "Many Hats."

Typically, in smaller agencies each employee wears more than one hat. Job descriptions will be less specialized as people are required to perform more job functions.

Smaller agencies also have fewer layers of departmental management, so a greater percentage of the employees report directly to the agency owner or president.

Large Agency = Specialization.

Usually, the larger the agency, the more specialized the individual job responsibilities. Large agencies are usually organized by communications disciplines (e.g., advertising, sales promotion, direct response), departments (e.g., account management, creative services, media), and sometimes by client groups (e.g., employees servicing a specific client account).

In larger agencies, departments may be as big as a small agency. Naturally, there are more reporting layers as well.

All Agencies Are Not Alike.

As mentioned earlier in this chapter, the traditional full-service advertising agency organization is in a state of flux. Larger organizations are faced with increasing competition from smaller, nimbler, and highly specialized agencies.

Provide a questionnaire to make sure that you receive the kind of input you need to manage the account.

You may also provide the client your assessment of the relationship.

12. Be Prepared to Resell the Agency's Merits Every Year.
Don't take things for granted; it's more economical to schedule an annual review meeting than to be tossed into a competitive agency review.

Present the agency's point of view and plans for the future.

Provide an update on the agency's best work for all its clients.

Remember, most account managers have more responsibility than "real" authority. That demands good leadership skills.

Finally, the only way to find real job security as an account manager is to provide strong leadership and a consistent flow of meaningful business-building contributions.

"We want people who are visionary, restless, endlessly curious, and love the thrill of building business."

— Roy Spence, GSD&M

A Day in the Life of an Account Supervisor.

Jodi Cary, Account Supervisor, Ogilvy & Mather/Chicago

A "typical" day? Every day is very different. Cliche, but true.

Our Marketing Calendar.

Generally, things depend on the time of year and my client's calendar.

Right now, I'm heavily involved in helping write next year's marketing plans. This includes:

- Analyzing last year's advertising
- Reporting competitive activity
- Working with the client to understand all issues facing the brand

After the plans are written and sold to management, we'll have a pretty good understanding of what the advertising must do and the budget.

Then, we'll devote the next six months to developing the objectives, strategies, media plans, and creative, so things can be executed in time for the client's peak business season.

One Campaign a Year.

I work on several major packaged-goods assignments. We generally produce one major campaign a year.

Since it only happens once a year, we spend a significant amount of time analyzing the business challenges, the role of the advertising, the brand's consumer, and what the brand means.

Once we begin to develop the advertising strategy and creative, we do a lot of research to make sure the message is as effective as possible with the brand's target consumer.

(Continued on next page)

In addition, there's more need for campaigns that offer consumers interactive opportunities and, of course, Web sites, which are not always a full service agency's strong suit.

As the number of media alternatives continues to expand, agencies are seeking new ways to effectively contact consumers. This need has led more companies to explore product placement in programming and films, and to develop their own branded entertainment content in broadcast and the Internet. These changes have led to some new thinking about how an agency should function and be organized.

New trends in agency organization will be discussed at the end of this chapter. First, let's review the traditional full-service organization and job functions, which still predominate the industry today.

The organization chart and job title responsibilities may vary from agency to agency.

However, large agency organizations, with all their specialization, offer the clearest way to understand what an agency does. For smaller agencies, just combine the functions. Or, eliminate a few.

As an agency grows in account billings and services, it is likely to adopt a more traditional full-service departmental structure.

Let's look at it department by department.

Agency Organization Chart.

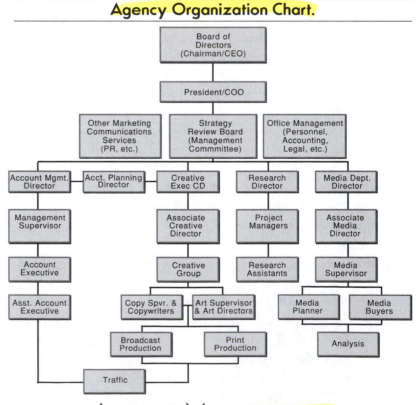

Account Management.

Account managers serve as the liaison between agency and client.

They are responsible for understanding their client's business, marketing needs, and representing the client's point-of-view with other agency departments.

Responsibility.

Account managers are responsible for developing the advertising plan and marshalling the agency's resources to accomplish the specified objectives on time and within budget.

David Ogilvy says the chief role of an account executive is, *"to extract the best possible work from the other departments of the agency."*

Since account managers work closely with their client counterparts (e.g., ad managers, brand managers, marketing directors), they tend to come from marketing and business backgrounds.

They need to understand their client's business thoroughly in order to assist in the planning effort and effectively interpret the plans for other agency personnel.

Account managers are in daily contact with their clients and, as a result, usually present the agency's recommendations and obtain client approval.

Then, they oversee and coordinate the planning and completion of the assigned work, including creative projects, media plans, and research studies.

Account management is the key coordinating force within the agency. They match up with every other department as the client representative within the agency.

Organization.

To some extent, the account management department organization may be influenced by the client organization.

For example, the agency will often structure management to parallel that of the client. Senior-level clients will have a senior agency counterpart, as will lower-level clients.

For larger accounts, it tends to be vertical.

In smaller client companies, the **Advertising Manager** is usually responsible for the advertising program and reports to the **Director**

of **Marketing** or **Director of Sales.**

In larger companies, advertising may be in a different department under a **CMO** or **Director of Marketing Communications.**

In larger consumer products companies, the key client contacts often are **brand managers**.

Again, client company organizations vary just as agency organizations do. P&G, for example, uses a combination of brand and advertising managers on some of its product lines.

Five Levels of Account Management:

Traditional large-agency account management consists of five levels. Naturally, there are fewer levels in smaller agencies.

1. Assistant Account Executive (AAE) or Account Coordinator.

A New Creative Agency

In 2004, Bernie Pitzel hit the ground running with Romani Brothers – his new agency and his new airline account – ATA. Those first few weeks, his office was his cell phone.

The ad agency business can be like that – explosive. But instant success had its roots in years of relationships.

"Boom Boom"

Bernie's best known campaign is probably *"Be Like Mike"* for Gatorade. But to ATA, it was a Midway Airlines TV spot he did a few years earlier.

"We need to put asses in seats," said the Midway client. Bernie created an ad that did exactly that.

It was called *"Boom Boom."*

An accelerating drum track showed destinations and fares. It was a great TV commercial.

However, other problems put Midway out of business. Clients went on to other airline jobs and Bernie went on to other ad jobs.

"Ring. Ring."

One day, the phone rang. The Midway clients were at another airline – ATA. They wanted Bernie. And *"Boom Boom."*

Bernie dug up the music and re-cut it for ATA. How good was it?

The first week it ran, it blew out ATA's new reservation center. (See the spot on in the AdBuzz theater.)

"You're on Vacation."

They also needed a new ad campaign. ATA flew to vacation destinations – low fares to Florida were a specialty. The theme? *"On ATA, You're on Vacation."* It was a hit.

Then things moved on, as they do.

Management changed at ATA – they got a big agency.

But everyone stayed in touch.

ATA wasn't happy with their big agency. They were paying a lot of money in fees and weren't getting the results they'd had with Bernie.

(Continued on next page)

At a large agency, the entry-level job title in account management is assistant account executive (AAE). New hires may start as account executives in smaller shops. The title of account coordinator is also often used.

The assistant account executive is normally a trainee position. AAEs learn agency procedures and their client's business through assisting the account executives.

They are heavily involved with coordinating projects and deadlines, keeping records, status reports, and monitoring budgets.

They have some direct client contact, but it's limited. AAEs need to demonstrate their analytical abilities in solving problems, organizational skills, and ability to contribute to a team effort.

2. Account Executive (AE).

Account executives play a crucial role at an agency.

They're responsible for the day-to-day operation of the account. AEs must demonstrate an understanding of the advertising function and a familiarity with the client's business.

AEs have almost daily contact with the client and are primarily responsible for the timely completion of all assignments.

They are involved with every agency department, scheduling meetings, obtaining client and legal approvals, budget control, and presenting agency viewpoints and recommendations.

AEs are partially responsible for the training of AAEs and the acceptance of the agency's work by the client.

3. Account Supervisors (ASs).

Account supervisors, like Jodi Cary, direct and supervise the planning and execution of account activities. They are an important contributor to the overall strategic direction.

The AS manages the activities of the members of the account team to ensure they deliver the agency's best product.

Account supervisors have frequent contact with middle to high-level clients, often to present the agency's work.

They are responsible for the effective training of AEs and AAEs, and partially responsible for the profitability of the account. They must demonstrate leadership.

4. Management Supervisors (MSs).

Management supervisors have the overall responsibility for total agency performance on the account as well as the client/agency relationship. They have regular discussions with high-level clients about the direction and performance of the business.

They provide leadership on important strategic issues and the servicing of the account.

MSs are responsible for staffing and training account personnel, as well as the account's financial performance. They report to senior agency management about the stability, growth, and profitability of the business.

Management supervisors review all the agency's work before it's presented to the client in order to ensure it is on strategy, of high quality, and that it is integrated with other marketing programs.

People in this position are usually officers of the agency with titles of vice president or senior vice president.

They must demonstrate superior management skills.

5. Director of Account Management.

Depending of the size of the agency, one senior-level (president or senior vice president) member of the agency will have the responsibility for the account management department or some portion of it.

This person determines the department's organization chart, reporting structure, policies, and procedures.

The director has periodic contact with the highest levels of client management in order to ensure the agency's performance is satisfactory. Directors, along with account group heads, set the direction and goals for the business.

This individual is also an important member of the agency's **Strategy Review Board.**

Field Account Groups.

In some instances, large agencies, particularly those that serve large national retail companies, organize supplemental marketing efforts on a regional basis.

Major franchises, such as McDonald's, Burger King, and Midas use this kind of organization. So do soft drink companies, such as Coca-Cola, and brewers, such as SAB.

Typically, the country is divided into a number of defined regions or markets, and both client and agency staff these areas with marketing and advertising support teams to assist local retailers or franchisees with their promotion plans.

In some cases, a number of different local agencies are also used to help localize the company's promotion plan.

Automobile companies also have some sort of field marketing or regional marketing. This varies widely and is often organized around some sort of franchise or dealer group.

Regional and field account executives work directly with client regional marketing, individual franchisees, and regional franchise marketing groups.

They receive direction and support from the agency's headquarters and, in return, provide information about local competitive conditions and the company's marketing performance.

The Account Planning Revolution.

The traditional agency organization is being affected by a trend called **account planning.** This approach to advertising development started in the United Kingdom during the 1960s at two rival London agencies, BMP and J. Walter Thompson.

In 1982, Chiat/Day introduced the discipline of account planning to the US. *"Account Planners are a new breed of researchers, skilled in personal interviewing and the understanding of social trends, who are charged with being the consumer's representative in the development of advertising campaigns."*

Creative Agency (Cont.)

At this point, ATA was fed up with agency bills and agency overhead.

They said to Bernie. *"We don't want the agency you work for. We just want you. Period."* Gulp.

Good News. Bad News.
The bad news was this client, with their own cost pressures, was no longer willing to pay normal agency fees. The good news was they were happy to hire Bernie with an offer too good to refuse.

In short order, Romani Brothers (Romani was his mother's maiden name) opened on April Fool's Day.

Successful Relationships.
Looking back, Bernie observes, *"It's all about relationships."*

"Most important, you need to have had some success together. That's critical – you can't just like each other.

"I'd say the three factors are: chemistry, mutual admiration, and mutual success.

"When that happens, at a certain point, you come to rely on each other."

And that put Bernie in the agency business.

But Things Keep Changing.
A new client can put an agency in business.

And then, things can change again.

As many observe, *"your inventory goes down the elevator every night."*

The airline business has its own ups and downs, and after a few great years and a well-regarded campaign, "Go Easy. Go ATA," good advertising wasn't enough.

ATA folded their tent and there was Bernie and Romani Bros. without their biggest account.

But elevators go up as well as down.

They'd been picking up new accounts. Peoples Gas, Rotary International, the PTA, and a few others.

They packed up their business, went down the elevator and then up the elevator at Schafer Condon Carter, a well-established integrated agency in Chicago.

And, just like that, the agency business keeps on rolling.

Whatever It Takes.

Mairee Ryan,
**Account Coordinator, Project
Director, Producer, Free-Lancer.**
PART ONE. 1999.

This morning, a client requested we use our creative director as talent in a college scholarship photo shoot for a recruitment poster.

Then, the creative director refused. My job is to deal with it.

Later that day, I was in a meeting where the entire concept was trashed.

Some days, that's my job – as an account services coordinator with PCG – Performance Communications Group – a marketing design firm.

Over 100 Accounts.

PCG handles over 100 accounts in not-for-profit and for-profit sectors.

My responsibilities included three big accounts: Robert Morris College, Bravo Restaurants, Inc. (Gino's East, Edwardo's Natural Pizza, and Ed Debevic's), and Thompson Hospitalities (Bob's Big Boy, TJ Austin's, and America's Best Diner).

(Continued on next page.)

Account planners work closely with the account managers and creative teams, advising both on consumers' perspectives and buying behavior. Charles Channon, former president of the Institute of Practitioners in Advertising, describes the account planner as *"the consumer's champion on the account team."*

Chiat/Day credits account planning for helping it grow from $50 million in billings in 1981 to $700 million by 1991.

Other agencies have taken notice, and today many have reorganized to adopt the account planning function – some call it by a different name, such as consumer insight, but they all have pretty much the same objective – insights that help develop better advertising and marketing and stronger brands.

The reason for account planning's success is quite simple.

The most effective advertising connects with consumers in a meaningful way. It stands to reason that a discipline that focuses on what is meaningful to consumers will be tremendously useful in the development of effective advertising.

While there is good and bad planning, just as there are good and bad marketing strategies, the overall trend toward developing a better relationship with consumers and brands makes planning a tool that will be used more and more by smart marketers.

Most of the well-regarded creative shops – Chiat/Day, Goodby Silverstein, Fallon, and Wieden + Kennedy – use account planners.

We'll cover account planning in greater detail in Chapter 11.

Creative Services.

Responsibility.

The Creative Department is responsible for creating and producing the print and broadcast advertising. And, more and more, non-traditional advertising. The department consists of:

➤ **Copywriters**
➤ **Art Directors**
➤ **Producers**
➤ **Support Personnel**
➤ **Supervisors**

These creative people work with account managers and clients to solve all kinds of marketing and advertising problems.

Their involvement is not limited to the creation of advertising alone. They may be asked to name a new company or brand. Other assignments might include a package design, point-of-sale display, product brochures, or a promotional event.

Good creative people are not only talented writers and art directors, but they also have a keen understanding of marketing and consumer behavior.

They understand consumer motivation and how to sell their clients' products. They have to wear many hats.

The Importance of Strategy.

Their efforts are always guided by a **creative strategy** that sets forth the objectives to be accomplished, the target, and the key message points to be communicated.

The creative product is critically important to the agency's business and financial performance.

First and foremost, clients hire agencies for their ability to create successful advertising campaigns.

Phil Dusenberry, BBDO Chairman, is fond of saying, *"I have always believed that writing advertisements is the second most profitable form of writing. Ransom notes, of course, is the first."*

Creative Department Organization.

Creative services in most medium-sized agencies is organized along the following lines.

Creative Director (CD).

The CD is the most senior executive in the creative department, responsible for the overall quality of the agency's creative product.

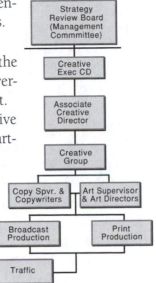

He or she determines the agency's creative philosophy, working procedures, and department organization.

The CD oversees all the agency's ideas and advertising executions in order to stimulate the department's best work and ensure that creative efforts are in synch with the established creative strategy.

The CD is likely to be a senior VP, member of the Strategy Review Board, and deeply involved with new business presentations.

Associate Creative Directors (ACDs).

In larger agencies with many client accounts, associate creative directors oversee a specific account or group of accounts.

This lightens the CD's management load and provides clients with more frequent involvement by a senior-level member of the creative department. ACDs report to the creative director.

They make sure that work for their clients meets the agency's standards and that it is delivered on time.

Executive and Group Creative Directors (ECDs).

In larger agencies, there may be even more senior CDs – executive creative directors (ECDs) may have a number of creative directors reporting to them.

If the agency is larger still, there may well be another level, most often called group creative director.

A number of group creative directors – each with CDs reporting to them – would report to the ECD.

"Title Inflation."

In some ways, agencies have only two things to give people – money and titles. In an area like creative, with egos on the line every day, there's a tendency to award titles liberally.

Whatever... (Cont.)

Project Oversight.

My job is "project oversight and coordination." It calls for managing projects by assessing client's needs, formulating work plans and budgets, and maintaining team relations.

What We Do.

The services we provide typically involve market research, strategic planning, advertising, media, promotions, and public relations.

For Example...

Let's take the Robert Morris (RMC) Scholarship poster. My job is to know what, how, who, when, and where.

What is the goal of the RMC project? To make potential students aware of scholarship availability.

How do we achieve that? We decided on print – initially a poster.

Who works on it? We needed to choose a graphic artist from our team. And, we needed to decide if we should use a copywriter who is better at long copy or in-your-face headlines.

Should we commission an illustrator who has a realistic or cartoon style? Or do we use photography?

And, of course, when does this project need to be completed?

Deadlines and Destinations.

After all these decisions are made, we set the completion date.

My job is to make sure the designer, copywriter, photographer, client, and printer meet their respective deadlines. Once 2,000 copies of the poster are printed, we get them delivered to high school counseling offices – all on time and within budget.

Every day, I do whatever it takes to get things done while juggling all the variables involved in the process.

And, yes, I really like my job.

PART TWO. 2004.

Well, I still really like my job. But it's a new job – jobs, actually. Let me tell you how everything has changed.

First, I freelance. If you're good, you can have fun and make money.

Improving My Skills.

Second, I'm now better at it. A lot.

(Continued on next page)

Whatever – Part Two (Cont.)

I improved my skills in these areas:

- **Writing** – You need to be clear about who's responsible, when things are due, and how much they'll cost. I write PR, too.
- **Production** – Now I'm good at producing print, broadcast, and live shows (a whole new area).
- **Sales** – I can make a call and make a friend.
- **Publicity** – I can write a release and I know who to send it to. This is a new skill for me.

I've become more "IMC."

Politics Are Tricky.

I don't know what to say about this – but you'll run into it – a lot.

Sometimes it's mediocre people just trying to hang onto a job.

Sometimes it's above-average people with really bad habits.

Sometimes I've handled it; sometimes not. And sometimes there's an ethical problem as well. Ouch.

Deal with it the best you can.

Miss Swiss Army Knife.

Now that I can do more things, it's made me more valuable – and I keep adding to my "Swiss Army Knife."

For example, I'm "the vacation replacement person." When people have extended leaves – for babies or vacations – I'm hired to take over.

It's fun. It pays well. And it often leads to still more project work.

It's a Freelance World.

In freelance, your insurance is your reputation and your relationships.

Right now, I'm doing a big project for a very big insurance company.

I've done major live events, helped introduce a franchise to Chicago, and even been the personal assistant to a well-known author/spiritual healer.

For fun, I helped run a rock-a-billy band and promoted events for a cool theater group. Now I'm on the board of another terrific theater group.

I still love what I do. My job keeps changing. I keep getting better at it.

So now when someone asks me, *"Whaddaya do?"*

All I say is, *"Whaddaya got?"*

So, you may find groups full of chiefs and hardly an Indian to be found. Yet, the functioning of creative departments is essentially the same – whatever the title.

Creative Groups at Work.

People work together in creative groups and get work done.

Reporting to the CD or ACD will be a creative group of **copywriters** and **art directors**. Usually, a writer and art director will work together as a **creative team** to conceive ideas and develop advertising.

Generally speaking, copywriters are responsible for what the message says, while art directors decide the design.

However, successful creative teams have a fluid working relationship where writers may have visual ideas and art directors may come up with headline and copy ideas.

Their goal is to create the best, most effective advertising – not to protect their own turf.

This team approach has been standard since the "Creative Revolution" at Doyle Dane Bernbach (DDB).

As you may recall, **Bill Bernbach** applied the visual/verbal principles of **Paul Rand** to the creation of advertising.

Writers and art directors work together to develop a selling concept that brings an additional level of surprise and interest.

The importance of TV, where visuals and words must work together, makes this team process even more important.

Teamwork at Work.

Typically, creative groups are assigned to certain accounts. This all depends on the size of the account. Large accounts like McDonald's may have many creative groups; other creative groups may have a number of smaller accounts.

Teams of copywriters and art directors will be assigned specific projects. In some cases, writers and art directors may switch around, in other cases, teams work together exclusively.

However, advertising tends to be more design intensive.

That is, once the concept has been jointly created, the art director often has to spend more time designing and finishing the ad for both presentation and final production.

The Creative Review Process.

For major projects, a lot of people can be involved in approval.

After copy and layout, scripts, and storyboards have been developed by a creative team, they are usually reviewed with the CD and, if it's a major campaign, the agency's Strategy Review Board.

With agency approval, the work is presented to the client.

Following the client's approval (including whatever revisions are called for), the agency's print and broadcast production departments become involved with the creative team.

We'll cover this process in Chapter Nine.

Print and Broadcast Production.

At most agencies, print and broadcast production are in the creative department; at others, they may be separate departments.

In either situation, these departments house the production specialists who assist the copywriters and art directors in the successful production of their creative work.

Print Production.

The print production department is staffed with experts in art buying, typography, computer graphic design, and all aspects of the printing process – particularly **pre-press.**

Electronic Studios and Pre-Press.

With the growth of computers and computer-based "electronic production studios," more and more print and even broadcast production functions are happening within the agency rather than being farmed out to production houses.

This is another example of new categories of job opportunities opening up in advertising and marketing. People in this growing part of the business have skills with specific computer programs.

Agency electronic studios and creative departments use Macs. (Other departments may be more likely to use PCs.)

Traffic – Account Coordination.

Yet another agency function, sometimes found within the creative department, is **traffic.** As the name suggests, the traffic department is responsible for steering various creative projects through the different agency departments.

Members of the traffic department, sometimes called **account coordinators** (like Mairee Ryan, wearing one of her hats) make sure the work flows smoothly through the agency and that projects are completed in time for client presentations and media closing deadlines.

Since the traffic department quickly exposes a newcomer to all the agency departments and procedures, many agencies hire entry-level employees as account coordinators.

Later, they may become account managers or producers. On most accounts, they're one of the most important team members.

Broadcast Production.

In the broadcast production department, **producers** are assigned to manage production of TV and radio commercials.

Producers assist in hiring film directors and the talent that appears in the commercials. They are responsible for getting bids, organizing the production, managing the budget, seeing deadlines are met, and buttoning up everything on the back end.

The cost of production can be quite substantial. It's important that these budgets are effectively managed.

For this reason, **broadcast business** is another important part of the broadcast department.

A Typical Day.

**Stephanie Buzan,
Media Supervisor,
Draft/FCB**

My job requires an understanding of how consumers use products and how media fits into their lives.

Planning when or where the target audience sees the commercial requires creativity and a good understanding of available resources.

My responsibilities are different day to day. It's part of what keeps the job exciting. Here's a recent Monday.

9:00 A.M. – Arrive at work and get myself organized for the week.

10:00 – Our S.C. Johnson media team holds a project status meeting.

10:45 – Work with the media planner on Raid to cost-out a budget for a possible new product test. The objective is to support a coupon in the Sunday newspaper. The plan also includes radio and newspaper, in addition to TV that will be running.

11:55 – The brand manager from S.C. Johnson calls about the media budget for Skintimate Shave Gel.

We review what has already been planned, then discuss the budget for the upcoming year.

12:10 P.M. – Lunch with *Parent's Magazine* sales representative. We discuss the Hispanic version and how my client can reach this growing market.

(Continued on next page)

Typical Day (Cont.)

1:30 – Conference call with the associate brand manager on Raid. We present the plan for the test market.

He's uncomfortable about the cost of the plan, including the cost of producing the ad. His budget only affords radio, but we feel strongly that the plan needs both radio and newspaper to be effective.

Unfortunately, he is not willing to invest and decides to investigate in-store opportunities through his sales force.

2:25 – Given the new budget for Skintimate, the media planner and I brainstorm different ideas for a creative media plan.

We discuss types of media, when the media schedule should start, and how the plan can increase brand awareness, particularly of the brand name. But we still have questions for the client...

3:45 – I touch base with the Skintimate account executive at FCB and ask her when we can schedule a pre-planning meeting with the client.

We want to better understand their objectives for next year before we evaluate the target audience and their media habits.

4:45 – Check my voicemail and e-mail and return a few messages.

5:30 – The agency's worldwide media director calls needing copies of pre-planning documents to send as examples to help our office in Venezuela.

Just one more project to be completed before heading home.

Broadcast Coordinators.

A **broadcast coordinator** (there are many titles, but the job is essentially the same) will keep track of the various types of paperwork associated with the business of producing TV and radio commercials – and there's a lot of it.

For example, the talent that works on a radio or TV commercial or a demo session (usually a soundtrack for presentation or research) must be paid – usually through one of the talent unions.

In addition, there is a complex bidding process that occurs with each piece of production. Again, coordinators have a lot to do to keep this organized.

Finally, each piece of production has elements – video and audio masters that must be stored and tracked – so that if a piece of advertising has to be revised, these expensive materials can be quickly brought out of storage for the necessary revisions.

It's an interesting and exciting area – and one that can lead to a full-time job as a broadcast producer or to a job as a broadcast production manager.

The Media Department.

As Marian Azzaro observes, media is *"the business end of the advertising business."*

And, as The Media Revolution built up steam, many media departments grew to become Media Agencies.

It made sense. Since the most amount of actual dollars spent were on the media buy, this business relationship could become more stable and, hopefully, more economical, as clients looked to save money wherever they could.

Meanwhile, the ads that ran – well, sometimes they were from the same agency, but now that marketers often had more than one agency at work on their brands, particularly with the growth of "projects," this could all be "unbundled."

Agencies objected, mostly in speeches that talked about the benefits of "integration." But, for the most part this became the new way of doing business.

Responsibility.

The media department performs a variety of important functions for the agency's clients. It analyzes and pinpoints the target market and researches the competitive media environment.

Using this data, it produces a **media plan** for investing the client's dollars in ways that will reach the best prospects most effectively.

Budgets and Objectives.

This department helps determine budgets and media objectives, in addition to selecting and contracting for media time and space.

Leo Burnett described the responsibility of his agency's media department as *"putting the ads in the right place at the right time so that the right consumers believe the story we are telling."*

Considering that the media plan usually represents, by far, the greatest percentage of the ad budget, clients are very interested in how their money is spent.

More than Number Crunchers.

As millions of dollars may be involved, media planning calls for a great deal of research and analysis.

But media people need to be more than number crunchers.

Their jobs require creativity and "big ideas," too.

They need to create new ways of identifying and reaching the target audience.

Perhaps it's through discovering some emerging medium or by arranging a cross-promotion with some other advertiser or media vehicle.

Good media planners get involved with all facets of their client's marketing efforts. As an example, in the previous sidebars, check out how Stephanie Buzan spends a typical day at FCB.

Media Agencies and Media Department Organization.

TODAY, MEDIA MAY BE HANDLED by either a traditional agency media department or by an unbundled media agency. More and more clients are choosing specialized media agencies. However, either way, the internal functions and operations are much the same.

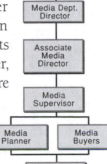

Two Functions: Media Planning and Media Buying.

Many agencies, but not all, organize the media department around its two main media functions: **planning** and **buying**.

- **The planning group** handles more strategic marketing and media issues, such as developing the media plan.
- **The buying group** handles implementation of the media plan – primarily buying.

In some cases, buying will be done by a media buying service. The media department will then be primarily planning.

Media Director (MD).

Similar to the organization of the creative department, one senior executive heads the department, serving as the agency's Media Director. Larger media agencies look like multiple media departments.

The Media Director is responsible for the staffing, policies, and overall performance of the department.

The MD is in contact with senior members of agency account management and the client. He or she deals with the larger strategic issues facing the campaign. Occasionally, the Media Director sits on the strategy review board.

As mentioned, with the increasing importance of media planning and buying as separate agency functions, many agencies have turned their media departments into separate companies. But the basic organization stayed pretty much the same.

Looking for New Business.

Here's an ad from Chiat/Day's early days. This one has them looking for a pet food account.

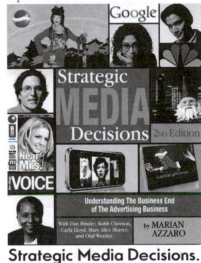

Strategic Media Decisions.

The Business End of the Advertising Business.

While we are all aware of the messages we see, the bulk of marketing dollars are spent, not creating those messages, but placing them in paid media.

This is the "business end of the advertising business."

If you'd like to know more, grab a copy of this book by Marian Azzaro, a former "Media All-Star" who now runs the IMC program at Roosevelt University.

She has pulled together her own all-star team of media teachers and media professionals to introduce you to this exciting part of the agency business.

Martin Sorrell on the Future.

Sir Martin Sorrell, CEO, WPP
These are Sir Martin's thoughts - from *Creativity* Magazine - May 2004.

#1 Geographic Shift.
First, geographically, the business will shift to Asia Pacific, Latin America, Africa, and the Middle East, and Russian and CIS countries.

Currently, WPP is roughly 40% US, 40% Europe, and 20% Asia Pacific, Latin America and Africa/MidEast.

Our objective is to be a third each. Among the reasons are population concentration: half the world's population is in Asia currently and it'll be two-thirds by 2014.

#2 Going "Outside Advertising"
Second, just over half our business is outside of advertising: in information insight and consultancy, (which is basically market research), in public relations and public affairs, and in branding and ID, healthcare and specialist communications, (by that I principally mean direct, interactive, and Internet).

Currently, it's about 50/50: we think it'll be two-thirds outside advertising in five to ten years.

Why? First, because network TV continues to increase in cost at a faster rate than general price inflation and second, because of the advent of new media and new technologies, the latest of which will be DVDs or video-on-demand.

#3 "Quantitative Media."
Third, quantitative media. The quantitative aids to decision-making, whether we like it, or whether creative departments like it or not, will become more important.

(Continued on next page)

Associate Media Directors (AMDs).

Reporting to the Media Director are Associate Media Directors (AMDs) who are responsible for all the media assignments on a given account or group of accounts.

AMDs work with account management and clients to set budgets, objectives, and strategies. They are responsible for overseeing the work of both the media planners and buyers.

Media Planners.

The media planners (and their supervisors, like Stephanie Buzan) report to the associate media director or director and work on strategic issues such as defining the target market, setting objectives, and determining when and where advertising will appear.

They are primarily responsible for developing the media plan for their accounts. Planners use a combination of analytical skills and creativity in preparing media plans that will effectively reach the target audience.

They also work with media buyers on the implementation and evaluation of their media plans.

An important new trend is more account planning–like behavior on the part of some media planners. This is one more example of the impact that the Media Revolution has had on the industry. We'll cover this in more detail in Chapter 10,

Media Buyers.

The department's media buyers are charged with implementing the media plan – negotiating rates and merchandising allowances and contracting for media time and space on behalf of clients.

Buyers work closely with planners to be certain budgets, objectives, and timing are clear and financial reporting is accurate.

They also assist in the monitoring of the media activity and post-evaluation of the media plan.

In order to do their job, media buyers need to be familiar with a variety of media research sources that cover media ratings, circulation, and pricing trends. Computers perform many of these tasks.

The Importance of Negotiation.

Almost everything is negotiable today – particularly media costs.

The buyer's primary role is to negotiate the best price, media placement, and merchandising possible.

While buyers must be comfortable with numbers, they also can exercise a great deal of creativity in structuring media deals and securing new advertising opportunities.

Media Analysts.

Assisting the planning and buying functions are media analysts.

These individuals help evaluate media alternatives by gathering and analyzing media and marketing research data.

More in Chapter Ten.

We'll cover this very important process in much more detail in Chapter Ten, "Media and the Marketing of Messages."

The Research Department.

Full-service agencies contain a research department.

Headed by a research director, research project managers are assigned to accounts, as needed, to gather and analyze research data important to the business.

Primary and Secondary Research.

Primary and secondary research methods are used to investigate a myriad of marketing issues: identifying prospects and markets of opportunity and measuring advertising effectiveness.

Secondary research is research based on other resources – such as preparing a summary of previous findings, collecting articles on the topic, or searching the Internet for information.

Primary research is research where you generate your own results – such as with a survey of consumers.

You do secondary research first.

When agency resources are limited, the research department may hire an outside research company to perform the service.

New Names, New Organizations, New Functions.

As discussed in Chapter Two, the research function has gone through major changes in the agency world.

During the 1980s, many agencies cut their research staff as clients assumed more control of the research responsibility.

The '90s saw a resurgence of agency research departments and a relatively new hybrid function called **account planning**.

Organizations shifted, some integrating planning into account groups, some replacing research departments with planning departments, and some, such as FCB, developing a "blended" approach, often called **Consumer Insight**.

We'll discuss account planning in the agency trends section of this chapter and in the Evaluation part of Chapter Eleven.

Other Parts of the Agency Also Do Research.

The account group and account planners are also responsible for collecting and analyzing secondary research.

New business efforts often involve quite a bit of research, either from the research department, account management, or a dedicated new business group which includes this as one of their functions.

Media research is another research function often performed by larger media departments.

The Strategy/Creative Review Board.

Most medium-to-large-sized agencies have some sort of formal advertising **strategy/creative review board**.

Members of the board include the agency's senior executives who serve as department heads and top management.

This group will convene to review all the major new strategies and campaigns being developed for the agency's clients.

Work is presented to the review board for approval before work is presented to clients. In this way, senior management can monitor and contribute to the effort on all accounts.

Sorrell on Future (Cont.)

From a Third to a Half.

In other words, two areas of our business in particular – information insight/consultancy and direct/interactive/Internet, which account for about a third of our business today – will account for about half our business in five or ten years .

The Three Most Important Things.

We still think that ideas and thinking are the most important things clients look for, and that's work or thinking in the broadest sense – not just advertising in the creative department of ad agencies.

It's in media, brand ID, creativity in all its senses.

Coordination and integration has moved up the client agenda to be a close second. You can see it in the biggest pitches going on in the industry now.

That is about trying to utilize the resources of these groups in the most effective way, in an integrated way.

And the third thing clients are focused on is price.

Source: *Creativity*, May 2004

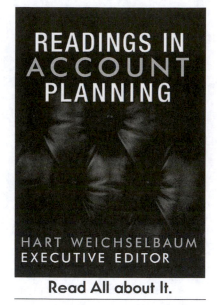

READINGS IN ACCOUNT PLANNING

HART WEICHSELBAUM
EXECUTIVE EDITOR

Read All about It.

Want to know more about this exciting and interesting part of research?

Compiled by Hart Wechselbaum, former head of Planning at The Richards Group, this book presents some of the classic articles on how Account Planning grew as well as fascinating new articles on where it's going in the future.

Contributing authors include Malcolm Gladwell (*Blink* and *Tipping Point*), Lisa Fortini-Campbell (*Hitting the Sweet Spot*) John Heilemann, and others.

Office Management.

Every agency has a staff of people to provide the operating and financial services that all businesses require.

Human Resources.

As Fairfax Cone noted, *"people are the assets of the agency... the inventory goes down the elevator every night."*

There is a department of human resources that handles personnel hiring and firing, insurance matters, and a relatively new range of responsibilities related to office behavior.

How an agency treats its employees will influence how successful it is in attracting the best talent – and keeping it.

Though some agencies have many long-term employees, advertising is a volatile industry.

Early advertising careers are typified by a number of job shifts, as inexperienced beginners with low salaries rapidly become experienced professionals worth much more in the agency marketplace.

Account shifts cause additional volatility, due to necessary hirings and firings by the winning and losing agencies. (Sometimes people who worked on an account that was lost are hired by the agency that won the account.)

Creative Recruiters.

Sometimes, a creative department has its own personnel function, primarily dedicated to finding new creative talent.

This is an industry in itself, with personnel firms across the country dedicated to the job placement of agency creatives and keeping in touch with a "feeder system" of portfolio schools such as The Portfolio Center, Miami Ad School, SVA, and Creative Circus, as well as art schools.

We'll cover this in more detail in the Careers section.

Legal Services.

Most clients and account managers are familiar with legal issues pertinent to their product category. Sometimes that is not enough.

At large agencies, a legal department advises on agency operations as well as the development of the advertising.

They may have one or two lawyers on staff.

Medium-sized and small agencies will have a retainer arrangement with a law firm.

If legal problems are large, lawyers specializing in advertising law are brought in to consult, represent, and even litigate.

Accounting.

An accounting department is responsible for billing clients and paying the media and other suppliers. This is a critical agency function. In the past, agencies often acted as "bankers" for their clients, assuming responsibility for millions of dollars in media.

A slow-paying client, a client who refuses to pay, or something as simple as inaccurate revenue projections by account management can quickly cause large problems for agencies.

So let's talk about how agencies make money.

Agency Income & Profit.

THE AGENCY BUSINESS BEGAN as soon as there was a way to make money creating and placing advertising.

The business has changed, but making money at advertising continues to be one of the primary goals.

As with any company, an agency needs to generate income and make a profit to stay in business.

Since agencies offer a variety of services, and client needs and budgets vary, agencies have developed several compensation methods.

Almost Everything Is Negotiable…

Today, almost everything is negotiable, and an agency-client contract can be written to cover virtually every situation.

And, standard agency-client behavior is changing.

As discussed in Chapter Two, many client-agency relationships are getting shorter. This includes more volatility on the client side – a new ad manager or director of marketing often brings a new agency into play.

One agency handling media while another handles creative brings yet another variable into play. There are now lawsuits and public comment on compensation and termination issues that never would have been raised just a few years ago.

Finally, company procurement departments have become involved.

Marketing budgets are large amounts of money and a company's procurement department is in charge of how money is spent. Usually, it's things like raw materials and office supplies. But, given the amounts of money at stake, it's one more way for clients to look at what they're getting for their money and, not surprisingly, further control costs.

Key Questions.

Be that as it may, the key questions remain the same:

* Can the agency make a fair profit?
* Are the terms reasonable for the client?

Three Ways to Make Money.

Typically, agencies charge for their services in three ways:

➤ **Media Commissions**

➤ **Markups**

➤ **Fees**

Let's take a look at them, one by one.

Media Commissions.

The earliest form and traditional method of agency compensation is the **media commission** system.

Since Cyrus H. Curtis instituted this system with his magazines at the turn of the century, this has been the way agencies were paid. But the world is changing.

The Traditional 15% Commission.

Traditionally, agencies retained a 15% media commission on the space and time they purchased for their clients.

Bell, Sorrell, and Wren on Agency Compensation.

Here are the thoughts of Howard Bell (IPG), Martin Sorrell (WPP), and John Wren (Omnicom) on this challenging topic.

Bell: There are pockets of best practices in compensation, there are pockets of horrible practice. The fundamental issue that the industry deals with and the clients deal with is moving from an input-based system to an output-based system. And an input-based system is the tone that for better or for worse in many instances we found ourselves in when we shifted out of commission, which was in effect a pay for performance.

Now, we're in an input-based system in an output-based business. The challenge for all of us to move toward models that provide serious upside. We have many incentive compensation plans with many clients. The amount of the upside generally depends on the amount of the risk rather than the value of the output. We'll get to a place where pay per performance in one form or another will be the way that we'll be compensated far more than it is now.

Sorrell: I'm not aware of any situation where the work is great that we haven't been paid well for it. I'm not aware of any situation where we do good work where the procurement department doesn't disappear into the background. So, I think clients will pay us if we do great work. Of course, I regret in a way the rise of the procurement department and the pressure that it's putting on our business. But that's a reality of life. Inflation is at a very low level. Our clients have no pricing power. That will continue, and the procurement department will continue to flourish and we have to continue to deal with them and work with them in an intelligent way.

(Continued on Next Page.)

Agency Comp. (Cont.)

Wren: We have 5,000 clients, so we probably have almost as many compensation arrangements. It comes down to the quality of the services that you provide. We're very consistent in our belief system, and then being paid a fair profit for the services that we provide. Oddly enough, when we first started to dislike procurement, we changed our corporate philosophy, and decided that it probably made more sense if we embraced procurement because it was kind of arrogant to think that we weren't going to learn anything if somebody came and challenged our premises.

We start off every conversation with the premise that we'll only continue to work for you if we both agree that we're going to be paid a fair profit on the services that we provide. If that's not a premise in which you're embracing us, we can shortcut this entire conversation and we'll depart. That's made us better.

For example, if an agency placed an advertisement in a newspaper with a $10,000 media cost, the agency would bill the client $10,000, but only pay the newspaper $8,500.

Thus, the agency would keep $1,500, or a 15% commission, for the creation and placement of the advertisement. This formula applied to all media.

The 15% media commission is still used in some cases.

Adjustable Commission Rates.
Today, however, clients will negotiate, and agencies will adjust the commission rate to match the client's budget so that the agency makes a fair profit and the client is not overcharged.

Often a **sliding scale** commission system is used to lower the commission rate as the media budget increases.

Criticisms of the Commission System.
While the commission system goes back to the late 1800s, it has its critics. Some say, and not without examples, that the commission system encourages agencies to recommend plans with high media expenditures in order to boost their own income.

Rather than be concerned with what marketing communications solution might work best, agencies are encouraged to recommend high-cost advertising media.

Furthermore, the system does not adequately monitor and adjust agency expenses on a cost-accounting basis. Expense and income may have nothing to do with each other. This is particularly true for new products and new accounts.

When Howard Gossage made this point in the '60s, it was generally rejected by the agency establishment.

Today, it is well accepted by clients and agencies alike.

Not surprisingly, there has been a turning away from the traditional performance-insensitive media commissions toward fee-based and performance-based systems.

Fee Systems – Four Types.
Again, everything is negotiable.

There are many different types of fee arrangements that are tailored to fit individual client needs.

Most fees can be grouped into one of four categories:

1. **Fixed Fee (Retainer)**
2. **Cost-Plus Fee**
3. **Performance Fee**
4. **Hybrid Fee and Commission**

As before, let's take them one by one.

1. Fixed Fee (Retainer).
Under a fixed-fee system, the agency and client agree to a fixed amount of money to be paid for certain services over a period of time – usually a fiscal year.

Often, a yearly agency fee or retainer is billed to the client in equal monthly installments.

Considering that work loads may vary month to month, and cost of service varies according to the different agency personnel assigned to the given projects (some people's talents command higher salaries than others), a fixed fee may be the simplest, though not always the fairest, method of compensation.

2. Cost-Plus Fee.

With a cost-plus fee system, the client agrees to compensate the agency for the costs incurred on each project, plus a fair profit margin (usually in the 20% to 25% range).

While this system is more complex and requires rigid cost accounting procedures, it is probably the fairest system of all.

The agency must keep accurate records of employee time spent on each account as well as expenses by project.

These costs are totalled by month and reflect the work load and level of involvement by different agency personnel.

All the costs (salaries, internal overhead, rent, travel, supplier expenses, etc.) plus the agreed-upon profit percentage are then billed to the client. The agency must make its cost accounting records available for periodic client audits.

There is usually some minimum monthly fee in this arrangement for an agreed-upon full-time level of account service.

3. Performance Fee.

In recent years, some agencies have built into their compensation agreement a performance or incentive fee.

If predetermined goals, such as awareness level or sales or market share are met, the agency's fee or commission amount is increased. If not, agency compensation is reduced.

While talk of pay-for-performance compensation is gaining in popularity, a strong direct link between advertising and sales is rare. Another problem is that it is implicit that the agency have some control over the advertising that runs if it is to be compensated on the performance of that advertising.

Most clients are reluctant to surrender this much control.

However, *Advertising Age* reports, *"in one of the purest examples of pay-for-performance, Drivers' Mart Worldwide plans to pay its ad agency a commission for every car sold."*

P&G is continually evaluating agency compensation so as to encourage agency performance and build in incentives that reward superior performers. In July 2000, they began formally rewarding their agencies based on brand performance and sales growth.

4. Hybrid Fee and Commission.

It is not uncommon for small-to-medium-sized advertisers to compensate agencies with a combination of commissions and fee.

In these instances, the media billings may not produce enough commission to fully compensate the agency for all its efforts.

So, a fee is included to cover specific services.

Originally, this arrangement was used for new product development, where media commissions might be some years away, and

Markups – Production & Service.

Another way agencies make money is to add a percentage markup to the cost of production and certain services.

For example, to produce a magazine advertisement, an agency usually buys type, photography, or illustrations, and other production services from outside suppliers.

17.65% of Net = 15% of Gross. Traditionally, the cost of these materials and services are marked up 17.65% of the net cost, which equals 15% of the gross cost ($10,000 x 15% = $1,500). Here's how it works:

Cost of Production

Materials & Services	$8,500
x Markup %	x .1765
= Markup	= $1,500

Billing to Client

Materials & Services	$8,500
+ Markup	+ $1,500
= Total Billing	= $10,000

Other production and service expenses are marked up in the same fashion, including television and radio commercials and research projects.

Agencies and clients negotiate and stipulate in their business contract what items can be marked up and at what rate.

Since many agencies have found the traditional markup of 17.65% not profitable, higher rates are often charged, or a fee system of compensation is used instead.

What Do Clients Want?

The ANA (Association of National Advertisers) produced a benchmark study identifying key issues in client-agency relations. They surveyed more than 100 major advertisers. Here are some of the key results:

Service and Responsiveness.
95% listed each of these as a key deliverable.

Three Key Attributes.
Advertisers want effective campaigns (56%). Outstanding ideas and implementation (40%), and strategic counsel and insights (35%).

Relationship Issues.
The top issues that advertisers feel affects client-agency relationships are: Disconnects from strategy to creative (24%), work that is not always on strategy (23%), and revisions and re-workings taking too long (21%).

What Do Agencies Want?

There is another side to the story.

100 agency professionals were also interviewed…

The Top Three Things…
agencies want from clients are: respect/trust (57%), followed by fair payment (41%) and clear communications – including criticism (39%).

Periodic Meetings…
Regular review was also viewed as necessary, 85% recommending periodic management meetings to review progress and identify problems. This was followed by defining clear expectations (65%) and participating in two-way evaluations (50%).

some of that as part of a test market, where billings were relatively small compared to the time involved.

Here are two examples of how agencies are evolving in terms of compensation.

A Balanced Workload.
Though one of the foremost Creative agencies in terms of crafting television commercials, the workload at Goodby Silverstein has shifted so that approximately half the fee income and account activity is digital. Their location in San Francisco, near Silicon Valley, helps make this model work – in terms of getting both the right clients and the right talent.

A Piece of the Action.
An interesting, though unproven, business model is CP+B taking over actual pieces of business, like Subservient Chicken action figures and negotiating an equity position with new client Haggar Slacks.

The Business of New Business.

A CRITICAL OBJECTIVE AND ROLE of any advertising agency is the generation of new business – it is the lifeblood of an agency.

As an agency adds accounts to its client roster, it becomes financially stronger and better able to hire the industry's top talent. And as the agency prospers, its reputation as a "hot shop" grows, which helps attract even more new business.

Start-Ups.

Along the way, we'll also be talking about start-ups.

Just as Roy Spence and friends started GSD&M right out of school, the agency business is still one where new people and new ideas can create a business almost overnight.

Bernie Pitzel did this with Romani Brothers.

Another person who did this was Wes Perrin, who helped start the "other" Portland, Oregon, agency – Borders Perrin & Norrander – later a part of the True North mega-agency group, then IPG.

New Business – Three Ways to Grow.

There are essentially three ways agencies can grow:

1. **Build Existing Clients' Businesses.**
2. **Add and Sell New Services.**
3. **Solicit New Accounts.**

In the sidebar, agency veteran Wes Perrin tells his story.

1. Build Existing Clients' Businesses.

By helping clients increase their brands' market share, and sales, the agency's billings and income increase.

As the two companies grow from within, together the bond of loyalty grows greater.

We saw this happen with Nike and Wieden + Kennedy, and, in the early days, with General Foods and Y&R.

2. Add & Sell New Services.

Agencies have expanded to offer sales promotion, direct response marketing, public relations, and other services in an effort to build their business and to provide integrated marketing communications to their clients.

Additional IMC Services.

This was Marion Harper's vision with Interpublic. Today every mega-agency group has a full range of services to sell their clients.

With the growth of IMC, many agencies are trying to add these functions. One of the more successful examples of an agency evolving into IMC has been Fallon. CEO Pat Fallon has committed the entire agency to solving marketing problems – not just doing ads.

3. Solicit New Accounts.

Building business by adding new clients is the most difficult and costly method, but necessary for the agency's growth and stability.

By servicing many clients, an agency is less vulnerable to a budget reduction or loss of one account.

In addition, with account turnover increasing, it is more critical than ever that agencies add business to protect themselves from what is an almost inevitable percentage of client losses.

New Business Presentations.

Most agencies have an organized and ongoing new business effort headed by its senior executives or a special new business team.

These people follow up on referrals and inquiries and actively solicit opportunities for the agency to meet with prospective clients.

They fill out the **RFPs** (this means Request for Proposal).

Account Reviews.

Usually, when clients consider switching agencies, they initiate a formal account review.

The client reviews a number of agencies and selects several to compete – inviting them to make one or more presentations on the agency's capabilities and its knowledge of the client's marketing situation. In agency jargon, this is **the short list.**

The presentation itself is called the **new business pitch.**

The New Business Pitch.

Preparing new business pitches may take a week or six months depending on the size of the account and client expectations.

Credentials.

One standard part of the pitch, the credentials presentation, tends to remain the same. Its purpose is to present the agency to its best advantage. Usually it details size, accomplishments, client list, key personnel, and appropriate case histories.

This part of the presentation may be changed slightly to emphasize agency experience in the relevant product category.

The process may involve one meeting or several. Typically, at least one meeting is at the agency and one at the client's office.

Sometimes a dinner or some other outing is scheduled so client and agency can get a better feeling of personal chemistry.

"Spec."

In many reviews, the agency is required to present **speculative creative,** or **"spec."** These are ads, commercials, and promotional

Start an Ad Agency and Live to Tell about It.

by Wes Perrin
(He's the one in the middle – co-founder of Portland's "other" agency, Borders Perrin & Norrander.)

You might consider the advice given to a colleague of mine.

He was working in New York for Ogilvy & Mather when he decided to move to Seattle to start an agency.

Before leaving he saw the great David Ogilvy and told him of his intentions, and asked for counsel.

Ogilvy nodded and smiled.

Two weeks later in Seattle, my friend received a postcard. In Ogilvy's unmistakable handwriting was a single word: *"DON'T."*

More Good Advice.

If you persist in the notion of starting an agency, many, like Ogilvy, will implore you to consider otherwise.

Starting with relatives and extending on to friends, neighbors, and acquaintances, people will warn you of high risk, lack of security, cut-throat practices, ulcers, and questionable social status.

Since there's a bit of truth in all this, I urge you to stop now – unless you really have a passion for the business.

Not Your Ordinary Opportunity.
Despite what certain capitalists might claim, this is not your ordinary business opportunity.

But let's say you are intense about the business, highly motivated to create great advertising, and committed to investing long hours and some stomach lining in the process.

Furthermore, you possess the classic entrepreneurship mentality: you consider risk a natural element of business life. How should one begin?

(Continued on next page)

Perrin (Cont.)

Five Key Steps.

In my view, there are five key steps:

1. Make sure you have at least one paying client in hand.

My partners and I formed BPN, with zero accounts, assuming naively we'd gobble up clients lickety-split.

Ha! It took us six months to gain the business we assumed we'd nail in a couple of weeks.

We'd read that Y&R began with *"clients none, cash meager, hopes high."* Sounds exciting. Don't.

2. Make sure you have enough money socked away to last at least one year on a starvation diet.

You need very modest capital to finance your start-up. (In 1977, we opened our doors after putting up just $5,000 each.) But you still need enough cash to look professional.

It's fine to start from your home, but don't stay there long… unless you plan to always be a small fish.

3. Nail down five professional allies: lawyer, accountant, banker, insurance agent, and landlord.

You will be very small potatoes to them for some time, but if you grow, you'll find them invaluable.

Plus, all, especially the banker, can be enormously helpful networking for prospective clients.

4. Recognize that you will not be able to succeed solo.

Join forces.

Here are key requirements:

- Don't echo one another; bring different talents to the party.
- Pledge allegiance to the same creative philosophy.

In my case, Borders was a great writer and Norrander a gifted art director. Without them, I never would have been able to retire early.

After that, write down all the names and phone numbers of the people you can use à la carte for copy, art, research, media buying, production, and PR.

Some will always be freelance category. Others are those you'll want to hire full-time.

(Continued on next page)

material which represent the agency's views on what the advertising should be. It can be very costly.

An agency is seldom fully reimbursed for these costs.

However, the investment is part of the cost of doing business.

Meanwhile, the client gets a sneak preview of the best thinking of the best agencies available.

Working on an agency new business team can be exhilarating, but the burn-out factor can be extremely high as well.

There are usually from three to five agencies in these pitches, so most agencies will lose more pitches than they win.

But, that's the business of new business.

Agency Trends

A 2006 "State of the Agency" study by the Winterberry Group found that the traditional marketing model is changing fast. Digital technologies and the proliferation of new media have diminished the impact of traditional platforms such as television and print. Consequently, the ad agency's role has been challenged.

The Winterberry Group conducted extensive interviews with over 70 senior agency executives around the country. The following quotations taken from several of these interviews gives you an idea about where the industry is and where it's headed.

"I have no idea of what the future will be, but I can guarantee you that three key ingredients will be needed: change, change, and change."

— *Maurice Levy, Chairman and CEO, Publicis Groupe*

"There are major changes happening in our industry, and we don't understand the speed and scale at which they're taking place."

— *Martin Sorrell, Chief Executive, WPP Group*

"Marketers are shifting away from advertising, which favors media, to direct marketing and promotion, which do not. While this has been happening for decades, the digital revolution has helped accelerate the shift. This means less advertising in the future and less money for media – all media. That's a reality."

— *Dave Morgan, CEO, Tacoda*

At the start of this chapter, we mentioned that this is an exciting time for everyone in advertising and marketing communications. Some rather large changes are occurring, and no one has a crystal ball to forecast exactly how this will all shake out. Here's one way of looking at it for those of you entering the job market: There are some wonderful new opportunities developing with few experts to fill the new job positions needed.

Let's look at a few more findings from the Winterberry study and look at some additional agency trends.

Winterberry reports that the agency has seen its portfolio of responsibilities fundamentally changed by the advent of non-traditional channels and by the growth of more nimble specialty companies.

Another significant development is consumers accustomed to the Internet now expect detailed product information to be readily available. This has led marketers and agencies to put much more emphasis on "below the line" promotional channels.

Finally, the effectiveness of television has been diminished by the growth of promotional activities and channels that generate more effective and measurable returns. As a result, tomorrow's key industry growth areas include direct response, event marketing, promotions, e-mail, online, and search engine marketing.

Briefly, we'll cover five of the most dynamic trends:

- **Increased Competition**
- **Mergers, Mega-Agencies, and Media Unbundling**
- **Non-Traditional Advertising**
- **More Kinds of Planning**
- **Re-engineering**

While we can't predict the future, it's easy to see that these important trends will affect tomorrow's advertising agency.

In fact, they're all having an impact today.

Increased Competition.

Year after year, competition continues to intensify in almost every product category. Every trend discussed in Chapter Two will continue as the modern marketplace evolves.

The result is an increasingly competitive playing field, which will feature a number of things.

It's not just marketing competition, it's message competition.

Clutter, Message Overload, and "Overchoice."
The channel changer defines the new consumer.

The amount of clutter is growing everywhere – on store shelves, in the media, and in consumers' minds. It's like confetti.

Network TV finds itself dealing with shorter and more fragmentary messages. And the list goes on.

While there may be no limit to the number of channels we can receive, there is a definite physical limit to what we can retain. Marketers now have to deal with message overload.

Alvin Toffler describes it as "overchoice." As the marketplace embraces segmentation and positioning, as technology allows more customized service and manufacture, we will find ourselves dealing with more and more choices.

Just managing choice becomes a major task. Agencies can play a key role in this, particularly as a strategic partner.

It is David Ogilvy who reminds us, *"Strategy is about choice."*

Message consulting is one response to this challenging new environment.

Audience Fragmentation.
On top of this, add the proliferation and fragmentation of media choices, the growth of TiVo, and the effect on audiences.

As cable choices increase, print alternatives grow, and the Internet expands, audiences fragment into smaller and smaller segments.

The result is that new combinations of media vehicles and marketing communications disciplines will be required to achieve marketing success.

Perrin (Cont.)

5. Understand that new business is the lifeblood of your business. It's comforting to have a client or two in the pocket when you start, but you must grow beyond that to succeed.

You need to have a systematic strategy in place to attract new accounts.

100 Top Prospects.
For me, that meant a list of 100 prospects. My criteria was basic:
- Legitimate, high-quality products,
- Belief in the value of advertising,
- Reputation for paying bills promptly.

From these, I selected a rotating Top Ten list – I'd seek a personal meeting with key decision-makers and maintain a constant contact via phone, mail, and association activities. Today, I'd certainly add e-mail to that list.

This did not result in overnight success, but over time we found patience and tenacity paid off.

Here are two examples:

Example #1: Ask for Projects.
Since most prospective clients were apprehensive about gambling on a new agency, I learned to close conversations by asking only for a project, not the entire account.

We could demonstrate our capability with minimum risk for the client.

We quickly discovered prospects were far more comfortable when they could "try us on for size."

The best payoff for this approach occurred nine months after opening.

Calling on a small manufacturer of outerwear and fishing vests, we learned they were anxious to create a new logo – and with good reason.

At the time, Columbia Sportswear had a curious amalgamation of a leaping fish and a large deer inter-twined with capital letters "C" and "S."

When I first called on the president, Tim Boyle, he was leaning toward a design with a drawing of a river bridge near their small plant.

My art director partner Mark Norrander got $500 worth of logo ideas from the best corporate identity designer in town.

(Continued on next page)

Perrin (Cont.)

We carried these out on a huge roll of art paper, presenting the options by slowly unrolling the paper the same way one would pull a window shade.

Happily, one design stood out as superior to the bridge concept.

That began our relationship.

We didn't have an account, but we had a beachhead.

Subsequently, we helped them with their dealer catalog then their first small-space magazine campaign – three ads with a $30,000 budget.

A Winning Position.

Our positioning statement said, *"We don't design outerwear, we engineer it."* In a year, we were agency of record.

Columbia Sportswear became our largest account. The "Mother Boyle" campaign has won a boxcar full of awards, and sales went from $2 million to hundreds of millions.

Example #2: Who's Got "The Vote?"

Another lesson: In a presentation situation there will always be one individual whose vote is bigger than all the rest.

Generally this is the owner or CEO, but it can be the director of marketing.

Learn who this person is.

I became acutely aware of this when pursuing Blue Cross/Blue Shield of Oregon. We were competing with four other agencies and knew we were not highly regarded by the ad manager.

However, we were favored by the new director of marketing – a former pro football player.

We made our presentation on a Thursday. It was not our finest hour.

We weren't optimistic. Friday, we heard rumors the account had been promised to one of our rivals. That afternoon, I received a call from the marketing director.

"Wes," he said in his best Vince Lombardi voice, *"I want you to get back over here Monday morning at 9 A.M. and SELL! Pull out all the stops."*

We found he'd persuaded the other managers to put off the final decision until they heard once more from us.

(Continued on next page)

The Growth of Database and Direct Response.

Advertisers and their agencies have learned a lot about **accountability** from improved database management techniques and the direct response disciplines.

Consequently, agencies will continue to be held more accountable in measuring performance and cost control.

The Need for Integrated Brand Images.

With this increasing market complexity, central integrated brand management by clients and agencies will become more important.

A unifying strategic vision will become more important.

Companies will need to concentrate on ideas and strong brand images that can be integrated into the various marketing communications disciplines and the many forms of new media.

More Mergers, Mega-Agencies, and Media Unbundling.

The acquisitions and mergers continue today.

The mega-agencies are committed to providing integrated services on an international and global scale. With the purchase of Bcom3 (Leo Burnett and DMB&B), and other specialty agencies, like Burrell (the leading Afro American agency) and Frankel (a leading sales promotion firm), Publicis became the #4 player. Now they're looking to succeed in the digital space with new plans and new agencies.

True North, then the sixth-largest agency network in the world, became part of IPG. The big keep getting bigger.

In June, 2006, IPG announced a new twist on mergers by combining two of its own companies. Draft, one of the country's largest direct response agencies, was merged with FCB, ending Foote Cone & Belding's 133 years as a stand-alone ad agency. The Draft/FCB Group is a new kind of agency that combines brand-building capabilities with behavior-based insights that are easy to measure with direct response techniques.

Today, the six holding companies (the five mega-agencies plus Dentsu) dominate worldwide ad revenue. Almost 75%!

Media Unbundling – A Way of Doing Business.

Now, almost every agency has accepted separate media agencies as a way of life. They are part of each and every mega-agency group, establishing it as an industry standard.

Another matching trend is client purchasing departments getting involved with the media function and media agencies.

Though we are seeing some interesting trends – with CP + B, viewing media as part of their creative thinking and some agencies taking an account planning-like approach to media thinking.

This is growing a new kind of advertising – non-traditional.

Non-Traditional Advertising.

Rick Boyko, former O&M Creative Head, now director of VCU's Ad Center has a presentation – it's full of unique creative work done by ad agency groups – but it's not quite advertising.

• There's a giant Hershey store in Times Square done by special O&M design unit – the next one is going up in Las Vegas.

• There's a long piece of video that ran as programming on *ESPN* – Wieden + Kennedy did it for Nike. It's a mood piece, not really a commercial, it's just... cool. *ESPN* ran it as is. Think about that, advertising where you don't have to pay for it to run... cool.

• Here's an oversize telephone. What? It was done by CP+B and it's sitting in an airport, and, if you can't quite read the board, it says *"Makes everything else seem a little too big."*

They turned an ad for the Mini into a bit of sculpture and performance art.

Cutting-edge agencies are breaking out of the box of paid media in traditional media vehicles and looking for dramatic new ways to connect with today's over-messaged consumers.

Smart clients are paying attention.

More Kinds of Planning.

The success of Account Planning is having an interesting impact.

The approach is growing into other areas – particularly media, but also having an impact on MarCom areas, such as Sales Promotion, and core processes, like strategic planning.

Media Planning Expands.

As covered in Chapter 10, the planning function, once a skill that was primarily quantitative – working to discover the best mathematical media efficiencies against specific target audiences – is becoming more qualitative.

Today, media planners are behaving more like account planners, tracking behaviors, lifestyles, gathering insights, and looking for the most effective apertures for messages.

The "p word," planning is attaching itself to more and more functions.

Communications Planning.

Sophisticated marketers like Unilever and Kimberly-Clark are looking to improve their performance on the millions of dollars they spend on media messages with internal and external resources that focus on the best channel of message delivery.

We have already mentioned – more than once – the classic example of Naked Communications pulling a British drug store chain out of advertising and being dramatically successful converting the efforts into an internal communications effort – having store personnel tell customers about the service as they were waiting to have prescriptions filled.

From Attitudes to Behaviors.

The insights offered by planners are also appealing to companies in the area of Sales Promotion. Instead of working to shift attitudes

I don't recall exactly what I said, but I remember I left the room soaked with perspiration.

The Vote that Mattered.

On Wednesday we were notified by a somewhat disgruntled ad manager.

"I have to confess you weren't my first choice," he said. *"But Dick (the marketing director) wanted you so much he won the rest of us over – after you came back a second time."*

It was Dick's vote that mattered.

In a room full of prospective clients, there will always be one person whose vote matters more than all the others.

Is It Right for You?

How do you determine if you're the right person to start an ad agency?

Start by answering the questions posed in a famous recruiting ad said to have been written by David Ogilvy:

"Can you stand up under pressure that would have most mortals climbing the walls? Are you willing to work hard?

"Do you have a good energy reserve?

"Do you have a good, strong backbone?"

How Bad Do You Want It?

To those words I'd add, *"Do you really want to give birth to advertising that breaks through today's enormous media clutter and is honest, human, memorable, intelligent, evocative, informative, and powerfully persuasive?"*

If you do, start an agency.

The future of this business will be bright if we attract those who insist on the highest standards.

The world, the country, the industry needs you.

About Wes Perrin...

With two stalwart partners, he founded an agency in Portland on May 1, 1977.

Their fledgling agency persevered, prospered, and sailed past its 30th anniversary.

Borders Perrin & Norrander, Inc. accounts include Columbia Sportswear, and Blue Cross/Blue Shield for Oregon and Washington.

Retired at 50, Wes is now Chairman Emeritus and a consultant to the agency and other marketing firms.

Re-Engineering in Action.

Two examples of work from the teams at Sullivan Higdon and Sink.

Most opportunities knock.
This one tears doors off hinges.

The Blue Team.

Here, the aerospace specialty group does work for their Cessna client and the Citation X.

I love you, Mom.
But I hate your smoke.

Let's take it outside.

The Green Team

This agency group specializes in consumer services.

with messages – always a tricky proposition – how about shifting behaviors with incentives?

Well, that's exactly what Sales Promotion does.

So the question is, "how much more effective might we be if we worked to generate additional insight into the consumers whose behavior we want to affect?"

The answer is quite clear and it should be no surprise that the planning function is being welcomed into this area of marketing communication.

Other areas, such as Web-based behavior, viral, and W-O-M (word of mouth) will also find themselves working to discover if planning can provide new levels of effectiveness.

Re-Engineering.

Other significant trends fall under the category of the re-engineering of the agency organization and the services it provides. Here are a number of issues we touched on earlier in this chapter that will continue to evolve and change the industry.

- **Need for New Business Models.** The old top-down marketing model has changed. Marketers can no longer tell consumers what they need. They must ask them what they want. The Internet, DVRs, iPods, iPhones, etc., have enabled consumers to create their own personal media networks that they can control and filter. Marketers and their advertising agencies must adapt by engaging and entertaining consumers on their terms.

- **Content Creation.** The commission system is gone, and agencies will need to evolve more into content providers for the Internet, media, and entertainment industries. The creative output of many agencies will expand well beyond pure advertising in order to provide new revenue streams.

- **Media Departments.** In some cases, the re-integration of agency media departments will help add back value to an agency's service. Many of the media departments that were spun off into separate subsidiaries in the 1990s will be reintegrated with many of the large agencies. The role of media planners will grow into a job much like account planners. They will play a critical role in creating new ways of reaching and engaging consumers. Media departments, whether re-integrated or functioning as stand-alone agencies with an expanding menu of services and capabilities will also become more involved with content development, including programming and new media forms.

- **New Media.** Interactivity and non-traditional forms of advertising will continue to flourish. No surprise here. Every marketer is looking for new ways to connect with today's over-messaged consumers. Those who discover new techniques will be rewarded with greater impact and stronger relationships between their brands and their users.

- **Globalization.** Like the good book said, "The world is flat." With the international growth of the Internet and social networking, marketers must think globally. People can research and shop around the world with a few key strokes and share their opinions with worldwide audiences. Moreover, expansion into more buoyant markets like China, India, Brazil, and Russia, where consumers are eager to enjoy their new prosperity, will reveal that the traditional advertising-driven business models can work in these markets.

New Challenges. New Opportunities.

As you can see from the previous discussion, there are a number of major trends affecting the ad industry and agency organization.

These changes will lead to new challenges and opportunities for future advertising professionals.

Agencies and their work will continue to evolve as they have with every major change in the media that carries ad messages.

Advances in computing, communication, and digital technologies will continue to provide many new career opportunities as new media forms and interactive communication evolve into the mainstream of the advertising industry.

And, it will still be about ideas... BIG IDEAS!

Summary.

HAVING READ THIS CHAPTER, you should have a clearer understanding of what advertising agencies do, how they're organized, and career opportunities available today and in the near future.

- The modern agency began to develop in the late-1800s.
- The role of an agency is to generate business-building ideas, provide brand stewardship, and build perceived value for its clients' brands.
- A full-service agency provides four departmental functions: account management, creative services, media planning and buying, and research.
- Agencies charge for their services three ways: media commissions, markups, and fees.
- Advertisers and agencies use a promotion mix of various communications disciplines and strive for an IMC campaign.
- Professionals with a range of experience in more than one communications discipline are valued for their ability to contribute to the IMC effort. There is a good deal of job description similarity and career mobility between advertisers, agencies, and other MarCom disciplines: sales promotion, PR, and direct response.
- While agency acquisitions and mergers continue worldwide, there always will remain a large number of specialized and local agencies and freelancers.
- Today, the digital revolution is having a huge impact on agency organization. Some agencies are developing digital capabilities. Digital specialists have become important partners.

References:

Ogilvy on Advertising.
You need to own this book. Period.

The New Account Manager
by Don Dickinson
The book for account execs.

Where the Suckers Moon
by Randall Rothenberg
The Subaru pitch – ultimately won by Wieden + Kennedy – and then lost.

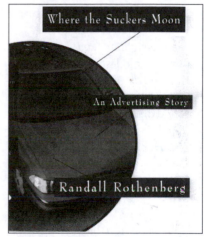

It's a great story – offering added insight into the agency business.

In a letter to *Ad Age*, Rothenberg (who also writes for the magazine) offered these observations.

"It's the agency business' overselling of advertising as a magic magnet capable of singlehandedly luring consumers to a brand against which the book stands.

"'Suckers' says advertising works – when it works – by capturing the inner mythology of a brand and reflecting it back to various constituencies in a way that turns them into true believers.

"That way, salespeople are galvanized to sell harder; line workers and service personnel are encouraged to be more productive, and consumers – the last ring in the concentric circles surrounding a brand – maybe, just maybe, will buy more."

Movies You Might Enjoy:

Here's a cool study project for this chapter – rent a video!

There have been a number of movies set in ad agencies. Here's our list of favorites – and not-so-favorites – the envelope please…

Agency – Perhaps the most unwatchable movie on advertising ever made. We're not sure – no one has been able to sit through all of it. Lee Majors is the creative director and Robert Mitchum is the agency head.

The Coca-Cola Kid – Probably the best movie ever made about an American corporate executive in Australia shot by a Yugoslavian director.

Crazy People – Pretty funny – Dudley Moore has a breakdown and the inmates start writing the ads.

Good Neighbor Sam – With Jack Lemmon – modestly amusing.

How to Get Ahead in Advertising – Actually, he gets a head – he grows a second one. Some like it, some hate it, you'll probably remember it.

The Hucksters – Clark Gable as an ad man and Sidney Greenstreet as George Washington Hill.

Kramer vs. Kramer – Based on the true story of an ad guy (he was in media in Chicago) – Dustin Hoffman plays him as a New York art director.

Lost in America – A modern day classic with Albert Brooks as an ad man who hits the road.

Mr. Mom – Written by ad man turned movie mogul, John Hughes.

North by Northwest – Really doesn't have anything to do with advertising, but it's cool that Cary Grant is an ad man. And did you know that Alfred Hitchcock was an art director before he was a film director?

Nothing in Common – Tom Hanks as an ad agency creative director. Hey, it could happen.

Picture Perfect – Part of the plot involved creating an ad campaign about being #2, and they got a real product to participate.

(Continued on next page)

• The major trends affecting the advertising industry and agency organization are: integrated marketing communications, acquisitions and mergers, media agencies, the expansion of the account planning approach, and continued re-engineering to improve effectiveness and profitability.

Remember, when media changes, advertising changes, and ad agencies are always changing.

Concepts & Vocabulary:

Account coordinators – Agency professionals with responsibility for keeping various aspects of an account or project on track. They may be part of the account management team, the traffic department, or in small agencies, they may even be a main source of client contact.

Account management – A department within an advertising agency staffed with different levels of managers (e.g., account executives, management supervisors) who serve as the liaison between the agency and client.

Account planning – A relatively new, hybrid approach to research. Account planners are a new breed of researchers, skilled in personal interviewing, who are charged with being the consumer's representative in the development of the advertising campaign.

Accountability – A combination of responsibility and results. As advertising expenditures have increased, agencies and clients are more and more concerned with accountability issues.

Art directors – Agency creatives with responsibility for the visual communication of the advertising.

Brand building – One of an advertising agency's major reasons for being – doing whatever is necessary for growing a brand and making it more successful in the marketplace.

Brand stewardship – A program of brand building practiced by Ogilvy & Mather.

Broadcast business – An important part of agency operations. It involves managing the dollars spent on broadcast, often including post-production issues such as talent payments.

Broadcast coordinators – Agency professionals with the responsibility of keeping track of costs related to broadcast production and then seeing that these projects are billed properly.

Business-to-business – A marketing or advertising plan that involves companies that sell products or services to other businesses.

Conflict of interest – A situation that occurs when an advertising agency is handling two or more clients that compete with one another.

Consultants – Professionals who offer their unique experience and advice. Consultants to advertising agencies may be used for agency operations, creative projects, strategy, cost-control analysis, or new business development.

Consumer insight – A research approach that focuses on generating unique and useful perspectives on consumer behavior, beliefs, and motivation.

Content development – Actions taken by advertisers and agencies to generate product placements and sponsorships, and to create original entertainment programs, films, sites, and games to serve as branded entertainment.

Copywriters – Agency creative professionals with responsibility for the verbal part of the communication.

Cost-plus fee – An agency compensation agreement whereby the agency bills its costs plus a fair profit margin to its client.

Creative boutiques – Agencies that limit their services to the conceptualization and production of creative executions.

Creative services – A department within an advertising agency staffed with copywriters, art directors, producers, and supervisors who are responsible for creating and producing advertising and promotional materials.

Creative strategy – A document that contains the objectives, target audience description, consumer promise, key copy support points, and brand personality that the advertising campaign must address.

Creative team – Usually two people – a copywriter and an art director, but there may be a larger grouping. Some agencies have added a computer professional to the team.

Design houses – Similar to creative boutiques, with more of a graphic design emphasis; work will include corporate projects such as corporate standards and annual reports in addition to marketing materials.

Fee system – A compensation agreement that specifies how and when an agency is to be paid without regard to media commission.

Fixed fee – Compensation agreement that specifies a fixed amount of money to be paid for certain services over a period of time.

Freelancers – Agency professionals, usually writers, art directors, or producers who are hired on a temporary or project basis. Some of these "temporary" relationships can last for many years.

Full-service agency – An advertising agency with the size, staff, and resources to provide four major departmental functions: account management, creative services, media planning and buying, and research.

Global agencies – Agencies that have offices in many different countries. They usually serve multi-national clients. They also have "local" accounts in those countries.

Ideas – An agency's primary reason for being – creating new thoughts that help brands grow.

Movies: (Cont.)

Putney Swope – Who will become the next head of the agency? Everyone votes for the guy no one else will vote for… the black agency music producer. Revolutionary in a '60s way.

Suits – This movie is about an ad agency pitching business and a writer with writer's block – not bad. Written by ex-agency CD Eric Weber.

What Women Want – Mel Gibson reads minds and creates (or steals) great ad campaigns. Kind of fun.

Will Success Spoil Rock Hunter? – With Tony Randall and Jayne Mansfield – surprisingly hip.

Income – The money an agency receives. It may be in the form of commissions on media and production, fixed fees, compensation based on hourly rates, or some combination of all three.

In-house agency – An advertising agency or advertising department owned and operated by an advertiser, having all the resources needed to create its own advertising campaigns.

Integrated marketing communications – The process of developing and implementing various forms of persuasive communications programs with customers and prospects over time.

Internet – An emerging media form that is creating new vehicles, new forms of marketing, and new kinds of advertising agencies.

Local agencies – Advertising agencies that serve clients in the markets in which they are located.

Markup – A way agencies make money by adding an additional charge to the cost of production and other services. Traditionally, agencies have marked up these materials and services 17.65% of the net cost.

Media billing(s) – The amount of money an agency or client account places in media.

Media buying – The implementation of the media plan; the purchase of media.

Media buying services – Companies that specialize in handling media planning and buying for their clients.

Media commission – A traditional system for agency compensation whereby the agency retains a percentage (traditionally 15%) of the media space and time it purchases for its clients.

Media planning and buying – The two primary functions of an advertising agency's media department.

Media plan – The document that states how media dollars should be spent. A written course of action that tells how media will be used to achieve marketing objectives.

National agencies – In the US, these are ad agencies that serve national advertisers. They may have a number of offices or only one.

New business pitch – May be a specific presentation to a client looking for an agency or a general presentation of agency credentials – or both. It usually refers to the meeting itself, but may refer to the materials prepared for that meeting.

Perceived value – The perceived unique value or brand personality of a product or service.

Performance fee – An agency compensation agreement that provides incentives for meeting the client's awareness or sales goals. Compensation is either increased or decreased depending on the results.

Pre-press – Preparation of print materials for production, often done in-house at the agency.

Primary research – Research that gathers and analyzes original information from a sample or population.

Producers – Professionals who have the responsibility of producing broadcast commercials. Producers work for advertising agencies and for production companies. You may have more than one producer on a job – one from the agency and one from the production house.

Production – A department within an advertising agency responsible for the production of the copywriter and art director's work. May refer to either print production or broadcast production.

Promotion mix – The various marketing communications disciplines a company may use to communicate with prospects and customers: advertising, public relations, sales promotion, direct response, packaging, and personal selling.

Re-engineering – The breaking down of traditional agency department walls and then forming service-cluster teams to meet the varying needs of clients.

Regional agencies – Advertising agencies that have strength in a certain region – they may have one office or a number of offices in that region. They serve local, regional, and national clients.

RFP – Request for Proposal. A request from a client to a number of agencies to prepare an initial credentials presentation, which usually includes initial qualifications for the requesting client.

Secondary research – Research that consists of collecting information from already-existing sources. You do secondary research first.

Service cluster teams – A team within an agency staffed to provide a client with the services which best meet the client's needs.

Short list – A list of agencies compiled by a client to compete for the client's account. Often, the second stage of a review.

Sliding scale – Agency compensation system that lowers the media commission percentage as the media budget increases.

Spec – Short for "speculative creative." Ads, commercials, and promotional materials that represent the agency's views of what the advertising should be.

Strategy review board – A group of agency senior executives responsible for reviewing major new strategies and campaigns being developed for the agency's clients.

Traffic – A department within an agency staffed with account coordinators who are responsible for steering the various creative projects through the different agency departments and making sure approval procedures are followed and deadlines are met.

Virtual office – Companies whose employees communicate with one another and their clients using the Internet, allowing them to complete work outside the office and regular office hours.

6

This chapter was originally written by Professor Carla Vaccaro Lloyd, an Associate Professor at Syracuse University's S.I. Newhouse School of Public Communications and the former Advertising Department Chair. Her students now work at such agencies as Kirshenbaum & Bond, Bozell, JWT, and Ammirati Puris Lintas – to name a few. She received her Ph.D. in sociology from Syracuse University and her master's from Northwestern. Professor Lloyd has taught advertising media for 15 years and specializes in media topics.

The update for this edition was done by Marian Azzaro. Named a Media All Star early in her career by MediaWeek *magazine, Azzaro is now Assistant Professor of Integrated Marketing Communications and head of IMC studies at Roosevelt University in Chicago, the largest IMC masters program in the US. Prior to joining Roosevelt, Marian worked in media planning at Foote, Cone & Belding/ Chicago and at Kraft General Foods. She is the author of* Strategic Media Decisions.

"Do you know why we publish The Ladies' Home Journal? *...to give you people who manufacture things that American women want and buy a chance to tell them about your product."*
— Cyrus H. Curtis, 1885

The World of Media

THE MEDIA ARE A CRITICAL COMPONENT of The Business of Brands. A huge business in its own right, most media depend on marketing and advertising dollars for their support.

And now, the Media Revolution is changing virtually every part of that world. So it's not surprising that the media industry is both the source of some exciting career opportunities in today's media-driven marketplace and the source of just plain excitement.

To Make a Long Story Short...

- **Lisa Weidman** worked at the University of California, Davis, college newspaper and thought she'd be a journalist. To make a long story short, she became Ad Manager of *THRASHER*, the skateboard magazine – one of our many **niche media**.
- **Bob Levin** began as an account exec at a big Chicago agency. After working on brands like McDonald's, he became President of Worldwide Marketing at SONY Entertainment. His responsibilities included marketing *Men in Black* and *Godzilla* – **entertainment brands.**
- **Brendan Kane** graduated from Syracuse in 1998 and decided to go into media sales after taking an advertising media course.
- In 1985, **Toby Trevarthen** graduated from Michigan State and started at an ad agency. Then he migrated to the media, becoming a specialist in integrating media programs for AOL Media Networks – a **media conglomerate.**
- It's a fast-paced world. **Mindy Cohen** graduated from Syracuse in 1993 with a major in advertising and a minor in psychology. In five years she went from Account Exec/Producer at Modem Media to *Disney Online* to her current role as Director of Marketing for *Cartoon Network Online*.

All of these jobs are brought to you by – advertising.

Advertising Makes Media Happen.

Without advertising, there would be no free "Must-See" TV. *Monday Night Football* would fail to hold the bottom line.

Without advertising, *Lost* would be, well, lost.

Sports Illustrated would cost a lot more than $3.50.

Super-Bowl Sunday, *The Simpsons,* and *Saturday Night Live* would, like, be swallowed up by pay TV *or wouldn't exist at all.*

There'd probably be no sports strikes, either.

Because there'd be no big bucks to strike for.

From 50% to 100%.

Advertising is vital to the American media.

"Advertising is the financial heart of the newspaper," states former Associated Press Vice President and author of *Strategic Newspaper Management,* Conrad Fink. It contributes about two-thirds of newspapers' total revenue.

"Advertising is the lifeblood of the magazine business, accounting for almost half of the industry's total revenue," says Magazine Publishers of America.

Advertising, by and large, pays for media. With commercial radio and TV, advertising is 100% of their total revenue.

A Monster Topic.

This is a monster topic for one chapter – it even covers monsters, like *Godzilla,* an **entertainment brand** (just like *NBC* is a brand, as is *Oprah Winfrey,* the Super Bowl, and *The Simpsons).*

Entire books have been written on topics we'll cover in a few paragraphs. But it's a great way to get started. So… let's.

How This Chapter Is Organized.

Here's how we'll cover the world of media.

1. **A Brief History of Media.**
   From Egyptian graffiti to the Internet, we'll see how each new media evolution changed the business of advertising.
2. **Today's Media World.**
   This is the longest section in the chapter.
   We'll cover the business of media one medium at a time.
3. **Consumers and the Media.**
   We'll look at how you and the media interact today.
4. **Media Conglomerates and Entertainment Brands.**
   We'll see how today's growing, fast-changing media companies are changing the media world we live in.
5. **Current Media Choices.**
   Finally, we'll take another look at each medium the way a marketer might – as an advertising vehicle.

And we'll see it all from the perspective of people who work for these fascinating companies.

First, let's look at how our world of media grew.

Medium/Media.

Here is how these words are used.

Medium = Singular.

This is the correct term for a single media channel, or a single media form, i.e., *"The recommended medium was magazines."*

Media = Plural.

This is a collective noun, the correct term for groupings of mediums, e.g., *"The media recommended were magazines and TV"* or *"Of all the media choices, we ended up recommending People Magazine."*

Medium Is/Media Are

Note that medium is singular and media is plural.

In the world of media, you will find a whole range of usages, some correct, some incorrect, and some slightly confusing.

Just remember, a medium *is* and media *are.* But, since we're dealing with a collective noun, "media is" is not all that incorrect – so don't go around correcting your boss.

Media Jobs.

Each of the disciplines discussed in this chapter offers a wide variety of job opportunities.

We'll tell you about some of these jobs, and the people who have them, in these sidebars.

What's a Rep?

As far as this chapter is concerned, it's a media representative.

Media Representative = "Rep."

A rep works for the media vehicle or a media company and calls on ad agencies or directly on marketers.

Media reps for newspapers and magazines are called space reps; their broadcast equivalents are media reps.

(Continued on next page)

A Brief History of Media.

THIS SECTION OF THE CHAPTER will briefly review how the American media system evolved, how advertising became the force it is today, and how consumer brands, like Campbell's Soup, profited from each major media development.

This was well covered in Chapter One, so we'll be brief.

The Big Picture Begins…

Three thousand years ago, ancient Babylonians put up posters to make announcements to their local community.

Graffiti was splashed across the walls of Pompeii and the stone obelisks of ancient Egypt, delivering the earliest messages.

The Word Goes Forth…

Just as much culture was in the oral tradition of folk tales and epic poems, most early advertising relied on sound, not images, to get the word out on goods and services.

Hawkers and their cries roamed the streets and markets of ancient towns promoting everything from medicinal "cure-alls" to hot cross buns. Each of these forms of advertising had strong local appeal and was based on the available technology – painted signs and the human voice.

Your Message Here…

One of the earliest recorded forms of advertising with a wider reach and more of a mass audience was a silver coin.

More than two thousand years ago, in the North African city of Cyrene, silver coins or tokens were minted to carry the image of a local plant grown specifically in Cyrene. This plant was a pain reliever and condiment, and the coins helped market this plant throughout the ancient world. And ancient Lydia advertised their local establishments.

Print and the Beginnings of Mass Media.

Newspapers made their debut in the early 17th century.

The first newspaper ad appeared around 1650.

Early advertising was more like our classified ads.

Even then, there was comment. Samuel Johnson said, in 1759, *"Advertisements are now so numerous that they are negligently perused, and it is therefore necessary to gain attention by magnificence of promise and by eloquence sometimes sublime and sometimes pathetic."*

The Rise of American Mass Media.

Though newspapers and magazines were published virtually everywhere, for a variety of reasons, both economic and political, mass media and mass advertising grew more dynamically in the US.

This was a government that granted freedom of the press. That freedom also created a much safer business environment for all media.

As was also discussed in Chapter One, it took the other basics of a modern economy to bring about the kinds of businesses that needed advertising for a country.

In every major American city, newspaper publishers were big businesses. They helped inform. They helped shape opinions. They helped sell goods. And they grew.

Cities and Retailers.

Newspapers were the perfect vehicle for growing urban centers. They contained local and national news, and provided an efficient and inexpensive medium for local retailers – a relationship that continues to this day.

$48 Billion. Over 1,400 Newspapers.

In 2006, newspapers amassed $48 billion from advertising.

The top seven newspaper companies have a daily circulation of over 20 million.

Daily newspapers reach 58.7% of all adults.

Readers had 1,437 newspapers to choose from.

Useful News.

A recent study by the Newspaper Association of America and the American Society of Newspaper Editors shows readers find newspaper advertising useful – 78% rely on newspapers for employment ads; 69% use newspapers to find an apartment; and 64% read the newspapers when looking for grocery ads.

Though habits are changing.

The Rise of National Magazines.

Around the turn of the century, with improved printing techniques and a literate middle class, magazines became a part of everyday American life.

Publishing started to become big business. It was a magazine publisher, **Cyrus H. Curtis,** who firmly established the agency's role by promoting agency commissions with a magazine started by his wife – *The Ladies' Home Journal.*

Meanwhile, exciting new consumer products – like soup in a can – began advertising.

While newspapers worked well for retailers, magazines were a far better medium for packaged goods.

Example: Campbell's – See Next Two Pages…

Campbell's Soup, a relatively new company, responded to the opportunities provided by the new technology.

By 1914, Campbell's had dropped newspaper completely from its advertising schedule, throwing the bulk of its advertising dollars into mass-market magazines, like the *Saturday Evening Post* and *The Ladies' Home Journal.*

Let's take a look at Campbell's…

Media History (Cont.)
1927 Farnsworth assembles complete electronic TV system (US).
1927 US Radio Act.
1929 50% of US homes own a radio.
1929 The car radio.
1932 Disney adopts Technicolor (US).
1933 FM radio invented (US).
1934 Communication Act creates FCC.
1936 Kodachrome.
1939 Regular TV broadcasts begin.
1948 LP record on vinyl (US).
1949 Network TV (US).
1952 Bing Crosby's company tests video recording.
1952 SONY transistor radio (Japan).
1958 The laser.
1959 Xerox.
1961 FCC approves FM stereo (US).
1962 FCC requires UHF tuners (US).
1963 Audio cassette (Holland).
1963 Communications satellite (US).
1964 Touch Tone (US).
1966 Fax machine.
1969 SONY U-Matic cassette (Japan).
1970 Floppy disc.
1972 HBO (US).
1975 Betamax (SONY) vs. VHS (JVC)
1979 ESPN
1980 CNN (US).
1981 MTV.
1982 USA Today (US).
1987 Jerry Seinfeld lands on HBO.
1992 First commercial text message.
1993 Howard Stern, Oprah.
1997 *South Park, Wired,* Web TV.
2002 TiVo.
2003 MySpace & Facebook.
2004 Google goes public.
2004 FTC CAN-SPAM Act.
2005 YouTube.
2007 iPhone

From Front… Here's a unique format – both sides of the same page – "Where Can You Turn for Simply Delicious Recipes?"

Soup in Print.

From the beginning, Campbell's found advertising an indispensable ingredient to its soup's success.

As early as 1899, they spent $10,000 on advertising. Two years later, the budget was up to $50,000.

In 1911, Campbell's increased its ad budget eight-fold to $400,000.

By 1920, Campbell's hit the $1 million mark – 5% of sales.

Today, they spend $130 million on soup alone.

Campbell's Soup, one of our nation's oldest brands, made it a common practice to test and eventually adopt each new medium.

Campbell's Cooks Up Posters.
Their first media blitz was posters.

In 1905, Campbell's ad committee decided to try a relatively new media form: streetcar cards (a type of poster).

After analyzing the media choices of the day *"paint, billboards, streetcars, magazines, and newspapers,"* ad committee members decided to place cards in streetcars splashed, for the first time, with *The Campbell Kids,* catchy rhymes, and the distinctive red-and-white cans – a design chosen after…

(Continued on next page)

One Brand Meets

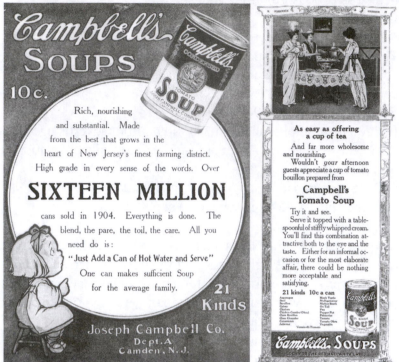

From early print (above) to streetcar posters (below).

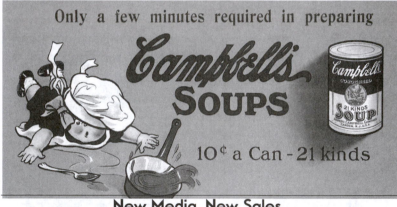

New Media. New Sales.

In 1905, streetcar posters helped increase sales 100%. Often, in the early days of advertising, the first use of a media form had a dramatic effect.

the Media.

"21 Kinds"

"Look for the Red and White Label"

With Such a Foundation a Grocer Can Perform Great Feats

1st. The publicity given **Campbell's Soups** is so extensive that everybody knows about them.

2d. The quality brings every customer back for more.

3d. The profit to you (33⅓%) and profit is the very foundation of your business, is big enough to make it worth your while to help our advertising with your salesmanship, to spread the good word about **Campbell's Soups**.

Joseph Campbell Company : Camden, New Jersey

Trade Advertising.

From the beginning, a key advertising target has been "the trade."

Here is an early ad encouraging grocers to stock Campbell's Soup.

Their benefit? Profits! The "foundation" the ad refers to is the 33.3% profit margin offered by Campbell's Soups. Another benefit is brand awareness. To the trade, advertising is a benefit.

Still at It. Campbell's still uses easy-to-prepare meal suggestions. Here, an Oscar Mayer tie-in with a simple recipe idea.

...to Back. Here, Campbell's reminds consumers that there are delicious (and simple) recipes on the back of each can.

Soup in Print (Cont.)

…someone commented on the look of Cornell's football uniforms.

At the bottom of the card were phrases like: *"6 plates 10¢"* and *"Just add hot water and serve."* The first contract called for cards to be used in one-third of all New York City street cars.

By the end of the year, Campbell's renegotiated its contract to include "every streetcar in New York City."

Sales had gone up by 100%.

They were so successful that Campbell's ad committee expanded its campaign to 372 cities and towns – 35,000 cards to blanket streetcars in each of the cities.

Discussion Question:

Why, in your estimation, do you think streetcar cards were so wildly successful?

An Early Magazine Advertiser.

As magazines developed, Campbell's made magazines a mainstay of its advertising, using eye-catching layouts, artwork, and copy to grab housewives' attention.

They also contributed magazine articles written by expert cooks offering helpful advice about using soup to fix meals.

They still do.

Top US Magazines:

AARP The Magazine
(24.2 million circulation)

Reader's Digest
(9.68 million)

Better Homes & Gardens
(7.68 million)

National Geographic
(5.05 million)

Good Housekeeping
(4.69 million)

Family Circle
(3.97 million)

Woman's Day
(3.92 million)

The Ladies' Home Journal
(3.92 million)

AAA Westways
(3.76 million)

People
(3.68 million)

Prevention
(3.39 million)

Time
(3.37 million)

(Source: magazines.org)

The Growth of Radio Networks.

Networks were a natural outgrowth of the technology.

The first network was born in 1923, when radio stations in Newark, New Jersey, and Schenectady, New York, linked together with a telegraph line to simultaneously broadcast the World Series.

Linking local stations with one another had all sorts of commercial potential, and stations were quickly connected to one another all the way across the country.

Huge and diverse audiences tuned into comedy, drama, and music – all broadcast by three major networks – NBC, CBS, and DuMont.

Shown here, *The Lucky Strike Hit Parade* broadcast on NBC.

Want to Know More?

Read Chapter 6, "The Queensboro Corporation: Advertising on the First Electronic Medium" in *20 Ads that Shook the World*, by James Twitchell.

As we discussed in Chapter One, magazines served a growing group of educated consumers with money to spend.

And they kept growing.

The Magazine Industry Today.

Today, Condé Nast, Hearst, and Time Warner are the largest US magazine publishers. They each publish 16 magazines.

Condé Nast publishes such recognizable titles as *Vogue, GQ,* and *Glamour.* Hearst titles include *Cosmopolitan, Esquire,* and *Good Housekeeping.*

Time Warner, a huge media conglomerate, publishes *Time, Sports Illustrated,* and *People* magazine to name a few.

The three top-circulating magazines in the United States are the *AARP The Magazine* (24 million subscribers), *Reader's Digest* (10 million), and *Better Homes & Gardens* (8 million).

The twelve largest circulation magazines are listed on the left.

Broadcast – Media Turns On.

In 1906, the first radio program of voice and music was broadcast in the US. Advertisers grew increasingly interested in radio as more people tuned in.

In the beginning, direct selling was forbidden. Advertisers were not allowed to quote prices. They were only allowed to mention their company or brand name.

Early radio commercials were "polite and unobtrusive," says mass communications professor, Joseph Dominick. Advertisers, as Dominick points out, were actually *"embarrassed to invade the privacy of the home with their sales messages."*

Known as indirect advertising, it was nothing more than product names incorporated into radio programs.

This ushered in the concept of **sponsorship.**

The Age of Radio.

But by 1930, audiences had grown. Radio was the undisputed king of the air waves, resembling network TV of not that many years ago – before the rise of cable.

Radio was big. As many as 88 million Americans followed the thrilling adventures of *The Lone Ranger* every week.

The Depression was also in full swing. Stations were ripe to sell their air time to companies. Direct advertising and 60-second spot announcements were born.

Commercials became slicker and hard-selling. The singing commercial, later known as the jingle, was developed.

Radio became a medium that got companies results.

For example, General Mills credits early radio for the success of its Wheaties cereal.

Great radio advertising then, like now, captures our imaginations – and builds brands.

Now Playing on the Internet.

Every year, the best radio advertising receives a Mercury Award from the Radio Advertising Bureau.

You can listen to some of these Mercury Award winning radio commercials by going to the jukebox on adbuzz.com – a link will take you to the awards, or you can go directly to their site: www.radiomercuryawards.com.

The Evolution of Radio after TV.

Let's skip ahead for a minute. When TV entered, the big-budget prime-time show – the mainstay of network radio, soon became a thing of the past. For a while radio was adrift.

But radio retained some strengths. You couldn't watch TV as you drove to work. A radio spot was a lot cheaper and quicker to produce than one for TV.

And, if you wanted to listen to your favorite music, there was usually a radio station eager to play it for you.

So, even as the focus shifted to television, radio evolved its own strong and unique role in the media mix.

Drive time became a key advantage for radio.

The ever-widening variety of music styles allowed radio to evolve into a uniquely powerful niche media.

Local retailers and national advertisers after niche targets, like teenagers, became heavy users of radio advertising.

About Amos 'n' Andy...

During the '30s, one of America's top radio shows featured two white guys from New Orleans playing two black guys from New York –Amos 'n' Andy.

Today, most Americans would be shocked by the racist humor and stereotyping.

It wasn't that long ago.

On the radio.

Campbell's on the Air.

Campbell's first used radio in 1931 – sponsoring a morning jazz show.

The advertising department was not pleased with radio's results. The jazz show was dumped and radio got the ax for two years.

By 1934, Campbell's was back on the air, this time sponsoring some of the most popular radio shows of the day, such as *The Burns & Allen Show* and *Amos 'n' Andy*.

As a matter of fact, the advertising on this last show played a significant role in the overall success of one of the Campbell's most popular soups.

Chicken with Noodles?

In 1934, Campbell's introduced a new soup: Chicken with Noodles.

Sales were lackluster despite the fine taste of this new soup.

This left Campbell's executives wondering why this "very good soup wasn't popular."

They turned to radio to give this soup the jolt it needed. After much discussion, executives decided that Chicken with Noodles would be showcased prominently on their wildly popular *Amos 'n' Andy* show.

A Slip of the Lip.

The commercial was written and handed to Freeman Gosden, who played Amos, to read live on the air. His tongue slipped.

Millions of listeners heard "Chicken Noodle Soup," instead of Chicken with Noodles.

And, as they say, the rest is history.

Demand Heats Up.

Amos' gaffe was Campbell's gold mine. In a few days, orders for this new soup came pouring in. A live radio commercial, with all of its spontaneity and room for error, made lukewarm sales red hot!

The commercial also gave this new soup the name it was searching for – one that still rings the cash register.

The Impact of TV.

"Television really transformed the American domestic center of gravity, moving it from the kitchen to the living room," says Robert Thompson, author and Director for the Study of Popular Television at Syracuse University.

"A Change in Domestic Geography."

"The 'domestic geography' of the postwar family shifted from the kitchen to the living room, because TV became the 'cultural heart beat' pulsing in the living room while families were eating," says Thompson. Families could hear the TV from the kitchen.

And *"TV, no matter what is on, keeps calling you,"* Thompson points out. *"It is not just audio noise,"* he adds.

The "town meetings" for families, which generally took place at the dinner table, shifted to the TV set.

The allure of TV worked in all geographic areas among all types of people, too.

"Good Midwestern families who came in for dinner at 5:00 pm were beckoned to the living room to listen to the news," explains Thompson.

"More urban, contemporary families who took dinner at 7:30 were lured in by prime-time shows."

Enter the TV Dinner.

Gathering around the television became one of America's favorite past-times in record speed.

Meal preparation and eating adapted with the advent of TV dinners.

Early TV dinners also paid homage to the medium – they were packaged in boxes that actually looked like TVs, complete with a screen, wood cabinet, and control knobs.

TV became the only medium to have its own food named after it.

Television Turns on America.

In 1933, **Philo Farnsworth**, a 16-year-old high-school student in Rigby, Idaho, patented "an electronic image dissector tube." Five years later, at 21, he transmitted the first television picture.

Ten years later, Americans saw their first TV commercial – for Royal Crown Cola on Schenenctady, New York's, WRGB.

Early Television.

Early TV didn't have mass appeal. There wasn't much mass.

Television sets were expensive. Programs and commercials only reached an upscale urban audience.

Live drama and opera suddenly cropped up in homes. This programming reflected the cultural tastes of those who could afford a set. And the taste of the sponsors.

From 10% to 90%.

In 1951, there were only 1.5 million television sets in the US. Soon, expanded production and department-store credit plans made purchasing a television set possible for more people.

By 1952, television had spread to 15 million households. Three years later, they were sitting in half the living rooms in America. By 1960, almost 90% of all US households had at least one TV set.

Multiple Advertisers and "SPOT."

Television programs cost more to produce than radio.

Therefore, advertising changed. Instead of one advertiser sponsoring an entire program, several advertisers sponsored small segments of that program.

TV Network Affiliation.

Local television stations benefit from **network affiliation.**

For starters, local stations receive high-quality programming that they could not afford to produce on their own. With high-quality network shows like NBC's *Heroes* or FOX's *24,* local affiliates attract large audiences.

This means local affiliating stations can charge higher rates. Local stations reap other benefits, too.

For instance, networks pay each of their affiliates 30% of the local advertising rate when a national ad runs. Nearly 10% of a local station's income stems from the network.

Early Growth of Cable.

By the late '70s, **network television** was the reigning champ of the airwaves and advertising revenue, but a young and rambunctious newcomer – cable TV – was on the rise.

Cable television had been around for quite some time.

It started about 1950, just after broadcast television began. Its role at that time was simple: improve the television reception of people living in remote areas.

Three Major Developments.

Three major developments allowed cable to gain strength:

- **The growth of domestic satellite relays**
- **Creation of TV superstations**
- **The introduction of pay cable services**

Again, technology reshaped the world of media, helping cable TV compete for audiences and advertisers.

Growth of Cable in the '80s.

Until 1980, cable had recycled old TV shows and movies. But no sooner had this decade begun than cable started producing its own programming.

Suddenly, a host of channels bounded into cable subscribers' homes. The new channels offered specialized programming on many subjects: health, finance, sports, and cultural events.

Advertisers discovered a new kind of TV, one that delivered **specialized audiences.**

Advertisers with specialized products (such as fly rods) could now use television without wasting ad dollars on viewers not interested in their products, just advertise on the fly fishing show.

Smaller local advertisers could now afford television – audiences weren't as big, but it was TV, and customers responded.

Today, cable is one of the fastest growing media.

By 1997, cable reached more than 70% of American television households. During the "upfront" for the 2005 television season, cable is starting to be compared with broadcast. It already secures a larger audience in two **dayparts**: late fringe and weekend day.

In 2006, advertising revenue cracked $19 billion. And cable revenue is expected to keep growing in double digits.

Example: *Nickelodeon*

For example, Nickelodeon, reaching 96 million US households, was the first cable network to appeal strictly to children and their parents.

Advertisers seeking to reach an audience of parents with young children can do so with the special programming offered by Nick, including age-specific cartoons, game shows, and sitcoms.

A Quick Question.

What cable stations do you watch? Hold that thought.

Then compare your viewing to the list of the top 10 cable networks by ad revenue on the sidebar on the next page.

An Interactive Future.

Now technology may change TV again. Television, long a passive medium, is now becoming interactive.

Most of today's television asks little of the viewer.

There are, of course, exceptions, like cable shopping channels.

And, of course, the channel changer gives viewers control.

But soon, viewers will program their TV to receive information and entertainment. They will be able to choose what they want to see when they want to see it – this is **video on demand.**

Campbell's Goes on TV.

Campbell's, and its agency, BBDO, were early believers in TV. They completely reshuffled advertising dollars to give television a major chunk of the total ad budget.

In 1954, Campbell's spent $11.5 million on advertising. TV received $4.5 million (39% of the budget).

The first television sets housed small screens – no bigger than 12 to 14 inches.

Families had to huddle around these small screens to get a glimpse of the flickering, black-and-white images of their favorite shows.

TV was actually changing the way American families ate.

Now Dad's an expert at "fryin' up" a chicken dinner!

Swanson TV BRAND DINNERS

Campbell's Buys a New Brand.

Families needed a quick food that was easy to prepare, convenient, and, perhaps most importantly, able to be eaten on a lap or a "TV tray."

The result was individual dinners in compartmental trays – TV dinners!

Seeing a need for a meal that would support this newfound behavior – TV viewing, Campbell's bought Swanson, the company that made TV dinners and other frozen-food items. (They owned Swanson until 1998.)

Robert Thompson noted, *"Soup is not a good TV food. It was a wise move on Campbell's part to buy Swanson's TV Dinners."*

Top 10 Cable Networks:

Here are the top 10 for 2002 – by dollar volume (in millions).

1.	ESPN	$920
2.	Nickelodeon	748
3.	MTV	737
4.	Lifetime	711
5.	TBS	667
6.	TNT	630
7.	CNBC	508
8.	USA Network	425
9.	Discovery	393
10.	CNN	352

News Corporation.

Here's a partial list of properties owned, or partially owned, by Rupert Murdoch's News Corporation:

Cable/Satellite
US: FOX News, FOX Sports, FX, FuelTV, FOX Soccer Channel
Latin America: Sky Entertainment
UK: British Sky Broadcasting
Germany: Vox
Australia: Foxtel
Asia: SkyB, Start TV, ZEE TV

Broadcast
US: FOX, FOX TV Stations, MyTV

Newspapers
Australia: the *Australian*
Hong Kong: *S. China Morning Post*
UK: *Sun & News of the World, Times and Sunday Times*
US: *NY Post, Wall Street Journal*

Publishing
US: Harper Collins, Zondervan

Magazines
US: *Weekly Standard*
Australia: Numerous titles

New Media
US: MySpace, Hulu, Photobucket, IGN Entertainment, Beliefnet

The Newest Edition.

The *Wall Street Journal*, purchased in 2008, is News Corporation's latest media property. We predict it will grow from just a newspaper to a multi-media brand. WSJ online is just the beginning.

This is all part of the world of media's next evolution.

Today's Media World.

EVERY YEAR, EVERY AMERICAN CONSUMES OVER $950 in media, and we spend about nine hours a day consuming it!

Our media world has grown into something pretty amazing – and pretty big.

Think about your own media budget. You receive about $950 a year in advertising-supported media (that's an average).

Now think about how much you spend to purchase media.

First, newspapers and magazines. Add entertainment brands like sports and movies (including the poster, T-shirt, and soundtrack album) and that number is even bigger.

Big Business!

The media world includes some of the world's biggest companies. While many media companies own more than one kind of media, it will be useful for you to look at the media world by category.

Three Major Categories.

For our purposes, there are two major media categories – print and broadcast – plus a number of other important types of media, which we will call "other." It looks this way:

- **Print.**

  Newspapers. Our oldest major medium. And, until very recently, our largest revenue generator.

  Magazines. Print media aimed at specific audiences.

  Out-of-Home. This is the oldest media form of all. It includes new technology, as well – from hand-painted billboards to new digital painting and electronic video signs.

  It includes the posters in your student union, your laundry rooms, and maybe even the walls of your dorms.

  Kiosks at bus stops and posters in subways are also included in this out-of-home category.

- **Broadcast.**

  Radio. This was our first electronic medium, and the first one fully sponsored. It's changed dramatically.

  Television (network, local, and cable). Television is the medium you probably know best. But you'll see there's a lot you don't know behind the scenes.

- **Other.**

  This catch-all category contains some big things you might not think of as media – your mailbox, telephone, and computer.

  Your Mailbox. Direct mail accounts for 23% of all ad expenditures. And it's growing. We'll read more in Chapter Seven.

  Your Telephone. Whether you call an 800 number (inbound), or someone calls you (outbound), telemarketing is big.

  Your Computer. You're already receiving ad messages on your computer, and now you're beginning to buy things by computer. This is one more part of today's media revolution.

Big Changes!

Media today is changing with the daily headlines.

In the past two decades, these changes have been radical.

Four Major Change Agents.

Four major factors have influenced these changes:

- **Media Technology.** Technology is changing the creation and distribution of media: from satellite feeds and digital broadcasting to the new niche media made possible by desktop publishing and the Internet. Tivo is an example of how fast media technology can make change happen.

  Each change in technology alters the playing field.

- **Media Competition.** Consolidations and mergers are the most obvious result, but the growth of media brands and entertainment brands is changing both the organization of media companies and the way they make money. The recent emergence of Clear Channel in radio, out-of-home, and concerts is an example of how fast things can change.

- **Media Audiences.** Change causes more change. Because of the new choices, media audiences are fragmenting. Major demographic and lifestyle changes combined with this abundance of media are also having impact. Recently, media buyers were surprised to discover young men were disappearing! Oh, they were still around, but playing video games and going on the Internet, not watching primetime network TV.

- **Media Expenditures.** With all this change, it's no wonder marketers are changing the way they spend money on media.

Trying to Keep Up...

And, with all this change, this chapter can't keep up either; we can only give you an overview of the changes going on.

But we do keep on top of things.

Just remember to check out our Web site at <u>adbuzz.com</u> for the latest developments – and, even better, the best way to keep track of change is through the media.

A Media Boom!

During the last two decades, for all these reasons, the media industry has boomed.

Here are a few facts about the media world we live in:

- **There are more than 1,300 commercial TV stations and 530 cable TV networks.**
- **Over 70% of American homes get cable.** They receive, on average, nearly 100 channels. This is up from only 11 in 1980.
- **There are presently 19,000 consumer and business magazines in print.** This is according to Magazine Publishers of America (MPA).
- **Almost 250 new consumer magazines were launched in 2007.** They come and go – but desktop publishing has made it easier than ever to start your own publication.

And the media options just keep on growing.

Media Technology.

TiVo is an example of technology that's changing advertising and the way we watch TV.

Media Competition.

ABC/Walt Disney brings out big guns to win Saturday morning.

TV Time.

A big chunk of Americans' time is spent parked in front of their TVs.

Women 18 and older spend more time watching TV than men. They tune in an average of 4½ hours daily.

On average, men watch 40 minutes less TV per day.

Think about it. Americans are spending about half-a-workday's worth of time in front of the tube.

"Encourage your children to read a newspaper every day. You'll be preparing them for the most important role of all...life."

My most important role is being a parent. My children aren't impressed by awards, they just want me to be there for them. That's why I've always loved reading to my kids (they think I make a very scary witch and a great duck). I urge you to read to your children every day—especially newspapers. Reading newspapers will give them the whole story of what's going on around them. And reading will prepare them for the most important role of all...life.
—Meryl Streep, Actress

It all starts with newspapers.
www.newspaperlinks.com

THIS MESSAGE IS BROUGHT TO YOU BY THE NEWSPAPER ASSOCIATION OF AMERICA

The Newspaper Association is using ads like this to encourage readership.

Major US Newspaper Companies:

Gannett, Inc.
90 dailies
$5.12 billion net revenue

Tribune Publishing
25 dailies
$3.96 billion net revenue

The New York Times Co.
17 dailies
$3.19 billion net revenue

McClatchey Co.
32 dailies
$2.36 billion net revenue

Advance Newspapers
27 dailies
$2.17 billion net revenue

Digital? Dig it!

Digital technology is further expanding channel line ups, bringing viewers multi-channel premium services such as: multiple HBOs; forty-plus music channels with CD-quality sound; and a variety of pay-per-view and on-demand offerings.

The digital compression of signals could increase the number of channels to 1,000 as TV in the US moves (by law) to digital in 2009.

Is it any wonder average daily television household viewing is up to almost seven hours? How much do you watch?

Riches in the Niches = Thousands of Magazines.

Magazine-based niche media are growing, as well.

On average, we still see about 20 new magazines launched every month, according to MPA.

Lisa Weidman discovered her niche in a job with a magazine, *THRASHER*, that hadn't existed a few years earlier.

We'll talk about her job later in this chapter.

Now, let's look at it one medium at a time.

The Scoop on Newspapers.

One of the most dramatic examples of media evolution is what is currently happening to newspapers.

Until 1995, newspapers were the #1 US ad medium, receiving over $38 billion in ad revenue in 1996.

From Number One to Number Three – But Still Growing.

Now they're #3, they were surpassed by TV and direct mail in total ad revenue, even though newspapers saw their own ad volume increase.

As of 2006, newspapers are up to $48 billion in ad revenue. About 85% of that comes from local advertisers.

Advertising = 67% of Revenue.

Advertising is critical to newspapers. Historically, advertisers have contributed two-thirds of newspaper earnings.

52 Million Households.

In 2006 there were 1,437 daily newspapers, and 907 Sunday newspapers in the US.

Daily newspapers reach 52 million households.

This is called **circulation.**

Two-thirds of adults 18 and older still read a newspaper.

According to a national readership study by the Newspaper Association of America, 58.8% of all people 18 and older read a daily newspaper and 68.5% of these folks read a Sunday paper.

Circulation Trends...

But the bad news is that the number of adults who read newspapers has declined sharply. In 1970, a significant 77.6% of all adults 18 and over read a daily newspaper and 72.3% of them read a Sunday paper. You can see the decline.

As you might guess, the big challenge facing newspapers today is trying to reverse this trend. An example from an ad campaign for the Newspaper Association appears in the sidebar.

Take a look. What do you think about it?

Newspaper Ownership.

Most newspapers are part of large ownership groups.

Some publish their newspaper nationwide, such as *USA Today* (Gannett), the *Wall Street Journal* (News Corp.), and the *New York Times* (Times Mirror).

Others specialize in media in their own market, such as the *Erie Daily Times* and *Morning News* published by Times Publishing located in Erie, Pennsylvania.

Some, like Gannett and Rupert Murdoch's News Corporation, are part of larger multi-media operations.

Newspapers Respond to the Marketplace.

Intense competition has forced all media outlets to become more aggressive. In an unprecedented move, Thomson Newspapers, one of the largest North American newspaper companies, broke tradition and began selling ads on the front page. This had long been considered a taboo.

Patricia Gillies, Director of Employee Publications at Thomson Newspapers, explained this bold strategic move *"recognizes the changing environment in which newspapers operate."*

Responding to Competition.

Severe competition has made media outlets more in tune with their audiences and more willing to adapt to their needs, wants, and interests.

In 1997, the *New York Times* was forced to adapt to the demands of the media marketplace – they would print some pages in color!

The Real Competition for Newspapers.

But the real competition is on your desktop. Classified ads for rentals, real estate, automobiles, and jobs were once huge "cash cows" for the newspaper industry.

Today, you're getting more of that information online. Why write a classified ad when you can go on eBay?

Some newspapers have been very aggressive going online.

But all of them know that the old ways are going.

However, as new media behaviors kick in, there has not been an effective new business model. So, newspapers are facing the loss of revenues from old behaviors (classified ads) without that revenue being replaced by new behaviors.

There's one more bit of competition – alternative newspapers.

Alternative Newspapers.

Another niche has grown in the newspaper industry, one you're familiar with – alternative newspapers.

These papers, often free, focus on entertainment and arts-driven features with ads targeted at a younger audience.

The first of these was the *Village Voice*.

Chicago Tribune: Gone to Zell.

Sam Zell, a tough, outspoken financier has a new investment – the Tribune Company.

Beset by declining revenues and a large group of shareholders that wanted to "cash out," Zell has taken over the media conglomerate that owns big city newspapers (the *Tribune* and *LA Times*, among others), radio and TV stations (including SuperStation WGN), and the Chicago Cubs.

Our advice? Watch this space!

In the months and years to come, you will see all of the aspects of The Media Revolution come into play as changing valuations, media traditions, and a blunt, often rude, business person collide on center stage.

Responding to the Marketplace.

Personal Ad. Personal ads and voice-mail services, like those advertised by the *Cleveland Plain Dealer,* have been real money-makers for traditional daily newspapers in recent years.

A Unique Newspaper. A Unique Audience. As their ad says, "It's so nice that homosexuals, Jews, and terrorists have a newspaper to read."

No,

I don't want to subscribe to The Village Voice. Who needs your crummy little radical, left-wing editorials, you Commie Pinkos, with your mud-slinging stories on politics and the government, why don't you just leave well enough alone? Quite frankly, I'm sick and tired of worrying about the homeless and corruption and injustice, why don't you stop stirring up trouble, anyway... hey, you know, this is America, love it or leave it... and your "scathing" reports on abortion and drugs and censorship and animal research, nothing's ever good enough for you is it, you, you, radical lunatic subversive radicals! ...Besides, you don't have any T.V. listings.

YES, I WANT TO BUY A ONE YEAR SUBSCRIPTION TO THE VILLAGE VOICE.

National Rate: $47.95 (Just 92¢ per copy)

To order, call toll-free 1-800-336-0686 Or mail this coupon to:
The Village Voice Subscriptions, P.O. Box 1905, Marion, OH 43302.

Name_____
Address_____
City/State/Zip_____
Amount enclosed $_____ Bill me___
Charge Me: AmEx_____ M/C_____ VISA_____
Credit Card #_____ Exp Date_____
Signature_____

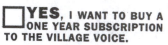

Rates good in U.S. only. Canadian and foreign subscriptions $79.20 per year; must have payment with order. Allow 4-6 wks for delivery. For address changes, call 1-800-347-6969.

America's First Alternative Weekly.

The *Village Voice,* America's largest weekly newspaper, was founded by Dan Wolf, Ed Fancher, and Norman Mailer in 1955.

It is considered the founding father of alternative weeklies.

The *Voice* introduced a new type of journalism that brought a *"free-form, high-spirited, and passionate journalism into the public discourse."*[28]

A Growing Category.

Some alternative papers are quite large. Chicago's *Reader* has a weekly circulation of 135,000.

Readers of the *Reader* tend to be better educated, single, and young. The inset shows who reads this alternative paper.

The *Austin Chronicle* boasts a readership of 243,500.

It provides stories that address the political and environmental concerns unique to Austin, the capital city of Texas.

"Reader" Readers:

Here's a profile of Chicago readers of the *Reader:*
  Median age: 40
  52% are 18–34
  62% are 25–44
  Median household income: $57,000
  93% have attended college
  49% professional/managerial
  60% male; 40% female
  70% are single

It also provides in-depth coverage of Austin's rich cultural scene.

The Onion, which began as a small humor paper in Madison, Wisconsin, now covers a number of markets, with advertising sales offices in Madison, Milwaukee, Chicago, Denver, and now New York.

Their outrageous humor has helped them establish a unique niche in the marketplace.

Check it out at www.theonion.com.

Example: Chicago Sees Red.

The success of Chicago's *Reader* did not go unnoticed by the *Chicago Tribune,* finally they stepped up with a bright weekday tabloid called *RedEye.*

In the beginning, it was available for 25¢ in unique little newspaper boxes all over Chicago.

Then, one more Chicago paper stepped in. The *Chicago Sun-Times* rushed to put out their version –same size, same price same attitude – named *Red Streak.*

Though the *Red Streak* folded in 2005, the Tribune Company continues to publish *RedEye,* as a now-free daily targeted at Chicago's young, urban commuters.

Magazines.

You Can Judge These Books by Their Covers.

In 2006, there were more than 19,000 magazine titles in the US.

Historically, magazines have devoted 50% of their space to advertising. The rest comes from subscriptions (which, not surprisingly, are about half price) and newsstand sales.

All these magazines generated $32 billion in total sales, and almost $11 billion in ad revenue. Magazines can be broken down into various types:

- **Consumer**
- **Business or Trade**
- **Newsletters and Journals**

It's a varied industry. There are big companies and small ones. Let's take a look at the various groupings.

Consumer Magazines – General or Specialized.

Consumer magazines are divided into two groups:

- **General Interest**
- **Specialized**

There are general-interest consumer magazines, such as *TV Guide* and *Reader's Digest*. These magazines carry editorial content that appeals to a broad variety of people.

Specialized magazines appeal to readers with specific interests, hobbies, and lifestyles. For example: *Ceramic Magazine, Becket Baseball Card Monthly, Keyboard,* and *Opera News.*

THRASHER is an extreme example of this type of magazine – it appeals to skateboarders.

Though general-interest magazines, like *People* and *Newsweek,* have circulations that are quite large, you might be surprised at how large some specialized magazines, such as *PC Monthly* and *Bride,* are in terms of ad pages and ad revenue.

And the largest circulation magazine is *AARP The Magazine!*

A Business Magazine for Every Business.

Trade magazines usually focus on some type of business with a specialized audience and a specialized advertiser base.

Condé Nast. This attractive montage from a trade advertisement shows the range of unique magazines they publish.

Trade Magazine Examples.

In the fields of advertising, marketing, and media, these are the major trade magazines: *AdWeek, Advertising Age, BrandWeek, Editor & Publisher, Media Decisions,* and *MediaWeek.*

If you think you might be interested in a career in this field, you should start reading them. Some have student subscription rates.

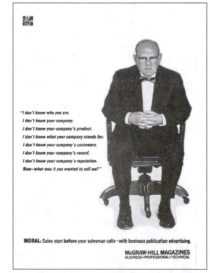

Good Reasons to Advertise. They are summed up in this classic ad from McGraw-Hill, which publishes Business Week *and many other specialized trade magazines. "Moral: Sales start before your salesman calls."*

SRDS.com.

Now you can get a feel for the information provided by *Standard Rate and Data Service* (SRDS) – on the Internet!

Additional Services.

Some of the things you can find:

• **SRDS Media Kit Link** – get media kit and Web site information for thousands of business publications.

• **Product Information** – more in-depth information from SRDS.

• **Industry Web Sites** – a hyperlink to leading media-related sites.

• And more.

Call 1-800-851-SRDS.

For media rates and data, contact SRDS offices.

SRDS Examples:

There's an example of SRDS at the end of this chapter for *Vanidades*, a magazine from Editorial Televisa, written for the particular interests of contemporary Hispanic women.

You'll also find a practice exercise using SRDS for Campbell's Soup.

Kiplinger Newsletters.

Kiplinger Washington Editors, Inc., publishes four different newsletters.

Kiplinger puts out a lot of other media products, too – a magazine, special reports, books, software, video, and television, but they're best known for their newsletters.

Each Kiplinger letter appeals to a different segment of the financial-interest group.

There's *The Kiplinger Letter* that makes weekly forecasts on business and economic trends. It also highlights what to expect from Washington.

The other three weekly letters include: *The Kiplinger Tax Letter, The Kiplinger Agriculture Letter,* and *The Kiplinger California Letter.*

If you'd like to view a sample of these letters to see just how different they are from magazines you read, go to www.kiplinger.com/letters.

Sometimes there's a grouping of magazines, sometimes two compete, sometimes there's only one.

Standard Rate and Data Service (SRDS).

You can find a complete breakdown of these magazines in *Standard Rate and Data Service (SRDS)*.

This directory breaks consumer and business magazines into different classifications.

SRDS then lists a brief description of each of the magazines, circulation information, advertising rates, and other important information critical in scheduling and running a magazine ad.

You can usually find a copy of *SRDS* at your local library and probably your school library. And on the Internet.

Newsletters and Journals: Controlled Circulation.

Newsletters are small publications that deal with the special interests of a particular group.

They may be sold by subscription, or they may be sent free of charge by the publishing group. Unlike magazines, you generally cannot buy a newsletter on newsstands.

Journals are supported by universities, grants, and institutions, and circulate to small groups of specialized readers.

Many journals do not include advertising.

These types of magazines are generally not advertiser supported in the traditional sense. They are paid for by:

• **Subscribers**

• **Dues-paying members** of the publishing organization

• **The company publishing the publication** may fund it for promotional and marketing purposes or for some other reason, such as employee relations.

How Magazines Make Money.

But, most magazines want to make a profit – and to do that, they need the right idea, a sales staff, and luck to help make it happen.

It's still an attractive, exciting business – even though success can be elusive. Here are two historical examples:

Examples: *SWING* and *George.*

Advertising revenue and subscriptions are especially important to new magazines, like David Lauren's *SWING* magazine.

Son of famed fashion designer Ralph Lauren, he started *SWING* magazine while attending Duke University.

He wanted to create an intelligent publication that dealt with the interests and concerns of twenty-something culture.

He couldn't swing it. *SWING* folded.

John Kennedy, Jr., co-founded *George,* a guide to the people and the process of politics as they relate to popular culture.

R.I.P. – A terrific magazine.

His magazine's aim was to *"bring politics to life with insightful reporting and cutting-edge commentary."* It was hugely successful, attracting both readers and advertisers.

For a while, it was quite successful.

But, sad to say, it did not last past his untimely death.

The Importance of the Sales Staff.

Advertising sales staffs, like the one in the sidebar for *Wired* magazine, are made up of account managers, sales managers, advertising coordinators, and regional sales offices directors.

They help service clients and get ads sold. This keeps the magazines on newsstands and coming to your mailbox.

Rate Cards and "Added Value."

Heightened competition has made media outlets more flexible and service-minded. For the past ten years, magazines, with the exception of the Condé Nast periodicals, have been very flexible about their advertising rates, making the price of advertising now fully negotiable.

Prior to this, advertisers paid the rates on the rate card.

Rate cards include a detailed listing of the various ways advertising can be purchased.

In *Glamour* magazine, for example, the rate card tells us that a four-color, full-page ad costs $161,220.

Three Free with Ten.

Some magazines will give advertisers three free pages of advertising if they buy ten pages.

Condé Nast magazines, such as *Glamour* and *Vanity Fair*, are willing to kick in all sorts of free promotional programs to advertisers paying the full price of advertising.

Instead of discounting the cost of advertising, Condé Nast magazines provide "added-value" to their clients by "organizing and subsidizing department store displays and mall fashion shows."

Other added-value deals that publications offer advertisers include "databases and marketing partnerships."

The Big 3 Make a Big Change.

Even the biggest media respond to the marketplace.

Newsmagazines, like *Newsweek, Time,* and *U.S. News & World Report,* often referred to as "The Big 3," have also had to adapt their editorial content to remain relevant to today's readers.

Facing fierce competition from broadcast sources and declining public interest in traditional news media, the Big 3 were forced to reinvent themselves.

As reported in the *Chicago Tribune,* what the Big 3 did was to critically examine the way they had been doing business.

They shifted their emphasis from traditional coverage of national affairs of government to an editorial product that newspapers and TV news were not serving. The Big 3 now cover more stories on business, technology, and healthcare.

Keeping Wired.

Here are some (not all) of the job titles on the masthead of *Wired* – jobs that have to do with the advertising-based economics of running a magazine:

Publishing Staff:
Publisher
Associate Publisher
Travel & Spirits Director
Strategic Sales Director
East Coast Account Managers (3)
West Coast Advertising Director
West Coast Sr. Account Manager
West Coast Account Managers (3)
Promotion Coordinator
Advertising Coordinator

Wired Market:
Premium Market Account Mgr.
Los Angeles Director
Detroit Director
Regional Representatives: Chicago, Boston, Southwest, Southeast, Asia, London, Europe
Marketing Services Director
Promotion Director
Strategic Marketing Director
Promotion Manager
Senior Promotion Associates (2)
Marketing Research Director
Marketing Design Director
Marketing Coordinators (2)

Consumer Marketing:
Sr. VP Consumer Marketing
VP, Retail Marketing
VP, Strategic Planning
Consumer Marketing Director
Advertising Services Manager
Sales Associates (8)
and more…

The Yellow Pages. A $15 Billion Business.

The *Yellow Pages* is a form of directory advertising – it's powerful because it delivers an audience ready to buy.

In 2007, businesses purchased $14.7 billion worth of *Yellow Pages* ads:

• Three out of four adults in the US turn to the *Yellow Pages*.

• Every month, *Yellow Pages* is used in 77% of all US households that are actively seeking product information and are ready to buy.

• 90% of *Yellow Pages* reference searches result in an actual purchase or intent to purchase.

Source: *Statistical Research Institute.*

Student Jobs in Outdoor.

We asked Chris Serrari, Office Manager at Lamar of Erie, PA. Here are some jobs to consider:

• **Graphic Artist/Creative Director.** Companies like Lamar have in-house creative departments. You can be a part of the process – even a part of sales calls.

• **Account Execs/Sales Reps.** The major career path is in sales. Selling the space available is hard work, but it can be rewarding.

The Sales Manager directs Sales Reps for the office. The General Manager continues to sell outdoor and is in charge of the entire office.

They also now concentrate on maintaining long-term relationships with their readers.

You'll notice throughout this chapter (and this book) that the marketplace is always changing, and many brands have to adjust to that change.

Next, another example of that change – newspapers.

Newspapers Become Magazines – The Domino Effect.

With the rise of TV, newspapers were no longer the source of the latest scoop on late-breaking news. The scoops were now for local TV news and the all-news stations like *CNN*.

So, newspapers focused more on depth and breadth, something TV news couldn't do. They became more magazine-like.

At the same time, the Big 3 weekly newsmagazines turned to more long-term in-depth articles – they became more like the once-popular monthly newsmagazines that provided in-depth discussion of issues. These faded.

However, monthly magazines that focused on an area of great interest to a specific group could still do quite well.

For example, *Wired*, featuring articles for "the modem generation," has prospered, going in-depth in the area of high-tech.

Inc. has connected with smaller companies and entrepreneurs. *Fast Company* is a hot new business monthly featuring cutting-edge issues for today's new corporate warriors.

Out-of-Home & Outdoor.

Outdoor ad revenue has grown 7% per year every year since 1993. 2006 ad revenues were estimated at $6.6 billion.

Place-based Media.

Traditional outdoor media include billboards and bus shelters, to name just two. New money is coming from nontraditional locales – health clubs, bathrooms, airports, restaurants, and bars.

Outdoor on the Move...

With new large-screen video technology, outdoor signs will start to provide more video images.

Technology is migrating everywhere.

Advancement in traditional technology now has truck-mounted rolling billboards in major markets. In addition, many companies are now putting more value on their own rolling stock, so you'll see more brand imagery on trucks and vans.

With improved flat-screen technology, there are major projects to replace the old posters at your movie theater, your McDonald's, and

even elevators with computerized video screens that can change quickly and flexibly… almost anything you can imagine.

You can find out more about this dynamic and changing industry, and see examples of award-winning work at the Outdoor Advertising Association of America Web site – www.oaaa.org.

Broadcast Media.

NOW LET'S LOOK AT THE BUSINESS OF BROADCAST – radio and TV. Television is a bit bigger than newspapers (a recent phenomenon) and radio, and like magazines, is now more of a niche medium.

Radio.

BETWEEN 6AM AND 6PM, more people spend more time with radio than any other medium – even TV.

The numbers tell the story. Radio's 10,000 stations reach 74% of all Americans over age 12 at least once a week.

The reason is simple. A full 95% of all cars have radios.

Drive Time Is Radio Time.

During morning drive time (6-10AM weekdays), 50% of Americans 12 or older listen to the radio. And, 42.2% of these people listen from 3 to 7PM on their way home from work.

The vast majority of those behind the wheel are also in the driver's seat at work. A recent study shows that 92% of professionals and managers tune into the car radio weekly.

Radio has become our companion medium.

It goes where we go, no matter where our lifestyles take us.

Among those 12 and older, 37.2% listen to the radio at home, 41.6% listen in cars, and 21.2% tune in at work and other places. At work, 65% of us have a radio nearby – though it's not always on.

Radio also accompanies people on their way shopping.

It is the last medium people hear before making a purchase.

Radio reaches 63% of adults 25–54 within one hour of making their largest purchase of the day.

Some people even listen while browsing through stores.

A Local Medium.

As you read earlier in this chapter, radio was once the major national network medium. Now it's a local medium.

From 1985 to 1996, advertising revenues nearly doubled.

Radio's real strength is now at the local level. It depends on local advertising for the bulk of its revenue.

In 2006, advertisers spent $19.7 billion. Only $1 billion was spent in network, the rest was in **spot radio.**

Of that spot revenue, $15 billion came from local sales and national spot accounted for $3.5 billion.

More Radio than Ever.

From 1983 to 1993, the number of stations grew by 22%.

For 2005, there were 10,659 commercial radio stations in the US.

How many stations in your market?

Making It in Radio.

At Syracuse, Brendan Kane was active in his fraternity – scholarship and PR chairman and house manager.

He majored in advertising and minored in marketing.

Brendan now works as Marketing Specialist in the sales department at WGRR radio (an Oldies station) in Cincinnati, Ohio.

A Cincinnati Powerhouse.
WGRR is a powerhouse station – #1 with the 35 to 54 segment.

Brendan interviewed at eight stations and chose WGRR.

It's owned by CBS. There was the opportunity for high visibility. (After all, the head of CBS started out in radio sales.) And Brendan noticed some nice perks. For instance, he noted that the sales staff got flown to Jamaica regularly.

Internships and Leadership.
Brendan, who's originally from Boston, had a number of internships while he attended Syracuse.

He interned at Ingalls Advertising in Boston. He also interned at Boston's KISS 108 in the promotions department.

When he studied abroad, Brendan secured an internship in London, working in account management.

These varied internship experiences gave Brendan a valuable insight into advertising's day-to-day operations.

His internship at Ingalls proved especially beneficial. Brendan notes, *"Now I know how ad agency buyers work. And I know how to approach them."*

Leadership positions at his fraternity also helped in broadcast sales. Brendan says, *"Those positions relate to what I'm doing now…*

(Continued on next page)

Making It (Cont.)

…networking, making cold calls, and establishing relationships. It helped me develop interpersonal skills and social capabilities."

Career Decision – Broadcast Sales.

A media planning course convinced Brendan to go into media sales.

Investigating the profession, he focused on broadcast sales.

There were a variety of factors – one was variety. As Brendan points out: *"Sales is not a daily grind. It isn't like the same thing every day. It's also good money. There's a lot of variety … sales proposals, promotions, and what is best for the customer."*

Brendan says he *"got turned off to the ad agencies because of the money aspect."* (Low starting salaries.)

He wanted *"the opportunity to make a lot of money in a short amount of time."* And Brendan also liked the variety media sales provides.

Cold Calls. Consultative Selling.

On any given day, Brendan may go out on *cold calls* – contacting potential clients for the first time.

Brendan sets up two appointments with new customers.

The first is a *needs analysis.*

He interviews customers to find out their specific marketing needs.

In this meeting, it's also crucial to find out who the sales pitch or proposal should be directed to.

After client marketing needs are identified, he works up a sales proposal with a demographic profile matching his station's listeners to the client's target audience.

It also contains station information and, often, promotional ideas.

Then he sets up a second meeting.

Brendan practices *consultative selling,* proposing plans and ideas based on marketing needs.

He views himself as a *"partner in helping clients grow their business."*

People & Promotions.

Brendan enjoys meeting new people and working for a variety of clients.

(Continued on next page)

Radio Formats.

Radio stations are categorized by various formats.

To appeal to specific segments, stations will select music, on-air personalities, and promotions to attract particular niches.

This is the radio station's **program format.**

Formats are constantly evolving. As Gary Fries, President of the Radio Advertising Bureau (RAB), states, *"There's something out there for everyone. Wherever people develop a new taste, radio develops a new format."* (Find out more about radio at www.rab.com.)

The Four Most Popular Formats.

The four most popular radio formats are:

- **Country – 19% of all US radio stations**
- **News/Talk – 12%**
- **Oldies – 9%**
- **Latino – 9%**

Radio formats break listeners down into highly targeted, very small portions of the population.

Growing Listenership – New Formats.

Radio listening is significant. Americans now spend 20 hours a week listening to radio.

A 1996 study done by Arbitron, a radio ratings firm, found that 95% of all Americans 12 and older listen to their radio every day.

Highly successful new programming like *Radio Disney* captures listeners' attention. A recent launch in Boston connected with 70,000 kids the first two weeks on air.

Radio is everywhere. Fully 99% of all households have radios. The average home has six. How many do you have?

Numerous Niches.

There are radio formats that fit almost every musical taste and political ideology.

WE SET RADIO BACK 40 YEARS.

"Fibber McGee and Molly." Sunday 6 p.m.
KSJN/1330 AM

That's why radio not only offers advertisers a steady flow of listeners, it delivers loyal audiences.

The programming and on-air personalities speak directly to you.

They tap into how you're thinking and feeling at a particular time in your life.

And we listen – to our favorite music, sports, and talk show celebrities. When you add it up, it's 20 hours a week.

Radio Networks.

Radio networks still exist, working much the same way as television networks, interconnecting local stations and providing affiliates with programming. But, for the most part, it's a looser affiliation. They're a lot smaller and less important.

Some are statewide, like the Yellowstone Network, listener-supported radio serving Montana and northern Wyoming. And some are pretty big. *ABC, CBS, ESPN,* and *Radio Disney* are some of the more important.

Networks offer local affiliates news, weather, talk shows, and children's shows. Local stations might even affiliate with several networks to get a variety of different programming.

That's why you may find stations in different cities with essentially the same playlists, station identification packages, and sometimes, even the same advertising campaigns.

Big News in Radio – Clear Channel and CBS/Viacom.

With a recent shift in ownership limits, radio has been reshaped.

Now there are two huge radio ownership groups.

Number two is Infinity Broadcasting, owned by CBS/Viacom which combined Infinity with Group W for a total of 183 stations in top markets across the country.

Number one is Clear Channel, a relative newcomer which owns, operates, or sells air time for over 1,200 stations and effectively controls rock radio. They're also one of the world's largest outdoor companies and a major player in concerts.

Ownership is just one more way that radio keeps on changing.

Want to Know More about Radio?

Visit the RAB site at www.rab.com and you'll find out more.

If you're like Brendan Kane, you may even find a career.

Television.

IN THE US, TELEVISION IS THE BIGGEST MEDIUM, and for the most part, it is commercially supported. In the US, commercial TV depends entirely on advertising for revenue.

Cable TV derives most of its earnings from subscriber fees.

In 2006, TV advertisers spent $66 billion.

This is the largest advertising media category.

Ad spending in cable television accounted for $19 billion, this was a 17% increase over 2005.

Advertisers Like Television.

TV stations and networks make money by selling time. (Print sells space, broadcast sells time.)

Television is prized by advertisers. Traditionally, they consider it to be one of the most effective and persuasive of *all* advertising media.

Viewers Like Television.

Over 99% of all US households own one television set; 81% have two. And 85% of all American homes have at least one VCR or DVR. (How many TVs in your home? And how many VCRs or DVRs?)

For years, TV has brought the news, big sports events, and broad-based entertainment into American homes. And we watch it all.

Social scientists report the average high school grad has spent more time with TV (15,000 hours) than in school (11,000 hours).

They're watching the commercials, too.

Media Synergy.

The fourth most popular magazine in the US used to be *TV Guide*. Americans do love TV.

Thousands of Messages Per Day?

No, we don't really see that many messages – but we are often exposed to that many.

For example, the number of messages you see on packages during a trip to the supermarket is staggering – as is the number of signs you see, but don't notice, when you walk into a convenience store (count them sometime, you'll be surprised).

Depending on which study you believe, researchers report that by the age of 18, the average American child has seen between 350,000 and 640,000 television commercials.

With More to Come…

In 1985, the average American family had 18 channels to choose from. By 1994, it had jumped to 38. Now, the average American family has more than 100 channels – with more to come.

Cable viewers spent $40 million on cable services. There are now six major broadcast networks.

More than 60% of American homes are hooked up to cable. And digital technology makes even more programming possible.

For all these reasons, television is attractive to advertisers.

Four Kinds of TV. Six Ways to Buy It.

Television can deliver a nation, a region, or a city.

Basically, there are four kinds of TV programming:

1. **Network**
2. **National Cable**
3. **Syndication**
4. **Local (mostly news)**

When it comes to buying television, advertisers can buy from the network or the producer of the syndicated TV show. Or… the advertiser can make a spot purchase from a carrier – a network, cable, local affiliate, or local cable carrier.

This results in these six options. Compare it to this chart:

National
  1. **Network**
  2. **National Spot**
  3. **National Cable**
Local
  4. **Local Spot**
  5. **Syndication**
  6. **Non-network Cable**

2007 TV (in Billions)	
TV Networks	$25.42
Spot TV	16.82
Cable TV	18.02
Syndication TV	4.17
Local TV	15.26
Total TV	79.69
(Source: www.adage.com)	

We'll cover the types of television now. Later in this chapter, we'll briefly cover the buying process. (We'll cover media planning and buying done by agencies in Chapter Ten.)

Network Television.

Network television comes into our homes free of charge.

There are currently four major national broadcast television networks in the US: the American Broadcasting Company (ABC), the Columbia Broadcasting System (CBS), the National Broadcasting Company (NBC), and FOX Broadcasting Company.

The first three have dominated broadcasting for 40 years.

FOX, a relative newcomer, has become the fourth network.

One New Network.

There is one new and growing network – the CW, which formed in 2006, combining the WB (Warner Brothers/Time Warner) and UPN (Paramount). This is all part of the trend of media companies developing their brands across media forms.

This is also a result of the fact there are now more stations broadcasting in virtually every major market.

Networks don't "rule the tube" anymore, but their prime-time hits – from *House* to *The Office* – still draw the biggest crowds.

Network ratings still dwarf all but the top-rated cable programs.

But even with diminishing audience share, *ABC, CBS,* and *NBC* are still the primary source of large mass media audiences.

A Dramatically Decreasing Share.

The older networks have seen their prime-time audience decrease drastically in recent years.

In 1980, three networks, *ABC, CBS,* and *NBC*, had a total audience share of 90%. By 1999, four networks, *ABC, CBS, NBC,* and *FOX* had a total audience share of 45.7%.

Why the big drop? Network TV's audience continues to decline because of cable, the Internet, and computer/video games.

Cable – More New Networks.

Cable has eroded network television's audience share. Look at the chart on the previous page. Cable ad revenue is now almost equal to that of the four networks.

And the younger the audience, the more it's true. Cable accounts for 43% of all TV viewing and claims about 29% of the ad revenue, according to *Electronic Media* reporter, Lee Hall.

And, it's *all* TV to kids. A recent survey found that 275 children ages 6 to 11 *"could discern little or no difference between broadcast TV and cable television channels."*

When asked which TV network they turn to first, 31% picked *Nickelodeon*, 14% picked *FOX*, followed by *The Disney Channel*, and *The Cartoon Network*.

It appears as if future generations of TV viewers will not see much of a distinction between cable, pay, and broadcast.

To them, it will truly be all TV.

Network, "O&O," and Affiliate.

Network TV consists of a group of local TV stations that are joined together electronically. Today, most networks rely on satellites to link all their local stations.

Until recently, regulations have allowed networks to **own and operate (O&O)** only five stations.

So, unless you grew up in one of the biggest markets, chances are the network station you grew up with was an affiliate.

But, with the Telecommunications Act of 1996, that may be about to change.

Here's how it stands today. Each local station signs a contract with a network that makes the local station an affiliate.

An affiliate agrees to air only that specific network's programming. Both parties benefit.

First, the network gets approximately 90% of the local station's commercial air time to sell to national advertisers.

Jobs in TV.

A job at a major TV station in a major market can be hard to come by, but there are a lot of jobs, and a lot of stations, that aren't major stations in a major market.

Look at all your options.

Here are some opportunities that may lead to jobs:

Internships.

Get a job before you get a job.

Lots of stations use lots of interns.

So find out who signs up interns and get on the list. You'll have a lot easier time finding out where the jobs are from the inside.

Assistantships.

A lot of people at TV stations need help – here are some of the areas that hire entry-level assistants:

Smaller Stations.

Everybody shows up at the big station with the downtown studio, but there might be a job for you at one of the stations you don't watch.

Cable Operators.

Finally, don't forget that all the cable operators have their own small station operations.

They do programs and they produce ads – lots and lots of ads.

Sure, some of them may have pretty small production budgets, but it's a great chance to get started.

Got Media?

Entertainment brands and marketing campaigns are teaming up. It's just one more way media is evolving.

Syndication.

Syndicated television sells, licenses, and distributes programs to stations.

It's a $3.5 billion business.

The process is worth reviewing.

First, Get a Program.

The first thing syndicators do is secure programming.

They can produce their own. Or, they can acquire programming from independent program producers.

Then, Get a Station.

After rights are secured, syndicators will offer the programs to stations.

The license lets stations use the programs for a fixed length of time. Once the license is signed, syndicators supply the station with a program tape.

Some Examples.

Original syndicated programming (called first-run syndication) includes talk shows (e.g., *Oprah, Jerry Springer,* etc.), dramas (e.g., the new *Star Trek*), and game shows (e.g., *Jeopardy*).

Hit Shows – Old and New.

Off-network shows (e.g., *Happy Days*) are syndicated programs previously shown on network TV.

Baywatch was perhaps syndicated TV's biggest success story – the world's most-watched TV show.

Barter.

Local broadcast and cable TV stations and syndicators generate ad revenue through a system called **advertising-supported syndication** or **barter syndication**.

In the 1980s, many stations were desperate for fresh programs but short on funds to pay licensing fees.

Syndicators devised an alternative payment method – barter syndication.

Under this system, a local station gave the syndicator some of its commercial air time – instead of cash.

Generally, barter syndication sells to local stations on a 50/50 basis.

Here's How It Works.

Let's say a syndicator sells *Home Improvement* to a local station with six minutes available on each episode.

The syndicator takes three minutes and the local station takes three.

(Continued on next page)

Through this collaboration, the network extends coverage.

Local stations come out ahead, too. All TV stations have a lot of air time to fill. You will recall that programming is the backbone of all TV stations, and it's expensive to produce.

A Shift in Policy.

Recent developments may alter these long-standing network/ affiliate payment arrangements.

First, Rupert Murdoch's FOX Network bought many more than five stations. A smaller, less-dominant network, they were allowed to buy as many as they could afford – they ended up with 22.

And, FOX was already in the programming business.

Growing Networks. Shrinking Audiences.

Meanwhile, audiences are shrinking at the same time the cost of producing shows is going up. That's why you're seeing more of those "reality" shows. They're cheaper to produce.

On average, it costs $1.2 million for an hour's worth of drama programming. *ER* costs even more.

You may need 22 episodes to fill a broadcast year. As audiences shrink, programming gets even more expensive.

Except for local news, programming has been the network's job. The three largest networks, ABC, CBS, and NBC each have approximately 200 local affiliates, covering close to 100% of the US.

Changing Production Relationships.

When there were only three networks, there were restrictions on those networks producing their own shows.

Now, with more network competition and a greater need to recapture production costs through syndication, networks are more deeply involved in producing shows and retaining syndication rights.

It all keeps changing – stay tuned.

Syndicated Television.

Syndicators supply programs to stations and some cable networks.

Demand for programming is always intense. But in the '80s, competition really heated up – as new stations came into the market.

Demand for original programming exceeded supply.

That's when syndicated shows, like *Oprah, Jerry Springer,* and *Wheel of Fortune* really came into their own.

The Advertiser Syndicated Television Association (ASTA) reported that *"in a little over 10 years, syndicated television has grown from almost nothing into a $1.6 billion advertising medium."*

Now that number has grown to more than $4 billion.

Syndication is explained it more fully in the sidebar.

National Cable.

National cable is now in about 60% of US TV households.

There are currently 7,090 cable systems in the United States servicing about 65 million TV households.

Unlike broadcast TV, where a local station airs only one channel and receives its programs from just one network, local cable systems offer subscribers multiple channels.

They get their programs from many cable networks.

That's why cable is often referred to as multi-channel.

Program Suppliers.

In order to fill all the available air time on their many channels, cable systems use a variety of program suppliers. They include:

- **Cable Networks**
- **Superstations**
- **Local Original Programming**
- **Pay-cable Networks**

When each local cable system has filled most or all of its channels with programming, it becomes a basic cable package marketed and sold to cable subscribers for a monthly fee.

The lowest fee gets "basic cable." Across the US, the average price for basic cable in 2007 was $42.76. Higher fees add various sport and movie "premium" channels, such as *ESPN* and *HBO*.

Cable Networks.

Local cable systems contract with many different cable networks. Cable networks consist of 24 hours of specialized programs appealing to practically every taste and interest.

Sports enthusiasts tune into *ESPN*; women watch *Lifetime*.

Superstations.

Cable systems usually include a few **superstations** in their basic package. A superstation is a local broadcast station that is distributed nationally to cable systems via satellite.

Superstations that have proven popular with viewers are Atlanta's WTBS and Chicago's WGN. They may have two-tier pricing for local and national advertisers.

Local Programming.

Some cable systems originate their own local programming – generally created by community or educational organizations – and show it on local access channels.

Pay-cable Networks.

Pay-cable networks offer commercial-free programming: premium movies, special events, concerts, and original series for a monthly fee beyond their basic cable service charge.

HBO and *Showtime* are examples of pay-cable networks.

Pay-cable networks are delivered to subscribers by the cable system in their local area. They do not carry advertising.

Though, as you are well aware, non-pay cable networks certainly do carry ads.

A Desirable Marketing Partner.

Cable's target focus, flexibility, and willingness to work with advertisers makes it a desirable marketing partner for advertisers.

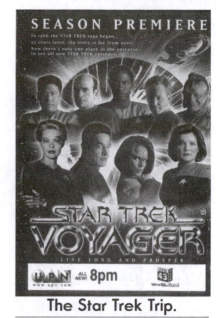

The Star Trek Trip.

It's gone from network to syndication to network – the *Star Trek* brand, originally a Paramount-produced network show, became successful in syndicated re-runs. Over time, this resulted in a number of new, syndicated spin-off series. Though all of these series have ended, you can still catch re-runs – in syndication.

Syndication (Cont.)

Variable Time Slots...

Advertisers who purchase syndicated TV buy programming, not time slots. Stations can broadcast whenever they choose. In Dallas, *Baywatch* might run 8 to 9 on Monday.

Denver might be 7 to 8 on Sunday.

...Mean Variable Ratings.

This is a big difference. A 30-second network spot will run in all US TV markets at essentially the same time.

Syndicated TV doesn't deliver that same consistency.

But It's Profitable.

Let's say 20 local stations buy *Home Improvement* through barter syndication. The syndicator has 60 minutes of commercial air time.

The syndicator packages the time for sale to national advertisers – usually at a very good rate.

Meanwhile, the local station sells its three minutes to local and regional advertisers. It's win/win.

And that's how it works.

MTV & the Growth of Niche TV.

Small Niche. Big Business.

In 1997, *Fortune* magazine reported MTV Networks — made up of *MTV* for teens, *Nickelodeon* for kids, and *VH1* for baby boomers — delivered close to $625 million in earnings to parent company Viacom.

This was 32% of Viacom's total earnings and a 25% boost in profit. MTV Networks' success depends on pleasing its many different groups of distinctive young viewers.

As a matter of fact, Tom Freston, CEO at MTV Networks, told *Fortune* that he's *"confident that MTV and Nickelodeon have room to grow, as long as they retain the loyalty of kids, teens, and twenty-somethings."*

Keeping in Touch with Your Target.

Earning this loyalty among fickle young audience members takes significant consumer research.

MTV does just that by studying the usual ratings, polls, focus groups, and online chats.

It also sends researchers into the field, to dig through dorm rooms, closets, and CD collections of 18- to 24-year-olds, to find out what this group wants and thinks is hip.

Unique Promotions. Unique Targets.

The unique promotions, programming, and packaging created by the MTV Networks are critically important to their success.

MTV's wacky promotions are driven home with graphic punch, creating a unique brand identity for the network.

(Continued on next page)

Your Media World Keeps Growing.

Newspapers, magazines, outdoor, radio, and TV are the media forms with which your parents are most familiar.

But as media interacts with today's fast-moving marketplace, it keeps changing and evolving. It's an exciting time to be in media.

For example, the Internet is congested with millions of new sites being added every year. It was estimated there were over 500 million sites in January of 2007. Today? A Google's worth.

It's a big world and getting bigger and more complicated, with new opportunities emerging all the time.

Let's talk about what that means to us as individuals, and the expanding range of media behaviors.

Consumers & the Media.

WE HAVE BECOME A MEDIA-SATURATED CULTURE. Professor James B. Twitchell notes in *AdCult USA*, *"the culture we live in is carried on the backs of advertising."*

He observes that *"much of what we share, and what we know, and even what we treasure,"* comes from ad messages created by ad agencies and delivered by vast and sophisticated media outlets.

From Stickers to Spectaculars – Indoors and Out.

Advertising is everywhere. Take a look for yourself: oranges, apples, bananas, and grapefruits affixed with little stickers used to promote the *Liar Liar* video, Snapple fruit beverage, *Hulk* cereal from Post, and the "Got Milk" campaign tying in with everyone.

New York Times reporter Carol Marie Cropper recently found that today's advertising gives consumers little privacy and even less room to escape.

Privacy? For $75 a month, Minneapolis-based AJ Indoor Advertising will plaster a page-size ad on 3,000 bathroom stall doors and urinal walls.

For $100 a month, Market Media of Massachusetts will place an ad in the form of a tile on the floors of grocery stores.

Escape? Ski Lift Media, Ltd., based in Banff, Alberta, mounts "advertising tubes" that include full-color ads on chair-lift safety bars to reach skiers and snowboarders.

From the fenders of a NASCAR racer to our favorite sports teams to toddler's T-shirts asking "Got Milk?", we now live in a media-saturated environment.

We're also media-saturated as individuals.

In 2006, a slow-growth year, advertisers spent $285 billion on advertising, an increase of almost $15 billion.

5,000 Messages a Day – or More.

This translates to approximately 5,000 messages confronting every man, woman, and child in the US every single day of the year.

City dwellers are bombarded with even more ads. Recent studies show urban dwellers exposed to an astonishing 13,000 ads per day.

What does this media glut mean for consumers?

Well, the first thing it takes is time.

The Great American Time Crunch.

Today's consumers feel like they are busier than ever before. They probably are. For example, in 1995, 59% of all American women were actively involved in the labor force, compared to 37% in 1967.

Married women, who juggle jobs, family, and household responsibilities may find little to no time to watch soap operas, daytime talk shows, or even read the daily newspaper.

The time crunch is severe. "*Americans currently spend an average of 9½ hours watching television, going to movies, renting videos, reading magazines, listening to music, or surfing the Web,*" reports Veronis Shuler and Associates, Inc. "*There are just so many hours in the day, and it looks like we've reached the saturation point,*" says President John S. Shuler to *Business Week*.

Studies show that as new media like the Internet emerge, Americans merely shift the amount of time they spend with other media – like television or magazines – to the new media experience.

Thus, many consumers do not expand the time they spend with the media, they just cut back on one to give to another.

Served or Delivered? Whose Media Are They?

We talked about this briefly in Chapter Three, but as we see the growing business of media, it's worth mentioning again.

They're *our* airwaves. Broadcast television, the driving force of our media age, comes to us over *our* airwaves. We own them.

Our government grants the use of the airwaves to broadcast stations – this is the basis for groups like the FCC judging how stations use the public trust.

It's the reason for those public service programs few of us watch. But whether we watch them or not, we should remember that these are our airwaves. They're our eyeballs.

The Evolution of Media.

Media guru Marshall McLuhan notes that we evolve as our media evolves. This is a point we've been making throughout the book.

Remember, when the printing press hit, we had the Reformation, the Thirty Years War, and, thanks to printer Ben Franklin, the American Revolution. We moved from "ear-driven" oral cultures to the printed page.

We've evolved again. Now we're literally swimming in media.

This new multi-media environment we live in is changing our consumption habits – greater amounts, greater variety, and greater sophistication. Today's viewer is not some passive victim.

We exercise our options as easy as a turn of the page, a thumb twitch on the channel changer, or a click of the mouse.

Today's Media Challenge.

This abundance has created a challenge.

How have media outlets themselves reacted to all of this change?

Niche TV. (Cont.)

Years ago, branding was extremely important in establishing it as a "cool place" and contending with the fact music videos were now everywhere.

Nickelodeon gets stamped in the minds of kids with bouncy music and the signature orange splat on everything from toys to macaroni.

A First for Cable!

Kids and advertisers alike are devoted to *Nickelodeon*, with the network controlling more than half the viewing of kids' television shows and with most advertising being sold out.

Nickelodeon made TV history during the 1997-98 television season by becoming the first cable network to top all the major broadcast networks for an entire season.

Nickelodeon also led the pack in the Saturday-morning ratings race among children's shows by rerunning its popular weekday programs.

VH1 – Another "Niche."

VH1, the network for "MTV graduates," gained recognition with its distinctive programming like its Pop-Up Videos.

Meanwhile, MTV produces most of its promotions and programming, since they feel they know their brands better than anyone else.

Branding is certainly helping these three cable networks stand out from the vast media crowd, maintain their loyal viewing audiences, and register continual strong earnings.

**The Double R-Bar —
An "Entertainment Brand."**

Movie cowboy Roy Rogers, here with movie and real-life wife, Dale Evans, was an early entertainment brand.

When he couldn't get a raise from Republic Pictures, Roy Rogers (his real name was Leonard Slye) got something else – his merchandising rights. Pretty sly.

Soon, his brand was on toy six-guns, comic books, lunch boxes, and all the other items kids buy.

It was more than he'd made making "B" cowboy movies.

Rogers expanded those rights into television – his TV show ran for years. He even leveraged his brand name into the restaurant business – Roy Rogers Family Restaurants, run by Marriott, became a major East Coast chain.

And *Roy Rogers, King of the Cowboys*, became one of our first modern entertainment brands.

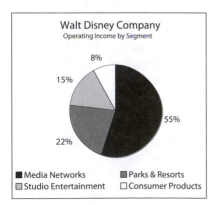

Walt Disney Company
Operating Income by Segment

- 55% Media Networks
- 22% Parks & Resorts
- 15% Studio Entertainment
- 8% Consumer Products

Media Conglomerates & Entertainment Brands.

NOW LET'S LOOK AT HOW MEDIA competes. Even in the early days, media companies were big. Today, they're huge.

Once media companies were defined by local newspapers – then by local media groups that added TV and radio stations.

Now, we are seeing media conglomerates that include everything from theme parks to film companies to jet engines. (GE owns NBC and Universal.)

Some, like News Corporation, already have global reach.

There will be winners and losers, but a revolution is always an exciting time to be doing business.

Big Stakes. Big Profits. Big Brands.

The media marketplace has always been one of high stakes and profit potential, where competition for consumers' attention and advertisers' dollars is fierce.

There's a lot of excitement in the world of media – there are a lot of interesting jobs and interesting brands.

Many of our most popular media outlets have become part of even larger media conglomerates.

These are massive media organizations. Rupert Murdoch's News Corporation includes everything from newspapers, magazines, books, 20th Century FOX film and video production, FOX TV, cable/satellite, and new media, like MySpace.

But big as they are, it's not an easy business.

Media Challenges.

As we discussed in Chapter Two, audience fragmentation and media clutter have also forced entertainment media companies to adopt *"cost-cutting tactics, layoffs, more sophisticated market research, and the formation of strategic joint ventures"* to survive in the overly crowded and competitive media world.

What this means to entertainment media organizations, like the Walt Disney Company and Time Warner, is the pressure to:

- Spend more to produce a product (like a movie, book, or television program) that exceeds the quality of other media producers, and
- Sell this product over and over again in different markets, venues, and formats to maximize profits.

Do it right, and your product becomes an **entertainment brand.**

The chart in the sidebar offers a breakdown of the ways the Walt Disney Company makes money from their creative properties.

Later, take a look at the *Lion King* sidebar to see what an entertainment brand can do when everything works together in the marketplace.

Splintered Media Audiences.

Size doesn't always help. Although they're big, media companies are finding that they have to spend more to capture segments of a splintered media audience.

They've added new divisions like record labels, and to leverage their entertainment brands, new movie studios, broadcast and cable networks, theme parks, and online ventures.

As we'll discuss in Chapter Ten, "it's all about the eyeballs."

Splintered audiences mean that properties that can accumulate big audiences (lots of eyeballs) are worth even more in today's media marketplace. When they can generate profits in more than one division, so much the better.

Big Brands. Big Bucks.

That's why media organizations also are paying more for producing the content or securing the rights to run certain programs.

NBC agreed to pay approximately $900 million to renew *ER* for three years. *CBS, FOX,* and *ABC* paid a staggering $17.6 billion for rights to broadcast NFL games for eight years.

These dynamic outlays translate to weakened profit margins. In 1987, Disney had operating margins of 25%; just over twenty years later, this has dropped to 13%.

FOX also knows how to go after other segments. The focus (some say bias) of FOX News consistently draws an older audience that feels comfortable with their presentation of "news" and opinion.

The Need for Branding Media.

Faced with intense competition, individual media outlets, like Viacom's MTV Networks, are finding that to connect with young viewers and attract ad dollars, they must handle their media property like a brand. In essence, to understand today's media environment is to understand branding.

FOX Builds Their Brands.

In the '90s, FOX became a major player.

In its 1997 financial report, FOX Broadcasting credits a strong brand identity for part of its phenomenal success, stating: *"Broadcast television remains the primary medium to reach a mass audience in the US, and FOX Broadcasting has one of the strongest brand images and attracts the highly sought after audience of young viewers."*

Revenues hit record levels at *FOX* in 1997, thanks to the network's unique strategy to distinguish itself from the older, more established networks (*ABC, CBS,* and *NBC*).

FOX's strategy focuses on targeting a younger audience with distinct programming and promotions.

In 1997, shows like *The Simpsons, King of the Hill, The X Files,* and *Melrose Place* made *FOX* the #2 network among the hip 18- to 34-year-old crowd during the lucrative primetime hours.

Strong brand identity and a focused strategy has won over even younger television audience members.

Integrated Media Rep.

For most of the last ten years, Toby Trevarthen has worked for Time Warner, *"the world's leading media and entertainment company."*

He's gone from marketing all Time Warner properties – to helping revitalize the AOL division.

He's also been an access point into Time Warner's assets. As he described it, *"My main objective is to provide integrated market solutions for our clients."*

An example – a program for a top hotel brand – Hilton.

Now Playing!

Time Warner Music connected with Hilton Hotels (Hilton features name entertainment) with an integrated promotional program.

A promotional CD, *"Jazz Happens at the Hilton,"* was created and used as part of a relationship marketing effort aimed at Hilton's top customers.

Hawaii Calling…

One of the marketing objectives was to stimulate traffic at Hilton's extensive Hawaiian properties.

A sweepstakes tied-in with *Message in a Bottle* and Time Warner's pay-per-view cable programming. It added up to millions in media value. Best of all, Hilton Hawaii bookings were up.

Media Migration.

How did Toby end up on the cutting edge of media integration?

He "migrated" there from his agency job because he found the media world more entrepreneurial.

(Continued on next page)

Toby (Cont.)

Toby notes, *"My selling style was such that I naturally integrated and packaged stuff. Then, in 1990, when Gannett started their integrated Gannettwork division, I just fell into it."*

Toby then went to Meredith (BH&G and other properties), *"where I helped package their home and family resources."*

Finally, Toby was hired by Time Warner to play on a larger stage as a Regional VP with *AOL.*

So Many Niches.

Asked for advice on connecting with today's media world, Toby has a simple answer – the Internet.

"When I started," he says, *"there were so many niches that I didn't know about, and I had to do a lot of research.*

Today, it's so much easier to find out about a company's resources – now you can just go to the Web site. Though you definitely need to be Net savvy today."

Toby invites you to visit www. timewarner.com.

Time Warner:

Broadcasting:
The CW, HBO, TNT, TBS, CNN, CNNSI, Cinemax, Headline News, The Cartoon Network

Movie and TV Studios:
Warner Bros., New Line Cinema, Castle Rock, Hanna-Barbera

Publishing:
Time, People, Sports Illustrated, Fortune, 28 other magazines, Warner Books, Little Brown

Music:
Warner Bros. Records, Atlantic, Elektra, Sire, Rhino

Recreation:
Atlanta Braves, Atlanta Hawks, WCW (World Championship Wrestling)

AdBuzz Note:

Read the Bob Levin PBS Interview, *"The Monster That Ate Hollywood."* www.pbs.org/wgbh/pages/frontline/ shows/hollywood/interviews/levin. html - Find link at adbuzz.com in Chapter Six Text Resources.

For example, after holding the number-one position among kids for the past four years, *FOX* continues to be extremely popular among youngsters. In May 1997, *FOX* secured the #2 ranking among the 2 to 11 set by averaging 1,385,000 kids with its *FOX Children's Network.*

Good Sports.

Accumulating small regional cable sports channels, FOX Sports Network presented pro baseball, basketball, and hockey.

Domination with local sport brands has made FOX Sports a strong player in TV sports almost overnight. They've even bought one more well-known entertainment brand – the *Los Angeles Dodgers.*

The Growth of Media Brands.

Media outlets, like MTV, have long understood the importance of branding when it comes to distinguishing a media vehicle in a competitive marketplace.

(You might want to review the earlier *MTV* sidebar.)

ESPN is a media brand on the move with everything from theme clubs (*ESPN Zone*) to a radio network, retail stores, a news-magazine, and some of the cleverest commercials on TV.

A Bigger Challenge for the Largest Media Companies.

An understanding of branding is helping some cable networks survive, even thrive, in a time of competitive chaos.

You will recall from previous reading that branding, as advertising agency Ogilvy and Mather describes it, *"is understanding the relationship between the product and its users."*

This is exactly what *MTV* is doing. (Look at the sidebar on Viacom's *MTV* and *Nickelodeon* brands.)

This takes keen consumer insight and a firm understanding that *"the brand's true owners are the loyal consumers who drive the bulk of profits."*

Ogilvy and Mather further suggests it is essential to *"understand the relationship between the product and its users, searching for the full significance of the product in the user's life."*

But this is much clearer for specialized media brands like *MTV, Nickelodeon,* or *ESPN* – they each stand for something with a key target. If you're NBC or Time Warner, the problem can be a bit more complicated.

The largest media conglomerates must act like multi-brand marketers. And, again, it's entertainment brands that can be the organizing concept for marketing efforts.

Entertainment Brands in Action.

In the fields of media and entertainment, new brands are popping up every weekend and every TV season.

Some will be here and gone in an instant, and others will become a major part of our media culture.

Godzilla's Brand Manager.

Bob Levin worked on big brands in Chicago. Then he went to brands that are blockbusters – *Jerry Maguire, My Best Friend's Wedding, Godzilla, Air Force One,* and *Men in Black.*

From there he moved to become president of worldwide theatrical marketing for Disney, and is now president of worldwide marketing and distribution for MGM.

Bob was President of Worldwide Marketing for Sony Pictures handling the marketing and tie-in efforts for the *Godzilla* campaign.

It was *big!* Size does matter.

Today's media world is big brands, big budgets, and a new appreciation for the value of a brand property. To make the most of that investment, SONY Marketing worked tie-ins with Taco Bell, toys, and an outdoor campaign that captured just about everyone's attention.

Size Matters.
Licensing, Spin-offs, and Merchandising Can Top $1 Billion.

To promote *Godzilla,* SONY spent an estimated $50 million. Marketing partners committed $150 million more.

A movie marketing blitz is sort of a mixed media work of art: publicity, movie  trailers, advertising, and merchandising create a six- to eight-week cultural event.

"When the public only sees things in advertising, they're skeptical," says Levin. *"But if it's in all the forms where they expect to see things, then it lifts [the campaign] to another level."*

Godzilla was More than a Movie.

It's an entertainment brand that can be used to sell lots of products. In all, 220 licensing partners signed up.

From there, Bob moved to MGM as President of Worldwide Theatrical Marketing and Distribution – a monster job.

And from there… well, it's Hollywood. Anything can happen.

Current Media Choices.

Now let's look at each medium the way an advertiser would – as an advertising vehicle. And let's see what working at these companies looks like from the people who work for them.

A Preview of Chapter Ten… and Chapter Twelve.

We'll come back to this one more time; we'll cover the topic of media selection in more detail in Chapter Ten – Media and the Marketing of Messages.

Understanding how to understand your media options is a key part of marketing in The Business of Brands.

In this next section we'll cover:

The Lion King.

Business Week reporters Ron Grover and Elizabeth Stevens show how valuable an entertainment brand can be.

In 1994, Walt Disney Company made *The Lion King* for $55 million.

Now look at the return on that initial $55 million investment.

$55 Million = $1.2 Billion…

The animated movie took in $313 million in US theaters and $454 million abroad, sold $520 million worth of videos, and was a main attraction on cable's *Disney Channel.*

That's just the beginning.

+ Merchandise…

Fans spent $3 billion on *Lion King* merchandise. A percentage of that went back to Disney as licensing.

+ Records and Television…

The soundtrack sold 11 million copies. Disney used the film again in September 1996 to boost the ratings of its struggling *ABC* network.

+ A Broadway Show…

The Lion King is still roaring.

In November, the Broadway musical debuted in a new Disney-run theater in Times Square.

Soon, tickets with a $70 face value were going for as much as $1,000 each.

After that, it went on tour.

+ Future Revenues.

By now sales are almost pure profit.

Stevens and Grover sum it up, *"Old movies such as* Casablanca *and* Star Wars, *TV shows such as* I Love Lucy, *books such as* Gone With the Wind, *or records such as Fleetwood Mac's* Rumours, *continue to sell well and attract new audiences long after they're created."*

The goal isn't merely to create a hit, but a cultural touch-stone that will earn revenue for many years.

That's the long-term economic power of an entertainment brand.

Newspaper Jobs.

Since most of their income depends on advertising, quite a few jobs at newspapers are advertising-related.

In general, both newspapers and magazines have these departments:

1. News/Editorial
2. Advertising Sales
3. Sales Support
4. Circulation
5. Production
6. Finance and Accounting.

The next part of this chapter will explain briefly how newspapers and magazines are organized.

It will also highlight a variety of entry-level job opportunities that exist within some of these departments for students who are studying advertising.

1. News/Editorial.

In newspapers, the news department is made up of editors, reporters, and photojournalists.

At magazines, the editorial department is editors, art directors, photographers, copy checkers, and researchers. (For the most part, magazine writers are freelancers.)

Those seeking entry-level positions in editorial departments should be strong writers, preferably having worked on college or university publications.

Internships and Entry-Level Jobs.

Although, the following three entry-level jobs are not directly related to advertising *per se,* they do employ some of the techniques and skills required in advertising, namely writing, graphic design, layout, and production.

According to the *Guide to Careers in Magazine Publishing,* co-produced by the Magazine Publishers of America (MPA) and The American Society of Magazine Editors, entry-level positions in magazine editorial include:

• **Editorial Assistant:** Works with an editor or several editors. Tasks include: answering correspondence, arranging photo shoots, typing, and proofreading.

(Continued on next page)

• Newspapers
• Magazines
• Out-of-Home
• Radio
• TV
• Movie Theaters
• Internet
• Mobile

Currently, those are advertisers' major media choices.

The Internet is a quickly evolving option – we'll cover it briefly here and then in more detail in Chapter Twelve – The Power of New Ideas.

Newspapers.

Wherever you live, the one media vehicle that ties a community together is still the newspaper.

Whether it's a Friday night movie, weekend shopping, complete sports scores, or more about an important news story, the newspaper is still the media vehicle that does the job.

And, as we said, advertising revenue represents about two-thirds of a newspaper's operating income.

Six Types of Newspaper Advertising.

Newspapers offer six different types of advertising:

1. Local Display Advertising
2. National (General) Advertising
3. Legal Advertising
4. Classified Advertising
5. Pre-print Advertising
6. Coupon Advertising

Let's briefly review them.

1. Local Display Advertising.

Local ads make up the bulk of newspaper advertising.

Local merchants, manufacturers, and distributors often use large type, graphics, and photos "displayed" in larger ad spaces.

This is called **display advertising.**

There are three types of local display advertising you should be familiar with:

    A. Retail or Price (Price/Item)

    B. Institutional

    C. Cooperative Advertising, aka "Co-op"

Let's take them one by one.

A. Retail (Price/Item) Advertising.

If you've ever seen a newspaper grocery store ad, then you're familiar with retail or price advertising.

Most stores use price advertising in their display advertising. This is also called price/item advertising.

These ads feature a variety of merchandise accompanied with a description and punctuated with a price.

They let consumers comparison shop – scanning the ads looking for merchandise that suits their tastes and wallets.

B. Institutional Advertising.

When retailers advertise the personality or image of their store, they are using institutional advertising. When you think of Banana Republic, Victoria's Secret, or Wal-Mart, an image or personality undoubtedly comes to mind.

Service institutions, such as banks and utility companies often use institutional advertising, too.

C. Co-op Advertising.

Local retailers cooperate with national advertisers (usually manufacturers – like Coke and Campbell's shown here).

This is cooperative (co-op) advertising. Local retailers will feature a manufacturer's product in a local display ad.

In turn, the manufacturer will pick up the cost of some or all of the local advertising.

2. National Advertising.

Advertisers who distribute their product nationwide sometimes use newspapers.

When they do, this is referred to as national advertising.

The national advertiser's in-house advertising department or advertising agency makes all the arrangements by preparing and shipping ads, as well as scheduling and buying ad space.

National rates are significantly higher than local retail rates – the argument being that coverage for a local retailer is a lower percentage of the market than for a national advertiser.

However, with national retail brands like K-Mart, Sears, and Walgreen's, it is a questionable one. Many national advertisers have trouble with this. Others, such as auto manufacturers, solve it by channeling the funds through local dealer groups.

3. Legal Advertising.

Legal advertising is included in the newspaper classified section. These ads actually fulfill certain legal requirements.

The US, state, and local governments are obligated to keep citizens up-to-date by publishing certain reports and statements.

Legal announcements cover a wide range of subjects: hearings, election notices, bidding opportunities for city contracts, etc.

Newspapers must meet certain qualifications to carry these legal notices and these requirements vary from state to state.

4. Classified Advertising.

If you've ever bought or sold a used car or bike through the newspaper, you're familiar with classified advertising.

These ads are "classified" into various categories and listed.

Classified ads are still a good source of newspaper revenue, though not the "cash cow" they were in the past..

Advertisers like them because they get results. Readers like them, too – when they're in the market.

Classifieds of the Future?

Here's one area where newspapers are making good use of new Web-based services. The Web is an excellent way to search.

Newspaper Jobs (Cont.)

• **Editorial Production Assistant:** Assists in coordinating the layout of various features and art written by the editors and designed by the art directors so that the magazine is appropriately prepared for printing.

• **Junior Designer/Art Assistant:** Functions as a junior artist or paste-up person under the supervision of an art director or design staff.

2. Advertising Sales.

The advertising department is made up of sales representatives (also called account executives) responsible for selling the ad space in the publication.

They do this by convincing advertisers their publication is the best possible way to reach the advertiser's chosen audience.

Advertising sales requires hard work, long hours, and, for magazines and national advertising, frequent travel.

However, if you're successful, you can make good money fairly quickly.

Preparation and Qualifications. To prepare for an advertising sales position, college students need experience in research and advertising media planning, buying and/or selling.

Excellent oral and written communications skills are a must.

Plan on taking a technical or business writing course – correspondence and business report writing is critical to the media sales profession.

The ability to make strong and persuasive presentations is key.

Speech classes are recommended, as is proficiency in PowerPoint.

Classes in marketing and advertising are beneficial. These courses not only orient students to sales, marketing, and advertising, but they help hone analytical and research skills.

Opportunities at Your School. Students should take advantage of local college media by working as a sales rep for their newspaper or radio station.

(Continued on next page)

An Ad for Classified Ads.

They bring in $18 billion a year to newspapers. But classifieds are moving to the Web – which has newspapers concerned.

Newspaper Jobs (Cont.)

3. Sales Support.

Larger newspapers and magazines often have a sales support department to assist sales representatives.

They may provide some or all of these services: marketing, research, promotion, and merchandising.

Smaller publications may not have any or all of these support activities.

4. Circulation.

This department has responsibility for getting the publication to readers.

Circulation executives work directly with the publisher to determine the rate base (the number of copies advertisers are told an average issue will sell).

They make sure the number of copies promised to advertisers are sold.

According to the MPA, these are the entry-level positions in the Circulation Department for those with general business or marketing backgrounds:

(Continued on next page)

We're already seeing combinations of traditional classified advertising and online searching with many newspapers. Though, as mentioned, the revenue stream has not quite caught up with the data stream.

5. Pre-Prints or Free-Standing Inserts (FSIs).
On any Sunday, give your newspaper a good shake. A variety of pre-prints will tumble out.

Notice who uses them.

It's a cost-effective way to get colorful coupon ads into the Sunday newspaper.

Companies will print the ads and pay to have them inserted into newspapers.

These advertisers take advantage of newspaper's efficient distribution while controlling production quality.

6. Coupon Advertising.
Advertisers use newspapers to deliver coupons – often using FSIs to do the job.

Food manufacturers may also take advantage of designated weekdays when newspapers feature food advertising.

This is known as **best food day** – usually Wednesday or Thursday.

Magazines.

WE'VE ALREADY COVERED a lot of the basics of the magazine industry, so we'll take a different angle here – let's take a look at a career in the magazine industry.

Lisa Weidman, Ad Manager, *THRASHER* magazine.

Lisa Weidman majored in English at the University of California at Davis. She worked for the college newspaper in her junior year, covering campus news and arts and entertainment.

The local Davis newspaper, the *Daily Democrat* (circulation 30,000), noticed Lisa's writing and hired her as a stringer in her senior year.

She reviewed music, modern art, theater, and performance art events; wrote features on artists and musicians; composed editorials; and put together the weekly event calendar, getting paid $7 per re-

view, $15 for a feature, and $19 for the calendar. Such is life as a stringer at a small paper.

Lisa ended up having to supplement her income with 32 hours a week at a coffee house. (Thanks a latté!)

She was afraid of getting stuck in her college town. So when her lease came up, she packed up and headed off to Berkeley.

Lisa worked at a clothing store in Berkeley for a year, while trying to find a job in publishing. No luck. So she left for San Francisco. Her luck changed as soon as she arrived.

THRASHER – All Aboard!

She landed an interview with a relatively new magazine called THRASHER – a skateboarding publication read by 350,000 teenage boys.

They are devoted readers who pass along the magazine to an average of seven friends. They tend to read the magazine in a group.

THRASHER also covers music and snowboarding.

Lisa's background in alternative music and pop culture, plus her ability to write, seemed like a good fit for the magazine.

She was hired as Advertising Manager.

THRASHER was a hot magazine when Lisa came on board.

As a matter of fact, there was a waiting list of advertisers who wanted to buy space and advertise in it. (WOW!)

Lisa started with a one-inch-thick binder filled with signed advertising contracts. These companies all wanted to jump on board the skateboard craze.

Smart Preparation and Dumb Luck.

Lisa admits the job was a complete fluke, but as you'll see throughout this book, many careers combine smart preparation (Lisa's writing skills) and dumb luck (showing up at THRASHER).

Lisa thought she wanted an editorial job, not one in advertising. She wanted a job where she could write. She took the Ad Manager position because THRASHER was a magazine she had read.

The publishers also convinced her that the magazine would be around for a while. Lisa saw this job offer as her big break – her foot in the door.

Small Company. Big Responsibility.

Working for a small magazine with a staff of just 25 allowed Lisa to do more than one job.

She was Ad Manager for six years and a Copy Editor for four.

She did the additional work because she wanted to.

The magazine needed someone to pick up the slack – and Lisa was that someone. Her job is far from boring because she is involved in so many projects that affect the vitality of the magazine.

In the early years, selling ad space for THRASHER was easy because the magazine was much in demand.

After the recession hit, selling ad space got a bit more challenging because so many small skateboarding businesses went under.

Lisa plotted a new strategy and went after large companies like Levi's, Nintendo, and Timex.

Newspaper Jobs (Cont.)

• **Circulation Promotion Assistant:** Assists in new promotion campaigns. Performs the analyses of subscription renewal approaches.
• **Subscription or Single Copy Analyst:** Analyzes data and prepares reports on subscription and single copy promotion efforts. Monitors promotion expenses and results.
• **Fulfillment Assistant:** Monitors renewal and invoice mailing.

5. Production.

Responsible for coordinating the editors, artists, photographers, and sales efforts into a finished product – a newspaper or magazine.
• **Electronic Pre-Press** is an area of increasing importance as computers have been deemed the central production tool for all print media.

It involves deep knowledge of computer programs and graphic formats – as source materials are converted from one graphic format to another.

And More…

Keep in mind that publishers across the board are exploring multi-media products and online services.

Virtually everything connected to the Internet is a hot area.

Many newspapers, such as the Chicago Tribune and the San José Mercury have large, active, and cutting-edge Internet operations.

The Internet has opened up all sorts of opportunities for students who understand strategic planning and Web development.

Entry-Level Positions at Magazines.

The Magazine Publishers Association (MPA) highlights these entry-level positions:

Ad Sales Coordinator:
Receives and logs insertion orders (requests for ad space). Responsibilities include receiving ad materials for each issue, working with production, and preparing information for billing.

Advertising Production Assistant:
Assists processing ad pages and special sections. Coordinates flow of ad proofs.

Sales Assistant/Administrator:
Manages account lists, communicates with clients. Prepares summary of reports submitted by sales reps.

Prepares and types analyses, reports, etc. Reviews billings for accuracy.

Junior Account Executives:
Local newspapers and magazines routinely seek assistant account execs to sell ad space.

They need to prepare presentations, and call on clients.

Other Entry-Level Positions:
The MPA identifies six other jobs that advertising students are suited for:

• **Marketing Assistant:** Assists with marketing programs. Edits, proofs, and maintains traffic flow within sales divisions. Maintains contacts with sales reps. Helps develop support materials.

• **Assistant Research Analyst:** Accesses and analyzes syndicated and primary research, prepares graphs and charts for presentations; assists in research analysis. Also responsible for staying current on competition.

• **Promotion Assistant:** Helps plan, write, and produce sales materials. Correspondence and filing.

• **Promotion Artist:** Helps on photo sessions. Does lay-out and design work on the computer.

• **Junior Promotion Copywriter:** Assists with promotional materials.

• **Merchandising Assistant:** Assists with merchandising tie-ins and special events.

Lisa also writes and designs the **media kit,** a comprehensive folder that introduces prospective advertisers to key facts and figures about the magazine's circulation, readers, and editorial. Most of her sales, however, come from convincing advertisers about the skateboarders and their unique lifestyles.

A Balancing Act.

Being advertising manager is also a balancing act. Each month, her publisher wants 45% of the magazine in articles and 55% in ads.

Ads are important to THRASHER's readers. They alert skateboarders to new products and retailers. Small ads are not very appealing to these youthful readers, however.

Lisa has to keep all this in mind as she approaches her sales responsibilities each month.

Promotions & More.

Lisa actively coordinates promotions for the magazine.

She even helps on fashion shoots.

But she finds that the most rewarding aspect of her job is working with clients, the actual advertisers in the magazine.

In her six years as Advertising Manager, Lisa has been in contact with each of her 100 clients at least once a month.

She works hard to build trusting relationships and forges year-round contracts with many of her clients.

Creating Ads, Campaigns, and Even Names.

Most of her clients are too small to hire an ad agency. So Lisa will help these advertisers create and produce the ads that will run.

For one new client, Lisa named the company and created the advertising campaign. She and THRASHER's art and production department became this fledgling company's ad agency.

It took some time, but it helped convince clients that Lisa is someone who can help them build their business.

$1.5 Million and More.

Lisa sells $1.5 million in ad space and services.

She also coordinates 65 to 90 inserts per issue, hires and trains sales assistants, oversees the printing of **second covers,** and in her spare time, because she loves writing, she copyedits the articles appearing in the magazine.

Creativity Is Where You Find It.

Lisa never thought she'd wind up in advertising – she thought there wasn't too much room for creativity. She says she was wrong.

She's learned that she has to be creative to produce ads, develop sales pitches, and negotiate and maintain relationships with her clients.

And she has to be creative in developing the media kit and all the other material needed to sell THRASHER.

Her job is interesting and challenging. Extremely.

Out-of-Home.

The Great Outdoors – and More.

"Outdoor advertising is a unique medium in that it communicates to an audience that's on the go – usually in transit, and always out of home," reports the Outdoor Advertising Association of America.

Outdoor advertising, or **out-of-home,** puts advertising right where consumers travel, gather, shop, and buy. As discussed previously, it is a growing and exciting area of the business.

According to Saatchi & Saatchi, *"out-of-home is a broad term referring to various forms of advertising that literally do not enter households, unlike print and broadcast. These include outdoor (billboards), transit, and place-based advertising."*

It's essentially all the advertising that can speak on behalf of a brand outside of the home.

Tactics and Technology.

An outdoor board is a tactic. It can tell you to turn at the next exit. It can build awareness by making big noise in your market.

Today, technology is helping outdoor make even more noise.

Huge computer-generated super graphics can cover buildings. Small screens in elevators can catch you in the middle of your day.

As the cost of big screens gets smaller (Moore's law at work), we will see more and more examples of video boards, and this oldest of media forms – the sign – will evolve into big TV screens with a variety of messages… and more.

Traditional and Place-Based.

There are two categories of out-of-home-advertising:
- **Traditional Outdoor Media**
- **Place-Based Media**

Traditional outdoor includes: aerial/inflatables, bus shelters, telephone kiosks, bus benches, outdoor (billboards), transit, and taxi ads.

Place-Based Media.

Place-based media provide advertising opportunities that can be purchased at places where advertisers might want their brand message to intersect with consumers.

Place-based media includes: airports, hotels, in-store, malls, stadium/arena/sport teams, in-flight, movies/theaters, trucks and truckstops, fitness/leisure facilities, and high schools and colleges.

Creative billboard ads can stretch tight advertising dollars.

The introduction of the Mini used outdoor creatively to help make a small budget for their small car have a big impact.

Tactics & Technology.

According to *American Demographics "many outdoor companies believe success depends on putting up more billboards, making them bigger, and loading them with more gimmicks."*

From Times Square in the East to the Seattle-Tacoma Airport in the West, giant TV screens make advertising's oldest medium state-of-the-art.

On the other hand, *"To ordinary Americans, more and louder billboards just add to the clutter, no matter how good-looking or creative they are."*

The Right Place.

Airports for Samsonite luggage.

Target Reaches Their Target.

New Yorkers are greeted with this clever high-impact, high-fashion outdoor from Kirshenbaum Bond & Partners.

Example: Brigham's Ice Cream.

Here's an example of how outdoor can work.

Lamar Advertising Company, one of the largest outdoor companies, helped Boston-based Brigham's Ice Cream fend off other brands that had aggressively entered the market in 1995.

Brigham's had a limited ad budget.

Its agency developed an outdoor ad campaign using imagery and humor.

Thirty-sheet poster panels and painted bulletins were strategically placed in high-traffic New England metropolitan markets. In one year, sales climbed 24%.

Sales Growth. Industry Growth.

The outdoor industry is growing again. Outdoor Systems, based in Atlanta, Georgia, purchased Gannett Outdoor for $690 million. They're now part of CBS Outdoor.

Consolidation is also occurring among outdoor companies and large media corporations.

Today's media conglomerates are diversified. They own a variety of media companies. Many of these media giants aim to become leaders in all media segments where they operate.

They see the money-making potential of outdoor and want to add leading outdoor companies to their portfolios.

Profile: Clear Channel.

In 1997, Clear Channel Communications, one of the world's largest media companies, bought Eller Media Company, the outdoor industry leader. Eller's holdings included:

- 100,000 domestic displays in 35 US markets
- 260 mall displays
- Convenience store displays in 25 states
- Coverage in many major airports
- 4,000 display Union Pacific Railroad outdoor portfolio

Today, Clear Channel owns over half a million displays around the world. To see the wide variety of out-of-home products they offer, visit their site at www.clearchanneloutdoor.com.

Board Scores.

Billboards make up a significant part of outdoor advertising's business. Let's review some basics.

Three Standard Formats.

There are three standard billboard formats:

- **Bulletin**
- **30-Sheet**
- **8-Sheet**

Showings.

Billboards are sold on a monthly basis and purchased according to **showing.** According to BBDO, *"showing refers to a collection of poster panels or bulletins that cover a specific market."*

Billboards that reach members of a market's population in one given day are called **daily impressions.**

A showing is rated on the number of daily impressions as a percent of the market's total population.

Showings are usually reported in increments of 25.

Here is an example of how showings are calculated for a market that has a population of 50,000.

Population	Daily Impressions	Showing
50,000	12,500	25
	25,000	50
	50,000	100

It's Show Time!

Outdoor advertising is typically sold using three types of showings: 100 showing, 50 showing, and 25 showing.

A 100 showing refers to the number of posters or bulletins needed to reach 100% of the market in one day.

A 50 showing is the number of posters required to reach 50% of a market, and a 25 showing is the number needed to reach 25% of a market.

The number of posters needed for each of these showings varies depending on the size of the market.

Let's say that you want to buy a 100 showing of king-size bus posters. These are the 30-inches-high-by-144-inches-wide posters that appear on the sides of mass transit buses.

To secure a 100 showing in Canton, Ohio, you'd need 20 buses. In Philadelphia, a larger market, you'd need 600 buses.

Billboards Come in Three Sizes.

Now that you have a general idea of how outdoor advertising is bought and sold, let's take a closer look at the different sizes of billboards advertisers can buy and how they use them.

1. Bulletins. These are the largest standard billboard structures, measuring 14 by 48 feet or 672 square feet. Bulletins are what you generally see on freeways.

Being the largest format means that bulletins deliver the biggest impact in the outdoor marketplace.

So, little wonder that they're built in the best locations to deliver high-density traffic, cropping up on major highways, by traffic lights, and next to road curves.

Bulletins are well suited for image-based advertising campaigns like *Apple's "Think Different."*

A Bulletin.

Painted or printed, it's always big – as large as 20 by 60 feet – usually in a prominent location. Extensions add extra dimension. Smaller ones are 14 by 48 feet.

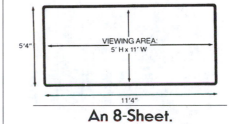

A 30-Sheet.

These are the standard-size outdoor boards located on primary arteries and local streets – about 10 feet high and over 20 feet wide.

An 8-Sheet.

This is a smaller outdoor board more suited for local neighborhoods, retail stores, and ethnic areas.

A Kiosk.

These are often found around bus shelters. They're about five-and-a-half-feet tall and about four-feet wide.

Great Outdoor.

Relieves gas pains.

FEW THINGS IN LIFE WORK AS WELL AS A VOLKSWAGEN.

Mass transit.

Volkswagen.

Pro create.
The new Power Mac G4.

Think different.

iPod

10,000 songs in your pocket. Mac or PC.

Apple.

Think different.

Messages appearing on bulletins may be either printed by a computer or hand-painted. Bulletins are usually bought in multi-month contract periods.

For even broader market coverage, **rotary bulletins** can be used, whereby an advertiser's message is moved from one location to another at stated intervals, usually every 60 days.

2. **30-Sheet.** Thirty-sheet poster panels are the next largest billboard structure, measuring 12 x 25 feet, or 300 square feet. They appear on high-traffic commercial areas on primary and secondary roads.

"Thirty-sheets" is a name dating back to the early days of billboards. It refers to the number of sheets of paper that needed to be printed to make up the complete poster.

Thirty-sheets are inexpensive, large enough to have impact, able to deliver frequency, and a good reminder or reinforcement message deliverer. Messages seen on 30-sheets are lithographed or silk-screened posters and generally bought on a 30-day basis.

3. **8-Sheet.** Eight-sheet poster panels are the smallest billboard structures at 6 x12 feet, or 72 square feet.

They can be found in high-density urban neighborhoods and suburban shopping areas and near convenience and neighborhood stores and gas stations to reach drivers and pedestrians. Messages seen on 8-sheets are printed on sheets of paper, then glued (posted) onto the face of the structure. Early printers used 8 sheets of paper to fill this size poster panel, thus the name.

Technology and larger presses have changed the posting process for both 8- and 30-sheets, but the names remain.

Kiosks.

Lower your sights. Billboards grab our attention overhead. There's another outdoor vehicle that hits us right at eye-level – **kiosks.**

Kiosks are the free-standing displays typically found in airports, rail terminals, malls, and stores. Telephone kiosks are displays that appear on the sides of many public telephones.

These eight-square-foot signs are backlit so that they glow from dusk to dawn, and in Manhattan, where sidewalks are jammed with pedestrians, telephone kiosks are decked out in eye-catching posters for such upscale fashion designers as Calvin Klein, Tommy Hilfiger, and Donna Karan.

Radio.

Radio Is Alive and Well.

As we discussed a little earlier in the section on mass media history, radio has taken some pretty big blows from emerging media – particularly TV.

On more than one occasion, media analysts have predicted radio's certain demise. But radio is a resilient medium that has survived and prospered by evolving and adapting.

Adaptability.

Some experts maintain that radio persists because of this personal, adaptable nature. *American Demographics* magazine reported that radio is still with us today because *"it has a tenacious ability to adapt to changes in popular tastes and to mold itself to a listener's lifestyle."*

When broadcast TV surfaced in the late 1940s, it stole most of the national advertisers away from radio.

TV was expected to consign radio to the dust heap.

Yet radio remade itself. Forced to search for new sources of revenue, radio went after the advertisers TV wasn't going after – local firms.

More recently, media competition has really heated up.

The emergence of cable TV might have been expected to contribute to radio's demise. But it didn't. Today, radio is a $19 billion industry – a favorite of advertisers and listeners alike.

Two More Evolutions.

As this book was written, two more evolutions were going on – online and high above our heads. Satellite radio – now delivered by Sirius and XM (trying to merge at present) – offers a wide range of options to a national audience. Streaming audio on the Internet brings an even wider range of stations into your home, through your computer. There's a lot to listen to besides your iPod.

A Fit with Our Lifestyles.

Radio finds a way to fit into our busy lifestyles. As American lifestyles have grown more hectic and mobile; people have less leisure time and are constantly on the go.

Radio fits. Want a change? Punch the button on the car radio and another station's ready to meet your mood.

Portability.

Radio is portable and immediate. Radios are in our homes and on our heads. We listen while we work, workout, and shop.

We even have our own radio network.

Your Own Radio Network: 2.5 stations.

Arbitron recently reported that the average person regularly tunes into only 2.5 stations daily.

Let's put this observation to the test. Do you have your car radio set to two or three stations? Are they the same ones you listen to when you're at work or home? Well, how big is your network?

Jobs in Radio.

Interested in making it in radio, like Brendan Kane? Here are some initial thoughts about getting that first job.

Breaking In.

One of the best ways to break into advertising is through advertising sales. And one of the best ways to break into advertising sales is radio.

The Good News.

First, the good news. Somewhere in your market, a radio station is looking for a new salesperson right now.

Successful radio sales people can make good money, and they can do it fairly quickly.

If you're tough, smart, and lucky enough to get with a good station, there might be a job for you.

The Bad News.

Now, the bad news. One of the reasons that station is looking for a new salesperson is that selling time on that station might not be easy.

At the early stages of a sales career, the casualty rates are, shall we say, a bit high. Getting that sales job can be pretty easy; keeping it might be another thing entirely.

Here are some of the places where you might find job opportunities.

Internships.

Get a job before you get a job.

Most radio stations are happy to use a few interns. Get on the list.

Sales & Promotion.

Radio stations are always putting together promotions designed to connect listeners, sponsors, and the station.

Putting together a promo is a great lesson in sales, sales promotion, and event marketing all rolled into one.

It's a great chance to see if you've got what it takes to make it in sales. If you do, you can make a lot of money – fast!

(Continued on next page)

Jobs in Radio (Cont.)

Production.

Most radio stations produce a significant amount of their own local advertising – another great opportunity to hear what you can do!

It's a chance to try your hand at writing, lend an ear to producing, and take a look at what it takes to make a radio commercial.

Call On 'Em All!

Don't just go to the stations you listen to. Branch out. It's a big world out there. Hear what it has to offer – it might include a job for you.

Radio: A Money-Maker.

Category: Coupons
Title: Frequent-User Coupon Book

Here's an idea that can generate lots of revenue for your station and create more and better radio advertisers:

• The station designs a coupon book that advertisers can redeem with the station's salespeople.

• The coupons offer discounts or value-added opportunities for advertising time. Examples: 10% off any schedule of $250 value or higher; buy a remote and get a discount on a weather dominator; sponsor a newscast, get a schedule free.

• The salespeople sell these coupon books for one day only for $299 (or whatever works in your market). The book is promoted as "Get $1500 worth of KXXX advertising for just $299."

If you have 10 salespeople and they each sell four coupon books, that's $12,000 in sales in one day. More sales are booked when advertisers redeem their coupons. This is a great way to upsell current advertisers and to get new or light advertisers to become more frequent users of radio.

(Source: Barb Salz, KGLO/KIA-FM, The Fox, Mason City, IA)

Further research shows that listeners develop a strong relationship with one station. Radio listeners are truly creatures of habit, and that makes them attractive to advertisers.

Consumer Reports notes that we *"listen habitually at predictable times to stations with narrowly targeted formats."*

This evidence shows that radio stations are capable of inspiring intense loyalty among their listeners.

Television doesn't spawn such devotion.

Unlike TV, radio listenership is based on stations, not programs. The big payoff for advertisers is that they can tap into a consistent and faithful audience that likes the medium.

A One-on-One Connection.

Radio is also an attractive and powerful medium to advertisers because it can speak one-on-one to consumers.

Think about it. What if you buy an ad on the second page of your local newspaper? Look at all the competition.

Your ad shares that page with news and other ads.

When you buy a 60-second spot on radio, you own that space.

For sixty seconds, that audience is yours.

An Over-Communicated Society.

In recent years, we've faced the boom of the Information Age and the din of the Electronic Rage – with no end in sight.

Today, there's more information than most of us know what to do with. This state of affairs has led some to deduce that we are "an over-communicated society."

This has some noticeable shortcomings for advertisers.

For starters, how can you break through the clutter to get your ad noticed and remembered?

This is a topic that advertising and marketing consultants Al Ries and Jack Trout wrestled with. Their thought-provoking findings have had some definite impact on radio.

Getting to the Mind through the Ears.

In this over-communicated era, Ries and Trout wanted to know *which type* of communication works best. Is it the stuff that reaches us through our eyes or ears?

Interestingly, they found that, in some ways, our minds work by our ears, not by our eyes.

People remember more when they *hear* than when they *see*. When the eye takes in information, it fades in a second or two. When the ear takes in information, it fades more slowly. It sticks in our minds for four to five seconds.

The ear is also faster than the eye. Ries and Trout note that, *"Repeated tests have shown that the mind is able to understand a spoken word in 140 milliseconds. A printed word, on the other hand, is able to be understood in 180 milliseconds."*

Radio offers advertisers a world of sound.

Nothing gets between listeners and their ears.

As Ken Roman, former Chairman of O&M, observed: *"Radio is fundamentally different from all other media. No pictures. No movement. Nothing to read. Pure sound."*

Ries and Trout point out, this pure sound has some real benefits for advertisers. Radio has no visual distractions. As Roman adds, *"Sound is a world of reality and of infinite possibilities."* This means advertisers who use radio can be heard and remembered.

Types of Radio Advertising.

Advertisers have three types of radio to choose from:

- **Local**
- **Spot**
- **Network**

Local, National, and Direct.

Radio is purchased on a local, national, and direct level.

National spot radio, like national spot TV, is used by national advertisers, agencies, and media buying services who purchase commercial time on a market-by-market basis.

Local radio is purchased by local advertising agencies and local advertisers. There is a small amount of direct radio time that a station sells directly to certain advertisers.

Resistance to Radio.

Radio stations get the most resistance from national advertisers' advertising agencies. Why do they resist buying radio?

Bob Bolte, Director, Advertising and Promotion Services at American Airlines, points out radio's greatest obstacle, which is echoed by other national advertisers: *"Our agencies are very successful in TV, the creatives know how to write and produce successful TV. With radio, they're not in their comfort zone."*

O&M's Roman has an interesting take on this: *"Among national advertisers, radio may be the most misunderstood, under-utilized medium. It is not hard to understand why. For one thing, it is not TV.*

"People who didn't grow up with radio just don't trust it."

The Appeal of Radio.

As we saw earlier, each radio station format appeals to a distinct group of listeners. These listeners are broken down into specific demographic characteristics: sex, age, psychographics, and lifestyle.

A radio station's audience description is called an **audience profile** or **listener profile.**

Advertisers review the radio station's listener profile.

Their task is to find a radio audience that most closely corresponds with their own target audience.

Radio Specialists.

Dick Orkin's Radio Ranch produces a lot of those funny commercials you like. Listen @ www.radio-ranch.com.

Radio Buying Strategy.

An advertiser considering radio should do so strategically. George C. Hyde, Executive Vice President of the Radio Advertising Bureau, suggests two simple strategic steps:

1. Identify Key Prospects.
Advertisers must have a clear description of who they intend to advertise to before purchasing radio time.

Use this target audience description to size up whether or not a radio station is appropriate for your brand.

2. Choose Station(s).
After a target audience is identified, select radio stations.

Let's say your target is risk-takers interested in buying sports cars. Stations with album-oriented rock might be a logical choice. Get it?

A Legendary Radio Promo – "Walking Naked."

This promotion stemmed from a bet.

Our morning man and PD (Program Director) agreed to walk "Naked" down one of our busiest streets at high noon. This generated lots of calls.

At noon on D-Day, people lined the street in anticipation as the two walked Naked down Mercer Street.

Naked was a Golden Retriever mix from the local animal shelter.

The event was part of a special promotion for the shelter to create awareness for animal adoption.

The publicity resulted in a number of new adoptions prior to Easter.

We had a lot of fun with this one!

(Source: *Small Market Radio Newsletter*)

The Reality of Reality TV.

As network audiences splinter, reality TV, which has a much lower cost per show than traditional sitcoms and dramas, has grown to fill additional programming slots.

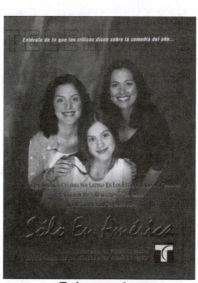

Telemundo.

This is one of two Spanish-language television networks in the US.

The other is *Univision*.

The *Telemundo* network provides around-the-clock programming to affiliates that serve 142 US markets. They reach nearly 93% of all US Hispanic households.

Television.

TELEVISION IS THE BIG GORILLA of the media world.

You've grown up with it, so you probably think you know it pretty well, and you do – from your side of the screen.

But now let's see how TV looks to advertisers.

It's for Free!

Broadcast TV is free and available everywhere.

What does this mean for advertisers?

With broadcast TV, advertisers have historically been able to reach just about every type of group in the US – young and old, male and female, rich and poor.

This is often referred to as **broadcasting**.

Television also offers a wide range of programming.

Advertisers can schedule their commercials on news programs, talk shows, situation comedies, police dramas, game shows, soap operas, and sporting events.

It's for a Fee!

Cable TV travels into people's homes through a special copper wire (called a coaxial cable) that is as thick as a pencil.

The same signals may also be received by a dish. With today's smaller dish antennae, this type of service, once common only in rural areas, is now found throughout America.

For simplicity's sake, we will refer to both cable and satellite delivery broadcast as cable TV.

Not everyone can get cable TV. Some cities aren't wired to receive cable signals. Some folks choose not to pay for them.

For advertisers, cable TV delivers a more select, usually up-scale audience. This is often referred to as **narrowcasting**.

Audience Measurement.

Television measures its audiences by using a television ratings firm, the A.C. Nielsen Company.

This audience measurement helps determine how much an ad on a certain station at a certain time will cost.

A rating is simply an estimate of the number of homes tuned to a program. Nielsen measures audiences by points.

One rating point equals 1% of the total US television households. In 1999, each rating point represented 994,000 TV homes (those households with TVs). In 2008, it's 1,125,000 US homes.

In 1998, the combined average audience rating for all four major networks during prime time was 35.

The overall rating for basic cable channels was 21.

In 1996, a typical 30-second advertising unit on network, prime-time TV cost $175,000. Audience size makes a big difference in how much an advertiser pays for a 30-second commercial.

A 30-second ad unit is far less expensive on national cable, with an annual average of $3,000.

The Importance of Programming.

Programming is what attracts viewers to particular stations. As a matter of fact, it is considered the *lifeblood* of this medium. After all, television programs attract the viewers advertisers seek.

Betsy Frank, Senior VP/Media Director at Saatchi & Saatchi states, "*Programming is still what this business boils down to. If a compelling program is somewhere out there on the dial, people will find it.*"

Media and advertising experts agree that a great television program will attract people no matter where it appears. Bob Alter, Cable Advertising Bureau Vice-Chairman agrees, "*Consumers don't care how they get their programming. They only care about the programming they get.*"

However, as audiences splinter, the reality is that more lower-priced programming will be featured.

Television Trends.

Viewers once dutifully waited to watch their favorite shows.

No more. Cable, VCRs, remote controls, and TiVo have entered people's homes. Now viewers with many channels to choose from don't have to change their schedules to watch their programs.

Zipping, Zapping, and More.

If people don't want to watch the TV commercials, they can zip, zap, or mute them with their remote control.

Viewers can now watch shows any time they please. (This is called **time shifting**.) VCRs were just the beginning. Then DVRs and VoD (Video on Demand) services expanded further the options available.

Viewers can now interact with their TV as never before. But as viewers have gained more control, advertisers have lost ground.

To a limited degree, scheduling has become somewhat of an unknown. Now, when a commercial comes on, viewers don't have to listen. And many don't. By punching the mute button on their remote control, they kill the commercial's sound.

Actually, viewers have never had to watch or listen to TV commercials. They could leave the room, strike up a conversation, or leaf through a magazine – with the TV on.

But before remote controls, viewers had to exert some kind of effort or modify their behavior to avoid commercials.

With the introduction of remote controls, television adapted to the dictates of viewers, as viewers briskly clicked from channel to channel (known as **channel switching** or **surfing**).

When viewers switch commercials off they are **zapping**. Or viewers might hit the fast forward button while watching videotapes (called **zipping**).

One of the newer developments now is video-on-demand advertising with which viewers can and do choose to watch product advertising. The most frequently watched VoD ads tend to be informational advertising about home furnishings, automobiles, and real estate.

Buying National Spot – Three Steps.

Purchasing national spot television can be divided into three steps.

Step One – Strategy.

First, national and regional advertisers choose the markets they want to advertise in.

Different advertisers will have different marketing objectives. Their spot market choices will coincide with these goals.

For example, a suntan lotion's marketing objective might be: "*to increase sales during summer months and, at the same time, sustain sales as much as possible throughout the year.*"

Responding to this marketing objective, the suntan lotion manufacturer advertises nationwide during the summer months.

In winter, TV ads are cut back to include only warm-weather markets where sun, fun, and sunburns reign.

National spot TV might be called upon to help achieve other marketing objectives. It can announce a sales promotion, support regional distribution, or fend off competition.

Step Two – Selection.

Once markets are chosen, the next step is to choose television stations within the designated markets.

The term used here is **ADI**, which stands for Area of Dominant Influence. (Do you know your ADI?)

Some markets will have an affiliate for all four networks. Some won't.

Bigger TV markets will have four networks and some independents.

Advertisers will evaluate each station by asking whether audience composition matches their target audience.

Advertisers might be willing to choose a station if it gives them added incentives. For instance, a station might throw in some billboards – free, short, 3- to 10-second announcements that identify an advertiser during breaks in the programming.

(Continued on next page)

National Spot (Cont.)

Step Three – Final Selection and Negotiation.

The third step in buying national spot includes selecting the specific programs on the chosen stations.

National spot television buying requires advertisers to purchase time directly from local affiliates.

These stations sell two different types of programming. Using their available access time, the half-hour preceding network primetime, local network affiliated stations produce their own programming and sell it to advertisers – generally, it's local news.

Then there is the programming supplied by the network.

(Remember, the networks keep the time within the program to sell to network advertisers.)

Mindy @ Cartoon Network Online

Mindy Cohen graduated from Syracuse with a major in advertising and a minor in psychology.

She began as an Account Executive and Producer at Modem Media. Then, after a year, she headed west to work at *Disney Online*.

Mindy is now Director of Marketing for *Cartoon Network Online*, supervising the entire marketing initiative for the network's Web site, CartoonNetwork.com.

A Degree in Disney.

Her senior year, she created a 120-page honors thesis detailing how Walt Disney World could create a totally new theme park.

Her thesis took a top prize.

(Continued on next page)

All this leaves advertisers scratching their heads, sometimes wondering who is actually watching their commercial messages.

Viewer Volatility.

Advertising and network TV executives are studying the problem of channel switching and this television viewer volatility.

The A.C. Nielsen Company tackled this topic by studying the viewing patterns of *ABC, CBS, NBC,* and *FOX* networks.

Nielsen attempted to find out just how channel switching affects TV commercial viewing.

Nielsen uncovered some pretty interesting results.

It appears as if some things haven't changed.

For instance, channel switching doesn't appear to lower the number of viewers who tune into TV commercials.

Nielsen found roughly equal numbers of viewers switch into and out of commercials This means that the size of the audience for each commercial remains pretty much constant.

The same cannot be said for viewer involvement. This is where channel switching creates headaches for advertisers.

Viewers who switch into commercials are just not as involved as those who see the TV spot from beginning to end.

And keep in mind that viewers do not automatically switch channels as soon as the first commercial break hits, either.

The upshot, says the Nielsen study, is that viewers do not become as absorbed with the commercials.

Reaching certain viewers has also become trickier, thanks to channel switching. For example, men really do switch channels more than women. Younger viewers switch more often than older viewers, according to Nielsen.

Trying to reach these "masters of the remote control" is like trying to hit a moving target.

For advertisers, viewer volatility has made delivering TV spots to viewers a much more complicated process.

More Channels to Choose From.

But this is nothing compared to what is now happening in the world of TV, thanks to technology. Now, viewers can have up to 1000 channels to choose from.

Some of these channels will be interactive.

There will be so many TV options that viewers will need a navigational system just to make their way through the maze of choosing what to watch. It's all coming our way.

Television Audiences – All Shapes and Sizes.

Television audiences have traditionally come in all shapes and sizes. This leaves advertisers with many options.

For instance, large national advertisers can sweep their messages across the entire US with the speed and efficiency of network TV. Likewise, this versatile medium can limit its scope and assist regional, even local, advertisers.

National Spot Television.

Spot TV refers to the buying of broadcast time on a **local market basis** as opposed to national network buying.

When national and regional advertisers buy local television in specific markets this is called **national spot television.**

Some of the reasons advertisers might use a market-by-market approach to their television advertising are highlighted in Jugenheimer, Barban, and Turk's *Advertising Media Sourcebook:*

- Advertiser doesn't have national distribution.
- Advertiser needs extra TV advertising to support a national advertising effort.
- Advertiser doesn't have a sufficient budget to buy national TV.
- Advertiser wants different advertising executions to run in different regions of the country.

Advertisers can buy any combination of coverage areas: 10 markets, 20 markets, or more, anywhere in the US.

The national spot buying process is covered in the sidebar.

Adjacencies.

Spot advertisers buy **adjacencies.** These are the units of time that occur just before and immediately after a network program runs. Advertisers can also buy time within station breaks.

This is the time available between programs that the network has authorized the local affiliate to sell.

Now, how do advertisers decide which program to buy from a local station? Some strategic questions an advertiser will ask include:

- What kind of ratings do the programs generate?
- What are the costs for these particular programs?
- What programs have availabilities, or units, that are still available to purchase?
- Does the program audience match my target audience?

Local Spot Television.

When broadcast stations are bought in only *one* market then advertisers are using **local spot television.**

Local advertisers such as car dealers, banks, grocery stores, and other retailers obviously need this limited coverage.

Advertisers using local spot television can buy any combination of the broadcast stations in their market.

Local spot buying follows the same process as national spot buying: stations are compared, evaluated, and chosen.

Then, programs are selected.

National or regional spot buying can involve many markets.

Local spot TV is much easier to schedule and buy since it involves only one market.

As mentioned earlier, there are only three to five TV stations within a given market. Therefore, there is considerably less time and effort involved in scheduling local spot TV.

Mindy Online (Cont.)

She was chosen to participate in Disney's World College Program.

In her spare time, she performed in musical comedies.

Thoroughly Modem Mindy.
Mindy launched her advertising career with Modem Media – at the time, a small agency of seven people.

The company's focus then, like now, is marketing and consulting for interactive media.

Modem Media boomed – it now employs over 250 people and has joined forces with TN Technologies, a division of True North.

Board Games in the Board Room.
Where did Mindy find out about this job? In her college's career newsletter.

Yet, it was creativity and willingness to go the extra mile that did it.

Here's what happened: After sending in her application, she went through three separate interviews.

Then came the wait.

Mindy thought the interviewers might need some help to make the decision to hire *her* – not someone else.

Mindyopoly!
So, Mindy set out to distinguish herself from the rest of the pack.

She did just that by designing her own board game – Mindyopoly.

It came complete with property cards detailing her previous experiences and accomplishments.

Once the executives received the game, Mindy immediately got a call from a company partner asking her to come in the very next day.

She was hired on the spot.

First Jobs Online.
At Modem, Mindy was asked to perform many tasks and roles – including coming up with creative ideas.

One of her favorite projects was designing the storyboard for Modem's first online game on *Prodigy* for *Coors.*

After a year, Mindy moved to the account side, where she assisted on the JCPenney account.

(Continued on next page)

Mindy Online (Cont.)

She worked on the production of Penney's online stores on *Prodigy* and *CompuServe*. She also handled all online promotions for this client.

In just five years, she's managed the marketing launches of four major Internet sites:

JCPenney.com

DisneyStore.com

DisneyBlast.com

CartoonNetwork.com

Mindy's Minnie Dress.

It was always one of Mindy's dreams to work full-time for Disney.

She'd participated in the Walt Disney World College Program.

One of her career moments was landing an internship with her first job interview ever.

"I had no clue what to wear," says Mindy. *"So, I opted for my pink polka-dotted Laura Ashley dress."*

She thinks she got the job because, *"I stuck out amongst all the suits."*

Mindy reckons it was either this or the fact that her dress paid tribute to one of Disney's corporate icons.

She says, *"Looking at the dress now, I think I must have looked like… Minnie Mouse!"*

LA Story.

After spending little over a year at Modem Media in Westport, Mindy headed west for Disney Online.

As Assistant Manager of Online Marketing and Promotions, Mindy managed the launch of two online venues: DisneyStore.com and DisneyBlast.com.

She created online promotions for *Hercules* ("Hercify the Web") and *101 Dalmatians* ("Spot the Web").

She coordinated all the marketing, planning, and Web site development for Disney.com's Family Fantasy Sweepstakes.

"Saturday Morning All Day Long!"

As we wrote this, Mindy was Director of Marketing for Cartoon Network Online, a division of Turner Entertainment in Atlanta, responsible for marketing and promotional initiatives for CartoonNetwork.com.

(Continued on next page)

Non-Network Cable.

Local and spot cable TV has become increasingly popular among advertisers. Advertising spending in non-network cable jumped 25% in 1996.

Non-network cable is bought on a market-by-market basis. Advertisers who purchase local cable TV buy one cable market using the programming provided by one or more cable systems.

Advertisers who use spot cable buy multiple cable systems scattered throughout the US.

Non-network has become more popular for two reasons.

First, cable is now in more homes. More advertisers can get the coverage they need by advertising on non-network cable.

Second, cable systems have made it easier and more cost efficient for advertisers to buy non-network cable.

In addition to local advertisers, national automotive and fast-food advertisers have started to take advantage of this economical and target-specific type of television.

It's just one more example of the ever-changing world of media.

Is it evolution or revolution? Stay tuned.

Movie Theaters.

Movie theater advertising has been around for many years, but, for the most part, it was just slides for local area restaurants you might want to visit after the movie.

Today, cinema advertising has really taken off. Today we have advertisers producing commercials specially designed for the big screen.

The entertainment industry reports there are 36,000 theaters throughout the US and almost 28,000 of them feature at least some form of pre-movie advertising.

In 2004, cinema advertising reached record-high levels with total advertising revenues of more than $480 million.

More importantly, advertising spending in movie theaters is projected to more than double to $1 billion by the year 2008.

In 2003, Arbitron, a major media research service, commissioned a study of movie-going audiences for cinema advertising clients. This study was updated and reported in 2007 indicating that 59% of consumers recall seeing commercials at movie theaters and 63% of movie-going adults (74% of teens) indicated that they don't mind seeing ads at the movie theater.

Advertisers have found success in movie theaters for two big reasons. The first is a captive (and usually bored) audience and the second is relevance to a product tie-in.

The Early Arriver Gets the Ad.

Whether anticipating crowds or just their personal nature, consumers arrive early for movies and once they sit down, they wait impatiently for the feature film to begin. The average adult spends about 24 minutes in the theater before the movie starts. They spend that time buying snacks, playing arcade games, or just sitting in the theater waiting for the show to start.

Coca-Cola was one of the first major national advertisers to take advantage of this captive and bored audience. The soft drink company created, and continually updates, a series of sponsored Coca-Cola Screen Play slides providing trivia and light information about movies and the movie business. This relationship between Coke and the theaters made tremendous sense, as Coca-Cola was the leading provider of soft drink fountain service in theaters.

Other advertisers have caught on and as product placements in movies have expanded, so has the corresponding cinema advertising. One of the more recent high-profile examples of this was the Ford Mondeo product placement in the James Bond film *Casino Royale*. The car manufacturer used this film as a platform to launch the new Mondeo product and then customized a commercial specifically to run in theaters prior to each showing of the movie.

We will certainly see more and more of this kind of movie tie-in advertising.

Internet.

The figure, 50 million households, is widely accepted as the base audience needed for mass media status. It took radio 38 years to reach a US audience of 50 million households. It took television 13 years and cable television just ten years to clear the 50 million households hurdle.

It took the Internet less than 5 years to reach that number.

Internet addresses come and go at a mind-boggling pace with an estimated 40,000 new Web sites added every day.

Despite the sheer quantity of sites out there, the average adult in America visits only a few sites on any given day. The most popular sites tend to be the larger Internet service providers like MSN and the bigger search engines like Yahoo! and Google, some of the big social networking sites like MySpace.com and FaceBook.com, and the big e-tailers like eBay and Amazon.

As you probably know, there are many different kinds of Internet Web sites. From simple news and information to interactive gaming and commercial sites, consumers have a vast number of choices to incorporate into their lives.

Similarly, for every different kind of Web site available, there is a different kind of advertiser use available as well.

Advertisers can and will do everything on the Internet. They can place advertisements on an existing Web site, they can create their own informational Web site, or they can create their own interactive or commercial Web site. Today, some advertisers are developing their own branded "friends" pages on social networking sites. For example, the Travelocity Roaming Gnome has a MySpace.com page and its own network of friends/users who visit regularly for entertainment and information.

Movie Trivia.

Coca-Cola was one of the early sponsors of pre-movie slide advertainment.

Movie Tie-Ins.

After years of driving BMW or Aston Martin, James Bond introduced the world to the all new Ford Mondeo in the 2006 film *Casino Royale*.

Mindy Online (Cont.)

Mindy says, *"this is the wackiest place to work, because everyone here is seriously a kid and loves cartoons."*

She says she couldn't have found a better environment. *"It's like Saturday morning all day long!"*

Who's the Boss?

Online media was rather new when Mindy entered the business. And she's had real fun teaching her bosses what this type of media is all about.

She says she's trained three bosses on the world of online media. *"As silly as it sounds, few people are totally up to speed on the Internet and its power as a medium,"* she explains.

At every job, she's been responsible for teaching her supervisors the ropes of online media.

And out of everything that Mindy's accomplished so far, the achievement she's most proud of is that she's always held true to her dreams.

For Mindy, dreams never end.

And some come true.

Networking Gnome.

Branding a relationship with friends, the Travelocity Roaming Gnome

Blogging GM.

The GM FYI blog shown here is written by and for car enthusiasts.

Evolution in Action.

How many times did you view something on YouTube this week?

It's part of the computer's evolution into a video delivery vehicle.

From an advertiser's perspective, there are many advantages and uses of the Internet as an advertising media.

All at once, the Internet provides any advertiser with cost effective, worldwide message delivery to a precision-targeted base of consumers. Production costs can be very reasonable, messages can be updated or changed at a moment's notice, and consumers can spend as much or as little time as they want with the message.

To Blog or Not to Blog.

Web Logs – or blogs – are one of the newer developments in the ever changing world of the Internet. Blogs are a hybrid – a kind of evolved version of a hosted chat room melded together into a sort of e-newsletter.

Blogs started as a voice in the wilderness; a place where people with strong opinions and perspectives could speak their mind. They've recently grown in popularity with several mainstream media now publishing material. Today, even the *Wall Street Journal* is host to a blog.

And, of course, as blogs have gained audience, they have also gained advertisers. Many major companies operate their own blogs on subjects relevant to their consumers. For example; McDonald's corporation maintains a blog about corporate social responsibility.

General Motors is another big corporate blogger with blogs on topics ranging from what's new and hot in the automotive industry to important social issues like ethanol/flex fuels and automotive safety.

As of this writing, some of the most popular bogs were taking in as much as $10,000 or more per month in advertising revenue. However, most of the 103 million blogs in existence don't even try to sell ads.

Mobile.

At the start of 2007 about 80% of the people in the U.S. had some kind of mobile phone service. Of those mobile subscribers, almost 40% indicate that they use their mobile phone to send and receive text messages. 40% may not seem like a lot but that is up from only 34% just one year earlier.

In this category, in terms of marketer use of mobile media messaging, the US is significantly behind the rest of the world. Total US spending on mobile advertising in 2006 was reported to be just over $400 million, a little less than one-third of worldwide mobile ad spending.

One big reason for this delayed development in the US is the US consumers' resistance to the whole idea of advertising on their mobile phone devices. A survey in 2006 asked US mobile phone subscribers if they would be willing to watch ads on their mobile phones in exchange for free access to mobile phone applications. More than half responded with a rating of only 1 (on a seven-point scale) saying they were "not at all willing" to do so.

In spite of this resistance and slow development in the US, it seems clear mobile services will be a very important part of the American mediascape at some point in the near future.

Summary:

This has been a quick tour through the media world.

You've viewed it from three perspectives:

- **The Media Company**
- **The Consumer**
- **The Advertiser**

And we've covered a lot of territory:

- **Media History.** You now have a good sense of how media and marketing have evolved and interacted.
- **Today's Media World.** You've been introduced to the business of media – a very big business. $300 billion big. You now have a sense of each of our media channels, their size, their power, and their changing ownership.
- **Consumers and the Media.** You now have a bit more of a feel for your role as a consumer of media and the emerging issues as the media marketplace continues to evolve.
- **Media Conglomerates and Entertainment Brands.** You've seen some of the evolution in the world of media.
- **A Deeper Look.** Finally, we've looked at media as an advertiser or an agency media department would.

We'll go even deeper in Chapter Ten – see you then.

Discussion Questions:

Let's exercise our brain cells with a few questions.

1. Media and Audiences.

If you were to start up a new magazine, who'd be the audience? Why would this audience be attractive to advertisers? What would your magazine offer readers and advertisers that current magazines do not? What would be the name of the magazine? Would it even be a magazine? Or would you use other media formats – like a CD?

2. Media History.

How did advertising media help build Campbell's Soup into a powerful brand? How does advertising media continue to make Campbell's Soup such a strong brand? What does it mean when we observe, "When media changes, advertising changes?"

3. Media Brands.

Why must today's media brand themselves? How would you create a brand for your campus radio station or newspaper?

4. Television.

What are the major types of television?

How is cable television like magazines?

What's the difference between syndicated and broadcast TV?

5. Your Media Network.

What is one of your favorite ads? Where did it appear?

Television? Magazine? Newspaper? Outdoor?

How did the medium enhance the ad's persuasive power?

6. Out-of-Home.

What type of outdoor would you use to advertise Twinkies?

7. Radio.

Compared to radio of yesterday, how does today's radio compare?

What are some of the differences and similarities?

Why is it still an attractive medium to advertisers?

8. Media and Society.

Do you think ads should appear everywhere?

Why or why not?

9. Media Jobs.

Your roommate has asked for some career advice.

He or she wants to know what kinds of jobs exist in ad media.

What do you tell him or her?

10. Newspapers.

Newspapers provide advertisers with six types of advertising opportunities. Can you identify an example of these types of advertising in your local newspaper?

11. Entertainment Brands.

What is one of your favorite entertainment brands?

In what media does it appear?

How does the medium enhance the brand?

Entertainment Brand Exercise:

A sports team is an entertainment brand. Your school has one. Here's your assignment.

1. **Describe your school's entertainment brand.**
   What are some unique aspects of your brand equity?
2. **List current ways your entertainment brand is marketed.**
3. **Think up a few new ways to expand your brand.**

VANIDADES
(Printed in Spanish)
An Editorial Televisa Publication

ABC　　　　　　**MPA**

Location ID: 8 MINT 49　　　　　Mid 001292-000
Published biweekly by Editorial Televisa, 6355 NW 36 St., Miami, FL 33166. Phone 305-871-6400 Ext: 327. Fax 305-871-7319.
For shipping info., see Print Media Production Source.

PUBLISHER'S EDITORIAL PROFILE
VANIDADES CONTINENTAL is edited for the particular interests of the contemporary Hispanic woman. It specializes in beauty, fashion and decoration and also has regular sections on food and cooking, travel and tourism, movies and TV, medicine, health and nutrition, and children. It contains in-depth articles and photographs of international and local personalities. Regionalized sections focus on local events and happenings. Rec'd 2/8/94.
U.S. advertisers only.

1. PERSONNEL
Pres/CEO—Laura D. B. De Laviada.
Intl Adv Dir—Enrique J. Perez.
US Adv Sales Dir—Roberto Sroka.

2. REPRESENTATIVES and/or BRANCH OFFICES
Miami, FL 33166—(Editorial Televisa), 6355 N.W. 36th St. Phone 305-871-6400. Fax 305-871-5026
New York, NY 10017—Leticia F. Cueto-Borsani, Editor, 780 Third Ave., 10th Fl. Phone 212-838-7220. Fax 212-838-8532.
Van Nuys, CA 91406—Miguel Sanchez, Editorial Televisa, 7710 Haskell Ave., Ste B. Phone 818-782-6188. Fax 818-781-9649.
Argentina—EDICO, Patricio Smith, AV Paseo Colon, 275 Piso 10, CAP FED, Buenos Aires, Argentina (1063) Phone 541-343-2225. Fax 541-345-0955, 541-334-0686.
Bogota, Colombia—Cecilia Rueda de Garcia, Editorial America, S.A. Transversal 93, No. 52-03. Phone 571-413-9300/9666. Fax 571-413-5009
Mexico—Editorial Televisa S.A. de CV, Miguel Ruiz Galindo Ave. Vasco de Quiroga #2000 Esq. a Fernando Espinoza Gutierrez, Edificio E. Col. Santa Fe, dela, Alvaro Obregon C.P. 01210. Phone 525-261-2600. Fax 525-261-2705
San Juan, Puerto Rico 00917—Grace Abascal,Editorial Televisa, Condominio Altagracia. Calle Uruguay 262, Oficina C1. Phone 787-758-1170. Fax 787-758-7670
San Isidro, Lima, Peru—Editorial Televisa, S.A., Jacqueline Orjeda,Edificio "Vanidades Continental" Ave. Republica de Panama 3631-3635, 3rd flr. Phone 5114-41-7853. Fax 5114-41-8546
Venezuela—Editorial Televisa, Luis Miguel Acetuno, Avenida Francisco de Miranda, Edificio Centro Plaza, Torre A, Piso 14, Caracas, Venezuela. Phone 582-286-7763.
Santiago, Chile—Editorial Televisa, S.A., Maria De los Angeles Swinburn, Reyes Lavalle 3194. Tel 562-366-7100/246-7204. Fax 562-246-4025
Guayaquil, Ecuador—Vanipubli Ecuatoriana, S.A., Maria Teresa de Solano, Avenida Jorge Perez Concha #306-A. Entre Diagonal y Todos Los Santos. Tel 593-4888-150/887-778. Fax 593-4887-776
London SW1V 3PS, England—John R. Boardman, Chm, Powers Overseas, Ltd., Duncan House, Dolphin square. Phone 44-071-834-5566. Fax 44-071-630-0696/44-071630-5878. TELEX 24924 Powers G.

3. COMMISSION AND CASH DISCOUNT
15% to recognized agencies. 2% 10 days. Net 30 days.

4. GENERAL RATE POLICY
90 days' notice given of any rate revision.

ADVERTISING RATES
Effective October 1, 1998.
Rates received October 21, 1998.

5. BLACK/WHITE RATES

	1 ti	4 ti	7 ti	13 ti	19 ti	26 ti
1 page	7500.	7310.	7125.	6750.	6375.	6000.
2/3 page	6000.	5850.	5700.	5400.	5100.	4800.
1/2 page	4685.	4565.	4450.	4215.	3980.	3745.
1/3 page	3375.	3290.	3205.	3035.	2865.	2700.
Junior:						
1 page	5625.	5480.	5380.	5060.	4780.	4500.

FREQUENCY DISCOUNT
Ads must be inserted within 1 year of 1st insertion to earn 4, 7, 13, 19, 26-time rate. 39-time schedule will earn 25% discount on the 1-time rate.

6. COLOR RATES

	1 ti	4 ti	7 ti
4-Color:			
Spread	20,000.	19,500.	19,000
1 page	10,000.	9,750.	9,500
2/3 page	8,000.	7,800.	7,600
1/2 page	6,250.	6,090.	5,935

	13 ti	19 ti	26 ti
Spread	18,000.	17,000.	16,000
1 page	9,000.	8,500.	8,000
2/3 page	7,200.	6,800.	6,400
1/2 page	5,625.	5,310.	5,000

	1 ti	4 ti	7 ti	13 ti	19 ti	26 ti
4-Color:						
1 page	7500.	7310.	7125.	6750.	6375.	6000.

7. COVERS

	1 ti	4 ti	7 ti	13 ti	19 ti	26 ti
4-Color:						
2nd cover	7475.	7285.	7100.	6725.	6350.	5980.
3rd cover	7475.	7285.	7100.	6725.	6350.	5980.
4th cover	8125.	7915.	7715.	7310.	6905.	6500.

9. BLEED
No charge.
Contracts and insertion orders must be specified wether ads bleed.

10. SPECIAL POSITION
Special inside positions, extra 30%

13a. GEOGRAPHIC and/or DEMOGRAPHIC EDITIONS
INTERNATIONAL EDITIONS
ARGENTINA
COLOR RATES:
4-Color:
1 page .... 4500.

CENTRAL AMERICA
COLOR RATES:
4-Color:
1 page .... 2500.

CHILE
COLOR RATES:
4-Color:
1 page .... 4500.

COLOMBIA
COLOR RATES:
4-Color:
1 page .... 3500.

MEXICO
COLOR RATES:
4-Color:
1 page .... 10,000.

PUERTO RICO
COLOR RATES:
4-Color:
1 page .... 5000.

LATIN AMERICA
Includes: Argentina, Central America, Chile, Colombia, Ecuador, Mexico, Peru, Puerto Rico and Venezuela.
COLOR RATES:
4-Color:
1 page .... 34,300.

CONTINENTAL
Includes: All Latin American and U.S. Editions.
COLOR RATES:
4-Color:
1 page .... 25,480.

MULTI-EDITION REGIONAL DISCOUNTS

2 countries	5%	5 countries	20%
3 countries	10%	6 countries	25%
4 countries	15%	7 or more countries	30%

15. GENERAL REQUIREMENTS
Also see SRDS Print Media Production Source.
Printing Process: Offset Full Run.
Trim Size: 8-3/8 x 11-1/16; No./Cols. 3.
Binding Method: Perfect.
Colors Available: 4-color process.

NON-BLEED
AD PAGE DIMENSIONS

Sprd	15-1/4	x	9-7/8	1/2 h	7-1/4	x	4-15/16
1 pg	7-1/4	x	9-7/8	1/3 v	2-1/4	x	9-7/8
2/3 v	4-3/4	x	9-7/8	1/3 sq	4-3/4	x	4-15/16
1/2 v	3-9/16	x	9-7/8				

NON-BLEED
JR AD PAGE DIMENSIONS

1 pg	4-3/4	x	7

16. ISSUE AND CLOSING DATES
Published biweekly.

		Closing	
Issue:	On sale	(+)	(*)
Mar 9/99	3/2	1/27	2/4
Mar 23/99	3/16	2/10	2/18
Apr 6/99	3/30	2/24	3/4
Apr 20/99	4/13	3/10	3/18
May 4/99	4/27	3/24	4/1
May 18/99	5/11	4/7	4/15
Jun 1/99	5/25	4/21	4/29
Jun 15/99	6/8	5/5	5/13
Jun 29/99	6/22	5/19	5/27
Jul 13/99	7/6	6/2	6/10
Jul 27/99	7/20	6/16	6/24
Aug 10/99	8/3	6/30	7/8
Aug 24/99	8/17	7/14	7/22
Sep 7/99	8/31	7/28	8/5
Sep 21/99	9/14	8/11	8/19
Oct 5/99	9/28	8/25	9/2
Oct 19/99	10/12	9/8	9/16
Nov 2/99	10/26	9/22	9/30
Nov 16/99	11/9	10/6	10/14
Nov 30/99	11/23	10/20	10/28
Dec 14/99	12/7	11/3	11/11
Dec 28/99	12/21	11/17	11/25

(+) Space
(*) Material

18. CIRCULATION
Established 1961. Single copy 5.00.
Summary data—for detail see Publisher's Statement.

A.B.C. 12-31-97 (6 mos. aver.—Magazine Form)

Tot Pd	(Subs)	(Single)	(Assoc)
89,436	37,912	51,524	

Average Non-Analyzed Non-Paid Circulation (not incl. above):
Total 1,198
TERRITORIAL DISTRIBUTION Dec 2/97—89,637

N.Eng.	Mid.Atl.	E.N.Cen.	W.N.Cen.	S.Atl.	E.S.Cen.
2,538	19,332	4,137	698	24,763	738
W.S.Cen.	Mtn.St.	Pac.St.	Canada	Foreign	Other
8,601	3,258	21,614	323	281	3,354

SRDS Exercise:

Let's get some practice with SRDS. Let's say you're a media planner and your job is to select and schedule media.

Your client, Campbell's, has decided to introduce a canned gazpacho soup to Hispanic women.

This tomato-based soup is served cold.

One of the magazines being considered for the introductory advertising campaign is *Vanidades* – above is an SRDS magazine profile.

Look at all the information this SRDS profile provides. Now see how helpful it can be by answering the following questions:

1. What language is this magazine printed in? The current Campbell's Soup campaign is only in English. Would you recommend creating a new ad specifically for *Vanidades* that will be in Spanish? Why or why not?

2. Taking a look at the Publisher's Editorial Profile, you will notice that *Vanidades* is made up of many different sections. Which section of the magazine will you choose for your Campbell's Gazpacho ad? Why have you chosen this section?

Vanidades. An SRDS Magazine Profile.

You'll be surprised at how much you can learn about a magazine by merely reviewing SRDS magazine profiles.
© SRDS

Bonus Question:

Let's say you are asked to schedule magazine ads over a three-month period for Campbell's new Gazpacho Soup in *Vanidades* in order to reach the Hispanic women's market living in the mid-Atlantic region of the US.

Which three months would you choose for the region?

Source Notes:

Here are the major sources used for this chapter. If you have any questions, post them on adbuzz.com.

List your message as Sources: 6.

Major Sources for This Chapter:

Newspaper Association of America Market & Business Analysis, 1998.

Editor & Publisher, 1997, 1998.

James B. Twitchell, "But First, A Word from Our Sponsor" (December 1996) *Current,* p. 15.

Robert J. Coen, "Ad Spending Tops $175 Billion" (May 12, 1977), *Ad Age.* p. 20.

Carl Marie Cropper, "Fruit to Walls to Floor, Ads Are on the March" (Feb. 26, 1998), *New York Times,* p. A1.

Brad Edmondson, "In the Driver's Seat" *American Demographics* (March 1998).

Ogilvy & Mather Worldwide Brand Stewardship brochure.

John Vivian, *The Media of Mass Communication* (5th edition), 1999, p. 178.

Marc Gunther, "This Gang Controls Your Kids Brains" *Fortune* (Oct. 27, 1997), p. 172.

Patricia Gillies, "Ads Step up to the Front Page," *Ideas Magazine* (October 1997), p. 21.

Robin Pogrebin, "The Number of Ad Pages Does Not Make the Magazine," *The New York Times* (Aug. 26, 1996), p. D1.

J. Linn Allen, "New Life for the Dinosaurs," *Chicago Tribune* (Sept. 29, 1997), p. 1 & 2.

Village Voice Web site, www.villagevoice.com/aboutus/history.shtml, December 5, 1998.

Audit Bureau of Circulation, Dec. 31, 1997.

(Continued on next page)

3. How often is *Vanidades* published?

4. Find the heading "18. Circulation." Your supervisor wants to know how many Hispanic women subscribe to *Vanidades*. Therefore, what is *Vanidades'* total paid circulation?
   4a. How much do Hispanic women pay for a single copy of *Vanidades*?
   4b. What's *Vanidades'* circulation in the mid-Atlantic region?

5. How much does a four-color, one-page ad cost in Mexico?

Concepts & Vocabulary:

ADI (Area of Dominant Influence) – Arbitron's mutually exclusive TV marketing areas defined by counties where the majority of total TV viewing occurs.

Adjacencies – In print, the editorial content next to the print ad. In broadcast, the programs that run next to a TV or radio commercial.

Afternoon drive – Weekday commuting hours from 4:00 to 7:00 P.M. when radio usage increases dramatically.

Alternative newspapers – Weeklies that present non-mainstream ideas, lifestyles, and viewpoints – usually in a tabloid format.

Arbitron – A national audience measurement service that provides ratings for radio and television stations.

Audience profile – Description of the demographics of a radio station's listeners.

Barter – The practice of selling advertising time and space in exchange for goods or services, not money.

Best food day – Designated day of the week (usually Sunday or Wednesday) when newspapers feature food product or supermarket advertising and coupons, frequently with related articles on health, recipes, etc.

Billboards – Large outdoor structures posted with advertising messages, erected in strategically chosen areas to reach the maximum number of passersby per day.

Broadcast – To transmit a radio or TV program to a mass audience.

Bulletin – The largest standard billboard structure, measuring 14 x 48 (672 square) feet, generally erected near high-density traffic areas.

Cable television – Signals received through either coaxial cable or satellite dish, as opposed to those sent via airwave and received through antennae.

Circulation – The total number of copies of a newspaper or magazine distributed by subscription, newsstand, and/or bulk.

Consultative selling – "marketing driven" sales approach used by media sales representatives who approach media sales as marketing consultants.

Controlled circulation – Publications that are distributed to select audience members and generally free of charge.

Co-Op (Cooperative Advertising) – Retail advertising that is partly or fully funded by a manufacturer.

Cost per thousand (CPM) – A method of comparing advertising vehicles. The CPM shows how much it costs to reach a thousand audience members.

Daily impressions – Billboards that reach members of a market's population in one given day.

Diary – Audience measurement technique where participants are asked to record in writing all their listening, viewing, or reading activities.

Drive time – Morning and afternoon time spent by commuters listening to their car radios.

Entertainment brand – A media property that stands out from its competition because it has a distinct personality, trademark, name, identity, or visual appeal.

Frequency – The number of times an individual or household is exposed to an advertising message over a certain period of time.

Free-standing insert (FSI) – four-color, pre-printed circular with coupons that is usually inserted into the newspaper for a fee.

In-bound telemarketing – Consumers use their telephones to initiate a call about information or purchase a product.

Kiosks – Free-standing displays typically found in airports, rail terminals, malls, and stores.

Media – Plural term used to refer to all means that can be used to speak on behalf of a brand. Traditional media include newspapers, magazines, radio, television, outdoor, and yellow pages. Nontraditional media can be far-reaching, from fruit stickers to T-shirts.

Media rep (representative) – A person who is employed by a media company that sells either time or space to advertisers.

Medium – One of the forms of communications that can be used to deliver advertising messages to consumers (e.g., magazine is a medium; newspaper is a medium).

Morning drive – Weekday commuting hours between 6:00 to 10:00 A.M. when radio usage increases dramatically.

Narrowcast – Specialized electronic programming or any other specific medium that is geared toward a specific target audience, thus delivering a narrow portion of the total media audience.

Newsletter – A type of publication that deals with the special interests of a particular group.

Newspaper – A publication that is issued for use by the general public at frequent and regular time periods.

Source Notes (Cont.)

The Austin Chronicle Web site, www.auschron.com/info/mission.html.

S. Watson Dunn and Arnold M. Barban, *Advertising: It's Role in Modern Marketing,* 5th edition, (1982).

Arbitron/RAB Media Targeting 2000 M Street Corporation, August 1998 Fall 1997 Arbitron National Database.

RADAR 53, Spring 1996.

RAB, "Radio — A Sound Investment" May 14, 1998.

Joseph R. Dominick, *The Dynamics of Mass Communication* (1994), p.181.

George Comstock, *The Evolution of American Television* (1989).

John R. Osborn, BBDO 1891-1991: Media Timeline.

Head & Sterling, *Broadcasting in America,* 6th Edition.

National readership statistics reported in the Newspaper Association of America publication "Facts about Newspapers," 1997.

Response Analysis Corporation. Printed in Newspaper Advertising Bureau's *Selling Against Broadcast.*

Leonard Mogel, *The Magazine* (1988), p. 208.

Paul Kagan Associates.

Broadcasting in America, 6th edition, p. 4. Head & Sterling, (1990).

Robert J. Coen, *US Advertising Volume,* 1997 and 2003.

Statistics reported in the *New York Times,* April 20, 1994 and provided by the A.C. Nielsen Co. for ratings period September 20 through 27, 1994.

1994 Guide to Advertiser-supported Syndication, Syndication: The Fifth Network.

(Continued on next page)

Source Notes (Cont.)

"Cable May Be Down, But Not Out," *Variety* (March 14, 1994).

"Reinventing Cable to Find Place on Converging Super-Highway" *Advertising Age* (April 11, 1994).

Categories taken from Jugenheimer, Barban, and Turk's *Advertising Media Strategy and Tactics.*

1993 Focus Marketing Promo Primer: A Compilation of Basics and Buzzwords for the Promotion Industry.

"Why Radio Thrives," *American Demographics* (May 1994).

"It's Not a New Medium, But Radio Still a Hot One," *Advertising Age* (May 9, 1994).

Advertising Age Fact Pack 2004 Edition.

Niche media – Specialized types of media that are geared toward distinct groups of viewers, listeners, and readers.

Nielsen (A.C. Nielsen Co.) – 1. Company that measures TV viewing as well as other marketing research. 2. TV ratings from Nielsen.

Owned and operated station (O&O) – A station that is owned and operated by a network.

Out-bound telemarketing – When a telemarketing firm initiates the telephone call to contact consumers about its product or service.

Outdoor – Billboard advertising that comes in three formats: bulletins, 30-sheets, and 8-sheets.

Out-of-home advertising – Forms of advertising located outside of the home, which include traditional and place-based media. Includes: aerial/inflatables, bus shelters, telephone kiosks, bus benches, outdoor (billboards), transit, and taxi advertising.

Place-based media – Advertising that occurs at places where consumers intersect with brand messages. This can include airport and in-store advertising opportunities.

Price/item advertising – Also known as display advertising – a form of local display newspaper advertising where a variety of merchandise is displayed in the ad with a description and a price.

Rate card – A listing published by print and broadcast media that show advertising costs, mechanical requirements, issue dates, closing dates, and circulation information.

Reach – The number of different individuals or households who tune into an advertising medium over a specified period of time.

Rotary bulletins – Billboard or other outdoor that can be moved from one location to another for maximum exposure in different locales.

Run of the press, or run of paper (ROP) – A newspaper ad insertion that runs anywhere in that paper. Position not specified.

Sheets – Poster panels printed with advertisements and affixed to billboards to display an advertising message.

Showings – A collection of poster panels or bulletins that cover a specific market. Usually referred to as 100, 50, or 25 showing (100%, 50%, or 25% of the market).

Space reps – *Rep* is slang for representative. A space rep is someone who sells print media.

Spot TV or radio – Purchasing television or radio on a market-by-market basis.

Standard Rate and Data Service (SRDS) – A service that publishes the advertising rates, discount structures, mechanical requirements, closing dates, production capabilities, and other important information about the media.

Superstation – Local independent television stations that uplink their signals onto a communication satellite, giving them national exposure.

Syndication – Television programs that are sold, licensed, and distributed to stations by independent firms.

Telemarketing – Use of the telephone to sell goods and services.

Time shifting – Process wherein TV viewers videotape a show and then watch it at a different time that is more convenient to them.

Zapping – Switching commercials off.

Zipping – Fast-forwarding through commercials.

7

This chapter features the following co-authors – each offering advice in their specialty.

Laurence Minsky (Columbia College Chicago), lead author of this chapter, specializes in Promotional Marketing. He is author of *How to Succeed in Advertising When All You Have Is Talent (2nd Ed.)* and other books.

Susan Jones (Ferris State) is author of *Creative Strategy in Direct Marketing*, and co-author of *Selling by Mail*, *Marketing Convergence*, and others.

Joe Marconi (DePaul and Columbia College Chicago) is author of over a dozen books, including: *Public Relations: The Complete Guide*, *Crisis Marketing*, *The Writing Book*, and more.

Kevin Adler (Engage Marketing) is the former head of the Leo Burnett/ Publicis Sponsorship Division – Relay Marketing – and is now President of his own event and sponsorship firm – Engage Marketing.

"Look for a business where the wind is at your back; where all the trends are working for you."
— Howard Draft
Chairman Draft/FCB

Marketing

THIS PART OF THE BUSINESS OF BRANDS will cover a wide range of companies, each supplying some key specialty.

It's an area where people with unique skills and strong motivation can make the most of their opportunities.

And just as The Media Revolution has impacted every business we've studied so far, this chapter will be no exception. Let's look at a few careers.

Making His Mark.

In college, **Mark Montoya** led a team of five from San Jose State to win a national collegiate advertising competition.

He saw opportunities in **event marketing.** The world's largest entirely free jazz fest is just one of his accomplishments.

Today, with media exploding, the basics of event marketing have new importance and provide new opportunities.

#1 Draft Choice.

In 1977, **Howard Draft** graduated from Ripon College in Ripon, Wisconsin. He was looking for "a business where the wind was at your back." He found it – **direct marketing.**

Today, he's in charge of DraftFCB, an Interpublic company, billing nearly $1 billion. Good choice, Howard.

Leading the Way.

As President of BSMG/PR in Chicago, **Barbara Molotsky**, drove **public relations** for Harley-Davidson and looked great in a milk mustache – repositioning a brand called "milk." We'll take a look at the growing business of marketing public relations, or MPR.

At the Top of the Arc.

Today, **Bill Rosen** is Chief Creative Officer of Arc Worldwide, traveling around the world overseeing the development of sales promotion and other integrated programs for blue chip clients like McDonald's, Procter & Gamble, and Coca-Cola.

He's just back from judging the Cannes Advertising Festival. Hey somebody has to do it.

"Currently, just over half our business is outside of advertising… we think it will be two-thirds in five to ten years…"

— Sir Martin Sorrell, CEO and Chairman of the Board, WPP

Services

How This Chapter Is Organized.

Here's how we'll cover the material in this chapter.

- **An Overview.** First, we'll help you get a handle on how marketers buy marketing services.

Then, we'll cover the major disciplines:

1. **Sales Promotion**
2. **Direct Marketing and Database Marketing**
3. **Public Relations**
4. **Marketing Research**
5. **Event Marketing and Sponsorships**
6. **Promotional Products**

Each topic is a book in itself, and each offers unique career opportunities, but this chapter will give you an introductory overview. And you may want to find out more.

Because, as traditional media become more expensive and less effective, these marketing tools are becoming more important.

We'll finish up with **The MarCom Manager** and how all of these specialties are integrated and coordinated.

You can also see how big this world is by taking a look at some of the things we won't be able to cover in this chapter:

- **Coupon Redemption and Fulfillment**
- **Game Management (e.g., scratch and win cards)**
- **In-store Sampling**
- **Information Processing Services**
- **Legal and Accounting Services**

They're also part of the world of marketing services. And, like everything else, The Media Revolution is having an impact.

For example, more and more coupons are being delivered electronically. But we've got enough to cover with these six.

Let's go!

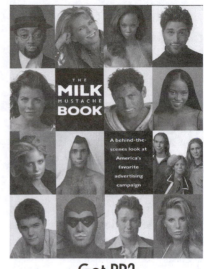

Got PR?

This great-looking book featuring the "Milk Mustache" campaign was prepared for the National Fluid Milk Processor Promotion Board by Bozell Advertising. It went to #5 on the *New York Times* bestseller list!

**In a Pickle?
Try Sales Promotion**

A smart sales promotion, with coupons and free-standing displays like this one, helped re-energize Nalley Pickles. There were ads, too. In a mature category, strong reminder advertising combined with a good retail promotion can often do the job.

When All You Have Is a Hammer.

There's an old saying… *"When all you have is a hammer, every problem looks like a nail."*

How you make your money can obviously affect your point of view.

As a result, many marketers believe ad agencies have a bias toward media advertising and solutions that are more profitable for them.

If an agency can make two or three commercials and run them in prime time TV, it may make millions in commissions and/or fees.

Not only that, but agency talent is good at making these TV ads – we like to do things we're good at.

Will that agency, clients ask themselves, counsel it objectively on the relative merits of the TV ad campaign versus a direct response campaign from which the agency may make only a modest profit – or, worse yet, have to "job it out?"

Getting the balance right – the marketing mix – is one of today's biggest challenges.

The Direct Approach.

Bose knows direct. Can direct work in general media?

If you really know what you're doing and you have a terrific product, you can do it.

An Overview.

WHAT ARE MARKETING SERVICES? This category comprises any and all additional services performed for a marketer besides the creation and placement of ads and commercials.

These services may be performed by an ad agency or, as is more common, by other specialized agencies or suppliers.

Some may be performed by the marketer. It varies.

There are many combinations and configurations.

Full-Service Agencies and Marketing Services.

In the past, a full-service ad agency might offer a more complete range of marketing services. In addition to media and research, some agencies might offer sales promotion.

Public relations was sometimes added to the mix, although most PR activities were carried out by the marketer, a specialized PR consulting firm, or both.

Some agencies developed specialized marketing services that were attractive to certain clients.

Grey Advertising offered excellent merchandising capabilities and Noble Advertising in Springfield, Missouri, was known for its strength in trade relations and trade promotions.

But, for the most part, it was not the major ad agencies that sparked the growth of marketing services; it was individuals with a unique vision who formed small companies offering these highly specialized services. And they grew.

Then, mega-agencies began to add these capabilities by purchasing the companies. Integration by acquisition.

Today's marketing services industry is a wide array of agency divisions and unique specialists, with almost every field experiencing dynamic growth.

Today's marketer has a lot to choose from.

From Collateral…

Collateral is a broad term that has traditionally been used to cover all non-media advertising work. It is most often applied to any print work done in addition to the advertising: brochures, signage, point-of-sale displays, direct mail, etc.

Years ago, the term "collateral" was spoken with a bit of derision at some full-service agencies.

At large agencies, this work was often done by a separate department or another agency entirely. At smaller agencies it was part of the advertising assignment. In some cases, it was done in-house by the marketer's own advertising department.

The client marketing or advertising manager, or the ad agency account executive, usually had the task of seeing that the collateral was coordinated with the advertising.

It was a simpler time.

...to Integration.

In today's more integrated environment, advertising is more correctly seen as one of several marketing communications disciplines all working toward the same marketing goal.

In many areas, particularly consumer packaged goods, advertising is still the largest item in the marketing budget.

But in other industries, there is a wider variance.

With that in mind, let's examine the services used, or at least considered, in every marketing communications program today.

Who Does What?

As marketers work to integrate and coordinate the marketing of their brands for optimal effectiveness, this is now a key question. There are many different answers.

Some services may be offered by the ad agency, or they may be contracted out to independent vendors.

The agency, in the interest of providing a truly integrated package to clients, may coordinate the services and the messages.

Indeed, in today's fluid (some would say volatile) movement away from the domination of mass media toward more targeted marketing and media, there are many opinions on what services should be offered by whom.

For all these reasons, "who does what" can vary widely from marketer to marketer and even from brand to brand.

For reasons of cost and control, coordination is most often done within the client's marketing department.

So it should come as no surprise that there are about as many combinations and configurations as there are clients.

A Wide Range of Solutions.

For all these reasons, several different models will be presented here – different ways in which marketing services are used to manage the marketing function.

Many of the marketing services can, and do, exist within the marketer's own advertising, research, public relations, or sales promotion departments. And, of course, each is featured at independent, highly specialized agencies offering only specific services.

Example: H-P Adds Insight.

For example, the marketing department at computer and printer manufacturer Hewlett-Packard (H-P) decided their efforts would be improved with more insight into their consumer.

They decided to add to this capability internally, but to develop expertise quickly, the best way is – get an expert.

So, they called Lisa Fortini-Campbell, one of the leaders in the field, and engaged her in a project. This long-term project involved getting a deeper understanding of the H-P target.

The result was not only advertising, but product development and services such as customer support.

How PR Drives Harley.

Harley-Davidson is a powerful marketing success story. Once near bankruptcy with a "Hell's Angels" image, it is now a powerful brand.

Improving Quality.

Improving product quality was the first job – but much of the marketing was PR-driven – by BSMG/PR.

It was a three-part program:

1. They Organized HOG.

The Harley Owners Group (HOG) became a powerful brand partner.

They helped improve the image.

Then, they helped promote it.

2. A Cause – MD.

Harley became a strong supporter of the fight against Muscular Dystrophy – helping to counter the Harley "outlaw" image.

3. Use PR to Show Harley Owners.

Finally, PR was used to profile Harley owners – Jay Leno, Malcolm Forbes, grandmothers, and RUBES (Rich Urban Bikers).

This critical third piece tied the program together – saluting Harley owners, reinforcing their relationship with the brand, and making the brand more mainstream.

This brand-building program was driven by PR – not advertising.

Example: 95th Anniversary

A nationwide road rally drove Harley's 95th Anniversary Celebration.

Beginning in five cities, from Spokane to New York, HOG members converged on Milwaukee for a week-long celebration.

(Continued on next page)

PR Drives Harley (Cont.)

This nationwide event involved:
• HOG
• The press
• The introduction of two new
 motorcycle models
• Harley's marketing partners

The rally provided a platform with news value that promoted Harley products and the Harley tradition.

Get with the Program.

A commemorative program let Harley dealers, merchandisers, and co-sponsors, like Dodge Ram Trucks, communicate with this target. You could even get your photo on a special commemorative Harley-Davidson Chrome Visa.

In the Beginning...

Careers in marketing services can have curious beginnings.

When Bill Rosen took his first job as a promotional copywriter, it was only supposed to be temporary – to make money while writing plays.

As you'll see, there are many opportunities – with new ones developing all the time.

Short-Term and Long-Term.

Many projects have both short-term and long-term effects in a marketing organization.

Short-term, Dr. Fortini-Campbell was hired to develop insights on a specific H-P product.

Long-term, H-P developed the ability to integrate consumer insight into a whole range of marketing operations – from product development to advertising to customer service.

In addition, they can now develop internal capability. Some of this they do with training – hiring Lisa's company to conduct seminars and other training sessions. These growing connections build a long-term relationship with the Fortini-Campbell Company.

A Two-Way Street.

This relationship is a two-way street. Fortini-Campbell now has unique experience and information about H-P.

So they are now even more valuable to H-P.

In addition, much of this information is confidential and proprietary – signing some sort of confidentiality agreement is standard procedure with most marketing services suppliers.

H-P has paid for their "learning curve." And they now have an investment in time and money that they would have to duplicate with another supplier.

When it works, client and supplier become more valuable to each other and work together even more efficiently.

Generalists and Specialists.

Most marketing services described here will be offered by some full-service ad agencies or as part of mega-agency groups.

Few smaller agencies offer more than the basics, with a bit of public relations and trade relations for specific industries. Services are often predicated on the needs of one or two large clients.

Major marketers have typically been more comfortable assigning tasks such as sales promotion, event marketing, direct mail, telemarketing, public relations, interactive marketing, and so forth, to specialists and dedicated agencies while controlling the strategic, planning, and integrating functions themselves.

But, as noted, there's almost any combination you can imagine.

It's also worth mentioning that, in certain cases, sub-contractors may also sub-contract. Specialization is key.

For example, a sales promotion agency may subcontract to another marketing services provider, such as a company that does in-store sampling.

And, as the Media Revolution continues to develop, new technologies and new combinations are growing even as you read this chapter.

Advertising Today – One More Tactic.

From this perspective, advertising becomes simply one more tactic or execution of the overall marketing communications plan. This is a view that many advertising executives may still resist.

Why? Because the advertising business model worked. Ad executives were able to recommend relatively simplistic media campaigns (e.g., primetime TV buys) that reached most consumers effectively and efficiently.

Comfortable with that strategy, many resisted change. But, as ad effectiveness waned, this resistance has gone out of fashion.

Now everyone needs better answers.

MarCom = Marketing Communications.

For many marketers, marketing communications (MarCom) in support of their brands has become a much more complex mix of services.

Today, marketers are putting a higher proportion of their total MarCom dollars into targeted, and more measurable, forms of promotion such as direct mail and sales promotions.

Marketers also have an increasingly wide range of options in the types of specialized agencies, suppliers, and media they select.

The needed expertise may come from in-house, from an agency, from a supplier, or from a combination of the three.

These services are often stand-alone, or conducted at the marketer's own offices, by its own staff.

When they are bundled at a full service ad agency, they will typically be within the marketing services department.

Now that you have a general sense of the variety of ways marketing services suppliers are used, let's take a look at the specific marketing services themselves.

The MarCom Industry.

It's a big business. Here are fee revenues from 2007 for marketing services and then all the categories for the sales promotion field.

The Marketing Services Industry. Here is the fee income of marketing services firms in public relations, sales promotion, direct, healthcare, and interactive.

In fees alone, it adds up to over $14 billion – about the same as ad industry income.

Category	Fees (Billions)
Digital	$3.36
Direct Marketing	3.36
Public Relations	3.20
Promotion	2.47
Healthcare	2.25
Total Marketing Services	14.64

(Source Ad Age Special Report 2008)

The Promotion Industry.

Now here's a breakdown of the over $338 billion spent in the sales promotion industry. And remember, this does not include trade dollars.

Category	Spending (Billions)
Direct Marketing	$67.2
Branded Entertainment	52.87
Employee Incentives	46.0
B-2-B	44.76
In-Store	44.25
Digital	26.53
Point-of-Purchase	19.33
Sponsorships	14.9
Coupons	7.1
Licensing	6.0
Product Placement	2.9
Sampling	2.0
Loyalty	2.0
Games & Contests	1.8
Event Marketing	0.68
Total	338.32

(Source: PROMO Magazine)

Classic MarCom.

This promotion for the original Macintosh computer combined advertising, publicity, in-store promotional materials, a contest for sales personnel, and a terrific consumer incentive – take home a brand new Macintosh computer and try it out.

Early Sales Promotion.

This was an early promotion success –
an in-pack with Wheaties – miniature
license plates – that encouraged
people to collect the whole set (and
buy lots of Wheaties).

Does Sales Promotion
Build Brands?

This is a controversial subject, and
the answer is "yes" and "no."

Traditionally, advertising has been
the discipline of choice for building
brand awareness and maintaining
brand value with consumers.

Traditionally, sales promotion was
seen as a discipline good at creating
an immediate sale, but not as good at
helping build long-term loyalty.

Ad executives maintained that
sales promotion would not build
brand awareness, and, furthermore,
it served as a deterrent to brand
loyalty by promoting price alone.

Today's attitude is that sales
promotion can contribute to brand
value when used correctly.

New Continuity Programs.
For example, one way today's sales
promotions can help build long-term
loyalty is through "continuity" or
"frequency" programs integrated with
consumer purchase databases.

Whether a marketer is an airline
with a frequent flier program or
a grocery store with a preferred
customer card, sales promotion
incentives can help marketers
"reward" customers.

(Continued on next page)

1. Sales Promotion.

THIS KEY MARKETING DISCIPLINE accounts for a larger share
of the marketing communications dollar every year. Since much
sales promotion expense comes in the form of trade discounts to
retailers, calculating an accurate total can be difficult. But it's big!

Much of the growth in sales promotion spending has come at
the expense of mass media advertising.

Consumer/Trade – Push/Pull.

Sales promotion falls into two areas:

* **Consumer Promotions**
* **Trade Promotions**

In general, consumer promotions are viewed as "pull." They pull
consumers into a retail store and pull product off the shelf.

Trade promotions are viewed as "push." They push merchandise
into the distribution channel and push displays into stores.

Push & Pull.

Sales promotions are usually divided between those normally
employed in consumer marketing (pull) and those employed in
business-to-business, or trade, marketing (push).

Most consumer promotions employ both.

In a *pull* strategy, consumer demand is stimulated with coupons
or other incentives. The demand from those purchases pulls the
product through the distribution channel.

In a *push* strategy, wholesalers, distributors, and retailers are given
incentives to push product – either on to the next member of the
distribution channel – or to the ultimate consumer.

Push and Pull Are Not Either/Or.

Push and pull strategies are not an either/or proposition.

Again, both strategies may be employed concurrently.

A copywriter might write a consumer coupon ad for *Good Housekeeping* in the morning – perhaps an ad talking about the good taste
or nutrition of Campbell's Soups, and offering a coupon to try the
new variety. That's a pull strategy.

That same day, another copywriter may have an assignment to
write an ad for *Chain Store Age*, or a sell sheet for the sales force
announcing a special display program.

That's a push strategy.

Marketer, Agency, or Sales Promotion Specialist.

Sales promotions in some form are done by just about everyone
with something to sell.

Selection of the appropriate promotion is more complicated.

Objectives may be in conflict; one may be to build the brand
long-term, another to stimulate sales short-term.

Sales promotion projects may be handled within the advertiser's
marketing department, by the advertising agency, or by a sales
promotion specialist.

With larger marketers, it would not be unusual for all of these
possible options to be going on at the same time.

Win. Free. Save. Incentive-Based Techniques.
Sales promotion provides some incentive – e.g., prizes, money off, or money back – to encourage immediate purchase.

Naturally, you're most familiar with consumer incentives, but those in the trade have incentives as well – such as sales contests.

That's one reason a marketer like P&G gets involved with NASCAR racing. It's the appeal of these events to the trade – a NASCAR event for a store manager is a strong incentive.

So, when you see Crisco, Folger's, or Tide on a NASCAR car, realize that the target isn't housewives who think about car races while baking pies, sipping coffee, or doing laundry – it's a store manager who may win a ticket and meet the NASCAR driver.

Act Now!!!
Sales promotions can be contrasted to ad campaigns by duration – sales promotions are short term, ad campaigns are longer term.

Sales promotions typically run no more than 90 days.

In fact, it's illegal to run a sales promotion indefinitely – a sale isn't a sale if it's the everyday way of doing business.

A dry cleaner in California was fined $75,000 for running a "second similar piece cleaned for one cent" promotion for years.

Other Differences between Sales Promotion and Advertising.
Sales promotion can be contrasted in other ways.

A sales-promotion strategy is based around the desired behavior – buy a larger size, buy more often, try the product, etc.

Sales promotions work to achieve specific, measurable sales or marketing objectives (units, dollars).

An advertising strategy is communication of a motivating message. Ad campaigns work to achieve specific objectives of brand or ad awareness that may be measurable, but, usually, these measures can't be directly equated with sales results.

For example, an ad campaign may generate high awareness of the brand, but other marketing factors, such as price, competition, and the product itself, may negate positive effects of the ads.

Getting Them to Work Together.
Sales promotion and advertising can be integrated.

For instance, an ad with a coupon in it is a sales promotion, although it uses print advertising to deliver the promotional device – the coupon. Additionally, traditional media advertising is often used to create awareness for a promotion.

The usual method of implementing sales promotions is to subcontract them to an agency that specializes in them – a sales promotion agency. These agencies are, by themselves, a huge business.

This selection is often done by the client. The ad agency may be involved for coordination of the targeting, the ad message to support the promotion, the graphics (which are usually provided to the sales promotion agency), and the timing, but the client is usually the driver.

Brand-Building (Cont.)

Incentives can help marketers achieve long-term brand loyalty: a discount for frequent purchases, a coupon for a preferred brand, or notice of an upcoming sale for products the customer buys often.

Another marketing activity that attempts to increase brand loyalty is "relationship marketing."

Done properly, it strengthens the bond between brand and consumer. The Harley-Davidson HOG program is an excellent example.

But is that PR or sales promotion or direct? Well, it's all of them.

It's marketing communication.

Shift in Strategic Planning.
This multi-discipline approach is one reason why strategic marketing communication planning has moved from ad agencies to marketing departments (cost is another).

Marketers are now reluctant to delegate overall responsibility for integrating communications to agencies, unless the agency has demonstrated both objectivity and a wide range of marketing capabilities.

When that can be accomplished, then *everything* builds brand value.

P&G Drives Sales with NASCAR.

Programs like this help P&G connect with both consumers and the trade.

Warm hearts without stretching budgets.

The simple, wholesome and wallet-friendly meal your family will love.

A Simple Tie-in.

As simple as tomato soup and toasted cheese sandwiches.

Here, Campbell's Soup and Kraft cheese slices share the cost of a coupon ad to promote these two lunchtime favorites.

Cooking up Extra Sales.

This Pillsbury Bake-Off promotion is delivered in an FSI as well as the package. It combines a contest, a premium (the cookbook), cents-off coupons, and tie-ins with other brands and a TV network.

And today, with more marketing communications options than ever, becoming familiar with every dimension of marketing communications is more important than ever.

First, let's take a look at various types of sales promotion.

Consumer Promotions.

First, let's look at the type of promotion you're most familiar with – those aimed at you as a consumer.

These include: coupons, contests, sweepstakes, cents-off, premiums, rebates, sampling, and tie-ins.

Reviewing these basic techniques is a good way to introduce yourself to the field. Then, see if you can identify them next time you go shopping or page through your local newspaper.

Coupons.

These are the most popular consumer sales promotion techniques among marketers. In 2007, it was a $7 billion business.

Usage is still strong, although growth of couponing peaked several years ago, and redemption rates have fallen off.

Free-Standing Inserts.

Free-standing inserts (FSIs) are preprinted pages of coupon ads most often found in your paper's Sunday edition.

Although they appear in your local newspaper, they are prepared well in advance and printed elsewhere by companies that specialize in preparing them. The two major FSI suppliers are Valassis and News America Marketing.

Other Ways Coupons Are Distributed.

Coupon ads appear on the pages of newspapers or magazines; they're sent directly to consumers via direct mail; coupons are placed in or on the package; and they can be distributed electronically at point-of-sale (e.g., cash register receipts).

Wired & Wireless Coupons.

With 200 million cell phone users, this is becoming a popular way to distribute coupons to people who request them.

You can also download and print coupons from manufacturer and retailer Web sites.

Contests, Sweepstakes, and Games.

Though they seem similar, they differ in important ways. There are legal issues involved, and mistakes can lead to severe penalties.

All can be solid performers.

Contests.

Contests require some skill (usually, not much).

Or, like The Pillsbury Bake-Off, they may require a lot.

Sweepstakes.

Sweepstakes, such as a simple drawing, are relatively inexpensive to administrate and are particularly good for large, national campaigns such as the perennial *Publisher's Clearinghouse* and *Reader's Digest* sweepstakes.

A sweepstakes is strictly based on luck. It cannot require a purchase to enter or it becomes a lottery and that's illegal – unless you're a state lottery.

Games.

These also are based on luck.

They are more involving than sweepstakes because they ask you to do something – scratch off, collect pieces, or enter a code online. They often require repeat visits to the retail outlet for game pieces.

That's why games are used as a continuity device.

Cents-Off Promotions.

These are perhaps the easiest to implement.

The marketer or retailer can implement this promotion quickly, without a great deal of planning required.

Premiums.

A premium is any additional item given free, or greatly discounted, to induce purchase of the primary brand by adding value to the overall purchase.

Premiums are effective at increasing sales, but they can also be used to enhance the brand image if the premium itself conveys the quality of the brand.

In-pack, On-pack, Near-pack.

Premiums can be offered **in-pack, on-pack** (attached to), or you can simply use the package as the premium (e.g., Planters Peanuts in a glass decanter).

In some cases, the premium is nearby.

This is a **near-pack.**

Self-liquidating Premiums.

A **self-liquidating premium** usually offers consumers a high quality product at a greatly discounted rate.

The marketer buys premium items in volume and passes the savings on to customers. The dispenser for M&Ms not only builds the brand, it encourages increased consumption.

A cosmetics company, like Lancome, for example, will offer customers who make a minimum purchase the opportunity to buy a travel case for $20 (marketer's cost) that retails for $40.

Marketers, retailers, and consumers all win in this type of promotion: the marketer makes the sale, providing the premium at no (or little) cost; the retailer makes the sale; and the consumer gets a quality product at a significant discount.

Premiums Can Also Enhance Brand Image.

Think of a Happy Meal or the glasses sold at McDonald's as a tie-in to a movie. They contribute to the film's exposure and remind people about their brands long after the visit.

Campbell's also does an excellent job in this area – everything from cookbooks and soup mugs to Christmas ornaments and refrigerator magnets, featuring *The Campbell's Kids.*

Packaging a Promotion.

Depending on how you slice it, your product's package can often be used as a vehicle to deliver a promotion – an incentive to purchase.

Here, the wrapper on a loaf of bread publicizes a Back to School Promotion.

A Self-Liquidating Premium.

M&Ms has built terrific equity in their "M" characters. Now, they can even charge for items that appeal to their heavy users and increase usage to boot.

Premiums.

Campbell's makes its brand part of the American kitchen with soup mugs and cookbooks.

Sampling by Coupon.

Here, a FREE TRIAL SIZE coupon delivers the sampling opportunity. It features the free trial-size in-store display, and the coupon can be used for either the trial size or for 50¢ off on a larger size.

Sampling.

This is the most powerful, and usually the most expensive, promotion.

If the product has a clear and easily demonstrable superiority to competing products, sampling is worth the considerable expense.

A great-tasting new soft drink or a new soap that smells great and leaves skin feeling clean is ideal for sampling. A paint that lasts for 30 years is not.

Distributing Samples.

Samples can be distributed a number of ways:

• door-to-door, a very expensive method;

• in-person in-store, also expensive;

• free with a coupon in the store, expensive;

• delivered via mail, also expensive;

• in a package delivered with your newspaper;

• by mobile sampling, where a marketer sends a vehicle to shopping centers, etc.; and

• for a minimal cost, a coupon redeemable for a free sample can be distributed. This method not only defrays the sampling expense, it can help qualify prospects and limit those who are not potential customers.

Rebates.

These are cash refunds for purchase.

Rebates raise some ethical questions.

On larger rebates, automobiles, for example, it is difficult to tell if the price is not added in elsewhere in the complex purchase or financing contract.

On smaller rebates, a large number of rebates go uncollected because of the hassle of filling out the form and mailing it in with proofs of purchase and receipts.

Some retailers nonetheless advertise the lowest possible price (after rebate) in large letters and sell the product knowing most people will not bother to collect the rebate.

Continuity Programs.

Trading stamps are an almost vanishing, continuity promotion. This is due to the inconvenience of collecting and pasting hundreds or thousands of stamps to earn relatively inexpensive premiums.

But other types of continuity programs are with us.

Programs by Local Retailers.

Continuity programs for local services often feature a free product (sub, coffee, bagel) or service (car wash, haircut) after nine or ten have been purchased and a card stamped. This encourages repeat business and builds customer relationships.

Now many supermarkets are developing "preferred customer" programs that will deliver discounts and added value as part of their incentive package.

Programs by Major Marketers.

Marketers, such as Marlboro and Pepsi, have developed continuity programs with branded items – some with great success.

Drink Pepsi – Get Stuff is a fairly recent example.

And, of course, frequent flier miles are now a part of almost all airline marketing, with many other marketers tagging along by offering free miles on a whole range of purchases.

Another form of the loyalty program is the "clipless coupon." Many grocery stores are now using "clipless coupons." The customer carries a membership card, swipes it at checkout, and automatically gets any applicable discounts.

This system removes much of the inconvenience of clipping and carrying coupons. It also creates a terrific *database* for the stores as it relates the entire purchase to the individual customer. The database becomes the basis for a good long-term relationship with customers.

Stores using databases can identify their best customers and their pattern of purchases, then reward those customers with special coupons tailored to their buying patterns.

Trade Promotions.

These promotions, invisible to the consumer, may typically account for a greater share of a marketer's promotional budget than advertising expenditure or consumer promotions.

They include contests, deals, point-of-sale displays, push money (also called **spiffs**), display allowances, and cooperative advertising, or simply "co-op."

Dealer Contests.

Here's an excellent way to make sure the message gets through.

An airline, for example, might promote a new route by running a contest for all travel agents, requiring them to write down key information on the new route as their "entry."

With a nice prize, like a two-week vacation for two, response rates will be high and the filled-out contest submission is proof that the message got through.

Merchandising the Advertising.

Telling your wholesalers, distributors, and retailers about your advertising and promotion plans is called merchandising the advertising (or promoting the promotion).

Once it was a powerful inducement for retailers to stock up and push your brand, because they knew your pull campaign would generate some traffic.

Now deals are so common that they're usually regarded as business as usual.

Today, when a salesperson calls on a busy retailer or wholesaler the first question might be simply, "what's the deal?"

Rebates.

Save 50¢ Now. Save $1.50 Later. Well, maybe that's what happens. Rebates often go uncollected.

Continuity and Premiums.

They combine in this frequency program for Pepsi Cola.

Below, an Early Kellogg's Trade Ad.

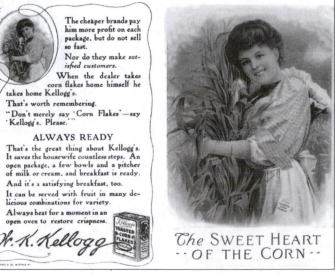

Bill Rosen's Career Path.

After graduating Phi Beta Kappa with a degree in Philosophy, Bill Rosen took a job at a not-for-profit managing and marketing programs for teenagers… teaching him how to connect with this fickle audience.

He then moved to a small Chicago-area consulting firm. "I learned how to create work that drives measurable action," he remembers.

"I also learned the importance of being able to clearly express my ideas and connect them to the strategy."

First Time at Frankel.

He then moved to Frankel, a big promotional agency, as a Senior Copywriter. He was soon put in charge of concepting and executing the national and local promotions for McDonald's, their largest account.

He recalls, "I really earned my promotional chops on local store marketing, where the ability to creatively leverage minimal budgets and assets were the keys to success."

A Breakthrough with Batman.

By applying those skills to national promotions, Rosen broke new ground, particularly with a *Batman Returns* tie-in. "We concepted a premium – one of the Batmobile's weapons – and managed to place it into the film."

His team also designed and executed collectable packaging (another first), all retail communications, including the first life-size Batman standee (many were stolen), and exterior banners that had characters from the movie descending on McDonald's.

A Promotional Promotion.

Rosen was then promoted to creative director on all of McDonald's adult national promotions and new product launches. He also established Frankel's Retail Design group, which included store design, store-within-a-store executions, mobile units, and dimensional design.

"It was a way to not only own the core creative idea, but to bring it to life at retail in a best-in-class way."

After being named Vice President, Group Creative Director, Rosen led the pitch that won GM business.

(Continued on next page)

A **deal** is usually a straight price discount offered to a whole-saler/distributor or retailer on a particular brand to help push it through the channel.

The trade deal is often a big part of the marketing budget — sometimes more than advertising. Deals may come in the form of **allowances.**

Spiffs.

This is an incentive from the marketer to encourage a retail sales-person to push the marketer's brand.

"Spiffs" are common in product categories where consumers ask for recommendations, such as cameras, audio and video equipment, cosmetics, etc. And they could be anything from the product itself to concert tickets to cash.

If there's a sales force involved, there's usually a spiff.

From Point-of-Sale…

Displays, often at the ends of aisles ("end-caps"), are provided by the marketers to the retailers.

Done correctly, displays can significantly enhance sales; however, if not merchandised to the retailer, many will go unused and this can represent a significant waste of promotional dollars.

Retailers guard their space jealously and will use only those displays that help them move product off the shelves.

Good displays usually offer a good deal to consumers. They may also have moving parts or other attention-getting devices.

Two Promotional Twists.

Promotions need a theme and a graphic device. Here, Snapple and Smirnoff Citrus Twist use similar themes. Unlike ad campaigns, promotional themes can come and go in 90 days or less.

End Cap with a Cap.

This end aisle display, an end cap – with Mickey Mouse ears on top – will get noticed and, hopefully, give sales a boost. It better. Because you have to pay extra to get this valuable display position.

...to In-Store Marketing.

With the fragmentation of media, retailers have realized the power they hold for creating exposure to brands.

Think of it this way: the highest rated show in 2008, *American Idol*, drew approximately 33 million viewers a week, while Wal-Mart draws roughly 100 million people a week in the US (170 million worldwide). This makes Wal-Mart the number one place for product exposure and awareness.

Other retailers realize this as well, and a new discipline was born – **in-store marketing**. With it, researchers look at consumer behavior in retail environments and the store itself as a medium. Floor graphics, in-store radio, and in-store TV are just a few of the many options that can be bought.

Product packaging is now thought of as billboards. The only difference – you can create awareness of a product among your target and get them to take it home in one step. In fact, approximately 70% of all purchase decisions are made in-store.

Co-op Advertising Programs.

In cooperative advertising programs (co-op), marketers pay a good percentage, often 50% or more, of the cost the retailer spends on advertising, provided the marketer's brand is featured prominently in the ads.

The rules vary by marketer, but usually the marketer will provide **ad slicks** (glossy product shots and suggested copy) and require a certain minimum percentage of the retailer's ad be devoted to the marketer's product. They usually require that no competitor's product be shown in the same ad.

A classic co-op campaign is still running in the media today.

It was a breakthrough campaign that crossed over the business-to-business/consumer barrier – Intel Inside!

Example: *Intel Inside*.

This brilliant branding campaign brought a pull strategy to a brand that isn't even sold to the average consumer.

That is, you can't go out and buy an Intel. (Well, you can, here in Silicon Valley, but you have to know an awful lot to be able to put it together and use it.)

Intel has people asking for computers of *any* brand *as long as they have the Intel processor inside*.

With this campaign, using the *"Intel Inside"* button on all packaging, in its own ads, and in the ads of any marketer using any Intel processor, Intel has become one of the most recognizable brands in the world.

In a complex formula based on processors sold, Intel pays for a percentage of the ad if the marketer uses the "button."

Bill Rosen (Cont.)

His team developed the idea of utilizing OnStar as a concierge service to build brand loyalty.

Consultant.

In 1997, realizing the power of truly integrated promotional ideas, Rosen launched a creative consulting firm – Integral Marketing and Creative.

The agency quickly grew. Client work included Nike, Anheuser-Busch, and Pepsi. But, in 2002, he had an opportunity he couldn't pass up.

Return to Frankel.

Rosen returned to Frankel as Chief Creative Officer (CCO), helping oversee its merger with other Publicis divisions to form Arc Worldwide. He was named North American CCO.

He led the development of four key marketing disciplines: promotion, direct, interactive, and retail.

These disciplines, working together, resulted in Arc Worldwide winning many blue-chip accounts, including Blackberry, Coca-Cola, Comcast, Miller, and P&G.

In a few pages we'll tell you about Rosen's and Arc's award-winning "Yellowball" campaign.

He's still creating dramatic stories, but they're playing on a bigger stage.

Draft's Choices.

Right out of Ripon College, Howard Draft became one of the first employees at direct marketer Stone & Adler.

He was an assistant AE on Hallmark and Illinois Bell – the first step on a journey that reflects the changing face of the overall marketing communication industry.

"This Is a Business."

Howard saw how direct marketing could deliver results. He says, "I realized, 'This is a business.'"

And he was good at it.

The company, now Kobs & Brady, sent Howard to open the New York office. He landed a new account few had heard of: HBO.

The First Buy-Out.

In 1986, Howard was named President and the agency was purchased by Ted Bates – then Bates was purchased by Saatchi.

He became Chairman/CEO of what was now Kobs & Draft.

When Saatchi ran into financial problems, he bought his company back.

Independent Growth.

Howard rode the growth in direct. He says, "Look for a business where the wind is at your back. Where all the trends are working for you."

Those trends were:

• more women now in the workplace (less time to shop);

• the increase in credit cards (easier to order).

(Continued on next page)

2. Direct Marketing.

WHILE THE DEFINITION OF DIRECT MARKETING (also called "direct response" or "database marketing") has broadened in recent years, the difference that has traditionally distinguished it from other forms of selling is that the final sale takes place without a retailer – *the customer orders directly from the marketer.*

As you might imagine, the Media Revolution has made this as easy as a mouse click.

An Ongoing Dialogue.

But what makes today's direct marketing programs really work is when they establish an ongoing dialogue with their customers to bring about more purchases and long-term loyalty.

This is Lifetime Value (LTV). You'll notice that there are a lot of acronyms in direct.

Direct marketing has its roots in mail-order companies and catalog marketers. While some companies continue to do their business in these traditional channels (think of some of the catalog marketers), direct marketing has become more than just a way of selling and, at almost every stage, the Media Revolution has powered exciting new approaches.

A Range of Promotional Tools.

Direct marketing, whether carried out by the direct marketing department of a company, an ad agency, or an independent direct marketing company, typically includes these services:

• **Direct Mail** – both electronic and "snail" mail.
• **Direct Response Television (DRTV)**
• **Telemarketing** (telephone marketing programs)
• **Database Services** – list management, lead-tracking, list and database maintenance, affinity marketing.
• **Interactive Marketing** – this can include everything from Web site development and e-commerce to viral videos.
• **Customer Relationship Marketing (CRM)**
• **Other Related Services** – for example, fulfillment.

Understanding Terms.

Sometimes direct marketing is thought to be synonymous with direct mail. But, as you can see, it involves much more.

Perhaps the easiest way to understand the difference is to remember that in direct marketing, merchandise can be featured in a variety of media – direct mail, print media, TV, radio, online advertising, and e-mail. The key is the *direct* order.

An Evolution to Relationship Marketing.

One more aspect is an evolution from getting the initial sale to building the relationship – **relationship marketing**. The result is more sales, but the focus is on the relationship – not just the sale. LTV=Lifetime Value.

For this reason, the communications should concern itself with more than merely selling merchandise.

For example, Similac's Strong Moms Club provides new mothers with a wide range of information related to their baby.

Certainly there are Similac savings (they use checks – quicker and easier to track), but the majority of the content of the best club mailings is useful information for mothers. In fact, there is some difference in content for mothers who currently nurse and those who use formula – since it's a different relationship.

Reasons for Growth.

A number of factors have sparked direct marketing's growth:

- **Changing consumer lifestyles.** The rise in dual-income, single-parent, and single-person households has increased the need for convenience.
- **More ubiquitous consumer credit.** Today's consumers are comfortable with credit card shopping, which has further contributed to the rise of direct marketing.
- **More and better lists.** Technology is more cost-effective. The information revolution has delivered many benefits. Because it's still true, "you're as good as your list."
- **Easier communication.** Beginning with 800 numbers, now direct marketing can take advantage of an ever-growing range of ways to connect and communicate. The Internet and e-mail are just the latest factors to power that growth.

Two Other Factors.

Besides consumer lifestyle changes, two other factors have helped trigger the growth of direct marketing.

- **Media fragmentation.** Whether print or broadcast, there exist today highly specialized vehicles that allow marketers   to reach people with very specific interests.
- **An increased valuation of current customers.** The increasing sophistication of computer-based information technology has helped reveal and reinforce an old truth of business – the value of current customers. LTV, remember?

Today, many marketers are able to maintain their best customers through databases that tell more about customers and predict their future buying behavior better than ever before.

And, of course, communicating through e-mail can make activities both more cost-effective and interactive. Now it's easier for consumers to tell us about themselves.

The Growth of Relationship Marketing.

Today, virtually all marketers are doing something based on the value of their current customers, and the Media Revolution has its impact here as well.

Direct marketing techniques are at the core of most relationship marketing programs. Combined with interactive platforms, you get a powerful result. For example, you've probably received a suggestion from Amazon.com based on previous purchases.

Draft (Cont.)

These trends turned direct response into a whole new kind of industry.

Draft developed expertise in direct response broadcast for companies like AmEx and GM.

It wasn't just running the commercials, it was measuring the lead-generating effectiveness of different media – and looking for new windows of opportunity.

International Growth & IPG. As is true in many marketing areas, US expertise leads the way. Howard became a partner with emerging direct marketing firms around the globe.

Soon, his agency came to the attention of Interpublic (IPG). It was "an offer too good to refuse."

Promotional & Event Marketing. While general agencies were moving into direct and sales promotion, Howard saw a strategic opportunity to grow from the other direction.

Working with IPG, he acquired capabilities in promotional, event, digital, and retail marketing as well as in general advertising.

Draft became a leader in "below the line" services – direct marketing and sales promotion.

His client roster grew to include British Airways, Kellogg's, Sprint, and the US Postal Service.

The New Day in Advertising. Then IPG ran into tough financial times. They needed to save cash and consolidate some of their agencies.

Meanwhile, Draft needed to open additional offices worldwide.

Howard was put in charge of a newly merged agency – Draft/FCB.

How did the two compare?

FCB was 133 years old, the world's third oldest ad agency (the successor agency to Lasker's Lord & Thomas), with approximately 6000 staffers. Draft had around 3000.

FCB had offices in 110 countries. Draft was in 24.

In 2006, the two agencies merged. Draft got top billing.

(Continued on next page)

Draft (Cont.)

In many ways, this merger can serve as a metaphor for the state of the entire industry – where the new is more valued than the old and where the promise of innovation is more important than tradition.

Lessons from the Merger.
This merger underscores the key trends within the advertising industry.

Clients are now demanding greater accountability, something both direct and promotional marketing firms are able to provide.

Media consumption is fragmenting. Marketers are recognizing that big television or print campaigns do not always provide a satisfactory return on investment. They're looking for more effective approaches.

A New Business Model.
You can see the results of these trends in how DraftFCB describes itself. Here's an except from their Web site:

"Being media-, discipline-, and channel-agnostic, DraftFCB recommends whatever mix of marketing communications options are best for building its clients' businesses – ranging from branding, advertising, direct and relationship marketing, promotions, retail, digital, search, sponsorship, and media – with a disciplined, relentless focus on creativity, accountability and metrics."

The Wind at Your Back.
Here's Howard's advice for those starting out. "Look for a business where the wind is at your back, where all the trends are working for you."

Today, DraftFCB has annual revenues near a billion dollars. Clients include Kraft, Dockers, Brown-Foreman, Coors, GM, Motorola, and HP. The agency seems to have the wind at their back.

What can you do to get going in the right direction?

Following his advice and catching the right trends in the fast-changing world of marketing communications might be your best first step.

One Thing in Common. Three Big Differences.

These different services all have one thing in common – they're targeted. They're aimed at very specific groups of people.

This direct target is not only smaller than a packaged goods target, it's much more defined.

There are three other differences worth noting:

- **Measurable payout.** You can tell quickly if direct marketing is working. You test and measure. Measure and test.
- **More expense.** On a per-person basis, direct marketing is much more expensive. Instead of **cost per thousand (CPM)**, it's **cost per inquiry (CPI)** or **cost per order (CPO)**.
- **The relationship begins with the first sale.** While ads also reinforce the feelings of existing customers, they tend to treat everyone as a potential customer. The database update that occurs when a customer makes a purchase from a sophisticated direct marketer begins a relationship – customers who spend a lot are offered many more perks and opportunities than those who spend a little.

Importance of the List.

Most critical to direct marketing success is list quality.

There are two main types of lists: internal and external.

- **Internal lists** are compiled by the organization itself – records of customers, donors, subscribers, inquirers, etc.
- **External lists** are rented or purchased from outside organizations, either **list brokers** or **list compilers.**

List brokers find sources of lists that match up with the marketer's needs and expedite one-time rentals or exchanges with list owners.

List compilers provide lists of people who have one or more things in common (profession, zip code, income range, etc. and sell that information to marketers.

Many external lists come from public records, e.g., car registrations. Others come from an individual's memberships, subscriptions, charge accounts, etc.

Keep in mind that, for marketers, lists represent not only a source of prospects, but also an additional source of income.

There's money to be made renting their own customer lists.

That's one reason you may be deluged with mailings soon after your name has been added to a new mailing list.

A golf enthusiast who has just started subscribing to a major golf magazine may soon be receiving mailings from golf resorts, golf equipment manufacturers, and even other golf magazines. And, if the e-mail address was part of that information, the golf enthusiast's inbox starts filling up as well.

List Enhancement and Merge/Purge.

List enhancement refers to the process of constantly improving mailings lists. One type of list enhancement activity is compiling additional information for an existing mailing list.

Here, data from a second list is incorporated into an existing list to provide a marketer with added information about people on his prospect or customer list.

Typically, this information might provide additional details about demographics, geodemographics (e.g., characteristics of the neighborhood they live in), and past purchasing behavior.

Another enhancement activity is "cleaning the list," the so-called **merge/purge** process of eliminating duplicate listings of names found on consolidated lists.

One Firm or Many. Contractors and Brokers.

One firm may offer all these services, or they may be contracted out. Some firms may do the list brokerage, others may do direct mail creative and list management.

Still another may provide **letter-shop** services, coordinating the addresses and mailing of promotional pieces.

Others Perform Database-Related Services.

While some ad agencies offer direct marketing services to clients, the majority subcontract to specialists. Let's see what they do.

Direct Mail.

This is any message sent directly to prospects by a marketer or other organization seeking to sell a product or gain support. It may be snail mail or e-mail.

In some cases, the mailing asks consumers to order the product or service advertised. Some ask for donations. Others urge a store visit. Often, there is some incentive involved.

In some, the mailing asks prospects to request additional information or to provide feedback. In others, it asks them to vote for a candidate or give to a cause.

The advantage of direct mail is it allows a marketer to send a personalized message to an already highly targeted audience – perfect for products or services that appeal to only a small group.

So, while the cost of sending out each message may be higher than mass media advertising on a per-capita basis, there's less waste in reaching prospects and more time to communicate in depth.

The lower cost of an e-mail is both good news and bad news. For the legitimate direct marketer, lower costs are a benefit. However, since it's so easy to enter this arena, the huge amount of spam and scams has drastically lowered the quality of that environment.

Direct Response Television (DRTV).

Certain kinds of businesses have found direct response television to be an effective way to advertise their products.

Most fall into the categories of health and beauty products, household appliances, financial products and services, self-help products, and music.

Most also lend themselves to demonstrations and testimonials, are not easily sold at traditional retail outlets, and have relatively high profit margins.

The New Triple Play.

The Internet, Direct Marketing, and Promotion are teaming up for a powerful marketing combination.

First, the Internet, often with some sort of traffic-driving incentive, collects the contact information – usually the name and e-mail address.

Then, direct marketing goes to work. Using the database generated by the initial effort, a combination of promotional offers and direct marketing techniques work together to develop and convert inquiries into customers.

Sometimes direct mail is also used. For example, a quarterly catalog may be mailed along with weekly e-mail offers.

As the information on customers accumulates, marketers can target and test e-mail offers with increasing accuracy and a relatively low cost per inquiry – compared to traditional direct mail costs.

As these three forces interact, programs can grow economically and become more effective.

It's one more example of how the Media Revolution is having an impact on virtually every aspect of the marketing mix.

"If direct is the future of advertising, certainly interactive is the future of direct."
— Steve Hayden
Vice Chairman,
Ogilvy Worldwide

Direct Mail Technology.

The direct marketing industry has always been at the cutting edge of database technology. Today, that technology can be on almost everyone's desktop.

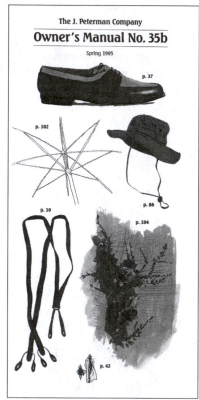

Direct Mail Tactics.

The copywriter who wrote the copy for the Peterman catalog not only made a lot of money, his client became something of a celebrity when he was portrayed by an actor on *Seinfeld*!

While some past products, like kitchen gadgets, featured in direct response TV commercials may have seemed bizarre, today we find many mainstream companies using such spots.

The traditional two-minute, direct-response commercial is still around, but it's difficult to convey both a sales message and ordering instructions in such a short time unit.

Infomercials.

As a result, some advertisers who use direct-response TV have gone to the 30-minute infomercial.

Most of these "programs" are essentially three 10-minute segments, each with its own "call to action" since few people will watch the entire 30-minutes.

One of the reasons infomercials have become a major advertising method is the extraordinary audience segmentation provided by cable television.

Advertisers can easily seek out niche markets on cable channels whose programming appeals to those markets' interests.

What better vehicle to promote a CD of a country star's greatest hits than *Country Music Television?* Where better to promote a *Sports Illustrated* subscription than *ESPN?*

And, since results are measured, you may find some you don't expect. Who would guess that beach volleyball on *ESPN2* would be a high performer for hearing aids? It was.

Better production values, use of infomercials by well-known companies, celebrity spokespersons, and the fact that consumers' purchases are protected through their credit cards are other reasons why infomercials have prospered.

Video Direct Mail = V Mail.

V-mail – either on DVD or CD-ROM – offers marketers another way to demonstrate their product visually. Web-based video is another option – as more and more consumers have broadband that allows for reasonable quality video. This, plus the lowering of video production costs (again, Moore's Law at work), means more video of all kinds as part of direct marketing.

With DVD penetration nearing 85% of US homes and the use of personal computers now almost universal, this method of promotion provides marketers a format with the combined strengths of mail and TV/VCR viewing: the ability to selectively reach a group of consumers with a powerful video message that can be viewed at a time that's convenient for the consumer.

Up-Selling.

While inbound calls deal more with taking orders and responding to inquiries, most marketers try to use that moment of contact to sell additional merchandise. As IBM said, *"every problem is an opportunity to demonstrate service."*

When a customer places an order for one product, the operator might ask whether they have interest in purchasing a related product.

This technique is called **up-selling.**

For example, if a parent is ordering a new robe for a son or daughter, the operator might ask if they need new slippers or pajamas.

Consumer Complaints about Direct Marketing.

The direct marketing industry faces serious issues and consumer complaints about privacy and fraud.

- Some people simply do not want to receive direct-mail pieces or telemarketing calls, regarding them as both an annoyance and an invasion of their privacy.
- Many are concerned about the amount of unsolicited "spam" e-mail that appears in their in-boxes.
- Others are uneasy about the information that is gathered about them and their behavior.
- Finally, a few are concerned about the unscrupulous practices of a few telemarketers, e.g., phony contests and investment scams targeted particularly at older citizens.

This has led to the following actions.

DMA List Removal.

Both industry and government have addressed these issues.

To give consumers the privacy they want, the Direct Marketing Association (DMA) allows people to have their names removed from all DMA member organization lists.

The FTC and Telemarketing Fraud.

Additionally, the FTC, in an attempt to reduce telemarketing fraud and abuse, has been enforcing a set of telemarketing guidelines passed by Congress in 1994.

Included in those guidelines are rules that:
- prohibit calls before 8 a.m. and after 9 p.m.;
- require prompt identification of the seller or organization;
- require full disclosure that the call is a sales call or a charitable solicitation before "making their pitch;"
- require telemarketers to disclose all material information about goods or services offered and terms of sale; and
- prohibit telemarketers from lying about any terms of their offer.

The National Do Not Call Registry.

Finally, the Do Not Call Implementation Act was signed in 2003, supporting the FTC's decision to establish the National Do Not Call Registry.

Beginning September 2, 2003, telemarketers were required to scrub lists of those who requested that telemarketers do not call.

In just the first few months, 55 million Americans registered.

And, despite appeals by the telemarketing industry, the constitutionality of this legislation has been held up in court.

The CAN-SPAM Act (Controlling the Assault of Non-Solicited Pornography and Marketing Act) went into effect on January 1, 2004. It establishes requirements for those who send commercial e-mail, spells out penalties for spammers and companies whose products are advertised in spam if they violate the law, and gives consumers the right to ask e-mailers to stop spamming them.

Telemarketing.

Telemarketing is the selling of products or services through telephone contact with the consumer.

Many telemarketing activities – especially inbound telemarketing communication – are closely tied to other marketing programs.

For example, Sprint realized they were spending lots of money getting new customers, but they were losing existing ones, because this key part of customer retention was not getting marketing attention.

Their marketers realized that they needed to upgrade this service.

Nearly all national firms engage in some type of telemarketing – from selling products to answering complaints or inquiries.

Whether it's another bank trying to get you to use their card or your own bank trying to get you to use another financial service, telemarketing is used to attract new customers *and* increase purchases among current ones.

Outbound vs. Inbound.

- **Outbound Telemarketing** refers to calls a marketer makes to sell its products or services. It may involve calls to prospective customers (asking about refinancing) or to existing customers (asking subscribers to renew early).

This part of the industry has had to deal with new limits due to the Do Not Call Registry, but telemarketing has always been creative in working around these limits.

For example, while working on this new edition, I received a call – even though I'm on the Do Not Call list. I'm pretty sure it was from India.

- **Inbound Telemarketing** usually refers to the "order-taking" operation of direct marketing.

Inbound calls also serve to maintain relationships with customers who may have questions or need service.

Some marketers encourage calls asking for catalogs or dealer locations.

It's one more dimension that needs to be integrated into a brand's plan.

Marketing is everything.

That includes telemarketing.

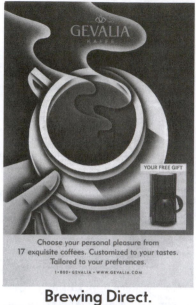

Brewing Direct.

Gevalia works to build a relationship with coffee drinkers.

What's your LTV in coffee? Let's try one year – take a typical week and multiply by 52.

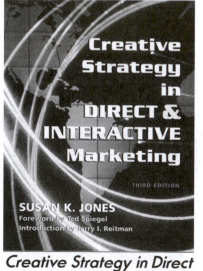

Creative Strategy in Direct & Interactive Marketing.

Third Edition, by Susan K. Jones.

Your chapter author is also the author of an outstanding book on direct marketing. Here's a review excerpt from Amazon.

"From the day I received "Direct & Interactive Marketing" my business has increased. This book has crystallized my thoughts and given me the grass root facts on the total marketing mix. My database for target markets is now complete and working like a dream."

Database Marketing.

Database marketing services range from the mundane to the advanced: from simple list maintenance to cross-selling programs that match demographic characteristics of two seemingly disparate groups in order to facilitate "mining" for prospects.

Typically, services include:
- **List Management**
- **Lead-Tracking**
- **List and Database Maintenance**
- **Affinity Marketing**

Setting up and maintaining a sophisticated relational database – one that contains properly set up customer information files and is useful for tracking customer histories and generating true marketing intelligence – requires a great deal of skill from both the technical and marketing people involved.

Relationship Marketing.

Relationship marketing is not database marketing, but it usually requires a solid database to be implemented.

Smart companies have always done relationship marketing: it consists of anticipating and meeting customers' needs in order to increase your business with them and realize their full **Lifetime Value (LTV)** – the estimated long-term revenue that can be expected from a particular customer.

LTV = Lifetime Value.

This concept asks a big question: "What is a customer worth to a company over the lifetime of that relationship?"

Whether it's automobiles or hamburgers, it's a lot. That's why every marketer is placing more value on relationships.

The LTV concept simply acknowledges that a customer will buy 10 or 12 automobiles, for example, in a lifetime.

Realizing this, marketers try to capture all those sales, not just one, by maintaining a strong relationship with that customer.

This relationship may work at more than one level:
- For GM, the customer is both the car buyer and dealer.
- For the dealer, the customer is the final consumer.

LTV is a strategic way of looking at the long-term value of a single customer, rather than the more common, tactical viewpoint of merely making the immediate one-time sale.

Good Examples.

Seabourn Cruise Lines maintains an almost unbelievable relationship with its clients.

For second-time clients, the upscale cruise line (average sale above $22,000) knows the type of pillow desired, the correct size of bed, and flowers, beverages, and foods favored for the cabin.

Land's End tracks who buys children's apparel and who buys bed linens. Subsequent catalog mailings are targeted to those who have purchased in that respective category.

3. Public Relations.

PUBLIC RELATIONS (PR) IS a very broad term that describes communicating – or "relating" – to the public.

PR's primary objectives are to generate *awareness* and to *influence* or *persuade* a defined audience or market to support a particular choice or point-of-view.

The PR department or agency's job is to present the client's story in a positive, persuasive way. It doesn't matter if the assignment is publicizing a brand, managing an announcement, writing a speech, or lobbying, that part of the job stays the same. The practitioner, whether new to the job or a seasoned pro, must learn all he or she can about the subject-company, organization, product, service, person, or brand.

Advertising vs. Public Relations.

For decades, many public relations pros have had a rivalry with ad agencies over which is more effective and provides the most bang for the marketing buck, particularly regarding brands.

Al Ries, one of the authors of *Positioning*, has (with his daughter Laura) made some interesting assertions in *The Fall of Advertising, the Rise of PR*. We cover his book in the sidebar.

The real point is that, in general, you want both.

You want good advertising *and* good PR.

Each has its advantages. Advertising allows you to have total control of the message, what it is, where it appears, how often, and in what form – funny, colorful, dramatic, or otherwise memorable enough to create national catchphrases.

PR costs a lot less than advertising and carries the added value of the implied credibility of the powerful media that chooses to present your story. But, of course, the marketer has no control over the content, tone, timing, length, or even whether the story ultimately leaves a positive or a negative impression of the subject.

Frequency is up to the PR professional's ability to merchandise a story once it runs – assuming it's favorable.

The best choice is usually an integrated marketing approach which can normally be managed to fit any budget.

CPR & MPR – Two Kinds of PR.

Some observe there are two kinds of Public Relations: **Corporate PR**, which focuses on corporate issues, and **Marketing PR**, a process that incorporates and supports marketing efforts.

While we are going to focus on public relations as part of an overall marketing effort, let's first take a quick look at CPR – Corporate Public Relations.

CPR = Corporate Public Relations.

These are the more traditional functions of a PR department.

They differ from MPR functions in that they do not contribute directly to the marketing of products, but rather have an effect on the overall image of the company and its reputation.

The Rise of PR?

According to this influential book, Al Ries and Laura Ries think we need to re-examine the roles of advertising and PR. It's very provocative.

Whether you're a PR major, an ad major, or think that maybe there's a way to do both, read this book.

Here are a few of the main points:

Credibility.

PR has credibility.

Advertising does not.

Advertising is the seller's voice.

PR has the power of third-party endorsement.

Two Major Functions.

Creating a brand and defending a brand are the two major functions of a marketing program.

PR builds the brand.

Advertising defends the brand.

The Role of PR.

Try to create the "Rosie Moment," the tipping point that pushes your brand to the top.

Understand the valuable role of the celebrity spokesperson. Products don't create publicity, people do.

The Role of Advertising.

The role is brand maintenance.

Advertising is the cheerleader that repeats what's already in the mind.

In general, clients overspend on advertising and underspend on PR.

The Fall of Advertising & The Rise of PR. by Al Ries and Laura Ries.

A Colorful History.

An early master of publicity and public relations was P.T. Barnum.

Because of questionable publicity techniques, most PR people cringe when Barnum is referred to as a pioneer in the PR field.

But regardless of his methods, he was a master at "press agentry" – getting "news" items into the media.

Promoting his circus, Barnum often staged unusual events, such as the fat lady marrying the thin man.

Bizarre events such as that were certain to generate lively news stories in the local newspaper.

Variations on these techniques are still used today by colorful entrepreneurs such as Richard Branson of Virgin, who will clearly do anything for publicity. Here, he poses with his new book.

Corporate PR people market the company's image and its interests as a brand, just as MPR markets individual products.

In combination, MPR and CPR provide a full and well-defined range of PR activities. We'll briefly cover:

* **Employee Communications**
* **Investor Relations**
* **Government Relations**
* **Crisis Management**
* **Community Relations**
* **Advocacy Advertising**

Each of these activities involves a variety of functions and positions. We'll cover them briefly and then focus on MPR.

Employee Communications.

PR departments often run an employee communications program within an organization.

While some companies assign this to the human resources area, the communications are generally managed by the communicators – the PR people.

Investor Relations (IR).

Sometimes this highly specialized function is assigned to a financial PR firm; sometimes it is handled by in-house staff.

Responsibilities include preparation and dissemination of the annual report, interim reports, and major financial information as it becomes available.

For publicly-held companies, particularly large ones, regular presentation of results to shareholders, the investment community, and the financial press is also a critical task.

Government Relations ("Lobbying").

Sometimes called legislative affairs and more commonly known as "lobbying," this PR function deals with all the levels of government that monitor or regulate relevant industries or organizations.

These specialists ensure that legislators understand the organization's position on current and prospective legislation or regulations.

In addition to making their client's position known, lobbyists can serve as an important information source for legislators.

Since few legislators have the time to read every piece of proposed legislation, they often rely on lobbyists to provide some of the information they need to consider, especially on how proposed legislation might impact their constituents.

Though lobbyists are often criticized and derided as "influence peddlers," most provide legislators and regulators with valuable facts and information.

Crisis Management.

Things happen. No company is immune to crisis. Large organizations often have plans in place to deal with both anticipated and unplanned crises.

Airlines, for example, have established procedures to follow and specific roles for all media contact people in the event of accidents; banks have procedures to implement in response to unforeseen negative news or experiences; chemical and petroleum companies have their own communication plans in place should any environmental or other disaster occur.

Good Example: Tylenol.

A crisis can take many forms. The 1982 product-tampering case that resulted in the deaths of seven consumers who bought Tylenol could have destroyed that brand, but the swift response by Johnson & Johnson reassured the public that this was an isolated situation that had been dealt with quickly. It became a textbook case of excellent crisis management.

Bad Example: Exxon Valdez.

In 1989 an Exxon tanker created an oil spill off the coast of Alaska that became the worst environmental disaster ever. It also became, to date, perhaps the worst example of crisis management, as the oil company's management failed to understand the scope of the problem, delayed its response, and ultimately reacted with a clumsy arrogance that damaged its reputation.

Going Global.

Today, something as seemingly small as a rumor on an Internet blog can keep customers away and put a stock in free-fall. The smallest businesses and the global titans all need to understand that major damage can come from a variety of situations and many directions. Being prepared with a crisis management plan is not only good PR; it could also end up saving a brand or the company itself.

Community Relations.

Large organizations, including corporations, are also "corporate citizens" and often take leadership roles in community activities by contributing to local libraries, underwriting local arts agencies and events, and supporting athletic programs.

Executives from large corporations are often encouraged to serve on local boards and commissions. Employees are encouraged to volunteer for civic programs and events.

Advocacy Advertising.

Sometimes an organization's messages are controversial. The news media will not carry it because they would then be obliged, by fairness, to give an opposing view equal time or space.

In such situations, companies or organizations may buy media space or time and run "advocacy ads" presenting their point-of-view or response to something that has appeared In the media.

These ads are not subject to editorial change.

Opposition organizations are free to buy their own space to refute the position taken by the group that placed the ad.

Exxon/Mobil Oil has done this for years with "op ed" ads placed in or near the editorial pages in major newspapers.

These ads generally present a position of the company on a topic of importance to the industry or the general public.

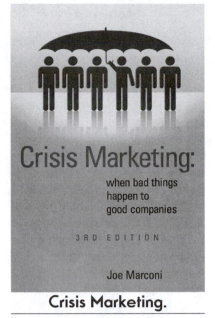

Crisis Marketing.

The definitive book on this topic, *Crisis Marketing: When Bad Things Happen to Good Companies*, was written by chapter co-author Joe Marconi. No business or organization anywhere in the world is immune to crises that have the potential to destroy reputations, careers and brands. This concise, readable guide explains what to do before, during and after the crisis happens.

P&G Evaluates PR.

While everyone acknowledges that good PR adds value, there has long been a concern about how to calculate that value.

P&G developed a program called PREvaluate that combines marketing mix models and measured media impressions.

They studied six brands.

For four of those brands, PR had the highest return on investment of any marketing tool.

For the remaining two brands, it came in second.

Motorola
Advocacy Advertising.

One of the more interesting advocacy projects was done by Y+R. Dennis Altman was the CD.

Japan had a key governmental group called the Ministry of International Trade and Industry (MITI) with a mission to coordinate Japanese incursions into Western markets. It was like a war production board.

Tactics, such as targeting and dumping (selling items below cost to put competitors out of business) are outlawed in world trade agreements. Yet Japanese industry, coordinated by MITI, attacked US electronics, German photography, and British motorcycle industries, establishing a firm foothold in each.

In general, US and European business leaders were unaware of Japanese tactics or that they were legal in Japan.

Tactical Steps.

"The Japan Initiative" resulted in a large-scale information campaign:

- Ads in business publications
- A PR speakers' bureau
- Regular press briefings

This campaign was not designed to "defeat" Japanese companies, but to arm industry leaders with information to compete more effectively.

At the right is one of the ads, "When Japan Waives the Rules, Japan Rules the Waves." There was also press coverage stimulated by the advertising.

The Results.

By the end of the campaign, electronics companies were competing on a "level playing field" in world markets.

Motorola became a key supplier to Japanese companies and was recognized as a world leader in international trade.

Advocacy in Action. Here's one of the ads Dennis Altman created for Motorola and an example of some of the editorial coverage that it helped generate.

Example: Fighting Back in the Media – Motorola.

Here is an example of advocacy advertising for Motorola.

Japanese industry was virtually declaring international war.

Bob Galvin, CEO of Motorola, decided to fight back by going public on the issues. Y&R was hired. They hired Dennis Altman.

MPR Duties and Functions.

Public relations, in the context of marketing and marketing communication, is typically MPR.

More and more, marketers are realizing the value of PR that is part of a marketing program. And, while the term "MPR" is not used everywhere, that is the part that we will focus on for the rest of this section.

The primary areas we will cover are:

- **Planning for MPR:**
- **PR Tactics:**
- **PR Evaluation**
- **IMC, MPR, and The Media Revolution**

PR is handled both by internal staff and by PR firms, usually on a fee basis. The more sophisticated the marketer, the more probable that an external PR firm will be used. In some cases, separate firms are retained for CPR and MPR functions.

MarCom & MPR

The MPR person or agency will likely work under the MarCom (the term some companies use for marketing communications) manager, along with advertising and sales promotion managers and other marketing staff.

Planning for MPR.

It's a structured process, very similar to the one you will see covered in Chapter 8.

Objectives, Strategies, Tactics.

It usually involves a situation analysis, where all aspects of the brand are examined – including, in a general way, the range of PR opportunities.

Then, objectives and strategies are set – sometimes in parallel to other functions like advertising and sales promotion. Sometimes the MarCom disciplines work together under an IMC umbrella.

From there, tactical programs are developed and timelines and budgets are set.

Remember, many PR programs depend on media response. That often means extended lead times.

Unlike advertising, where content and schedules are under the control of the marketer, a PR program has to develop messages that are interesting to the media.

Unlike advertising plans, where budgets insure that messages are in the media, results of the PR plan are less certain. Not every plan, no matter how well thought out, results in PR exposure.

However, when successful, PR can be hugely cost-effective.

MPR Tactics:

This is a fairly lengthy section – but even so, it will only summarize. A book like *Public Relations: The Complete Guide* will cover the topic in more detail.

However, let's take a summary look at the following:

- **Press Kits**
- **Press Releases**
- **Media/Press Tours**
- **Technical Articles**
- **Feature Article Development**
- **Event Management**
- **Product Publicity.**

That final topic, product publicity, is an umbrella for a wide range of activities.

First, let's talk about ways to connect with the working press.

Press Kits.

By themselves, they may just be stacks of fact sheets, photos of key personnel, and a bit of brand history. But when a PR program is up and running, they can be valuable resources. Because they become a valuable information resource about your company.

As you might imagine, more and more are using their Web site to duplicate the basic information provided by a press kit.

"When *Newsweek* Showed up, the Light Bulb Went On."

When Barbara Molotsky graduated from Northwestern with a degree in English literature, she wasn't sure of her career path – so let's follow it.

She started in the promo department of a so-so department store… *"Here comes Helen in a polyester suit, a great buy for Mother's Day at $49.95…"*

Then she got a real PR job – at a hospital – fundraising and answering reporters' calls if the latest ER trauma victim seemed newsworthy.

Chocolate Can Cause Headaches.
Then, she wrote a provocative news release for the hospital's headache seminar. *Newsweek* ran the story. For Barbara, *"The light bulb went on."*

Head to Toe.
With new focus, she went on to do PR at a small ad agency and then to a bigger PR-only agency.

She began doing product publicity on everything from Helene Curtis Hair Care to Dr. Scholl's Foot Care.

She liked it. She then moved on to Chicago's foremost product PR firm.

Three weeks after she joined, they lost the account she was supposed to work on. Careers can be like that.

Talking Turkey.
Barbara connected with Swift Butterball Turkeys. There was a glut of turkeys that Thanksgiving.

Swift was worried. But Barbara and her agency created a hotline for cooks traumatized at cooking turkey.

(Continued on page 347)

Molotsky (Cont.)

Live home economists answered calls. It was a winning program.

Then She Got a Call...

...to work at Hill & Knowlton, the top PR firm in the world. It was great.

Then the top guy left, resulting in an uncertain office situation – careers can be like that.

The Phone Rang Again...

This time, it was for a small 13-person business-to-business PR agency that wanted to grow.

Barbara became President of Bozell/PR (now BSMG/PR) in Chicago.

Ten Years Later...

Chicago's BSMG/PR was a 120-person office.

One of her most visible PR efforts surrounds the "Milk Mustache" for the Fluid Milk Advisory Board.

Barbara gives a lot of the credit to Chuck Peebler, then President of Bozell.

"He insisted 10% of the marketing dollars be focused on PR. Support at the top gave us a seat at the table from the beginning, to leverage PR as part of the overall strategy."

Milk Brand Repositioning.

Milk is a brand. It competes with soft drinks and other beverages. The brand image was – milk is for kids.

The job was *"to reposition milk as a contemporary adult beverage."*

"On a large scale, it's a public education campaign to drive Americans to increase calcium, but it really works on a different level – entertainment.

"Using popular contemporary entertainment figures is a powerful way to endorse the benefits of milk. And, given the inherent news value of the people in our ads, we can leverage that in entertainment-oriented media venues – like Entertainment Tonight, *and print venues like advertising columns."*

BSMG/PR conducts targeted media initiatives that communicate meaningful health benefits to different audiences – from teen girls to adult males.

(Continued on next page)

The term electronic press kit is coming into more common use. It is more easily updated and can be, depending on management's strategy, quite comprehensive and complete, or very narrowly focused.

Press Releases.

This is the PR person's primary tool for communicating news to appropriate consumer and business media, reviewers, editors, radio and TV producers, bloggers, and other centers of influence. Press releases can be about new products and services, changes in features, brand extensions, events, and promotions. They are relatively inexpensive to prepare and distribute.

When written well and managed properly, a press release can be the single most cost-effective communication in the entire spectrum of marketing communications, including advertising.

Unlike advertising, which encourages clever language and dramatic presentation of product benefits, public relations materials have to present a more journalistic approach.

A press release that comes off as too self-serving quickly finds its way into the circular file. Again, effective public relations must be concerned with a story angle that is interesting to the media.

A minor modification in packaging or ingredients does not merit a press release – it just wastes the time of the reporters or editors and makes them wary of future press releases from the sender – even though it may make a great bit of "new and improved" advertising.

Significant product news, on the other hand, or a product's connection with a human interest story, may be of high interest to audiences and, when presented well, offer an extremely cost-effective way of gaining mass visibility awareness.

Wanted: An Objectively Written News Story.

A **press release** is an objectively-written news story about a company or its product. It is written in professional journalistic form and sent to the news media for possible use.

Traditionally, releases are in print form, but electronic versions are e-mailed and posted online routinely.

Video news releases (VNRs) – both in hard copy form and online – are also produced when appropriate.

The primary requirements are that the release effectively present the subject's message and contain something of value for the media and its constituent audience.

Press Release Requirements.

This is worth restating. A press release should be written and presented in professional journalistic style. This means it can be used exactly as written or presented in the publication or blog or on the broadcast outlet to which it was directed.

A press release, posting or VNR should always have contact information. That way, writers, editors, and producers can get more information if they feel it is necessary.

Media/Press Tours.

A media tour gives editors and writers with whom PR people work an opportunity for face-to-face questioning. It's a chance to meet their PR contacts and perhaps interview key executives, technicians, and financial experts who are critical to in-depth stories.

These tours can take place at the company or at the news organizations' offices and can be as formal or informal as the parties prefer.

Inviting Press to the Company.

When a company has a story that is interesting to the general press or the particular trade press that covers it or its industry, they can invite writers and editors to visit the facility. This gives the company an opportunity to show itself at its best on its "home field" and provides media with an "up close" and potentially more colorful or dramatic look at an organization, its people and products.

Taking the Company to the Media.

Another version of the press tour is to have PR people and their experts visit the editorial offices of the key magazines, TV and radio stations, newspapers and blogs.

Getting Technical.

You may remember that "business-to-business" or BtoB is still a major part of the marketing world. Most specialized industries have trade journals that feature news and information on that particular specialty.

Companies that are involved in technology – whether high-tech, or agriculture, or aviation, or running a restaurant, stay involved in the news of their industry. Here, PR can help in a big way.

While some of these technical topics might not be of interest to the average reader, those who read these magazines and trade journals are very interested. This focused editorial environment, combined with the relatively small staffs of these journals, provides an important public relations opportunity.

The sidebar on Articles covers this in slightly more detail.

Feature Article Development.

Cuisinart was a relatively unknown French kitchen appliance.

Then an article in *Gourmet* magazine spoke its praises as the key to many interesting recipes. That started the ball rolling.

Cuisinart sales personnel can point to that article as the "tipping point" that started growing sales in the US.

Magazines and news shows need to fill in those spaces between the ads. If you can develop a story that is truly newsworthy, one of those articles could be about you and your company.

Event Management.

Often, staff members at a PR firm will find themselves, creating, organizing, promoting, and running events. This area has grown into its own marketing specialty.

We'll cover event marketing a bit later in this chapter.

Making Whoopi.

Ads featuring Whoopi Goldberg address lactose-intolerance, which has a higher incidence among African Americans.

Whoopi says, *"Lucky for us, there's lactose-free milk with all the calcium of regular milk."*

"And you know," says Barbara, *"when I see a piece of ours on* Entertainment Tonight, *or in a marketing column, I still get the same buzz I did when that* Newsweek *reporter showed up at the headache seminar."*

What Does It Take to Get into PR?

Barbara Molotsky says she looks for three things when people come in looking for a job:

1. **You Need to Be a Good Writer.**
   "Writing is critical.
   "PR works to find a hook, to make a product newsy."
2. **You Need to Be Smart.**
   "You need an upfront knowledge of PR. It will show up in the way you answer questions in an interview. Please, don't say, 'I'm a people person.'"
3. **You Need to Be Creative.**
   "In PR we have to do everything (not like you advertising people).
   "You need to be a good manager, a budgeteer, a detail person, and, of course, a good sales person."

Articles.

Article placement is part of PR's job.

There are two kinds of articles – technical articles and feature articles.
Technical & Case History Articles.
Technical articles are "soft," rather than "hard" PR: they typically contain little direct product mention, but enhance the prestige of the company.

Merchandised correctly, reprints can be some of the hardest working pieces in the MarCom mix.

(Continued on next page)

Articles (Cont.)

A technical article program recognizes that the logical authors (engineers and scientists) are too busy developing products to write articles.

Freelance technical writers create the article, while the engineer reviews and approves it. It is then sent to a trade magazine or journal.

Some PR people may be qualified, but using tech writers is common.

Feature Articles.

These are softer articles about the company or people in the company.

If you have a good story angle, they should not be overlooked.

Exclusives.

While press releases concerning any general news items about a company are sent to all media outlets, technical and feature articles are usually given on an "exclusive" basis.

This assures the publication agreeing to run the article that the same story won't be sent to a competing publication.

The end result is a "protected" story for the publication and excellent publicity for the company.

However, particularly when it's an event that's a relatively small part of a marketer's overall program, like staffing a trade show booth, a PR firm may find this as part of their task. Or, the firm may have an entire division that specializes in events.

Product Publicity.

Here, we have a wide range of creative opportunities – everything from holidays and Top Ten Lists to celebrity endorsements and street corner stunts. We've put an alphabetical list of this kind of activity – courtesy Thomas Harris – in the sidebar.

These are the broad categories:

Awards, Lists, and Holidays. These help create a brand "resumé." A good example is the Rolaids award for best relief pitcher – a tie-in with their long-running advertising theme "how do you spell relief?"

Books, Blogs, and More. Literary activity – from short informational brochures to ongoing electronic dialogue to full-length books can provide useful support. And, they fit nicely in press kits. A good example is the book made by ad legend Howard Gossage for the Scientific-American Paper Airplane Contest. Thirty years later, it's still available.

Contests, Competitions, Created Events. The line between MPR and Sales Promotion and Event Marketing? Well, actually, there is no line. They overlap. The key is if it is a good idea that supports the brand. These activities could be handled by any of a number of suppliers – the PR firm, the Sales Promotion firm, the Event Marketer.

This underlines the need for good IMC management. If it's a good idea for the brand, that's the important thing. The rest is detail.

Media Appearances. The ultimate is appearing on *Oprah* or the *Today Show*. But there are abundant opportunities to connect the brand or brand spokesperson with the public through the media. After all, that's what public relations does.

Whether it's appearing on a local radio talk show, being quoted in an article, or getting on *Larry King*, it's all about connecting the right message with the right media vehicle.

Merchandising the PR.

Visibility and positive awareness doesn't just happen. Send reprints of major published articles about the company or its products as soon as possible after they appear to promote or enhance the image of the company or product.

This is especially important for several reasons.

- *First, don't assume all the publication's readers saw the article.* Mail reprints to important members of the target market. Reprints of media stories have much higher credibility than brochures.
- *Second, reprints should be given to the sales force.* Sales people love to show up at a customer's office with a reprinted article about the product they're trying to sell – especially when the story is from prestigious journals, which can carry a lot of weight in among industry professionals.

PR Evaluation: Research, Tracking, Measurement, and Feedback. Traditionally, public relations has a good record in publicizing its own value. That is, keeping track of how the program performed and informing the client/brand of the results.

Here are the primary ways PR programs evaluate their own performance and communicate that performance to management.

Research. Pre and post awareness studies can track things such as attitudes and awareness of such things as brand leadership or the need for calcium.

Tracking. Sometimes, this research is an ongoing process – so that, month after month, or year after year, we see how we're doing. We tend to be more aware of this sort of ongoing tracking in things such as political races, where candidate preference is tracked by the media like a marathon.

Measurement. PR firms, don't just accumulate tear sheets of published articles, they add up all the mentions, multiply those mentions by the size of the media vehicle's audience, and present a rough measurement of the overall media impact of the PR program.

Feedback. The marketplace can make us smarter – whether it's hits on a blog, letters to Consumer Affairs, or inquiries to a Butterball Turkey Help Line. PR professionals are always looking for ways to engage the public and understand what and how they're thinking.

IMC, MPR, and The Media Revolution.

As IMC – Integrated Marketing Communications – becomes the standard operating philosophy for brand management, MPR – Marketing Public Relations – will become more and more important.

First, successful programs consistently demonstrate their value to management – whether it is the direct and obvious benefits from trade shows and industry publications, or the wider world of consumer media.

The traditional CPR – Corporate Public Relations – functions are still important, but there is growing appreciation for the value MPR can add to a marketing program.

Second, remember that the other side of fragmentation is an expansion of media opportunities. That means there are more media vehicles out there with more time and space to fill.

That's why smart and effective MPR professionals are highly valued – they know how to connect brands with the growing menu of media opportunities. And that's why finding out more about a career in MPR might be something that interests you.

4. Marketing Research.

LARGE MARKETERS AND FULL-SERVICE AD AGENCIES typically have a marketing research department or a research department that will help marketers in any number of ways.

We'll cover the process in more detail in Chapter 11.

But, if you're interested in this field, there are many other support companies you should know about as well.

Most Popular Types of MPR Tactics:

What can you do in Marketing PR? Here are thought-starters – A to Z – from *Value-Added Public Relations* (NTC/McGraw-Hill) by Thomas L. Harris, co-founder of Golin-Harris:

Awards – for example, "Best-Dressed" for a fashion marketer.

Books – like Campbell's recipes.

Contests – an opportunity for more product involvement – like a Bake-Off.

Demonstrations – can you present product "demos" in an interesting way?

Events – yours or someone else's.

Festivals – ditto.

Grand Openings – Great for retailers. Remodeling? It's a Grand Re-Opening!

Holidays – can you tie-in with a day, month, or week or create your own?

Interviews – do you have a spokesperson who can make media appearances?

"Junkets" – is there a reason to bring the press to you? A fancy press tour?

Key Issues – can your brand connect with or support an issue or worthy cause?

Luncheons – feed 'em and pitch 'em.

Museums & Memorabilia – does your brand have a history? Publicize it.

Newsletters – these can double as direct mail to a variety of "publics."

Official Endorsements – does someone famous like your brand? Could they?

Product Placement – can put your brand in a movie or TV show.

Questionnaires – do a survey. Then, publicize the results. Think about it.

Radio – "Trade for Mention" contests.

Sampling – look for opportunities

"Thons" – marathons, telethons, bike-athons, walk-athons, and etc. link brands to worthy causes.

Underwriting – sponsorship of events

Vehicles – cars, trucks, hot-air balloons.

"VNR" – this stands for Video News Release. We'll talk about these later.

Weeks – like a holiday, only longer.

eXpert Columns – these are written by real (or invented) spokespersons who write about and answer questions about the product category.

Youth Programs – kids, teens, babies.

"Zone" Programs – target local areas.

Want to Know More about Research?

One of the best connections is the Advertising Research Foundation (www.thearf.org).

They offer research internships at places like ESPN, MRI, Interpublic, and Millward Brown.

Their site will keep you in touch with numerous seminars, papers, and other resources.

They feature Webcasts, seminars (often with student rates), and the participating members of ARF represent some of the best in marketing research – at agencies, specialized suppliers, and marketers.

Qualitative and Quantitative.

How can you prepare? Think about it.

Market researchers have to understand facts and feelings – you'll need to become an applied consumer behaviouralist, combining quantitative data with qualitative input like interviews and focus groups.

You may find yourself at the cutting edge of the Media Revolution, discovering new ways to use emerging technologies like online focus groups and surveys, and discovering new ways of tracking behavior.

First, Get Good at Secondary.

Secondary research skills are key.

Don't just look at the first page when you Google – learn to dig.

It's out there.

Learn to find the kind of useful data that can help make marketing more effective.

Tough times. A bright future.

Companies need to know what works – particularly in tough economic times. So knowing what works in market research can be a smart move.

Why not do some research on market research?

Internal Departments.

Often, a large advertiser will maintain its own marketing research department, responsible for most marketing research functions.

When Scott Bedbury moved from Nike to Starbucks, the one key person he brought along was his consumer insight expert.

The marketing research people at Kraft engage Lisa Fortini-Campbell around the world to improve their consumer insight.

Typically, an internal department will be concerned with the analysis of the company's own sales data and in reviewing data purchased from syndicated suppliers such as A.C. Nielsen Company, which tracks sales and market share data of package good products nationally.

Additionally, the internal marketing research department will be expected to provide management with short- and long-term estimates of market trends and market potential to assist the company in its future planning.

The internal marketing research department also hires independent marketing research firms to carry out large-scale primary research studies – from initial focus groups to eventual large-scale surveys. Research conducted for a new product falls into this category.

Finally, the internal marketing research department at the client or agency hires other research firms that specialize in advertising research to test the effectiveness of advertising messages, both before and after these ads and commercials appear in the media.

Outside Research Companies.

There are two major types: Limited-Service and Full-Service.

Limited-Service Research Suppliers.

Limited-service research suppliers specialize in a particular type of research activity.

- **Syndicated Research Suppliers** such as A.C. Nielsen make data available to any firm willing to pay.
- **Standardized Research Suppliers** such as Gallup & Robinson, which use a specific, standardized method to test advertising effectiveness. In Gallup & Robinson's case, the effectiveness measurement method is "recall."
- **Specialized Research Suppliers** are firms that deal only in one facet of research, e.g., telephone interviewing.

Full-Service Suppliers.

A full-service research supplier is hired to do a total marketing research project, from start to finish.

These firms will carry out custom research as opposed to offering a standardized methodology.

One of the major differences between a customized research project and syndicated or standardized research is the advertiser works closely with the research company from the outset of a custom project and does not simply purchase stock research data.

We'll introduce you to the basics of this critical function in Chapter Eleven – "Evaluation and Integration."

5. Event Marketing.

Even though it may entail a lot of hard work, Event Marketing can be a fascinating job – connecting a brand with an audience by tapping into their passions. Those passion points include not only sports, but arts and entertainment, cause marketing, and many other consumer passions.

Some view the proper terminology as "sponsorship agencies" where "event marketing" is listed as one area of focus within a broadened "sponsorship consulting" offering. This also includes: sports marketing, guerilla marketing, youth marketing, cause marketing, and experiential marketing.

In broad terms, most event marketing agencies package their service offering into 3 main "buckets" – strategy, execution, and measurement.

A Very Big Business.

It's hard to put a value on event marketing, though many measure it as over $100 billion. Everyone can agree it's big, but it's hard to place an exact value on the event marketing part of events – particularly the major ones.

For example, the Olympics. Clearly, it's a major event, and sponsorship dollars provide a major amount of the dollar value. But so does the government of the host country and all the government sport teams that participate – not all with 100% sponsorship funding.

The Olympics and professional sports are sponsored events, but, when you look at the numbers, most of the support is in traditional paid advertising.

Another major category is trade shows, which feature relatively little in paid advertising. Yet, they deliver very high value and, as you will see, are highly regarded by most marketing executives. After all, trade shows often bring together a high percentage of your best customers – value that's hard to beat.

That said, event marketing, in some shape or form, is an important part of almost every brand's business plan, for a lot of good business reasons.

Working Backward.

Often, event marketers are forced to "work backward."

That is, they have to deal with an existing event, whether it's a trade show, sporting event, or rock concert and look to develop the best "fit" for the brand and the attending target.

This can range from huge global events, like the Olympics, to more regional and local events like NASCAR races, concert tours, sporting events, street festivals, or charitable activities.

Here, the dates, location, and logistics of these are already set and the task is to find the optimal way for the brand to connect with the "passion points" of the audience that attends or, in some cases, stimulate attendance with an appropriate program.

Children's Miracle Network.

Even though the event may be just once a year, cause marketers still have to communicate year-round.

All the World's a Stage.

In 2008, Arc's work for the Center for Disease Control, "Yellowball," won three Cannes Lions: Gold and Silver in Direct, and Bronze in Media.

Bill Rosen explains, "The campaign was designed to combat teen and tween obesity by encouraging physical activity. As part of the campaign, we dropped 500,000 real yellow balls all over the country, in parks, playgrounds, and schoolyards – anywhere kids could find them."

Each ball had a special code, creating a 'chain letter' of play. Over 16,000 Blogs were created. More than 5 million kids participated.

Of the program, Rosen notes, "Individual media executions are nothing without an innovative, organizing idea that connects with consumers and gives each execution a purpose for engagement."

Profile: Mark Montoya, Montoya Productions.

In 1990, Mark Montoya graduated from San José State with a B.S. in advertising.

He was President of the student chapter of the Business Marketing Association. In 1989, he led a team of five and won a national collegiate competition for DuPont.

Mark also picked up a $2,000 individual scholarship.

He went to work with his brother's design firm for a few years, but grew restless and set up his own company.

He saw a need for someone to market sponsorship of cultural and sports events in San José – including the San José Jazz Festival.

He packages sponsorships at several levels, verifies audience demographics, and guarantees media exposure.

Today, the San José Jazz Festival is the world's largest entirely free jazz festival, running five stages over a two- or three-day weekend each August.

He also handles sponsorships for a performing arts summer series (see www.PASSINFO.com for the Web site) and many other events.

"I learned it all in that (advertising) program," he says. *"How to focus on the core message and repeat it... how to see the world and my product, my brand, from my target market's point of view... how to put together a coherent, compelling presentation.*

"I couldn't do what I do without that foundation, that understanding of what has value and what doesn't."

Working Frontwards.

As event marketing grows, there are more opportunities to address event-based sponsorship opportunities more strategically.

In this case, event marketers become engaged in the strategic planning process. As the industry continues to evolve, there is a concerted effort on the part of event marketers to be perceived as more than strictly tacticians – hence, the growth in prominence and depth of "strategy" as a service offering.

A Similar Process. Strategy, Execution, Measurement.

The initial steps in the strategy development process look much like they do in other marketing disciplines:

1. Gain a solid understanding of the client's business. Establish clear, actionable, and measurable business objectives.
2. Gain a solid understanding of the target consumer segment(s).
3. Gain a solid understanding of the brand positioning/message.

From this point forward, the unique nature of the sponsorship / experiential strategy development process truly takes shape.

Strategy.

With objectives and audience (and, of course, budget) in mind the sponsorship strategy team identifies the consumer passion point(s) that best align with the consumer target(s).

The team then takes a comprehensive look at the available opportunities in the marketplace (e.g. Golf / a review of all available golf sponsorship opportunities) and then makes a recommendation to the client as to which opportunities to pursue.

As part of this process, the agencies may also make recommendations on the creation of proprietary events created specifically to meet the brand objectives.

Proprietary events are recommended when no existing opportunity is suitable or when the brand needs something "ownable" that cannot otherwise be purchased through a traditional sponsorship.

Execution.

Now it's time to put the recommended strategy into action. This involves negotiating the approved sponsorships and implementing the "activation plan" (the marketing plan that turns the sponsorship into an integrated marketing platform).

On the event side of the table the service offering becomes MUCH more detailed and labor-intense.

It is common for event marketing agencies to have dedicated event execution teams who specialize in the many aspects of making events happen.

Services include basic account management functions as well as those specific to the event.

Measurement.

As the event marketing industry has come of age over the past 10 years, it has been held (much like its counterparts in other marketing disciplines) to ever-increasing levels of accountability for real results and tangible business impact.

The industry responded. You won't find a sponsorship agency today that doesn't list measurement as a service offering, though the way in which this service is delivered varies from agency to agency.

Some agencies have measurement teams as self-contained units within their organization. Others outsource the lion's share of the work to 3rd party measurement specialists.

Measurement Pays Off.

The results of these measurements have had a very positive result.

In 2004, a Global Events Trend Survey found that 44% of marketing executives believe that event marketing provides the greatest return on investment.

In an interview on this survey, Kevin Adler, then head of sponsorships and event marketing at Publicis' event specialist, Relay, noted, *"People aren't giving up on advertising, but they are starting to... funnel some of these marketing dollars into tactics that cost infinitely less and can, in many cases, deliver infinitely more."*

The survey also noted that not all events are created equal.

Trade shows, conferences, and seminars were rated highest.

So, for example, auto manufacturers will cut ad budgets before they cut back on their participation in an Auto Show.

A Two-Way Street.

There's good reason for this high opinion. As Adler notes, *"The continued fragmentation of media choices makes it harder to reach consumers. The passive nature of advertising as a medium, almost by definition, necessitates a complimentary method that allows for two-way marketing, and that's what event marketing does."*

Unique Challenges

There is nothing "turnkey" about a sponsorship and event plan.

The best ideas, poorly executed will ultimately fail to deliver, and the level of ongoing detail management and hands-on involvement necessary is much greater than that for traditional media and advertising agencies.

While a media buy can be trafficked and then a post-buy report generated without excessive agency involvement between the trafficking and the delivery of the post-buy report, the event marketer's job really just begins once the "buy" is made.

Certainly some sponsorships do serve as turnkey audience delivery vehicles, but the real value in sponsorships is the access to exploitable marketing assets that then need to be "activated" to actually see that value. That work is incredibly labor-intensive and requires long hours and frequent travel by the account teams to ensure that the program is actually delivering once it hits the market.

Integration & Coordination.

The Super Bowl reminds us how many IMC can be coordinated.

From advance planning of Super Bowl-themed sales promotions, PR programs that publicize various Super Bowl spots, to the CRM (Customer Relationship Management) effort imbedded in every Super Bowl ticket, this event is a supreme example of marketing teamwork.

We're not talking about the NFL teams, but the coordinated and integrated efforts of marketers, agencies, the NFL itself, the media companies involved, and all the suppliers of marketing services.

By the way, you can even read about Super Bowl commercials in *The Super Bowl of Advertising: How the Commercials Won the Game* by Bernice Kanner.

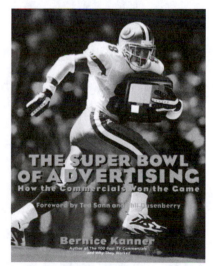

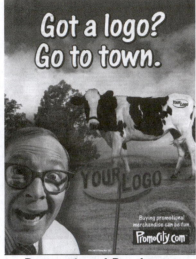

Promotional Products.

Here, a new Internet-based company advertises how it can put a logo on almost anything.

Business Gifts.

Land's End found an additional market for its products in the promotional products business by selling high-end sportswear to companies wanting personalized clothing items bearing their own brand names – high-value items that can be given to employees and important customers.

Want to Know More?

Visit the PPAI, the Promotional Products Association International: www.ppa.org

6. Promotional Products.

ALSO KNOWN AS ADVERTISING SPECIALTIES, **promotional products** are articles of merchandise, usually carrying an imprinted message or logo given to customers or prospects free of charge. In 2007, it was a $19.4 billion business.

Often, the products have some functional value (e.g., pens, note paper, T-shirts) to encourage use in the work or home environment in hopes of achieving a connection with the target market.

Types of Promotional Products.

Promotional products fall into three main categories:

1. **Advertising Specialties**
2. **Business Gifts**
3. **Recognition Awards**

Let's look at them one by one.

Advertising Specialties.

The pens, key chains, hats, and T-shirts we all have with a logo or a message have the following characteristics:

- **Imprinted with a promotional message or logo**
- **Useful, either for work or pleasure**
- **Given with no obligation**

Some people confuse advertising specialties with premiums (see "Sales Promotion"). Premiums are used specifically as an incentive to purchase another product.

For example, if we give away an Eddie Bauer windbreaker with the purchase of an expensive racing bike, the windbreaker would represent a premium and not an advertising speciality. (And, the Eddie Bauer windbreaker would not necessarily carry our logo.)

If we were the bike store and we gave our best customers free calendars featuring scenes from the Tour de France (with our store's name on the calendar), that would be an advertising specialty.

Business Gifts.

Business gifts are more expensive items given to customers or employees in order to show appreciation of past loyalty or performance.

Unlike advertising specialties, these gifts may not carry the organization's message or logo, or it is more discreet, making them more appropriate for home or office use.

Recognition Awards.

Recognition awards include plaques, trophies, service pins, and other items that are purchased by organizations to recognize performance of their own employees or their distributors.

Wearables = 30%.

The most popular category of promotional products today is wearables (T-shirts, sweatshirts, golf shirts, hats). Wearables account for more than 30% of all promotional product sales.

Other top five categories are: writing instruments, glassware, calendars, and office accessories.

Specialized Distributors and Suppliers.

Companies purchase promotional products by contacting specialized distributors or agencies who serve as both a counselor and a source of information on available merchandise.

The distributors offer advice on what would be the most appropriate items to use, maintain product catalogs on merchandise from a variety of suppliers, and then place the order to the supplier, including the specific message or logo to be placed on the item.

Some suppliers are companies that sell their own brand of a particular type of merchandise, e.g., you may wind up ordering advertising specialty pens from Bic or PaperMate.

"The Products That Remain to Be Seen."

Promotional products are an excellent way to put your brand and a brief message before your customers.

If they are functional and people use them in their homes or offices – promotional products provide good continuity, keeping the brand before the target market.

The Promotional Products Association positions these advertising specialties as *"the products that remain to be seen."*

Properly used, they can play a role in overall marketing strategy.

Companies will often distribute less expensive products to groups that haven't been qualified as prospects yet, saving the more expensive items for current customers or those with exceptional potential.

The MarCom Manager.

WITH ALL OF THESE SPECIALTIES and the need for an integrated approach, it is no surprise that there is an individual within the organization charged with overseeing them – the MarCom Manager.

As with many jobs in marketing, the titles may vary, but the job is the same – coordinating the growing variety of tasks in marketing communications.

The Role of the MarCom Manager.

The MarCom manager plans and implements a coordinated marketing communications program supporting a brand or product line.

This involves integrating advertising, sales promotion, PR, interactive, and direct, in support of marketing goals and objectives.

This position requires a generalist familiar with the strengths, costs, and weaknesses of all marketing communication disciplines.

He or she almost always works within the marketer's organization, though many marketing services organizations are trying to offer balanced and integrated MarCom management.

This person typically rises through the corporate or agency ranks, starting as a specialist and gradually assuming wider responsibility.

The problem is that one's initial area of expertise may overshadow decisions on the relative worth of related disciplines – a MarCom person who comes out of PR may have a very different point of view from one who comes out of advertising.

But the ones who succeed learn to use all the tools.

Our Conceptual Model.

This is a useful way to think about The MarCom Matrix, with six major forms of MarCom: Advertising • Public Relations & Publicity • Sales Promotion • Direct Marketing • Event Marketing • New Media (which includes the Internet).

They all revolve around the "Idea."

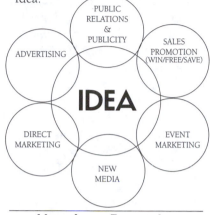

Here's an Example.

Let's say our idea is to combine Domino's Pizza and the game of dominoes. Here's what you'd write:

- **Advertising.** An ad with the headline "The Domino Theory." History of Domino's pizza, history of game. Ads would have coupon offer and some sort of game involvement.

- **Sales Promotion** (Win/Free/Save). Give domino pieces with every purchase. Find some way to build continuity – add "Lucky Domino" for extra value/prizes.

- **Public Relations.** Do giant toppling domino designs, have contests, film the event for a news release.

- **Direct Marketing.** Send free domino and coupon to every customer in your database – or every student on campus.

- **Event Marketing.** Sponsor a big Domino Tournament, have demonstrations at student centers.

- **New Media.** Build a Web site with a downloadable domino game and an on-line tournament. And don't forget a downloadable discount coupon.

Jack of All Trades?

With few, if any, exceptions, companies have yet to demonstrate expertise across all forms of marketing communications.

But in today's marketplace, there's an easy way to get the best expertise money can buy. You buy it.

That's what we've seen in this chapter – groups of companies leveraging their specific expertise into success in a marketplace with an almost insatiable demand for first-rate marketing skills.

In every discipline, companies and individuals have grown by focusing on doing one thing very well.

This has also created a new breed of company – mega-agencies that offer their large clients the full range of marketing services.

We all know the best-case scenarios and the success stories.

But how much do those business models and case histories match up with our unique combination of resources and market conditions?

Not as much as you might think.

Try as we might, coordinating all of the options and specialists is still more of an art than a science.

Today, you don't have to be a jack of all trades; you just need to know where to find the skills you need and the job you need done.

That's the task of the MarCom manager.

Future Issues.

THERE ARE MANY ISSUES. The ones we will discuss briefly are: Integration and Coordination, Convergence and Emergence, the Rise of PR, and the MarCom Explosion.

Integration and Coordination.

The new integrated marketing communications (IMC) environment is, in many respects, a reflection of economics.

As money has become tighter, and mass media more diversified and less efficient, many see IMC as an opportunity to make marketing more effective. But it's often easier said than done.

As new industries emerged, public relations, the necessary marketing tool of a start-up company, became a driving marketing force. As media fragmented and database capabilities grew, new possibilities in direct marketing emerged.

And, as sophisticated consumers and retailers became better informed, tougher-minded, and less brand-loyal, promotional incentives had to become a more important part of the marketing mix.

Convergence and Emergence.

The specialists are changing, too. Two opposite trends are generating exciting activity in the world of marketing services.

Leading-edge companies are growing and converging.

Everyone's evolving into full service – but with a big difference.

The Convergence Factor.

The unbundling of marketing services has had a new result. The more successful specialists grew and added capabilities – converging back into a new breed of full-service marketing companies – since, after all, clients need every kind of service.

But there's a difference. Each company is leveraging its specialty to position itself as a unique type of full-service agency.

This is presenting exciting new combinations.

Now any given service might be provided by the marketer, the ad agency, an independent supplier, or even the media.

The Emergence Factor.

With each marketplace change, new opportunities emerge for new marketing-services specialists.

Direct specialists like DraftDirect evolved, adding sales promotion capabilities. DraftDirect became DraftWorldwide. Then, in 2006, it merged with Foote Cone & Belding, and is now DraftFCB, offering traditional media advertising services as well.

And new players enter the game – sometimes spectacularly.

For example, a design firm, CKS, cut the traditional design shop implementation time for United Airlines by almost 75%!

With performance like that, new opportunities come naturally.

Then additional clients and capabilities are added.

And the emerging company converges on the full-service model. See what's happening?

The MarCom Explosion.

It's everywhere. It's in the Super Bowl, the Olympics, planning meetings at the largest marketers, and in the business plan of every start-up with a chance of success.

It's not only an explosion of companies, specialties, and media choices, it's an explosion of jobs and career opportunities.

Discussion & Exercises:

1. Sales Promotion.

A. Select five nationally branded products you buy. What would be some particularly relevant premiums or self-liquidating premiums that might be offered by each of these brands – premiums that will hopefully attract new buyers to your brand and not current customers?

B. For those same five products, create a theme and a concept for a promotional game.

2. Relationship Marketing.

You're the promotion manager of a high-end men's or women's clothing store. Set down a year-long relationship marketing program you'd establish to maintain good relations with your best customers. Some may be ongoing, others may be short-term.

3. Public Relations.

You're the top PR officer at your college or university. You're trying to get the local newspaper to have a better sense of what's happening at your school. You think the school's doing some exciting things the community should know about.

You've had no luck getting press releases or stories run by the paper. So, you decide to have a press tour on campus to let some of the top people at the paper learn first-hand what's happening at your school that's truly newsworthy.

Using your own school for this exercise, describe the following:

A. The specific topics or issues you want your people to cover in the sessions and tour you'll hold.

B. Tell where you'd hold the session and what places on campus you'd have these newspaper people visit.

C. Explain who at the college you'd have them talk with for each of these topics or stops. Explain why you've selected each topic to discuss, place to see, or individual who should appear. For this scenario, make it real.

4. Event Marketing.

Select five national companies that don't market beer, soft drinks, or fast foods. For each one, come up with an idea for a major event that they could sponsor.

Explain why that particular event would be particularly appropriate to reach the company's target market.

Further, tell us what it is about each of these events that will make them particularly newsworthy.

The Rise of PR.

We're going to mention this influential book again – *The Fall of Advertising and the Rise of PR.*

Is this really happening? Well, yes and no.

It is certainly true that major marketers are taking a hard look at how marketing PR can help advance company goals.

And, just like in advertising, everyone's a genius in retrospect.

That is, the big PR success stories are always identified after the fact – we just take note of the programs that made it into the media – we forget all the ones that didn't.

We don't agree with everything in the book, but we think it's important enough to recommend that you read it and, whatever else you do, make PR one of your competencies.

A Micro-Macro Trend.

We are now seeing new marketing services specialists emerge.

These range from cutting-edge technology suppliers to traditional specialists – such as promotional products suppliers with new high-tech items and online ordering capabilities.

The world of marketing public relations is also growing, and it's one more field where entry is relatively easy and reputations can be made fairly quickly.

And through it all, someone has to integrate and coordinate the growing range of options in marketing services – the MarCom manager. After all, every specialty is, in one way or another, working with other specialties.

It's all part of the new specialties, new combinations, and new job opportunities happening at every turn – in marketing services.

References:

Here are some of the leading books in the categories we've discussed:

Sales Promotion.

Sales Promotion Essentials: The 10 Basic Sales Promotion Tech-niques… and How to Use Them.
by Don Schultz et. al
    A good introduction to the basics.
Best Sales Promotions
by William A. Robinson
    Excellent examples with comments by a sales promotion pioneer.

Direct Marketing.

There are a huge number of books in this field, covering everything from direct-mail copywriting to advanced database techniques. Here are a few to get you started.

Being Direct
by Lester Wunderman
    The founder of Wunderman, now a part of Y&R/WPP, wraps the lessons he's learned into interesting stories.
Direct Mail Copy That Sells!
by Herschell Gordon Lewis
Herschell Gordon Lewis on the Art of Writing Copy
by Herschell Gordon Lewis
    You're not going to believe this, but before he became the guru of direct-mail copywriting, Lewis was the director and producer of gross and ultra-low-budget "bucket of blood" movies.

(Continued on next page)

5. MarCom.

Using the MarCom Matrix as a model, see how you might be able to expand any and all of the previous ideas into other MarCom specialties.

Concepts & Vocabulary:

Ad slicks – Pre-printed ads, or pieces of ads, used to create local ads or co-op advertising.

Advocacy advertising – Advertising that attempts to influence public opinion on a political, environmental, or social issue of special interest to the organization doing the advertising.

Affinity marketing – Marketing that aims at certain targets based on beliefs or affiliation – like a credit card with your school logo.

Allowances – System of funding advertising or marketing programs to be implemented by participating retailers or distributors.

Business gifts – A type of gift usually given to highly valued customers, most often as a year-end expression of appreciation.

Cause marketing – A type of sponsorship that links an organization with a social or charitable cause.

Collateral – All promotional materials not associated with major media; usually catalogs, point-of-sale, direct mail pieces, etc.

Consumer promotion – Sales promotion activities designed to stimulate immediate sales by "pulling" consumers into a retail store through incentives such as coupons, added value offers, and games.

Co-operative (co-op) advertising – Usually refers to advertising for a nationally advertised product that is shared by the national advertiser and one of its local retail outlets.

Corporate public relations (CPR) – Non-marketing related PR, such as investor relations, employee communications, government relations, crisis management, community relations, etc.

Database marketing – A process of systematically gathering information about individual customers and their purchasing behavior to help marketers target these customers' needs.

Direct mail advertising – Any form of advertising that is sent to prospective customers via mail.

Direct marketing – Selling products and services without retail stores. Merchandise may be advertised through any media. The purchase is by phone, mail, or Internet order.

Direct response television (also known as DRTV) – Advertising that sells a product "through TV" only.

Displays – Can be as simple as stacked cartons or custom manufactured shelves or other type of merchandising unit that display items offered for sale – often at a special price.

Display allowance – A monetary allowance given to retailers by national manufacturers in order to obtain point-of-sale displays and/or guaranteed shelf space for their products.

End cap – Display at the end of the aisle – a valuable location.

Event marketing – Promotional activity in which a marketer provides financial support (sponsorship) for an event in exchange for the right to have its name or logo displayed at the venue.

Exclusive – Highly newsworthy technical or feature article originated by an organization's PR department offered to a publication on a protected, or "exclusive," basis. Provides publication with an important story while giving organization substantial publicity.

FSI (free-standing insert) – Preprinted advertising units that are then inserted into the paper. Most widely used in Sunday papers.

Frequency programs – Type of consumer promotion that rewards customers for repeated patronage, e.g., frequent flier programs.

Governmental relations – Also referred to as "lobbying" or "legislative affairs." PR activity in which organization representatives try to inform legislators of organization's positions on issues that may impact their business or interests.

Green marketing – Business practices engaged in by an organization that demonstrate its concern for environmental issues.

Inbound telemarketing – Most often refers to the "order taking" of a direct marketer using a toll-free 800 number.

In-pack – Premium inside of a package – like a toy in a cereal box.

Legislative affairs/lobbying – (See "governmental relations")

Lettershops – Specialists in producing and preparing direct mail.

List brokers (compilers) – Companies that prepare and provide lists to direct marketers.

List enhancement – Process of improving lists.

LTV (lifetime value) – Direct marketing concept of determining the long-term value of an individual customer.

MarCom manager – Title for person responsible for planning and implementing coordinated, integrated marketing communications.

Marketing public relations (MPR) – Functions of public relations that support the marketing efforts for a product or service.

Marketing services – Any service that enhances marketing efforts: such as advertising, public relations, promotion, research, etc.

Merge/purge – A system used by direct-response marketers to eliminate the duplication of names in lists.

Mining – Extracting desirable prospects from lists and databases.

Near-pack – Premium displayed near the package.

On-pack – Premium attached onto package.

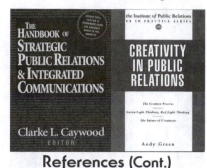

References (Cont.)

Public Relations.
PR! A Social History of Spin
by Stuart Ewen
An entertaining history of the development of PR in US society.

Handbook of Strategic Public Relations & Integrated Communications
by Clarke Caywood et. al
Solid summary edited by one of the PR leaders in IMC.

Creativity in Public Relations: Green Light Thinking. Red Light Thinking.
by Andy Green et. al Approaches for bringing creativity into PR.

Career Opportunities in Advertising and Public Relations
by Sally Field
Useful information on connecting to the PR job market.

Guerrilla PR.
by Michael Levine
Good advice for the small business.

Marketing Research.
Here are a few books. Covered in more detail in Chapter Eleven.

The Market Research Toolbox: A Concise Guide for Beginners
by Edward F. McQuarrie

Market Research Matters: Tools and Techniques for Aligning Your Business
by Robert Duboff and James Spaeth
(Spaeth is head of the Advertising Research Foundation.)

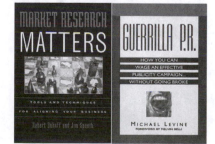

**Stedman Graham
Joe Jeff Goldblatt, C.S.E.P.
Lisa Delpy, Ph.D.**

Foreword by Dick Ebersol, President, NBC Sports

The Ultimate Guide to SPORT EVENT Management & Marketing

References (Cont.)

Event Marketing.

This field is growing rapidly.

Here are two of the latest books.

The Ultimate Guide to Sport Event Management & Marketing
by Graham, Goldblatt, and Delpy

Know who Stedman Graham goes with? Oprah! An excellent introduction with a sports emphasis.

Event Marketing: A Management Guide

Sponsored by the Event Marketing Committee of the Association of National Advertisers.

The ANA prepared this book to help member marketers manage this growing area.

You might also look for a copy of the *Sports Marketing Journal* – your school's sports department might have one. Or check their Web site.

Promotional Products.

There are currently no books on promotional products, though you might want to contact the Promotional Products Association International (www.ppa.org) and look at the Web sites and catalogs of promotional products suppliers.

Outbound telemarketing – That part of telemarketing that involves the contacting and selling of prospective buyers by phone.

Premiums – An "extra" item that the consumer receives when purchasing a product during a promotional period.

Press conference – A meeting arranged by the PR staff of an organization at which a newsworthy announcement is made to media.

Press kit – Folder containing news releases, photographs, and background information.

Press release – News story about an organization (or one of its products or services) written by a public relations staff writer and sent to a news medium as a possible news item. Resulting "publicity" represents free exposure for the company, product, or service.

Press tour – Occasion when members of news media are invited to tour a company's facilities and meet with company executives.

Promotional products (formerly known as specialty-advertising items) – A useful item given free to consumers that carries the name or logo of the company giving out the item.

Public relations – Activities designed to generate news coverage or other positive impact with the "public."

Publicity – Free media exposure on a company, product, or service.

Relationship marketing – A marketing strategy that emphasizes an ongoing relationship with customers through periodic assessment of the customers' purchasing patterns and through regular contact that rewards them for their continued patronage.

Sales promotion – Use of various types of incentives to encourage consumers or distributors to make immediate purchases. Sales promotion activities are generally classified as being either consumer promotions or trade promotions.

Self-liquidating premium – Premium item offered at cost – the marketer recovers some or all of the money used to produce the item.

Spiffs (also called "push money") – Monetary incentives given to retail salespersons who "sell" customers on a particular manufacturer's products; during these promotions, the salespersons earn additional money by making a sale on that brand.

Telemarketing – A form of direct marketing that uses the telephone to deliver the selling message and to take the sales order.

Trade promotion – Sales promotion activities that provide incentives for distributors to purchase additional quantities of a product and to promote that product to the ultimate consumer.

Trade show – Events where manufacturers of related products (e.g., companies that sell products to home builders) display and demonstrate their products for members of the trade (e.g., home builders) in a large exhibition hall.

Up-selling – Direct marketing technique in which an operator taking an order attempts to sell the customer on an additional item.

III The Brand-Building Process

THIS SECTION WILL COVER how advertising is planned, implemented, and evaluated in today's marketplace.

You'll see how marketing thinking is "manufactured."

You'll see how marketers, agencies, media, and marketing services work together to build brands.

8 Marketing & the Planning Process

PLANNING & STRATEGY DEVELOPMENT is the focus of this chapter. Planning begins with evaluation.

You'll see how marketers and agencies work together to define and refine objectives and then develop strategies.

9 Creativity & the Communication Process

FROM IDEA TO IMPLEMENTATION. This chapter will cover the key element of implementation, the way an ad agency creates, presents, and then produces the communication.

It's one of the most fun parts of advertising.

10 Media & the Marketing of Messages

MEDIA IS THE CRITICAL CONNECTION. It delivers the message in the marketplace. Media costs are usually the largest part of an advertising budget.

This chapter will cover the ways agencies determine the most effective way to deliver their brand's message.

11 Evaluation & Integration

BRAND BUILDING IS an ongoing process of learning, evaluating, and improving – in a continual dialogue with the marketplace.

This chapter will survey the way programs are evaluated – providing critical information as the process begins anew.

You'll see how marketers improve their programs by integration – coordinating the full range of marketing activities.

Think different.

Marketing Plan.

This describes *what* a marketer wants to accomplish. It covers:

Product
Pricing (and budgets)
Distribution (place)
Promotion (including advertising)
Marketing Objective & Strategy
Advertising Objective & Strategy
and more.

Creative Strategy.

The creative strategy describes *how* you will achieve your advertising objective, covering such things as:

Brand Essence or Personality
Target Audience
Consumer Benefit

To help develop creative work, there may be some sort of "creative brief" that briefs the creative department on the advertising task and the target.

There may also be strategies in areas such as sales promotion and PR.

Media Plan.

The media plan includes:

A Media Objective – A goal which focuses on a target audience.

A Media Strategy – How you will meet that objective in terms of reaching the target audience.

A Media Plan – Tactics (media buys) that help you achieve your goals.

Ad Campaign.

The advertising itself is a result of this planning. Each ad is a *tactic* that helps achieve the advertising objective.

The advertising may be:

A TV or Radio Commercial
Print Advertising
Direct Mail
Or a combination of all the above.

& More...

Today, advertising is more than advertising. A complete marketing program for a brand might include event sponsorship, a sales promotion event, and product publicity.

Putting them together is IMC – **Integrated Marketing Communications.**

8

This chapter was written by Professor Jim Avery of the University of Oklahoma. Professor Avery is a former Management Supervisor at Wells Rich Greene, where he supervised the Midas Muffler account. He is the former head of the AEJMC Advertising Division, author of the text Advertising Campaign Planning, *and was appointed a member of the National Advertising Review Board (NARB) in 1997. He consults internationally.*

"Strategy is about choice."

—David Ogilvy

Marketing
The Planning Process

THIS CHAPTER on advertising campaigns will cover:
- **The Campaign Concept** – who does what, plans, and the need for organized action
- **The Language of Marketing** – missions, objectives, strategies, tactics, and other useful definitions
- **The Marketing Campaign** – some real world examples
- **How Advertising Works** – an introduction to basic communication theory
- **The Campaign-Planning Process** – a useful framework for building an advertising-based marketing campaign

As we start this chapter, let's meet four professionals and see how they develop advertising campaigns for their brands.

The first, **Casey Davis,** is a client. The other three work for agencies: **Alicia Hale,** a media person; **Bob Rickert,** a creative; and **Anders Pers,** an account guy.

Each is involved in the planning process; they all have a common objective – a winning advertising campaign.

Casey at the Bank.

Casey is the Marketing Manager for PNC Bank in Boston. He made the transition from agency account management to being a client and is a veteran of many advertising campaigns.

As you review what PNC had to do to re-establish themselves after a name change, you'll start to get the flavor of what is necessary to establish a brand and develop the plan for an ad campaign.

Rising in the Airline Industry.

Many of you will be able to identify with Alicia. We know this because, statistically, more students who read this book (our target) are female and under 30. So is Alicia.

She has risen quickly in the ad agency business because she works hard and loves advertising. She'll tell you how her discipline – media planning – contributes to the overall advertising campaign, which leads to the branding of American Airlines.

A Kodak Moment.

Anders Pers is an Account Manager on the *Kodak* business at O&M in New York – not bad for a kid who went to high school in Sweden and college at the University of Kansas.

Anders will tell us how account management contributes to planning an advertising campaign.

From Account Work to Creative.

Bob Rickert made his own interesting career change. He made the transition from the "suit" side as an agency account exec to the creative side a half-dozen years ago.

He re-evaluated his own objectives and strategies.

He became a copywriter at one of the top creative agencies in the country. Bob will tell us about the planning necessary to develop the creative part of the advertising strategy and how this will help to brand his client, Nicor, an energy utility.

As deregulation hits the utilities, advertising and branding will become increasingly important to Nicor – as well as its competition.

This is another example of how marketing has become a critical function for virtually every business – even a utility!

Each Plays a Part in Plans and Strategies.

Each of these have written a little about how they contribute to planning an advertising campaign.

Though the planning process may vary among agencies and marketers, there's one thing that is certain – many different people will contribute.

So this is also a good way to give you a tour through the factory, so to speak, as advertising is planned, then "manufactured," and then distributed through the media.

As we take you through the process, perhaps you'll be able to see where you might fit into the advertising business.

The Single Most Important Thing.

Even though there are more alternatives than ever, the advertising for a brand is still one of the most important thing that can be done to generate sales for that brand. It may also be the most fun.

Even with the growth of IMC, advertising is usually the key component of the branding process. And, even when a related field, such as sales promotion, becomes more important, you'll find that you'll still be using the same kind of strategic thinking

It is one of the biggest budget items, and it is the item most controlled by the marketer.

Promotional costs may be equally large (or larger), and public relations may be critical as well – but advertising is still a key driver for most marketers. And, as we said, you're still using the same kind of thinking. So, for these reasons, we'll focus on *the planning for an advertising campaign.*

When a series of advertisements runs, that is called an **advertising campaign.** This chapter is about planning that campaign.

**The Right Product.
The Right Message.**

This campaign for *Lever 2000* took it to #2 in bar soap, outperforming many established brands like Zest, Safeguard, Irish Spring, and Coast.

Background.

The bar soap category was relatively flat. Dial was the #1 brand, and P&G was the overall category leader.

There was general dissatisfaction among deodorant soap users regarding skin care, but most doubted a soap that "did everything" would deliver.

Two Objectives.

The primary objective was to get a 7% share – competitive with the other established brands.

A second objective was to give the Lever name consumer exposure. There was no inherent meaning or benefit in the name nor was it "consumer-friendly."

Lever wanted to become a higher profile brand in the US, where P&G dominated.

Strategy.

Strategically, the goal was to position *Lever 2000* within the deodorant segment. Research showed the way to communicate the skin care benefit was through the absence of a negative (harshness).

This avoided turning off those who didn't want a "complexion bar," while addressing a common complaint – deodorant bars dried the skin.

Creative.

The creative strategy was to position *Lever 2000* as better for your skin.

The advertising idea gave meaning to the name by linking the name and the benefits.

(Continued on next page)

Lever 2000 (Cont.)

The selling idea was expressed in a memorable ad theme...

"The deodorant soap good for all your 2000 parts."

The "2000 parts" television featured a montage of body parts communicating both the deodorant benefit and the skin care benefit.

The "better for your skin" benefit was further communicated with a commercial using a montage of baby parts. This also communicated all-family suitability.

Media.

The objective of the media plan was to generate brand awareness leading to initial trial and repeat purchase.

The target was women 18–49 with a household size of three or more.

A secondary target was men 18–49.

The media mix was network TV and national consumer print.

Share of voice was estimated to be in the 8-9% range.

Consumer and professional direct marketing plans were also used:

• A consumer-sampling program delivered products and coupons.

• A medical sampling program educated doctors about the brand's dual benefits.

Results.

Lever 2000 was the first and only successful new bar soap in the last 15 years.

• Within a year, *Lever 2000* grew to be the #2 brand with a 6.6% dollar share.

• Almost every other deodorant brand experienced share declines.

• Despite launching at a premium price during a recessionary year, the brand exceeded its original sales plan by 25%.

• Lever overtook P&G as the dollar share leader in bar soap with 34% total to P&G's 32%.

(Source: *Effie Awards Case Study – Lever 2000* by Bill Knees, Unilever HPC)

From Marketing Plan to Advertising Plan.

As we discussed in Chapter Four, marketers prepare a marketing plan, which involves the Five P's – including promotion.

This chapter will focus on how planning is done for a key part of that larger plan – an advertising campaign.

We'll review who is involved and what they do – though you should be familiar with this from previous chapters.

Key Concepts – Almost a New Language.

We will first discuss how advertising works and introduce you to a number of key concepts. It's almost like learning a new language – and a new way of thinking.

Along the way, we will give you a few real-world examples to illustrate the points we've made – like the Lever 2000 campaign in the sidebar.

Then, we'll take you step-by-step through the theoretical process of developing an ad campaign up to the time the creative objective is presented to the creative department and the media objective is presented to the media department.

We'll cover those steps in Chapters Nine and Ten.

First, Examples. Then the Theory.

Now we're going to take you through some real-world examples and then give you the underlying theory.

This is the reverse of some books. But we think it's important to understand that in ongoing businesses some steps are sometimes eliminated or shortened and others inserted due to the circumstances.

For example, a new product will take more planning than one more year of a successful program.

A software introduction might spend more time on PR and a big trade show, while a small, local pizza restaurant might let the sales rep for a newspaper, radio station, or direct mail service help create the advertising.

But even with all those variations, you'll see that there is a similar underlying planning process involved. Once you get a feel for this, it will be easier for you to understand the underlying theory.

When you do the reverse, you end up having to memorize a lot of abstract concepts that don't seem to relate to anything.

Got it? Okay, let's get going.

The Campaign Concept.

MARKETING IS FULL OF PLANS, and strategies. In fact, two people can be in a meeting and talk about "the strategy" and actually be referring to very different things. Here, look at some of the different kinds of strategies that may be used in developing a campaign.

- **Marketing Strategy** – This is the overall marketing of the brand, including all Five P's. This is the core organizing concept of the marketing plan. Saturn's strategy, for example.
- **Advertising Objective and Advertising Strategy** – This is usually the part of the promotional "P" given the most attention. There may also be sales promotion and PR strategies, as well as some sort of digital strategy.
- **Creative Strategy** – This strategy focuses on determining the right message. It may be referred to as a communication strategy, creative strategy, or some other variant, such as Creative Work Plan, or Creative Action Plan, etc. There is often a preliminary document called a **creative brief,** which serves to brief the creative department.
- **Media Objective and Media Strategy** – This deals with reaching the target audience most efficiently through paid media. This is often the largest part of the marketing budget. Again, with the emergence of digital alternatives, these message delivery options may show up here.
- **Other Plans and Strategies** – The above strategies are the four most common. If other disciplines are brought in, you may have other strategies as well: merchandising strategies, promotional strategies, design strategies, and research strategies are all possible. So are plans in the same disciplines.

It is critical to keep your specific discipline in focus and to understand how it relates to the larger picture.

For example, Y&R, a very successful ad agency asks, *"What is the role of the advertising as a subset of the marketing strategy."*

Who Is Involved?

Now that you see there can be a number of strategies, it may be helpful to review who does what in developing and approving all of these plans and strategies.

Marketers Write the Marketing Plan.

Generally, marketing plans will be written by the marketing department and approved by either a management committee or the COO (chief operating officer). In some cases, the ad agency may write or help write the marketing plan.

Upper management may or may not be involved in approval of various aspects of the programs.

Sometimes, management signs off on the budget once a year.

Other times, management is continually involved, doing things such as approving or revising recommended advertising.

Saturn's Strategy.

To you, Saturn has probably always been around. But, it's a relatively new brand that was the result of much planning by General Motors.

GM planned to recapture a part of the market lost to foreign-built cars and hold on to those who were considering a foreign car, but still feeling American loyalties.

The Saturn brand's job was to accomplish that objective. And, in many ways, it succeeded.

The Coke Brief Is Brief.

It's just one sentence: *"Only the unique sensory experience of a nice, cold Coca-Cola brings a magical delight to the real moments of my life."*

This is, however, a key piece of guidance for the development of the Creative Strategy.

The Agency That Wrote the Book.

If you can find it, here's a clear and readable introduction to the Y&R Creative Work Plan written by longtime Y&R creative guru Hanley Norins.

Early chapters take you through the original Work Plan, step by step.

Then, Norins examines great Y&R campaigns in print, TV, direct, sales promotion, public relations, and event marketing.

There's a concluding session on "The Whole Egg," Y&R's pioneering approach to IMC.

Some of this has been covered briefly in Chapter Four.

Other aspects will be covered in more detail if you decide to take a marketing course.

Agencies Write the Advertising Plan.
This will be the main area of emphasis in this chapter.

While an agency generally works with the marketer developing the plan, it is one of the agency's primary responsibilities.

The advertising plan will include sub-strategies, primarily the creative strategy and the media strategy.

These are then approved by the marketing department.

There Are Many Ways to Develop a Creative Strategy.
At some agencies, like Y&R, the creative director is responsible for the Creative Work Plan, though the entire agency participates – particularly account management.

At other agencies, it is even more collaborative.

Some sophisticated brand groups, like Coca-Cola, may provide the brief themselves – particularly since they work with more than one creative supplier.

At agencies with account planning, the process generally includes a **creative brief** (to "brief" the creative department) and the planner is deeply involved in strategy development.

After the strategy is developed, the creative department then moves on to developing the advertising message. That's Chapter Nine – "Communication & the Creative Process."

Media Departments Write Media Plans and Media Strategies.
Media involves the expenditure of a substantial amount of money – it is usually the largest part of the advertising budget.

This is the responsibility of the media department.

Media plans are first approved by agency management and then submitted for approval to the client. Smaller agencies may have the account manager write the media objectives and strategies.

At most agencies, it is done by the media department.

Larger client organizations may have a specialist with the primary responsibility of monitoring the expenditure of these funds.

Some New Variations.
CP+B and others take a wider view of message delivery – so the message and the channel may themselves become part of the strategic process.

With new approaches to message planning, thinking about the message "window" may come before working on the message itself.

As you can see, it can be a complex process where many have to work together.

A Team Working Together.
An advertising campaign (in fact, any kind of communication campaign) involves many different functions and even different companies working together – many people working to fulfill one objective. Even though they may work at different companies, or in different departments, they all play on the same team.

At the client, there is an advertising manager, brand manager, or marketing manager, such as Casey Davis at PNC Bank.

Depending on the size of the company, there could be a layering of people matched by the hierarchy at the agency.

This is one more reason the brand concept is so important – it is the organizing force for all these people. They are working on behalf of the business unit – the brand – that is responsible for how they make their living.

The Leader of the Team.

While the process may be complicated, the team organization is usually pretty straightforward. At the agency, the account manager manages the resources of the agency to develop the brand's strategic direction.

The media planner writes a media plan and the buyer buys the media. This is true whether the media function is inside the agency or at a separate media agency.

A research director and/or account planner finds information about attitudes toward the brand and how people make purchase decisions.

Account Managers Also Write Strategy.

The account management team is the link between the agency and the client, but that's only a small part of their job.

The account group is also responsible for writing strategy. They must work with the client brand group and the agency media, research, and creative departments to arrive at the correct strategy to move the brand ahead and fulfill agreed-upon objectives.

The real difference between a brand manager at the client and an account manager at the agency is small.

Both are interested in the same thing – developing the strategic direction necessary to build the brand.

Agencies Turn Ideas into Ads.

The creative people actually make the advertising.

If you think of an advertising agency as a manufacturing concern, then the creative people run the factory. They generate the ideas for what the factory makes, and then they actually produce the work.

Account management is exactly that – management. They are deeply involved in managing the process and making sure that the "product" will sell.

Generally, the copywriter writes the ad and the art director creates the visuals, though they usually work together as a creative team – with a creative director deeply involved.

Print production helps turn the copy and layout into a print advertisement. Broadcast production helps turn a storyboard into a television commercial. And, if there's a digital component, those specialists will add their own kind of production expertise.

Advertising. "It's a Team Sport."

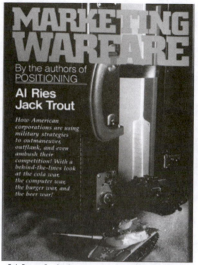

Worth Mentioning Again.

This book by Jack Trout and Al Ries makes a useful comparison between successful military strategies and tactics and successful marketing.

The War Room.

These days, you may be familiar with James Carville on a TV talk show, or in a commercial with his wife (she's a Republican, he's a Democrat).

Carville was a major political operative/strategist for Bill Clinton.

"It's the Economy, Stupid."
During the 1992 presidential election, he was the primary strategist in a campaign where a former governor of Arkansas, one of the smallest and poorest states in the US, beat an incumbent president – George Bush – who, at one time, had an approval rating of almost 90%.

Whatever your views, this is quite an accomplishment.

A documentary, *The War Room*, follows Carville and the rest of the Clinton team. It's worth watching.

Billy Bob Thornton's character in *Primary Colors* is loosely based on Carville.

But take a look at the real thing.

A Team Sport.
As the previous graphic indicates, a lot of people are involved.

A traffic manager makes sure the ad travels through the system and is sent to the media in time for it to run.

Printing plates or film are sent to the magazines and newspapers, and tape is sent to radio and television stations.

A media estimator provides estimated costs to the media planner. A media researcher may prepare a competitive report to aid in the development of strategy.

And these are just the people at the advertising agency.

It's a team sport where people work together to build the best thinking possible.

Other Team Members.
There may be sales people from the media involved, or specialists serving the client's sales force.

As the advertising is planned and placed in the media, other media people also become involved. A promotion may be developed and sales promotion suppliers involved.

The point is, many people and many organizations are involved. Think of it as a team sport – the whole organization is working together for victory in the marketplace.

Two other analogies are also appropriate – a military campaign and a political campaign.

Campaigns That Are Not Advertising.

Military campaigns and political campaigns are the two most common references we have to the term.

Military Campaigns.
The advertising industry probably adopted the term "campaign" from both military and political roots.

For example, the British campaigns of the Revolutionary War: The campaign of 1777–78 was made up of Howe's Philadelphia campaign and the British campaign of the South, etc.

Each of these were military campaigns.

While Howe's Philadelphia campaign took place when he marched on Philadelphia, it was also part of the larger campaign of 1777, which Howe hoped would end the war. It didn't. Remember, not all campaigns accomplish their objectives. And others, such as George Washington, were running campaigns of their own.

Political Campaigns.
A political campaign is similar.

In the 1960 national election, both John F. Kennedy and Richard Nixon had multiple campaigns that could be described as media campaigns, seasonal campaigns, and other kinds of campaigns, each contributed to their overall presidential campaigns.

In recent years, every US presidential candidate has had an Iowa campaign, a New Hampshire campaign, a campaign for each of the states, and a national campaign. And, as recent political campaigns demonstrated, the early front-runner is not always the winner.

Each individual geographic campaign contributes to the overall political campaign to win the presidency.

Many Individual Campaigns.

Just as in a large war, a political campaign is made up of many individual campaigns with one unifying objective.

It works just like an ad campaign.

This illustration shows how each media campaign, or each campaign designed for a specific time period, contributes to the overall campaign.

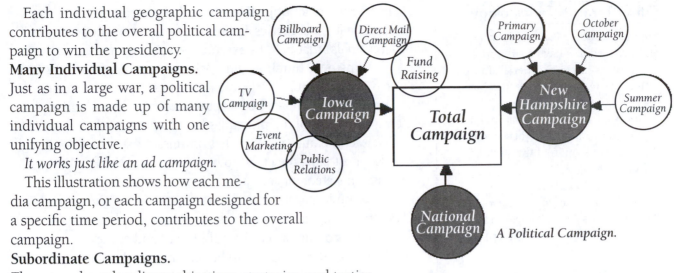

A Political Campaign.

Subordinate Campaigns.

There may be subordinate objectives, strategies, and tactics.

Each state campaign is made up of individual media campaigns.

It is common to have campaigns identified chronologically. There will be a caucus or a primary campaign or even a summer campaign or an October campaign.

It is easy to see that soon there is a campaign (time) within a campaign (state) within an overall campaign.

So, for example, you could describe the Iowa campaign as containing a TV campaign or a billboard campaign or a direct mail campaign. Like strategy, the word is used a lot and may have more than one meaning, depending on the context.

The Language of Marketing.

Marketing and advertising use some of the same language as war and politics.

In their classic book, *Marketing Warfare,* authors Trout and Ries applied the military principles of Carl Von Clausewitz (a 19th century Prussian general) to today's marketing.

The analogies were useful, and their book was a best seller.

Because the same type of thinking needed to win on the battlefield is needed to win in the marketplace.

The Need for a Common Vocabulary.

Effective communication depends on a common vocabulary.

It's critical on the battlefield, in the heat of a political campaign, and in the complicated process of planning a successful campaign for your brand.

As you enter the world of marketing and advertising, you need to understand what these words mean and use them properly.

Here are commonly accepted definitions of important words:

Mission, Objectives, Strategies, Tactics = MOST.

These are key words that describe and define the intellectual framework of the process. Each is clear yet complex.

They are locked together in a logical structure.

Saturn's Mission:

Recapture American car buyers who had switched to foreign-built cars with *"A new kind of car. A new kind of car company."*

Other Terms & Terminology.

Support, Tone, & Brand Character.
Strategies usually have a support or "reason-why" section, generally indicating the reason that the product delivers the selected benefit.

Support – Facts or information that support the claim or benefit stated in the objective section of the strategy.

Examples:

Mac Book. Easy to use.

Mott's Apple Sauce. In Easy-Serve Jar.

Reason Why – A specific reason that a product delivers a benefit or that proves an advertised claim.

Permission to Believe – A piece of information, factual or otherwise, that allows a person to believe the delivered benefit or advertised claim.

Nine-Wheel Logic – Type of support which seems to prove a point, even though it doesn't.

Example #1: *"Daddy, why does the train go so fast?" "Because it has all those wheels."*

Example #2: New colors may be added to a product to symbolize a new ingredient or feature which may be colorless and technically difficult or uninteresting to explain.

Example #3: The respective characters of the actors who represent the Mac and the PC.

Brand Character/Tone & Manner.
Ad strategies often have Tone, Brand Character, or Tone and Manner Statements designed to describe and define qualitative aspects of the brand or the advertising.

Brand Character – This is a statement about core values of the brand itself.

Examples:

Mac is friendly and easier to use than a PC.

Mott's Apple Sauce is nutritious and easy-to-serve.

Tone (Tone and Manner) – Statement about the kind of advertising that will appeal to a certain target.

Examples:

Advertising will appeal to computer users. (Apple)

Advertising will appeal to mothers concerned about their children's nutrition. (Mott's)

For example, an **objective** is a goal and **strategy** is the way we achieve that goal. **Tactics** are individual actions (like battles or TV commercials) that help us execute the strategy or win the war.

As Winston Churchill said, *"War is my strategy. Victory is my objective."* Individual battles are the tactics.

A **mission** is a related concept that operates on a higher plane. It is a statement of the principles by which a company is run.

Some companies are founded on mission statements, though, for the most part, they tend to be written after the fact.

Mission statements can also change over time.

An example, Apple's stated mission was once: *"Our goal is to put Macintosh computers in the hands of as many people as possible."*

This mission impacted their objectives and strategies.

Objective – A specific task to be accomplished.

P&G believes objectives should be: Specific, Measurable, Achievable, and Compatible (with other objectives and policies).

The P&G acronym is SMAC.

Defining objectives is key to good strategies. An example of an objective statement for a marketing strategy might be: *To increase unit sales of low-end computers next quarter by 15%.*

Strategy – How you will meet an objective.

There are many types of strategies: advertising strategies, communication strategies, marketing strategies, promotional strategies, and design strategies, to name a few.

Alternate Strategies – There are often alternate strategies available even when the objective is clear.

Example: *Our strategy will be to: (a) increase advertising; (b) offer price-off incentives; (c) provide easier financing; (d) lower the retail price; and (e) some or all of the above.*

The chosen strategy tends to be the best hypothesis as to how to meet the objective.

Sometimes this is based on experience, sometimes not.

When something is "on-strategy" it conforms to the hypothesis. When it is "off-strategy" it may fail to meet the objective or it may represent an alternate hypothesis.

Having a strategy is no guarantee you will accomplish your objective, but it increases your chances of success.

Tactics – Specific planned actions that execute the strategy. Ads, sales materials – the whole range of marketing communications tools are tactics. So is a sales call.

Example: *TV commercials comparing aspects of the Mac vs. a PC.*

Strong strategies beget strong tactics. In theory, mediocre execution of a correct strategy is better than an excellent execution of an incorrect strategy. In theory.

Key Fact (Y&R Creative Work Plan) – Based on analysis of all pertinent facts, the key piece of information that defines the business problem.

Problem – In this context, the specific issue that marketing communications must overcome to meet our objective.

Much of the work we do in developing strategies is aimed at overcoming problems.

In the Y&R Creative Work Plan, they look for *"The Problem the Advertising Must Solve."*

Solving that problem often becomes the objective.

Example: *People perceive it as difficult to switch from a PC to a Mac.*

Mandatories – Legal requirements or corporate policy.

Example: *Macintosh is a registered trademark of Apple Computer.*

Target Talk.

Target alternate descriptors are: **target audience, target consumer, target customer,** and **prospect.**

Whatever you call it, this is the person (or group) most likely to buy or influence purchase, or the person (or group) at whom the marketing communication is usually aimed.

Secondary Target – Some other key group in the sales or distribution process. Example: grocery trade.

Demographics – Specific quantitative facts about the target: age, income, etc.

Psychographics – Qualitative information about the target, sometimes based on quantitative information, sometimes based on smaller qualitative studies, sometimes based on considered judgement. Lifestyle, attitudes, etc.

Usage – Information based on use of product, product category, or competitive products.

Examples: *Bifocal wearers, owners of a PC.*

Attributes, Benefits, Features, and Laddering.

Strategic discussion begins with focusing on the benefit a product offers the target. Sequencing these factors is called **laddering.**

Here are generally agreed upon factors listed bottom to top:

Attribute (Product Attribute) – Characteristic of product, usually inherent or natural.

Applesauce comes in wide-mouth glass jars.

Product Feature (Feature) – Aspect of product, usually based on some manufactured or designed aspect.

Applesauce spoons smoothly out of the jar.

Product Benefit – A benefit to the consumer, usually based on a product feature or attribute.

Applesauce is easy to serve.

Customer Benefit (Consumer Benefit) – A benefit to the consumer, usually based on how the product benefit delivers a positive result to the consumer.

Some Important Terms with Varying Definitions:

"Campaign" and "strategy" are two critical terms that may be used with different meanings.

Here are a few others:

Event Marketing.

1. Marketing an event.

2. Treating advertising or promotional programs as events.

Position.

1. Place product resides in mind of consumer (Trout and Ries – *Positioning: The Battle for the Mind*).

2. Relative position in market i.e., leading mid-price laser printer.

Positioning.

1. The process of determining the correct position.

2. The process of achieving that position in the marketplace.

Re-Positioning.

1. Changing position in market or mind of consumer. Costly, time-consuming, doesn't always work.

2. Changing the advertising. Quick, easy, and sometimes it works.

The Ladder:

Value.
The powerful human dimension reinforced by the Benefit.

Consumer Benefit.
Usually based on how the Product Benefit delivers a positive result to the consumer.

Product Benefit.
Benefit to consumer, usually based on Product Feature or Attribute.

Feature.
Aspect of Product, usually based on manufactured or designed aspect.

Attribute.
Characteristic of Product, usually inherent or natural.

The Big Issue – Where to Focus.
Generally, the lower on the ladder you are the more product specific you are. Higher on the ladder = more generic.

Every food reinforces nurturing values. Every business product allows us to "be our best."

Remember, strategy is about choice.

Ad A: "Talking Stuffer."
This was prepared for the Christmas season – a major gift-giving time.
It emphasizes low-cost calling plans.

Ad B: "Love Connections."
This ad was done for Valentine's Day, with gift-oriented offers and a Candy Bar Phone.

I save time and my children get extra nutrition (which they enjoy), because I serve applesauce.

Values – The human dimension reinforced by the benefit.

I'm a good mother because I serve applesauce.

Laddering is the process of moving through this sequence.

The general method is to ask people why is that feature (or benefit, etc.) important and the answer generally moves you to the next level of the ladder. See sidebar.

A Question of Emphasis.

Many things may be true about a product, a target market, and a marketing situation.

The critical factor is determining what is most important.

As you examine the factors represented in laddering, you must choose – you must determine what must be emphasized to make your advertising message most effective.

The Advertising Campaign.

WHAT IS AN ADVERTISING CAMPAIGN?

Advertising is paid communication for an identified sponsor. Usually this advertising is distributed through mass media.

It is a series of, or multiple, advertisements that are part of a coordinated effort for an identified sponsor.

The American Marketing Association's *Dictionary of Marketing Terms* defines it as follows:

"A group of advertisements, commercials, and related promotional materials and activities that are designed to be used during the same period of time as part of a coordinated advertising plan to meet the specified objectives of a client."

This is consistent with the thinking in the industry and is consistent with how we got the term "advertising campaign."

Now let's look at three campaigns: One is for MACtel, a local telecommunication supplier; one for PNC, a New England bank; and one for Nicor, a new brand with no product to sell – yet.

By the way, some of these ads were done a while ago (we know you can tell by the stone-age cell phones), but the principles are solid, and the campaigns worked.

Example #1: MACtel – A Campaign in the Marketplace.

These ads were done for MACtel, an Alaskan company specializing in cellular phone service. It is a subsidiary of the local telephone company, Anchorage Telephone Utility.

These ads were created when cell phones were first being introduced to the market. It was a successful campaign.

Their agency, Porcaro Communications, created this campaign to convince Alaskans to buy cellular service from MACtel. The ads communicate the benefits of a cellular phone.

Benefits were written to coincide with seasonal events.

Four Ads – Creative Consistency.

Take a look at the four ads, A through D, in the sidebars.

This advertising campaign shows creative consistency.

The layouts are all similar and uniquely recognizable.

Every ad shows the telephone with some element that communicates the seasonal event.

A Brand-Building Theme Line.

They all use the same logo and campaign theme line, *"MACtel: The Alaskan Company."* They all have the address, phone number, and services offered.

Of course, this is an advertising campaign defined creatively, but it is also an ad campaign defined by medium.

It is a newspaper advertising campaign.

In fact, if MACtel had only had sufficient budget to run two ads in the local newspaper, it would still be an advertising campaign because it is a series of ads.

They also had a radio campaign which is compatible with the newspaper campaign, using the same theme line, *"MACtel: The Alaskan Company."* And, the campaign was effective.

Let's look at the thinking behind this campaign.

MACtel – Creative on the Mark.

Here's the view from Mark Hopkin, Creative Director for Porcaro Communications: *"When the agency started working with MACtel Cellular, cell phones were still viewed as toys for the status conscious – or electronic leases for workaholics. Furthermore, MACtel was in a distant second place in sales and name recognition."*

Two Goals.

"Through regular meetings with our client, we determined that we had to accomplish two goals:

"First, we needed to increase name awareness and recognition, so MACtel could get its share of the market.

"Second, we needed to educate the public of our product's day-to-day usefulness to ordinary people.

"To build name recognition, we decided that we would not refer to it as a cellular phone. It was a MACtel phone.

"We used newspaper and radio advertising to reach the target group. The newspaper advertisements you see on these pages."

Radio – Our Second Medium.

"The radio was used to reach people when they were out and about during the time when they were most likely to recognize the need for a cellular phone.

"We then created ads featuring cell phones in everyday situations with everyday people and a wise cracking announcer who celebrated mundane situations that ordinary Alaskans could relate to.

"These included a housewife getting a call from the school nurse about a sick child and a businessman leaving work early to go salmon fishing.

"We took it out of the realm of the status conscious, gave it to regular people, and showed how MACtel made life easier.

Ad C: "Better Get Hoppin."
This ad was for Easter, another Candy Bar phone promotion.

Ad D: "Don't Be Left Out…"
This ad was used to convince the target audience that a cell phone can be necessary safety equipment during an Alaskan winter.

Casey and the PNC Team *working to build a winning marketing and advertising plan.*

PNC Background.

Until 1993, the company known today as PNC Bank, was called The Massachusetts Company.

Founded in Boston in 1818, the Massachusetts Company pioneered the concept of financial specialization for individuals and was the first money management and trust company of its kind in the United States.

The company served the financial interests of many well-known New Englanders such as Daniel Webster, Henry Wadsworth Longfellow, and Oliver Wendell Holmes.

It also managed a portion of Benjamin Franklin's bequest to the city of Boston.

The Massachusetts Company was acquired by Pittsburgh-based PNC Bank Corp. in 1993.

At the time of this program, PNC was the 11th largest commercial bank in the United States, competing head-to-head with the largest financial services and money management companies in the world.

"The production for both the newspaper and radio were inexpensive enough that we could produce new work to fit each season, so they were always fresh and timely."

Triple-Digit Growth.

"The results were phenomenal. MACtel enjoyed triple-digit growth for the next few years, Anchorage achieved one of the highest cellular phone penetrations in the US, and MACtel had become the dominant provider in the market."

Background and Planning for an Advertising Campaign.

Now let's take a look at the campaign for Casey Davis' PNC Bank. Remember, before we take you through the theoretical process, we're going to examine a real one.

Notice how and why words are used.

In the real world, all sorts of existing factors, like brand history, competitive marketers, existing business organization, and limitations on resources play a part in the decision-making process.

Once more, as David Ogilvy said, *"Strategy is about choice."*

Let's take a look at some of the choices Casey had to make.

Example #2 – PNC Bank.

The Mission.

PNC Bank's mission is to provide private banking services through premier client service to high net-worth individuals and businesses in the New England region.

The Target Audience – 3–5%.

Their target consumer is defined as individuals and businesses with $1 million or more in investable assets.

This comprises 3–5% of all New England households.

The Products.

With corporate headquarters in Boston and a branch office in Greenwich, Connecticut, PNC tailors financial solutions to meet each client's individual investment needs and objectives.

Their most successful and profitable product lines were portfolio and investment management (stocks, bonds, mutual funds); estate planning and trust services; mortgages; construction loans; lines of credit; home equity facilities; and personal banking services such as retail deposit products (checking, money market accounts, CDs, IRAs).

The Problem.

Within virtually every marketing and advertising campaign is a problem. *Often, defining that problem clearly is a critical part of the planning process.*

Here's how Casey viewed the PNC problem in 1997:

"Although the company was founded over 179 years ago, we have only been doing business in New England as PNC Bank since 1993. Four years is hardly a corporate financial tradition by Boston standards.

"Moreover, some of our most formidable competitors can trace their corporate roots back to the mid-1700s. This is an accomplishment not

lost in the minds of the wealthy establishment in New England. These affluent individuals and families make up a significant portion of our target audience.

"Market research studies have shown that lack of awareness among target consumers is our highest marketing obstacle."

The Solution.

PNC set out to define a marketing solution to the problem with the knowledge that generating the right kind of awareness among target consumers was of major importance.

Initial Objective.

Part of their initial objective was to establish the base awareness measurement as documented by two market studies.

Then they set goals to measure the increase in awareness over time using future market studies. As they move ahead, this will allow PNC to measure quantitatively if they are meeting their goals.

Positioning *PNC*.

Casey and the marketing team developed several marketing strategies to meet their awareness goals.

The first was to establish an advertising positioning strategy that provided PNC Bank, with a niche in the market they could defend, a niche no other competitor could occupy.

In the end, their positioning statement became the following:

> **Position:** With a long standing tradition of customized individual service, PNC Bank offers the superior client service of a boutique private banking organization combined with the vast resources of one of the nation's largest financial services companies.

Armed with this positioning strategy, PNC set out to communicate it to target consumers using several marketing vehicles.

Perhaps the most market-visible and successful of these marketing vehicles is a print advertising campaign.

From Creative Brief to Tactical Plan.

The agency followed up initial conversations with a creative brief for review.

After a few revisions to this creative brief, it then became the tactical plan by which the print advertising was developed.

Working closely with Ketchum, the print advertising was developed to execute the primary strategy – at the tactical level this was corporate image-oriented rather than product specific.

The *PNC* Media Plan.

While the advertising was being produced, client and agency looked at media. The goal was to expose target consumers to the new advertising as many times as possible within budget.

PNC used the following publications to reach affluent individuals in New England: *Wall Street Journal* (New England Edition), *Boston Globe* (Business section), *Boston Business Journal*, *New York Times*, *Connecticut Weekly*, *Stamford Advocate/Greenwich Times* (Conn.).

PNC's Agency Partner – Ketchum Communications.

The print ads were developed by the agency of record, Ketchum Communications' Pittsburgh office.

Working via phone, fax, and e-mail, PNC communicated the awareness problem and the proposed positioning statement.

This provided the agency staff with the information it needed to craft a compelling advertising execution.

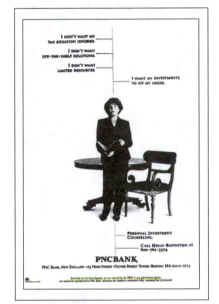

These ads have a sophisticated look and message. *They connect with the needs and concerns of PNC's target of high net-worth customers.*

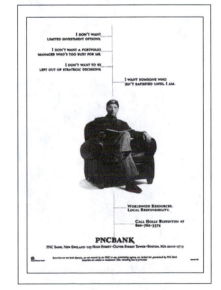

*"Nobody's ever branded
the warmth of your house
or the hot water that comes
out of the pipes."*
— Bob Rickert

Nicor. 30 second TV: "Gnome"

On a snowy Chicago winter evening…

a little lawn gnome comes to life…

goes in the house to make a cup of tea…

*…and takes a nice hot shower.
The announcer then reminds us*
**ANNCR (VO): "Generations have
relied on us for their energy needs…**

They also selected weekly New England newspapers serving selected affluent communities and magazines for various New England theaters and performing arts centers.

PNC and the agency also plan to add two to four additional consumer magazine publications to the 1998 media plan, all of which target high net-worth individuals.

Evaluation – Results Tracking.

So far, many believe the advertising has been successful.

Customer Service now fields more initial inquiries from potential clients than before the advertising, and many of those calls have resulted in new clients to the bank.

PNC will complete a quantitative analysis of their next market awareness study scheduled for late first quarter 1998.

At that time, they will measure any change in target consumer awareness versus base levels.

Ahead of Plan.

Although the bank is ahead of their plan, they certainly cannot attribute all of their success to the print advertising campaign.

However, it is an important and visible part of the marketing mix, and Casey believes it has done a great job of implementing PNC's positioning strategy.

Results in the Real World.

This is a good result, and a good summary of how planning works in the real world.

They set objectives, developed a positioning strategy, and executed an advertising campaign to meet their goals.

Now they are ahead of plan and working to evaluate their program so they can improve it next year.

That's how planning looks from the client side.

Now let's see how it looks from the agency side.

Example #3: Nicor – Building a Brand in a Hurry.

Bob Rickert was the writer and lead creative for a client named **Nicor**. They'd spent over four decades as the natural gas company (Northern Illinois Gas) that serves the suburbs of Chicago.

With the deregulation of the utility industry coming, they had to create a brand in a hurry.

In Bob's words, here's what they had to deal with…

The Mission.

"Our mission has been to take the former company, Northern Illinois Gas, and relaunch the company with it's new name, Nicor."

Nicor Strategy and Position.

"Because our client doesn't want to compete on a pure price basis, the strategy we presented and sold took the high road.

"Our position is to create a brand that stands for 'an unconditional supply of energy and the service to back it up.'

"This means that whenever, wherever, and however you need energy, you can count on Nicor *to provide it for you. It also means every type of energy, from natural gas to electricity."*

The Nicor Media Plan.

"Nicor is a broad-based product – a utility – with fairly broad objectives – building awareness. TV was a logical media choice.

"While there is some supporting print and other collateral materials, such as bill-stuffers, the major part of the advertising budget will be in TV.

"A major focus is the development of these TV commercials."

The Team.

Here's where the real world differs from theory. Getting people to work together can be an imperfect process.

New teams, whether student ad teams or new agency client relationships, may be less than ideal. Here's Bob's view…

"Our team consists of all the usual players. Extremely busy executives without enough lead time to understand the nuances of the client's business. An account person who, because the business was new with a tight due date, had to accelerate all of our learning.

"Creatives who had to keep reminding the others that TV is essentially an entertainment medium. And, of course, the client who, in this case, has been exceptional."

Imperfect as the real world may be, they got the job done.

Evaluation before Production.

Before the TV commercials were produced, some evaluation was done – in this case, focus groups.

"I spend a lot of time protecting work that's already been presented to our clients. To present the work to focus groups, I wrote audio scripts to be taped and played while storyboards were shown.

"Our lead account person has been extremely helpful in gauging the mood and the expectations of our client.

"There is nothing more important to have than good account management while you're trying to keep all parties focused on the big picture of creating and protecting the brand image."

The Production Team.

"The producer on this project has been helpful because he hasn't attended any of the meetings or research groups that led to approval of the work. Because of this, we believe his opinion has perhaps been much more consistent, since he sees the work more like consumers than will any of the other team members."

The Product – An Advertising Campaign.

The commercials were produced and run throughout Chicago.

"To date, the advertising has grown the brand's awareness to nearly the level of its goliath competitor. The high-quality commercials were generally well-regarded and accomplished their objective of introducing the Nicor brand to the market.

"In every piece of research, consumers have said they'd be comfortable choosing Nicor. Not bad for an 18-month-old brand."

When suddenly, he hears a noise!

The family is back. And Dad notices…

Our little gnome has his cup of tea.

ANNCR (VO) *Given a choice, seems everyone would. Energy from Nicor. Make yourself comfortable.*

Now Showing…

This is a lovely little spot, with nice music and great storytelling on film.

See it for yourself as a QuickTime movie on <u>adbuzz.com</u>

Branding & Advertising.

As you've seen from these examples, a brand is built by individual people becoming familiar with how the product (or store or service) performs in a competitive marketplace and then teaming up to create work that improves that situation.

Building Brands with Plans.

In every case, they're all focused on building their brands –improving the brand's performance in the marketplace – one of the main activities of The Business of Brands.

Brand Linkage.

On a basic level, the linking of the brand name and that marketplace performance (hopefully, with "functional superiority") is branding.

Think of the other links you can build. The fortunate linking of Nike with Michael Jordan just as was taking the basketball world by storm added great power to the brand. Likewise, Nike linking with Tiger Woods gave them instant credibility in golf.

Added Values.

As you build a brand, there is a further linking of other related values – for a perfume or fashion product, these values might include a certain edgy look or attitude.

For a food product it might be any of a number of things:
- It might be old-fashioned and nurturing
- It might support a certain flavor, such as spicy
- It might support a nutritional benefit
- It might support values of an ethnic heritage

Whichever values are selected, these **added values** can build the brand further.

Consumer Criteria.

The values addressed in the advertising must be what consumers expect from the product, or what they may judge to be consistent, or relevant.

Another way to think about values in advertising is that they must contribute to the satisfaction for why people buy the brand.

We addressed that issue earlier as the *"factors that motivate purchase behavior."*

The Importance of Advertising.

For most products, the linking of name, performance, and added values is performed by advertising.

For MACtel, it was communicating the product's appropriateness for the Alaska market.

For PNC, it was reinforcing existing values of the bank in a way that connected with a very specific target – well-to-do New Englanders.

For Nicor, it was building awareness of a brand-new brand name across an entire market – without a product to sell!

More Marketing Activities.

Other parts of a campaign designed to brand a product might be a sales promotion event or even a public relations program. This is where marketers examine other IMC opportunities.

For example, the Rolaids Relief Pitcher Award is PR that reinforces *Rolaids' "How Do You Spell Relief?"* advertising.

We've provided other examples throughout this book.

In these cases, advertising had to do most of the work. There's a good reason for this. For advertising-driven brands, PR or sales promotion is really part of the ad campaign.

And today, even with all the emphasis on other forms of marketing communication, and all the opportunities for "brand contact points," it is still advertising that does most of the job communicating with consumers.

Now that we've seen a few brief real-world examples, let's take a look at the process from a theoretical perspective.

How Advertising Works:
An Introduction to Communication Theory.

ADVERTISING IS ABOUT SELLING. Advertising is a replacement for or adjunct to a company's sales force and it does virtually everything a sales force might do – except take orders.

Advertising is also a replacement for or a supplement to **word of mouth** – which is still an important way that all of us collect product information.

Primarily, advertising is about trying to influence people to buy the brand. It includes any paid communication that would be intended to generate sales:

1. immediately or in the future;
2. to potential or current customers;
3. as reinforcement to past customers;
4. in any other way possible.

As we've said, for most products this means advertising.

Other Requirements – Functional Superiority.

As we've also mentioned more than once, the product must have some form of functional superiority to be successful.

Remember, this is *functional* superiority.

Example: *Suave*

A new shampoo may have some new ingredient or fragrance, but many will still select the leading price brand, Suave – still the volume leader in the shampoo category.

Suave has maintained acceptable performance while delivering on price. This adds up to "value," which is Suave's functional superiority – it's "reason for being."

Factors That Influence Purchase Behavior.

One of the early tasks in developing your advertising plan will be determining *"factors that influence purchase behavior."*

Many Roles of Advertising.

Advertising can perform many roles:

- It introduces a new brand, product, or service to its desired customers.
- It helps build existing brands in three ways.
  √ by providing perceived performance differentiation versus the competition;
  √ by providing added-value and therefore avoiding unprofitable price discounting;
  √ by building some measure of customer trial, repeat, and loyalty, thereby stimulating both short-term and long-term demand.
- It helps build an extendible asset, either the brand or company name.
- It helps build pride in the company and its products and services with employees and business associates.

Source: *Advertising Works II*

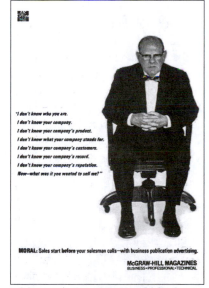

"I don't know who you are.
I don't know your company.
I don't know your company's product.
I don't know what your company stands for.
I don't know your company's customers.
I don't know your company's record.
I don't know your company's reputation.
Now—what was it you wanted to sell me?"

MORAL: Sales start before your salesman calls—with business publication advertising.

McGRAW-HILL MAGAZINES
BUSINESS • PROFESSIONAL • TECHNICAL

How Advertising Works.

Remember this ad from Chapter Six? The grumpy guy says, *"I don't know who you are. I don't know your company. I don't know your company's product. I don't know what your company stands for. I don't know your company's customers. I don't know your company's record. I don't know your company's reputation. Now – what was it you wanted to sell me?"*

This classic ad is an excellent argument for advertising.

Karma Queens, Geek Gods, & Innerpreneurs.

In the newly released book *Karma Queens, Geek Gods & Innerpreneurs*, branding expert Ron Rentel with Joel Zellnik creates nine new consumer types. Here are a few of them:

Karma Queen. Identified as a woman in her 40s or 50s who tends to buy organic food, wear Birkenstock footwear, practice yoga, and buy high-end bath products.

Geek Gods. Identified as men aged under 35 who can't live without the latest gadget and are eager to help others understand their electronics. They are considered the most benevolent of the consumer types.

Innerpreneurs. Rebels, people who ignore trends and focus on their own peace of mind. Such consumers may be in the market for a life coach or a wilderness vacation.

Denim Dads. Active in raising children. Embrace a balance between life and work. They might buy expensive jeans and pick the same music player their kids use.

Parentocrats. Upper middle class parents consumed with their children's well-being who may invest heavily in music lessons or videos promising to make children smarter.

A hint. When developing marketing communications, an insightful and thought-provoking target description – either one that exists or one that you have assembled – can help provide focus for the whole team. It helps to visualize who you're talking to.

This will help you determine the basis on which you will compete – a critical planning decision.

Two Primary Functions.

While the planning process has many steps, such as developing an overall marketing plan, the part we will focus on is the way the brand is communicated to potential customers – this is the advertising plan.

In its most narrow definition, advertising is made up of two primary functions:

1. **The Advertising Message.** This is also often referred to as **advertising creative**, which includes production.
2. **Media Planning and Placement.** After all the planning is done, the ads must be created and placed in paid media.

In a broader definition, delivery of the marketing message would include every aspect of the promotional function, such as sales promotion, event marketing, merchandising, direct marketing, and public relations.

Importance of Target Audience Definition.

These functions, creating the ad and placing it, require identifying a **target audience** with as much detail as possible.

Demographics could include age, gender, income, education, profession, and many other physical characteristics.

Psychographics are also used to get a grasp on the values and lifestyles held dear by the target group most likely to buy.

On a deeper level, researchers, account planners, and all advertising people look for meaningful consumer connections that will make the advertising more persuasive.

The Creative Function – Creating the Advertising Message.

The advertising message is the advertising creative product.

The more correctly the advertising message is stated, the fewer times the advertising will have to be placed in the media to have the same impact as a less powerful advertising message.

Logic and Emotion.

Most successful advertising operates on two levels – logical and emotional.

The logic is based on the right message – usually focusing on some factor that motivates purchase behavior.

The emotion is based on the right emotional connection with the target group. This connection will usually reinforce some aspect of the brand's values. This is an oversimplification which we promise to complicate further in Chapter Nine.

Advertising Goals.

The goal of most advertising is to impart some information to a specified group of people. But since we live in an over-communicated society, if the information is something people have heard before they often use selective perception to tune it out.

If it is a new and fresh presentation, there is a higher probability the message will be more memorable and persuasive.

That's why advertisers, and the people who create advertising messages, go to great lengths to develop a fresh way of stating an old premise.

Songs and jokes are written with a commercial bent to entertain audiences. Research is conducted to determine what criteria the target group uses to make purchase decisions.

If the research reveals that a decision to purchase a car is based on color, then new television commercials will show colorful cars and the copy will clarify the color options.

Advertising – A One-Sided Conversation.

When selling communication is between a salesperson and a potential customer, the effectiveness of the message is easier to evaluate because feedback is immediate.

Advertising communication through the mass media is more difficult because the message is received by the intended audience at remote locations.

Therefore, a message sent by the advertiser receives little feedback from the receiver of that message.

The Communication Process of Advertising

Feedback

Advertiser
Sender
(Encoder*)

Audience
Receiver
(Decoder†)

Message
*Brand advertising
†Current or potential customers, stakeholders

Here is one model of how advertising communicates.

Notice that it is more difficult for the audience to communicate back to the advertiser. Feedback is hard to come by.

This feedback usually takes place through market research – the Evaluation part of the process.

Factors That Motivate Purchase Behavior.

The message will be strong if it addresses the criteria that are important for decision-making. (Note: both "influence" and "motivate" are used. Either is correct.) These factors are determined through feedback from the target audience.

Example: Airlines.

For example, in the case of airline selection there are three criteria that motivate purchase behavior: scheduling, ticket price, and airline mileage clubs.

If there is only one airline flying at the time you want to go, and the prices are similar, chances are you will choose that airline rather than adjust the time when you want to go.

If there are many different carriers flying at the same time, you will likely choose the airline on which you have accumulated

Today's Targets.

Think of some of the groups that advertisers wish to reach today – and the product categories that can most efficiently be sold with advertising.

"Boomers."

Americans born in the '40s are now in their 60s. And whole new categories of products have arisen to meet their needs: health and pharmaceutical products, retirement programs, travel, financial products and services, etc.

College Students.

Did you know that you're in perhaps the largest college enrollment market ever? Why not list some of the product categories that should be advertising to you.

The Apple Purchase Decision.

The Mac vs. PC commercials use emotion and logic and actually communicate to both current PC users and current Mac users.

To PC users, they repeat the simple ease-of-use message, which Apple has used for years, along with an emotional message – Mac = Cool, PC = Not Cool.

The logic plus the cool/not-cool message goes to PC users who may consider switching. And it also provides Mac users with the emotional pay-off that they are cool and made the right choice.

United Airlines: "Training Room"
(Airport SFX under) Woman: (VO)
Didn't this training start at six?
Man I: (VO) Where is he?
Man II: (VO) What's the deal?
Man III: (VO) I got things to do.

Trainer: Feeling a little frustrated?
Tired of waiting? You don't understand
what's going on? Well, hang on to that
feeling the next time a frustrated cus-
tomer comes to you with a problem.

*Make it **your** responsibility to fix the*
problem. Act like you own the place.
'Cause you know… you do.

ANNCR: (VO) Compared to the rest of
the industry, United Airlines is heading
in a different direction.

Trainer: Tomorrow, we'll talk about seat
assignments. Oh, don't be late.

miles – or, depending on who is paying and the promotional rate structure, the price might be a factor as well.

Many other things are true about airlines. They have flight attendants and pilots, many of whom have nice smiles.

They fly to interesting places that you may want to visit some-day. They serve food of varying quality.

However, these factors usually do not have much to do with which airline you choose. You must know what's important.

The Importance of What's Important.

You might want to recall some discussion in Chapter Two about United Airlines switching agencies. A competing agency stated that United had *"the world's best irrelevant advertising."*

That competing agency won the business.

United had done some research and received feedback that revealed deep dissatisfaction among their target audience – business travelers.

One way United tried to connect with this audience was by ac-knowledging their dissatisfaction. They did it in ads, and even in their annual report, featuring complaints from disgruntled fliers.

Why are they doing this?

First, because negative factors can also motivate purchase behavior. If they can overcome some negatives, they will have a competitive advantage over other airlines.

Second, they may be able to change their product – to make it one that actually delivers a better experience to their target – or at least communicates that they're trying to do it.

This will improve their functional superiority.

All things being equal on the major factors that influence pur-chase behavior – schedule, price, and frequent-flyer points – this approach may add important values to the United brand – building a position as the airline that understands the business traveler.

The Importance of Feedback.

Remember, all of this was based on feedback, in this case research with the target audience – business fliers.

Feedback is a major component of the evaluation part of our Planning/Implementation/Evaluation process.

In the case of MACtel, our first campaign example, this feedback information was acquired through research.

The Media Function – Delivering the Message.

This topic deserves a brief mention right now, though we'll cover it in more detail in Chapter Ten.

Here, the goal is to deliver as many ad messages as possible to the target in the most efficient and effective way achievable.

Reach is the percentage of audience we expose to our message.

The number of times the audience is exposed to the message is called **frequency**. (Yes, this will be on the test.)

Frequency is *not* the number of times the ad is placed.

Media Measurement.

The results of the media plan can be quantitatively measured through the use of ratings. Nielsen and Arbitron have been the two key providers of program rating information.

When we read that the Super Bowl had a rating of 68, that means that 68% of all American households had their TV sets tuned to that program (sometimes called a vehicle).

GRPs = Gross Rating Points.

When multiple advertisements are run on television, the sum of the ratings generated by each individual vehicle in which an advertisement may appear is called a GRP.

That stands for **gross rating points.** This is a very standard term in advertising. (Yes, this will also be on the test.)

TRPs = Target Rating Points.

If the target is a critical subset of the overall audience, the more specific term "TRP" may be used.

TRP stands for **target rating points.** So if the Super Bowl rating is 68, but only half the audience is in the target, the TRP is 34.

Media Effectiveness.

Using these measurement tools, effectiveness is usually defined by the quantity of advertising pressure exerted on a given target group.

Three Measures of Effectiveness.

Three measures of effectiveness are:

- **GRPs** – gross rating points
- **Reach** – the percentage of different people who have had the opportunity to see the advertising
- **Frequency** – the average number of times those people have had the opportunity to see the advertising

And, as you might imagine, this material might be presented in a variety of combinations.

For example, in addition to TRPs, both reach and frequency may be stated in general terms or, more specifically, related to the target audience for the brand.

High Reach/Low Frequency or Low Reach/High Frequency.

This is often a key media decision.

High reach/low frequency or low reach/high frequency can be achieved from the same quantity of GRPs by adjusting strategic direction and the type of media purchased.

We learn through repetition.

Advertising works best when it is repeated.

Efficiency is evaluated based on the quantity of advertising messages that can be delivered for a given cost.

CPM = Cost per Thousand.

Often, in advertising, this information is expressed in the reverse; that is, the cost to deliver a message to a thousand members of the target audience.

This is called cost-per-thousand or **CPM** (the "M" is the Roman numeral that stands for thousand).

Our Changing Media Behavior.

We still watch a lot of TV, listen to a lot of radio, and read a lot of newspapers.

But our behavior is changing.

Recently, the 4As, ANA (Association of National Advertisers), IAB (Interactive Advertising Bureau), and the consulting firm of Booz Allen Hamilton, completed a major study on our changing media behavior.

They identified six trends:

Marketing as Conversation. Marketing has become less about pushing messages and more about co-creating experiences with consumers.

Media: The New "Creative." Marketing message distribution – timing, context, and relevance – is as important as creative execution.

Marketing + Math. New digital tools have brought a new generation of math to marketing.

Mind the Gap. Marketing spending in digital media is way behind consumer behavior shifts. There is still a major gap between traditional and nontraditional media.

The "Digitally Savvy" Organization. Functional technology skills are rising to the level of brand strategy.

The Network Effect. Partnerships and collaborations will grow in number and depth.

Remember, our media habits are changing even as you read this.

What's your media behavior?

Note: The Study "HD Marketing 2010" can be downloaded by going to http://www.boozallen.com/news/39486580 and then clicking on Marketing and Media Ecosystem 2010 Study.

Lavidge-Steiner Learning Model.

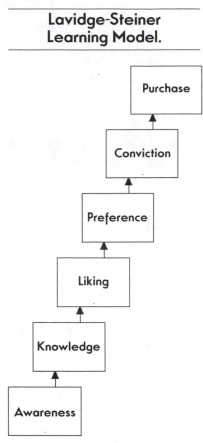

The model shows you that learning begins with awareness and then moves from knowledge to liking to preference to conviction and then to purchase.

This process can sometimes be quite rapid. In some circumstances, purchase may seem to occur at the awareness level – particularly if some incentive is used.

Media Strategy.

The intent of strategy on the media side of advertising is to first determine in which medium advertising messages will be the most likely to influence the intended target audience.

This will usually be the medium consumed by the target audience. The second intent is to place advertising for the brand in that medium or vehicle as many times as possible.

On a very basic level, when repetition takes place in advertising, you are beginning to reach people.

We repeat. People learn through repetition.

Advertising works best when it is repeated.

How People Learn…

While there are many models of how people learn about the brands they buy, the model in the sidebar – the Lavidge-Steiner Learning Model – is one example of how awareness, through advertising, ultimately leads to purchase.

Learning is clearly enhanced by multiple advertisements through a series of advertisements.

If this point seems a bit simple, it is.

Advertising works by placing a message that motivates purchase behavior into a media vehicle in which the intended target audience has interest.

As each advertisement is placed in the path of the target audience, more and more advertising pressure is exerted against that target audience. As these multiple advertising messages are placed in the media, the series of advertisements becomes an advertising campaign designed to reach people.

The increased frequency of messages delivered to the target audience results in increased awareness, which in turn can lead to increased knowledge, liking, and so on.

Advertising is a tool. It is not a "magic magnet" luring unsuspecting consumers into the store to buy a product.

When it is used well for a good product, it can work very well.

When used poorly, or if the product doesn't have the functional superiority necessary to compete, it is a waste of money.

Short-Term and Long-Term Effects.

As John Phillip Jones points out, effective advertising usually has a measurable effect in the short term. Powerful long-term campaigns are usually powerful in the short term, as well.

Much of the effect of advertising is part of a building process.

For example, the mere fact that a product and its advertising have been around for a while is a signal to many hard-to-persuade customers that the brand must be doing something right.

A frantic changing of ad messages may send another signal to sophisticated consumers – perhaps something is amiss.

Either way, over time the total impact on the consumer for a brand is the result of multiple advertising campaigns.

Each individual advertising campaign works with the other

advertising campaigns to impact potential consumers' awareness and to potentially change their purchase intent toward the brand in a positive (or negative) fashion.

And, of course, other "brand contact points" may play a role.

The Campaign Planning Process:
Writing an Advertising-Based Marketing Plan.

JUST AS BRAND NAME, product performance, and added values are linked together in the branding/advertising process, marketing, advertising, message development, and media placement are linked together in the planning process.

A Logical Sequence.

The marketing plan helps determine the role of the advertising strategy. The advertising strategy, in turn, helps determine the message strategy and the media strategy.

At each step, new thinking and new expertise are needed.

In a general way, you've seen how individuals at MACtel, PNC, and Nicor wrestled with these issues.

Now let's go through the planning process step by step.

The world being what it is, not all marketers or agencies go through every step and make every connection – but most try.

Often, a lack of time, a lack of information, a lack of resources, a lack of ability, or even a lack of luck can result in plans that are not done properly – or, even if done properly, they still may not perform.

It's not a certain world, but as Louis Pasteur once said, *"Fortune favors the prepared mind."* So, let's prepare ourselves.

Overview – A Ten-Part Process.

The following process and structure is not the only way to do things, but it is one that you can depend on.

Briefly, there are ten steps we'll cover.

1. **A Situation Analysis.** This is an Evaluation process. To begin, we see where we are – we find out what we know.
2. **Research.** We may evaluate further, and we may want to find out anything else we do not know.
3. **Problems and Opportunities.** Here, we look for the good news as well as the bad news.
4. **Marketing Objective.** Based on what we know, we then determine our marketing goal.
5. **Budget.** Here's a very tough part of the process. Now we must determine how much it will take to achieve our objective and build a rationale for getting the budget approved.
6. **Strategies.** Now that we know our goal, and how much we can spend, we then determine how we will get there, with advertising and media objectives and strategies.
7. **Advertising Creative.** Here, we develop our message based on our advertising strategy. If we have other messaging, in sales promotion, PR, or digital, the core benefit message developed here is usually very useful.

Read All about It.

Advertising Campaign Planning: Developing an Advertising-based Marketing Plan
by Jim Avery.

If you want to know more, read the whole book.

It is a more complete presentation and explanation of the advertising planning process we are covering in this chapter.

It is based on a format developed by P&G and one of their agencies.

Published by The Copy Workshop.

8. **Media.** Next, we develop our media plan, which is based on our media strategy. As media options have expanded, this area, not surprisingly, has become more complex and creative.

9. **Sales Promotion.** This section can also include any other appropriate marketing communications tactics, such as PR, event marketing, and digital efforts.

10. **Evaluation.** Once we're done, we want to see how we've done.

Now let's go through the process a step at a time in a bit more detail.

The First Step – A Situation Analysis.

The first step in creating an advertising campaign is collecting information to determine your current situation. That's why the first part of a plan is called the **situation analysis**.

Some call it a **background review.**

In planning, one of your first challenges is to determine what you do not know. This allows you to go out and conduct research so you will know what information you need.

Hopefully, this is what you do not know but soon will.

The goal of the situation analysis is, simply, to determine the current situation for the brand. After all, in order to get to where you want to be, you need to know where you are.

Most of the time, it covers the following areas:

• Current Users,
• Purchase Cycle,
• Geographical Emphasis and Seasonality,
• Creative Requirements, and
• Competitive Review.

Okay, one at a time.

Current Users.

We start with a review of the current users of the brand and those who use the competition – including their demographics and psychographics.

This is the beginning of the target audience definition – the more you know about your customers, the better.

In general, your future customers will be very much like the customers you already have.

Purchase Cycle, Geographical Emphasis, and Seasonality.

Next, we want to know how often they buy (sometimes called **purchase cycle**), where they are located (**geographical emphasis**), and what season, if any, has the greater consumption of the brand, etc. (sometimes called **seasonality**).

Seasonality.

For example, an ad campaign will be quite different if 90% of the purchase of the brand takes place in five days, as is the case with fireworks; or five weeks, as is the case with Christmas cards; or if seasonality is virtually flat throughout the year, with products such as milk or bread.

Seasonality Part One.

Some products have a very definite seasonality. Here's one. Hallmark advertises for a once-a-year selling opportunity.

Geographical Emphasis.

It is also quite common for national products to have very different sales levels in different parts of the country.

Whether those reasons are regional tastes, brand history, a stronger distribution network, or climate, they can be very important factors in planning.

Once you know that desserts and baking are more common in the Southeast, it will dramatically affect your national plan.

Creative Requirements.

Though you will not have the final answer, some find it helpful to provide an initial indication of creative needs and opportunities.

This would go here.

Competitive Review.

The last part of the situation analysis is a review of the sales, share, and competitive spending of the category. This generally requires the purchase of information from a specialty research company like LNA/Competitive Media Reporting.

Nielsen has been in the business of providing competitive sales information on brands sold at retail for over forty years, but only since the mid-eighties have they used scanners to gather the information.

Before that time, packages had to be counted by hand. The introduction of the UPC code dramatically changed the quality and the quantity of information for both retailer and manufacturer.

There are other services, such as IRI, that provide UPC-based share and sales data.

In other categories, there are other forms of tracking services.

Share of Market and Share of Voice.

You should know your competitors' **share of market** and their share of media weight (called **share of voice**).

This can be critical information in planning for your brand.

Assuming we know our situation, let's assume we're all part of a marketing team and work through the rest of the process together.

The Second Step – Research.

Much of the information that will have been gathered for your situation analysis will be **secondary research** – research drawn from existing sources. (In the sidebar, we cover the difference between secondary and **primary research**.)

Usually, the research segment of the planning has to do with primary research. Naturally, there may be situations where time and resources are simply not available.

However, it's important that key learning is identified, as there may be other ways to achieve the goal – for example, implementing a survey or a series of one-on-one interviews with current customers.

Research Goals.

The goal of this research will be to help with the development of overall strategy. For this reason, the information sought will most likely be in these three areas:

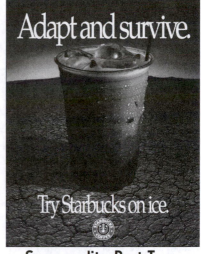

Seasonality Part Two.

Here, Starbucks works to counter the seasonality of hot beverages, like coffee, in the summertime.

Primary Research & Secondary Research.

This is important – and it will probably be on the test.

There are two types of research – primary and secondary.

The first thing to remember is that secondary research comes first!

Secondary Research.

Secondary research is drawn from existing sources – all company data, industry data, government data, media source data, trade association data, or commercial source data such as syndicated research.

It's anything already compiled.

Secondary research should always be done first.

This is research that most of us can do ourselves, with a little guidance and a lot of common sense.

It's also wise to remember the admonition: *the world is full of lousy research!*

When and where – and why – data were collected is important.

If data are too old (in marketing, two-year-old data can be too old), from the wrong demographic, or collected merely to justify or validate a program, they're worse than useless; they're misleading.

(Continued on next page)

Research (Cont.)

Marketers are better off thinking they have no information than feeling confident about faulty information.

Primary Research.

In general, you do primary research only after you've done secondary research.

Primary research is the gathering and analysis of original information from a sample or population.

It can be expensive and it needs to be done right.

So, before you do any type of quantitative research, such as a survey, you should have done exploratory primary research – e.g., focus groups or depth interviews.

Chapter Eleven.

This topic will be covered in more depth in Chapter Eleven.

"In retail, it's location, location, location. In business, it's differentiate, differentiate, differentiate."

— Robert Goizueta,
former CEO, Coca-Cola

Factors that Motivate Purchase Behavior.

People buy Lava Soap for one reason – to get very dirty hands clean in heavy-use situations, like workshops.

1. The Target Audience:

This is quite often made up of the people who currently use the brand, or people like them, but it could be people who influence the purchase. Young children, dogs, and cats don't actually buy brands, but they have a strong influence in the cereal and pet food categories.

For example the target might be the **primary grocery shopper** (**PGS**). For peanut butter, even though kids eat it, mom buys it, thus the campaign *"Choosy Mothers Choose Jif."*

2. Factors That Motivate Purchase Behavior:

We can't repeat this point often enough. How consumers make purchase decisions is critical to the success of the ad campaign.

For example, people who use bar soap may use criteria like color, aroma, price, "rinse-ability," longevity, or natural ingredients to decide which brand to actually buy.

Notice that it is not common for consumers to list cleaning as a reason for purchase behavior since this is a generic benefit of the entire category – all soaps clean.

Yet, some differentiation of cleaning might be a factor, even though it might not show up in research. Judgment is key.

If current or potential consumers want an aqua-colored bar to match the decor of the bathroom, there is little probability that they can be sold a bar of Lava. On the other hand, if getting hands clean is key for the bar of soap in the mud room or garage, then Lava may be the brand of choice.

3. Unique Brand Characteristics:

This may be key to what is unique to the brand.

Rosser Reeves at the Ted Bates agency called this a **USP**, or a **Unique Selling Proposition.** This is the key point of difference in the marketplace. M&Ms have a candy coating, Burger King is broiled not fried, and Visa is accepted virtually everywhere.

This allows those brands to make consumer-oriented claims like: *"M&Ms melt in your mouth, not in your hands"; "Have it your way";* and *"Everywhere you want to be."*

The key in the Research segment of the campaign plan is to make certain that the brand has all the necessary information in these three areas: Target Audience, Factors that Motivate Purchase Behavior, and Unique Brand Characteristics.

This is true whether you're dealing with a large brand and a big research budget or with a small start-up doing it on a shoestring.

Research Techniques.

Generally, the advertising agency or client will use a combination of qualitative and quantitative research tools to gather the information necessary to have the necessary information for the brand.

This will be covered in more detail in Chapter Eleven, but it will be helpful to offer a brief summary here.

Focus Groups.

The most common research tool used to gather qualitative information is the focus group.

Its correct name is the **focused group session** because it is a group of people in a session focused on one subject.

In our case, we would probably focus on the product category and the brand; how it is used, opened, and purchased.

We may do groups with both users and non-users.

One-on-One Interviews.

Another way to gather information qualitatively is one-on-one interviews. This can be more expensive, but has less probability of a few members of the group becoming opinion leaders during the group session.

Surveys.

The most common quantitative information gathering technique is the survey. The questionnaire can be administered through the mail, in malls via intercepts, or over the telephone.

Preparing the Research Plan.

The criteria for deciding which method to use is based on what information it will yield, how reliable it will be, and the resources available.

Qualitative information will usually give you positive (or negative) reinforcement for something you already believe to be true.

The brand will be able to glean rich quotes from consumers, called verbatims, on how they view the brand.

Quite often, advertising campaign lines or headlines come from focused group sessions.

At a minimum, the brand should expect to gather some key copy points. (Don't fall into the dangerous trap of conducting research without knowing what information is sought.)

Again, this will be discussed in more detail in Chapter Eleven.

The Third Step – Problems & Opportunities.

This segment of the advertising campaign summarizes the key problems in the category or for the brand.

Most of the time, there is at least one opportunity for every problem, but not always.

For example, Arm & Hammer baking soda knew their key problem was that women did not bake as many biscuits in the latter half of the 20th century as they did when the brand first came out.

There was no obvious opportunity to go with that problem. They either had to convince women to start cooking biscuits from scratch again or they had to find another use for the brand.

They did the latter. They uncovered a major usage opportunity.

There may be a box in your refrigerator right now.

Also called SWOT.

Another name for this section is SWOT. This stands for "Strengths, Weaknesses, Opportunities, and Threats."

It's another way of organizing Problems and Opportunities.

The Problem of Problems.

The most difficult part about trying to determine what you will do to advance the brand is often isolating problems.

Tums – Finding a New Problem to Solve.

Tums is an old low-tech brand, competing in a low-interest category with lots of competition – most making similar "fast relief" claims.

A new generation of heartburn products were about to come into the market. That was the situation.

The Insight.

The growth in awareness of osteoporosis among women was receiving more and more attention.

Tums is pure calcium carbonate, a form of calcium which the body can absorb.

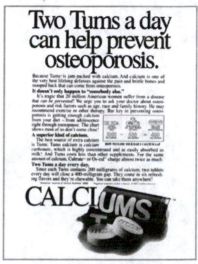

The Point of Difference.

Calcium provided a compelling point of difference that could separate the brand from the rest of the category.

The Strategy.

The strategy was a dual promise –get rid of heartburn with something your body needs – calcium.

Tackle heartburn with something your body needs anyway.

(Continued on next page)

Tums (Cont.)

The Support.

• Tums is the only antacid made with pure calcium carbonate, a great antacid and a source of extra calcium.

• Every time you take a Tums you're giving yourself something your body needs every day – calcium.

• Major competitors like Mylanta contain no calcium.

The Signature Visual.

It's based on two words. Calcium ends in "um" and Tums ends in "ums." By combining the two words visually, the point is made in an engaging way.

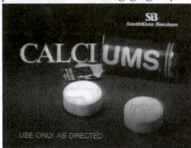

A TV commercial tells the Tums story in a place everyone can relate to – a diner.

Beyond Traditional Media.

There were additional dimensions to this idea – new markets and new communications opportunities.

• Hispanic advertising
• A 30-minute healthcare documentary which aired in 90% of the US

(Continued on next page)

For example, it was found in blind testing and in group sessions, that Nestle chocolate was preferred over Hershey.

But awareness of Nestle was significantly below that of Hershey. The problem was awareness, not taste.

The opportunity married to that problem was anything that would raise that low level awareness – advertising, increased distribution, sales promotion.

In some ways, virtually anything would help solve the problem if the result was more consumer trial and then the "functional superiority" of preferred taste would give the brand traction.

One of the key skills you need to develop for this stage of the process is an understanding of problems.

And this means an understanding and interpretation beyond the obvious of "we need to sell more" or "we have low awareness."

"The Problem the Advertising Must Solve."

In Y&R's Creative Work Plan, one of the better planning formats, a key component is "The Problem the Advertising Must Solve."

Identify the right problem, and you're on your way to finding those opportunities and solutions.

This is also a good place to put all the bad news.

No one particularly likes bad news, but in the tough world of marketing and advertising, it must be acknowledged.

The Problems and Opportunities section is where you do it.

This is the section where the Tums opportunity may have first appeared. For years, they'd been advertising as a traditional antacid. A change in the marketplace – an increased concern with osteoporosis – generated this worthwhile new opportunity.

The Fourth Step – The Objective.

There is much that you will want to accomplish. But when it's all said and done, your marketing objective will be a number.

Most likely it will be a statement of your sales goal. There may be other numerical goals as well – such as a brand awareness goal.

Though getting there can be demanding, and figuring out the right goal can be time-consuming, the final objective will probably be quite simple and straightforward.

It will be a number – a profitable number.

Because, when it's all said and done, the company that owns the brand wants to make money on the brand.

To do that, you need to accomplish some goal.

That goal will be your marketing objective.

The Fifth Step – The Budget.

The purpose for this part of the process is to provide substantiation for the amount of money you wish to spend.

As you might imagine, budget meetings are important. This is where management approves, or does not approve, the money you need to run your marketing and advertising programs.

A lot of things come into play during a budget meeting. If other divisions are having a bad year, you may find some of your budget taken away to help other brands. And vice versa.

Historical Expenditures.

Much budgeting is done by taking the volume projection and simply calculating the budget as a percent of sales.

If the brand spent 5.25% on advertising last year and the year before, something in that area will probably continue.

A-to-S Ratio.

This is a critical issue. It is the Advertising to Sales ratio.

This varies widely from category to category and often from brand to brand. (We listed some in Chapter Four on page 201.)

For example, in the shampoo category, a price brand like Suave will have a much lower A-to-S ratio than a brand-new luxury shampoo or the restaging of Pert Plus.

This can also be an area where marketers work for competitive advantage. For example, Nike changed A-to-S ratios when they began to dominate the sporting-shoe category.

LensCrafters needed to pull many more customers into their in-store lens-grinding labs than a frames-only eyeglass store.

They increased their A-to-S ratio dramatically.

Elements of the Budget.

The budget will have to break out expenditures by category.

The most common categories are:

- **Advertising** – Primarily media and production.
- **Sales Promotion** – This covers trade and consumer events and production. Discounts are handled in a variety of ways.
- **Public Relations** – This is primarily related to marketing public relations. Some include event marketing here.

Though you may begin with round numbers and projections, at a certain point this part of the plan must become quite detailed.

There are also fairly rigorous procedures within each company for final approvals and the expenditure of budgeted funds.

In every company, this is serious business.

The Sixth Step – Strategies.

As we mentioned in our initial definitions section, objectives are what you want to do and strategies are how you are going to accomplish those objectives.

In a marketing plan, objectives are usually numbers – something specific that can be a yardstick against which to determine success or failure.

Objectives & Strategies.

The marketing strategies state how you will fulfill the marketing objective. Here, in very simple terms, you can see the creative and media subsets. Now look what happens…

Tums (Cont.)

- Direct marketing to 70,000 health professionals
- The Calcium Information Center, through an 800#
- Community outreach programs in hospitals and women's health clinics
- Doctor office detailing

The Results: Tums Is #1.

- #1 antacid
- #1 branded calcium supplement
- Highest brand loyalty in category
- Highest share of doctor recommendations for calcium
- The brand women most often report taking for supplemental calcium.

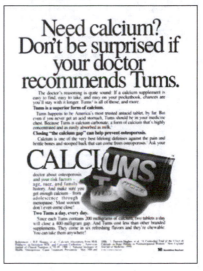

All this for a brand that was over 60 years old. Who says you can't teach an old brand new tricks?

(Source: *"Instilling Life in a New Brand,"* by Stephen Badenhop. In *30 Years of Winning Effie Campaigns.* From the *American Marketing Association.*)

Consider the *Campbell's Kids* advertising campaign. These ads formed a consistent campaign because they used the same illustrated style and consistently communicated the same two key selling points:

- **21 kinds**
- **10¢ a can**

Finally, they used repetition of the message with a variety of executions – keeping it fresh, but consistent.

A Balanced Ration

A food which is first of all delightfully appetizing. And also a food that combines in just the right proportions the various elements which your system needs to keep you in vigorous trim.

It would be hard to name a better-balanced food than

Campbell's Vegetable Soup

The rich stock is made from choice Government-inspected beef. In this we blend thirteen different vegetables. Among these are carrots, yellow turnips, white potatoes and sweet potatoes—delicately diced,—small peas, baby lima beans, green okra, and tender corn.

"Alphabet" macaroni adds to the attractive appearance. And we flavor this wholesome combination temptingly with celery and parsley and a delicate hint of leek and sweet red peppers.

As nourishing and satisfying a dish as you ever tasted. It involves no labor for you; no waste of time nor fuel. And you will find its regular use a constant benefit to your family's health and condition.

Hadn't you better order a few cans from the grocer and start your dinner with it today?

21 kinds

10c a can

Campbell's SOUPS
LOOK FOR THE RED-AND-WHITE LABEL

Marketing Objectives	
Sell 1,000,000 of the brand	
Market Strategy/Creative to establish the brand as superior to all competition	**Market Strategy/Media** to deliver advertising to a target audience of W18-49
Creative Objective to establish the brand as superior to all competition	**Media Objective** to deliver advertising to a target audience of W18-49
Advertising Creative Strategy to be determined	**Advertising Media Strategy** to be determined

The Strategy Becomes the Objective! These two marketing strategies become discipline-specific objectives which are then accomplished through other substrategies that need to be developed.

The Seventh Step – Advertising Creative.

The plan for advertising creative usually has only one objective.

If it starts with the words "to establish" then the person writing the objective has to say what the advertising is intended to do.

The advertising creative strategy will then address how that objective will be accomplished.

An entire creative platform is divided into segments.

There are many different ways to structure a creative platform. Here's an example for Campbell's.

Campbell's Soup Copy Platform:

> **Target Audience:** Women 18 to 49
>
> **Objective:** To establish Campbell's Red and White Label condensed soup as a delicious meal.
>
> **Strategy:** To convince women 18 to 49 to buy Campbell's Soup instead of other mealtime alternatives because Campbell's Soup is healthy and good tasting.
>
> **Considerations:**
> 1. Campbell's Soup is always served warm.
> 2. Campbell's Soup is inexpensive.
> 3. Campbell's Soup is available at virtually every grocery store.
>
> **Support:** Campbell's soup is nutritious and tastes good because it is made with the highest-quality ingredients from recipes developed by top-quality chefs.
>
> **Tone:** Lighthearted and fun.

A Creative Strategy Template.

As can be seen above, this strategy uses the template:

> To convince _____
>
> to use _____
>
> instead of _____
>
> because _____.

This template forces the strategy to recognize competition and a reason for the brand's being. It was originally developed by one of the agencies I worked for – Wells Rich Greene.

Sometimes Called a Copy Strategy.

After this creative platform, sometimes called a creative, copy, or communications strategy, is agreed to by both client and agency, the creative team at the agency starts to create advertising.

The creative platform also becomes part of the written annual planning document.

The Creative Brief.

A related part of the strategy or platform is the creative brief.

Its purpose is to "brief" the creative department and help them focus on the task.

It usually wraps the creative platform in additional information about the target and their relationship with the brand or product category. Its purpose is to provide insight and inspiration.

The Creative Action Plan & Other Strategy Formats.

Advertising agencies are concerned with brands. That includes their own brand. So it's not surprising that they even try to brand their strategy systems. That's why it's important to understand the underlying principles of all these message planning systems.

If, in your career, you move from one agency to another – or from one marketer to another – you may very well be working with a slightly different format.

They all tend to have the following characteristics:

- **An objective** is stated.
- **A target audience** is defined.
- **A strategy** – a way of selling the target, a proposition – is offered. In every case, this is a persuasive way of connecting the product to the target. It usually has some relationship to the factors that motivate purchase behavior.
- **And more.** There are other aspects to this kind of planning. For example, the system I prefer uses "considerations." Y&R's Creative Work Plan places great emphasis on defining "The Problem the Advertising Must Solve."

  Many of these systems use some sort of Tone and Manner statement, addressing some aspect of brand character.

  You'll see some of this in more detail in Chapter Nine.

The Eighth Step – Advertising Media.

The media plan usually has objectives which address the target audience, the geography, the seasonality, and whether there will be a reach or a frequency objective.

The media plan is just part of the advertising campaign – it's a specific discipline used to accomplish the marketing objective.

For example, if the marketing objective is to ship five million cases during the coming year, one of the strategies may be to advertise to a target group of women 18 to 49.

Alicia Hale Talks about Media Strategy.

Right now I'm an Associate Media Director on American Airlines at Temerlin-McClain. My responsibility is the strategic development of media.

From an "A" to AAF to AA.

I graduated from the University of Kansas with an advertising degree. I decided to pursue a career in media after getting an "A" in my media strategies class as a junior.

After the course, my professor encouraged me to participate in the AAF National Student Advertising Competition (AAF/NSAC).

Though we spent all night in the computer lab during spring break, it was one of the best experiences of my life.

I then spent two years at JWT/New York before moving to Dallas.

Now, I determine in which media to place ads for American Airlines.

I manage five other people – a supervisor, two planners, and two assistants.

When putting a plan together we follow a step-by-step process.

Objectives and Goals.

The media selected to generate awareness for each campaign is based on objectives and goals agreed upon by the agency and brand.

We begin the process by gathering information from our media buyers, if we're intending to use broadcast media, and print sales reps if we propose to use print media.

(Continued on next page)

Alicia on Media (Cont.).

Gathering information is often the hardest part of the job.

You may have to rely on people who don't have your same time constraints.

When all the information is available, a strategy and the tactical means for implementing that strategy are developed.

A Good Career Choice.

Overall, media has been a good career choice for me. I have the opportunity to be creative as well as crunch numbers.

Some of the perks of the job when you're broke and just starting out are free lunches and tickets to the theatre and sporting events.

Of course, now I can buy my own.

This, then, would lead to a media objective of delivering advertising to a target audience of women 18 to 49.

The media strategy might be to advertise in daytime television and in women's magazines. Though, with changing lifestyles, the media department might also want to look at other options as well.

Media Flow Chart.

Below is a media flow chart that shows the advertising media used for the University of Alaska in the 1997–98 fiscal year.

The university will use cinema, transit, newspaper, radio, cable TV, and magazine advertising.

Selling messages will be delivered during three key periods leading into registration – fall, spring, and summer.

Often, the flow chart will also have costs listed in a column on the right and delivery numbers in a row across the bottom.

Multi-Tiered Media Flow Charts.

Some marketers have a number of tiers.

For example, automobile marketing includes a national brand campaign – sometimes more than one, for various nameplates – plus a regional dealer effort, plus local dealer advertising.

Large fast food franchises often have national, regional, and local programs going on – virtually simultaneously.

Media Flow Chart: University of Alaska.

	July	Aug	Sep	Oct	Nov	Dec	Jan	Feb	Mar	Apr	May	June
Cinema (slides):												
Fireweek (7)		▓				▓					▓	
Totem (8)		▓				▓					▓	
University (6)		▓				▓					▓	
Dimond (9)		▓				▓					▓	
Denali (1)		▓				▓					▓	
Eagle River (6)		▓				▓					▓	
Wasilla (3)		▓				▓					▓	
Fairbanks (9)		▓				▓					▓	
Kenai (3)		▓				▓					▓	
Transit (poster panels):												
Bus Rear (10 buses)	▓▓▓▓										▓▓	
Bus Side (10 buses)	▓▓▓▓										▓▓	
Newspaper:												
Anchorage Daily news		▓				▓					▓	
Radio (:60):												
KBear ?, 18/wk		▓				▓						
KLEF ?, 18/wk		▓				▓						
KNIK ?, 18/wk		▓				▓						
KYMG ?, 18/wk		▓				▓						
Cable Television (:30):												
50 Spots/week (100 GRPs)		▓				▓						
Magazine (P4CB):												
Time			▓			▓						
U.S. News & World Report			▓			▓						
Newsweek			▓			▓						
Sports Illustrated			▓			▓						

A flow chart helps them keep track of programs.

For smaller franchise groups, the flow chart will tell them when national programs are going on, and when they're on their own.

The Ninth Step – Sales Promotion, Public Relations, & More.

This part of the plan addresses: sales promotion, public relations, and other appropriate IMC programs.

With the growth of IMC, we will be seeing these aspects play a more and more important role in the planning process.

Sales Promotion.

This is the part of the plan that provides tangible motivation to the consumer to buy the brand with some sort of incentive (a small bribe).

The purpose of a sales promotion event is to increase the value to the consumer so that she or he will be more interested in purchasing the brand.

We discussed sales promotion techniques in Chapter Seven.

Smart marketers work to integrate their sales promotion efforts with the advertising, so that the theme and message add value to the brand at the same time they provide that incentive.

Sales promotion should work in concert with the advertising.

Here, Gerber capitalizes on the unique relationship and feelings that parents have for their newborn children to create involvement in a successful sales promotion program.

An advertising campaign for a packaged food product will quite often use television advertising to create branding and a coupon, an FSI for example, to create trial.

Trade Promotions.

Trade promotions seek to do the same thing. But the target audience is members of the trade – dealers, retailers, wholesalers, franchisees, etc. Some trade promotions may include such things as co-op advertising or advertising allowances, display allowances, free goods, etc.

Occasionally, there is some confusion among students about sales promotion. For example, a 50¢ coupon that is part of a full page Right Guard magazine ad in *Men's Journal*. Clearly, this is an ad.

But the sales promotion costs include the coupon, the money the advertiser pays for the redemption of that coupon, and a fee to the clearing house. Some of these costs, other than media expense, may show up elsewhere in the marketing budget.

The Media Flow Chart.

Alicia Hale now does media planning for Temerlin McClain, the agency for American Airlines.

She talked briefly about some of the issues she deals with.

The Need for a Flow Chart.

One of the best ways to address these issues is with a media flow chart – a way to visually communicate a complicated media program.

The flow chart can then be used as a reference for overall discussion of the media plan as well as specific concerns such as weights, start dates, and scheduling.

The flow chart helps make the abstract strategic concepts of a plan easy for all to visualize.

Powerful Emotions. Powerful Promotions.

Here, Gerber creates a continuity program – *Gerber Rewards* – that includes both big prizes and small incentives.

The incentive leverages both logic and emotion. There's a nice "bribe," a college scholarship, that also hooks into the feelings a parent has for their new baby.

Event Marketing.

Some industries have critical trade shows. Other product categories need sampling and outreach.

On your own campus, you may see some examples on your way to class.

Public Relations.

The public relations segment of the plan starts with an objective that states the goal. Strategies are then written to plan the method and tactics for fulfilling the objectives.

Unlike sales promotion, most marketing planning still does not take public relations into account – yet.

But as Integrated Marketing Communications becomes more important, integrating this powerful marketing communication discipline into the marketing plan will become more important – and more common.

Public relations is usually performed by a public relations agency. This is separate from an advertising agency. The public relations strategy will usually seek to build publicity for the brand or for the advertising. The specific press releases are the tactics of the plan.

As discussed in Chapter Seven, public relations in this context usually refers to MPR, or marketing public relations.

& More.

Newly emerging digital opportunities may play a role. Don't pass them by. Here is a place to integrate them into your plan.

The Tenth Step – Evaluation.

An advertising campaign starts and ends with research.

In the beginning, a situation analysis is conducted to determine where you are, in order to understand what you need to know.

From there it is research, problems and opportunities, objectives and strategies, advertising media, advertising creative, sales promotion, and public relations.

This last segment is named Evaluation.

The Evaluation segment is there to make sure that a method is in place to determine the quality of the plan so that learning can be had in the following period.

For example, the Evaluation objective might be *"to determine how the plan can be improved during the coming fiscal year for implementation into next year's plan."*

In some ways, this is always the objective, though the methods may change. And you should note that Evaluation also has its own objectives and strategies.

This portion of the plan is a built-in mechanism to find new ways to improve the plan each year. It helps to eliminate the tendency to use the same plan year after year.

The knowledge gained from this segment is one of the primary tools for improving marketing efforts.

This aspect is so important that Chapter Eleven will emphasize Evaluation. Though Evaluation occurs at the beginning and end, we felt you would appreciate it more at the end, since you now will have a better idea of the need for evaluation.

Some Common Methods of Evaluation.

The Evaluation is divided into methods of evaluating the brand and ways to evaluate the advertising.

Tracking Studies.

In general, any research that tracks some factor or factors over time is called a **tracking study.**

Brand Evaluation – Attitude and Usage.

Strategically, when evaluating the brand, it is common to use an **attitude and usage study** or some other quantitatively based measure of consumer attitudes.

If they're continued over time, they become tracking studies.

Advertising Evaluation – Recall, Persuasion, Entertainment.

Evaluation of the advertising can be broken down into measurements of consumer recall, persuasion, and entertainment as a result of the advertising.

Recall is the consumer's ability to remember the advertising, including key points within the advertising, at some point after the advertising is placed in the media. Twenty-four hour recall is common.

Persuasion – Pre/Post.

Persuasion is a measure taken to determine the advertising's ability to change consumer buying intent.

While there are many research methods to do this, it is common to just ask people if they intend to buy the brand.

The change from what respondents said before the advertising, and what they said after they saw the advertising can be attributed in a large degree to the power of the commercial message.

Entertainment – A Topic of Debate.

There is much discussion as to the importance of entertainment in the evaluation of advertising.

Clearly, we all prefer entertaining commercials.

But it is not as clear what role entertainment plays in a successful advertising campaign. The nature of the product and the nature of the consumer connection are two key variables.

This explains why talent and good judgment are always critical for the development of a successful campaign.

In recent years, advertisers and their agencies have seen the value of advertising that is entertaining to the target audience.

The idea here is that if the advertising is entertaining, then people will watch it, read it, or listen to it.

With the average American being exposed to between five hundred and three thousand messages a day (depending on which research you believe), the advertising must get attention.

The entertainment value of the advertising is usually discussed qualitatively, and some research suppliers can provide benchmark scores. This allows advertisers to know if their advertising is more or less entertaining than other advertising.

This is one more factor in the complex process of planning an effective advertising campaign.

Attitude and Usage.

This Effie-winning campaign provided a new generation of women with relevant and meaningful new usage for Reynolds Wrap and dramatically reversed a declining sales trend – one that had stretched nearly 20 years!

Recall and Persuasion.

This Effie-winning campaign for Lubriderm capitalized on the brand's heritage while dramatizing the problem of dry skin in a memorable and persuasive way.

The campaign helped generate double-digit growth in both shipments and consumption.

Summary:

The Importance of Advertising in Brand-Building.

MARKETERS AND ADVERTISERS jump through all these hoops because, in many cases, an advertising campaign can build brands faster and better than any other business tool.

And even many of the other marketing tools – digital programs, events, PR blasts, and sales promotion – are initiated with an advertising mindset.

Done well, there is no better way to build awareness or improve public perception than a hard-hitting advertising campaign.

Done badly, there is no faster way to waste large amounts of money and put your career in jeopardy.

Effective advertising begins with an intelligent plan.

But this is only the beginning.

The creative message must be crafted exceptionally well.

And then the message must reach the target effectively.

Those are the next two steps in the brand-building process.

Creative message development and marketing those messages.

And, they're our next two chapters.

Discussion & Review Questions:

1. An Advertising Campaign.

What is the definition of an advertising campaign?

2. Objective and Strategy.

Define, order, understand, and explain the hierarchy:
- A marketing strategy
- Advertising objective and advertising strategy
- Creative strategy
- Media objective, strategy, and tactics.

3. A Team Sport.

Why is advertising a team sport?

4. Campaign Origins.

What is the genesis of the term "campaign?"

5. MOST

What does the acronym MOST stand for?

6. Attributes and Benefits.

What is the difference between an attribute and a benefit?

7. Feedback.

How do we get feedback from advertising communication?

8. Select a Brand for Discussion.
- What is the single most important thing that can be done for that brand?
- What are the factors that motivate purchase behavior?

9. Media Flow Chart.

What is a media flow chart?

10. Media: Reach and Rating.
What is the relationship between reach and rating?

11. Media: CPM.
If a magazine advertisement costs $125,000 and it reaches 8 million people, what is the CPM?

12. Situation Analysis.
What are the key steps in a situation analysis?

13. Strategy Development.
What three things do you need to know before you can create advertising?

14. Consumer Research.
How do one-on-ones differ from focus groups?

15. A-to-S Ratios.
What is an A-to-S ratio?

16. Creative Strategy.
Explain the elements in an advertising creative strategy?

17. Sales Promotion.
What is the difference between advertising and sales promotion?

18. Evaluation.
Why is the evaluation step important in an ad campaign?

Concepts & Vocabulary:

Account manager – Sometimes referred to as an account executive or account supervisor. This advertising agency person is responsible for strategy development, managing the resources of the agency, and communication with the client

Added value – 1. In sales promotion terms, it refers to an approach where something is added instead of discounting the price. 2. In advertising terms, it usually refers to some aspect of brand equity.

Advertising agency – An agent hired and authorized to take care of advertising matters for a client. A full service agency will plan, set objectives and strategies, create, place, and evaluate the advertising. A limited service agency may only create or place the ad.

Advertising budget – The quantity of money available for an ad campaign. It is often divided into advertising, sales promotion, production, etc. There are a number of ways to develop a budget.

Advertising campaign – A group of advertisements, commercials, and related promotional materials and activities designed to be used during the same period of time as part of a coordinated advertising plan to meet the specified advertising objectives of a client.

Advertising effectiveness – A measure to determine the extent that the advertising campaign met the objectives that were established.

References:

Here are some books you may want to read to develop better strategies and more effective advertising.

The Mind of the Strategist: Business Planning for Competitive Advantage
by Kenichi Ohmae
Classic insight into the mental process behind winning strategies was written by the head of McKinsey/Japan.

It's a salute to *"that ultimate non-linear thinking tool, the human brain."*

How Advertising Works: The Role of Research
Edited by John Philip Jones
Professor Jones worked for JWT in London before becoming a professor at Syracuse. He offers one of the best professional perspectives around.

Some of the latest and best thinking on getting good research into the planning process.

Strategic Brand Communications Campaigns.
by Don Schultz and Beth Barnes
Some of the best current thinking on how to make Integrated Marketing Communications work.

(Continued on next page)

References (Cont.)

Advertising Works II
by Alan Middleton, John Dalla Costa. A very well-written and useful book published by the Institute of Canadian Advertising.

Canada is a market that has always had to work under extra challenges of cost and scale. The result is a conceptual approach combined with some very interesting case histories that few of us have ever seen before.

It's out of print, but you can probably find a copy on Amazon.

The New Positioning: The Latest on the World's #1 Business Strategy
by Jack Trout
Solid update on a classic.

22 Immutable Laws of Marketing
by Al Ries and Laura Ries
An excellent easy-to-read compilation of good common-sense marketing advice. Many of these things seem simpler and more obvious in retrospect, but Ries and Ries help tie the threads together.

(Continued on next page)

Advertising evaluation – A process to evaluate the effectiveness of the advertising campaign. Four measures used include: recall, persuasion, entertainment, and sales.

Advertising objective – What the advertiser hopes to accomplish as a result of the advertising. It is the same as a marketing strategy.

Advertising plan – A written document designed to outline the advertising objective, the rationale for the objective, and how it will be fulfilled.

Advertising strategy – How the advertiser plans to fulfill the objective. It can be written for media, creative, sales promotion, public relations, production, etc. Contained within the advertising plan.

Background review – Sometimes called a situation analysis, it is a recap of what is currently known about the brand. It includes: current users, geographic, seasonality, purchase cycle, creative requirements, competitive sales, and competitive spending.

Budget – This can mean either sales volume or spending allocation.

Consumer – The people who will buy the brand.

Consumer orientation – To think about the brand from the consumer's point-of-view instead of the manufacturer's viewpoint.

Creative brief – This is used to brief the creative department. It usually contains a creative strategy and other background information needed to write and visually create advertising.

Creative objective – What the advertiser hopes to accomplish as a result of the creative product. The creative objective is linked to the marketing strategy. It can start with the words "to establish."

Creative platform – Similar to a creative brief. The parameters contained are usually target audience, benefit, support, and some type of tone and manner or brand character statement.

Creative strategy – How the advertiser plans to fulfill the creative objective. A good template is: to convince _____, to use _____, instead of _____, because _____.

Creative Work Plan – Refers to a method to create and produce advertising and advertising strategies developed by Y&R.

Customer – The people who currently buy the brand.

Decision grid – A quantitative weighting system used to make complicated decisions.

Frequency – The number of times an individual or household is exposed to an advertising message over a certain period of time.

IMC – Integrated marketing communication.

MarCom – Marketing communications.

MOST – Mission, objectives, strategies, tactics.

Marketing plan – A written document designed to outline the marketing objective, the rationale for the objective, and how it will

– 420 –

be fulfilled. It contains elements for the Five P's – price, product, promotion, place, and people.

Media objective – What the advertiser hopes to accomplish as a result of the media plan. It is the same as the marketing strategy.

Media plan – A written document designed to outline the media objectives, rationale for the objective, and how they'll be fulfilled.

Media strategy – How the advertiser plans to fulfill the media objective. There are media strategy for media mix, types, formats, geography, seasonality, and flighting/continuity.

Mission – This is an overall goal, a company's reason for being.

Objective – This is a specific goal to be accomplished within a certain defined period.

Primary research – Gathering and analysis of original information from a sample or population (see *secondary research*).

Positioning – The art of arranging the mental picture of your brand maintained by the target audience. Positioning is done to the mind, not the product.

Public relations – Part of the Promotion "P." It seeks to use publicity and other forms of non-paid communication to influence attitudes and buying behavior.

Reach – The percent of the target group which has been exposed to the advertising at least once. It is an unduplicated number.

Sales promotion – Part of the Promotion "P." It seeks to use small rewards to change the value relationship of the brand. An example is a fifty-cent coupon.

Secondary research – Gathering and analysis of information which is available in published form, i.e., printed or online sources.

Situation analysis – See *Background review*.

Strategy – This is how you get there – the way you accomplish your objective.

SWOT analysis – This is similar to Problems and Opportunities in a Background Review. SWOT stands for "Strengths, Weaknesses, Opportunities, and Threats."

Tactics – These are specific actions to fulfill strategies.

Target audience – This is the group of people most likely to purchase the product. These people can be users, those who influence the users, and actual buyers.

Trade – Retailers and wholesales in the distribution channel who will resell the product to the end users or consumer.

USP – Unique Selling Proposition. An advertising approach developed by Rosser Reeves.

Word of mouth – In terms of marketing and sales, this is another important way that we all get information about products.

References (Cont.)

Books by Trout & Ries. This was the writing team that put out some of the classic books on marketing thinking.

Each of these books still offers useful advice for the marketing and advertising professional:

Marketing Warfare by Jack Trout and Al Ries
Bottom-Up Marketing by Jack Trout and Al Ries
Positioning: The Battle for Your Mind by Jack Trout and Al Ries

These are some of the books that started it all. And, if you decide to go into the business of brands, you'll eventually need to read them all.

Advertising Campaign Planning: Developing an Advertising-based Marketing Plan by Jim Avery

One thing I guarantee – if you finished reading this chapter, you'll already be familiar with this book.

There's a very simple reason for this – I am the author. It lays out the planning process we've just covered much more completely.

One of the main uses of this book is to help develop plans books for the AAF/NSAC, but it works well for most types of advertising planning.

And, if you have the good sense to participate in the AAF/NSAC competition at your school, you may not be able to avoid this book.

Jim Avery,
University of Oklahoma

9

This chapter was written by Tom Fauls, Associate Professor and Director of the Advertising Program at Boston University. He teaches creative courses plus Interactive Marketing Communication, New Media Strategies & Design, and Digital Brand Dialog.

His students have gone to most of the top-10 agencies and interactive agencies including Digitas, neo@Ogilvy, and R/GA, plus Google , Microsoft, and Yahoo!

He's worked at NWAyer, Leo Burnett, TLK, JWT, FCB, C-K and Atkinson Marketing as Copywriter, ACD, CD, and ECD. Tom has a BA in Communication Arts from Notre Dame, an MS in Advertising from the University of Illinois, and completed the Web Commerce Program at DePaul University School of Computer Science, Telecommunications and Information Systems.

> *"Advertising is the greatest art form of the twentieth century"*
>
> — Marshall McLuhan

Creativity & Communication

THE MEDIA REVOLUTION has had major impact on the creative side of the Business of Brands – to say the least.

One of the most exciting changes is a huge expansion in the number of opportunities. Now, high-level creativity and creative technology are everywhere – not just the largest markets.

Best of all, while this chapter will focus on creative specialists, you might want to remember one other piece of very good news – now all of us have the power to be creative.

Four Creative Careers.

Let's take a quick look at four creatives and The Media Revolution.

Rewriting the Rules of the Road.

In 2001, as Exec Creative Director and President of Fallon, **David Lubars** knew the car-buying market was changing. He saw BMW's segment spending more time online. BMW owners, perhaps more than most, wanted to be in control.

The result? BMW Films. High-octane creativity online.

Shaping the Digital Age.

Armed with her BFA from the Rhode Island School of Design, **Pegeen Ryan** was prepared for everything. Virtually. Good thing, too – because the traditional direct agency she joined morphed into one of the world's premier interactive agencies – Digitas.

Now she's at Mullen, developing ideas in every conceivable interactive channel. Microsites. UGC (user generated content). Games. Mobile alerts. Social networking. She's not just creating new ads, but totally new marketing concepts!

Building Blogs.

Since 9th grade **Liz Gumbinner** knew she'd be in advertising. After graduating from Boston University, she worked her way up to CD on brands like Mitsubishi, Universal theme parks, and Old Navy.

Then she combined her writing talent, marketing experience and new "mom" status to become co-founder and editor of the CoolMomPicks.com site and newsletter. Creativity *can* start at home.

Moving out. Moving in. Moving up.

During his internship at Crispin Porter + Bogusky, **Thomas Kemeny** gave up his Chicago apartment and moved into the agency's Miami office. He did more than that.

He developed a TV spot during this unpaid internship that won a One Club Pencil. And that paid off in a job at Goodby Silverstein in San Francisco. Way to go.

From Advertising to Almost Everything.

The Media Revolution is causing creative careers to undergo some pretty exciting changes – revolutionary changes.

Once upon a time – when I was your age – a successful creative had to understand how to craft advertising in the traditional media: print, television, radio, outdoor, and collateral – usually a brochure. Sometimes, there was something extra ("other") like your slogan on a button or a T-shirt for the sales meeting.

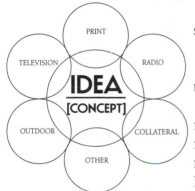

Fig 1. Traditional Media Advertising

Figure 1, on the left, kind of describes it – traditional media.

That was pretty much it.

It sure seemed like a lot at the time, but it's nothing like today.

Today, creative careers not only range across all media – but they range across almost all forms of marketing communication: Ads, Public Relations, Sales Promotion, Direct, Event/Environmental, and New Media – which usually starts with a Web site, but then grows into almost anything you can imagine.

Now it kind of looks like Figure 2. In this book, we're calling it the MarCom Matrix.

Fig 2: The MarCom Matrix

For this chapter, we'll be looking two ways – forward and backward.

We're going to be looking forward at the ways people are meeting today's challenges – and we'll take a look backward at how those challenges were met in the past.

We think you'll see that great work is still great work, even though the channels may be changing.

It can be a great outdoor board or a banner ad, a direct mail piece or a Web site, a TV commercial or a viral video on your phone.

Creativity? Some Definitions.

"The supreme task of the physicist is to arrive at those universal elementary laws from which the cosmos can be built by pure deduction.

"There is no logical path to these laws; only intuition resting on experience can reach them."

Albert Einstein

"Creativity is the art of establishing new and meaningful relationships between previously unrelated things... which somehow present the product in a fresh new light."

Leo Burnett

"All great innovations consist of sudden shifts of attention and emphasis onto some previously neglected aspect of experience... They uncover what has always been there [yet] they are revolutionary."

Arthur Koestler

Creativity in Advertising.

Reach the target with a benefit in a persuasive way. That means the right attitude as well as the right message.

Here, a high-flavor food product of dubious nutritional value sells with a spicy, fun-loving attitude.

Hints, Links & Resources.

At the end of each section, look for this sidebar, which will tell you where to find out more.

More Good Advice

"You must have inventiveness, but it must be disciplined. Everything you write, everything on a page, every word, every graphic symbol, every shadow should further the message you're trying to convey."

Bill Bernbach

"An advertisement is creative when a consumer looks at it and sees something in relation to himself that he would not have seen without the advertisement.

"I find nothing more tiresome than a maudlin display of brilliance of how bright a writer or art director thinks he is."

Carl Ally

How This Chapter Is Organized:

First, we'll discuss Creatives, Concepts, and Challenges – who they are, what they do, and some of the unique challenges facing creatives in the Media Revolution.

1. **The Creative Challenge** – New channels and the need for new business models.
2. **"Creatives"** – Who they are – and who's joining the team.
3. **Concepting** – What creatives do.

Then, we'll take a walk around the MarCom Matrix, and briefly cover everything from traditional advertising to new media.

4. **Traditional Media Advertising**
5. **Public Relations & Publicity**
6. **Sales Promotion**
7. **Direct & Database Marketing**
8. **Event & Environmental Marketing**
9. **New Media**

Finally, we'll deal with a few practical matters.

10. **Selling Your Ideas**
11. **Producing Your Ideas**

That's quite a bit for one chapter and, as you might imagine, we'll just skim the surface. But if you'd like to know more, we'll also provide **Hints**, **Links**, and **Resources** we think you'll find helpful.

Ready? OK, let's go!

The Creative Challenge:
Communication Models. Channels. Challenges.

We're going to start by covering some pretty big thoughts, which add up to some pretty big challenges.

- **Creativity and Marketing**.
- The need for new **Communication Models**.
- The growth of new **Communication Channels**.
- **Clutter and Culture** – Shifts in everything from the number of messages, to the way we relate to them.
- **The Rise of Digital Marketing**. We no longer just consume media – now, with digital media, we can interact with it and even create it.

By the way, when you're in the middle of a Revolution, you often lose the old rules without having quite figured out the new ones.

That's pretty much what's going on right now.

Basically, creativity is *"new combinations of old elements."* That was James Webb Young's classic definition.

It may be a straightforward idea that takes an unexpected turn of logic, or something that comes from left field.

It may, at first, appeal to our reason and later on be found making itself at home with our emotions. Or vice versa.

It's the puppy with the bent ear that made us stop and somehow ended up going home with us. And now it's everywhere.

Marketing Creativity – Art with a Business Objective.

Creativity is everywhere. It's in our music, in art, in fashion.

It's in architecture, movies, books, and so on.

Of its many uses, creativity in marketing is unique.

Here, creativity serves a business objective. It's why we aren't artists in the same sense as Picasso or Hemingway.

True artists may not worry about how you respond to their art. However, in marketing the response of the audience is critical – in fact, it's the whole reason for that creativity.

The Need for Effective Creativity.

In most cases, creativity in some form is essential to do the job, whether it's merely clarity of design in a simple sign, or all the things that make a Web site "sticky."

Most smart marketers know you can't bore people into buying, so that means persuasive communications that make things interesting. Over-communicated consumers demand it.

Sure, they understand ads pay for most information and entertainment, and if they need a locksmith, they'll take the trouble to find one. But in their daily lives, they won't stop in their tracks for an ordinary brand message.

However, in exchange for a little entertainment or information relating to real needs, they may give your message a first glance.

A Few Other Differences.

A number of other factors present a challenge:

- **Time.** It's creativity on demand with schedules and deadlines.
- **The risk of the unknown.** If it's truly new, how will it connect? Will it work? We don't know for sure.
- **The risk of "been there/done that."** If it isn't new, will anyone notice? Has it stopped working, or can we keep it fresh?
- **Fear.** If it's new, will it work? If it isn't new, will I keep my job? By now, you've gathered that sometimes marketing can be a bit of a tough business to say the least. On the other hand…
- **Fun.** It can be fun and exciting, and you work with people who are pretty interesting. Other kinds of creativity are often pretty lonely. Here, it's a team sport. And we have wonderful tools to work with. The idea. The visuals. Wordplay. Layout. Typography. Copy/scripts. Drama. Humor. Empathy.

That may explain why many love it and hate it at the same time.

Communication Models and Business Models.

Though the messages vary, we work off some basic communication models and business models. And they're changing, too.

The Decline of the Interruption Model for Messages.

Once, the default communication model was **interruption**. Ads were interruptions on TV or in a magazine.

If it was interesting, we paid attention, and we understood that our media cost less because of advertising.

Media economics made this model work. Advertising costs were low enough, audiences were big enough, and enough people

Effective Surprise.

Make surprise work for you.

"Grab life by the beans."

Entertainment. Good.

Here, the Colombian Coffee Council says, *"Grab life by the beans."*

Information. Better.

A low-priced restaurant tells you they put more beef in their burgers.

Benefits. Best.

Ads like these helped establish Volvo – as durable. Safety came later.

Pop Culture.

CP+B looks for "cultural tension" to get traction for its message.

Upscale Culture.

David Ogilvy used this to become "the Rolls Royce agency."

Pink Air.

An early example of ironic humor. Ad legend Howard Gossage announced a campaign to color the air in your tires.

responded to the ads so that the whole thing worked.

For about 100 years, this business model worked.

Well, as you've read in other chapters, those economic factors are changing – higher costs, smaller, more fragmented audiences, lower response levels.

It all adds up to a search for new answers – new models.

That's why you're seeing work on all sorts of new communication models – some based on search, on interaction, on involvement, and even on new ways to interrupt.

That's one huge creative challenge. But wait. There's more.

Changing Channels. Creating Channels.

Now we choose from an amazing new menu of media choices.

Many of them have been around for less than ten years – some for less than ten months.

Podcasts. Online video. Sponsored blogs. Smart phones.

As if it weren't hard enough to figure out what the message should be, today's creatives have to become conversant with all sorts of new communication channels – or we have to become conversant with new experts in those new channels.

A New Kind of Challenge.

Put it all together and you've got a brand new adventure and a brand new set of challenges for the "creatives" who still have the same job – to create messages that work in the marketplace.

Today's creatives have more opportunities than ever before. More TV channels. More tools on your desktop. More ways for your words and visuals to reach people. And, since it's not all good news, more competition for attention than ever before.

Clutter and Culture.

In this kind of environment, how do we create messages that "stick." How do we connect? Think Velcro.

Mixed together, we find pop culture, media, clients who want messages that work, the client's brands – and another activity we call "branding" – and, of course, the agencies and their "creatives" who have to make sense of all this and create the work that works.

If that sounds just a little bit wild and complicated, you understand perfectly. This is a business that travels at the speed of pop culture, sometimes even playing a role shaping it.

Look around. You'll see ads, PR campaigns, and promotions that reflect or derive from popular news and entertainment trends.

It's always been that way – from David Ogilvy's Rolls Royce ad with a headline pulled from a British car magazine to the latest car ad based on anything from a JD Power survey to a superspy movie.

The Bad News about the Good News.

Clutter. The blizzard. Call it what you will, all those terrific new media channels and messaging opportunities create their own problem.

Sometimes the world looks like the side of a NASCAR racer, with logos and messages on every square inch.

How do we connect with all that going on?

This is the final part of the creative challenge.

Two things that help us: culture and personal decisions.

Swimming in a Media Culture.

That media stew isn't just ads – it's news, news about the news, entertainment, our favorite sports teams, and all the other things we watch, read, and listen to.

As Howard Gossage said, "People read what interests them. Sometimes it's an ad." Make that "read, watch, and listen" and it's still true. We have more choices and, more and more, they're *our* choices.

Relevance. What's Interesting to You?

We all have different lives, agendas, and shopping lists.

Our bookshelves, video collections, and refrigerators reflect that.

In the winter, some go to the beach for sun, some go to the mountains to ski, and some stay home in front of the fire. All those individual differences add up to a pretty interesting marketplace.

If we can find ways to connect things that genuinely interest people, we're on the way to meeting some of those challenges.

Different Folks. Different Strokes. Different Jokes.

As a creative, it's your responsibility to get into the lifestyle of the people who'll be seeing your ideas. You must understand what makes them tick and, sometimes, what makes them laugh.

You have to learn to connect with people who may not be at all like you. Successful creatives learn how to do that. It's fairly easy to understand your own generation. How would you sell a retirement community to people over 55? What media channel would you use?

Remember, we each consume a different media stew.

In many cases, you'll have to research these differences. Or the agency will have done it for you.

The Rise of Digital Marketing... and More.

With the rise of digital marketing, we're seeing the effectiveness of traditional advertising decrease (though there are still some pretty terrific exceptions) without any dependable new answers.

Naturally, everyone wants accountability and ROI (Return on Investment). After all, we all want to know what worked.

So even though we can show instances where something worked, we no longer have the steady record of performance that was once common to most ad programs.

But the big change is, you're no longer a passive media consumer. More and more, you're in control.

Yesterday. Today. Tomorrow.

Meanwhile, marketers love the seemingly impressive numbers they get with almost everything they do online (more on that later).

But they also realize that this new world doesn't always deliver.

Sometimes, they see traditional advertising working – just like the old days – then, just as quickly, things change.

Business minds want dependability. Marketers look for measured results on all elements of their campaigns, on- or off-line.

And, simply put, these days it's just not that simple.

Want to Know More...

about the first modern art director?

This book surveys the amazing 50-year career of Peretz Rosenbaum – better known as Paul Rand, the primary influence on Bill Bernbach and virtually all the art directors at DDB.

Is Great Creative Enough?

Sad to say, it often isn't. Horn & Hardart hired some of New York's top creative talents to produce ads that would save their failing chain.

This ad, with candles and light bulbs as the main course, won awards. But the award-winning ads weren't enough to keep the chain in business.

New Yorkers were familiar with Horn & Hardart. They had newer and better choices. They enjoyed the ads. Then went somewhere else to eat.

"Persuasion is an art, not a science."
— Bill Bernbach

Creative Teams.

Teaming up is very, very important.

You'll find many aspects of the creative arts where teams work together.

Songwriting is one of them.

Creative Department Organization:

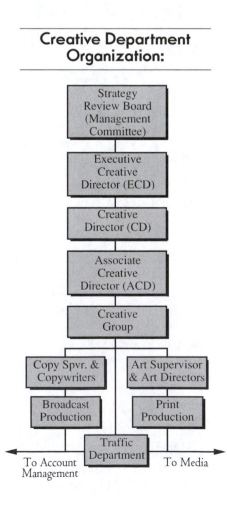

So even business is getting creative in surprising ways.

For example, many of the most boutique-y, high-concept agencies are hiring experts in "analytics," the quantitative analysis of every measurable variable. Meanwhile, traditional marketers, like P&G, are rubbing elbows with creatives at Cannes.

And marketers around the world are looking for creative solutions to the Creative Challenge. It adds up to big opportunities for those who can meet the challenge with creativity that works.

"Creatives."

It may seem like an odd-sounding term, "creatives." But that's what we often call people whose job is creating marketing communications – particularly advertising. It usually refers to: **copywriters**, **art directors**, **designers**, **musicians**, **Web designers**, and **creative directors**.

Simple Organization. Complicated Job.

As you can see by the chart on the sidebar, the organization of a creative department is pretty simple, though the job is complex.

Basically, it's a hierarchy – top to bottom.

Big creative departments have a lot of people, smaller agencies, just a few in the creative department.

Big departments have a lot of titles, small departments, just a few.

Some typical titles – Copywriters, Art Directors (AD), Associate Creative Directors (ACD), Creative Directors (CD), Executive Creative Directors (ECD), and Chief Creative Officer (CCO).

Plus Free-lancers.

More and more agencies use free-lancers to staff up for heavy workloads. Some work for more than one agency.

It's a Team Sport.

This chapter will focus on copywriters and art directors, who will report to a creative executive – usually a creative director.

These are still the primary entry level jobs – though we are now seeing many with digital skills becoming a part of 21st Century creative teams. Now, let's add a strong shout out to all the talented people they team up with who also work and think creatively.

Here are some examples:

- Print, broadcast, and interactive **producers** may or may not be organized under the creative department, but they're full-fledged creatives, with calculators. In print, there's a whole area called "**electronic pre-press**" that deals with taking graphic files into the various channels – from old-fashioned newspaper to the latest high-tech computerized press, and then over into the Web. We'll get back to them in the very last section – Producing Your Ideas.

- **Graphic designers** typically specialize in brand logos, package design, brand and corporate identity – though their influence is becoming more wide-ranging.

In the past, designers spent little time collaborating with copywriters on ad concepts and much more time thinking about the brand from a visual perspective. As channels broaden, more and more creative projects are being approached from a design perspective – CP+B's Mini Campaign would be a good example.

A number of top creative executives, Alex Bogusky and Rich Silverstein are two, came from design. Some marketers, like Apple, are showing how design can build a competitive marketing advantage.

- **Interactive developers** often make major creative contributions when their talent enables complex Web-based interactivity and functionality. The germ of the idea may start in an agency but blossom in surprising and wonderful ways once developers begin working on it.
- **Planners**, with one foot in creative, one in account management and another (they're unique) in research, must think creatively.
- **Other team members**. Agency account managers, media planners, research professionals, and client brand managers are also expected to think creatively in their work. Not all the "big ideas" come from the creative department.
- **Other MarCom Specialists.** Other members of the team also have to think creatively. In event marketing, project managers better have their creative hats on, and in many sales promotion organizations, the initial creative thought for the promotion comes from the account manager – the creative team then executes with the account manager acting like a creative director. Meanwhile, over in public relations, the creative spin in the press release will be coming from the PR team – they have to do the creative work as well as the client contact.

Remember, marketing needs creativity in many different ways. And you may need to wear a creative hat from time to time, even if you aren't a "creative."

New Kinds of Creative Suppliers.

To no surprise, new shops have emerged with business models designed to answer clients' desire for fresh approaches.

Not all succeeded, but all one needed to start were a few new computers, the people who knew what to do, a smart new business plan, and a cool new Internet address.

It's still pretty easy to form a new agency. Even though much has been written about the consolidation of agencies under the major holding companies, there remains a steady stream of seasoned professionals splitting away to form their own shops.

In New York, Robert Greenberg and RGA are showing the way. In San Francisco, the tall, talented, and female Amazon Advertising is making their mark.

Example: Amazon Advertising.

The agency was founded in San Francisco in 1996 by big agency creatives Millie Olson and Lynda Pearson – tall, female, and talented. Thus, Amazon.

From a small "boutique" specializing in products targeted to women, they grew to gain a national client list and a strategic and financial alliance with Leo Burnett/Publicis.

Now they do work for Kashi, which became part of Kellogg's (a Burnett account). They have become a valued creative resource for Leo Burnett client Procter and Gamble. They recently became the agency for Mondavi Wines in the San Francisco area.

Here is their philosophy.

We believe in ideas sustained by human truths. We believe that strategies should feel like stories waiting to be told.

We judge work by the fact that it must work or die. In the end, we don't know if starting with women made the difference, although we are quite certain that on any given day you will find more interesting shoes here than in any agency in America.

Find out more: www.amazonadv.com

Specialties.

As discussed in Chapter 5, there are numerous types of shops dedicated to special targets, media, categories, issues, and specialties.

Here are just a few examples:
- Multicultural (Asian, etc.)
- Generational (Gen Y, etc.)
- Event/Entertainment
- Technology
- Branded Content Development
- Green Issues
- Social Marketing
- Healthcare
- Mobile Marketing
- Automotive
- e-mail Marketing
- Search Engine Optimization
- Business to Business
- Video Game Marketing (plus specialists in casual games, advergames, etc.)
- Agricultural
- Trend Spotting/Cool Hunting
- Local Retail

As you can see, there are many types of small and medium-size niche shops. They are usually relatively independent, even if part of a larger holding company.

Some Career Advice.

Given the growing number of agency types and creative job opportunities, don't limit your career aspirations to only the top-twenty agencies. You may find a very interesting fit with a specialty agency.

Tony the Tiger.

The original concept:
Frosted Flakes have sugar.
Sugar equals energy.
Tiger symbolizes energy.
Tigers go G-r-r-r…

In the sidebar is a list of some current agency specialties.

David and Goliath.

Actually, that's the name of one of the newer agencies (Kia is one of their accounts). Most claim unique business models, usually involving a pledge to be media neutral.

Others tout their independent nature and ability to generate ground-breaking work. Most promise quality creative, which, after all, is what marketers are looking for. Quite a few now exist as part of one of the giant ad holding companies.

Concepting – What We Do.

IT'S SIMPLE, BUT COMPLICATED. The business of creatives is to come up with ideas that have the potential to sell the product.

Their brains are idea factories. **Words + visuals = concept**.

Left Brain. Right Brain.

Naturally, writers will tend to be "left brain," focusing on verbal expressions. Art directors and designers will tend to be "right brain," focusing on visual and graphic solutions.

But, when it's working, they're interacting.

There are a lot of words and phrases related to what they do… brainstorm, think, create, ideate. Many describe it as "**concepting**." And it's a "whole brain" activity.

When a creative team is concepting – developing original ideas – art directors are free to think verbally and copywriters visually. Or, both simply think "conceptually." The roots of this are in the ways the legendary art director **Paul Rand** and copywriter **Bill Bernbach** worked together.

It's an interesting dynamic. When the two work together, art directors can and do come up with headline or script ideas, and copywriters might have the visual inspiration.

But sooner or later we see why their titles differ. When longer copy assignments happen, someone with great writing chops has to make the words sing. Ditto for the details in art direction.

If you feel you're one of the very rare creatives with the talent to go all the way in both areas, congratulations. But, more often than not, it takes two.

Concepts and Concepting – Some Quick Definitions.

First, let's define "**concept**." As a noun, it's the key idea of your creative solution. It's usually a visual element and a verbal element in some interesting combination.

As a verb, "to concept" simply means the act of developing all the ideas you can before your deadline runs out. So, you concept (verb) to come up with a concept (noun). Get it?

In a print ad, for example, the concept would be the combined effect of the visual and headline. Sometimes it's wild and out there, sometimes it's simple and basic.

When you were a kid, you probably remember Tony the Tiger saying, "*They're G-r-r-reat!*" Simple. But it's a concept.

With appropriate variations, the same thought applies to all the other marketing tactics out there – from video to digital to match book covers – and the back of a cereal box.

aka "Selling Idea."

Another phrase that is commonly used is "selling idea." After all, a concept is an idea that helps fulfill a marketing objective which, more often than not, involves helping to sell something.

The **concept stage** is usually an early time in development when you see what the idea is, but it's not fully worked out.

Usually, the problem you're working on gets initial approval at the concept stage. That is, the basic idea is approved before you work out details such as a full script and storyboard for a video idea.

Concepting 101.

How to Get Ideas and What to Do with Them.

You may or may not become a "creative," but, since every job in the Business of Brands has some creativity in it, you should probably become familiar with what they do and how they do it.

Briefly, here are some of the ways creatives work.

Preparing to "Concept" – The Creative Brief.

All agencies like to believe they're unique, from their core philosophies down to the way they launch new projects. Sometimes they'll even emphasize these distinguishing differences while presenting their credentials to prospective clients.

It's all part of the "special sauce" that differentiates one agency brand (e.g., Ogilvy, JWT, Leo Burnett, etc.) from competitors. This usually includes important agency processes. We covered this somewhat in Chapter Eight.

The project launch is a critical stage, since the quality of the creative output is influenced by the quality of the input. While every agency has its procedures, virtually all include some version of a **creative brief** (We talked about this in Chapter Eight and we'll tell you more in Chapter Eleven).

Often, you'll get the brief presented to you during an internal "kick-off" meeting. You'll ask questions and discuss background details with others working on the account.

A Good Brief Needs a Good Planner.

Ideally, agencies using the British-pioneered planning system give you a planner with a deep understanding of the consumer and the consumer's relationship with the product category and the brand. A good brief won't weigh you down with too much information – only what you need to understand the assignment.

Planners pride themselves not only on being able to clearly craft the creative brief, but also to inspire a creative team to develop smart, original, relevant solutions.

A good brief should include:

• Current category and brand situations
• Target audience profile – with genuine insight
• Objectives (and how your success will be measured)

P&G and Selling Ideas.

P&G found successful Selling Ideas have "Three Principle Variables."

1. **Substance.** This has to do with meaningfulness or desirability to the consumer.
2. **Credibility.** Capable of being believed. However, it's OK if it's a bit of a challenge.
3. **Provocativeness.** The way the idea is expressed is "a thought-provoking method of expression."

The Before-We-Fall-In-Love-with-Our-Concept Checklist.

❏ Is it original? Everything's been done before. But we can often find fresh new combinations.

❏ Is it unexpected? Or is it surprisingly familiar? You want to go either "Aha!" or "Oh yeah!"

❏ Is it relevant to the brand's key benefit? Better yet, does the idea come out of that main benefit?

❏ Will typical readers or viewers get some clue as to why your product is different and better?

❏ Is it appropriate for both ends of the target audience range?

❏ Is it clear? Fast? Memorable? Campaignable? On strategy (or at least close)?

❏ Does it differentiate your brand? If not, it's a generic ad for the whole category, including your competitors. But, sometimes you can own it anyway.

Example: Energizer

Durability was the only meaningful category benefit for batteries. Energizer's competitor was Duracell. They had to **out-execute** the category leader. Ouch! (It's a tough business.) But you gotta keep going…

and

going.

Three Brief Briefs.

Asking the right questions is key to getting the right answers.

Here's how three smart agencies ask those questions:

JWT (They Call It a Point of View)
What is really going on?
Whose time are we after?
What are they interested in?
What is the brand going to do?
What do we know that might help?
Thought starters.

Wieden + Kennedy London
Background
Audience
Creative challenge
Practicalities Inspiration/Stimulus

Crispin Porter + Bogusky
At-a-Glance. What is the most relevant and differentiating idea that will surprise consumers or challenge their current thinking or relationship with the brand?

Tension. What is the psychological, social, categorical, or cultural tension associated with this idea?

Question. What is the question we need to answer to complete this assignment?

Talk Value. What about the brand could help us to start a dialogue between the brand and our target, among our target, and/or within popular culture in general? It could be the little rationalizations that people use to support their emotional decision.

Free Strategy Seminar.

If you'd like to dig into strategy a bit more, we've posted a Strategy Seminar on adbuzz.com. This seminar was originally prepared for Apple Computer. It surveys a number of agency strategy systems and contains additional definitions and examples. Go to www.adbuzz.com and click on CAFÉ. There are also PowerPoints for most of the chapters of this book and some other interesting things (sorry, no test answers).

- Key benefit (most likely to trigger choice of our brand)
- Key emotional motivator
- Any new agency insights
- The strategy

There may be some research results as part of your brief.

In the sidebar, we've posted a few sample brief formats

Learning to Work to a Strategy.
"Strategy" is how the agency recommends achieving the objective. The creative concept you're about to develop will, in some way, relate to that strategy.

How to Get Ideas. And More Ideas.

Okay, you've been briefed and you have the strategy.

It's time to have an idea – a concept.

Isn't it amazing how good ideas will pop up out of nowhere – except when you're really desperate to find one?

Most of us will take one anywhere we find it, and run with it any way we can. Problem is, we're hired to go beyond a single, merely "good" idea. The goal is "great" ideas, so anything good is just a starting point. And yes, that is pressure.

When we get one great idea, we're expected to do a couple more, only completely different. For added excitement, how about an impossible deadline?

It's often said, the best way to get a great idea is to get many ideas. But you'll rarely be given the time to play with hundreds of visual-word combinations to find one that's surprising, smart, relevant, and doable. Just as photographers seldom have time to try every combination of lenses, speeds, angles, and compositions.

You need a plan. A technique that speeds the process and helps you work through maximum possibilities in minimum timeframes.

Some Ideas about Getting Ideas.
The following steps are not new. Variations can be found in many books, beginning with a timeless little book published in 1940 by James Webb Young, *A Technique for Producing Ideas*. They combine the best techniques I've learned working with many amazing partners at seven agencies. Here goes…

1. **Absorb the background material.** Typically your project launch meeting and creative brief plus any research. Follow your instinct and do your own online search until you've satisfied your curiosity and filled gaps in your knowledge.

2. **Have a quick follow-up session.** Get with your partner and share first reactions plus any starter ideas. Make sure you agree on the one benefit most likely to make prospects remember your brand (a good briefing should make that clear). This is the one single thing consumers should remember if they forget everything else. Write it in a clear, one-sentence statement. Don't try to make it clever, just crystal clear. That's your first headline. It won't be good, but it's a beginning.

3. **Split up.** Individually, start compiling visual and verbal elements that flow logically from either the problem your brand solves or the key benefit it provides. These ingredients form the matrix your ideas will spring from – your creative worksheets. Write or sketch the basic (most obvious) elements defining the situation, problem, and benefit.

Look for "top-level themes" (see sidebar).

Okay. Now What?

Under each top-level theme, record every related word or image that comes to mind, from silly to serious – single words, phrases, quotes, sentence fragments, scenes, images, visual metaphors.

Use any style – handwritten, sketched, your Mac – whatever feels right. Wherever you can, think of the opposite of the word or image. Ideas are often based on an opposite or negative of a key thematic element.

I like to cram as much as possible on each page so I can look later for surprising connections between separate items.

If you have a big wall, sometimes it helps to put the ideas up on that wall.

From Bad Ideas to Good Ideas.

Thoughts may occur to you that seem too stupid or simple to write down. Add them anyway. Really. Bad ideas lead to good ideas, especially after a little time passes and you see new possibilities in a fresh light. Even a creative mind like Leonardo da Vinci gave himself permission to chase whatever ideas popped into his head, as they popped into his head.

When you look at his notebooks (check it out online), you can see verbal notations and small sketches on completely different topics, all on the same page.

Finally, go back over your worksheets. Circle or highlight anything that feels promising. If some time has passed, you may be surprised at the new relationships you missed first time through.

Pencil-in your notes or draw lines where two parts combine to make something new.

To once again quote James Webb Young, "*...an idea is nothing more nor less than a new combination of old elements.*"

Those circled/highlighted ideas are what you'll share with your partner. You cannot return to your partner with nothing. You must have at least a few ideas.

Okay, time to team up again. We're ready for steps 4–6.

4. **Share.** Now it's time for you and your partner to get back together and share. This is where the magic happens. Your partner looks at some of your half-baked but promising fragments, is inspired with ways to finish them, and the air begins to crackle with electricity. You react to your partner's ideas. Together, you paper the walls with your most promising stuff.

Top-Level Themes.

For example, let's say it's a campaign for a dog food that helps older arthritic dogs stay active. Your basic elements/themes might look like this:

<u>dog</u> <u>food</u> <u>age</u> <u>arthritis</u> <u>action</u>

These top-level themes are so obvious, it may seem pointless to write them down.

But if you don't include the word "dog," you might never think of "dog-tired." Or any of the dozens more that could eventually become part of something brilliant.

<u>Dog</u>

Breed	Lap dog
Canine	Leash
Bowl	Dog star
Canine patrol	Dogleg
Collar	Tags
Pant	Bark
Bite	Paw
Roll over	Doggedly
Fetch	Retriever
Dog's life	Four-legged
Tail-wagging	Old dog new tricks

Beating the "White Bull."

It's easy to get hung-up staring at the blank sheet – what Hemingway called the "White Bull."

That obvious word or image can also be a way to beat the empty page.

When you're trying to be creative, rejecting thought after thought because they aren't quite right is a losing strategy.

By simply writing the most obvious themes, you defeat Hemingway's White Bull – an important psychological victory in concepting.

When Two Things Come Together…

They can create a unique new concept.

Naturally, not every combination is a win – just like not every ingredient improves a recipe.

You have to be the judge.

Try this: Look at ideas that appeal to you. What was the combination that made them work?

The better you understand how good ideas work, the better you will be at coming up with them.

Branding as Magic?

You might want to read "Black White and Pango Peach Magic" by Howard Gossage which talks about how we use cultural communication in advertising.

It's an excerpt from *The Book of Gossage* posted for you in Readings at www.adbuzz.com.

Go to AdBuzz. Go to the Study Hall. Go to the pulldown menu and get Readings and Chapter 9. (Yes, yes, we know it's a bit complicated, but it's the best way we could figure out to organize all of the resources we've provided.)

---

5. **You're exhausted.** Your brains now have all the thinking power of crème brûlée, with none of the delicious caramelized coating. But it feels good knowing you've got some good stuff, even if there's no gold yet. This is when you get away from it and go somewhere else.

6. **Let your subconscious keep working.** Amazingly, even though you left the work behind while you went away to do other things, the wheels continued – subconsciously – to work.

    All of this leads to…

7. **Yes. That's it!** Suddenly, an idea wells up into your conscious brain. A new way to express some of those idea fragments you'd been playing with. The clouds lift, revealing a brilliant solution. The Eureka moment.

Of course, it doesn't always go exactly like that. Sometimes darts, video games, or a little hall-ball become necessary. If you're thinking this technique isn't glamorous and sounds like hard work, you're right. But it does work.

Remember, no matter how big or small the project seems, your reputation is on the line. Who knows? Maybe this is the "What-did-we-do-to-deserve-this?" assignment that turns into a career-changing achievement.

Now, let's put those ideas in context – that crowded media world where your communication will run.

Traditional Media Advertising.

The Media Revolution has cooked up an exciting stew for those in marketing. That's where your message has to live.

But that can be easier said than done, because today's media environment is highly fragmented. We're building snowflakes, and it's a blizzard out there.

This will be the largest section of the chapter, because we're going to cover *all* the traditional media.

There are whole books devoted to just one aspect of this job – print or branding or even outdoor. As quickly as possible, we'll cover:

• Overall Considerations
• Print and OOH (Out-of-Home)
• Television
• Radio
• Collateral

Then we'll cover the rest of the MarCom Matrix.

Overall Considerations.

In every media, your creative has to consider the following.

• Branding
• The Media Environment
• The Strategy (Product/Target/Benefit)

If you think that's a lot to think about, you're right.

Brands and Brand Contact Points.

We began this book with a number of brand definitions, based on where you were in the Business of Brands. Now let's look at a brand through the eyes of a creative team with an assignment.

The creative team would start with this question about the brand: *What does it mean to a consumer?*

In the end, the brand is what the consumer believes the product or service stands for. This is usually a combination of consumer attitudes reacting over time to several factors:

• What differentiates the brand within the category?
• What intangibles are associated with the brand?
• How strong are key brand associations?

Marketers may have their own idea of what the brand should stand for, but ultimately it's no more nor less than the consumer's perception of it.

Let's take a specific example – Tiffany, the luxury jewelry retailer.

Example: Tiffany.

One of the few brands that needs little more than its name comes in a distinctive robin's egg blue box. But its meaning is so ingrained into the culture, you "see" the brand value.

• How can you leverage that famous blue box?
• What else differentiates the brand?
• The Tiffany brand stands for a collection of intangible, but real, values: tradition, exclusive designs, timeless beauty, uncompromising quality, romance, emotional surprise, etc.
• Do any other key brand associations come to mind when Tiffany is mentioned?
• What qualities does this brand transfer to the giver?

Opening a Media Window.

Even the most powerful brands need reinforcing.

So let's keep thinking – not just about what we say, but who we say it to and what media windows we can open.

For example, people who are already Tiffany customers will deserve extra attention. Are there secondary groups of potential customers?

How about husbands who need to be reminded of anniversaries? Newborns? (Tiffany has a pretty little silver bell with the baby's name and birth date engraved – nice baby present.)

Are there new media opportunities?

How about an online catalog?

How about a Gift Registry with an application that helps you remember anniversaries and birthdays? (They have one.)

Hmmm… How do we create a message that gets people to sign up? (Bet they'd like an idea like that.)

Example: Mac vs. PC.

Here's another good example. We discussed the Mac vs. PC strategy in Chapter Eight. Now let's take a look at how a creative vision executed that competitive strategy.

Something to Think About.

Brand Contact Points.

Whatever brand you're working on, it can be very helpful to think about all the places that your target consumers touch the brand – and vice versa.

Role Playing: Walk through a typical day, when might someone come into contact with the brand – or something that reminds you of the brand or brand category. For example, if working on a detergent, what about the display areas around laundromats.

Category Extensions: Think like McLuhan, who calls things "extensions." Example, a car is an extension of your legs. Clothes are an extension of your skin. Paper dolls? An online site where you can dress an image of yourself?

Basics: Packages. Check out lines. T-shirts. Pocket Protectors. Is there some simple and obvious contact point opportunity?

Keep Thinking: Who knows – you might have the next great branding idea.

This Box Is Robin's Egg Blue.

But you already knew that.

Whatever is inside has the added value of the Tiffany reputation.

Mac vs. PC.

I'm a PC.　　　I'm a Mac.

You can see a range of Mac/PC TV commercials at:

http://www.apple.com/getamac/ads/

Cultural Cues.

When you consider using cultural cues, you'll have to make a few judgment calls:

- Does it relate at all to the reason the brand is different?
- Is it merely gratuitous borrowed interest (a common argument for killing an idea)?
- Is a high percentage of your audience familiar with it?
- Is it consistent with the brand's personality?

- The Mac and PC campaign managed to contrast the brand with its more powerful competitor without appearing to be too cruel or mean-spirited (well, maybe a little cruel).
- While both brands came off as likeable, which seemed confident, smart, unassuming, friendly, approachable, and useful?
- Note how they use metaphors to make technical claims.

Fragmentation, Clutter, and Culture.

Okay, let's talk some more about all the media bits in the stew. With every new media channel, our target audiences fragment into smaller and narrower segments.

That can be good if we take advantage of that specific media environment and make the message more relevant to their special segment. It may mean tailoring more message variations, and that's part of the evolving reality for creatives.

Even though it means there are more opportunities, this is a big problem for advertising.

Remember, advertising grew as a cost-effective way to reach and persuade large audiences.

As costs rise and audiences shrink, make no mistake, this is a big challenge – particularly for mass marketers who are seeing a hundred-year old business model lose its punch.

It's also the reason that effective creative communication is more important than ever.

Pop Culture and Marketing Concepts.

Sometimes, not often, the marketing concept actually leads the culture. Years ago, there was a Wendy's campaign called "Where's the Beef?" It actually worked its way into a Presidential debate.

Nike is a brand that has occasionally been able to lead the culture.

But, more often, marketing takes its cues from the culture, and media leads – with the music and fashions, and graphic styles, and all the other things we do that seem to add up to "culture."

That said, let's take a tour through the various forms of traditional media – Print and OOH, TV, and Radio.

Example: Concepts with Cultural Cues.

These Altoids outdoor boards use sly movie and cultural references. Because they worked their way into pop culture, the concepts still worked for some time after the popular films ran.

By the way, in both these examples the wording was so clever there was no need to get permission nor to license intellectual property.

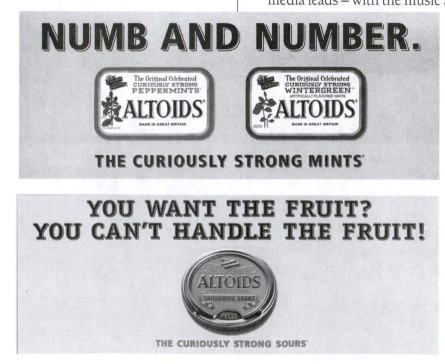

Working with Strategy.

When a creative talks about strategy, he or she is almost always talking about a Communications Strategy – which may also be called a Creative Strategy or a Copy Strategy.

This will be a subset of the Marketing Strategy and focus on what we want to communicate to our target audience as part of meeting the Marketing Objective.

Even though the strategy is a firm, disciplined document that focuses on the communications job to be done, there are still many, many ways to accomplish that goal.

Propositions, Enemies, Aspirational Images, & Nine-Wheel Logic.
Briefly, here are a few ways to approach a strategy in the development of a concept.

The **proposition** is, usually, a straightforward **reason why** approach. The classic USP for M&Ms, "*M&Ms melt in your mouth, not in your hands*" is an example. P&G's Bounty Paper Towels are "*the quicker picker-upper.*" "*Choosy moms choose Jif.*" It helps if you are able to put that proposition into a memorable piece of language.

Now what's this about enemies? Well, sometimes you can create drama for your brand by positioning it in some conflict.

So, for example, those chocolates that melt in your hand – even though you don't go around holding pieces of chocolate in your hand – are M&Ms' "enemy." Red eyes for Visine, which "*Get the Red out*" would also qualify. Listerine and other mouth washes fight bad breath, or "halitosis."

In terms of developing an ad concept, an **enemy** is a construct which serves to dramatize the product benefit by creating conflict.

Aspirational images are idealized visions connected with the brand. The Marlboro cowboy and the models used by the Gap and Abercrombie & Fitch (and most fashion advertising) are good examples of this kind of imagery.

Nine-wheel logic? It's when one thing represents something else.

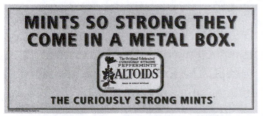

"So strong they come in a metal box."

Why does the choo-choo go so fast? See all the wheels. Think we don't do that in advertising? Think again. How about Altoids.

Metaphors, similes, analogies, icons, and more. We use all sorts of creative ways of thinking to create concepts out of strategies.

Now that we've briefly covered the idea of brands and the job of coming up with a concept, let's continue our tour of the creative craft.

First we'll cover the basics of print, which have been around since the invention of the printing press and then the rapidly expanding options in electronic media.

STAVROS COSMOPULOS

Nail the Concept.

Thumbnails – small (generally one or two inches), rough sketches only you and your partner see – have been around forever. Leonardo daVinci made good use of them in his notebooks (the last one of which sold for over $30 million). Because they're low tech and fast, thumbnails give you creative freedom in early concepting that computers can't match.

The reason for thumbnails? It's unlikely your first layout will be your best. So good thumbnail skills help you quickly visualize which of several variations work best.

Thumbnails let you work faster than sketching in actual size. And since the drawings are never meant to be good art, there's no pressure to draw carefully. You're free to focus on trying different composition, spacing, sizes, formats, copy grids, etc.

Once you've narrowed the layout choices, you can spend more time on a larger, more detailed rough layout to show your creative director (CD). Or you can take it straight to computer. Because you worked through a lot of variations in thumbnail stage, you'll be able to present your work with greater confidence. When your CD asks, "Did you try . . . ," you may be able to truthfully answer yes.

For client presentations, comps (comprehensive layouts) are much more detailed, sometimes resembling fully produced ads. Many art directors jump right to the computer and work in one of the standard "page layout"

(Continued on next page)

Nail the Concept (Cont.).

apps – InDesign or Quark. Photos and graphics you manipulated in Photoshop, Illustrator, et al, are imported into the page layout file, where you can fine-tune typography and position graphics with amazing precision.

But, when you only have a half hour to whip a new idea into something presentable, a few quick thumbnails will get you to a better layout faster.

**4 Thumbnail Layouts with
5 Elements in 60 Seconds.**

Try this one-minute experiment. Give yourself 60 seconds to sketch the four different thumbnail variations below, to organize these five elements in a one-page ad: 1) six word headline, 2) visual (coffee cup + donut), 3) two paragraphs of copy, 4) logo, 5) package of coffee beans.

Four Thumbnail Variations:

1. Large visual with small headline surrounded by white space.
2. Bigger headline and reposition the logo/package.
3. Change position/size of visual and break headline into two lines.
4. Change position of items in visual then change copy position and number of columns.

Jell-O believes you've taken enough lumps in your life.

TRY NEW, CREAMIER JELL-O PUDDING & PIE FILLING ... AND SMOOTH THINGS OUT.

Visual/Verbal Collaboration.

Remember, words and pictures can work together – or they can work against each other.

Here, a photo of smooth-pouring Jell-O Pudding contrasts with words about lumps.

Print and OOH (Out-of-Home)

If you're not going into creative, you can read this section once, get a general idea, and move onto the next chapter.

But… if you're going into creative, you'll probably read this over and over again – and it still won't be enough. Here goes.

Hold That Thought.

In the beginning, most creatives start by working with print.

There's a simple reason for it – print holds still.

Even though you may eventually want to be creating TV, music videos, and dancing hamsters on your cell phone, it's just a bit easier to get started with ideas that stay in one place while you look at them – and while you think them up.

So that's where we'll start. Wait. One more thought.

A Look Backward and a Look Forward.

We need to make one more point about print and OOH.

Everything old is new again – and vice versa.

Many of the old forms of advertising are being reborn. That's the Media Revolution for you.

Billboards now show up on your computer as banner ads and at the rock concert as posters and T-shirts.

Direct mail may still be in your mailbox – but we'll bet there's a lot more of it sitting in your e-mail – even though the "junk" percentage is pretty high.

Catalogs and brochures? Sure, there are still plenty of those around – but now Web sites and pdf attachments are doing the same thing – without the printing or mailing costs.

Print ads – you still see them – because there is a whole explosion of new alternative newspapers and magazines for special interests.

And maybe some of them turn into Internet platforms with a place to click for a nifty brochure or catalog.

Today, there are a lot more ways to be in print than print.

Now, a few more thoughts.

Print.

As discussed, art directors and copywriters need to work together to create that winning concept. The jobs are complementary, but each brings something unique to the process.

Let's look at art directors first.

Art Direction.

Art directors' work gets more challenging each year. As always, they're expected to be full big idea partners to help brands work their way into consumers' hearts and minds.

They're also counted on to play a part in the production of those ideas. Though they do get help from another group of specialists – electronic pre-press.

And even though art directors don't have to know every new app, they have to know enough to talk to those who do.

The added irony is, young art directors are assumed to be skilled at running a variety of applications, often from page design, graphics and photo manipulation to Web design and interactive ads. Yet, the higher they climb up the creative department ladder, the less they do on computers.

It's not unusual for young art directors to "break in" on jobs emphasizing computer formatting, graphics apps, and Web scripting more than concepting. As they prove their concepting ability, responsibilities shift in that direction.

Art with Words – a Knowledge of Typograhpy.

The vast majority of marketing involves the printed word, so you'd think readability would be a no-brainer. "Readability" is a measurement of how easily and comfortably text can be read.

If the art direction and typography makes it possible only with effort, it's merely "legible." That's not exactly the gold standard of communication.

The Importance of Typography.

Great art directors never stop learning the art of typography. Every decision they make is a judgment call involving many variables. But the first and most important is readability. If reading is effortless, the typography is successful.

Page design software makes it easy to manipulate type with great precision. It's so easy you have to be careful not to over-think it with things like forays into "fringe fonts" (using unusual type faces that are hard-to-read or distract from the message), setting type on an angle or curve, in colors, skewed three-dimensionally, or with drop shadows.

In other words, it's very tempting to set type in ways that draw attention to the type.

Thoughts on Type – "The Crystal Goblet."

Famed typographer Beatrice Warde gave us a metaphor illustrating how to think of type. In *The Crystal Goblet: Sixteen Essays on Typography*, she imagined two wine goblets and compared them:

"You have two goblets before you. One is of solid gold, wrought in the most exquisite patterns. The other is of crystal-clear glass, thin as a bubble, and as transparent . . . if you are a member of that vanishing tribe, the amateurs of fine vintages, you will choose the crystal, because everything about it is calculated to reveal rather than to hide the beautiful thing which it was meant to contain."

This is the basis for the idea of "transparent" type – the thought that good typography is invisible.

If you have a vague feeling your idea lacks something and an urge to experiment with type, it's usually a sign your concept needs more work. Playing with typography – unusual fonts, size variations, odd columns, etc. – will not make subpar concepts great.

If your layout lacks a distinctive campaign "look," drawing attention to the type itself is not the solution.

Know Your Fonts, Points, and Picas.

Learn to identify some of the most common font groups:

- serif: Times New Roman, Georgia, Palatino, Century Schoolbook
- **sanserif:** Arial, Helvetica, Trebuchet, Verdana
- *fringe or script fonts like Mistral are hard to read – a poor choice when readability counts.*

Learn points and picas: 12 points in a pica. Six picas in one inch. So, 72 points equals one inch.

Headlines and line breaks: When a print headline needs to be broken into two or three lines, discuss where the line break(s) should be. The best break for balance may be different than the best one for the line's rhythm.

Leading: (Pronounced "ledding") the space between lines of type.

Kerning: Space between characters

Ligatures: The way any 2 characters join together

Tracking: Adjusting the kerning over multiple lines of copy

Line length: Copy is very difficult to read when it's set too wide. Here are two common rules of thumb for line length:

1. Nine words, max, to a line
2. Between 35 characters (minimum) and 65 (maximum)

Now get familiar with your fonts so you can identify the most popular. There are important differences that will help you in your work. For example, how does **11pt Helvetica** differ from **11pt Times New Roman**? Yes, it looks bigger.

Using ALL CAPS slows reading, and uses more space.

For headlines: **Cap/lower case (designated by C/lc) in bold sans serif is very readable. Big Cap/ Small Cap Is Also a Readable Style.**

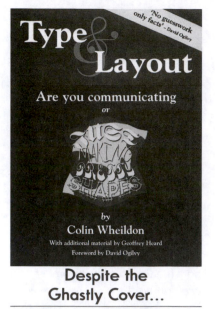

Despite the Ghastly Cover...

The book inside, *Type & Layout: Are You Communicating or Just Making Pretty Shapes*, by Colin Wheildon, is actually a pretty useful book.

For a start, it will stop you from making dumb rookie mistakes.

Some Copywriting Books We Like.

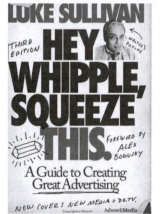

Helps you hit the heights.

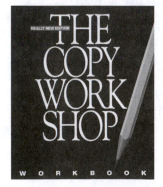

Helps you learn the basics.

For example, setting a headline in a color (assuming there's no logical reason) only results in drawing attention to the color. Which, in turn, becomes another graphic element forcing readers to ponder its significance. And distracting attention away from the concept.

Copywriting.

It seems the more that's out there, the less we read. Average copy length seems to drop. In media that targets younger demographics, it might seem like it's disappearing altogether.

However, there are still lots of reasons why you need smartly-crafted copy. "Reason why" is one of them.

Rest assured, despite the campaigns covered in ad industry publications or what you don't hear in TV spots, copywriters have plenty to write, in every medium.

Writing That Cuts Through, Hits Home.

Your first copywriting challenge is "becoming" the target audience. It takes some effort to review your work as the reader, not yourself. The real test comes when busy readers give the page you've worked on for hours or days two seconds of their time to see if it's relevant to their lives.

About That First Sentence...

Good copywriters put quality time into crafting the first sentence. Readers who don't get past it are gone. So it's worth writing several just to see which gets you into a good rhythm.

Great first sentences usually do four things:

- Smoothly follow the flow of the concept.
- Tell us something we didn't already know from the concept.
- Continue the concept's stylistic "promise" – whether it's dramatic, full of attitude, or just funny, readers will be disappointed if that vibe is missing in sentence one.
- Do it quickly. Keep it short.

Once you've got an opening that works, respect the reader's time. Make the first paragraph crisp.

If you have two interesting examples or funny bits, choose one.

Don't make the reader wait long before getting to the point.

As you write, in the back of your mind remember the motivator most likely to drive the brand decision.

Turn Features into Benefits.

When you have product features, convert them to benefits.

Do you understand this? If the feature is a better braking system, the benefit is keeping your family safe.

Smart, Spare Copy Editing – *Now With 20%* ***More Restraint!!!***

Most assignments work well with a conversational style: talking to one reader as you'd chat with a friend.

Have you noticed it in this chapter?

Contractions simplify and shorten for easier reading.

I wouldn't say, "If you are going for coffee, I will go with you."

I'd say, "If you're going for coffee, I'll go with you." Got it?

Part of this breezy style comes from cutting words we automatically leave out of casual speech.

Put the Second Person First.

As a general – but not hard – rule, write in a second-person voice (you, your) rather than a first-person voice (we, our, us). The ad is paid for by the brand, but the decision to read is all about you – the reader.

To check how well your copy flows, it helps to read it aloud. Awkward or illogical transitions from one sentence or paragraph to the next are often easily fixed.

Other "flow" problems may be stubborn and require more rewriting. In the end, reading your copy – the way your audience reads it – should feel like being pulled effortlessly from beginning to end.

"Approachable" Copy – Making It Easier to Read.

Successful copywriters make their copy "approachable." If it's more than four or five sentences, they create a paragraph break or two, or let the copy wrap around a visual.

The alternative, a single text-heavy block, offers no escape.

A long paragraph feels like too much of a commitment. It'll scare readers off, no matter how great your first sentence was.

Finally…

One of the most challenging tasks in copywriting is crafting an end. A lot depends on whether you have a specific call-to-action.

That aside, there are two common schools of thought:

1) Reward readers who get this far with a clever new twist on the concept. But NOT the same wordplay as your headline.
2) Reward readers by giving them the url/toll-free number so they can "find out more" and then let them go.

Like most creative decisions, one strategy won't fit all situations. It's your judgment call. Have a reason for your choice.

Tips on Taglines.

To get a jump start writing taglines, try starting with these, then keep going with whatever seems to work for you:

Where… Where data becomes information.

When… When it absolutely, positively has to get there overnight.

Because… Because everything is riding on your tires.

Now let's look at another form of print – the outdoor board.

Global Evolution.

Once, Japanese manufacturing stood for poor quality. Now, Korean cars are viewed as almost as good as Japanese cars.

Top Ramen.

Make your claim. Make it clear. Make it interesting.

Advertising Yiddish.

By the way, show business and advertising use a few Yiddish words.

Chutzpah – Being bold with attitude.

Maven – An expert.

Schtick – A piece of business. Groucho Marx's cigar was his schtick; Madonna's dramatic changes in look are hers.

Clitchik – Well-turned phrase at the end of an ad.

Doggone Nice Copy.

Student work from Creative Circus.

She's won $200,000 and a room full of trophies. But she'd rather have one of those rubber squeaky toys.

She's never known love. She's never known affection. And she's never known what it's really like to be a dog. But she's about to find out that after five-years of training and hard work, her owner would rather put her to sleep than be burdened with finding her a home. And we're quite sure she doesn't know why.

Please call and make an appointment to come visit our kennel. Once you look into the eyes of these extraordinary animals, you will see why we work so hard to save their lives.

Fine-Tuning Your Ideas.

Now that you've got some winning ideas, you're ready to tweak. Few emerge ready for prime time. Most have to be pushed.

Let's say it's a print ad with a visual and headline. You make a quick sketch. That's one solution – just your first attempt.

But is it the one? How do you know? What if your creative director takes a quick look, changes a couple words or alters the image and makes it three times better? Making you feel three times smaller?

To prevent that painful condition, you'll do a bunch of layout variations. The fastest way is thumbnails. [See thumbnail sidebar.] They'll help you see which of several layouts work best. You may also write headline variations. You either find one that's better or prove it can't be beat.

Your idea might go from good to great in the seventh variation. You weren't going to stop at only the third, were you?

Try to Make It Unique to Your Brand.

If the tagline isn't exclusive to your brand, will consumers remember?

Hummer: *Like nothing else.*
Porsche: *Nothing else comes close.*
Sony: *Like no other.*
Nissan: *Driven.*
Mini: *Let's drive.*
VW: *Drivers wanted.*
Lufthansa: *There's no better way to fly.*
Singapore Airlines: *A great way to fly.*
United Airlines: *It's time to fly.*

A Taxi Top.

From the Miami Ad School.

OOH? Aah!

Want to see some great outdoor? Go to www.oaaa.org/creativelibary/ for award-winning outdoor.

Outdoor/Out-Of-Home (OOH)

Signs are the oldest form of advertising.

Many view it as the most difficult form of print – you have to do the whole job with fewer words and less time.

Yet technology is making this oldest ad form new again.

Old Meets New.

After a decade of growth, Out-Of-Home (OOH) continues to expand through new digital formats. In addition to traditional static boards, a liberal definition of OOH includes just about any message, in any form, displayed in a public setting.

From taxi tops to gas stations, stadiums, restrooms, transit stops, elevators, and malls, boards with dynamic digital updating are spreading into new environments every day. Inside and out.

Some even feature interactivity.

Meanwhile, static displays are getting more 3D extensions of every size and shape above, below, and beyond sign frames.

Mini USA created a board that displayed personal greetings when Mini drivers with special RFID keychains passed by.

For all the electronic and kinetic possibilities in OOH, there's still no greater creative coup than a killer board using only a visual plus a few words.

Sure, it's great to have a budget for costly special effects. But if that had been available, your CD would've cherry-picked the assignment in the first place.

As in other media, when one part (either the line or the visual) is unexpected, the best complement can be something straight and simple as a contrast from the other (see earlier Altoids boards).

Overcoming the Outdoor Challenge.

Great outdoor is a big achievement. Many factors are against you.

- **Time.** Drivers have only a quick glance to see and "get" your idea.
- **Clutter.** Your board competes with visual and audio distractions inside and outside of drivers' cars.
- **Brevity.** You're usually limited to a visual and seven or eight words (not many budgets will let you do extensions and special effects).
- **Place.** If you don't know your locations in advance, your board has to work in any situation with all backgrounds.

Not surprising then, that your best concept strategy is speed – lightning-fast ideas that are quickly comprehended.

In OOH, any lack of clarity equals lost opportunities.

When in doubt, bold, san-serif fonts are highly visible from a distance. Keep contrast (between type and background) high for low-light viewing. And let the logo/package be proportionally a bit bigger than you'd show it in print.

When you're done, go back one last time and strip every word and graphic element that isn't absolutely necessary.

For simplicity, taglines can usually take the day off in OOH. If you find yourself adding subheads or extra details for "more impact" in OOH, go back to the drawing board.

And while you're working to develop that stronger concept, maybe these tips will help.

Bonus! Top Secret Insider Tips.

Wish I'd known these before having to learn them the hard way:

- If the visual is unexpected, the headline can be straightforward. And/or vice versa. In some cases, the more unclever the headline, the more dramatic its contrast with the surprising visual. And/or vice versa. There are countless great ads with plain product shots as visuals. They all have surprising headlines.

- If the headline is unexpected, the first line of copy should help make things perfectly clear.

- If your concept helps answer the consumer's first question about any ad — "Is there anything here for me? Anything I care about?" — you're on the right track.

- Not all ads have to be funny. But interesting is good.

- Writing or sketching a stream-of-consciousness description of your assignment is a great way to trick yourself into some quality concepting. The key is getting it down on paper. Say it any way that feels good. Imagine you're explaining the project to your dog. Your dog knows you're brilliant and will never give you negative feedback.

- When you and your partner meet to develop original ideas, don't say, "I got nothing." Force yourself to say "What if…" without having any idea how you'll finish it. Then think of a way to finish it. A great partner will use improv comedy techniques in response, never negating, but returning your "What if…" with something added to get you a little closer to the reason why your brand is different. After a couple of back-and-forths, you may actually have something.

- Look for secondary levels of meaning. If readers can quickly "get it," they'll enjoy and remember the message.

- Humans are wired to solve puzzles. Most great ads leave a part of the puzzle missing so consumers must complete it. That invites involvement and makes the idea far more satisfying. Even when it takes a nano-second to complete, the effect is powerful.

- Don't get so excited about your first idea that you start working up all the details. Keep looking for ideas two and three.

- One of the hardest things to give-up is a favorite concept that almost works. If you haven't figured it out in a couple of hours, move on. If it's preventing you from finding ideas that do work, drive a stake through it. In *On the Art of Writing*, Sir Arthur Quiller-Couch said it well: "Murder your darlings."

- Far more ideas are rejected than accepted. No one likes that part. Give yourself a few minutes to mourn your fallen concept, then focus on proving you have many more.

Ads with No Message, Rules, or Copy.

It's ironic that the most discussed and awarded work — ads celebrated in industry magazines and award competitions — is a tiny fraction of the industry total.

Often, these are ads with no apparent brand message. More often than not, they're for successful brands aimed at the hip and the young people, like you. Here are some places to look:

- The first six to eight pages of fashion and youth-culture magazines.
- TV spots for high-profile brands targeting young adults.
- Branded content in microsites and viral videos.
- Super Bowl spots.

Ads with no copy or brand "sell" do have a strategy. They start with the assumption that the target dislikes pushy product messages. The strategy is to show respect for the audience by:

- Not assuming they can be manipulated by conventional marketing
- Giving the gift of entertainment
- Being consistent with the target's sense of humor, style, and values
- Featuring people with attitudes (facial expressions and body language) audiences can relate to

If the brand can do that without seeming like it's trying too hard, the target might consider it worthy of consideration.

If you fall into a job working only on brands targeting the hip and young, you might never have to write a word of copy. For the other 95% of accounts, it's good to know accepted standards and techniques.

Because everything is riding on your tires.

Taglines.

Taglines give consumers something memorable and relevant about the brand.

A great tag can be a defining moment for a brand, and for a career. Not everyone believes they're necessary. Certainly, some campaigns do succeed without them.

Here are some good ones:

Memorable.

Alliteration:

Don't dream it. Drive it.   Jaguar

Rhyme:

Taste. Not waist.   Weight Watchers

Double meaning:

We bring good things to life.   GE

Nothing runs like a Deere. John Deere

Simple.

Got milk?   ADA

Think different.   Apple

Fresh Mex.   Chevy's

Original and Ownable.

Parallel structure gives these lines nice rhythm and memorability:

It takes a licking and keeps on ticking.
                    Timex

The quality goes in
    before the name goes on.   Zenith

Lowering Competitors.

No-nonsense tone implies negative about competitors.

They make money the old-fashioned
    way. They earn it.   Smith Barney

Live a Cutty above   Cutty Sark

Related to Key Benefit.

Alarmed? You should be. Moss Security

Kills bugs dead.   Raid

The quicker picker-upper.   Bounty

(Continued on next page)

And while you're working to develop that stronger concept, maybe these tips will help you give it another try.

Video and Audio.

The Craft of Electronic Communication.

Here's where the Media Revolution is really making an impact.

Most video platforms – and more emerge each year – are ad-supported in some way. That adds up to more ads in more platforms, formats, lengths, and screen sizes than ever before.

A Growing List of Electronic Platforms.

This list is probably already out-of-date. Look at the opportunities.

- Conventional "broadcast" TV – still huge
- In-store networks at mass merchandisers or "big box" stores
- Video Web sites – growing
- Video microsites – and growing
- Internet video viewed on TV set via game console
- Commercial VOD (video on demand) channels via cable or satellite – could also be termed "branded content"
- In-store displays and kiosks
- Short IDs of any length or style
- 10s, 15s, 30s, 45s, 60s, 90s, 120s, etc.
- Long-form DRTV (direct response TV, aka informercial)
- Long form branded content video (BMW rampenfest.com)
- Movie theatre pre-roll
- Mobile spots or branded video content
- Podcast spots or brand placement/integration in content
- Video as an element in an alternate reality game (ARG)
- Video as part of a user-generated mash-up campaign
- Pre, post, or mid-roll spots on social media or other sites
- On social media brand profile pages
- Viral branded content on video sites, social media, etc.
- Bluecast via Bluetooth short wireless technology
- Overlay across screen bottom

Any idea you can imagine, you can create. Whether it's on film, video, computer generated, or a combination, you and your creative partners can make it happen.

In fact, if you can't find the platform or format you need, you might invent a new format or platform. Today, who knows?

What Does All This Mean?

Since consumers have so many choices for video content and so many ways to avoid commercials, the need for compelling, relevant messages has never been greater.

That's easy when the target viewers are just like you and much more challenging when they're not. Use the same method for getting ideas laid out earlier in this chapter.

Video projects are big investments in money and time, so you could present many rough ideas at the agency before one gets green-lit for full-up, client presentation (spending time/money for detailed, color storyboards).

Key Frames and Key Visuals.

When concepting time is precious, you can float ideas for your CD quickly in a simple format: a single frame representing the primary theme along with a short description (not a script).

From there, depending on your agency's presentation style and format, there are many ways to present video.

The Traditional Storyboard.

The old-school technique usually shows a 30-second spot in six to twelve panels.

The script is shown under each panel so the audio corresponds with the action. Here's one Dennis Altman did for the fictional island of Toomba, shrunk to fit.

Usually, each large board has six panels 8"w x 4.5"h (16:9 ratio) or 8"w x 6"h (4:3 ratio). Modern TV screens are 16:9 (which is also the HD format) but often display content in 4:3.

Working together, sketch a mini 12-panel thumbnail (on one 8.5" x 11" sheet) before spending time/money on detailed, full-size panels. Stick figures are all you need at this stage. Though that changes quickly once you get initial approval.

It's worth the effort to spend some time thinking through the content of each panel because you may only get one chance to present and sell your idea.

Look at your storyboard as the brand manager will look at it – how strong is the brand's visibility in your panels?

Don't be surprised if it takes you several 8.5" x 11" mini board versions to get it right. That's "boardsmanship," and it can make the difference between success and failure.

Toomba :30 TV

TUBBY: Toomba? What's that a dance? Nobody goes to Toomba!

TANYA: We like… oh, more popular places. TUBBY: Take me to the action, baby…

TUBBY: …24 hours a day. It's showtime! TANYA: And shopping, don't forget shopping!

TUBBY: Drinks in pineapples this big! Pin-ya-col-ada por-favor

TANYA: And you can have your nails done right on the beach! MUSIC UP

ANNCR VO: Toomba Island. Nobody goes there. Isn't that nice? 1-800-PRIVACY

TOOMBA
nobody goes there
1-800-PRIVACY

Taglines (Cont.).

Position and Differentiate.
The dependability people.   Maytag
The Uncola   Seven Up

Leverage Attitude.
The few, the proud, the Marines.
   Marines

Link to Brand Name.
First relationships last.
   First National Bank

Near Claim.
Quite possibly the world's perfect food.
   Chiquita

Competitive.
Don't be satisfied with less than Lennox
   Lennox

Parody Literature/Language.
Squeeze the day.   Tropicana
What foods these morsels be.
   J.N.Adams Tea Room

Solve a Problem.
Prestone, and the rust is history.
   Prestone Engine Coolant

Parody Competitor's Line.
The right price.   US Telecom
(parody of AT&T's *The right choice.*)

Gen Y (low/no-sell).
Image is nothing. Obey your thirst.
   Sprite
Impossible is nothing.   Adidas
Just show me the jeans. Arizona Jeans

Aspirational, Philosophical.
Just do it.   Nike
Do amazing things   Microsoft

Connect with Target.
Choosy moms choose Jif.   Jif
You're worth it.   L'Oreal

Fresh Mex.

Here, the media is also the message – with fresh-made TV spots.

Imagine the Possibilities.

Here are a few of the many possibilities for video:

- Voiceover monolog
- Testimonial (satisfied customer on camera) monologue
- Dialogue with two or more characters (often plus voiceover)
- Product demonstration
- Slice of life
- Music-driven or sound effects (SFX) only, with copy supered (superimposed on screen)
- Interactive video with user-initiated audio followed by companion landing page
- DVR-immune, live-to-tape commercial (usually by show host or cast members, often co-written by the show's writers)
- Brand integration into content

A TV Success Story.

When the Martin Agency started doing TV spots for GEICO, they wrote about 26,000 premiums annually.

In 2008, GEICO moved past Progressive to become the third-largest auto insurance company behind State Farm and Allstate. GEICO has quadrupled in size in the last 12 years going from just under $3 billion in premiums in 1996 to $12 billion in 2008.

They've constructed an interesting campaign with a simple claim/tagline – "15 minutes can save you 15%" – and a wide variety of executions to keep it fresh.

For client presentations, you can show hand-drawn storyboards – usually rendered by a pro – while doing your best dramatic performance of the script.

You can also create an "animatic" or "previsualization" of the idea by editing video of each storyboard panel against a "scratch" audio track (perhaps your own voice) of the script.

Or you can build an animatic using Flash or other software.

Writing for Television.

For all the many formats, styles, and video genres, here's a handy formula for writing video scripts for short form video (screenplays use a different format).

Writing print ads does not prepare you for the video scripting challenge. The biggest challenge is getting used to 15 or 30-second time restrictions.

Thirty Seconds of Video – Twenty-Eight Seconds of Audio.
To begin, you don't even get a full thirty seconds because you can't count on the first and last half-seconds.

Then you quickly learn the talent you've cast can only do so much with tight scripts.

That is, if you've written "wall-to-wall" with little time for pauses and creative performances.

The more time your talent has to interpret their lines, the better their performances and the better your spot.

Economical scripts also give editors time to work their magic, with space for SFX and musical punctuation – not to mention the importance of pauses, which are the "white space" of audio tracks (giving greater impact to audio before or after the silence).

Scripts that are written wall-to-wall reduce all those possibilities. Perform your scripts out loud, time them carefully, and edit them down to a "breathable" length using the average of at least five readings.

A good goal for a :30 is a maximum timing of :275. You'll need that two and a half second pad (at least) to add the unscripted nuances you're certain to get from talented performers.

It also gives your editor space, sometimes fractions of a second, to insert a small improvement that can make a big difference.

With practice you'll learn to time scripts accurately, managing each line, beat and pause down to hundredths of a second. And you'll savor every redundant word deleted and syllable cut.

And Your Point Was?
Remember focusing on benefits over the features?

Throw in the fact that busy consumers won't take away more than one point and you have a simple reminder: boil concepts down to a single theme.

It may seem like a good idea to throw in extra points, but "mission creep" can be a spot killer. Stay on point.

At the end of your spot, it's common to "ask for the order." The common call-to-action (CTA) for many ads – "pointing to" Web sites to continue consumer-brand dialogs – creates a flow from general to specific. It can also reduce the average amount of copy in your TV spot.

Remember, you don't have to pack tons of info into scripts if the details are online. That's one reason why there are so many ads with minimal copy targeting younger demographics.

Just Checking: Time for a Bit of Research.
Multitasking also affects scriptwriting. Studies show that many "viewers" are engaged in one or more activities with the TV on.

When viewers aren't actually looking up at the screen, you can't rely on visuals only. Hey, looks like it's time for some research.

Researching Your TV Commercial.
If you're developing concepts for a big brand, don't be surprised if your spot is measured carefully, often before it's approved for production.

Usually, they'll take a rough version of your spot and test it with a group of people, and find out how they respond.

Typical metrics include unaided and aided brand recall, likeability, message recall, key brand associations, and purchase intent.

If your objectives involve driving viewers online, weblogs should show spikes in traffic matching the media schedule.

Before you finish your script and boards, ask how strong you've made the brand's presence. Is strong brand identification part of the last three-second takeaway?

You may feel frustrated at this last obstacle, but if the client is going to spend a lot of money on your concept, it's not unreasonable to do a bit of testing with consumers.

While that's going on, looks like it's time to turn on the radio!

Radio.

Boo hoo. No pix. No visual metaphors. No special effects. Just sound.

Don't let anyone tell you that. And don't believe it's hard to write good radio. The key is letting the listeners' imagination help you.

You want to design sound so listeners build their own mental visions – the images that work for them. A different image, in fact the perfect image, for each listener.

The Opening.
In radio it's important to open with something surprising, dramatic, or intriguing in the first few seconds.

Listeners sense when commercial breaks are approaching and may have plans to avoid them. Your opening must foil that plan.

In addition to unyielding time limits, radio punishes writers who fail to experience their scripts the way listeners must – with zero prior knowledge.

If you give no clues about where we are, who characters are, or what the product category is, listeners have no way to know.

If you make them wait too long to get to the point, they'll lose patience and move on down the dial or just turn you off. If you use subtle SFX – she drops the sponge – it's lost under road noise.

"The Straw Man."

Steve Steinberg, who taught radio at The Portfolio Center, suggests creating an imaginary competitor for your product – a "Straw Man" – to dramatize your advantage. Here, Dick Orkin (Radio Ranch) sells McDonald's breakfast at Chateau Le Foof.

McDonald's "Chateau Le Foof." :60
SFX: Bell
Waiter: Good morning, Mr. and Mrs. Whifflebottom.
Whifflebottoms: Good morning.
Waiter: Enjoying your stay at Chateau Le Foof?
Whifflebottoms: Quite.
Waiter: I assume you'll be joining us for breakfast.
Whifflebottoms: Breakfast?
Waiter: Yes, one boiled egg covered with poached salmon bits and set on a slice of dry toast all for the very reasonable price of seventeen dollars and forty-nine cents.
Mrs. Whifflebottom: No, no, we'll be going to McDonald's.
Waiter: McDonald's?
Mrs. Whifflebottom: They have a breakfast special for ninety-nine cents.
Waiter: Ninety-nine cents?
Mrs. Whifflebottom: Two farm fresh eggs scrambled in creamery butter, a toasted English Muffin, and crispy crunchy hash brown potatoes…
SFX: Feet exit
Waiter: I see, well have a good day then… Ah! Mr. HodNoggin!
HodNoggin: Morning.
Waiter: You'll be enjoying our delicious breakfast special?
HodNoggin: Breakfast special?
Waiter: Yes, an enormous boiled egg, smothered in a sea of poached salmon bits and set on a massive slice of dry toast all for only twelve dollars and forty- nine cents.
HodNoggin: No!
Waiter: Nine dollars and seventeen…
HodNoggin: No!
Waiter: Four dollars…
HodNoggin: No! I'll be having scrambled eggs, an English Muffin, and hash browns at McDonald's.
Waiter: Ah! Very good! (softly) You supercilious twit.
Mrs. McFarfel: Good Morning!
Waiter: Ah! Mrs. McFarfel, you'll be having breakfast here?
Mrs. McFarfel: No, I… But I…
Waiter: I've locked all the doors… You won't be going to McDonald's!
Mrs. McFarfel: Help! Help!
SFX: Clatter, yelling & commotion (continues underneath).
ANNCR: The incredible ninety-nine cent Breakfast Special – at participating McDonald's.

Radio has the power *to create unusual yet memorable mental images.*

The Soul of All Radio Dialogue...

is **conflict**. Think about it. If the characters agree, there's no drama.

Keep the conflict alive and don't forget to use contrasting voices.

Tip of the Freberg.

Jeff Goodby calls him *"a martial arts master of advertising."*

In the '50s and '60s, Stan Freberg had Top Ten records – comedy records. His parodies of pop tunes were hilarious – his ads outrageous.

Not only that, but those ads built brands. From *"Who put eight great tomatoes in that little bitty can?"* for Contadina (and Howard Gossage) to his work for Sunsweet Prunes (*"Today the pits, tomorrow the wrinkles. Sunsweet Marches On!"*)

In the age of anti-advertising, we should note that Freberg did it first – almost fifty years ago.

A Tip. Get Tip of the Freberg, *a 4-CD boxed set* (Rhino). *One disc is full of his revolutionary radio spots.*

Jeff Goodby notes, *"The brilliant ones, like Stan, realize that the mundaneness of what must be conveyed [in an ad] can actually augment the humor when placed in an unfamiliar context."*

"I SAW IT ON THE RADIO."

Tools You Can Use.

On the plus side, you have an amazing arsenal of weapons.

- Great voice talent that not only brings characters to life, but also invites deep listener involvement.
- Experienced studio engineers can cut the best parts of different takes together when talent can't nail it in one take.
- Music houses can work wonders.

Consider, for example, the many ways music can make a difference. You and the composer you select have total control over many elements that can telegraph meaning faster than words.

Here are just a few examples of what music can do:

- Use tempo to control pacing and heighten script effects
- Pitch (high or low)
- Melody or lack of
- Dynamics (loud or soft)
- Placement of musical "buttons" for punctuation
- Sudden pauses create "white space" to frame important words
- The "color" of various instruments, signals, attitudes, or emotions
- Certain chords and keys are often linked to emotions
- Music tone contrasting with script tonality can signal satire
- Musical shortcuts (e.g., summer action film trailer's music, psycho-thriller violins, a foreboding string bass, happy trumpets, eerie sci-fi, etc.)

Call in a Specialist.

Radio seems to be one of those things that some people – usually those who LOVE radio – do better than others.

As a result, we find a number of specialists out there.

Two you might want to listen to are Dick Orkin, who runs the Famous Radio Ranch (http://www.radio-ranch.com). Once you hear some examples, you'll probably recognize his voice from some very funny commercials you've heard over the years.

Jeff Hedquist is another radio specialist (www.hedquist.com), and on his Web site he offers a number of excellent articles on writing good radio – plus more good examples.

By the way, a lot of radio writing is done at the local radio station – so if you think you're interested in this area, you might try looking for an intern job at your favorite local radio station.

Taking It All Apart & Putting It All Together.

Now we're about to leave the traditional media and move into creativity in a variety of marketing communications channels.

This takes a new kind of creativity – it's more than just developing a concept for a print ad or TV commercial, it's thinking about how to communicate.

To help you get started, here's a look at how a brand you're familiar with – McDonald's – looks at the communications playing field.

New Thinking. "Brand Journalism."

Here is a way of looking at the transition from traditional advertising to the new world of the Media Revolution – "Brand Journalism."

In 2004, McDonald's CMO Larry Light addressed some of these very large issues with some dramatic new thinking. He took a step back from the traditional media laundry list and spent some time thinking about key aspects of the McDonald's brand and how we connect with it.

So, before you embark on our journey through public relations, direct marketing, sales promotion, event marketing, and video games, take a look at Larry Light's observations on brand journalism.

"Mass Marketing No Longer Works."

Though McDonald's is certainly a big brand, Light's view is that *"McDonald's is not a mass brand."* In his opinion, *"no single ad tells the whole story."* He didn't stop there.

For McDonald's, *"Communicating in a repetitive manner is old-fashioned, out-of-date, out-of-touch brand communication,"* he said.

"We don't need one big execution of a big idea," he said. *"We need one big idea that can be used in a multi-dimensional, multi-layered, and multi-faceted way."*

Four Cultural Languages.

Here's an example of this multi-dimensional new thinking working with McDonald's *"I'm Lovin' It."* Light said the fast food giant wants to deliver that message worldwide in four cultural languages: sports, fashion, music, and entertainment.

An expression of the cultural language of music is introducing their new jingle in a hip-hop style, engaging "edgy" musical performers, and rolling out a dramatic new music promotion – *Big Mac Music Tracks* – in conjunction with global marketer SONY.

A Dramatic Shift in Spending.

To branch out, he said, the company is using many platforms and has shifted the ad budget. Two-thirds of that budget was once dedicated to prime-time TV, now it's only one-third.

The money has gone to "all other media."

Larry Light. McCMO.

A graduate of Canada's McGill University, Larry Light has made a career of understanding how marketing works worldwide.

And he teaches.

He has held marketing positions as Executive VP for Marketing and Media Services at BBDO Worldwide, and was Chairman/CEO of Bates Advertising's international division.

He has also taught at NYU, the Wharton School, the Kelley School of Business at Indiana University, and the Executive Program at Northwestern's Kellogg School of Business.

At McDonald's, he is responsible for global marketing and overall brand development efforts.

In 2003, McDonald's moved to a unified global advertising strategy, based around the line *"I'm Lovin' It."*

It looks like people did.

Sales were up dramatically.

And, as Light said, *"We've gone from the brand they merely know to the one that's suddenly cool."*

McDonald's spends an estimated $1.5 billion on advertising worldwide.

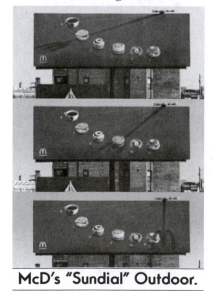

McD's "Sundial" Outdoor.

Taking an environmental view, the sundial moves to indicate various menu items.

"We're asking media to come to us with creative ideas," Light said, *"just like the (ad) agencies compete, why don't media compete?"*

A Dramatic Shift in Thinking.

Light had more revelations. *"Beware the so-called 'positionistas,'"* he warned. *"They say that a brand can only stand for one thing... this may make some sense for small brands. But for big brands... like McDonald's, it's nonsense!*

"Customers... want a dynamic creative chronicle.

"Journalism is the collection and communication of news, events, and happenings. Our brand means different things to different people. It does not have one brand position.

"It is positioned differently in the minds of kids, teens, young adults, parents, and seniors. It is positioned differently at breakfast, lunch, dinner, snack, etc.

"No one communication tells the whole brand story.

"Each communication provides a different insight into our brand. It all adds up to a McDonald's journalistic brand chronicle."

And that's Brand Journalism in action.

New Media (Interactive & More).

Is interactive marketing still in its formative stages? Or is it so naturally flexible it'll never stop evolving?

Either way, it's an amazing gift to creatives – a virtual universe with millions of parks and new rides appearing daily. It's a playground where everything's connected and anything's possible.

Best of all, compared to big budget TV campaigns, groundbreaking interactive can be far more cost-effective.

And it's fast! Measurable results are often returned so fast, the penalty for failure is trumped by a string of surprise hits scaling from nothing to monster success overnight.

For this section, I'm going to give you a bit of history.

From Fringe to Mainstream.

In 1994, when the first banners appeared on computer screens, it was impossible to forecast where it would all lead.

Web sites hard-coded banners into their HTML and everyone hoped for the best. To major marketers, it was a quaint experiment run by propeller heads.

The attitude on Madison Avenue wasn't much different.

Meanwhile, graphic design studios were being asked to help design Web sites for forward-thinking clients. Eventually, those studios morphed into interactive agencies as the Internet grew, and no one wanted to be the last marketer without a presence online.

The Ubiquitous Click.

As the Internet grew, banner ads became ubiquitous. People were intrigued by the idea you could click and be taken to a page where the pitch continued. It was more than an ad. With that simple click, you could "interact" with an ad in a way that was never possible with traditional advertising, and it was fun.

In the beginning, click-through rates soared and each was reported to advertisers who then knew precisely how well their ads were working. It was like direct response marketing with better measurements, much faster results, and none of the printing or postage costs.

This ad phenomenon grew rapidly through the nineties along with a financial explosion called the "Dotcom Bubble." Along the way, agencies realized they needed interactive capabilities or they'd lose business. So they began buying those independent interactive studios. But they didn't integrate them into the mothership, the home office.

In many cases they remained in their small high-tech offices and consulted with clients through the parent agency. They continued to conceive and produce the creative work, which was still a tiny fraction of overall marketing budgets.

By the height of the dotcom boom in late 1999-early 2000, some traditional agencies were growing their own interactive departments, but few interactive staffers were invited to the grown-ups' table for key meetings.

Senior agency executives were still unfamiliar with interactive and unlikely to recommend it to clients. Traditional creatives were also unfamiliar with interactive options. They were dependent on strangers in the interactive units.

The interactive marketing industry slipped backward during the dotcom meltdown from 2000-2002. Many marketers and agency people felt it was a flash in the pan, at best a minor marketing channel. As more and more users went online, it became a true mass market – but with a big difference. It was a mass market of individuals – each with the power to interact.

Here's what happened:

- By 2001, broadband service began to penetrate US markets at a more rapid clip. Faster access speed meant consumers could download or stream richer, larger files. That meant marketers could use "rich media" ads with video, sound, and interactivity beyond mere clicks. These highly visual ads, especially with Flash and video, are much more like the ads traditional agency staffers knew and loved (and could get excited about). They also get much higher clickthrough and engagement rates, which makes them attractive to clients, albeit with higher media costs than static banners.
- By 2004, the marketing industry realized search marketing could be incredibly cost-effective. Serious marketers got involved in building paid search programs with the "Big Three" search providers, Google, Yahoo, and Microsoft.
- Video kicked in. YouTube and other social networking sites made sharing and finding videos easy and fun, fueled by a limitless supply of original, entertaining shorts.

Branded Content on YouTube. Example: Jumpin' In.

Many brand managers are encouraged to experiment, especially online. Because it's difficult to predict exactly which video content has the secret sauce to go viral, current practice is to produce several quirky, short entertainment videos and hope one of them hits the jackpot.

When they do, they can catch fire with millions of views, plus any bonus exposure when newspapers or TV shows pick up the story.

In the case of Levis "Jumpin' In" video, produced by a small West Coast boutique, teens showed off several amazing ways to jump into their jeans. The (intentionally) amateurish viral footage even upstaged the launch of a major brand campaign by a much larger New York agency.

These client-side experiments show the growing range of creative opportunities, even if many of them may be short-lived.

Marketing Evolution.

Now an Internet release of the movie trailer is part of every movie's marketing.

Rich Media at Work.

Here's a simple sequence using rollover and click-through for a DVD of the movie *Juno*.

• Behavioral and contextual targeting technology finally began to work, delivering more relevant ads, while testing software made it easier to find the best among several ads.

• "Engagement" described a variety of rich media ad measurements like time spent within the ad, rollovers, number of individual interactions (play video, pause, rewind, activate sound, replay, forward to a friend, etc.).

• Classified ads, commercial e-mail campaigns, microsites, social media marketing, branded content campaigns, user-generated campaigns, and many other formats are all part of a powerful menu of fully integrateable tools in an ever-expanding interactive toolbox.

That's what happened. And it changed everything.

By 2007, it became clear that it was not enough to have an interactive division or a sister agency to handle that part of a brand's advertising. Clients demanded their agencies adopt a media-neutral approach to every campaign.

Agencies began to realize that separate teams for traditional and interactive media were counter-productive.

But interactive concepting can't be separated from the process of actually creating or scripting the code that makes everything work. In fact, the developers who know what can be done and who create the content and functionality often contribute significantly to the concept itself.

From 2004 through 2007, many traditional and even some digital agencies had been farming out complex interactive programming to independent third-party shops. That even led to some bitter disputes over creative credits when awards were won.

In 2007 and 2008, many agencies that had been relying on third-party partners began to build more serious in-house developer capabilities.

In new media, there's room at every step to enhance or even recast an idea. While the art director and copywriter don't have to know coding to come up with interactive ideas, those who do the coding can also be a creative part of the concepting.

This has created a new set of creative relationships in advertising that will become smoother and more productive over time.

Okay, now let's take a look under the hood.

Rich Media Formats for Display Ads.

Online display ads that result in deep viewer involvement have actually created a new type of marketing. They're a powerful form of branding not only because they're so entertaining that users spend more time with them (compared to TV or print ads), but also because users can control multiple levels of interaction. They have aspects of direct, print, and broadcast.

When users land on a Web site publisher's news or entertainment page, serious publishers who respect their readers won't give an advertiser free rein to distract (or irritate) readers. That would eventually drive readers away.

The ad might be allowed to use motion or floating graphics to attract attention for a limited time after which it would cease in order to let readers access the content they seek.

But when a user mouses over an ad, that proves interest. By definition the user is focused on the ad. At that point the ad can come to life and invite all kinds of interaction. That's a powerful branding opportunity because it's all user-driven.

By 2004 the Interactive Advertising Bureau (iab.net) had begun posting the standards (size in pixels, dimensions, file size, animation restrictions, polite ad standards, etc.) for all universally accepted formats. Visit www.iab.net if you'd like to review the current standards. Then, as you visit the major category pages of major Web publishers, look for variations of these formats:

- Corner pulls
- Expanding ads
- Streaming video
- Leaderboards (with animation, video, interactivity)
- Skyscrapers
- Leaderboards with companion skyscrapers or rectangles
- Floating, overlay or takeover ads
- Interstitials (in separate windows that load between pages)
- Wallpaper ads
- Widget ads
- Instant message ads
- Wireless ads

Pioneering the New Creative Frontier.

As you can see, the creative options in new media are more than art and copy. And things are evolving even as you're reading this.

New projects, new techniques, and new answers to new problems are all part of this fast-growing field.

The boundaries are expanding, even as new channels are opening up with more mobile options, more ubiquitous Wi-Fi, and faster-than-ever processors all creating new opportunities.

Let's look at one – games.

Creative Opportunities in Game Marketing.

When I started working on the Activision account in the early days of video games, I never dreamed how important they'd become to advertising.

But where consumers go, brands follow. Today, consumers are spending lots of time playing games. Online, on consoles, handheld consoles, and cell phones. In movie theatres, an entire audience can play as a group (see "NewsBreaker Live" on p. 455). Each year brings more ways to use games in marketing, which means there's a good chance you'll be creating in, and around, games.

What's Old Is New Again.

Take a look at how the Internet has brought back some of the classic forms of advertising.

The Poster = The Banner Ad.
Posters and billboards have been around for centuries.

Now, like it or not, they're back again – bouncing around on your computer screen.

Sometimes noisy and loud, sometimes well-designed and classy.

The Direct Mail Letter = The E-mail.
Junk mail isn't just for your mailbox any more. Now, direct marketers have found a better way.

Sometimes it's e-mail of dubious quality, just like some of the early ads for patent medicines. And sometimes, it's mail we want – from a specialized retailer, or our favorite club telling us what bands will be showing up next weekend.

Brochure/Catalog = Web site.
Catalogs and brochures used to generate lots of work for writers and art directors – now it's all online.

And, if you're good at it, they'll be lining up to pay you.

The TV Spot = The Viral Video.
When was the last time you looked at a cool piece of video on the Internet?

Yesterday? Less than an hour ago?

Now there are more and more opportunities for everyone.

Once upon a time, you needed lots of money to do a great TV commercial. With today's equipment and software, there's more and more you can do yourself.

So as media evolves, and the Media Revolution rolls on, some of the newest opportunities may look a bit familiar.

And remember, everyone is always looking for that combination of hard work and talent.

Good luck.

In-Game Placement.

In this screencap from *Burnout Revenge*, the player cruises past a Carl's Jr. truck – a quick ad for fast food.

$9 Billion and Growing.

Video games have become a $9 billion business – some predict it will double by 2012.

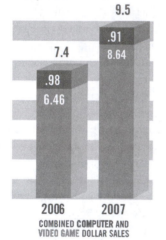

COMBINED **COMPUTER** AND
VIDEO GAME DOLLAR SALES

Source: NPD Group / Retail Tracking Service

Casual Game Sites.

Casual games, like the famous Bejeweled from PopCap games, are quick, free entertainment. Though you'll likely have to hear a bit from some sponsors (like Sprint, in this screenshot) before you can get to your gaming. And just in case the ad went by too fast, you've got another chance to learn more by clicking on the always-present banner ad up top.

So let's look at some formats and see how game marketing can lead to big ideas for any target demographic. We're going to look at:

- In-Ad Games
- Casual Games
- Advergames
- Mainstream Video Games
- Alternate Reality Games (Args)

Let's play!

In-Ad Games.

A common objective of online display ads is engaging users, and few platforms do that better than games.

With a little imagination you and your partner can adapt almost any traditional campaign to micro game play inside a standard IAB rich media format.

It's not the only rich media strategy, but it's worth considering when it makes sense for your creative brief. A little animation entices users to mouse into the ad and play. You've probably seen examples using golf or baseball.

Once a user mouses in, every little action is a point of engagement with the brand, and measured proof of success.

When game action involves (or simply hints at) the reason why your brand is different or better, you're moving the needle, as researchers say.

Casual games.

These are mostly free, simple, ad-supported games. Unlike popular console titles, casual games have fast learning curves so you can have fun playing for just five or ten minutes.

They're perfect for killing time or short work breaks.

On a casual game site's home page, several ads may be visible. Then while a selected game downloads, large ads may appear, followed by banners of various formats and sizes during play.

For a full sponsorship or special promotion, you can even integrate your brand into some games. Since people play casual games for a quick escape, your ads should be playful and fun.

Advergames.

Can you imagine being paid to create games? Art directors and copywriters are doing just that, adapting their client's brand values to build entertaining, and usually casual, games.

It's a form of branded content. Or "advertainment."

Like casual games, advergames are easy to master, with fewer levels than major titles. Think of them as extremely interactive ads.

The branding can be strong – brand characters can star in games. Or light – logo/product above, below, or off to the side of game action.

Ideally, the product or service plays a key role.

Players should be able to jump in and play immediately.

The objective is to reinforce awareness and associations with key brand values or benefits.

The games are like little gifts that strengthen consumer bonds.

Examples of advergames in various consumer categories can be found on many of the Web sites of brands marketing products for children (e.g. Kraft, Nabisco, Kellogg's, Pringles, etc.).

Your goal is building fun, playable games with just the right amount of branding. If they're addictively fun, users not only play, but pass games virally to friends. It's clearly a form of advertising, and there should be no attempt to disguise that fact.

Since advertising to children is a very sensitive area, many brands include messages for children explaining that a game is also advertising:

From Nabiscoworld.com:

Hi kids, when you see "Ad Break" it means you are viewing a commercial message designed to sell you something.

AD BREAK *Remember, if you are under 18 years old, you should get a parent's permission before you submit any information about yourself or try to buy anything online. [www.Nabiscoworld.com]*

Two more elaborate and very successful advergames show how a great result can be multiplied many times when the news media and the blogosphere get in on the game.

Example: King Games.

The King Games promotion from Burger King (described in more detail later in this chapter) became a runaway hit, selling over 3 million copies, lots of Value Meals, and countless other food items. The real payoff was far greater. When customers end up playing and liking the games (they were generally considered well worth the modest price), you can imagine the media value of all those minutes and hours spent with the King.

Example: NewsBreaker Live.

NewsBreaker Live was an interactive cinema advergame developed by agency SSK for client MSNBC.com. The 2007 global premier of "crowd gaming" used motion sensors and computers to transfer filmgoers' group motion onto the big screen and "catch" headlines falling from the colorful MSNBC campaign graphics. The campaign earned more than 65 million global media impressions, over a quarter million YouTube views, and hundreds of posts to the blogosphere. It's a bit difficult to capture the essence of the NewsBreaker game in black-and-white print, so have a look at: http://ssk.com/awards08/webbys/msnbcdotcom_campaign/

Mainstream Video Game Advertising.

There are several ways to involve brands with major video game titles. Like the first banner ads on the Web, the first video game ads were hard-coded into games.

Later, companies like Massive figured out how to dynamically serve and change ads in real time in online game scenes.

For example, your ad concept can be adapted to a virtual billboard or transit poster and viewed through the eyes of a first person shooter prowling the urban landscape.

Nabiscoworld.

Race for the Stuf is one of many advergames on nabiscoworld.com. This game is a tie-in to the Oreo "Double Stuff Racing League" promotion.

Now Creepy on Multiple Levels.

The quality of the King Games made them addictive and well worth the small price (compared to most console titles).

In Sneak King, players guide the King as he surprises famished folks with his famous hot sandwiches.

Human Joysticks.

The NewsBreaker Live game SSK created for MSNBC used motion sensors to turn theatergoers' collective movements into game action. Acting as human joysticks, the crowd moved in unison to "capture" headlines falling from the MSNBC graphic on the big screen.

ATTENTION:

If you have any information regarding the location of a 2006 Audi A3 with VIN WAUZZZ8P65A045963, please contact Audi of America at audiusa.com/A3 or call 1-866-OK-RECOVER.

Name of the Game.

Alternate Reality Games (ARG) can be an involving way of getting consumers to connect with your brand.

Here's a poster from Audi's famous ARG, The Art of the H3ist, which was used to promote their new A3.

You can learn a lot more about this ARG from one of its creators, the marketing firm McKinney, at www.mckinney.com/A3_H3ist/

McDonald's The Lost Ring.

This is an ARG McDonald's developed for the 2008 Beijing Olympics.

Here's how it starts:

"I woke up in a labyrinth on February 12th they call me Ariadne… My memory is gone. I have a strange tattoo – It's my only clue. Doctors say I'm an Olympic-caliber athlete. So far nobody recognizes me…"

From the "Terms of use:"

"By accepting these terms and conditions, you agree to enjoy the adventure of a lifetime. You agree to immerse yourself in solving a global mystery and help us in our mission to bring the world together through play. You agree to have fun. McDonald's is proud to sponsor The Lost Ring and bring the spirit of the Olympic Games to people around the world."

It's over, but you can read a case study at findthelostring.com.

In fact, virtual boards showing real time ads for real brands can enhance game action and make it feel more realistic.

As an online game subscriber's known profile becomes richer, games could use that data to target more relevant ads.

Of course, this probably doesn't work that well with period games taking place in the first century BC. Hmm. Cave paintings? Tavern signs?

Old-fashioned product placement can work just as well in games as it does in films and on TV. You may someday find yourself creating plot variations that enable your client's brand to be part of a game scene.

If the client is willing to pay for better exposure, you can concept ideas that integrate the brand into the game's story. Game developers can write code guaranteeing the brand is on-screen for a minimum number of seconds before the game character moves on.

In addition to appearing in his own video games, the Burger King also appears in the EA boxing game, Fight Night 3, as part of a boxer's posse.

Burger King also appears in Need for Speed 3, and game coders made sure players can't pile their cars into the building.

Alternate Reality Games (ARGs).

ARGs are virtual mysteries solved by many players pooling their ideas and clues online.

The games avoid selling language, but clues or evidence may involve the brand or the brand's values.

The values experienced during the game will end up being associated with the brand.

A combination of Web sites, live staged events, blogs, traditional media, wild postings, and user-generated content create an alternate reality with brand connections.

The intrigue is meant to be so engaging a mere handful of early "players" will help it become viral.

By following leads, searching for clues planted in the real and virtual worlds, and pooling their knowledge on community sites, players close in on the endgame.

For those following closely, extra entertaining "Easter egg" events (e.g., new Web sites or videos) can be found and enjoyed.

Depending on the game, players may win prizes or special access to restricted sites/events. For most, the entertainment value of the game is the reward for playing.

It's not even important that all who get involved eventually use the brand, as long as they spread the buzz.

Fictional characters are sometimes also portrayed in real world events by actors. There may be surprises dropped on the players at any time, and the actual storyline may even be open to change as the game plays out.

Wanted: New Media Revolutionaries.

If you have a taste for the cutting edge and are willing to add technical skills to your creative skills, there are amazing opportunities waiting for you.

As you might imagine, those opportunities are growing and changing every day, but there's one constant.

If you can develop the interactive platforms that build brands, the Media Revolution wants you.

Take It to the Streets with Guerilla and Ambient Marketing.

This should be the most fun a creative can have, because you're not confined to standard formats. You can use live performers, parts of the landscape, "street furniture" – trash cans, benches, cracks in the sidewalk, etc. Anything suitable for public viewing and consistent with the brand's values.

The actual terms are loosely defined. "Ambient" or "place-based marketing" usually means an unexpected outdoor installation. You and your partner brainstorm using the same concepting techniques outlined earlier in this chapter. The difference is, now you're working with real locations or props and a live audience. You can do almost anything imaginable (with permission from the city or property owner).

A popular tactic is installing graphics or three-dimensional objects around existing objects (lamppost, manhole cover, water fountains, etc.). Passers-by should be entertained, intrigued, or amused with a memorable "Aha!" moment involving the brand.

"Guerilla" is an umbrella term that can cover ambient tactics as well as live demonstrations or street theatre. The Truth anti-tobacco campaigns staged elaborate street theatre performances in front of the headquarters of big tobacco companies, usually to the amazement of stunned on-lookers. The entertaining and sometimes shocking "performance art" is filmed and released online and on TV for a young target audience.

Other guerilla tactics have included:
- Renting foreheads for temporary tattoo ad messages
- Using stencils and power cleaners to "print" sidewalk messages
- Molds for pressing amazing sand-sculpture designs on popular beaches

The beauty of an inspired guerilla idea should be in a cost-effective Return On Investment, multiplied exponentially through the viral buzz online.

Where There's Opportunity, There Are Risks.

Ad pundits jumped all over Folger's manhole street graphic, suggesting that, while a clever juxtaposition, the aroma of subterranean steam would be counterproductive.

A more notorious example, though quite successful in raising awareness, was the infamous *Aqua Teen Hunger Force* caper. In Boston, small battery-powered signs were attached to public structures like bridges where their LEDs would illuminate the "Err" character from the Adult Swim cable show. However, the police weren't told in advance and no one got permission from the city. When folks reported the strange electronic devices, it triggered a widespread bomb scare.

The PR Mindset.

In public relations, it's important to think in terms of getting media attention.

Here, TIDE finds a very appropriate role to play that connects the brand in a positive way to newsmaking disasters, such as hurricanes.

The TIDE brand group assembled traveling Laundromats on trucks so that hurricane victims can wash their clothes. A small supporting advertising budget – with testimonial-style commercials – publicizes the effort.

Product Placement that Makes Fun of Product Placement.

Here, in one of Will Ferrell's irreverent comedies, he simultaneously makes fun of athletes doing commercials and does a very effective job of advertising.

Two of the participating products – Old Spice and Miller Lite used Ferrell in broadcast advertising and used the Internet to do some "you can't do that on TV" versions.

Public Relations and Publicity

More and more marketers are valuing "PR" as a cost-effective way to get product publicity.

Like *advertising* and other MarCom channels, *public relations* is about creatively taking advantage of all media and the cultural change they create. So much, in fact, that many traditional definitions are becoming less relevant with every new, hybrid form of communication blurring the boundaries.

Public relations demands its own form of creativity.

After all, just announcing that you have a new product formulation or a new package design isn't going to get you coverage on *Oprah* or the *Today Show*.

Effective public relations not only demands that you understand what the client wants to say, but that you understand what the media considers newsworthy.

When you see "Real Beauty" models from Dove on *Today* and fun-loving product tie-ins in a Will Ferrell movie, you know it can be done – but it's a different kind of creativity.

Another interesting aspect of public relations agencies – there is seldom a separate "creative" department. In PR, the account managers usually have to do the creative thinking.

That said, let's take a quick look at creativity in public relations.

From Media Space to Cyberspace.

As noted in Chapter Seven, there are many forms of PR. And while corporate PR also involves highly creative projects, our focus here is on *marketing* PR, designed to build brand awareness and key brand associations.

Practitioners, either on the client or PR agency side, historically focused on unpaid or "earned" exposure gained by interesting editors and broadcast producers in positive stories involving the brand. Developed in a journalistic style, print and video news releases tell the story of major brand developments.

The Importance of Journalistic Style.

Remember, in PR, your audience is *the media*. They have to decide whether or not it's a good story.

And nothing will turn off the media quicker than a press release that reads like ad copy.

Some can make the switch between PR and advertising writing styles, and others find they are best at one or the other.

But these days, you have to do more than press releases.

The time is past when brands only had to effectively manage public perception through a handful of mainstream media. The social media revolution, consumer-generated marketing, search, and the expansion of media outlets have changed the game.

More Tools. More Channels.

Yet every interactive way consumers can control information and news online gives PR practitioners tools as well.

Social media – blogs, microblogging, chat rooms, social networks, branded content, etc. – are all rich opportunities for creating brand dialog.

However, PR professionals must also keep up with the industry's most current ethical codes and standards, including the obligation to reveal sponsors of interests or causes they represent as well as avoiding deceptive practices.

Among the tools PR creatives can use are services like www.nielsenbuzzmetrics.com, enabling real time monitoring of brand mentions across all blogs and most other interactive channels.

This can help you quickly spot and react to negative buzz before the brand is flamed all over cyberspace. It also lets you monitor and measure results from proactive initiatives without waiting weeks for surveys or reports.

Today branded content videos, social network brand profiles, widget development, corporate blogs and microblogs, consumer-generated blogs, user-generated content, promotional microsites, and alternate reality games (ARGs) are just a few of the channels PR practitioners use to tell the brand's story and manage reputations.

Consumers and Creative Content.

To appreciate how much the PR industry has grown in recent years, consider declines in newspaper readership. When newsrooms cut staff, editors had fewer reporters. This opened up room for content generated by public relations professionals.

At the same time, print and broadcast media saw a chance to recapture lost revenue by following readers and viewers online. They built out their sites and experimented with new styles of content.

Why are Web site publishers and editors especially eager for content? Unlike newscasts and newspapers, there are no time or space limits to the content online. More content means more traffic.

As long as editors can access a steady stream of new, interesting, and informative content, that traffic can be "monetized" with ads across an unlimited number of pages.

Better targeting can even monetize the farthest page from the home page (the "long tail") with ads relevant to either the user's clickstream or the content on the page.

That means editors eager for good content will take advantage of well-written press releases, graphics, and video news releases (VNRs).

Birth of the Blog.

Today, news online isn't limited to mainstream media.

Bloggers of all stripes are attracting impressive traffic and also rely on new content to keep users returning.

PR practitioners now have a new set of online opportunities.

Whether information begins with a press release, blog entry, social network brand profile, eNewsletter, or Web page, it's still all about the approach.

Microblogging.

Similar to a blog or weblog, the practice of posting numerous, short text updates that can be automatically sent to "followers" who have subscribed to receive them.

Just as a social network can host the profile pages of both individuals and brands, so can both create microblogs. For example, this microblog "Tweet" from GM's Twitter microblog:

While we're on cool pics of the Pontiac G8. Check out this one from http://tinyurl.com/68ze7h about 1 hour ago from web…

Consumer-Generated Media.

Marketers can track CGM for their brand at nielsenbuzzmetrics.com.

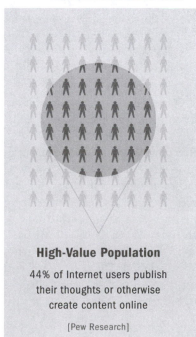

High-Value Population

44% of Internet users publish their thoughts or otherwise create content online

[Pew Research]

Public Relations &
The Media Revolution.

Here are some more examples of new media technology and good, old-fashioned PR.

Podcasts.

Podcasts are especially useful for corporate PR: analyst/investor calls, speeches, webinars, or audio/video versions of white papers. Package these for busy people who couldn't see events live or just prefer to review them at their convenience.

e-Newsletters.

A brand's permission-based e-mail or **e-newsletter** is a marketing channel that could involve PR, advertising, sales promotion, and relationship marketing professionals. Take, for example, the elaborate e-newsletters from Tide offering articles, a "quick tip from Mary," "stain solutions," polls, free samples, "where to buy," and a link to a web site for a reality TV show sponsored by a Tide brand.

Coca-Cola sent subscribers an e-mail newsletter during the 2008 Olympics, featuring graphics and links to:

- A sweepstakes
- The brand's special page celebrating its sponsorship of the games
- Videos on a brand web page
- Podcasts with titles like hydration & children or the science of taste
- A flash-based global virtual vending machine
- The brand store
- A recipe
- The rewards club

Of course there was also a link to forward the newsletter to your friends.

Buzz.

Buzz or **WoM (word-of-mouth)** involves a variety of social networking tactics in addition to blogs and chat rooms. Some agencies specializing in buzz use large (hundreds of thousands) panels of unpaid consumer volunteers to spread news about a brand. The practice is based on the idea that the most effective messages are those heard within social networks from friends or family members—"connectors" we trust.

(Continued on Next Page.)

PR Is for the Public.

Smart PR cannot sound self-serving. If stories felt the way consumers *imagine* PR would feel, you've lost. However, if written and designed in a journalistic style, the release can serve readers, publishers, and your client.

Regardless of the medium, editors, reporters, writers, and producers should be able to take your well-organized and clearly prioritized facts – who, what, when, where, and why – and craft surprising, intriguing, or entertaining leads.

Provide lots of specifics and remember what's most interesting to readers – their problems, their needs, and their desires, and how to find out more. If you find brand puffery working its way into your release, cut it.

PR in the Social Media Era.

The Media Revolution also means you can create your own media and your own PR. Most of these are familiar to you, but let's take a quick survey of what you can do from a creative perspective.

Blogs and Chat Rooms.

Blogs and **chat rooms** symbolize how PR evolved from a one-way flow of communication to include more dialog.

Monitoring an industry's blogs offers a window into consumers' real-time issues and feelings. Brands can then host conversations in a *somewhat* controlled way on their own blogs. Or you can use them along with other tactics like videos in a broader buzz marketing campaign.

Blogging can be both risky and time-consuming. What goes on the site will be instantly public worldwide, so you must take the time to know your stakeholders and communities inside and out. And you have to be ready to respond quickly to a variety of opinions.

If entries feel too canned or slick, the blog won't have that spontaneous charm or *feel* of the unscripted blogosphere. Stick to the topics you've mastered and err on the side of facts vs. opinion.

Plan topics in advance so they can be researched and discussed.

Imagine the toughest challenges and organize your strongest evidence before posting that entry.

You may even want legal departments to review blog entries.

SEO or Search Engine Optimization.

A somewhat technical but very important aspect of using interactive tools – especially blogs – is **SEO** or **Search Engine Optimization**. Search is the key tool people use to find things online, and SEO is the strategy for making your pages findable.

SEO is a very big, detailed science and can't be learned overnight. Even though most serious marketers hire SEO experts, it's important enough to study until you've learned the basic principles.

When you write a blog, for example, think in terms of one important theme per entry or page.

If your copy has such original, focused, useful content that others will want to link to it, the page will earn a high placement on natural (unpaid) search engine results for the keyword or phrase that best describes it.

You should also make blogs findable with submissions to appropriate blog directories and search engines like technorati.com, et al.

Something Not to Do.
Finally, the one thing you must never do is to disguise a blog or a corporate voice in any way.

There are many examples that demonstrate deceptions *will* be discovered. And the result *will* be a train wreck (e.g., *Wal-Marting Across America*, Wal-Mart and Edelman's fake blog).

Corporate blogs can humanize even the biggest corporations. GMblogs, for example, give executives a chance to get out of the home office and share views in a more informal setting. You could even go along (with the driver's eye view) as GM Vice Chairman Bob Lutz took a Chevy Cobalt SS for a fast lap around the test track.

McDonald's corporate blog lets executives air out even the toughest issues, using anecdotes with videos to discuss challenges, respond to reviews or complaints, show progress, and promote civil consumer dialog.

Best of all, these blogs can also act as an early warning system when new issues appear. Prepared starts with "PR."

Sales Promotion.

From Chapter Four, we know about the Four P's of marketing (product, price, promotion, and place, and, of course, that fifth P – people), but how often does *promotion* steal the creative spotlight? Actually, more than you'd think.

Most of the time, sales promotions involve concepting offers to save, win, or sample.

The objective? To promote sales. No surprise there.

But the long-term goal can also be building brands – establishing and raising awareness, or creating strong brand associations.

The tactics you create can take many forms and can work in most media channels. Here's a quick review from Chapter Seven.

- POP (point of purchase)
- Contests and Sweepstakes
- FSIs (free-standing inserts) and Coupons
- Direct Mail (e-mail or snail mail, acquisition and retention)
- Broadcast, DRTV and In-Store and Interactive Video
- Interactive Marketing
- Out-of-Home
- Employee Cross-Selling and Up-Selling Strategies
- And More

PR & The Media Revolution (Cont.).

Examples are BzzAgent and the P&G-owned Tremor for teens and Vocalpoint for moms. When spreading the word, agents and connectors are required to state their brand affiliation.

Social Networks.
MySpace and Facebook began pulling a lot of traffic from Web portals around 2006. These community sites let groups of related, acquainted or like-minded individuals create profile pages with some measure of privacy control so ideas, news, information, graphics, games, or videos can be shared with invited friends/colleagues.

A brand profile page on a heavily trafficked social network can be a big opportunity to stretch your creativity.

Most pages feature multiple interactive activities and freebies so fans can have fun and get tones, videos, or wallpaper while spending quality time with the brand.

A brand profile can also be a powerful social platform for consumer dialog. Because it's not hosted on your own site, friends of the brand may feel more comfortable and open to a closer "relationship" and exchange of information. The combination of animation, audio, video, rewards, widgets, and interactivity gives you almost unlimited creative freedom.

Widgets.
These are small apps anyone can put on almost any Web page. The code behind widgets can import real time content from other sites without making users leave the page.

You can create rich branded content (slideshows, videos, stock quotes, games, horoscopes, music, weather, purchases, etc.).

When social networks opened their platforms and let developers offer widgets to anyone (and let them keep profits), they added yet one more channel for creative marketers.

Playing for Talk Value.

Burger King's agency, CP+B, is concerned with connecting their brands with popular culture. They ask the question, "What about the brand could help us to start a dialogue between the brand and our target, among our target and/or within popular culture in general?"

Here, the King character becomes a major participant in video games.

A bit of ironic humor is also part of the recipe.

Hints, Links, & Resources.

To view and read about current promotions, visit *promomagazine.com.*

 And here's a pretty good book (even if we don't publish it) on promotional marketing – *How to Sell More Stuff* by Steve Smith.

Creating Effective Sales Promotion.

Creativity is crucial, not only in the way you present offers, but also in the creativity of the offer itself.

Example: Burger King's Xbox Games.

The 2006 Burger King/Xbox *King Games* were a successful promotion that could be described in several different ways.

They were a promotion because they could be bought at BK for only $3.99 with the purchase of a Value Meal.

This was when most console video games sold for about $50, and there had never been a brand game developed for consoles before. At the same time they could be called advergames, because they were developed around strong brand themes and presence.

Featuring characters like The King and Subservient Chicken, they were definitely entertaining enough to drive traffic and cause several million players to actually pay for them. So they could also be called "branded content," being much more like expensive console games than the simple advergames hosted on brand sites.

Not surprisingly, the collaborative effort involved many: ad agency CP+B, in-house Burger King marketing experts, promotions agency Equity Marketing, and Microsoft's Xbox 360.

Coke: Creating Their Own Video Network.

Coca-Cola wanted to take full advantage of its investment as a major sponsor of the 2008 Beijing Olympics. They partnered with Chinese marketing firm Pioco and created a promotion to engage tens of millions of consumers in Beijing and Shanghai.

Through thousands of Bluetooth short-range wireless hotspots, consumers could download Coke's highly entertaining Olympics video ads. Signs told them to activate the Bluetooth feature on their phones. Then results were multiplied through viral distribution to friends and family.

Like the BK promotion, the Coca-Cola Olympics campaign can be described in several ways. It was definitely a promotion because it offered free downloads, which generated awareness and brand associations with a source of great national pride.

It was also branded content because consumers found the ads entertaining enough to motivate downloads. The campaign was event marketing, Out-of-Home *and* video. Viral *and* mobile marketing.

Most of all, it was brilliant creative thinking.

A Different Creative Organization.

In Sales Promotion, you will find creativity popping up in many different places.

Sales promotion specialists, agencies, entrepreneurs, and media companies all offer creative solutions.

Sometimes, all at once.

In Sales Promotion, account managers are much more deeply involved in developing the creative concept. So, if that's where your interests lie, you might want to find out more. For a start, take another look at the Sales Promotion section in Chapter Seven.

Direct, Database, and Relationship Marketing.

Direct marketing (DM), which also encompasses database and "relationship" marketing, is one of these specialized disciplines that used to work in isolation.

Basically, it's the art and science of acquiring, nurturing, and managing customer relationships (again, see Chapter Seven for details).

Marketing elitists unkindly called a major part of direct marketing "junk mail." Others are equally rude about infomercials.

Yet, this is creativity that pays its own way. More recently, brand managers have begun paying more attention to data showing the discipline's highly measurable cost-effectiveness and the unique contributions it can make to an integrated marketing effort.

Most DM is defined by a combination of characteristics:

- It is highly targeted and segmented, in contrast to "spray and pray" media strategies
- It includes some kind of offer or incentive
- It urges consumers to act or respond immediately in a specific way
- It relies on continual testing in small quantities to "optimize" every variable (list, offer, and multiple creative variables)
- It provides precise, measurable results

The 40/40/20 Rule.

For decades, many in traditional advertising saw DM as the ugly cousin in the marketing family, perhaps because the creative factor was less important than the list or the offer.

This was expressed as the 40/40/20 rule, which described how much each variable contributed to a campaign's success:

- list = 40%
- offer = 40%
- creative = 20%

That is, a great offer sent to the perfect list of prospects could do well even with mediocre creative. But if either the list or offer were wrong, the world's best creative couldn't save the campaign.

That was then.

Interaction and Integration.

Through the first half of the 1990s DM was primarily direct mail, telemarketing, ads with toll-free numbers or reply cards, and direct response TV (DRTV or infomercials).

Then, the power of interactive marketing started to kick in. Now interactive marketing has dramatically changed the image and the effectiveness of DM. It's the hub integrating everything.

Direct mail, e-mail, online display ads, text alerts, search results, and traditional media can all point to Web sites where consumers "respond" in a variety of ways.

In fact, whenever there are links to be clicked, it's DM.

The List of Marketing Channels Continues to Grow.

- Direct Mail
- Inbound and Outbound Telemarketing
- DRTV
- OOH
- Commercial E-mail
- Viral Video
- Product Placement
- Branded Content
- Magazines
- Newspapers
- Social Networking,
- Online Display Ads
- Pos (Point-of-Sale)
- Sponsorships
- Promotions
- Blogs
- Podcasts
- Search Marketing
- Ambient Marketing
- Word-of-Mouth
- Event Marketing
- Network/Cable/Spot TV
- Radio

Brewing up Direct Response.

Making direct work as a distribution channel demands a full-time commitment to creating results-driven communication.

There's a constant challenge to generate new leads and new customers and to maximize the relationship with existing customers.

Creatives who are successful in this demanding field can have long and lucrative careers.

And How About...

All the other ways there are to connect in the Media Revolution.

- **Telemarketing** – inbound and outbound.
- **Direct Response** – in television (infomercials and more), radio, and every click here on every Web site.
- **Print** – every 800#, url, and snail-mail address, and all those response cards – even the ones that fall out of the magazine (they're called "blow-ins").
- **Take-One Brochures**.
- **Take this Survey**.
- **Free Sample**.
- And more.

Today, it's easier than ever to build a direct and interactive relationship into your marketing.

Classic Direct Mail.

Experienced direct mail fund-raiser, Sierra Club, packs a lot into one mailing.

The envelope asks us to *Help Save the Endangered Species Act*, and get a FREE Sierra Club Rucksack.

Here's some of what's inside:

- A 4-page "Dear Friend" letter.
- A high-value offer – a nice back pack.
- A postage-paid envelope, with a message reminding you to put on your own stamp.
- Some FREE 4-color Post Cards of endangered animals.

All at a non-profit postage rate of 11¢!

And online, the response mechanism can easily grow into a dialog that combines branding strategy with DM.

Test for the Best.

In direct, you're always trying to improve your performance – testing new offers and new appeals.

Using traditional direct mail, this was expensive and time-consuming. Online DM gives you many more ways to efficiently and quickly test for maximum results. Clients love seeing the hard Return On Investment (ROI) numbers. And creatives learn more quickly about how their ideas and executions work.

It's no wonder the top ad agency holding companies now get over half their revenue from "non-traditional" media or "marketing services," the majority of which use DM tactics.

Advertising and public relations students might not expect to be working on direct mail or e-mail projects right away, but many will find themselves with at least a few during their first years.

While we can't cover the vast storehouse of knowledge surrounding major DM channels like direct mail and e-mail, let's note some key elements that creatives have to work with.

Direct mail.

In the design of direct mail, there are more creative variables in addition to the list and the offer. Some can have a surprising effect on response levels.

- Format (postcards, self-mailers, outer envelopes of all sizes, 3-dimensional mailers, etc.)
- Outer envelope "teaser" concepts to maximize the "open rate"
- Use of color and images
- Number and style of pieces inside (letters, brochures, Business Reply Card or BRC, buckslips, lift notes, Business Reply Envelope or BRE, etc.)
- Use of personalization
- Length (in many cases, long copy beats short)

You might want to start paying attention to how direct marketers create messages – and start collecting examples that you think work.

e-Mail.

Commercial e-mail (as opposed to personal) uses variables like these:

- **Format** – text only vs html, which permits images
- **Subject Line** – equivalent to the outer envelope teaser
- **Preview Pane** – small window seen in many e-mail apps in which the user can see the upper portion of the e-mail before deciding to open it

e-Mail vs. Snail Mail.

There are also significant differences, pros and cons, between "snail" direct mail and e-mail:

- e-Mail can be more cost-effective because there's no printing, paper, or postage
- Direct mail doesn't have the spam problem
- e-Mail lets you test and optimize all your variables faster

- List brokers don't always have e-mail addresses, which change more often

Legal Considerations.

Even though the spam problem made permission-based e-mail marketing more challenging, it's still a cost-effective and growing direct marketing channel. The 2003 CAN-SPAM law requires:

- subject line clearly stating offer (nothing misleading)
- clear, working link to unsubscribe
- actual contact or company name and physical address somewhere in the e-mail

For copywriters and art directors, e-mail success starts with the "open rate," usually determined by the combined effect of subject line and the visual + headline visible in the preview pane.

When opened, the full e-mail displays in a separate window. Then the "click rate" measures those so moved by the message that they click-through to a landing page developed to "convert" through a sale, registration, info request, sweepstakes signup, coupon download, etc.

The landing page is the final key to success and, for art directors and copywriters, an important responsibility.

And, of course, if you want to know more, take a visit back to Chapter Seven.

Events and Environments.

No new product launch? No millionth customer gala? No Grand Opening? No anniversary to celebrate?

No problem. We'll just create an event and get the brand out there. We'll get it out where your customers live and work. For brands, there must be 50 ways to leave your marketing plan.

Actually, hundreds. You'll find ideas hidden in your brand's traditions, values, and benefits, while others appear after a little street-level cool-hunting. There's a never-ending pool of clever ways you can involve your brand with pop culture and events.

Thinking Up New Connections.

Brainstorming for event ideas is actually easier because you can work with ideas that play out in real time, in real places.

Sometimes you can piggyback your idea onto a larger existing event like Fashion Week in New York. Or perhaps the Rutabaga Festival in Cumberland, Wisconsin (free recipe books, a concert, and, of course, Miss Rutabaga). And remember, you don't have to wait for someone to give you an event assignment.

Check out the Pepsi example in the sidebar.

That was big. This is bigger. Talk about a chance to create something larger than life. Have you ever seen the Energizer Bunny® Hot Hare Balloon, six stories tall, going and going and going?

Since 1994 it's been the star attraction at balloon races and festivals from coast to coast. I saw it lift off in St. Louis' Great Forrest Park Balloon Race. If I ever had doubts about the power of a live event,

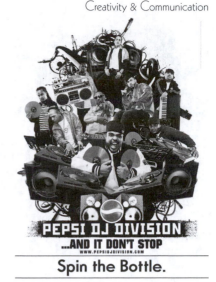

Spin the Bottle.

For decades the Pepsi brand has been all about youth and fun. But how do you get those values out to "the hood" (picture old ad guy making air quotes) where ads can't go?

Solution: the Pepsi DJ Division, "... *an association of the premier DJs in the country's top urban markets...*" That's how they described it in a press release to editors and journalists. But if you searched online, you'd find "...*home to the hottest DJs in Hip Hop.*" That was the subject line of the first non-paid search result for the keyword "pepsi djs." The link was Pepsidjdivision. com, the official site. That search listing was followed by more links to YouTube videos of Pepsi DJ Division-sponsored battles in New York. And those links were followed by over three million more hits, all for the keyword "pepsi djs." Think these events connected with the street?

Juxtaposing the Pepsi brand with popular DJs was a terrific start. Taking it a step further, August was dubbed "Month in the Mix," with Pepsi-sponsored events around the country drawing spillover crowds. Each event was magnified many thousands of times by images and videos uploading to the Web. There were launch parties. Remote radio broadcasts. Coverage on Pepsidjdivision.com. And sweepstakes where Pepsi Stuff Points could win you a trip to a live sponsored concert.

You can see how an event's impact can be pumped up – before, during and after – by promotion, search, PR, interactive, and advertising.

Driving Sales Since 1936.

That's when the original Oscar Mayer's nephew created the first Weinermobile.

Originally, the Weinermobile was driven by "Little Oscar" who would visit stores, schools, orphanages, children's hospitals, and participate in parades and festivals.

They created a media vehicle that was an actual vehicle. And its popularity grew.

Hotdoggers for Hire.

Today, the fleet of seven Weinermobiles is piloted by graduating college seniors – officially known as "Hotdoggers." Each Weinermobile holds two Hotdoggers.

It is an open position to US citizens and the duration of the job lasts for one full year: from the first of June until the following first of June. Every March at Kraft and Oscar Mayer headquarters in Madison, Wisconsin, there are final round interviews held for the hotdogger position. The Weinermobiles are then assigned to various regions of the USA – there is also some international travel.

Now in Its Fourth Generation.

Over the years, Weinermobile designs have been updated.

The most recent version of the Wienermobile, built in 2004, includes a voice activated GPS navigation device, an audio center with a wireless microphone, and a horn that plays the Wiener Jingle in 21 different genres from Cajun to Rap to Bossa Nova.

The Weinermobile has become a valuable part of Oscar Mayer's brand heritage.

they were erased as the awestruck crowd watched a 166-foot pink, battery-powered bunny, with sunglasses and drum, ascending into the blue. Just in case, little branded souvenirs went home with children and adults to sit on dresser tops or swing from backpacks in school hallways. I'll bet every one of the thousands of kids there remember that spectacle today. Even while shopping for batteries.

From Wienermobiles™ to Bullseye Bodegas.

Events and environments have grown into a huge marketing channel – with ideas that can be created anywhere and by almost anyone. PR, promotion, and ad agencies. Event marketing agencies. In-house agencies. Trade show agencies. A host of hybrid marketing consultancies. And maybe even your local ad team.

Smart branding with events creates buzz, but it's also about drawing concentrations of the prospects and customers most likely to have high lifetime value (LTV) for the brand. That is, those who'll be our most loyal and highest-spending customers over their lifetime with the brand.

Driving Traffic. Pulling Brands.

As we look at just a few of the endless possibilities, ask yourself, "Would I have come up with an idea like that?"

An event can be as simple as drawing crowds with your branded vehicle or moving display. Can anyone forget a Wienermobile™ sighting? Do I even need to write the brand name or show the pic? Wouldn't you visualize it on hearing the name?

How many brand impressions has it generated since it first hit the streets in the 1930s? Plus all the media coverage.

What if I mentioned the word "Clydesdales?" Would anyone come to an event you build around that part of another brand?

Target helped popularize the "pop-up" (this is a term coined by trendwatching.com) retail event around 2002.

There were no Target stores in Manhattan, so they created the USS Target and docked it at Chelsea Piers for two weeks. Tiny in terms of sales, it was huge in the press.

In the hot summer of 2004, a sizeable Target truck parked its giant bullseye logo at a well-trafficked SoHo corner.

Imagine the effect as the *"Deliver the Shiver"* ambassadors began selling hundreds of small air conditioners, complete with Target-branded pull carts, for $75.

During Fashion Week 2008, limited-run Target *Bullseye Bodegas* appeared in several Manhattan locations to offer their home and fashion designer labels. These events were much more about re-inforcing brand values than making retail profits. Needless to say, the value of spreading the brand's image of fun, surprise, and chic-with-value (along with the press coverage) far exceeded costs.

Co-Branding – Sharing the Cost, Sharing the Success.
Creating and executing events gives brands the chance to share visibility by partnering or co-branding with a cause. The excitement helps draw crowds and raise donations (along with one from the brand itself) for worthy non-profit organizations. Whether partnering with a national or local cause, the co-branded event model has become the standard.

This is due in part because it reminds everyone – from the city permit office to the traffic cops – the event isn't just self-serving and that the brand has its heart in the right place.

Trade Shows.

Trade shows can be very important events for many companies. There are hundreds of trade shows, and most brands are involved in at least one. Unlike consumer expositions, trade shows are where businesses in and servicing the same category sell products/services to each other.

Each show is a huge opportunity for a memorable event. The challenge is out-thinking all the other brands trying to steal the show. Not easy.

Tatts and Buzz.

There'll be buzz at every show, but it *will* be dominated by one or two ultra-clever ideas. So, it might as well be yours. Events don't have to be at the show booth, either. Brands often host off-show parties or build environments to boost awareness, drive booth traffic and capture attendees' data.

Depending on the brand and the event, you might be amazed how many people will become walking billboards in exchange for something free and a few minutes of fun or attention. Branded t-shirts, bags, temporary tattoos, and other giveaways have all been used successfully, but they're a dime a dozen at trade shows.

Example: Hell's Highway.

When game publisher Ubisoft wanted to generate buzz for the WWII-themed first person shooter *Hell's Highway* at the Penny Arcade Expo (PAX), they offered Army-style buzz cuts. The catch: the word "hell" was visible when you left the booth.

After a hundred and fifty plus recruits, you couldn't walk anywhere around the huge show without being reminded of the game's debut.

Arguably, this idea was more impactful and memorable than an ad in the official expo publication, even before the press picked it up.

Teaming up for a Tour.

In 2008 Courvoisier and LRG apparel launched a national tour of 3-day-only popup events. They featured popup boutiques, celebrities, launch parties with music and cocktails, and showcased new products and designs. Videos were posted and the designs were auctioned with proceeds going to a non-profit cause.

Buzz with Buzz Cuts.

There are many ways to get a "3rd Party Endorsement."

Game marketers Ubisoft went for an extreme version – which was an excellent match for the audience they were after – hard core game players.

Remember, catching the right fish, means using the right bait.

Condensed Connections.

Unlike mass media, where the audience and your connection is very diffuse, a trade show is a concentrated connection opportunity.

A high percentage of your audience is usually in your target.

Often, there are "supercustomers," either influencers or those, like buyers, who purchase large quantities.

When dealing with an audience like this, you need to abandon the equations of mass media, with cost per thousand, and focus on cost per customer. It is not unusual to spend tens of dollars or hundreds of dollars on each of these supercustomers. Maybe a few get taken out to dinner. At a very nice restaurant.

And, remember, even these message windows need to be served up with brand appropriate creativity.

Because the marketer at the next booth is trying just as hard as you are – and spending just as much money.

Creativity can make the difference.

The Challenge: Prove It Worked.

Every marketer wants proof of performance. The more clearly you can demonstrate it, the better. Even working with buzz cuts, it's important to measure event success. You can count impressions (in the case above, estimate the number of people who saw guys with "HELL" on their scalp).

You can also mention digital buzz in the form of blog mentions and press stories.

With a little foresight you'll be able to prove successful events in many ways:

- Samples or freebies distributed
- Media impressions (earned media)
- Site visits, (length of visits, conversions, etc.)
- Attendance
- Consumer interactions or contacts
- Database entries (e.g., names from sweeps entries, etc.)
- Charitable donations raised
- Coupons distributed

A Great Way to Start.

Event marketing and sports marketing can be a great way for you to get a taste of marketing in the real world.

First, events tend to be treated as projects. And learning to organize and execute a project is not only a great resume builder, it helps you develop skills with a wide range of applications.

Second, events and sports marketing tend to touch on all aspects of IMC. There's often advertising, promotion, media sales, public relations, some sort of interactive component, and often a direct component as well.

It can be a door that opens up many other doors.

Best of all, there are events and sports marketing activities virtually everywhere.

A world of opportunity – because events are happening!

Okay, two more things we need to cover – selling your ideas and, once you've learned to do that, getting them produced.

Selling Your Ideas.

After all your hard work developing killer ideas, it can all go down the drain without a great presentation.

Yeah, you have to do that, too.

Presenting creative work can be the most exhilarating, fun, frightening, exhausting, unfair, or puzzling process you've ever encountered.

But worry not. Chances are you'll get to watch others presenting before you're in the spotlight. And a more senior creative will probably tag along to support you at your first client presentations. Or, you get to watch someone else present your work. Hey, it happens.

First let's realize, most major campaigns go through multiple presentations on both agency and the client sides. The early, internal (within the agency) presentations are informal, yet big opportunities to shape, refine, and get ready for prime time.

Depending on agency size and organization, art director/copywriter teams probably meet with their ACD and/or CD before making a more "buttoned up" presentation to account management.

Every agency is different, but even on minor projects you might want to do a quick "disaster check" with your ACD or CD before meeting with the account team.

Be prepared to go through a number of rejections and revisions before getting the OK to show your stuff to account managers.

If it's a big project, get ready for multi-tier presentations as you work your way up to top executives.

When two or more teams work against the same brief, the process can be lengthy. That's good. It prepares you for every possible question, including the one from the heavy breather (senior executive) with the power to pull the trigger on your production.

Once work is green-lit for client presentation, that may be a multi-tier process, too. For example, on major brand campaigns you could present to an assistant or associate brand manager before getting to the brand manager.

Or, you could present to a brand manager before the CMO or other C-level executives. The reason is, lower-level managers will be in hot water if they don't filter off-strategy or inappropriate campaigns.

Leaders on both agency and client sides have all experienced their own train-wreck meetings, so they want to be reasonably sure your stuff is ready. The last complaint they want to hear from a high-level executive is, "Why did you waste my time with this?"

I'll Never Be a Killer Presenter Like _____.

Unless you're that rare, naturally gifted presenter – and there's usually at least one in every agency, you'll have to develop and polish your personal style over time.

Even the quietest creative can present well with the right preparation and support. Rather than radically change your personality, work on building around your strengths.

I've seen immensely talented but painfully shy creatives earn respect by being genuine and letting their passion for the brand and the idea show through.

Because, when you believe in the work, you can be yourself and make the sale.

I've also seen internal shootouts where slick creatives who knew how to work a room edged out far better work that was underpresented. So, if you're naturally a bit laid back, it doesn't hurt to let your caffeinated alter-ego show through.

Get Ready, Get Pumped.

There are many dynamic factors to consider when presenting:

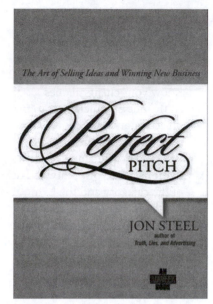

The best book on presentations is Jon Steel's *Perfect Pitch: The Art of Selling Ideas and Winning New Business*. Lots of great presentation stories and backstories.

Presentation Check List.

If you want to sell those unexpected concepts, keep this check-list handy:
- Know your clients' names.
- At the outset, quickly recap the objective and strategy to show you understand them.
- Pre-plan comments that demonstrate your knowledge of the category and the brand.
- Pre-heat the room for your first idea by telling a story connecting the target's world to your conceptual approach.
- Plan a multi-media presentation and use props or techniques like a mood board when appropriate.
- Present with energy, confidence and enthusiasm.
- Don't be afraid to be dramatic with your voice and body language.
- Be prepared for the dead silence that often creeps over the room at the end of presentations (many clients practice the dark art of showing no emotions pro or con). One technique is to break the silence with an easy question that gets the discussion going without forcing clients to give you a thumbs up or down right away.

- How well do agency and client players know each other?
- How important is this project? How many people will be there?
- Does the brand have well-established values?
- What's the objective?
- Who's presenting *before* creative (if a big meeting, creative often presents last, after research, media, strategy and planning – creative is always the dessert)?
- How broad a range of work are you presenting?
- Has the agency decided on a favorite concept to push?
- How well do your materials explain the ideas?

We all want to create unexpected ideas, but that can mean ideas that make clients nervous.

If you can show how the edgy part of your idea is related to the consumer's emotional state or the reason the brand is better, you have the beginning of a good presentation.

If the idea is gratuitously outrageous – say, for pure shock value – and the brand is *not* already associated with that style, your challenge is bigger.

Planners Can Help.

If you're working with a planner, you already have a strong ally. Good planners help you anticipate how a target audience will relate to an idea. The planner can also help explain the connection. And it wouldn't hurt for you to connect the planner's key insights to your concept.

But if you wander into territory that could damage the brand and the client-agency relationship, your planner will help you ride that fine line between risky-great and risky-we're-gonna-get-fired.

Of course, *two* less edgy concepts presented with *one* that's over-the-top (client visualizes her job or bonus sprouting wings) is easier than presenting *three* high-risk ideas.

When you're working out at the end of the limb, it can break. Which might be ok, if you have a record of more hits than misses.

Fact is, if you don't present a concept that bombs every once in a while, you may be working *too* safe.

That's just as true for agencies as it is for creatives.

You're On!

Your introductory comments should set-up the emotional motivator behind the brand decision, so the client easily sees the connection when you reveal it.

As you perfect your presentation, don't let it feel too rehearsed. Keep it loose enough to feel more spontaneous than memorized.

Also, expect the client (or, as often happened to me, your own boss) to interrupt with challenges, just to throw you off balance.

I had one creative director who had a great relationship with the client's Chairman of the Board.

The two of them thought it was great fun to heckle me mercilessly. "Fauls, you're losing control of the room!" But my partner and I always made the sale.

If the client says something you completely disagree with, find a way to agree with it: "Ya know, Bob, it's *interesting* you would bring that up, because we kicked that idea around, too, and…"

Stay extra alert while you're not talking so, when your partner gets stuck, you can fill in the blank.

Sometimes clients ask challenging questions just to see how much you believe in your idea.

That's when you enthusiastically explain your approach, while also acknowledging the client's point of view.

Remember, the more you and your partner rehearse, the more your confidence will show. And the more your show will sell.

Producing Your Ideas.

Art directors and copywriters have a talent for "blue sky" thinking and crafting compelling messages.

But would you put us in charge of planning, organizing, and managing a Verdi opera? How about a society wedding?

Let's be frank. You wouldn't ask some of us to manage a two-player air-guitar throwdown.

That's why producers are so important.

Producers are creatives with big-time project management talent, production knowledge, and serious responsibilities.

There are other reasons.

Most campaigns, regardless of the medium, involve many players from the agency, client, and multiple third parties. Not to mention unbending media specifications, tight deadlines, and even tighter budgets.

For that you want someone who's creative *and* detail-oriented. You want someone great at managing rooms full of oversized egos. Someone who gives you game-changing creative insight one minute and answers potentially explosive technical questions the next.

As other roles in branding change, no one has to pedal faster than producers to keep pace with emerging technologies.

It's a tough challenge.

In my career, I witnessed the transitions from film only to film and tape, from flatbed to digital editing, and finally high definition digital video.

Every advance brings new challenges, but producers are always there to make it work and bring it in on budget.

Broadcast Producers.

Those producing TV and radio spots have traditionally been called "broadcast" producers.

This is a bit of a misnomer now because so much of the film, video, animation, CG or CGI (computer graphics and computer generated imagery), and motion capture produced today is distributed via the Internet, cable, podcasts, and other marketing channels.

Broadcast Producer Responsibilities.

- Recommending directors, production "houses," and editors (often while screening their reels with the creative team).
- Recommending music houses.
- Contacting and sending bid packages to preferred directors and production houses.
- Setting up Q&A sessions with production houses and editors.
- Reviewing bids with agency and client.
- Creating schedules and production notes (these can fill large binders with details of the shoot as well as post-production editing, music, etc.).
- Working with a counterpart producer at the production house to coordinate:
  - Schedules
  - Location Scouting
  - Casting Sessions
  - Wardrobe
  - Set Design
  - SFX
  - Talent Issues
  - Dealing with Sticky "Issues" (there are always sticky issues), especially during the shoot.
- Managing and advising during long casting sessions.
- Being the liaison between all agency/client people and the director during the shoot.
- Coordinating deadlines and distribution of the finished spot with agency traffic people.

Detroit's Virtual Garages.

Virtual garages add flexibility and cost-savings to digital 3D production.

As long as we've had cars, we've spent much time and money creating gorgeous print and film imagery in every conceivable setting.

Now three-dimensional Computer Generated Imaging (or Computer Graphic Imagery) is changing the production of static and motion imagery both on- and offline.

CGI has been around for over a decade, but until recently, wasn't ready for prime time.

Agencies began using it instead of through-the-lens imagery in the early 2000s, but only in applications like TV, where resolution was not as high as in print.

In earlier versions, even the best CGI couldn't quite nail lifelike reflections and highlights. Now, however, the software makes it possible to create dazzling images suitable even for high-resolution print.

Modeling this Year's Model.
In CGI, 3D wireframes are constructed from a car's engineering data, enabling the creation of each model in any color, lighting, or angle.

The money-saving potential is so great, car makers have built virtual garages housing all their models. In fact, the trend is so strong it has seriously hurt the businesses of formerly successful auto photographers.

Agencies with auto accounts generally have access to these virtual garages and can use them not only for faster, more accurate comps, but also for final art. This is one of those areas requiring specialists, since the software can't be learned quickly.

(Continued on Next Page.)

Most large agencies have at least some broadcast producers, often hiring freelance producers to handle the overflow.

Broadcast producers stay with the creative team from the time a project is greenlit through distribution to the media.

They may also advise you in your concepting phase on various details and possibilities to help with your presentation to the client.

In the sidebar, I've listed some of broadcast producers' responsibilities:

Typically the producer will go to every meeting involving the shoot with the creative team.

Even with a degree in film, video, or production, it takes time to master the role of producer.

Experience is often gained in the traffic department or as an assistant producer.

Interactive/Digital Producers.

Interactive or digital producers focus on video/animated content, rich media ads, widgets, social media campaigns, e-mail/e-newsletters, advergames, and site development.

That also covers mobile technologies, including SMS and MMS alerts.

They may also be involved in SEO and PPC search campaigns.

Like broadcast producers, they may produce film or video.

But when it comes to adding interactivity, accountability, and digital distribution, everything is different.

These producers must have sufficient knowledge of the many technologies to be able to advise other agency staffers and communicate with developers scripting the content. They must also be up-to-date on accepted IAB ad format standards.

Outside Developers.

Even experienced digital agencies may call on specialists. As US broadband penetration grew from 2000 through 2007, agencies frequently relied on outside developers to create the more complex sites, ads, and content conceived by agency creatives.

These so-called "third parties" often contribute important strategic and creative ideas in addition to building the finished work or, in some cases, even proprietary applications.

Many independent digital shops also create project work from concept through finished product.

As more ambitious digital projects were created to take advantage of new technology and users' ability to view richer content, individual agencies began to increase in-house capabilities to reduce dependency on third parties (the client is the first party and the agency is the second).

Production Specialists.

However, production is also an area of great specialization, continuing a Hollywood tradition.

For example, if you're shooting a car in LA, you'd have no trouble finding someone whose specialty is polishing the chrome.

You'd also probably find more than one go-to specialist for creating realistic-looking ice cream that won't melt under studio lighting.

Today, you have many new digital wizards who specialize in production applications so complex, they require exclusive focus in order to master the technique.

And because film or video shot today is so often re-purposed for various online marketing campaigns, producers must be fully versed in a variety of editing, content delivery, and content management technologies.

It's the same with interactive.

There are numerous companies that have developed proprietary rich media ad formats (e.g., expanding ads, corner pulls, floating ads, etc.). These rich media companies assist agency producers and creatives in producing interactive ad concepts that work flawlessly across all the sites on the media schedule.

"Preditors" and More.

Since many marketing plans now involve branded content (mainly videos), hybrid producer-editors called "preditors" have emerged. As the name implies, they can produce, shoot, and edit video on a more cost-efficient, faster timetable.

Holding companies also began to reorganize their digital assets in the 2000s. Large holding companies like Omnicom, WPP, Publicis, and IPG count many "digital" shops among their assets.

They are spread across the globe from India to Central America, North America, South America, Europe, Asia, Australia, and Africa.

In 2007 Publicis created Prodigious Worldwide to organize their digital production assets under the same "umbrella" and provide more cost-effective ad and content development.

This "distributed production" is important in interactive marketing because a big part of optimizing campaigns involves testing many ad variations. It also allows more cost-effective use of resources, shifting work to the shops that aren't busiest, regardless of the location.

This system will also help create many scores of versions of campaigns reflecting local dialects and cultural nuances.

WPP's digital production group was reorganized in 2008 under a unit called Deliver. It also includes many global assets.

Print Producers.

The two major types of print production are publications (magazines and newspapers) and direct mail.

And printing is still an art. Maybe it looks great on your computer screen, but you don't want to discover that the color is muddy after thousands have been printed. You need these people.

Those producing print ads advise creative teams on specs, illustration and photography, develop estimates, and manage bidding

Detroit's Virtual Garages.

At first, automakers hired studios working with data under tight security to create these virtual cars.

Now their agencies are hiring CGI specialists who can assist producers and art directors in adapting CGI for layouts or final production.

Imagine you're an art director or producer working with such a specialist to place your client's car at a certain angle, in a particular color, at a killer location during magic hour (sunrise or sunset).

Of course, this digital revolution is not confined to cars. Today you can see examples everywhere, including online 360° displays that let users rotate products for a view from any angle.

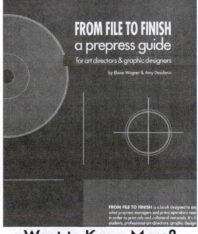

Want to Know More?

From File to Finish: a Prepress Guide for Art Directors and Graphic Designers by Elaine Wagner and Amy Desiderio. Available from the Copy Workshop at www.adbuzz.com.

Creative Resources.

Want to know more about good creative?

You're in luck. There are lots of terrific award books around.

The top three are:

One Show Annual – published every year by The One Club. www.oneclub.org

Communication Arts – *CA* has an Advertising Annual that you should get every year, if you're serious about the best in creative.

www.commarts.com

CMYK – Want to see the best in student work? Subscribe to *CMYK* – you might even want to enter some of your best work.

www.cmyk.com

for photo shoots or illustrations.

They're responsible for making sure the electronic pre-press output is in compliance with publishers' specs. Print producers may also produce OOH and collateral.

Since most print publications have unique sets of specifications and materials deadlines, print producers and traffic managers have their hands full.

Direct mail producers manage many different mail "packages," formats and folds. Their duties can include managing electronic pre-press, and keeping track of daunting numbers of test cells and source codes – sometimes hundreds per mailing – on elaborate spreadsheets.

They ride herd on countless printer specs for complex packages and travel the world to conduct press checks.

Print runs of over a million aren't uncommon, which is why producers need to assure accurate, flawless output.

Many press runs involve high-speed, eight-color presses and in-line processing (printing, imaging/personalization, merging components, spot-gluing, trimming, folding, sealing, etc.) the length of a football field.

It's a skill in itself. And first-rate print producers and electronic pre-press people are priceless.

Summary:

We've covered a lot of ground in this chapter.

And the ground keeps changing – particularly in creative.

But let's take a minute to go over what we covered.

The Creative Challenge.

We talked about the need for effective creativity – to help craft marketing messages that connect in today's over-messaged marketplace.

"Creatives."

We briefly reviewed the jobs in an agency's creative department and the new kinds of agencies that are emerging in the Media Revolution.

In fact, while you were reading this chapter, there were probably two new kinds of agencies created.

Concepting.

Some call them Selling Ideas. We talked about the ideation process that art directors and copywriters go through together to come up with those ideas needed to make messages memorable and effective.

Fighting Fragmentation.

It's hard to make memorable snowflakes when there's a blizzard going on.

We discussed the growing number of challenges and some of the ways creatives work to develop concepts that get noticed.

Print and OOH.

Next, we covered the craft of developing materials in the print media.

You got a feel for the challenges faced by art directors in type, design, and production and some of the ways copywriters developed and edited their messages.

Video and Audio.

You took a quick tour through the growing range of electronic options that a good creative team have to work with.

Interactive.

Next, we talked about connecting through the digital media that are a growing part of our lives.

Guerrilla, Ambient, and Promotional Communications.

The ways to connect keep expanding – from product placement to events and messages that show up in surprising places.

Public Relations, Events, Blogs, Social Marketing.

Again, we are seeing new environments for messages everywhere we turn.

Here we covered another sample of that growing media environment.

Selling Your Ideas.

Creative careers are built by selling those creative concepts.

We can't just think of them – we have to get them to work in the marketplace.

Part of that comes from effective presentation techniques, and the other part is learning what connects in today's fast-changing media marketplace.

Discussion Questions.

1. In your own words, why do you think messages have to have extra entertainment value? What is a marketplace message that you've seen in the last two weeks that has stayed with you?

2. Would you like a creative career? Why or why not? If you would, which creative career most appeals to you?

3. When you have to think of a new idea, what process do you go through?

4. What advice would you have for someone who has to connect with you?

   What media would they use? How would they get your attention?

5. What print media do you read regularly?

6. Where do you regularly see signs and billboards? Do you remember any of them?

7. Name your favorite television commercial – new or old.

8. Can you remember a single radio commercial you've heard recently?

9. Have you purchased anything online in the last month? Did you research a purchase?

10. Name some sites you visited this week. Why did you visit and would you go back?

11. Surprise! Where would be a good place to get your attention that isn't part of the regular media world?

Concepts and Vocabulary.

Advergames – Video games commissioned by a brand and developed around a strong brand theme and presence.

Alternate reality game (ARG) – Elaborate and realistic online multi-player mysteries designed to gradually generate buzz while also subtly involving the brand, usually leading up to a staged conclusion.

Annual report – This is an elaborate publication prepared for publicly traded companies and other types of organizations (like non-profits). Its main purpose is to present pertinent financial data of the past year to stockholders and stakeholders describing the activities and plans of the organization. Financial PR, a specialized type of PR, usually has this responsibility.

Apps – abbreviation for "applications," or computer software.

Bed (or "rug"): In radio, the sound or music under the announcer or dialogue.

Benefit – What the advertiser promises the consumer. Every good ad should have one. (Sometimes called the *claim* or the *promise*.)

Bluetooth marketing – Using Bluetooth short distance wireless technology to transmit data, content, music, video, coupons, offers, etc., to Bluetooth-enabled wireless devices. You might also hear the term "BlueCasting™," a term that is trademarked by Filter UK Ltd.

Branded condition Web site – Also know as "disease-awareness" or "help-seeking" sites. Developed and administered by individuals or pharmaceutical marketers to create or reinforce a brand identity for a medical condition defined by certain symptoms.

Branded content – Content is usually branded in a more subtle way than conventional ads. Also called advertalment or branded entertainment.

Branded integration – The practice of working a brand into the fabric or plot of a film or video, in a more significant way than a simple product placement. Involving multiple mentions or scenes.

Business return envelope (BRE) – The postage-paid, pre-addressed envelope furnished in the mailing. The self-mailer return card is called a BRC – Business reply card.

"Call to action" (CTA) – Ad statements urging specific actions such as a purchase, registration, sweepstakes entry, coupon download, store/site visit, viral message to friends, request for info, etc.

Cause marketing – An emotional aid – often a charity that relates to the target profile. Famous Amos cookies donated a share of sales to inner city reading programs. American Express gave part of expense account items to "Charge on Hunger."

CG or CGI – Computer generated, computer graphics, and computer generated imagery.

Chutzpah – (Yiddish) Bold, with attitude.

Clitchik – (Yiddish) Well-turned phrase at the end of an ad.

Closer – The finishing touch on an argument. Example: "If you can read this, thank a teacher."

Comp – Short for *comprehensive layout,* an almost finished layout, with type set and a tight representation of graphics.

Companion ad – One of two or more online ads working to extend or reinforce the message in other ads on the same Web page.

Concept – The "idea" of an ad. That is, a communication idea that helps a brand achieve its goal of persuasion.

Control package – The package to beat; the mailing that got the highest return. Using that as a standard, you now can vary the list, offer, and creative to see if you can beat it.

Corner pull – Online ad format showing a virtual page corner that can be pulled with the mouse to open a larger ad unit.

Creative team – Usually an art director and a copywriter, but the team can be any two people who will put a creative idea on the table.

Database – This is the list. It could come from returned guarantee cards, magazine subscribers, residents of a certain Zip Code, a societal membership, or simply bought from a "list house."

Demographics – Quantifiable data pertaining to the target such as age, gender, income, education, and occupation.

Dimensional mailings – Something other than an envelope – a package of some sort. The container for a gift that comes with a letter, or a cassette that comes with a booklet, etc. If it has length, width, and depth, it's a dimensional mailer (also known as 3D mailing or Impact mailing).

Dingbat – Decorative font characters (✇□•◻✜✐✔◆❋✳✿○✼✪ ✳✺▲↝•✔✗✍§) often used to set off or separate ad elements or sections of copy.

Donut – In radio, music with a hole in the middle for an announcer.

Drive time – A premium buy, from 7-10AM, and 4-6PM. This is when most people are driving to and from work – and listening to the radio.

Drop – This is the actual act of mailing the direct marketing material. Drop dates are part of the tactics plan and are listed on every schedule.

80/20 Rule – Rationale for concentrating on most important customers (like airline Frequent Flyer programs). Important to most direct marketers. 80% of a company's business (often) comes from a key 20% of its customers.

Expanding ad – Online ad format with the ability to expand down or out, usually when users mouse over it. It remains open for a limited time before snapping back to original size (for details, see: www.iab.net).

Geographics – Data about the target concerned with tastes and style preferences dictated by climate, topography, local customs, regional fashions, and lifestyles.

Imaginative divergence – The surprising part of the concept. It takes an aspect of the problem or the brand or the strategy and builds on it in a surprising way.

Interactive Advertising Bureau (IAB) – An industry association that promulgates and maintains standards for all forms of Internet display advertising. See: www.iab.net.

Interruption model – Advertising interrupts broadcast viewers or print media readers in the middle of content.

Jingle – A song that sells.

Johnson box – Usually a box or section at the top of a DM letter which headlines the subject matter and flags it in an intriguing way.

Justified, justification – In typography, the practice of aligning lines of type along an unseen vertical grid line, usually left, "justified left," and often both left and right "justified left and right."

Landing page – Destination Web page where users land after clicking on an ad or link.

Layout – A representation of a piece of print: ad, brochure, etc.

Leaderboard – Large horizontal rectangular ad unit usually shown at the top of a Web page. Can show animation or video. Can also expand downward or work with companion ads below. See www.iab.net.

Letter – A direct mail package can contain many pieces, but the letter is the heart of the mailing.

Letter shop – This is where the hands-on people work – the stuffers, addressers, ink-jet personalizers, and finally, the people with the trucks who make the drops (mailings).

Lift note – A note or added small piece in the mailing which adds urgency and extra incentive to prompt reply.

List – It is now possible to get a list of any likely prospects you can imagine. Commercial list brokers are in the business of supplying specialized mailing lists in countless forms. Marketers can shop for lists by name, age, gender, income, geography (Zip Code), occupation, interests (via magazine subscriptions), lifestyle (RV owners, skiers, divers, etc.).

Maven – (Yiddish) An expert.

MarCom – Marketing Communications. A general term encompassing all advertising and PR marketing channels, traditional and digital.

Media neutral – Marketing strategy or media planning with no predisposition or preference towards one or more media. Also termed "media agnostic."

Mobisodes – Short, episodic videos produced specifically for the smaller screen of handheld wireless devices.

Monetize – The process of making money from Web traffic through the sale of ads sold on a PPC (Pay Per Click) basis or CPM (Cost Per Thousand) views.

Mood board – Sometimes used during presentations, a collage or collection of images/objects intended to suggest the cultural context of a target audience.

Motion capture – In filmmaking, the process of digitizing (usually) human movements via special magnetic or reflective elements positioned at key points on the skeletal frame. The direction and speed of motion is captured on multiple cameras and, through software, adapted to show 3D motion.

Multimedia messaging service (MMS) – For handheld devices, similar to SMS but including images and/or audio/video.

News release – A news story about the brand in a form that editors of print and broadcast outlets can use.

Outer – The exterior of the envelope, wrapper, or cover of the letter, kit, or package that is the mailing.

Overlays – In the context of video, an ad that occupies the lower portion of the screen, superimposed over the video beneath (for details, see: www.iab.net).

Patch/Window – In direct mail, the hole in the envelope through which the address or teaser material can be seen. Sometimes an essential part of the artwork.

Pay per action (PPA) – An online display ad payment method in which advertisers pay only when a click-through results in a defined action such as a purchase, registration, appointment for a test drive, etc.

Pay per click (PPC) – A popular online display ad payment method. Advertisers only pay when a user clicks (as opposed to CPM or PPA).

Pitch letter – Before a story is fully developed, many practitioners test the waters with a pitch letter to a reporter or a publication, describing a story angle or upcoming event. This avoids sending material to an outlet which may not want it and often results in feedback that helps form the actual story.

Premium – A gift. Rule of thumb – when you offer something worth getting, response is greater.

Pre-roll ads – The practice of forcing online video viewers to screen an ad before gaining access to the content they seek. Mid-roll ads run in the middle of content while post-roll ads run after the content is finished (for details, see: www.iab.net).

Press conference – When an important announcement is to be made, the PR department may invite coverage from interested media. This gathering usually offers opportunities for questions from the floor, photo opportunities, and well-prepared handouts.

Press kit – The most elaborate handout is a kit of all sorts of useful material. It may include the essential statement and quotes from the press conference, photos, back-up information, brand and personnel histories, and even video footage.

Product placement – Brief mention or cameo appearance of a product/brand/logo in films, TV, online video, etc.

Psychographics – Qualitative data about the target, such as personality traits, buying habits, hobbies, special interests, ideas, ethnic modes, and personal values.

Publics: We all know who we mean by "the public," but PR professionals segment that mass group into areas of special interest. They call each segment a "public." Some of the publics are: External Publics, Internal Publics, Sales Outlets, Financial Analysts.

Relationship marketing – The practice of building relationships with existing customers, for greater LTV. That's Lifetime Value, right?

RFID – "Radio Frequency Identification." Electronic chips small enough to be placed almost anywhere, including on products for inventory tracking purposes. The chip can respond to an electronic signal with a short distance broadcast of data identifying itself.

Roughs – Layout which is larger and more detailed than a thumbnail but not yet finished. Art directors often do a series of ever more detailed roughs as they work out aspects of the layout and/or graphic design. (Sometimes spelled "ruffs.")

Sans-serif – Typefaces with no serifs (thin "tails" found on the ends of many letters in serif fonts), e.g., **Helvetica**, **Verdana**, Futura, **Arial**, etc.

Schtick – (Yiddish) A piece of business.

Search engine marketing (SEM) – also known as Pay Per Click (PPC) or sponsored search results. Typically 3-line text ads appearing above or in a column to the right of the first page of search engine results. The sponsor is charged (by the search engine) only when a user clicks to be sent to a landing page.

Search engine optimization (SEO) – the practice of editing both content and underlying code to cause a page to be among the top listings on the first page of search results for its most important search engine terms.

Self mailer – A one-piece mailer which requires no envelope. The outer has the teaser and address. When you unfold it, you have the letter.

Serif – Typefaces characterized by small, straight or curved tails at the top and bottom of letterforms. Serif fonts are often preferred for long copy because the serifs facilitate the smooth flow of vision from one letter to the next. The type you're reading here is a serif font (Berkeley). E.G., **Times New Roman**, Garamond, Baskerville, **Century Schoolbook**, Palatino.

SFX – Sound effects.

Short message service (SMS) – For handheld devices, commonly known as "texting," these opt-in messages or alerts may be sent as part of a mobile marketing program. Usually limited to 160 characters.

Skyscraper – Long vertical rectangular ad unit on the right or left side of a Web page (for details, see: www.iab.net).

Slice of life – Short video scenes showing everyday events in the lives of the characters involved.

Social media – Online channels enabling communities of users with common interests to exchange dialog and information. Blogs, social networks, chat rooms, social bookmarking (digg, del.icio.us, reddit, etc.), user reviews and ratings, wikis, etc.

Spoilage – The waste in every mailing: misdelivered, misaddressed, or "address unknown." A certain percentage is expected to be waste. As technology advances, spoilage diminishes.

Structural connectedness – The logical part of a concept. It connects with the strategy, with target audience perceptions, and other aspects of keeping the campaign organized.

Tags: Usually, retail information at the end of a radio spot, such as "*…In Jonesville, see the new High Definition TVs at Vantage Video, in the Chesapeake Mall.*"

Target – The person, group, or organization that is addressed by the advertising.

Target sketch – A fictional glimpse into the lifestyle of a prospect, usually built on hard data.

Teaser – That's the message on the outside of the envelope, which entices the recipient to open. The teaser can simply state the offer, or it can make a creative appeal to people with special interests. One of the most successful teasers for a mailing that solicited subscriptions for the magazine, *Psychology Today*, had this line on the outer: "*When you're home alone and you go to the bathroom, do you lock the door?*" Prospects for a magazine about psychology found it very hard *not* to open that envelope.

Thumbnails – Small sketches of possible ad ideas or layout approaches done by either the art director or copywriter. Today, that sequence may be dramatically altered depending on the computer, the computer operator, and the **"scrap,"** or reference material.

Video news release (VNR) – A press release that a TV station can use. It may cover the essential information, show a new model of merchandise, and even contain an advance copy of a TV commercial. There may or may not be a sound track to this footage. Sometimes, additional views of the subject or product are added to the package, which may be adapted by the TV news outlet. This additional material is called "B roll footage."

Webisodes – A series of typically short videos developed for the Web. They can be lightly branded content or sponsored with separate ads.

Widgets – Small applications – usually within framed rectangles – easily inserted on Web pages, blogs, social network profiles, etc., enabling remote content delivery (weather reports, product info, etc.) or actions to be taken (transactions, data requests, etc.) without leaving the page.

10

"Today's toughest question is how to find your customers at the most strategic time — that's why media is the new creative frontier."

— Keith Reinhard, Chairman, DDB

Media
& The Marketing of Messages

COMMUNICATING THE COMMUNICATION is the next step in the process. You saw how an agency media department was organized in Chapter Five – now you'll see what all those people do.

The Message Must Go Through…

After the marketing plan is developed and the ad message is created, it has to get to the target audience – this is the role of the ad agency's media department.

But even though all these people are organized around the same task – delivering ears and eyeballs to marketers – they've had very different career paths.

From Bike Path to Career Path…

Back in 1982, **Debra Becker** went from Hofstra University to a family business – Meltzer's Bicycle Store– with a $10,000 ad budget.

A few years later, Debra pulled up stakes and moved to Portland, Oregon, as a media director at INS Advertising, creating media plans for Shilo Inns and local auto retailers.

She's been a media director, a retail ad manager, and now she's back in Syracuse as media director of a leading agency, Latorra, Paul & McCann. She'll talk about local and regional media planning.

Planning Priorities.

Alfred Gilbert became Senior Media Planner at Draft/FCB in New York. His career path was more direct.

After graduating from Syracuse, he found an entry-level position as an assistant media planner on Oil of Olay. Now he's using his skills on a $40 million national account.

From Grunt to Cutting Edge.

Steve Klein is Managing Partner, Director of Media and Interactive Services, for Kirshenbaum, Bond & Partners (kb&p) – one of the most exciting agencies in New York and home of the Media Kitchen.

It wasn't always that way.

This chapter was also written by Professor Carla Vaccaro Lloyd, Associate Professor at Syracuse's S.I. Newhouse School of Public Communications, and Marian Azzaro of Roosevelt University. Professor Lloyd is Chair of the Advertising Department. Professor Azzaro is a former Media All-Star and head of the IMC program at Roosevelt.

Media Building Blocks.

Alfred Gilbert is pushing the envelope and fighting a war.

His media planning for the US Postal Service has to battle tough competition – FedEx. His competition created a hard-hitting newspaper campaign.

Why did they choose newspapers? What should Steve do?

We'll cover the strengths and weaknesses of various media choices.

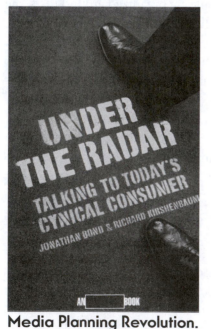

Media Planning Revolution.

You can read more about Steve Klein's exploits at the cutting edge of media with Kirshenbaum & Bond in the *AdWeek* book *Under the Radar: Talking to Today's Cynical Consumer.*

An English major in the class of 1981 at Columbia, Steve got his first job at Grey doing *"all the grunt work of an assistant media planner in a monster agency."*

Five years later, he became Director of Strategic Media Development at another agency. From there, he moved to the cutting-edge – setting up a full-service media department at kb&p.

Then, he moved his department onto the information superhighway and began delivering interactive services to clients.

We'll give you an insight into his activities, which are featured in Richard Kirshenbaum and John Bond's book, *Under the Radar.*

Welcome to the Next Level.

Alissa Agisim graduated from Syracuse in 1995 with a dual major in advertising and marketing. Her internship was with David Letterman's writers, and her first job was at *The Carnie Wilson Show* as a production secretary.

She answered phones, heard complaints, and listened to stories from people who wanted to be on the show – scary.

In 1996, she got her first job in advertising – as a Junior Media Planner on Wendy's. A little over a year on the job, she was promoted to Media Planner.

Alissa said, *"It was very exciting for me when I left Carnie, I was beginning my career."* A year later, she was promoted to media planner. *"It was nice to know that my career was advancing and Bates had confidence in me to bring me to the next level."*

Now let's see what it will take to get you to the next level.

How This Chapter Is Organized.

In Chapter Eight, you saw how an overall plan is developed.

In Chapter Nine, you saw how messages were created.

Now, we're going to roll up our sleeves and see what it takes to get those messages in front of our target.

This will be the most "how-to" chapter in the book.

Here's How We'll Cover the Material.

❶ **Media Speak.** First, we'll show you how to talk media. There are a lot of important terms. We'll put them in context. You'll have to learn them. And, they'll be on the test.

❷ **The Media Building Blocks.** This section will look at media from a media department's point of view – including the **Strengths and Weaknesse**s of each major medium.

❸ **The Media Plan.** What it is. How to create one. Media strategies and objectives made simple

❹ **The Media Planning Revolution.** Throughout, you'll see new ways planners are leveraging the explosion of new media opportunities.

From network TV to cable to out-of-home to hanger tags at a local clothing store, you'll see how media planning is at the cutting edge of our Media Revolution.

When we're done, you'll know what it takes to make those first steps into the world of media.

Media Speak.

GRPs? CPMs? HUTs AND PUTs AND DOUBLE TRUCKS – OH MY! Wandering into the media department can be like crossing the border into a foreign land.

Until you learn the language you might need an interpreter.

So that you don't cross your BDIs with your CDIs, let's take a moment to crack the code of the media world.

Commonly Used Media Terminology.

There are some key terms in media that you have to know and use correctly to avoid confusing yourself and others.

Let's review some basic, yet critical, media terminology.

Media and Medium.

Let's start with **advertising media**. This term refers to all the channels of communication used to deliver advertising messages to consumers. It is also the plural of *medium*.

Primary Media, Mediums, and Vehicles.

Advertising media come in many forms, with the primary media including newspapers, magazines, television, radio, directory advertising (i.e., yellow pages), direct mail, business and farm publications, outdoor, and point-of-purchase.

A single type of media, such as magazines, is called a **medium**; a single carrier, such as *Sports Illustrated,* is a **vehicle**.

These are the three major terms used to refer to the various categories of media delivery.

Now let's look at how media professionals define and categorize the people actually reached by media.

Audiences.

What about all of those curious media acronyms (HUTs, PUTs, and GRPs)? Not to mention the infamous "double truck?"

Some of these will be discussed later on in this chapter, others won't. (After all, this isn't a media planning textbook).

But just in case you find yourself working as an intern in the media department of an ad agency and need to know what a "double truck" is, we've attached a whole glossary of media terms at the end of this chapter, courtesy of TBWA Chiat/Day.

Now, let's examine how media professionals define the folks they try to reach with their ad messages.

The Eyeball Business.

Media planning boils down to advertisers investing in "eyeballs."

They strive to get their messages in front of the eyes (and ears) of those most predisposed to buy their product or service.

In media speak, these pinnacle people with real purchasing power are called **prospects**.

As a matter of fact, media professionals have a variety of key terms to define the folks they want to reach with their messages.

Let's review a few of these important terms now, starting with the concept of audience.

**Many Channels.
One Objective.**

This chapter is focused on one thing – getting media messages to the target in the most efficient and effective way possible.

Driving Eyeballs.

VW's offering of uniquely painted VWs caused a media buzz.

TV commercials featured the unique colors. At the end of the spot, you discovered that only 2,000 VWs were available in the special colors – and you had to shop for them over the Internet.

When you did, you were directed to your closest VW dealer.

From production to media plan to follow-through, this campaign drove traffic and stimulated interest.

Niche Media.

ABC/Disney focuses on a small target – kids – with a weekly audience of 1.6 million kids 6–11 and 600,000 moms. Got a niche? Scratch it.

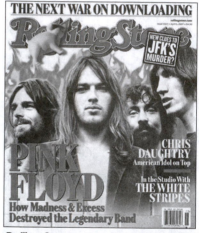

Rolling Stone: Circulation: 1,400,000
Page Rate: $157,880

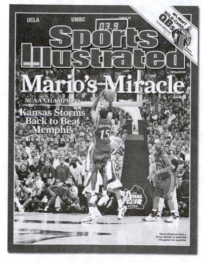

Sports Illustrated: Circ: 3,150,000
Page Rate: $320,680

Audience refers to the number or percent of homes or people exposed to a media vehicle or advertising message.

Audience coverage is a term that tells us the number or percent of people or homes who are reached by a single insertion of a particular media vehicle in a specified area.

On Target.

Thanks to the ability of technology to give us detailed information on consumer attitudes, preferences and behaviors, specialized media, and databases, advertisers can be more precise in terms of defining, and ultimately reaching, their audience.

In *The New How to Advertise*, Ken Roman and Jane Maas state that **precision marketing** is *"increasingly possible."* They describe it as *"marketing aimed at specific segments or even individuals."*

The benefit? *"Less waste and a more personalized message."*

The terminology that matches this more exacting approach to marketing and advertising starts with **target market.**

This is the group who has been identified as having real sales potential for the brand and can be defined, not only in terms of demographics (age, education), but by other distinguishing characteristics such as psychographics (attitudes, behavior) and product usage (heavy users, light users).

A *target consumer* is a member of the target market.

Prospecting for Prospects.

Advertisers pay big bucks to reach prospects.

For instance, a 30-second spot, called a **unit,** on the 2008 Super Bowl cost $2.8 million. The same spot on the Academy Awards boasted a $1 million price tag.

Print can also be costly, with a full-page ad in *Rolling Stone* magazine costing $157,880 and the same insert in *Sports Illustrated* going for $302,680.

With those kinds of dollars involved, you can see why media companies are so concerned with both the quality and the quantity of the audience they deliver.

Because advertisers are spending so much money to reach these "pairs of eyeballs," they demand measurement statistics to both quantify and define the people they are reaching with the advertising media they're buying.

In other words, advertisers demand that the media be accountable for delivering a specified audience. In their quest for **accountability,** one of the first things that advertisers want to find out is who reads, listens, or tunes into a particular media vehicle.

Audience composition gives advertisers this statistical breakdown by spelling out the demographic classification of individuals within a media vehicle's total audience.

Reach and Ratings.

The next thing advertisers are concerned with is finding out how many people are being reached by a particular media vehicle. This varies depending upon the type of media that is being measured.

Broadcast media use **rating points** to report the percent of the target audience reached by a media vehicle.

Seinfeld was the top-rated television program in 1997, with a 22% audience rating. In 2007, *American Idol* had a 17.3% rating.

Print media, on the other hand, relay target audience statistics through **circulation** figures that tell advertisers precisely the number of copies of a publication sold or distributed.

Spin had a circulation of 450,000 in 2007.

Then again, some copies of *Spin* have more than one reader. That is computed as **passalong**, and it's quite controversial (see sidebar).

The Buck Stops Here: Advertising Spending.

Marketers spend billions of dollars every year trying to coax people into buying their products and services.

As a matter of fact, advertising has grown right along with the economy in the United States.

For over 150 years, American business has used mass media.

Advertising and ad revenues continue to grow, though there are interesting changes in the mix.

In 2006, US advertisers spent $285.1 billion on advertising.

This was a 5.2% increase over 2005. However, with problems in the US economy, a 3.2% decline is predicted to $270.8 billion. Overseas, growth is expected to continue, growing 3.3% to $372 billion for a worldwide total of $642.8 billion. (You can find updated industry totals and projections at www.mccann.com.)

Above-the-Line and Below-the-Line.

The revenue that is spent on paid advertising in **mass media**, like broadcast network TV and newspapers, and on **specialized media**, like cable and magazines, is called **above-the-line**.

Below-the-line is all promotional expenditures that are not allocated in above-the-line media. It consists primarily of sales promotion, public relations, and event marketing.

$4,300 per Household. $1,600 per Person.

When you add below-the-line expenditures, the number gets even bigger. According to *American Demographics* magazine, private and public agencies spend almost $400 billion a year to bring above- and below-the-line messages to every person in the United States.

Consequently, these agencies spent $4,300 on every American household, or $1,600 per person.

79% Consumer. 21% Business to Business.

US advertisers spend their ad budgets trying to reach either consumers or businesses.

Typically, 79% of all money plowed into advertising is spent on media that is aimed at the consumer.

The remainder is appropriated to **business-to-business advertising media**, like specialized business periodicals that are geared toward professionals working in specific industries or businesses, such as Putman Publishing's *Chemical Processing*, which is aimed at chemical engineers.

Nielsen TV Ratings:

12/08/08 – 12/14/08

Rank	Name	Ratings/Share
1	NBC Sun. Night Football	13.7/21
2	CSI	12.7/20
3	60 Minutes	11.6/18
4	Two and a Half Men	9.5/14
5	Criminal Minds	9.3/15
6	The Mentalist	9.0/14
7	CSI: Miami	8.9/14
8	CSI: NY	8.7/15
8	Eleventh Hour	8.7/15
10	NCIS	8.6/13
11	Sun. Night NFL Pre-Kick	8.5/14
12	House	8.4/13
13	Survivor: Gabon Finale	7.8/12
14	Survivor: Gabon	7.7/12
15	Law and Order: SVU	7.2/12
16	Survivor: Gabon Reunion	7.0/12
17	Worst Week	6.7/10
18	The Big Bang Theory	6.5/10
18	Football Nt America Pt 3	6.5/11
20	How I Met Your Mother	6.4/10

Nielsen TV ratings represent the percent of the audience watching a particular TV program at a particular time.

Audiences are of a different size and composition at different times of the day. That's why prime-time ratings points (shown here) are more valuable than daytime, fringe, or late-night ratings points.

The "Passalong" Controversy.

Many media research companies report "passalong" readership figures in addition to circulation.

This number includes people who get the magazine passed along to them by regular subscribers.

For example, *Spin* has an estimated 5.56 readers per copy.

How many people read your copy?

Now you understand why most agency media executives question the validity of passalong.

Largest Advertisers:

		Ad $ (in billions)
1.	P&G	$5.23
2.	AT&T	3.21
3.	Verizon Comm.	3.02
4.	General Motors	3.01
5.	Time Warner	2.96
6.	Ford Motor Co.	2.53
7.	GlaxoSmithKline	2.46
8.	Johnson & Johnson	2.41
9.	Walt Disney Co.	2.29
10.	Unilever	2.25
11.	Sprint Nextel	1.90
12.	General Electric	1.79
13.	Toyota	1.76
14.	Chrysler	1.74
15.	Sony	1.74

(Source: *Advertising Age*, 2008)

"Ambush Marketing."

Chiat/Day produced some great outdoor for Nike. The boards were posted during the LA Olympics – though Nike was not an Olympic sponsor.

Reebok was the "official shoe."

But that didn't keep Nike from blanketing the area with every available bit of outdoor in LA during the games. Ambush!

So even though Reebok was the official sponsor, it seemed like Nike was sponsoring the Olympics.

This caused great concern and complaints – affecting policies on media availabilities in every Olympic venue from then on. For Nike it was a big win – with a big assist from smart media planning.

There was even a music video-style TV commercial featuring the billboards – with Randy Newman singing "I Love LA" and the Nike boards and athletes being featured throughout. Reebok hated it.

Between 1% and 3%.

The investment that advertisers make in media is the largest chunk of their advertising dollars, far surpassing the money spent on advertising production.

On average, US companies spend between 1% and 3% percent of their annual earnings on advertising.

The Largest Categories.

Companies that spend the most on advertising tend to be the largest manufacturers of food, soft drinks, automobiles, tobacco, and beer, as Competitive Media Reporting points out.

For example, in 2007, media conglomerate Time Warner, the fifth largest US advertiser, spent $3 billion on media advertising. P&G, the nation's largest advertiser, shelled out $5.2 billion.

Telecom giants AT&T and Verizon were the country's second and third largest advertisers, spending over $3 billion apiece – a large portion, no doubt, spent to compete with one another.

Advertisers spend half of their ad dollars in local media.

Newspapers have historically been the largest medium for local advertisers and continue to be so today, even with revenues declining.

Traditional and Non-Traditional.

Today, advertising media are often categorized as traditional or non-traditional.

Traditional media, made up of newspaper, magazines, TV, and radio, still control the vast majority of advertising spending. This started to change in 2005, when interactive technology began having a significant impact on how media budgets are appropriated.

Non-traditional media are often driven by technology and can be any new media form that allows for commercial expression.

These unconventional media forms are far-reaching and include everything from truck advertising – where sides and backs of freight trailers or vans are leased to advertisers – to Internet advertising, where destination sites, micro-sites, or banner campaigns can be used to interact with consumers.

Digital technologies are forcing marketers to rethink how they advertise to their consumers.

And, as the options have expanded, the planning process has become more complex.

Let's take a deeper look at the pros and cons of various media forms.

Traditional Ad Media = 50% of All Ad Dollars.

Traditional advertising media are booming, receiving over 50% of all advertising dollars.

In 1996, television inched out newspaper for the first time.

In 2007, Network TV (broadcast plus cable) accounted for 29% of US ad spending.

Magazines were second with just over 20% of spending.

And newspapers ran a close third with 19% of ad spending.

The US Media Dollar.

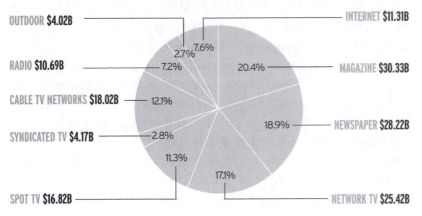

OUTDOOR $4.02B — 2.7% 7.6% — INTERNET $11.31B

RADIO $10.69B — 7.2% 20.4% — MAGAZINE $30.33B

CABLE TV NETWORKS $18.02B — 12.1%

SYNDICATED TV $4.17B — 2.8% 18.9% — NEWSPAPER $28.22B

11.3%

SPOT TV $16.82B — 17.1% — NETWORK TV $25.42B

(Source: 2007 Spending from 2008 Advertising Age Fact Pack)

But, the Media Revolution is causing great dislocations.

For example, as we took this book to press, many newspapers were experiencing sudden, double-digit declines.

The Growth of Direct.

With the growth of the Internet, it's easier than ever to provide some type of direct response capability – such as a Web address.

Think of it, have you seen a message recently without one? So, it's not surprising that this area is experiencing healthy growth.

Increasingly, direct marketing and one-to-one target marketing are becoming part of general advertising campaigns.

Spending on direct marketing reached over $60 billion in 2007.

There is more concern of accountability across the board.

Follow the Money.

All media – whether traditional or non-traditional – have to be measured, priced, negotiated, and bought to stay afloat.

Advertisers only invest their dollars where there is opportunity to make sales or to meet some other objective – like bolster the stock price or get elected. So when it comes to media, advertisers invest in audience. When purchasing prime-time TV, advertisers don't just look at ratings, they look at audience composition.

According to advertising agency BBDO, the term **audience** refers to the persons (or homes) reading, listening to, viewing, or seeing a particular media vehicle.

With that general overview of media terms, let's move onto reviewing where the media world is heading and what exciting things are in store for those who use them.

These Numbers Change Every Year.

To get the latest update on US media spending, go to www.mccann.com, where Robert Coen tracks the latest in media spending patterns.

Here's the data for 2007, with spending shown in billions and the percent change from the previous year indicated:

1.	Direct Mail	$60.99	+4.0
2.	Newspapers	42.93	-7.1
3.	Broadcast TV	45.75	-1.2
4.	Radio	18.59	-5.3
5.	Cable TV	20.48	+6.0
6.	Yellow Pages	14.54	+1.0
7.	Magazines	13.70	+4.0
8.	Out of Home	7.28	+6.5
9.	Internet	10.92	+20.0
Other		41.42	+3.8
Total		**$283.88**	**+0.7**

(Source: www.mccann.com)

What Kind of Media Is Google?

It's a search engine that adds advertising in a unique way.

It delivers an audience that is simultaneously broad and highly targeted.

How many times a day do you use Google?

It's easy to understand why our behavior has added an exciting new dimension to media planning.

Suddenly, media planners are interested in things like key words.

Some of those key words are available for almost nothing – others are the subject of a bidding war between various competitors in the category.

It's just one example of how our media behavior and the media planner's job keeps changing.

Nissan: Branding and the New Media Frontier.

Traveling on a Road Less Traveled.

TBWA Chiat/Day is known for its breakthrough media strategy – bringing you those ads for Absolut Vodka and Apple Computer and, year after year, a fresh Nissan campaign.

On the Edge.

Their edgy media planning routinely captures headlines and startles the competition. They don't play it safe.

Inside Media magazine noted, "*The agency can be obsessive at times about breaking rules, sometimes with spectacular success.*"

Let's follow their approach over the years.

For example, in 1996, with no new models, their *"massive new branding campaign"* for Nissan stirred up the marketplace.

Over the Top.

In 1996, they spent *"$200 million on network television alone"* for Nissan. It left "*industry players and rivals shaking their heads even more than usual.*" They were putting out the message before they had the cars.

The objective? Convince consumers that brand Nissan stands for the ultimate "youthful" and "fun" car.

All this went on while Nissan was involved in a massive retooling.

So they ran a commercial starring action figures and a toy model of their Z car – not yet for sale.

They worked to shift attitudes.

(Continued on next page)

Media Building Blocks.

WE REVIEWED THE WORLD OF MEDIA in Chapter Six. Now we're going to look at it from an advertiser's perspective.

It's a Whole Different Media World.

Thanks to new technologies, media mergers, media and audience fragmentation, and recent federal court decisions, media have been evolving and are continuing to evolve into a burgeoning, and not yet clearly understood, complex communications system.

An Unprecedented Number of Choices.

Nowadays, there are an unprecedented number of media choices that advertisers can choose from.

See for yourself. Stop reading for a moment. Look around.

Come on now, be thorough… are you in your dorm room? Is the radio or TV on? Okay, that's easy. But keep going.

Did you count the rock concert poster above your desk?

How about that baseball cap worn backwards? The people behind you can see the logo.

Did you remember to include the T-shirt with your school's mascot? How about the candy bar wrapper or energy drink can next to your notebook? Did you count these packages? You should.

Brand Contact Points.

Increasingly, marketers are thinking in terms of product packaging and in-store advertising as **brand contact points**. They are becoming extremely important as we consumers become less brand loyal, and as our media options expand.

Not only that, but, more and more, planners are looking at *all* contact points – not just those in the media. For example, did you know we make more than two-thirds of our brand decisions right at the grocery store shelf?

Throughout this chapter, we'll remind you that even cereal boxes can become an important media vehicle.

How about the pen or pencil you're taking notes with?

Is there any specialty advertising on it?

What about your roommate, besides being a friend and part-time pain in the neck, he or she is a living, breathing billboard – as well as a narrowcasting communications channel (remember "word-of-mouth?").

Check out the logos on his shoes, jacket, sweatshirt, watch, cap, and jeans. Not to mention his notebook.

Okay, the break is over, let's get back to reading.

How many different advertising messages did you locate? What were some of the more unusual places?

The purpose of this little exercise is to help you understand what we mean by advertising media in today's media world.

Now, to get you started on your own course of action to understand media, let's begin with the fundamentals of where it all starts: media delivery and what it means.

Media: It's Everywhere Your Brand Needs to Be.

There's never been so much advertising media.

Advertisers are using them, sometimes abusing them, to splash their ads everywhere.

Consumer Reports recently reported, *"Advertisers are putting their messages in public lavatories, on the sleeves of pro athletes, on TV screens in kids' classrooms – even on clouds."*

The list of new media is growing at a startling rate. *Business Marketing* points out: *"There's a proliferation of new-media options just waiting to be tapped,"* such as, *"CD-ROM catalogs and magazines. On-line commercial services. Interactive floppies. Electronic niche publications. E-zines [digital magazines delivered directly to the recipient via e-mail]. Internet newsgroups and real-time chat sessions. Electronic public relations. Kiosks. Interactive TV tests. The World Wide Web."*

And this is just the interactive stuff. The media list continues to swell, sprawling to some pretty unlikely places, where advertising sprouts up on everything from shower stalls to sailboats.

Five Media.

Until recently, advertisers basically relied on five media to make their brands thrive: television, radio, newspaper, magazines, and outdoor.

Compared to some of the new media forms, using these five media isn't too complicated. As Renetta McCann, Senior VP-Media Director at Leo Burnett USA, points out *"[They]… were sitting right there in front of you."*

Challenges.

With all of these new media opportunities come real challenges for the media professional in charge of selecting and scheduling the media.

Today's media professional is having to change to deal with the complex media world. They *"must become more flexible, have more tools and more placement options,"* says McCann.

Because today's advertising media are much more than magazine ads and television commercials.

Today's media have been expanded to refer to *any opportunity* that speaks on behalf of a brand to any consumer.

All the World's a Media Buy.

It's everything from a Fortune-500 corporation sponsoring a black-tie dinner to a local automotive parts store's sky writing. (These ideas come from Keith Reinhard, CEO of DDB, the sixth largest advertising agency in the world.)

"Wherever the Message Is, That's the Medium."

Arthur Anderson, Principal at the management consultancy Morgan, Anderson & Company, sums it up:

"Wherever the message is that's the medium: the Internet, event marketing. . . All of these things, if you look at it, are media."

And as advertising continues to embrace integrated marketing strategies, the definition of media is stretched even more to include

Nissan (Cont.)

A Strange and Brutal Future.
When the campaign began, Nissan was caught in a difficult situation which forced TBWA Chiat/Day to rethink media strategy and buying. *"Nissan's objective is not to recapture past glory but to prepare for a strange and brutal future."*

"Continuous Impact."
Media Director Monica Karo notes that market forces changed the way she approached media for Nissan.

"We went to a continuous, significant, impactful strategy all in premium prime and sports, which is very, very different for Nissan. There's no syndication, no fringe, no tonnage prime. We're looking for a certain point level, so we're on the air 49 out of 52 weeks with pretty much the same weight."

This strategy of continuous media drilled in Nissan's new attitude.

Time for a SHIFT__
Then, when the new models were ready, TBWA Chiat/Day and Nissan shifted gears, with a new worldwide campaign that introduced a wide range of Nissan models with a unifying word…

They paired *"a globally powerful word,"* with complement words that allowed the customization of marketing efforts for specific models.

From *"SHIFT__ Exhilaration"* for Altima to *"SHIFT__ Power"* for the reintroduced Z-car.

Their XTerra launch earned a Grand Effie in 2001.

Innovation in media strategy has been a key part of Nissan's success.

(Continued on next page)

Nissan (Cont.)

New Audiences. New Partners.
As the brand grew, Nissan added audiences.

Two important new audiences were Hispanic Americans and college students.

Another internal audience is the Nissan dealer network.

Zimmerman and Partners, a large agency (15th in the US – a division of Omnicom) became more and more important, developing dealer programs with their approach, which they call "brand-tailing," an approach that works to energize sales while nurturing the brand.

For example, Regional Assistant Media Planner Megan Lattus, a 2006 Syracuse grad, developed a program to target college seniors.

It featured an integrated strategy using different media platforms to drive traffic to local Nissan dealerships in top Mid-Atlantic markets.

She spent four months researching and developing a regional plan that would fit both Zimmerman's goals of maximizing advertising spending and Nissan's objective to reach more students.

The campaign utilized the Nissan Sentra, Versa, Altima, and Xterra as its focus in all advertising.

It featured college newspapers, posters, location media, and e-mail blasts, targeting graduating seniors across 44 schools in the Mid-Atlantic.

Plus a New Multi-Cultural Marketing Partner.
In 2008, they named Hispanic shop Dieste Harmel & Partners in Dallas, to handle the multicultural marketing business for its Nissan and Infiniti.

Duties for Dieste include creative, media planning, and buying for the US Hispanic, African American, and Asian American markets.

New models, new markets, new partners, new media.

event marketing, product publicity stunts, and computer hookups, to name a few.

Debra Goldman in *Media Quarterly* supports this claim. *"Potentially everything can be an [ad] medium: schools, sport stadiums, calling circles, shopping malls."*

Ad messages placed in these unconventional media have the potential of making immediate, if not intimate, contact with consumers right when these consumers are most predisposed to think about purchasing and using the brand.

And that's powerful communication.

Perception or Reality – Your Media Aperture.
Are these professionals' perceptions our media reality?

Let's put their observations to the test. Suppose you're on a ski trip in Utah. While riding the ski lift, you see an advertisement that reminds you how nice a piping-hot cup of chocolate would taste.

This ad appears as a small billboard affixed to both the back of the chair in front of you as well as the ski-lift tower.

A company called Ski View posts these billboards for clients. What an imaginative and effective way to communicate to a group of consumers who have an immediate need for the product as soon as they whisk their way down the chilly ski slopes.

Bite-Size Media: Fragmentation and Clutter.
Advertising messages have generally appeared as commercial interruptions in electronic or print media.

There are two major reasons why some advertisers are turning away from traditional media to some pretty unconventional methods to deliver ad messages to consumers.

The first has to do with media and audience fragmentation.

The second has to do with advertising clutter.

Let's take a look at both.

Audience and Media Fragmentation.
Yesterday's mass media once attracted large numbers of diverse audience members. These media have been blown to pieces – fragmented. And so have their audiences.

Take broadcast network TV and mass-circulation magazines, once the media darlings of the nation's advertisers.

Years ago, if you wanted to be seen and heard, you bought network TV ads and printed big spreads in magazines.

Now, these media superstars have lost some of their shine as audiences have shrunk and spun off to more specialized media.

Some Examples.
Take broadcast network television for example. Twenty-five years ago, a whopping 42 prime-time shows delivered a 15% household rating. In 1997, there were only five broadcast-network prime-time shows that delivered a 15 rating or better. In 2007, just one.

Where have the numbers gone? A lot have gone to cable TV.

And what about mass-circulation magazines?

Their large audiences have been eroded by the dramatic growth of specialty magazines.

As a result, American media are fragmented as never before. Advertisers are no longer capturing mass audiences. They are chasing after small niches to secure enough target-audience members.

Clutter Clutter Clutter.

Another reason why advertising messages are cropping up in all sorts of noncommercial areas, like laundromats and health clubs, is because of advertising clutter.

Clutter refers to an overabundance of advertising within a particular advertising medium.

If the September issue of *Vogue* is overflowing with 800 ads, how is your ad going to stand out?

The reason clutter has advertisers concerned is that it can lower overall consumer awareness levels. It can also get in the way of establishing favorable brand attitudes.

Clutter can even suffocate some pretty good ads.

Broadcast Clutter.

Relaxed codes in the broadcast industry and elsewhere have created more advertising in traditional commercial media.

By the end of 1999, commercials and promo spots on *ABC* and *NBC* took up over 15 minutes per hour.

Some of the nation's advertisers have found that their messages can no longer communicate effectively to consumers in these cluttered media. Their advertising messages get lost.

Advertising clutter in the traditional media have forced advertisers to search for new, more intrusive media vehicles.

They've started inserting ads in some pretty unexpected places.

Blimps, Wienermobiles, and Other Media Vehicles.

For example, Goodyear hovers in the sky with a blimp.

Oscar Mayer prowls the roads in the Wienermobile.

One of the more ubiquitous images in the Super Bowl is Budweiser One – a helium-filled logo hovering above the stadium. This was the visual that the Fox Network cut to after virtually every group of commercials.

Consumer Reports magazine says that advertisers can now rent space on garbage cans, bicycle racks, and parking meters, even the bottom of golf cups.

Coca-Cola once even stamped its logo on eggs.

Bristol Myers Squibb has made it an annual tradition to dole out free samples of aspirin at post offices on April 15 to soothe the jangled nerves of late income-tax filers.

Absolut Vodka carved its bottle into a 20-acre crop next to the Kansas City airport. *Carro-Sell,* a revolving media company, sells ad space on the moving metal plates of airport baggage carousels.

RJR Nabisco, the makers of Camel cigarettes, hands out sandals with the word "Camel" embossed on the soles, so that beachgoers can leave "camel tracks" in the sand.

A New Media Sampler.

In addition to the traditional mass media of television, magazines, radio, newspaper, and out-of-home, a wealth of new or alternative media are emerging or becoming more prominent.

Advertisers are seeking new ways to avoid clutter or simply hit their target market without the waste associated with much of the mass media. Here's a brief sampler:

Supermarkets.
Supermarket TV
Supermarket carts
Supermarket belt dividers
Supermarket receipts
Scanner-sensitive coupons
Grocery bags

The New Outdoor.
Mobile billboards
Flying signs, blimps, etc.
Inflatables
Outdoor video panels
Public restroom stalls

Traveling with the Target.
Airline ticket jackets
In-flight magazines and video

More New Video Opportunities.
Home shopping networks
Long-form commercials
(infomercials)
Leaders on video rentals
Movie theater advertising
Product placements in movies
and TV

Other Brand Contact Points.
Coupons on ATM receipts
Ads at the bottom of golf holes
(talk about tightly targeted!)
Stick-on ads on the front page of
newspapers
Directory advertising
Town crier

Communication Trix.

How many forms of communication can you spot on this Trix box?

Up-Front Media.

This package works to distinguish itself from the dozens of other cereal brands on grocery shelves.

The front extends TV advertising featuring the *Trix Rabbit*.

It also features the movie *The Lost World,* in a unique sweepstakes offer.

If you saw the movie you probably heard a lot of noisy dinosaurs.

To win the grand prize of eight round trip tickets to New Zealand and Australia, as well as $24,000 in travel money, you need to find a box that roars.

Yes, a roaring box. (And you thought radio was the only medium that delivered sound effects.)

Back Up.

The back of the box (not shown here) continues to advertise *The Lost World* sweepstakes.

But there's one more communications message – sort of a direct mail solicitation – where they want you to help General Mills decide on the newest color Trix: wild cherry red or blueberry blue.

There's a whole lot of communicating going on here.

Trix didn't miss a trick.

Driving Brand Awareness for Peanuts.

Now, if a blimp is too small and a billboard too stagnant, then the sky is truly the limit – CTA Lasers has beamed laser images for Doritos, Coors beer, American Airlines, and other advertisers on the California clouds. The lasers can also generate ad images onto walls, buildings, bridges, and even mountains.

And, as you can see, the Wienermobile is no longer alone on the road to greater brand awareness. They're not playing for peanuts.

In the new world of media there are *no* missed opportunities.

Not even when you duck inside a restroom. WeeWee Advertising of Jackson, Mississippi, is just one of the companies that will place an ad in a strategic spot in public bathrooms.

But no matter where advertising eventually crops up, its purpose will remain steadfast. Advertising, no matter if it's splashed on health-club shower curtains or beamed across LCD display units in urinal stalls, will continue to try and solicit positive attitudes.

Strengths & Weaknesses.

WE'VE LEARNED ABOUT MEDIA COMPANIES as businesses. Now let's talk about them as advertising vehicles.

In this section, we'll emphasize the traditional media vehicles.

But we should be clear that new media opportunities are an exciting and growing area that may provide the right extra impact in delivering the message for your brand – as Max Racks did for Altoids.

We'll walk through the traditional media forms in the same sequence as before – and what you'll see is that each medium is unique, offering advertisers a variety of strengths and weaknesses.

You'll discover newspapers and radio are powerful local media.

You'll read that magazines and cable are some of the best media around for delivering specialized audiences.

You'll become aware that outdoor grabs consumers' attention right before they make a purchase. We'll be pointing out the plusses, as well as the minuses, of each of these five media.

Here are the sorts of considerations you will have to make if and when you create or evaluate a media plan. And, yes, it will probably be on the test.

Print – Strengths & Weaknesses.

This section of your text will also discuss how indoor print media, founded on journalistic principles, distinguish themselves from other media in a variety of ways.

Print advertising is an effective way to reach consumers both inside and outside of their homes.

As advertising vehicles, newspapers and magazines share some common strengths. First, we'll highlight common characteristics these print media share and why advertisers find them attractive.

Some Unique Characteristics.

Advertising media professionals and print sales representatives agree that newspapers and magazines possess some unique characteristics that can enhance advertising messages.

Of course, newspapers and magazines have their own individual strengths and weaknesses, which we will explore later. But let's begin by taking a look at the plusses these two print media share.

First, we'll look at the traditional print media that readers use indoors: newspapers and magazines. Then, we'll take a short look at the "other" print advertising – outdoor and out-of-home.

Newspapers and Magazines.

Newspapers and magazines contain different editorial content that make reading either very urgent, somewhat pressing, or downright unhurried.

It all depends on the timeliness of the subject matter.

Newspapers are usually read and gone in a day or so, while magazines tend to hang around awhile.

Newspapers and magazines are both members of the journalism family. They rely on advertisers for financial survival.

Through advertising, newspapers and magazines supply important consumer information that readers depend on.

Print editorial content affects:

1. how long readers hang onto a print medium, and

2. how advertisers use the print medium.

Newspapers and magazines share 11 characteristics that appeal to advertisers. Let's take a look at them.

Advantages of Print – 11 Shared Characteristics:

1. Print is portable.

Newspapers and magazines go where people go.

Let's put this statement to the test. What do you do with your school newspaper when it's time for class and you're not quite done reading the last few paragraphs of a good story? Don't you stuff it in your backpack and take it along to class?

What about when you head off to the gym? Does a magazine tag along and help you pass the time while climbing the Stairmaster?

Magazines and newspapers are portable. They're compact, bendable, and lightweight. They can go anywhere.

So you can find it both inside and outside your home.

Max Racks.

Here's how Leo Burnett exploited synergy and got extra mileage out of its wildly successful Altoids campaign.

They added *Max Racks* to the media plan – they dispense free postcards.

Max Racks is a new medium that's popped up on college campuses, restaurants, and bars – complete with *"Curiously Strong"* postcards.

Holders are affixed to entry ways of major buildings, student newspaper stands, and any other high-traffic area students pass by daily.

An extra bonus is the fact that the postcard can be sent along to another person at no cost to the advertiser.

Now that's curiously strong.

Print Accommodates Complex Copy.

Here, the target is dog owners (and vets). Print makes it easier to make more than one point.

Story Value.

This ad from Chiat/Day for the Nissan Pathfinder connects the story value of an off-road experience with the features of the SUV.

It's complex but interesting.

Print can keep you company. And you don't have to turn it on.

When a magazine or newspaper is on a waiting room table, or in an airplane seatback, it can be read by many different people other than the subscriber.

When this happens, advertisers get more readers than they bargained for, although passalong readers are generally not as committed to the publication as subscribers.

2. Print is "time independent."

Unlike TV, print doesn't have a schedule. Readers choose the time and order of what they want to read. Print is convenient.

Advertising messages aren't bound by time, either. Ad messages can be longer, more detailed, and tell an entire story.

3. Print is not a fleeting medium.

Reading is an active and involving mental process.

Print media engage people's minds. Consumers tend to glean more accurate information by reading than by viewing a rapidly changing image on a screen. They can study the body copy, stare at the photography, and even reread the entire ad.

If a consumer needs to find an address or phone number, or compare prices, print makes it easy.

4. Print media accommodates complex copy.

Products that are expensive, complex, or technical tend to require a more comprehensive sales message. Print is great for that.

Print advertising can deliver the whole sales message.

If you've got a lot to say, like Nissan does for their Pathfinder, print is the way to say it – and the place.

As Howard Gossage said, *"People read what interests them. Sometimes, it's an ad."* Gossage loved doing ads in magazines like the *New Yorker,* where people were involved with what they read.

For example, laser printers are a **high-involvement** purchase – complicated and expensive. Print can help tell that story.

They're not like cheeseburgers, a **low-involvement** purchase.

Newspapers and magazines deliver readers – people who like to read. They enjoy reading articles – long and short.

Ads with complete sales messages help readers make informed buying decisions. Of course, whether that ad gets read or not depends to some extent on how involving it is.

It also depends on other things. For example, think of tire and battery ads. Not terribly interesting. But when you suddenly need a tire or battery, they become fascinating literature.

5. Pictures can be better in print than broadcast.

Pictures are static in print media. They hold still. They can be held and studied. You can examine expressions on faces or focus on certain product features.

Pictures can sometimes look better in print than broadcast. Of course, a lot has to do with the press and one's television set, and we've all seen our fair share of bad newspaper photos.

But still, if newspaper photos are cropped just right, and the black-and-white tones are near perfect, the results can be pretty dramatic and sometimes even arresting.

Think about the black-and-white photos that Calvin Klein uses in magazine ads. Pretty attention-getting, aren't they?

6. It's easier to feature more than one product in print.

Broadcast's shorter ad units often limit advertising messages to saying just one thing. In print you're not as confined.

Advertisers can feature their entire product line.

Fashion designers can run 10 to 12 pages of magazine spreads to announce their fall clothing line.

In specialty print, specialized advertisers have advantages. Capezzio can run four consecutive pages in a dance magazine.

On a local level, grocery stores can use four or five pages of the newspaper to advertise 50 to 60 of their products.

Small budget advertisers can leverage smaller print units.

And, because you, the reader, are in control of what you decide to look at, it's very easy to scan the many items advertised until you find what interests you.

7. Print media are versatile.

Print media can be bought in a variety of sizes. And advertisers can choose from an enormous range of editorial content.

There's also geographic flexibility. Often, print can be bought on a local, regional, or national basis.

Print advertising media offer all sorts of creative and promotional opportunities as well. Flexible. Flexible. Flexible.

Print Is Versatile.

Even small budgets and small ads can work hard.

Print puts words to work.

More Versatility.

Print media can be bought in a variety of sizes.

"People read what interests them. Sometimes, it's an ad."

— Howard Gossage

**Print Lends Credibility
and Prestige.**

Here, sophisticated humor for the local YMCA.

Print Can Deliver Coupons.

It can also deliver many other sales promotion devices, including…

Product Samples.

To the right, a sampling packet helps P&G introduce a new, improved version of Always.

8. Print ads can be preserved and reread.

Print ads can have long lives. They can be saved for days, months, even years. They can be torn out, stored, and studied.

Do you have any stuck on your bulletin board? See?

9. Print advertising is personable and intimate.

Print advertising communicates on a one-on-one basis.

What do we mean by that? When you sit down to watch TV or listen to the radio, are there any other people in the room?

At school, you might watch TV in a big room along with a host of others or… just a few friends.

When you sit down to read, it's a whole different matter because, as we've said, reading is a lot different from viewing.

This makes print advertising rather intimate and certainly personable. Advertising copywriters can take advantage of this.

10. Journalistic content lends credibility and prestige.

Advertisers prize print media for its fact-based content.

Good journalism and good writing tend to give advertising in newspapers and magazines an added dose of credibility.

Then again, you might not feel the same way about these ads if they appeared in a supermarket tabloid next to an article titled "Aliens Ate My Head."

For example, AT&T might choose the *Wall Street Journal* to make a hard-hitting ad even more authoritative.

An over-the-counter drug manufacturer might run an ad in *Time* to give its product added credibility.

11. Print can deliver coupons and other promotion devices.

Print is a tangible medium. As such, it can often lend sales promotion endeavors a helping hand.

Coupons, samples, and premiums all take advantage of print. Coupons can be clipped, filled out, and sent in. They can all be delivered quite inexpensively through print media.

Example: Kellogg's.

Kellogg's delivered two free samples plus coupons to Sunday newspaper subscribers in select markets. It placed a small box of cereal and a cereal bar along with the Sunday newspaper in a plastic bag. Kellogg's supplied the bags.

The outside of the bag was printed with pictures of the samples and announcements of the offers inside.

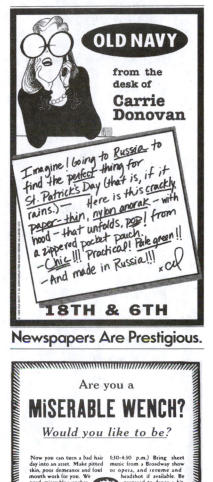

Adjacencies.

On the right, Target does print advertising that's right on target.

Their inside front cover position connects them with the editorial content of this special issue of *Newsweek*.

Newspapers Are Prestigious.

Readers Tend to Be Upscale.

What a creative media effort for Kellogg's!

First, people have leisure time on Sunday. They spend it reading the paper. As a matter of fact, newspapers secure their highest readership on Sundays.

Second, people are not running to work, they have time for breakfast on Sunday. Kellogg's brought it to them.

Third, two samples were delivered right to people's doorsteps without any mailing lists or additional postage.

Newspaper Strengths & Weaknesses.

Now let's take a look at newspaper strengths and weaknesses.

Newspaper Strengths:

1. They're considered a prestigious place to advertise.

Newspapers carry significant clout in local communities.

Many local business owners take this into consideration and believe newspapers add a certain degree of believability and prestige to their advertising.

2. Newspaper readers tend to be upscale.

Newspaper readers tend to be older, more educated, and have better jobs. They tend to be people advertisers want to reach — they have more money to spend.

Where else would you want to advertise for a "miserable wench" for an upcoming production of *Pirates of Penzance* (see sidebar)?

3. Readers really use advertising.

A study showed 60% of people said they look forward to newspaper advertising.

Only 28% said that they look forward to receiving direct mail, 20% mentioned magazine, 7% TV, and only 6% said radio.

Newspaper advertising spurs people to buy. Sixty percent of people reported that after seeing a newspaper ad, they went out and shopped for the item.

Newspapers Have Immediacy.

An ad like this can capitalize on the news value of the news itself.

Readers Really Use Newspaper Advertising.

They use it to find out about things to buy – cars, homes, and more.

4. Newspapers require less lead time than other media.
Newspaper advertising doesn't require as much preplanning as some other media.

It can be placed or canceled within a matter of days.

This allows advertisers all sorts of scheduling flexibility.

5. Newspapers have a strong local emphasis.
Newspaper editorial content predominantly focuses on the local community it serves.

Regional and national advertisers who want to concentrate in certain local markets can effectively do so by using newspapers.

6. Newspapers have a strong sense of immediacy.
The editorial content contained in newspapers is perishable.

It gives advertisers immediacy. This is particularly beneficial to advertisers who need an immediate response.

7. Newspapers have "cataloging value."
Newspapers' editorial content and advertising are organized and categorized into different sections (e.g., sports, lifestyle, etc.).

This "cataloguing value" helps advertisers reach specific demographic or lifestyle groups – in the right frame of mind.

Newspaper Weaknesses:

It's not a perfect world. Here's some of the downside.

1. Newspaper reproduction can vary.

Some newspapers have old presses, some have new, but the real issue is that when you're printing hundreds of thousands of pages every day, even the best newspaper presses may have variable reproduction quality.

2. Newspapers have small passalong readership.
Magazines reach larger audiences because they are passed along to other readers.

Newspapers publish perishable material; they have a very small passalong readership.

3. Newspapers can be costly.
This is particularly true for national advertisers, who are charged higher rates than local advertisers.

Additionally, national advertisers have to use numerous newspapers to build the kind of audience coverage they may need to effectively reach a certain region.

Newspaper advertising can be expensive for local advertisers, too. Newspapers publish frequently. The cost of buying ads on a continuous basis can mount up.

4. Newspapers may carry adverse editorial.
Newspapers report news that is tough, gritty, and unsettling.

Some advertisers might not want their products associated with this type of editorial environment.

5. Newspapers are cluttered.
Newspapers carry a wealth of information.

Advertising competes with many other ads and articles.

It's sometimes difficult for a small ad to stand out.

6. Newspapers are not read thoroughly.

Americans have hectic and demanding schedules.

They are pressed for time and often do not read the entire newspaper. This can mean money wasted for an advertiser.

7. Newspapers have poor demographic selectivity.

Newspaper readers are older. Many younger people don't have the daily newspaper habit, although they may still read certain sections – such as the Entertainment section before the weekend.

In general, a complete demographic cross section of the population will not be available.

Newspapers and magazines are in the business of producing editorial content that engages, enriches, and educates specific and desired readers.

And there has been a lively growth in "alternative" newspapers in many parts of the country.

Magazine Strengths & Weaknesses.

Although they're both print media, magazines are usually used quite differently from newspapers.

Overall, magazines have some unique characteristics that advertisers view as both good and bad.

We'll examine these next.

Magazine Strengths:

1. Magazines deliver specialized audiences.

With more than 9,000 magazines to choose from, there's a magazine to suit practically everyone.

Magazines break the population down into tiny niches based on lifestyles, hobbies, and interests. This lets advertisers target specialized groups with very little waste.

2. Magazine ads are long-lasting.

Magazine ads can hang around for months, even years.

This means advertising has real staying power.

3. Repeat advertising exposure.

Magazine audience coverage builds over time. Readers pick the magazine up over the course of the week, two weeks, or a month.

As such, advertisers have the opportunity to have their ad seen multiple times.

4. Magazines have high passalong readership.

Magazine articles are interesting, thought-provoking, and not immediately perishable.

They are read by multiple members of the household.

They make the rounds in waiting rooms, too.

Of course, the size of the passalong audience is different for each magazine. And numbers claimed are probably excessive.

Example: Diamond Publishing.

Diamond Publishing, based in Gravette, Arizona, publishes printed materials exclusively for people who have to wait. The magazines offer readers two features: trivia and advertising.

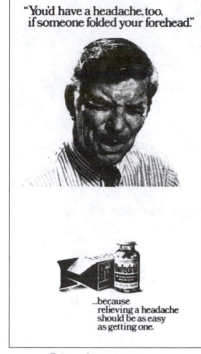

Disadvantages.

Newspapers have disadvantages, too, as this humorous ad points out.

Specialized Audiences.

If you want to hook fishermen...

...or people with crabgrass.

Creative Flexibility.

Quality reproduction for a quality image and a subtle and humorous message for Purina. *"Sparky opted instead for a quiet dinner at home."*

Spread Out.

Here, Mazda uses the extra space offered by a two-page spread to emphasize the extra cabin space offered in the Mazda 6.

Diamond says that the purpose of its magazines is to give readers *"All the News You Never Knew That You Never Needed to Know."* Diamond circulates its materials at lunch counters, doctor's offices, hospitals, lube shops, and pharmacies – practically anyplace where people have to wait for services or goods. The publications circulate in 29 states. And, as you might guess, these publications are passed along to more than one reader.

5. Magazines offer creative flexibility.

Advertisers can buy different sizes of ads and run them anywhere within the publication.

The use of vivid color or stark black and white can enhance the effectiveness of ads – and magazines are a good medium for each.

Advances in production have made magazine ads more active.

Magazine ads can take on three-dimensional qualities with special die-cuts and assembly. These pop-up ads are dramatic and grab readers' attention.

Magazine ads can include sound with special microchips that play a tune or have a voice-over read the advertising message.

Posters and "scratch and sniff" ads give ordinary magazine ads added value. **Gatefolds** make regular size ads extra-large.

A gatefold is a magazine insert which is usually made up of an oversize page with extensions on both the left and right sides.

These extensions fold toward the center of the page – like a gate. Readers open the extensions to reveal portions of the ad.

Magazine ads can even fade in and out like TV.

Stoli Vodka ran a heat sensitive ad that only appeared after coming in contact with readers' body temperature. Readers had to hold their hand on the *Stoli* bottle to make the ad appear.

Magazine Weaknesses:

1. Audience accumulation takes time.

Magazines lack immediacy. Audience builds over time.

Therefore, this medium is restricted to those advertisers who do not demand an immediate response from consumers.

2. Magazines can be cluttered.

Magazines can include significant amounts of advertising.

Some advertisers may find themselves fighting against their main competitors within the same issue.

3. Early closing dates.

Advertising in most magazines does not allow for spontaneity.

It requires significant preplanning.

For example, if advertisers want to include an ad in the January issue of *Architectural Digest*, they have to submit the ad and purchase order by October 20 of the previous year.

Out-of-Home Strengths & Weaknesses.

Outdoor advertising offers some distinct advantages.

As you might guess, outdoor advertising that's plastered on everything from buses to railcars has some drawbacks, too.

Let's take a quick look at each.

Out-of-Home Strengths:

Marketing AD Ventures (MAV), a large outdoor advertising supplier, offers five reasons why advertisers should use outdoor:

Extensions give outdoor extra dimension.

1. Outdoor can have great *visual impact*.

Outdoor advertising delivers a powerful visual message.

Advertisers can't buy a bigger print ad than billboard.

Outdoor advertising provides bold, beautiful images printed on paper or vinyl using a computer printing process.

This means vivid color with all sorts of detail.

Outdoor ads that feature few words and compelling photos or art have real stopping power, even if we are driving down the freeway at 65 miles an hour.

As the glue billboard on the right demonstrates, there are a number of very creative things you can only do with outdoor.

If you have one of those creative opportunities, an outdoor spectacular can be hard to beat.

2. Outdoor can give you *blanket coverage* of a market.

Everyone who steps outside their door to work, shop, or play sees outdoor. According to MAV, *"Outdoor reaches a large percentage of the population between the ages of 18 and 45."*

Outdoor advertising can be placed in certain neighborhoods delivering upscale, ethnic, or professional markets.

3. Outdoor provides *frequency* and *repetition*.

Outdoor advertising is a medium that can't be turned off. These ads are *"on display 24 hours a day, 7 days a week, 30 days a month. It can't be shut off, tuned out, thrown in the trash, or used as a coaster on the coffee table,"* says MAV.

Outdoor is a high-frequency medium.

Some ads are seen over and over again by commuters driving to work, pedestrians walking to the office, and bus (and train) riders traveling in and out of the city.

Outdoor advertising serves as a constant reminder that can reinforce the advertising campaign's message.

Great Visual Impact.

Outdoor works best with simple impactful messages.

Blanket Market Coverage.

Frequency and Repetition.

Due to regular traffic patterns, many people see the same outdoor every day — allowing messages to build up.

Large Audience. Low Cost.

Remember these?

Outdoor made the idea work.

Large Audiences for Large Ideas.

Outdoor Can Be Almost Anywhere...

Here, a Times Square Moment.

4. Outdoor delivers *large audiences* at a *low cost.*

Reaching a thousand people with outdoor costs less than reaching that same group in television, radio, and newspaper.

Simply put, the CPM (cost per thousand) is far less expensive for outdoor than other types of advertising.

The numbers speak for themselves:

In 1998, a 50-showing of 30-sheets in the top 100 US markets had a CPM of $3.50.

Compare this to a $9.90 CPM for a 30-second network TV spot; a $5.30 CPM for a 60-second drive-time radio spot; and a $21 CPM for a half-page newspaper ad in the same markets.

Outdoor is extremely cost efficient.

Properly used, it can really stretch tight ad budgets.

5. Outdoor has *versatility.*

Outdoor advertising is versatile.

It comes in many shapes, sizes, and formats.

Let's just use one example – buses. An advertiser can buy vinyl posters in king-size (30"h x 144"w); super king-size (30"h x 240"w) or queen-size (30"h x 88"w). The advertiser can even wrap the entire bus – not to mention using the interior bus cards.

Outdoor's versatility goes beyond variations in size.

It moves and talks.

Thanks to technology, outdoor offers advertisers real flexibility. Outdoor can be equipped with moving parts or video projection.

A two-story sized container of *Cup of Noodles* on Times Square spews a constant blast of welcome steam.

Planter's Mr. Peanut waves to bustling New Yorkers.

Outdoor ads don't have to stand silent. Outdoor boards can tie to a toll-free cellular number or ask listeners to tune into a low-band radio frequency being broadcast from that board!

It can be almost anywhere.

Outdoor ads also come in many formats that reach people in all sorts of places. An outdoor board may be the last message people see before they shop.

Out-of-home is unsurpassed at providing directional and location information.

An outdoor board can extend the borders of a retail location. A strong visual with directional information can be extremely effective in capturing an audience for a restaurant, gas station, or tourist destination.

It's "poor man's TV."

A combination of outdoor and radio is called "poor man's TV." One delivers the audio, the other delivers the visual.

This can be a powerful combination: outdoor plus drive-time radio. It may be why one of the largest radio station operators just bought the largest outdoor company.

Out-of-Home Weaknesses:

Outdoor advertising has the potential to be the ultimate "in your face" medium.

It dares to be noticed.

Yet, outdoor poses five distinct drawbacks to advertisers. Let's review them.

1. Poor demographic selectivity.

Outdoor advertising reaches just about everyone.

When a bus rumbles by with a big display on its side for Arrow dress shirts, everyone stuck in traffic sees the ad.

Arrow wants to reach businessmen.

This outdoor display may very well reach male commuters going to and from work, but it may reach a lot of nonprospects, too.

That's one of outdoor's drawbacks. It isn't a specialized medium.

It doesn't deliver a specific niche like cable or magazines.

Its reach is far-reaching.

Practically anyone who steps outside is part of the audience.

2. Limited time. Limited copy.

Outdoor is read as people pass by.

It doesn't get full attention.

As a result, most outdoor is easy to ignore.

The Seven Word Rule.

How much can an advertiser say on an 8-sheet poster?

Messages have to be kept to no more than seven words if they want to be read and comprehended. No complex copy for these ads.

Outdoor delivers simple messages with minimal copy.

3. Out-of-home has complicated logistics.

Getting those vinyl wraps up on the corner of Sixth and Main needs a lot of money and lead time.

You can do it, but it's not like buying a newspaper ad.

Which side of the road are you on? The coming-to-work side or the going-home side? That can make a big difference.

While it seems simple – an ad on a stick – it can be anything but. Inexperienced people often have a bad experience.

4. Out-of-home can be expensive.

Over time, outdoor delivers a great CPM. But, on the front end, material preparation and scheduling isn't cheap.

5. It's subject to increased restrictions and availability.

Outdoor is often viewed as environmental clutter.

If you have the wrong message at the wrong time, you could find yourself on the wrong end of a picket line.

Limited Time. Limited Copy.

Complicated Logistics.

Outdoor at Work. Above, Chick-fil-A does a good job with outdoor.

Reward Yourself.

Go to radiomercuryawards.com and listen to some award-winning radio commercials. You can hear more on the jukebox at www.adbuzz.com.

And Here's a Script…

for one of our favorites – the radio series "Real Men of Genius."

ANN: *Bud Light presents…Real Men of Genius*

MVO: *(Singing) Real men of genius.*

ANN: *Today we salute you, Mr. Stadium Scoreboard Marriage Proposal Guy.*

MVO: *(Singing) Mr. Stadium Scoreboard Marriage Proposal Guy.*

ANN: *You've combined the three things you love most in this world: your girlfriend, your team, and lots and lots of attention.*

MVO: *(Singing) Everyone look at me.*

ANN: *Your first proposal: her hand in marriage. Your second proposal: two more jumbo chilli dogs.*

MVO: *(Singing) Chilli cheese!*

ANN: *It's the perfect plan unless her name is spelled wrong, she's in the bathroom, or she says 'no'.*

MVO: *(Singing) Pretty please.*

ANN: *So, crack open an ice cold Bud Light, Mr. Bachelor on the Big Screen, and remember that even if she says no, we'll always say yes.*

MVO: *(Singing) Mr. Stadium Scoreboard Marriage Proposal Guy.*

ANN: *Bud Light Beer. Anheuser Busch. St. Louis, Missouri.*

Radio's Strengths & Weaknesses.

Now let's tune into radio's strengths and weaknesses. Advertisers who use radio feel it offers some distinct advantages. Here are some of its strengths.

1. Radio's various formats help advertisers reach special target audiences.

Radio's program formats help pinpoint specific groups of consumers that advertisers might want to target.

For example, Rush Limbaugh's program attracts the 35–55 crowd. Radio experts state that formatting does such a good job of targeting that advertisers don't have to worry about reaching the wrong audience.

Gary Fries from the Radio Advertising Bureau (RAB) explains, *"Radio is such a diverse targeting vehicle that you're able to be very successful by reaching a very small element of the population."*

Howard Stern's audience was key in the success of Snapple.

2. Radio can be inexpensive, making it a frequency medium.

Compared to television, radio's advertising rates are less.

Even if CPMs are comparable (radio is usually lower), radio's smaller audiences mean that each spot costs less. This makes radio relatively inexpensive.

This lower cost per spot means advertisers can afford to advertise repeatedly (known as **frequency**). Most people feel that a bit of frequency is needed for ads to be effective.

This low-cost frequency is also attractive to advertisers wanting to maintain brand name recognition.

3. Radio reaches the mobile market.

Radio sits in the dashboards of nearly all cars and trucks.

Radio can connect just before consumers make a purchase.

According to R.H. Bruskin's *Media Targeting for the '90s*, radio is the number-one medium adults listen to closest to the time of purchasing a product or service.

4. Radio is a flexible medium.

Radio's round-the-clock broadcasting allows advertisers to choose from a variety of different **dayparts**.

Formats can change throughout the day, as well.

Radio offers a variety of advertising opportunities.

Sponsorship, live remotes, and varied unit lengths are available.

Local firms can join with a national advertiser and share the expense of the radio commercial (**co-op advertising**).

Producing radio ads is not as involved (or as expensive) as television commercial production. Last-minute changes can often be accommodated, and new creative can be done quickly.

5. Radio also offers creative flexibility.

Radio can put many possibilities into the hands and minds of clever copywriters.

As discussed in our creativity chapter, radio is the "theater of the mind" medium. It is not restricted by visuals like TV.

Copywriters can conjure up all sorts of extraordinary scenarios through words, sound effects, and music. Listeners use their imaginations to give characters and situations meaning.

In addition to its many vivid creative capabilities, radio also offers geographic flexibility in that it can be bought locally, regionally, or nationally.

6. Radio offers advertisers immediacy.

Radio plays current music and news that's up-to-date.

Consequently, this medium offers people *immediate* and fast-breaking entertainment and information all day long.

The radio dial is one of the first things people reach for in the morning. They flip the radio on to listen to the news. As a matter of fact, radio is often the first source of news. Forty-two percent of all Americans tune into radio in the morning to get their dose of news, compared to TV at 30%, and newspaper with 16%.

Local retailers who have sales to announce benefit by placing advertising with radio's direct, instantaneous environment.

Radio's Weaknesses:

As you've already seen, every medium also has weaknesses.

Radio has a few, as well.

1. Radio is a cluttered medium.

There is a possibility of radio commercials getting lost.

First, there are many radio stations in most markets.

Second, most people are doing something else while they're listening to their radio.

For example, at some time during morning drive time, 50% of adults listening to the radio are driving, 37% are eating breakfast, and 25% are cleaning up the house. (Some multi-task.)

Only 23% of them are just listening to the radio.

Radio carries a lot of advertising.

2. Radio commercials are fleeting.

Radio commercials are short-lived.

And given the fact that this medium does not have visuals, it is sometimes limited to delivering simple messages.

Radio Offers Creative Flexibility.

Big ideas in 60 seconds. You've heard and laughed at commercials done by Dick Orkin's Radio Ranch.

They create and produce radio commercials for clients across the country – both local and national.

Go listen to some of them at www.radio-ranch.com.

No Medium for Old Men.

Or maybe so. Here are three classic campaigns that featured old guys: Dave Thomas, founder of Wendy's; actor Wilford Brimley selling the cholesterol-reducing benefits of oatmeal; and the Charmin guy.

Dave Thomas
Founder of Wendy's

"The Personal Selling Medium."

Television connects with people. The personable style of founder Dave Thomas played a powerful role building Wendy's business and brand personality in its TV advertising.

TV Covers the Marketplace.

Television is a powerful visual medium that can reach a mass audience.

TV Is Intrusive.

TV has become our cultural reference frame. Here's another older actor at work. Mr. Whipple!

Everybody remembered his plea: *"Please don't squeeze the* Charmin."

This intrusive campaign became part of a brand's equity.

Television Strengths & Weaknesses.

First, we'll discuss the major strengths television offers advertisers. Then, the various weaknesses.

Cable TV has some unique characteristics of its own.

These will directly follow the general overview of television.

Television's Strengths:

1. Television has impact.

Television is called the personal selling medium. To some extent, TV replaces a salesperson at a store.

For example, Dave Thomas, the avuncular owner of *Wendy's* fast-food chain, really exploited the personal selling power of television. Amiable and persuasive, he simply told us about the merits of his menu.

There are other examples.

What about local car dealers? Celebrity endorsers?

Television also has impact because of its ability to combine sight and sound, motion, color, and graphics.

All these devices make TV an excellent medium to demonstrate, persuade, and create instant product identification.

How many times have you seen products effectively demonstrated on TV? What about all of the effective infomercials that crop up on late-night television?

Finally, TV is a great storytelling medium.

In the hands of talented creative people you can tell an interesting and engaging story in just 30 seconds. Stories have impact.

2. Television covers the marketplace.

Network television has mass appeal and large market coverage.

(Cable has more narrowly defined targets which we'll review later.)

Network television has traditionally been considered a mass medium. Its broad realm of programming – from sitcoms to the Olympics – tends to attract a wide range of viewers from all different age groups, occupations, and income levels.

3. Television is intrusive.

Television reaches most people every day. It's part of the American landscape and certainly a part of our daily lives.

In 1950, the A.C. Nielsen Company reported people watch TV an average of 4 hours and 35 minutes each day.

By 1987, viewers were spending nearly as much time viewing TV (7 hours and 10 minutes) as they spent at work.

As cable TV, VCRs, videos, and video games entered, they helped keep Americans in front of their TV screens.

In 2006, the total daily viewing for all household members was 8 hours and 14 minutes.

With so much time spent in front of the tube, viewers have the *opportunity* to be repeatedly exposed to commercials.

This repetition helps build brand familiarity.

4. Television is flexible.

Television can be used in many different ways. It offers advertisers flexibility in how they buy and schedule commercials.

They can choose from 10, 15, 30, or 60-second units.

Even longer units of time can be negotiated.

In 1985, BBDO bought the first three-minute commercial. Pop music performer Lionel Richie performed in a commercial for Pepsi, which aired during the Grammy Music Awards.

Television can be purchased nationally (network TV) or bought in only certain areas (national spot TV) or locally.

When it comes to scheduling ads on TV, advertisers have a number of options. The broadcast day is broken into a variety of different time periods (called dayparts).

Particular programs are clustered into a number of time slots and are generally grouped during the morning, afternoon, early evening, night, and late night.

Television also offers a wide range of programming.

In terms of creating and producing the advertising message, television is also very flexible.

Advertisers can choose from a wide variety of production techniques and advertising formats to get their message across to consumers: slice-of-life scenarios, extreme close-ups, voice overs, jingles, humor, animation, and the list goes on.

5. Television is a cost-efficient medium.

Television is considered cost efficient.

CPM is the general standard used for TV, as it is for other media. It's a handy yardstick.

Compared with other media, TV can deliver a thousand audience members at a relatively low cost.

Network broadcast TV is expensive in absolute cost, but when you compare it to other media on the basis of audience delivery and cost, TV comes out a value.

To make media cost comparisons, advertisers calculate how much it costs to reach one thousand target audience members.

Analyzed this way, broadcast television's big audiences tend to make this medium worth the investment.

However, the overall cost of producing and buying television commercials can require large ad budgets.

6. Television is considered a prestigious medium.

The programs on television tend to lend this medium prestige, credibility, and authority.

Especially at the network broadcast level, large budgets are spent on production and celebrities. Consumer reaction to these lavish productions is powerful.

Viewers overwhelmingly think TV advertising is the most exciting. Compared to other media, 81% of people say that television advertising is the most exciting, compared to magazines at 6%, radio at 5%, and newspaper at 3%.

The Whopper Virgins Media Plan.

CP+B calls it "Creative Content Distribution."

You can see their philosophy at work with many of their campaigns.

The legendary Subservient Chicken, where a garter-wearing chicken on a Web site (www.subservientchicken.com) obeyed typed-in commands.

More recently, they produced a long Web-based "mockumentary" combined with shorter TV commercials around the slightly controversial theme "Whopper Virgins."

In theory, CP+B sought people in foreign lands who had never tried a Burger King Whopper. Ironic humor and a post-modern attitude tends to be typical of the CP+B approach.

The television works on its own, but it's just weird enough that you just might want to see what else they're up to — and you go to a well-produced, fast-loading video that involves you with the Whopper in a humorous way.

More CP+B Irony – The VW "RoutanBoom."

Using celebrity presenter Brooke Shields, CP+B creates another "mockumentary" that combines TV commercials and longer-form Web-based video.

Here, the premise is that people are having babies just so they can own a VW Routan minivan.

Ridiculous? Of course. But since we get the humor right away, we can be amused as we are pitched the benefits of this VW model.

Again, a smart, efficient combination of traditional media and the Internet – with just enough humor to develop curiosity-driven Web traffic.

Flexibility + Interactivity.

The Internet has made TV even more flexible. Here, Nike lets you go to a Web site and pick the ending in this entertaining series of commercials. Watch out for the chain saw!

People also feel that TV advertising is more authoritative.

Fifty-seven percent of people believe TV advertising is most authoritative. Twenty percent feel newspaper advertising is the most authoritative, followed by magazines at 9%, and radio at 6%.

Television's Weaknesses:

1. Television messages are fleeting.

Television commercials do not last long.

They normally last 10 to 60 seconds. This means that viewers do not have the luxury of analyzing the message.

2. Television advertising is expensive.

Network television is expensive.

A 30-second spot on NBC's *Law & Order* is $264,889.

If an advertiser buys three prime-time spots for four days on *Law & Order,* the bill quickly adds up to a hefty sum of nearly $3.2 million (of course this can be negotiated).

Television production is also costly, adding to the expense.

3. Popular TV programs can have limited time available.

Newspapers and magazines sell pages or "space." TV sells time. Time cannot be expanded to accommodate all advertising requests.

Television is confined to a 24-hour day with just so much time devoted to commercial air time.

Therefore, demand for commercial time on a highly rated show or daypart may exceed supply.

Some advertisers may be closed out of the program, daypart, or season they'd like for their advertising.

Cable TV Strengths & Weaknesses.

Remember, cable is narrowcasting. And many of the cable channels are niche media, with smaller audiences but higher concentrations of certain types of viewers.

Cable's Strengths:

Today, advertisers consider cable television a strong and vital advertising medium for several different reasons.

1. Cable offers advertisers geographic flexibility.

When it comes to coverage, cable has any type of small, medium, or large advertiser *covered*.

Local advertisers can buy commercial time from local cable systems and run on a range of top cable channels.

Regional advertisers can take advantage of the more user-friendly buying that can be done with the larger cable carriers.

2. Cable is inexpensive.

Compared to broadcast TV, cable advertising is a bargain.

Although you should keep in mind that when advertisers buy cable, they are getting a lot less audience for their money.

First, while almost 100% of US TV households can receive network broadcast TV, only about 60% of these homes have access to cable television.

Therefore, cable has a smaller coverage area nationwide. Cable also costs less because its fragmented audience is spread across a variety of channels. Remember that broadcast networks concentrate their programming on one channel. In doing so, broadcast networks are able to capture mass audiences.

Cable networks consist of multiple channels. Smaller audiences are dispersed across a variety of different cable networks.

Consequently, cable costs less than broadcast TV.

3. Cable programming is varied.

As a result, it delivers specialized audiences.

Cable networks don't try to be everything to everybody.

Rather, they concentrate on one particular group of people and strive to be absolutely everything to that one particular group.

Cable offers advertisers specialized programming and narrowly defined audiences. This allows advertisers to target specific markets without wasting ad dollars on nonprospects.

VH-1 delivers music-loving adults who are professionals.

Financial News Network (FNN) reaches investors and money managers. CMT covers country-and-western fans.

In cable, if you've got a niche, you can scratch it.

4. Cable delivers upscale audiences.

Cable subscribers tend to be higher-educated and have a higher annual income than broadcast TV viewers.

These upscale consumers are attractive to advertisers because they have more disposable income.

5. Cable television allows a wider variety of ad formats.

Advertisers have many choices when it comes to buying commercials on cable television.

Cable offers advertisers the shorter advertising units found on broadcast TV and, at the same time, provides much longer commercial unit lengths – primarily infomercials, which can range from 2 to 30 minutes in length.

Cable Television's Weaknesses:

1. Cable has low network ratings.

Compared to broadcast television, cable ratings are much lower. This is a drawback to some advertisers.

Many times they have to buy multiple stations to obtain an acceptable reach level. There's small, and then there's invisible.

Some stations just don't deliver enough viewers.

2. TV audience ratings reports are inadequate.

The current ratings system has some drawbacks in measuring cable audiences.

Small sample sizes and a system that was set up to measure broadcast instead of cable TV are called into question.

Agencies are sometimes reluctant to use the cable audience measurement statistics that are presented to them.

TV Messages Are Fleeting.

This TV commercial for Century 21 makes the point that your message is seldom the only one out there.

Digital. The New TV Frontier.

Digital TV is going to mean a lot of changes.

They might not happen all at once, but the big news, from a marketing standpoint, is that you will, eventually, be able to make TV almost as interactive as your computer.

Certainly, you'll be able to imbed ordering and e-commerce information.

But wait, there's more!

Smart techies will be able to download that information – dancing hamsters and all – into your e-mail inbox.

And more channels overall will provide more opportunities to provide content.

You'll probably get more than TV as well.

Your digital TV will be able to download data – whether it's a directory, your daily newspaper, or the latest upgrade for Guitar Hero.

Time-Shifting Made Easy.

We're already seeing major changes in viewing habits.

Digital TV will provide additional opportunities – and maybe some of them will be opportunities for you.

TV broadcasters will be working to discover new ways to leverage the digital advantage.

One more way the Media Revolution is having an impact on The Business of Brands.

Want to Know More?

Right now, one of the best places to go is DTV.gov.

New Media
Strengths and Weaknesses.

This part of the media world is changing even as you read this.

But here, in a general sense, are the strengths and weaknesses of the entire category of new media technologies.

New Media Strengths.

1. It's new.

Often, the first stone makes the most noticeable splash. Being an early adopter of any new media technology may not generate much awareness all by itself, but it is often very merchandisable – as a publicity program in other media.

With that in mind, any and all new media programs make a certain sense.

2. The media itself is often low cost.

With most traditional media forms, you are paying for some sort of high-cost component – newsprint, network air time, local air time, a billboard at the corner of 3rd and Main. A Web site, banner, or search listing is not, in itself, inherently expensive.

3. Interaction and involvement.

Most new media efforts provide a "next step," whether it is a click-through, a Web address, database sign-up, or an online ballot. We know that the more inviting we can make our message environment, the better we will do both short-term and long-term.

4. Buzz and excitement.

If you have a hit, millions may visit your site or watch your video.

Add to that the values that accrue to being "the new thing," and a successful new media effort can feel very rewarding.

5. It's measurable.

You can count every click and track every journey through your site. What did they watch, what did they do, and where did they go. Now you can know. Instantly.

But, despite these obvious strengths, there are some weaknesses.

New Media Weaknesses.

1. It's hard to get there and hard to find.

Driving traffic to a site can be a high-effort, low-success type of task.

Whether a matter of relevance or convenience, it can be hard to generate the series of actions necessary (remember the URL, enter it in a browser, find time to visit and get involved) to end up with a successful experience.

2. Production can be expensive and time-consuming.

New technologies can absorb great amounts of time and resources without necessarily generating an equivalent payout.

So, even though the Web site might not cost you much, getting it up and running in terms of all the staff time, programming, and the general inefficiency of doing something new... well, you might find yourself catching mice with a cheese truck.

3. Many new media audiences are small to invisible.

The core idea of mass marketing and mass media involves working with large audiences.

With new media programs, sometimes it's difficult to impossible to generate enough critical mass.

4. That great new media program? It's not yours.

The new media environment is also hugely cluttered. Many are called, few are clicked.

5. It's hard to get good quantitative data.

Hard to measure before the fact. Impossible to predict. And, even with high levels of traffic, it can be hard to discern, much less measure, any sort of sales lift.

Still, new is new, and we all see many examples of those who have developed a new approach, an involving site, or a viral video that shows up on everyone's desktop.

It's an exciting new part of the media world and there are literally thousands of things happening at once. That said, it's hard not to believe there's not "a pony in there somewhere."

The Media Plan.

THE ADVERTISING MEDIA WORLD HAS CHANGED, and it will continue to rapidly evolve. In this fragmented media world, branding becomes even more important.

To resonate with and ultimately be remembered by consumers, a product or service needs to speak in a single message, a unified voice. It needs one theme to cut across today's fragmented media and be heard through the din and clutter of all the other competing messages.

To maneuver through this fragmented and tangled media world takes talent, smarts, strategic thinking, marketing savvy, and a tenacity to continue to learn.

Most of all, it takes a plan. And that takes a planner.

Do You Have a Plan?

Media planners are specialists who select and schedule the media that will carry messages to particular audience segments.

Most media planners work at advertising agencies or independent media agencies. And their job is being significantly affected by this media revolution.

They are becoming more and more like account planners as they search for insights that will make their media plans more effective.

New Expectations.

New expectations loom ahead for these professionals.

For instance, media planners will be expected to keep up on the hundreds of media possibilities and to know when it is appropriate to use them to help achieve clients' marketing goals.

Planners will no longer be thinking just about TV, radio, or magazines. They'll have to select and schedule all types of media.

Going Postal.
Media Strategy in Action!

Al Gilbert
Senior Media Planner
Foote, Cone, & Belding, NY.

After working at Wells two-and-a-half years, Al was promoted to a media planner. Soon after, he moved to a larger agency – Foote, Cone, & Belding/New York (now Draft/FCB).

Moving Up.

He was hired as Senior Media Planner on Nabisco. Within two years, he was transferred to the United States Postal Service (USPS) account and promoted once again, this time to Media Supervisor.

Foote, Cone, & Belding was awarded the Priority Mail business after a competitive agency was unable to produce advertising that sufficiently grew the business.

Planning to Win.

During his time on the USPS account, he wrote and implemented media plans that have captured the client's imagination because of their solid strategic thinking and unparalleled creativity. (He was also promoted to Senior Media Planner.)

These media plans helped provide unprecedented results for USPS in terms of positive business growth in the highly competitive two-day expedited delivery market.

Al's media plans have also managed to put the competition on the defensive – forcing competing mail delivery services to lower their rates and reconsider how they plan and execute their media.

And Moving West.

Sometimes your reward is a promotion, and sometimes it's a brand new job. In this case, Al moved to Y&R/San Francisco where he was brought in to handle the Clorox business.

Planning for the Future.

The ANA study "Marketing & Media Ecosystem 2010" identified six key trends.

The first, "**Media: The New Creative** – Marketing message distribution – timing, context, and relevance – is as important as creative execution."

Here are five others:

- **Marketing as Conversation.** Listen, facilitate, and create advocacy. Marketing is less about pushing messages *at* consumers and more about co-creating experiences *with* consumers.

- **Marketing + Math.** Data quality, quantity, and accessibility have brought math to marketing. New digital tools, predictive models, and behavioral targeting will turn insight into foresight.

- **Mind the Gap.** Marketing spending in digital media is far from commensurate with consumer behavior shifts – when will the divide between traditional and nontraditional media end?

- **The "Digitally Savvy" Organization.** Technology without an aligned organization, the right talent, and a progressive culture is inadequate. Functional skills are rising to the level of brand strategy.

- **The Network Effect.** Partnerships and collaboration among agencies, media companies, and marketers will grow in number and depth. New players will assume important roles and continue to reshape the value chain.

Jayne Spittler, Leo Burnett's Director of Media Research, offers this advice: *"It will be more challenging to work in advertising in new media. Do you, for instance, support a video menu or do you have a branded home-shopping store? It's a 'sky's the limit' type of thing. And advertisers have to know all of the possibilities. That's my job."*

Yet media planners do not see traditional advertising media, such as network TV and magazines, going the way of typewriters and leisure suits.

Spittler echoed the sentiments shared by other media directors, stating in a recent *Mediaweek* article, *"There will always be a place for good old 30-second TV spots."*

So how do these media planners go about doing their job? How do they combine the conventional with the unconventional when it comes to scheduling media?

That's what the next section of this chapter will tackle.

Media Planning.

MAKING SENSE OF THE BOUNDLESS NEW MEDIA WORLD is the real challenge facing today's media planners. Some experts contend it's a real balancing act between the old and new media.

In a *Business Marketing* editorial, today's media planning was described as: *"Getting a handle on emerging forms of media. That's what today's world of media planning is all about. Thinking out of the box. Pushing the envelope. Creating new standards."*

A recent study by the ANA concluded, *"Marketing message distribution – timing, context, and relevance – is as important as creative execution."* As a result, media strategy and planning have developed a higher profile among marketers. One more example of the Media Revolution at work.

Where to Begin.

So where do media planners begin? What process do they follow to get the advertising messages delivered to target consumers?

Successful media planning is the task of selecting and scheduling media that will reach as many of the target audience as frequently as possible for the least amount of cost.

After being assigned a client's product or service, media planners turn to devising a written course of action – a **media plan.**

A media plan strategically shows how an advertising budget will be used to buy media that will reach the maximum number of prospects for the brand with the greatest effectiveness at the lowest costs.

All media plans must work hard to help achieve the client's **marketing objectives**.

They are, in fact, a key part of the marketing plan.

Donald Evanson reported in *Mediaweek* that *"80% of media plans submitted for Mediaweek's Plan of the Year Award were anchored to a client's marketing situation."* He says, *"The media plan of today contains specific references to the marketing problem that the strategy of the media plan will attempt to address."*

Keep in mind that clients hand over their hard-earned money

to media planners with the expectation that these dollars will be judiciously invested in media that will deliver target audiences who will react positively to the brand's message.

Media Planning Old & New.

Media planning is a hot topic. This wasn't always the case. Until recently, media selection and placement *"played second fiddle to... creative development,"* as Junu Bryan Kim noted in *Advertising Age*.

The Way It Used to Be...

For years, when it came to campaign development, the spotlight was really on *what* was said (ad message) not on *how* it was delivered (media plan).

Nor was advertising media planning considered all that exciting or, for that matter, creative. Back then, calling media planning creative was like saying Howard Stern is subtle. You get the point.

Sue Oriel, Media Director at Zenith Media, outlined the changes she has seen in the media planning process over the past 10 years.

Oriel observed, *"Planners have finally shaken off the image of Neanderthals with calculators – not that there's anything wrong with the odd Neanderthal attitude when it comes to buying – and replaced it with that of the consumer-sensitive ideas-merchant at the numbers end of the business."*

From Clerical to Creative.

Media planning in the old days was mostly a clerical task, with planners caught up in all sorts of numbers and forms.

With fewer media choices and lower costs overall, clerical accuracy was the most-needed skill.

They were the behind-the-scenes players in an advertising agency, and their job consisted mainly of filling out insertion orders and wrestling with reams of CPM figures (which we'll talk about later) and audience delivery statistics.

Planners had little face-to-face contact with the client, and the media plan tended to be sifted through the account executive to the client. Well, all that has changed.

The Way It Is Now...

As previously discussed, media fragmentation and the adoption of IMC have, as Kim points out, *"Necessitated looking at advertising from the media standpoint sooner than was done before."*

The result has been a revolution in media planning. Let's look at how they're doing it today.

Trends in Media Planning.

So what are the trends? The big one is that media planning has risen to become an essential component of the client's marketing plan.

Today, it is not uncommon for media decisions to be made before a creative concept has even been born. And, in some cases, these decisions will have an impact on the entire creative ad development.

A related interesting development is that media planners are fast becoming more involved with the creative department's copywriters and art directors.

This is something pretty much unheard of years ago.

Brand Contact Points.

Don't forget that your media plan may contain more than media.

Think Brand Contact Points – all the different ways consumers connect with your brand.

Impact and Involvement.

Here's a promotion that leverages Wheaties sports hero brand equity – a special offer that lets you become the hero on a Wheaties box!

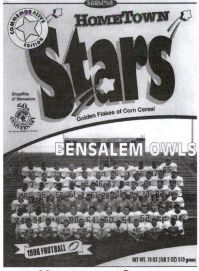

Hometown Stars.

Carlisle Cereal Company takes another approach – packaging a cereal that really hit close to home.

This "Hometown Stars" cereal box actually featured the 1996 local high-school football team, complete with the season roster.

That's target packaging.

Local and Regional Media Planning.

Remember Debra Becker's first job – for the family bicycle store? It was a great way to understand what it takes to succeed in a local market.

Handling advertising for a small, local retailer was both rewarding and a great learning experience.

"*It was exciting to try advertising and promotion strategies and see them work,*" says Debra.

Other retailers in town began copying Debra's unique approaches and clever ideas.

Overall, she feels that this first job gave her the experience to compete in the larger, more competitive advertising job market later on.

Other experience helped, too.

After getting her master's degree at Syracuse, she joined the Roberts Group located in Syracuse, New York, as a media buyer.

A year later, she was promoted to Media Director, where she supervised the John Deere national co-op advertising program.

Growing Business with Garden Way.

A year later, Debra worked as Media Director and Branch Manager for Multi-listing International located in Albany, New York. There, she designed media plans for *Troy-Bilt* and *Bolens* lawn and garden equipment.

Her client, Garden Way, coaxed Debra to come over to its side, which meant a move to Troy, New York.

So she became Garden Way's Retail Advertising Manager, expanding her division so much that it led Garden Way to record growth and profits.

Prior to Debra's arrival, Garden Way's main income came from direct response advertising.

Debra expanded this media effort by planning and placing advertising for Troy-Bilt dealer groups and factory stores.

(Continued on next page)

David Martin, CEO of Penta-Com, a BBDO division that does Chrysler's media planning, explains: "*The creative people and the media people must intertwine their work as much as possible. They have to understand the overall project is part of a targeting process.*"

Today, media planners are being pushed into the spotlight that once only shined on the account executives. Gone are the days when media planners were left back at the ad shop, giving their plans to account executives to present to the client.

Now, more than ever, planners are mixing it up with clients by going to important strategic planning meetings and making key presentations.

Zenith's Oriel describes this change, saying: "*Media planners now take for granted their ability to contribute above and beyond the targeted placement of spots and spaces.*

"*They regularly enjoy the business confidences of their client in order to make sure their ideas are relevant and actionable.*"

Reasons for the Change.

Why the change? For starters, clients are more media savvy.

Second, media is a hefty expense and prices have been on the rise for years. Clients want that biggest bang for their buck and are fast realizing that a smart media plan can save them money.

Third, there are so many more choices – and qualitative considerations are making decisions even more complex.

Just 10 years ago, the process of media planning was mostly driven by advertising costs and audience deliveries.

Traditional media planners had to think more about numbers than strategies. (Mind you, it is still important to find the best media prices for your client.)

But today's media planning demands that far more attention be given to media strategy and planning.

Andy Tilley of Zenith Media says, "*As media choice increases and the number of messages proliferates, then what will be required is media planning working hand in hand with account planning.*"

He notes that the ad business needs "*people who understand communication from the consumer's viewpoint. And that means both the content of the creative work and the context in which it appears.*"

He goes on to explain, "*If you do media planning correctly and account planning correctly, you answer the same questions – how is the communication going to work and how can we make it more effective?*"

Tilley observes that it all boils down to having a keen understanding of the consumer, saying: "*And in a rapidly-changing media world, an understanding of the consumer/media relationship is of fundamental importance to the process.*"

Later in this chapter we'll see how DDB has found a strategic process that allows the media planner to gain magnificent insight into the consumer-media relationship.

For now, let's turn our attention to where media decisions are spelled out by examining the media plan. Step by step.

Creating the Media Plan.

According to BBDO, a media plan is *"a blueprint for future action that is a means of organizing a brand's advertising into media objectives and strategies that are*

1. *goal oriented – increase sales and marketshare*
2. *make sense – effective and efficient*
3. *manageable – can be executed, are flexible, and are developed before the media buy."*

Media Objectives and Media Strategies.

The **media objectives** tell us *what* your media plan hopes to achieve. **Media strategies** tell us *how* the objective will be implemented.

Media plans grow out of a solid marketing plan that is developed by the client's brand management group in tandem with the advertising agency's account team.

You were exposed to the process of developing a situation analysis and marketing plans in earlier chapters.

Media plans flow directly out of this work.

The Media Planning Team.

The media plan is created by the **media planning group**, which can be made up of an associate media director, media planners, and assistant media planners.

At smaller ad agencies, the plan may be put together by just one person. And if the planning group members are not also responsible for media buying, then they will work along with the media buying group to get the job done.

There are also new titles and job descriptions entering the game. CP+B calls Jim Poh (their media director) "director of creative content distribution."

The media buying group can be responsible for buying national or local media.

For any kind of media planning team, the process of creating a media plan includes five distinct steps.

Step One – Evaluation & Analysis.

All media plans begin with a thorough analysis of the brand's market situation and marketing objectives.

You'll notice some of these factors are similar to those in the Situation Analysis done for the marketing plan in Chapter Eight.

According to BBDO, these factors include:

1. **Brand History** – The brand's past track record, including sales history, past creative and promotional endeavors, prior pricing policy, distribution practices, etc.
2. **Purchase Cycle** – The purchase pattern for the brand during the course of the day, week, month, or year.
3. **Prime Prospect** – The target consumers who will be most receptive to what the brand has to offer
4. **Budget** – The size of the budget, especially in relationship to the competition.

Debra (Cont.)

She also designed and implemented a co-op ad program for dealers throughout the US and Canada.

In 1994, Debra returned to her hometown to assume the media helm at Syracuse's Latorra, Paul, & McCann.

As the agency's Media Director, Debra currently works for a wide variety of clients – including *Agway, Carrier*, regional Chevy dealer groups, and the New York State Fair.

Although it's certainly not the largest account she's worked on, the State Fair is one she's very proud of.

While she handled the media planning, the New York Sate Fair set record attendance figures.

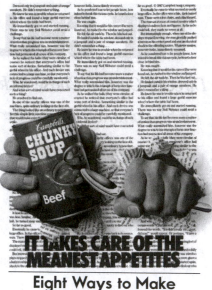

IT TAKES CARE OF THE MEANEST APPETITES

Eight Ways to Make Media Impact.

With today's new media environment, achieving impact is a bigger challenge every day.

Briefly, here are eight ways to do it.

1. Saturation.

Concentrate your dollars for overwhelming presence in a single medium.

The *"Got Milk"* celebrity milk mustache campaign put all of its dollars into print – for a dominant presence with its arresting ads.

2. Omnipresence.

This is the opposite approach. Try to achieve a presence in all media. There is some evidence that hearing the same message in a variety of media vehicles is more effective than hearing the message repeatedly in just one media vehicle.

3. Match Media to the Message.

Find media that add value to your message. Think about how those Keri transit posters on dirty subway cars dramatized the importance of fighting bacteria.

Ugh! But it added value.

4. Do the Unexpected.

This is the opposite of the previous approach. Choose someplace you wouldn't expect to see your brand. Surprise adds impact.

5. Extra Continuity.

Find some way to extend your presence over a long time.

(Continued on next page.)

5. **Seasonality** – The time of year that a brand experiences real sales increases.

6. **Geography** – The specific areas of the country broken down into regions and markets that show an opportunity for sales success for the brand.

7. **Competition** – Competitors identified and analyzed.

8. **Promotional Activity** – An analysis of marketing communications activities, such as sales promotion, direct marketing, public relations, and personal selling for the brand and its competitors.

Problems and Opportunities.

Studying and carefully analyzing these marketing variables, the media planner is searching for problems and opportunities.

This analysis becomes the foundation for the media plan.

After this analysis is complete, it's time to move on to creating media objectives – deciding which course of action is optimal based on the current conditions of the marketplace.

Step Two – Planning Media Objectives.

According to Saatchi's media department, media objectives can be broken down into four basic components:

1. **Target Audience**
2. **Seasonality**
3. **Geography**
4. **Reach and Frequency**

Notice how certain aspects interlock with the initial Evaluation and Analysis stage of the plan. And, even with all the new media choices, these four basics are still solid.

Using Saatchi & Saatchi's four basic media objectives, let's discuss each and look at some of the ways media planners go about addressing each important strategic area.

Let's start with the most critical decision media planners have to make: deciding *whom* to advertise to.

1. Target Audience – To Whom Should You Advertise?

The first decision an advertising media planner must make is determining just exactly who should receive the messages.

Media planners will grapple with trying to determine which audience group will be most receptive toward the client's advertising and most inclined toward purchasing the brand.

Essentially, media planners need to determine with which group clients should invest their advertising dollars in order to get the biggest return.

For media planning purposes, the target audience is quantified and defined in terms of demographics, psychographics, product usage, and media usage. This is the **target profile.**

Developing the Target Profile.

To craft this detailed target profile, media planners rely on syndicated media research sources and proprietary research.

Media planners depend on **syndicated research** like Simmons Market Research Bureau (SMRB) and Mediamark Research Institute (MRI) to find out who the target audience is in terms of:

- **Demographics** (gender, age, income, household size, presence of children, household income, education, geography, race)
- **Product Usage** (heavy, medium, and light users)
- **Media Usage**

Psychographic information helps media planners gain critical insight into the target audience's lifestyle, mindset, groups it relates to, and neighborhoods. It can be provided by syndicated research companies like PRIZM.

Here is where the new variety of media choices begins to be evaluated. As the media landscape has continued to become more complex, cluttered, and fragmented, new tools are being developed to do a better job of precisely targeting consumers in today's complicated media marketplace.

PMN – The Personal Media Network.

Some agencies are trying to develop strategic methods that will help them find the most efficient times, places, and vehicles to reach the best prospects.

Mike White, Executive VP Media Director at DDB Chicago, and Page Thompson, Executive VP Media Director of DDB New York, have created and developed a system called the **Personal Media Network (PMN).**

PMN allows *"agency personnel to get a more vivid and comprehensive picture of the most receptive target consumers, the most relevant media vehicles that play a part in the consumer's life, and those that are the most relevant and persuasive."*

The PMN system is built on three factors:

- **Individual Media Consumption Patterns**
- **The Core Audience**
- **Aperture®**

Let's take a quick look at how this system works.

Media Consumption Profiles and Media Paths.

At the center of the PMN system is the media consumption pattern of 4,000 individuals. These profiles show how individuals consume media, from when they wake up in the morning to when they retire at night, based on needs, interests, and moods.

What DDB has found, and worth noting here, is that these media choices constantly change throughout the day and are driven not by broad media, such as television or radio, but by specific vehicles such as *Seinfeld* or *Glamour* magazine.

DDB found that the media paths people follow throughout a typical day include both traditional and new media vehicles driven by their desires.

How can you gain better consumer insight into understanding your key prospects? DDB suggests you begin with charting prospect behavior three different ways:

Impact (Cont.)

6. Short-Term Blitzes.
Again, the opposite. Concentrate all your efforts in an intense outburst.

7. Unusual Use of Medium.
Pop-ups, fold-outs, extremely large space print, and extended length broadcasts are examples.

Hal Riney developed a 30-minute show on Spring Hill, where the Saturn was built, as part of the brand's introduction.

8. Shifting Media.
Shifting media choices can add impact. High-impact decisions may have a combination of these characteristics.

For example, Nike's famous LA Olympic "ambush" billboard campaign was an unusual and unexpected short-term blitz in a new media choice for athletic shoes.

Fashion Institute of Design & Merchandising.

Suppose you were an admissions director at a fashion design school and your job was trying to reach fashion-conscious women 16–19?

Your ad budget won't support ads in *Sassy* or *Seventeen*.

Besides, your campuses are concentrated on the West Coast.

What's more, you have to reach these fashion-minded, artistically inclined young women in the spring so they can take advantage of the scholarships your school has to offer.

Is this is a tall order? You bet.

But look at how the bright marketing and media minds at the Fashion Institute of Design and Merchandising (FIDM) solved this communications challenge.

Consumer-Driven Media Planning.
FIDM took a consumer-driven approach to their media planning and joined forces with Rampage, a clothing company that manufactures hip contemporary clothing that is moderately priced and geared for junior-sized women who aren't afraid to wear cutting-edge fashion.

Ads and Promotion on a Rampage.
Rampage clothing is distributed nationwide in discount stores.

So in this case, the clothing company became the ad medium.

(Continued on next page)

1. **Time** – by day, week, month, year, season
2. **Place** – commuting, office, home, store
3. **Circumstances** – happy, worried, hungry

The PMN system also identifies the readers, viewers, or listeners that are devoted to certain magazines, TV shows, or radio stations. They wouldn't think of missing an issue of their beloved magazine or an episode of their "must-see" TV shows.

The Importance of Your Core Audience.

This group of extreme loyalists to a particular media vehicle is called the **core audience.**

And why is it important to know who your core audience is? Research has shown that advertising has a better chance of actually reaching and having an impact on this group.

Aperture®

Another factor the PMN system identifies is Aperture®. This refers to the time, the place, and the frame of mind that cause a consumer to be open to a message.

More importantly, Aperture® identifies the exact point when a prospect's *"mind is open through which the message can pass."*

DDB believes prospects are willing to pay attention to advertising if it is on their own terms.

This means advertising has to intersect people in places they have chosen, when they are open to persuasion, and with relevant and arresting messages.

The trick is finding where all three of these intersect – this is the consumer aperture for your brand.

The Need for Media Insight.

To get ad messages seen and heard in today's fragmented, cluttered media world means moving beyond quantitative definitions of the target audience to more in-depth qualitative descriptions in order to gain more complete consumer insight.

In so doing, media planners have a better chance of making sure their messages are received and received favorably.

An excellent example is the Fashion Institute of Design and Merchandising (see sidebar).

2. Seasonality – When Should You Advertise?
A media planner looks at the calendar year and decides the best times to advertise in order to maximize sales for the brand.

The media planner is looking for peak sales seasons. As an example, BBDO media planners establish when to advertise based on a variety of factors, including:

1. **Seasonal Sales**
2. **Media Efficiency**
3. **Competitive Presence/Spending**
4. **Promotions Scheduled**

In considering the four factors above, planners try to coincide their client's advertising during peak sales periods.

An Example...

For example, a planner assigned to *Gertrude Hawk Chocolates,* a premium chocolate retailer, might want to schedule ads prior to St. Valentine's Day to take advantage of seasonality.

Planners also have to consider how cost efficient certain media vehicles are during certain times of year.

So, even though children's TV programs might be more expensive prior to the December holiday gift-giving season, it makes all sorts of sense for a planner working on a toy account to swallow these higher-prices to cash in on the heightened enthusiasm kids have toward toys during this time of year.

Competitors' presence and spending are other factors that affect when to schedule advertising.

Direct or Differential Scheduling.

Two basic marketing approaches dictate how planners will deal with the competition.

If the brand's overall marketing objective is to go head-to-head with competitors, then the brand has opted for a **direct strategy.**

To help implement this strategy, media planners must schedule media during times when the competition is advertising.

If, on the other hand, the brand's overall marketing objective is to develop a unique presence in the marketplace that is separate from the competition, then the brand has opted for a **differential strategy.**

To help implement this strategy, media planners will schedule a different course of action for the plan.

If the brand's budget pales in comparison to the competition's, the planner may concentrate bursts to get the messages heard.

Sales promotions like contests, sweepstakes, and event sponsorships are activities you learned about in earlier chapters.

You will recall that they are short-term incentives. As such, they also have an effect on how the media will be scheduled.

A planner must make sure that extra media are bought and scheduled to generate enough noise about the sales promotion activity that consumers or the trade will know enough to take advantage of the offer.

The moment the campaign begins is called **time-zero start up.**

3. Geographic Considerations – Where Should You Advertise?

A media planner must decide whether to advertise a brand nationally, regionally, locally, or in a combination of these three.

Here is how Saatchi & Saatchi looks at factors that influence where a media planner chooses to advertise:

1. **Distribution** – Is the product distributed nationally, regionally, or locally?

2. **Budget** – Does the advertising budget support a national media effort or merely a regional media plan?

3. **Competition** – Do you want to avoid competition and develop your own distinctive marketing action? Or do you want to go head to head with competition to increase marketshare?

FIDM (Cont.)

It makes a lot of sense, doesn't it?

The clothes are appealing to exactly the same audience FIDM wants to reach.

Now look at how inexpensively FIDM was able to deliver its message to its intended target audience.

The 22¢ Connection.
The media vehicle for FIDM became a postcard that attached to the Rampage tags hanging on the apparel.

The postcard hang tags were attached to all of the spring apparel line – which meant the message got delivered when young women were applying to college.

Did FIDM locate its Aperture®?

Did it find the opening in the consumers' minds when they were thinking about fashion and their future?

I think so.

Catching the Right Aperture®.
Look at how the ad message grabs the reader's attention by announcing a chance to win a full-tuition college scholarship.

The ad message intersects with the target audience when she is interacting with trendy clothing.

If she has bought the clothes and is now at home removing the tags, the FIDM ad message cashes in on the positive frame of mind the young woman has about just getting a new outfit. A clever and effective media delivery that really hits the target audience.

Keri Antibacterial Lotion.

Talk about effective media planning working with powerful creative messages – check this out.

Bristol-Myers Squibb Company used transit advertising on gritty New York City subways to introduce its new Keri antibacterial hand lotion.

The brand found the perfect time, place, and group of people to talk to about germs. I guess you'd say the media planners found the perfect Aperture® for this new product entry.

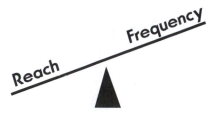

4. Sales by Market – Do you want to place additional ad dollars in markets where your brand is doing particularly well? Or would you like to consolidate dollars in sales regions where the product category is experiencing high sales growth?

Insight into Different Geographic Approaches.

Planners pay attention to a brand's geography. Saatchi's media department provides some reasons why advertisers take different geographic approaches.

Why National?
- Brand has national distribution
- Brand has broad skews of product usage throughout country
- Brand currently does not have any geographic sales history available, as with a new product

Why Spot?
- Brand has a concentration of sales in particular areas
- Brand has regional appeal
- Brand has part of a regional roll-out
- Brand has a small budget

Why Both?
- Brand has national distribution with high regional sales
- Brand is adopting an offensive or defensive strategy on top of a national base of media

Offensive or Defensive Strategy.

When it comes to choosing certain markets for concentrated advertising focus, media planners may choose an offensive or defensive approach for a brand relative to its competitors.

With the offensive approach, the media planner will recommend a geographic focus that matches up head-to-head with a key competitor.

In a situation where a brand campaign is designed to maintain or build on its existing strengths, the media planner will opt for a more defensive approach of allocating advertising to markets/regions where the brand has strength.

As you can see, a lot of consideration goes into making the decision on where to advertise.

Once this decision is made, the media planner moves on to the third major objective, which involves deciding when to advertise. Let's now see how planners arrive at this objective.

4. Reach and Frequency – How Many of Your Target Consumers Do You Want to Reach and How Often?

Another strategic decision media planners have to wrestle with is deciding how many target consumers they want to reach and how often (**frequency**) they want to reach them.

Reach and frequency are quantitative terms used to describe the size and repeat exposure of an audience to a media schedule over time.

Taking many competitive, budgetary, and communication factors into consideration, a media planner will set the reach level by specifying the percentage of members of the target audience to reach.

The planner sets the frequency level by choosing how many times to show the advertising message to the target audience.

Reach or **ratings** refers to the percentage of an audience who are exposed to an advertising vehicle at least once, usually over a four-week period.

Gross rating points are the summation of all ratings for an advertising schedule. GRPs show how much media weight, or emphasis, a media planner has put into a specific day, week, or month. It is a duplicated figure.

Reach is always expressed as a percentage – some number less than 100%. Rating points are accumulated and can therefore add up to numbers much higher than just 100.

Media planners have often been nagged by the age-old question of how much advertising frequency is enough?

In an *Ad Age* column, media guru Jim Surmanek, then Senior VP and General Manager of International Communications Group, provided these perspectives on how media planners can come to grips with finding an answer to this daunting question.

He recommends advertisers consider the following points when it comes to setting frequency levels:

1. **Consumer Motivation**
2. **Purchase Cycle**
3. **Purchase Decision**
4. **Message Complexity**
5. **Advertising Effectiveness or Memorability**
6. **Commercial Length**
7. **Time of Day or Attention Levels**
8. **Competition**

The Great Reach/Frequency Trade-off.

In media planning, because budgets are a fixed constraint, the planner has to make a choice to emphasize either reach or frequency.

A planner can create a media plan that achieves a high audience reach with some acceptable level of frequency. Or, a planner can create a media plan that achieves a high level of frequency for some acceptable level of reach.

Very few clients have budgets big enough to accomplish both high reach and high frequency. The budget constraint thus makes reach and frequency a key trade-off in media planning.

Step Three – Media Strategies (Planning Continues).

Once the media objectives are decided upon, planners turn their attention to the media strategies, which include:

1. **Assessing the Nature of the Media and the Message**
2. **Comparing Strengths and Weaknesses of Various Media**
3. **Comparing Media Efficiencies on a CPM Basis**
4. **Eliminating Media That Do Not Fit Brand Personality**
5. **Considering the Various Selling Environments and Creative Opportunities the Media Offer**

A CPM Comparison.

Here is a comparison of CPM efficiencies for different media. In this case, the target is women 18–49.

Medium	Unit	$CPM
Network radio	:30	2.81
Day net radio	:30	5.35
Cable	:30	6.05
Print	4-color page	7.67
Early AM net TV	:30	11.14
Late-night TV	:30	12.22
Syndication	:30	13.29
Evening news	:30	17.80
Prime network	:30	18.31

Do You Know Where Your ADI Is?

ADI is a broadcast term that stands for **Area of Dominant Influence.**

It divides the country into TV markets, which may overlap cities and cross state lines.

For example, the Cincinnati ADI includes northern Kentucky.

Here is a list of the Top 85 ADIs.

1. New York
2. Los Angeles
3. Chicago
4. San Francisco-San Jose-Oakland
5. Philadelphia
6. Detroit
7. Dallas-Ft. Worth
8. Boston
9. Washington, DC
10. Houston
11. Miami-Ft. Lauderdale
12. Atlanta
13. Puerto Rico
14. Seattle-Tacoma
15. Phoenix
16. San Diego
17. Minneapolis-St. Paul
18. St. Louis
19. Baltimore
20. Pittsburgh
21. Tampa-St. Petersburg
22. Denver-Boulder
23. Cleveland
24. Portland, OR
25. Cincinnati
26. Sacramento
27. Kansas City

(Continued on next page.)

ADIs (Cont.)

28. Milwaukee
29. San Antonio
30. Providence
31. Columbus
32. Salt Lake City
33. Norfolk
34. Charlotte
35. Indianapolis
36. Raleigh-Durham
37. Orlando
38. New Orleans
39. Greensboro
40. Buffalo-Niagra
41. Nashville
42. Hartford
43. Memphis
44. Raleigh-Durham
45. Austin
46. Rochester
47. Jacksonville
48. Louisville
49. Oklahoma City
50. Dayton
51. Birmingham
52. Boca Raton
53. Richmond
54. Albany-Schenectady
55. Honolulu
56. Tulsa
57. Toledo
58. Greenville
59. Tucson
60. Akron
61. McAllen-Brownsville-Harlingen
62. Wilkes Barre-Scranton
63. Fresno
64. Grand Rapids
65. Allentown-Bethlehem
66. Knoxville
67. El Paso
68. Ft. Myers-Naples-Marco Island
69. Albuquerque
70. Omaha
71. Montery-Salinas-Santa Cruz
72. Syracuse
73. Wilmington
74. Harrisburg-Lebanon-Carlisle
75. Sarasota-Bradenton
76. Springfield, MA
77. Greenville-New Bern
78. Baton Rouge
79. Little Rock

(Continued on next page)

6. **Determining National vs. Local Spending**
7. **Determining Scheduling Strategies**
8. **Considering Synergy Between the Media and the Ad**

We will go over each of these briefly, but please keep in mind that the process of devising media strategy is a complex and involved one. A full discussion can be found in Marian Azzaro's fine text, *Strategic Media Decisions*.

With that said, let's move on to an abridged version of this strategic development as it relates to media planning.

1. Nature of the Media.
Which of the media are most appropriate for your product and service? Which mix of media will do the best job to help deliver ad messages to the target?

Media planners can choose to advertise their brands in one medium, which is called a **concentrated media effort,** or use a variety of media to get the brand's message out, which is known as a **media mix.**

In determining which media to use, planners consider factors such as marketing objectives, budget, and target audience.

Individual characteristics unique to each medium, such as broad or specialized reach, cost, and geographic selectivity, are weighed to determine how they will fit into the entire media plan.

And, of course, as new options enter into consideration, the comparison becomes more complicated.

2. Compare Strengths and Weaknesses of Each of the Media.
We covered this in depth earlier in the "Media Building Blocks" section of this chapter. Each medium offers advertisers certain advantages and disadvantages.

For example, television offers advertisers the dynamics of sight, sound, motion, and color. In many ways, this advertising medium comes the closest to personal selling.

Radio lacks sight and motion but makes up for this with its specialized audience delivery and loyal listeners.

The Internet offers sight, sound, and low-cost, but small and uncertain audiences.

It is important to consider each medium's strengths and weaknesses relative to the needs of the client's message strategy when determining which media to use.

3. Compare Media Efficiencies on a CPM Basis.
One of the ways media planners can compare different media vehicles, such as a Web site banner against, say, a four-color, full-page ad in *Spin* magazine, is by taking a look at how much it costs to deliver one thousand audience members for each vehicle.

CPM allows media planners to compare which media vehicle is delivering a thousand target audience members with the greatest cost efficiency.

For example, if a Web site charges $15,000 per ad banner and reports 100,000 visits per month, then it has a CPM of $150.

In turn, if *Spin* charges $29,700 for a four-color, full-page ad and reports a circulation of 1,111,000, then it has a CPM of $26.77. *Spin* magazine is the more cost-efficient buy here.

Although the price of the ad is more expensive, the cost of purchasing 1,000 audience members is significantly lower at $26.77 than the banner ad at a much higher $150 CPM.

4. Eliminate Media That Do Not Fit Brand Personality.

Today's media planners move beyond the numbers and make sure that each media chosen really fits the personality of the brand.

A planner working on a caffeine-charged cola with an in-your-face brand personality may want media with the same attitude such as MTV and *Spin*.

5. Consider the Various Environments and Creative Opportunities the Media Offer.

The overall media environment is also an important factor. This is the general selling atmosphere the medium lends to the brand.

For example, early-morning TV is a perfect media environment for oatmeal, mouthwash, orange juice, and coffee.

Outdoor advertising, especially billboards on the way to the airport, is a strong place to advertise airlines. Food magazines create a persuasive environment for an advertiser's recipe offer.

Strong media environments can help attract consumer's attention and sometimes motivate action.

6. Determine National vs. Local Spending.

Media planners need to decide how to allocate the budget to national and local media and how to justify these decisions.

If local media are included, planners need to spell out which markets have been chosen and why.

7. Determine Scheduling Strategies.

When scheduling advertising, media planners work within the time frame of the campaign period. Some product categories, like frozen pizza for example, have a long campaign because they can be used and purchased year round.

Other product categories, like fly fishing rods and reels, may only have five month's of usage and purchase potential – thus their campaign period is shorter.

Taking other items into consideration, such as creative, budgetary, and competitive factors, planners schedule media in order to support the usage and purchasing patterns of their clients' products in an effort to maximize sales.

Four Types of Ad Schedules.

According to BBDO, planners have four types of ad schedules to choose from: continuity, flighting, pulsing, and blinkering.

Continuity refers to a continuous ad schedule where media weight has been scheduled constantly throughout the period with no variation in the amount of advertising and no hiatus.

As long as the budget will support it, products with year-round usage potential might opt for continuity.

ADIs (Cont.)

80. Wichita
81. Stockton
82. Bakersfield
83. Charleston
84. Mobile
85. Columbia, SC

What's Cooking at the Media Kitchen.

Darren Herman is a cutting edge part of the media scene at Kirshenbaum & Bond. Their media group is called the Media Kitchen.

The Media Kitchen is an innovative media company designed to invigorate the role of creativity, inventiveness, and ideas in developing ground-breaking brand media solutions across the spectrum of media disciplines.

Here's how they serve it up.

"The Media Kitchen will expand the palate of traditional media fare "Meat and Potatoes" (Media Planning and Buying) to offer a more extensive and unique blend of dishes including Under the Radar (Guerrilla) media, media brand planning, brand exposure planning, branded media, media test kitchen, cross platform media management, econometric modeling, online and convergence media and inter-national management."

The Media Kitchen Philosophy.
We define media as *"anything that can carry a branded message and impact on the consumer,"*

Media strategy should be an essential component of any brand's message, not merely a means of distributing it.

This definition goes hand in hand with our commitment to media neutrality, creativity, accountability, and innovation.

Darren has added his own perspective to the media world in his book, *Coloring Outside the Lines: Confessions of a Digital Native*. It's available as a book or as a download for only 76¢ (at www.lulu.com). It offers genuine insights into digital media startups.

The Media Kitchen Recipe:

Here are the operating principles at the Media Kitchen – sort of their "cookbook." Now that you've had an introductory chapter on the art of media planning, this may start to make sense to you.

1. **Remember, it's communication, not exposure.** Develop the media (channel) brief before or, at worst, in parallel with the brand plan/creative brief.

2. **Seek and develop media relationships and contexts that position brands.** The medium is often the message.

3. **Always put the customer at the center of our communications universe.**

4. **Create new research agendas – quantitative and qualitative.**

5. **Ensure every campaign provides learning on how media contributes to effectiveness.** What are the marketing drivers and their relationships?

6. **Evolve ways to pretest and post-test media and communications strategies and new methodologies.**

7. **Create new buyer-seller relationships.** Have an approach more akin to partnership marketing.

8. **Exploit, adapt, and adopt best media and communication practice.**

9. **Media is pivotal to communications.** Use all the tools in our kitchen.

10. **Always remember, we are not a commodity.**

11. **Start to restructure jobs and roles now.**

12. **Beware of rules; they don't stimulate, they stifle.**

(Source: Kirshenbaum, Bond, + Partners, www.kb.com.)

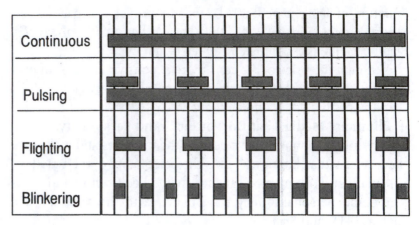

Flighting includes periodic waves of advertising followed by long periods of total inactivity. Products with seasonal emphasis might adopt flighting schedules.

Goods and services with year-round usage potential but small ad budgets may also flight their advertising.

Pulsing combines these two schedules. Pulsing includes a continuous base of advertising that is reinforced by periodic bursts of heavier media action.

Brands that have year-round usage potential that layer on additional promotional activity will pulse.

A fast-food retailer may use image advertising year round and add more media to support a promotion.

Blinkering includes short in-and-out bursts of advertising throughout the campaign period with all hiatuses being approximately the same length and brief.

Blinkering can provide an illusion of continuity without the hefty price tag. Therefore, it is favored by advertisers who may require continuity but cannot afford it.

8. Consider the Synergy Between the Media.

Synergy refers to the cooperative interaction that chosen media have on each other. As Saatchi & Saatchi point out, *"One medium can spark recall of an ad in another medium."*

Here are some of the examples Saatchi & Saatchi provided:
- Add outdoor near supermarkets to remind people of the TV message on their way to the store.
- Add newspapers to give a recipe idea for a brand you sell on TV.
- Add radio to reinforce the jingle from your TV spot.
- Add the URL address to drive Web traffic.

With Synergy, all elements of the plan work together.

Step Four – Implementation – The Media Buy.

The next step in the process is getting the buy made.

You may work at an agency that has specialists.

You may work in a small agency, where you have to put your media buyer's hat on, roll up your sleeves, and do it.

Or, you may have the job done for you by a media buying service.

One of the Toughest Jobs in Advertising.

As you might imagine, buying and negotiating can be a fairly tough-minded field. Everyone has some leverage.

The media companies want to get the most for their perishable product (an unsold minute is gone forever), and you want to pay the least (remember, you have your buyer's hat on now).

However, you should also remember that buyers and sellers have been doing this for years. They're able to be tough negotiators, each working to get the most out of the deal for the people they work for – and still have lunch. The media company buys.

Step Five – Evaluation – The Post-Buy Analysis.

While all of the rating services work very hard to make the numbers as accurate as possible, past performance is never going to be a perfect predictor of future performance.

And, very often, when a media buy is made, certain guarantees are also made – remember TRPs and GRPs?

Electronic media may make some overall audience guarantees. Print media may have some circulation guarantees.

If those numbers are made – or exceeded – everybody's happy.

If not, it's time for a **make-good.** That means the medium has to "make good" on the shortfall in audience guarantee with another ad.

Another Tough Job.

As you might imagine, a lot of work can go into evaluating a media buy. But it's often worth the effort.

If the buy performed as planned, this is good news that can be shared. If the audience guarantee fell short, the make-good can be merchandised as proof of the agency's diligence and the media company's commitment to keeping their promises and delivering value.

Long-term, the make-good can make good relationships.

Summary:

The process of creating a media plan has changed radically in recent years. Some marketers, like UniLever, now consider media planning to be a driving force in their international marketing.

This "other agency service" has become a key growth area, with agencies now marketing their branded media capability.

There's more emphasis on strategy than ever before. Media planners are now expected to develop total communications plans.

Media plans are a concerted effort that increasingly come out of integrated teams made up of account planners, media planners, and creative personnel, along with brand management groups.

The future of media planning is brighter than ever as our media universe grows. The Media Revolution keeps on rolling.

Exercise:

Media plans can make advertising campaigns more powerful and persuasive.

What Are Your Favorite Advertising Campaigns?

1. Where does this advertising campaign appear? Which media does this ad campaign use?

2. How are the media being used to enhance the creative messages of this advertising campaign?

3. Why do you think these media were chosen for this advertising campaign?
Why were some left out?

4. In analyzing just the media effort behind this advertising campaign, why is the media plan effective?

Discussion Questions:

1. Radio.
What are the strengths and weaknesses of radio?
Why is this medium a good choice to advertise a second-level soft drink brand, like Hires Root Beer? What are the drawbacks?

2. Magazines.
Magazines offer advertisers some real strengths and some real weaknesses. What are they?
How could Pop Tarts toaster pastries use magazines in a creative way to reach the college market?

3. Media Audiences.
Who are the most likely prospects for Welch's Grape Jelly?
Who is the audience for ESPN's *Sports Center*?
Which TV program has the largest audience coverage right now?

4. Choose a Magazine That You Normally Don't Read...
By looking at the ads and the editorial content in this publication, can you make some educated guesses about the magazine's audience composition?
Who is this magazine being aimed toward in terms of demographics, lifestyle, hobbies, and interests?

5. Below-the-Line.
What is the best example of below-the-line activity that you've seen recently? Why was it so good?

6. Brand Contact Points.
Can you recommend a brand contact point for Bic Razors that would happen sometime during the summer months?

7. Media Clutter.
Where have you seen media clutter occur? What are the downsides of clutter? What could an advertiser do to contend with this?

8. Newspapers.
Pick up a copy of your local newspaper. How would you tell a local photo developer to use newspaper advertising throughout the year?

9. Media Plans.
What are the steps of putting together a media plan?

10. Target Audiences.
What are some of the ways media planners approach selecting target audiences?

11. Seasonality.
Seasonality affects media strategy. Let's say you're creating a media plan for a new line of children's sunscreen. What media strategies do you recommend?

12. Offensive and Defensive.

What is the difference between offensive and defensive strategy? Can you provide an example for each?

13. Geographic Considerations.

What geographic considerations should a media planner think about in developing media strategy?

14. Scheduling.

What are the various ways media planners can schedule media? Which of the patterns would be best for a national fast-food chain with a large budget?

A national fast-food chain with a limited budget?

A national fast-food chain with a very large budget that needs to reach a variety of target audiences?

A local ski shop?

Concepts & Vocabulary:

Above-the-line – All expenditures appropriated to advertising media.

Accountability – To be held responsible for recommendations and show that these actions help contribute to the overall marketing communications goals.

Advertising media – All the channels of communication used to deliver advertising messages to consumers.

Audience composition – A description of a media vehicle's total audience in terms of demographic classification of individuals.

Below-the-line – All promotional expenditures which are not allocated to paid media advertising.

Blinkering – One of four types of ad schedules that is characterized with short in-and-out bursts of advertising throughout the ad campaign period. Hiatuses are approximately the same length and are brief.

Brand contact points – An IMC concept referring to every instance in which a consumer interacts with a brand – seeing the package on the shelf, the logo at a sporting event, a mention in an article, or an ad. Each of these is a brand contact point.

Business-to-business advertising media – Media which specialize in business-based communication, primarily trade magazines.

Circulation – The total number of copies of a newspaper or magazine that is distributed by subscription, newsstand, and bulk.

Clutter – Quantity of messages which compete for attention within a media vehicle, a medium, or in the media environment overall.

Continuity – Refers to a continuous ad schedule where media weight is scheduled constantly throughout the year with no variation in the amount of advertising and no hiatus.

Gross Rating Points (GRPs).

A rating point is the percent of the target audience reached by a media vehicle.

Gross rating points are the summation of the all of the rating points generated by a media buy or schedule.

This is a duplicated figure.

Example:

Adults 25-54 Rating

National Geographic	16.5
New Yorker	2.0
Daytime/In-home radio	7.2
ABC Mon. Night Football	11.2
Academy Awards	23.0
Total GRPs	59.9

Gross rating points are most useful in comparing different media schedules, buys, or plans to one another.

The GRP number will identify which media schedule, buy, or plan is the most efficient in generating the most exposures or impressions.

Source Notes:

"Targeting Marketing," in Kenneth Roman & Jane Maas', ed., *The New How to Advertise.*

The cost for a single announcement in broadcast media is called a unit cost and can be expressed as a :30 or :15 in television or a :60 or :30 in radio.

In outdoor, the number of people passing who have a reasonable opportunity to see the poster (DDB).

Prepared for *Advertising Age* by Robert J. Coen, McCann-Erickson Worldwide.

Inside Media, August 14, 1996.

A New Resource:

This chapter (and Chapter Six) are also part of a brand new media book, *Strategic Media Decisions,* a complete look at all the exciting things going on in the growing world of media as well as all the career opportunities.

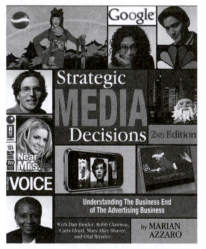

Strategic Media Decisions, 2nd Edition by Marian Azzaro, with Carla Lloyd, Mary Alice Shaver, Dan Binder, Robb Clawson, and Olaf Werder. Available from The Copy Workshop (www.adbuzz.com).

Co-op advertising – Retail advertising that is partly or fully funded by a manufacturer.

Cost per thousand (CPM) – A method of comparison whereby the cost of an advertising vehicle is multiplied by a thousand and divided into the vehicle's total audience. The CPM shows how much it costs to reach a thousand audience members, and thus it can be used to compare which advertising vehicles are most cost efficient.

Daypart – The part of a broadcast day when a particular program is either seen or heard. It also refers to how advertising time slots are grouped, with the most common being morning, afternoon, early evening, night, and late night.

Double truck – A two-page spread in newspapers where the editorial content or the advertising runs fully across both pages.

Flighting – One of four types of ad schedules which includes periodic waves of advertising followed by long periods of total inactivity.

Frequency – The number of times an individual or household is exposed to an advertising message over a certain period of time.

Gross rating points (GRPs) – The summation of rating points. A duplicated figure that shows how much weight a particular media buy is delivering.

High-involvement – Refers to a product that requires considerable thought and consideration from consumers when it comes to purchase – a computer, for example.

Households using television (HUT) – A Nielsen term that refers to the percentage of households tuning into television at a given time.

Low-involvement – Refers to a product that requires little thought and consideration from consumers when it comes to purchase – a package of gum, for example.

Media fragmentation – The splintering of mass media audiences into small, specific groups.

Media objectives – These are the goals of the media plan that specifically state what the course of action will be to help achieve the marketing goals.

Media plan – A written course of action that tells how media will be used to help achieve the marketing objectives.

Media strategy – Statements that specifically outline how the media will be used to help achieve the marketing goals. They flow directly out of the media objectives.

Media vehicle – A single media carrier, such as a magazine, newspaper, or cable channel.

Medium – One of the forms of communications that can be used to deliver advertising messages to consumers (e.g., a magazine is a medium; a newspaper is a medium).

Mediamark Research, Inc. (MRI) – A national company that supplies syndicated information on media audiences' demographic characteristics, audience media exposure, and product usage profile data.

Non-traditional media – Media that are often driven by technology; can be any new media form that allows for commercial expression.

On target – A media recommendation that has succeeded in reaching its specified target audience members.

Passalong readership – A magazine reader other than the subscriber or the purchaser of the magazine. Pass-along readers are those who get the magazine secondhand – patients in a doctor's reception room, for example.

Precision marketing – Marketing aimed at a specific segment or even individuals.

Prospects – Individuals identified as those most predisposed to buying a company's product or service.

Pulsing – One of four types of ad schedules which combines continuity and flighting. Pulsing includes a continuous base of advertising that is reinforced by periodic bursts of heavier media action.

Person using television (PUT) – A Nielsen term that refers to the percentage of individuals who tune into television during a given time period. It reports the total persons tuned into TV, not to specific programs.

Rating points – The percentage of individuals who tune into a particular program for a specific time.

Reach (or rating) – The number or percentage of different individuals who tune in, listen to, read, or interact with the media over a specific time period.

Readership – A term used to refer to a publication's audience which tells the total number of different persons reading an average copy of a magazine.

Run-of-paper (ROP) – An advertising insertion that runs anywhere in the newspaper. The position is not specified.

Simmons Market Research Bureau (SMRB) – Another national research company that provides syndicated information on media audiences' demographic characteristics, audience media exposure, and product usage profile data.

Syndicated research – Data that is sold to companies by independent research firms.

Target market – A group of individuals that has been identified as having real sales potential for the brand and can be defined in concrete terms that can include demographics, psychographics, product usage, etc.

Target profile – For media planning purposes, the target audience is quantified and defined in terms of demographics, psychographics, product usage, and media usage.

Traditional media – These include newspapers, magazine, television, radio, outdoor advertising, and Yellow Pages – media that are established and have been in the marketplace for a long time.

Unit cost – The amount of money charged for a specific unit of time or space in the media.

This chapter was written by Alice Kendrick, *Professor of Advertising at Southern Methodist University. Alice believes that life, whether of the personal or the marketing communications variety, is one big series of questions. She teaches about the value of making informed decisions and the tools and processes necessary to generate needed information. In 2008 she was named Educator of the Year by the AAF, and in 2007 received the Research Innovation Award from the Advertising Research Foundation. She is coauthor of two books and has published more than 30 refereed research articles, and acts as a research consultant to agencies, clients, and media companies.*

"We're not sure who discovered water, but we're pretty sure it wasn't a fish."

— Howard Gossage

Integration & Evaluation

PLANNING, IMPLEMENTING, AND EVALUATING a marketing campaign can take anywhere from a few weeks to a year. Through it all, evaluation and optimizing is everybody's job.

Researchers and account planners aren't the only ones who should engage in research and planning in today's ad world. Everybody can benefit from insights. That includes media planners, client account executives, copywriters, Web masters and mistresses – EVERYBODY.

I asked some of my former students to share their views on research, account planning, evaluation, and integration. Jill Imig, Ashley Watson, Brian Kress, Crystal Anderson, Augustin Jalomo, and Jabari Hearn all took some of the same classes at SMU. Each was good at getting to know the consumer. And each has found interesting employment in the Business of Brands. We'll hear from them throughout this chapter.

Whether they've gone to work for big advertisers like Nike, media companies, online advertising consultancies, or "traditional" advertising shops, they all believe strongly in the power of good information to make their marketing communication efforts better.

Evaluation – a Broader Definition.

This book uses a wider definition of the word "evaluation" – it's the ongoing process of evaluating progress – not just the evaluation that occurs after the job is done.

As Jack Haskins, former Ad Research Director for Ford Motor Co., would say, *"Post-campaign research is like a 'post-mortem' inquiry – it's really too late to do anything for the victim."*

Today, advertising and marketing can benefit from evaluation every step of the way – you can't wait till it's over to see how you're doing. Sometimes the process is, as marketing guru Tom Peters described it, *"Ready. Fire. Aim."*

Integration – An Ongoing Process.

This chapter also surveys what we call integration – a process of prioritization and optimization. Today, there are more choices.

To make those choices, effective evaluation is critical.

Time Is Money.

To make things even more interesting, choices must be made and challenges met under extreme time pressures.

For many marketers, waiting can be an expensive proposition.

We want good information and we want it fast.

The Problem with Scorekeeping.

In this chapter, and in your career, you will encounter various advertising evaluation tools that rely exclusively on numbers – strictly quantitative measures applied to either the creative or media efforts. Though such "scorekeeping" tests can be useful in certain circumstances, this chapter will not emphasize them.

The problem with post-campaign "scorekeeping" is that it's basically too late to do anything about whatever problems might be found with the advertising.

And the problem with obtaining pre-campaign "scores" is that research is not a crystal ball – quantitative scores always need interpretation and explanation, which often requires a more qualitative approach, and they are seldom definitive. Research can inspire good ideas and help you make better decisions. It may even give you some pretty good indications. But it does not necessarily predict the future.

Scorekeeping is OK. Winning is better. And to win, you usually need useful information sooner rather than later.

So, throughout this section, we'll be talking about ways we can bring good research into each step of the process. Quickly.

How This Chapter Is Organized.

In this chapter, we'll cover:

❶ **When to Gather.**
   We'll identify key "apertures" or opportunities where research can play a valuable role.

❷ **How to Gather.**
   We'll introduce you to various available research tools.

❸ **What to Gather.**
   We'll discuss the types of information that need to be gathered and how to prepare a Research Plan.

❹ **Evaluation in Action.**
   We'll show you some real world examples of how it works.

❺ **Integration in Action.**
   As they say, *"when all you have is a hammer, every problem looks like a nail."* We'll show you instances where integration outside of traditional advertising helped marketers succeed.

❻ **Challenges for the Future.**
   Computers put out incredible amounts of data.
   Learning how to get useful information out of this data is a critical skill for tomorrow's marketers and advertisers.

"(Planning is) absolutely the most intriguing and though-provoking part of the advertising process. I'm always learning new things, digging for more information and then creatively presenting meaningful data which becomes the foundation of a campaign."
Jill Imig – Zenith Media

"Consumers are constantly changing, which causes the consumer/brand balance to constantly shift."
Ashley Watson – The Designory

"Day in and day out, I look at consumer trends, emerging technologies and use the forces of my inner geek to solve my clients' marketing problems."
Brian Kress – Click Here
(Richards Group)

"My job as an Account Planner is to creatively solve business problems with insight-driven strategies."
Crystal Anderson – Energy BBDO

"As an Hispanic marketer, I use the principles of account planning and research every day when putting together new business initiatives or providing points of view or recommendations to clients."
Augustine Jalomo –
Latino Marketing Consultant

"The art of account planning is not only for advertising. It's useful in any product or experience creation."
Jabari Hearn - Nike

A 10 Point Research Planning Process :

1. Become aware of an advertising problem.
2. Define and clarify the problem.
3. Secondary research: review existing knowledge.
4. Primary research: define one specific problem.
5. Prepare a detailed research plan.
6. Implement the research.
7. Process the data.
8. Interpret the data.
9. Communicate the results.
10. Apply the results to solve the advertising problem.

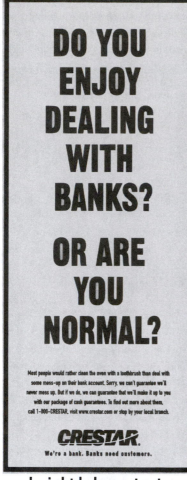

Insight Is Important.

Insight into the consumer and the product category is one of the ways great advertising gets produced.

Above, an insight into how people feel about banks leverages a campaign with the theme line "We're a bank. Banks need customers."

Below, insight into the purchase decision for a piece of jewelry.

So, let's get going.

A Practical Definition of Research.

A practical definition of research is simple: *"systematic gathering of information to answer a question or solve a problem."*

Conducting research can be as simple as looking up a word in a dictionary (hey, that's systematic).

It could involve observing consumers as they shop for or use a product (we call that **ethnography**).

It could be engaging in a quantitative demographic analysis of government census information, as you plan a campaign, to find out where your best prospects live and how many of them there are.

It could be obtaining feedback on a number of concepts or copy approaches for your new campaign.

It could be conducting a post-campaign online survey of consumers to determine their usage of and attitudes toward your brand and its advertising.

As you can see, that simple definition covers a lot of activities.

Insurance, Information, Insight, and Inspiration.

One way of viewing research is as "insurance" – insurance against making the wrong decision. The primary way we do this is to get very specific kinds of information that help us know more about the decisions we must make.

Throughout, we've talked about the importance of informed decision making. Research can, and does, help reduce the many uncertainties that surround something as complicated as the planning of an integrated campaign. It won't predict the future for you, but you'll have a better general idea of what might (or might not) happen tomorrow.

But it's not just avoiding negatives. Good research can give you true insight into the problem you're trying to solve. We'll take a look at how The Richards Group did it for Motel 6.

Finally, when you do get it right, you have a better chance finding the vision and inspiration that can result in a big win.

And it's a lot more fun to keep score when we're winning!

1. When to Gather.

THE STEREOTYPICAL VIEW OF ADVERTISING RESEARCH held by many is that of scorekeeping after a commercial or a campaign is up and running in the marketplace.

Sort of like the Nielsen overnight ratings – or the most-liked commercials the day after the Super Bowl – the next day you get a number, a score. One of the most common methods of keeping score is to measure product sales – but there is so much more to the research puzzle than that.

Four Ways to Get Smarter.

We always want to get smarter. Here are four critical research stages in the advertising development process that help us do that.

A. Planning Research. The information needed for upfront planning is critical. It may include last year's "scorekeeping" but more importantly it involves a substantial amount of additional new work and new thinking.

B. Developmental Research. Research can help develop thinking, strategies, insights, and advertising. With the now-widespread use of account planners in the US and the growing popularity of ethnographic and other social science approaches to studying consumer behavior, research has become an even more active partner in the advertising development process.

C. Implementation Research. With the increasing cost of television production and media, insurance can be a smart investment.

Here, we can test the implementation of the strategy we developed – usually tests of ad concepts or rough ads.

Sometimes there is a complete market test.

D. Measuring Results. Finally, when we've done our best in the marketplace, we need to see how we've done.

It's time to see what the score was. Maybe we won big, maybe we lost, or, more likely, it was somewhere in between.

We'll use that information to make next year even better.

Now, let's take the four "whens" one by one.

A. Planning Research.

THIS IS ALSO KNOWN AS BACKGROUND RESEARCH. Planning research, or background research, is critical to understanding the environment in which your next ad campaign will compete.

Essential to this environmental evaluation is a document generically referred to as the **situation analysis,** or marketing situation analysis – the compilation of material from a variety of sources gives us a firm idea of "what is" with respect to the marketplace and our product.

This was also covered in Chapter Eight on planning.

The brand-analysis checklist on the right is a useful starting point for developing background on your brand.

Electronic Resources.

You can gain access to much of the information you need for producing your situation analysis through electronic resources such as online databases or via the Internet.

Typically, the information will come from a combination of printed sources available in places such as libraries or company archives, customized research reports available through research vendors, competitive information gathered from the Web, and periodical articles and industry reports from online databases available primarily through public or university libraries.

Examples are *LexisNexis*, *Infotrac*, and *Hoover's*

These and other online resources are described on an advertising research wiki produced by SMU librarian Amy Turner. You can access the wiki at http://smuadresearch.pbwiki.com/.

"[I look at] tracking studies, attitude and usage data, or [conduct] consumer research that helps you understand where your communications can help impact the business."
Crystal Anderson – Energy BBDO

Brand-Analysis Checklist I:

This is a good way to get started collecting information on a brand:

I. Company.
- Location
- Organization and major activities; subsidiaries
- History
- Financial data
- Annual report
- Key personnel/managers
- Recent news from online database sources, newspapers, etc.

II. Category.
- Category definition
- Size of category in units, dollars, etc.
- Category history and growth
- Category growth projections
- Distribution channels/methods of distribution
- Major manufacturers/players
- Seasonal factors
- Regional factors
- Other relevant category factors
- Legal considerations
- Major trade publications/trade organizations in category

III. Products within Category.
- Share of category by product
- Product-form description (size, flavor, model, etc.)
- New product introductions
- Benefits and appeals of new products
- New packages, innovations, etc.
- Recent news about/affecting product category

Brand-Analysis Checklist II:

This is the second part of the brand-analysis checklist, focusing on the collection of marketing and advertising information for a brand.

Brand Analysis.
- Top brands by dollar or unit sales
- Growth trends of top brands
- Category share by country and by region
- Pricing trends
- Recent news about/affecting brand

Consumer Profile.
- Demographics of users
- Frequency of purchase/usage
- Place of purchase
- Heavy-user profile
- Awareness and attitudes toward brand
- Decision maker vs. purchaser
- Normal purchase cycle
- Brand loyalty/switching

Advertising.
Messages.
- Creative strategies of top brands
- Specific promises, appeals, claims, special effects
- Examples of past and current executions

Media.
- Category and brand spending
- Seasonality (by quarter)
- Regionality (spot buying)
- Media employed by top brands
- Spending patterns – flighting, continuous, etc.
- Spending compared with market share

Promotion.
- Promotions used in category
- Major brand promotion types and examples
- Success rates of promotions

Other Pertinent Information.
- Personal interviews
- Other information sources

Although you would need a special password to access specific subscription online databases through the SMU wiki, there's a good chance that your university subscribes to the same sources.

The Web: A Word of Warning.
Internet Web sites contain widely varied content produced by a wide array of individuals and organizations – some are more credible than others, as the SMU wiki points out in a section titled "Research Hygiene."

Always be careful to check the original source of the information you are quoting in your research. Is it simply someone's opinion, or is it the result of objective empirical research, etc.

Many Web sites contain highly filtered information that reflects the point of view of their publisher – take this fact into consideration when evaluating the information therein.

As You Read in Earlier Chapters…
Much of this has already been introduced to you in Chapter Eight. The planning process involves getting a lot of specific information about your brand and your category.

This is often the first kind of research you do.

Different Kinds of Information.
Campaign planning requires several different kinds of information:
- **Competitive Activity**
- **Market Share Data**
- **Current Examples of Advertising in the Category**
- **Advertising Expenditures**
- **Marketplace Trends**
- **Demographic Data**

The list goes on. Ultimately, this information must be organized into a coherent report.

Brand-Analysis Checklist.
An example of how to organize planning information is included in the Brand-Analysis Checklist on this page and the previous page.

The checklist (which has two parts) includes a series of topics for which secondary and primary research can supply information.

Taken together, these pieces of information form the backdrop for the upcoming ad campaign.

Remember, Secondary Research Comes First.

B. Developmental Research.

A FUNDAMENTAL SHIFT IN THINKING about the ability of research to contribute to better and more effective advertising came in the late 1980s and 1990s with the introduction of the account planning discipline in US agencies.

This British approach to planning an advertising campaign (see Chapters Two and Five) placed research emphasis squarely on the *development* of the creative and media strategies.

The underlying belief is that the gathering of information from consumers will lead to insights.

These insights will then lead to more relevant advertising concepts. This will lead to more effective messages, which will increase the chances that the advertising will accomplish its objectives as determined by post-campaign (evaluative) tests. You get the point.

Developing Strategies as Well as Ads.

Developmental research ultimately contributes to the formulation of the creative strategy, usually taking the form of a creative brief. Increasingly, though, US account planners are mining consumer insights not only for creative message development, but also for media strategies and development.

The major types of research activities which can be useful at the developmental stage are:

- **Focus Groups**
- **One-on-One Interviews**
- **Observation and Other Techniques.**

These will be discussed later in this chapter.

Creative Briefs and Planners.

A creative brief reflects the consumer insights determined through the developmental research and employs them as the basis for a creative strategy, which then acts as the blueprint for the creative executions to follow.

Account planners are responsible for making sure that all ads produced by the creative department are "on strategy."

Sometimes it takes a lot of thinking and work on the front end to get it right. On the right is an example of a creative brief and the creative approach that resulted for Motel 6.

The brief is all of that thinking, why we're advertising, who we're selling to, what is the single most persuasive idea…

That black box in the corner – a print ad with just that great headline in the center – is the result.

Note that even the very minimal production values of the ad reinforced some of the brand values of Motel 6.

As you can see, it takes a lot of work to get it right.

But if the information is good, creative people like David Fowler and The Richards Group creative team can take that information and make powerful advertising.

C. Implementation Research.

THE THIRD "APERTURE" FOR CONDUCTING RESEARCH gives us the opportunity to gather consumers' reactions to one or more creative or media strategies. This can be done by using focus groups, preliminary copytests (described in the next section), or experiments such as test markets or even laboratory tests.

Two Basic Forms.

Implementation research is likely to take two basic forms: Pre-tested concepts or ads and test markets or "pilot tests."

1. **Concepts or ads are pre-tested:** consumers are allowed to react to ad concepts or rough executions to determine which is

---

Motel 6 Creative Brief.

Warning: People don't like ads. People don't trust ads. People don't remember ads. How do we make sure this one will be different?

Why Are We Advertising?
To make people feel good about their decision to stay at Motel 6.

Who Are We Talking To?
Medium-income (HHI between $30,000 and $50,000) business and leisure travelers who pay for their own accommodations.

They intend to spend only a short amount of time in their motel room (either crashing for the night or planning to be out for the entire day).

They either don't have a lot of money to spend on a room, or they feel virtuous in saving money.

What Do They Currently Think?
"I feel embarrassed about staying at Motel 6 because it's the lowest price."

What Would We Like Them to Think?
"Staying at Motel 6 is the smart thing to do."

What Is the Single Most Persuasive Idea We Can Convey?
Motel 6 is the smart choice.

Why Should They Believe It?
At Motel 6 you get all you really need: a clean, comfortable room at the lowest price of any national chain.

You won't get any of those unnecessary features that cost you a fortune, like french-milled soap, chocolates on your pillow, or fancy drapes.

Are There Any Creative Guidelines?
Continue folksy down-to-earth style and tone of the current campaign.

(Source: *The Richards Group*)

When you're sleeping, we look just like those big fancy hotels.
Motel 6

Which Ad Pulled Best?

Ad A. *"Colgate Plus was designed by a team of scientists to accurately fit the shape of the human mouth…"*

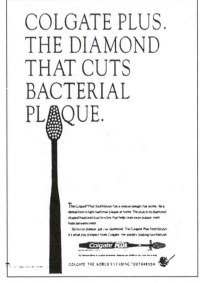

Ad B. *"The Colgate Plus toothbrush has a unique design that works like a dental tool to fight bacterial plaque at home…"*

Example 22 from Which Ad Pulled Best? *©NTC Books. Want to find out which ad worked better?*

Guess you'll have to buy the book!

most likely to have the greatest impact in the marketplace. Though it is the exception rather than the rule, sometimes mechanical devices can be used to obtain feedback from consumers. Researchers at NeuroFocus, located in Berkeley, California, use a combination of data from neurological and physiological equipment to determine which elements have the greatest effect on people who see them. Among the tools in their high-tech toolbox are an electroencephalograph, or EEG, which measures brain waves; an eye movement camera to track visual engagement; and galvanic skin response to gauge emotional reaction.

2. **Test markets or "pilot tests"** are set up to compare the effectiveness of the creative message, the media strategy, or both. Once common, test markets are less used because of the speed of competitive response. They also take time – check out the "good food" example on the following page.

D. Measuring Results.

THE FINAL OPPORTUNITY for gathering information regarding the advertising campaign is after the advertising is up and running in the marketplace.

Periodic measures of effectiveness can be taken during the course of the campaign, or as an after-campaign measurement.

Types of Post-Campaign Research.

Some of the most common ways marketers quantitatively evaluate the results of their ad campaigns are:

- **Standardized Copytesting**
- **Attitude, Awareness, and Usage (AAU) Studies**
- **Dollar Sales or Volumetric Analyses**
- **Behavioral ROI**

Standardized Copytesting.

Determining whether ads are on strategy is one of the most important activities in the creation of a successful campaign. Measuring the communications impact of an ad is known as **copytesting**.

Here is an argument for the importance of copytesting from *Advertising Works II* (from the Institute of Canadian Advertising).

"Copy is usually a more important decision than media or budget.

"Up-front decisions on advertising and promotion roles and objectives, market strategy, and positioning are all synergistic with effective copy generation.

"Top management should organize the advertising and promotion areas so that they can spend more on generating and testing highly varying creative program alternatives.

"Management should encourage variability in creative output by not overly constraining the creative teams and using creative teams that are most likely to have different creative approaches."

With all the possible variables, consistency of measurement and evaluation can become quite important.

If you've ever weighed yourself at home, then weighed in at the doctor's office and been told you're five pounds heavier, you can appreciate the value of consistent instrumentation and measurement.

Two scales, side by side, may not yield the same result. Just as a doctor might advise you to keep using the same scale to more accurately gauge your gains and losses, so advertisers often choose to stick with a particular type of measure to judge the effectiveness of their advertising over time.

Copytesting Services.

Examples of major national and international standardized copytesting firms are Starch Research, Gallup & Robinson, and Millward-Brown. Each has its own way of assigning a numeric score to an ad based on its ability to be noticed, understood, and liked.

For Starch, the measures of "noted" (those who remember seeing the ad in the magazine), "associated" (those who can associate the brand name with the ad), and "read most" (those who claim to have read most of the ad's copy) are used.

Colgate-Palmolive used the standardized copytesting services of Gallup & Robinson to test print ads in major national magazines over a period of years.

On the previous page are two examples for Colgate Plus toothbrushes from a great little book called *Which Ad Pulled Best?*

Can you guess which ad pulled better? That's the point.

You really do need some evidence from consumers to measure the relative strength of different appeals – fits the shape of your mouth or works like a dental tool at home.

For more information on advertising research services, see www.greenbook.org or starchresearch.com, gallup-robinson.com, or millwardbrown.com.

AAU Studies.

Periodic assessments of how a brand and its advertising are being perceived in the marketplace are useful in establishing brand presence, competitive noise, and market share.

An example of such a study is commonly called an **Awareness, Attitude, and Usage** survey (AAU), and is conducted among a

Questions:

These were the questions asked in the Amdro AAU study.

"Now, thinking about fire ant control products, which one brand of fire ant control product first comes to mind?"

"What other brands of fire and control products can you think of? What others?"

"For which brands of fire ant control products have you seen or heard advertising in the past two to three months? What others?"

Base = Total Respondents
Wave I	n = 525
Wave II	n = 525
Wave III	n = 526

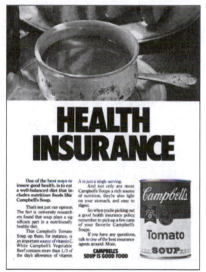

Test Marketing.

Test markets can be good insurance. The *"Soup Is Good Food"* campaign was put into test market by Campbell's.

There were no quick dramatic results, but the campaign remained in test market for over a year.

Slowly, it became clear that the new approach was generating increased sales and improved attitudes.

Based on the test market results, it became the national campaign for a number of years.

Read the whole story in *The Care and Feeding of Ideas* by Bill Backer, founder of Backer & Spielvogel – the agency that created the campaign.

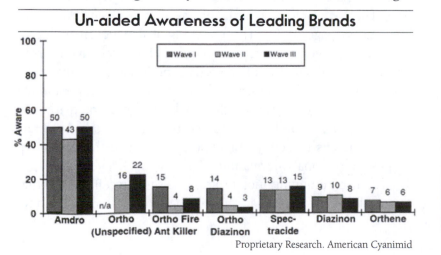

Un-aided Awareness of Leading Brands

Proprietary Research. American Cyanimid

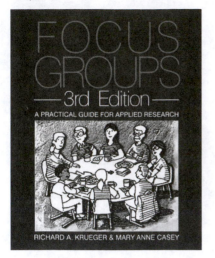

Focus Groups: A Practical Guide for Applied Research, by Richard A. Krueger, contains a step-by-step approach for planning and conducting a successful focus group – from recruitment and discussion design through analysis. From Sage Publications.

Focus Group Agenda.

Fire Ant Killer:

There were seven segments:
1. The Self-Treatment Process
2. Category Evaluation/Brand Awareness
3. Brand Evaluations
4. Advertising Awareness
5. Purchase Decision Process/ Influencers/Retail Environment
6. Packaging
7. *Amdro* :30 TV commercial

Here is the detailed outline:

1. The Self-Treatment Process
   - What is it like to have fire ants on your lawn?
   - What are the challenges/issues you face in treating for fire ants?
   - How did your experience with fire ants last year compare with previous years?
2. Category Evaluation/Brand Awareness
   - What are the product choices for treating fire ants? Types: liquid, bait (probe for level of understanding of bait vs. contact), powder, granules, etc.
   - Which brands have you used? (probe for loyalty)

(Continued on next page.)

random sample of consumers, sometimes by telephone interview, but increasingly by online panel surveys.

The preceding chart is an example of the results of an AAU study for Amdro fire ant killer. This chart shows the "un-aided awareness" of leading brands through three waves.

The result of this research is that *"Amdro continues to dominate un-aided awareness of fire ant pesticide brands, with half of the respondents mentioning it on an un-aided basis."*

This research also monitors the competition. *"Ortho also has high un-aided awareness, with more than one-third of the respondents mentioning the brand name by itself or a specific Ortho product."*

Sales or Volumetric Analyses.

All clients "keep score" by way of periodic sales reports, which can take the form of retail sales figures, warehouse removal data, or orders placed to a central facility. Results can be expressed as dollar amounts or in terms of volume of units sold.

Although advertising is rarely the only factor in sales success (or failure), it is common for advertisers to look at how advertising expenditures and sales figures correlate.

Test Marketing.

Test markets are an important way to see how products and advertising messages perform in the marketplace on a limited scale, such as a single city or area or several cities. Results of these real-world trials are used to evaluate and adjust campaign elements before rolling out nationally.

The speed of competitive response has made this tougher.

Today, competitors can "read" a test market quickly, and by the time the test is over, a competitive response or product improvement has been prepared.

Behavioral ROI

Today, more than ever, communicators in the digital marketing world have the tools and metrics that allows them to gauge almost immediately the effectiveness of their online advertising and promotion. Services now offer data about whether creative messages result in online transactions, search, or other behaviors on the part of consumers who are served (translate "exposed to") them (see "The New Gold Standard," Brian Morrissey, *Adweek*, February 4, 2008, page 30-31). This matching of ad exposure with user behavior is providing enormous amounts of data for advertisers to use in fine-tuning both online ad distribution and creative strategy alternatives. This deluge of data brings with it some unique analytic challenges, as we will discuss later. Behavioral marketing also has raised a number of important issues for both marketers and researchers related to consumer privacy and the ownership and use of personal information.

Of course, communication professionals in direct mail and other forms of direct-response advertising, such as infomercials, have always been able to gather behavioral feedback from their efforts. An infomercial runs, the phone at the fulfillment company rings, and if the infomercial was the only piece of marketing communication used to promote the product, a cause-effect relationship can be made between the running of the commercial and the resulting sales. Such scenarios have long provided instant data regarding the commercial's Return-on-Investment for the advertiser. (They do not, however, provide insight into the specific reasons why a consumer picked up the phone, or didn't. Neither do the online analytics, for that matter. For this type of diagnostic information we may need Developmental or Implementation Research as discussed earlier.)

2. How to Gather.

EARLIER WE DISCUSSED THE IMPORTANCE of using secondary research to form the situation analysis. This section will focus on primary research – that which we produce ourselves by employing one or more research designs or data-gathering methods.

Qualitative and Quantitative.

Two basic types of primary research are available.

Qualitative research, which typically is conducted in a relatively short period of time among relatively small, non-random samples.

Quantitative research, which is typically conducted using large and preferably randomly selected samples.

Qualitative Approaches.

Here are some interesting ways research people have developed to discover consumer opinions about products and brands.

Since people don't usually go around thinking about these things, these techniques help them focus or uncover their feelings and attitudes. In fact, the first technique we'll discuss is called the **focus group.**

Focus Groups.

Focus group research is one of the most commonly used qualitative data-gathering methods.

Though definitions may vary slightly, a basic focus group consists of a group of 8 to 12 carefully chosen members of the target audience who are convened for an interview/discussion of up to two hours led by a moderator who follows a pre-approved discussion guide.

Often these sessions are conducted in focus group research facilities whose interview rooms can be viewed by client or agency personnel through a one-way mirror.

A focus group can be quite versatile – in addition to discussing a product, participants can also view existing or prospective advertising, sample new or existing products, or engage in a number of projective techniques discussed in the section below.

Focus Group (Cont.)

- Overall, are fire ant treatments effective?
- How do you define effectiveness?
- How long does it take to treat fire ants? Are some products faster/more effective?
- What are the major brands of fire ant treatments?

3. Brand Evaluations
- Probe for images of Spectracide, Amdro, Ortho Fire Ant Killer, GreenLight, Orthene
  a. present board featuring each brand name
  b. first words that come to mind for each
  c. brand collages (as time permits)
- Does the cost of fire ant products affect your purchase decision?
- Which are the most expensive? Least expensive?
- Which are the best value?

4. Advertising Awareness
- Have you heard/seen any ads in the past year for _____?
- Describe advertising heard/seen
- What was the major message the ad was trying to communicate?

5. Purchase Decision Process/ Influencers/Retail Environment
- How/when do you go about purchasing fire ant treatments (when problem occurs, beforehand, etc.)?
- How/when do you typically decide which brand to buy? (beforehand, in store, etc.)
- Where do you purchase fire ant treatments?
- Describe the "fire ant section" of the store (shelves, displays, etc.).
- Do you consult with store clerks for information? Are they knowledgeable?
- Are there other sources you consult? Probe for influencers/ sources of information.

6. Packaging
- Participants examine current category packages

(Continued on next page)

Focus Group (Cont.)

- Which type of package do you like the best? Why?
- Could packaging be improved? How? (Note: Participants may resume brand discussion upon encountering packages.)

7. Amdro :30 TV commercial

- What is the main message this TV commercial is trying to communicate?
- What do you like or dislike about this commercial?
- Is this message relevant to you?

Proprietary Research
© American Cyanamind

"My role is a fusion of account planning and media planning. We analyze media touchpoints and provide consumer insight through research and focus groups."

Jill Imig

Why We Buy.

Paco Underhill has built quite a career by observing how shoppers shop.

In his book, *Why We Buy*, he talks about various social behaviors that occur in a store.

You can read more about it in Malcolm Gladwell's "The Science of Shopping" at www.malcolmgladwell.com.

This article is also featured in *Readings in Account Planning*, courtesy the author.

One-on-One Interviews.

In situations where it is either difficult to convene a focus group or when the topic might not be one easily handled in a group setting, a researcher might opt to conduct one-on-one interviews (sometimes called depth interviews) with selected members of the target audience.

Upper management personnel or doctors or other busy professionals are often interviewed one-on-one at their convenience, though obviously it is more time-consuming to hold a large number of individual interview sessions than a small number of group interviews.

Another instance where one-on-one interviews might be recommended would be when the subject might be considered personal or sensitive – e.g., financial planning for retirement, or halitosis.

Observation.

Anthropologists, and, more specifically, ethnographers, have long used the technique of observation to study groups of people and their habits. Advertisers, too, are keenly interested in studying groups of consumers and their habits, for somewhat different reasons.

Advertising, of course, is built on the pillars of the social sciences, so the fact that ad researchers and account planners would employ ethnographic techniques such as observation is not surprising. True ethnographic studies usually involve a researcher engaged in field work that takes the form of living among people and experiencing their surroundings, interactions, language, rituals, and so on. And true ethnographic studies are normally conducted for a year or more, sometimes decades, whereas advertising related studies rarely are fielded for longer than a month, and many times take a week or less.

Advertising researchers and planners who borrow from this interpretation of ethnographic data collection can record their "field notes" in writing, and also can record their experiences, surroundings, conversations, and interviews by way of audio tape, video cameras, or still photography.

Working for Chupa Chups USA, manufacturer of Pop Rocks, Crazy Dips, and other candy brands, Southern Methodist University ad research students observed dozens of 9- to 11-year-old children as they made candy purchases in mass merchandise outlets and convenience stores.

Four Eating Styles.

Later, they observed the children as they consumed the candy.

Four eating styles were observed.

A number of ways of opening the Pop Rocks package were also observed. This sort of information can be very helpful as you're working to find advertising and product approaches that appeal to your target.

Projective Techniques for Qualitative Interviews.

While a direct line of questioning is useful for gathering certain types of information from consumers (e.g., *"What was the last brand of jeans you purchased for yourself?"*), sometimes the real brand insights are gleaned from less direct, more creative responses to projective lines of questioning.

Projective techniques allow an interview participant to express brand attitudes indirectly through pictures or words or picture/word combinations.

Examples of projective techniques are:
- **Brand Collages**
- **Storytelling**
- **Word Association**
- **Drawing**

Let's take a look at these interesting approaches.

Brand Collage.

Few exercises hold as great a potential for zeroing in on the often subtle differences among brands than the brand collage.

Respondents are provided with hundreds of assorted images clipped from magazines and are asked to choose and mount on a blank sheet of paper those which *"best represent your idea of Brand X."*

At the end of the collage exercise, participants are encouraged to explain why they chose the images they did.

In evaluating and interpreting collages, the researcher looks for themes and trends across responses.

Storytelling.

It may sound silly to ask a focus group respondent to write a story about a pair of Reebok basketball shoes visiting the grocery store – *"What time of day did the shoes go food shopping? What conveyance did they arrive in? Which brands did they buy?"* – but it's actually a highly calculated and disarming way of communicating the nuances of brand image and personality using grocery aisles as the responsorial canvas.

If similar grocery shopping stories were produced by consumers for Nike, Adidas, or other brands of athletic shoes, imagine the opportunity for comparison of brand images.

Word Association.

One of the most instructive methods of getting to the bottom-line evaluation (i.e., *"Tell me what you really think?"*) of a product, service, person, or advertisement is to give a consumer a one-word opportunity to size up the entity in question.

One useful way to structure the word association exercise is to ask the consumer to write or say out loud the *first* word that comes to mind after being presented with the brand name, product, or ad.

In marketing communications, first impressions may mean the difference between consumer acceptance or rejection, so the importance of "first-word" associations should not be underestimated.

Four Eating Styles:

Eating Styles

The Exhibitionist

Tight-Lipped

Tingly Tongues

Sticky Fingers

Ways to open Pop Rocks

The Perfectionist

The Terminator

The Shredder

Lobster Claws

Developing New Ad Ideas.

Above is a brand collage from a "Got Milk?" focus group.

Below is an award-winning ad in the series.

got milk?

Word Association Gets "Good Vibrations."

You might not remember the "Good Vibrations" campaign for Sunkist Orange Soda, but it was very successful. Teens on the beach enjoyed Sunkist Orange Soda to the classic tune of the Beach Boys "Good Vibrations."

Word association helped them get there. First, they asked the target – teens – what Sunkist meant. The answer – California – made sense. Sunkist was a California-based orange-growing co-op.

Then, they asked teens what images were inspired by California – answer – the beach. Finally, they asked what thought "the beach" inspired. Answer – The Beach Boys.

That's the logic that created "Good Vibrations" for Sunkist.

Internet Questionnaire:

from Decision Analyst, Inc.

Types of studies available include:
• Advertising tracking studies
• Awareness, trial, and usage studies (ATUs)
• Conceptor™ new product concept testing
• CopyTest® for radio
• CopyTest® for print ads
• CopyTest® for TV storyboards
• CopyCheck® for early-stage creative
• Customer satisfaction monitoring
• Employee satisfaction tracking
• Package graphics testing
• Optima™ product testing
• Market segmentation studies
• New product concept testing
• Promotion concept testing
• Brand name evaluation
• Strategic positioning studies

If "confusing" is the first word used to describe a new ad or strategy statement, the advertiser needs to rethink how to effectively communicate the brand message.

Drawing.

Qualitative research presents a situation in which the expression *"a picture is worth a thousand words"* most definitely applies.

Allowing participants to express ideas about products or brands through paper-and-pencil illustrations often prompts a quality of response that might not have occurred with direct questioning.

Illustrating is particularly useful when interviewing young children who are not yet adept at verbalizing experiences.

Quantitative.

Quantitative techniques are designed to produce results and information in which you can have a high degree of confidence.

Part of this is due to the larger numbers (quantities) of respondents. The other factor is the design of the research.

Surveys.

A sample survey involves measuring a part of a population (called a **sample**) in order to estimate the characteristics of the entire group (as opposed to a census, which involves measuring each member of the population).

This enables a researcher to obtain information about products, consumers, and markets by measuring a relatively small percentage of the overall group.

Sample surveys are referred to frequently in the advertising industry for information about audience sizes, product usage, and total market size.

There are a number of syndicated research reports. There are three, in particular, you should become familiar with.

Nielsen, MRI, and SMRB.

The Nielsen ratings, which are intended to represent the national audience for network programs, are based on a sample of only a few thousand television households.

Nielsens are the current standard for television audience measurement. They also produce other important marketing research related to product sales.

Mediamark Research, Inc. (MRI) and *Simmons Market Research Bureau* (SMRB) provide this information through annual surveys of 20,000 randomly selected households.

Samples: Random vs. Non-Random.

In order to ensure the **projectability** of findings from a sample to the larger population, a randomly selected sample should be used and a sufficient number of responses should be collected.

Randomness ensures that each member of a population has an equal chance of being selected for inclusion in the sample – that no bias is employed in choosing who will be interviewed or measured.

An example of a population could be women 25–49 who have ordered children's clothing through specific mail-order catalogs.

An example of a sample would be 500 such women randomly chosen from a list of the children's clothing catalog databases.

Professional survey research firms can advise an advertiser about types and sizes of samples and the acceptable degree of sample error that will result.

A list of sources to consult about the technical aspects of sample surveys is included at the end of this chapter.

Questionnaire Design.

Once the sample specifications are decided upon, a questionnaire can be used to measure the desired characteristics of the group.

A **questionnaire** is an instrument of measurement and, as such, consists of individual items designed to measure specific variables (e.g., awareness of particular brands of children's clothing).

Writing items for a questionnaire begins with formulating question objectives, such as *"to measure brand awareness of cellular telephone services."*

After specifying the objective for the question or questions, then an appropriate questionnaire item can be created.

The section titled "3. What to Gather" gives examples of specific questions used in advertising surveys.

Advertising Surveys on the Internet.

The Internet has made possible almost instantaneous concept and copytesting possibilities for advertisers.

Through pre-screened Internet panels, target-audience consumers are invited to view advertising or advertising concepts over the Internet and then answer a series of questions online.

An advertiser can receive topline results of the Internet survey that same day.

You can look at an example of Internet advertising survey research by Decision Analyst, Inc., featured on the previous page.

Experiments.

When the research question asks about cause and effect (e.g., *"Does twice as much advertising result in twice as many sales?"*), experimental design is needed.

An experiment is a highly choreographed research study in which the effects of one or more independent variables (such as ad spending levels) are measured by noting changes in one or more dependent variables (such as ad awareness, brand attitude, or sometimes sales).

Controlled Environments or the Real World.

Some experiments take place in controlled environments such as laboratories – to determine, for instance, whether certain layout formats achieve the desired eye movement around the page, on the computer screen, or on the store shelf (for an example, see Perception Research Services, www.prsresearch.com).

Experiment: Ad Specialties vs. Discount.

Table I. Group Activity by Month.

Active for	Ad Spec. Group (%)	Discount Group (%)	Control (n=97) (%)
1 mo.	39.4	32.3	58.8
2 mo.	16.0	12.9	12.4
3 mo.	6.4	14.0	8.2
4 mo.	7.4	12.9	6.2
5 mo.	4.3	6.5	1.0
6 mo.	6.4	4.3	3.1
7 mo.	7.4	8.6	7.3
8 mo.	12.8	8.6	7.3
Activity in 5 or more months	30.9	28.0	14.5
Activity in 6 or more months	26.6	21.5	13.5
Total active months	317	315	231

Table II. Avg. Spending per Mo.

Group	$ per active month ($)	Total spending months ($)
Ad Spec.	66.82*	317
Discount	51.75*	315
Control	38.69	231

* Indicates significant differences at 0.05. Ad Specialties group had significantly higher spending than the Discount and Control groups. Discount Group had significantly higher spending than the Control Group.

Table III. Avg. Total Spending.

Group:	Average Total ($)
Ad Specialties	218.95*
Discount	172.85*
Control	91.73

* Indicates significant differences at 0.05. Ad Specialties and Discount groups had significantly higher total spending figures than the Control Group.

(Source: Kendrick, 1998 *Journal of Services Marketing*.)

People Who
Aren't Like Me.
(and What I Learned from Them)

A Qualitative Research Assignment. The purpose of this project is to study behavior, motivations, language, and other issues associated with product usage or behavior you do not engage in yourself.

It's an opportunity for you to immerse yourself in something you have no personal experience with.

The assignment involves interviewing and observing participants, analyzing the information you gather, and communicating findings.

Keep in mind this isn't a large-scale sample survey. You're looking for insights, trends, motivations, processes, consumer "rituals," consumer language for the product/category, and so forth.

Suggested Activities:

1. Determine the desired product usage/behavior you wish to study. (Playing computer games if you do not play, coloring one's hair if you don't, shaving one's face if you don't, etc.) NOTE: Cigarette smoking – or other addictions – are NOT good choices. Trust me on this.

Depending on how extensive this assignment is, your instructor may wish you to conduct secondary research before participant selection and interviews.

2. Interview a small number of people. Since you'll only be required to interview a small number, consider ways you might refine your screening questions to obtain a more homogeneous group of subjects. For instance, try not to mix heavy users (professional skydivers) with light users (jumped out of a plane once).

Go with one or the other.

3. Write a series of screening questions to qualify your potential participants based on the criteria established in #1 and #2 above.

4. Recruit your participants. Arrange visits/interviews with them, as well as observation of others. You need to find a balance.

(Continued on next page)

These types of research studies are rather expensive and, not surprisingly, they are fairly rare.

They may involve the use of a mechanical measurement device, such as an eye camera – which tracks and records eye movement around a page.

Many experiments in advertising and marketing communication are conducted in the real world, so the effects of independent variables can be gauged under actual marketplace conditions.

Such field experiments are expensive, and sometimes they can be quite time consuming, but their results can be very instructive and strategically useful.

Example: Price Promotion versus Promotional Products.

One such field experiment was conducted for the purpose of determining whether price promotion (using discounts) or imprinted promotional products (also known as specialty advertising) would result in greater consumer loyalty to a dry cleaning establishment.

Using a field experiment design involving two treatment groups and one control group, researchers monitored the number of dry cleaner visits and the dollar amount of each visit for nine consecutive months.

The results were almost counterintuitive to what one might expect in the heavily price-promotion oriented dry cleaning business.

The experimental group that periodically received imprinted promotional items (such as sewing kits, stress relievers, and notepads) visited as frequently or more frequently than did the experimental group that received periodic discounts, and they spent as much or more per month than the discount group.

Both the promotional product group and the discount group demonstrated more loyalty (in both sales and visits) than the control group, who received only a letter thanking them for being a customer.

As you can see from the tables of results, the control group fared far worse than either the promotional products or the discount group.

Results convinced the management of the dry cleaning business to initiate customer retention programs, several of which involved the distribution of promotional products.

The Importance of Good Information.

A lot of time and trouble goes into designing, executing, and then measuring the results of an experiment like the one just described.

But, if you were running a dry cleaning business, or any kind of business, and wanted to know how you could improve it, this kind of information is tremendously valuable.

3. What to Gather.

VARIABLES THAT CAN BE MEASURED in the course of conducting advertising research range from simple awareness of a brand or an ad to actual purchase, and all steps in between. Behavioral ROI, discussed earlier, is considered the ultimate way of assessing an ad's impact, but many other advertising- and brand-related measures also provide important pieces of the planning puzzle.

Much advertising research is involved with determining what if any communication impact an advertisement might have had.

Such measures include:
• **Brand Awareness**
• **Ad Awareness**
• **Brand Knowledge/Information**
• **Ad Knowledge/Information**
• **Attitude Toward the Brand**
• **Attitude Toward the Ad**
• **Purchase Conviction/Intention**
• **Actual Purchase/Sales.**

Let's take a look at these measures.

Ad/Brand Awareness.

Question Objective: To measure awareness of television advertising for high-tech companies.

Recall Question: *"Please list the names of the cell phone company or companies you remember having seen advertised on television during the past week."*

Recognition Question: *"Which of the following cell phone companies do you remember seeing television advertising for during the past week?"*

___AT&T
___T-Mobile
___Sprint Nextel
___Verizon
___U.S. Cellular
___other (please specify: _____)

Ad/Brand Knowledge/Information.

Question Objective: To measure the perceptions of price promotion for cell phone calling plans.

"Which of the following cell phone calling plans is currently offering unlimited calling after 7pm?"

___AT&T
___T-Mobile
___Sprint Nextel
___Verizon
___U.S. Cellular
___other (please specify: _____)

"Not Like Me." (Cont.)

The balance will be between talking to people, observing their behavior and the behavior of others, and whether to participate in the activity yourself (not required, do so at your own risk!).

I suggest five depth interviews of at least 30 minutes each with some additional observation.

5. Compose a discussion guide. Your guide should include sections addressing: detailed description of behavior/product usage (including use occasions), specific language associated with the behavior/product usage, motivations involved in using the product, history of involvement with the product, brand considerations, and issues associated with product usage.

Often the use of a deprivation-type question is useful. It's also helpful to use one or more projective techniques such as word association, storytelling, collage, etc. to add texture and depth to your analysis.

6. Conduct your interviews. I suggest one-on-ones or dyads. Consider tape recording, photos, videos, or taking notes to facilitate your report-writing.

7. Compile and analyze your "data."

8. Write your report. Use a standard research report format such as the following:

Title

Study Objectives

Method – How participants selected, how information was gathered.

Findings – Main "learnings" and INSIGHTS (Follow the discussion guide outline for this section, which will be longer than other sections).

Conclusions

Suggestions for Future Research

• **Papers will be 5-10 pages.**

• **Oral reports need not be boring.** Successful reports have included "dressing the part," video segments, audio interviews, role-playing... the list goes on. Use your imagination to communicate your insights!

Going Global for Nike.

I work in the Global Consumer Cultures Department as a Global Consumer Strategist at Nike Global Headquarters in Beaverton, OR.

I work on the Basketball and Athletic Training categories in partnership with the Global Brand Management to help them define, develop, and maintain an ongoing relationship with their core consumers. I also assist with any qualitative research and strategy needs.

So far, in my year and a half at Nike, I've worked on everything from Brand and Athlete positioning to new product development to retail consumer experience design.

The Consumer Decides.

At Nike we've created several company maxims. Number 5 is "The Consumer Decides," which means that with today's sophisticated and empowered consumers, we need to make sure we maintain a two-way dialog in order to understand the infinite variety of their cultural views.

When we understand our consumers and the context in which they live, we can confidently create products and experiences that speak to kids on a practical and emotional level.

The art of account planning is not only for advertising. It's useful in any product or experience creation.

—Jabari Hearn

Brand Attitude.

Question Objective: To determine which flavor of a new ice cream is preferred in a taste test.

"Which flavor of ice cream did you enjoy the most overall?"

___Banana Nut Crunch
___Mocha Roca Munch
___Chocolate Bungee Marshmallow
___Caramel Peanut Topple
___Cherry Almond Avalanche

Conviction/Purchase Intent.

Question Objective: To determine purchase intent at the current retail price.

"How likely would you be to buy the flavor you enjoyed the most if it were available at your local grocery for $4.59 per half-gallon?"

___I would definitely buy it
___I would probably buy it
___I'm not sure whether I would buy it
___I would probably not buy it
___I would definitely not buy it

Purchase/Sales.

In an average month, how much do you spend on professional laundry and dry cleaning services?

___none – I do not use these services
___less than $10
___$11–$20
___$21–$30
___more than $30

4. Evaluation in Action.
A Case Study – Visit Florida.

Now we'd like to show you how it works when it all works together. The first example we're going to show you was done by students just like you.

It was done by the 2004 winners of the American Advertising Federation National Student Advertising Competition (AAF/NSAC) – Southern Methodist University (SMU). The client was Florida Tourism. The faculty adviser was Dr. Peter Noble.

Let's take a look at how they put it together.

Background.

Florida, already one of the most favored destinations in the US, challenged the 250 AAF university chapters to devise an integrated marketing campaign designed to increase travel to Florida's wide range of destinations (not just Disney World) by a wide range of travelers (not just the typical family with 1.7 smiling children).

Florida has quite a few different places to go – two coasts, with great diversity in accommodations, attractions, and lifestyle.

It attracts a wide range of demographic and psychographic groups – grandparents, families, gay/lesbian groups, and, of course, college students on spring break.

What unified these diverse groups and destinations?

And then, how could you communicate to this varied and wide-ranging audience in a focused and inclusive way?

Now you start to see the research challenge. Here's how the more than 150 schools accepted Florida's challenge, and the SMU student ad agency approached the problem.

The Research Plan.

The Plans Book (a big deal in AAF/NSAC) first developed a Situation Analysis. Just like in Chapter 8.

Then, they developed a Research Plan.

Research Objectives.

- Determine the current perception of the state of Florida and what target market best fits the state.
- Detect the lifestyle and purchase trends in order to gain insight into traveler psychology, leisure, travel trends, and the tourism industry.
- Identify influences on target market travel purchase behavior which may encourage choosing Florida as a leisure destination.
- Discover which characteristics of Florida most appeal to the target market.
- Determine media that impact the target market leisure destination decisions.

Research Strategies.

- Gather information from traditional and online surveys.
- Conduct focus groups and one-to-one interviews with previous Florida visitors and travel industry influencers.
- Analyze published information relevant to the travel industry.

Secondary Research.

- Determined the trends and niches within the market.
- Identified influences of the target market who chose Florida as their leisure destination.
- Investigated traveler psychology, purchase cycle behavior, consumer leisure expenditures, experiential and destination marketing trends, and tourism promotion and marketing tools.
- Researched consumer decision-making behaviors.
- Conducted formal content analysis of creative and media strategies in destination advertising.

Primary Research.

- Conducted nationwide online leisure travel survey with 500+ previous Florida visitors.
- Interviewed Generation Xers, Baby Boomers, and families.
- Held key speaker sessions with travel industry experts and marketing veterans.
- Conducted interviews with a variety of leisure travelers.

It's the Behavior, Stupid!

The Next Stage of IMC Evolution. UNC professor Robert Lauterborn, co-author of the influential *Integrated Marketing Communication: Pulling It Together And Making It Work*, makes some observations on where it's all headed.

His current concern is that IMC has become more of a MarCom/media selection process – management of an expanding menu of MarCom options.

And, in many ways that is true.

Today, IMC is very much a process of prioritization and selection. And, given the continually expanding menu of options, it's hard to argue against this approach.

But Lauterborn thinks there's a better way.

Enter ICBM.

His acronym is for Integrated Customer Behavior Management.

Programs should have specific, measurable, behavioral objectives.

Hard to argue.

While IMC was originally developed as a problem-solving approach, it has become a comparison of the relative effectiveness of different marketing communications solutions.

In addition, the inertia of whatever was done last fiscal year usually has huge impact on the plans for this fiscal year.

The key? Truly integrating the consumer into the process. Moving from MarCom integration to organizing around the desired behavior.

Naked Thinking.

In a way, the approach taken by planning group, Naked Communications, is getting at this problem from a slightly different direction.

They focus on message – but messaging with a behavioral outcome. They ask, What is the right message communicated in the right way through the right channel to effectively reach the right consumer. It is a short, but critical, step from there to motivating the right behavior.

(Continued on next page.)

It's the Behavior (Cont.)

As a beginning, we probably need to address the behavior within agencies and marketing departments, where an ad is the answer almost before the question is asked.

But, Professor Lauterborn is right.

What is the behavior we wish to inspire?

It's the behavior.

Creative for a Reason.

Good research makes it easier to explain good creative.

Here, the silhouettes are designed to let people tap into their own memories – as opposed to having them try to relate to smiling models.

The print, television, and outdoor executions had good graphic consistency and the media plan concentrated the dollars on the right audiences in the right markets at the right time.

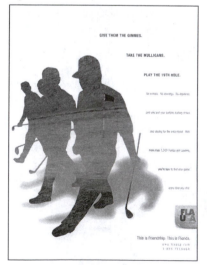

A group of golfers in silhouette. Copy is golf-oriented and ends "This is Friendship. This is Florida." Ads like this would go in magazines with an upscale male skew.

(Continued on next page.)

Research Results.

And here's what the team discovered.

Leisure Travel Index.

- 90% of participants have previously visited Florida.
- 62% of previous visitors fly to Florida and 49% stay in moderately priced hotels.
- 77% of participants travel with their immediate families.
- 73% of participants are influenced by vacation recommendations of their family and friends.
- 95% of participants tell their family and friends about their leisure vacations.
- 86% of participants feel that activities and attractions are more important than price (48%), convenience (46%), and accommodations (58%), when choosing a leisure destination.
- 71% of participants plan their vacations 1–6 months in advance.
- 92% of participants agree that the money spent on their vacation was "worth it."

Insight: The target market must address previous Florida visitors that are most likely to fly to their destination, travel with family, and prefer a vacation experience over price, convenience, and accommodations.

Focus Groups & One-to-One Interviews.

- Previous visitors, who have not vacationed in Florida within the past five years, have a "been there, done that" attitude.
- Most previous visitors are unaware of the variety of activities and attractions in Florida.

Insight: Get previous Florida visitors to come back to Florida and show them through advertising, promotions, and public relations what they can do in Florida.

Key Observations.

Florida needs to recognize the changing demographics of American leisure travelers and identify with their needs.

This shift in focus will set Florida apart from its competitors.

Targeting leisure travelers who vacation in party sizes will more likely result in increased paid lodging while in Florida.

An advertising campaign that recognizes and speaks to the value leisure travelers place on relationships will encourage them to come back more frequently or stay longer.

Developing "Togetherness."

The SMU Team chose a proprietary research approach – the Praxis Denominator Model™ to work their way to the next step. It's a research-based creative tool.

It assists in studying diverse groups to determine common problems, interests, or desires in order to help focus creative strategies. The model illustrates the process of identifying the VISIT FLORIDA target market. The demographics, leisure travel motivations and vacation behaviors of the target market demonstrate how the demographically diverse target market shares one common goal.

They called this group "Relationship Travelers" and the common bond was simply stated as "Togetherness." Here's how it looks as a presentation model.

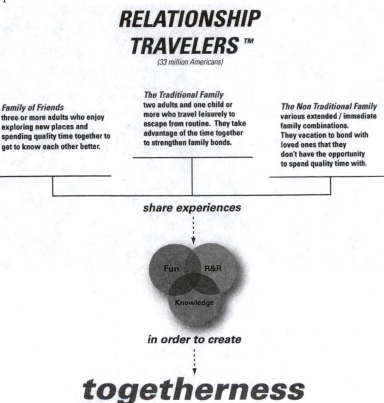

RELATIONSHIP TRAVELERS ™

(33 million Americans)

Family of Friends
three or more adults who enjoy exploring new places and spending quality time together to get to know each other better.

The Traditional Family
two adults and one child or more who travel leisurely to escape from routine. They take advantage of the time together to strengthen family bonds.

The Non Traditional Family
various extended / immediate family combinations. They vacation to bond with loved ones that they don't have the opportunity to spend quality time with.

share experiences

Fun R&R Knowledge

in order to create

togetherness

Research led to a clear description of the target mentality and values that all these groups held in common.

The Creative Solutions.

Focused research doesn't really limit effective creativity.

Rather, it provides a solid platform, so that you can reach in the right direction.

In this case, the creative team came to some fairly simple, but unusual answers.

For example, they didn't end up using either people or destinations – kind of surprising for travel advertising.

Rather, they focused on the idea of Florida being the place where you could be with the other people who were important in your life.

They worked to develop ads where that wide variety of potential travelers could read themselves – and their family or friends – into the thought of a Florida vacation.

And remember, research told us that they were already familiar with Florida.

We didn't have to teach them something new, we had to remind them of what they already knew and felt.

It must have connected with what the client already knew and felt, because of all the proposals by student agencies coast to coast, this is the one they chose.

Smart research had a lot to do with it.

Cooperative advertising with other related marketers (such as Alamo car rentals) was also recommended to expand the impact economically.

The FLA/USA graphic was another consistent device that was used on everything from ads to orange peels.

Relationship Traveling & IMC. In addition to traditional media, there was a comprehensive Internet campaign and some unique PR and promotional tactics.

For example, there were palm tree heat lamps in Northern cities, peel-off FLA/USA stickers on oranges – with the chance to "Win a Slice of Florida Life," and special promotions aimed at key influencers, like travel agencies.

Want to Know More about the AAF/NSAC?

Go to the American Ad Federation (AAF) Web site: www.aaf.org.

Know about ARF?

It's the Advertising Research Federation (ARF). Their Web site is: www.arfsite.org.

Learjet Creative Brief.

Warning: People don't like ads. People don't trust ads. People don't remember ads. How do we make sure this one will be different?

Why Are We Advertising?

To create excitement about the Learjet 60 as a cost-effective solution to prospects' need for a trans-continental jet and to reinforce Learjet's high performance mystique.

Who Are We Talking To?

High-level corporate executives, corporate fleet managers, and chief pilots who need a corporate jet with trans-continental capability. Learjet buyers are motivated by emotion, but must justify their decision to peers and constituents in rational, financial terms.

What Do They Currently Think?

"I'd love to own a *Learjet* and get that kind of high performance. But you pay a price: either in dollars, in range, or in comfort. I think they have a transcon jet now, but it's probably just a longer version of their old 55."

What Would We Like Them to Think?

"*Learjet* does have a jet that will fly my longer missions, and it's not just a stretched version of the 55. And it's cheaper to fly than any transcontinental Hawker, Falcon, or Citation 10."

What Is the Single Most Persuasive Idea We Can Convey?

Learjet performance in a cost-effective transcontinental jet.

Why Should They Believe It?

- Transcontinental range (2,750 nautical miles) is the highest of jets with comparable performance.
- Seats up to eight, stand-up room for passengers, stand-up private lavatory.
- Learjet allure.

Are There Any Creative Guidelines?

- Call to action: "Call Ted Farid, VP Sales and Marketing."
- Consider a new themeline.

(Source: *The Richards Group*)

In the sidebar, I've put in another creative brief from The Richards Group. And, below, here's the ad that resulted.

How to Save Money on Your Long Distance Calls.

This ad looks absolutely gorgeous in four colors.

And it integrates everything we understand about the product, the target, and the task from the creative brief.

Along the top of the ad, small well-crafted icons deliver key selling points (range, stand-up cabin, and economical fuel consumption), while allowing plenty of room to show the beauty of the plane. It sells hard. But with the right tone for the target.

Good advertising like this doesn't just happen.

The clarity of the background information used to brief the agency team about the product, the target, and the task helped great advertising take off and fly.

5. Integration in Action.

THIS BOOK IS *ADVERTISING & THE BUSINESS OF BRANDS*. But, as we've said, "*advertising is more than advertising.*"

As Bob Levin (*Godzilla's* brand manager) noted, "*When the public only sees things in advertising, they're skeptical. "But if it's in all the forms where they expect to see things, then it lifts [the campaign] to another level.*"

Throughout this book, you've seen examples of brands that established themselves because they used more than advertising.

Some brands have established themselves in surprising ways.

But, perhaps nothing has been as surprising as the dramatic change in the media marketplace itself. The Media Revolution has forced a wholesale change in the way marketers go to market.

Integration and Disintegration.

The big reason for the growing need for "integration" is the disintegration of once large and relatively low-cost media audiences.

Let us be clear about this. There was no desire on the part of marketers to make their job more expensive and more complicated, it was a necessity forced upon them as a relatively simple and straightforward business model – advertising on mass media vehicles – became less effective.

We covered the reasons for this in Chapter Two. Simply put, the increase in cost per thousand in mass media, the growing maturity of various product and service categories, where brand preferences and behaviors are increasingly "locked in," and the overall proliferation of messages into a "blizzard" of individual communications has created an environment where only the very exceptional programs succeed.

Marshall McLuhan and "The Flip."

The Canadian media guru noted that "extensions," a word he used for many things (a car is an extension of your legs, the TV is an extension of your perception) had a number of effects. He used the hard-to-remember acronym E.O.R.F.

First, something is extended. E is for extended. E-mail extends our connections, the channel-changer extends our reach across the room.

Second, some things become Obsolete. O is for obsolete. E-mail makes regular mail obsolete and the channel changer makes getting up out of the chair and a magazine like TV Guide (once a huge circulation magazine, now a relic) no longer necessary.

R is for retrieval. Certain skills and behaviors are recovered. E-mail actually brings back written communication – since it's so much easier. The channel-changer, to some degree, recovers our curiosity (we call it "channel-surfing") as we are no longer locked into limited choices in our viewing. And then there's the "F" word. McLuhan calls it "The Flip." Certain things are reversed. As we connect via e-mail, we turn our back on those in the same room. As we travel hither and yon in the stimulation of our channel-surfing, we vegetate and stagnate. And, perhaps, instead of being stimulated to consume products by the messages of advertising, we merely consume advertising!

Think about it. How many clever commercials do you consume on any weekend? How many of those actually stimulate you to do what they want you to do? Perhaps a few. But, for the most part, they are a calorie-free, and consumption-free part of your media diet.

You've built up an immunity to marketing messages.

An Expanding Marketing Menu.

The first stage of Integrated Marketing Communications, though not everyone calls it IMC, some call it simply "marketing," has brought a growing awareness of the many ways that marketing can communicate.

Each method has its success stories: sales promotion, public relations, direct marketing, cause marketing, sponsorship, and unique combinations of all of them have shown that they can be effective.

Integration and Promotion.

Entertainment brands add new levels of cross-promotion while brands add entertainment value. *Austin Powers* is promoted – so is milk.

Reinforcing Brand Values.

Cheeky British humor reinforces the brand values of both Virgin Atlantic Airways and *Austin Powers*.

The Massage Is the Message.

Here, a very cheeky *"I was admiring your Heinie"* promotes *Austin* and Heineken to an adult audience.

Because of the many roads to marketing success, the art of IMC has become the effective management of an abundance of choice. And, to that end, advocates of each and every form of marketing communication whisper in the ear of marketing decision-makers.

"OverChoice" and "Coping Strategies."

In his prescient book, *Future Shock*, Alvin Toffler talked about "overchoice," a situation where there was, perhaps, too much to choose from.

Around that time, we asked consumer insight expert Lisa Fortini-Campbell, what, in a broad scale way, she saw in the consumer marketplace. Her answer, "coping strategies."

"What you don't understand," said a woman in a focus group on low-fat foods, *"is that before we never thought food could hurt us."* She was speaking of a change in her world, where instead of supermarkets filled with an array of good-for-you food that would care for her family, she now faced a more hostile nutritional world with mine fields of nutritional and ingredient information to be negotiated and large looming problems from childhood obesity to Type II diabetes ready to invade her family by way of the knife and fork.

As a classic TV commercial once asked, "What's a mother to do?"

And, on the other side of the focus group mirror, they are asking, "What's a marketer to do?"

That question has more and more interesting answers.

Let's look at a few.

In First Place with "The Third Place."

Starbucks "Third Place" is an understanding of their brand based on consumer insight. Starbucks is an integration-driven company, originally begun with Howard Schultz's "Milan Epiphany."

That "third place" is a private time between work and home that the consumer has with his or her cup of coffee.

Reading, listening to music, and taking that cup of coffee with you – to those other places. In retrospect, it's easy to see why Starbucks has been driven by in-store merchandising, with reading and music as promotional options, and lots of fresh new ways to take home your Starbucks.

And, remember, much of their marketing costs are tied up in location, location, and location.

Hardly Anyplace... and Then...

Meanwhile, Lands' End, established by a Chicago ad executive who loved to sail, became a large-scale clothing retailer almost without being anyplace – they did it by going direct to you. Now they're working to make the Internet work harder for them.

Unlike Starbucks, Lands' End spent little on locations – they wanted to be in your mailbox, in the catalogue by your easy chair, and, hopefully, as one of the bookmarks on your Internet browser.

But they had one more big customer. Sears. Lands' End had built up such brand value that Sears added it to their stores.

New Marketing Equations.

Nike established themselves with big ad budgets that were affordable because of their business strategy: lowering costs, raising prices, and using the margin to fund an unprecedented level of unprecedented advertising.

Harley-Davidson revitalized their brand with marketing public relations that engaged its desired target audience and now the brand is powered by a growing base of loyal and enthusiastic customers.

"The Battle for Your Attention."

Now media companies have become a new force in marketing. New entertainment brands are popping up all the time.

The largest? *Star Wars!* As Joe Plummer, former research director of the Advertising Research Foundation, observes, *"The biggest new brand has been Star Wars – bigger than Microsoft, bigger than Nike."* Next time you visit a younger brother or sister, or a niece or nephew, take a look at the role entertainment brands play in their young lives.

Take a look at how entertainment brands now market themselves – like *Austin Powers.* When they had a brand new entertainment brand, they leveraged each movie with engaging product tie-in advertising that utilized their unique brand personality to connect with a wide range of products – milk, beer, airlines, and Mini.

The Entertainment Economy.

There's a lot at work here. Michael Wolf's prescient book, *The Entertainment Economy: How Mega-Media Forces Are Changing Our Lives,* gives you a window into new dynamics in the world of media.

Fragmented audiences mean more audiences.

New Products. Old Products. New Ways. Old Ways.

Coming up, you'll see how PowerBar grew into a significant new business (number one in a brand new category) with a strategy tied into event marketing – as they connect with their core target, runners, and leverage that reputation to a larger market.

And then, at your neighborhood store, you can see how the marketplace has created an entire category of nutrition bar products.

Even Campbell's Soup, a brand built on advertising, works to make the most of their mature brands with a continuing program of sales promotion. When you look at Campbell's, you can see a traditional brand integrating by continually searching for the optimum mix for its marketing efforts.

Campbell's knows that the marketplace is a moving target.

They've watched as their original bit of marketing genius – condensing soup to reduce shipping costs – had become increasingly obsolete as a desire for convenience combined with more and more solitary eating situations changed something as simple as soup.

Recently, they made a small but significant change in their Chunky Soup advertising. Their continual evaluation of soup

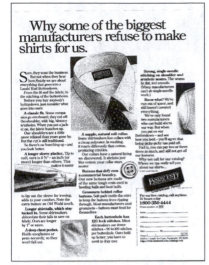

The Direct Route.

Lands' End became a major national clothing brand by connecting directly with its target.

Apple Computer – Integration by Design.

Everyone knows about Apple's cool iPods and iBooks. You should also know that Steve Jobs and Apple use design for competitive advantage.

Branding.

Apple uses design to differentiate – it's not just the advertising.

This helps give them the ability to keep their margins higher.

Usability.

Consumers intuitively understand Apple products. Their design group uses anthropological tools to research the best way to do this.

The result – easy to use.

(Continued on next page)

The Next "Third Place."

Starbucks evaluates and re-evaluates. Here, another version of Howard Schultz's vision for Starbucks. Today, evaluation is an ongoing process.

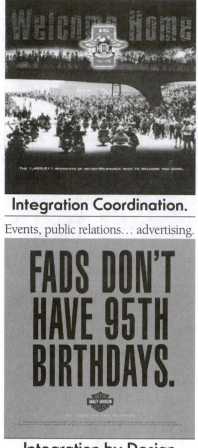

Integration Coordination.

Events, public relations… advertising.

FADS DON'T HAVE 95TH BIRTHDAYS.

HARLEY-DAVIDSON

Integration by Design (Cont.)

Display.

Information design is another Apple core competency. They work at it.

The entire Graphic User Interface (GUI), originated by Xerox but popularized by Apple, is based on designing machines so that humans can work with them intuitively.

Technology.

"Apple uses design to select and apply new technologies." There has always been a high design quotient in Apple products.

Design pays off on the bottom line.

Conceptualization.

They're always thinking about new ways to connect with the consumer through both emotion and hardware.

& More…

Finally, Apple design is a part of popular culture – it's cool.

They integrate that consumer connection in a way that represents how their products work – by design.

(Source: *Business Week* 7/31/2000)

---

consumption discovered that their target market – men in their 30s – had finally figured out how to make soup.

So the commercials that had the mothers of NFL stars preparing soup changed.

Now, after a hard day at work, the NFL stars make their own soup.

Evaluation loops back into integration and implementation.

Taking Advantage of Strategic Advantages.

Each brand is leveraging the growing range of marketing communications opportunities to grow their brands in ways that take advantage of their strategic advantages.

Nike in sports. Starbucks in your neighborhood. Lands' End in your mailbox (and now your e-mail box). Harley-Davidson on the road and in the news. And *Austin Powers* on the telly.

Each one is integrating, and then optimizing, their communications for success in the marketplace. Which, of course, is the whole point of integrating in the first place.

Integration and Optimization.

First, integration is about optimization. It's about making the best of your resources and your alternatives.

We've evolved from a few relatively efficient media channels to a wide range of marketing communications options.

And, whether you're a dry cleaner or a multi-million dollar media corporation, the concern is finding the best way to spend those precious marketing dollars in communicating with the customer.

Integration and Information.

Effective integration is about information. In this chapter, you've seen how the right information at the beginning of a project can help in the creation of effective messages.

Our dry cleaner discovered promotional products would generate greater sales than discounts – and that both would be more profitable than the least expensive thing – doing nothing.

What should you do? You usually need some sort of information to help establish a goal, to measure your progress, and to judge alternatives objectively.

That means you have to integrate ongoing evaluation into whatever you do. The *"systematic gathering of information to answer a question or solve a problem"* has to become something you do all the time – whatever you do.

So that when new information emerges, your antennae are already out and ready to pick up the signals.

Whether you're a top executive at a huge company (someday) or a lower-level assistant trying to figure out how to get ahead, getting the right information and knowing what to do with it is key.

In the next chapter, you'll meet Lynne O'Shea. When she was a sales trainee at P&G, a run in her stocking was the catalyst for a profitable national promotion for P&G.

Integration and the Customer.

Integration is about the people who support your business – the customer. As marketing consultant Anders Gronstedt notes, *"The path to business success is built on long-term customer relationships. Treat customers as friends. Send thank you letters. Offer value...*

"Integrated marketing is about integrating messages at all the points where customers have contact with a company.

"That's how one builds long-term brand relationships."

Throughout a brand's operations, the right kind of customer information can help management deliver a better return on their marketing investment by connecting with the right customers – and keeping connected.

Just as Lands' End sends you more mail when you write an order, with new database technology, companies can know more about their customers and improve the connections that build real value for a brand.

Integrated marketing means organizing around customers.

Integration Is about Vision and Values.

You need to know where you're going.

Optimization only works when you have a goal.

Information only helps when you know what you need to know.

And that means, somewhere in the equation, a brand organizes around core values and a vision of the future.

You saw it in the early days when King Gillette and John Dorrance had visions of disposable razor blades and condensed soup.

You see it today in the visions of Howard Schultz of Starbucks, Phil Knight of Nike, and George Lucas changing the technology of entertainment with one of the biggest brands of all – *Star Wars*.

When you have a vision, much of what it takes to do the complex jobs of integration is operational. When you know you want to create a third place, it's merchandising that place.

When you're Harley-Davidson and you know you need to reconnect with a whole new kind of customer and become part of their lives, you form H.O.G. – Harley Owners Group – and let the love of your brand shine through.

From Information to Inspiration.

And that means you have to add one more "I" to your information – Inspiration. Remember? From data to information to insight to inspiration.

The visions that helped create important new brands were often based on just a few bits of information.

Pattern recognition helped those visionaries see a picture of the future – and then they worked to make it come true.

Often, over much adversity.

New Information...

shows consumers more concerned with germs and bacteria.

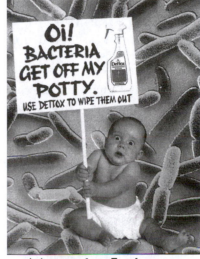

Messaging Evolves...

as it uses this new information.

Products Evolve...

and that new information creates still more effective messaging.

"D.O.G." Exercises:

What does "D.O.G." stand for? It's "Daily Observational Grist."

These can help make you a better observer of the world around you.

They were first developed as part of an SMU summer program in London where we worked on improving account planning skills.

We were in a new culture – even though everyone spoke English – and we all made "DOG Books."

Becoming a DOG Detective.

Account planners take on the role of professional observer, sleuth, and purveyor of insight.

Sometimes it simply means being a bit more observant than usual, and trying to understand something you've never really given a lot of thought to or just taken for granted.

Every day for a period of one week, you demonstrate your observational and information-gathering skills by producing (and presenting) a DOG.

At the end of the week, compile your DOGs into a brief report.

What's a Good DOG?

Here are some examples:

• **Process DOG:** This is about how things work behind the scenes. How does a commercial dry cleaner clean clothes without using water? How and when do 24-hour grocery stores clean and wax their floors?

• **DOG Decoder:** What things mean, expressions you've heard. What words do sixth-graders use for "cool"? What words do 60-year-olds use for "cool"? Visit a local printing or paper company. Ask for some samples. What words are used to describe the various types of paper?

• **Name that DOG:** Account planners try to communicate consumer learnings to a host of others in the agency – creatives, media planners, and account executives – quickly and creatively.

(Continued on next page)

Tools for Success.

When you face adversity, you want all the help you can get.

That's what this chapter has been about – getting the information you need to solve today's problems and have tomorrow's visions.

There's a lot of opportunity for you to do both in The Business of Brands. And, as long as we're talking about adversity, let's mention a few other challenges you may run into along the way.

6. Challenges for the Future.

Usually, we evaluate what we're asked to evaluate.

When you're writing a book, you have a little more latitude –sometimes you can actually pick what you want to evaluate.

Here are some things we think you should evaluate as you deal with information in tomorrow's marketplace.

• **Data Overload**
• **Innumeracy**
• **Low-Quality Qualitative Information**
• **Information Cost**

The Blur of Diversity.

Alvin Toffler observes that once, in a mass market economy, it was "one size fits all."

Today, in our diverse economy and diverse society, information is also diverse – you can find an example of almost everything.

This diversity of opportunity is a wonderful thing, but for marketers concerned with accumulating good-sized audiences and markets, it can make finding the right answer even more daunting. As marketers, we'll all have to deal with this.

It's all the more reason you have to be very clear-headed about the information you're going after – because there's a lot of information lying around, but it might not be the right information.

Let's look at some other challenges you may have.

Data Overload.

When there were only three networks, it wasn't that tough to know what was on TV every night.

With more than a hundred, it's impossible. Today, we often have to deal with too much data – without a channel changer in sight.

In business, where we have to turn that data into useful and actionable information, that can be a real challenge.

Data in the digital world, though often touted as the ad measurement Holy Grail, can be particularly confusing to work with, as issues of which measurement criterion (clicks, sales, Web site audience, search behavior, or simply exposure to an ad?) are not entirely agreed upon.

Konrad Feldman, CEO of digital media measurement firm Quantcast, argues that raw data does not translate into competitive advantage for a company. *"The valuable asset is the processed data that provides insights"* (Adweek, The New Gold Standard, Feb. 4, 2008, p31).

Quantcast uses a "tagging" system that enables Web publishers and others to measure audience size, demographics, and other information on their sites.

Quantcast offers basic audience data from thousands of sites for free on its own Web site. You might want to impress your advertising professor by going to Quantcast.com and check to see if the demographics of your university's Web site (just enter the site under Advanced Search) or your other favorite sites are analyzed.

The good news is there are a lot of jobs out there for someone good at turning all of those numbers into something useful.

The bad news is there sure are a lot of numbers out there.

And, sad to say, there are a lot of people who aren't as good at working with those numbers as you might hope.

Click-through studies, UPC scanning data, survey data, and all those other bits of information we can generate in our information-rich environment means we'll all have to get real good at managing all that data – and editing it into the information we need.

Innumeracy.

Innumeracy is like illiteracy – only it's with numbers.

When we're "GAF" (Good at Figures), numbers on a spreadsheet mean something. We can extract what we need to know.

When we're not GAF, it's a blur. And, for a lot of people out there, that's what it is – a blur.

Don't let one of those innumerate ones be you.

That said, becoming GAF isn't all that easy.

Because data overload means we often get a lot of numbers – but not exactly the numbers we need.

We have to know how to work with those numbers – and recognize what's useful and what isn't.

Work to make sure you don't grow up innumerate. One way is to become familiar and comfortable with good numbers. By that, we mean, the kinds of worked-out data that are clear and useful.

Learn to read a Nielsen study. And one from IRI (to learn more about IRI, visit us.infores.com).

Look at readership scores.

Get a feel for how good information looks and feels.

Then start to get involved in generating your own information. The AAF/NSAC is a great place to start.

Design a survey for a class project. See what you discover.

You'll find that 100 opinions on a survey will really open your eyes about how others view the world.

And the fact that you helped create that information… well, you just might like the way that makes you feel.

Low Quality Qualitative Information.

Everybody has an opinion. And, you can probably find at least one example that "proves" almost anything.

Should we drive more slowly? You can show where someone driving too slowly caused an accident.

Build Your Own Brief.

Below is the Creative Brief format. Why not use it?

It might be a brief which would serve as the strategic basis for your favorite student activity – or perhaps an ad campaign for your ad class.

Here's the format.

Creative Brief Format.

Warning: People don't like ads. People don't trust ads. People don't remember ads. How do we make sure this one will be different?

Why are we advertising?

Who are we talking to?

What do they currently think?

What would we like them to think?

What is the single most persuasive idea we can convey?

Why should they believe it?

Are there any creative guidelines?

Courtesy, The Richards Group

References:

Besides my book, you might enjoy:
Hitting The Sweet Spot:
How Consumer Insights Can
Inspire Better Marketing
and Advertising
by Lisa Fortini-Campbell, Ph.D.

Truth, Lies & Advertising:
The Art of Account Planning
by Jon Steel
A wonderful, easy-to-read book from the "Got Milk?" agency. It tells that story and more. (AdWeek Books)

Should we wear seat belts? You can probably find an example where, under some circumstances, it was a problem.

Still, we shouldn't speed and we should wear our seat belts.

Focus groups are one place where it's very common for marketers and advertisers to have "information accidents."

A loudly held opinion can sway a room full of people who don't care that much. A distracted moderator can let things get off track.

An important executive watching the focus group may only be capable of hearing what he or she wants to hear.

That lady on the end agrees with you – she's smart, represents the consumer, and proves that you've got the answer – even though it's only one opinion.

And, no surprise, you might not like that other person at the other end of the table who didn't much like your ad – and you manage to tune out what he or she is saying.

Getting qualitative information, while it is fun and stimulating, can also be imprecise and contradictory. Be careful.

Don't have an accident. Don't just go out to prove your bias by finding a few agreeable folks in a mall.

Remember, we often learn more from the people who disagree with us a bit. Listen. Buckle up and figure it out.

The real gift of qualitative research is when it can open our eyes and help us see the world in a whole new way.

The Cost of Information.

Good information can be expensive – in money and time. And, since the payoff is sometimes distant or uncertain, and resources are always a little tight, it's an easy expense to cut.

This is another challenge – and it's one you might be able to meet early in your career.

First, good information doesn't have to be expensive. Digging into secondary sources might get you just the help you need.

Can't afford a focus group? Go talk to some customers informally.

One-on-one interviews done by someone who really cares (you) and who isn't afraid of a little hard work (you again) can really get a project rolling.

And it's just amazing, when a little bit of good information gets everyone feeling a little bit smarter, you can often find the money to get a little more.

Because, after all, who doesn't want to feel smarter?

Keep Doing It.

Nike, one of today's smart companies, has an ongoing commitment to staying in touch with their customers – and staying ahead of their competition.

The same commitment to winning that old runners (like Nike founder Phil Knight), or young runners bring to their job is a big part of what it takes to win in the marketplace.

Evaluation, like athletic training, is what smart companies do.

Scorekeeping is OK. Winning is better.

Summary:

In this chapter, we covered ways that the systematic gathering of information can help answer questions and solve problems.

- The key "apertures" or opportunities where research can play a valuable role.
- Various research tools available to answer those questions and solve those problems.
- The types of information that need to be gathered.
- We showed you how this information can be the key ingredient in inspiring better marketing and advertising.
- Finally, some answers may not be advertising at all. As you look at the inherent advantages of your brand, information and inspiration might lead to exciting new territory.

We began by defining research as, *"the systematic gathering of information to answer a question or solve a problem."*

Now let's finish with a few more ways to develop those skills.

Things to Do:

Here are some ways to get some exercise on these topics:

1. Questionnaire Questions.

Write four questionnaire objectives for a survey research project whose purpose is to determine what is considered "cool" among undergraduate students at your university.

After you've written the objectives, write 10 (total) questions that correspond to the four objectives.

2. Four Research Stages...

Using the brand of your choice, discuss possible research efforts at each of the four research stages or apertures:

- **Planning Research**
- **Developmental Research**
- **Implementation Research**
- **Measuring Results**

3. Internet Information Search.

Using search engines on the Web, locate, summarize, and analyze five information sources about a product or product category. In your analysis, be sure to ask, "How current is this information?" and, "What is the original source of the information?" Does the information appear to be credible/believable?

4. Brand Collage Exercise.

Clip up to 300 images and words from magazines. (This actually takes less time than you think and can be mildly enjoyable.) Ask five people to choose and tape down any three of those clippings which they believe illustrate what a specific brand, television show, etc., is like.

Ask participants to explain why they chose the images they did.

Magazine Cover Assignment:

Here's a consumer research assignment you might really enjoy.

The final product is a mocked-up magazine cover complete with title, cover story and "art" (suggested visuals are fine if your art direction skills aren't completely honed). Plus additional teaser headlines indicating other stories inside.

Every element of your magazine cover must indicate understanding and familiarity with your target audience. A one-page explanation of each editorial decision (each cover element) accompanies the cover.

Research Your Target.

To gather information and insights for your new magazine, conduct personal interviews (use a discussion guide) with at least five members of a particular target market.

Examples might be: high school juniors/seniors thinking about college, students who eat in the campus cafeteria, customers of a local coffee shop, etc.).

Review what you've learned and distill your information into "stories" or topics that reflect the activities, interests, motivations, information needs, desires, and fears of your target market.

Now you're ready to be an insight-driven magazine publisher.

Create Your Magazine.

First, name your magazine (Use your creativity, but remember everything must be dictated by learnings – not clever plays on words).

Look at our list of learnings and insights and start to write headlines or blurbs for each. It's fun!

Consider what you should use for your cover photograph/art.

What would draw your target audience in? What appeals to them?

Finally, in the address label on the cover, create a fictitious name and address that's also on strategy (example: A.B. Student, 18 Crossroads Lane, Upwardly Mobile, AL).

5. Application of Data and Information From Online Sources

Go to Hoovers.com and enter the name of a company or brand. Click on a listing of competitor companies or brands. Now find the Web sites of your original company and its competitors. Enter each of those Web sites on Quantcast.com in the "Advanced Search" field. Study the data from the Quantcast analysis. Write a one-page report summarizing your findings, as well as a list of five potential applications of the data – how might you put the data to work for your advertising or marketing campaign? Note: If you find it challenging to get your head around the competitive information and data from the free versions of these sites, imagine what it might look like if you were a paid subscriber, or simply click on paid subscription options to get a taste of the data deluge you might be in for.

Bonus: Choose a campus program, philanthropy, or even your university Web site as your "brand" and diplomatically share the results with the program administrator. You'll be surprised at the undivided attention you will get for your research efforts.

Concepts & Vocabulary:

Account planning – System of planning advertising. Relies heavily on qualitative consumer research and representing the consumer at all stages of ad development; originated in London in the 1960s.

Anthropology – The study of differences and similarities, both biological and cultural, in human populations.

Apertures – Term borrowed from photography to refer to opportunities or "openings" for results of research to be applied to the development of effective advertising messages. (A different definition related to media appears in Chapter Two for Aperture®.)

AAU (Awareness Attitude Usage) – Survey of consumers to determine knowledge and use of brands and brand advertising in a category of products or services; also called **tracking studies**.

Brand collage – Qualitative research exercise. Focus group participants select and arrange images cut from magazines to represent their impressions of a specific brand.

Copy testing – Consumer evaluation of rough or finished advertising; can be conducted in focus groups or in large-scale surveys.

Creative brief – Agency document which contains advertising strategy, specifically the reason for advertising, the target market, consumer perceptions, and how advertising can change them.

Demographic data – Quantative information describing age, income, education, marital status, employment, etc., of target audience.

Developmental research – Information gathering among consumers to determine appropriate advertising strategy; takes place before advertising is created.

Ethnographer – A person who spends some time living with, interviewing, and observing a group of people so that he or she can describe their customs.

Ethnography – A description of a society's customary behaviors, beliefs, and attitudes*

Experiment – Highly structured research method which involves determining the effects of a stimulus (independent variable) on the behavior of a particular sample (dependent variable); can be conducted in a research laboratory or under marketplace conditions (field experiment).

Feedback– Responses of a target audience to marketing communications messages; used by advertisers to gauge effectiveness of advertising and to take steps to make it more effective.

Focus group – Gathering of up to 12 members of a target market for a discussion of a brand and its advertising. Led by a moderator who follows an agenda of questions/topics. Usually lasts two hours.

Innumeracy – Numerical form of illiteracy; can't use numbers.

Lexis/Nexis – A proprietary database, available by subscription, which includes periodical articles and press releases about new product news, marketing developments, and market share.

One-on-one interviews (also called **monadic** or **depth interviews**) – An in-depth data-gathering method which requires that an interviewer question one participant at a time; specified in situations where the topic being discussed is considered sensitive to the participant or where convening a focus group is not possible.

Pattern recognition – The ability to see the whole picture based on just a few points of information.

Primary research – Gathering and analysis of original information from a sample or population (see *secondary research*).

Projectability – The ability to generalize or extrapolate findings from a relatively small study or survey to a larger group or population; random sample surveys have the highest projectability.

Qualitative research – Systematic information-gathering activities which do not involve the assignment of numbers to results (see *quantitative research*); includes focus group interviews, one-on-one interviews, observation, and other techniques.

Quantitative research – Systematic information-gathering activities which result in analysis of numerical data collected from a sample; includes sample surveys, experiments, analysis of sales data, etc.

Questionnaire – Instrument of measurement used in a survey research effort; contains items (questions) which result from a list of objectives arranged in a way easily understood by a respondent.

Randomness – The principle that each member of a specified population or group had an equal chance of being selected for inclusion in a sample to be studied.

Research – The systematic gathering of information to answer questions and solve problems.

Sample – A subset of a population or large group designated for measurement; samples can be selected randomly or nonrandomly.

Secondary research – Gathering and analysis of information which is available in published form, i.e., printed or online sources.

Situation analysis – Written evaluation of marketplace factors affecting a specific brand and its category competitors; this document is used as a basis for marketing and advertising strategy.

Storytelling – Qualitative research technique. Participants create a fictional scenario involving a specific brand in order to provide insight into brand personality (e.g., Describe what would happen if L'Oréal and Suave shampoos went on a double date with two brands of beer—please specify which brands of beer would be involved).

Survey – Systematic measurement of a subset of a population for the purpose of projecting the results to the entire population.

Word association – Interview technique. Participants are asked to write or say words or phrases which come to mind when a specific brand name is mentioned; used to obtain insight into brand personality and status.

12

The Power of New Ideas

This chapter was written by Dennis Ganahl and Joe Bob Hester. *Dennis was on the faculty at Southern Illinois University Carbondale when he wrote this. He has owned and published newspapers, been a consultant with Pulitzer, Capital Cities, and Newhouse Publishing, and advised political campaigns for the US Senate and state office holders. Joe Bob (also known as "Joe Dot Bob") teaches in the Advertising Sequence at the University of North Carolina including graduate seminars on the Internet. Joe Dot Bob also created the original architecture for the adbuzz. com Web site.*

"FORTUNE FAVORS THE BOLD," the Roman poet Virgil observed in about 30 BC. It's still true. The focus of this chapter is the power of new ideas to reshape The Business of Brands.

Brian and **Jennifer Maxwell** teamed up to create and market PowerBar. They're **new product marketers.**

Eliot Kang started a new agency, Kang & Lee – one of the new Asian-American agencies arising to serve this important and expanding segment of the American marketplace.

At Procter & Gamble, already a smart company, they wanted to become better at having ideas. They put **Jim Stengel** in charge.

We'll take a look at the media career of **Bob Pittman,** who helped introduce a cable channel you may have heard of – *MTV.* Then, he helped manage one of the premiere online brands – AOL – part of the new medium that's changing everything – the **Internet.**

And, since we all want to know what's cool, we'll meet someone who makes her living tracking it down – **DeeDee Gordon,** the "coolhunter."

How This Chapter Is Organized.

Here are some of the topics we'll discuss:

❶ **The Challenge of Change.**

We'll begin with a discussion of change itself and introduce you to the Four C's – a new way to look at the Five P's.

We'll look at new products and how marketers bring them to market – like PowerBar. And we'll see how an established marketer like Campbell's works to keep their brands fresh.

❷ **New Agencies for a New World.**

We'll take a look at Eliot Kang's Kang & Lee.

Agencies are quick to respond to a changing marketplace, and this exciting new agency is an excellent example.

❸ **The Internet.**

From the beginning, we've seen how new media forms changed advertising – and we're seeing it again.

All by itself, the Internet is creating new marketers, new kinds of agencies, and more new media combinations, like MSNBC, Google, Yahoo!, eBay, and Amazon.

We'll look at a media revolutionary who's had ups and downs – Bob Pittman of *MTV* and AOL.

❹ Managing Change.

Next, we'll look at a big brand marketer, Jim Stengel of P&G, who's now a marketing revolutionary!

❺ Innovation in Marketing Services.

Finally, we'll look at how the need for innovation is driving a growing range of additional opportunities in the marketplace.

You'll meet a traditional marketing consultant who has been in the innovation business since she was a P&G trainee.

You'll meet DeeDee Gordon, "coolhunter," who took a knack for spotting trendsetters and turned it into a business.

She tracks down trends for some of America's top marketers.

The Challenge of Change.

THE CONCEPT OF "TRADE" has been around as long as there have been two people – each with something the other wants.

Each person negotiated the value of their product in a trade for the other's product. That's how the marketplace began.

Mass Marketing – One Size Fits All.

The Industrial Revolution changed everything as mass manufacturers shipped their products widely to those who sold them.

At that time, the manufacturers who developed these products controlled the marketplace – because few mass-manufactured razor blades or condensed soup.

During times of economic expansion, early manufacturers simply had to place ads that trumpeted the benefits of their unique brands and keep up with growing demand.

Except for wars and economic depression, this wealth-building formula continued for 100 years.

In Chapter One, the story of marketing was the story of manufacturers and their ad agencies.

Tangible products with tangible features and benefits – such as *"an amazing new way to make toast"* – was the primary formula for success.

Then, in the late 1980s, an "indigo beep was heard round the world."

In Chapter Two, you read how the power of information changed the relationship between manufacturer and distributor.

International stock market information changed the ownership of agencies.

And information changed your desktop.

Driven by Innovation.

In many ways, this entire book has been about the power of ideas.

P&G's 1931 introduction of brand management was an innovation that made multi-brand marketing possible.

Chiat/Day's 1982 introduction of British account planning was an innovation that enhanced agency contributions to brand building.

The media world is constantly innovating to build their own brands and create new ones.

Meanwhile, new entertainment brands compete for attention with every channel change.

In this chapter, we'll focus on the new idea process itself.

Because, whatever you do tomorrow, innovation and its consequences will be a part of it.

A Toast to New Ideas.

Something as simple as toast can start a whole new industry. Here, one of the first of the home appliances for something we all take for granted.

There's big business in little things.

An amazing new way to make toast

You don't have to watch it—
—it comes out automatically
when it's done

Every piece perfect every time

It happens in the "best of regulated families" whenever toast is made. Everyone depends on everyone else to watch the toaster—with the result that everyone forgets until a thin column of smoke rises toward the ceiling.

Or the toast is made in the kitchen and arrives at the table either pale in color—scraped—stone cold —or dried out and hard.

Now an amazing new way of making toast has been perfected. You do not have to watch the bread after you put it into the toaster. You do not have to turn it. There is no danger of its burning. Yet every slice is done to perfection. An even golden-brown. Deliciously crisp. And so hot that the butter melts instantly.

Now—automatic toast

You've really never eaten toast quite so luscious as the new Toastmaster makes *every* time. And all you have to do is: 1. Drop a slice of bread into the oven slot. 2. Press down the two levers. This automatically turns on the current and sets the timing device. 3. Pop! Up comes the toast automatically when it's done, and the current is automatically turned off.

Both sides are toasted at the same time in an enclosed oven. Thus all the goodness and flavor of the bread are sealed in—the toast is always piping hot when served—and it is delivered to you twice as speedily as with the ordinary toaster which toasts each side of the bread singly.

At your dealer's—or order direct

The Toastmaster is a small brother of the big Toastmaster, used for years by famous restaurants, hotels and sandwich shops. It's a little beauty. Finished in flashing nickel, it makes an attractive piece for the server or dining table. So you can make toast right at the table the minute you want it.

See this novel toaster at your Electric Light Company, department store or electric dealer's. In case your dealer cannot supply you, send us a money order for $12.50. We will ship you a Toastmaster postage paid, on 30 days trial. Money back if it doesn't win you at once. Waters Genter Company, 231 No. Second Street, Minneapolis, Minn. Toastmasters are distributed in Great Britain through Hector C. Adam, Limited, Phoenix House, 19-23 Oxford Street, London, W. 1.

The TOASTMASTER

The Power of Information.

This is the beep heard round the world. The UPC (Universal Price Code) provides an incredible amount of detailed marketing information.

Whole companies, such as Information Resources, Inc. (IRI), have been built on collecting and analyzing this scanner data.

Other companies, like Wal-Mart, grew by leveraging the power of this information.

Information Goes Global.

"The mark is strong!" That's what it says in German, as Wal-Mart (or, as they say, "Val-Mart") introduces their brand of aggressive retailing to the German market.

"To create the future is to be the enemy of today."

— Peter Drucker

Information changed everything.

And it powered The Business of Brands.

The Power of Information.

With that beep, computer information began changing the marketplace. Computer-based information was no longer confined to big mainframes. It was everywhere.

It was on your desktop and at the checkout counter.

Something as simple as the UPC code dramatically affected the relationship between retailers and manufacturers.

Now retailers have up-to-the-minute information on the value of their shelves, what's hot and what's not. Those who have been better at using that information have developed big advantages.

For example, Wal-Mart has changed the marketplace in ways that include how *"small-town America does business,"* the way P&G operates, and, now, German retailing.

That's power that reaches around the world.

The Power of the Individual.

While we may sometimes feel overwhelmed, the result can be very empowering for all of us as individuals.

It has given us access to the power of information.

That information gives us more power to get what we want.

As we exercise that power, the mass market is fragmenting into more options for more individuals.

And that is changing marketing. Again.

The End of the Five P's?

Professor Robert Lauterborn of the University of North Carolina and one of the co-authors of the influential book, *Integrated Marketing Communications*, has even suggested brand managers, professors, and students bury the Five P's (product, price, place, promotion, and people) which has been taught for several generations.

He suggests we replace them with the Four C's to reflect the changes in the marketplace. Let's look at what he's talking about.

The New Four C's Are...

CONSUMER, COST, CONVENIENCE, COMMUNICATION.
Let's go through them one by one.

Consumer.

"Consumer" replaces "Product." Today's marketplace is driven by the consumer, not the manufacturer or the retailer.

Today, an outside-in consumer-focused perspective is necessary to build products the way consumers want.

Dell now tailor-makes each computer they sell to meet the needs of individual customers. (Henry Ford once said, *"You can have a Model T in any color you want as long as it's black."*)

How far can this go? The interactive media and an independent product delivery system have put the control of the marketplace directly into the hands of the consumer.

Even mass marketers are looking for ways to respond as they work to look at the world from the consumer's point of view.

Cost.

"Cost" replaces "price." A major part of the choice consumers make is the total they want to spend for the product or service.

Today, customers have a lot of options and strategies. They can shop with coupons or other sales promotions to lessen the final price of the product. They have alternatives – including not buying anything. It's not just about money, either.

For example, some of a customers' choices are:

- **Time they will spend shopping**
- **Distance they will travel**
- **Cash cost for the product** (and payment options)
- **Sales tax, extended-warranty cost, special services**
- **Finance costs**

All of these options can reduce or increase the final cost of the product. Often, the consumer even has the power to affect the cost by a choice of shipping options.

Convenience.

"Convenience" replaces "place." Today retailers and manufacturers know they must make their products and services easily available to the consumer.

This has spawned *"drive-through dining, banking, photo developing, medications, product pick-up, and free home delivery."*

The number-one reason people select a bank is convenience – which puts emphasis on the customer's convenience.

Banks need to provide services like financial grocery stores, ATM cards, electronic banking, and whatever's next.

Now, even Wall Street is looking at changing its hours, because of trading being done after-hours on the Internet.

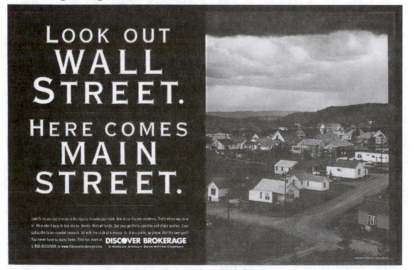

A Change in Distribution. A Change in the Marketplace.
Sometimes the real driver of change may be hidden from view.

The wide-spread distribution of computers with Internet connections was the change that made new business models – such as managing your own stock trading – possible.

IDEO: Organized for Innovation.

Let's look at IDEO – the Innovation Company. Located in Palo Alto, California, they're considered one of the world's most influential product development companies.

90 Products a Year.
Innovation is quite a business.

On average, its design teams create over 90 products a year – ranging from sophisticated medical equipment to the 25-foot mechanical whale in *Free Willy*.

Company leader Dave Kelly described IDEO's motto as *"fail often in order to succeed sooner."*

"Focused Chaos."
The atmosphere is *"focused chaos."* Kelly says innovation must, *"stay focused, encourage wild ideas, defer judgment, build on the ideas of others."*

An innovation culture is playful. Office surroundings and decor encourage a free-wheeling ambiance.

Diversity at Work.
The innovation culture starts and finishes within a team comprised of diverse specialized expertise.

Diversity is important. It ensures multiple perspectives. The culture is egalitarian, nurturing, and accepting.

The team seeks expert opinions from all sources. Team members are forbidden to criticize the ideas of others... the culture is non-judgmental and accepting.

All recognize that innovation is the result of intense commitment and plenty of hard work.

Sounds like a fun place to work, doesn't it?

Strategy by Design.
Want to find out more?

Visit www.ideo.com. Or read the *Fast Company* article "Strategy by Design" at www.fastcompany.com/magazine/95/design-strategy.html

Or... keep reading this chapter.

Something Old.

Constant execution and improvement can still build success.

Only today, company communications strategy will have to go top to bottom to be effective.

Here, a good example from UPS.

IDEO. Something New.

IDEO redefined design by creating experiences, not just products. Now its changing innovation itself.

At Kaiser Permanente – IDEO designers and social scientists teamed up with nurses, doctors, and facility managers. They came up with surprising insights.

For example, checking in was a nightmare. Waiting rooms were uncomfortable.

Doctors and medical assistants were too far apart. (See how they're gathering information?)

(Continued on next page)

Communication.

Finally, "Communication" replaces "promotion."

Now businesses need to think about all of the ways they make **customer contacts –** not just what their ads look like.

Ads may be the most visible element of the communication plan, but non-planned contacts may have equal or even greater impact on the consumer. For example, IMC guru Tom Duncan notes that often the lowest-paid employees have the most frequent contacts with customer and prospects.

What happened to your communications plan when it left the corner office? What effect does a littered restaurant location or an unhappy employee have on a prospect? This is communication even more powerful than *"Do you want fries with that?"*

How many ads does it take to overcome those negative aspects? More to the point, advertising may not have that much power.

Companies need to continually assess and evaluate the way they're communicating – top to bottom. This also needs to be integrated into the marketing communications plan.

Tomorrow's Marketing Models.

Will the Four C's become the marketing model of the future?

Or, just as traditional marketers added a fifth P – "people," will some other system develop the consumer perspective even further? One thing is certain – innovation will be part of it.

"The Dilemma of Success."

People constantly search for answers to their life's problems. Many of these answers are available commercially from marketers.

Answers to everyday questions like, "What's for dinner?", "What's the best type of vacuum to buy?", "What's wrong with my car?", "Who can fix my computer?", and "What kind of bugs are those?"

Successful marketers solve consumer problems. They develop products or services and sell them, hopefully, for a profit.

But, this also creates the "dilemma of success."

The dilemma is this – the longer a business is successful and the more successful it is, the more likely it is that factors will emerge that will diminish that success.

This is inevitable for a number of reasons:

• **Maintenance Personality**
• **Competitive Innovators**
• **Savvy Consumers**

Let's examine these factors of "creative destruction."

Maintenance Personality.

A marketer begins business as an innovator of a new product or a new product design. Once the marketer becomes successful his or her concern becomes the maintenance of that success.

That can be difficult – as a Palm PDA (Personal Digital Assistant) suddenly has to deal with a BlackBerry, and then the BlackBerry meets the iPhone.

Meanwhile, business can stay so busy keeping its first place today that it forgets to think about what it is going to take to be first place tomorrow.

Innovative Competitors.

Get too successful at being #1, and soon the marketplace creates a #2 and a #3. Maybe more.

This creates a competitive environment.

As we've discussed, there are many ways to compete.

Starbucks Success Brews Up Competition.

Starbucks innovation inspired other retail coffee chains, new distribution strategies, like Gevalia, and new store brands and flankers from large coffee marketers like P&G and KGF. And from large chains like McDonald's and Dunkin' Donuts.

Remember, strategy is about choice. And there are always a number of choices available to a marketer. Innovative strategic choices and aggressive competitors are a fact of life of the marketplace.

Savvy Consumers.

The marketplace changes us, too. Today's "Samurai Consumer" is tough and experienced from years of battling the marketplace.

For example, if you grew up in the US, you can't remember a time when you weren't a target for some marketer – starting with your breakfast cereal and your holiday toy list.

You learned. You learned to watch with skepticism, not believe everything you were told, and to pick what you really wanted from the non-stop parade of wonderful things to buy.

You learned. We all did.

Today, we all know who these savvy customers are. They're you.

Innovate or Die.

It's a tough world – for companies, for products, for brands, and for all of us as individuals. One way we make it easier is by learning – and innovating. That's the whole point of education, if you think about it – to give you the tools that will help you innovate.

This is at the root of Paul Romer's observations (remember him in Chapter One?) about the power of ideas to build a vital economy.

Some will be big lifetime innovations. Others will be the little day-to-day innovations that make life easier and friendships richer.

Even little innovations can lead to big business opportunities.

A shoe. Nike. A place for coffee. Starbucks. An auction. eBay.

A directory. Google. A calendar/address book – the PDA.

Or all of them together in the iPhone – or whatever's next.

Innovation to solve "new" life challenges is so desired that successful marketers are in a constant search for innovative answers – though it means a constant battle with the "maintenance personality."

As Howard Schultz at Starbucks observes, *"The way to stay on top is to reinvent yourself."*

Competitive Innovators.

There's always a company like 3M looking over your shoulder – and into the future.

They know that it's hard to keep innovating – and it's hard to keep making money at it.

3M knows that having new ideas is easy. But it can be hard to have new ideas that also make money.

IDEO (Cont.)

After seven weeks with IDEO, they realized they didn't need state-of-the-art buildings, rather, they needed to overhaul the patient experience.

The Experience.

"IDEO showed us that we are designing human experiences, not buildings." noted Adam D. Nemer, Kaiser's medical operations services manager.

As the economy shifts from the economics of scale to the economics of choice and as mass markets fragment, it's more important than ever for corporations to improve the consumer experience.

Yet, after decades of market research and focus groups, many marketers realize they still don't really know their consumers – or know how to connect with them.

Now IDEO has developed a methodology – a way of doing it –that we all can learn from.

It's a five-step process.

(Continued on next page)

Success = Competition.

Above, an ad for the Palm Pilot. (IDEO helped develop it.)

On the right, one of the many new competitors.

And then, it's time for BlackBerry!

IDEO (Cont.)

The IDEO Way.
Here are the five steps:

1. Observation. IDEO uses tools like shadowing, behavioral mapping, "Consumer Journey," "Extreme user interviews," storytelling, and what they call "UnFocus Groups."

2. Brainstorming. Remember brainstorming? Invented by Alex Osborn.

3. Rapid Prototyping. Mock-ups speed up decision making.

4. Refining. IDEO narrows the choices to a few possibilities.

5. Implementation. IDEO brings strong engineering, design, and social-science capabilities to bear in creating the product or service.

Innovation by Design.
Instead of looking at the world through a business-school prism, IDEO is teaching companies to look at the world like anthropologists, engineers, psychologists, and as designers – the result is innovation.

From *The Power of Design*
Business Week, 5/17/04

New Products. Evolution & Revolution.

LET'S LOOK AT SOME INNOVATIVE MARKETERS. A commitment to new ideas can bring new products into the marketplace.

First, we'll meet the team that developed PowerBar.

Then, we'll see how Campbell's, a company with a long history of both innovation and "taking care of business," integrates new ideas into a business that's over a century old.

PowerBar™

Bonk! Brian Hits the Wall.
Brian Maxwell liked to run marathons.

When Brian Maxwell "hit the wall" running a marathon and lost first place, he did something about it.

He invented the PowerBar.

In fact, he did more than that – he invented the entire energy snack bar category!

Brian, along with his wife and partner, Jennifer, filled a need for a non-filling, high-energy food which enabled athletes to perform at a peak competitive level.

They realized the original name, "Energy Bar," didn't dramatize the benefit of their product.

So they took a look at a better description of the benefit – *POWER!* They changed the name to PowerBar and grew their brand into the national champ.

Building on PowerBar's success, they translated this discovered need into a product line which exceeded $100 million in sales in 1999. And in 2000, he and his wife sold the company to Nestlé for $375 million. That's the good news.

The sad news is that Brian died recently. But his legacy lives. There are numerous tributes to him on the Internet.

In addition to those on the PowerBar site, there is an interesting one by inline speed skater Jonathan Seutter (www.skatelog.com/skaters/jonathan-seutter/brian-maxwell.htm).

That tribute honors both Brian's quality as a person and some of his innovative marketing techniques.

Entrepreneurs in Action.
PowerBar's success was a classic entrepreneurial tale.

They took their savings and his small teaching salary – and went for it. Thirteen years later, they employed 250 people.

In the beginning, they gave away product samples at competitive events. They took orders from dedicated runners.

In fact, they still sell PowerBars via mail order.

Competition in Action.
Since inventing the energy bar food category, PowerBar has acquired competitors like Quaker Oats and M&M Mars.

But, like Nike, this was a company founded by competitive athletes – some estimate PowerBar market share to be 60%.

A Team Sport.

Expanding the Brand.

PowerBar just completed a full-product line extension:

- a liquid food: power gel
- a newly flavored and textured PowerBar – Harvest
- a line of competitive sports drinks – Perform
- a line of snack energy and protein bars called Essentials and Protein Plus.

Outside-In – Listen to Your Customers.

PowerBar's built around an **outside-in strategy.**

They listened to their consumers and developed a product to answer the needs of their core customer – the high performance athlete (primarily runners and triathletes).

Though their usage may broaden, their brand is built around the relationship with this core group. PowerBar is committed to enhancing an athlete's performance through nutrition.

Even if you grab one for a quick snack – instead of a marathon – the added value of the brand's image helps.

Fully Integrated Grass-Roots Marketing Communication.

Jennifer and Brian's original goal was *"to help people tap the science and spirit of sports through nutritious healthy products."*

Here, their communication strategy is executed through a fully integrated grass-roots campaign.

PowerBar sponsors over 4,000 sporting events, including the Tour de France, Boston Marathon, Olympics, and thousands of small and regional events.

A "green marketing" program is called D.I.R.T. (Direct Impact on Rivers and Trails).

The Power of Grass-Roots Promotion.

Their promotional mix includes event marketing, endorsements, and promotional products (their logo on athletic gear is perfect for event sponsorship).

Word-of-mouth and an Internet address list the schedule of many of the world's competitive athletic events.

This focus on events allows one-to-one relationship building.

Brian and Jennifer Maxwell are an excellent example of what you can do – with the power of two.

They did all the marketing and sales themselves and didn't take a salary for the first two years.

Innovation can be a lonely job, and, like so many things, it's better when you do it together.

From the time Cyrus Curtis turned his wife's helpful articles into Curtis Publishing's first hit, *The Ladies' Home Journal,* partnership has been a force in The Business of Brands.

D.I.R.T.-Level Marketing!

Here's an example of their mission-centered approach to marketing – Direct Impact on Rivers and Trails (D.I.R.T.). It's a grant program.

Supported activities include:

- Efforts that improve access to wilderness – like hiking and bike trails
- Efforts that improve and restore natural areas
- Efforts that increase the number or size of local parks, recreation, and wilderness areas.

This is an excellent example of developing a marketing program out of the core values of a brand.

Here's what Jennifer and Brian have to say: *"Trail runs and hikes continue to be an important part of our family's favorite weekend activities. This is why at PowerBar we are excited to support access to trails and rivers…*

"Our goal is to ensure that no one runs out of trail before they run out of energy!" Nice Mission Statement.

TV from PowerBar – based on Brian's real life experience – insight in action.

In-Store Innovation.

This gravity-feed display provides better organization and product information. In stores where it replaced the old-fashioned stack display, sales lift averaged 5% and the long-term sales improvement was 3%. In a mature category, that's terrific!

Brand Values and Distribution.

Not only does this program reinforce the values of their brand, it is also the foundation for multi-tiered distribution, which includes: sporting goods stores, grocery retailers, and mail order.

Don't Bonk! Truth in Advertising.

In 1999, PowerBar increased their advertising. Wieden + Kennedy created a TV spot that relived the experience that caused Brian to develop the PowerBar in the first place.

It features a runner about to win a marathon.

As the runner hits the tape, he hits a wall – *bonk!*

"Bonking" is a runner's term for totally running out of gas.

The runner falls backward, unable to break the tape, and lies there as other runners pass him to win.

The brand message comes on the screen: "Don't Bonk!"

Since being purchased by Nestlé, PowerBar moved to Publicis, a more traditional agency. But you can still see the original W+K commercial on our adbuzz.com Web site.

Campbell's Keeps Simmering.

"INNOVATION IS CRITICAL TO OUR GROWTH AGENDA. We are making our brands more contemporary, more relevant, and more convenient to consumers of all ages... we are thinking inside and outside of the can. Growth will come from being better connected to our customers and consumers than ever before."

That's what it said in a Campbell's Annual Report.

Since then, they've tried to evolve their offerings to match today's more fast-paced and convenience-driven lifestyle. (Remember The Four C's? Condensed soup is no longer convenient.)

The Challenge of Change never ends. And sometimes the bad news is good news.

5% to 8%.

In 1998, Campbell's Annual Report further noted that, *"Powerful advertising is an essential part of our new marketing strategy.*

"In our US soup business, our new "Good for the Body, Good for the Soul" campaign captures perfectly Campbell's *nurturing and nourishing qualities. We remain committed to raising advertising spending as a percentage of sales from approximately 5% in 1998 to at least 8% over the next few years."*

Campbell's marketing and selling expenses increased from 19.6% in 1996 to 22.7% according to their 1998 Annual Report.

But more ad weight was not enough to fight consumer trends.

Condensed soup was no longer "convenient." Even the small step of adding water could be a problem – particularly in an office lunch room.

And, there was more individual eating of soup – it was no longer a family meal.

Those were the challenges Paul Anderson faced when he joined Campbell's from P&G.

We briefly mentioned some of the things he did in Chapter Four. We'll take a bit more time here, because he had to find the right mix between innovation and tradition.

As you review his activities, you'll see he moved in three directions.

1. He innovated products to make them more compatible with current lifestyles.

2. He recognized a key secondary target – kids. More and more he dedicated marketing efforts and product development efforts to this key demographic.

3. He faced up to a long-term in-store problem. With all those varieties, the soup aisle was pretty darn confusing. It could take you a long time to find the soup you were looking for – and you couldn't find out much about a new variety.

Just that one basic change in the in-store display had a positive impact on sales. Let's take a look at some of the other things they did.

Campbell's New Product Focus.

Developing an effective strategic corporate plan and an accompanying communication plan is like making dinner.

Here's the strategic menu for Campbell's innovations:

• **Convenience**

• **Kids**

• **Premiums and Promotions**

• **Easy-to-Use New Products**

And, to maintain their existing loyal customer base, they are shifting to promotions with "mega-events."

Convenience.

As mentioned in Chapter Two, Campbell's realized that, in today's market, trying to change the nature of their condensed soup business was "pushing water uphill."

Their new focus is on more convenient ready-to-serve soups.

Kids.

Campbell's sales depend on maintaining consumer brand loyalty, and their future lies with creating loyalty among kids – and their mothers. "Mouth Fun" was a separate sub-campaign aimed at kids and moms.

Kids products like Spaghettios received continuing attention. And all their brands get a solid level of promotion.

A Promotional "Mega-Event."

Twenty-five years ago, Campbell's developed an integrated "mega-event" promotion called *Labels for Education.*

Students' families collect labels to receive free educational and athletic equipment for their school.

Strategic Change.

Changes in lifestyle – like the microwave – create new "Factors that Influence Purchase Behavior."

Here, Campbell's promotes their new Soup to Go!

Product Change.

Even old favorites need innovation.

Here, Tomato Soup goes ready-to-serve in a classy glass jar.

Keep Doing What Works.

Campbell's found that they have a brand that works well on premium items. They continue to push this strategic advantage.

Now Being Served Online.

The *Campbell's Community* is more than recipes. There's a company history, updates on their *Labels for Education* program, and even e-commerce (now it's easier than ever to get an official soup mug). Just go to www.campbellsoup.com.

An important new brand.

Prego®

Prego and Gallo...
Pasta Made Perfect

TRY! *Campbell's*
Creamy Potato *with Roasted Garlic*

Great Taste Never Looked Better!

Recipe for Change.

Campbell's has to keep cooking up new brands and new product ideas to meet the challenge.

This is a powerful combination of cause marketing and a continuity program. Twenty-five years later, it's still going strong.

Add it all up and it's easy to understand the all-encompassing theme that also combines old and new.

"M'm! M'm! Good! Possibilities!"

Fully Integrated Promotions.

Campbell's fully integrated promotions utilize national and international umbrella advertising, prominent on-shelf supermarket displays, coupons, new products, new packaging for established products, and specialty sales promotions like NFL tie-ins.

The promotion above utilizes tie-ins with out-of-home advertising. In fact, a billboard with your face on it is one of the prizes. It's a relatively unique promotion with interesting consumer involvement opportunities. And, of course, it serves as a vehicle to deliver more ordinary values as well – such as coupons.

Cooking up Easy-to-Use New Products.

Campbell's has always been about convenience. It's more important than ever with today's "time-poor" consumers.

Prego – A Growing Brand.

Convenient Italian cooking is a growing category, and Campbell's Prego brand has become a major player.

Home Cookin' – A Brand New Brand.

With the steam going out of condensed soup, Campbell's needed to develop other sub-brands.

And then came the bad news. It was "M'm! M'm! Good!" news.

America Comes Back to Soup.

When the economy and the stock market took a nose dive, guess which was the only S&P 500 stock to escape a huge sell-off in 2008? Campbell Soup Company.

They had hiked their dividend again – the fifth time in five years.

Healthy eating habits – and solid marketing – meant they had to increase production of their V8 Vegetable Juice. Their upscale soup, Select Harvest, was making solid gains, and, a bad economy looked like good news for their traditional condensed soups.

Soup was even a weapon against one other social trend – obesity.

Want to eat less at your meal? Have soup or a salad first.

Campbell's hit a perfect storm of good news. Their dedication to innovation paid off – and economic and social trends beyond their control made things even better.

As they say, *"fortune favors the prepared mind."*

New Agencies for a New World.

WHEN AGENCIES OFFER MARKETERS new skills and insights, agencies grow. These new skills and insights are the kinds of agency innovations that usually bring success in the marketplace. And nothing attracts clients like success.

Internet Agencies…

One example of innovation in the agency marketplace has been the growth of **Internet agencies** – agencies that specialize in Web site design as well as Internet-based marketing programs.

They offer skills in Web site construction and a whole range of related services. Their computer-based skills are often far superior to those of traditional agencies.

In the '90s, Mark Kvamme's CKS stunned the design community by doing a complete redesign for United Airlines in a fraction of the time, and at a fraction of the cost, of traditional design firms.

Today, most design firms have these capabilities – and so do more and more traditional advertising agencies.

Integrated Marketing Communications Agencies.

As Don Schultz noted, smaller business-to-business marketers and agencies have been practicing IMC for years.

The scale of their business, the relatively clear communications options, and value and sophistication of each individual customer provides a marketing environment conducive to IMC practices.

Ninety Miles West of Toronto…

One place with a conducive environment is Waterloo-Kitchener, a vital part of Ontario, Canada, about ninety miles west of Toronto. It's Canada's version of Silicon Valley.

Quarry Integrated Communications, located in Waterloo/Kitchener, has grown to become Canada's leading agricultural agency – with additional expertise in financial and high-tech.

They combine this expertise with cutting-edge capabilities that serve clients like Sprint, FedEx, HP, and Blackberry.

Eliot Kang.

Eliot Kang
President and CEO
Kang & Lee Advertising

He arrived in New York at the age of 11. A dedicated student, Eliot thought he'd be a social worker.

While studying at Cornell, he took a year off from studies to visit Korea – and connect with his Asian roots.

After working there as a translator, he hooked up with some American ad executives to do ethnic marketing.

Putting that same dedication to work, he built his own firm from the bottom up – literally. He started with a cousin in the basement of his father's antiques showroom.

Entrepreneur Turned AdMan.

"I see myself more as an entrepreneur than advertising person," says Kang.

"Our policy is, 'If it doesn't exist, we'll create it.'" It's exactly what he's done.

The 5A's.

Kang created the first guide to Asian-American media.

He was a driving force organizing the 3AF – the **Asian-American Advertising Federation** (www.3af.org).

Now a part of Y&R and WPP, he has built what is generally regarded as the largest US advertising agency for the Asian-American market.

And now he's also leveraging his expertise the other way, helping WPP grow in Asia.

New Markets.

New ad opportunities = new agencies.

Korean

Chinese

Japanese

Vietnamese

From AAAAA to 3AF.

In 1999, 15 agencies founded the 5A's – the Association of Asian-American Advertising Agencies.

Then, they rebranded themselves as the 3AF – the Asian-American Advertising Federation.

Shown Here, Left to Right: Wei-Tai Kwok, secretary; Zan Ng, board member; Eliot Kang, president; Shelley Yamane, board member; Greg Macabenta, board member; Joe Lam, treasurer; and Greg Chew, Creative Director of Dae Advertising (also an advertising instructor in San Francisco).

Example: Technical Writing.

They've leveraged other skill sets as well. Quarry has combined communications skills and high-tech expertise, to add a technical writing division.

In addition to providing a much needed service for their client base, integrating this service into their client's communication organizations serves tom generate other projects.

An integrated organization that matches up with client needs generates new business. It's a new version of an old formula.

And you don't have to go to Canada to visit, there's always www.quarry.com.

New Agencies for New Markets.

The US is becoming a world country.

Once primarily European, new groups are now becoming major parts of American society. Diversity is more than a social policy, it's a fact of life – one that now comes in many flavors.

Profile: Kang & Lee.

Kang & Lee Advertising, established in 1985 as AMKO Advertising, boasts over $65 million in capitalized billings and is part of the Young & Rubicam family of companies.

Today, Kang & Lee Advertising is the largest full-service marketing communications company linking corporate America to the Asian-American marketplace and other diversified markets, including the Russian and Polish community.

A Blue-Chip Client Base.

As a pioneer in the Asian-American market, Kang & Lee provides solutions for its blue-chip clients, among them AT&T, Bank of America, Prudential, Sears, Seagrams, the *New York Times*, United Airlines, United States Postal Service, and others.

Multicultural, Multilingual, Multifunctional.

Kang & Lee's staff consists of over 100 multicultural, multilingual individuals in New York and Los Angeles.

Capabilities include creative development, account management and production, media planning and placement, direct marketing, database management, community and event marketing, and public relations.

They were the first-place winner of the O'Toole Multi-cultural Advertising Awards given by the 4A's.

Eliot offers this advice, *"If you're going to be a pioneer in a market, you have to spend at least half of your time selling that market.*

I used to spend 70% of my time selling the potential of the Asian-American marketplace, and many other agencies do the same kind of thing. You sell the market first and your company second.

"The first thing that you have to do when you start a company in a new market is to look at whether that market is big enough. In the ad business, a market needs to include at least 10 million consumers before you can convince a company that it should target those people."

The Asian-American Market – Six Cultures, 12+ Million.

Approximately 89% of Asian-Americans are from six cultures: Asian-Indian, Chinese, Filipino, Japanese, Korean, and Vietnamese. Unlike the Hispanic market, languages vary widely.

The 3AF estimates the market as 12.7 million (over 4%), expected to double to a projected 10% of US population by 2020.

Average household income is the highest for any ethnic group ($46,695) and total spending estimated at $344 billion.

Education is the highest of any group in the US.

And, of course, one US state already has an Asian majority.*

Diversity and Adversity.

The market impacts diversity in more ways than one.

Third- and fourth-generation Asian-Americans are much different from recent immigrants.

In some cases, they share few of the traditional values of that country. Family members are all in the US – not quite the lucrative target for long-distance companies as recent immigrants.

Historical and cultural issues also complicate matters. Some Asian groups, for a variety of reasons, are not the best of friends.

An Entrepreneurial Heritage.

It's a powerful new market with an abundance of opportunity.

Eliot Kang's father came to the US and started a business; his son followed in that tradition.

Asian-Americans start a higher percentage of new businesses than

the general population, so we should be seeing more growth.

That includes opportunities for a whole new group of advertising agencies, helping marketers find innovative ways to deal with a changing world.

And, in advertising and marketing, where talent, new ideas, and innovation always have a chance for success, America and Americans will continue to lead the way.

* Hawaii, of course.

Vietnamese promotional piece from Kang & Lee for Bank of America.

Just in time for Chusok!

The frostier the winter, *the more fragrant the plum blossom will be.*

Kiero no hi.

Changing Everything.

It's changing how you book a trip, how you look for a book, and how you search for a house or apartment.

With SABRE, American Airlines was able to achieve strategic advantage in the airline industry, based on the delivery of information to travel agents. Today, we can all get that high level of information.

How did you book your last trip?

Invest in Change.

Now, investments are being made over the Internet. It may even change the hours that Wall Street is open.

People once worried about making a small purchase on the Net.

Now they are buying stocks.

The Internet

Background · — · — · — · — = 0 1 0 1 0 1 0 1 0 1 0

THINK ABOUT MORSE CODE. In the 1800s, the invention of the telegraph made it possible to transmit messages across the country using a simple series of dots and dashes.

By today's standards it was extremely slow, but it wasn't all that different from the **binary system** (zeros and ones) computers still use to communicate today.

Now, instead of a single telegraph line, today's computers can communicate with virtually any other computer over the Internet, a vast collection of computer networks.

1969. ARPAnet – The Internet Is Born.

Many authors cite 1969 as the birth of the Internet, when the US Department of Defense commissioned the Advanced Research Projects Agency (ARPA) to develop an experimental network to support military research.

This network, called ARPAnet, was designed to function when portions of the network were inoperable or even destroyed.

1971. E-mail.

Two years later, **e-mail** was invented. Though it was one of the first methods developed for sending messages, it's still the primary method used for inter-person Internet communication.

Next. NSFNET.

Access to ARPAnet was primarily restricted to computer science researchers, government employees, and government contractors.

In 1986, the National Science Foundation commissioned a new network called NSFNET.

This network, using technology developed for ARPAnet, connected five supercomputer centers using telephone lines.

The NSFNET networking effort resulted in an explosion of new connections, primarily from universities. As a result, virtually anyone attending a university could become an Internet user.

1987. UUNET.

One of the first commercial Internet providers, UUNET, was formed in 1987. UUNET provided commercial USENET access.

USENET, founded in 1989, is a collection of discussion groups or news groups. Still thriving today, virtually any topic you can think of now has a discussion group.

1991. Open for Business with HTML.

In 1991, two major events occurred.

First, the National Science Foundation lifted remaining restrictions on commercial use of the Internet.

Then, what was probably the most important development in the history of the Internet (so far) occurred…

The World Wide Web.

As Thomas Friedman recounts in *The World is Flat*, "*The actual concept of the World Wide Web – a system for creating, organizing, and linking documents so they could be easily browsed – was created by British computer scientist Tom Berners-Lee. He put up the first Web site in 1991, in an effort to foster a computer network that would enable scientists to easily share their research.*

Berners-Lee had developed a system for using networked hypertext to transmit documents and communicate among members of a network.

Hypertext is simply a method of electronically linking documents. A hypertext document contains links to another document, and selecting a link will automatically display that second document. The World Wide Web suddenly provided easy access to any form of information anywhere in the world.

1993. Mosaic. The Internet Goes GUI.

At this point, the World Wide Web was primarily text based. That changed in 1993 with the development of Mosaic, a **graphic user interface** (GUI), or browser.

Mosaic was designed at the University of Illinois' National Center for Supercomputing Applications (NCSA).

For the first time, there was a widely available multimedia **(hypermedia)** tool that could handle **hyperlinked** audio, pictures, and video in addition to text.

Mosaic later developed into the browser Netscape Navigator.

1993. 600 Web Sites.

The World Wide Web revolutionized modern communication. In 1993, there were approximately 600 Web sites.

In 1994, there were 10,000 Web sites, and the Web became the second most popular service on the Internet.

1995. 100,000 Web Sites.

By 1995, there were 100,000 Web sites, and the Web became the most popular service on the Internet.

In 1996, there were 500,000 Web sites, and in 1997, one million.

2000. Seven million Web Sites – and still growing.

A few years ago, World Wide Web researchers at Ohio College Library Center (OCLC) determined there were seven million unique sites – about 40% with content freely accessible to the public.

New Web sites now appear at a rate of about one per minute.

It's Changing the News.

The Internet has started to make profound changes in our media habits. Now we can subscribe to newspapers online.

What's next?

Here, an ad for www.abcnews.com.

Maybe Not Everything.

Is this really the way you're going to buy a tie? Then again, were you going to buy a tie?

The Banner.

As the Internet emerged, so did new forms of Internet-based advertising – a new size, new functions (like click-through), and a new way to deliver advertising.

Ad Webonomics 101.

"Not someday, today – advertising on the Web makes economic sense. You just have to forget everything you ever learned about the business."

A New Advertising Economy.

Evan I. Schwartz argues that an entirely new publishing and advertising economy is taking shape on the Web. He calls it Webonomics.

Four Main Groups.

This economy consists of interactions among four main groups:

- **Consumers** (the millions of people "surfing" the Web)
- **Content Creators** (publishing companies, TV networks, movie studios, and hybrid media outlets creating sites to inform and amuse)
- **Marketers** (companies promoting products and services)
- **Infrastructure Companies** (the hardware and software producers, ISPs, ad agencies, and the others who contribute)

Five Principles:

Schwartz identifies five principles:

Principle 1: Consumers will rarely pay a subscription fee for access to a Web site.

Principle 2: The old models of selling advertising do not apply.

Principle 3: Marketers are not on the Web for exposure but results.

Principle 4: Customers must be rewarded when they disclose information about themselves.

Principle 5: It's not the quantity of people you attract to your site that counts most, but the quality of their experience there.

(Source: *Wired*, February 1996)

Shopping **online** beats standing **in line**.

LANDS' END
DIRECT MERCHANTS
www.landsend.com

From catalog to the web, the store is yours.

www.landsend.com/1-800-627-4104

The Web reached 10 million consumers faster than any other technology (pagers, telephones, fax machines, VCRs, cellular phones, PCs, and CD-ROMs) in history.

The Internet as an Ad Medium.

THE INTERNET IS THE FASTEST-GROWING MEDIUM in history, and it continues to grow even faster.

50 Million in Five Years.

The Web took only five years to penetrate 50 million US homes, compared to 10 years for cable television, 13 years for broadcast television, and 38 years for radio.

And audiences from other media are migrating to the Internet.

According to Forrester Research, 78% of computer users report taking time away from watching television to use their computer.

This phenomenal growth made advertisers take notice, because wherever there are audiences, there will be advertisers.

Prodigy Tries It First.

When the commercial online service *Prodigy* started in 1990, it was the only online company to adopt advertising as a revenue source. Being first isn't always the answer.

The early interface was slow, and the early adopter *Prodigy* audience was not lucrative for the initial investors. Other major online services did not seriously address advertising until 1995.

***HotWired* Sets the Trend. The Birth of the Banner.**

However, Internet advertising really began when the first banner ads were sold on the *HotWired Network* in October 1994, and Netscape Navigator 1.0 was released in November of the same year.

At this time, the majority of the Web's early adopters were somewhat hostile to advertising, so *HotWired* allocated a rather small portion of the area within the browser frame to advertising.

The **banner** was born. Soon, sites across the Web were using this "standard format" for advertising.

Five Choices for Internet Advertising.

As the Internet has evolved, five distinct choices emerged for marketers and advertisers on the Web.

1. **Portals**
2. **Destination Sites**
3. **Micro-Sites**
4. **Banner Ads and Similar Types of Sponsorship**
5. **Search-Based Text Ads**

Let's look at them one by one.

1. Portals are the gateways to the Internet.

AOL is a portal.

So is MSN.

Others, like *Yahoo!*, established themselves with

VACANCY

YAHOO!

A nice place to stay on the Internet.

FREE E-MAIL. ALL U CAN EAT BUFFET

convenience, good design, and the magic word –"Free!"

Others, such as Microsoft, have not had great success.

This is one of the battlefields of the Internet, with large media companies working to become the portal of choice.

2. Destination Sites.

Destination sites use information, entertainment, and high production values to attract users and bring them back again.

Some companies are now spending significant amounts of time and money to develop original content, with every technological feature available.

For example, Nabisco has invested a lot in a kid-oriented site with features like the *Oreo Dunking Game.*

The Need for Web Strategies.

Advertisers now understand the need for Web strategies that not only provide information, but work to turn potential customers from information seekers to qualified leads to buyers.

Example: Web-Based Service.

Companies have found success by using their Web site to provide customer service. Both FedEx and UPS allow users to track packages online. Airlines now offer e-tickets.

Other companies did not have the quick success they hoped for. Lands' End discovered online sales would not replace catalog sales quickly, though their online business is growing.

The Dockers site was designed to allow you to purchase clothes online, but complaints from retailers caused re-evaluation.

3. Micro-Sites and "Magpies."

A **micro-site** is simply a small cluster of brand pages hosted by content sites or networks.

Micro-sites are also called "brand modules," and in Europe they're called "magpie pieces," after the bird that sneaks its eggs into other birds' nests to hatch.

These sites allow advertisers to provide information and collect customer information without the cost of a complete Web site.

As Web usage and bandwidth has grown, most marketers now realize that they have to step up to running a site of their own.

4. Banners, Buttons, Etc.

Web advertising really began with banner ads, and they continue to be a primary form of Web advertising.

Banners and **buttons** are simply rectangular graphics located on pages in high-traffic Web sites.

Users click on the banner and link to the advertiser's Web site. This is called **click-through.**

This "click-through" provides advertisers with a measurement of response – the objective of most banner ads.

In the beginning, click-through rates were as high as 20 or 30%; however, these rates have declined to less than 1% in many instances.

Will It Kill Advertising?

George Lois, Richard Kirshenbaum, and the *Pillsbury Doughboy* pose for this cover on one of the early issues of *Wired* magazine, which examines the impact of the Internet, interactivity, and media fragmentation on the advertising business.

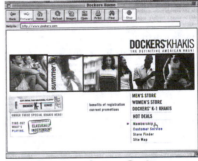

Not for Sale Online.

You can't buy Dockers online. They will send you to their retail partners.

Banner Size Guidelines.

The Interactive Advertising Bureau (IAB) has developed a set of recommended standards for banners.

Unit	Weight Limits GIF/JPEG	FLASH	Animation	Border
728x90				
300x250	40K	40K	15 Sec.	None
160x600				
180x150				

Interactive Advertising Bureau
www.iab.net

Spam, Spam, Spam, Spam.

E-mail spam got its name from a *Monty Python* comedy sketch. In the 1970s, the British comedy troupe performed a sketch featuring a diner menu consisting of *"egg and bacon, egg sausage and bacon, egg and Spam, egg bacon and Spam, egg bacon sausage and Spam, Spam bacon sausage and Spam, Spam egg Spam Spam bacon and Spam, Spam sausage Spam Spam bacon Spam tomato and Spam, Spam Spam Spam egg and Spam, Spam Spam Spam Spam Spam Spam baked beans Spam Spam Spam, etc."*

As the waitress recited the menu, Spam-loving Vikings sang in the background.

Since the practice of "spamming" forces readers to see the same message over and over and over again, the repetition of "Spam" in the sketch provided the perfect moniker.

The Hormel Company may have mixed feelings about the use of their trademarked brand name.

But they're making the most of it, leveraging Spam as a "cool" Internet brand.

In fact, you can get "Spam Stuff" by going to their site. At www.spam.com, of course.

The Google Ad Strategy.

While everyone else was heading towards splashy "splash pages" and tricky banners, Google went the other way.

Their strategic choice was fast-loading text only ads. This was 1998, the heyday of animated brand-toting banners dancing at the top of almost every portal.

(Continued on next page)

5. Search-Based Text Ads.

Do you Google? Of course you do. The Google search engine has become one of the standard tools of the Internet.

And the recent public offering of their stock was an upbeat re-surgence of "dot.com" stocks after the spectacular crash of Internet and technology stocks.

One of the reasons that Google was so successful is that it is already a $600 million advertising business. Big and profitable.

Those simple text ads on the right side of your search are there by way of a relevance algorithm called AdWords.

Now other sites are signing up to make a few pennies per click with these simple unobtrusive text-based ad listings.

More than 180,000 have joined so far.

E-Mail as a Marketing Tool.

Web sites, banner ads, and text-based ads are only part of the Internet advertising mix. E-mail, the most popular online activity, has emerged as a powerful tool.

However, using e-mail for marketing got off to a poor start.

The Birth of Spam.

In 1994, two Arizona attorneys sent thousands of repeated messages to Usenet news groups. The messages advertised legal assistance for obtaining green cards.

This process of sending the same message to large numbers of news groups without regard to group content is called **spamming**. (See sidebar.) The reaction to the spam was swift.

Large volumes of e-mail complaints, known as flames, poured in to the lawyers' Internet service provider (**ISP**). The ISP's computers crashed repeatedly, and finally the company terminated the lawyers' account. (But the lawyers generated business with it.)

A recent feasibility study on a "no-Spam" list, similar to the Do Not Call Registry, generated the opinion that it would merely generate and attract more Spam.

However, we now have Spam filters.

E-Mail Strategies – *Hotmail*.

Today, Internet marketers use e-mail in a variety of ways.

Some companies, such as *Hotmail*, provide free e-mail accounts to users. The *Hotmail* e-mail reader displays paid advertising.

Other companies sponsor e-mail newsletters or mailing lists (commonly known as discussion groups).

Still others sponsor e-mail games and sweepstakes.

E-Mail Strategies – "Opt-In."

The fastest growing use of e-mail is direct, or **opt-in**, e-mail. Consumers register at company Web sites and agree (opt-in) to receive future e-mail messages.

These messages may contain information about sales items, new products, site enhancements, or special offers.

Since consumers usually provide specific demographic information along with their e-mail addresses, marketers can better target their messages.

Technological Advances.

One of the things that makes Internet advertising and marketing so exciting is the constant development of new technology.

Technology promises more exciting ways to reach and interact with consumers. Sometimes they work; sometimes they don't.

Push Technology.

The use of opt-in e-mail is a simple example of push technology. **Push technology** delivers messages directly to users, rather than waiting for the user to come to the advertiser.

Companies like *PointCast* hoped to make push technology work. The idea was a free Internet news source supported entirely by advertisers. Special software would "push" the latest headline news and information from a variety of sources – plus ads.

Demographic information provided during registration would allow advertisers to target more precisely. Great idea. It didn't work.

"Push" Is Hot. Then It's Not.

When push technology arrived on the scene, many "experts" said this was the advertising solution for the Internet.

But push technology never lived up to its hype.

There were two major problems:

- Push technology works best with dedicated Internet connections – generally available only in work environments.
- The second problem is content. Without adequate quality control, push quickly turns into spam.

  Those who opt-in soon want to "opt-out."

Rich Media.

Another promising technology is known as **rich media.**

This refers to the use of new technology to provide streaming video, audio, and other enhancements to banner ads. Using Shockwave, Real Audio, Windows Media Player, and other enhancements, you now get more than just a Web site.

Example: *BMW.*

As bandwidth expanded, marketers became more interested in delivering Internet-based video experiences for their brands. The first to really do it right was BMW.

They produced a series of Net films called "The Hire." It wasn't just the media that was rich – so was the budget. The idea was a series of six- to eight-minute films about a hired driver (Clive Owen) in dangerous situations. The best of them is by Guy Richie (Madonna's husband). Just the idea of an action film for the Internet created a lot of buzz and "The Hire" caught on.

Find out for yourself at www.bmwfilms.com – and you'll be one of over 12 million (so far) who tuned in.

Read more in the sidebars on the next two pages.

BMW's Online Strategy.

The Problem: BMW felt they had to get back to their original performance positioning.

Research showed that BMW had become more of a status car than a performance car with drivers just entering the luxury-car market.

Goals: The goals were simple: make BMW relevant and cool to young purchasers 25–44.

Strategy: *"We wanted to showcase the cars in a fun and exciting way, and show them as the ultimate driving machine without selling anything."* said Karen Vondermeulen, BMW Group Marketing and Events Manager.

Insight: James McDowell, BMW North America VP of Marketing said, *"We saw, in 1999 we were trying to climb a mountain on the wrong side... we asked ourselves, 'What if we throw out some of our core assumptions – for instance, that we have to do brand image advertising on network TV."*

Tactics: Fallon Worldwide was hired. Their campaign, "The Hire," was a series of short films done by top action directors for the Internet. (www.bmwfilms.com)

One key was that the target group would not perceive the films as ads.

Everything about the communication said "film."

Guerrilla PR posted information about the films on movie sites.

Postcards as movie posters and movie promo-style radio ads supported the introduction of the films.

(Continued on next page)

But rich media comes at a price – in bandwidth and dollars. Most Web publishers limit banner size to 10 to 12 kilobytes.

Anything larger than that increases the time needed for a Web page to load, this increases the chance users will click away rather than wait for the download.

Rich-media banners reach well above the 12 kilobyte threshold. And, rich-media ads can be expensive to produce, costing as much as six times more than traditional banners.

Interstitials, Daughter Windows, Splash Screens.

One popular form of rich media is the **interstitial**.

An interstitial is a Web page, usually containing a promotion or ad, that appears in a separate browser window.

A **pop-up window** opens and appears automatically when a user enters a Web page. A **daughter window** opens only when a user clicks on an accompanying banner.

There are other names for interstitials: splash screens, parent windows, extramercials, transitionals, and child windows.

MarketAdviser predicted spending on interstitials would grow to 15% of ad spending. However, as search-based ads grew dramatically, interstitials and rich media together were about 15%.

Keyword search ads are now about 40% of revenues.

Industry Growth. Key Industry Issues.

In 1998, the IAB reported that Internet advertising revenues reached $1.92 billion. They surged to $4.62 billion in 1999 and peaked at $8.09 billion in 2000.

Then, the "irrational exuberance" ended. Spending declined to $6 billion (still a big number) by 2002, volume began to recover as marketers found out what worked.

2003 revenues were $7.3 billion. For a more complete picture, visit the Internet Advertising Bureau site (www.iab.net).

FAST. An Internet Advertising Summit.

In 1998, P&G used its position as the world's largest advertiser to bring together key groups to address major issues facing the Web as an advertising medium.

The Future of Advertising Stakeholders (FAST) summit participants identified four key issues:

- **Gaining Consumer Acceptance**
- **Standardizing Measurement**
- **Defining Ad Models and Creative Formats**
- **Making Online Media Easier to Buy**

Advertising Age named P&G Interactive Marketer of the Year, primarily for their leadership role in the FAST summit. And the Internet has become more realistic in what it promises and what it delivers.

But it is still an industry of volatility and dramatic ups and downs.

With that in mind, let's meet a former leader of the Internet – one who has had a dramatic input on a wide range of media.

Bob Pittman – Media Superstar.

IN THE FIRST EDITION, we saluted one of the top talents in media marketing – Bob Pittman. Terms applied to him at various times in his career include: *"radio whiz kid," "cable wonderboy," "MTV wunderkind," "neo-legend,"* and *"marketing prodigy."*

They may all be true. But after the rise and fall of AOL, they've said other things as well. Here's the story; judge for yourself.

Flying Lessons.

Growing up, Bob Pittman wanted to fly airplanes. His father wouldn't pay for lessons. So, he paid for the lessons himself, at 15, with a part-time job as a deejay at a Mississippi radio station.

Three Colleges Later...

He attended Millsaps College, Oakland University, and the University of Pittsburgh, but never finished.

Then again, radio programming isn't taught many places.

Bob learned on his own. At the age of 21, he was the highest-paid radio programmer in the country, guiding *WNBC* to the top AM radio spot in New York City by the time he was 23.

Then he moved over to television. And helped launch *MTV*.

The Birth of MTV.

MTV: Music Television was launched in August 1981 by Bob Pittman along with David Horowitz. It was an idea that almost wasn't.

The idea itself had been around for a while. Pittman produced and hosted *Album Tracks* in 1978 (it ran for two seasons).

Nickelodeon ran a video music show in 1980.

There was even a video music network before MTV.

According to Pittman, *"The success of MTV was the execution of the idea – our particular vision of the programming and the unique attitude and culture of the network that we developed."*

Impact of MTV.

Briefly, here are some of the effects of MTV's introduction:

- **It changed the cable industry**
- **It changed the music industry**
- **It revolutionized TV graphics**
- **It transformed advertising** – MTV rock-videos popularized a new quick-cut style for TV spots

The Journey Continues...

In June 1988, Pittman went to Time Warner, and managed their Six Flags theme park operations.

He went to Century 21 in 1995. There, he encountered *AOL*.

He bought ads and sponsored the real estate section. He says, *"I saw a place I could advertise where my competitors weren't, yet."*

He became the service's first million-dollar advertiser. *"On the TV advertising, we were spending tens of millions of dollars. I got about three thousand leads a week.*

"When we launched on AOL, which at the time had about 6 million subscribers, we got about 16 thousand leads a week."

Pittman was ready for a new media revolution.

BMW Online (Cont.)

Marketer McDowell continues, *"we wanted it to be about entertainment, not advertising."*

Media. There was some traditional media support – print, radio – to lead people to the Web site. There were faux movie posters and postcards.

Publicity was used, just as it would be for a movie, placing stories in *Time, Entertainment Weekly,* and the *New York Times* among others.

Fallon ran 15 second teasers on TV, directing viewers to the Web site. It didn't feel like advertising. *"It wasn't a hard decision at all,"* notes McDowell. *"It was strategically correct. BMW owners are early achievers who consider technology their friend."*

"We asked ourselves if we could get one million (people) to watch these films and make it as cost-effective as a traditional broadcast TV campaign."

Results: The films were downloaded 10 million times and appeared on *Bravo* and *Independent Film Channel.* Season #1, budgeted at $9 million gave BMW an estimated $20 million worth of promotion.

It was judged cost-effective.

It was also judged persuasive. Before/after awareness and attitude among those who viewed the films and those who hadn't showed signficant shifts.

Purchase receptivity was up 64% and planned dealer visits up 550%.

Overall BMW sales were up 12.5% in 2001 and sales of the 3-series jumped 37% during the four-month promo period.

Awards: BMWfilms.com cleaned up: Best of Show at the One Show, a Grand Clio, and the Cyber Grand Prix Lion at Cannes. Dan Wieden and the Cannes Festival even created a new award, the Titanium Lion. Wieden explained it was to be given to work *"in any category, or any combination of categories, that causes the industry to stop in its tracks and reconsider the way forward."*

Bob Pittman Says: "Brands Win!"

Pittman is well known for his ideas about the impact of visual imagery upon the post-TV generation.

He says they process information simultaneously, not one piece at a time, as did previous generations.

Here are some of the other things he has to say... on brands, hard work, the Internet, and more...

"The number one trend in this country is that brand buyers control the economy.

"A second trend – convenience is king...

"Finally, you find technology literacy emerging."

"There is absolutely no substitute for hard work."

"The mass market is moving to the interactive medium. I bet my career on this."

"We're the first company to hit critical mass in cyberspace. Our strategy is to take advantage of that."

"Understanding – and delivering – what the consumer is looking for, and not so much the technology itself, is the key to the interactive business."

"The reality is TV is the competition for anything in the home."

"It's not about what you think is cool. Listen to what consumers want."

About Online Media:

"It's like TV, print ads, editorial, direct marketing, telemarketing, catalogs, stores, all added together."

"Coca-Cola doesn't win the taste test and Microsoft is not the best operating system, but in America BRANDS win."

The Rise of AOL.

As a big AOL advertiser, Bob became acquainted with Steve Case and others at AOL. And they became acquainted with him.

He became President/COO of AOL in October 1996.

And, in the tradition of revolution, he started changing things.

He brought a new revenue model to AOL – more dependence on advertising and e-commerce, with no connect-time revenues.

This was all part of the incredible rise of AOL which included the stratospheric rise in the value of AOL stock.

AOL-Time-Warner.

Remember how the stock market drove agency mergers?

It happened again. This time the high value of AOL stock allowed AOL to use the value of their stock to finance a merger/take-over of traditional media giant Time Warner.

There were problems. One was merging the cultures as a well-established media company found itself the junior partner.

But the real problem was the meltdown in the value of AOL stock, as the "dot.com explosion" became a stock market disaster.

In July of 2002, Pittman resigned as COO of AOL.

Steve Case, CEO, also left around that time.

Two years later, Pittman re-emerged with a market research company called OTX, which allowed marketers to test film trailers, commercials, and consumer products. From there, he evolved to an Internet investor with his Pilot Group. Stay tuned.

The Internet & The Business of Brands.

THE IMPACT OF THE INTERNET, and particularly the World Wide Web, is being felt throughout The Business of Brands. New marketers, new kinds of agencies, new media, and new specialists have emerged.

And with them, a variety of new opportunities for advertising and marketing graduates who understand this exciting new medium. This section takes a brief look at some of the players in the Internet advertising game.

New Issues.

Spam and Privacy. Cookies and Hackers.

The Internet has brought new problems – from consumer privacy to computer piracy.

Particularly after a mailbox full of spam, many consumers are concerned about what marketers plan to do with all the data that is so quickly and easily gathered in cyberspace.

A **cookie,** is a unique data file that a site leaves on your computer. These data files contain information the site can use to track your behavior on that site.

Security is also a concern, especially for e-commerce. The ability of unlawful elements to clone cell phones and use phony credit card information makes consumers understandably concerned.

That's not all. It's the World Wide Web. Everything is everywhere.

Globalization.

Perhaps this should be a book in itself, not just a short subsection, but the macrofact is that the Internet has connected us all.

Whether it's a computer scam based on another continent, a US company moving their "back room" to a place where programmers and telemarketers are one-third the cost, or just you saving money booking your own trip and getting a real deal at a nifty little hotel in Barcelona. Wherever you go, it's a new world.

And we all have to live in it.

As Marshall McLuhan noted, when media changed, we changed. And this change is profound.

Larry Grossman, former president of NBC News updated McLuhan for us. *"Printing made us all readers. Xeroxing made us all publishers. Television made us all viewers. Digitization makes us all broadcasters."* Think about that.

It's not just bmwfilms.com. You can put video of your own on your own Web site. Some of you already have. Many of you will.

We all affect each other more and more – as we connect through the World Wide Web – which truly is worldwide.

New Marketers.

We've already seen important new brands emerge.

Yahoo! The Super-Portal.

In 1994, two Stanford University graduate students, Jerry Yang and David Filo, created Yahoo!, an Internet portal.

A portal is simply a gateway through which many Internet users will pass. By adding value to that portal through features and services, Yahoo! became an Internet mega-brand.

Business Week defined four different types of portals:

- **Doorways**
- **Channels**
- **Programs**
- **Marques**

Yahoo! fits all four definitions. Do you Yahoo!?

Amazon.com.

Intelliquest asked 10,000 randomly selected Internet users to name the brands they associate with books. 56% named Amazon.com.

Not bad for a company that has a five year return on capital of minus 51%. But Wall Street believes in Amazon.com.

Founded in 1995, Amazon.com became the fastest growing e-commerce retailer on the Internet.

In 1999, Amazon.com founder Jeff Bezos went from the cover of *Wired* to the cover of *Time* as their Person of the Year.

In 2003, not ten years old, sales were over $5 billion. Depending on how you do your accounting, they made a profit.

In 2007, he made a move to change how we read books with a new piece of media technology – an electronic book with a wireless connection to books, magazines, newspapers, and more. The revolution keeps rolling along.

"Today, we are beginning to notice that the new media are not just mechanical gimmicks for creating worlds of illusion, but new languages with new and unique powers of expression."

– Marshall McLuhan
(He said this in 1957)

"Printing made us all readers.
Xeroxing made us all publishers.
Television made us all viewers.
Digitization makes us all broadcasters."

– Larry Grossman, NBC News

Cover Story.

Jeff Bezos makes the cover – before he makes a profit. And he keeps on making news as Amazon grows.

Permission Marketing.

Seth Godin of *Yahoo!* believes you have to give it away to get it – so he gave away the first four chapters of his book – on the Internet.

His brand philosophy *"Turning strangers into friends and friends into customers."*

Instant Competition.

Amazon.com has competition, too. Barnes & Noble, the leading bookseller, has clearly seen the advantages of search-engine-based technology.

Once again, it's the marketplace at work. As you can see by the ad on the right, B&N is promoting their online brand, barnesandnoble.com.

Meanwhile, B&N's big retail competitor, Borders, has its own strategy. They teamed up with Amazon.com!

Google – The New Big Dog.

The Internet is still full of volatility. Today's winners can be tomorrow's losers. And the game keeps changing.

As *Wired* notes, Larry Page and Sergey Brin called their company Google because it was the biggest number they could imagine.

But it wasn't big enough. Today, their brand has become a verb, with more than 200 million requests a day.

A New Advertising Model.

As we noted earlier, advertising is one of the big revenue drivers for Google, as search-based text ads became the dominant form of Internet advertising – hitting 40% of all volume in 2003 according to the Interactive Advertising Bureau.

Advertisers tell Google how much they want to spend, then "buy" pertinent keywords. When users type in a matching term, the ad appears near the search results under the heading "Sponsored Links." You've seen it yourself dozens of times.

Here's the beauty part. Only if a user clicks on the sponsored link does the advertiser pay. Google simply subtracts the small "cost-per-click" amount from the advertiser's account. When the daily budget is met, Google stops displaying the ad.

It's cheap. It's measurable. It's efficient. And it works.

Best of all, numerous marketers are pointing to very real results based on Google click-throughs, and now other sites are using Google's business model (and their search algorithim that matches the sponsored link with the search).

The Internet – Back in Business.

Revenue growth is back on a solid footing.

More important, so are the business models.

After failed (so far) experiments like push technology, multi-million and billion dollar winners are emerging.

Successful Internet business models like Amazon.com, eBay, and Google are bringing solid growth to this dynamic new medium.

That includes the growth of interactive agencies.

Managing Change.

As the pace of business accelerates, organizations have to become better at managing an accelerating constant – change.

The technological change driven by Moore's Law – as chip speed doubles every 18 months while the cost decreases.

The change in communication driven by the Media Revolution – as we move from a one-way to a two-way communication model throughout society.

The change in business as new ideas replace older ones, through "creative destruction."

And, finally, the transforming power of new ideas.

How do organizations, which are often built on getting something right and then repeating that behavior, also learn how to do something new?

It is a challenge facing every business and everyone who works.

The Arc of Change.

Sometimes even rapid change takes a bit of time. For example, the IT revolution didn't lead to better productivity right away.

As Paul Romer notes (remember him from Chapter One?), "you needed more than new computers. You needed new business processes and new types of skills to go with them."

It's one thing to know things are changing. It's another to know what to do about it. Two large companies that are working hard to do this are GE and P&G.

"An Old Economy Dinosaur."

That was how P&G was being described at the dawn of the 21st Century – not that long ago. The CEO resigned, earnings goals were missed (a rare thing for P&G), and the stock was down by 50%. Ouch.

As new CEO A.G. Lafley moved into his new responsibilities, he placed big responsibilities on the shoulders of Global Marketing Officer Jim Stengel.

This isn't introducing a PowerBar, P&G is big. Worldwide, there were over 200 brands and more than 3,500 marketing people.

How did a mature complicated organization manage to re-invigorate itself and achieve sales growth more than double the growth rate of the categories they compete in?

Complexity and Technology.

The beginnings of this change were established in the 90s, under a previous CEO. The immediate results were not what everyone wished, but the matrix organization put in place by Durk Jager began to pay off.

Under the new organization, business units got authority to develop new products, plot rollouts globally and develop the marketing programs around them, eliminating the need to get signoffs from regional bosses at every turn. Speed to market improved – and so did the connection with local markets worldwide.

Big Brand Revolutionary.

"So many things have changed… with the rise of new forms of communications.

"Obviously, consumers have changed a lot. We're trying to capture all that and integrate it." — Jim Stengel
Global Marketing Officer, P&G

Here are some of the ways that P&G evolves and innovates. They are dedicated to paying attention to their customers. This is what happens when you listen to the marketplace.

Febreze

It started as a fabric refresher in 1998, but it became clear that Febreze would never become one of P&G's coveted billion-dollar brands in such a limited category. So P&G took cues from consumers to turn Febreze into an air freshener, too, spurring rapid growth. The takeaway: Brand equities can be broader than marketers imagine.

Naturella

The old P&G model was to build premium brands in the US and export them. Naturella, a mid-tier-priced feminine protection brand featuring the herbal ingredient chamomile, started in Mexico, where it helped  P&G regain category leadership. P&G transplanted the concept in Latin America, Russia, and Poland within three years. Lesson: Developing markets and lower-income consumers can be launching pads for brands, too.

(Continued on next page.)

Brand Revolutionary (Cont.).

Pampers

As the brand fell behind Kimberly-Clark Corp.'s Huggies in the 1990s, technical innovations like Pampers Rash Guard fell flat. A product and advertising overhaul built around baby development and seeing the world through babies' eyes revived Pampers globally. Lesson: Emotional connections can trump benefit claims.

Tide & Downy

Detergent-softener combos had come and largely gone before Tide with a Touch of Downy hit stores in 2004. But the co-branded iteration scored an 8% market share and helped push Tide to record sales without significantly hurting Downy or the fabric softener category. Lesson: Roll out the brand matrix; co-branding works.

Olay

A once dowdy brand built around the pink beauty fluid Oil of Olay, the brand has gotten a makeover. The "Oil" is gone, and such products as Daily Facials cloths, Regenerist age-defying products, and Quench body lotion have turned Olay into a $2 billion global powerhouse growing at more than 20% annually. Lesson: Innovation can make even "Oil of Old Lady" young again.

(Souce: *Advertising Age*, 12/12/05)

With new champions, brands that had been low priorities began to flourish with local and regional attention.

There were big hits, but also some expensive misses.

Stengel noted, "*We had kind of gotten ourselves into a strategy where we were focused more on high end and more on pretty amazing technological things — like Dryel and Febreze and Swiffer. And we weren't really thinking about what it would take as a company to be the best brand builder with low-income consumers in countries like China and India… and that is a profound change… I think it shifted our consumer research, changed our mentality, challenged our paradigms.*"

Simplicity and Focus. Complexity and Dreams.

Stengel went in "*with a dream of turning P&G into the best marketing company in the world.*" He implemented Marketing Framework 3.0.

The framework included the seemingly contradictory dynamics of dreams and process, of multiple initiatives and single-minded focus.

All he had to do was get 3000 marketing people to work together.

Some of it centered around simple but powerful thoughts like "the consumer is boss" and his company-wide communication that there were two "moments of truth:" the first was in the store and the second was when the consumer used the product at home.

This company-wide effort included "on the ground" activities of even higher-level marketing executives spending time in homes and stores every quarter.

Big Brands Worldwide.

As you can see in the sidebar, the results are wide-ranging.

The initial focus was big brands and big markets, expanding down the list as the big things got fixed. The result? More big brands. The portfolio of billion dollar brands expanded from 10 to 17,

Search and Re-apply.

P&G has also become a better learning organization.

They use their global marketing intranet to share best practices.

They publicize these best practices with an expanding array of internal rewards as well as some well-publicized external activities, such as the Cannes Film Festival where they have become an award-winning presence.

Finally, as marketing options have expanded, P&G has expanded the range of their marketing expertise, implementing long-term programs in Marketing Public Relations and New Media to go with their already proven expertise in Advertising, Sales Promotion, and Event Marketing (remember, they were one of the first to understand the potential of NASCAR).

GE Goes Green.

A large complex company, with manufacturing businesses ranging from light bulbs and kitchen appliances to thermoplastics and nuclear reactors. GE also has services business like long-term insurance and consumer credit.

With all of their divisions, they've been committed to a high-level of performance. What's more, as a company they've made an additional commitment to "green marketing" with additional concern over the environmental impact of their business. It's helped them grow into new areas – like wind turbines.

As CMO of GE, Beth Comstock had to evolve her background in public relations to turn marketing from what was perceived as a cost to a revenue-generating profit center.

A Partnership between Marketing and Technology.

One of GE's divisions developed an innovative scanner for the medical profession. GE marketing made a suggestion that improved its usage in the medical marketplace by raising the bar for GE technology – adding software that made this scanner more user-friendly for a variety of medical specialties.

A Commitment to Manage Change.

This commitment came from the very top, GE CMO Jeff Immelt wanted an initiative that showed what marketing can do. As Comstock noted, "*He wanted us to become as comfortable with ideas as we are with process.*"

Think about that. Process is easy for an organization, we figure out a way to do it and then we keep doing it.

Ideas are different. They can be disruptive. They can even be, as Schumpeter pointed out, "destructive."

Comstock brought in change agents, including consultants specializing in the field (yes, there are companies that help other companies manage change), and she made her divisions look outside themselves at what was going on in the markets they served.

As change agent Dev Patnaik of Jump observes, "Marketing is broken in many companies. It's a bunch of 25-30 year olds who think they can tell you what's going on based on a spreadsheet. That's not understanding the value chain."

Learning to Learn from Failure.

Not all ideas work. But all experience is a learning opportunity.

Understanding how to work with new ideas also demands learning how to handle failure.

Adding this necessary but complicated component to a culture based on success and performance is, again, easier said than done.

But it seems to be working – because the successes are starting to mount up.

A Strong Agency Partnership.

One of the major partners in this effort is GE's long-time agency, BBDO.

Together, they launched an agency-client collaboration called Project Inspire.

It started internally at BBDO as a way to come up with ideas (remember, the "O" in BBDO was Alex Osborn, the inventor of "brainstorming").

Then, it integrated with GE's mandate to innovate.

Quaternary Economic Activity?

What is quaternary economic activity? We'll take you quickly through the economic history of the world, and you'll understand.

Primary Economic Activity. A few thousand years ago, the lives of everyday hunter/gatherers changed when we learned how to grow crops. It was the Agricultural Revolution, and people were able to stay in one place and develop a new level of civilization.

Secondary Economic Activity. A few hundred years ago, another big change made an impact on our lives – the Industrial Revolution. Mass produced goods, mass transportation, and all that went with that changed everyday lives.

Tertiary Economic Activity. Not that long ago, "The Third Wave," the Post-Industrial Revolution, made another big change. Information and services provided new kinds of jobs and new levels of prosperity. This is the revolution we're living now.

But there's a new one coming…

Quaternary Economic Activity. It's things done for their own sake.

Today, more and more individuals have the resources and opportunity to pursue activities that offer personal and social satisfaction.

This is more than the volunteerism and social connection, such as church work and charities, that have been a part of human society of centuries. It is the power of individuals to pursue activities that offer pay-off in terms of personal satisfaction. A song. A novel. A music video. Restoring a piece of land for ecological reasons. Building a Web site, starting a blog, and doing your own "cause marketing."

Today, more and more of us can go for a different kind of "green."

Sure, it's work, sort of. But it's directed at the things we want to do – not the things we have to do.

As you plan your economic future, don't forget to include a bit of quaternary economic activity.

McDonald's Innovation Menu.

As a global brand, this is McDonald's perspective on agency relationships. *"We view each network as a global creative community. Just as global TV networks rely on reporters stationed around the world, we expect our agency networks to take advantage of creative resources stationed around the world."*

Some Global Examples.

McDonald's is now using:

- Dramatic outdoor from Brazil
- Store decor developed in France
- Salads developed in the US
- An ad campaign developed in Unterhaching, Germany

This demonstrates the "borderless" approach to creativity they want to encourage – using the best ideas from all global affiliates.

Previously, McDonald's had used many different themes in their many different markets.

- Yao Ming, the NBA star from China, will be featured prominently in ads in that country.
- Even Ronald McDonald has had a makeover – changing to cargo pants and a loose-fitting shirt.

Ronald will be used more extensively in promotions with more frequent personal appearances, as they pursue more unconventional marketing tactics.

Event Marketing – The Olympics.

Sports is one of the "cultural languages" McDonald's will use.

This included sponsorship of the Summer Olympics in Beijing.

As companies go global, events such as the Olympics begin to generate huge efficiencies and unique opportunities.

Nearly 300 crew members from 33 countries served athletes, coaches, and fans as part of *McDonald's Olympic Champion Crew* program.

Local competitions measuring service, speed, accuracy, personality, and teamwork determined team selection.

PROUD PARTNER

One result was the shift in GE's advertising, from *"We Bring Good Things to Life,"* which had a 24 year run, to *"Imagination at Work"* which actually has a powerful impact on brand value in a surprising way. It reinforces the value of GE stock – positioning them as a company that will be at the heart of responsible and successful growth.

Innovation in Marketing Services.

WHERE DOES INNOVATION COME FROM? Two people we'll profile here address innovation and change in dramatically different ways. Lynne O'Shea started inside marketing and advertising and moved outside to consulting.

DeeDee Gordon started outside the industry and moved inside. Each brings innovation to whatever they do.

Missouri, Texas, Washington D.C., Cincinnati…

Lynne's journey in innovation started in 1968.

Graduating from the U of Missouri with degrees in journalism and political science, she first went to help a Texas Congressional candidate named George Bush – and helped him win. After a short stint in D.C., she got her master's and then to P&G in Cincinnati.

The Ivory Palace.

Innovation can start anywhere.

In this case, it started with a run in a stocking.

Lynne was on a sales training visit when it happened – at a supermarket. She asked the store manager if he carried pantyhose. He pointed to flat boxes stacked somewhere near the magazines (this was many years before L'eggs).

She found out something else – those boxes delivered huge margins to the grocer; he just didn't have anywhere else to put them. One of P&G's brands was Ivory Liquid, which was good for washing fine fabrics – like pantyhose.

Lynne went to Tom Laco with her idea – and the "Ivory Palace" was born. It was a round end aisle display (remember, the world hadn't seen a L'eggs display yet).

On the lower level were small sizes of Ivory Liquid (they'd been having trouble getting distribution for that size). At eye level, the store could display pantyhose, etc… any brand.

On top, there was a free small pamphlet on fine fabric care, which Lynne wrote. It was a big success.

The promotional program ran for three Nielsen periods, grew Ivory Liquid business, and took a good-sized hunk out of the competition – Woolite.

FCB, IH, AA, IPG…

Feeling more in tune with Chicago and the agency business, Lynne went to work for FCB/Chicago. She helped develop the global campaign for First National Bank of Chicago.

Then she moved on to International Harvester (IH) as Director of Communication. IH was a company that didn't make the turn.

A strike and a shrinking market for expensive farm equipment gave her a taste of crisis management – with an unhappy ending.

She had a better time as Director of Marketing at Arthur Andersen & Co (AA&Co), then a leading accounting firm.

She worked in strategic planning at Interpublic (IPG). Next, Gannett Media, where she helped develop the *Gannettwork* – an innovative project to integrate Gannett's media properties.

Ad Woman of the Year.

In 1989, while at Gannett, she was named Ad Woman of the Year by the Women's Advertising Club of Chicago.

Today, she's with ATKearney, one of the country's top consulting firms. She's not in advertising any longer, but the lessons she learned are serving her well. Her comments...

"What I got from advertising was an ability to understand – and fall in love with – the consumer. In every business, you have a target customer of some kind, but in advertising, the good agencies are better at generating the insights and the emotional connection.

"I believe that ability has helped me across a range of businesses.

"A related skill is a passion for business, business problems, and for finding the heart of the communication you need to make.

"Because when we communicate with real feeling, this adds a richness – a value – to all of our communication.

"Now, I'm intrigued with internal employee communications – because people have to believe in their brands.

"With Kearney, we deal with a whole other kind of information – with IT (Information Technology) capability that is cutting edge.

"Right now, I feel agencies are kind of limited in that area. The medium is the message and we know the new medium – the Internet."

From Placid Planet to Planet Hollywood.

DeeDee Gordon started working in a store in Boston called Placid Planet. It was very hip, and, for a small unique lifestyle boutique, very successful.

She sort of designed her own major – she took some accounting courses and textile courses (*"so I'd have a better understanding of how things are made. I wasn't sure if I wanted to buy, or design my own."*)

One day a woman came in showing her some products *"and asking me tons of questions... what's cool and how do you know... she came in a couple of times and then she showed up with the agency."* This was DeeDee's "light bulb" moment.

"I realized I was helping them make decisions – and that I could shape their line and make money doing that.

"I was helping them understand what their target was – which in one case was completely different from what they thought.

"For example, they had a product they thought boys would buy – and I told them, 'a lot of women will want this style and you'd better make enough in smaller sizes.'"

Cutting Costs for Kellogg's.

A current project for Lynn O'Shea has been Kellogg's operations and marketing.

She refers to the 4 C's mentioned earlier in this chapter.

*"Our job is cost. Peter Drucker refers to the difference between **cost-driven pricing**, where you add up costs and that's your price, and **price-driven costing**, where you focus on a target price, and then you work to get there.*

"We're doing that right now.

"It's as important as the advertising – because if we do our job, after those wonderful ads run... when you go to the store, you'll see a better price on that Kellogg's cereal box."

From Inside to Outside.

From inside The Business of Brands to becoming an outside advisor – the experience you gain one place can often be used to good advantage at the next.

It helps Lynne add value – with change and innovation.

Innovation makes a difference wherever you are – and whatever you're doing.

Not too flakey. Here's a souvenir from Lynne O'Shea's Kellogg's consulting project.

Featured in Fast Company...

...and Premiere...

...and the New Yorker *and...*
you can read her story at
www.malcomgladwell.com

Her journey took her to working for Converse and then on to marketing projects too secret to mention.

The L Report.

Since 1994, she's been tracking trends in the teen market and reporting them in *The L Report,* which is offered by the company she works for, Lambesis Advertising.

It's $20,000 a year. (Sorry, there's no student rate.)

DeeDee works for top retailers, movie studios, car companies, packaged goods marketers, apparel and cosmetic companies, and others in the entertainment industry.

The Importance of Information for Innovation.

The kind of information DeeDee brings to the table is key.

Because new information is one of the ways we are able to develop new insights. She realized the need as she looked at the research that was available.

"We were given a lot of money to get research – and everything we got was a rearview mirror, it was all what had already happened. We needed to figure out how to get in touch with the kids who were making the decisions."

DeeDee's Secret Database.

DeeDee tracks down the trendsetters – the first kid in your high school to create a totally new look – or get excited about a band that becomes a hit – someone whose taste is a little bit more ahead of the curve.

DeeDee finds them and listens to what's on their minds.

Keeping an eye on, and interacting with, these trendsetters is the key to predicting, rather than following, teen trends.

From a global pool of about 10,000 young people, she chooses about 2,000 and works to find out the ever-changing answer to what's hot and what's not.

Frequent Flyer.

To keep the data coming in, she pretty much lives out of her suitcase. When we called her on her cell phone, she was in New York, working on a very secret project.

"What's happening?" we asked, reading through articles on DeeDee in *Fast Company* and *Premiere.*

"First, there's a huge shift in perception. Kids can and do see everything. Future generations will have to be expert editors.

"And the world that kids are living in is radically different from the one companies understand. Every day, kids see violence and destruction... sleazy political officials... autopsy pictures... there's more pessimism than adults understand.

"That's why editing is so important, they're dealing with so much information that one of their basic life skills will involve scanning, sorting, and editing lots of information.

"You already see this in retail, music, and movies that mix a lot of different styles, eras, and influences."

The Power of Insights.

Finding those new insights provides a way to connect.

"The goal is that when teens look at a piece of communication, they say, 'this company understands me. This company isn't talking down to me – it's talking to me.'"

"My job is to help with the conversation."

The Geography of Change.

Empirical evidence is based on observation and practical experience rather than theory. After doing a lot of observation and having a lot of practical experience, DeeDee noted something interesting about where trends tend to come from:

"Fashion tends to go east to west, while lifestyle tends to go west to east. Music happens all over the place, but surprisingly often, it goes from the center out."

For example, the *Smashing Pumpkins* broke out of the Midwest.

The Coolhunt Project – Coming Soon.

"People are looking for more meaning," said the coolhunter.

They're also looking for cool ideas for movies.

Jersey Films (Danny DeVito's company) even looked into developing a movie script based on Malcolm Gladwell's famous *coolhunt* article in the *New Yorker*. It was called *The Coolhunt Project*.

Go to www.malcolmgladwell.com and you can read it yourself. Cool.

coolhunt. It's not just what kids think is cool. It's what cool kids think is cool.

Conclusion: The Business of Innovation.

WHETHER IT'S FINDING "THE NEXT BIG THING" or lowering the cost of a box of corn flakes, innovation plays a part. Because our antennae are always tuned for something new.

The Business of Brands is always working to add value to their brands. Innovation is one of the ways to do it.

Once upon a time, Tide brought a new kind of technology to getting clothes clean. Today, part of their long-term heritage is based on the fact that they've continually improved their formula.

Then again, when there is another major detergent technology, this might also be a reason to develop another brand.

When P&G developed the capability to put flourescers into a detergent formula that actually made the colors in clothes look brighter, they introduced a new detergent – Bold.

They were able to introduce a new brand because of another innovation – Neil McElroy's brand management system, which allowed a company to compete with itself.

This continuing cycle of competition – competing with other companies, as well as with your own performance – drives today's marketplace. It's a continuing challenge, where the standards are always getting higher.

DeeDee helped make this shoe happen for Converse.

Changing the Game.

Yet innovation has the ability to change the game.

…Buzz.

*"Because its purpose
is to create a customer,
any business enterprise has
two — and only these two —
basic functions —
marketing and innovation.
Marketing is
the distinguishing,
the unique, function
of a business."*

— Peter Drucker

The Web as Research Tool.

The impact is everywhere.

The Internet — the worldwide communications structure on which the Web runs — was started to serve military and university researchers.

It's a natural for research.

Today, the Web has become the logical starting point for almost all secondary research searches.

It's a gold mine of demographic data. And it's more than *Google*.

Start with Statistics.

You might want to visit the Federal Statistics site www.fedstats.gov.

Anyone with a modem can get publicly available statistics (such as the Statistical Abstract of the US), from more than 70 government agencies, including the Census Bureau.

From the Stanford Research Institute (SRI) site, www.sri.com, Web surfers can fill out the Values and Lifestyles II (VALS II) questionnaire and get their personal VALS II type done within a few minutes.

VALS II is psychographic or lifestyle information on consumers that is highly regarded by many in advertising and marketing.

It helps target people by more than geographic and demographic parameters.

This ready availability of secondary research is a potential boon to those who know how to use it.

Just as the coffee industry was grinding away as a commodity business with declining consumption, the innovations that started with *Starbucks* revitalized the whole coffee category.

As ever-faster, ever-larger computer chips deliver greater performance, new products, and new information changes the game.

After reading this book, each of you will be able to turn to more information and more information processing power than all the scientists of the world had twenty years ago.

Yet, even in this world of high-tech computers, the high-touch techniques of DeeDee Gordon and Lisa Fortini-Campbell are still needed to develop insights into what Kenichi Ohmae refers to as *"that ultimate non-linear thinking tool, the human brain."*

And even in the world of high-tech computers, someone with a paradigm-changing vision, like Michael Dell, or the guys from *Google,* can take on the big boys — and win.

Come Out and Play.

And that's the world that's out there waiting for you.

You can help innovate.

You can help innovations turn into reality.

You can help a company keep on track — improving things project after project and year after year.

It can be "the next big thing" or those little daily improvements and innovations that help a company's operations as they build brand equity.

Finding the place that's right for you is what the next section is about. We hope you find it helpful.

Because you have an exciting bit of innovation ahead, growing and building an untested brand in today's marketplace.

It's your career.

Good luck.

Discussion Questions & Activities:

1. The Challenge of Change.

Paul Romer notes, *"there are goods that are complementary."* For example, paper is more valuable when you have pencils. What complementary goods do you think we could use more of?

2. New Agencies in a New World.

Identify a demographic group. Unlike Eliot Kang's advice, it does not have to be a group of 10 million or more. After you identify this group, create a name for an agency that specializes in communicating to that group. What products or services would be on your agency's new business list? In other words, what could you profitably advertise to this demographic group?

3. The Internet.

Describe your recent behavior on the Internet.

What new sites or experiences have you had in the last few months?

If you were designing a site or service, what would it be? What would you call it?

4. Managing Change.

In your own words, how would you describe the barriers to change in a large organization?

Select your favorite new product in the last six months. Did it come from a large company or a small entrepreneurial organization?

5. Innovation in Marketing Services.

How would you do your own "cool hunt?"

What areas in your life do you think are going to change dramatically?

Does that inspire any business ideas?

Concepts & Vocabulary:

Here are some of the words and concepts from this chapter:

ARPAnet – Advanced Research Projects Agency network. Much of the technology developed for ARPAnet is used on the Internet.

Bandwidth – This refers to the size of the "pipe" that carries your Internet signal. More bandwidth, means more information moving faster from the Internet to your computer.

Banner – Rectangular graphic located on pages in high-traffic Web sites. Users can click on the banner and link to the advertiser's Web site.

Binary system – A numbering system based on twos (2s) rather than decimals (10s). Each element has a digit value of either zero (0) or one (1) and is known as a *bit*.

Button – Smaller version of a banner.

CERN – European Particle Physics Laboratory where the World Wide Web was developed.

Click-through – When a user clicks on a banner. Used to measure response to banners. Also called *ad clicks*.

Click-through rate – Percentage of impressions that result in click-through. Also called *ad click rate*.

Communication – Replaces "promotion" in the Four C's.

Consumer – Replaces "product" in the Four C's.

Content aggregator – An Internet provider, like *AOL,* that adds value by bringing together a number of features and services.

Convenience – Replaces "place" in the Four C's.

Cookie – A unique data file that a site leaves on your computer. These data files contain information the site can use to track your behavior on that site.

Cost – Replaces "price" in the Four C's.

References & Resources:

Ad Resource – Internet Advertising and Promotion Resources
www.adres.internet.com/

Advertising and the World Wide Web. (1999). Edited by David W. Schumann & Esther Thorson.

CiAd (formerly AdMedium) – The Center for Interactive Advertising
www.utexas.edu/coc/admedium/

ClickZ Network – An online resource for media buyers and planners, Web and e-mail advertising firms, list vendors and agencies, ad and commerce-based site publishers, and Web developers.
www.clickz.com/

CyberTimes – This *New York Times* Online section offers a look at the Internet, computers, and other technologies that are changing the way people live. Features daily news and original columns produced expressly for the Web.
www.nytimes.com/yr/mo/day/tech/indexcyber.html

EMarketer – *"e-telligence for business."*
www.emarketer.com/

Iconocast – The definitive source for facts, figures, trend analysis and in-sider information in the Internet marketing industry.
www.iconocast.com/

The Interactive Future – *Advertising Age's* look at the future of interactive advertising. www.adage.com/ifuture/

Interactive Marketing: The Future Present. (1996). Edited by Edward Forrest & Richard Mizerski.

Internet Advertising Bureau – The first global not for profit association devoted exclusively to maximizing the use and effectiveness of advertising on the Internet.
www.iab.net/

(Continued on next page)

You need to read more than Ad Age. *Here are two magazines that can keep you in touch with the changing marketplace.*

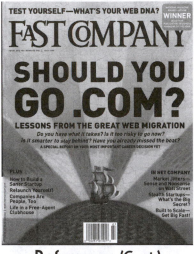

References (Cont.)

Media Central – "News and Info for Media and Marketing Professionals." www.mediacentral.com/

Online Advertising Discussion List – Focuses on professional discussion of online advertising strategies, results, studies, tools, and media coverage. www.o-a.com/

Selling on the Net: The Complete Guide. (1997). By Herschell Gordon Lewis & Robert D. Lewis.

The Standard – *"Intelligence for the Internet Economy"* www.thestandard.com/

Wired **Magazine** – *"The journal of record for the future."* www.wired.com/wired/current.html

Fast Company – about businesses that "get it." www.fastcompany.com

Cost-driven pricing – Traditional approach to pricing. Manufacturer determines costs of manufacture, adds desired margin, and establishes price.

Customer contacts – Another phrase for "brand contact points." Simply put, it refers to any time a customer interacts with a brand or people who work for the company that provides the brand.

Daughter window – Interstitial that opens only when a user clicks on an accompanying banner.

Destination site – Web site that uses information, entertainment, and high production values to attract users and bring them back again.

E-mail – Computer-to-computer electronic mail.

Graphic user interface (GUI) – Computer operating system which uses visual icons to communicate functions to the user. This was first developed by Xerox at their PARC facility, then "borrowed" by Steve Jobs and Apple. The Apple interface was then "borrowed" by Microsoft. You might want to catch the made-for-cable movie *Pirates of Silicon Valley* for a bit more of the story. Most consumer computer programs now have a GUI front end.

HTML – Hypertext Markup Language – the language of Web design.

Hyperlink (or link) – Text or graphic that users can select to electronically link to another document.

Hypertext – A method of electronically linking documents.

Hypermedia – Hyperlinked audio, video, images, and text.

Impression – Opportunity to see an advertisement. Also called *ad view.*

Internet – A vast collection of computer networks.

Internet agency – Marketing services supplier specializing in Internet-related services: Web site design, e-commerce strategies and applications, banner advertising, etc.

Interstitial – A Web page, usually containing a promotion or ad, that appears in a separate browser window.

ISP – Internet service provider.

Micro-site – A small cluster of brand pages hosted by content sites or networks. Also called *brand modules* or *magpie pieces.*

Mosaic – First graphical user interface for the World Wide Web. Later became Netscape Navigator.

New product marketers – This may be an entire company, or marketing or brand group personnel with new product responsibilities. They may have responsibility for existing products under the brand umbrella, part of the marketing department, a free-standing group within the company with additional functions, such as product development, or it may be the company's entire reason for being.

NSCA – National Center for Supercomputing Applications at the University of Illinois. Developed Mosaic.

NSFNET – National Science Foundation network. Forerunner to the Internet.

Opt-in – Consumer agrees to receive future e-mail messages.

Pop-up window – Interstitial that opens and appears automatically when a user enters a Web page.

Portal – Gateway through which many Internet users will pass.

Price-driven costing – Marketing-driven approach to pricing. Marketer determines desired price of item and works to deliver manufacturing costs and efficiency that deliver that price, including margin. Examples: In the automobile industry, Japanese manufacturers delivered a high-quality relatively low-cost auto by targeting the final cost. Currently, Kellogg's is working to deliver lower prices on their cereal products without sacrificing quality.

Push technology – Delivering advertisements directly to users rather than waiting for the user to come to the advertiser.

Rich media – Technologically enhanced online advertisements, usually containing video, audio, interactivity, etc.

Spam – Unsolicited e-mail message(s) sent repeatedly to large numbers of people or newsgroups. Also a trademarked product of Hormel Foods.

USENET – An online collection of discussion groups, or newsgroups.

World Wide Web – A hypertext-based system for finding and accessing Internet resources.

The Discipline of New Product Marketing. Here's an introduction to the topic by one of the experts – Tom Kuczmarski. From Innovations Press.

You

This chapter was written by Professor Jim Marra of Temple University, with invaluable assistance from Ed Letven. Professor Marra is in the Advertising Sequence at Temple and former Head of the AEJMC Ad Division. He is author of Advertising Creativity: Techniques for Generating Ideas *and* Advertising Copywriting: Techniques for Improving Your Writing Skills *and co-author of* Advertising Campaign Strategy.

Ed Letven is founder of LD&B Marketing, one of the largest full-service agencies in the Philadelphia region.

Major contributions were made by dozens of former students of all the authors of this book.

Thanks to everyone.

LET'S BEGIN WITH A FEW FORMER STUDENTS who used to sit in classrooms – just like you.

One Saturday Morning, **Dawn Vaughn**, a graduate of Ball State, packed up a 14-foot U-Haul and headed out of Muncie, Indiana, to Atlanta, Georgia, and *took her product to market*.

Before she packed up the U-Haul, Dawn had contacted – and followed up with – 20 Atlanta advertising agencies. That's part of *understanding your market*.

Cody Aufricht graduated from Texas Tech in 1981. He majored in advertising and for his college years was an All-Southwest Conference swimmer.

Twenty-five years later, he's grown his career into Marketing Director of a franchise operation with 120 offices.

Cody's *increased his market value*.

One night, **Heather Roe-Day** sat down in her dorm room and evaluated herself – she thought about her strengths and weaknesses as the first step in her job search.

And that's one of the first steps we'll discuss – *understanding yourself as a brand*.

Each of these students took the steps necessary to get that first job – and launch their career.

Not Too Early.

Even though you're just finishing up an introductory course, if you think you might want to do something in The Business of Brands – even if you're not sure what – this section is for you.

As you will see, it's not too early to start getting ready for that career – even if you don't know what you'll be yet.

And once you connect, as Dan Hadel, one of the people you'll meet, put it, *"It's the most fun I ever had while getting paid."*

*"If I were starting life over again,
I am inclined to think that I would go
into the advertising profession
in preference to any other."*

— Franklin D. Roosevelt

& Your Career

Introduction.

THE FIRST TWELVE CHAPTERS in this book lasted a semester. This section may last a few years.

In some ways, it will probably last your whole career.

This section is about preparing for your career – you know, the one you don't have yet – the one you're thinking about.

The Business of Brands.

The Business of Brands is a big one. It includes virtually every company in America – every package on every shelf.

It includes virtually every service – every hospital, bank, and organization in your community.

It includes every newspaper, TV, and radio station – and more – in the expanding world of media.

It includes all the agencies, old and new, that help build all those brands. It includes all the marketing services companies that help make the connections that make marketing work.

That's a lot of jobs.

One of these companies probably has a job that's right for you. Your first job is to figure out which one it is.

Focus and Expand.

From that huge list of opportunities, you need to find a way to focus on those that make sense for you – at the same time you should probably expand your horizons – so that you catch as many of those opportunities as possible.

Which ones seem to align themselves with your meaningful points of difference? Which ones match your interests, your skills, and your talents?

You're probably still at the beginning of your explorations.

But we can help you organize that exploration.

"The Brand Called You."

This is a how-to for "The Brand Called You."

That's the way you should think about yourself.

In the first issue of *Fast Company*, that was the title of the cover story by marketing guru Tom Peters (you can read the whole thing at fastcompany.com/keyword/118brand).

Here's some of what he has to say: "*Regardless of age, regardless of position, regardless of the business we happen to be in, all of us need to understand the importance of branding.*

"*We are CEOs of our own companies: Me, Inc. To be in business today, our most important job is to be head marketer for the brand called You.*" Peters continues…

"*You're every bit as much a brand as Nike, Coke, Pepsi, or the Body Shop. To start thinking like your own favorite brand manager, ask yourself the same question the brand managers at Nike, Coke, Pepsi, or the Body Shop ask themselves:*

"*What is it that my product or service does that makes it different?*"

Your Big Question.

During this semester you've been introduced to a lot of businesses. You've acquired a general idea about how they work together in the marketing marketplace.

Along the way, you've learned a few concepts and grabbed a few quick snapshots of possible jobs and careers.

As you went through the chapters of this book, you probably asked yourself a question.

That question – the big one – was, "Where do I fit in?"

You probably asked yourself a few more questions like…

• **Would I like that job?**

• **Could I do that job?**

• **Where do I find that job?**

And, of course…

• **How do I get that job?**

This section will help you get started on some answers – answers that can help position you for that first job and a successful career in The Business of Brands.

How This Section Is Organized.

This section is a simple four-part plan to help you get started:

1. **Understanding Yourself as a Product**
2. **Understanding Your Market**
3. **Increasing Your Market Value**
4. **Bringing Your Product to Market**

In each part, we'll show you what it takes to get started, add a few tips to make it easier, and share some good advice from students who were walking in your shoes not too long ago.

The Three R's of Job-Hunting.

In the back, we've added a few more things for you:

- **Resources.** The names (and phone numbers) of some useful resources in your search.
- **References.** A master list of the most useful materials for building a marketing plan for your career.
- **Résumé Development.** Don't wait till you're getting ready to graduate. You should have a great résumé – starting now!

And, to help put those Three R's in perspective, we have a four-stage program to help you develop that "Brand Called You."

The Tiger, the Phoenix, the Turtle, and the Dragon.

As we were writing this section, someone pointed out that each stage of the process sort of matched up with one of the Celestial Animals in Chinese mythology. Check it out.

The Tiger is the strongest of the Celestial animals – it represents human nature – good and bad. Control the tiger.

Understand yourself and your strengths and weaknesses.

The Tiger represents *understanding yourself as a brand.*

The Phoenix is in a constant state of rebirth. It represents the "creative destruction" of our modern marketplace.

It also offers some clues to the importance of being on the right part of the cycle. The Phoenix represents *understanding the market.*

The Turtle protects and strengthens. With slow steady steps, he is the symbol of increasing your own strengths and advantages.

The Turtle represents *increasing your market value.*

The Dragon can bring you inspiration, wealth, and great good luck as you strive toward your goal – and we assume that is your goal. The Dragon represents *bringing yourself to market.*

If you do your part, they're all on your side, helping you prepare for the world ahead.

For, as they say, "*fortune favors the prepared mind.*"

Good News and Bad News.

First, here's some good news. The Business of Brands is full of rewarding, fulfilling, and exciting careers. There are a lot of jobs in the field. And you really might like the work and the people.

But there's also bad news. The business of marketing and advertising is tough – make no mistake about it.

But the rewards are there – that's why a lot of people just like you want to get a start. But you may have to start at low pay.

More bad news. It may take some time for you to get that job. That's why you need to start as early as possible.

Finally, a job in this field may not be right for you. The best jobs are inherently competitive, stressful, and insecure.

It's not for everybody. But even that is something you might want to find out sooner rather than later.

So, let's get started.

The Tiger
Understanding yourself as a brand.

The Phoenix
Understanding the market.

The Turtle
Increasing your market value.

The Dragon
Bringing yourself to market.

The Tiger Is West.
The color is white.
The Tiger is animal spirit.

T.I.G.E.R.

Talents
Interests
Goals
Experiences
Resources

My name's Kevin.

I don't **sleep.**

For **every** day you work,
I work two.

Those thirty concepts you came up with?
I had sixty billion.

When you head for the bathroom,
I hold it.

So the next time you pause to catch your **breath,**
Ask yourself:

"What was Kevin doing last **night,**
while I was **sleeping?"**

Here's Your Competition!

Kevin, in the ad above, is telling you he's giving something extra on every project. In the creative field, everyone works to outdo everyone else. Deal with it.

Look around you in class. That's your competition – not to mention those who are already in the industry.

Competition is a vital part of today's marketplace. It's how your potential employers think. They'll like it that you think that way, too.

Understanding Yourself as a Product.

WHEN YOU FIRST ENTER THE JOB MARKET, you'll be a commodity – a product like all others – a student with an undergraduate degree in advertising or marketing.

You've got a lot of competition.

Second, you're unique. You have talents, interests, and experiences that are distinctive.

Your first step is sort of a Situation Analysis (remember that from the planning chapter?).

We'll be doing some evaluation, some planning, and then, of course, some implementation.

Let's start with a bit of evaluation.

We call this little formula **T.I.G.E.R.** It stands for:
Talents, Interests, Goals, Experiences, and Resources.

It's a beginning for understanding your potential as a unique product – a brand. So let's work through our formula and see what kind of brand you are.

T = Talents.

Even though no one is good at everything, everyone's good at something. Over time, why have you been congratulated? What have you been praised for? What have your parents, friends, and teachers told you you're good at?

In short, what are your talents and skills?

Start a T.I.G.E.R. worksheet.

What do you have under talents?

Writing? Math? Leading and organizing people? Presenting in front of groups? Planning? Time management?

Here's Heather Roe-Day to tell us about some talents that have helped her as a product manager at Unicover.

"The position of product manager requires marketing skills, an understanding of basic accounting principles, analytical skills, and extensive organizational skills.

"The greatest skill I use every day is the ability to organize my tasks and orchestrate the activities of others in the company to help all promotions grow from the concept stage to the finished product stage.

"My involvement in outside activities while in high school and college built the foundation for time management and helped me learn to set intermediate goals in order to complete large tasks."

Heather was actively involved in school organizations. The things she learned developed into one of her special talents – a key to her latest success.

Still another was analytical ability, something you use every day – the ability to understand the problem and solve it.

The same is true with you. What are those things you do well? What do you think are your special and unique talents?

Note them in "T" for Talents.

I = Interests.

In many cases, your talents are related to your interests. Because, chances are, you're talented in whatever interests you.

Now, of course, this isn't totally true. We can have lots of interest in music or sports without having the talent to play professionally.

The next useful insight is to identify your interests.

Example: Craig Fry, Car Guy.

Craig Fry liked cars. He knew how they worked, and he knew how to fix them. This was his special interest.

When Craig prepared his portfolio, it was probably no surprise that the ads about automobiles were the best in his book.

Craig discovered, and was discovered by, agencies that worked in the "automotive aftermarket" – companies that market all the things you need to keep a car running.

Craig combined his talent as a writer with his car-repairing hobby and became an award-winning copywriter in the field of automotive-aftermarket advertising.

A Tip from Tracey.

Tracey Aurich has a suggestion about how your talents and interests might be applied to your first job.

"Know that your favorite hobby or activity, no matter how obscure, probably has an industry that supports some form of advertising. So, contact the director of marketing at the company that manufactures your favorite product or provides a service aligned with your favorite hobby.

"Join the industry's trade association network.

"Read the industry magazines to become familiar with the companies, the language, and the people."

Identify your interests, and you've gone a long way to identifying your talents as well. They tend to go together.

Not Interested? Try This.

What if you don't know what you're interested in?

You may decide that your world-class bottle cap collection doesn't qualify you for a career.

Or, you may decide the fact that you like pretty much the same clothes, music, and movies that your friends do isn't going to differentiate you. You might be right.

But the problem may be not really knowing what you're interested in. Try this question exercise.

- **When the pressure is off and when others aren't telling you to do something, what is it you do?**

  Buckminster Fuller, one of the twentieth century's most inventive and original minds, was once asked by a student how you can know what it is you should do.

  Fuller observed that you can know the answer by tracing your own history and identifying what it is you did and continue to do when others (parents, friends, teachers) aren't telling you what to do.

  So what is it you do? What are your interests?

  Jot them down next, under "I" for Interests.

Match Your Talent.

Another good way to expand your horizons is by matching specific talents with specific jobs.

The following list is an example.

You need to know what kinds of entry-level jobs exist, so you can match your talents to the job type.

Talents: Imagination, Writing, Conceptualizing.

- Assistant/Junior Copywriter or Writer (ad agency, promotions company, marketing company, direct and telemarketing companies, PR firm)

  Note: Be sensitive to getting specific here, including concentrating your attention on various forms of writing, such as public relations or television scripts.

Talents: Interpersonal, Organizational, Analytical.

- Media Sales (all media, including print and electronic)
- Product or Service Sales (various product or service companies)
- Personnel (various product, service, advertising, promotions, PR/publicity, and marketing companies, for training, education, counseling, organizing, coordinating)
- Assistant AE (ad agency)

Talents: Design, Computer Graphics, Art Production.

- Graphic Artist, Illustrator, Art Director (ad agency or other communications companies or marketers)
- Production Assistant (print or electronic)
- Traffic Manager (oversee workflow in ad agency and other communications companies)

Talents: Mathematical, Analytical, Strategic.

- Assistant Media Buyer (ad agency, media agency)
- Traffic Manager (see above)
- Research Assistant (ad agency, specific product or service company, marketing companies)
- Trade Show/Event Planner or Representative (marketing and communications firms, including PR)

T (Talents)

_____
_____
_____
_____
_____
_____

I (Interests)

_____
_____
_____
_____
_____
_____

G (Goals)

_____
_____
_____
_____
_____
_____
_____

E (Experiences)

_____
_____
_____
_____
_____
_____

R (Resources)

_____
_____
_____
_____
_____
_____
_____

- **What is it you do that makes time disappear?**
Some of the things we do seem like they'll never end.

Other things we do we don't want to end.

What are the things you do that you don't want to end? These are your interests, those things that take up time but that also make time disappear.

Note those things that make time disappear.

- **What would you like to talk about on the phone?**
Regardless of what career you pursue, once in it you'll spend time on the phone. In many cases this will be significant time. So, if you had your choice, what is it you would like to talk about with someone else on the phone?

These are your interests. Jot them down – "I" for Interests.

G = Goals.

They say, _"When you don't know where you're going, any road will get you there."_ We all need goals.

And, when you think about it, goals are one of the things that differentiate marketers – and their brands.

Short Term and Long Term.

Your goal may be simple. Like "Get a job that doesn't suck."

Not bad for a start.

But even that goal may be a year or two away.

So you may need more than one goal.

You probably need a long-term goal – a great job.

And you probably need a few short-term goals, too.

These short term goals may seem contradictory (for example, they may necessitate taking a job that sucks), but they should be steps on the road to your long-term goal.

Not Easy Being Green.

Steve Green was working as a PA (production assistant) on commercial shoots. Then he quit. He said, _"I realized that I didn't want to be in the film industry. And the only reason you should take a PA job is if you think you want to work in the film business._

"I realized that it wasn't for me – it was just a job where you stood around in the cold and got people coffee. But, if I wanted a career in film… hey, then it'd be a great job."

Goal Setting – A Messy Business.

Now Steve is reworking some of his long-term goals.

Remember, goal setting can be a messy business. You won't be right all the time and some goals may be out of reach.

There's one more problem. When we put that goal down in writing, in public, it can get weird. If we don't reach that goal, we can feel like some sort of failure. That stops a lot of people from setting goals and committing to them.

Well, get over it. Get used to it.

People in business fail all the time.

That's one of the ways we get smarter.

It's why evaluation is such an important part of the process.

Some ads don't work. Some brands fail.

Some companies go out of business – or change ownership.

It happens. A lot.

Part of the excitement and the energy of our marketplace has a bit to do with the fact that when you're trying to do something new, well, you never know.

You may fail at some jobs. But a job isn't a career. And as you build your career, you're going to have some ups and downs.

Deal with it. That's part of finding your way into a career.

False Starts and Backtracks.

There may be false starts. You may have to backtrack.

You may end up somewhere totally different than you thought. But that's part of building your brand.

Arm & Hammer Baking Soda thought they made something for baking. But the world changed. Now it deodorizes refrigerators. There may be a box in yours (or maybe there should be).

Steve Green, after a few days as a PA, saw that this was not the road he wanted to travel. Good news. Steve just got a job selling for a recording company. It's a better fit. And that's how it works.

Take a pencil. Write down some goals. "G" for Goals.

And remember, pencils have erasers.

E = Experiences.

Most potential employers are more interested in your experiences than your interests. They want to know where you've worked and what you've done.

And even though you're probably young, you've probably had experiences relevant to the field, experiences that count.

Ideally, those experiences will be connected with your talents and interests. It stands to reason. You have a talent for something because you're interested and then you actualize that talent, which results in your experiences.

Now is the time to list those experiences. If you feel they're in short supply, well, that tells you something right there. (Remember, you still have a bit of time to get your "brand" in shape for the marketplace.)

When you get to Step Three – Increasing Your Market Value, you can take a look at the kinds of experiences you may need to add.

Goals, Dreams, & Wishes.

Sometimes it's hard to keep them straight. Goals are things you might be able to achieve if you work hard.

Dreams can come true (maybe) if you happen to be very, very lucky.

And wishes, well, we all have them, but they're usually pretty much out of our control.

We won't tell anyone to give up on their dreams. And none of us could stop wishing if we tried.

But goals are something we can all work toward. And we might reach them.

If your wish or dream is winning the lottery, we won't tell you not to, but if you're doing that with the rent money, we'd suggest a bit of restraint.

You know what we're saying.

Why are we talking about this?

Because sometimes it's hard to separate the three – we want all three to happen, and maybe, just maybe, if we work real, real hard that dream can come true.

But, while you're wishing, having a goal you can work for is a great way to pass the time while you wait for those dreams to come true.

Get a goal. And if one of those goals might seem sort of like a dream, well, what's wrong with that?

Goals = S.M.A.C.

The folks at P&G have some guidelines for objectives: "S.M.A.C."

Goals Should Be Specific – It should be clear what they are.

Goals Should Be Measurable – You should be able to know whether you did it or not.

Goals Should Be Achievable – No wishful thinking. Your objective should be something you have a chance of actually doing.

Goals Should Be Compatible – That means they should be a good fit with everything else going on.

P.S. What's Your E-mail?

Sometimes we have fun-loving e-mail addresses. Hint: boozehound or n00bpwnr are probably not right for a résumé. If necessary get a new one now.

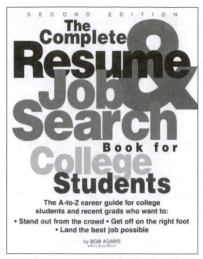

There are many good books on

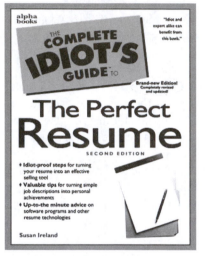

résumés.

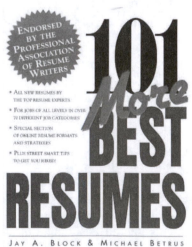

Get one – the sooner the better.

By the way, résumé has two "é's" in it, even though these book titles don't.

A Classic Résumé.

These are *your* experiences. You can serve them up any way you want. There's a classic example from Maxine Paetro's *How to Put Your Book Together and Get a Job in Advertising*.

Take a look at these experiences as listed in a résumé:

June to Present. Part-time chauffeur/word processor for New York consulting firm specializing in non-profit organizations.

- Transport President to and from appointments.
- Edit and type staff associates' fund-raising proposals.
- Deliver and recover Blanche (President's cat) to and from vet.
- Claim President's fur from furrier.
- Bring in President's pearls for repair.

June to February – Mr. B__, New York. Live-in companion/ cook to 90-year-old man.

- Accompanied Mr. B__ on walks through United Nations Park. Often stopped to see Moon Rock.
- Coordinated and prepared Sunday lasagna luncheons.
- Initiated subscription to *New York Times* large print edition.

September to May – New York. Au pair for divorce lawyer and her 12-year-old son.

- Laundered their dirty clothing.
- Washed their filthy dishes.
- Cleaned their stinking kitchen.
- Prepared their wretched meals.
- Never complained once.

Get the idea? On one level, these experiences were ordinary – they were commodities on the low-end of the job market.

But this person made them extraordinary.

This person communicated life lessons and this little résumé was a window into the quality of the person who had those experiences. In addition, it demonstrated he or she could flat-out write.

This is an outstanding example of what a brand personality can do to add value. The actual jobs were ordinary.

The presentation made them extraordinary.

Look at your experiences through the lens of your brand personality. When you do that, you're beginning to position yourself in the crowded job marketplace.

R = Resources.

Marketing Strategy is the search for advantage in the marketplace. Let's look for and list some of your initial advantages:

Two E's, Three F's.

The first two will usually be:

- **Education**
- **Experience**

For the most part, your resources will fall into three categories:
- **Family**
- **Friends**
- **Friends of the Above.**

These are resources that can work to your advantage.

"Don't Send Nobody Nobody Sent."

That's a saying they have in Chicago.

It means that who you know counts.

Is this fair? Not particularly.

But it's exactly the way things work. Deal with it.

Summer internships. Entry-level jobs. An interview.

In many cases, resources can make the critical difference.

Melissa's dad called a friend he knew. The friend scheduled an interview. A job had just opened up. Melissa got the job.

She got the job on her merits. But she got the interview on her relationships. Resources can make the difference.

Later, you'll be putting some of these resources to work as you bring your brand to market.

But let's not get ahead of ourselves.

For a start, all you need to do is begin building a list of anyone and everyone you and your family know who has a job in marketing or advertising – with name, address, phone number, the name of the company, and that person's job title.

You might want to talk to your parents, some of their friends, and maybe a favorite aunt or uncle – see who they might know.

Do your first draft now. You'll be developing it further as you bring your brand to market.

"R" is for Resources.

Put Them All Together.

So, how do you look?

More there than you expected? Or less?

You may not have the answer yet, but we bet you've got a clue. Either way, you're starting to get a clearer picture of "The Brand Called You."

Need a little work? That's OK. We'll save that for Step Three.

You can probably find a way to build each of these areas. Next, we need to take a look at how your initial brand profile matches up with the marketplace. Time for Step Two.

The College Baseball Story.

A freshman pitcher on a college baseball team was having a tough time.

It was his first start.

He was getting shelled.

The pitching coach walked out to the mound for a little talk with the obviously upset young pitcher.

"I don't understand it, Coach," the pitcher said. *"In high school I used to strike out eight out of every nine guys."*

"Don't worry, son," said the coach. *"That ninth guy? They're all here."*

You've probably seen this already. You may have been at the top of your class in high school. Then you get to the next level and look around.

It's everywhere. In the art school, everyone got an A in art.

On your college sports teams, almost everyone there was All-Conference at their high school.

Maybe these things are more obvious in sports than in education or the job market, but the same thing is true.

People are better, standards are higher, and the competition is a lot tougher.

And don't worry. When you're out there in the working world, the same thing will happen.

That ninth guy.

They're all there.

Deal with it.

The Phoenix is South.
The color is red.

2:

The John Sutherland Exercise.

Here's a way for you to match up your Talents and Interests with the Marketplace.

1. Write down a few categories of activity that interest you – car racing, musical comedy, rock and roll.

2. Now, identify some job opportunities in that category – they may be local or they may be national. For example…

- Car Racing – where's the closest NASCAR event? Do they need an intern? Look at some of the publications and advertisers. Make a phone call.

- Musical Comedy – Where is your closest venue? Do they need someone to help sell season tickets – maybe outline a direct response campaign, or identify some local marketing partners. Get a poster designed. Does the Web site need help? Is there a new young audience (like you) that can be attracted?

- Rock and Roll – Does your favorite radio station need an intern? Is there an alternative newspaper that features bands and concert listings? Will there be a big festival this summer?

(Continued on next page.)

Understand Your Market.

THE PHOENIX IS IN A STATE OF CONSTANT REBIRTH – much like today's marketplace.

It's not too soon for you to start to get in touch with that marketplace. Get a feel for the changes going on and look for those that work to your advantage. Here are two examples.

Vergara's Vision.

Marcelo Vergara graduated from the University of Kansas.

As you will read, Marcelo had an excellent sense of the marketplace he was going job-hunting in. Check it out.

"I landed a great job at the moment desktop publishing became a real advertising tool, much like the Web is today.

"I did it by turning my résumé into a campaign for me. It showed I could think, execute, and ultimately market myself.

"They like that, and it makes for cost-effective hiring.

"Pick your target employers. Be selective. Choose quality firms. Research them thoroughly. Learn about their top managers. Check the trade press (online and off). Check local business papers. Call the local ad club. Ask for their newsletter. Learn all you can about your top choices.

"Develop a strategic marketing plan for your own campaign.

"Execute this plan and be creative with the media you choose.

"You're objective is to get an interview.

"Create your Web site/print campaign, but instead of putting a normal résumé online, design a real site. Make yourself the product or service. Brand your skills. Brand your personality.

"Get your target to interact with you before you even meet.

"Figure out a way to get them to send you an e-mail instead of the other way around. This business is all about relationships.

"When you get an interview, tell them how you did it and show them your strategy. It shows you have discipline, maturity, and understanding. Those are good things."

Note how important it is to target.

Marcelo had a strategic focus and plan for his "brand."

Notice how he matched his brand up with the marketplace and emphasized values like "interactivity."

Also notice that he set achievable goals – get an interview, build relationships. *His brand planning had a target customer focus.*

Marcelo knew what he wanted.

Our next example, Tracey, wasn't quite so sure.

Here's what happened.

Not-So-Spacey Tracey.

Tracey Aurich, a Penn State grad, found her first advertising job a bit outside that "box" that says all ad agencies create ads for the Nikes of the world.

"When you think about getting a job in advertising, you probably think about creating commercials and print ads for sport utility trucks and shampoo at a big city agency or selling ad space for a local newspaper.

"Well, it turns out there are other products and services that need to be promoted, not to 'Joe Consumer,' but to specialty markets.

"And within these markets, you can find a career in advertising.

"It's just a matter of knowing if an opportunity exists.

"Case in point. . . I fell into my first account services position at a pharmaceutical advertising agency – a specialty I didn't know existed.

"As recently as five years ago, pharmaceutical advertising involved promoting prescription and over-the-counter medications to healthcare professionals only. But recent legal changes have made the field even more interesting.

"Now that direct-to-consumer advertising is permitted, this specialty is becoming better known."

Note How Fast Things Change.

Tracey entered a field that didn't do consumer advertising.

Now she's involved in it in a big way – participating in a revolution in pharmaceutical marketing.

Keys to Finding Market Opportunities.

If you have a crystal ball, turn it on, and skip this next section.

But if you're not so sure about how to get a handle on that fast-changing marketplace, here are a few specifics: five to be exact.

1. Advertising-to-Sales Ratios.

Take a look at the advertising-to-sales (A-to-S) ratio of various companies. It's a good measure of where some of your best opportunities might be.

For example, a steel company will probably have larger sales volume than a company that manufactures blue jeans.

But the jean company spends a higher percentage of its sales on advertising and marketing.

In addition, the brands with the higher A-to-S ratios in their category tend to be the leading brands and the better marketers.

You can find A-to-S ratios in trade magazines like *Advertising Age*. Their "Leading Advertisers" issues contain a lot of useful information. Get the *Ad Age* FactPack pdf at www.adage.com.

2. "SIC 'em!" Go to SIC Codes.

SIC stands for Standard Industrial Classification, which is a way of looking at companies by industry.

Almost all businesses fall within its broad categories.

Standard Rate and Data, the bible of the agency media department, also shows these SIC codes in terms of description of the industries the publications serve.

For example, a publication about farm agri-business might be read by farmers, chemists, agri-chemical executives, farm machinery salespeople, and a whole host of people who interact within this vast marketing category.

Remember what Tracey said about hobbies being businesses, too? For fun, why not find out about companies that are involved in the things you're interested in? SIC 'em!

The John Sutherland Exercise (Cont.)

In virtually every market, in virtually every category, there are people who need to do marketing and advertising. Why not find out what's going in areas that you're already interested in? You'll start to see patterns and you'll be getting smarter about what's out there in the marketplace.

Give it a try – even if you just write a few things down and spend a little time Googling, it'll still be time well spent.

John Sutherland is Chair of the Department of Advertising at the University of Florida.

Thanks, John.

No More Secretaries – Better Know How to Type!

In general, entry-level jobs belong to juniors, assistants, or coordinators.

The secretarial job is pretty much a thing of the past. Still, there is quite a bit of word-processing, chart and spread sheet organizing, and general duties that need to be done.

They're good jobs for becoming familiar with all a company does – and a path to higher positions.

That's how Dan Pastuszak, a Temple graduate, began his account exec career at Ogilvy & Mather/NY.

Dan has this to say: *"Chances are your first agency job will be administrative. Learn to type. I'm not kidding.*

"Don't let your ego blind you.

"That's how some of the best in the business started out."

Dan describes who makes it and who doesn't. *"Agency people can see the difference between someone who wants a career and someone who just wants a job.*

"The latter will receive a form letter thanking them for their time.

"The former will be recognized as someone with a desire to be the best, to go above and beyond what's expected, and will be asked to start in two weeks."

Stacy's Story.

Stacy Smollin, a Penn State grad, had this experience at DoubleClick, an innovative Internet firm she'd tracked down – a firm about to emerge.

"'*But does it matter that I don't know anything about the Internet?*' I remember asking when I was offered my first position at DoubleClick.

"I'll never forget the answer: 'If you knew how a television worked, you would watch it for the dots behind the screen rather than the content on it. I'm looking for a bright, confident person who is eager to learn. You're it.'"

The point of Stacy's story is that the Internet was a new, fast-growing medium, and DoubleClick needed qualities and skills in a person that could be applied.

If Stacy's vision had only been ad agencies, she would have missed out on this job opportunity.

The Mirror Test.

Know what the Mirror Test is?

It's an old personnel joke.

"*We hold a mirror up to a candidate's nose, and if it fogs up, he's breathing and we hire him.*"

Sometimes you can find situations where they are doing so much hiring they use the Mirror Test.

But most of the time, you need a few more qualifications.

3. Focus on High-Growth Industries and Businesses.

When we think high tech, we think high growth.

Maybe we also think high risk – but, as we've said all along, the marketplace can be a dangerous place.

Look for areas where things are happening. Consider that the financial industry, the wine industry, the travel industry, and many more industries are experiencing huge expansion.

Remember Mark and his insights into desktop publishing?

Sometimes it's just certain companies within the industry – you'll want to know which companies those are. And where.

The world business community continues to benefit from the information and communications explosion.

To learn about high-growth industries, go to the Web and look up thestreet.com. This is a powerful place to get ideas about high growth businesses. The site was rated number one by the *New York Times* and gives wide-ranging opinions about the world's business opportunities and stock market projections. You can get a one-month free trial subscription by logging on.

Another valuable resource is motleyfool.com with an idea a minute plus droll humor and sharp analysis of emerging markets.

4. Consider Emerging Markets.

When companies are literally inventing themselves, it's sometimes impossible to get someone with experience. So, as they say in football drafts, go for "the best available athlete."

Stacy Smollin made that decision and she got in on the ground floor of an exciting Internet company.

If you're smart, aggressive, flexible, and resourceful enough to track them down (they're too busy to look for you), you'll be who they're looking for – if they had the time to look.

Emerging Companies Need to Tell Their Story.

Emerging companies and emerging markets can't emerge without communications. They need advertising and publicity to tell the world their story. Your career will go further faster when you're in a business where the rules are being written as you live it.

So you might want to segment some of your target marketing to include the emerging market firms, those that will define the first years of the new millennium.

Read All about It.

Read the trade and business magazines. *Marketplace,* the second section of the *Wall Street Journal (WSJ),* is usually a good place to turn to when you see a copy.

Get familiar with some of the cutting-edge business magazines like *Wired* and *Fast Company,* as well as the standbys *Business Week* and *Fortune.*

At first, only bits and pieces will make sense to you – but then the connections will start to kick in.

The opinion pages on the Internet and your local business paper can help you see what's coming and who might be hiring.

5. List and Learn about the Top Companies in Your Town, City, or Region.

Many major markets now have business newspapers. You might also use your local chamber of commerce and business associations as resources to help you do this.

You may be surprised how much opportunity is right there.

Check out each relevant category in The Business of Brands.

Marketers: Discover the leading companies in your area, and major branches of national companies in categories that interest you – as well as the hot new players.

Agencies: You can find advertising agencies in virtually any market by searching the 'Net. Then, go visit their Web sites.

Media: Don't stop with the obvious – the newspaper and the leading TV and radio stations.

Don't forget specialty magazines (some may be published in your market) or cable TV providers. Or the local suburban newspapers and "shoppers." And you might as well find out who sells the out-of-home media in your home town.

Marketing Services: Go to the business yellow pages (that's not the consumer yellow pages where you look to see who delivers pizza – this is a separate book entirely). Look under "Marketing," "Marketing Services," and "Public Relations."

See what you find. You might be surprised.

The more you learn about your market, the better you'll understand it and your place within it.

The Power Example.

Let's take the power industry as a test example for a target marketing exercise. Why power?

First, it's a large capitalization business, to use a stock market term. Though it is a mature industry, it is now in a high-growth phase again, mainly due to de-regulation.

Advertising and marketing are now becoming absolute necessities because of all the new competitors.

We shared one example with you in Chapter Eight – Nicor, a gas supplier getting ready for the new energy marketplace. (Enron would probably be a bad choice in this category.)

This new marketplace means new suppliers of energy are coming to town – each with their "brand" of energy.

And this means there may be opportunities for you.

Second, the industry has long-term career advantages.

People will always need energy (light and heat).

Third, power companies are usually publicly traded, so there is lots of information about them.

This example can be applied to your selection of industries and business, since it gives you steps for understanding your market.

Job Title Overview.

Here's a look at job titles. They're arranged by levels (e.g., junior, senior) and job function.

As a beginner, you'd normally start at the assistant or junior level, then work your way up.

This holds true regardless of your company type, such as an ad or PR agency, marketing-services firm, manufacturer, or media company.

In all departments, there may be a need for interns.

Account Services.

Good with people? Talented in creating resolution and common ground? Fine organizational skills? Got proof? Then this may be for you.

Assistant Account Executive
Assistant Account Representative
Junior Account Executive
Account Coordinator
Research Account Assistant
Account Executive or Planner
Sr. Account Executive or Planner
Assistant Account Manager
Manager Account Services
Account Supervisor
Group Account Supervisor
Vice President Account Services

Creative Department: Art/Graphics.

Like to draw? Good at it? Quark no problem? Got proof? Imaginative? This is for you.

Junior Production Artist
Junior Creative Coordinator
Assistant Production Services
Junior Graphic Designer
Assistant Art Director
Junior Art Director
Art Director
Senior Art Director
Assistant Digital Services
Digital Designer
Graphic Artist
Senior Graphic Artist
Manager Digital Services
Web Site Internet Designer

(Continued on next page)

Understanding the Job Market.

The marketplace isn't just industries, it's the jobs within those industries. By now you know that any list we print will be a bit out-of-date as soon as we print it.

But the following summary will provide a useful framework. It lists entry-level jobs by category within The Business of Brands.

Job Title Overview and Review.

Make a quick review of your basic options and opportunities.

By referring to the chart and the book, you'll be able to identify most of the jobs and their titles at the entry level.

There are also additional links and resources at adbuzz.com.

Marketers.

• Review Chapter Four for ideas about jobs in marketing departments and jobs in field marketing, such as staff assistant, marketing coordinator, or assistant brand manager (notice the words assistant and coordinator – these denote entry level).

• Don't forget field marketing. This is needed in various companies, such as franchise groups and beverage marketers and openings happen often as people move up.

Agencies.

• New types of advertising agencies are developing, such as ethnic agencies, Internet agencies, and don't forget creative boutiques.

• Review Chapter Five for jobs in ad agencies, such as junior copywriter, account executive, or production assistant.

Media Companies.

• Review Chapter Six for jobs with various media, such as circulation promotion assistant, fulfillment assistant, or sales assistant with a newspaper. They also tend to use lots of interns.

Marketing Services.

• Consider marketing-services companies that perform agency-like functions, creative departments at media companies, design firms, interactive agencies, production companies, sales promotion agencies, public relations agencies, database marketing firms (a "hot" field), direct marketing firms, or even Web site developers.

Developing Your Target.

By now you have an initial understanding of what it takes to understand your market.

Now let's dig in a little deeper and narrow your target.

Target Marketing Yields Understanding.

By digging into your potential target markets, you'll start to crystallize your sense of yourself as a brand even more.

And you'll start to develop some thoughts on where you can make the best connection.

• You don't know everything, but you're making a start.
• You're beginning to understand your market.
• You're beginning to understand what you have to offer.
• You're beginning to understand the entry-level jobs.

You want to work to form a better match between what you can offer and what the market needs.

GO = Geography and Opportunity.

Now let's add two other things to your target definition:

- **Geography**
- **Opportunity**

There may be a particular part of the country where you want to work – or need to work. And there may be a unique set of circumstances that creates an opportunity that you can leverage.

Geography – Where Is Your Target?

You may find them in the following places:

- Your hometown.
- Your college town – if it's not your hometown.
- Your college or department's alumni directory. Think hard about this one, because you can immediately establish a common ground with the target.

    Identify a number of your college or department's graduates who are now working in the field.

    They're likely to help you, even if only to give you some good advice or maybe a person to contact.

    If you're going to school in a big city, maybe your job is right where you're going to school. But maybe not.

Target Marketing Yields Opportunities.

Without knowing a single thing about you, we know there will be companies or places where you have better opportunities than others. Watch for them.

In researching prospective target markets be on the lookout for opportunities that match up well with your T.I.G.E.R. profile.

Opportunities will surface the more you learn about the possible targets. For example, if there's a place to live while you look for a job, that place will have better opportunity.

You know what we're saying.

Target Marketing Creates Matches.

By digging into your potential target markets, you'll also crystallize your sense of yourself as a brand even more.

You'll start to feel where to make the best connection.

What you're looking to do is create a better match between what you can offer and what the target needs.

And you can find potential targets in the minds of family, in the minds of friends, and in the minds of their friends. They know people. They can help you locate potential targets.

As you consider potential targets, always search for a match between your T.I.G.E.R. profile and key companies.

As You Focus, Expand Your Job Horizon.

This isn't contradictory. As you focus on what you want to do, you need to expand your horizons about where you can do it.

Later, in the section called "Bringing Yourself to Market," you'll be creating a strategy for "The Brand Called You."

Job Titles (Cont.)

Creative Department: Copy Services.

Like to write? Are you all about words? Read for leisure and with skill? Imaginative? Able to visualize? Got proof? Here's the list.

Proofreader
Researcher
Junior Copywriter
Senior Copywriter
Copy Chief
Copy Creative Director
Associate Creative Director
Creative Director

Audio/Video/Broadcast.

Into sound? Sight? Technology? Can't stay away from the camcorder? Got proof? Maybe you're in here somewhere.

Production Assistant
Producer
Assistant Audio Engineer
Assistant Cameraman
Assistant Computer Service
Assistant Film/Tape Editor

Traffic Production Services.

Like to keep track of things? Room neat and orderly? Known for having things together? Like looking over shoulders? Maybe you're here.

Traffic Assistant
Traffic Coordinator
Traffic Manager
Assistant Production Coordinator
Assistant Estimator
Estimator

(Continued on next page)

Target Marketing Creates Matches.

Going Public. Looking at her options, Joy Farber found that a small public relations firm was the best fit. She gets to write – and do a lot more.

Job Titles (Cont.)

Media Services:
Broadcast and Print.

Like digging into data? Like spending money. . . wisely? Organized? Like detective work? Got proof? This might be for you.

Media Assistant

Media Researcher

Media Coordinator

Assistant Media Planner

Media Planner

Assistant Media Buyer

Media Buyer

Agency Marketing Department.

Like digging? Probing? Planning? Marketing? This might be it for you.

Research Assistant

Researcher

Senior Researcher

Assistant Planner

Planner

Public Relations.

Great with people? Like making lemonade from lemons? Good at presenting? Writing? Conceptualizing? Planning? Maybe you're here.

Administrative Assistant

Research Assistant

Proofreader

Account Coordinator

Assistant Account Executive

Account Executive

Account Supervisor

(Continued on next page)

For now, let's consider some examples of how to expand and then narrow your target. Here's what we mean.

Example: Writing Jobs

For example, assume you want a writing job – because you love to write and think you're good at it.

The most obvious writing job is advertising copywriter – but don't stop there. Look at the other writing opportunities.

Marketers: If you do good business and technical writing, there may be a job at a marketer. Don't forget their corporate communications department – companies need newsletters.

John's daughter was a technical writer moving to Portland. He had a friend who knew Dan Wieden. Dan got her an interview at *Nike* and she got a job there – as a tech writer.

Agencies: In addition to advertising, consider sales promotion (one of the text resources in the adbuzz.com study hall is an article called "How to Get a Job in Sales Promotion" by Coleen Fahey).

Don't forget Direct – a field that depends on good writing.

And, now that you think of it, so does the Internet.

Media: There's selling and writing at a lot of media companies. Got an ear for radio? See what the stations need. Got an eye for TV? See what your local cable provider might offer.

And don't forget the smaller media – the city business magazines, the regional shoppers and alternative newspapers – they use writing. Of course, there will probably be phone answering and "go-fer" work attached – that's true in most entry-level jobs.

But, if it's consistent with your long-term goals, there's nothing wrong with a stepping-stone job.

Marketing Services: We already mentioned Sales Promotion and Direct. There's one more rich area – Public Relations.

Now there's a field that needs a lot of writing.

Joy Farber, a former Temple student and now a PR account executive with BSMG Worldwide in New York City, tells how she landed in public relations.

"My plan was to be a copywriter – though toward my senior year in college I had the nagging suspicion that, as much as I enjoyed writing, if I had to do it all day, every day, it would drive me bonkers.

"So when I finished school, I decided to freelance while conducting my job search. It allowed me to sample different jobs, and that's how I ended up in a small but visible PR firm.

"In PR I could be on both the creative side and the business side. I could develop strategy. I could plan campaigns. I could write, and I could be the client contact. This diversity is why I chose PR.

"In a small firm I could learn a lot quickly, gaining responsibility by grabbing it. Even if your aspirations are to work in a large agency – which mine always were – consider the benefits of starting small."

In short, there are lots of writing opportunities in The Business of Brands – if you expand your horizons.

Increasing Your Market Value.

THE TURTLE CARRIES A LOT ON HIS BACK. He offers protection and strength. The steps are slow but sure.

There are several ways for you to increase your market value.

Chances are, you have almost two years to prepare for a career in the marketplace – two years to find the right match between your "brand" and the marketplace.

That's two years to do a bit of "brand-building."

Here are four areas you can work on right now:

A. Making the Most of Your Degree
B. Internships and Summer Jobs
C. Networking
D. Extras

Each can increase your value in the job market.

A. Make the Most of Your Undergraduate Degree.

There are a number of ways to make the most of your degree so that you increase your market value.

1. Take the right courses
2. Get the right minor with your major
3. Get involved and volunteer
4. Look into student advertising competitions
5. Comb your campus

These are things you can get started on right away.

Let's look at them one by one.

1. Take the Right Courses.

When you're a freshman in college, things seem pretty much laid out for you. Your advisor tells you to take certain courses, and you do. But what your advisor might not tell you is that you should be mapping out future courses according to your career interest.

That sounds fine, but the problem is, do you really know what that interest is or even will be?

Much like anything else, there's a learning curve here regarding your courses and career interest. The curve begins as a freshman.

- You start with prescribed and required courses because you must. During this first year you begin to learn what subjects you like, and perhaps more importantly, what subjects you don't like (be careful not to have your liking or disliking dependent too much on the profs, but rather have it dependent on the actual subject matter).

- The curve continues into your sophomore year, when your interests are probably coming more into focus. You're still taking required courses, but now is the time to begin considering, and even taking specific courses in, your interest area.

- When you're a junior, you may be well into your major field of study, but even if you're not, you at least begin to recognize things that interest you, things that you can see yourself pursuing in the years to come.

3: *The Turtle is North.*
The color is black.

Job Titles (Cont.)

Administrative Services.
Like keeping track? Organized? Good with money? Like collecting money? Like paying it out? Good at math? Maybe this is it.
Assistant Bookkeeper
Receivables Clerk
Payables Clerk
Comptroller

Corporate Communications.
Like to manage? Like to see things grow? Solid business writer? Good at organizing? Try this field.
Junior Product Manager
Product Manager
Assistant Marketing Manager
Marketing Manager
Assistant Marketing Services
Marketing Director

Sales/Communications.
Sold anything lately? Everyone sells in one form or another? Family members in sales? A people person? A lot of young people start here and find they like it.
Salesperson
Service Representative
Sales Trainee
Sales Representative
Sales Manager
Sales Director

Ask Audra?

Check out Audra Smith's good advice on good courses for ad majors.

Each is a way to increase the value of "Brand You."

Specific Courses. The following will provide you with a broad spectrum of knowledge for the advertising world:

• Graphic Design • Sociology • Psychology • Marketing • Creative Writing • Public Relations • Media Planning • Media Buying • Ad Campaigns • Public Speaking • Computers

Of course, you can only learn so much in a textbook.

Audra's Activities for Ad Majors. The best experience is hands-on. Combine the course knowledge you've acquired with hands-on experiences, and you're ready for the job hunt and your first interview:

• Internships • Advertising or Marketing Clubs • College Media • College Yearbook • Alumni Relations • Campus Events

Remember, each item has its own means of expansion.

For example, if you're interested in marketing, whether it's your major or not, you should include marketing, research, consumer behavior, and organizational management.

Similarly, if you're interested in writing, various departments around campus probably offer beginning writing courses.

Even within the creative writing course of study, you're liable to find beginning poetry, scriptwriting, or technical writing courses offered by the same or an aligned department offering creative writing.

And don't forget newswriting and journalism. Even in this electronic Internet Age, good writing skills will serve you well – even if you're not a writer.

• In your senior year you're settled well into your major and career interest. At least that's the way it's supposed to work.

People Change.

True, it may not always work that way, especially when you consider that many people change not just jobs but careers three or four times in their lifetime.

Consider yourself fortunate if you're one of the few who knows exactly what you want to do for your career.

And don't be upset if you've changed your mind once or twice already – maybe you're still not sure.

Take heart. If you keep focused and productive, chances are you'll find the niche in the marketplace that's just right for you.

Meanwhile, the courses you take can go a long way toward sharpening your talents and interests.

2. Get the Right Minor with Your Major.

As an added bonus, consider a minor. Often a minor to go along with your major degree (advertising, marketing, etc.) can help differentiate you from others and sharpen your talents.

In most cases, a minor may only require satisfactory completion of six or seven courses.

If you've been dabbling in a particular subject area with certain course selections, by the time you're a junior you may already have completed two, three, or more of those courses.

Obviously, you should check carefully with your advisor and an advisor in the department of your minor. But here are some thoughts as to the kind of minors that can help:

- If you're interested in account services work, then psychology, sociology, or marketing may offer valuable minors.
- If you're interested in creative work, then English, art, computer graphics, photography, or psychology may be suitable minors.
- If you're interested in media or research, economics, statistics, marketing, psychology, or sociology may be good minors.
- This is a business where presentation is key, whatever you do. If you enjoy theater, improv comedy, or want to become a better public speaker, develop those skills as well.

But there's even more you can do to increase your market value.

Because there's more to school than taking classes.

3. Get Involved. Volunteer.

You want to make the most of your undergraduate degree, and the way to do that is by getting involved. Join clubs and organizations, particularly those in the field.

Most have events that need advertising and promotional programs – projects that will help you develop time-organizing skills.

Of course, once you get in the habit of volunteering your time, you might find you like it.

That's what Dawn Vaughn does now as a professional in the industry. Read what she has to say in the next sidebar.

By getting involved and volunteering, you'll serve your practical need for getting that good first job, but you'll also "serve your soul," as Dawn put it, by contributing and making a difference.

And don't stop once you've started work.

Often the advertising or marketing group in your area will have some sort of charitable effort – it's a good way to help, and it's a good way to network.

From Alderman to Oval Office.

At the beginning of his career, Bruce, your editor, volunteered to write copy for a local aldermanic candidate in Chicago.

That led to other freelance work – most of it for free.

Eight years later, that led to a paying job as Creative Director for the President of the United States. Hey, you never know.

4. Look into Student Advertising Competitions, Particularly AAF/NSAC.

One experience that is extremely valuable for advertising majors is the American Ad Federation National Student Advertising Competition (AAF/NSAC), "The College World Series of Advertising."

It's a competition participated in by most of the ad programs at US colleges and universities. A lot of people think it's the best real-world advertising experience offered at universities.

How the NSAC Works.

A prominent national advertiser presents a case. Past sponsors have been American Airlines, Chevrolet, Chrysler, Florida Tourism, Hallmark, Kellogg's, Nestle, Pizza Hut, Toyota, and Visa.

They provide the initial input.

Each school forms an agency-like advertising team.

Then the "fun" begins. First, market research, then a complete marketing and advertising plan, and, finally, creating a full-fledged advertising and promotional campaign for a prestigious client.

It's sort of like all the things we talked about in this book. Only, instead of talking about them and taking a test, you really do it.

The plan and campaign are coordinated into a plans book and actually presented to the client and a panel of nationally renowned judges at the opening district competitions.

Then see how you measure up. Each district winner goes on to compete at the "world series" final competition. It's pretty cool.

How It Benefits Your Career.

It's no secret that students whose teams do well at the district and especially the national world series competition also do well in the job marketplace.

Their experience with AAF/NSAC is one of the main reasons they have value in the job marketplace.

In fact, right now, you might want to find out when the district competition is in your area. If it's close enough, you might want to consider taking a day off and see seven ad teams in action.

You'll see what we mean.

The Brand Called Dawn.

Dawn Vaughn believes in giving back something a little extra – now that she's unloaded the U-Haul.

"As you finish up this book, you may or may not know what's in your soul.

"You may know that you want to work for a large corporation or make lots of money or clean up children's TV or work in special event planning or work for a nonprofit organization.

"That's great. But if you don't know what's in your soul, that's okay too, because you will in time.

"As you look for the answer you'll 'try on' each agency and see which one or which clients work for you, giving you a confident feeling that you're doing what your heart desires.

"For some people, like myself, it's important that they make a difference in the world.

"That's why I donate my time and account service knowledge to the Georgia Eye Bank.

"I donate my time and knowledge to help them with calendars, donor cards, annual reports, and promotional folders.

"In return, I feel that I help make a difference, and that's what's in my soul."

What's the Deal, Mack?

Competing in AAF/NSAC helped Mack Owen prepare for winning in the real world.

"I made some decisions in college that had a major effect on my career.

"One of the best was to try out for the AAF competition team.

"This year-long project brought together 15 ad majors as a student agency to work on one campaign.

"I learned through the competition about working together and the considerable challenges there are in putting together an ad campaign."

Our Intern.

Here's Copy Workshop summer intern Adria Kornick, helping on an instructional video.

Want to see the videos? Check out the Theater portion of adbuzz.com.

Mack Attack!

Mack Owen is a graduate of Texas Tech University and now in charge of his own in-house advertising department for a major chain of car dealerships in western Texas.

In the sidebar, see what he has to say about AAF/NSAC.

5. Comb Your Campus.

Beyond participating in competitions, search out, work for, or volunteer your time to key campus organizations and groups.

• Campus media may include your campus newspaper, radio station, or even an allied department on campus that works with the media, such as your sports information, university relations, or communications departments. They may need your help.

• Work study programs often allow you to work within your major or minor department while going to school.

• Internships. Remember, it may be possible to take more than one internship over the course of two or three years.

• Join various campus organizations that will help differentiate you as a brand, while simultaneously improving your skills in a particular area. For example, if you're interested in a "people" job position, then think about becoming a campus counselor or tour guide for new or prospective students on campus.

Think about becoming involved with your student activities center on campus, as well.

• Start a student agency. Remember Roy Spence and GSD&M? Maybe you want to be the next student agency that turns into a real ad agency. Why not find out?

Form a student agency – work for the student paper or student groups. Make some noise. Have fun. Create great samples.

Almost everything you do will be increasing your market value.

B. Get Practical Experience.

There are two good ways to get it:

1. Internships
2. Summer Jobs

And you have a chance to get more than one of each.

1. Internships.

Try to get at least two before you graduate. Internships often provide valuable work experience and contacts.

Remember, it's not uncommon for student interns to continue working for the sponsoring company after the internship is over.

Differentiating a "Commodity."

As we've said, your degree will be, in many ways, a commodity. It's very similar to all the other degrees from your classmates at your school and other schools.

Activities that differentiate you from those classmates are often considered the most valuable by those making decisions about who gets the jobs.

For example, production companies look for someone who has done apprentice or intern work in the production field.

Larger media companies, such as major local TV stations, often look for sales people who have trained at smaller media companies, such as local cable TV stations and radio stations.

Make note of these special experiences. You should also consider adding those you plan on developing in the near future. This will help keep you on course in your career pursuit.

Differentiating Your Résumé.

Bruce Bendinger believes internships differentiate – because they *"introduc[e] you to the student behind the résumé."*

In addition, Bruce says, *"be ready to tell me the story of your background in an engaging way."* We'll talk about stories a little later.

Internships Get You Connected.

The Business of Brands is inter-connected.

Here's what happened to Mack Owen when he interned in a business he didn't think he'd be interested in. *"Though I didn't have any real interest in the newspaper business, I decided to accept an offer to intern at a small newspaper in West Texas. With the small paper I was able to work directly under the advertising manager.*

He gave me the opportunity to sell on the streets just like every other sales representative at the paper." As a result, Mack learned to sell.

By the way, David Ogilvy says that, at some point, virtually everyone in advertising should be in sales. The sooner the better.

Create Your Own Internships.

The importance of digging up internships, literally creating them, is dramatized by Gregg Friedmann, a Penn State graduate now a copywriter for the Torre Lazur pharmaceutical advertising agency.

"Odds are that somewhere near you, there is an ad agency or marketing department willing to give you an internship.

"During my junior year I called a wide selection of ad agencies close to where I live and asked about internships. One local agency gave me a shot, even though they never had an intern before.

"Thanks to the contacts I made during that summer internship, I not only got a lead on my first job, but I am now working at the same agency I had interned at years before.

"Here are some ways to make this happen for you:

• *"When you call the agency, you'll get the receptionist. Ask to speak to the person in charge of internships. If there is no such person, ask to speak to the creative director or the account planner or someone in the field you're suited for.*

• *"Don't let go of this contact, even if they don't return your call. Send an e-mail, a letter, or tell your story on voicemail. If it seems fruitless after awhile, move on to the next person and agency.*

• *"Beyond arranging for an internship yourself, go to your school's career placement office or your department's internship office or director. Make your plans known and make repeated visits to obtain the latest information on available internships."*

Need to Produce for Bruce?

Here's what Chicago ad exec (and book editor) Bruce Bendinger has to say about internships and summer jobs on your résumé.

Differentiating a Résumé.

"Student résumés are hard to read, because they usually don't do a good job of introducing you to the person behind the résumé.

"That's why I look for internships and summer jobs.

"For me, people with the initiative to get good internships and summer jobs are a cut above the generic grade point, major, summer job, ad club, 'I'm a people person' résumé that is the fate of most students.

"I look for interests and enthusiasm. Any projects, like a fundraising concert or an extracurricular that demands a lot of time and dedication – a student publication, for example.

"This tells me the person likes to work and isn't afraid to do something extra.

"Finally, I really want to know a little more about you, the person.

"It doesn't matter to me if your parents were marketing executives or you're the first in your family to finish college. But I want to know either fact.

"I want to get a sense of the life that shaped you. Be ready to tell me the story of your background in an interesting and engaging way."

Making Your Network Work.

Shawn Kelly connected with mentors to get an extra edge. Here's his network news – get more from your professors!

"One of the most important steps you can take, aside from making a complete commitment to your college education, is surrounding yourself with the right professors.

"Use your professors as role models and try to establish a solid mentor/protégé relationship with at least one of them.

"Mentors can offer tremendous insight into your future career.

"Let them share with you some of the mistakes they made along the way.

"Have them introduce you to other walking success stories.

"You will soon discover that they can be great sources for business leads.

"My own mentor not only acted as my academic adviser, but also served as a constant source of motivation.

"Through my mentor, I landed scholarships, academic honors, and the internship that became the job of my dreams.

"If you're serious about a career in advertising or marketing, then understand the importance of a mentor and of networking with your professors and peers alike.

"Seek out the best and brightest of your faculty and fellow students and make them your personal support group."

Whether you secure an internship from your school, department, or through hitting the streets on your own, the main point is to get at least one during your college career.

2. Summer Jobs.

Don't get just any summer job. Get one in advertising or marketing. Even if you're sweeping floors, making copies, sitting in meetings only occasionally, or answering the phone.

Here is where your real first job may be.

And here is where you'll expand your own experiences, adding more bulk and substance to "The Brand Called You."

And Summer Trips.

If you need to work most of the summer to help with school costs, consider what you can do in a week or two.

More from Bruce – he took a week during one of his summers and stayed with a friend to do informational interviewing.

"I spent a week in New York the summer after my junior year.

"I knocked on doors, got advice from strangers, and tried to understand what they were looking for. It was hugely valuable.

"By the time graduation rolled around, I knew the agencies. I also knew by then that I wanted to work in Chicago – not New York.

"They were seeing me with my third sample book, completely changed from front to back.

"It worked. I had offers from Chicago's three biggest agencies.

"That early start made a huge difference. And going to New York really helped me know I wanted to work in Chicago."

So, when you plan your summer trip, think about the long-term payoff, too. Even if you don't end up there.

C. Networking.

On some levels, it's as simple as the law of averages.

The way to get connected is to get connected. Build your knowledge. Build your connections. Build your relationships.

The more people you know, the better your odds. You'll have more to choose from, you'll be able to make better judgments.

Here are some useful guidelines for building your network:

1. Find a Mentor
2. Get to Know Important Others
3. Look for People from Whom You Can Learn

Let's take them one at a time.

1. Find a Mentor.

Still another vital concern for you is to begin developing your contacts and references – your network.

Some will come from your own personal networking, which means you should be active in your local advertising or marketing organizations, including those in your college and regional area.

But others will come from those people you have contact with daily, your professors.

In the sidebar, Shawn Kelly, a graduate of San Jose State, mentions the importance of his mentor, Professor Tom Jordan.

You should remember, too, that finding contacts, mentors, or a network of colleagues won't work if you wait until you're a senior.

You need to begin developing those relationships early on.

2. Get to Know "Important Others."

Start by targeting key people, such as your profs or those you meet at professional meetings in your local area.

Write them. Keep up with them and what they're doing.

Maintain their contact. Don't lose touch. Got e-mail? Use it.

Terryl Ross, a 1990 graduate of Syracuse University, has this to say about the importance of networking,

"Establishing a network with people in your field is the key to starting and maintaining a successful career.

"Of the jobs and contracts I have had in my eight years in recreation, 85% have come from the networks I created.

• "Establish networks by joining clubs, attending conferences, meeting alumni, and volunteering for projects related to advertising.

• "Keep in touch with people you meet. Send e-mails, cards, and examples of what you have produced. Ask for advice.

• "Establish networks in other fields where you have an interest.

"Remember, it's never too early to start building your network, and your network can never be too large."

3. Look for People from Whom You Can Learn.

During your first few jobs, it's critical to find people to learn from.

At the beginning of your career, learning is even more important than earning. And these days, it's not as easy as it used to be.

Everybody's busier, so it's harder to find that time when you can really hear what more experienced people can teach you.

But it's one of the most important things you can do.

D. Extras.

It doesn't stop there.

Here are a few more ways you might consider adding to your value – though some of them might cost a bit.

1. Interview Extras
2. Building Your Book
3. An Advanced Degree

Remember, you're competing against a lot of other smart, dedicated people. And your target market is looking for people who have something extra. Give them what they want.

1. Interview Extras.

When you go on an interview, you want to be able to show something more than your diploma, grade point, and a résumé. Here are some thoughts on giving your presentation something extra.

Testimony through Letters and Commendations.

As you work or volunteer throughout your college career, you'll develop references, those who can and will speak kindly of you as a coworker and person.

Often they're pleased to write you letters of recommendation.

Networking Gets You Connected.

The Strength of Weak Ties.

In his classic 1974 book, *Getting a Job*, Mark Granovetter had fascinating insights based on a survey.

• 56% of the people who got jobs got them through some sort of personal connection;

• 20% got them through a formal hiring process;

• 20% applied directly.

Now it gets interesting.

Connections = Better Jobs.

Personal connections tended to result in better jobs at better salaries.

But those connections were not necessarily strong or close. They tended to be weaker, "friend of a friend" type connections.

But even though they weren't close or strong, they were close enough and strong enough to open the doors – and that was the key.

So don't be bothered if some of the connections you connect with are a bit distant – that's normal.

People Like to Connect.

One more thing. While it is a bit of an imposition, most professionals enjoy making the connections that result in someone getting their start.

It's a source of satisfaction.

And, years from now, when you're asked to help the son or daughter of "a friend of a friend," you may get the same satisfaction.

Simple Advice.

Chris Smith's craft is copywriting. His advice? "Start yesterday!"

If you've been particularly successful on a certain project, get a letter of commendation to add to the letters of recommendation.

Produced Work.

Through your classes and experiences, what work have you actually produced that warrants notice?

Are there posters and support materials for some project you worked on? They can help dramatize the event.

• Did you put together a marketing plan for a campus group that helped stimulate the group's constructive thinking about its future?

• Did you spearhead the fraternity recruitment drive?

• Have you helped someone solve a marketing or advertising problem? Be ready to show or discuss these achievements.

Consider one-page case histories that highlight those projects.

Look for ways to visualize and dramatize accomplishments.

Don't have any accomplishments to visualize and dramatize?

Looks like you've got one more goal.

2. Building Your Book.

For those interested in the creative side of advertising, showing something when you're done means your "book."

Gregg Friedmann offers some more advice. *"If you've already told any of your professors or anyone in the ad business that you want to be a copywriter, that person probably told you that you'll need to put your book together.*

"Allow me to tell you a few things about that book.

"First of all, when you graduate, no one will care that you aced Bio-mechanics of Basket Weaving or Small, Meaningless Mammals 101. Because whoever interviews you will want to see what you can do.

"That's where your book comes in.

"Your book is a binder or portfolio case filled with samples of your work. It's the one thing that will make or break you more than anything else. Your book can speak volumes about your conceptual ability and your writing skill. So make the most of it.

"You should start thinking about it as early in your college career as possible. I highly recommend Maxine Paetro's How to Put Your Book Together and Get a Job in Advertising, *which will give you specific guidelines for your book."*

More Book Tips.

Chris Smith, a copywriter in Houston, has some more specifics.

"When should you start working on your book? Start yesterday.

"You can stop the same day you accept the Rolex at your retirement party. Never stop hammering your book into shape."

Here are some tips from Chris:

• *"Take what you think is currently your strongest campaign and work on new ones until it's your weakest.*

• *"Team up with an artist (if you're a writer) or a writer (if you're an artist). That way, both your books will be better.*

• *"Focus on ideas and only finish the great ones.*

• *"Don't waste time polishing waste. Waste the bad ideas.*

• *"Show your work to as many industry people as possible and then heed their advice.*

• *"Keep your eye on CMYK Magazine and student competitions. That's the kind of work being done at the portfolio schools, and that's what you'll be competing with when you graduate.* (Order your copy at www.cmykmag.com.)

• *"Fill your book with ads that reflect your style. The really great creatives make each ad their own without straying from a clients' appropriate tone or strategy."*

Go to www.cmykmag.com.

The advanced advertising schools make it a point of having you leave their programs with a book good enough for a job.

What If You're Not Creative?

For a start, if you were on an AAF/NSAC team, you'd have a plans book you can show.

Add Post-Its™ on parts where you contributed. Be sure to have a summary – verbal or written. AAF Plans Books can be a bit daunting to interviewers who aren't familiar with them.

3. Think About an Advanced Degree (Maybe).

An advanced degree isn't for everyone, nor does it guarantee career success. But for some people, it helps.

Advanced degrees like MBAs, MAs, and MFAs can provide you with additional skills, prospects, and a certain degree of prestige – depending on who you're talking to.

Going into marketing? Consider an MBA.

For ad agency work, an MBA for account execs or a portfolio school for creatives may be a good decision.

Advanced Degrees in Marketing.

Many market research companies prefer advanced degrees and most marketing companies look for MBAs in marketing.

Good News! Your Company Might Help with Your MBA.

You've just finished paying tuition for your undergrad degree, and you want to get started on your career.

So two more years of school may not be quite what you had in mind. Don't worry, a lot of people feel that way.

In fact, quite a few get their MBAs while they're already working.

Most cities have MBA programs designed for people working 9 to 5 – with lighter course loads and evening classes. And many companies have programs where they'll pitch in and help with the tuition.

You might even let people know you're interested in getting an MBA during your interview.

You need a powerful book to get a job.

The Book for Your Book.

It's *How to Put Your Book Together and Get a Job in Advertising* by Maxine Paetro. Available from The Copy Workshop at adbuzz.com.

Student Work.

For *Waffle House.*

A Student Ad.

It's for the Atlanta Hawks. Two of the top portfolio schools are in Atlanta.

More Student Work.

Today, many advertising creative portfolios are polished and professional – the product of advanced creative training schools.

For good entry-level jobs at top ad agencies, you'll probably need to spend a little time at one of these schools.

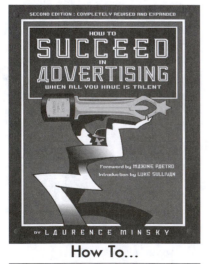

How To...

Succeed in Advertising When All You Have Is Talent by Laurence Minsky. Available on www.adbuzz.com

Even though you don't have that MBA on your résumé yet, the fact you want to get one will show prospective employers that you want to keep moving ahead.

Advanced Creative Degrees.

In advertising education today, one of the most coveted advanced degrees isn't traditional; it's the completion of intensive creative advertising work, including strategic planning, account planning, ad campaign development, design, and copy.

The following is a fairly up-to-date list of the major programs in this field – in alphabetical order:

Creative Schools.

This list does not include a number of very fine art schools – though these programs do include art direction emphasis as one of the major areas.

⭐ **Creative Circus (www.creativecircus.com), Atlanta.**

For aspiring copywriters, the Creative Circus Web site claims, *"At the Circus, writer's don't just write – they take 26 letters and turn them into magic. By the time they graduate, a blank sheet of paper isn't a wall. It's a doorway."*

The Creative Circus offers advanced work in design, photography, art direction, and copy.

⚙ **Miami Ad School (www.adschool.edu), Miami** (plus programs in Chicago, Minneapolis, and New York).

Their Web site states, *"No Bull. No nonsense. Only 'in touch' professionals earning their paychecks as creative directors, art directors, graphic designers, copywriters, illustrators, or photographers . . . You take on the Mac and win. You learn how to strategize. You develop a photographer's eye and writer's ear. You bang out copy. You draw roughs."*

The Miami Ad School also offers course work in account planning and a unique network of schools that allow students to work in New York, Chicago, and Minneapolis after the first year.

✏ **Portfolio Center (www.portfoliocenter.com), Atlanta.**

"Portfolio Center is a competitive, highly motivated and energetic environment… Our alumni win the most awards. They make the most money. They are among the most revered creatives in the country."

The Portfolio Center offers course work in design, photography, art direction, copy, and illustration.

☆ **University of Texas (www.utexas.edu/world), Austin.**

In addition to offering an excellent undergrad program, this university has added a grad program with a creative emphasis.

Go visit their Advertising World Web site, it's one of the most comprehensive advertising sites anywhere.

❣ VCU Brandcenter (<u>brandcenter.vcu.edu</u>), Richmond, Va.

This innovative program developed by Virginia Commonwealth University, has students work in agency-like groups.

Their Web site describes the program's distinguishing characteristic as *"practical, real-world expertise with a true academic understanding of advertising and marketing and how they work... Students at the Brandcenter will be equally divided among concentrations in art direction, copywriting, and account management."*

The VCU Brandcenter is one program that vigorously includes the account services side of the industry in its curriculum in addition to account planning, art direction, and copywriting.

They are now adding a media track, funded by some of the top media agencies. Their advisory board includes some of the top ad executives in the US. Their director is Rick Boyko, former creative head of Ogilvy & Mather in the US.

Admissions works to keep a balance among all disciplines.

And Others...

The Academy of Art College in San Francisco, Advertising Arts College in San Diego, Art Center College of Design in Pasadena, Brainco in Minneapolis, AdEd and Columbia College in Chicago, and SVA (School of Visual Arts) in New York are other places where you can keep growing your creative skills.

There are excellent new programs opening up all the time and many are growing.

Keep Increasing Your Market Value.

Once you graduate and get that first job, your brand-building doesn't stop. Here's an example.

Cody's Career Path.

Cody Aufricht's first job was with a small agency – Snelson Advertising in Midland, Texas – a fairly small business-to-business ad agency specializing in oil and gas and financial advertising.

Cody spent his first two years as an account exec, moving up to Senior AE in 1983 and then to Vice President/Partner in 1985.

By 1988, he was Ad Manager of International Telecharge, Inc., a $300 million publicly held telecom company. By 1990, he was that company's Manager of Marketing Services.

After marketing management positions for PHH Vehicle Management Services, Inc., Cody moved to Director of Marketing for Todays Temporary, Inc., a $180 million staffing company.

Now, he develops and directs overall marketing strategy for 120 company-owned and franchise offices, directs all market research programs, and manages all marketing communications.

The lessons to be learned from Cody's career growth:
- He started small where he could learn the business
- He proved himself enough to move up (to manager)
- He moved up again, this time to director

Cody of the West.

Cody Aufricht, whom you met at the chapter's beginning, worked his way up to Director of Marketing

He offers some nice advice on getting started.

First, think of your task as a marketing problem. You are a product. Your features, benefits, and price are unique – you're a brand!

Your Brand Positioning Statement.
Start by writing a brand positioning statement. Copy this formula:

**To (market target),
I am the brand of
(frame of reference)
that (point of difference).**

Now answer these questions:

Your Target Market.

With what group do your interests and unique attributes match up best?

Are you a tenacious salesperson?

Are you creative like a writer?

Or are you methodical – like a researcher?

Do you match up with Midwest ad agencies, top-market radio stations, or creative boutiques?

Where do you have leverage?

Who are good potential consumers of you, the product?

Answer these questions. You're on the way to focusing on your target.

Next, you need to establish your frame of reference.

(Continued on next page)

The Dragon is East.
The color is green.

4:

Cody's Code (Cont.)

Your Frame of Reference.

Your frame of reference is how your target market categorizes products, or in this case, job candidates.

Are you an entry-level candidate with an internship to your credit?

How are you viewed by your prospective employers?

Show them that you understand how they are thinking and making the decision.

Your Point of Difference.

Your meaningful point of difference is the specific benefit you want your potential employers to associate with you.

Are you a talented copywriter?

Are you willing to travel four days a week? Have you worked closely with clients while in school?

Put Them All Together.

A final positioning statement might look like this:

To Dallas-based, business-to-business ad agencies with telecom clients.

I'm a top performing ad graduate with solid telecom knowledge and a track record that demonstrates I can help on your telecom accounts.

(Continued on next page)

The entry-level job was as an account executive (at larger agencies his title probably would have begun with junior, or assistant, or ended with coordinator).

The jobs showed increasing responsibility – from AE to ad manager to director of marketing – a fairly common pattern for career success in The Business of Brands – step by step, up the ladder.

And you can get a head start while you're in school.

Bringing Your Product to Market.

ACCORDING TO CHINESE MYTHOLOGY, the Dragon is the most powerful of the celestial animals. Chi – the Dragon's breath, flows all around us. The Dragon brings good luck and inspiration. You'll need all you can get as you work to connect.

Let's start with two examples – Dawn and Bruce.

Dawn's Marketing Campaign.

Remember Dawn Vaughn and her U-Haul truck?

She'd sent résumés to over 20 Atlanta advertising companies during her senior-year spring break. She then followed up with each company before she headed south.

Her first position came from a newspaper ad – an entry-level job as Account Coordinator for a small agency.

She did everything for the company, including layout, answering the phone, and coordinating services for the accounts.

In 1995, she moved on to Fahlgren Advertising (a larger agency with 30 employees) as Account Coordinator. She quickly moved up to Account Executive, working on McDonald's Atlanta.

In 1997, she moved on to Fletcher Martin Associates, a hot Atlanta agency employing 85 people.

As this book was written, she was an Account Manager working exclusively on the Arby's Midwest restaurant account – but don't be surprised if her career keeps growing.

The lessons to be learned from Dawn's career growth:

- Her campaign had a target. She followed up. And she followed up on her follow-up. Then she moved up.
- Move on and up when the opportunity presents itself. For Dawn, this meant going from Account Coordinator to Account Executive to Account Manager.

Bruce's Early Start.

Bruce again. He started early. As a writer, musician, and cartoonist in college, he also focused on the right target – at the time.

He recalls when he was a student like you.

"It's funny. Even though my father was in advertising, I didn't really consider it until my junior year.

"But once I decided, I really focused – and it gave me a big advantage.

"I spent a week in New York the summer after my junior year.

"I knocked on doors, got advice from strangers, and tried to understand what they were looking for.

"My opening story was that I was looking to be the kind of person they'd want to hire a year from now. I remember getting excellent advice from Dave Ochsner at Hoffman LaRoche and Bill Casey at Papert Koenig & Lois, who had started up one of the early copywriter courses.

"They may not know how much they helped me early on, but they were hugely helpful– in visits of less than an hour.

"For a variety of reasons, I decided on Chicago, the second biggest ad market. A fraternity brother's father was exec AD at a Chicago agency.

"I imposed myself on their hospitality over the Christmas holidays and tried to connect with as many major agencies as possible.

"I think I got in for interviews at eight of the top twelve agencies.

"My story had evolved to one where I was working to become the person they wanted to hire. I was first in line for campus interviews for all the agencies – plus P&G. (I had a different story for them – I told them that I was probably going to be an agency guy, but that I sure was interested in their company, the #1 advertiser. Somehow, that was enough to get them to fly me to Cincinnati for an interview.)

"By the time graduation rolled around, I knew the agencies.

"In turn, they were seeing me with the proof of my dedication – my third sample book, completely changed from front to back.

"I had offers from Chicago's three biggest agencies.

"That early start made a huge difference. And getting acquainted while I learned what they were looking for helped me get it right."

Bruce had a story, and he had a campaign.

Well, Dawn and Bruce have their jobs. What about you?

Your Pre-Launch Checklist.

Launching your brand in the marketplace will take a few things. Here's a quick checklist.

- **Your Résumé and More.** You'll need a résumé that does the job – plus a few other things to differentiate yourself from every other résumé-packing graduate. These days, you need an online version of that résumé.
- **Your Brand Story.** This is an interesting way of presenting your brand and your brand personality. We'll help you get started on your story in a few pages.
- **Your Market.** We'll review Step Two and talk about some ways to define your target and hit it effectively.
- **Your Campaign.** Finally, we'll talk about how to put all of the elements together into a winning campaign.

The day may be a few years off – but it's not too early to start talking about it and thinking about it.

Your Résumé & More.

Where's your résumé? You should have one right now.

You should be growing your résumé regularly – watching it build as you add value to your brand. And you need a pdf version and a word-processor version so you can e-mail it as well.

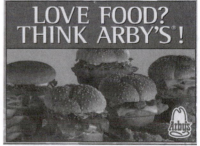

Take Action and Produce Things.

Now that you have a plan, you need to put it into action. And that means producing things. Here's a list:

- **Cover Letter**
- **Memorized Story**
- **Résumé**
- **Book** – if you're on the creative side of things. Samples of what goes into your book are shown earlier in this chapter.
- **Extras**

At the heart of this list is your résumé. It presents you as a brand that will fit with your target. You may not have it yet, but it's not too early to start working on it.

Getting the Job In a Tough Economy.

Getting that first job is always tough. But some times are tougher than others. Here's some good practical advice.

1. Find Ways to Prove Yourself. Is there some project you can take on at a reduced rate. Show your prospective employer you really want to help make his (or her) business a success. And then do exactly that.

2. Consider Opportunities at a Small Business. Whether you look for one that's going great guns, or one with problems, they all need help. And they can hire you faster with fewer interviews and more flexibility.

3. Expand Your Networking. That's particularly true if the sector you're looking at (for example, traditional ad agencies) is suffering in this economy.

4. Market Your "Personal Brand." We've been talking about this throughout this chapter. The tougher it gets, the more you need to put your own personal brand out there – to differentiate yourself in a difficult marketplace.

Tight and Right.

A résumé does more than list what you've done.

It also represents how you present yourself.

It should have clarity and purpose.

Have a few people look at your résumé and get suggestions.

If you want a few more tips, check the resource section in the back and look at a few basic formats. And then develop the résumé that's right for you.

Your résumé is a summary of your knowledge, experiences, and skills. It's chock full of facts about you.

On one page, you should be able to present – in writing – why you are qualified for an entry-level job at a company in your target.

And because it's one of the first and most important ways your target will get to meet you, it's important.

It should be brief, pointed, dynamic, and well organized.

- **Brief.** Use one side of one sheet of paper.
- **Pointed.** It should note the experiences and skills tailored to your target and the position you're applying for.
- **Dynamic.** Select your words carefully. Use action verbs – they're the writer's best friend.
- **Well Organized.** There are two basic formats for résumés: chronological and functional.

The Chronological Résumé.

The most common format is to present information in reverse chronological order, with the most recent experience first.

A good outline for the résumé would be the following:

- **Contact Information.**
  Your name, address, and phone number.
- **Objective.**
  A single, brief statement of the professional goal you have for that first job.
- **Education.**
  Your degree, major and minor, month and year of graduation, and name of school.
- **Special honors or achievements.**
  This may include dean's lists, high GPA, leadership roles in organizations, or special commendations from faculty or professionals.
- **Experiences and Employment.**
  Your title, name and location of employer, and dates of employment.

  If possible, include brief descriptions of those jobs that reflect well on you and relate to your objective or what you believe fits well with your employer's need.

  If you paid for a large percentage of your college costs, you may even want to state that percentage, since this will reflect well on you as an ambitious and self-sacrificing individual.

If appropriate, you may want to break your experiences or employment out into two sections: related experience and additional employment.

- **Activities and Interests.**

  Very brief lists or descriptions of those activities that personalize you for the employer and also reflect well on how you would fit with the company.

- **References.**

  Generally, the rule is to avoid listing references on your one-page résumé; however, if you have strong references who have enthusiastically agreed to support you, then you should seriously consider including them on a separate piece of paper, urging the employer to contact them.

  Of course, you should include name, title, address, and phone number for each reference. And you should always make certain that your references agree in advance to your request to use them as part of your job search.

The Functional Résumé.

The functional résumé is based on your skills, rather than chronology *per se*. It is meant to highlight the match between your skill set and what the employer needs. Still, for the most part it follows the basic chronological résumé format.

- **Contact Information**
- **Objective**
- **Education**
- **Experiences**
- **Skills** – Note those skills you've gained from previous experiences or employment that relate to those desired by the employer. For example, you may title one of the sections, "Organizational Skills."

  Then describe those skills as they have been developed and refined in your previous jobs.

And More?

What else do you have along with your résumé?

For example, do you have your own stationery?

Do you have any examples of the work you've done – a business card for your lawn-mowing service.

The poster for the school fundraising drive you headed up.

Even if you aren't looking for a creative job, using writing or graphic samples, you should look for ways to make your accomplishments tangible.

Remember, one of the big jobs of services marketing is to make the benefits tangible. You should work to make the benefits of hiring you exactly that – tangible.

Your Emotional IQ.

In today's workplace, you'll be judged not just for your technical skills and how smart you are – but by how well you handle yourself in the modern work environment.

More and more, we need to develop "emotional intelligence."

What Is It?

Based on what it takes for success in the workplace, many managers are looking for (and promoting) people with the right emotional habits as well as technical skills.

What are these abilities?

Some of the abilities considered vital for success are emotional competencies, like trustworthiness, adaptability, and a talent for collaboration.

Some Sample Questions.

How persuasive are you? How would you answer these statements?

- I hold myself accountable for meeting my goals.
- I can handle multiple demands and changing priorities smoothly.
- I can change tactics quickly when circumstances change.

Becoming Emotionally Smarter.

Emotional IQ can be improved. We can get better at balancing priorities and keeping our temper.

You have to work to do it – many emotional habits were established early in life. Here's the general approach.

- Identify areas where you can become emotionally smarter.
- Practice new responses.
- Find a role model with habits you admire – try to copy them.
- Many school activities can be good ways of developing emotional competencies – both as a leader and as a team member.

Emotional IQ is a combination of learned behaviors – habits with some emotional responses attached.

Changing can be hard work – you're dismantling an old habit and building a new one.

In a market dominated by change, one thing you can change is *you*.

Enjoy being the brand.
It's the most important product
you'll ever promote.

*"When you get your first job in
the business, don't be concerned
with salary, because you're really
continuing your education."*

— Lee Clow

From T.I.G.E.R. to Target.

Remember that T.I.G.E.R. profile?
Let's see if we can use that to identify
some targets. Hopefully, by now
you've got an initial handle on where
you're aiming.

Many Roles.

Now think of the different roles
associated with that talent.

Take entertainment, for example.
There are many kinds of businesses
in the entertainment industry —
movie production, movie theaters,
live theaters, television, radio, or
even comedy clubs to name a few.

Each is looking for a variety of
skills, and marketing is a part of their
business.

You have to find the targets for
your talents within them.

Your job is to achieve a deeper
understanding of the match between
you and your target market.

(Continued on next page)

B. Your Brand Story.

Your story will give a focus to "The Brand Called You." In a few
comfortable sentences, you should be able to introduce yourself
and position yourself in a memorable way.

Every brand needs a story. For you, it's a way to focus on how
you'll introduce yourself to people who might want to hire you.

Why is this important? Bill Dauphanis of Pricewaterhouse/Coo-
pers LLP has some insights. *"Brands are built around stories. And
stories of identity – who we are, where we've come from – are the most
effective stories of all. This is a powerful way to bring them to life."*

Stories help us connect with each other as human beings.

They're a great way to make lessons tangible and real. So, instead
of saying "plan your campaign," we tell you the story of Dawn and
her U-haul truck. Get it?

So, What's Your Story?

Those employers understand that a brand has a story behind it,
one that's meaningful to the customer. It's also a story that creates
a "point of difference" for the brand, something that makes the
brand unique in the marketplace.

This is part of what goes into their many advertising decisions.

Before they hire you, they'll want to know your story. At least
part of it should come from what you learned about your position
among your competition.

Here's what Lee Clontz, a graduate of the ad program at the University of South Carolina, has to say about building your own story.

*"The quickest way not to get a job is to bore an interviewer. Nothing
is worse than a boring applicant. College is a tremendous opportunity to
do different things, explore exciting options, and take interesting classes.
Do something different, something impressive.*

*"Have an interesting story ready that will set you apart from the
hordes of other people your interviewer will meet.*

*"Do something others aren't doing. You've got to build your story. Be
ready with concrete ways you can demonstrate your leadership skills,
your talents, your initiative, and your versatility.*

*"There's nothing wrong with an interviewer thinking of you as 'that
Peace Corps person' or 'the newspaper editor.' In a pile of résumés,
you're trying to be more than just a name. To do that, you've got to be
different, and you've got to be interesting."*

How to Build Your Story.

What is a key event or accomplishment that dramatizes your brand
personality? How do you fill in the blank?

A Story Builds Your Brand. "The _____ person."

How you fill in that blank will define your brand. Remember
what Lee Clontz said, *"There's nothing wrong with an interviewer thinking of you as 'that Peace Corps person' or 'the newspaper editor.'"*

For your target, that means you need a story that says "Peace
Corps" or "newspaper editor."

Your story should convey a single strong meaning the same way Heinz Ketchup's story is "slow," and Volvo's says "safe."

This story will be yours and yours alone.

It should be organized and memorable.

What Is a Story? Five Steps.

Structure. First, know the main structure of a story. A story has a beginning, middle, and end, and usually flows through time.

In the movie *Good Will Hunting,* the end is very much like the beginning (same scene and characters). It's like a circle.

Motifs. Second, a story has motifs – threads that wind their way through the story details so that, in the end, the viewer, listener, or reader can see a discernible pattern. The motifs can be repeated images or words, those central to the story's meaning.

Drama. Third, a story has drama. Action that rises and crests in the mind of the person on the receiving end.

Anchor. Fourth, a story has an anchor, which is its dominant meaning or theme. It is the single most important message you want remembered. And the beginning, middle, end, motifs, and drama should all be tied to that anchor.

Surprise. Fifth, there's a bit of a surprise, a punch line, some sort of reward to the story that makes it worth remembering.

During and after a story is told to someone, that person should be able to condense and wrap it into a tight package of meaning.

The Potato Chip Story.

For example, consider the storycrafting power of Chris Pultorak, a Temple graduate, now an Account Executive with Foote, Cone & Belding (FCB) in Chicago.

"In college I interviewed for a combination scholarship/internship program that was being offered by a local advertising organization. Right in the middle of my interview, the four board members were delivered their lunch. Everything was fine until they realized that the delivery guy stiffed them on their potato chips.

"You can imagine the panic. I don't think they heard a single thing I said after that. I talked. They ate.

"And they grumbled about not having potato chips.

"Then they nodded and thanked me for coming.

"On my way out, I noticed the next candidate waiting in the lobby for his interview. I also noticed a food vendor who was parked right in front of the building. So, I bought four bags of chips, handed them to the next candidate, and said, 'Here, they'll love you for it.'

"The next day I received a call from the review board awarding me the scholarship. And I became known as 'that potato chip guy.'"

But notice his story and how it positions Chris as that "potato chip" guy. How it flows through time. How it contains a beginning, middle, and end. How it carries a motif of potato chips throughout. And the simple surprise of the punch line.

And finally, how all of these story-building elements are anchored to the main message of making Chris memorable.

T.I.G.E.R. to Target (Cont.)

You can't think enough about this.

And much of your thinking should combine expanding potential targets while narrowing your focus based on the match. All at the same time.

There, we said it again, focus and expand. You have to do both.

Developing Target Categories. Here are some ways to develop categories as you narrow your targets and expand your opportunities.

#1. Think across Industries and Businesses.

You need to think openly and creatively about a possible first job.

Often, college students think only narrowly about that job and where they believe they'll fit in.

For instance, since so much of an ad education in school is from an ad agency perspective, the inclination is to believe that an agency is a logical starting point.

Quite often that's not the case.

For example, if you want control, you might try product management.

As a product manager, you can still apply promotional skills and talents in helping market the brand – and you'll have more control than an ad agency account exec.

Broaden your perspective.

#2. Think across Media.

Apply your profile across the whole range of media – old and new.

What specific talents, interests, experiences, or resources do you have that relate to the need for that talent in those media?

Are you a whiz at writing radio spots? Or magazine ads?

If you like retail, can you see yourself working in a newspaper advertising department designing or writing ads?

If you adore magazines, can you see yourself working on a specific magazine's next promotion?

That should tell you something.

And, especially today, do you see some opportunities that may fit you in today's new media?

(Continued on next page)

T.I.G.E.R. to Target (Cont.)

#3. Think across Agencies.

Now that you've gotten broad enough to keep open to job possibilities that at first seem removed from the obvious choices in marketing or advertising, take another look at agencies.

Not only are they considered the ultimate supplier of ad-related jobs, but one agency connects to a lot of marketers, media companies, and marketing services suppliers.

They're at a central point in The Business of Brands.

Obviously advertising agencies head the list. But there are many kinds of agencies: sales promotion, public relations, trade exhibit, event, and direct marketing agencies.

Each has a focus and expertise in particular industries.

High-tech agencies are one example, as are marketing agencies, which have splintered off into many directions, such as event marketing, direct marketing, or telemarketing.

Another point to consider beyond agency type is agency size. There are large, medium, and small agencies. Each requires similar skill sets such as interpersonal ability, writing, or art.

And some, such as is common with smaller advertising agencies, may require a range of skill sets.

Smaller Agencies?

Wyatt Urmey (shown above), a South Carolina grad, gives you some insight into the smaller agency.

"Of the roughly 250,000 people employed in advertising, only about 15% are at big agencies. There's opportunity in the small agency arena.

(Continued on next page)

Building Your Story.

First, you have to decide what you want remembered as that single-minded meaning about you.

Of course, that meaning should be vital to how you want to position yourself in the mind of your target. And it should sell you in a memorable way.

Second, that single-minded meaning should relate instantly to the interest of your target. That's what Chris did.

They wanted potato chips. He provided them.

You may want to role-play as your target – so you craft your story with the target in mind.

Third, select an experience that best relates to the meaning you want conveyed and then give it shape and form.

For Example:

First this happened. Then that happened.

Then there was a problem. And things weren't looking good.

But after working on it and visiting the right people, things began looking up. Until another problem.

But working on it again produced positive results. Until the work made it through and got published and now my name is on it because I was *"the writer who wouldn't say no."*

Short Stories and Long.

Notice how short the story can be. A brief paragraph or two.

It leaves room for a motif – perhaps a recurring problem.

It builds a bit of drama by creating some tension as to whether things will work out.

Finally, with a bit of surprise, it positions the person as a certain type of writer, a type that would be memorable.

The story of your life might be long and interesting.

But the interview won't be.

Bruce's story was he wanted to become someone they wanted to hire. That's a pretty short story.

Yours can certainly be longer than that, but it's not a novel – save the long version for your memoirs.

C. Your Market.

There are a number of ways to narrow down your target market. Chances are, you're already starting to do that.

And, since the market match is so different for each individual, it's hard for us to give you specific advice.

So let's review what we've already discussed.

A Brief Review.

First, you have your T.I.G.E.R profile of you as brand.

You've identified your talents and interests, stated your goals (short- and long-term), described your experiences, and tapped into those resources needed to find that first job.

You're now closer to understanding yourself as a product.

Second, you also understand more about your potential market. The different types of organizations where you may fit, such as ad agencies, marketing services firms, or individual media.

You know how to look for them.

Your Initial Target.

In your local area, you've already taken a look at advertising-to-sales ratios, SIC codes, emerging markets, and specialized fields, such as event marketing or retail.

Third, you know what it means to increase your market value while in school. Taking the right courses. Working as an intern. Volunteering. Finding a mentor. Increasing your value through the work you produce, the people you know, and the experiences you've had.

Market Match-Ups: Skills, Regions, Categories, Companies.

Based on what you know about yourself and your market, find the matches between the two.

To do that, think creatively about those matches.

These are some of the categories most of us use:

- **The Skill:** What do you bring to the party? Where would your skills fit in The Business of Brands? Verbal? Visual? Managerial? Marketing? Advertising? Sales?
- **The Region:** Where do you want to be working? There are a lot of hours when you're not on the job. Where do you want to be when you get out of work?
- **The Category:** Where in The Business of Brands do you fit? Sports marketing?
- **The Company:** Is there a company you want to work for more than anything? Does your family own it?

Think about Making Those Connections.

After you've identified your targets, you might want to start planning your strategy for contacting them. It might not happen for a while, but it never hurts to think ahead.

To do this, think like they think and do as they do.

Be creative here as well.

What are they impressed by? What do they like? What are they like? Put yourself in their place.

For example, if you were an agency executive with hiring power, would you be interested in hiring someone who knew specific details about the advertising your agency was currently running?

Would you be interested if that someone knew the agency's history? Its client base? Its manner of doing business?

Knowing the answers to such questions will help you impress your target at the outset.

Plus, answering those questions will go a long way toward giving you something to say when you contact your targets.

Now you need a fourth thing – your campaign.

T.I.G.E.R. to Target (Cont.)

"Experience. Small agencies provide employees with a large diversity of work experience. Art directors often have to write copy.

"Media people may be involved in research, accounting, or even payroll.

"Creative Flexibility. In a smaller agency, employees have input on and creative control of their work, generally because there are fewer people involved in the approval process.

"Work Appreciation. A small agency is like a family. Close ties develop. When someone has a success, it's hard to miss, though it's hard to miss the failure, too.

"Then again, it could be that the big agency is where you'll find that first job. The big agencies (by now you know the names) are always looking for fresh talent and youthful, trend-savvy people, but you have to be good, very good. Their regional offices may be excellent places to begin your job search. Again, though, you should look within them to determine their needs for certain skills and the kinds of industries and businesses they serve."

Bigger Agencies…

This same kind of enthusiasm for the business can be heard from Dan Hadel, at Y&R in New York.

Dan graduated from the University of Kansas in 1991 and took his first job in Y&R's media department.

He's worked on a range of accounts, including Jell-O Pudding Snacks, International Home Foods, Met Life, and Colgate toothpaste.

"What makes this business so exciting for me is the fact that advertising is an ever-evolving business always opening up opportunities to "try your hand" in different arenas.

"In my almost six years at Y&R NY, my experience already includes managing the media buying for sports marketing packages, developing Internet sites, and working on new business pitches.

"My agency experience has been the most fun I've ever had while getting paid.

(Continued on next page)

T.I.G.E.R. to Target (Cont.)

"Make no mistake, though, the average starting salary is fairly low and the hours can be long. Very long.

"But the long-term rewards, both personally and professionally, can become exponential in the long run."

To this point you've been considering certain skills, a range of industries and businesses, and potential roles those skills can fit within those industries and businesses.

You've been thinking across industries, across media, and across agencies.

By now, you should be convinced that there are jobs.

But that you have to think openly and creatively about what and where they are, and how they match with your skills.

Keep looking for the best fit. This ad for a job-hunting service aims at people who don't feel like they've made the right career decisions. All the more reason to start early.

D. Your Campaign.

Planning Your Launch.

It's a process – sometimes a long one.

While a few are lucky enough to know right off what they want to do and where they want to do it – for most of us it's the process of a year or two.

Putting It Together.

Here's where you put it all together. While every campaign is different, since you have a different product (you), and a slightly different market (your target), the details will vary.

But most campaigns have these building blocks:

1. **Your Résumé.** On one page, you should be able to present, in writing, why you are qualified for an entry-level job at a company in your target.

2. **Your Brand Story.** In a few comfortable sentences, you should be able to introduce and position yourself in a memorable way.

3. **Extras.** You should have more than a résumé. No stupid pet tricks please, and don't bring a musical instrument, but whether it's a bit of writing you did, or a letter or article about you, try to bring something extra.

4. **Your Target List.** Names and addresses of the companies on your target list. Plus the people you should contact. Plus some information about them.

5. **Your Initial Contact.** Some sort of written communication to introduce yourself and present your résumé. Tell them you will contact them. And do it. It's not their job to contact you.

6. **Follow-Up.** Now you have to do what you say you'll do. Follow-up and try to schedule some sort of initial interview – if there's no job, try to schedule an informational interview.

7. **Follow-Up Your Follow-Up.** Pleasant tenacity should be one of the skills you develop at this stage of the game. We'll talk about how to project a feeling of being positive and organized – rather than a desperate nag.

8. **The Roll-Out.** Finally, whether you've got a U-Haul, a portfolio, or a one-page résumé, you're ready to make connections that will ultimately lead you to that first job – the first step on your career path.

Deep Breath…

OK, let's go over the campaign game plan. If you've just finished up the intro course, you should think of this section as something you'll skim for future reference.

Relax and enjoy it.

Get the concepts into your head and let them cook.

They can simmer for up to a year.

But…

If you took the course a year or so ago, it's time to get serious. So let's dig in together. We've got work to do.

Here are some areas of your launch that might need work.

Extras.

You should really consider extras not so extra. They're necessary. And they should demonstrate your talent. You may want to use them when contacting targets. Or, you may want to bring them with you when you visit or interview.

Here's a list of some extras to consider:

• Your own stationery and business card
• A mini-brochure/résumé for handouts

You really should have more than a résumé.

Think of it this way: you're a product, a brand. Doesn't every brand deserve a bit of a promotional brochure? Of course it does!

The Mini-Résumé Promotional Piece.

Bruce remembers going to a finals for the "College World Series of Advertising" (aka the AAF/NSAC).

"The West Florida prof, Tom Groth, had encouraged every student to develop a small pocket-size promo piece – and to hand them out.

"Within fifteen minutes, I had five or six of them in my pocket – and I looked at them the next day. They were simple little one-fold brochures that dramatized the benefits of hiring that person.

"Each one was different – different type, different design, different message – but they all worked."

You should consider developing one for yourself.

Work Samples.

• Student advertising competition entries or submissions, especially if you've done well at the competition level.
• Ads or campaigns you've worked on as an intern or in school.
  For example, have you organized a recruitment campaign for a school organization or for your sorority or fraternity?
  If so, is it worth showing? If yes, then show it.
• Commendation letters for work performed. Many times "mentor" profs will be glad to write a commendation letter.

Your Initial Contact.

Decide what you're going to say before you say it. Make sure what you're going to say is in your target's best interest, as well as your own. Just like the advertising for brands, you need to consider the benefits for your target if they hire you. These should be the centerpiece of what you say.

Some Initial Contact Tactics:

Here are some choices of how to contact them:

• **Send a letter.** Make it short. Make it good. If you want to sell yourself as a writer, there's no better opportunity than the cover letter. Make it creative, energetic, FUN!

  Joy Farber wrote her first letters in the third person, signing them "Joy's Agent." Why?

  "So I could spout my attributes without sounding cocky." Cool.

Helpful Habits for "The Brand Called You."

Some recommendations from Tom Peters' book *Re-Imagine! Business Excellence in a Disruptive Age.*

Think Like an Entrepreneur.
Even as you work for someone else, you should, in a good way, "be the boss of your own show." How you do your current job should enhance your market value.

Always Be a Closer.
As Peters notes, "As all true business people know. Life is sales. The rest is details."

For your job, you should be concerned with implementation, things that get done.

Embrace Marketing.
He observes, "You need to master much more of the marketing puzzle than you did in the past." Market your point of view. Market your value.

Thrive on Ambiguity.
Mixed signals. Uncertain circumstances. Don't just "deal with it."

Work to thrive in that environment – it could be with us for a while.

Nurture Your Network.
Peters believes that "Loyalty is more important than ever."

He also notes that, "the old loyalty was vertical." Loyalty to a hierarchy.

"New loyalty is horizontal."

He concludes, "You must build – and deliberately manage – an ever-expanding network of professional contacts throughout your field."

Relish Technology.
A Media Revolution thought…

"You must instinctively appreciate the unequivocal fact that the Internet and everything that comes in its wake will turn business upside-down in an astonishingly short period." The prospect should make you "tingle with joy and anticipation."

Re-Imagine! Is packed with useful observations about surviving – and thriving – in today's business world.

Management Skills.

Do you have management skills?

Consider Heather Roe-Day, a U of Wyoming graduate.

Here, she describes the skills she needs for her Product Manager position for Unicover Corporation.

"It's my responsibility to coordinate the efforts of all segments of our business to create promotions and finished products that appeal to our customers. For instance, I...

• *"Develop promotion concepts fully into marketing plans, complete with product costs, advertising costs, expected sales, and expected profits.*

• *"Convey the marketing focus to the promotion designers and copywriters.*

• *"Order all product materials or products from vendors and coordinate deliveries.*

• *"Ensure all promotions and manufactured products are produced in-house in a cost effective and timely manner.*

• *"Analyze promotions to determine more profitable products and more effective designs for future products.*

"The position of product manager requires marketing skills, an understanding of basic accounting principles, analytical skills, and extensive organizational skills.

"The greatest skill I use every day is the ability to organize my tasks and orchestrate the activities of others in the company to help all promotions grow from the concept stage to the finished product stage.

"My involvement in outside activities while in high school and college built the foundation for time management and helped me learn to set intermediate goals in order to complete large tasks."

• **Pick up the phone and call.** Get names and titles. (Note: secretaries, executive assistants, and receptionists are worth their weight in gold generally, and when it comes to helping you contact someone, they're the key.)

• **Go there.** Don't just drop in. Arrange for an information-gathering session, being right up front with who you are and your interest in the company.

Once there, ask for advice. This makes those being asked feel good, and you'll be getting smarter about your market.

By the way, don't forget to bring a few intelligent questions.

• **Consider guerrilla marketing.** Since you're an unknown commodity in the marketplace, you may need to be especially creative in how to make contacts.

Example: The Tuesday Campaign.

Here's what Tuesday Poliak did to get interviews for jobs.

She wanted to work for a large ad agency in a major California market, but she knew it would be difficult to get interviews.

What Tuesday did worked for her.

Tuesday duplicated photos of key agency CEOs and put them into simulated driver's licenses. She then put the licenses into wallets and placed the wallets on the floors of restrooms of agency offices. When the wallets were found, they were promptly given to the respective CEOs, who upon opening them, found Tuesday's story inside.

Tuesday was given three interviews within a week.

Are You Ready?

By now you know the main message from this chapter. Start formulating the marketing of "The Brand Called You" right now.

It will take work. But it will be worth it.

You'll probably be going back over this chapter a number of times as you get your brand ready.

Are you ready? How about a quick review of the things you have to do? You can make certain you've covered all your bases by answering these questions:

• Do you understand yourself as a product and brand? Have you completed your T.I.G.E.R. profile? Do you think you know how to differentiate yourself as a brand?

• Do you understand your market? Do you think you know which companies are in your target? Have you begun looking for them? Can you think like they think?

• Do you have plans to increase your market value? Internships. Course selection. Networking. Summer jobs.

• Do you have a plan of action for bringing yourself to market? Is your résumé ready? How about those not-so-extra things that can demonstrate your talents?

Get Ready to Roll...

As we said, if you've just finished up the intro course, think of this section as something you'll skim for future reference.

But as we also said, the sooner you start, the better you'll do.

So think about getting started.

Even if you start early, you've got some work to do.

Tom Peters has a few well-chosen closing words.

"It's this simple. You are a brand. You are in charge of your brand. There is no single path to success. And there is no one right way to create the brand called **You.**

"Except this: Start today. Or else."

Job-Hunting's Three R's.
Resources, References, and Résumés.

Here's an initial list of places to find out the things you'll need to know. And, of course, you'll want to see what you can find at adbuzz.com – see you there.

Job Finding Resources.
Advertising-Specific Publications.

- *AdWeek* (adweek.com)
  770 Broadway, 7th Floor, New York, NY 10003
  Features agency jobs. Has agency directory.

- *Advertising Age* (adage.com)
  220 E. 42nd. St., New York, NY 10017
  Special edition listing ad agencies.

- *BrandWeek* (brandweek.com)
  (Address same as AdWeek)
  Features marketing jobs. Has client directory.

- *MediaWeek* (mediaweek.com)
  (Address same as AdWeek)
  Features media jobs. Has media directory.

- *Standard Directory of Advertisers* (redbooks.com)
  National Register Publishing, P.O. Box 31
  New Providence, NJ 07974

- *Standard Directory of Advertising Agencies*
  (same as above)

Advertising-Specific Organizations.

- **Advertising Research Foundation** (thearf.org)
  641 Lexington Ave., New York, NY 10022

- **Advertising Women of New York** (awny.org)
  153 E. 57th St., New York, NY 10022

Analytical Skills.

Do you have analytical skills? Consider what Lynn Carlson, a graduate of the U of Wyoming and now a Researcher for IRI (Information Resources, Inc.), tells you about what it's like to work in market research.

"Don't let the word 'research' turn you off to the field of marketing.

"Marketing research is simply finding ways to get people to buy your brand.

"I work in the Client Service Department of IRI, analyzing data to assist our clients' marketing information needs.

"We are able to provide this service through the use of databases based on UPC codes at your grocery store. When items are scanned, a computer gathers the information and assembles it into customized databases for our clients.

"They're the key to marketplace information, and its timely delivery makes the data very actionable.

"The fun part about marketing research is the interaction between our company and our clients.

"I often feel as though I work for the client company more than my company, because we are incorporated into their daily events and decisions.

"It's rewarding to assist in a major business decision, such as a new product launch or an acquisition.

"The information is fascinating, and the speed at which we get new data every day is different because of the fast-paced, ever-changing market.

"So, next weekend when you buy something at the grocery store, chances are I'll be looking at the results of your purchase a few weeks later."

Getting the Job In a Tough Economy.

Getting that first job is always tough. But some times are tougher than others. Here's some good practical advice.

1. Find Ways to Prove Yourself. Is there some project you can take on at a reduced rate. Show your prospective employer you really really want to help make his (or her) business a success. And then do exactly that.

2. Consider Opportunities at a Small Business. Whether you look for one that's going great guns, or one with problems, they all need help. And they can hire you faster with fewer interviews and more flexibility.

3. Expand Your Networking. That's particularly true if the sector you're looking at (for example, traditional ad agencies) is suffering in this economy.

4. Market Your "Personal Brand." We've been talking about this throughout this chapter. The tougher it gets, the more you need to put your own personal brand out there – to differentiate yourself in a difficult marketplace

Web Resources.

As you know by now, it's easy to surf the Net and find information about any one of a number of organizations or publications.

Through your search engine (e.g., Yahoo!, Excite, etc.) you can do key word searches, that will generate numerous sources for more information.

You can also search the following Web sites for job and career information:

- www.adage.com
- www.ipa.co.uk
- www.resumepls.com
- www.monster.com
- www.careermart.com
- www.careers.org

- **American Advertising Federation (aaf.org)**
  1101 Vermont Ave., Ste. 500, Washington, DC 20005
  Has education division. Can help put you in touch with the local ad clubs in your area.

- **American Association of Advertising Agencies (aaaa.org)**
  405 Lexington Ave., 18th Floor, New York, NY 10174
  The 4As can be an interesting resource. Go to their site and find information on Careers in Advertising, Professional Development, Internship and Scholarship Programs, and a Bookstore with some unique publications.

- **Point of Purchase Advertising Institute (popai.com)**
  1600 Duke Street, Suite 400, Alexandria, VA 22314

- **Promotional Products Association International (ppa.org)** 3125 Skyway Circle N., Irving, TX 75038

- **Local Advertising Clubs and Organizations**
  (Contact those in your area, or check with the AAF.)

The Yellow Pages.

We don't have to tell you how to use the Yellow Pages, do we? However, be sure to use the *Business* Yellow Pages, rather than the Consumer Yellow Pages.

You might be surprised at the categories of companies that you find listed in your area.

Leading Advertising-Allied Organizations.

- **American Marketing Association (marketingpower.com)**
  311 S. Wacker Dr., Suite 5800, Chicago, IL 60606
  Note: Publishes the important Marketing News *trade magazine to keep you current on the industry's trends.*

- *Promo Magazine* **(promomagazine.com)**
  This is a terrific resource on the sales promotion industry. Their Promo 100 list provides great leads for top performers in this exciting field. You can also find out more about some of the interesting specialties: Events, Interactive, Retail, Premiums, Licensing, Sweepstakes, and Viral.

- **Public Relations Society of America (prsa.org)**
  33 Irving Pl., New York, NY 10003

Leading Advertising-Allied Media Organizations.

- **Newspaper Association of America (naa.org)**
  4401 Wilson Blvd, Suite 900, Arlington, VA 22203

- **American Society of Media Photographers (asmp.org)**
  150 N. Second Street, Philadelphia, PA 19106

- **Magazine Publishers of America (magazine.org)**
  810 Seventh Ave., 24th Floor, New York, NY 10019

- **National Cable Television Association (ncta.com)**
  25 Massachusetts Ave. NW, Suite 100, Washington, DC 20036
  Their site has a "Careers in Cable" page.

- **National Newspaper Association** (nna.org)
  2020 N. 14th Street, Suite 300, Arlington, VA 22201

Campus Resources.

Make yourself known in the offices and with the people who can help you on campus. Here are places to look:

- **Career development or job placement center**
- **School advertising offices**
- **College relations department**
- **College media and publications** (e.g., newspapers, radio stations, university press, alumni magazine)
- **College news department**
- **College recruitment office**

References.

And here are some books to get you started.

Your Local Bookstore.

There's nothing like a big modern-day bookstore for combining business with pleasure.

Stores such as Barnes & Noble, Borders, and Walden Books make it easy for you to search out books on jobs and careers. Their shelves are well stocked.

Check the careers and the marketing and advertising sections.

Advertising Career Books:

We've highlighted some of our favorites in the sidebars, but there are many, many more. For example, in searching for advertising career books on Amazon, you'll find the following:

Approach an Advertising Agency: And Walk Away with the Job You Want (Here's How)
by Barbara A. Ganim

Breaking into Advertising: How to Market Yourself Like a Professional (The Breaking Into… series)
by Jeanette Smith

Career Opportunities in Advertising and Public Relations (Career Opportunity Series)
by Shelly Field and Howard J. Rubenstein

Careers in Advertising
by S. William Pattis

How to Succeed in Advertising When All You Have Is Talent
by Laurence Minsky

The Insider's Guide to the Top 20 Careers in Business and Management: What It's Really Like to Work in Advertising…
by Tom Fischgrund

Vault Career Guide to Advertising
by Ira Berkowitz

It's easy to find books...
on getting a job in advertising.

They're all pretty good.
Just remember, after you read them,
you've got to do the work.

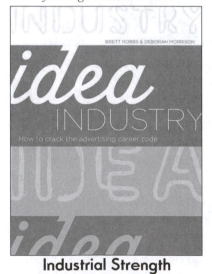

Industrial Strength

Based on over 100 interviews with professionals at top agencies across the country, *Idea Industry* gives you an insider's view of what each area of an agency does and shows you how to get the advertising job you want.

Idea Industry is available from Amazon and from the online store at The One Club (*www.oneclub.org*).

Careers Vocabulary:

Here's a short concept and vocabulary list for this chapter.

AAF/NSAC – This is the American Advertising Federation's (AAF) National Student Advertising Competition (NSAC).

Advertising-to-sales ratio – The A-to-S ratio identifies industries and companies with large advertising expenditures relative to sales – good targets in your job search.

Book – Also referred to as a portfolio. This is how aspiring creatives (writers, artists) demonstrate their wares. Student books contain speculative examples of ads and ad campaigns.

Brand story – A memorable narrative with 5 characteristics: 1) a beginning, middle, and end, 2) surprises, 3) motifs, 4) drama, and 5) an anchor. The story should be succinct and could be no longer than a paragraph.

Creative degrees – Advanced degrees for aspiring copywriters and art directors.

Emerging markets – Likely targets for a beginning job. Companies or industries currently experiencing rapid growth.

Internship – A form of student apprenticeship or understudy, where students can learn the workings of the industry. Internships may be semester, year-long, or summer-term experiences. They may count for credit. They may or may not be paid. Many communications programs (advertising, public relations, journalism, etc.) and marketing programs within those colleges or universities have their own internship relationships and resources. It is not uncommon for students to create their own internships, as long as they are sanctioned by the school.

Network – Can be an action verb, as in "You should network throughout school." Can also be a noun, as in "You should develop a network while you're in school."

Résumé – A one-page document profiling and highlighting you as a brand – your objective, achievements, experiences, and, if room, references.

SIC codes – Standard Industrial Classification. A way of looking at companies by industry. Can be found in *Standard Rates and Data*, the bible of agency media departments.

Target – Can refer to target marketing or target list. In this chapter, it refers to the group you judge to be the best source of that first job.

Notes & Resources:

Key Dates & Notes:

YOU CAN USE THESE PAGES FOR YOUR CLASS.
If you want to make copies, you have permission
to make copies of these calendar pages.

_____
_____
_____
_____
_____
_____
_____
_____
_____
_____
_____
_____
_____
_____
_____
_____
_____
_____

MONTH_____ YEAR_____

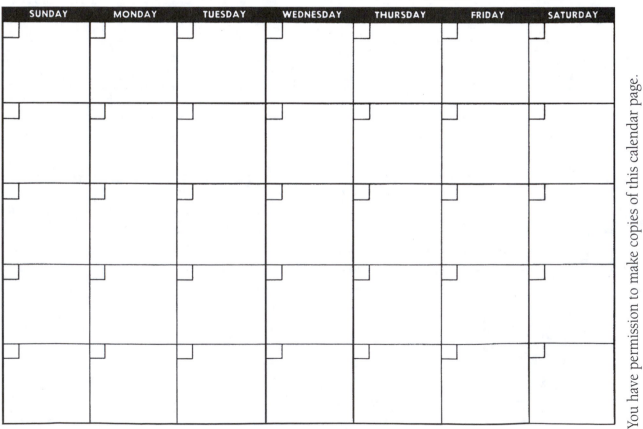

SUNDAY	MONDAY	TUESDAY	WEDNESDAY	THURSDAY	FRIDAY	SATURDAY

MONTH_____ YEAR_____

SUNDAY	MONDAY	TUESDAY	WEDNESDAY	THURSDAY	FRIDAY	SATURDAY

MONTH_____ YEAR_____

SUNDAY	MONDAY	TUESDAY	WEDNESDAY	THURSDAY	FRIDAY	SATURDAY

You have permission to make copies of this calendar page.

MONTH_____ YEAR_____

SUNDAY	MONDAY	TUESDAY	WEDNESDAY	THURSDAY	FRIDAY	SATURDAY

MONTH_____ YEAR_____

SUNDAY	MONDAY	TUESDAY	WEDNESDAY	THURSDAY	FRIDAY	SATURDAY

Index:

Two words not in the index are **advertising** and **brands,** since they appear throughout the book on virtually every page.

Other words, such as **advertising agencies, marketers, marketing services,** and **media,** which are also chapter headings, are only mentioned related to key items, (as in advocacy advertising or media plan).

Finally, not every brand name, agency or ad topic is indexed, particularly if the purpose was to reinforce the text, rather than serve as a case history example or key concept.

If there are topics you think should also be indexed, send us an e-mail. Thanks.

Acknowledgements:

HERE'S WHERE WE THANK all the people who helped make this book happen. Next edition, one of them might be you.

For Starters, We'd Like to Serve Up Thanks to...

The Campbell's Soup Company, for providing copies of *America's Favorite Food* as an initial resource. *Campbell's* wide-ranging marketing activities provided a unifying point for all authors.

Thanks to Shannon Jordan for help at a difficult time and P&G public relations for their usual efficient job.

Thanks to Alex Bogusky and CP+B, Wieden + Kennedy, Jeff Goodby, GSD&M, Kang & Lee, KGF, Bob Levin's office at SONY, Barbara Molotsky, Howard Draft, Dennis Holt, DeeDee Gordon, Mark Goldstein at BBDO, the Martin Agency, and Linda Kaplan Thaler.

There's more – David Peacock at A-B, Mairee Ryan, Adam Seever, Todd Holscher, Wes Perrin, and Bernie Pitzel.

Janet Champ, thanks for being you.

Thanks to all the chapter authors for their skill and hard work, particularly Tom Fauls, Laurence Minsky's Chapter 7 team, and our Editorial Board, Jim Avery and Jim Marra, who were long-distance partners in more ways than one.

Thanks to WDCB for keeping us company.

Beyond the Call of Duty – Our Class-Testers.

There was a Class-Testing version of this book. We'd like to thank the professors and the students who helped make this a better book – not without a bit of pain. (You know what we mean.)

Those who survived that early edition get a free copy of this one.

Thanks go to **Alan Holliday** and **Chris Cakebread** at Boston U, **Bonnie Rega** and **Daniel Ng** at Bradley, **John Dahlberg** at Canisius, **Ricci Fuller** and **Frank Gallucio** at Fayetteville Technical Community College, **Bev Atkinson**, **Jane Bongers**, **Joanne Lehman**, and **Barbara Smith** at Humber, **Richard Nelson** at LSU, **Pam Mickelson** at Morningside College, **James Cleary** at Northwood, **Kim Rotzoll** at University of Illinois, **Jason Berger** at UMKC, **Bob Pfingstler** at U of Pa/Edinboro, **Patricia Orman** at University of Southern Colorado and **Jim Avery** at Oklahoma University, whose walk matched his talk. And to the students who taught us.

Thanks to Pat and Eugenia for helping keep us together, and Kevin Heubusch for finishing us up with professionalism and precision. And to Lorelei for always making it happen.

Bruce Bendinger

Editorial Staff:

Lorelei Davis Bendinger: Publisher
Bruce Bendinger: Executive Editor
Jim Avery: Consulting Editor
Jim Marra: Consulting Editor
Patrick Aylward: Production Editor
Gregory S. Paus: Cover Design
Mike Zitt: Electronic Pre-Press
Stefanie Crawford: Proofing
AdBuzz Design: Bruce Bendinger, Joe.Bob Hester, and Casey Stockdon

BOOKS FROM **THE COPY WORKSHOP**

adbuzz.com | 773-871-1179 | FAX 773-281-4643 | thecopyworkshop@aol.com

INFORMATION	DESCRIPTION

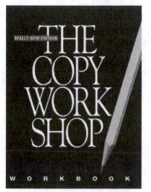

The Copy Workshop Workbook
by Bruce Bendinger

440 pages, $37.50

ISBN# 978-1-887229-12-8

This is the #1 book on copywriting. Agencies use it as a training resource. It's used by universities, art schools, and the American Management Association (it's the basic book for their copywriting seminar). The Really New Edition features more great examples of ads that work, a practical approach to integrated communication - The MarCom Matrix - and new chapters on Sales Promotion, Direct, and "MPR" (Marketing Public Relations). Also available in Chinese and Korean.

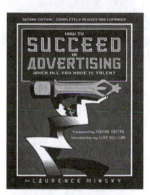

How To Succeed In Advertising When All You Have Is Talent
by Laurence Minsky

480 pages, $47.50

ISBN# 978-1-887229-20-3

From the Beetle to the Mini. From "Eat Mor Chikin" to the AFLAC Duck. From "Think Different" to "Got Milk." This completely revised and expanded 2nd edition includes life lessons from 18 of advertising's most important talents.

Advertising Campaign Planning:
Developing An Advertising-Based Marketing Plan
by Jim Avery

264 pages, $32.75

ISBN# 978-1-887229-06-7

This book is designed for student ad agencies and college campaign "teams" for the AAF/NSAC College World Series of Advertising. The basis of the book is a powerful interlocking marketing plan, based on the P&G/WRG (Wells Rich Greene) system. Best practices presented in a clear and easy to follow sequence.

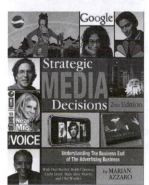

Strategic Media Decisions, 2nd Ed.:
Understanding The Business End Of The Advertising Business
by Marian Azzaro, w. Carla Lloyd, Mary Alice Shaver, Dan Binder, Robb Clawson, and Olaf Werder
556 pages, $67.50

ISBN# 978-1-887229-33-3

Welcome to the $300 billion business of media. Learn how it works from some of media's top professors and top professionals. This is a book in touch with today - packed with genuine substance and contemporary best practices in a clear, easy-to-read format.
FREE WORKBOOK. A student workbook is available on the MediaBuzz Web site, which also features additional material and information.

BOOKS FROM THE COPY WORKSHOP

adbuzz.com | 773-871-1179 | FAX 773-281-4643 | thecopyworkshop@aol.com

| INFORMATION | DESCRIPTION |

Hitting the Sweet Spot:
How Consumer Insights Can Inspire Better Marketing and Advertising
by Lisa Fortini-Campbell

257 pages, $29.95

ISBN# 978-1-887229-09-8

The Consumer Insight Classic. Clear and engaging - written by one of the top professionals in consumer insight. The book takes you through the process step by step - from Data to Information to Insight to Inspiration. This book is used worldwide by both students and professionals.

The New Account Manager, 2nd Ed.
by Don Dickinson

524 pages, $47.50

ISBN# 978-1-887229-37-1

A smart book about one of the most challenging jobs in business - account management.
Use as a core text for a management course, or as a supplement for your student agency.
The 2nd Edition includes a new chapter on Account Management in the Era of IMC, featuring contributions from top professionals in a variety of fields.

Take A Stand For Your Brand:
Building A Great Agency Brand From The Inside Out
by Tim Williams

220 pages, $29.95

ISBN# 978-1-887229-25-8

Agencies need to do for themselves what they do for their clients: build a distinctive brand. But they are usually so eager to be a "full-service integrated agency" that they try to stand for everything. Take a Stand for Your Brand shows how agencies can develop a clear positioning that builds on the agency's unique strengths, differentiates the agency in the marketplace, and makes the agency more intensely appealing to prospective clients.

The Book of Gossage
by Howard Luck Gossage
Introduction by Jeff Goodby, w. Stan Freberg, Kim Rotzoll, John Steinbeck, and Tom Wolfe.

2nd Edition - Includes the Disc of Gossage. 400 pages. $50.00

ISBN# 978-1-887229-28-9

This is a book about and by *"The Socrates of San Francisco,"* Howard Gossage, the copywriter who introduced the world to Marshall McLuhan, helped start Friends of the Earth and brought interactivity to his unique brand of advertising.
He was 30 years ahead of his time, so the world may be ready.
The Second Edition also features **The Disc of Gossage** - packed with extras; a radio address, an ad gallery, and more.

BOOKS FROM THE COPY WORKSHOP

adbuzz.com | 773-871-1179 | FAX 773-281-4643 | thecopyworkshop@aol.com

INFORMATION   DESCRIPTION

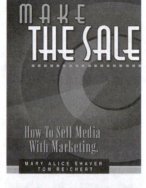

Make The Sale:
How To Sell Media With Marketing
by Mary Alice Shaver
and Tom Reichert
296 pages, $27.95

ISBN# 978-1-887229-16-6

Even in today's tough economy, a successful media salesperson can do very well. This is the first book that's a comprehensive introduction to Media Sales. Learn "The 4 M's:" Market, Marketer, Message and Media. Great advice useful for all media, with an emphasis on local media: newspapers, radio, TV, outdoor, Yellow Pages and more... From prospecting for those first clients, to making that first presentation, to building a successful sales career - this book helps beginners become winners.

Creative Insight:
The Researcher's Art
by Jeffrey F. Durgee
233 pages, $29.95

ISBN# 978-1-887229-26-5

The search in Market Research is often the search for new insight. Professor Durgee's book combines practical experience for top marketers and ad agencies with his own unique insights into what it takes to find the path to actionable insights. Today, leading-edge writers and researchers such as Gladwell and Rapaille note the power of insight. Durgee offers practical steps on the road to discovering them.

From File To Finish:
A Prepress Guide
by Elaine Wagner &
Amy Desiderio

282 pages, $37.50

ISBN# 978-1-887229-32-6

We are pleased to present Professor Elaine Wagner's clear and reader-friendly book clarifying the often complicated process of preparing computer-based graphic files for printing or for sending to a publication.
This is a critical issue and Professor Wagner, with the assistance of printing professional Amy Desiderio, makes this complicated area crystal clear with principles that apply while technology evolves.

What Do You Mean I Can't Write?
A Practical Guide To Business Writing For Agency Account managers
by Norm MacMaster

74 pages, $11.75

ISBN # 978-1-887229-29-6

Years ago, top ad agency executive Norm Macmaster wrote a guide for beginning account executives.
It became legendary - with copies handed down from generation to generation. With the author's permission, we bring this underground classic to light - clear and practical, it provides beginners with the information they need to do the job.

BOOKS FROM **THE COPY WORKSHOP**

adbuzz.com | 773-871-1179 | FAX 773-281-4643 | thecopyworkshop@aol.com

INFORMATION   ## DESCRIPTION

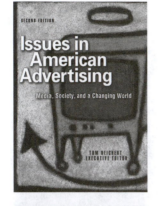

Issues in American Advertising:
Media, Society, and a Changing World
by Tom Reichert, et al.

328 pages, $45.00

ISBN# 978-1-887229-35-7

Professor Tom Reichert felt he needed a small supplement for his large intro class – one that exposed beginning students to a few of today's important issues. It was reader-friendly and contemporary. Then we decided to turn it into a full-blown adverising and society text – with contributions from top people in each area. 18 timely topics written for a student audience.

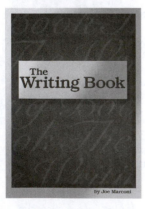

Readings in Account Planning
Edited by Hart Weichselbaum

328 pages, $47.50

ISBN# 978-1-887229-36-4

As Head of Planning for the Richards Group and one of the founders of the US Account Planning Group, Hart Weichselbaum has been one of the key players in the growing profession of account planning. He has selected some of the best articles in the field for this outstanding collection.

The Writing Book
by Joe Marconi

312 pages, $42.00

ISBN# 978-0-9819095-0-9

Joe Marconi is one of our most important business writers – author of over a dozen (last time we counted) books, including Beyond Branding, Creating the Marketing Experience, Crisis Marketing: When Bad Things Happen to Good Companies, Public Relations – The Complete Guide, and more. He conducts seminars and workshops internationally and teaches at the university level.

Save 20%
When you buy from the bookshop on www.adbuzz.com